Twentieth-Century Literary Criticism

Guide to Gale Literary Criticism Series

For criticism on	Consult these Gale series
Authors now living or who died after December 31, 1999	*CONTEMPORARY LITERARY CRITICISM (CLC)*
Authors who died between 1900 and 1999	*TWENTIETH-CENTURY LITERARY CRITICISM (TCLC)*
Authors who died between 1800 and 1899	*NINETEENTH-CENTURY LITERATURE CRITICISM (NCLC)*
Authors who died between 1400 and 1799	*LITERATURE CRITICISM FROM 1400 TO 1800 (LC)* *SHAKESPEAREAN CRITICISM (SC)*
Authors who died before 1400	*CLASSICAL AND MEDIEVAL LITERATURE CRITICISM (CMLC)*
Authors of books for children and young adults	*CHILDREN'S LITERATURE REVIEW (CLR)*
Dramatists	*DRAMA CRITICISM (DC)*
Poets	*POETRY CRITICISM (PC)*
Short story writers	*SHORT STORY CRITICISM (SSC)*
Literary topics and movements	*HARLEM RENAISSANCE: A GALE CRITICAL COMPANION (HR)* *THE BEAT GENERATION: A GALE CRITICAL COMPANION (BG)* *FEMINISM IN LITERATURE: A GALE CRITICAL COMPANION (FL)* *GOTHIC LITERATURE: A GALE CRITICAL COMPANION (GL)*
Asian American writers of the last two hundred years	*ASIAN AMERICAN LITERATURE (AAL)*
Black writers of the past two hundred years	*BLACK LITERATURE CRITICISM (BLC-1)* *BLACK LITERATURE CRITICISM SUPPLEMENT (BLCS)* *BLACK LITERATURE CRITICISM: CLASSIC AND EMERGING AUTHORS SINCE 1950 (BLC-2)*
Hispanic writers of the late nineteenth and twentieth centuries	*HISPANIC LITERATURE CRITICISM (HLC)* *HISPANIC LITERATURE CRITICISM SUPPLEMENT (HLCS)*
Native North American writers and orators of the eighteenth, nineteenth, and twentieth centuries	*NATIVE NORTH AMERICAN LITERATURE (NNAL)*
Major authors from the Renaissance to the present	*WORLD LITERATURE CRITICISM, 1500 TO THE PRESENT (WLC)* *WORLD LITERATURE CRITICISM SUPPLEMENT (WLCS)*

ISSN 0276-8178

Volume 249

Twentieth-Century Literary Criticism

**Criticism of the
Works of Novelists, Poets, Playwrights,
Short Story Writers, and Other Creative Writers
Who Lived between 1900 and 1999,
from the First Published Critical
Appraisals to Current Evaluations**

Lawrence J. Trudeau
Project Editor

GALE
CENGAGE Learning™

Detroit • New York • San Francisco • New Haven, Conn • Waterville, Maine • London

GALE
CENGAGE Learning™

Twentieth-Century Literary Criticism, Vol. 249

Project Editor: Lawrence J. Trudeau

Dana Barnes, Sara Constantakis, Kathy D. Darrow, Matthew Derda, Kristen Dorsch, Dana Ferguson, Jeffrey W. Hunter, Michelle Kazensky, Jelena O. Krstović, Michelle Lee, Marie Toft, Jonathan Vereecke

Content Conversion: Katrina D. Coach, Gwen Tucker

Indexing Services: Laurie Andriot

Rights and Acquisitions: Margaret Chamberlain-Gaston, Mari Masalin-Cooper, Tracie Richardson, Sarah Tomasek

Composition and Electronic Capture: Gary Leach

Manufacturing: Cynde Lentz

Product Manager: Mary Onorato

For product information and technology assistance, contact us at **Gale Customer Support, 1-800-877-4253.**
For permission to use material from this text or product, submit all requests online at **www.cengage.com/permissions.**
Further permissions questions can be emailed to **permissionrequest@cengage.com**

Gale
27500 Drake Rd.
Farmington Hills, MI, 48331-3535

LIBRARY OF CONGRESS CATALOG CARD NUMBER 76-46132

ISBN-13: 978-1-4144-7029-0
ISBN-10: 1-4144-7029-0

ISSN 0276-8178

Printed in the United States of America
1 2 3 4 5 6 7 15 14 13 12 11

Contents

Preface

Since its inception *Twentieth-Century Literary Criticism* (*TCLC*) has been purchased and used by some 10,000 school, public, and college or university libraries. *TCLC* has covered more than 1000 authors, representing over 60 nationalities and nearly 50,000 titles. No other reference source has surveyed the critical response to twentieth-century authors and literature as thoroughly as *TCLC*. In the words of one reviewer, "there is nothing comparable available." *TCLC* "is a gold mine of information—dates, pseudonyms, biographical information, and criticism from books and periodicals—which many librarians would have difficulty assembling on their own."

Scope of the Series

TCLC is designed to serve as an introduction to authors who died between 1900 and 1999 and to the most significant interpretations of these author's works. Volumes published from 1978 through 1999 included authors who died between 1900 and 1960. The great poets, novelists, short story writers, playwrights, and philosophers of the period are frequently studied in high school and college literature courses. In organizing and reprinting the vast amount of critical material written on these authors, *TCLC* helps students develop valuable insight into literary history, promotes a better understanding of the texts, and sparks ideas for papers and assignments. Each entry in *TCLC* presents a comprehensive survey on an author's career or an individual work of literature and provides the user with a multiplicity of interpretations and assessments. Such variety allows students to pursue their own interests; furthermore, it fosters an awareness that literature is dynamic and responsive to many different opinions.

Every fourth volume of *TCLC* is devoted to literary topics. These topics widen the focus of the series from the individual authors to such broader subjects as literary movements, prominent themes in twentieth-century literature, literary reaction to political and historical events, significant eras in literary history, prominent literary anniversaries, and the literatures of cultures that are often overlooked by English-speaking readers.

TCLC is designed as a companion series to Gale's *Contemporary Literary Criticism, (CLC)* which reprints commentary on authors who died after 1999. Because of the different time periods under consideration, there is no duplication of material between *CLC* and *TCLC*.

Organization of the Book

A *TCLC* entry consists of the following elements:

- The **Author Heading** cites the name under which the author most commonly wrote, followed by birth and death dates. Also located here are any name variations under which an author wrote, including transliterated forms for authors whose native languages use nonroman alphabets. If the author wrote consistently under a pseudonym, the pseudonym is listed in the author heading and the author's actual name is given in parenthesis on the first line of the biographical and critical information. Uncertain birth or death dates are indicated by question marks. Single-work entries are preceded by a heading that consists of the most common form of the title in English translation (if applicable) and the name of its author.

- The **Introduction** contains background information that introduces the reader to the author, work, or topic that is the subject of the entry.

- The list of **Principal Works** is ordered chronologically by date of first publication and lists the most important works by the author. The genre and publication date of each work is given. In the case of foreign authors whose works have been translated into English, the English-language version of the title follows in brackets. Unless otherwise indicated, dramas are dated by first performance, not first publication. Lists of **Representative Works** by different authors appear with topic entries.

- Reprinted **Criticism** is arranged chronologically in each entry to provide a useful perspective on changes in critical evaluation over time. The critic's name and the date of composition or publication of the critical work are given at the beginning of each piece of criticism. Unsigned criticism is preceded by the title of the source in which it originally appeared. All titles by the author featured in the text are printed in boldface type. Footnotes are reprinted at the end of each essay or excerpt. In the case of excerpted criticism, only those footnotes that pertain to the excerpted texts are included. Criticism in topic entries is arranged chronologically under a variety of subheadings to facilitate the study of different aspects of the topic.

- A complete **Bibliographical Citation** of the original essay or book precedes each piece of criticism. Source citations in the Literary Criticism Series follow University of Chicago Press style, as outlined in *The Chicago Manual of Style,* 15th ed. (Chicago: The University of Chicago Press, 2003).

- Critical essays are prefaced by brief **Annotations** explicating each piece.

- An annotated bibliography of **Further Reading** appears at the end of each entry and suggests resources for additional study. In some cases, significant essays for which the editors could not obtain reprint rights are included here. Boxed material following the further reading list provides references to other biographical and critical sources on the author in series published by Gale.

Indexes

A **Cumulative Author Index** lists all of the authors that appear in a wide variety of reference sources published by Gale, including *TCLC*. A complete list of these sources is found facing the first page of the Author Index. The index also includes birth and death dates and cross references between pseudonyms and actual names.

A **Cumulative Topic Index** lists the literary themes and topics treated in *TCLC* as well as other Literature Criticism series.

A **Cumulative Nationality Index** lists all authors featured in *TCLC* by nationality, followed by the numbers of the *TCLC* volumes in which their entries appear.

An alphabetical **Title Index** accompanies each volume of *TCLC*. Listings of titles by authors covered in the given volume are followed by the author's name and the corresponding page numbers where the titles are discussed. English translations of foreign titles and variations of titles are cross-referenced to the title under which a work was originally published. Titles of novels, dramas, nonfiction books, and poetry, short story, or essay collections are printed in italics, while individual poems, short stories, and essays are printed in roman type within quotation marks.

In response to numerous suggestions from librarians, Gale also produces a paperbound edition of the *TCLC* cumulative title index. This annual cumulation, which alphabetically lists all titles reviewed in the series, is available to all customers. Additional copies of this index are available upon request. Librarians and patrons will welcome this separate index; it saves shelf space, is easy to use, and is recyclable upon receipt of the next edition.

Citing *Twentieth-Century Literary Criticism*

When citing criticism reprinted in the Literary Criticism Series, students should provide complete bibliographic information so that the cited essay can be located in the original print or electronic source. Students who quote directly from reprinted criticism may use any accepted bibliographic format, such as University of Chicago Press style or Modern Language Association (MLA) style. Both the MLA and the University of Chicago formats are acceptable and recognized as being the current standards for citations. It is important, however, to choose one format for all citations; do not mix the two formats within a list of citations.

The examples below follow recommendations for preparing a bibliography set forth in *The Chicago Manual of Style,* 15th ed. (Chicago: The University of Chicago Press, (2003); the first example pertains to material drawn from periodicals, the second to material reprinted from books:

Cardone, Resha. "Reappearing Acts: Effigies and the Resurrection of Chilean Collective Memory in Marco Antonio de la Parra's *La tierra insomne o La puta madre.*" *Hispania* 88, no. 2 (May 2005): 284-93. Reprinted in *Twentieth-Century Literary Criticism.* Vol. 206, edited by Thomas J. Schoenberg and Lawrence J. Trudeau, 356-65. Detroit: Gale, 2008.

Kuester, Martin. "Myth and Postmodernist Turn in Canadian Short Fiction: Sheila Watson, 'Antigone' (1959)." In *The Canadian Short Story: Interpretations,* edited by Reginald M. Nischik, pp. 163-74. Rochester, N.Y.: Camden House, 2007. Reprinted in *Twentieth-Century Literary Criticism.* Vol. 206, edited by Thomas J. Schoenberg and Lawrence J. Trudeau, 227-32. Detroit: Gale, 2008. The examples below follow recommendations for preparing a works cited list set forth in the Modern Language Association of America's MLA Handbook for Writers of Research Papers, 7th ed. (New York: MLA, 2009. Print); the first example pertains to material drawn from periodicals, the second to material reprinted from books:

Cardone, Resha. "Reappearing Acts: Effigies and the Resurrection of Chilean Collective Memory in Marco Antonio de la Parra's *La tierra insomne o La puta madre.*" *Hispania* 88.2 (May 2005): 284-93. Rpt. in *Twentieth-Century Literary Criticism.* Eds. Thomas J. Schoenberg and Lawrence J. Trudeau. Vol. 206. Detroit: Gale, 2008. 356-65. Print.

Kuester, Martin. "Myth and Postmodernist Turn in Canadian Short Fiction: Sheila Watson, 'Antigone' (1959)." *The Canadian Short Story: Interpretations.* Ed. Reginald M. Nischik. Rochester, N.Y.: Camden House, 2007. 163-74. Rpt. in *Twentieth-Century Literary Criticism.* Eds. Thomas J. Schoenberg and Lawrence J. Trudeau. Vol. 206. Detroit: Gale, 2008. 227-32. Print.

Suggestions are Welcome

Readers who wish to suggest new features, topics, or authors to appear in future volumes, or who have other suggestions or comments are cordially invited to call, write, or fax the Product Manager:

Product Manager, Literary Criticism Series

Gale

27500 Drake Road

Farmington Hills, MI 48331-3535

1-800-347-4253 (GALE)

Fax: 248-699-8884

Acknowledgments

The editors wish to thank the copyright holders of the criticism included in this volume and the permissions managers of many book and magazine publishing companies for assisting us in securing reproduction rights. Following is a list of the copyright holders who have granted us permission to reproduce material in this volume of *TCLC*. Every effort has been made to trace copyright, but if omissions have been made, please let us know.

COPYRIGHTED MATERIAL IN *TCLC*, VOLUME 249, WAS REPRODUCED FROM THE FOLLOWING PERIODICALS:

American Indian Culture and Research Journal, v. 19, no. 1, 1995. Copyright © 1995 Regents of the University of California. Reproduced by permission of the American Indian Studies Center, UCLA.—*Ariel,* v. 5, July, 1974 for "James K. Baxter: In Quest of the Just City" by Charles Doyle. Copyright © 1974 The Board of Governors, The University of Calgary. Reproduced by permission of the publisher and the author. *James K. Baxter* (Twayne's World Authors, 1976).]—*Colloquia Germanica,* v. 21, 1988 for "Uses and Misuses of Language: Uwe Johnson's 'Ingrid Babendererde' as a GDR Novel" by Robert K. Shirer. Copyright © A. Francke AG Verlag Bern, 1988. Reproduced by permission of the author.—*Germanic Notes,* v. 18, 1987. Copyright © 1987 *Germanic Notes.* Reproduced by permission.—*The Germanic Review,* v. 64, winter, 1989 for "History in Uwe Johnson's 'Jahrestage' " by Sara Lennox. Reproduced by permission of Taylor & Francis Group, LLC, http://www.taylorandfrancis.com.—*Journal of New Zealand Literature,* v. 23, 2005. Copyright © 2005 University of Waikato. Reproduced by permission.—*ka mate ka ora,* v. 8, September, 2009 for "Baxter's Burns" by Dougal McNeill. Reproduced by permission of the author.—*Seminar,* v. 10, May, 1974. Copyright © 1974 The Canadian Association of University Teachers of German. Reproduced by permission.—*South Atlantic Bulletin,* v. 33, November, 1968. Copyright © 1968 by the South Atlantic Modern Language Association. Reproduced by permission.—*Southwest Review,* v. 68, autumn, 1983. Copyright © 1983 Southern Methodist University. All rights reserved. Reproduced by permission.—*Studies in Short Fiction,* v. 36, fall, 1999. Copyright © 1999 by *Studies in Short Fiction.* Reproduced by permission.—*Studies in the Novel,* v. 30, spring, 1998. Copyright © 1998 by the University of North Texas. Reproduced by permission.—*The Virginia Quarterly Review,* v. 13, spring, 1937. Copyright © 1937, by *The Virginia Quarterly Review,* The University of Virginia. Reproduced by permission of the publisher.—*Western American Literature,* v. 27, spring, 1992. Copyright © 1992 by The Western Literature Association. Reproduced by permission.—*World Literature Written in English,* v. 22, autumn, 1983. Copyright © 1983 *World Literature Written in English.* Reproduced by permission.

COPYRIGHTED MATERIAL IN *TCLC*, VOLUME 249, WAS REPRODUCED FROM THE FOLLOWING BOOKS:

Baker, Gary L. From *Understanding Uwe Johnson.* University of South Carolina Press, 1999. Copyright © 1999 University of South Carolina. Reproduced by permission.—Bond, D. G.. From *German History and German Identity: Uwe Johnson's* **Jahrestage.** Rodopi, 1993. Copyright © Editions Rodopi B.V., Amsterdam 1993. Reproduced by permission.—Boulby, Mark. From *Uwe Johnson.* Frederick Ungar Publishing Co., 1974. Copyright © 1974 by Frederick Ungar Publishing Co., Inc. Reproduced by permission of The Continuum International Publishing Group.—Carew-Miller, Anna. From "Mary Austin's Nature: Refiguring Tradition through the Voices of Identity," in *Reading the Earth: New Directions in the Study of Literature and Environment.* Edited by Michael P. Branch, Rochelle Johnson, Daniel Patterson, and Scott Slovic. University of Idaho Press, 1998. Copyright © 1998 by the University of Idaho Press. Reproduced by permission.—Harrison, Elizabeth Jane. From "Zora Neale Hurston and Mary Hunter Austin's Ethnographic Fiction: New Modernist Narratives," in *Unmanning Modernism: Gendered Re-Readings.* Edited by Elizabeth Jane Harrison and Shirley Peterson. The University of Tennessee Press, 1997. Copyright © 1997 by The University of Tennessee Press. Reproduced by permission of The University of Tennessee Press.—Hirsch, Marianne. From *Beyond the Single Vision: Henry James, Michel Butor, Uwe Johnson.* French Literature Publications Company, 1981. Copyright 1981 French Literature Publications Company. Reproduced by permission.—Hoyer, Mark T. From *Dancing Ghosts: Native American and Christian Syncretism in Mary Austin's Work.* Copyright © 1998 by University of Nevada Press. All rights reserved. Reprinted with the permission of the University of Nevada Press.—Karell, Linda K. From "Lost Borders and Blurred Boundaries: Mary Austin as Storyteller," in *American Women Short Story Writers: A Collection of Critical Essays.* Edited by Julie Brown. Garland Publishing, Inc., 1995. Copyright © 1995 Julie Brown. All rights reserved. Reproduced by permission of Routledge/Taylor & Francis Books, Inc., and the author.—Klimasmith, Betsy. From "'I Have Seen America Emerging': Mary Austin's Regionalism," in

Gale Literature Product Advisory Board

The members of the Gale Literature Product Advisory Board—reference librarians from public and academic library systems—represent a cross-section of our customer base and offer a variety of informed perspectives on both the presentation and content of our literature products. Advisory board members assess and define such quality issues as the relevance, currency, and usefulness of the author coverage, critical content, and literary topics included in our series; evaluate the layout, presentation, and general quality of our printed volumes; provide feedback on the criteria used for selecting authors and topics covered in our series; provide suggestions for potential enhancements to our series; identify any gaps in our coverage of authors or literary topics, recommending authors or topics for inclusion; analyze the appropriateness of our content and presentation for various user audiences, such as high school students, undergraduates, graduate students, librarians, and educators; and offer feedback on any proposed changes/enhancements to our series. We wish to thank the following advisors for their advice throughout the year.

Mary Austin
1868-1934

(Full name Mary Hunter Austin; also wrote under pseudonym Gordon Stairs) American nature writer, novelist, short story writer, autobiographer, playwright, essayist, critic, poet, and translator.

The following entry provides an overview of Austin's life and works. For additional information on her career, see *TCLC*, Volume 25.

INTRODUCTION

Mary Austin is an early twentieth-century American author, remembered for her portrayal of the landscape and culture of the American southwest. A nature writer in the tradition of Henry David Thoreau, Austin is best known for her first book, *The Land of Little Rain* (1903), a collection of sketches depicting the southern California desert. In this and other works, the author eschewed the longstanding tradition of romanticizing the land, particularly the desert, instead evoking the grandeur, vitality, and indifference of the southwest landscape in elaborate detail. While the influence of the environment on the character and fate of humankind is a predominant theme in her writings, Austin explored a variety of subjects, including the artist's struggle to express reality, the confines of prescribed gender roles, and folkloric and religious traditions, as well as differences between Native American and Euro-American cultures. A well respected and popular figure of her era, Austin suffered significant critical neglect for several decades after her death. Among her admirers, she is appreciated for her innovations in numerous genres, as well as her contributions to feminism, modernism, regionalism, and Native American studies. Writing in 1983, James Ruppert asserted that Austin was "foremost among the writers concerned" with "a revitalization of the arts through a return to American materials," noting that during her forty years as an author and scholar, "she was continuously involved with American Indian culture and literature, the southwestern environment, and the insights to be garnered from cultural and environmental interface."

BIOGRAPHICAL INFORMATION

Austin was born September 9, 1868, in Carlinville, Illinois, to Susanna Savilla and Captain George Hunter, a lawyer and town magistrate, who had served with distinction in the American Civil War. In her youth, she was an avid reader and began composing poetry at a young age. When Austin was ten, her father and younger sister both died, and she was left in the care of her mother, with whom she had a strained relationship. Several years later, the author attended Blackburn College, where she studied mathematics and science, and graduated in 1888. After completing her studies, Austin moved to California, where her brother had relocated in search of better opportunities. She and her mother set up a homestead near Fort Tejon, and although the venture failed financially, it provided Austin with her first introduction to the western landscape and culture that would dominate her later writings. In California, Austin began teaching and met Wallace Stafford Austin, whom she married in 1891. The couple settled in Owens Valley but suffered numerous financial setbacks and incurred significant debt, which Austin struggled to pay off through various teaching appointments. In 1899, the author taught at the Normal School, later known as the University of California at Los Angeles, and returned to Owens Valley after a year. During this time, Austin also began to gather material and hone her writing skills. She sold several stories to *Overland Monthly* and joined a circle of writers around Charles Lummis and his magazine, *Land of Sunshine*. In 1900, the *Atlantic Monthly* began publishing her western-inspired material, and in 1903 her first book, *The Land of Little Rain,* was published.

The first decade of the 1900s was a productive and happy period for Austin. While researching material for her first novel, *Isidro* (1905), the author became involved with a colony of writers in the village of Carmel, which included novelist Jack London and poet George Sterling. During this time, she composed another collection of sketches, *The Flock* (1906), as well as a second novel, *Santa Lucia* (1908). After being diagnosed with terminal cancer, Austin left Carmel for Italy but made a remarkable recovery, which she attributed to prayer. In 1909, she traveled to England and met several important writers, including H. G. Wells, George Bernard Shaw, and Joseph Conrad. In 1910, Austin traveled back to the United States for the New York production of her play *The Arrow-Maker* (1911). Over the next thirteen years, the author divided her time between New York and Carmel and produced several more novels, including *A Woman of Genius* (1912), *The Lovely Lady* (1913), and *The Ford* (1917). She also worked for feminist causes and various war projects, and even returned to England to lecture before the Fabian Society. Her marriage to Wallace Austin, which had suffered for several years, was dissolved in 1914. After a visit to New Mexico in 1918, Austin was drawn to the southwest, and during the 1920s she settled permanently in Santa Fe, where she lived for the rest of her life. This region inspired several later works, including a book of sketches, *The Land of Journeys' Ending* (1924), and another novel, *Starry Adventure* (1931). In 1932, the author produced her last major work, an autobiography, titled *Earth Horizon.* That same year, she was diagnosed with coronary disease. Austin died on August 13, 1934, in Santa Fe, after suffering a brain hemorrhage.

MAJOR WORKS

Among Austin's most recognized writings are her autobiography and her stories and sketches depicting California and the American southwest. Her first major work, *The Land of Little Rain,* is now considered a classic text in the field of American nature writing. The work is comprised of fourteen sketches, which detail the author's observations as she journeys through the Tejon and Bakersfield region, Owens Valley, and the Mojave Desert. In these pieces, Austin highlights the various cultures that populate the land, including European, Hispanic, and Native American communities, but the primary focus of the work is the effect of the land on the people, flora, and fauna that populate it, particularly the ways in which it draws out qualities of hardiness, frugality, and adaptability. One of the best-known chapters from the work, "The Basket Maker," features a Paiute Indian woman named Seyavi, an independent female artist who struggles to maintain her values and aesthetic integrity as she interacts with people of disparate cultures. Austin's later work, *The Land of Journeys' Ending,* was inspired by the western landscape of New Mexico and Arizona. Similar in structure to *The Land of Little Rain,* the volume relates the author's observations of the natural and cultural life of the southwest, and more fully explores the relationship between humanity and the land. The cactus is an important image in the collection, providing the ultimate example of adaptation and survival in the arid desert environment. In addition to ruminations on the natural world, Austin also explores differences between Native American and European cultures. Utilizing imagery from the Tewa rainmaking ceremony, the author describes the individualistic orientation of European Americans, in contrast to the communal consciousness that distinguishes Native American society. The power of the land is another important theme in the work, particularly in relation to the individual, whose patterns of thought and actions are effected by nature's rhythms, topography, and

seasons. In her last major work, *Earth Horizon,* Austin defies traditional conventions of the autobiographical form to recount her life. Focusing on her youth and early years as a writer, the author creates three distinct voices to depict different aspects of her identity: Mary Austin the author; "I-Mary," a mystical and independent self; and "Mary-by-herself," a vulnerable personality that seeks the approval of others. As the work progresses, the voices converge and interact with figures from Austin's past, including writers, intellectuals, artists, Native Americans, and Hispanic settlers, as well as voices that originate from the land itself. In *Earth Horizon,* the author identifies several primary forces in her life, most notably writing, mysticism, an awareness of the natural world, and appreciation for folk experience and patterns of life.

Although not as well known as her other writings, Austin also produced significant works of fiction. Her first novel, *Isidro,* is a romantic tale depicting the mission days of California. The novel centers on several characters, including a *haciendado*'s son on a quest to join the Franciscans at Carmel and a missing heiress, who poses as a boy, as well as a villainous character who ultimately redeems himself by sacrificing his life for others. Although noted for its formal construction, the novel has been particularly praised for its evocation of the pristine California landscape and insightful portrayal of the tension between the ordered structure of the mission and the freedoms of Native American life. In *Lost Borders* (1909), a collection of short fiction, Austin returns to the themes of *The Land of Little Rain,* particularly focusing on the ways in which the land shapes the character and destiny of its human inhabitants. In this collection, she also explores themes related to relationships, such as motherhood and marriage, and portrays the desert as a powerful, primal, and mysterious maternal presence. Considered one of Austin's best novels, *A Woman of Genius* borrows themes and circumstances from the author's life in its exploration of protagonist Olivia Lattimore's struggle to become an actress. Throughout her life, Olivia is faced with restrictive gender expectations, which conflict with her desire to pursue an artistic career. Despite the disapproval of her mother, friends, and romantic interests, however, Olivia chooses to follow her own path. Published posthumously in 1988, *Cactus Thorn* is a novella that explores themes similar to those presented in *A Woman of Genius,* including restrictive gender roles and the difficulties of heterosexual relationships. In this work, protagonist Dulcie Adelaid is a young vibrant woman from California, whose emotional honesty and passion are directly linked to the mystic power of the desert. Dulcie is betrayed by her lover, Grant Arliss, a politician from New York, who ultimately succumbs to his own hypocrisy and cowardice.

CRITICAL RECEPTION

Austin first began to win recognition in the 1890s and early 1900s, when popular magazines such as *Overland Monthly* and the *Atlantic Monthly* began publishing her stories and sketches inspired by the California desert. Her first major work, *The Land of Little Rain,* was enthusiastically received after its 1903 publication, establishing Austin as a significant new voice of American western literature. Over the next two decades, Austin wrote prolifically in several genres, gained notice with the publication of several novels, and forged connections with prominent literary figures in the United States and abroad. During this time, she also became increasingly involved with feminist causes and promoted herself as an authority on Native American culture. In 1932, Austin finally achieved the stature and acclaim she had sought throughout her career, with the publication of her autobiography, *Earth Horizon,* which was chosen as a Literary Guild selection. But after her death in 1934, her works gradually fell out of favor, and the author was largely forgotten except among scholars of western literature. For several decades, Austin was relegated to the margins of American literature and pejoratively labeled a regionalist writer.

After decades of neglect, Austin's writings once again garnered critical attention following the 1985 reissue of *A Woman of Genius.* With the rise of feminist scholarship during the 1980s and 1990s, the author gained a new following, particularly among critics interested in her treatment of gender issues and cultural themes. Commentators such as Faith Jaycox, Karen S. Langlois, Linda K. Karell, and Beverly A. Hume emphasized the feminist themes in Austin's writings, particularly "The Walking Woman," *A Woman of Genius,* and *Lost Borders.* While Jaycox focused on Austin's use of "Western conventions" in her effort to "give voice, deliberately and positively, to feminist issues," Hume described the author as an "ecofeminist" pioneer and noted the ways in which she exposed patriarchal power systems and explored the fundamental connection between nature and womanhood. Janis P. Stout, however, questioned the view that Austin was an unwavering feminist. Stout, writing in 1998, argued that the author's fiction reveals "uncertainties and tensions" regarding woman's role in society and show both "undeniable feminist strains" and "traces of ideas that might even be called counter-feminist." Other scholars, such as Langlois and Noreen Grover Lape, began reevaluating Austin's reputation as an authority on Native American cultures. In her 1995 essay, Langlois suggested that the author was more concerned with self-promotion than cultural scholarship, and that her understanding was "intuitive" rather than scientifically based. Lape also identified problematic aspects of Austin's portrayal of Native American society, claiming that while her efforts to reclaim these cultures threatened "their free agency,"

her work was nevertheless important to "the resurgence of Native American art and culture" in the United States. In more recent scholarship, critics have also emphasized the importance of environment in Austin's writings. Anne Raine, Carol E. Dickson, Betsy Klimasmith, Heike Schaefer, and Corey Lee Lewis, among others, have addressed several issues related to the author's representation of the American southwest, including the relationship between the land and its inhabitants, the challenges associated with using language to portray the natural landscape, and Austin's theories of regionalism. As a result of these and other studies, Austin is increasingly appreciated as an important and relevant figure in American literature, whose achievements as a naturalist and social commentator deserve further recognition. Heike Schaefer, writing in 2004, argued that "Austin went beyond the romantic conceptions of her predecessors," and that her "environmentalist awareness and sensitivity to social imbalances of power" enabled her "to contribute an innovative regionalist vision to American literary history."

PRINCIPAL WORKS

The Land of Little Rain (sketches) 1903
The Basket Woman (juvenilia) 1904
Isidro (novel) 1905
The Flock (sketches) 1906
Santa Lucia (novel) 1908
Lost Borders (short stories and sketches) 1909
Outland [as Gordon Stairs] (novel) 1910
The Arrow-Maker (play) 1911
Christ in Italy (essays) 1912
A Woman of Genius (novel) 1912
The Lovely Lady (novel) 1913
California: The Land of the Sun (sketches) 1914; also
    published as *The Lands of the Sun,* 1927
Love and the Soul Maker (novel) 1914
The Man Jesus (nonfiction) 1915; also published as *A
    Small Town Man,* 1925
The Man Who Didn't Believe in Christmas (play) 1916
The Ford (novel) 1917
No. 26 Jayne Street (novel) 1920
The American Rhythm (criticism and translations) 1923
The Land of Journeys' Ending (sketches) 1924
The Children Sing in the Far West (poetry) 1928
Experiences Facing Death (essays) 1931
Starry Adventure (novel) 1931
Earth Horizon (autobiography) 1932
Can Prayer Be Answered? (essays) 1934
One-Smoke Stories (short stories) 1934
Mother of Felipe, and Other Early Stories (short stories)
    1950

Cactus Thorn (novella) 1988
Beyond Borders (essays) 1996

CRITICISM

Dudley Wynn (essay date spring 1937)

SOURCE: Wynn, Dudley. "Mary Austin, Woman Alone." *The Virginia Quarterly Review* 13, no. 2 (spring 1937): 243-56.

[*In the following essay, Wynn emphasizes Austin's "Folk" philosophy and her mystical orientation to life, noting that despite the inconsistencies in her thought and writings, she remains an important cultural figure in America "for extending the range of our consciousness of our environment and our social possibilities."*]

"It was clear that I would write imaginatively, not only of people, but of the scene, the totality which is called Nature, and that I would give myself intransigently to the quality of experience called Folk, and to the frame of behavior known as Mystical." Thus Mary Austin wrote in the introduction to *Earth Horizon,* her autobiography, published two years before her death in 1934. The pattern of her life, she wrote, had been distinctly clear in her consciousness before she had lived the first third of a normally long life. From the moment she communicated with God under a walnut tree in the orchard in Carlinville, Illinois, when she was between five and six years old, there were intimations that she was to have an important destiny. The details were yet to be filled in, but the pattern was there. That destiny led to lonesome, rebellious, but profitable years in a California desert, to association with Pacific Coast radicals and poets such as Jack London and George Sterling, to some years of activity in the suffragist movement, to association with the Fabians, to a study of prayer-techniques in Italy, to a championing of the American Indian against "the folly of the officials," to years of studying and writing about the cultural resources of the Southwest, to a career as writer of novels, plays, poems, stories, and articles of great variety of subject and worth. If, throughout such amazing activity as the cyclopedic account indicates, she went unhurriedly and reflectively, it was perhaps because of the pattern. Knowing so clearly what she had to do, and wanting to do so little else, she achieved unity in her life. This is not to say that her ideas were always consistent. The unity is in the method of approach more than in the results reached.

Throughout the thirty or more books and fifty or more articles in periodicals, there runs an intense moralizing and an eager search. She was a born pragmatist and radical, she said, never believing anything that was told her but always wishing to bring belief into line with innate moral sense. She rebelled against the Methodist Church, and spent the rest of her life seeking, out of experience, an answer to the religious problem. She rebelled against the status of woman in the 'eighties and 'nineties, and never rested until she had worked out her own naturalistic and empirical defense of women's rights. She rebelled against the bleakness of life in America, and was never content until she found roots for a more expressive American life. Her approach to every problem was a double one. First there was plain introspection to discover what seemed most right and most life-giving. Then there was a testing of all in the light of what primitive, well-adapted peoples had to show. "The frame of behavior known as Mystical" and "the quality of experience called Folk" are nearly always inextricable; they work together to some fruitful conclusions. They also account for whatever is called Rousseauistic, primitive, absurdly mystical, and inaccurate in Mary Austin's thought. Despite all her learning in some fields, she was always an amateur, the pioneer who believes nothing, hardly knows where to go to find out, and finally has to discover everything unaided, by looking deeply within and observantly around. That is why all her ideas seemed, to her, so original, and still seem, to her devoted readers, so powerful.

A radical in an Illinois town in the 'eighties was a lonesome person. *Earth Horizon* and *A Woman of Genius* are evidence of it. Her own family was frightened by her disrupting insights. In the small settlements of the California desert and mining regions, a woman who wanted independence, who wanted to be judged by her intrinsic worth and not by what she could make some man feel, and who wished that life might give outlet for play and for impulses to self-expression—such a woman was strange and misunderstood. There was no one for her to talk to but herself. Some stories clearly autobiographical, such as **"Frustrate,"** other stories in *Lost Borders,* the novel *Santa Lucia,* and *Earth Horizon* all attest this. In the eastern metropolis, a woman who stood up and told the critical cliques that they were woefully ignorant of America, who told economic radicals that their radicalism and most of their morality were "topsy-turvy," was tolerated but misunderstood. When she said that New York re-discovered her about every seven years, she should have said that New York was only made aware of her every seven years. She saw to that herself. She was never at home there, except possibly in one brief period when she was a problem-solver and could enjoy the stir that New York was making in introducing a little realism into the discussion of American life. Even in Santa Fe, she was suspect, because she was often erratic, irascible, and egotistical. "Woman Alone" she called herself.

One does not need any fancy psychology to see that her aloneness was a great impulsion toward the Folk. She wanted to belong, to be one of a race, to have a home, to express herself and be understood. But she was not at home in the America which emphasized a repressive morality, worshiped bigness, and divorced its living from its way of getting a living. She could find her cultural home among the Folk, who were still immune to the evils of the dominant American culture and whose qualities pointed a way for the whole American future. Sometimes, indeed, she could not wait upon that future; her aloneness drove her to see the dominant American way itself as a folk way. For example, she once saw in the 1926-1929 era a fine cultural movement led by "Sat-EvePost" and men with a good "medicine for Things." Usually, however, she saw that she would have to wait, and she spurned the dominant American way and looked to the Folk for a future. Mary Austin's ideas about the Folk and their possibilities are very complex, but they will reveal a very representative Mary Austin. "Folkness" was central in her method of thinking, and led to all her regional activities and whatever regional philosophy she had.

From the time of some of her earliest works, **"The Land of Little Rain"** and *The Flock,* a great part of Mary Austin's power lay in a sense of what people gain from a complete adjustment to the land they live upon. The desert Indians and sheepherders in the high pastures of the Sierras had taken a fresh start in the land, had integrated morality, religion, and economics into a pattern that was wise because it was naturally adapted to the physical environment. Before the California days, as a girl of fourteen, Mary Austin felt that the American community, as she knew it in the Middle West, lacked this wise adjustment. She tells of first going to the house which her mother had built, shining and new, and of being "struck with a cold blast of what she [Mary Austin] was to recognize long after as the wind before the dawn of the dreary discontent with the American scene, which has since been made familiar to us all by the present generation of writers in the Middle West." When she turns from primitives to a representative Anglo community on the California frontier, she has her heroine, Serena Lindley of *Santa Lucia,* feel the lack of co-ordination in her life, the gap between the means to life and the living, which lets in boredom and the sense of frustration and rootlessness. By contrast, Dr. Caldwell, who has been in this land thirty-five years, finds contentment in the ramshackle old house where living has gone on. Dr. Caldwell exacts a promise from his prospective son-in-law that the old place will be kept and children brought up there. "'. . . it is my belief that here in the West, perhaps in all America, we do not take enough account of the power of our inanimate surroundings to take on the spiritual quality of the life that is lived in them, and give it off again like an exhalation, and not pains enough when we have made such a place,

to preserve it for those who come after from generation to generation. . . .'" It is no wonder that when, some ten or more years later, such members of the eastern "radical-intellectual" group as Waldo Frank and Van Wyck Brooks rode through the Middle West and reported that America was a land of shacks which appeared never to have been lived in, Mrs. Austin's scorn was derisive. She had beaten them to the observation, made it from the inside, with pity and tolerance, and with something to offer besides more and more rootlessness.

Criticism of American rootlessness is implied in almost everything Mary Austin wrote. A folk-like adaptation to the new land is the cure that is offered. A philosophy of Folk-ness develops by the time she is settled into the life at Santa Fe, but it does not appear explicitly in her books so much as in periodical writings. Originally, she says, the term "Folk" included all of us; recently it has come to mean "those minority groups whose social expression is the measure of their rootage in a given environment . . . people whose culture is wholly derived from their reactions to the scene that encloses, taking nothing from extra-tribal sources except as these forcibly constitute themselves factors of that scene." "To be shaped in mind and social reaction, and to some extent in character, and so finally in expression, by one given environment, that is to be Folk." The Folk have a sounder, better-rounded view of their group destiny than world-aware sophisticates have. Indeed, she continues, the lack of receptivity to the multiple influences that flow through the world is the mark of Folk-ness. Both the founders of the Republic, following the egalitarian ideal, and their successors, with their public schools and newspapers, failed to take proper account of this quality. Isolation from the main stream of world thought and world influences, an impenetrability and obtuseness, and a natural adaptation to the physical environment, are the requisites of Folk-ness. Two groups in America, she says, have had these conditions in perfection, the Anglos of the Appalachian highlands, and the Spanish-speaking peoples of the Southwest. The former have given us a poetic style in balladry and dialogue which reveals "touches of splayed Elizabethan rugosity," its imagery displaying "an immortal freshness." The latter, having taken over the Indian food-crop, the architecture, and the whole economic complex of Indian life, developed in their folk-product "an objective superiority" based on pictorial and plastic elements.

Naturally, one who insisted so constantly and so volubly upon the worth of the indigenous and well-established folk groups in the Southwest had to meet the charge of escapism, even of sheer mystical nonsense. Out of desperation and disgust with the obtuseness of many critics, Mary Austin's final plea was on a basis of utility. The poetry of the Indian is not for our imitation; it is simply an indigenous object lesson, an example of how a true poetry reflects the landscape line and the native rhythms, and how its suggestive power is greater when it grows out of the integrated experience of a people. It should be collected, translated, explained, studied, and the way of life that produced it kept as nearly intact as possible. On this last point, Mrs. Austin was a fighter. Stupid officials, officious missionaries, and an indifferent public were targets of her wrath; loud progressivists who assumed that the dominant Anglo culture was superior in every way to the Amerind were victims of her most ironic thrusts. Of all folk groups in America, the Indian was the one which most needed to be encouraged in keeping its integrity, for the simple reason that the Indian would suffer most and profit least from being dissolved into the huge current of the usual American life. She could admit, however, that the Indian's tribal life was breaking up, his arts of dance and decoration dying (at least until resurrected by sympathetic groups of artists in the Southwest), his ceremonies and religion becoming meaningless conventions and formalities even to many Indians. This is the point at which her common sense came in. She bowed to nobody in respect for Indian culture and in comprehension of the wholeness and beauty of the Indian way of life, but she could nevertheless see that the concrete pattern of Indian life would ultimately be broken, the religious and esoteric meanings of the poetry, decorative design, and dance-drama lost. That was why, she felt, the Indian must be encouraged in his arts before all was lost. Let the forms continue, since they still existed, so that Indian life might make the contribution to an indigenous American culture that it was, to her notion, destined to make.

Despite the fact that Mrs. Austin's later years were greatly devoted to the arts and the folk-lore of the Spanish-speaking people of the Southwest, the Indian was central in her thoughts. She hailed the political changes in Mexico, beginning in 1921, as evidence that Mexico was awakening to her fundamental Indian heritage, one of intense communal and artistic instincts, overlaid too long with the Conquerors' culture. As long as her attention was directed specifically toward Mexico, she saw the Indian as the basis of a new Western culture, taking in both North and South America. The "wantlessness," the innate community sense and artistic sense, the incorrigible Folk-ness (both in the sense of "environmental rootage" and "limited range of social perception") of Spanish-Americans in New Mexico, she attributed chiefly to their Indian heritage. She recorded with glee the way in which the villagers in Mexico, as soon as the revolution had given them opportunity, seized again the *ejidos,* originally communally-owned strips of land. This was evidence, she thought, of their clinging to a pattern of social life older than the Spanish conquest. It was a folk manifestation, the resurgence of a loyalty that had lived, sub-

merged, through generation after generation. To Mexico and south she looked for the re-establishment on the American continent of the basic patterns of American life—not a state socialism, but an informal, spontaneous, small-scale communism enhancing Folk-ness. At one time, the best plea she could make for the revival and encouragement of Indian arts in the Southwestern United States was that the Indian pueblos and the villages of New Mexico could help Mexicans to find their way more directly to the old Indian patterns which, strangely, had been more broken up in Mexico than in New Mexico.

A rejuvenated Mexico was, for a time at least, the symbol which co-ordinated Mary Austin's enthusiasms. But she never let enthusiasm for exotic Folk-ness carry her away from considerations of how Folk-ness was to operate among her own kind. True, after talking with Diego Rivera in Mexico, she came away feeling that his painting "came forth with charm such as is missed by Nordics." "It was a relief to me," she wrote, "to discover that there was no Nordic taint in Diego Rivera." This may mean, in its full context, that she was glad to find her intuitions about the American rhythm and pattern corroborated by one of a different race. More likely, it means that she was sick of Nordic progressiveness, maladjustment, and assertiveness. Nevertheless, Mary Austin was a pioneer American, of Anglo and Nordic stock. Folk-ness was not an exotic means of entertainment to her; it was a way of looking at and interpreting the life of the United States. If Mexico as a symbol most completely co-ordinated her enthusiasms and seemed to be the completest fulfillment of her prophecies, the next best symbol was the aridity of the Southwestern United States and the need there for irrigation. The Colorado River controversy focused her attention upon this physical fact and its implications.

The controversy was long and involved, as battles over water rights always have been. It began when Boulder Dam was projected, and it involved the seven states that had territory in the watershed of the Colorado River and its tributaries. It resulted in a fight between California and Arizona. California wanted half the water, although she could supply little to the drainage into the proposed reservoir, and wanted it because she could prove she needed it *now,* to supply electric power to Los Angeles and water to valleys lying hundreds of miles from the dam. Arizona wanted a good proportion of the water held for the other less populous states, with a view to their future development. For Mary Austin, it became a fight hazarding everything she held dear. It was the California cult of bigness, based on a short-sighted cultural and economic view, against her own idea of regional autonomy. She envisaged hundreds of small communities in valleys along the whole Colorado course. Isolated, well-integrated, having the fundamental Southwestern communal pattern enforced by the sharing of water-rights, these communities would be the focal points of the new American social pattern: industrialism on a small scale, community-mindedness, integration of the economic pattern with the physical background, a spontaneous, folk-like development of the capacities necessary to the functioning of such communities. For one of the greatest evils in American life, as she saw it, was that such hordes of people "benefit by, without understanding, the mechanistic basis of modern society." "The proportion of any community which has only a button-pushing, spigot-turning acquaintance with its material advantages, is the measure of that community's cultural inertia." Small communities scattered throughout the Colorado basin would keep the population "on the stretch," would call out "invention and foresight, *among the people.*"

Mary Austin took an active part in the struggle, wrote articles, attended the seven-states conference as representative of New Mexico. She was aware that her views seemed poetic and impractical to economists, legislators, and business men; that California was not practising any economic atrocity, but a good economics, widely approved. What she was fighting for was the cultural future; her opponents, for the economic present. Mrs. Austin's point was lost sight of in the final settlement. But the fight co-ordinated her views. All her writing at the time of the controversy and immediately afterwards reveals that the following implications of her regionalism, heretofore somewhat diffused, were brought together: her definition of culture; her belief that the Southwest was to be, or had the proper conditions for being, the seat of the world's next great culture; the belief that the dominant Anglo culture, progressive and mechanistic, would be great only by the infusion of traits from a more poetic, leisure-loving, artistic, and religious-minded people; her advocacy of an essentially rural, spontaneous communism over against an urban-industrial state socialism. And one might hazard the speculation that the set-back her ideas received in this affair, their first practical test, was a great impetus towards her enthusiasm later for Mexico, where she was able to see in Diego Rivera and certain social movements in Mexico the village Folk-ness and communalism she admired. A practical set-back, of course, was for her only a delay, not a defeat. She turned, in the last years of her life, from an all-inclusive speculation about regionalism to finding out all she could about Indian and Spanish-American Folk-ness; from prophecy, to put it roughly, to collecting. And, of course, to "the frame of behavior known as Mystical," explicitly.

Mrs. Austin's views, however, are not often so well co-ordinated as when she was thinking about the future of the Southwest in relation to the development of water resources, or about Mexico. There are contradictions and confusions in her thinking. Folk-ness happens to lead on occasion to a regional philosophy, but Folk-

ness, as a method of approach, a way of prophesying through intuition, often leads to concepts that do not readily fit together. The native communism of the Mexican village which she once discovered as the very pattern of the indigenous American life and the hope of the future, is in another place thought to bring in the "menace of cultural arrest through the perfection of economic adjustment." Aboriginal communalism, whether in Mexico or in the pueblos of New Mexico, is traced from security to complacency to inertia to desuetude. The economic pattern forced a like rigidity on the whole cultural complex, which made the Indian incapable of coping with more individualistic peoples. Of course, Mrs. Austin was dealing in well-known anthropological fact; nevertheless, there is inconsistency between this view and the later enthusiasm for the Mexican pattern; also between this and the usual implication that the beauty of the folk way of life is in stability and resistance to change.

The greatest paradox of all perhaps lies in her wavering attitude towards "Big Business"—what other regionalists call finance-capitalism. Mary Austin usually found the dominant mores of American society, built around ideas of progress and rapid expansion and supported by the finance-capitalist régime, the enemy of all she had fought for. And yet we find her in 1920 writing that Mr. Herbert Hoover was a man "in travail with an idea," feeling his way toward a deeper, more intuitive prepossession of the American people, the idea that "self-government means the release of the personal drive: liberty to perfect the technique of action. . . . Law-making and policing are relatively futile in the presence of working power." And late in 1928 she wrote that she had found "the thing worth waiting for." Eighteen years among Indians, and more years of study tracing social institutions from the Stone Age to the present, had revealed that all radicalism was wrong. She had discovered the "inescapable tendency of Things to accumulate about certain types of personality." The discovery was contemporaneous with her finding The Saturday Evening Post America's great folk voice; it helped her "return to the high-priesthood of man's economic conquest of the earth," to see "the spiritualization of business." Spirituality for business men was a "specialized type of energy, working from within," a subconscious mastery of business, a good "medicine for Things." Accordingly, the solution for economic maladjustment was to take all the chains off and let Mr. Ford, Mr. Hoover, and their type exercise their medicine. Not to divide the heap but to increase it, everybody getting a larger share and admitting the rights of the leaders, the "good medicine" men, to inordinately large shares. It was, to her, a new spiritual insight for America. Today it sounds like Mr. Walter Lippmann's "benevolent capitalism," and one suspects that Mrs. Austin only gave anthropological and mystical support to a none-too-original idea. Folk-ness as a method, that is, exercise of the prophetess's and witch-woman's function, led to what is almost a betrayal of the Folk, even if "Folk" is taken to mean the dominant horde which had just voted for prosperity. If "Folk" is taken to mean those submerged minorities which cling desperately to non-progressive ways, there is decidedly a betrayal. The paradox can be explained only by saying that "Woman Alone" could not resist the temptation for once to get on the bandwagon. She failed to see that in modern society the men with "medicine for Things," the producers, the small merchants, the technologists, are not necessarily the ones to whom Things gravitate. Between the more abundant production of things and the methods of modern finance-capitalism is a gap that Mrs. Austin's primitives probably did not have to contend with. Of course, she was right in seeing, in 1928, that solutions offered by "topsy-turvy radicalism" were inimical to the American temperament; but she was absurd in calling this a new folk insight, the spiritualization of a national impulse.

There are other paradoxes. A regionalist whose philosophy was to a great extent founded upon primitivism and an advocacy of the "limited range of the social perceptions" of the Folk, would not be expected to be a worker in progressivist causes, clamoring for more popularizations of science and history and journalistic re-writes of Freud and Jung, clamoring for woman suffrage, telling federated women's clubs that they represented a new and valuable stirring of the American consciousness, excoriating American small-townness, advocating a court for domestic relations in terms that called out the satire of even her friends the Fabians, and generally conducting herself like either a metropolitan rationalist trying to bring enlightenment to the provinces, or an American business man believing that culture can be bought. Not that a regionalist is expected to be pure primitivist and against everything that world-aware sophisticates stand for. But in the light of her pronouncements on the impenetrability of the Folk, her tirades against intellectuals, and her challenge to the cult of Bigness, all her progressivist activities and ideas are inconsistent, to say the least.

Some of the inconsistencies can be explained away by chronology. On the whole, Mary Austin evolved from a progressivist, a radical, an intellectual problem-solver, to a regionalist whose faith was in the Folk; from a general desire to save America by lecturing at it, to an obsession that it had to find its roots, not necessarily by retreat, but by a poetic and mystical absorption in some elements of the past. Some of the inconsistencies disappear when her ideas are put into their proper period and long, gradual changes are plotted; but Mary Austin can never be made simple. There are back-trackings and reversions, and inconsistency holds all along the chronological line. Whatever pattern emerges is that enforced by the *method* of her thinking, the intuitional way of the Folk. The champion of Folk-ness, of course, had

not the limited social perception of the Folk. She was world-aware. Indeed, she wrote of a future "folk-fixation," and the implication is that the whole nation in that time will have the awareness and the state of consciousness that are now only for intellectuals, but will have them by automatic, subconscious means. She said that highly self-conscious and sophisticated artists were the Folk of the great world, as much at ease among world-ideas as is an Indian medicine-man among tribal myths and legends. Such a straddling of the gap between the universalizing tendency of radical intellectualism and the localizing tendency of out-and-out regionalism, leaves no room for any argument. Mrs. Austin stands everywhere, mystically divining. Her Folk-ness, therefore, was not altogether primitivism, or escapism, or a systematized regionalism, or anything that can be labeled. She is valuable not for giving a system but for making us more aware, for extending the range of our consciousness of our environment and our social possibilities.

It has long been the fashion to say that Mary Austin was greater as a woman than as a writer. Her personality did have, according to all reports, a "seminal" quality (the adjective was once applied to Rousseau's mind). It created a stir in other people, in a way that her books alone perhaps never will. But ultimately she will have to be judged by her writing. And she seems to have divined well there. **"The Land of Little Rain,"** *The Flock, The Land of Journey's Ending*—she was sure that these would be remembered. Her practical life closed with an absorbing interest in the arts and crafts of the New Mexican Folk. But one of the last things she wrote was a poem, **"When I Am Dead,"** full of nostalgia for such days and scenes as are portrayed in **The Flock.** Could it be that she recognized that such work as **The Flock** would ultimately be of much more importance than all the years she served as the oracle of Santa Fe and prophet-at-large to America? Her best mode was that of aloneness, when with quiet patience she set down the glamorous, cruel, strange beauty of the land, the great Sierra pastures, the desert, the cañons and mesas. As for her attempt to predict the means and method of our adaptation to the land, she was perhaps as good a prophet as any.

James Ruppert (essay date autumn 1983)

SOURCE: Ruppert, James. "Mary Austin's Landscape Line in Native American Literature." *Southwest Review* 68, no. 4 (autumn 1983): 376-90.

[*In the following essay, Ruppert analyzes Austin's concept of the "landscape line," which she proposed in her critical essay included in* The American Rhythm, *asserting that while this idea remains vague in the au-*

thor's argument, it is nonetheless valid as an "intui-
tive" device that seeks to demonstrate the influence of
the environment on Native American song and poetry.]

While the literary exiles at the beginning of the century
sought to flee American life, another group of writers
became convinced that under the changes of modern
life, a true ancient American spirit existed. Both groups
saw numerous historical examples of the creative welding of the arts, culture, and the environment. The arts
exploded with attempts to reforge those connections.
Imagism, Vorticism, oral poetic forms, and *vers libre* attempted to liberate poetry from the superfluities of the
recent past, while the new subject matter ranged from
psychological probings of the American character and
the human impact of technology to the study and translation of New and Old World literatures in order to find
the true and eternal power of poetry. Many artists and
poets felt that in the distant past, art—especially song/
poetry—had been more powerful, more affective, and
that the modern spiritual and artistic wasteland invali-
dated the Victorian world view. Amy Lowell capsulizes
this attitude toward an artistic revitalization in a letter
to Mary Austin (April 24, 1923) concerning Pueblo poetry: "The extremes of sophistication and the aboriginal
are not so far apart; man returns to simplicity when he
has gone along the road of sophistication far enough."

Foremost among the writers concerned with what Harriet Monroe called "The Great Renewal," a revitalization of the arts through a return to American materials,
the American landscape, and aboriginal American arts,
was Mary Hunter Austin. During her forty years as a
poet, writer, dramatist, essayist, and folk arts specialist,
she was continuously involved with American Indian
culture and literature, the southwestern environment,
and the insights to be garnered from cultural and environmental interface. She wrote prolifically during her
sixty-six years of life. Her bibliography includes over
thirty books, well over a hundred articles, hundreds of
poems and short stories, numerous introductions and
forewords, and many translations from American Indian
materials as well as four "Indian" plays. She was a
popular author who today is often relegated to the position of a regionalist or nature writer.

Her continual concern, however, was to map the influence of environment on the people who lived in it. In
American Indian society she saw an artistic tradition
forcefully welded to culture; a clear, mutually beneficial
totality established by the American Indians with the
American environment. Amerind cultures exemplified
an ideal of interdependence. Central to her vision was
the conviction that the land and the people who inhabited it were intricately bound together. She encouraged
American artists to understand the ways that American
landscape may have already influenced American art
and to study American Indian art as an example of a

true American folk art expressive of the American environment and the cultural adaptation which had irrevoca-
bly taken place.

In this view of cultural adaptation, Austin never excluded such practical and basic levels of interpenetra-
tion as food and water, but her main concern was with
mystical and spiritual levels. She wanted to know how
the spirit of man and the creative spirit of the land were
welded together to form culture; how this fusion influenced man's thought and art. In particular, she wanted
to know how and where this welding had happened in
American Indian culture and art, and how she could encourage contemporary America in that direction. She
believed that America really had no choice about adaptation to the land, that in the long run through the process of mutual adaptation of the land and the people,
the land always won. It always shaped the culture more
than the culture shaped it. In southwestern culture, and
in the clearest witness for the land's influence—art—
she found the most consistent and unqualified examples
of the environment's influence:

> But to be a part of a musical culture would mean to
> have produced a kind of music which is not only ex-
> pressive of life as it is being lived among us, but is at
> the same time spiritually satisfying. And the only
> people among us who have done that are the Indians
> and the Negroes. People who study such things inti-
> mately say there are signs that, beginning with these
> two folk methods of music, we are gradually evolving
> a mode of musical expression which is recognizably
> American. Similarly, beginning with the architectural
> pattern developed among our Indian pueblos, adding
> steel and adapting it to urban conditions, we are creat-
> ing an American architecture. In literature we are ap-
> proaching forms that are natively expressive. By the
> time we have developed all these things to the point at
> which they are instinctive, and complement one an-
> other in a generic relation to American life, we will
> have an American culture.[1]

([**"Regional Culture in the Southwest"**])

This progression of thought brought Austin to a position that might be described as geographic determinism,
where all aspects of culture are formed under the pressing influence of the environment. Though societies may
vary in the manner in which they accept this influence,
none may avoid it. The arts, as the most expressive and
sensitive cultural aspect, reveal most clearly this determining force. Especially do the ritual dance-dramas of
the American Indians, an all-encompassing art form,
show the student most persuasively the permeating influence of the land. As the dance-dramas combine
dance, drama, design, costume, song, music, and poetry,
they completely express the tribal culture's physical, artistic, and mythic relationship to the environment. When
asked to give the sources of poetic influence in the
Southwest for *Poetry* magazine (December 1933), Austin responded: "There are invariably two sources of po-

etic influence in any given region; one of them the shape, the rhythm and procedure of the land itself, and the other, the contribution to the life lived there made by the experience and racial qualities of the people, out of whom the body of native verse proceeds." In her answer, the second aspect is designed to incorporate the influence of transplanted cultures, but since the racial qualities will eventually lose to the land, only one fundamental force exists—the land. There are other forces, but their range is severely limited. "Art, considered as the experience of any people as a whole, is the response they made in various mediums to the impact that the totality of their experience makes upon them, and there is no sort of experience that works so constantly and subtly upon man as his regional environment."[2] [**"Regionalism in American Fiction"**]

Austin felt that the ritual dance-drama of American Indian peoples most clearly expressed the regional environment of the tribe. Since the dance-drama combines a variety of arts which western culture normally separates, and since it is created by a number of people over a long span of time, it is capable of translating all the complexities of a natural environment into a coherent structure. This structure then becomes the essence of literature because poetry, music, storytelling, dance, and design may develop from it.

Austin sought the common ground for all artistic aspects of the dance-drama in rhythm. She felt it was the most immediate, and yet most evasive, influence of the land. The rhythm of the land affects us so completely and so unconsciously that it is difficult to isolate. "The suggestibility of the human organism in the direction of rhythmic response is so generous that the rhythmic forms to which the environment gives rise seem to pass through the autonomic system, into and out of the subconscious without our having once become intellectually aware of them. Rhythm, then, in so far as it affects our poetic mode, has nothing to do with our intellectual life."[3] [*The American Rhythm*] Austin saw American Indian cultures as having allowed that flow of rhythmic forms to effect their art completely, from the flow of their stories and designs to the culminating flow of the dance-dramas.

Austin considered American Indian arts more affective, familiar, and physical because they were concerned less with intellectual distancing. They incorporated rhythm and movement. Austin saw movement, both the movements of necessary social labor in the environment and the movements of personal response, as playing an important role in the transmission of the rhythms of the land into the rhythms of the dance-drama and, ultimately, song/poetry:

> That these movements have been, in the main, the measure by which man has accommodated himself to the contours of the earth, may be due to the salience of

such contours over every other feature of what in the main takes place on them. . . . What we have to deal with here is the certainty that although the country [the Southwest] has been successively lived in by three groups of people long enough to put its imprint on their types of verse, it has in no case failed to do so, and that in every case it has been the contour of the land and the gesture by which it has been overcome that has been recorded.

> [*Poetry,* December 1933]

Around 1915, after years of collection and study of American Indian ritual, song, and poetry, Austin became convinced that she could, to a limited extent, decode those recorded rhythms. She concluded that American Indian dance-dramas, especially song/poetry, expressed through poetic form the rhythms of the cornlands, the Great Plains, the desert, the mountains, and the wooded ranges. Even more interestingly, she felt that by listening to an American Indian song/poem from a ceremony, even in an unknown language, she could identify the landscape which nurtured the expression. Through this she became convinced of the power of the environment in determining rhythmic modes, and she even postulated the eventual influencing of modern American literature by the American landscape:

> It was when I discovered that I could listen to aboriginal verses on the phonograph in unidentified Amerindian languages, and securely refer them by their dominant rhythms to the plains, the deserts and woodlands that produced them, that I awoke to the relationships that must necessarily exist between aboriginal and later American forms.

> [*The American Rhythm,* p. 19]

The link between modern American literature and Native American literature was sparked by the flash of personal illumination derived from the American landscape.

Austin's flash of understanding formed the basis for one of the most interesting and enigmatic of all her conceptualizations, the idea of the "landscape line." This idea became her classification tool, her analysis tool, her translation principle, and her criterion for true American poetry. Since the rhythms of the environment "produce" the poetic rhythms which are used by the true poets of the land and the people, and which are reflected in oral tradition, one might expect that the poetry of all people in a given region should be similar. Austin writes conclusively in *The American Rhythm,* "We have seen how native rhythms develop along the track of the rhythmic stimuli arising spontaneously in the environment and are coordinated by the life-sustaining gestures imposed upon us by that environment." Yet modern American poets and aboriginal poets in the same location have used wildly different metrical rhythms to express their experience of the land. What then does she mean by the geographical determinism of environmental rhythms?

Unfortunately, in explaining the landscape line, Austin is never clear enough to make the concept readily accessible to her readers and critics. Almost certainly she is not specifying a new analytical tool, but voicing an insight created on the personal, intuitive level. Readers are asked to follow with common sense, trust her prophetic realization, and validate the concept of the landscape line in their own study. Still, the average reader is left wondering where to begin because the author (who was occasionally referred to as "God's mother-in-law" because of her inclination toward prophetic pronouncements) has not shown us the path, though I contend she has given us some clues.

As readers in the western tradition, we expect her use of the word "rhythm" in song/poetry to mean the cadenced flow of sound similar to rhythm in music. The land's influence is then in the nature of some pattern or recurring stress, rhyme, and sound elements. This is, however, precisely the assumption that Austin tries to combat when in *The American Rhythm* she argues against the melodic line as the primary mold of aboriginal verse. She argues that if the melodic line is more important than the words (a view she attributes to translators Natalie Curtis Burlin and Alice Fletcher), then why does the aboriginal poet fill out the line with nonsense syllables instead of changing the text so that it can fill out the melodic line? She cites Indians' making up new melodies to fit her translations, while making distinctions between aesthetic repetitions and religious repetitions. All this brings her to a point of insisting that the thought in the words is primary. In seeing the Indian's idea of rhythm as something larger, involving also melody and ideation, she is rejecting the sophisticated idea of rhythm as recurring stress patterns and rigid forms that dictate the structure of the words:

> But I have never met with the slightest disposition to force the words into a predetermined mold. Mold or rhythm-pattern, so far as its exists for the aboriginal, exists only as a point of rest for the verse to flow into and out of as a mountain stream flows in and out of ripple-linked pools. It is this leap of the running stream of poetic inspiration from level to level, whose course can not be determined by anything except the nature of the ground traversed, which I have called the landscape line. The length of the leaps, and the sequence of pattern recurrences will be conditioned by the subjectively co-ordinated motor rhythms associated with the particular emotional flow.
>
> This landscape line may, of course, involve several verse lines as they appear on the printed page, and is best described by the modern term, cadenced verse. In the placing of this line, and the additional items by which it is connoted and decorated, the aboriginal process approaches closest to what is known as Imagism, unless you will accept my term and call it glyphic.
>
> [*The American Rhythm,* pp. 55-56]

If the landscape line can run over several printed lines, then it has little to do with rhyming structures, and if

meter exists only as a resting place while the landscape line leaps with the poetic inspiration, then meter is not essential to it. These thoughts describe the essentials of free verse or, as Austin called it, "cadenced verse." Clearly the concept of the landscape line is not something that the traditional tools of poetic analysis can grasp.

We are not dealing with anapests for the desert and couplets for the plains, but a deeper idea of the structure and flow of emotion and idea. The structure of a thought and the rhythm of its development, as molded by the environment and the emotion, more closely describes what Austin meant by the landscape line.

Perhaps the only concrete illustration Austin gives of the landscape line in all her works is in her article on **"Non-English Writings"** for the *Cambridge History of American Literature.* Here she discusses American Indian thought as expressed in song and poetry, and elaborates on the process she calls "glyphic," which she compares to Imagism. She proposes that in both systems a small kernel of suggestive expression "states a thing apprehended through the external sense; something seen, heard, or done, enclosing a spiritual experience as in the thin film of a bubble." She implies that the woodland songs do not merely describe, but open up the singer's soul. She then gives an example of an Ojibway Mide'Wiwin song, where the woman sings:

> We are using our hearts

meaning in full:

> With deep sincerity
> We join our hearts
> To the hearts of the Midé Brethren
>   To find our sky again.
> With our hearts
> Made pure by singing
> We uphold the hearts
>   of our Midé Brethren
> Seeking our sky.

Any number of interesting observations of the co-ordinate development of writing and poetry could be made from the study of this single ceremony, and the relation of both to their forest environment. In both there is that tendency, always so clearly marked in a complicated environment, to take the part for the whole, the leaf for the tree, the track of the bear's foot for the bear, the reaching hand for the aspiring spirit of man.

It is this suggested relation between literary form and the land which produced it, which gives point to a choice of the Hako ceremony of the Pawnees for analysis.

What Austin seems to be saying is that in this five-word line of the Ojibway ceremony, we have one of those "small suggestive kernels"—an external sense experience enclosing a spiritual experience, conditioned by environment. The line "We are using our hearts" is made to stand for a much larger concept of uniting with the shaman brethren, supporting them and using the heart to unite with the Allness. She implies that in complicated environments like forests, we can expect the landscape line to take the form of short, suggestive, symbolic structures similar to Imagism. The part—using the heart—is taken for the whole, uniting with the brethren and Allness. The rhythm of development is expressed by the tension created in an attempt to move from that part to the whole. All this is conditioned by the emotion of joyful expansion and union. Of course, a song or sequence can be created by a series of these kernels, but the basic structure of the thought is that of taking the part for the whole.

Austin goes on to expand on how the land can influence those rests and leaps of poetic inspiration in the landscape line, by discussing in **"Non-English Writings"** the Pawnee Hako ceremony.

> But there are some features that distinguish it as a literary production, which must be mentioned. Each movement is complete in itself, but indispensable. There is a closer relation between the emotional episodes and the rhythm, a finer web of words. Progressive stanza structure characterizes every movement. The verse forms are dramatically logical and rhythmically descriptive, the action leading and largely determining the form. To a very remarkable degree the verse contours conform to the contours of the country traversed, either actually or imaginatively, throughout the performance. . . . The Pawnees and cognate tribes who use the Hako have lived so long exposed to the influence of the open country about the Platte River that their songs unconsciously take the shape of its long undulations . . . the following, one of a series of songs describing the journey of the Father group to the group called The Children:

> Dark against the sky younder distant line
> Runs before, trees we see, long the line of trees
> Bending, and swaying in the breeze,

which accurately represents the jog trot of journey across the rolling prairie. A little later comes the crowding of ponies on the river bank:

> Behold upon the river's bank we stand,
> River we must cross.
>
> Oh Kawas come, to thee we call,
> Oh come and thy permission give
> Into the stream to wade and forward go.

Finally, on the other side, after stanzas representing every stage of the crossing, there is the flick of the ponies' tails as the wind dries them.

> Hither winds, come to us, touch where water
> O'er us flowed when we waded,
> Come, O winds, come!

Again, as the visiting party draws up from the lowlands about the river, we have this finely descriptive rhythm:

> The Mesa see, its flat top like a straight line
>   cuts across the sky,
> It blocks our path, and we must climb, the mesa
>   climb.

> What work in any language more obviously illustrates the influence of environment on literary form? Other examples there are of much subtler and more discriminating rhythms, but they only announce themselves after long intimacy with the land in which they develop. The homogeneity of the Amerind race makes it possible to detect environmental influences with a precision not possible among the mixed races of Europe.

In this long passage, Austin tries to fit a picture of the landscape with the thought rhythms. In this manner she hopes to expose the environmental influences on the verse.

In the first section cited from the ceremony, these "verse contours" are likened to the "long undulations" of the prairie country around the Platte River. The first song section is one long run-on thought that continues to unfold and expand. The sight of the horizon in the distance brings the searching singer to the trees on it, and then to the complementary motion of the trees. We might be justified in saying that the continuous, expanding, swelling development of the thought is like the rolling undulations of the prairie.

The second song section is sung as the travelers reach a river. Their halting is mirrored in the way the words seem to stop and come back upon themselves. The river must be crossed, and the thought keeps coming back to that fact while emotionally the singers are open and respectfully waiting for a response to their supplication.

The third song section, sung after the travelers have passed the river, calls for the wind to dry them. Here the small quick phrases thick with repetition and alliteration are likened to the action of the wind on the wet bodies and to the anticipation of the travelers.

In the last song section, the long line of verse is likened to lowlands rising up to the mesas. The line is stopped by the idea of climbing, and the repetition brings the obstacle quality of the mesa into verbal complement. Emotionally the repetition prepares the singer for the climb, and we are soon back again on the undulating of the prairie.

I think it is clear from this example that the landscape line for Austin is a function of how the thought of the line reflects the landscape in form. Repetition, development, phrase size, and phrase breaking are some of the formal qualities in which we realize the landscape line. The rhythm of development is closely allied with the structure of the thought itself. Both mirror the singer's sense of time and perception. After being colored by emotion, they are passed on to us, or as Charles Olson says: "Rhythm is Time." Our sense of time is molded by the manner in which the thought unfolds itself. The formal qualities of meter and rhyme may or may not aid the expression of the landscape line. The primary questions for Austin are how the thought wrestles with the language and how the result reflects the environmental influences.

In the few published attempts to come to terms with Austin's sketchy description of a principle she considered very important, the reviewers do not discuss the landscape line as thought structure and development. Thomas Ford, in an article entitled "The American Rhythm: Mary Austin's Poetic Principle" (*Western American Literature,* 1970), presents a halfhearted attempt to elaborate upon the similarities she saw between certain American poets and Amerind poetry, based on similar environmental influences. After starting out with a gross misrepresentation of Austin's ideas by implying she saw a continuous development from Amerind poetry to modern American poetry, he reviews the nature of rhythm and states Austin's belief in the determining and influencing power of environmental stimuli. He goes on to discuss three American poets singled out by Austin as occasionally expressing pure American rhythms: Carl Sandburg, Vachel Lindsay, and Sherwood Anderson. In order to find these similarities which Austin postulated, Ford compares an Anderson poem with a section from a Pawnee corn dance, ostensibly because they both deal with corn growing. He finds both having the common idea of corn as a goddess; both are unrhymed and are in an unaccented pyrrhic meter. Ford draws no conclusions from this: "Whether the likenesses are the result of common responses to the natural energy and rhythm in the land, one can only wonder."

Again he compares an early poem of Sandburg's to a Washoe love song translated by Austin. He observes: "The mode of expression in the two poems is certainly similar. According to Mary Austin, the Indian lover 'sings for the purpose of bringing the soul of the beloved into communion with his soul.' . . . Both poets have used the same mode of realization." Though Ford may see some similar ideas here, nothing is really built on an attempt to understand the landscape line, since the questions of thought structure, development, and verse form are not considered.

He compares Lindsay's Congo poem with a Pima emergence song. Ford sees little in common as far as rhythm goes, except for one element:

> Lindsay's [poem] has a driving accented beat that can be scanned, and he makes considerable use of rhyme.

His poem moves headlong toward a resounding climax in the last line. The Pima ritual, on the other hand, does not have definite accent or rhyme, and does not move so rapidly. There is, however, one distinct similarity, and that is in the use of repetition, which, incidentally, seems to have both rhythmical and ritualistic significance for the Indian.

Ford then goes on to Austin's translation method without clearing the waters he has left so murky.

Though we do not know why certain poems are selected, other than that some have similar topics and some are characteristic of a given region or poet, Ford might have been fruitful if he had approached the idea of similarities from the basis of thought development in the structure. Perhaps an even more fruitful approach would have been to compare poems of these authors with Amerindian poems that deal with the same landscape. Comparing a Lindsay poem about the Congo with a desert Pima emergence song seems to represent a basic misunderstanding of Austin's ideas. The truest analysis might come from discussing these poets in relation to their landscape. The similarities Austin saw between American poets and Amerind poets were that they both reflected the American environment and, thus, American rhythms through the landscape line.

Still another critic, T. M. Pearce, summarizes briefly the idea of the landscape line in a short chapter on Austin's Indian poems in his *Mary Hunter Austin* (1965), saying that the phrase applies to cadenced verse governed by the motor impulses created by actions and emotions of a particular region. Pearce also mentions the idea of American rhythms, quoting mainly from **The American Rhythm** and Austin's introduction to *The Path of the Rainbow,* yet he does not attempt to tie the two together. He expands by quoting her views of different poets' work. She criticized Stanley Vestal's western ballads because they did not reflect the western environment, and yet she praised Niehardt's "Song of the Indian Wars," for, "although it followed the standard model of pentameter rhyming verse, the lines flowed past the metered and rhyming length to reach the freedom of a 'landscape line.'" He continues by quoting Austin's praise of Frost's "long, undulant conversational line, reminiscent of the New England landscape." Pearce continues to list the critical pronouncements from Austin's articles concerning American rhythm, and the response by her critics, without ever attempting a complete definition. He concludes by implying that Austin tried to incorporate the principles of the landscape line into her translations, a correct observation, but one, since it is not based on thorough analysis, that gives us little more than the most surface description.

Critically more important is Dudley Wynn's dissertation for New York University, "A Critical Study of the Writings of Mary Hunter Austin (1868-1934)," which is by far the most detailed and analytical discussion of Austin and her ideas of the American rhythm and the landscape line. Though written in 1939, it is still an important evaluation of Austin and her place in American literature.

In his section on *The American Rhythm,* he follows Austin through her discussion of rhythmic stimuli to the idea of the glyph and finally to the landscape line. Trying to place this concept in the framework of the book's main argument, he is disappointed to conclude that there are no concrete criteria for the explanation and identification of the landscape line in either Indian or contemporary poetry. Assuming a literalist position, Wynn takes the suggestive guiding statements by Austin verbatim and decides:

> For the landscape line turns out to be nothing but "cadenced verse" with an infusion of imagism—something glyphic. The "landscape line" is nothing inherently Indian, has nothing to do with the rhythmics dictated by the contours of the country; it is the free-versifiers' definition of organic and natural rhythms and their expression of revolt against the thralldom of formal metrical patterns.

Austin would have voiced her rebellion against metrical formalism if that were her only goal. Many other writers had already so rebelled, after all. Her goals were larger. She wanted to push the reader into admittedly unexplored territory. Wynn reasons that since Austin proclaimed her ability to discern a poem's geographical origin through an analysis of the landscape line, the reader is justified in expecting her to give us a literal formula for determining these origins. He concedes that this formula does not need to be merely metrical, but could incorporate line length and stanza spacing on the page. Still, his analysis suggests his own bias in favor of classical European metrics.

Retreating from the question of the landscape line to the overall idea of *The American Rhythm,* Wynn does see some similarities in the approach of the contemporary poet and the Indian poet, but not in their forms. He feels each is free in choosing the medium "in accordance with the innate rhythm of his emotion." Since he assumes that Amerind poetry is locked into highly formal rhythm patterns, he sees no evidence of the landscape line's influence in that poetry. Wynn decides that Austin is just using this concept to establish that there was a debt owed by contemporary writers to the aboriginal. From this base, she could more effectively push the ideas of the necessity and inevitability of cultural adaptation to the land. Yet Austin said that the landscape line runs on past the end of the printed or sung line. This statement alone rules out Wynn's effort to confine Austin's idea to a metrical form.

It barely needs noting that Wynn is being far too literal here. He seems to expect a precise metrical formula from someone who is working out the concept of the landscape line on a much more mystical, intuitive plane. When, in *The American Rhythm,* Austin says that the landscape line "is best described by the modern term, cadenced verse," she does not intend that we take her literally, but the concept of cadenced verse will best help us understand the landscape line. In *The American Rhythm,* she does not attempt a complete discussion of the concept, but rather is content to suggest and then move on to the other ramifications of her main idea— geographic determinism. Austin sees no necessity of a complete working out of all topics she brings up in *The American Rhythm.* In a letter to Arthur Ficke (March 27, 1930), she explains her position:

> I recognize no such objection as you lay upon me to demonstrate an American Rhythm "by means of vast documentation, special reference and detailed analysis." This is a matter I had out with myself many years ago, after I discovered myself in possession of a field of scholarly research that had not been entered by many of my contemporaries. I see myself, primarily, as a creative thinker—or creative writer, whichever term suits you best—which I feel to entail a higher obligation than that of stodgy and meticulous demonstration for the uninitiated, of what has come to me through the regular channels of scholarly experience. I felt that I couldn't be faithful to my primary obligation if I must go dragging after me all the fructifying sources, as a queen bee trails the entrails of her mate.

Still, there is little in the book that would bring us to a useful understanding of the landscape line as thought structure and development in poetry. Wynn and the general reader can hardly be blamed, however, if they expect a clearer and more direct statement of such a new and confusing idea. Austin herself seems to have had trouble clarifying this idea. She says, "The marks of this distinction are too subtle to define or describe, but they do not fail."[4]

Austin hoped to give the writers of her day guidance in their struggle to revitalize their art. She saw in Native American dance, drama, music, architecture, poetry, and design an artistic response to the American environment which was socially and culturally effective. She encouraged artists to explore Native American materials and to draw lessons from a true folk art, lessons which would weld the searching American arts to their true source, the experience of the American landscape.

We can lament the fact that Austin was not a trained academic, ready and willing to work out every intricate knot in the web of her thoughts, but that was not her purpose or mode of understanding. If we invalidate her ideas on these grounds, then we stand to lose rich theoretical treasures. Her ideas may not be practical tools for literary analysis, but she was opening new territory and, to this day, few have followed her. A critic might question the value of all this for contemporary poetry, but such a critic would be forgetting the importance of "place" as emphasized by the poets of the last thirty years, the concern today with ethnopoetics and oral forms, and the impact of the land as expressed by so many contemporary writers. Another critic might suggest that exploring the intertwining of the land and the writer requires an unusual depth of penetration and synthesis which only a mystical understanding can create. If so, then Austin becomes even more important to study, for, from the few who have this depth, others must learn. Though Austin believed in instinct over logic, insight over calculation, she can still provoke a vital probing of the American writer and the American landscape.

Notes

1. Mary Hunter Austin, "Regional Culture in the Southwest," *Southwest Review* 14 (July 1929), p. 476.

2. ———, "Regionalism in American Fiction," *English Journal* 21 (February 1932), p. 97.

3. ———, *The American Rhythm* (New York, Houghton, Mifflin, 1930), p. 4.

4. ———, "John G. Neihardt's Expression of the West," *Southwest Review* 13 (January 1928), p. 258.

William J. Scheick (essay date spring 1992)

SOURCE: Scheick, William J. "Mary Austin's Disfigurement of the Southwest in *The Land of Little Rain*." *Western American Literature* 27, no. 1 (spring 1992): 37-46.

[*In the following essay, Scheick studies Austin's* The Land of Little Rain *and argues that while her purpose in writing about the California desert is to convey its transcendent power, her narrative is repeatedly "frustrated" by her position as a self-conscious observer, which results in a text that is riddled with intimations, not of transcendence, but of death and her own mortality.*]

Although *The Land of Little Rain* (1903) was created to earn money,[1] [**"These Modern Women, Woman Alone"**] Austin also had higher motives. Earlier in her life, she had moved to the desert of southern California, where (her friend tells us) she had "felt the rigors and bleakness of the desert denied her a vocabulary and her mysticism."[2] In time, Austin tried to appreciate better the strange beauty of this desert. *The Land of Little Rain* records her attempt to express this revised perception, especially of the "strange," which for her implies "a criticism of the familiar." The familiar "lack[s] any criterion of authority other than that it is ours," Austin

observed.[3] [*Earth Horizon*] Her first book challenges "the familiar" not only in its setting but also in its search for the transcendent there. The sheer minimalism of the austere desert terrain presumably might facilitate the detection of the transcendent; in turn, her book further suggests, this detection presumably might facilitate a revision in her readers' perception of reality.

Conveying the "strange" in this instance apparently did not require inordinate attention to style. Austin noted that "nothing was further from [her] mind when writing" *The Land of Little Rain* than "the question of style"; she had not considered style to be "a writer's problem."[4] [**"How I Learned to Read and Write"**] If we take her at her word, her first book may be read as a relatively unguarded account of her experiences. Austin's sections on the desert, even more than her few entries on the mountains, reveal not only the search but also the frustration of her desire for a transcendental encounter.

The fact of human mortality is the principal cause of this frustration. This actuality contravenes Austin's attempt to detect the eternal in her temporal encounters. Symptomatic signs of Austin's unfulfilled desire surface in her art, especially in her tendency to transform descriptions of nature into autobiographic and anthropomorphic associations. This manner of association amounts to a rhetorical dis-figurement and re-figurement of Austin's experience with nature. In short, Austin appropriates metaphorically (through dis-figurement) what is resistant to her metaphysically. This stylistic manner in effect replicates and reenacts the physical disfigurement of the landscape that Austin explicitly denounces in her book.

In *The Land of Little Rain* Austin particularly appreciates the minimalism of the desert. For her, the desert surpasses all other terrains. It intimates some eternal force at the core of the material world. "None other than this long brown land lays such a hold on the affections," she explains in her introductory sketch, "the rainbow hills, the tender bluish mists, the luminous radiance of the spring, have the lotus charm" and "trick the sense of time."[5] This sentiment is reprised in the final sketch of *The Land of Little Rain*. There Austin reports that in the desert one may detect "a sense of presence and intention," an intimation of "eternal meaning" (246, 262). For Austin, the desert reflects a transcendent timelessness that she would like to believe redeems temporal experience from its tragic transience and materiality.[6]

However, if nature conveys hints of the eternal, it also resists Austin's quest to close with the transcendent. Everywhere in nature she senses "purposes not revealed" (184)—something infinite that is intimated and at the same time resistant to human apprehension. The desert in particular always at once allows for "communion" with the "clear heavens" and, contrarily, takes a "toll"; it does so by suggesting in various dire ways that every viewer is "of no account" within the context of divine "imperturbable . . . purposes" (21, 186). The sempiternal "nature" she detects in this landscape is seemingly near to her spatially; but at the same time it remains apparently remote metaphysically. The spiritual fulfillment she seeks in the desert is rebuffed. As a "land that supports no man" and "sets the limit" (3) beyond what any human law might decree, the desert may metonymically reflect the eternal in nature, but it also especially seems antagonistically Other to Austin. She must remain a mortal viewer confined in time.[7]

As her allusion to the land of the lotus-eaters suggests, the Odysseus-like stranger must somehow forget the realities of the present, must somehow escape time if she is to merge with "the lotus charm" of the desert. Such "bewitched" evasion (17), such forgetting, would mean the end of the viewer as a viewer. It would mean going "mad in time" (69), as she says at one point about the old miners who try to live in the desert. It would mean dying away from the physical world not only spiritually but also physically.

Indeed, however much Austin seeks to focus her book on the intimations of transcendental wonder expressed in landscapes, her vision is cluttered with iterated signs of nature's "elemental violence" (109; cf. 6). She finds reminders of mortality through violence everywhere in nature. As her imagery suggests, she detects death even in "the terrible keen polish" and "saw-tooth effect" of majestic mountains with "long shark-finned ridges" (186). She especially emphasizes the signs of death evident in the southwestern desert, where she cannot help but notice, significantly in the first sketch of her book, an ominously representational "line of shallow graves" (18).

Austin reads each of these graphic signs as a *memento mori*. These signs serve as emblems of her own physical mortality. They indicate her personal insignificance before nature's reductive "elemental violence" and, especially, point to her temporality. This temporality necessarily excludes her (as viewer) from the eternal. To fulfill her desire to encounter the transcendent apparently reflected in nature, to truly participate in "the splendor of the apocalypse" evidently revealed in the material creation (248), she would have to "forsake . . . most things but beauty and madness and death and God" (184). Austin would have to succumb to the desert's lotus-charm of forgetfulness. This forgetfulness would in effect be an apocalyptic obliviousness typical of death. To be the very perceiver she is in her book, however, she must be a temporal self confronted by the circumstance of her mortality. In other words, to have a self, an identity, a consciousness, she must remain es-

tranged from the eternal. However much she yearns for closure with the divine, her temporality, her mortality prevents her from being an Emersonian "transparent eyeball" with "the currents of the Universal Being circulat[ing] through" her.[8]

Austin, accordingly, tried in her book to embrace aesthetically this mortal opacity of her eye. She tried to accept her Odysseus-like foreign presence in the lotusland of nature. She hoped to redeem this experience of exclusion through a documentary verbal art that might somehow serve, in a secondary way, to capture and convey a sense of the eternal in nature. She thus sought to be "a mere recorder" (112), as she called herself at one point in *The Land of Little Rain.* Given the mortal opacity of her eye, its lack of transparency in a metaphysical sense, "a mere recorder" was all Austin believed she could be. Her experience taught her that she could not become a primary Emersonian transparent eyeball. So, perhaps, she hoped that the narrative objectivity of the "mere recorder" might at least provide a secondary kind of transparency.

Austin's use of the word *mere* reveals more than her humility before the majesty of nature; it also reveals her hesitant and unhappy acknowledgement of the barrier of temporality. Mortality, as signed in a land of "elemental violence," "sets the limits" of human perception. Besides the word *mere,* the disjointed narrative segmentation, the ellipses within paragraphs, the periphrastic sentences, and the anxious shifts in point-of-view (between an individualistic *I* and a communal *you*)[9] collectively suggest Austin's discomfort with and antipathy to the limited role of observer in *The Land of Little Rain.*[10] This observation is perhaps substantiated by the fact that her next book, *The Basket Woman* (1904), does not relate her personal encounters with nature and, pertinently, does not evidence the stylistic limitations evident in *The Land of Little Rain.*

Austin prefers a more elemental and effulgent art than that of the "mere recorder." In *The Land of Little Rain* she idealizes art that originates in "the satisfaction of desire" (171), not in its frustration and limitation. Any explanation of art other than satisfaction of desire, she says explicitly, is a contrived "house-bred theory" (171); that is, it is not a *natural* explanation. In fact, reflexive theorizing, as Austin herself is compelled to do in her book at this very moment of self-consciously commenting on art, strikes her as a symptom of her own opacity, of her own alienation in a lotusland of ideal forgetfulness and lack of consciousness.

She accordingly idealizes Native Americans, who seem to her to be like the desert plants and animals. Each plant and animal, Austin observes, inherently "knows its purpose" (221) and intrinsically mimics its "land [which] will not be lived in except in its own fashion"

(88). Native Americans, in Austin's opinion, experience the divine mirrored in the land by "a sort of instinct atrophied by disuse in a complexer civilization" (234). Austin's book, thematically and aesthetically, registers her unrequited desire for a similar intimate, instinctive association with the "purpose" infusing whatever she reports in her limited capacity as a self-aware outsider behind opaque eyes.

It is hardly surprising, moreover, that she longingly records her belief that "every Indian woman is an artist,—sees, feels, creates, but does not philosophize about her processes" (168-69). These women seem closer to the timeless eternal within nature; they seem more nearly to be the Emersonian transparency Austin wishes herself to be. Austin makes these observations while reporting on the baskets made by Seyavi, a Native American weaver, whom Austin admires for achieving "wonders of technical precision, inside and out" (169). Seyavi's Native American art manifests this gracefulness because it is informed by "the satisfaction of desire" (176). Nevertheless, it is important to note Austin's metaphor of mysterious, laborious, and possibly painful extraction when speaking of this aesthetic attainment in the metaphysical desert of mortal temporality: "Seyavi had somehow squeezed out of her daily round a spiritual ichor that kept the skill in her knotted fingers long after the accustomed time, but that also failed" (176).

Austin, too, tries to squeeze out of her temporal experience some transcendental ichor that will flow from her hand into her writing; but in contrast to Seyavi, she remains a frustrated "recorder" who produces a "knotted" work that is no wonder of technical precision. Austin's problems with written expression, noted earlier, are features of aesthetic decomposition in her narrative that correspond to the many signs of physical decomposition in the desert. Each of these limitations in expression, too, is a *memento mori*; each suggests that "decomposing" mortality frustrates the human (and specifically Austin's) wish for closure with something transcendent. It is important to note, however, that what spiritual ichor even Seyavi "had *somehow* squeezed out of her daily round" had "also failed" her finally (emphasis added).

That her temporal identity is a barrier to detecting the divine may be the painful truth Austin's reflexive theorizing mind unearths for itself in the metaphysical desert of human experience. But this self-consciousness, which only fuels Austin's longing for what she cannot have, becomes more of a problem than she knows. She senses that this reflexivity occludes the sort of instinct she admires in Native Americans, the instinct that would lead to a greater recollection of the transcendent in her own life and art. But she only senses this problem. Her unrequited yearning, intensified by her reflexivity, refuses to

be contained within her self-declared role in the book; and finally, this yearning subverts her conscious effort to accept the lesser avocation of being a mere observer. Ironically, her desire becomes an agent of her failure to achieve even the secondary, and second-best, transparency—that of an objective reporter of the "nobler plan" expressing the "long and imperturbable . . . purposes of God" (186, 201).

One indication of her failure as a documentary artist surfaces in her tendency to inscribe herself on and to read herself in the landscape she describes. Austin, as is well supported by her biographers, was an unhappy person. Enduring a troubled childhood, a failed marriage, the birth of a retarded daughter, recurrent awkward social interactions, a seemingly unpromising career, lingering illnesses, and a sense of herself as physically unattractive and frail, she felt unloved and, perhaps, unlovable. In *The Land of Little Rain* she mentions that she possesses "a poor body" (106). Later in life she described herself as "under the average height, not well filled out, with the slightly sallow pallor of the malaria country." She similarly confessed, even more intimately, that Jennie, her sister who died in 1878, "was the only one who ever unselfishly loved" her.[11] Given these features of her personal experience, it is not surprising that in *The Land of Little Rain* she identifies emotionally with the desert terrain, its "thirsty soil," its "land of lost rivers, with little in it to love," that "cries for" a redemptive rain (5-6). Typically, Austin identifies with the "demoniac yuccas," which form "tormented, thin forests" of "unhappy growth" in "a lonely land" (10-13).

The words *cries, demoniac, tormented, unhappy,* and *lonely* indicate Austin's tendency to project human, specifically her own, sentience and emotion upon the landscape in *The Land of Little Rain.* Such expressions of emotional coloration abound in her book and defy any critical claims for her objectivity or reliance upon descriptive "details to exercise their own energies."[12] And these autobiographical traces merge with a second indication of Austin's failure as a documentary artist: her tendency to anthropomorphize her descriptions. In her book, animals are "hill-folk," "foolish people," "little people" (28, 34, 138); meadowlarks nest "unhappily" or "pitifully" (15); coyotes make a "dolorous whine" or seem "ashamed" (29, 55); buzzards are "full of a crass and simple pride" (52); and mountain streams are like human "tears" (205).

Altering the figures of nature rhetorically in this manner may seem in one sense to elevate (possibly in Native American fashion) the status of the land and the animals beyond social convention. Yet in another sense this procedure obliterates their distinctiveness from humanity. Such obliteration of difference, in contrast to what an ideal documentary method presumably would emphasize, becomes in effect an act of appropriation by means of perspective. Austin, in short, unconsciously resorts to a form of colonization of the land.

This is, perhaps, an unexpected development, given the Preface of *The Land of Little Rain.* In the Preface Austin explicitly remarks her general avoidance of names found in geographies (vii). In contrast, she reports the names Native Americans have attributed to various places; these names "always beautifully fit" the site and do "not originate in the poor human desire for perpetuity" (viii). However, when Austin says, "by this fashion of naming I keep faith with the land and annex to my own estate a very great territory" (ix), her metaphor of annexation is telling. The word *annex* conveys a nuance that conflicts with her intention to separate her own spiritual appreciation of nature from others' material exploitation of the landscape. In this instance, Austin's analogy is unfortunate. It implicitly insists that the way of the spirit is akin to, not really different from or even opposed to, the way of proprietary colonization. Although Austin explicitly deplores the subjection of nature to the proprietary human self, her use of the word *annex* rhetorically replicates this behavior; for it territorially fences in, rather than emancipates, the transcendent.[13]

Whenever Austin alters the figures of nature rhetorically (by autobiographizing and anthropomorphizing) she annexes the landscape through a verbal act akin to proprietary naming by colonizers. She seizes metaphorically what has been resistant to her metaphysically. The language of anthropomorphism and autobiography confiscates the land through a rhetorical figuration that amounts to a dis-figurement of what is Other. When Austin linguistically displaces what is objectively outside the self through a language of subjective appropriation—through a rhetorical dis-figurement—she in effect reenacts the human disfigurement of the landscape that she specifically decries in her book. Austin may denounce both mental acts of naming and physical acts of violence against nature; but her rhetorical disfigurement replicates the "human occupancy of greed and mischief" that leads to "disfigurement," that leaves a "mark on the field" that "banishe[s]" the wild (60, 128, 131). Such physical disfigurement, like Austin's rhetorical dis-figurement, reveals an "obsess[ion] with [one's] own importance in the scheme of things" (281). It does not signify one's submission to the universal.

The universal mattered to Austin throughout her life. As her letters testify, she marvelled over such mystical incidents as the communication between her daughter and a dead playmate. Especially important were her own "singularly vivid impression[s]." In 1917, she spoke of these impressions as "something like a free verse poem, in rather obscure imagery." This, she noted further, "is almost always the way foreknowledge comes to me."[14]

During the writing of her first book, we may accordingly surmise, Austin apparently hoped to recover (in some sense) the sort of mystical rapture she occasionally knew during her childhood and later felt she had lost in the desert. Such sublime occasions, however, tend to be moments of confiscation. They tend to be experienced as emanations from the margins of thought, from some seemingly anonymous exteriority beyond consciousness. These rare junctures of transfigured insight, as Augustine's *Confessions* paradigmatically suggests, are generally perceived as something that happens to one, not something one deliberately seeks out. As her comments on foreknowledge indicate, Austin recognized this requirement of passivity. Nevertheless, her longing for the experience had become too self-conscious during her travels in the desert and during her recollections in her first book. Austin could not recuperate, by the force of her conscious thought, such mystical moments.

Austin's ostensible ideal of sympathy for and submission to the universal did not guarantee her mystical fusion with nature either as an Emersonian transparency or even, secondarily, as an objective observer of nature. If *The Land of Little Rain* thematically insists upon the impossibility of being a mystic, it aesthetically discloses, as well, the failure of a mere recorder. Throughout *The Land of Little Rain,* Austin fails as an objective reporter. She instead remains a lonely outsider delimited by her subjectivity. As an outsider, her insistent, unfulfilled search for divine assimilation finally dramatizes only its own subjective frustration. In *The Land of Little Rain,* this drama of frustration includes the transformation of an ideal into its abjured opposite. The sympathetic abandonment of self to sempiternal "nature" becomes the self's dis-figuring appropriation of an otherwise metaphysically resistant natural landscape.

Notes

1. Mary Austin, "These Modern Women, Woman Alone," *Nation* 124 (March 1927): 229.

2. Peggy Pond Church, *Wind's Trail: The Early Life of Mary Austin* (Santa Fe: Museum of New Mexico, 1990), p. 8.

3. Mary Austin, *Earth Horizon: An Autobiography* (Boston: Houghton Mifflin, 1932), p. 230.

4. Mary Austin, "How I Learned to Read and Write," *My First Publication,* ed. James D. Hart (San Francisco: Book Club of California, 1961), p. 65. Even the title of Austin's first book may not have been her own choice: see *Literary America 1903-1934: The Mary Austin Letters,* ed. T. M. Pearce (Westport, Connecticut: Greenwood, 1979), p. 16.

5. Mary Austin, *The Land of Little Rain* (Boston: Houghton Mifflin, 1903), p. 16. Page references

for subsequent quotations drawn from this edition appear parenthetically in the discussion.

6. In *The Beloved House* (Caldwell, Idaho: Caxton, 1940), pp. 64-77 and in *Mary Hunter Austin* (New York: Twayne, 1965), pp. 19-23, T. M. Pearce documents Austin's early mystical experiences.

7. This observation raises a caveat to unqualified statements concerning Austin's association (by way of connection, learning, and emulation) of human life and landscape in *The Land of Little Rain*: e.g., most recently, Jacqueline D. Hall, *A Literary History of the West,* ed. J. Golden Taylor (Fort Worth: Texas Christian University Press, 1987), pp. 359-69; and *Stories from the Country of "Lost Borders,"* ed. Marjorie Pryse (New Brunswick: Rutgers University Press, 1987), pp. vii-xxxviii. On Austin's later sense of the impact of landscape on the structure and expression of emotion and thought, see James Ruppert, "Mary Austin's Landscape Line in Native American Literature," *Southwest Review* 68 (1983): 376-90.

8. *Emerson's Nature: Origin, Growth, Meaning,* ed. Merton M. Sealts, Jr. and Alfred R. Ferguson (New York: Dodd, Mead, 1969), p. 8. In his later career Emerson revised his earlier position by taking into account what he, too, came to feel as a resistance to the sort of pure communion with nature that he had earlier celebrated. Commentary on Austin generally alludes to the influence of Transcendentalism on her thought, which is succinctly noted in Esther Lanigan Stineman's statement that "Emerson remained a model for Mary's own work" (*Mary Austin: Song of a Maverick* [New Haven: Yale University Press, 1989], p. 12). See also, "The Feel of the Purposeful Earth," *New Mexico Quarterly* 1 (1931): 17-33, in which Henry Smith traces several themes in Austin's work that were nurtured by Transcendentalist tradition; and *A Critical Study of the Writings of Mary Hunter Austin* (New York: Graduate School of Arts and Sciences, New York University, 1941), in which Dudley Wynn suggests that Austin departed from systematic Transcendentalism.

9. That Austin's narrative voice emerges as an imposing presence, like that of the characters in her books, is remarked by J. Wilkes Berry, "Characterization in Mary Austin's Southwest Works," *Southwestern American Literature* 2 (1972): 119-24.

10. The irresolute shifts in viewpoint raise difficulties with the suggestion that Austin clearly identifies with, exalts, and aesthetically replicates the "communal rather than [the] defensively isolated": A. Carl Bredahl, Jr. *New Ground: Western American Narrative and the Literary Canon* (Chapel Hill: University of North Carolina Press, 1989), p. 54.

11. Austin, *Earth Horizon,* pp. 87, 170. Austin's state of mind is also suggested in her dedication of *The Land of Little Rain* to Eve Lummis, "the comfortress of unsuccess." Despite her misgivings, her book was critically well-received (Stineman, p. 74). That Austin used an "aesthetic of repetition" to "recover the mother," to empower the "maternal past" as especially represented by Seyavi, is observed by Elizabeth Ammons, *Conflicting Stories: American Women Writers at the Turn into the Twentieth Century* (New York: Oxford University Press, 1991), pp. 91-99.

12. Bredahl, p. 53. It is also doubtful that Austin departs from "the eastern imagination" that "seeks to impose itself upon the land" (p. 53).

13. In *The Fall into Eden: Landscape and Imagination in California* (Cambridge: Cambridge University Press, 1986) David Wyatt also notes Austin's analogy, but he stresses her use of style (syntax and rhythm), in lieu of naming, as her alternative claim to fame (pp. 81-86).

14. Pearce, pp. 25-26, 110-11.

Mark T. Hoyer (essay date 1995)

SOURCE: Hoyer, Mark T. "Weaving the Story: Northern Paiute Myth and Mary Austin's *The Basket Woman*." *American Indian Culture and Research Journal* 19, no. 1 (1995): 133-51.

[*In the following essay, Hoyer examines the stories and adapted Paiute Indian tales in Austin's collection for children,* The Basket Woman, *asserting that the stories in the book that portray the friendship between adolescent boy-figures, such as Alan, and the Paiute basket woman are remarkable not only in their presentation of the natural world "to an audience of children" but in their attempt "to mythologize the 'natural history' of white-Indian relations."*]

Piudy, a member of a Northern Paiute band often designated as "Snakes," is said to have told the following story in the summer of 1930:

> Almost everything was Coyote's way. The Indian planted the apple. When he planted it, he said for all the Indians to come and eat. When he told them that, all the people came.

> The white man was a rattlesnake then, and he was on that tree. The white people have eyes just like the rattlesnake. When the Indians tried to come to eat the apples, that snake tried to bite them. That's why the white people took everything away from the Indian, because they were snakes. If that snake hadn't been on the tree, everything would have belonged to the Indian. Just because they were snakes and came here, the white people

took everything away. They asked these Indians where they had come from. That's why they took everything and told the Indians to go way out in the mountains and live.[1]

What interests me most about this myth is what most anthropologists at the time would have called its "inauthenticity"; that is, it is clearly a product of postcontact Paiute culture, as seen in the devastating critique of Anglo culture by means of Piudy's reconstitution and deployment of one of Christianity's foundational myths. For that very reason, most anthropologists at the time excluded such myths from their collections, even though, as Jarold Ramsey points out, "it [is] precisely at the moment when [the storyteller] beg[ins] to invent and borrow stories and adapt them to [his or] her native tradition (proving its vitality and no doubt revealing its formal 'rules') that the ethnographer should have been most alert—and most grateful. He could have been studying mythology-in-progress."[2]

Current ethnographic theory gives us plenty of ammunition with which to question the accuracy (or "authenticity") of even such clearly "inauthentic" myths—by making us aware, for example, of the role the anthropologist may have played in the final "product" as it comes to us, of the lack of information given us as to its context and performance, and of the possible results of the myth's textualization. Nevertheless, Piudy's myth would seem to be able to tell us something about one Paiute's imaginative strategy: his adapting of Christian mythology to a "traditional" Paiute form, and his use of this form in a "traditional" way—to teach.

The pointedness of the lesson, moreover, is underscored by one of the very elements obscured by the myth's textualization: its context. According to the ethnologist's preface, these myths were collected in the summer of 1930. A prohibition exists in many tribal traditions against telling certain types of stories in the summer; the reason sometimes given, especially in Great Basin and Plateau cultures, is that the snakes are about and are liable to hear the stories. In light of these facts, the lesson in Piudy's telling of this myth takes on an added layer: Piudy seems to be saying that, not only was "the white men . . . a rattlesnake then"—in the past—but, more to the point, you, the anthropologist, by coming here trying to collect myths without regard to our people's customs, are showing that you, as a representative of white culture, are still a snake.

The sense that Piudy's manner of teaching his listener a lesson is "authentic" is strengthened when we compare his deployment of Biblical imagery to that used by another Native American storyteller, Gertrude Bonnin/Zitkala-Sa, a Yankton Sioux, in a story written some thirty years earlier. Her book, *American Indian Stories,*

a collection of autobiographical and fictional pieces, contains a chapter entitled "Impressions of an Indian Childhood," in which she tells of hearing from some visiting missionaries about the big red apples that grew plentifully back East and that could be had for the taking.[3] This image becomes fundamentally associated in her account with the mission school to which she goes at the age of eight, located to the east in Indiana, in what she later calls "the land of red apples."[4] For Zitkala-Sa, the fruit turns bitter. By associating the apples with the whites' school, Zitkala-Sa not only evokes the Biblical symbol for the knowledge of good and evil but implies what Piudy has stated unequivocally, that "white men are snakes."

There are stories not only behind those told by Piudy and Zitkala-Sa, but behind my commentary on them as well. How we adapt and shape our own histories to suit private purposes; how we often borrow from others' stories in ways that transform and distort them; how we combine these two activities in order to create our own mythologies; and ultimately, how, once these mythologies are recorded in some form, they are adapted by others to their own histories and purposes—such issues are part of that story. Furthermore, my choice of subject matter and my approach to writing about it necessarily imply something about my attitudes toward particular mythological traditions and the syncretisms that result from their contact, although what precisely they imply remains subject to interpretation.

For me, as a literary scholar, such considerations crystallize in the writings of Mary Austin, an early twentieth-century Euro-American author who evidenced, throughout her career, a deep interest in both Native American and Christian mythologies and religious traditions. Austin's body of work includes twenty-seven books and scores of articles in such popular journals as *The Overland Monthly* and *Harper's*. Among these, her writings focusing on Christian themes include **Christ in Italy** (1911); **The Man Jesus** (1915); and articles such as **"Can Prayer Be Answered," "Do We Need a New Religion,"** and **"Religion in the United States."** Her writings focusing on Native American cultures, themes, and issues include two "Indian dramas"—one, **The Arrow-Maker** (1911, 1915), was the first ever produced on stage with an all-Indian cast—in addition to a number of articles on Indian drama; a volume of "re-expressed" Indian verse, **The American Rhythm** (1923);[5] her contribution on indigenous "literatures" to *The Cambridge History of American Literature* (1919); articles in support of Native American autonomy, such as **"Why Americanize the Indian";** and two collections of stories patterned after Native American stories, **The Basket Woman** (1904) and **One-Smoke Stories** (1934). Her first and best-known book, **The Land of Little Rain** (1903), a collection of sketches about the Owens Valley of California, profiles in separate chapters a Shoshoni medicine man and a Paiute basket weaver, the latter becoming the title character of her second work, *The Basket Woman: A Book of Indian Tales for Children.*[6] It is to this second book that I would now like to turn, since it is an early work and thus its Native American influences are more clearly attributable to the tribes with whom Austin became acquainted while living in the Owens Valley of California: the Paiute and Shoshoni.[7]

In the preface, Austin clearly indicates that her purpose is "not so much to provide authentic Indian Folk-tales, as to present certain aspects of nature as they appear in the myth-making mood, that is to say, in the form of strongest appeal to the child mind. . . ." This purpose is informed by the author's conviction that myths are "the root and branch of man's normal intimacy with nature."[8]

Austin goes on to present a variety of myths, some adapted directly from the Paiute, others clearly invented by the author herself. At least one of them might be said to capture the spirit of Piudy's and Zitkala-Sa's stories. In **"The Coyote Spirit and the Weaving Woman,"** Austin repackages the idea that white men who chase Indian women are "coyotes," the functional equivalent of Piudy's snakes, a term that, in other Paiute sources, was a common designation for such men.[9] The irony of the fact that a Paiute term is used against men of her own race is underscored by the ambiguity of the figure of the Weaving Woman. She is the first woman to show Coyote that he is indeed a man, but she ultimately is thrown over for a younger woman. The figure of the Weaving Woman seems not only to be an incarnation of the Basket Woman of the title but to represent the author herself, the weaver of tales—both of whom experience hardships that turn out to be fundamental to their skill as artists and craftswomen. This identification between author and Paiute basket weaver has been hinted at in the earlier book, *The Land of Little Rain,* in the chapter devoted to Seyavi ("The Basket Maker"); later it is developed more explicitly in Austin's autobiography, *Earth Horizon.*[10]

Viewed in this way, the Weaving Woman of this tale is one of a series of transitional figures that play a key role in Austin's writing. These characters typically move across the borders erected by such categories as race, gender, and ideology, and, in so doing, create a dual identity. Examples from other Austin works include the main female character in her first novel, *Isidro* (1905), who is not only a woman passing herself off as a man but a Mexican-American believed (mistakenly, it turns out) to be half-Indian; many of the stories in *Lost Borders* (1909) feature women characters who are either half-breeds or full-blood Indians who have relationships with and are then abandoned by white men.

In *The Basket Woman,* although approximately half of the stories are etiological myths with titles such as **"The Cheerful Glacier"** and **"The Crooked Fir,"** just under one-half portray the developing friendship between two central characters, the Paiute basket woman and an Anglo youth named Alan, whose parents employ the Indian woman as a laundress. The remaining two myths also have as central characters boys of about the same age as Alan. The preadolescent boy in this book is another of the transitional figures who move across borders—in this case not only between childhood and adulthood, but also between the separate worlds of Indian and white. It is these stories that provide narrative and thematic continuity within the book, in that, through them, we witness the evolving relationship between a Euro- and a Native American—a relationship mirroring that between the author and her Indian subject. Through these stories, we recognize the complexity of the book's project, which is not only to present nature to an audience of children but also, I would suggest, to mythologize the "natural history" of white-Indian relations. You will note that I have just claimed that two figures function as mirrors of the author—both the native basket weaver and the preadolescent Anglo boy. To see these reflections, we must turn to the stories themselves.

In the first story in the volume, Austin introduces us to Alan and the Paiute *mahala.* Alan is a newcomer to the country. As such, he is initially afraid of the Indians generally and of the Basket Woman in particular. He believes she might throw him into the basket she carries over her shoulder "and walk away across the mesa," a fate suggested to him by the teamster who had brought his family to their new homestead.[11]

Of what is Alan afraid? The fact that the Basket Woman is "the only Indian that he had [ever] seen" makes it clear that Alan is reacting to a preconceived image of the Indian based on white lore, such lore being transmitted not only through stagecoach drivers but also (undoubtedly) through books Alan has read about the West.[12] Alan's parents, by contrast, assure him that there is nothing to fear. His mother's attitude is perhaps attributable to the fact that, since she employs the Paiute mahala as a washer woman, their relationship is constituted strictly in economic terms. His father, who also employs Paiute laborers, tells Alan that the Indians "are not at all now what they were once."[13] The father's words imply a belief that the Paiute, like the stereotypical Indians of the nineteenth century, were once "a proud, war-like race." This stereotype, when applied to any Native American tribe, is at the very least a distortion, fixing as it does on one attribute among many; moreover, applying such an attribute to the Paiute represents an egregious fabrication, since the Paiute were generally peaceful with both their Indian and their white neighbors.[14]

Like his parents, Alan has his preconceptions; however, lacking awareness of the clear, economically defined roles that seem to guide his parents' feelings and behavior, Alan registers a marked ambivalence toward the Paiute. He tells his father, "I do not like Indians the way they are now," but he remains troubled by the conditions in which he sees them living.[15] Alan's ambivalence is shattered when, in a dream one night, the Basket Woman comes to him and carries him away in her basket. This marks the first of several journeys during which Alan sees a particular band of Owens Valley Paiute at different points in their history, learns their customs and myths, and comes to understand something of their culture and to appreciate their resilience as a people. Thus, for Alan, the basket begins to undergo a transformation: His attitude shifts from a fear of it as a vessel of capture to a desire for it as a vehicle of the imagination. This shift suggests that Austin is not only playing on the stereotypes promulgated by popular nineteenth-century literature, such as captivity narratives, but also implying that her book, like the basket, is itself a vehicle of an imagination that is narratively transported rather than a vessel of capture that is narratively embodied.[16] The book thus comes to equal the basket.

Since it is through such figures as the preadolescent boy and the Paiute woman that we best see Austin's manner of mythologizing white-Indian relations in the "land of lost borders," we might well want to examine the form that such mythologizing takes. Her first book, *The Land of Little Rain,* gives us a clue. In it Austin juxtaposes Christian and indigenous Great Basin religious mythologies. In one chapter we journey, via Austin's imaginative re-creation of the medicine man Winnenap's syncretic vision, to **"Shoshone Land,"** a journey that is cast as an analog to a return to Eden. She alludes to the Biblical story of Naboth's vineyard in framing **"My Neighbor's Field"** and places within this frame the Owens Valley Paiute tale of Winnedumah. These tales, which are about keeping faith with one's "brothers," may be read as commentary on relations between Euro- and Native Americans. In **"The Basket Maker,"** she compares Seyavi to the Biblical prophet Deborah in a description reminiscent both of a passage in *Lost Borders,* in which the desert-as-woman becomes a mythic figure, and of her self-depictions in *Earth Horizon.*[17]

Just so in *The Basket Woman,* where Austin creates her own syncretic mythology by mixing native- and Christian stories and forms. The importance of syncretism in Austin's writing is emphasized not only by the myths and their position in the volume, nor the similar handling of mythology in her first book, but also by the circumstances of her life at the time. In the late 1890s, Austin experienced a personal crisis that forced her to reform her spiritual identity. This crisis was brought on by her increasing sense that her life did not in any way

correspond to what she had envisioned for herself when she had married Wallace Austin a few years earlier. The most poignant disappointments resulted from a growing frustration with her daughter Ruth, who was developmentally disabled and prone to uncontrollable outbursts, and with her husband Wallace who, according to her, failed to communicate or work with her to achieve the stability that would enable her to do what she had always wanted—to write. This identity crisis eventually led to her first awareness "that she couldn't, in the orthodox sense of the word, go on calling herself a Christian" and that, while "the experience called the Practice of the Presence of God" had returned, it was accompanied by "a profound movement of spiritual growth away from the orthodox Protestant expression of it."[18]

There are indications that experimentation with Paiute ritual began to play a role in Austin's "practice." Helen Doyle, a Bishop doctor who treated Ruth, tells us, in her biography of Austin, that her friend would travel frequently to Round Valley to visit the Birchim family, who operated one of the largest sheep ranches in the Owens Valley. Nearby was a Paiute encampment, from which the Birchims, as was the custom, would have hired laborers. During the Austins' visits, the son, Will Birchim, who is said to have been conversant in Paiute language and lore, often performed songs and chants he had learned from his Indian neighbors.[19] Austin's interest in learning Paiute ritual even led her once to "lay out all one cold night on the mountains at the risk of her life to watch the P[a]iutes dance their Dance of Death."[20] [**"How I Would Sell My Book, 'Rhythm'"**]

When her mother became ill, Austin sensed that traditional Protestant modes of prayer were wholly inadequate to the situations she was facing. In *Earth Horizon,* Austin writes that, during an earlier conversation, she asked her mother whether she got what she prayed for, and her mother responded that she felt the presence of God, which was enough. To one such as Mary Austin, whose circumstances differed so greatly from expectations and who held the conviction "that life is essentially remediable, undefeatable; the thing was to discover the how of it," feeling the presence of God was not enough: She wanted results; she wanted to effect outcomes.[21] And so she turned to a Paiute medicine man. When Austin asked him the same question she had put to her mother, he replied, "Surely, if you pray right."[22]

Austin's emerging sense of the difference between native and Christian modes of prayer and ritual is captured in *Earth Horizon.* She writes about learning from the medicine man that

> [p]rayer had nothing to do with emotion[,] [but was] an outgoing act of the inner self toward something, not a god, toward a responsive activity in the world about

you, designated as The-Friend-of-the-Soul-of-Man. . . . This inner act was to be outwardly expressed in bodily acts, in words, in music, rhythm, color, whatever medium served the immediate purpose, or all of them.

Man is not alone nor helpless in the universe; he has toward it and it toward him an affective relation. This, precisely . . . was probably what Jesus meant with his figure of the branch and the vine, the Son and the Father. The illuminating point, the thing that Protestant Christianity had utterly failed to teach her, was the practice of prayer as an act, a motion of the mind, a reality. . . .

The experimentation, she continues, "began as adventure and became illumination. It went on . . . for years, and gradually embraced all the religious gestures accessible. . . ."[23]

The reference to "what Jesus meant" shows her tendency to reinterpret Christian mythology in light of what she had learned from the Paiute, something that she does more self-consciously in the books written immediately after leaving California.[24] Additionally, the last lines of the passage above reveal Austin's willingness to combine "religious gestures." Another incident from this period in her life indicates her capacity to believe seemingly disparate views simultaneously. In San Francisco, at a gathering of some of the group she would later live with in an artists' colony in Carmel— Jack London, Ambrose Bierce, James Hopper, and George Sterling—she tells of meeting John Muir and being entertained by the tales of his wilderness forays. Comparing Muir's to Sterling's spiritual or philosophical attitudes, she writes that Muir

told stories of his life in the wild, and of angels; angels that saved him; that lifted and carried him; that showed him where to put his feet; he believed them. . . . Sterling didn't believe in angels; but he believed in aliveness; sensitivities of stick and stone, of communications of animals, and I believed them both.[25]

Austin believed in both Christian and Native American mythologies. The mixing of mythologies in *The Basket Woman* attests to her belief and can be seen most clearly by juxtaposing two stories. The seventh of the fourteen tales in the book, titled **"The Christmas Tree,"** employs a central Christian image marking the birth of Christ, an image that, significantly, is thought to have been adapted in medieval times from even earlier "pagan" ritual. The final tale, titled **"Mahala Joe,"** uses one of the most well-known and frequently told Owens Valley Paiute myths as an intratextual commentary on one of the most significant local events in the history of white and Indian race relations. Both stories use as their central characters preadolescent boys, the transitional figure referred to earlier, who can thus be read as succeeding incarnations of Alan and of Austin herself.

In **"The Christmas Tree,"** Mathew, a boy whose mother has died, moves with his father out of the booming mining town where they had previously lived to a cabin on Pine Mountain, thus carrying out the dying wishes of his mother. The town is described with particularly hellish images that stand in stark contrast to the tranquility of Pine Mountain, "a strong, red hill" that the local Indians call "The Hill of Summer Snow." Mathew, who shares his name with the first gospel writer, grows up on the mountain, free to explore and play while his father is employed cutting wood for the mine at the base of Pine Mountain. The boy comes to know the plants and animals there as friends. He forms a special attachment to a particular silver fir tree in a small cluster of firs, which becomes a mother figure to him: "In the spring . . . it gave out a pleasant odor, and it was to him like the memory of what his mother had been." When he longed most for his mother, he would hug it and nestle among its branches, "[telling] it all his thoughts."[26]

When Mathew turns twelve, his father sends him to the newly built church school in the booming town below, where Mathew is instructed in the practice of Christianity. As a result, he begins to fear the time he will have to return to the mountain, where he will have "no one to tell him about this most important thing in the world" (i.e., the gospel message).[27] As he approaches his first Christmas in the town, Mathew is asked to supply the church with a Christmas tree, since his father is the wood cutter. He chooses his favorite tree. This decision causes him ambivalent feelings, which intensify into guilt as he looks upon "his" tree in the church on Christmas Eve. While the minister tells the story of the Christ child's birth in Bethlehem, Mathew can only look at the tree, until he sees it "tremble . . . , moving its boughs as if it spoke; and the boy heard it in his heart and believed, for it spoke to him of God." Mathew loses his fear of returning to the mountain; in fact, he begins to yearn for his return when he realizes that "he might find more in the forest than he had ever thought to find, now that he knew what to look for, since everything speaks of God in its own way and it is only a matter of understanding how."[28]

This story at first seems motivated by a rather standard kind of Transcendental panentheism,[29] but the way in which it presents Mathew's emerging spirituality and mirrors Austin's own spiritual development undercuts that kind of simple reading. Early in the story, Mathew realizes intuitively (though perhaps not consciously) his connection to a sacred quality within the tree. This realization is evidenced when he lays garlands of flowers and berries on its branches and creates an altar-like cairn of stones at its base, in which he stores all his treasures.[30] The story implies that this worship occurs on a mountain that is sacred to the local Indians. Mountains, it should be noted, are associated with power in both Biblical and Paiute mythology. For example, flood myths in both traditions depict a high mountain as the only ground remaining above the water; this mountain becomes the central point from which people and all other beings populate the world. Two features of Austin's Pine Mountain suggest that she is taking pains to highlight its sacredness to the Paiute Indians. First, its Indian name, the Hill of Summer Snow, shows that it is one of the more prominent features in the vicinity and thus implies its importance in the local mythology, perhaps as the central peak.[31] Furthermore, its red color is sacred to the Northern Paiute (and to many other Great Basin cultures) and often is used, along with white, by doctors in healing ceremonies. Since the mountain and the tree are holy, when Mathew personifies the tree as a concomitant step in developing his relationship to it, he is performing a move characteristic of native mythology. Additionally, although Mathew's intuitive sense is temporarily lost in the context of his Christian education, its eventually return is signaled by a desire to share his sacred experience of nature with other Christians. When the tree, laden with its "pagan" significance, is literally transplanted into a Christian church, it marks Mathew's return to this original sense that spirituality inheres in all things. Metaphorically, then, the intuitive experience of sacredness corresponds to the "pagan" mythology that is then grafted onto Christian mythology, and the result is a kind of syncretism that leads Mathew, significantly, back to the mountain, the sacred place of the local Paiute people. When we consider that Austin joined the Methodist Church at the age of thirteen (approximately Mathew's age) and that, when she wrote this story, she was undergoing a spiritual crisis that turned her away from the practice of institutionalized Christianity to a practice of Paiute religion as she understood it, we see the preadolescent male figure equated with his author.

This reading of the story is further strengthened when we consider that, in *The Land of Little Rain,* Austin's first move in acknowledging the sacredness of the land is to adopt the Indian practice of name-giving.[32] [*Stories from the Country of Lost Borders*] This practice is tied fundamentally to a belief in the power of language as a creative force. Early in the book, it enlarges to include not only the use of names but also the telling of stories.[33] In light of that tendency, let us turn to an examination of the final story in *The Basket Woman,* "Mahala Joe," which superimposes the local history of race relations over the backdrop of a well-known Owens Valley Paiute myth. Actually, the myth is more than just a backdrop; as in most of Austin's writings, backdrop, in the form of a landscape that is at once physical and mythical, is both the most prominent and the most powerful character, exerting its influence on human endeavor. For Austin, then, the point becomes to match the mythical landscape to the physical; from this attempt arises the need for reconstituting Christian mythology in light of Paiute oral tradition.

Although Austin, in keeping with her desire to make her story "mythic" (i.e., enduring), does not precisely place it in history, we can deduce from historical sources that the events take place in the early 1860s, just before the most significant conflict between the Owens Valley Paiute and the white settlers. The conflict is sometimes referred to as the Owens Lake battle; it occurred in 1862 as part of the fallout from the more infamous Paiute Indian War of 1860, which took place farther north and east in Nevada.[34] Austin's story involves two boys, Joe and Walter, a Paiute and a white, respectively, who are raised together as brothers after Walter's mother dies in childbirth and his father, a prominent rancher, gives him up to be raised by a young Paiute woman who herself has just given birth to a boy. The two boys are thus "both nursed at one breast"—literally as well as metaphorically.[35] The mother figure here, as in the earlier story, becomes a type of "earth mother." The implication is that both white and Indian are sustained by the same mysterious life-giving power that is concentrated in the land itself.

The most significant events in the relationship between the boys begin when they hear the arrow maker tell the story of Winnedumah, the Owens Valley Paiute culture hero. The legend is an etiological myth explaining the presence of a highly visible rock monolith atop the Inyo Range and of some unusual pines along Independence Creek. Winnedumah and his brother Tinnemaha, forebears of the Paiute, are engaged in a war with a neighboring tribe to the west. The last of their tribe to stand and fight, they are leading their enemies eastward toward their own tribe's territory. At the moment when Winnedumah—who has vowed that he will always remain faithful to his brother—reaches the top of the Inyo range, he looks back over his shoulder and sees Tinnemaha, who is trailing him, hit by an arrow; in that instant, the pursuers are turned into the long-leaved pines along the creek, and Tinnemaha and Winnedumah are transformed into large boulders. Thus the rock monolith, locally called the Winnedumah monument, preserves the memory of Winnedumah's devotion to his brother.[36]

After Joe and Walter hear this story, they decide to visit the site. Around this time, minor skirmishes have begun to occur between whites and Paiute people in the valley. During the trip, two key events set the stage for the final climactic scene. First, the boys get lost and, inspired by the example of the story, swear a vow on Joe's elk's tooth that, come what may, they will always stand together. After they fall asleep, a powerful Indian appears out of nowhere and carries Walter back to his own people. After Walter returns home, he and Joe again visit the arrow maker, who, when told the story, identifies the mysterious Indian as none other than Winnedumah himself. The arrow maker then formalizes and ritualizes the vow the boys swore on the mountain by mixing their blood.[37] When the hostilities between whites and Indians escalate to a point where war seems inevitable, Walter's father sends him back East to his mother's family, something Joe is not told. It is implied that Walter, in contrast to Winnedumah, never looks back. Joe rides with the other Paiute warriors, but, when he realizes that they are to attack the ranch of Walter's father, he turns and flees. As a result of this act, he is forced to wear the woman's dress as a badge of shame. As a matter of principle, he continues this practice even after the duration of the imposed penalty has passed, for the rest of his life.

In the context of the Paiute myth at the heart of this tale, the message is clear as both a moral and political statement: Although both white and Indian people are sustained by the same land, the whites break their promises to the Indians, whereas the Paiute, following the example of Winnedumah, stick by their word, whatever the cost. This lesson is inscribed not only in the story but in the land itself—in the figure of Winnedumah. The complexity of this particular lesson is reflected in the figure of Joe, who seems to combine the two central figures of the earlier part of the book. In Joe, the adolescent boy is transformed into a Paiute mahala. I would venture that Austin's **"Mahala Joe"** may well be based on a locally famous Paiute transvestite basket maker of the 1910s, Joe Eugley. If my speculation is true, it reinforces the sense that Austin has made Joe the book's final amalgamation of the two central figures, who are also mirrors of the author.[38]

In the contexts created by both that association and the positioning of the stories in the book as a whole, the moral and political messages of this final story blur into a spiritual one. If the word spoken by the whites cannot be trusted by the Indians, it does not guide the actions of the whites themselves either; if the word here, as elsewhere in Austin, is linked not only with individual utterances or names but with stories as well, then whites must turn to Native American mythologies as a guide to reinterpreting Christian mythology—a move implicitly made in the earlier story.

Rather than advocating a rejection of Christian mythology, Austin encourages a syncretic blending of it with the indigenous mythology. Only in this way, the book implies, can Euro-Americans begin to understand the land in which they have come to live. In *The Land of Journey's Ending,* a book that more explicitly advocates a syncretic blending, Austin writes that "no man has ever really entered into the heart of any country until he has adopted or made up myths about its familiar objects."[39] In this sense, then, *The Basket Woman* is addressed to the larger audience of Euro-American readers who, like the children for whom it is explicitly designed, are thus placed in a transitional position in regard to their relation with indigenous races. By re-

creating and deploying both native and Christian myths in a fashion similar to that used by Piudy and Zitkala-Sa, the book attempts to teach readers the lesson that both assimilation and extermination, the polarized terms guiding the "Indian debate" at the turn of the century, are morally and spiritually inadequate to the situation of the races. This lesson is carried through the book—the metaphorical equivalent of the Paiute woman's basket. In order to understand more specifically how this equivalency works, we need briefly to consider the nature of Paiute basketry.

Baskets in Paiute culture traditionally are made in one of two styles—twined or coiled—with the former far more common up until the early part of this century. In the Owens Valley, coiled baskets are created by winding up to three individual strands—typically of willow or rye-grass—one after the other in a downward and leftward spiral, so that each strand remains separate and recognizable; twined baskets have strands interwoven over one or, more usually, two warps, called by anthropologists "plain twining" and "twill twining," respectively. The large-type burden baskets, carried by a tumpline and traditionally used to collect pine cones or nuts (a vital nutritional source collected in the fall) and to transport household items when camp was being moved, often found service after contact as laundry baskets.[40] It is this kind of basket, typically of the twill-twined variety, that the basket woman in Austin's story—who, we remember, was employed as a washer woman—presumably would have carried.

The fact that it is in this basket that the preadolescent figure of Alan is imaginatively transported in the book's opening tale becomes doubly significant when we consider the historical context. Both the laundry that the Paiute woman carries and the basket itself—a popular item that could be sold to whites—are economic staples for the Indian woman. Furthermore, the pine nuts constitute a nutritional staple—one that carries symbolic or ritual weight, since the fall Pine Nut Festival is one of two major Paiute tribal gatherings.

Because her husband tended to switch jobs frequently, Austin was constantly struggling to support her family by writing; thus her book, like the Paiute woman's basket, was a means not only of maintaining economic stability but also of carrying her stories—the seeds of a new religious mythology. Just as the basket's predominant pattern is composed of two strands woven together, the new mythology offered by the book is made from two of the area's prominent religious traditions. The seeds of these traditions are carried, via the author's imagination, to be planted in her readers' minds.

In closing, let me turn to the spiritual association of baskets and basket-weaving in a Native American context, as recorded from two famous Pomo weavers. In the words of Mabel McKay—a healer who has been described as "a traditional basket-maker, a weaver whose work is associated with power and prophecy"—we see the creation of the basket in the larger context of Native American spiritual traditions: "Everything is told to me in my Dream. What kind of design, what shape, what I am to do with it—everything about the baskets—is told in my Dream."[41] In a similar vein, Essie Parrish offers a prayer that begins with a standard Christian address to God and then continues with a blessing that must be considered traditional Pomo. In it, Parrish links the power of the baskets she made with the power of speech; both come from the same source and flow through her, the artist. Just as significantly, she draws on the figure of the Christian-derived male deity, who is transformed (or who transforms himself) into a female power that is then manifested through an Indian woman. Through this figure, Parrish shows that the opposites that many people would see—male and female, Christian and Indian—are, for her, actually complements, united in her baskets no less than in her prayer:

> Our Father, the good power
> The power of good words
> The good power hand. She made this basket. . . .[42]

Notes

1. Isabel Kelly, "Northern Paiute Tales," *Journal of American Folklore* 51:202 (October-December 1938): 363-438. Reported in Jarold Ramsey, ed., *Coyote Was Going There: Indian Literature of the Oregon Country* (Seattle: University of Washington Press, 1977), 258.

2. Jarold Ramsey, "The Bible in Western Indian Mythology," *Journal of American Folklore* 90 (October-December 1977): 442-54.

3. Gertrude Bonnin/Zitkala-Sa, *American Indian Stories* (1921; Lincoln: University of Nebraska Press, 1985), 41-42.

4. Ibid., 47ff.

5. Arnold Krupat uses this work as an illustration of one "of those moments in the history of translation when the intentions of poet-translators from the dominant culture more nearly seemed to approach the intentions of Indian performers . . . ," in an act that he terms "translation-as-criticism." Krupat continues: "[T]he fact that translation-as-criticism to some extent mirrors the Native American way of doing 'criticism'—critical practice, that is, only as internal to an evolving literary practice—it may do somewhat less violence to the literatures it 'criticizes.'" Krupat, *Ethnocriticism: Ethnography, History, Literature* (Berkeley, CA: University of California Press, 1992), 193-95. (Krupat also refers to Austin in *For Those Who Come After* and *The Voice in the Margin*.) For a

contrary view on Austin, see William Bevis, "American Indian Verse Translations," in *Literatures of the American Indians: Views and Interpretations,* ed. Abraham Chapman (New York: New American Library, 1975), 308-23, whom Krupat footnotes on the pages cited above.

6. Mary Austin, *The Basket Woman: A Book of Indian Tales for Children.* (1904; Boston: Houghton Mifflin Company, 1910). Hereafter cited as *BW.*

7. Lying on the east side of the Sierra and stretching somewhat more than eighty miles in a south-north direction, the Owens Valley begins about 175 miles northeast of Los Angeles, with Death Valley to the southeast and Yosemite to the northwest.

Today, the Paiute and Shoshoni of Owens Valley call themselves the "Paiute-Shoshone Tribe of Owens Valley," reflecting the extent to which intermarriage has occurred. (Intermarriage, from what we know, has always been common between the two cultures.) Many other Northern Paiute groups, particularly in Nevada, prefer the term *Numu* ("People"), their traditional name for themselves. In my discussion, I use *Paiute* and *Shoshoni* because my focus is on the way these peoples and cultures have been perceived and understood by Austin in her own time.

8. *BW,* iii.

9. See, for example, Judy Trejo, "A Paiute Commentary," *Journal of American Folklore* 87 (1974): 66-71, in which Trejo tells us that "Paiutes refer to young Anglo boys who sneak around gawking at young girls as coyotes (*e-etza*)."

10. Austin, *Earth Horizon* (New York: The Literary Guild, 1932). See, e.g., 289. Hereafter cited as *EH.*

11. *BW,* 5.

12. Ibid., 4.

13. Ibid., 6.

14. *Peaceful* is, of course, a relative term, and whether the neighboring Washoe or Shoshoni, for example, might describe the Paiute as such—especially before the time of Euro-American contact—is open to debate. My point here is that "war-like" activities, such as raiding, seem not to have been central to Northern Paiute culture in the same way that they were in some other Indian cultures.

15. *BW,* 7.

16. Although to develop an argument about another book is beyond the scope of this paper, I would suggest that, in her later, fanciful novel, *Outland* (New York: Boni & Liveright, 1919), Austin reworks the conventions of captivity narratives.

17. *Stories from the Country of Lost Borders,* ed. Marjorie Pryse (New Brunswick, NJ: Rutgers University Press, 1987), 160. Pryse comments on the parallel between Austin and the desert-as-woman passage in her introduction but not in the context of the reference to Deborah (p. xxix).

As hinted at in Austin's later work, Winnenap seems to have been, for her, a model of Native-Christian syncretism. In *California: The Land of the Sun,* after recounting an Owens Valley Paiute etiological myth explaining how California came to have its shape, she tells us that "Winnenap . . . was eclectic in his faiths as in his practice." That his wife "was a tall brown woman out of Tejon and her mother was of that band of captives taken from San Gabriel by the Mojaves, Mission-bred" suggests that the sources for Winnenap's spiritual philosophy and practice may have come not only from Indian cultures but also from Catholicism. Thus the syncretism in the earlier book should be seen as an attempt to reflect Winnenap's beliefs rather than just a wholly fictional projection of the author's beliefs onto an Indian figure. See *California: The Land of the Sun* (New York: The Mac-Millan Company, 1914), 3-4.

18. *EH,* 267. Austin's characteristic habit of "borrowing" freely from diverse sources can be seen in her use of the phrase, *the Practice of the Presence of God,* which comes from seventeenth-century French monk, Brother Lawrence of the Resurrection.

19. Helen MacKnight Doyle, *Mary Austin: Woman of Genius* (New York: Gotham House, 1939), 190.

20. Austin, "How I Would Sell My Book, 'Rhythm,'" in *The Bookseller and Stationer,* 1 May 1923, 7. The "Dance of Death" to which she refers is most probably what is often called the "Cry Dance," a mourning ceremony for those who have died during the previous year.

21. *EH,* 268.

22. Ibid., 274-76.

23. Ibid., 266-67.

24. In *Christ in Italy,* for example, she explains how she came to understand the Jesus portrayed in the art of the great Italian masters at the same time that she was being tutored in Christian prayer by Sister Veronica—an experience that, incidentally, she claims cured her of breast cancer. *Christ in Italy—Being the Experiences of a Maverick among Men* (New York: Duffield and Company, 1912). At the same time that *Christ in Italy* was being published, she was working on drafts of a play, *Fire,* which begins with a dramatization of the Owens

Valley Paiute myth about the origin of fire and then grafts this myth onto the basic plot of the gospel story, with the Paiute fire-bringer as rejected savior. *Fire* was published serially in *The Play-book* II, Nos. 5-7 (October-December 1914) and was performed at the Forest Theatre in Carmel sometime between 1912 and 1914. In *The Basket Woman,* the story entitled "The Fire-Bringer" is another adaptation of this myth, presented without the subtext of the gospel story.

I might also suggest that Austin's tendency to re-interpret Christian mythology is parallel to and consistent with her insistence that American poetry be understood in light of Native American verse forms. See, for example, *The American Rhythm* (1923; New York: AMS Press, 1970).

25. *EH,* 298; my emphasis.

26. *BW,* 93-94.

27. Ibid., 99.

28. Ibid., 103-104.

29. *Panentheism* differs from *pantheism* in that, while both terms denote that God is suffused throughout nature, the former term denotes that God's presence is not exhausted in nature—that is, He is both immanent and transcendent, a portion of his reality continuing to exist outside of material nature.

30. *BW,* 93-94.

31. Jay Miller, for instance, comments that "[t]hroughout [a] region, people can point out a particularly high or prominent peak as the sacred center where creation began or an Immortal lived." He goes on to discuss one of the most powerful of these peaks in the south and central Basin, Charleston Peak in the Spring Mountains west of Las Vegas, noting that its native name is Snow-Having. I am not arguing that Austin is drawing on the name of this specific peak, but I believe that her use of a name that keys on the same characteristic suggests that she most likely got it from a local native source and that she is aware of its spiritual implications. See Jay Miller, "Basin Theology and Religion: A Comparative Study of Power (*Puha*)," in *Journal of California and Great Basin Anthropology* 5:1-2 (1983): 66-86.

32. *Stories from the Country of Lost Borders* (New Brunswick, NJ: Rutgers University Press, 1987), 3. See also footnote 31.

33. The importance placed on "the Word" is a characteristic of both Christian and many Native American traditions. Consider creation accounts, for example. Just as the God of Genesis speaks the

world into existence, so, too, does the creator figure in many Native American tales speak beings into existence by giving them their names. Contemporary Indian authors also emphasize this characteristic—for example, N. Scott Momaday in "The Man Made of Words" and Leslie Marmon Silko in *Ceremony.*

34. For a history of the Paiute Indian War of 1860, see Ferol Egan, *Sand in a Whirlwind: The Paiute Indian War of 1860* (Garden City, NY: Doubleday & Company, 1972); for Owens Valley history, see William Chalfant, *The Story of Inyo,* rev. ed. (1922; Bishop, CA: Chalfant Press, 1933); and, more recently, William H. Michael, "'At the Plow and in the Harvest Field': Indian Conflict and Accommodation in the Owens Valley 1860-1880" (M.A. thesis, University of Oklahoma, 1993).

35. *BW,* 202.

36. Julian Steward, "Myths of the Owens Valley Paiutes," *University of California Publications in American Archaeology and Ethnology* 34 (1934-36): 355-440.

37. *BW,* 201.

38. Reported in Catherine S. Fowler and Lawrence E. Dawson, "Ethnographic Basketry," in *The Handbook of the North American Indians,* vol. 11, *The Great Basin,* Warren L. d'Azevedo, ed. (Washington, DC: Smithsonian Institution, 1986): 705-37.

39. Austin, *The Land of Journey's Ending* (1924; Tucson: University of Arizona Press, 1983), 302.

40. Fowler and Dawson, "Ethnographic Basketry."

41. Greg Sarris, *Keeping Slug Woman Alive* (Los Angeles: University of California Press, 1993), 51.

42. Quoted in ibid., 60.

Linda K. Karell (essay date 1995)

SOURCE: Karell, Linda K. "*Lost Borders* and Blurred Boundaries: Mary Austin as Storyteller." In *American Women Short Story Writers: A Collection of Critical Essays,* edited by Julie Brown, pp. 153-66. New York: Garland Publishing, Inc., 1995.

[*In the following essay, Karell maintains that in her short story collection* Lost Borders, *Austin uses the "recurring metaphors" of "borders and boundaries" as a means to resist "the dominant white culture's definitions of femininity, literature, and cultural superiority." Austin further demonstrates that spirituality "is an essential component of female subjectivity," and that storytelling "is itself a spiritual act capable of radical reconceptions of gender and identity."*]

> Out there where the borders of conscience break down, where there is no convention, and behavior is of little account except as it gets you your desire, almost anything might happen; does happen, in fact, though I shall have trouble making you believe it.
>
> Mary Austin, *Lost Borders*

In her 1932 autobiography, *Earth Horizon,* Mary Austin records an experience from her childhood that sets the tone for her writing as an adult. Austin writes that her creative storytelling angered her mother, who interpreted her young daughter's "storying" as a "wicked" insistence on relating imagined events as if they had actually happened: "Mother said she supposed she'd have to punish you or you would grow up a storyteller. Well, you *did* see them. If you got punished for it, you'd simply have to stand it" (42, 43). Austin's textual reconstruction—her story—of her resistance emphasizes that storytelling capable of challenging rigid definitions of truth may evoke punishment, particularly for women whose speech may be interpreted as lies and whose resistance is measured by their ability to endure. Austin locates another form of resistance in the act of writing the autobiography itself. In some places, as in the above passage, Austin erodes the distinction between author, subject, and reader by aligning reader with subject through her use of the second-person pronoun "you." Elsewhere in *Earth Horizon,* she frequently splits the autobiographical subject into the first-person "I" and the third-person "she." In each case, Austin prevents the stable opposition of subject to object that is a prerequisite to relationships of dominance and submission. In *Lost Borders* (1909), as its title suggests, storytelling performs similar acts of boundary blurring, thus revealing the debilitating conventions of domination that the enforcement of stable boundaries helps to construct and maintain.

Austin was born Mary Hunter in 1868 in Carlinville, Illinois. After her graduation from college, she traveled to southern California with her mother and brothers in order to homestead. Like her fictive narrator in *Lost Borders,* Austin interacted with the region's diverse populations. She visited Native Americans and was politically active to help secure fair legal treatment for the Native and Hispanic cultures she valued. In California, Austin met and married Wallace Austin, embarked upon a teaching career, and encountered the landscape and cultures that would dominate her thinking and writing throughout her life. Although she left the desert in 1906 (and was later divorced from Wallace Austin), her time there had a formative influence on her writing and helped to encourage her independence as a feminist and an activist.

Austin wrote and published in almost every conceivable literary genre and was widely known and respected as a literary artist at her death in 1934. However, Austin's work has received little sustained critical attention, and today it is generally excluded from the American literary canon. At best, a small selection of Austin's early fiction, including *Lost Borders,* is granted moderate respect as "local-color" writing. In both her fiction and nonfiction, Austin crafted an authorial voice that tended toward both the confidently transcendent and the feminist. She explicitly described herself as a storyteller, a mystic, a prophet, and a maverick, and with the determination of the female child who elected punishment over silencing, she repeatedly challenged cultural expectations about what a woman should write. To assist her in this challenge, she claimed the literary authority of an essential female spirituality that was dramatically influenced by her understanding of Native American spiritual beliefs and oral storytelling traditions.

Austin's acknowledgment of Native American influence in her writing, her typically brash confidence, and her articulate self-presentation have resulted in her writing often being read through the related critical lenses of Western Christian assumptions and disappointed gender expectations. For example, distinctions between the author and her characters are often elided entirely in the criticism, subjecting Austin to parody during her lifetime and to personal insult and condescension since then. References to her weight, physical appearance, and unconventional spiritual beliefs regularly intrude into assessments of her writing. Even sympathetic readings that attempt to reexamine Austin's contributions to literature and feminism tend to be "marred by the war between affection and exasperation, respect and dismissal, that appears to overtake many who try to write about Austin" (Porter 307). Alternating affection and exasperation may be reasonable responses to Austin's work. Particularly in *Lost Borders,* Austin's graceful poeticism edges into a mystical obliqueness while her biting wit occasionally lashes out to reassert cultural stereotypes of female incapacity. However, dismissing Austin because she can be essentialistic and even contradictory is a self-defeating gesture of academic protectionism that ignores the contributions Austin's writing makes to contemporary feminist debate. By drawing on Native American spiritual beliefs in *Lost Borders,* Austin challenges the ethno- and intellectual centrism that construct the boundaries of much contemporary feminist theorizing that cleaves feminists into what appear to be two opposed camps: essentialists and everyone else. Throughout *Lost Borders,* Austin's claims to essentialism prove valuable as a form of identity politics, as a strategy to obtain legitimate and necessary cultural power, and as an aspect of her understanding of the relationship between female subjectivity and spirituality. At the same time, Austin displays a consistent awareness that identity is constructed and fragile.

In *Lost Borders,* a collection of 14 short stories set in the desert region of California, Austin explores a series of oppositions rigidly enforced in Western culture: male/female, self/other, sacred/secular, and oral/written literature. In my examination of a selection of stories from *Lost Borders,* I argue that Austin attempts to claim a spiritually authorized power for marginalized characters by employing borders and boundaries as recurring metaphors of resistance toward the dominant white culture's definitions of femininity, literature, and cultural superiority. Central to my reading of this collection is my belief that Austin's claim is grounded in her conviction that storytelling is itself a spiritual act capable of radical reconceptions of gender and identity. I argue that *Lost Borders* embodies Austin's insistence that spirituality is an *essential* component of female subjectivity, an insistence that authorizes female agency by privileging the female storyteller who narrates and unifies the collection. Paradoxically, however, Austin's essentialism reintroduces the troubling conflation of femininity, spirituality, and nature that has historically authorized attempts to master the female.

In the closing passage of **"The Land,"** the first story in *Lost Borders,* Austin describes the California desert as the site of an essential femininity:

> If the desert were a woman, I know well what like she would be: deep-breasted, broad in the hips, tawny, with tawny hair, great masses of it lying smooth along her perfect curves, full-lipped like a sphinx, but not heavy-lidded like one, eyes sane and steady as the polished jewel of her skies, such a countenance as should make men serve without desiring her, such a largeness to her mind as should make their sins of no account, passionate, but not necessitous, patient—and you could not move her, no, not if you had all the earth to give, so much as one tawny hair's-breadth beyond her own desires.
>
> (160)

Austin simultaneously represents the desert landscape of *Lost Borders,* the physical site of the stories her narrator tells, as a sexualized, desirous, female body and as a figure of mystical spirituality. Austin explicitly rejects the patriarchal construction of feminine "otherness" based on the oppositions between sexual and spiritual that was so intensely a focus of her midwestern Methodist childhood. Instead, her image of the desert emphasizes their integration; borders between sexuality and spirituality are fluid. Throughout *Lost Borders,* Austin represents the desert landscape as an active and central character whose power derives from her spiritual authority.

Before examining more fully the ways in which Austin grants her *Lost Borders* characters agency through spiritual authority, I want first to explore the basis of her spiritual understanding. Her autobiography gives us insights into the ways in which Native American spirituality influenced Austin's adult understanding of spirituality and helps to clarify its relationship to authorial production. In *Earth Horizon,* Austin describes visiting a Paiute medicine man, and subsequently defines her experience of spirituality as involving a reciprocal relationship with a responsive power that she designates as the Friend-of-the-Soul-of-Man:

> The Paiutes were basket-makers; the finest of their sort. What Mary drew from them was their naked craft, the subtle sympathies of twig and root and bark; she consorted with them; she laid herself open to the influences of the wild, the thing done, accomplished. She entered into their lives, the life of the campody, the strange secret life of the tribe, the struggle of Whiteness with Darkness, the struggle of the individual soul with the Friend-of-the-Soul-of-Man. She learned what it meant; how to prevail; how to measure her strength against it. Learning that, she learned to write.
>
> (289)

The passage is simultaneously a metaphor for the writing process and a description of a spiritual initiation Austin credited with teaching her to write. In the Paiute culture Austin describes, as in Native American cultures generally, the valorized distinction in Western culture between secular and spiritual disappears. As Austin's description suggests, tasks of everyday artistry such as basket-weaving are both functional and spiritual. In this context, storytelling must likewise be understood as both a functional and a spiritual act. As Leslie Silko insists when she writes, "You don't have anything / if you don't have the stories," Native Americans understand the power to shape the world that inheres in stories (2). Until the emergence of deconstruction, Western understandings of language insisted on word/meaning stability, while in traditional Native beliefs, the question is not one of the putative stability or instability of meaning but of the effect of language in the world. Words have spiritual power; they are living entities that have a manifest effect on the world. Storytellers may be healers; certainly they are historians and culture-bearers.

Austin, then, like the narrator of *Lost Borders,* grounds her authority to speak in a spiritual understanding that is dramatically influenced by Native American spiritual and literary traditions. James Ruppert has shown that "Austin hoped to give the writers of her day guidance in their struggle to revitalize their art" by returning to a consideration of the interdependent effects of the land and spirit evident in Native American literary forms (Mary Austin's **"Landscape"** 389). By crediting the Paiutes with her growing talent as a writer, Austin both attempts to legitimate an ancient literary heritage largely unrecognized within Western culture's valuation of written literature and to assert that her own authority as a storyteller implicitly derives from the spiritual potency of the literary models she follows. Nonetheless, her representations of Native Americans in the above passage from her autobiography are marred by stereotyping and insistent gestures of appropriation and colonization. Austin reinforces oppositions between tame/wild and whiteness/darkness, producing a primitive "other" in service to a white culture. Her allusion to a "strange secret life" encountered with Native Americans recapitulates the stereotype of an alien and exotic race whose mysterious knowledge is harnessed to revitalize white culture.

Austin's reliance on essentialistic conceptions of gender and racial identity here and in her representations of the desert landscape is troubling. However, it is important to consider the complexities of Austin's Native American influence before pejoratively branding her "essentialist." In *The Sacred Hoop,* Paula Gunn Allen writes, "We are the land. To the best of my understanding, that is the fundamental idea that permeates American Indian life; the land (Mother) and the people (mothers) are the same[;] . . . the earth *is* being as all creatures are also being: aware, palpable, intelligent, alive" (119). The stories in *Lost Borders* consistently present the desert as just such an active being. In **"The Hoodoo of the Minnietta,"** for example, we read that "the desert had [McKenna], cat-like, between her paws" (164); in **"The Return of Mr. Wills,"** the desert's "insatiable spirit . . . will reach out and take Mr. Wills again" (187); and in **"The Ploughed Lands,"** Gavin is lost in the desert "in the grip of another mistress who might or might not loose his bonds" (177). While Gavin becomes "his own man" only after he leaves the desert behind for "white people, towns, farms" (179), other white male characters never escape the desert's power: "Out there beyond the towns the long Wilderness lies brooding, imperturbable; she puts out to adventurous minds glittering fragments of fortune or romance, like the lures men use to catch antelopes—clip! then she has them" (182). Conceiving and representing the land as feminine is a central aspect of Native American spiritual belief. Unlike inscriptions of a feminine landscape common to American literature produced by whites, however, Native American conceptions of a feminine landscape work to prevent the exploitation of the land and its inhabitants by positing an ongoing relationship among them. Austin's essentialism is grounded in her awareness of this difference in spiritual understanding and results in representations of a female desert who is dangerous mainly to those men who attempt to master her.

Allen and other Native American women writers have criticized feminism for its failure to acknowledge how different cultural positions affect feminist theorizing: in this case casting the land as female is not inevitably a reinscription of essentialism, nor does essentialism itself necessarily perform the same cultural work of defining women as "other" in Native American literary traditions. Of course, Austin is not Native American nor does she write from within that literary tradition. However, in **"Regionalism in American Fiction,"** Austin does align herself with Native American understandings of the land when she insists that all literature must reflect "in some fashion the essential qualities of the land" (106). Like Allen, Austin believes those essential qualities are linked to a particular definition of femininity that includes activity, intelligence, independence, and mystical power. Here as elsewhere, however, Austin deconstructs her own essentialism with her belief that writers must acknowledge that there is "not one vast, pale figure of America, but several Americas, in many subtle and significant characterizations" (98). *Lost Borders,* then, is Austin's challenge to literary and cultural representations that create "one vast, pale figure of America."

Both the structure and subject of *Lost Borders* enact its title. For instance, the 14 separate stories are unified by a single female narrative voice, eroding the borders between them. Clear demarcations between beginnings and endings of the stories collapse as individual stories may include within them several other stories. While she is neither omniscient nor universalized, the unnamed narrator provides a unifying voice. She acts as a distinctive trail guide through *Lost Borders,* maneuvering the reader through the stories that comprise the desert landscape, privileging her own interpretations, as in **"The Fakir,"** when she begins with her own point of view: "Whenever I come up to judgement, and am hard pushed to make good on my own account (as I expect to be), I shall mention the case of Netta Saybrick, for on the face of it, and by all the traditions in which I was bred, I behaved rather handsomely" (211). Austin's narrator is a witty, bitingly ironic cultural interpreter, a confident trail guide, and a woman compelled to tell the stories of the land: "I had long wished to write a story of Death Valley that should be its final word. It was to be so chosen from the limited sort of incidents that could happen there, so charged with the still ferocity of its moods that I should at last be quit of its obsession, free to concern myself about other affairs" (203). As James Ruppert has pointed out, Austin's understanding of storytelling is influenced by Native American oral poetic traditions ("Discovering America" 256). In *Lost Borders,* the context of the story's telling is emphasized and its origin carefully noted; the reader's participation in determining the story's meaning is valued; and privileged Western ideals such as chronological progression, climax, and resolution are less apparent and dramatic. The collection is structurally calculated to refuse Western models of literature as timeless, self-contained products of individual genius. Instead, Austin's boundary blurring creates indistinct textual divisions and reasserts the importance of context and audience for a story's meaning.

Austin's "Borderers" are Native American women and men, sheepherders, pocket hunters, and the female storyteller patterned after Austin's own biography. Marginalized within the Euro-American culture newly settled in California, these characters safely roam the desert beyond the boundaries of the homesteads and towns that are occupied by these white settlers. In **"The Land,"** their marginal status gives them knowledge that enables them to survive:

> First and last, accept no man's statement that he knows this Country of Lost Borders well. A great number having lost their lives in the process of proving where it is not safe to go, it is now possible to pass through much of the district by guide-posts and well-known water-holes, but the best part of it remains locked, inviolate, or at best known only to some far-straying Indian, sheepherder, or pocket hunter, whose account of it does not get into the reports of the Geological Survey.

> (159)

The narrator aligns herself with marginal figures whose knowledge of the land surpasses the limits of official knowledge and is a component of their claim to a spiritual authority necessary for survival. Relying on stable boundaries is a dangerous strategy in Austin's desert landscape, where the privilege of masculine entitlement that such boundaries preserve is especially vulnerable: "Out there, then, where the law and the landmarks fail together, the souls of little men fade out at the edges, leak from them as water from wooden pails warped asunder" (156). Although Austin grants her narrator a spiritual authority to speak, she does not privilege her speech as universal. Any pretensions to represent universal truths are deliberately undercut. Elsewhere in **"The Land,"** for example, she responds to a challenge to "find a story" about a piece of pottery with a vow to "make a story," and discovers immediately the impossibility of speaking universally. Stories shift and change to accommodate the needs of their tellers and hearers:

> Next winter . . . a prospector from Panamint-way wanted to know if I had ever heard of the Indian-pot Mine which was lost. . . . I said I had a piece of the pot, which I showed him. Then I wrote the tale for a magazine, . . . and several men were at great pains to explain to me where my version varied from the accepted one of the hills. By this time, you understand, I had begun to believe the story myself. . . . Now it only needs that some one should find another shard of the gold-besprinkled pot to fix the tale in the body of desert myths.

> (158-159)

In this passage, oral and written literature have storytelling in common as their source, and the distinction between them blurs as Austin's narrator relates her story. Moreover, history is revealed as a series of competing interpretations, where gender determines authority. Male knowledge of the story is enough to invest it with the illusion of truth; the male miners display no hesitancy—are "at pains" in fact—to correct the narrator.

"The Land" also contains a macabre warning of the dangers female storytelling can pose to rigid definitions of truth and certainty. The narrator retells a story of settlers who are killed when the salt crust over a lake collapses. She first hears the story from another character, Long Tom Bassit, who heard it from "a man who saw it":

> [The story] was of an immigrant train all out of its reckoning. . . . [N]ear the middle of the lake, the salt crust thinned out abruptly, and, the foreward rank of the party breaking through, the bodies were caught under the saline slabs and not all of them recovered. There was a woman among them, and the Man-who-saw had cared—cared enough to go back years afterward, when . . . long before he reached the point, he saw the gleam of red in the woman's dress, and found her at last, lying on her side, sealed in the crystal, rising as ice rises to the surface of choked streams.
>
> (157)

In this, the most ambiguous and disturbing story within a story in the collection, Austin figures the border between safety and death as literally unstable, with a brightly clothed but unnamed woman as a visible marker of instability and border collapse. Silent, this woman entombed in salt is also a symbol of unspeakability, as Austin emphasizes when her narrator attempts to "make a story of it" at dinner:

> I never got through with it. There, about the time the candles began to burn their shades and red track of the light on the wine-glasses barred the cloth, with the white, disdainful shoulders and politely incredulous faces leaning through the smoke of cigarettes, it had a garish sound. Afterward I came across the proof of the affair in the records of the emigrant party, but I never tried telling it again.
>
> (157)

Race and class determine who may speak and what may be said: White shoulders and the affluence signaled by wine, cigarettes, and leisurely candlelight create a privileged space into which stories about collapsing borders are not allowed to enter. Although the response of an incredulous and disbelieving audience threatens hereafter to silence this storyteller and erase the story, her claim to have "never tried telling it again" is, of course, false. Austin subverts the social constraints on women's speech by having her narrator retell the story within **"The Land,"** and it is retold with each new reader.

The feminized, essentialized landscape of *Lost Borders* is the linchpin of Austin's gender critique. As Annette Kolodny demonstrates in *The Lay of the Land,* feminized landscapes have had a long shelf life in American literature, and in *Lost Borders,* Austin accentuates that tradition by figuring the feminized, eroticized desert as both the testing ground and the hoped-for trophy of many of her white male characters. White women's relationships with the land in *Lost Borders* are sometimes equally troubling in their representation: "Women, unless they have very large and simple souls, need cover; clothes, you know, and furniture, social observances to screen them, conventions to get behind; life when it leaps upon them, large and naked, shocks them into disorder" (165). Yet Austin counters these generalizations with representations of individual women who reject precisely those "social observances" and "conventions."

In **"The Walking Woman,"** Austin presents a particular instance of a marginal character who rejects social observances and challenges conventional demands of femininity: "By no canon could it be considered ladylike to go about on your own feet, with a blanket and a black bag and almost no money in your purse, in and about the haunts of rude and solitary men" (256). Yet even with the Walking Woman, Austin posits an authentic female identity located beneath "the looking and seeming," a phrase that refers to a wide range of incapacitating social behaviors coded feminine: "She had walked off all sense of society-made values, and, knowing the best when the best came to her, was able to take it" (261). Freeing herself from "the looking and seeming" releases the Walking Woman to receive "the best," which in this case means work overseen and valued by men, heterosexual love, and motherhood. Finally, however, ambivalences lodged in **"The Walking Woman"** undermine these valorized components of institutionalized femininity. The story **"The Walking Woman"** concludes when the narrator disagrees with the Walking Woman's assertion that freedom from convention requires a woman have work that is valued by men, a heterosexual relationship, and a child, saying, "At least one of us is wrong. To work and to love and to bear children. *That* sounds easy enough. But the way we live establishes so many things of much more importance" (262). The indeterminacy of this passage is characteristic of Austin's skillful ability to undermine the certainty of interpretation. The conclusion refuses final resolution in favor of evocative uncertainty, allowing Austin to privilege the tension between an essential female identity and a socially constructed one.

Austin's inscription onto the landscape of both an essentialized female identity and a spirituality conceived as irreducibly feminine does more than merely invert the historical literary maneuver by which men have celebrated mastery of the female "other" and eroticized their assault on the land. In *Lost Borders,* Austin establishes her alliance with marginalized groups, including women, Native Americans, and the few white men who reject constructions of masculinity that privilege dominance, exploitation, and aggression. For Austin, those who occupy a position of marginality are not situated there exclusively because of their race *or* gender *or* class. Instead, Austin's understanding of marginality as a site of spiritual authority derives largely from individuals' and groups' relationships with the land. Cultural attitudes regarding gender certainly shape the contradicting interpretations the narrator receives of the Walking Woman's potential insanity, but Austin asserts her sanity by presenting her speech as containing "both wisdom and information" (257). More important than the Walking Woman's gender alone, her status as a "Borderer" is established by her relationship with the land. She lives with the land without attempting to master or control it, and therefore has privileged knowledge of it.

By drawing on Native American oral storytelling traditions, Austin is able to challenge boundaries between oral and written literature, and sacred and secular expressions, although she does so at the expense of exoticizing the cultural group to which she is indebted. Nonetheless, I want to suggest that Austin's representation of the desert as female anticipates current feminist debates over the political potential of a "strategic essentialism." For Diana Fuss, deploying essentialism as a method of resistance can grant authority to speak. While Fuss wonders if "calls . . . for a strategic essentialism might be humanism's way of keeping its fundamental tenets in circulation at any cost and under any guise," she points out the need to consider cultural and institutional differences: "The question of permissibility, if you will, of engaging in essentialism is therefore framed and determined by the subject-positions from which one speaks" (86). Austin's insistence on spirituality as enabling female authority allows her to grant agency to the marginalized characters that populate her stories, and her forthright acknowledgment of Native American influence reveals that spirituality is not transcendent, raceless, or universal. Instead, Austin's claims to spiritual authority draw their power to perform cultural critiques from their difference from the universal.

Works Cited

Allen, Paula Gunn. "The Feminine Landscape of Leslie Marmon Silko's *Ceremony*." *The Sacred Hoop: Recovering the Feminine in American Indian Traditions*. Boston: Beacon, 1992, pp. 118-126.

Austin, Mary. *Earth Horizon*. Boston: Houghton Mifflin, 1932.

———. *Lost Borders*. New York and London: Harper & Brothers, 1909. Rpt. as *Stories from the Country of Lost Borders*. Ed. Marjorie Pryse. New Brunswick, NJ: Rutgers University Press, 1987.

———. "Regionalism in American Fiction." *The English Journal* (Feb. 1932): 97-107.

———. "Woman Alone." *The Nation* 124 (March 2, 1927): 228-230.

Fuss, Diana. "Reading Like a Feminist." *Differences* 1 (Summer 1989): 77-92.

Kolodny, Annette. *The Lay of the Land: Metaphor as Experience and History in American Life and Letters*. Chapel Hill: University of North Carolina Press, 1975.

Porter, Nancy. Afterword. *A Woman of Genius*. By Mary Austin. Old Westbury, NY: The Feminist Press, 1985, pp. 295-321.

Ruppert, James. "Discovering America: Mary Austin and Imagism." *Studies in American Indian Literature: Critical Essays and Course Designs*. Ed. Paula Gunn Allen. New York: Modern Language Association, 1983, pp. 243-258.

———. "Mary Austin's Landscape Line in Native American Literature." *Southwest Review* 68 (1983): 376-390.

Silko, Leslie Marmon. *Ceremony*. New York: Penguin, 1977.

Karen S. Langlois (essay date 1995)

SOURCE: Langlois, Karen S. "Marketing the American Indian: Mary Austin and the Business of Writing." In *A Living of Words: American Women in Print Culture*, edited by Susan Albertine, pp. 151-68. Knoxville, Tenn.: The University of Tennessee Press, 1995.

[*In the following essay, Langlois addresses the issue of Austin's reputation as an authority on Native American culture, which the author vigorously promoted throughout her career, ultimately claiming that her "understanding of Indians was, in part, an imaginative journey," that her expertise was "intuitive" rather than scientifically based, and that her primary goal was not her writing but her "highly marketable image."*]

In 1932 the American western writer Mary Hunter Austin published her autobiography with Houghton Mifflin Company. Heralded by her publishers as the greatest autobiography since Benjamin Franklin's, Austin's book was chosen as a Literary Guild selection and became the capstone of her writing career. The title, **Earth Horizon,** was a reference to an Indian rain symbol. Included in the autobiography were Austin's memories of her life in California at the turn of the century and her experiences with the Owens Valley Paiute Indians. It was during this period, she confessed, that she first discovered "there was a part for her in Indian life." As she explained, "she entered into their lives . . . the strange secret life of the tribe" (289).

Austin's claims about her familiarity with Indian culture were frequently met with disdain. Among her severest critics were various friends and professional associates who thought she fabricated her expertise. As Ina Cassidy, a member of the Santa Fe, New Mexico, artists' colony, observed: "It is very amusing to me and to others who know the Pueblos and the Navajos, to hear Mary claim to be an authority . . . for we know from personal observation and intimate knowledge that she knows very very little, at first hand" (Nov. 4, 1933). Nevertheless, Austin had largely built her career on her claims as an expert on Native American life. Her writing on Indians made up one-third to one-half of her oeuvre. Without any formal training in anthropology or ethnology, she repeatedly managed to disarm her critics and market her work to the American reading public.

Austin was born in 1868 in Carlinville, Illinois. In 1888 she graduated from Blackburn College, a small Presbyterian institution. She moved west with her widowed mother and brother to homestead in Fort Tejon, California, once the site of a large Indian reservation. After her marriage to Wallace Stafford Austin, a speculator, she lived in a series of small desert towns in the shadow of the Sierra Nevada.[1] These frontier communities were in close proximity to scattered Indian camps where the remaining Paiute Indians lived. At the turn of the century there were four to five hundred Paiutes in the Owens Valley. Their chief art was the weaving of baskets to store foodstuffs such as pine nuts, roots, and berries. They lived in conical structures made of willows and sealed with mud, called "wickiups."

Although burdened with her responsibilities as a frontier housewife and the care of her retarded daughter, Austin aspired to a life as a professional writer. But in the desolate town of Independence, where she and her husband finally settled, there seemed little hope of a literary career. Bored by the usual round of small-town activities, she became interested in the life of her Paiute housekeeper and "a handful of Paiute Indians" living nearby. As she later confessed, she become acquainted with Indian culture because there was literally nothing else to be interested in. During a trip to Los Angeles she met Charles Lummis, a former "Harvard man" who had come west and established himself as a nationally known authority on the Indians of the Southwest and as the editor of the California periodical *The Land of Sunshine*. A poem Austin submitted for publication in his magazine reveals her attraction to Indians as a potential literary subject. However, the conventional verse, **"Little Light Moccasin,"** indicates a naïve, superficial notion of Indian life. The following is a short excerpt from the poem, which appeared in April 1899:

> Little Light Moccasin swings in her basket
> Woven of willow and sinew of deer
> Rocked by the breezes and nursed by the pine trees
> Wonderful things are to see and to hear.

At the Lummis home Austin met Dr. Frederick Webb Hodge, an experienced ethnologist, who told her how to collect information about Indians. (The Bureau of Ethnology, a division of the Smithsonian Institution, had been created in 1879.) He also furnished her with an "alphabet" to use in the study of Indian languages. With this rudimentary instruction in the elements of field research, Austin pursued her interest in Indian culture. She attended the Indian celebrations, or "fandangoes," as they were called, at Fort Independence and recorded two Paiute war chants on a wax cylinder with an Edison home phonograph. She quickly informed Hodge that she had collected some "scraps of information" about Indians, including a "pretty fair account of their myths and domestic economy, incomplete accounts of their dances and secret rites, and a translation made by one of their number of some songs." In addition, she added, "I can give some description of their artifacts [*sic*]." She hoped to utilize the material for her literary work and "in that way . . . make my bread and butter" (letter to Hodge, Nov. 5, 1899).

We have only Austin's word for how intimately she knew Indians, and her later claims differ significantly from the statements she made during this period. Unlike her contemporary James Mooney, the "Indian Man," and other white Indian experts of her day, Austin never submerged herself in Indian culture by living like an Indian or among the Indians.[2] Rather, she lived for a portion of her life in frontier areas where Indians were. She was not a professional ethnologist or anthropologist. Although she claimed to have mastered some Indian sign language, she knew no Indian languages or dialects. She was an aspiring professional writer in search of good marketable material.

Austin used some of her impressions in her first book, **The Land of Little Rain** (1903), a well-received collection of picturesque essays about the California desert. It contained two sentimental sketches that reflected her idealized notions of primitive life and her belief in the nobility of Indian character. Utilizing the Paiute women's reputation for basketry, she wrote an essay on Seyavi, an aged basket maker, who like "every Indian woman [was] an artist" (168).[3] A second sketch focused on Winnenap, a tribal medicine man, who, after his death, went to "no hymn-book heaven, but the free air and free spaces of Shoshone Land" (101). The Indians in **The Land of Little Rain** are virtuous and high-minded and have lost much of their "savageness" (Austin's term). Her next work, **The Basket Woman** (1904), a collection of folktales for children, also contains variations on the image of the "good Indian."

Austin's early work was easily marketed to an eastern audience because of its picturesque natural charm and romantic aura. However, her writing was not without its critics. Playing the role of the mentor, Lummis addressed a problem which would plague her literary career—her scattered attention to detail and her disregard for "factual" knowledge. He chastised her ("Dear Child" as he called her) for not giving the reading public what he called "a fair bargain." While complimenting her on her "great gift," he admonished her not to "swindle" her readers by writing about things she was ignorant of, or in his words, not to "feather your nest with stolen plumage" (letter to Austin, Nov. 24, 1904).

In 1905 Austin left her husband, placed her daughter in an institution, and abandoned the borders of Death Valley for the seaside literary colony of Carmel, California. As a budding Indian faddist, she appears to have "gone native" to some extent. Her professional activities were accompanied by a penchant for wearing the beaded leather gown of an "Indian Princess," and arranging her knee-length chestnut hair in long Indian braids (Genthe 75).[4] Exhibiting a Victorian affectation of Indian ways, Austin typed her manuscripts and received her guests in a studio built in a tree, which she called her "wickiup," and wrote to her friends and associates on personalized stationery monogrammed "Mary Austin, The Wickiup, Carmel by the Sea." It was an early expression of Austin's unique myth of the self as Indian expert.

Austin had a theatrical personality and a flair for the melodramatic. She perceived Indians as romantic figures despite the harsh realities of Indian life. She was fascinated by their "mystical" religion, a spiritual orientation in stark contrast to the midwestern Methodism in which she had been raised. After eighteen years in the California desert, she craved novelty and stimulation. Her identification with Indians was a way to escape the restrictive mores of white middle-class life. It was also an opportunity to enhance her literary persona and to advance her professional career. Having lived for years on the fringe of civilization, she could turn her isolation into an asset. She could exploit the ways in which her experience set her apart.

Austin's next effort was a contemporary California novel, *Santa Lucia* (1908). But she returned to her Indian material in a collection of regional short stories entitled *Lost Borders* (1909). It contained three tales about Paiute and Shoshone women and their ill-fated relationships with white men. Possessed of some stereotypical Indian traits, Austin's Native American heroines are Anglicized, romanticized figures, as is frequently the case in her writing. They have many of the qualities representative of the traditional "Indian Princess" motif—beauty, grace, and a childlike devotion to their white lovers. For example, Turwhasé, the "gray-eyed" Shoshone in **"A Case of Conscience,"** is described as being "never weary nor afraid. She was never out of temper, except when she was jealous, and that was rather amusing. Saunders himself told me how she glowed and blossomed under his caress, and wept when he neglected her. . . . Turwhasé had the art to provoke tenderness and the wish to protect, and the primitive woman's capacity for making no demands upon it" (31).

Austin also began to collaborate on an Indian play, *The Coyote Doctor,* with the dramatist Elmer Harris. Its melodramatic storyline concerns a Paiute woman and her lover, who are forced into exile by the tribe after he is accused of practicing "coyote" witchcraft. (Plays with Indian themes were a popular form of entertainment. Donald MacLaren's *The Redskin* had been successfully produced in New York in 1906.) Negotiations to place *The Coyote Doctor* were unsuccessful, although the actress Florence Roberts had tentatively agreed to play the female lead. Nevertheless, Austin astutely saw the commercial possibilities of an Indian play, and without any technical knowledge of stage craft or dialogue, plunged forward as an aspiring playwright on her own.

By 1910 she had completed her own play, **The Arrow Maker,** which was accepted for production at the New Theatre on Broadway.[5] Her overly poetic story of "primitive domestic life" centers on the plight of a Paiute medicine woman, or "Chisera," who loses her spiritual power when she is scorned by her lover, the tribal arrow maker. Although the drama was mounted by the producers as an Indian extravaganza, all of the parts were played by white actors. To lend authenticity, costumes and properties were copied from artifacts in the Metropolitan Museum of Natural History. Photographs of the play, with its spectacular stage settings, were featured in the Sunday *New York Times* (Pictorial section, Mar. 12, 1911). However, the production closed early amid harsh reviews which criticized it as "ridiculous" and "pretentious" because of its phony dialogue and unimaginative plot. As one critic lamented, the play "belong[ed] to the a b c's of dramatic art" ("New Play" 106-7).

Nevertheless, the publicity surrounding **The Arrow Maker** boosted Austin's reputation as "an authority on the red man of the Southwest" ("To Produce Indian Play"). Catering to the public's interest in the vanishing frontier (Buffalo Bill Cody was still touring the country with his Wild West Show), she found new ways to add to her status as an Indian expert. This included lecturing on one of her favorite topics, "primitive woman." Taking every opportunity to, as she phrased it, "talk Indian," she found ample occasion to exploit her acquaintance with Native American life and to cultivate a unique identity in New York.

As part of her self-promotion, Austin was given to fictionalize or exaggerate certain aspects of her past. In an imaginative recreation of her own experience, she embellished her reputation as an Indian expert in **Christ in Italy** (1912). In a little bit of nonsense, she claimed to have studied with Tinnemaha, a Paiute medicine man, and announced that she had drunk from Hassayampa, a secret river in California that gives Indians visionary powers (x-xviii, 68-69).[6] Austin may have been inattentive to details, or she may have been deliberately manipulating her readers' ignorance of the West. In either case, Hassayampa is a well-known river located approximately fifty miles west of Phoenix, Arizona. Austin's eastern publishers, who were primarily interested in marketing her writings as light entertainment, seldom questioned her claims or her accuracy. Her work had artistic merit, whether or not it was authentic.

In the next few years Austin supported herself on an unsteady income as a professional writer. However, the First World War undermined the sale of her work, including her California novel *The Ford* (1917), and she despaired over the poor sales of her books during wartime. Hard-pressed, she proposed a collection of Indian legends for children, entitled *The Trail Book,* arguing that the subject matter of American Indian trails was appropriate to the patriotism the war had engendered. She explained that she had begun her children's book because of "the lack of imaginative material with the American stamp." The "time was ripe," she proclaimed, for a literary movement back to "American sources" (letter to Greenslet, Sept. 29, 1917).

Austin had established herself as a creative writer and essayist. In addition, she decided to try her hand at academic nonfiction, to "capture . . . the intellectual audience" (letter to Van Doren, July 14, [1921]). For example, she accepted an assignment from Carl Van Doren to contribute a six-thousand-word essay on **"Aboriginal Non-English Writings"** to the *Cambridge History of American Literature* (1921). The other contributors were an illustrious group of male university professors, and Austin was clearly out of her depth as a professional writer and nonacademician. Her numerous book and magazine deadlines left her little time to pursue original research. She wrote in desperation to Frederick Hodge for suggestions on what she might read, and pored over the information he sent her, which included his own scholarly papers. Commenting later on her practice of availing herself of other people's hard-won expertise, he privately complained that she was "always a sponge" (Gordon 181). Nevertheless, Austin met her deadline. Ever mindful that writing was a business, she sent off a letter reminding Van Doren to send her a check.

Partly as a result of her association with Hodge, in 1918 Austin was given an appointment at the School of American Research in Santa Fe, New Mexico, as an associate in Native American literature. She was confident that the appointment would add stature to her reputation as an authority on Native American life. She had exhausted her material on California Indians, and would now be able to gather information about Indian tribes of the Southwest. One wonders about Austin's sensitivity in setting an Indian prayer-meal bowl on the desk in her office to hold her pencils and pens. Soon she began to hold "friendly court" with the local Indians and to investigate the Indian pueblos near Santa Fe. It was re-

ported by the local press that she was touring the region, getting "local color" for a series of stories.

Austin's diverse interests soon focused on the translation of Indian songs or poems, an interest she shared with many amateur and professional ethnologists. Beginning in 1911 she published several "transcriptions" or "re-expressions" of Indian poems or songs, which appeared in *McClure's, Harper's,* and *Poetry.* She was dependent on bilingual translators, and the ethnographical authenticity of her Indian material was frequently questioned. For example, she identified "A Song in Time of Depression," one of two "Medicine Songs" which she published in *Everybody's Magazine,* as a Paiute poem "transcribed from the Indian Originals." However, the lines "Return and sing, O my Dreams, / In the dewy and palpitant pastures" suggested Austin's own penchant for florid language (415). As she admitted, some publications, such as the *Atlantic Monthly* and the *Century,* refused to publish her Indian material unless she "confessed that I had made it up, but never on the assumption that they were Indian" (*Earth Horizon* 333). In stark contrast to its rejection of Austin's "re-expressions," the *Century* had published the translations of the anthropologist Alice Fletcher as early as 1894.[7]

Although highly imaginative, Austin often exhibited a limited capacity for careful, analytical thinking. At Blackburn College she had taken classes in the natural sciences, but she lacked training in modern social science research methods. Hindered by her inadequate academic background, she depended on her creative instincts and "feminine intuition." She sometimes drew unwarranted conclusions on the basis of inadequate evidence and frequently paraded her theories as fact. Concerning the results of her research on Native American songs, she explained: "Then I made some further inquires into Indian song forms with a view to local influences. I find them derived very largely from dramatic forms, and had [sic] some new light on drama in relation to the food quest. That in turn threw light on the so called 'sex drama' which turned out to follow a food curve" (letter to MacDougal, Jan. 28, 1919).

Despite the dubious nature of her "re-expressions," Austin became a leading pioneer in the burgeoning field of "Amerind" verse. Proclaiming her theory that poetic cadence is a function of the environment, she completed an abstruse if imaginative introduction to accompany her collection of Indian poems. She submitted *The American Rhythm,* as it was called, to Ferris Greenslet, her editor at Houghton Mifflin, who had previously assured her that his company wanted the rights to all of her Indian material. Expecting something romantic and picturesque along the lines of her earlier work, Greenslet was put off by her theorizing. He expressed his doubts that his company could successfully market the book, and rejected it for publication.

Published by Harcourt, Brace and Company in 1923 and reissued by Houghton Mifflin Company in 1930, Austin's idiosyncratic "criterion of American rhythms" caused an outcry in some circles, as represented by the poet Arthur Davison Ficke, who accused her of making it all up. Dismissing the legitimacy of his concerns, she made the sweeping observation that she was the final authority on the study of Indian poetry as "my own field, first staked out and preempted by myself" (letter to Ficke, Mar. 27, 1930). Nevertheless, Ficke noted, as a poet he "simply [did] not believe a word of it" and was "absolutely stumped" by her assertions. Referring to her well-known reputation for attacking her critics, he taunted, "if you want to print this somewhere, and slay me in your reply to my objections, you have my permission."[8]

His response was, to Austin's way of thinking, a manifestation of traditional male superiority. As she complained, "my men readers in particular seem pent [*sic*] on taking me down a peg or two" (letter to MacDougal, May 16, [1923]). Indeed, she had received "a number of long letters from College professors . . . pointing out that . . . I would have written [the book] quite differently if I had not been a woman."[9] She was criticized for her blatant disregard of academic methods and her obliviousness to the proper use of facts. Outraged by questions concerning the scholarly value of her work, she combated her critics with charges of sexism. She defended her intuitive approach as perfectly sound, and lashed out at the chauvinism of male experts who relied on "formal intellectualization" and an "ivy league education."

Austin may well have been right in her charges of gender discrimination, but she was also guilty as charged. The issue was the extent of her expertise. By way of illustration, in 1907 the musicologist Natalie Curtis had published *The Indians' Book,* a well-received collection of Native American songs. Curtis had studied at the National Conservatory of Music in New York and abroad and had collected her translations by traveling by train, wagon, and horseback to visit Indians in remote locations across America. Obviously Austin was self-taught, but how much did she know? Had she exploited her intuitive understanding of Indians, a superficial acquaintance with their culture, and the borrowed expertise of more knowledgeable people to develop a career as an Indian savant?

By the 1920s Indians were Austin's stock in trade. She kept her name before the public with a steady stream of articles and book reviews about indigenous American culture. There was growing popular interest in the subject of Native Americans, and Austin was indefatigable in persuading editors to accept her expertise on practically every aspect of primitive life and to give her space in their periodicals.[10] She also continued to publish her

Indian short fiction. In 1922 she contracted with Harry Payne Burton, the editor of *McCall's,* to write three stories with an Indian theme for $750 each, an extremely high fee in that day. Caring less about the authenticity of her work than its exotic appeal to his female reading audience, Burton instructed her to "seize every opportunity that you artistically can" to add "touches of glamour" and alleviate a "grim atmosphere."[11] In the world of commercial magazine publishing, as in the commercial theater, the marketing of Native American life was a white person's game that frequently had little to do with real Indians. As a market product they were irrelevant.

Austin's name was sufficiently linked with Indians in the popular mind that she was invited to become consulting editor to the Camp Fire Girls, an organization whose symbols were derived from Indian lore. Her appointment included the likelihood that some of her stories would be serialized in their publication, *Everygirl's Magazine.* Sizing up the matter from a strictly commercial point of view, her publisher noted that he could envision "widespread publicity for your books in your connection" with the periodical (Houghton Mifflin, letter to Austin, Feb. 18, 1922). Unfortunately, Austin was never inclined to reject opportunities that enhanced her visibility, no matter how ludicrous. She agreed that the venture would be good publicity for her Indian work, although she was a little dubious about using "my position in Camp Fire to sell my own books" (letter to Pratt, Feb. 15, 1922).

In order in increase her income and professional recognition, Austin also attempted to sell the motion picture rights to her Indian work. The "celluloid Indian" was the new fashion. D. W. Griffith had successfully adapted *Ramona,* Helen Hunt Jackson's romantic novel about the California mission Indians, into a popular silent film starring Mary Pickford. As Austin confided to her publishers, she had already received a "number of nibbles" on her play **The Arrow Maker.** As Austin explained, "I do really mean to make a serious effort to get my Indian stories on the screen. Nobody living is so well prepared to do this authoritatively." Noting that the Santa Fe area was "crammed with movie people," she hoped to place a story that would "go over big." She pinned her highest hopes on her 148-page manuscript "Thinking White," the tale of an educated Navajo Indian who marries a white woman. Convinced that it was "a good screen story," she hoped to tie the film rights in with book publication, and to reap the agent's selling commission and the screenwriter's fee (letter to Greenslet, Apr. 5, 1927).

To broaden her sources of income, she also exploited her flair for the dramatic in a career as a public lecturer with the Louis J. Alber World Celebrities Lecture Bureau, which promoted such well-known personalities as

Harry Houdini. She saw lecturing as a useful way to "try out" her Indian material on the public. Her standard fee was two hundred dollars for her presentations at Chautauqua meetings, women's clubs, Rotary associations, literary and poetry societies, and university forums. Among her lectures, which included talks on Native American dance, drama, and literature, the most popular was that on aboriginal poetry, accompanied by readings from her own Indian verse. Bewailing the impossibility of trying to type on passenger trains, she crisscrossed the country on her annual winter lecture tour. On occasion her lectures were simultaneously broadcast to a radio audience. To increase her financial return, she tried to organize her tours in conjunction with the publication dates of her books, and to arrange for extra promotion and bookstore displays in all the cities and towns on her itinerary.

In addition, Austin attempted to curry favor with important people who could help advance her professional career. Besides copies of her books, she frequently sent gifts of Indian cornmeal, pottery, and jewelry, including rings that her New York acquaintances nearly "pried" off her fingers. Exhibiting her penchant for Indian religious symbols, she also sent fetishes, sometimes with mixed results. She mailed the writer Louis Adamic "the foot of a little furred animal," with instructions that he should carry "Mokiach, my Lord Puma" on his person to release his "subconscious forces." As Adamic recalls in his autobiography, *My America,* he wondered if Austin was a "vague folk-cultist" or a "crackpot" (479).

"The country has almost seemed to go *indian* [*sic*]," the apologist Mabel Dodge proclaimed in 1922, and Austin was in the vanguard.[12] As a leading enthusiast, she was frequently criticized for her flamboyant "Amerindian airs." Indeed, there appears to have been considerable playing for effect in her appearance at a publisher's banquet in her honor at the National Arts Club in New York City. Her choice of companion for the evening was the well-known young Chickasaw Indian artist Overton Colbert, who wore quill-embroidered buckskin, a full-length black, white, and flamingo feather Indian headdress, and a necklace made out of alligator teeth. The middle-aged woman writer and Native American escort were a variation of the popular Indian sidekick motif.[13] Capitalizing on her reputation as an authority on Indians, Austin was creating something more than her writing to be noticed. She was producing and aggressively promoting a highly marketable image.

In a review of one of her books, Van Wyck Brooks reflected on what he perceived as the decline of Austin's serious career and the ascendance of her personal psychodrama. In an account that seemed straight out of a silent film, he described how, while researching *The Trail Book,* she would go to the Museum of Natural History at midnight,

and, standing among the Indian relics, fall into a trance that placed her in a mystic communion with the Great Spirit and the souls of the dead. And once, by daylight, to the alarm of the guard who supposed for a moment that she had designs on the collection, she took several relics from a case that had been opened for her and placing them in her bosom fell into a state of silent ecstasy. Great was the guard's relief when, after a few minutes, she returned the relics to the case and explained that she had been in communion with the gods of the red men.

(310-11)

Austin was indignant at Brooks's review, and lashed out at the story as "false and discrediting" (letter to editor, June 8, 1920). While admitting that she had gone into the museum at night with a lantern, taken Indian artifacts and costumes out of the cases, and, in some instances, tried them on, she was outraged at seeing her actions belittled in print. Yet she often engaged in what was perceived as odd behavior. It was another aspect of her creative approach to expertise—a kind of Aristotelian mimesis. As she explained in *The American Rhythm*: "I have naturally a mimetic temperament that draws me toward the understanding of life by living it. . . . So that when I say I am not, have never been, or offered myself, as an authority in things Amerindian, I do not wish to have it understood that I may not, at times, have succeeded in being an Indian" (37-41).

Putting aside the issue of Austin's outrageous denial of having ever claimed to be an authority, her comment sheds new light on her work as an Indian expert. Her understanding of Indians was, in part, an imaginative journey. She believed that she knew about Native American culture because she perceived it intuitively and had tried to imitate it. In so doing, she had entered into the "Indian consciousness." Is it possible to find value in such a nonintellectual approach? If so, Austin was a creative artist who tried to achieve a perfect fusion of art and life; if not, she was a classic example of the "wannabe Indian" only too well known to the Native American community.

For example, in preparation for her book *The Land of Journeys' Ending* (1924), Austin undertook an automobile trip across the Southwest. Temporarily inconvenienced by a sandstorm, she left her car, wrapped herself in an Indian blanket, and after positioning herself under a large rock, made "good medicine" to improve the weather (Fink 227). One wonders at Austin's acting out the traditional "blanket Indian" stereotype. As an Indian faddist, she freely adopted religious and cultural aspects of "Indianness" that she believed were superior to those of Western civilization. However, she may have been guilty of more than a little arrogance when she self-servingly co-opted only those practices which particularly intrigued her. As she once observed (in a comment that was hardly to her credit), she liked to "play" Indian.

Austin was frequently guilty of a similar offense in her writing. As she observed, she was not interested in the "exactitudes" of the ethnologist.[14] She freely blended factual information, descriptive phrasing, Indian stereotypes, and the workings of her imagination to create her own conception of Native American life. The following passage is taken from *The Land of Journeys' Ending,* published by the Century Company and serialized in *Century* magazine:

> The evening meal at the pueblo is taken before the fire, with the smoking food-bowl in the middle, the platter of bread beside it, the swinging cradle within reach, the children leaning on their parents' knees and taking their portions by the only rule of table manners the pueblo knows, with slowness and dignity. After supper the sack of native tobacco and the heap of soft corn husks, and the quiet stealing away of one or another of the house group for the hour of meditation and the last salute to the Sun Father; then the voice of the *pregonero,* sounding from the housetop, with directions for tomorrow's labor. If it should be evening at Taos, you will hear the young men, ghostly in their white sheets, on the bridge between the north and the south houses, singing their wordless moonlight melody, or at Zuni they will foregather on the terraces to moan melodiously until the protest of some sleepy elder cries them silence.

(243)

Obviously, the above passage gave a romantic picture of the beauty and humanity of Pueblo culture, but it also belied its complexity. Her descriptions were frequently idealized and impressionistic, crafted for the white imagination. Generally speaking, she did not write for professionals. She popularized a primitive, indigenous culture for a middle-class, mass-market audience. As a self-proclaimed intuitionist she advocated those aspects of life that were nonrational, nonscientific, and nonanalytical. As an outspoken neoprimitivist she promoted certain features of Native American culture that she found absent in white civilization and that she perceived to be of value.

In 1925 Austin permanently relocated to New Mexico. She built a house with her royalties and the money from her lecture tours, outfitted it with the latest innovation in Santa Fe—gas heating—and decorated it with Native American baskets and rugs. Santa Fe was the center of a thriving tourist trade, and she devoted much of her time to the preservation of Indian arts. As she observed in an unguarded moment, such activities also vindicated her against her critics. "The easterners used to be afraid of me," she explained, "afraid that I might be mistaken [about Indians]. . . . And, of course, the part I play in the new museum and the Indian Arts Foundation at Santa Fe make a difference" (letter to Greenslet, Feb. 1, 1929). She was soon active in a variety of reforms to ensure the preservation of Indian arts and the protection of Indian lands. Her impressive ef-

forts on behalf of Native American rights inspired the *Los Angeles Times* to dub her "Little Mother to 350,000 Indians."[15]

Regrettably, Austin also spent a lot of time promoting herself in innumerable newspaper interviews. As her interest in Indians became legendary so did her grandiosity. One of her more outrageous statements was that all Americans would eventually look like Indians—"flat back, high chest, square chin" (a comment guaranteed to reinforce stereotypes).[16] Alluding to Austin's pompous habit of making visionary, "prophetic" declarations, her friends snidely referred to her as the Chisera, the Paiute name for a medicine woman. In a pointed criticism regarding her divine self-importance, a writer for the *Forum* compared her overbearing manner to that of the priestess at Delphi delivering the oracles. As one reviewer dryly concluded, Austin's pretentious observations might "be important without being quite all-important."[17]

Austin's unbounded enthusiasm for Native Americans was no doubt motivated in part by spiritual, aesthetic, and cultural values. But throughout her life she also evinced a habitual pattern of excessive emotionality and flamboyant, self-dramatizing behavior. As she frequently complained, her own life "bored" her. She was driven by an insanely intense need to be noticed and to be associated with grand causes. Often neglecting her writing, she was distracted by her various roles as Indian enthusiast, propagandist, and reformer. As she informed an editor at Bobbs-Merrill who asked about acquiring one of her manuscripts, "I have no time for a mere publisher" (letter to Chambers, June 9, 1928).

Nevertheless, Austin wanted her Indian books to be "money makers" and was frequently disappointed in her royalties. On occasion, she reprimanded her publishers for their inexcusable "stupidity" in marketing her Indian books, claiming that they could have "gotten [more] out of them, if you understood them and the rapidly increasing interest in the subject" (letter to Greenslet [Feb. 3, 1929]). Periodically, she hounded them to expand the consumer interest in her work by trying to exploit the British market and by obtaining German and French editions. Overwhelmed by the endless list of her suggestions and complaints, the editor Ferris Greenslet cast her career as an Indianist as a mock-heroic play, and offered to convene "a grand pow-wow on your future work as a whole" (Greenslet, letter to Austin, Oct. 24, 1927).

Despite her efforts at promoting her work, Austin remained financially insecure throughout much of her career. She added to her income by republishing her Indian poems in anthologies, giving second serial rights on magazine stories to newspapers, and pocketing twenty-five-dollar royalties from various university and little theater productions of *The Arrow Maker* and a second Indian play, *Fire.* Her determination to make her work profitable is illustrated in the publication of *Taos Pueblo* (1930), completed in collaboration with Ansel Adams. His twelve original black and white photographs of the pueblo were accompanied by Austin's text, which was completed in one week without her ever having seen his photographs. Although the country was in the midst of the depression, the work was published as an expensive art book by San Francisco book designer John Henry Nash. Lamenting that a costly book could not possibly stay in print, Austin took her personal copy to New York on her annual lecture tour to show to her publishers, in the vain hope that they would publish a less expensive edition. In a dogged attempt to make more money, she asked Adams if he had any leftover photographs that could be marketed with her inscriptions. She also inquired if he had any moving pictures of Taos or "any other Indian movies" for which she could supply the text. As she observed, her agent, Ann Watkins, could "sell anything" (letter to Adams, Mar. 13, 1931).

Austin frequently seemed to want a monopoly on Native American material. Although she was generous in offering help to her friends, she damned many of her competitors as "ignoramuses." As she complained, some of the authorities on Native American culture had never been closer to an Indian than a cigar store. Faced with an avalanche of important new books on Indians, she resorted to making exaggerated, even fantastic, claims about her own work. In an application for a Guggenheim to help pay for a typist and a translator, she grandly observed, "One possible objection to my getting the award this time is that I do not know any authorities on Indian Art to refer to, I being the only authority who has written anything on that subject" (letter to Hodge, Oct. 24, 1932). It was hardly the kind of statement that would endear her to other white experts or to Native Americans. Unfortunately there is no record of what Indians thought of Austin.

Although Austin wrote in a wide variety of genres on a vast array of subjects, she consistently promoted herself as *the* authority on Indians. "Practically everybody at work in this field refers to me sooner or later," she noted. Somewhat as an afterthought, but perhaps more to the point, she also admitted that "the public seems to be willing to accept me on this subject with less criticism than on any other" (letter to Greenslet, Nov. 10, 1926). Nevertheless, for all her extravagant claims, she could not silence her critics. Responding to some of her writings, Franz Boas, the leading academic anthropologist, "gave me an unpleasant quarter of an hour," she complained, "attacking my personal integrity" (letter to Dear Friend, Apr. 13, 1930). Her former mentor, Charles Lummis, was one of her most avid detractors. At first sympathetic to her efforts, he was now appalled, and he

condemned her "oracular impudence" and "incalculable nerve." Contrary to her claims of expertise, he observed, "she never would study anything for it all comes to her by divine revelation" (Fiske and Lummis 106). In his comments on *The Land of Journeys' Ending,* he berated her for her careless use of language, in particular, her use of the word *Pueblēno* to refer to the "inhabitants of the Indian towns of New Mexico and Arizona" (*Land of Journeys' Ending* 456). "There is no such word in any language, and there can not be such a word in Spanish. A skilled writer is entitled to make words in his own language, if he gives them the parentage of Clarity and of Legitimacy. But 'Pueblēno' isn't even a bastard word" (Lummis, "Pueblo Myth" 171).[18]

In 1934, the last year of her life, Austin published *One-Smoke Stories,* a collection of piquant Indian tales. She described the work as "one of my pet books the only genuine book of Folk Tales, in the Folk manner that has yet appeared in America" (letter to Bender, Jan. 27, 1934). However, she was quickly forced to refute charges that her "authentic" Indian tales were "worthless to the student interested in exact observation." In response to yet another expert, she angrily threatened to "remove [his] scalp and wear it in my belt." However, she was given to privately admit that not only was her work in *One-Smoke Stories* not original, but that "in forty years I have published but two tales not previously published by other collectors" (letter to Canby, Apr. 1, 1930).

In a second book published that same year, *Can Prayer Be Answered?* Austin attempted to silence her detractors forever by asserting that she had "Indian blood," an imaginative embellishment on her earlier claim of a "somewhat mythical Indian ancestor" (*Can Prayer* 12; *Earth Horizon* 267). As Ina Cassidy caustically observed, Austin no longer needed to "talk to Indians, or to be with Indians in order to *know them.*"[19] A claim of Indian ethnicity automatically confers knowledge and power. There is no way to document the truth of Austin's statement, but clearly she had become her own art. Nevertheless, non-Indians cannot be Indians. If it were simply the case of an individual adopting an Indian persona, it would be a relatively harmless matter. However, it becomes more problematic if Austin made such a claim to enhance her status as an Indian expert. Then again, perhaps she had half-begun to believe it herself.

Throughout her career Austin's association with Indians made for good publicity and for good copy. Her work as an Indianist brought in money and advanced her professional life. The country's continued infatuation with Native Americans provided a receptive market for a commercial product—her literary output. She was selling something that the general public was willing to buy, and with some effort she was always able to place her work. Austin's writing contributed to a certain idea of Native Americans—a variation of the "Noble Savage." Her Indians were artistic and spiritual, living in harmony with nature, in stark contrast to the usual "cowboys and Indians" motif. Thus, she stressed a vastly more positive image. She accomplished a great deal in fostering sympathetic, popular interest in indigenous culture and in giving added legitimacy to a part of western life that was largely neglected and unknown. Nevertheless, a large part of her writing was in the tradition of Euro-American ethnocentrism, whites creating and imagining the American Indian. Her work, when compared to photographs and ethnological reports, evidences cosmetic "improvements" on real Indians.

Austin's infatuation and identification with a picturesque, romanticized idea of Indian life reveals as much about her creative temperament as it does about Native American culture. Indians, as America's resident exotics, provided the richness and drama her own life lacked. They served her artistic and psychic needs. Through them she made her professional career more colorful. They became projections of her personality and her artistic alter ego. Austin was a gifted writer with an absolute genius for self-promotion. While she had a certain knowledge of primitive life, she was also something of a charlatan. Nevertheless, her imaginative self-mythology as the leading authority on Indians was unusually successful by any standards of her day. If her work was criticized by more knowledgeable experts and others of her contemporaries, it was accepted by most publishers and by the American reading public.

Notes

1. For additional information on this period of Austin's life see Austin, *Earth Horizon*; Fink; and Stineman.

2. For a discussion of ethnology, professionalism, and field research, see Moses.

3. For a discussion of the marketing of Austin's western work, see Langlois, "Mary Austin and Houghton Mifflin."

4. See also Ted Gale's cartoon of Mary Austin in her Indian braids, *Los Angeles Times* [1910], Braun Research Library, Southwest Museum, Los Angeles, CA. In response to Austin's identification with Indians, as well as her stubborn personality, her Carmel associates nicknamed her Sitting Bull.

5. For additional information see Langlois, "Mary Austin and the New Theatre."

6. See also Austin, *Can Prayer Be Answered?* 3-6.

7. See Alice C. Fletcher, "Indian Songs—Personal Studies of Indian Life," *Century* Jan. 1894: 421-31.

8. Ficke, letter to Austin, Mar. 11, 1930, qtd. in Pearce 241-42.

9. Austin, letter to Luhan, May 16, [1923]. For additional comment on Austin's expertise on Native American poetry, see Howard; and Castro 5-45.

10. For a list of Austin's publications, including those on Native Americans (books, journalism, short stories, essays, poetry, and contributions to collections), see bibliographies in Stineman 249-52; and Wynn 399-412.

11. Burton, letter to Austin, Sept. 23, 1922. In 1925 Austin won the O. Henry Memorial Prize for "Papago Wedding." For a selection of Austin's short stories, see *The Land of Little Rain*; *Lost Borders*; *The Basket Woman*; *The Trail Book*; *One-Smoke Stories*; and *Western Trails*.

12. Luhan, letter to Austin [Dec. 1922], qtd. in Pearce 172.

13. Alice Fletcher was frequently accompanied by her collaborator and adopted son, the Omaha head chief's son and ethnologist Francis La Flesche. For an illuminating discussion of their relationship, see Mark 307-9.

14. Austin frequently described herself as a "folklorist" as opposed to an "ethnologist," as in her letter to Canby, Apr. 1, 1930. This distinction was frequently, if incorrectly, employed to validate both her status as an "authority" on Indians and her right to make unsubstantiated claims regarding their life and culture.

15. "Mary Austin Little Mother to 350,000 Indians, Says Coast Paper," Oct. 31, 1933, unidentified newspaper clipping, Bancroft Library, U of California, Berkeley. Among Austin's many activities on behalf of Native American rights were her efforts to defeat the Bursum Bill, which threatened Pueblo land rights. She also organized the Indian Arts Fund, bequeathing it her home in Santa Fe following her death in 1934.

16. "Race of Future Like Indians." One example of Austin's numerous stereotypes occurs in her depiction of Turwhasé, the Shoshone heroine in "A Case of Conscience" (*Lost Borders* 32-33). Following the birth of her first child Turwhasé is described as being "hopeless. She had never left off her blanket, and like all Indian women when they mature, had begun to grow fat." Another example appears in *Earth Horizon* 246, wherein she refers to a Paiute baby as a "beady-eyed brown dumpling."

17. "Miss Austin Defines One Hundred Per Cent American Poetry," unidentified newspaper clipping, Cassidy Collection, Bancroft Library, U of California, Berkeley.

18. For a defense of Austin see T. M. Pearce 35-40.

19. Diary, Jan. 19, 1934. Cassidy also noted that she had never seen an Indian in Austin's home, with the exception of Tony Luhan, who was married to Austin's friend and confidant, Mabel Dodge.

Works Cited

Adamic, Louis. *My America, 1928-1938.* New York: Harper, 1938.

Austin, Mary. *The American Rhythm.* New York: Harcourt, Brace, 1923.

———. *The Basket Woman.* Boston: Houghton Mifflin, 1904.

———. *Can Prayer Be Answered?* New York: Farrar and Rinehart, 1934.

———. *Christ in Italy.* New York: Duffield, 1921.

———. *Earth Horizon.* Cambridge, MA: Houghton Mifflin, 1932.

———. *The Land of Journeys' Ending.* New York and London: Century, 1924.

———. *The Land of Little Rain.* Boston: Houghton Mifflin, 1903.

———. Letter to Ansel Adams. Mar. 13, 1931. Huntington Library, San Marino, CA.

———. Letter to Albert Bender. Jan. 27, 1934. Mills College Library, Oakland CA.

———. Letter to Henry S. Canby. Apr. 1, 1930. Huntington Library, San Marino, CA.

———. Letter to D. L. Chambers [Bobbs Merrill Company]. June 9, 1928. Lilly Library, Indiana U.

———. Letter to Dear Friend. Apr. 13, 1930. Braun Research Library, Southwest Museum, Los Angeles, CA.

———. Letter to Arthur Davison Ficke. Mar. 27, 1930. Huntington Library, San Marino, CA.

———. Letter to editor [*The Freeman*]. June 8, 1920. Van Pelt Library, University of Pennsylvania.

———. Letters to Ferris Greenslet. Sept. 29, 1917; Nov. 10, 1926; Apr. 5, 1927; Feb. 1, 1929; [Feb. 3, 1929]. Houghton Mifflin Co., Boston.

———. Letters to Frederick Webb Hodge. Nov. 5, 1899; Oct. 24, 1932. Braun Research Library, Southwest Museum, Los Angeles, CA.

———. Letter to Mabel Dodge Luhan. May 16, [1923]. Yale U Library.

———. Letter to Daniel Trembly MacDougal. Jan. 28, 1919. Arizona Historical Society, Tucson.

———. Letter to Daniel Trembly MacDougal. May 16, [1923]. Huntington Library, San Marino, CA.

———. Letter to Mr. Pratt [Houghton Mifflin]. Feb. 15, 1922. Houghton Mifflin Co., Boston.

———. Letter to Carl Van Doren. July 14, [1921]. Princeton U Library.

———. "Little Light Moccasin." *Land of Sunshine* Apr. 1899: 261.

———. *Lost Borders.* New York: Harper, 1909.

———. "Medicine Songs." *Everybody's Magazine* Sept. 1924: 413-15.

———. *One-Smoke Stories.* Boston: Houghton Mifflin, 1934.

———. *The Trail Book.* Boston: Houghton Mifflin, 1917.

———. *Western Trails: A Collection of Short Stories by Mary Austin.* Ed. Melody Graulich. Reno and Las Vegas: U of Nevada P, 1987.

Brooks, Van Wyck. "A Reviewer's Notebook." *Freeman* June 9, 1920: 310-11.

Burton, Harry Payne. Letter to Austin. Sept. 23, 1922. Huntington Library, San Marino, CA.

Cassidy, Ina. Unpublished diary. Bancroft Library, U of California, Berkeley.

Castro, Michael. *Interpreting the Indian: Twentieth-Century Poets and the Native American.* Albuquerque: U of New Mexico P, 1983.

Fink, Augusta. *I Mary: A Biography of Mary Austin.* Tucson: U of Arizona P, 1983.

Fiske, Turbese Lummis, and Keith Lummis. *Charles F. Lummis, the Man and His West.* Norman: U of Oklahoma P, 1975.

Genthe, Arnold. *As I Remember.* New York: Reynal and Hitchcock, 1936.

Gordon, Dudley. *Charles F. Lummis: Crusader in Corduroy.* Los Angeles: Cultural Assets P, 1972.

Greenslet, Ferris. Letter to Mary Austin. Oct. 24, 1927. Huntington Library, San Marino, CA.

Houghton Mifflin Company. Letter to Mary Austin. Feb. 18, 1922. Huntington Library, San Marino, CA.

Howard, Helen Addison. "Mary Hunter Austin (1868-1934)." *American Indian Poetry.* Boston: Twayne, 1979. 67-86.

Langlois, Karen S. "Mary Austin and Houghton Mifflin Company: A Case Study in the Marketing of a Western Writer." *Western American Literature* 23.1 (1988): 31-42.

———. "Mary Austin and the New Theatre: The 1911 Production of *The Arrow Maker.*" *Theatre History Studies* 8 (1988): 71-87.

Lummis, Charles F. Letter to Mary Austin. Nov. 24, 1904. Braun Research Library, Southwest Museum, Los Angeles, CA.

———. "Pueblo Myth and Ritual." *El Palacio* Mar. 3, 1928: 171-72.

Mark, Joan. *A Stranger in Her Native Land: Alice Fletcher and the American Indians.* Lincoln: U of Nebraska P, 1988.

Moses, L. G. *The Indian Man: A Biography of James Mooney.* Urbana and Chicago: U of Illinois P, 1984.

"The New Play." *Theatre Magazine* Apr. 1911: 106-7.

Pearce, T. M. "The Literary Idiom of Mary Austin." *Mary Austin: A Memorial.* Ed. Williard Hougland. Santa Fe, NM: Laboratory of Anthropology, 1944. 35-40.

Pearce, Thomas Matthew, ed. *Literary America, 1903-1934: The Mary Austin Letters.* Westport, CT: Greenwood, 1979.

"Race of Future Like Indians Seen by Author." New York *Herald* Nov. 13, 1932.

Stineman, Esther Lanigan. *Mary Austin: Song of a Maverick.* New Haven, CT: Yale UP, 1989.

"To Produce Indian Play." *New York Times* Nov. 14, 1910.

Wynn, Dudley Taylor. "A Critical Study of the Writings of Mary Hunter Austin (1868-1934)." Diss. New York U, 1939.

Noreen Groover Lape (essay date 1997)

SOURCE: Lape, Noreen Groover. "'There was a part for her in the Indian life': Mary Austin, Regionalism, and the Problems of Appropriation." In *Breaking Boundaries: New Perspectives on Women's Regional Writing,* edited by Sherrie A. Inness and Diana Royer, pp. 124-39. Iowa City, Iowa: University of Iowa Press, 1997.

[*In the following essay, Lape discusses the issue of Austin's "appropriation" of Native American "cultural expression" and her frequent posing as a "transethnic" in order "to foster her own creative goals," contending that while her efforts to reclaim Indian and Mexican cultures sometimes threatened "their free agency," her work was important to "the resurgence of Native American art and culture."*]

In **"Regionalism in American Fiction"** (1932) Mary Austin declares that the reading public's "insistence on fiction shallow enough to be common to all regions . . . has pulled down the whole level of American fiction" (98). The strength of her claim originates from her belief that regional difference defines the American literary tradition. Moreover, she views Native Americans as consummate regionalists since "everything an Indian does or thinks is patterned by the particular parcel of land which is his tribal home" (**"Regionalism"** 104). Austin uses regionalism to answer the demand for a national literature as well as to reclaim Native Americans into American society and art. However, her theories raise critical questions about the appropriation of Native Americans by Anglo culture. Although of Anglo descent, Austin seeks to cross ethnic boundaries and become a native. While it is impossible to escape one's own ethnic perspective and identity, Austin's southwestern writings reveal her efforts to empathize and identify with natives. Despite the fact that she never completely frees herself from colonial ideology, her essays and short stories agitate for the resurgence of Native American art and culture.[1]

The region, Austin maintains, is both an active and passive participant in shaping American literature. As she states, "The region must enter constructively into the story, as another character, as the instigator of plot" (**"Regionalism"** 105). The land in Austin's regionalist philosophy is a character with agency that moves throughout a story and motivates plot. In addition, Austin asserts that fiction must "come up through the land, shaped by the author's own adjustments to it" (**"Regionalism"** 101). Living on the land, people adopt its rhythms and symbols, and so cultural self-expression is always geographically determined. For Austin, then, regionalist fiction is shaped by the writer's adaptation to the land, and the land is the central "character" in the regional tale. Since American writing literally emerges from the soil and environment, she directs her white audience to embrace the aboriginal roots of the American tradition, to cease looking to Europe for forebears, and to "handle our American material in generic American metres" (**"New York"** 129). By asserting that the land is the formative influence on American art, Austin creates a causal link between region and culture and divorces the American tradition from its European roots.

Answering Ralph Waldo Emerson's challenge to define a national literature germinating in America, many have proffered a monolithic American tradition replete with a canon of shared ideals. Austin opposes an American monolith, promoting instead a "genuine regionalism": "[w]e need to be prompt about it, before somebody discovers that our resistance so far has been largely owing to intellectual laziness which flinches from the task of competently knowing, not one vast, pale figure of America, but several Americas, in many subtle and significant characterizations" (**"Regionalism"** 98). Austin finds futile the search for the "great American novel" and "absurd" England's insistence that Babbitt is the consummate American character. Making regionalism the aesthetic basis of American literature, she argues that no single novel can account for the "fine and subtle distinctions" among America's many regions (**"Regionalism"** 99). While Austin stresses the need to recognize "several Americas," she locates the cultural center of America in the Southwest, the seat "of the *next* great and fructifying world culture" (**Land** [*The Land of Journey's Ending*] 442).

Diversity for Austin reigns across the multiregional continent, but unity exists among persons within a common region. Since Austin maintains that region shapes culture, American literature is implicitly multicultural. The land, much more than race, she insists, is the determining factor in the lives of people. In **The Land of Journey's Ending** she states that at frontier points of contact, racial strains "run together" and create a new race which the land determines in "design" (438). Hence, as groups merge or melt, racial factors are less significant than regional ones. Similarly, she construes race in terms of the land: race is "a pattern of response common to a group of people who have lived together under a given environment long enough to take a recognizable pattern" (**"Regionalism"** 97). Austin never totally discounts the effects of race on culture and identity, but she does delimit its influence.

Because race is the effect of region, Austin can strongly identify with the Native Americans and Mexicans who are her neighbors in the Southwest. Identification with regional subjects is characteristic of regionalists who, as Judith Fetterley and Marjorie Pryse explain, portray "regional experience from within, so as to engage the reader's sympathy and identification."[2] Austin's attempts to locate herself within regional experience often results in her acting as an anthropologist, or a transethnic when she fancies that she can become a native.[3] Consequently, her writings provoke questions about intercultural regionalist empathy that involves the appropriation of Native American cultures by white Americans. Does a distinctly American literary tradition necessitate the appropriation of aboriginal elements? Can Anglos approach Native Americans without fetishizing their cultures? To what extent should white authors conserve regional experience, the cultural and social lives of Native Americans? Austin holds that native cultures must be preserved, in her view because Native and Anglo Americans are inextricably entwined. Politically, she denounces the unjust "Indian policy" and deems it "unsound, expensive, inefficient, and injurious—not only to the Indian but to us" (**"Why Americanize"** [**"Why Americanize the Indian?"**] 167). The "Indian policy" harms both cultures, because Native Americans are the origins of a distinctly national literary tradition rooted in the American continent. Desiring to prevent the destruction of aboriginal cultures, Austin employs and modifies Franz Boas's theory of cultural relativism and his project to salvage dying Native American tribes.[4]

Inspired by Boas's anthropology, Austin shares his preservationist agenda. Boas shaped the discipline of anthropology in the twentieth century as he critiqued the evolutionism of nineteenth-century ethnologists. Evolutionary ethnologists adopted Spencerian Darwinism, which offered them "a sequential theory of social advancement" (Dippie 102). Through their investigation of recovered artifacts, they argued that humans rose in intelligence and evolved unilinearly in ascending steps (Faris 164-66). Hence, for evolutionists human development across cultures was "uniform" and "systematic" (Hyatt 43). In addition, they held that whites occupied the highest and people of color the lowest rungs on the evolutionary ladder. Concerned about the racist and imperialist implications of evolutionism, Boas challenged its hierarchism.

In place of the unilinear paradigm of evolutionary ethnology, Boas introduced the ethnographic method, which he employed in his life's work studying tribes of the Pacific Northwest. He stressed the necessity of conducting fieldwork in order to understand the "customs, language, and social systems" of a culture. Boas's recent biographer, Marshall Hyatt, reasons: "[s]uch a methodology would . . . highlight the impact of environment on cultural elements" (43). As I have shown, Austin causally links environment to cultural expression in her regionalist philosophy and aesthetics. Boas, however, resisted geographic determinism, claiming only the limited effect of environment on human cultures (Hyatt 43).

In his ethnographic fieldwork, Boas found a more democratic method than evolutionary ethnology offered. Whereas evolutionists proposed hierarchies, Boas asserted that culture is relative (Dippie 282; Rohner and Rohner xiv, xviii). He professed that "cultural improvement . . . is not an absolute, with Western man representing the apogee" (Rohner and Rohner xviii). Instead, each society possessed its own integrity and rationality against which its customs should be interpreted.

Although Austin did not personally know Boas, her writings reflect his theories in cultural anthropology. Like an anthropologist, Austin studied and wrote about Native American and Spanish colonial cultures. Because of her proclivity to empathize, she often blurred the line between anthropologist and transethnic in her self-fashioning. In other words, she not only studied but also identified with Native American cultures. Presuming an aboriginal connection, Austin would sometimes pose as a transethnic, willingly appropriating the culture and aesthetics of Native Americans to foster her own creative goals. She even would go so far as to wear

Spanish and Native American dress in public. In an essay memorializing her death, Mabel Dodge Luhan, who at times had a tempestuous relationship with Austin, derisively describes one such masquerade by Austin: "[s]he had never cut her hair and it fell to her knees. She braided it and built it up around her head in a coronet. At parties she felt like a Spanish duchess with a high tortoise shell comb stuck behind her coils and a black lace mantilla thrown over the whole, so sitting down, she was as impressive as she felt herself to be, but as soon as she stood up, there she was, ridiculous" (20). Besides adopting the costume of a Spanish duchess, Austin also liked to wear Native American clothing. When she lived in Carmel, she would don "the leather gown of an Indian princess" and write in a Paiute wickiup perched in a tree (Stineman, *Mary Austin* 95). In *The American Rhythm* she states: "when I say that I am not, have never been, nor offered myself, as an authority on things Amerindian, I do not wish to have it understood that I may not, at times, have succeeded in being an Indian" (41). Not only did Austin mimic the clothing of southwestern native cultures, but she actually claims (albeit tentatively, given her negative declaration) to have become a Native American.

Another way she sought to get within regional experience was to replicate the anthropologist-native relationship. She learned the role of the anthropologist through her friendships with experts in the field. Austin, who often deemed herself an "ethnologist" (a term she used rather broadly to describe those who study people and culture), corresponded with the well-known ethnomusicologist Frances Densmore and obtained informal, methodological training from Frederick Webb Hodge, the expert in Native American culture (Stineman, *Mary Austin* 172). Further, throughout her autobiography she describes her folklore-collecting excursions in Tejon and other places in the Southwest.[5]

Austin was also immersed and well read in anthropology. She studied Bureau of Ethnology reports and constructed a personal "library covering the general subject of Anthropology," which she bequeathed to the library of the Laboratory of Anthropology in New Mexico (Austin, *Earth* [*Earth Horizon*] 288; "Indian Arts Fund" 61). She acknowledges in *The American Rhythm* the influence of "ethnologists" on the development of her Amerindian aesthetic:

> I would unfairly conclude this record of my work if I omitted to return acknowledgments for the help I have had from the ethnological studies of such scholars as Fletcher and Densmore, Goddard and Boaz and Kroeber, Mathews [sic] and Cushing and Harrington. In admitting the contribution of their scholarship, I should fall short if I did not also acknowledge the generosity of their personal assistance in elucidating the creative process as it exhibits itself in the aboriginal mind. Though they do not always take me so seriously as I

take them, it would be unfair not to admit that they always take me good-humoredly.[6]

(65)

Austin admits that these anthropologists did not view her work seriously. Perhaps this was because "atheoretical, descriptive, and unscientific" popular anthropology—the kind written by Austin and a number of other southwestern women writers at the time—was "stigmatized and peripheralized" by academic anthropologists (Tisdale 311, 330). And Austin's approach to ethnographic writing was admittedly unscientific. She rather poetically muses: "I felt myself caught up in the collective mind [of the tribe], carried with it toward states of super-consciousness that escape the exactitudes of the ethnologist as the life of the flower escapes between the presses of the herbalist" (*American* [*The American Rhythm*] 41). Loosely situated within the anthropological tradition, Austin attempts to transcend scientific objectivity and achieve a spiritual, mystical understanding of her subjects. Nevertheless, between her correspondence to anthropologists and her library of sources, she was steeped in the discipline of anthropology and, I argue, adopted the subject position of the anthropologist to fashion her self-presentation as an artist and to understand southwestern cultures from within.

In her desire to "go native," to don the trappings of Native American and Spanish colonial cultures, Austin duplicated the methods of the ethnologist Frank Hamilton Cushing, to whom she pays tribute in the passage above from *The American Rhythm.*[7] Though Austin purports a very strong identification with Native Americans in claiming to "have succeeded in being an Indian," the much-mythologized Cushing was the first recognized anthropologist to "go native." He was sent by the Bureau of Ethnology to study the Zuni and in a novel move resided with them, "a privileged insider," for five years. He even earned high office in the Society of the Bow, one of the Zuni Secret Societies (Gronewold 44). Similarly, in *The Land of Journey's Ending* Austin describes how in Spanish colonial New Mexico she, a white woman, was allowed to witness the secret ritual, Los Hermanos Penitentes, and later gained entry to the private chapel of the Third Order of St. Francis.

Besides imitating Cushing by acting the participant-observer, Austin also adopted his approach to understanding cultural artifacts. Another early-twentieth-century anthropologist, Alice Fletcher, who similarly lived with the Missouri Valley Native Americans she studied, characterized Cushing's archaeological method as one of "unconscious sympathy," which arose from his "power of thinking his way along the lines of aboriginal thought" (qtd. in "In Memoriam" 370). By immersing himself in the material conditions of aboriginal culture, Cushing tried to replicate the ways in which the Native Americans created their material artifacts and discovered their technology.

Although the aboriginal artifact is literary for Austin, she simulates Cushing's archaeological method in translating Native American literature. The ability to form an empathic bond with native cultures is central to Austin's translation method, which she terms "re-expression." Studying aboriginal tribes, Cushing seeks to "surround [him]self with their material conditions," and Austin attempts to "saturate [her]self . . . in . . . the environment that cradled [native] life." Cushing's goal is to "restore their act and their arts," and Austin's is to produce "a genetic resemblance to the Amerind song that was my point of contact" (Cushing, qtd. in "In Memoriam" 368; Austin, *American* 38). Cushing and Austin share Boas's assumption that "the most important task in ethnography is to present the culture of a people from their own point of view, as perceived by the people themselves" (Rohner and Rohner xxiii). They flirt with the boundaries of anthropological authority in romantically striving to transcend their own Anglo cultural positions.

Further, Austin often pushes the limits of the "ethnologist" role to become the transethnic. In so doing, she explores the outer limits of regionalist empathy. Historically, in Austin's time the notion of participant-observation developed for fieldworkers in anthropology. While participant-observers recognized that their personal experience and subjective authorship were central to ethnographic inquiry, they strove for objective distance from their subjects (Clifford, "Introduction" 13). Clifford Geertz sums up the role of the participant-observer when he states: "[w]e are not, or at least I am not, seeking either to become natives (a compromised word in any case) or to mimic them. . . . We are seeking, in the widened sense of the term in which it encompasses very much more than talk, to converse with them" (13). Austin is a transethnic precisely at the moments when she mimics and seeks to become a native.

Related to this point about Austin's transethnicity, Elizabeth Ammons raises a significant question which is also applicable to the white, transethnic, regionalist writer: "[w]hat are the ethics of advantaged white women adapting other people's cultural perspectives to their own personal ends?" Ammons maintains, "In the history of modernism the appropriation by white artists of the cultural perspectives of people of color has almost always been racist and exploitative" (*Conflicting* 101). Austin, Luhan, and countless other writers and artists of Santa Fe and Taos, New Mexico, celebrated "primitivism" and adopted the perspectives of people of color. Primitivists found in the Southwest "exotic" women of color; an absence of distinction between material and spiritual worlds; and "natural" political and social forms, which were preferable to highly developed "civilizations." Though adapting the perspectives of people of color is problematic, is it always racist, exploitative, and socially irresponsible? Austin certainly appropriates

native cultural expression; she uses native tropes throughout her writings, seeks to enter aboriginal experience via her translations, and employs Native American and Mexican folklore as the basis of her *One-Smoke Stories.* Yet, as I will show, at a time when the pleas of Native Americans in their struggle for human rights went unheeded, Austin claimed access to their culture and communicated its beauty, spirituality, and humanity to whites.

Occasionally, however, Austin's appropriation of natives threatens their free agency. Arguing for the development of a more sensible and humane Native American policy by the Indian Bureau, she concludes: "we want this policy in the hands of a group of properly qualified people who will remember that the Indians do not belong to them, but to us, and will hold themselves reasonably sensitive to public opinion on the subject" (**"Folly"** [**"The Folly of the Officials"**] 288). This "us," presumably, refers to the public sympathetic to the Native American cause; nevertheless, she objectifies the tribes as national assets, possessions of philanthropic and humanitarian groups.

Austin does not swallow wholesale the potential racist implications of primitivism. She refers to the Native Americans as "simple primitives" but asserts that primitive does not mean "a savage or a degenerate or even a mental dwarf" (**"Why Americanize"** [**"Why Americanize the Indian?"**] 170).[8] Lois Rudnick states that D. H. Lawrence, who sojourned for a time with Luhan in Taos, adopted a Native American mythos to effect the rebirth of modern humanity. Yet he was ambivalent about Native Americans, exhibiting a "latent racist paranoia" toward people of color in general (*Mabel* 194). Austin, however, was unlike many white, modernist artists who appropriated the perspectives of people of color in an era in which Freud made primitivism attractive by professing that civilized people repressed primitive desires to their detriment (Dippie 290). Austin did not come by the Native Americans via Freud, primitivism, or dime novels. She apprenticed with them before she embraced their perspectives and their art. In *Earth Horizon,* referring to herself in the third person, she asserts:

> There was a part for her in the Indian life. She had begun the study of Indian verse, strange and meaningful; of Indian wisdom, of Indian art. The Paiutes were basket-makers; the finest of their sort. What Mary drew from them was their naked craft, the subtle sympathies of twig and root and bark; she consorted with them; she laid herself open to the influences of the wild, the thing done, the thing accomplished. She entered into their lives, the life of the campody, the strange secret life of the tribe, the struggle of Whiteness with Darkness, the struggle of the individual soul with the Friend-of-the-Soul-of-Man. She learned what it meant; how to prevail; how to measure her strength against it. Learning that, she learned to write.

(289)

As opposed to the modernist writers whom Luhan took on "guided tours" of the land and its people (Rudnick, *Mabel* 293), Austin "consorted" with Native Americans and attempted to learn their culture from the inside. Like the anthropologist, she "entered into their lives"; she did not merely borrow from them, but "she learned to write." She states in *The American Rhythm* that the Native American influence "has given to my literary style its best thing" (39). By appropriating the point of view of Native Americans, Austin believed she invigorated and refined her art, her personal self-expression.

Although Austin adopted Native American art as her own, her goals were not entirely personal. Unlike Boas, who instituted ethnography as a salvage project and accepted the passing of cultures as inevitable, she desired to preserve *and* to revivify the native cultures that were vanishing. James Clifford discusses the politics of ethnography that aims to salvage dying cultures in his essay "On Ethnographic Allegory" (1986). The native or "disappearing object" is a "rhetorical construct," asserts Clifford, which authorizes the "representational practice" of salvage ethnography. Clifford critiques the assumptions of salvage ethnography: that a culture's "essence" is lost with change and that purportedly weak cultures need to be represented by an outsider, the anthropologist, who then becomes "custodian of an essence." Finally, he speculates about how the ethnographic genre might change if the focus was placed on the future of these societies and not their vanishing past ("On Ethnographic" 113, 115). Clifford's points illuminate Austin's writings in interesting ways, although it must be remembered that the vanishing native was much more than a "rhetorical construct" to Austin, who witnessed the active cultural and even physical extermination of Native Americans. Nevertheless, does Austin see herself as custodian of an essence? Is she future or past oriented regarding aboriginal cultures? To what extent does she reinforce the belief in the Vanishing American? In other words, what are the politics of her salvage operation as she reclaims natives into the American tradition?

While Austin admits that Native Americans are vanishing in most parts of the United States, she ultimately seeks to prevent their demise by arguing their artistic worth. Yet she struggles with the colonizer's rhetoric of vanishing throughout many of her writings. For instance, she rather dismissively states:

> It is not, however, the significance of Amerind literature to the social life of the people which interests us. That life is rapidly passing away and must presently be known to us only by tradition and history. The permanent worth of song and epic, folk-tale and drama, aside from its intrinsic literary quality, is its revelation of the power of the American landscape to influence form, and the expressiveness of democratic living in native measures.[9]

> **("Non-English" ["Non-English Writings II"]** 633)

Given the gradual demise of Native Americans, Austin suggests, their artistic culture is less significant to their own society, which is "rapidly passing away," than to the conquering society, which it serves as a model of genuine American literature.

Elsewhere Austin is less willing to concede the native's disappearance. Echoing the language of early ethnologists, she summons her audience to remove the barriers from the "evolutionary progression" of Native American dance drama so that it can develop into a "legitimate theatrical expression":

> What [the average American] does not realize is that with his and the government's connivance, a steady propaganda has been going on for the past thirty years in Indian schools to overcome both the religious and the art values of Amerind drama. . . . What is required for this, as for any other cultural salvage, is the cooperative activity of an enlightened group. And it may as well be stated here as anywhere that any Indian dance drama which the miscellaneous public is permitted to attend has already lost most of its religious implication. If the schools and missionaries will let him alone, the Indian is perfectly able to maintain his own spiritual integrity.

> **("American Indian" ["American Indian Dance Drama"]** 744)

Austin redefines "cultural salvage" in a broader, political context, making it more than the preservation of raw data in a paper record. She urges the schools and missionaries to eschew interference in Native American life and allow the Native Americans to salvage their own spirituality and thereby redeem and invigorate their dramatic practice.

In the desert Southwest, where ancient art survives, Austin discovered an enduring native population, the hope for the future of American culture. *The Land of Journey's Ending* prophesies that the Southwest will be the region in which resides the next great world culture. According to Brian Dippie, the southwestern tribes, who persisted amidst genocide, historically represented the hope for Native American endurance. The plains tribes were the true Vanishing Americans, because their hunting and raiding culture died with the demise of the buffalo and the emergence of the reservation system. The Navaho and Pueblos, however, retained their cultural integrity largely because the Southwest desert held little attraction for Anglo settlers (Dippie 286-87). The desert Southwest is the land of journey's ending where New Mexican and Native American art flourishes. It is a place to witness "Art Becoming," where "art renews itself" (*Land* 445, 444).

Austin intervened to prevent the extinction of Native American art by establishing museum collections in the Southwest. She inaugurated one of her major salvage projects by cofounding the Spanish Colonial Arts Society with Frank Applegate (Austin, *Earth* 358). This society dedicated itself to preserving and rebuilding New Mexican culture. Similarly, she established the Indian Arts Fund, which sought to preserve the essence of native Southwest cultures and also to perpetuate dying cultures. True, as Vernon Young observes about Austin's work, "[m]useums of anthropology and Indian ceremonial do not constitute the tools of new culture; they memorialize a vanishing culture" (161). As opposed to the salvage ethnographers, whose goal is only to preserve the past, Austin's museums anticipated the future of Native Americans and of Anglos. Rudnick argues that Austin's patronage of the arts, though well intentioned, is just another form of colonization, as Austin appropriates native symbols for her own tradition ("Re-Naming" 25). According to Austin, the Indian Arts Fund began when "a score of Americans . . . found themselves sighing over the rapid disappearance of the exquisite *tinajas* of the Pueblo Indians, being struck with the value of their decorative schemes, and their pertinence to the evolving American aesthetic" (**"Indian Arts"** [**"Indian Arts for Indians"**] 381). But Austin transcended the colonialist objective by creating a museum "dedicated to the needs of the Indian artist, rather than to the American crowd vaguely curious about Indians" (**"Indian Arts"** 381). Further, the museum's goal was "not merely to anticipate their [Native Americans'] complete demise but to keep the arts alive" (**"Indian Arts"** 388). Austin stimulated the Native Americans' economy by keeping their arts alive and encouraging them to make crafts (Rudnick, "Re-Naming" 25).

Yet in reanimating native art and economy, Austin acted as custodian of an aboriginal aesthetic essence. Esther Lanigan Stineman claims that by encouraging the people to reproduce traditional crafts, Austin imprisoned them in a nonindustrial past (*Mary Austin* 178). Austin is not a cultural purist who wishes to return the tribes to their precontact states; she advocates the adoption of certain Anglo cultural practices. At the same time, incorporating Boasian cultural relativism into her views, Austin abjures extremist assimilation policies which seek to turn Native Americans into white men.

In **"Why Americanize the Indian?"** Austin takes to task the government boarding schools for Native American children. She critiques the philosophy of the Indian school, which presumes that the Native American student is an inferior white who must be transformed, through education, into an "imitation poor white" (Austin, **"Why Americanize"** 168). Consequently, the student, who is both unfit for Native American life and rejected by white society, becomes "a social outcast and an economic drifter" (Austin, **"Folly"** 285). Given this cogent analysis, Austin questions whether Americanization, the eradication of regional/cultural differences, is the answer to the "Indian Problem" as she adopts a stance of cultural relativism in her writings. In other words, she continually dismantles the hierarchy that ranks Anglos above natives. Viewing individuals within their cultural contexts, she asserts the value of native traditions and questions the universal applicability of Anglo customs.

Hence, cultural relativism with its insistence on the worth of individual societies becomes her means of arguing for the conservation of regional cultures, which are the components of a genuine American tradition. For instance, in **"White Wisdom"** from *One-Smoke Stories,* Austin adopts a stance of cultural relativism when she depicts the absurdity of white education for Native Americans. The story also questions the wisdom of white society's racial biases. Through the character of Dan Kearny, the gray-eyed Ute, she maintains that regardless of physical appearance and cultural demeanor, the white-educated Native American will always be a pariah in Anglo American society.

The frame of the story portrays a Ute speaker, offering his tale as a caution to the Navaho, "a tree of protection" as they "pray Washington to build schools for them" (*One-Smoke* [*One-Smoke Stories*] 182). The speaker warns them not to be "twice-bitten" by white wisdom—bitten by their desire to obtain it and then again when it betrays them. The protagonist of the story, the gray-eyed Ute, was "twice-bitten." The speaker's aunt helped nurse the elder Dan Kearny's wife on her deathbed and then later married him and raised his son, Dan Kearny. Although Dan is educated in a white school, his Ute relatives attend to his education in Native American traditions; hence, as a child he is "two-minded." However, when he is older, his Ute mother sends him to a white school according to the wishes of his departed father.

The story is set on a reservation, and its political backdrop is institutionalized assimilation. The speaker complains, "Washington will have all Indians to live wholly in the White way." They may choose only from "among the White man's religions" and are debarred from performing their ceremonial dances. In all aspects of life they must follow the white way "except for the one thing of living according to their heart's need of living" (*One-Smoke* 189). The "one thing" the speaker refers to is intermarriage. The story examines the absurdity of acculturation without the possibility of amalgamation.

The newly "whitewashed" Dan Kearny serves a purpose for the reservation agents, who seemingly admit him to their society and then use him to control the tribe. Dan Kearny is "as one painted with Whiteness" (*One-Smoke* 187): in physical appearance he is white and is treated with the deference accorded a white man. The traders on the reservation call him Mr. Kearny; he often eats meals with the white missionary agents; and on his rides around the reservation he is accompanied by their daughter. Kearny speaks to the Utes on behalf of the agents, mocking the tribe's customs and affirming the need for assimilation: "[a]s for dancing, it is nothing to me that you dance buffalo trot or fox trot. . . . But if you dance, saying to the rain or to the corn, obey me, that is the talk of savages" (**One-Smoke** 191). Having become a privileged participant in white life, Kearny renounces the culture of the Ute.

Kearny learns, though, that there are definite limits to this liberal acceptance on the part of whites. After he asks the missionary's daughter to marry him, he discovers his outsider status. She is "sickened" at his proposal and cries to her mother, "[D]on't let him touch me!" Her mother responds with anger; despite having treated him as one of her children, she objects when he dares to propose to her daughter "as though [he] were White" (**One-Smoke** 196). Austin suggests that while white education does not make Native Americans equal to whites, its purpose is to make them less different and more tractable.

Kearny rebels against their control and runs away to join the Ute dance at Big Meadows. When the speaker, who is Kearny's cousin, and the speaker's mother discover him, he has adopted the Ute dress and married a Ute wife. The story momentarily seems to endorse the fixity of race and the fluidity of culture. However, in an ironic twist the speaker's mother reveals to her son that although Kearny was brought up by her Ute sister, he is actually the son of his father's white wife, who died. The story, then, depicts the arbitrariness of race categories that are not innate but socially constructed. Though Kearny looks and acts white, the missionary's daughter is revolted by him because she supposes him to be part Ute. Her reaction to his proposal is based not on his projected cultural identity but on his assumed Native American heredity. By disclosing that Kearny is white, Austin satirizes the girl's bigotry and reveals the irrationality of society's racial prejudices. The story completely deconstructs race and culture as a carnival of signifiers devoid of any fixed signification. At the story's end, Kearny, who remains deceived about his racial identity, is no longer manipulated by white wisdom but uses it defiantly, as "a shield under which tribal use flourishes, and a thorn in the side of the Agency which they can in no wise pluck out" (**One-Smoke** 182).

"**White Wisdom**" discloses Austin's skepticism about the viability of assimilation policies when Anglo Americans continue to endorse an ideology of difference. Proffering the perspective of cultural relativism, the story asks, What is the virtue of white wisdom for its own sake? Similarly, Austin questions the assumption that so-called civilized white customs are more rational and valid than Native American ones. In "Why Americanize the Indians?" she worries that schools have "saddle[d]

upon these simple primitives some of the most ridiculous fetishes of our complex civilization—the fetish of bundling up the human body in cloth, the fetish of steam-heated houses, the fetish of substituting the fox trot and the bunny hug for the buffalo and deer dances, the fetish of high-heeled shoes for women and $9.98 custom-made suits for men" (169). Through these comparisons, Austin makes white customs appear primitive. As whites foist these customs upon the Native Americans, the reasons for them "are completely hidden from the Indian" ("**Why Americanize**" 169). By repeating the word "fetish," Austin accentuates the fact that undisputed reverence is attributed to white culture, arbitrarily making high-heeled shoes more "civilized" than moccasins.

Somewhat moderate in her views about the coerced Americanization of Native Americans, Austin advocates fluid acculturation or biculturality. "Mixed Blood," for example, is the story of Venustiano, a half-Spanish, half-Native American man who is educated Presbyterian. Ironically, though he is of "mixed blood," he adopts a Presbyterian identity and renounces his Native American self, even "refusing to let his hair grow." Venustiano had "no occasion for instruction in his own tribal rites" and so "was glad to call himself by their [the Presbyterians'] name." In addition, Venustiano is ethnocentric in his religious belief, proclaiming to his uncle, the cacique, "I got me a God that is the true one, and not no old people's story." He disowns his Native American heritage but with unconscious irony reminds his mother "that he was of mixed blood and no Indian." Despite his disavowal of his Pueblo roots, Venustiano exploits his heritage by marrying Abieta of the Turquoise Clan and claiming his "allotment of pueblo land" (**One-Smoke** 286, 288).

Venustiano's ethnocentric Presbyterianism causes the tribe to spurn him. Although he marries a Native American wife and lives on tribal land, to the chagrin of the Pueblo people he refuses to partake in any Native American ceremonies or even to wear native dress when working with the tribe. When the people alienate him, he complains to his wife "that they ought to remember that he was of mixed blood and proper Indian feelings" (**One-Smoke** 289). Venustiano acknowledges his Pueblo ancestry and avails himself of his "mixed blood" identity when it benefits him.

The tribe, however, isolates Venustiano because he is consistently unable to embrace his mixed identity and view ethnicity as flexible. To the tribe Venustiano is in "bad form" since "nothing in Pueblo custom inhibited the utilization of as many rites as a man found served his purpose." The "good Catholics," for example, did not let "making the Roman sign inhibit the salutatory pinch of sacred meal on entering a friend's house" (**One-Smoke** 288, 287). The Pueblos scorn Venustiano for failing to syncretize his mixed identity yet wishing to live among the people whose culture he repudiates.

In the end, through the "witchcraft" and machinations of his wife and her aunt, Venustiano learns tribal pride and respect for native customs and is eventually readmitted "to the community of labor" (*One-Smoke* 294). The story resists making value judgments about cultural traditions and illustrates that only by viewing culture as fluid can Venustiano capitalize on the potential of his "mixed blood" identity.

Besides depicting the "mixed blood" character who resists fluid biculturalism, Austin portrays the difficulties some Native Americans have with the uncompromising assimilation policies of whites. **"Hosteen Hatsanai Recants"** faults Christian assimilationists with being inflexible and fetishistic. Hatsanai converts to Christianity when he meets and falls in love with Tuli, a Native American Christian. When Tuli goes blind, Hatsanai seeks a second wife, pending the approval of Tuli, to assist her at home. The missionaries are enraged when the threesome request that they marry Hatsanai and his pregnant second wife according to Christian law.

Austin reconciles Christianity with the polygamy of Hatsanai by radically suggesting that biblical doctrines, rather than being fixed in meaning, are interpreted within cultural contexts and are, therefore, fluid with culture. The missionaries deem Hatsanai a sinner and rebuke him: "You have a wife whom you married in the sight of God, and would you insult her by bringing into her house a ———?" Further, they call his wife Tuli a "pagan and a backslider" (*One-Smoke* 233). Interpreting Hatsanai's polygamy from their own cultural perspective, the missionaries deem his second wife a "whore," imply that their relationship is purely sexual, and accuse him of insulting Tuli. However, Tuli is not "insulted," for he has married the second wife to honor her, not satisfy his sexual appetite. He complains that he has practiced monogamy "according to their [the missionaries'] convenience" (*One-Smoke* 228). In other words, monogamy is not an absolute moral standard, and within certain cultures it is even an inconvenience. Hatsanai dumbfounds the missionaries when he challenges them to cite any sayings of Jesus that forbid him to marry his second wife, the mother of his child. Although he has honored his wife, Hatsanai is berated by the missionaries and accused of sinning. Because Christian doctrine is not flexible but culture bound, Hatsanai cannot reconcile his Native American lifestyle to Anglo Christianity.

Austin does not so much object to introducing Christianity to the Native Americans as she does to the dogmatism of the missionaries who are unable to see that from Hatsanai's cultural perspective finding a mate to assist his blind wife and then wishing to marry this new bride when she becomes pregnant are acts of love and kindness within his own culture. Fearing that they are doomed to Christian hell, Hatsanai and his wives recant their Christianity. Hatsanai relates, they "threw into the Cleft all our fetishes that we had from the Mission," including "Sunday-school cards, a silver cross . . . a Bible . . . our writing of marriage" (*One-Smoke* 235). Along with these "fetishes," they expel white cultural prescriptions which ascribe unquestioned reverence to Anglo American practices. Instead, the story endorses cultural relativism by judging the morality of polygamy within its cultural context. Like Dan Kearny, the gray-eyed Ute, Hatsanai and his wives return in the end to the more amenable Native American spirituality.

From within his native religion, Hatsanai can somewhat reconcile his spiritual beliefs. Although he renounces Christianity, Hatsanai dreams of Christ: "it is His face I see, and yet as though it were also one of the Dine, and the face is kind." He dreams of a syncretic Christ, the European God with the face of a Native American. Moreover, he appeases himself with the knowledge that "*there is no Saying*" of Jesus that makes his act of polygamy sinful and defiant (*One-Smoke* 236). Similar to **"Mixed Blood," "Hosteen Hatsanai Recants"** depicts Native American religion as flexible and accepting of other religious beliefs.

Since the existence of "several Americas" is central to Austin's "genuine regionalism," **"White Wisdom," "Mixed Blood,"** and **"Hosteen Hatsanai Recants"** argue for the preservation of regional cultures. Austin rejects the complete Americanization of the tribes; rather, her solutions to the "Indian Problem" are syncretic ones, based on a "more rational Americanization" (**"Why Americanize"** 171). For instance, she asserts that the Native Americans should be given their religious freedom and the liberty to create their own art, rather than mimicking European forms. Also, Native American family and village life should be restored but with improved sanitation. Upon reinstituting family life, village schools should replace government boarding schools, and an adult education program should be coordinated in the village to lessen the alienation between parents and their white-educated children. Children should attend classes until they are approximately sixteen and then be allowed to choose whether they would like to continue their education at a white school. Normal schools should be established for any students wishing to become teachers and craftsmen among their own people. Instead of paternalistically denying Native Americans access to an industrialized future (Stineman, *Mary Austin* 178), Austin declares, "Open all the doors to civilized opportunity . . . but neither nag nor compel them to enter" (**"Why Americanize"** 170, 171). While Austin endeavors through her salvage project to preserve the aesthetic essence of the region, politically she does not attempt to fix Native Americans in a sentimental past. Instead, she locates their cultural essence in their art and without force or coercion welcomes them to all other aspects of white life.

Austin's intercultural relationship with Native Americans raises complex questions about the politics of white regionalists identifying with nonwhite cultures. Can white writers ever respectfully speak on behalf of non-white cultures? (And for that matter, can scholars who study such writers ever adequately depict them?) Austin employs Franz Boas's anthropological methodology and attempts to study Southwest native cultures empathically from their own perspectives. But she does not transcend the critical problems arising from her writing other cultures. However, she does make an effort to carve out a respectful subject position for herself by redefining "primitivism" and adopting a position of cultural relativism in order to revalue Native American regional cultures and claim for them a place in American life and art. Ultimately, she extends the concept of regionalism beyond the effects of locality on individuals. For Austin, region determines the forms of cultural self-expression, and multiregionality characterizes the American tradition.

Notes

1. Dudley Wynn has commented about Austin's oeuvre: "Mary Austin can never be made simple. There are back-trackings and reversions, and inconsistency holds all along the chronological line" (225).

2. Fetterley and Pryse contrast regionalists to local colorists who "hold up regional characters to potential ridicule by eastern urban readers" ("Introduction" xii).

3. Sollors uses the term *transethnic* to describe the writers Waldo Frank and John Howard Griffin ("Literature and Ethnicity" 664).

4. In a longer version of this article, I analyze how Austin ranges between the discourses of evolutionary ethnology and Boasian cultural anthropology.

5. For example, see Austin, *Earth Horizon* 237, 238, 247, 251, and 258.

6. Frances Densmore was an ethnomusicologist who studied and translated the songs of the Teton Sioux, Choctaw, Menominee, and British Columbia tribes. Pliny Earle Goddard was a linguist and the foremost Athabaskanist of his time. He was also in close intellectual alliance with Franz Boas, the influential German anthropologist who rebutted the theories of cultural evolutionists. Alfred L. Kroeber was a student of Boas; he made contributions in all four fields of anthropology. Kroeber studied the Zuni, Arapaho, Mohave, and Yurok tribes. John Peabody Harrington, through Kroeber and Goddard, developed an interest in Native American languages, especially those of the Southwest. He was the first ethnologist to realize the import of Native Americans' knowledge of the world around them. Washington Matthews was a collector and translator of Navajo myths, prayers, and songs. Alice Fletcher, a pioneering fieldworker in anthropology, studied Native American music and Plains Indian religious ceremonies. Her best-known works are *The Hako: A Pawnee Ceremony* and *The Omaha Tribe.* Frank Hamilton Cushing lived with the Zuni for five years while he studied them.

7. Austin praised Cushing for obtaining parts of the sacred tribal epic of the Taos Pueblo, which had never before been shared with whites. With Hodge she prepared a second edition of and wrote an introduction to Cushing's *Zuni Folk Tales,* which was reissued in 1931 ("Indian Arts Fund" 60). Many scholars today find problematic Cushing's sojourn with the Zuni. They charge that he obtained the trust of the Zuni people only to betray them by revealing their sacred ceremonies. Austin applauds Cushing in "The Folk Story in America" 18. For critiques of Cushing, see Dippie 285 and Gronewold 42.

8. Similarly, in "The Aims of Ethnology" Boas states: "I have used here throughout the term 'primitives' without further explanation. I hope this has not conveyed the impression that I consider these tribes as living in an original state of nature, such as Rousseau imagined. On the contrary, we must remember that every primitive people has had a long history. . . . There is no primitive tribe that is not hemmed in by conventional laws and customs" (633).

9. Austin declares the importance of western American art to the national tradition. She laments in her conclusion: "[n]ot until this vanishing race attains the full dignity of extinction will its musical themes and decorative units pass into the artistic currency of the West" ("Non-English" 833).

Works Cited

Ammons, Elizabeth. *Conflicting Stories: American Women Writers at the Turn into the Twentieth Century.* New York: Oxford University Press, 1991.

Austin, Mary. "American Indian Dance Drama." *Yale Review* 19 (1929-30): 732-45.

———. *The American Rhythm: Studies and Reexpressions of Amerindian Songs.* 1923. New York: Cooper Square, 1970.

———. *Earth Horizon.* Albuquerque: University of New Mexico Press, 1932.

———. "The Folk Story in America." *South Atlantic Quarterly* 33 (1934): 10-19.

———. "The Folly of the Officials." *Forum* 71 (1924): 281-88.

———. "Indian Arts for Indians." *Survey* 1 July 1928: 381-88.

———. *The Land of Journey's Ending.* New York: AMS Press, 1969.

———. "New York: Dictator of American Criticism." *Nation* 21 July 1920: 129-30.

———. "Non-English Writings II." *The Cambridge History of American Literature.* Ed. William Peterfield Trent et al. Vol. 4. New York: Putnam's, 1921. 610-34.

———. *One-Smoke Stories.* Boston: Houghton Mifflin, 1934.

———. "Regionalism in American Fiction." *English Journal* 21 (1932): 97-107.

———. "Why Americanize the Indian?" *Forum* 82 (1929): 170.

Boas, Franz. *Race, Language, and Culture.* Chicago: University of Chicago Press, 1940.

Clifford, James. "Introduction: Partial Truths." *Writing Culture: The Poetics and Politics of Ethnography.* Ed. James Clifford and George E. Marcus. Berkeley: University of California Press, 1986. 1-26.

———. "On Ethnographic Allegory." *Writing Culture: The Poetics and Politics of Ethnography.* Ed. James Clifford and George E. Marcus. Berkeley: University of California Press, 1986. 98-121.

Dippie, Brian. *The Vanishing American: White Attitudes and U.S. Indian Policy.* Middletown: Wesleyan University Press, 1982.

Faris, Robert E. L. "Evolution and American Sociology." *Evolutionary Thought in America.* Ed. Stow Persons. New Haven: Yale University Press, 1950. 160-80.

Fetterley, Judith, and Marjorie Pryse, "Introduction." *American Women Regionalists, 1850-1910.* xi-xx.

Geertz, Clifford. *The Interpretation of Cultures.* New York: Basic Books, 1973.

Gronewold, Sylvia. "Did Frank Hamilton Cushing Go Native?" *Crossing Cultural Boundaries: The Anthropological Experience.* Ed. Solon T. Kimball and James B. Watson. San Francisco: Chandler Publishing, 1972. 33-50.

Hyatt, Marshall. *Franz Boas: Social Activist.* New York: Greenwood Press, 1990.

"The Indian Arts Fund." *Mary Austin: A Memorial.* Santa Fe: Laboratory of Anthropology, 1944. 59-61.

"In Memoriam: Frank Hamilton Cushing." *American Anthropologist* n.s. 2 (April-June 1900): 354-80.

Luhan, Mabel Dodge. "Mary Austin: A Woman." *Mary Austin: A Memorial.* Santa Fe: Laboratory of Anthropology, 1944. 19-22.

Rohner, Ronald P., and Evelyn C. Rohner. "Introduction: Franz Boas and the Development of North American Ethnology and Ethnography." *The Ethnography of Franz Boas.* Ed. Ronald P. Rohner. Chicago: University of Chicago Press, 1969. xiii-xxx.

Rudnick, Lois Palken. *Mabel Dodge Luhan: New Woman, New Worlds.* Albuquerque: University of New Mexico Press, 1984.

———. "Re-Naming the Land: Anglo Expatriate Women in the Southwest." *The Desert Is No Lady: Southwestern Landscapes in Women's Writing and Art.* Ed. Vera Norwood and Janice Monk. New Haven: Yale University Press, 1987. 10-26.

Sollors, Werner. "Literature and Ethnicity." *Harvard Encyclopedia of American Ethnic Groups.* Ed. Stephan Thernstrom. Cambridge: Belknap, 1980. 647-65.

Stineman, Esther Lanigan. *Mary Austin: Song of a Maverick.* New Haven: Yale University Press, 1989.

Tisdale, Shelby J. "Women on the Periphery of the Ivory Tower." *Hidden Scholars: Women Anthropologists and the Native American Southwest.* Ed. Nancy J. Parezo. Albuquerque: University of New Mexico Press, 1993. 311-33.

Wynn, Dudley. "Mary Austin, Woman Alone." *Virginia Quarterly Review* 13 (1937): 243-56.

Young, Vernon. "Mary Austin and the Earth Performance." *Southwest Review* 35 (1950): 153-63.

Elizabeth Jane Harrison (essay date 1997)

SOURCE: Harrison, Elizabeth Jane. "Zora Neale Hurston and Mary Hunter Austin's Ethnographic Fiction: New Modernist Narratives." In *Unmanning Modernism: Gendered Re-Readings,* edited by Elizabeth Jane Harrison and Shirley Peterson, pp. 44-58. Knoxville, Tenn.: The University of Tennessee Press, 1997.

[*In the following essay, Harrison demonstrates the ways in which Austin and Zora Neale Hurston employ the concepts of the anthropologist in their respective autobiographical works, but she argues that while their writings "valorize 'primitive' cultures and question innate racial characteristics," they also introduce "narrative strategies" that "critique the relationships among narrator, subject, and audience," and in this respect "function as precursors for contemporary, postmodern writers of ethnic fiction."*]

As twentieth-century "regional" or "ethnic" writers, Zora Neale Hurston and Mary Hunter Austin have suffered from a neglect of their literary strategies in favor of an analysis of the cultural context of their narratives. By focusing on the incorporation of this content, we might reconsider the place of each author in the modernist American canon. Far from simply recording or romanticizing "primitive" African and Native American cultures, these two authors critique the relationships among narrator, subject, and audience, and construct complex narrative structures which incorporate oral forms. Their narrative techniques, what I define as "ethnographic fiction," link them to so-called high modernists like James Joyce, Virginia Woolf, and William Faulkner, whose experiments with multiple points of view and oral narratives can no longer be considered unique.

Although modern psychology's influence on the development of stream-of-consciousness narrative is widely recognized, anthropology's effect on fiction writers of the modernist period is often overlooked.[1] Many people know that Zora Neale Hurston trained under anthropologist Franz Boas at Columbia University in the late 1920s, and some literary critics have studied Hurston's anthropological writings. But few have focused on how Hurston used her training in ethnography to develop new fictional forms. Likewise, critics analyze Mary Austin's stories about Native American cultures in the southwestern United States without considering seriously how her theories of what she termed "Amerindian" folklore may have affected her own literary methods. Unlike Hurston, Austin never studied anthropology in an institution; nevertheless, as I will demonstrate, the two authors were influenced both directly and indirectly by new anthropological concepts developed by Boas and his contemporaries.

During the early part of the twentieth century, a schism was occurring in anthropology between the evolutionists and the historians. Franz Boas and his school represented the latter approach, which stressed what today we call "cultural relativism," or the idea that no race or culture is inherently superior to another.[2] Boas's *The Mind of Primitive Man* (1913) was a remarkably influential book, which no doubt affected Hurston's ethnographic research, since she studied under him, and must have been familiar to Austin as she completed work on Native American literature and traditions for ***The American Rhythm*** (1930).[3] Both Hurston and Austin demonstrate and challenge the idea of Boas's cultural relativism in their narratives. Following the anthropologist's concepts, their writings valorize "primitive" cultures and question innate racial characteristics. But

through their own research and reading in the field, the authors developed narrative strategies which also question ideas of "objective" knowledge and "accurate" reportage, ideas which, as a trained social scientist, Boas could ill afford to reject.[4]

As women, moreover, the two authors establish a different perspective than their male contemporaries who had previously dominated the social sciences. Occupying a unique stance as female researchers and literary artists, Hurston and Austin ultimately subvert Boas's method of participant-observer ethnography.[5] The following pages will discuss Hurston's *Mules and Men* and *Tell My Horse* and Austin's ***Land of Little Rain, Lost Borders,*** and ***One Smoke Stories*** to demonstrate how both authors create a new genre of "ethnographic fiction" from their knowledge and incorporation of anthropological methods. As committed cultural relativists, Hurston and Austin prepared literary audiences for an acceptance of new social science tenets and thus helped disseminate changing views of culture. In this way they function as precursors for contemporary, postmodern writers of ethnic fiction.

One of the major methods of modern anthropology popularized by Franz Boas was a more interactive model of collecting material called participant-observer ethnography. Instead of remaining an aloof, "objective" outsider, the collector might actually enter into the culture to take part in its rituals. Participant-observer ethnography posited a new relationship between narrator/ observer and subject/material. In her first book of folklore, *Mules and Men* (1935), Hurston uses this strategy. The author began her project of collecting African American folklore in 1927 while she was Boas's student at Columbia. The narrator, Zora, who simultaneously does and does not represent Hurston herself, takes part in storytelling sessions on the porch of the local store, rather than passively describing only what she sees. At first this narrative technique appears as a simple framing device. The reader follows Zora on her folklore-collecting journey from Eatonville to Polk County, Florida, and finally on to New Orleans to observe hoodoo. But the relationship between the narrator and the tales she collects is complicated by the slippage that often occurs between the frame and the material. The narrator tells as well as reports jokes and folktales in the frame story; the act of observation is not separated from the reportage of data as in traditional ethnography.

Hurston represents herself in the text as both educated ethnographer and as one of the "folk" whom she travels to study. In the introduction she intimates that as a native of Eatonville she will be able to gather stories there "without hurt, harm or danger." But collecting from "the Negro," she tells us, is difficult "because he is particularly evasive" and "offers a feather-bed resistance" to outsiders. The point of view of the introduction then shifts to "we"—Hurston places herself as one of the observed: "we let the probe enter, but it never comes out" (2).[6] Constantly shifting perspectives throughout *Mules and Men,* the narrator Zora manipulates her audience and implicitly asks her readers to question the accuracy of the material she collects. Whose voice, after all, do we trust?

To become an "insider," Hurston the narrator hints, an observer must surrender "objectivity," revealing a problem with Boas's participant-observer method. However much her mentor stressed surrendering aloofness, he maintained traditional scientific attitudes toward "accurate" reportage. Hurston's shifting points of view challenge the efficacy of such a method. "Subjects" will only reveal when and what they want to, perhaps never to outsiders, no matter how much researchers try to enter into the culture they wish to study. The narrator's final tale, which closes the book, confirms Hurston's skepticism about objective reportage. The story of Sis Cat conflates narrator, author, and material into one. The tale teller who invents the "lie" and the author who records it are Sis Cat; and the Rat, who has been doubly duped by her "lies," represents Hurston's presumably white audience. The tale itself becomes both folklore material and a gloss of the text's ultimate purpose. The "manners" that Sis Cat learns to use after catching her Rat demonstrate the narrator's method of gathering and reporting data. As an anthropologist, it seems, Hurston has learned a new way of storytelling ("lying") rather than adopting Boas's "scientific" method.[7] However, the author can only reveal her strategy indirectly through analogy and symbol so as not to threaten the anthropological label of her study or risk rejection from her teacher and sponsor.[8]

In Hurston's second collection of folklore, *Tell My Horse* (1938), the author modifies her narrative strategy. Unlike *Mules and Men,* an academic investigation supported by Boas, the research for *Tell My Horse* was funded by two successive Guggenheim Fellowships and developed as a project expressly for Mrs. Osgood Mason, Hurston's wealthy white patron. Mason literally owned the material Hurston collected. Consequently, Hurston's purpose and audience shifted. She was not to appeal to a scholarly reader but to one who held more popular, or stereotypical, views of African American and Caribbean culture. Furthermore, Hurston was more of an outsider herself in Jamaica and Haiti than she had been on her native territory in the United States.

The author's relationship with her "subjects" is represented in the curry goat feed incident in chapter 2 of *Tell My Horse.* First, Hurston must assure her audience that although she is not Jamaican, she can still offer her reader "inside" information. She reports: "They did something for me there that has never been done for

another woman. They gave me a curry goat feed. That is something utterly masculine in every detail. Even a man takes the part of a woman in the "shay shay" singing and dancing that goes on after the feed" (11).

Not only is she privileged to take part in an authentic cultural event despite her outsider status, but her gender is also overlooked. In fact, it is perhaps because of her academic status that she is able to overcome her gender. As Hurston soon reveals, Jamaican society is patriarchal and denies independent action for women. Ethnographer Zora must convince her audience that she has not been denied access to the culture she has come to study. Later in the chapter she makes another intimate appeal to her audience, inadvertently revealing her anxiety about the role she has assumed: "The band began playing outside there in the moonlight and we ran away from the table to see it. *You* have to see those native Jamaica bands to hear them. . . . As I said before no woman appears with the players, though there is a woman's part in the dancing. That part is taken by a man especially trained for that" (14; emphasis added). In *Mules and Men* Hurston does not address her reader in the second person, nor does she emphasize her trespassing on male territory when she attends storytelling sessions on the porch. Perhaps in unfamiliar territory, outside her native Eatonville, she is less sure that she can overcome her inferior female role.

Also in *Tell My Horse,* the narrator's position as sympathetic listener is mediated. As a black American, Hurston makes it clear that she does not necessarily share or agree with Jamaican and Haitian values, particularly those concerning the treatment of women. A frequent criticism of *Tell My Horse* is that Hurston abandons her cultural relativism for a kind of female chauvinism.[9] In chapter 5, "Women in the Caribbean," the author makes generalizations about the low status of women in the two cultures and compares their situation unfavorably with American women. Gwendolyn Mikell points out that as a black woman anthropologist, Hurston's life experiences caused her to intertwine an outsider's and insider's viewpoint. Even though "we may wish to accuse her of patronization," Mikell explains, "the skill with which she unmasked these social sensitivities reminds us that, as an intellectual, she was the contradictory product of the class-and-race conscious American society of the 1930's" (222). Though the author may seem ethnocentric here, I believe Hurston is defending her own tenuous status as social scientist by distancing herself from the cultural practices she observes. Furthermore, blending outsider and insider perspectives enables her to mediate between objective and subjective viewpoints without privileging either. Her criticisms of Caribbean culture in chapter 5 are counterbalanced by an equally honest appraisal of the context from which she operates. She addresses her audience at the beginning of the chapter as "Miss America, World's champion woman" (57), a lighthearted but critical epithet which indicts herself as well as her readers as snobs.

In representing "data" to an educated, and most probably, white audience, Hurston had to confront skepticism and even hostility toward her depictions of unfamiliar "primitive" cultural practices, especially native religions. She developed fictional strategies for valorizing African American hoodoo and Haitian voodoo. (Later we will see Austin using similar strategies for Native American mysticism.) Hurston surrounds her discussions of New Orleans' hoodoo with an aura of mystery. She explains in *Mules and Men* that hoodoo is more a "suppressed religion" than a foolish superstition. "It is not the accepted theology of the Nation," she states, "and so believers conceal their faith. . . . The profound silence of the initiated remains what it is" (185). Likewise, in *Tell My Horse,* part 3, "Voodoo in Haiti," is devoted to a description of voodoo loa (gods) and ceremonies. Hurston compares voodoo rites with Catholicism and shows how the two have become amalgamated in Haitian culture (230-31). She explains that it is a religion of "the mysterious source of life," but "the symbolism is not better understood than that of other religions and consequently is taken too literally" (113). In *Mules and Men,* narrator Zora travels to New Orleans to become initiated herself into this secret faith, then gives her eyewitness account of her experiences. The strategy of withholding then giving information, telling the reader of the secrecy of the rites then only partially revealing them through personal reportage allows readers to experience the confusion of being immersed in a different culture. Throughout part 2 of *Mules and Men,* the narrator alternates between describing hoodoo rituals such as those she learns under hoodoo doctor Luke Turner (198-202) and omitting discussion of them: "I studied under Turner five months and learned all of the Leveau routines," she states, but does not tell what they are, for, she claims, "in this book all of the works of any doctor cannot be given" (202).

Before revealing her experiences with Kitty Brown, another New Orleans hoodoo doctor, the narrator cites several conjure stories not only to "illustrate the attitude of Negroes of the Deep South" (231) but also to testify to the effectiveness of Kitty's spells. All the evidence in this section of the book is circumstantial—the narrator does not give proof or offer any additional explanation or analysis of the phenomena. Letting other eyewitnesses testify first, the narrator can both claim and disclaim the efficacy of hoodoo—and the accumulation of testimonies prepares her audience for her own eyewitness account. As on the porches of Eatonville and Polk County, the narrator again mediates a position between educated observer and curious participant in order to dispel her audience's skepticism.

In *Tell My Horse* Hurston extends her strategy to confront the audience's disbelief in voodoo. First, she insists that the religion is too complex and comprehensive to explain in one book: "This work does not pretend to give a full account of either voodoo or voodoo gods. It would require several volumes. . . . Voodoo in Haiti has gathered about itself more detail of gods and rites than the Catholic church has in Rome" (131). Then, like the narrator in *Mules and Men,* she corroborates her observations of zombies with personal testimonies, "but without using actual names to avoid embarrassing the families of the victims" (192-94). Third, she narrates her own witnessing of a zombie in a hospital and verifies the account with a photograph. Throughout the text, photos of voodoo ceremonies and dances are interspersed, giving the book a kind of travelogue appearance. Hurston can assert that she was actually present at these events with the pictures to prove it.

Finally, the author uses another, more subtle means of challenging the reader's skepticism which she embeds within the narrative itself. The reader identifies with Hurston as narrator/character in her travel adventure as she first remains doubtful about the existence of voodoo. At one point in the book, she explains how she is assured by upper-class Haitians that zombies are only a myth (181). Soon after, of course, she observes one, and the word of her educated hosts is in doubt. Later in the book, before she goes to visit a bocor, or voodoo priest, her yard boy, Joseph, is frightened by what he tells her is the "cochon gris," a secret society he claims wants to eat his baby. When another upper-class Haitian visits Hurston, he learns what Joseph has told her, and Hurston overhears him berating Joseph for "tell[ing] a foreigner, who might go off and say bad things about Haiti such things" (203). The scene closes with the visitor and Hurston assuring each other that they understand "figures of speech," and the reader is left to wonder whether, again, the upper-class Haitians are trying to hide something from the narrator. Sure enough, in the next few pages Hurston describes her horrifying experience at a secret society meeting. Throughout the narrative, Hurston is dissuaded by her hosts from pursuing information about voodoo or the cochon gris, which only makes her—and the reader—more curious and determined in the search.

Another way Hurston reveals the complexity of the "primitive" cultures she documents is to foreground oral expression in her narratives, implicitly questioning the perceived superiority of written literature. In *Mules and Men,* we see a blurring between oral and written language in the construction of the narrative frame. The "conflict" of the plot, the competition among tale tellers, dramatizes the African American practice of "the dozens," or what Henry Louis Gates defines as "that age-old black ritual of graceful insult" (293). The tales often reflect the nature of the "talking game" on the porch. For example, in chapter 2, the men and women of Eatonville compete for linguistic primacy. The sexual battle on the porch is replayed in the tales. One story-teller, Gene, asserts, "her tongue is all de weapon a woman got" (30), prompting Mathilda to tell "why women always take advantage of men" with the well-known "keys to the kingdom" folktale. In this tale, woman might control man's access to the bedroom, the kitchen, and the cradle with the keys the Devil teaches her to use, but her power is strictly limited to the domestic sphere. Furthermore, Hurston makes the next performance in the chapter a song by Jack that describes one man courting three women. Although the narrator of the song might be "in hell" with "that pretty Johnson gal" in the last verse, he has still enjoyed the attentions of three different lovers with impunity. It seems that even in the content of the tales they tell, the women lose.

But the tale-telling sessions also reveal women subtly resisting the patriarchal culture. The chapter ends in a dialogue and exchange of insults between a brother and sister, which the sister wins. She has the last word while he, finally overcome by all the coon-dick has drunk, "mumbl[es] down in to his shirt and [goes] to sleep" (37). In this particular tale-telling session, as in others throughout the book, Hurston's literary construction mirrors and comments upon the verbal gaming the narrator observes, revealing complex linguistic practices of oral expression, as well as documenting the relative roles and status shared between the sexes.

The overall narrative structure of *Tell My Horse* appears deceptively simpler than Hurston's earlier ethnography, since it is mostly straightforward, first-person travelogue. But here as well, the author incorporates orality into the written account of her observations. She does this by breaking codes of standard ethnography—she includes her own opinions and reactions to the cultures in a kind of breezy, conversational style that defies objective reportage.[10] With her side comments and matter-of-fact generalizations, she might be a precursor to today's roaming television commentators. More significant, Hurston introduces postmodern ethnographic techniques after discarding Boasian models. She includes dialogues and scenes in *Tell My Horse* which reveal her interference in the cultures she observes. In Jamaica she insists upon going on a wild boar hunt (31) and even builds a stove for her hosts who have never owned one (23). Surely these actions would be considered unauthorized influence by ethnographers of the modern period. But Hurston includes the interaction and dialogues she engages in with her hosts to reveal not only the mutual exchange of cultural information, but also her self-reflexive stance. *Tell My Horse* becomes part diary in addition to travelogue, political commentary, and ethnographic description. This loosely structured, mixed genre represents a different way of transmitting oral data by replicating the ethnographer's reactions instead of censoring them for an illusory, "objective" style.[11]

By validating the "primitive" cultures she studies, Hurston implicitly questions Western cultural practices which deny supernatural experiences in favor of rational, objective knowledge—and, thus, her narratives begin to challenge the validity of Boasian ethnography itself. In the last two chapters of *Tell My Horse*, Hurston visits Dr. Reser, a white American man who has become a revered voodoo priest throughout Haiti. He is loved and trusted by the Haitians because he acts as their friend, not their superior (247). He tells Hurston about his belief in voodoo gods from "several instances of miraculous cures, warning, foretelling of events and prophecies" (256). Then he describes to her his experiences of being possessed:

> Incident piled on incident. A new personality burned up the one that had eaten supper with us. His blue-gray eyes glowed, but at the same time they drew far back into his head as if they went inside to gaze on things kept in a secret place. After awhile he began to speak. He told of marvelous revelations of the Brave Guedé cult. And as he spoke, he moved farther and farther from known land and into the territory of myths and mists. Before our very eyes, he walked out of his Nordic body and changed. Whatever the stuff of which the soul of Haiti is made, he was that.
>
> (257)

Here Hurston not only illustrates the doctor's willingness and ability to experience mysticism but also the relative nature of culture itself. Under Franz Boas, Hurston had helped to prove that race and culture were not synonymous. In this scene Reser becomes Haitian by fully accepting his adopted society's cultural practices: his "race" is culturally constructed.

Nevertheless, despite Hurston's eager participation in Jamaican and Haitian culture, she does not take the final step of becoming part of the culture as Dr. Reser does. In *Tell My Horse* and in *Mules and Men*, she maintains the status of outside observer, interested and sympathetic, but still removed. Both books close with folktales—or primary ethnographic data—(*Tell My Horse* ends with Dr. Reser's tale, "God and the Pintards") and Hurston affirms her position as cultural interpreter: "But the most important reason why I never tried to get my information second-hand out of Dr. Reser was because I consider myself amply equipped to go out in the field and get it myself" (252). So although throughout her narrative she questions accepted ethnographic techniques and challenges assumptions of objectivity, she still represents herself as a fieldworker in the end, a consummate outsider-insider.

While not celebrated as an ethnic or ethnographic author like Hurston, Mary Austin, nonetheless, uses ethnographic methods in her fiction. An autodidact, she immersed herself in Native American culture through participating in its rituals and studying its literature. She familiarized herself with anthropological terminology and methods. Like Hurston's *Mules and Men* and *Tell My Horse,* Austin's first two collections of short fiction, *The Land of Little Rain* (1903) and *Lost Borders* (1909) depict the relationship between narrator and tale as a function of the participant-observer relationship. It is important to note that Austin, while sympathetic and knowledgeable about Native American culture, was nevertheless Caucasian and thus unable to participate or validate her experiences as completely as Hurston could in studying her own Eatonville neighbors for *Mules and Men.*[12] To overcome the handicap of her outsider status, Austin often poses as witness and listener. She does so not only in individual narratives like **"The Land"** and **"The Woman at the Eighteen Mile,"** but also to introduce collections of tales. *The Basket Woman* (1904), subtitled *Fanciful Tales for Children,* establishes the author as listener in the preface: "I know that the story of the Coyote-Spirit is true because the Basket Woman told it to me, and evidently believed it. She said she had seen Coyote-Spirits herself in Saline Valley and at Fish Lake. I know that the story of the Crooked Fir is true, because if you come up the Kearsarge trail with me I can show you the very tree where the White Bark Pine stood; for I was one of the party that took it on its travels over the mountain: and the rest of the stories are all as true as these" (vi-vii). By establishing a relationship with her "subjects" through listening and watching, Austin attempts to shift the emphasis away from her own ethnicity; still, her anxiety about an authentic voice is evident. Contrary to Hurston, whose shifting viewpoints often playfully tease the skeptical audience (as in the Sis Cat tale), Austin's multivocal narratives become a means of validating the original sources of the author/narrator's information.

Austin's stories often contain multiple layers of narration through hearsay and gossip. Like Hurston's Zora, Austin's narrators call into question the "truth" of the "data" presented, but instead of challenging the accuracy of the tales themselves by calling them "lies," they withhold crucial information from the audience or claim incomplete or contradictory knowledge. By doing so, Austin hopes to tempt her readers into the mystery of her tale in the same way that Hurston teases her audience by conflating narrator and character "Zora."

In **"The Walking Woman,"** the last story in *Lost Borders,* the narrator learns of the elusive wandering woman about whom she writes "by report" when she stops at various places on her travels. She wants to meet the walking woman in person, to verify for herself whether or not she is comely or if she limps. In this story and in others, the narrator pursues a "trail" of hearsay in order to find her plot and confirm the truth behind it. In **"The Woman at the Eighteen Mile,"** a story earlier in the collection, the narrator confesses, "[F]rom the moment of hearing of the finding of Lang's body at Dead Man's Spring, I knew I had struck upon the trail of the story" (203). Often the story the narrator wants to tell is not the typical male adventure of a lost explorer or a discovery of a mine in the desert; instead, as in **"The Walking Woman"** and **"The Woman at the Eighteen Mile,"** it is a portrait of a mysterious individual, whose life may not be glamorous but whose survival on the harsh desert landscape is remarkable. Following trails to stories becomes the overall plot structure or frame of Austin's story collections. Through these shifting and mediating points of view, Austin foregrounds the act of collecting their story material as much as the tales themselves.

Like Hurston, Austin reveals the unreliability of her narrator. We see this strategy especially in the opening story of *Lost Borders,* **"The Land."** The narrator recounts an incident in which a friend brings her a potsherd and tells her that she "ought to find a story about [it] somewhere" (158). She replies that she will rather invent a story about it, which she proceeds to do. Later, after telling the story and publishing it in a magazine, strangers approach her and confirm its truth. The narrator then admits, "By this time, you understand, I had begun to believe the story myself" (158). This revelation reverses the narrative act: life imitates fiction instead of fiction deriving from life. The audience's trust in the narrator is lost if the very nature of the tale telling is called into question at the beginning of the book.

Hurston's careful depiction of hoodoo as an arcane but not ersatz religion affirms her stance as cultural relativist. Austin, likewise, celebrates Amerindian cultural practices and mysticism through her invocations of the mysterious influences of the desert and her depictions of wise Native American women. In the preface to *The Land of Little Rain* she writes: "I confess to a great liking for the Indian fashion of name-giving: every man known by that phrase which best expresses him to whoso names him. . . . For if I love a lake known by the name of a man who discovered it, which endears itself by reason of the close-locked pines it nourishes about its borders, you may look in my account to find it so described. But if the Indians have been there before me, you shall have their name, which is always beautifully fit and does not originate in the poor human desire for perpetuity" (3). Naming instead of possessing land is a repeated motif in Austin's short fiction. "Not the law, but the land sets the limit," the narrator asserts in **"The Land of Little Rain"** (9). The desert is associated with Amerindian culture and figured as impenetrable by Austin. Her characters are often overcome by "desertness" which moves them beyond the boundaries of "civilization" or white man's culture. In **"The Land,"** the interaction of two cultures is again emphasized by the dichotomy between law and nature. Out there where "the law and landmarks fail together . . . almost anything might happen" (156). Actually, beyond the borders is where Austin gathers her stories. But the land that Indians inhabit, the desert, is also treacherous, for it claims both lives and souls. While celebrating its beauty, the narrator also cautions against its power. Austin's narrative strategy, like Hurston's, invites readers to identify with the mysterious allure of the landscape and the people who inhabit it while simultaneously undercutting their own bias of cultural superiority.

In her stories about Native American women, particularly **"The Basket Woman,"** Austin makes implicit cultural comparisons in order to authenticate Amerindian culture. Seyavi, the basket woman, has "set her wit to fend for herself and her young son" (*The Land of Little Rain* 93) after the death of her mate, and she does so by selling baskets. The narrator compares Seyavi's art of basket making to white woman's hairstyling: "In our kind of society, when a woman ceases to alter the fashion of her hair, you guess that she has passed the crisis of her experience. . . . The Indian woman gets nearly the same personal note in the pattern of her baskets" (95). The irony here is unmistakable; Austin elevates Native American art by recontextualizing it in familiar terms that trivialize white culture as a result.

The narrator describes Seyavi's basket designs, which have "a touch beyond cleverness" (95), and explains how when Seyavi cuts "willows for baskets the soul of the weather [goes] into the wood" (96), something readers can only understand by owning one of her creations. At the end of the story we are given what might seem to be a pitiful picture of Seyavi, old and blind, sitting by the fire in the "campoodie" sharing gossip with her three other blind companions. But in this description is also a tribute to her "spiritual ichor" (98) as well as to the Indian way of life which allows her dignity to the end. Seyavi remains part of the campoodie, and if her only privacy is in her blanket, she still "sits by the unlit hearth of her tribe and digests her life, nourishing her spirit against the time of spirit's need" (99).

Throughout Austin's fiction, in fact, the figure of the Indian basket maker functions as a kind of *chisera,* or wise woman, for the narrator. In *The Basket Woman* Austin introduces her as the real narrator of the text who retains primary authority over it; the author is only a recorder of the stories she is told. As for Hurston, who learns secrets of hoodoo from Kitty Brown, Austin's narrators are initiated into the mysteries of Native American culture through women.

Austin's stories also reflect the literary techniques of the culture she observes. In *The American Rhythm,* she describes the effects of her study of Amerindian speech on her writing. It has "given to [her] literary style its best thing, a selective economy of phrase, and its worst, a habit of doubling an idea back into its verbal envelope" (390). Here, I believe she is explaining the structure of her stories as "trails" without traditional plot development. The motifs of landscape imagery in individual stories coupled with the reappearance of characters like the basket woman and the pocket-hunter constitute the "doubling back," a Native American literary technique Paula Gunn Allen discusses in "The Sacred Hoop." One instance of recurrence can be noticed by juxtaposing Austin's first two collections of stories, *The Land of Little Rain* and *Lost Borders.* The first story in each describes the desert in essentially identical terms. In both, the land is first invoked from the outsider's perspective as a wasteland then revealed from the native view as mysterious and powerful. Another motif reinforcing what Allen calls the "mystical and psychic" in Native American thought is Austin's image of the wise woman, who though not always Native American, seems to subscribe to Indian cultural values. In *The Land of Little Rain* this character is represented by Seyavi, the basket maker, and in *Lost Borders* she is transfigured into the walking woman and the woman at the eighteen mile. Such motifs in themselves are not peculiar to Native American literary techniques, but their mystic quality underlines the cryptic aspects of the culture the author describes.

Austin's highly descriptive language conforms to her own study of Native American poetic form, which uses the "glyph" or "type of Amerindian song which is lyric in its emotional quality and yet cannot be expressed by the simple lyric cry" as its primary form (*American Rhythm* 53-54). The lyricism of Austin's narrative with its sometimes diffuse and even transcendental imagery simulates the form of the glyph. Both the glyph and the "inter-communicative silences" the narrator describes in **"The Walking Woman"** highlight aspects of Native American mysticism.

Austin's narrative frame also demonstrates the transference of tales from spoken to written form. *One Smoke Stories* (1934), the author's final collection of short fiction, is a group of tales literally meant to be told during the length of time it takes to smoke a ceremonial cigarette. Genre is determined by the combination of content plus culture, not the other way around. For instance, she explains in the introduction, "one-smoke stories are common to all who live in the area: the form is so admirably conceived for oral telling that all anecdote in the Indian country tends to fall into that shape, which accounts for my including in this collection tales of other peoples than Indians" (xiii-xiv). The author develops her theory of the origins of genre further in *The American Rhythm,* when she explains the effects of landscape and environment on literary form.

Like Hurston in *Tell My Horse,* Austin questions scientific objectivity and affirms the relative nature of culture in her fiction without rejecting her own position as interpreter of it. **"White Wisdom,"** a tale in **One Smoke Stories,** epitomizes the author's ethnographic fiction. The story is narrated by a Ute Indian, an outsider to his audience of Navahos, yet like the author herself, no stranger, but another "tribesman" who has sympathetic reasons for sharing his "telling" (182). White "wisdom," as to be expected, is treachery for the Indians. Dan Kearny, the protagonist, is a supposed mixed-blood who never fits completely into either white or Ute culture. Ultimately his offer of marriage is rejected by a white woman and he accepts his Indian name of "Twice-Bitten." But while the story makes clear how white culture threatens Amerindian survival, it does not affirm Indian culture unequivocally, and thus avoids reverse ethnocentrism. Instead, the wisdom of the tale is represented through the foreknowledge of the *chisera,* the narrator's mother, who divines all along that Dan is not Ute at all by blood, for his parents were both white. The twist at the end of the story is not this revelation, however, but rather that Dan's ethnic origin is irrelevant. He has lived as a Ute most of his life; therefore, he has become one. Like Hurston's Dr. Reser in *Tell My Horse,* Austin's character illustrates the relative nature of the culture. One's race or membership in a particular culture is not biologically determined.

Finally, despite her deep, personal involvement with Native American mysticism, as an author, Austin, like Hurston, remains apart from the culture she records in order to maintain the delicate balance between her subject and her audience. As adopted outsiders, Dr. Reser and Dan Kearny represent the extreme of assimilation into another culture. Posing as ethnographer/narrators in the text, Austin and Hurston circumvent the complete subjectivity of cultural immersion experienced by their characters.

Thus incorporating oral and literary techniques from the cultures they studied, Zora Neale Hurston and Mary Austin developed original and complex literary forms. Their experiments with narrative form constitute part of a new tradition of writing by women regionalists in the modern period—ethnographic fiction. In addition to Hurston and Austin, many of their contemporaries were influenced to a greater or lesser degree by the developing social science of anthropology.[13] Tracing narrative strategies among these writers might help reveal how the reading public received and accepted ideas of cultural relativism. With new immigration restrictions and a rising tide of xenophobia occurring in the 1920s in the United States, the nation faced crucial decisions about whether to become a "melting pot" (cultural assimilation) or a "salad bowl" (cultural relativism and multiculturalism). Authors Hurston, Austin, and others through their ethnographic narratives questioned the ethnocentrism of their dominant Anglo-European culture. These questions have resurfaced in the 1980s and 1990s with a new generation of ethnic writers.

In fact, an important connection might be established between regional writers of the modern period and contemporary ethnic authors. Critics have explored Zora Neale Hurston's influence as a literary foremother for a generation of black women writers from Alice Walker to Toni Morrison, but they often overlook her narrative strategies in favor of her heroic female plots. Mary Austin is often recognized as a precursor for Willa Cather and her novels about the Southwest, but she is perhaps as much a model for Louise Erdrich and Barbara Kingsolver, who depict Native Americans interacting with white society. Today's ethnic authors can assume their audience is already familiar with multivocal narratives that question objective reportage and challenge ethnocentrism.

One example of the parallel between modernist and contemporary ethnographic literature is Gloria Naylor's *Mama Day* (1988), which explores the family and ancestry of an urban African American woman. In the first few pages of the novel, the narrator introduces the main characters and adds an anecdote about "Reema's boy," who leaves his rural home on the island of Willow Springs to become "educated":

> Look what happened when Reema's boy—the one with the pear-shaped head—came hauling himself back from one of those fancy colleges mainside, dragging his notebooks and tape recorder and a funny way of curling up his lip and clicking his teeth, all excited determined to put Willow Springs on the map. . . . And then when he went around asking us about 18 & 23, there weren't nothing to do but take pity on him as he rattled on about "ethnography," "unique speech patterns," "cultural preservation," and whatever else he seemed to be getting so much pleasure out of while talking into his little gray machine.
>
> (7)

One problem with Reema's boy, the narrator explains, is that he fails to listen to the people of Willow Springs to understand their stories, but instead arrives with predetermined categories of analysis. Naylor's introduction is a cautionary tale for would-be ethnic authors. Zora Neale Hurston and Mary Austin avoid the trap that Reema's boy falls into of treating their subjects as objects. Like Naylor's narrator, they know the pitfalls of appropriating the voice of the "other." Affirming cultural and narrative relativity, their ethnographic fiction not only charts a more complex territory in literary modernism but also illustrates a vital link between regional literature and postmodern multicultural texts.

Notes

1. See Manganaro's introductory chapter to *Modernist Anthropology: From Fieldwork to Text,* a collection of essays on modernist anthropology. He

traces the cross-disciplinary influences between the humanities and social sciences to show how "anthropology vitally participated in the century's most important cultural and . . . literary movement" (Preface vi). Also included in this volume are essays considering Ruth Benedict's poetry and ethnography (Handler) and Margaret Mead's and Zora Neale Hurston's innovations in ethnographic reportage (Gordon).

2. See Torgovnick's chapter, "Defining the Primitive/ Reimagining Modernity," in *Gone Primitive: Savage Intellects, Modern Lives,* for a discussion of the development of the Malinowski and Boas schools of anthropology and how cultural relativism affected Western assumptions about and ideas of the "primitive," that is, non-Western societies anthropologists often chose to study.

3. According to her biographer, Esther Stineman, Austin was a self-educated ethnologist; she sought out scholars in the field and corresponded with them (172). Austin was probably familiar with Boas's theories from her wide reading in Native American ethnography. In "Discovering America: Mary Austin and Imagism," Ruppert confirms that in her contribution on aboriginal literature in the *Cambridge History of American Literature,* she quoted frequently from scientists such as Densmore, Fletcher, and Boas (255).

4. Later Hurston suffered for working outside accepted scientific methods. When she wanted to begin work for her Ph.D. in anthropology in 1935, her funding source, the Rosenwald Foundation, withdrew its support when it was discovered that she would spend only three semesters in classes before fieldwork. Edwin Embree, the foundation's president, felt she needed more "discipline" in learning ethnographic methods. See Hemenway (208-10).

5. For a relevant discussion of postmodern ethnography and its relation to feminist theory, see Mascia-Lees, Sharpe, and Cohen. They argue that unlike male anthropologists, feminists have been aware of the presence of the "other" for forty years. Only now are postmodern ethnographers (i.e., post-Boas) recognizing the need for the "other" to speak. Participant-observer anthropology, while concerned with the relationship of the dominant to the culture observed, nonetheless, still spoke from the position of the dominant (11).

6. I am indebted to Johnson for this critique of Hurston's outsider/insider status in *Mules and Men.*

7. See Willis's chapter on Hurston, "Wandering: Zora Neale Hurston's Search for Self and Method" (26-52). Willis explains how *Mules and Men* repre-

sents Hurston's "specifying," or verbal one-upmanship, in written form (31). She equates the author's "manners" in the Sis Cat tale with her aggressive writing strategy (29). Johnson and Boxwell also analyze this tale. Johnson concludes: "To turn one's own life into a trickster tale of which even the teller herself might be the dupe certainly goes far in deconstructing the possibility of representing the truth of identity" (289), while Boxwell uses the image of Sis Cat to underscore Hurston's self-representation as ethnographer in her text (613).

8. According to hooks, Hurston's strategy is to make her data more accessible by masking her true relationship to her academic mentors. Rather than operating under Boas's instructions, as she claims in the introduction to *Mules and Men,* in actuality she compelled him to support her study of African American folklore (137-38).

9. See, for instance, Hemenway, who considers *Tell My Horse* as Hurston's "poorest book, chiefly because of its form." He objects to naïve political analysis, her chauvinism, and her inclusion of legend instead of historical fact (248-49).

10. See Gordon for more on how Hurston departs from standard ethnographic genre in *Tell My Horse.*

11. This focus on self as both interpreter and creator of "data" resembles current postmodern ethnographic techniques more than modernist methods. See, for instance, Clifford.

12. See Rudnick and Ammons. Rudnick acknowledges Austin, Mabel Doge Luhan, and Alice Corbin Henderson's Anglo "patronizing" control over a subordinate culture but also affirms the positive exposure these artists gave Native American political and social issues (25). Ammons asks whether it is ever possible for "a member of a dominant group honestly to cross cultural boundaries," then answers her own question by saying that Austin came closer than most. She never assumed that she could completely understand or represent "Amerindian" art and culture (102).

13. Other writers I consider part of this tradition include Anzia Yezierska, Mildred Haun, and Sui Sin Far.

Works Cited

Allen, Paula Gunn. "The Sacred Hoop: A Contemporary Perspective." *Studies in American Indian Literature: Critical Essays and Course Designs.* Ed. Paula Gunn Allen. New York: MLA, 1983. 3-22.

Ammons, Elizabeth. "Form and Difference: Gertrude Stein and Mary Austin." *Conflicting Stories: America*

Women Writers at the Turn into the Twentieth Century. New York: Oxford UP, 1992. 86-104.

Austin, Mary. *The American Rhythm: Studies and Reexpressions of Amerindian Songs.* New and enlarged ed. Boston: Houghton Mifflin, 1930.

———. *The Land of Little Rain.* 1903. Rpt. *Stories from the Country of Lost Borders.* 1-149.

———. *Lost Borders.* 1909. Rpt. *Stories from the Country of Lost Borders.* 151-263.

———. *The Basket Woman.* Boston: Houghton Mifflin, 1904. Rpt. New York: AMS, 1969.

———. *Stories from the Country of Lost Borders.* Ed. Marjorie Pryse. New Brunswick: Rutgers UP, 1987.

Boxwell, D. A. "'Sis Cat' as Ethnographer: Self-Presentation and Self-Inscription in Zora Neale Hurston's *Mules and Men.*" *African-American Review* 26 (Winter 1992): 605-17.

Clifford, James. *The Predicament of Culture: Twentieth-Century Ethnography, Literature, and Art.* Cambridge: Harvard UP, 1988.

Gates, Henry Louis, Jr. "Afterward: Zora Neale Hurston: 'A Negro Way of Saying.'" *Mules and Men.* New York: Harper & Row, 1990. 287-97.

Gordon, Deborah. "The Politics of Ethnographic Authority: Race and Writing in the Ethnography of Margaret Mead and Zora Neale Hurston." Manganaro 146-62.

Hemenway, Robert E. *Zora Neale Hurston: A Literary Biography.* Urbana: U of Illinois P, 1977.

hooks, bell. "Saving Black Folk Culture: Zora Neale Hurston as Anthropologist and Writer." *Yearning: Race, Gender, and Cultural Politics.* Boston: South End, 1990. 135-43.

Hurston, Zora Neale. *Mules and Men.* 1935. Rpt. New York: Harper & Row, 1990.

———. *Tell My Horse.* 1938. Rpt. New York: Harper & Row, 1990.

Johnson, Barbara. "Thresholds of Difference: Structures of Address in Zora Neale Hurston." *Critical Inquiry* 12 (Autumn 1985): 278-89.

Manganaro, Marc, ed. *Modernist Anthropology: From Fieldwork to Text.* Princeton: Princeton UP, 1990.

Mascia-Lees, Frances, Patricia Sharpe, and Colleen Ballerino Cohen. "The Postmodernist Turn in Anthropology: Cautions from a Feminist Perspective." *Signs: Journal of Women in Culture and Society* 15 (Autumn 1989): 7-33.

Mikell, Gwendolyn. "When Horses Talk: Reflections on Zora Neale Hurston's Haitian Anthropology." *Phylon: The Atlanta University Review of Race and Culture* 43 (Sept. 1982): 218-30.

Naylor, Gloria. *Mama Day.* 1988. Rpt. New York: Vintage, 1989.

Rudnick, Lois. "Re-Naming the Land: Anglo Expatriate Women in the Southwest." *The Desert Is No Lady: Southwestern Landscapes in Women's Writing and Art.* Ed. Vera Norwood and Janice Monk. New Haven: Yale UP, 1987. 10-26.

Ruppert, James. "Discovering America: Mary Austin and Imagism." Ed. Paula Gunn Allen. *Studies in American Indian Literature: Critical Essays and Course Designs.* New York: MLA, 1983. 243-58.

Stineman, Esther Lanigan. *Mary Austin: Song of a Maverick.* New Haven: Yale UP, 1989.

Torgovnick, Marianna. *Gone Primitive: Savage Intellects, Modern Lives.* Chicago: U of Chicago P, 1990.

Willis, Susan. *Specifying: Black Women Writing the American Experience.* Madison: U of Wisconsin P, 1987.

Janis P. Stout (essay date spring 1998)

SOURCE: Stout, Janis P. "Mary Austin's Feminism: A Reassessment." *Studies in the Novel* 30, no. 1 (spring 1998): 77-101.

[*In the following essay, Stout offers readings of Austin's novels, from* Isidro *to the posthumously published* Cactus Thorn, *to suggest that the accepted view of the author as an unwavering feminist is incomplete, for these works reveal "uncertainties and tensions" concerning woman's role in society and show both "undeniable feminist strains" and "traces of ideas that might even be called counter-feminist."*]

> There rose up like a wisp of fog between me and the glittering promise of the future, a kind of horror of the destiny of women.
>
> —Mary Austin, *A Woman of Genius*

Mary Hunter Austin, best known for her book of essays **The Land of Little Rain** but also a prolific novelist, is customarily regarded as an ardent feminist. Dudley Winn, writing shortly after her death, stated that she "rebelled against the status of women in the 'eighties and 'nineties, and never rested until she had worked out her own naturalistic and empirical defense of women's rights." More recently she has been characterized by T. M. Pearce as "a feminist before all else" and by Augusta Fink, with significant ordering, as "feminist, naturalist, mystic, writer."[1] Both her nature writing and her use of Western materials and conventions have been insightfully read in recent years, the first by Elizabeth Ammons and the second by Faith Jaycox, as strategies for "giv[ing] voice, deliberately and positively, to feminist issues."[2]

Certainly the biographical record provides a sound basis for this assessment. Indeed, Austin called herself, in a 1927 essay, a "fighting feminist." She marched and spoke for suffrage and rebelled against prescriptive notions of what women ought to want and do, adopting unconventional behaviors that shocked her small-town neighbors in California and startled even New Yorkers. She defied the then-prevailing resistance to married women as schoolteachers and, after leaving her husband, made her own way in the world. Her insistence on her own and other women's right to pursue careers (one of the hallmarks of the New Woman identified by Carroll Smith-Rosenberg) is indeed one of the strongest of the "feminist ideas" that, as Blanche Gelfant says of *A Woman of Genius,* shape much of her fiction.[3] The ardency of her expression of such ideas, which certainly worked to Austin's detriment commercially, has also been seen by recent scholars as a cause of the long critical neglect of her work. Nancy Porter, for example, believes that it is because of their assertive feminism that her novels have been "dismissed" in favor of her nature writing.[4]

Despite this critical consensus, I want to present a different view of Austin's novels, one emphasizing tension and conflict more than consistency in her advocacy of feminist views. This reading, too, is anchored in Austin's biography. She was in many respects a person shaped by conflicting urges. At their best these constituted complementarities in her personality and goals—for example, her insistent restlessness and her powerful homing impulse. But with respect to what she wanted for her own life and what she believed women in general wanted, she was often ambivalent, both advocating reforms that she considered essential if women were to live as equals, especially in marriage, and at times expressing seemingly contrary, more traditional views. Her novels, too, are marked, as I read them, by inconsistencies and reversals—the kind of "narrative splits" and "breaks" that can be seen, as Margaret Higonnet writes, as "forms of [feminist] resistance" to "narrative wholeness and closure" or as evidence of Austin's reluctance to be bounded in a single literary (or personal) space.[5] Their vision of gender issues is by no means singleminded.

My purpose here is to propose a sequential rereading of the nine novels—*Isidro* (1905), *Santa Lucia* (1908), *Outland* (1910 in a pseudonymous British edition, 1919 in the American edition bearing Austin's name), *A Woman of Genius* (1912), *The Lovely Lady* (1913), *The Ford* (1917), *No. 26 Jayne Street* (1920), *Starry Adventure* (1931), and *Cactus Thorn* (1988)—that will accommodate both their undeniable feminist strains and their traces of ideas that might even be called counter-feminist. Such counter-impulses sometimes appear as balancing complementarities implying fullness of vision and experience, but sometimes erupt into texts in unrec-

onciled or even unacknowledged ways. By re-reading Austin's novels in this way, I resist foreclosure and recognize both ambivalence within individual works and fluctuation from novel to novel. Such a reading reveals the uncertainties and tensions of a complex and imaginative mind confronting both its own insecurities and those of its historical moment and allows us to see that Austin's novels are not at all univocal tracts but multivalent fictional structures, more interesting and perhaps more important than they have sometimes been thought.

* * *

A Woman of Genius, the most noted of the nine novels, has been called a "dress rehearsal for Austin's autobiography."[6] In fact, Austin's novels are all to some degree autobiographical. For that reason, and since a basic level of awareness of Austin can still not be assumed, it may be well to summarize some aspects of her life before turning to the works themselves.

Austin's life was a troubled one both in personal and in professional ways, but it was also a life of feminist emergence and achievement. Melody Graulich, one of the strongest voices in the recent surge of scholarly interest in Austin, calls her biography "a classic in the pathfinder tradition."[7] The path she forged for others to follow was in part a geographical one more commonly associated with males, that of westering into freer territory. It was also very specifically a path of release and independence for women. The image of the wilderness trail characteristically served Austin as an emblem of movement along paths of discovery and freedom, and thus an expression of her feminism. She herself linked the two, spatial movement and feminism, in recalling that she "found the pointers of her own trail going in the direction of women who desired the liberation of women."[8] [*Earth Horizon*]

As a member of what Nancy Porter calls "the first tide of career-minded new women to pull at the shores of middle-class convention," Austin made a series of departures both geographical and social.[9] The first of these was her departure at the age of nineteen from the bastion of conventionality, Carlinville, Illinois, where she had spent an unhappy and lonely childhood as the daughter of a sickly father who died when she was ten and an unloving and severe mother. This first departure, a family migration to arid Southern California, was actually involuntary; Mary was merely acquiescing in her mother's decision to join her son, Mary's older brother, in homesteading there. She would later interpret it, however, as the first and most dramatic of a series of departures in pursuit of personal freedom. A sense of the blessedness of having escaped Carlinville permeates her autobiography, *Earth Horizon* (1932), as well as *A Woman of Genius.*[10] Significantly, perhaps, upon arrival in Los Angeles she chose to ride horseback to her brother's homestead rather than go in the wagon with her mother. Soon she began to roam about the southern tip of the San Joaquin Valley, learning the terrain and developing the skills of observation that would later characterize her nature writing.

Austin's second departure was her escape from the family home. Despite failing the state teacher examination, she found work as a private teacher that entailed residence at the ranch home of a nearby family. When her employers moved away and her mother withheld her portion of the inheritance from her father on grounds that such resources should be kept for sons, she escaped once again by marrying a restless and apparently ineffectual man who surely had no idea what a strong person he was taking as a life partner. She was twenty-three at the time.

Mary Hunter's marriage to Stafford Wallace Austin proved unsatisfactory in ways that would later appear in her novels. Wanting closeness, she found her husband inexpressive. Wanting personal fulfillment through individual endeavor, she found prevailing assumptions about married life restrictive. During their years together, as Mary increasingly centered her attention on the development of a writing career that disrupted the housewifely role he expected of her, Wallace pursued shifting moneymaking schemes that he could never manage to bring off, entailing moves from one small town to another in mountainous south-central California. He drifted into debt that he failed to tell her about, with the result that she was at one point evicted from their lodgings while pregnant and was served with a notice of debt while recovering from childbirth. It is easy to understand how the repeated shocks of her father's death when she was ten years old, her mother's inadequate emotional nurturance, and her husband's failure to provide either financial or emotional support might leave her with a conviction that women had to be able to make their own way but, at the same time, with a lingering wish to be taken care of. These motifs would form a counterpoint in her work.

Austin's main interest during these years was in the land and its native and Spanish people and in her writing. She rambled and visited Indian villages, leaving household chores undone, and went away intermittently for stays in Los Angeles or San Francisco in the company of literary figures from whom she was learning her profession. Once she accepted a teaching job some sixty miles from home despite having no provision for the care of her retarded daughter. After the success of *The Land of Little Rain* (1903) gave her reason to believe she could support herself, and the placement of her daughter in permanent private care allowed her to believe that she had adequately fulfilled her maternal role, she was able to make these temporary absences from her husband permanent. In 1906, in the most deci-

sive of her departures, she signaled her commitment to her career by moving to Carmel as an early member of the writers' colony there that included Jack London, poet George Sterling (with whom she developed an intense but probably platonic relationship), and Lincoln Steffens (for whom she conceived a great passion). When she later settled in New York, following an extended trip to Europe, the move would be made partly in pursuit of Steffens, who soon dropped whatever interest he had felt in her in favor of another woman. This incident is the root of Austin's longlasting concern, evident in several of her later novels, with equal rights in love relationships and with the necessary connection between public principles and private morality.

It was during her early years in New York, after returning from England in 1910, that Austin became active in feminist causes. Before leaving California she had come to know Charlotte Perkins Gilman, whose election of a career after a torturous experience of marriage and mothering gave her confidence in her own similar choice. While in England she met May Sinclair and other feminists and socialists and marched in a suffrage parade. Now she joined the National American Woman Suffrage Association, speaking at a rally on October 13, 1911. She seems also to have occasionally attended the newly formed Heterodoxy Club, a "meeting place for activist women" and a "sympathetic female support group."[11] During this same period, 1911-12, she completed and published her most consistently feminist novel, *A Woman of Genius.* Four years later, along with thirteen others, she would contribute to the group-written suffrage novel *The Sturdy Oak.*[12]

Austin's novels, even when they assume heavily romanticized forms, draw on these various elements of her own experience. They deal with life in the West and in New York, with water rights, business ethics, the loss of a child, labor organization, career-building, theater. They manifest women's yearning for romantic love and a secure home but also their determination to fulfill themselves in work as self-reliant intellectual and moral beings. Repeatedly, even obsessively, they depict women's discovery either that the men with whom they are entangled are weak or venial, as Austin found her husband, or that, as she observed of Lincoln Steffens, their public professions do not govern their private actions. The one point of thematic consistency in her novels is their concern with the nature of marriage. The effort to "imagine the foundations for an egalitarian marriage" that Graulich locates in *A Woman of Genius, The Ford,* and *Starry Adventure* actually extends, in some form, to all nine of the novels.[13] As we will see, the degree to which that effort can be called feminist varies from one book to the next, reflecting Austin's attempt to advocate simultaneously two options commonly regarded as being mutually exclusive: more active roles for women in public and professional endeavors *and* greater security in domestic roles. It is a duality that Austin experienced in her own life and never fully resolved.

* * *

The first of Austin's novels, **Isidro,** published just two years after the book of nature essays that is still usually regarded as her finest work, might well be dismissed as simply a historical romance deploying such tiredly conventional motifs as disguise, a lost child, uncertain identity, and daring rescues (in this case, from Indians).[14] At the center of this elaborate romance, however, is a story of a woman's conflicted sense of gender roles. The heroine, a spirited girl named Jacinta, first appears in male disguise as a boy called El Zarzo (the thorn—thus an early anticipation of Dulcie Adelaid, in **Cactus Thorn**). She carries this off so well that Isidro, the prodigiously handsome scion of a fine old Spanish family to whom she attaches herself as a servant and traveling companion, is completely fooled. After being reunited with her long-lost father (a romance incident of particular power for Austin) she begins to dress and behave like a lady, but takes to that "new life" the way a "caged animal takes the cage and the hand that feeds it." When Isidro is captured by Indians, Jacinta resumes her boy's clothes to attempt his rescue. As she rides off on horseback, thus assuming the male's traditional role of traveler or explorer rather than the female's passive "mapping" as goal or space to be explored, she draws "deep breaths of freedom and relief."[15] Clearly, for Jacinta as at times for Austin herself, the outdoors and escape from en-housement are an invigorating release associated with self-definition as a capable and effective person. Even so, in an ending that reinscribes what Rachel Blau DuPlessis calls the conventional story of "romantic thralldom,"[16] the novel leaves her happily married and staying at home with her children while Isidro goes on trips. It is a first novel of mixed messages.

The ambivalence evident in the love-and-marriage plot of **Isidro** is even more clearly evident in Austin's second novel, **Santa Lucia.** A work more in the vein of social realism than **Isidro, Santa Lucia** turns away from the romanticizing of California's Spanish history (a mode in which Austin was following popular interest and the example of her mentor Charles Lummis) to the treatment of contemporary experience. The title refers to an actual California town in present time. Here the central female role is split among three characters, all to some extent autobiographical, at times in wish-fulfilling ways, yet all three to some extent marked by traditional stereotypes, despite traits that call such stereotypes into question. For each of the three the central question is the possibility of happiness in marriage, and the answers are by no means so idyllic as for Jacinta.

The first of the three heroines to be introduced, surprisingly named William,[17] is a jumble of contradictions. Typecast for much of the book as silly though amiable and delightfully energetic, she is gently mocked for her impulsiveness and the wearing of frills and curling paper. Yet, like Austin herself, she likes the outdoors and natural science, and as her masculine name indicates she has a potential for freedom from conventional femininity. Austin reconciles the apparent inconsistencies of the characterization in part by ignoring them—she seems to enjoy offering readers an unexpected mixture—but in part, too, by presenting William's sillier qualities as bits of childishness that she grows out of. Along with her other qualities, she has a beautiful and charming presence that Austin was only too aware she did not possess herself, and her doting father and retiring (rather than domineering) mother are clearly wish-fulfilling parental figures. Like Jacinta, William demonstrates her strength by rescuing her man from a murder attempt, yet once again the end of her story is the conventional happy ending, marriage—but a marriage-ending couched in unconventional terms, in that William's marriage is expected to be one of equality.

The second heroine, Julia, has been the focus of most discussions of the novel. A bored and frustrated wife, she seeks to escape her marriage through adultery and ultimately does escape through suicide. It was this second-heroine plot, with its sensationalism and its direct assault on the myth of marital bliss, that caused the book to become, in a small way, a scandal. In California, where it had been expected to sell best, **Santa Lucia** was refused by at least one public library and was pulled from bookstore shelves after a store owner reportedly said that his wife found it morally objectionable. An indignant letter from Austin to her editor, F. A. Duneka, dated June 24, 1908, while she was traveling in Europe, indicates that friends had let her know what was happening and that she was outraged by having "the stigma of impropriety" put on her work "in a way to stop sales." A later letter to Duneka mentioning "other criticisms" such as "loss of power and finish" (a phrase adapted from a New York *Times* review) concedes that there is some truth to such criticisms.[18] But we might well wonder if these criticisms were not motivated by the prior moral objections.

Whereas William is mostly fantasy, Julia is only marginally so. Her beauty and her power to lure men seem to have been qualities Austin coveted, but her desperate wish to escape a dreary marriage and her stimulation of gossip in a suffocating small town are drawn directly from experience. Her suicide after the failure of her efforts to escape her marriage is a melodramatic version of Austin's own escape by way of divorce—a displacement that, in keeping with common childhood fantasies, ensures others will be sorry. Julia reflects, then, Austin's conflict between defiance of repressive conventions and desire for fulfillment (even if that meant victimhood) in conventional terms.

The third heroine, Serena, is also in some respects a self-portrait of Austin. She is orphaned (of both parents, however, not just the father), is a person of conspicuous capabilities, and has not only prepared to be a school-teacher but been pressured into doing so, as Austin was, despite her own lack of interest. Her aunt tells her explicitly that teaching and nursing (which was Austin's mother's occupation during her widowhood in Illinois) are "the only creditable employments" for women (*SL* [*Santa Lucia*], p. 53). Serena wants to make her way in some artistic activity but, reflecting a complaint that Austin voiced against both her mother and her husband, gets no encouragement along that line. Her husband, Evan Lindley, is a thinly disguised version of Wallace Austin, who lives beyond his means in the hope that he will make a major coup in various business endeavors, one of them being water-resource development, and can't bring himself to inform his wife that they are deeply in debt until the repossessors actually appear at the door when she is recovering from the birth of their first child.[19]

This third-heroine plot steers a middle course as to the likelihood of happiness in marriage in that Serena's marriage, which begins in dismal conventionality, moves toward a happy equality-of sorts. Despite Lindley's feckless improvidence, he is painted not as a villain but as an unenlightened man trying to carry on received traditions. In the belief that he should maintain control and be the protector of the weaker vessel, he excludes Serena not only from any decision-making role in their affairs but even from any knowledge of them. Condescended to despite her superior abilities, bored, chafing against enforced propriety and idleness, she yearns for her "share in the world's work" (*SL*, p. 81)-a complaint that astonishes Evan—and complains that she doesn't see why it should be "so taken for granted" that married women are "not intellectual" (*SL*, p. 61). Just as Jacinta, in *Isidro*, found ladylike behavior a cage, Serena finds marriage on such terms a prison: "a doorway into which she had stepped in a day of rough weather-and now, suddenly, the door had swung upon the latch, and she saw the whole procession of life go by her in the street" (*SL*, p. 76). From this despairing point, Austin presses her story toward a qualified happy ending of compromise and reconciliation hinging on the male's reform.

Evan comes to accept the fact that Serena runs household matters better than he does and solicits her to draw on her artistic ability in designing a tract of houses that will add substantially to their income—another rescue of the husband by the wife. (We can guess how keenly Austin must have wished that Wallace would similarly ask her to rescue him from his improvidence by pursuing her writing ability for the good of the family, and thereby reconcile her conflicting impulses.) He also shows a newfound enlightenment by voicing the sen-

sible but unconventional opinion that since the Julia and Antrim Stairses' marriage is making both parties unhappy and it does not seem to contribute to the happiness of society in general to keep a bad marriage going, they should be able to part and try to find happier arrangements. Serena also moves toward compromise, beginning to take an interest in creative household shifts, gaining contentment in her maternal role, and— the aspect of the matter that gives one pause—giving herself up to admiration of Evan's masculine virtues. In the concluding passage, one of those counter-elements in Austin's fiction that I have referred to, as she stands at an open window looking out on the Stairses' now darkened house, she reconciles herself to marriage and to masculine leadership in the world despite having envisioned "herself and all women" suffering "unfulfilment" because of "colorless, unimpassioned marriages . . . childbirth and sorrow and denial—oh, a common story!" Saved from these morose musings by a "sense of saving commonness," she turns her thoughts to her husband's involvement in business affairs and, beginning to understand this interest as a "relish for life," is flooded by an admiration for "the undaunted male attitude which begot great achievement on the West." This admiration "shame[s]" her by its "largeness" out of her own "complicated futility." Hearing the "quick, nervous step that announced him," she turns excitedly to go let him in, but first, "smiling, she turned and drew the blind" (*SL*, pp. 345-46). Today's readers might be inclined to see intentional irony in this encomium to male superiority and marital tranquility, accompanied by the emblematic closing of the window, but it might more accurately be read as another expression of wishfulness on Austin's part. She had not been able to have a marriage like that herself, but she could entertain a wish to surrender the burden of self-reliance.

Despite Serena's conversion to idealization of the male, *Santa Lucia* can best be seen as a novel advocating the reform of marriage on a basis of equality. Julia's inappropriate and unsuccessful marriage, which she is able to escape only by suicide, makes an argument for easier divorce laws and greater social tolerance. The kind of marriage Serena and Evan have at first, in which the wife "spen[t] herself" solely on the husband's comfort (*SL*, p. 81), is also seen to be wasteful of human capital, causing a woman not only to be "spent" but to be squandered. Only William's marriage of equality glimpsed prospectively at the end of the novel promises not to be either utterly destructive or at minimum frustrating. Two out of three marriages, it seems, are likely to be unhappy—a point made by the novel's subtitle, *A Common Story*. It was perhaps this subtitle, seeming to attribute not only marital frustration but adultery, suicide, and even abortion (it is murkily implied that Julia has obtained an abortion in San Francisco) to the general run of human lives, that ruined the book commercially, since it can reasonably be supposed that the reading public would have tolerated or even sought out such novelistic sins if they had been presented as scandalous exceptions to general practice. What Austin's indignant audience apparently did not recognize was that, in embedded ways, the novel actually reinforced some of the very attitudes toward marriage that it putatively condemned. Serena's realization at the end that her husband knows best and masculine occupations are, after all, superior is a distinctly counter-feminist note, a return to an only moderately revised form of "romantic thralldom."

Elizabeth Ammons has observed (in a discussion of *The Land of Little Rain*) that Austin had greater success with "experimental structures" than with "conventional inherited narrative forms."[20] The ending of *Santa Lucia* demonstrates, however, that in her fiction she tended not so much to abandon as to invoke—with variation—inherited forms that end, for women characters, either in marriage or in death. *Santa Lucia* ends in both, Julia's death and William's marriage. Just as the death is unconventional, however, in being a chosen death to *end* a marriage, William's marriage promises to be an exceptional one. In a sense, Austin attempts to "write beyond" the conventional ending she has chosen. Her proposal that marriage can be happy only when based on some degree of equality between the sexes can be seen as an attempt to "construct" an "oppositional strateg[y]" to the depiction of gender institutions in narrative," an approach to narrative that DuPlessis has defined as feminist.[21] Even so, the language of submission in marital bliss invoked at the end with respect to Serena and Evan's reconstructed marriage is a troubling counter-strain to this feminist strategy.

* * *

After *Santa Lucia,* the sequence of Austin's work as a novelist becomes somewhat confusing. According to dates of U.S. publication, her third novel was the noted *A Woman of Genius,* in 1912. Actually, however, the third was *Outland,* which appeared in England in 1910 under the pseudonym Gordon Stairs (adapted from the name Antrim Stairs in *Santa Lucia*). Austin was already working on *Outland* when the failure of *Santa Lucia* became evident—that is, before the writing of *A Woman of Genius.* This fact is significant for understanding the place of that work in Austin's varying development of a feminist voice in the novel. She completed *A Woman of Genius,* but not *Outland,* after she became active in feminist causes in New York following her return from Europe.

In *Outland* Austin once again gave a large role to romantic love despite the thrust of the novel toward other matters. In part, this may have been due to her desire for a financial success with the book and a sense that a love interest was essential to such a success. Her letters

to Duneka about this and other projected works (like her later letters to her editor at Houghton Mifflin, Ferris Greenslet) show a keen interest in commercial appeal.[22] But we have no reason to believe that the novel was not also shaped by her own interests. Love relationships were important to Austin throughout her life. Perhaps because the fantasy genre in which she was working freed her to disregard realistic probability, she achieved in *Outland* much more of a reconciliation of female independence with romantic satisfaction than in *Santa Lucia,* where the two are in conflict. The central female character, Mona, is a self-supporting professional woman who has quit her job as a professor in order to give full time to writing. She has rejected repeated proposals of marriage from Herman, a professor of sociology, because he regards marriage dispassionately, as a convenient arrangement. She holds out for romance and gets it, after he undergoes a change of heart. But she does not have to abandon her professional goals simply because she and Herman will be married. The book envisions, though sketchily, a romantic relationship based on equality and respect for the work commitments of both parties.

While *Outland* awaited a publisher, Austin pushed ahead with work on *The Ford,* a novel of business practices and manipulation of water rights in California, matters she had become familiar with during her marriage. Sixth in order of publication, or fifth in order of U.S. publication, *The Ford* was thus her fourth novel in order of first writing. In many ways this novel echoes the ending of *Santa Lucia,* with its tribute to the "largeness" of the "undaunted male attitude which begot great achievement on the West" (*SL,* p. 346).[23] Austin wrote to Duneka that she was planning "a novel of contemporaneous Californian life called *The Ford,* in which a man is put to the three great temptations, money, power, passion."[24] She does not mention any interest in women's issues in her conception of the book at that time. When *The Ford* was published, however, in 1917, it included a strong component of feminist affirmation. In the interim she had produced the ringing feminism of *A Woman of Genius,* which reflected her growing involvement in women's issues while also continuing the lifelong duality of her vision of what women want.

By 1912, when *A Woman of Genius* appeared, Austin's personal outrage at the lack of equality between the sexes in daily life was of long standing. As a girl at home, she had reacted with astonishment and indignation to what she perceived as her mother's deference to her older brother for no reason except his sex, a deference that extended even to household policy regarding how long eggs should be cooked at breakfast. If James decreed four-minute eggs, then all lesser beings must get four-minute eggs! For his part, James seems to have accepted this role with equanimity and to have made lordly pronouncements on Mary's failings. Later, Austin's defiantly unconventional behaviors occasioned disapproval among her neighbors in the small towns where she and her husband lived, much as Julia, in **Santa Lucia,** becomes a scandal as she beats her wings against the cage of matrimony and propriety. She organized theatricals, she cultivated the acquaintance of Indians and sheepherders, she was a freethinker in religion, she hiked instead of staying at home to cook and clean, and she went away for extended periods leaving her husband to shift for himself. These evidences of unwomanliness and immorality caused her to became a scandal and to suffer isolation.

In *A Woman of Genius* Austin drew on her cumulative dissatisfactions to create an argument for change. For the most part, however, that argument is an individualistic rather than a systemic one. As the title indicates, she fully adopted the premise of the genius's difference from people in general—an inherently isolating vision that, in Du Plessis's words, is a "particular exaggeration of bourgeois individualism" that "increases the tension between middle-class women as a special group and the dominant assumptions of their class."[25] Accordingly, the novel traces through much of its considerable length the solitary growth and emergence of Olivia Lattimore, a woman of exceptional ability and determination who achieves success on the stage. In the novel's later chapters, however—apparently written after Austin became involved in the Suffrage Association, Mabel Dodge's liberal-to-radical salon, and probably the Heterodoxy Club as well—the isolating force of genius theory yields to advocacy of feminism as a group movement.[26] Olivia's achievement is generalized to the status of an achievement for women in general by being claimed as an example and an inspiration to all. Austin's depiction of Olivia, then, directly reflecting her involvement with feminist activists, becomes doubly feminist in that it both offers a vision of an achieving woman and espouses solidarity and a larger movement of change.[27]

Following closely the course of her own early life, Austin begins with her genius's childhood in a small midwestern town that she calls Taylorville, Ohianna. Olivia, narrating her story in the first person, recalls how intensely she longed to escape Taylorville and experience "the sustaining fairy wonder of the world" (*WG,* [*A Woman of Genius*] pp. 7-8). Even as a child she was "stirred" by the "allurement of travel and adventure" whenever she saw wagons and teams hitched around the town square. The linkage here of departure and geographic movement with self-fulfillment and self-definition is one of the first premises of the novel. Like Austin's own involuntary migration to California, Olivia's first departure from home is scarcely volitional. Manipulated into marriage by her mother, she feels "pushed out of the nest" (*WG,* p. 72). Even so, that first

departure makes possible her later launching of herself toward her "Shining Destiny," a journey on which she is more fully in control.

Olivia's demurral from conventional gender roles begins early and grows into a specific focus on independent work. By adolescence she has developed a "horror" of the demand for women to "defer and adjust, to maintain the attitude of acquiescence toward opinions and capabilities that had nothing more to recommend them than merely that they were a man's!" (*WG,* p. 44). That Austin herself felt such a "horror" is evident in a letter to Witter Bynner where she stated her "antipathy to the ministering angel type of woman."[28] This does not mean, either for her or for her character, that romantic love and marriage hold no appeal, but rather that marriage must accommodate equality and a woman's right to pursue self-definition through work. Most emphatically, they want both. Olivia feels that if she could only have her husband and her work, both, she would have no more to ask of life. Unfortunately, he cannot understand or support her artistic ambitions. Even so, once her first experience of professional theater gives her a vision of "a country of large impulses and satisfying movement" (*WG,* p. 86), there is no question but that she must set out to find the way there. When Tommy (the conventionalism of the name is appropriate) fortuitously dies, she gains the autonomy essential to the pursuit of her career. Looking back from the vantage of her later success, she regrets that most of her family and friends "couldn't have walked in the way with me," but since their attitudes were firmly set against such a departure from convention she has had to "wal[k] in the way . . . alone" (*WG,* p. 70). Even when she is later reunited with her one true love, she refuses to marry him unless he will also marry her work.[29] He won't.

Olivia is not finally alone, however, even if others have refused to walk the path toward her destiny with her. Not only does she make a late marriage with a man who shares her professional interest, she is also given solidarity with other women. Her actively feminist younger sister (a grown-up version of the beloved sister Austin lost in childhood, drawn along the lines of her activist friends in New York) tells her, in the most overtly exhortatory passage in the book, that she constitutes a "forward movement" in herself. "Every time I see a woman step out of the ranks in some achievement of her own," she says, "I think, 'Now, Olivia will have company'" in the "conscious movement of us all toward liberty" (*WG,* p. 261). If Olivia's second marriage, at the end of the book, seemingly lacks passion, it is at any rate a mutually supportive bond, enabling her to enjoy both emotional and professional satisfaction. Such an ending—a culminating marriage, but with a difference—reflects the duality of Austin's own nature. She may have "alternately avoided and celebrated as socially useful" the domestic culture that in some ways represented the mother toward whom she had such strongly ambivalent feelings, but she sought to develop "models for combining two careers with a common domestic life." The received notion that "the man alone must 'support' the family" was an idea she regarded as one of the "sex superstitions" that had to be shaken off if men as well as women were to achieve "emancipation" in a democratic society.[30]

A Woman of Genius has continued to attract the attention of scholars and critics, especially as a likely influence on Willa Cather's noted *bildungsroman* of another woman artist, *The Song of the Lark,* published three years later.[31] At the time of its initial publication, however, it was another serious disappointment. Like *Sonta Lucia,* the book was found morally objectionable by the wife of a man involved in its sale, this time a member of the publishing company, and Doubleday dropped it after four months.[32] Once again Austin had been given a pointed message about the peril to her career posed by writing that was controversial in its dealing with women's issues. Whether as a result of that warning or as a result of her own ambivalences about home and freedom, in her next novel, *The Lovely Lady,* she conveyed an astonishingly different view of what women want. Indeed, of her five novels published after *A Woman of Genius,* none except the posthumous *Cactus Thorn* would continue the pitch of concerted feminism she had reached there.

* * *

It is the kind of inconsistency represented by *The Lovely Lady* that leads me to question the prevailing view of Austin's fiction as voicing a "thorough-going insistence on and assertion of a feminist perspective."[33] In this novel, published only a year after *A Woman of Genius,* her attention is centered on a love story in the context of a man's, rather than a woman's, pursuit of a career. In a direct narrative pronouncement, the novel pays tribute to "that essential essence of maleness, the mutual power of work well accomplished."[34] Women, in the world of this novel, are not interested in careers, but almost solely in marriage and possessions. Those who are beautiful are also menacing; they are the "charming ambuscades" from which "the arrows of desolation might be shot" at a man (*LL* [*The Lovely Lady*], pp. 222-23). It is hinted that the "plain" girl who gains the hero's love at last may be somewhat an exception—he tells her jocularly that instead of waiting for a knight to kill a dragon for her, she would probably have killed it herself (*LL,* pp. 209-10). We are given little evidence of such spiritedness, though, and in any event the bulk of the novel does not include her. The world of business and financial struggle that so occupies the hero simply does not involve women except in the role of almost invisible "typewriters" whom he could never consider

loving. The readiness of his supportive sister and his partner's wife to concede that "much as their several lives had profited by the partnership, they were still and *naturally* outside of it" (*LL,* pp. 114-15, emphasis added) is simply astonishing when one recalls the Mary Austin who believed that she *naturally* had a right to work and who fought for that right.

Not until 1917, four years after the anomaly of *The Lovely Lady,* would Austin publish *The Ford,* which she had begun before *A Woman of Genius.* As completed, the novel is considerably less centered on masculine endeavors than Austin had indicated in the plan that she sent to her editor in 1908. It offers, in fact, overt feminist rhetoric comparable to that found in *A Woman of Genius.* Such rhetoric is undercut, however, by the implications of certain incidental details in the working out of the love plot. The central interest of *The Ford* is the business world of California, especially with respect to water rights, and the readiness with which economic power-brokers fall into corrupt practices that destroy players who may be rich in principle but are poor in capital. Combined with this, through the roles of several characters involved in the complex business dealings traced out in the novel, is a strong secondary concern, once again, with the nature of marriage. Here Austin again reveals counter-impulses toward modes of life that can only with difficulty be accommodated to a feminist vision.

The difficulty of accommodating the wishes of both men and women within the institution of marriage is first illustrated in the marriage of Ken and Anne Brent's parents. The children's mother is utterly miserable on the isolated sheep ranch that they and their father love. Not only is she shown as a disagreeable complainer, but the language in which natural beauty and healthy outdoor work are presented makes it clear that the locus of primary narrative sympathy is with the father's rustic values. Even so, the book respects the urgency of Mrs. Brent's wish to find "a Way Out" of the situation that entraps her.[35] After her death Mr. Brent tells Ken that men "*can't* make a woman's life for her" and should not blame wives who leave: "They've got to have their own life, Kenneth, they've got to make it themselves" (*Ford,* pp. 154-55). He exemplifies Austin's hope, strongly expressed both here and in the later *Starry Adventure,* that men can and will learn. Even the children, however, are uncertain that women can really "make it themselves." As Ken and Anne, with their friends Virginia Burke and Frank Rickart, discuss what they want to do when they grow up, Anne says she wants to "keep house and have children," a wish that Frank approves because, as he says, that is "what women are for" (*Ford,* p. 46). Only Virginia insists that some women can do other things; they don't have to get married. Actresses, for example, "are always Miss." As an adult, Virginia marries and divorces, then becomes, indeed, an actress and a labor organizer and fiery speechmaker. Clearly, she has achieved a more public life than that of keeping house and having children. But Frank, still distrustful of such innovations, speaks "portentously" about "what was likely to happen if somebody somewhere didn't put a firm, restraining hand on women." Divorce, in particular, "gave them a sense of being free to do *any*thing!" (*Ford,* p. 194).

Precisely where Austin, as narrator, stands on these issues is not so clear as we might suppose, given her own divorce and the fact that she did make a life and a living on her own. Clearly, Frank's conservative rhetoric is undercut by its shallow expression and his equally shallow characterization. But Virginia's espousal of change and personal freedom would also seem to be undercut by her depiction as being flighty and manipulative. Of the four characters established in the novel's opening scene of childhood play as the centers of narrative interest, Anne is probably the most fully endorsed. Rather than growing up to be a housewife and mother as she had said she wished, she becomes a businesswoman of impressive acumen and daring, demonstrating the truth of Virginia's insistence that some women can do other things. It is Anne's insight into the complex machinations of Frank's business tycoon father, the sometime villain of the piece, that shows Ken what he needs to do to save the water rights of the neighboring ranchers. Yet Anne cannot be taken altogether as a model of what Austin wants women's lives to be, since her life, too, is shown as being incomplete and rather lonely without love and marriage. The possibility that her competence may itself lead to satisfaction of her more conventional emotional needs is raised when Old Man Rickart, the tycoon, muses in amazement at her courage, "I'd marry her myself if I thought she'd have me. I don't know why men don't marry women like that" (*Ford,* p. 426). But at novel's end she remains alone, interested in her work and finding satisfaction in it but wanting more.

The ending of Anne's story shows that, as in *A Woman of Genius,* Austin was working to revise narrative conventions in ways that would accommodate a wider range of female desires. In her working out of Ken's story, however, she once again invoked a blatantly conventional love-story ending. *The Ford* is an interestingly innovative novel in its realistic dramatization of business conflicts and in its examination of Anne's maturation as a businesswoman. By inserting a love interest into this material at all Austin complicated and undercut her feminist force. Worse, the terms of the culminating scene between Ken and his one true love, Ellis, reinforce stereotypes of female passivity and male dominance. Seemingly with no authorial irony calling the scene into question, Ellis stands, in the final chapter, passively waiting and looking "as though she had just risen . . . out of the earth" as Ken, the mobile force,

approaches. Assuming a conventional masculinity considerably at odds with his behavior during most of the book, he walks up and "tak[es] a firm *proprietary* hold upon her" (*Ford,* pp. 439-40; emphasis added)—a particularly troubling gesture in that it enacts and seemingly validates Frank's earlier insistence that someone should "put a firm, restraining hand on women."

This concluding scene is disquieting, too, in the way it invokes what was for Austin a characteristic trope, earth-as-woman, or here, woman-as-earth. That traditional trope appears as early as *The Land of Little Rain,* with its "full-bosomed hills," and continues to *Cactus Thorn.*[36] In those works, the metaphor posits the female principle as one of vitality and creative energy. Here it reinforces the passivity of Ellis's stance and her manhandling by Ken. She has been identified with the soil through her love of plants and gardening and her assistance in Anne's innovative real estate business that matches buyers with available farmland on the basis of whether the properties of the soil at that particular place are suited to what the would-be purchaser wants to grow. These associations not only offer a horticulturally satisfying vision, but put woman into a position of foresight. Earlier in the novel, however, the earth-as-woman trope has appeared to different effect when the ordinarily amiable Mr. Brent expresses what sounds like a raw urge to conquest: The land "laughs—*she* laughs. I tell you . . . we've got to master *her*—we've got to compel *her*" (*Ford,* p. 62; emphasis added). Ken's gesture in seizing Ellis enacts just such a compulsion—and Austin does not question it textually. At its terminal point, then, the novel undercuts its own vision of female vitality, freedom, and leadership.

If *The Ford* reveals, once again, a tension between Austin's feminism and her lifelong yearning for what Augusta Fink calls (perhaps reductively) "emotional fulfillment" and "the simple joys of hearth and home,"[37] her next novel, *No. 26. Jayne Street,* reveals a tension of another kind: her prolonged sense of aggrievement against Lincoln Steffens. To be sure, the motive force of the novel goes well beyond her brooding over that resentment to express a very serious conviction of the need to put the private relations between men and women on the same basis of ethical idealism that are espoused in public discourse. But if "the personal was the political" for Austin as a matter of principle,[38] it was also a literary practice: her personal concerns and her political principles equally shaped what she wrote. In *No. 26 Jayne Street,* as in the posthumous *Cactus Thorn,* Austin treats a young woman deeply in love with a man publicly esteemed as a reformer, who is unwilling to tolerate his deviation from public principles of honesty and equality in the conduct of his amorous life. In *Cactus Thorn* the woman's reaction is clear and vengeful: she kills him and returns to her space of freedom in the West with a sense of relief and vindication.

In the more complex structure of *No. 26 Jayne Street* it is less clear that Neith Schuyler's soundly feminist refusal to accept Adam Frear's disregard of women's rights in his private morality brings her satisfaction or fulfillment.

Austin never allows us to question the rightness of Neith's principles. She herself described the main question of *No. 26 Jayne Street,* in a letter, as "whether there can be any genuine democratic reform while the private lives of the reformers deny the democratic principle."[39] The novel firmly endorses her insistence that Frear's private conduct be consistent with "all those principles of conduct to which he was publicly committed" (*No. 26* [*No. 26 Jayne Street*], p. 269)—an insistence he dismisses as "perversity" (*No. 26,* p. 299). Democracy, Neith says, is what she came to America for, and democracy in private affairs means "not to bring on anybody a set of conditions in which he or she hadn't the full equality of decision" (*No. 26,* p. 296). It is a kind of no-taxation-without-representation principle: no emotional disruption without consultation. When a man abandons a woman without her consent, he is acting by an "autocracy of personal feeling" (*No. 26,* p. 290) rather than democracy. Under that autocratic system—which Austin saw as being prevalent in her society—women are set against each other as competitors for men's affections. Not only does such a system work against community among women, an essential component of a feminist vision, it corrupts the social order, she believed, in other respects as well. Precisely how it does so is not clear, but Neith, at any rate, believes that this "perpetual battle of the hearth" becomes extended in society in general in the forms of "militarism" and "Capitalism" (*No. 26,* p. 188).

The canvas of *No. 26 Jayne Street* is very large, encompassing views through Neith's eyes of labor conflict, socialist and syndicalist ferment, and opposition to the war effort. Female solidarity is displayed throughout; as in the later chapters of *A Woman of Genius,* women are, Stineman observes, "a class" and their interests are "class interests."[40] Some of the many women characters in the novel find satisfaction in political activism or else manage to set aside their griefs from love relationships as they press for social reform, among them the singleminded reformer/visionary Rose Matlock, the woman Frear had jilted when he proposed to Neith.[41] Neith is more centered in romantic love than these other women. At the end she is left in stasis, waiting to see if Frear will learn and come back to her but determined not to ask him to do so. Even though this determination is endorsed by the novel, however, it does not bring her happiness: "She felt the future at her heart like a small, gnawing worm" (*No. 26,* p. 353). Once again the desire for romance and marriage undermines female freedom and independence.

* * *

For all its effectiveness in depicting the unsettlement of the times, *No. 26 Jayne Street* was such a commercial failure that it discouraged Austin from making any further efforts in long fiction for several years. At last, however, in 1927, she wrote *Cactus Thorn*—if anything, even more vehement in its advocacy of equality of the sexes in amorous relationships—and in 1931 she published *Starry Adventure,* the sequel to *The Ford* that she had long had in mind, which proved to be her last novel. In both of these late works she returned to the topic that had caused her such personal misery and on the basis of which she had worked out a forward-looking ethic, the issue of equality in amorous relationships. *Starry Adventure* not only advocates the reform of romance and marriage but envisions, through a striking transformation of the language of traditional masculine conquest itself, a redefinition of masculinity.

A symbolism of motion and of houses, the two poles of Austin's sensibility, is pervasive. The central character, a young man named Gard, has come to maturity in the immediate post-World War I generation, a time of speed-up in technology and social mobility. The times, he thinks, are "torn apart, swirling together."[42] From their ranch home in New Mexico, his family members have scattered in all directions, his grandfather to the war as a chaplain and then to Mexico as a missionary, his mother to Arizona for her second husband's health, his sister Laura to the East Coast and then to Geneva to work as a secretary to a diplomat engaged in postwar negotiations. Gard has stayed at home as a partner in a business restoring old houses. Hired by a wealthy patron of the arts from New York, Eudora Ballantin (a recognizable portrait of Mabel Dodge Luhan), to restore an eighteenth-century house she has purchased, he falls in love and has an affair with her despite the fact that in a strictly pro forma way he is already married to his childhood friend Jane. Restlessly, he drives the highways and back roads of New Mexico trying to decide what he wants to do in life and how to deal with the imperious Eudora, who, like Adam Frear in *No. 26 Jayne Street,* has felt no compunctions about initiating a new love affair without first obtaining Gard's agreement to breaking off their relationship. Austin's principle of equal consent, it appears, applies equally to women as to men; her interest is in reform of the sexual relationship, not just reform of men.

For many years Gard has had a sense that he is destined to some great endeavor, which he thinks of as a "starry adventure," a phrase with overtones of a stereotypical masculine tradition of adventure and conquest. But in this novel such stereotypes are overcome. It is Eudora who makes conquests, though they are scarcely "starry." It is Gard's sister who takes part in exciting endeavors in public affairs. Jane, too, is an adventuring woman, so independent that when she wants to get away and think she spends hours "off in the car" or takes lone horseback rides along "untraveled road[s]" or in "high track-less country" (*SA* [*Starry Adventure*], pp. 408-11). Yet her primary goal is to have a marriage of real sharing with Gard and to establish a permanent home with him. Except for the largely behind-the-scenes sister who pursues important public work, *Starry Adventure* does not offer a portrayal of the New Woman. Instead, liberation from gender inequality enters the novel primarily in the portrayal of a new man. Gard, a kind of guardian angel of home and tradition, finds ways of restoring not only old dwellings but old relationships as well. After an ordeal of self-examination, he realizes that he wants a real marriage with Jane and wants to live permanently in the house where he grew up. Once he realizes that, he "know[s] himself his own man" and feels himself "subtly welcomed by his own land" (*SA,* p. 390)-figuratively, a welcome to the female principle. The impetus of the novel is characteristically dual, since the farflung motion of the others is fully accepted and celebrated, though the greater emphasis is on homing, continuity, and reconciliation of sexual opposition.

Even after their romantic *eclairecissement,* however, when Gard realizes that his "starry adventure" is to be shared with Jane, he wonders what the adventure is to be and continues to feel that, like heroes of tradition, he should be going out and doing something momentous. He feels a need to undertake something more, and more manly. It is Jane who helps him gain a new understanding of himself and his destined adventure by asking, what if the adventure is not something to do but something to experience, an inner adventure? What this may mean she explains by invoking an analogy that when applied to a male is both startling and original: gestation and birth.

> "Suppose I should be going to have a baby. I might be any time. And I wouldn't know anything about it for weeks. And then it would be only a kind of sick feeling. And no other feeling for months. They say you don't. And what I would feel wouldn't make any difference; wouldn't stop it, or make it go faster. And when it came, no matter how glad I was to have it, it would be something terrible to go through. I might even die of it . . .
>
> "How do you know your adventure isn't going on in you this minute?"
>
> (*SA,* p. 417)

Masculine endeavor is recast as, not an endeavor of conquest or a thrill, but a quiet inner growth like a pregnancy. Gard's "starry adventure" is perhaps to be the establishment of his life in the home, coming to know himself, nurturing life and the tradition of his own particular place—a destiny of a traditionally feminine quality but one he finds immensely satisfying. For their belated honeymoon trip (another end-of-novel variant of the conventional marriage ending) Gard and Jane

have planned a car trip around the state making observations in preparation for writing a co-authored "history of the House." A profoundly and innovatively feminized hero, he is last seen on the night before they leave on this home-centered journey, making a last "circuit of the house" before going to bed, an action that is always a "deep delight" to him (*SA,* p. 419).

Once again, then, Austin attempted to structure an ending that would incorporate the marriage motif of narrative convention yet revise it to accommodate a vision of gender equality. She had done so in *A Woman of Genius,* with Olivia's concluding marriage to a professional peer who respected her work, and in *Outland,* where the male has to change to suit the woman's expectations, and she had attempted similar variants less successfully in *The Ford* and *Santa Lucia.* Seeing liberation for women as entailing liberation from constraining preconceptions for men as well, she defines equality in marriage, at the end of *Starry Adventure,* in such a way as to include domestic identities for men as well as outward endeavors for women.

* * *

Mary Austin may have thought of her life as "a road mark, a pointer on the trail" (*EH* [*Earth Horizon*], p. 279), but she also said of herself that "few intellectuals of her generation have clung more obstinately to the idea of a home, a house, a garden" (*EH,* p. 274). This essential duality of her character and mind was captured by Mabel Dodge Luhan in commenting that she was "one of the best companions in the world in a house or on a trip."[43] It was a duality that leant her thinking a distinctive subtlety and richness, but could also lead to a degree of ambivalence that undermined her noted feminism. When her imagination turned toward houses, it tended also to turn toward a conservative vision of relations between men and women. In her sequence of nine novels she worked toward fictional structures encompassing a complex duality in which both freedom of movement and security of em-placement were valued, symbolizing a reconciliation of traditional values of masculine liberty and feminine homing, but with the two polarized values distributed according to less rigid gender lines. Never, however, did she structure a narrative that completely dispensed with the convention of the marriage ending. The result is an *oeuvre* that exhibits considerably less consistency with regard to feminist vision than critical assessments have sometimes implied. At times, through their plot structures, her novels engage in the "process of resistance, revision, and emancipation" with respect to traditionally dominant plot patterns that Nancy K. Miller defines as a feminist poetics.[44] At times they are rhetorically insistent on feminist values of liberation and empowerment. But at times, especially at particular moments in *Santa Lucia, The Lovely Lady,* and *The Ford,* they are self-questioning, uncertain, self-deconstructed by details and incidents that imply values counter to those being overtly endorsed.

In her last works of long fiction, however, Austin achieved credible visions of androgyny and gender equality. In **Starry Adventure** she did so by addressing not so much the classic question of what it is that women want (and have a right to expect) as the question of what men who are freed of their preconceptions may want. It seems that they may want a portion, at least, of what women have had all along. The shared values and mutual respect that are implied at the end of **Starry Adventure** are the basis Austin proffered for the realization of equality and harmony in relations between men and women. A vision of that equality and harmony was the essence of her own kind of feminism. It was not, in the end, a consistent vision of liberation and empowerment for women so much as a vision of cooperative equal partnership of the sexes—a vision in which the journey of liberation was reconciled with the security of em-placement in a "circuit of the house." A possible result of that circuit is, of course, the reinscription of patriarchal domesticity. In that event, Austin's feminist vision would prove not to have been feminist at all. She places a great deal of confidence in the prospect of reform of the male.

If he is not reformed, the remedy she envisions is that of the "thorn" employed by Dulcie Adelaid in **Cactus Thorn**—the dagger. It is no doubt significant that this daring and defiant work did not find a publisher during Austin's lifetime. The recourse to violence that she seems to espouse in **Cactus Thorn**—and after which her female hero is not shown as repentant, but as serene—could scarcely have failed to startle editors. Her hope for equality in women's relationships with men becomes women's right to demand that equality without quarter. But the vision she asserts so boldly here was modulated by her ambivalence toward the need for balance between self-assertion and secure anchorage in the Beloved House (as she called the home she built in Santa Fe in 1925). Accordingly, her views and her novelistic imagination were always more supportive of the complete or primal woman than they were of the new, liberated woman. No doubt a feminist, she recognized a multiplicity of human needs. We can only speculate as to whether, had she lived to complete yet another novel, she might once again have vacillated in her vision of how to achieve satisfaction. As it stands, she reached in her final novel, **Starry Adventure,** a vision of harmonious resolution of gender roles that relies on feminization of the male, as well as liberation of the female.

Notes

1. Dudley Winn, "Mary Austin, Woman Alone," *Virginia Quarterly Review* 13 (1937): 244; T. M. Pearce, *Literary America, 1903-1934: The Mary Austin Letters* (Westport, Conn.: Greenwood Press, 1979), p. 251; Augusta Fink, *I-Mary: A Biography of Mary Austin* (Tucson: Univ. of Arizona Press, 1983), p. 1.

2. Elizabeth Ammons, *Conflicting Stories: American Women Writers at the Turn into the Twentieth Century* (New York: Oxford Univ. Press, 1992), p. 87; Faith Jaycox, "Regeneration through Liberation: Mary Austin's 'The Walking Woman' and Western Narrative Formula," *Legacy* 6 (1989): 5.

3. Austin, "Woman Alone," *The Nation,* 1927; rpt. *Beyond Borders: The Selected Essays of Mary Austin,* ed. Reuben J. Ellis (Carbondale: Southern Illinois Univ. Press, 1996), p. 113. Smith-Rosenberg, *Disorderly Conduct: Visions of Gender in Victorian America* (New York: Oxford Univ. Press, 1985), p. 176; Gelfant, "'Lives' of Women Writers: Cather, Austin, Porter / and Willa, Mary, Katherine Anne," in *Women Writing in America: Voices in Collage* (Hanover: Univ. Press of New England, 1984), p. 246. Regarding the New Woman's involvement in public issues, see Ammons, *Conflicting Stories,* pp. 6-7, 169-70.

4. Porter, Afterword to Mary Austin, *A Woman of Genius* (Old Westbury, NY: Feminist Press, 1985), p. 307. Esther Lanigan Stineman agrees that "when Austin allowed herself the luxury of speaking contemptuously of men in her most realistic fictions . . . she laid herself open to the most severe criticism"; *Mary Austin: Song of a Maverick* (New Haven: Yale Univ. Press, 1989), p. 40. Vera Norwood links genre hierarchy with resistance to the more obvious feminism of Austin's novels in commenting that her reputation has been "based on her naturalist writings because they were perceived to fit comfortably into the male canon of natural history"; Norwood, Introduction to Austin, *Heath Anthology of American Literature,* 2nd ed. (Lexington, Mass.: D. C. Heath, 1994), p. 918.

5. Margaret R. Higonnet, "Mapping the Text: Critical Metaphors," in *Reconfigured Spheres: Feminist Explorations of Literary Space,* ed. Higonnet and Joan Templeton (Amherst: Univ. of Massachusetts Press, 1994), p. 196. On literary space and feminism see, for example, Ruth Salvaggio, "Theory and Space, Space and Women," *Tulsa Studies in Women's Literature* 7 (1988): 261.

6. Stineman, *Mary Austin: Song of a Maverick,* p. 136. For the biographical information that follows I have relied primarily on Stineman and on Fink's *I-Mary.*

7. Melody Graulich, Introduction to *Western Trails: A Collection of Short Stories by Mary Austin,* ed. Graulich (Reno: Univ. of Nevada Press, 1987), p. 2.

8. Austin, *Earth Horizon* (1932; rpt. Albuquerque: Univ. of New Mexico Press, 1991), pp. 2, 274, and 279. The use of the third-person pronoun is frequent in the autobiography, which as Graulich points out is "like all of [Austin's] work . . . filled with imagery of walking and trails"; Afterword to *Earth Horizon,* p. 376.

9. Porter, Afterword to *A Woman of Genius,* p. 295.

10. It is difficult to understand T. M. Pearce's statement that Austin "never joined in the attack upon the Middle West which grew from *Main Travelled Roads* into the Prairie School of Middle Western writers." Pearce, "Mary Austin and the Pattern of New Mexico," in T. M. Pearce and A. P. Thomason, eds., *Southwesterners Write: The American Southwest in Stories and Articles by Thirty-Two Contributors* (Albuquerque: Univ. of New Mexico Press, 1946), p. 309.

11. Scholars have differed in their dating of Austin's entry into feminist causes. Pearce, *Literary America,* p. 63, states that she moved to New York and joined the Association in 1912, but prints a letter dated October 9, 1911 in which Anna H. Shaw invites her to speak. Austin's address shown in the letter is 456 Riverside Drive, New York City. Nancy Porter states that Austin became involved in social causes in 1911; Afterword to *A Woman of Genius,* p. 304. Mary Fink places the beginning of her activity in public causes in the late fall of 1914; *I-Mary,* p. 172. On the Heterodoxy Club, see Dee Garrison, *Mary Heaton Vorse: The Life of an American Insurgent* (Philadelphia: Temple Univ. Press, 1989), p. 67. See also Judith Schwarz, *Radical Feminists of Heterodoxy: Greenwich Village, 1912-1940* (Lebanon, N.H.: Victoria Publishers, 1982). Schwarz does not mention Austin.

12. Elizabeth Jordan, ed., *The Sturdy Oak* (New York: Henry Holt, 1917).

13. Graulich, Introduction to *Western Trails,* p. 6.

14. Austin's treatment of Indians in *Isidro* is more than a little startling, considering the time she had spent among them, her later claims to friendship with Indians, and her championing of Indian rights. She refers to them as rascals and judges that the recall of the Dominicans left them "far sunk in original savagery" (p. 424).

15. Austin, *Isidro* (Boston: Houghton, Mifflin, 1905), p. 353. The 1970 reprint by Gregg Press includes a brief biographical note containing many errors. See Karen R. Lawrence, *Penelope Voyages: Women and Travel in the British Literary Tradition* (Ithaca: Cornell Univ. Press, 1994) on the gendering of narratives of travel.

16. Rachel Blau DuPlessis, *Writing Beyond the Ending: Narrative Strategies of Twentieth-Century Women Writers* (Bloomington: Indiana Univ. Press, 1985), pp. ix-xi and 1-3. Similarly, Estella Lauter, in *Women as Mythmakers: Poetry and Visual Art by Twentieth-Century Women* (Bloomington: Indiana Univ. Press, 1984), p. 95, comments that for "female protagonists" the quest "requires a rupture with the values that confine them within ordinary life situations."

17. The name William signals a set of parallels with certain attributes of Austin's sometime friend Willa Cather. Cather called herself William during her adolescence and took a shortlived interest in biological science, as does the young William of Austin's novel. The physical description of Austin's William evokes photographs of the young Cather in her "face that was too round, too red and shining" and figure "round and tight." Her friends don't know whether she "would like to dress well and couldn't" or "knew how and didn't care." (Mary Austin, *Santa Lucia: A Common Story* [New York and London: Harper and Brothers, 1908], pp. 3-4.) She is outdoorsy, like Cather, and is doted upon by her physician father; Cather had a fond older friend in Red Cloud who was a doctor. Most startling is the similarity in source of the name: Although Cather's christened name Wilella was chosen for an aunt, when she later changed Wilella to Willa and adopted the middle name Sibert she was memorializing an uncle who was a casualty of the Civil War, dying of wounds received at Manassas. Austin painstakingly explains that her William was named for an uncle killed at Antietam. The parallels seem too numerous to be merely coincidental. Yet Austin's acquaintance with Cather is usually dated from about 1910, two years after *Santa Lucia* was published. Moreover, Cather did not ordinarily share such personal details with casual acquaintances. There is much to be learned about the interactions between the two writers. On the sources of Cather's name, see James Woodress, *Willa Cather: A Literary Life* [Lincoln and London: Univ. of Nebraska Press, 1987], pp. 18, 21.

18. Mary Austin to F. A. Duneka, June 24, 1908 and October 28, 1908; The Pierpont Morgan Library, New York. The *Times* review is quoted by Stineman, p. 105.

19. Fink sees both Lindley and Antrim Stairs, Julia's husband, as renderings of Wallace's "most infuriating traits"; *I-Mary,* p. 120. Cf. Stineman, pp. 98 and 101.

20. Ammons, *Conflicting Stories,* p. 87.

21. *Writing Beyond the Ending,* p. 34.

22. Austin's editor at Harper & Brothers, her U. S. publisher, had expressed interest in the book when she mentioned it to him, but seems to have discouraged her after reading the manuscript. To judge by Austin's reply, he considered it overly poetical. He may have meant by that that it was insufficiently realistic—as, being a fantasy, it assuredly is, if realism is what one expects. Austin chose not to press for U.S. publication, believing that she could not survive two commercial failures in succession. F. A. Duneka to Mary Austin, November 12, 1908; Mary Austin to F. A. Duneka, January 30, 1909; The Pierpont Morgan Library, New York.

23. When the order of first writing is established, this puzzling echo of the 1908 *Santa Lucia* in the 1917 *The Ford* becomes understandable, and in addition we can see that Austin was alternating between modes of fantasy (the first and third novels) and realism (the second and fourth).

24. Mary Austin to F. A. Duneka, n.d. but apparently written between November 12, 1908, when Duneka asked to see the manuscript of *Outland*, and January 30, 1909, when Austin expressed disappointment that he had not liked the fantasy work; The Pierpont Morgan Library.

25. DuPlessis, *Writing Beyond the Ending*, p. 85.

26. Garrison numbers both the Heterodoxy Club and Mabel Dodge's salon among the "five organized groups [that] gave birth to the prewar Village spirit" (the other three being the staff of the *Masses,* the Liberal Club, and the Provincetown Players) and calls Heterodoxy a "nursery of modern feminism"; *Mary Heaton Vorse,* p. 67.

27. Other very powerful works developing a vision of women's strength and independence, not treated in this article, are the short stories "The Walking Woman" and "Kate Bixby's Queerness." Elements of the latter story are embedded in *Santa Lucia.*

28. Mary Austin to Witter Bynner, n.d. but by internal evidence 1928; Houghton Library, Harvard Univ., bMS Am 1629, quoted by permission.

29. Stineman observes that Olivia's refusal to marry Helmeth "advances the plot of 'the new woman' to a new plateau, for Olivia's choice is one of affirmation rather than unadulterated renunciation"; *Mary Austin: Song of a Maverick,* p. 143.

30. Porter, Afterword to *A Woman of Genius,* pp. 309, 303. Austin, "Sex Emancipation Through War," *Forum* (1918); rpt. *Beyond Borders,* p. 46.

31. Nancy Porter asserts that Cather's novel was "directly influenced" by Austin's work; Afterword to *A Woman of Genius,* p. 296. Blanche Gelfant com-

pares the two novels in "'Lives' of Women Writers," p. 246. Sally Allen McNall examines parallels of both novels to Mary Wilkins Freeman's *The Butterfly House* (1912), but does not suggest influence; McNall, "The American Woman Writer in Transition: Freeman, Austin, and Cather," in *Seeing Female: Social Roles and Personal Lives,* ed. Sharon S. Brehm (New York: Greenwood Press, 1988), pp. 43-52. Since both are strongly autobiographical and the life experiences of the two writers were similar in many respects, it might seem that the textual parallels could be coincidental. Considering how numerous and how close they are, however, it seems more likely that Cather had read Austin's book and that it remained in her mind when in late 1913, the year after its publication, she began work on material with similar themes.

32. Stineman, *Mary Austin: Song of a Maverick,* p. 139.

33. Porter, Afterword to *A Woman of Genius,* p. 307.

34. Austin, *The Lovely Lady* (Garden City, N. Y.: Doubleday, Page, 1913), p. 114. Other illiberal narrative pronouncements in *The Lovely Lady* include antisemitic slurs. Given the dates of publication and her practice of working on a variety of projects at once, it is possible that Austin wrote much if not all of *The Lovely Lady* before she wrote the later and more overtly feminist chapters of *A Woman of Genius.* I am not aware, however, of any documentary evidence to date her actual work on the manuscript.

35. Austin, *The Ford* (Boston: Houghton, Mifflin, 1917), p. 27.

36. Austin, *The Land of Little Rain* (1903; rpt. Albuquerque: Univ. of New Mexico Press, 1974), p. 171.

37. Fink, *I-Mary,* p. 1.

38. Pearce, *Mary Hunter Austin,* p. 13.

39. Mary Austin to Roger Scaife, June 11, 1920, Houghton Mifflin Collection, Bancroft Library, Berkeley; quoted by Karen S. Langlois, "Mary Austin and Lincoln Steffens," *Huntington Library Quarterly* 49 (1986): 380.

40. Stineman, *Mary Austin: Song of a Maverick,* pp. 146-47.

41. One of these is a lower middle class young woman named Sadie Comyns, "part Russian" and "maybe a little Jew" who is "a Syndicalist"; *No. 26 Jayne Street,* p. 79. In keeping with Austin's regular practice of incorporating real persons and incidents into her fiction, Sadie may be a portrait of

leftist writer Josephine Herbst, who came to New York in 1919 and immediately became involved in labor issues. Rose Matlock, the magnetic reformer whom Adam Frear jilts when he begins to pursue Neith, was probably drawn on the labor organizer Rose Schneiderman, who spoke at a meeting at Cooper Union on February 20, 1914 organized by members of the Heterodoxy Club (Schwarz, *Radical Feminists of Heterodoxy,* pp. 24-25). Schneiderman may have contributed, too, to the character Virginia, also a labor organizer, in *The Ford.* Moreover, the dramatic pageant Virginia helps to organize, depicting a massive labor strike-called "The Battle" and intended to "strike the very roots of Capitalism" (*Ford,* 303)-was probably based on a dramatic spectacle organized, in part, by Austin's friend Mabel Dodge Luhan.

42. Austin, *Starry Adventure* (Boston: Houghton, Mifflin, 1931), p. 383.

43. Luhan, in *Mary Austin, A Memorial,* ed. Willard Hougland (Santa Fe: Laboratory of Anthropology, 1944), p. 22, quoted by Shelley Armitage in her essay "Mary Austin: Writing Nature," in Peggy Pond Church's *Wind's Trail: The Early Life of Mary Austin,* ed. Shelley Armitage (Santa Fe: Museum of New Mexico Press, 1990), p. 3, and by T. M. Pearce, *Mary Hunter Austin* (New York: Twayne, 1965), p. 51. Few people would have agreed that the imperious and waspish Austin was one of the best companions in the world, in any setting.

44. Nancy K. Miller, *Subject to Change: Reading Feminist Writing* (New York: Columbia Univ. Press, 1988), p. 8. See also Marianne Hirsch, *The Mother/Daughter Plot: Narrative, Psychoanalysis, Feminism* (Bloomington: Indiana Univ. Press, 1989), p. 8, in agreement with both Miller and DuPlessis.

Mark T. Hoyer (essay date 1998)

SOURCE: Hoyer, Mark T. "'To Bring the World into Divine Focus': Syncretic Prophecy in *The Land of Little Rain.*" In *Dancing Ghosts: Native American and Christian Syncretism in Mary Austin's Work,* pp. 19-48. Reno, Nev.: University of Nevada Press, 1998.

[In the following essay, Hoyer notes the ways in which "the syncretic vision" offered by Austin in her The Land of Little Rain *and, specifically, her structural and thematic use of "a mythical journey to a Promised Land foretold in both Native American and biblical traditions" transform the work into one "that is simultaneously spiritual autobiography and cultural, as well as biophysical, ecology."]*

Independence—March 30, 1994

I sit on the porch of the Circle K Trailer Court and Motel, facing south. Sun is already warm at 7:20. Traffic whizzes by, north and south along 395. Toward the sun rise the Whites and the Inyos, some snow lingering which at the moment I cannot see in the glare of the sun. To the west, Sierra peaks, snow-clad, rise above the white picket fences, white houses, and green of the trees—young cottonwoods. The Sierra peaks shine with snow in the sun. Southward, a brown house gives way to a brown-grayish sagebrush plain, extending to the edge of the Inyos and coming to a point where they seem to meet the Alabama Hills jutting eastward from the Sierra.

Birds flit and call everywhere, their voices mingling with the rain-bird which waters the small patch of green lawn in the motel's front driveway. They fly with the passage of a truck. T-T-T-T-T-T-T-TTTTTTTTT: the song of the rain-bird.

In this valley, it's hard not to think in terms of opposites. The Sierra—lush, snowy, welcoming, westward—and the Inyos—brown, dry, forbidding, eastward. But that's probably mostly an aesthetic response. After all, the Sierras were seen by pioneers as forbidding in a very practical sort of way. And the mountains held a different significance to the local Indians, who personalized them with names from myth and saw them as their home in certain seasons, a shared home with deer, cougar, badger, bighorn sheep, bear, fish, and pinyon nuts.

Today David and I will go to the Eastern California Museum, stop by Mary Austin's house, and, using a list of place-names that David has compiled, try to figure out where her neighbor's field, the campoodie, the mesa trail, and the other landmarks she mentions are located.[1]

First published in 1903, **The Land of Little Rain** is a classic in the field of American nature writing. Its status has prompted critics to compare Austin as an environmental thinker with Henry David Thoreau and John Muir, and as a literary regionalist with Sarah Orne Jewett and Willa Cather.[2] Such comparisons and generic designations of the book have tended to confine discussion of Austin's ideology to feminists and ecocritics, who focus, respectively, on such features as Austin's strong, unconventional women characters and an environmental philosophy that repeatedly insists that humans must live within the bounds set by nature. This book, which first brought Austin to national attention, prominently features two Indian characters: Winnenap, a Shoshone medicine man who married into a Northern Paiute band, and Seyavi, a Paiute basket weaver. The two stories devoted to these characters, **"Shoshone Land"** and **"The Basket Maker,"** along with **"My Neighbor's Field,"** which is situated directly between them, form the crux of Austin's syncretic vision and nourish speculation that the book's cultural commentary extends further and is decidedly more complex than previous analyses indicate.

Critics often focus on the importance to the book of the latter two of these stories. In his essay "The Moral in Austin's *The Land of Little Rain*," for example, James C. Work sees Austin's description of the field's composition as a metaphor for the entire book, pointing to the implications for detecting the book's environmental philosophy and thematic unity without exploring the social and cultural implications that the mixing of native and introduced species may hold for the mixing of native and Euro-American peoples. Although several critics have explored the ways in which Austin's art is modeled on that of Paiute basket weavers, they provide little on the cultural context of the Owens Valley Paiute-Shoshone people, information that would help us more fully appreciate the *specific* ways in which that context helped mold Austin's feminist ideology and artistic aesthetic.[3]

Placing **"My Neighbor's Field"** and **"The Basket Maker"** into the context of **"Shoshone Land,"** a story featuring an Indian doctor's syncretic paradisiacal vision, reveals a more complicated picture with broader social implications. These stories situate "Naboth's field"—and by extension Austin herself, for her house sits directly across from it—at a crossroads between the two dominant Indian cultures of the area. The juxtaposition tells a story that seeks both to expose the history of whites' dealings with the Indians and at the same time to point to the commonalities between native peoples and Euro-Americans. Within each story, moreover, Austin juxtaposes the religious mythologies of the Bible and the Owens Valley Paiute—Shoshone oral tradition in ways that reveal their fundamental congruity, thereby offering readers her own syncretic vision.

Shelley Armitage reminds us that both thematically and stylistically, Austin often structures her stories as "ongoing pilgrimage[s]" based on myths, which "offer new versions of old [mythic] patterns." This mythmaking is crucial in creating what Austin describes in *The Land of Journey's Ending,* her last desert book, as a work that is both prophecy and ritual. Likewise, her classic of the California desert, *The Land of Little Rain,* revises an established mythic pattern in a rhetorical act that can be read as both ritual and prophecy. Though generally classified as nonfiction and variously described as a book of "charming" regional sketches, descriptive essays, and natural history, *The Land of Little Rain* is structured by a mythical journey to a Promised Land foretold in both Native American and biblical traditions, and specifically in Wovoka's Ghost Dance religion.[4]

My argument in support of this thesis derives from several factors both biographical and literary. Recall that we can trace Austin's knowledge of the Ghost Dance to 1895, by which time she had begun experimenting with Paiute ritual; that Mooney's encyclopedic study of the Ghost Dance was published the following year; and that

there is evidence that Austin carefully read and took notes on that work (though precisely when is not clear). In addition to models from Paiute culture—Wovoka's father, Tavibo, and the earlier prophet Wodziwob foremost among them—Mooney delineates Wovoka's biblical exemplars in a substantial section on the Ghost Dance's "parallels to other systems." He compares Wovoka specifically to the Hebrew prophets generally, and to Moses, Elijah, Ezekiel, and Jesus in particular.[5] These four prophets, among others, all make ghostly appearances via Austin's allusions in *The Land of Little Rain.* In the contexts of the syncretic vision offered in the book, of the possible ties that a central figure in the book, Winnenap, has to the Ghost Dance religion, and of the journey to a Promised Land that, via these allusions, forms the book's implicit trajectory, these parallels nourish speculation about the influence of the Ghost Dance on Austin's first major work. Animating the book's more overt themes, their appearance ultimately transports *The Land of Little Rain* beyond the boundaries imposed by the generic designations typically assigned to it and transforms it into a work that is simultaneously spiritual autobiography and cultural, as well as biophysical, ecology.

THE PROPHET ENVISIONS THE JOURNEY

The Land of Little Rain opens with the narrator's confession that she prefers and has adopted for her book the Indian fashion of name giving. According to Christian and many Native American mythological traditions, naming is intimately tied to the act of creation, an act that is in turn linked to storytelling. Austin moves us quickly from specific place-names—Sierra Nevada, Panamint, Amargosa—to the name she prefers for the region, the one used by the Indians: "The Country of Lost Borders." We are thus placed simultaneously in a specific geographical region and in the imaginative realm of the author, a place where "[n]ot the law, but the land sets the limit."[6]

We can get a more complete sense of the nature of that place by taking a brief excursion into Austin's personal notes. In one of her many Bibles she densely annotated Acts, a chronicle of the ministry of the Apostle Paul, and Romans and Corinthians, two of the epistles Paul wrote. One of the most interesting annotations is beside the verse that recounts Paul's conversion: "And as he [Saul] journeyed, he came near Damascus: and suddenly there shined round about him a light from heaven." After this event Saul changed his name to Paul and began to preach the gospel of Jesus as he understood it. Austin wrote in the margin, "'a light'—the white light of the desert—the 'flash' at Cottonwood Creek."[7]

Although there is a Cottonwood Creek draining east from the Sierra Nevada just south of Mount Langley, the Cottonwood Creek to which Austin refers lies in the

White Mountains east of Big Pine and drains southeast into Fish Lake Valley. It is one of the few year-round spring-fed streams in those mountains, which form the Owens Valley's eastern border. Fish Lake Valley was home to Wodziwob, the Ghost Dance prophet of 1870, and, according to Austin in **"The Divorcing of Sina,"** to Tinnemaha, the model for her character Winnenap. Did Austin have a conversion experience there like the one described by Paul, and if she did, was it this experience that precipitated her spiritual awakening in the 1890s? A reference in Austin's journal of 1909, written when she was in London after having just left California, suggests that the answer to both questions is yes: "Paul by his own account says that he did not receive the gospel from eye witnesses and apostles but directly from Christ (*as I*)."[8]

In this context, and in the light of Austin's own lifelong attempts to syncretize native and Euro-American mythologies, we now turn back to the practice of naming adopted for *The Land of Little Rain.* The name Austin invariably uses for the White Mountains, the location of the revelation recounted above, is Waban. One of the few Indian names I have been unable to trace in the ethnographic literature to a local source, Waban was one of the earliest Indian converts mentioned by John Eliot, whose *Indian Dialogues* was published in 1671 "as a sort of training manual and model for new Indian preachers."[9] Considering the change in her spiritual orientation, which began in the Owens Valley under Tinnemaha's guidance and moved her away from conventional Protestant expression toward experimentation with native religious forms, Austin's use of that name for the mountains in which she experienced her great awakening can be seen as a way of marking a turning point in her own spiritual evolution—a turning in the opposite direction from that of Eliot's converts—and as testimony to her impetus to syncretize native and Christian names, stories, beliefs, and rituals.

In *The Land of Little Rain,* then, the statement "not the law but the land sets the limit" stands as both an artistic creed and a spiritual one. With its echoes of a fundamental Judaic tenet, the statement announces its author's revisionary impulse: instead of privileging the law as handed down by Yahweh, she will privilege the Land as the giver of all right law. If the Land speaks the law, then it may also, like Yahweh, depend on prophets to translate what it is saying, to tell its stories. Just as the biblical prophet seeks to return Yahweh's people once again to an ongoing communion with their God by warning them of the consequences of their inattention to that law and to those stories, so Austin seeks to effect the people's return to the law imposed by the Land. She here establishes a clear proto—deep ecological model for what is to follow in the book, a model that conceives of the biological and cultural integrity of the land as inextricably bound.[10]

Although the narrator spends most of the first story describing the land's topography, inhabitants, weather, and seasons, she leads us by story's end to "the fabled Hassaympa, of whose waters, if any drink, they can no more see fact as naked fact, but all radiant with the color of romance. I, who must have drunk of it in my twice seven years' wandering, am assured that it is worth while."[11]

Water is indisputably one of the key symbolic elements in the mythologies of desert cultures; it holds an importance that even a cursory scan of Paiute myths makes clear. Indigenous Great Basin cultures hold water to be the keystone of religion and liken it to the human breath.[12] Biblical stories likewise reveal the central symbolic function of water. In her reference to Hassaympa, Austin combines these bodies of mythology. Since *Hassaympa* is an Indian word,[13] we can assume that a Native American story led her to the spring; but she ties the Bible into Paiute mythology by using the phrase "twice seven years' wandering." The number seven always carries a heavy symbolic load in biblical stories. The time span of *twice* seven years, however, occurs only once.[14] When none of Pharaoh's advisers can interpret his dreams, he calls in the slave Joseph, who has won his captors' trust, to tell him their meaning. Joseph tells Pharaoh that God has decreed seven years of plenty to be followed by seven years of famine. He is immediately put in charge of storing grain during the seven years of plenty so that the seven years of famine will not destroy Egypt. Moreover, later in Genesis, Joseph is referred to as "a fruitful vine near a spring." Even more important, he is one of the first of the biblical prophets to keep alive the dream of Yahweh leading the tribes of Israel to a Promised Land, a dream that comes to fruition in large part because of Moses' reluctant leadership.[15]

The "twice seven years" span also resonates with Austin's personal history. The seven-year period from 1888 to 1895 roughly corresponds to the period between Austin's arrival in California and her move to Independence. The year 1896 marked a spiritual turning point in her life that precipitated a second seven-year period of artistic plenty—most of it spent in Independence—beginning in 1897, when Austin began to publish regularly in national journals, and ending in 1903, the year *The Land of Little Rain* was published.[16] Austin's use of the phrase in the context of her arrival at Hassaympa is more than a poetic way of indicating the length of her residency in California. Its reversal of the biblical pattern of plenty to drought shows the author's revisionist tendency, and its evocation of both biblical prophecy and Native American mythology announces the book's prophetic and syncretic purpose. Further, these time spans control the unfolding of the book, which is divided into fourteen ("twice seven") chapters. The early chapters are full of images of drought—

"Scavengers" is the prime example—but the book ends, in **"The Little Town of the Grape Vines,"** in images of plenty. Thus, the reference to Hassaympa at the end of the first chapter is a clue that our journey through the book will end at a spring of water arrived at by means of story, fable, or (more broadly) mythology.[17]

An allusion to Hassaympa elsewhere points to its connection in Austin's mind with Jesus and to the reasons she was inspired by the "Indian Messiah," Wovoka. In *Christ in Italy* she writes that the images of Christ as depicted in the writings of the saints and in the art of the Italian masters indicate that others raised in the Christian tradition "had come by the same trail" to the Friend-of-the-Soul-of-Man as had the Indians from whom she borrowed the term. Although she "couldn't perceive the stair by which [these Christians] climbed," the source was the same: "Hassaympa goes round and about Lost Borders; it flows and sinks and rises again in unnamed canons, loops about desert ranges and is lost in the sand. Only Indians know where to find it with any certainty. Once there was a White man who thought he could guide people to its shallows—but that was a long time ago and he has been judged quite harmless. . . . What happens to you if you have drunk Hassaympa is that all place and time dissolve." In the context of her discussion later in *Christ in Italy* about why and how, in the Owens Valley, she rejected "churchianity" and yet still had visions of "Christ walking in the desert dust," the "[w]hite man who thought he could guide people to [the] shallows" of Hassaympa stands as an oblique reference to Christ.[18]

Because Hassaympa possesses sacred powers, our arrival there at the end of the first chapter of *The Land of Little Rain* sets the stage for the book's first overt act of syncretic prophecy, which occurs in **"Shoshone Land."** Showing the author's tendency to collapse place and time, the vision offered there is the first of two precisely situated incarnations of the "fabled Hassaympa."

The Prophet is Shown Paradise

Winnenap, a Shoshone doctor who married into a Paiute band, is the fictional character Austin creates to lead her narrator to Shoshone Land in the chapter of that name. Winnenap is based on the historical figure Tinnemaha (Te-ni-ma-ha, Te-ni-ma-ha-te), whom Austin met sometime around 1892 in the village of Captain George near Lone Pine. Tinnemaha was a Paiute—or, like the early Ghost Dance prophet Wodziwob, a Paiute-Shoshone—healer who tutored Austin in native forms of prayer. Both the paradisiacal vision and the historical context Austin establishes in this chapter imply that the source for Winnenap's/Tinnemaha's vision—and in turn the source for Austin's own prophetic vision as offered in her book—was Wovoka.

The syncretic nature of Winnenap's faith and its possible link to the Ghost Dance are apparent when we turn to a brief reference in a later work. In *California: The Land of the Sun,* Austin first recounts a Paiute etiological myth explaining how California came to have its shape and then writes that "Winnenap . . . was eclectic in his faiths as in his practice." His wife, she continues, "was a tall brown woman out of Tejon and her mother was of that band of captives taken from San Gabriel by the Mojaves, Mission-bred." This information suggests that Winnenap's spirituality may have drawn both from traditional Indian religions and from Catholicism. Furthermore, since the Mojaves are said to have sent delegates to a Ghost Dance ceremony in 1890, it also suggests that Winnenap/Tinnemaha may have been exposed to Wovoka's syncretic religion through his wife's kin.[19]

Other historical documents point to the possibility that even before Wovoka's Ghost Dance of 1890, Tinnemaha may have been involved with Wodziwob's Ghost Dance of 1870. According to Austin in **"The Divorcing of Sina,"** Tinnemaha, like Wodziwob, hailed from Fish Lake Valley, just east of the Owens Valley. Recall, too, that Wovoka's father, Numu Tavibo (Northern Paiute White Man), was a follower of Wodziwob and may have received his name after being taken prisoner in the aftermath of the Pyramid Lake War of 1860 or during the Owens Valley War of 1862-63.[20] He would have been incarcerated at the regional post, Fort Churchill, outside Reno. On August 18, 1862, it was reported that Te-ni-ma-ha and Chief George were among the five Paiute chiefs who had turned themselves in as hostages to a cavalry brigade dispatched from Fort Churchill to secure peace in the Owens Valley. According to instructions given by Major R. C. Drum, assistant adjutant general in San Francisco of the Pacific forces, these hostages were to be held at Fort Churchill.[21] Thus, Tavibo and Tinnemaha might have been held at the fort at the same time.

We should bear in mind Tinnemaha's possible ties to the Ghost Dance as we examine how Austin's narrator in **"Shoshone Land"** recounts Winnenap's syncretic paradisiacal vision and establishes a historical context for it. Like many of the chapters in *The Land of Little Rain,* **"Shoshone Land"** begins with a symbolic entry into a landscape that is both literal and imaginative. Although the narrator has visited this land personally many times since, she admits that she first encountered it "through the eyes of Winnenap in a rosy mist of reminiscence," seeing it "with a sense of intimacy in the light that never was." Every spring, in a ritualistic act of renewal, Winnenap would travel "east and east" until he came to a place where "the earth falls away in a wide sweeping hollow which is Shoshone Land," a land of "pure desertness" that "no man knows the end of." The medicine man weaves the magic of Shoshone Land around his listener with words, "[drawing] up its happy places one by one, like little blessed islands in a sea of talk," just as Austin herself is simultaneously re-creating this journey for us as we read her words.[22]

This re-creation requires the narrator to manipulate images as well as words, and Austin's use of both depends on synthesizing Native American and Euro-American elements. In Shoshone languages, as Richley Crapo points out, the words for "power" (*puha*), "water" (*paa*), and "path" (*po'ai*) are closely related. But there is also an association between "water" and "breath," and a further association between "breathing" and "thinking" in the word *sua,* which hints at "the overall mediation of the mind and memory."[23] Austin's description of how Winnenap presented this vision to her partakes of the same linguistic associations.

These words and images, moreover, have sacred significance. The image of the places in Shoshone Land being "little blessed islands in a sea of talk," for instance, evokes the world creation myth of the Owens Valley Paiute-Shoshones, with words here substituting for the dirt Coyote carries in his mouth and drops in the primordial sea until there is enough land to satisfy his co-creator, Wolf, and to support all other beings. Winnenap's words may also represent a call to one of his personalized powers, or spirit helpers. In Great Basin religions, animals are the most frequent helpers, but inanimate objects or places can also grant power. According to Owens Valley Paiute William Piper, the strongest power, which has the name "day-light side" (*ta-vi-ha-na-wa-ti*), comes from the east. The best doctors are able to utilize this power, and its presence can be seen in the healer's ability to sing "of places unknown."[24] When Winnenap pictures for Austin a place "no man knows the end of," and when she in turn pictures it for us, both are "singing of places unknown" and in so doing are manifesting their power. We can imagine, then, that Winnenap's words translate for the narrator his own experience of entering into sacred space, an experience the author re-creates for her readers. The images depicted represent places in memory to which she has been led on a sacred trail that is simultaneously literal and imaginative.

Following this trail, we journey toward Shoshone Land; it is a journey linked with a return to paradise. *This paradise, however, is not the Eden of Judeo-Christian tradition.* The biblical garden is not congruent with the nature of the land here, and so it must be revised if it is to maintain symbolic power and presence. Here, the mesquite, not people, is "God's best thought." Here, "there is room enough and time enough," but no forbidden fruit, for "every plant has its perfect work"—not because there are no "noxious weeds" but rather because the inhabitants find "a use for everything that grows in these borders." Mostly, however, this land is paradisiacal because the inhabitants have learned the secret of living "like their trees, with great spaces between."[25] They have learned the law dictated by the Land in which they live.

In this paradise, water need not be produced by supernatural means, as it was for the Israelites when Yahweh showed Moses where to pound his staff on the rock; it is sufficient to pay close attention to mourning doves, local inhabitants who voice the presence of the desert spring. The doves revivify in an ecosystem-specific way the biblical image of the Holy Ghost, often pictured as a dove descending from on high, most memorably when Jesus was baptized by John in the River Jordan. In her notes, Austin refers to the dove that descended on Christ as a "Totemic animal." And she here implies that the Shoshones in effect hunted the divine when she remarks that they once hunted doves at these very springs.[26] Having been first to the source, the Shoshones, through Winnenap, now serve as her guides to spiritual nourishment and fulfillment.

The paradisiacal images used in both traditions are of more than just spiritual significance, however; they have political implications as well. Austin writes that "when the rain is over and gone [the Shoshones] are stirred by the instinct of those that journeyed eastward from Eden, and go up each with his mate and young brood, like birds to old nesting places." This ancient impulse is shared by all who live in the desert region, plant-people and animal-people no less than humans. Even in the "years of scant rains, some plants lie shut and safe in the winnowed sands, so that some species appear to be extinct," until in "[y]ears of long storms they break . . . thickly into bloom." Because the Shoshone "liv[e] like their trees," and because every "Shoshone family has in itself the man-seed, power to multiply and replenish," this passage can be read as an implicit prophecy of Indian resurgence.[27] Like the plants, the Shoshone survive unnoticed and will, according to nature's ways, make a comeback.

This is the same prophecy—using similar imagery—that the Ghost Dance offered its believers, as can be seen in these lines from a Paiute Ghost Dance song: "The cottonwoods are growing tall / They are growing tall and verdant."[28] Thus it is interesting to note that in telling the conclusion of Winnenap's story, Austin invokes the struggle occurring in Paiute communities between, on the one hand, the Ghost Dance with its syncretism and its hope of Indian resurgence and, on the other, a rejection of such native spiritual practices.

Austin writes that in the year of "the big snow," when a pneumonia epidemic killed hundreds of Indians across the region, the Paiutes called a council and decided to exact the ancient penalty: suspected of practicing witchcraft, the medicine man of each camp, Winnenap among them, was to be killed. Trying to impress on the Paiutes the severity of the penalty for murder, the whites in nearby towns called on Indian leaders to turn their people away from such pagan superstitions. "At Tunawai," Austin writes, "the conservatives sent into Nevada for that pacific old humbug, Johnson Sides, most notable of Paiute orators." Along with the Winnemucca family, Sides was among Wovoka's chief rivals for political and spiritual leadership among the Northern Paiutes in western Nevada.[29] Into the earlier paradisiacal picture has come a tempter, and the temptation, reversing our expectations, is not that the Indians will return to ancient ways but that they *won't,* that such "pacific old humbug[s]" as Johnson Sides will turn the Indians away from their own tribal wisdom.

An account written by William A. Chalfant, the editor of the *Inyo Independent,* sheds light on what is at stake. Chalfant reports that an epidemic broke out in the winter of 1900-1901 and that Johnson Sides came with "some of the local chief Piutes . . . to the writer's office and explained the situation at length." Sides, who was wearing a silver medal given him by the government "inscribed with his name and the title Peacemaker," "requested that his words be written down exactly as he gave them—being apparently doubtful about newspaper accuracy." In the parts of this speech extracted by Chalfant for a later article, Sides seems most concerned to use the occasion to lobby for help from the whites in the form of education for his people, thus solidifying his role as "Peacemaker"—the same role that put him in conflict with Wovoka, who claimed that God had made *him* president of the West. As to the situation at hand—the desire of some of his people to kill their medicine men—Sides is reported to have said, "Old times pass way—no use talk old times."[30]

Sides, then, saw no utility in paying attention to "old times," to tradition. But for Austin, as for Wovoka, tradition formed the basis of the new medicines and rituals of Indians and whites alike. Austin reinforces this point by showing the wisdom of the tradition that Sides rejects but Winnenap accepts. After Winnenap was killed, "his women buried him, and a warm wind coming out of the south, the force of the disease was broken, and even they acquiesced in the wisdom of the tribe." Thus, by pitting Sides the "humbug" against Winnenap the visionary, Austin re-creates the regional situation of the conflicts over the Ghost Dance, thereby implying the ties between the visions offered by Wovoka in his Great Revelation and by Winnenap (through Austin) in the book.

Those ties are reinforced in the chapter's final paragraph, which begins, "Since it appears that we make our own heaven here, no doubt we shall have a hand in the heaven of hereafter." The image Austin sees as heavenly is the one Winnenap painted for her, the one that has been confirmed by her own experience there. It is not otherworldly in the least, but "tawny gold underfoot, walled up with jacinth and jasper, ribbed with chalcedony, and yet no hymn-book heaven, but the free air and free spaces of Shoshone Land."[31] It is thus aligned with native tradition, where heaven, or the other world, is but an idealized copy of conditions in *this* world, as it is in Wovoka's prophetic visions. Recall that a key feature in those visions is the image of a regenerated world of peace and plenty where all share in the bounty. Austin's portrayal hints that such a vision is accessible to all. With her characterization of the "free air and free spaces" of Shoshone Land, Austin covertly points to the contrast between the land that exists only inside a Euro-American geopolitical frame of reference—a land that epitomizes the *lack* of Native American religious freedom at the turn of the century—and the land that exists inside the imaginative realm of Native American religious vision. Like Wovoka's revelation, and in line with the revision of the biblical pattern announced in the earlier allusion to Hassaympa, Winnenap's vision as Austin depicts it subverts reality—a historical situation marked by a drought both material and spiritual—and establishes in its stead an image of the plenty to come as foretold in the native prophetic tradition. It is precisely such a vision that animates **"The Little Town of the Grape Vines,"** to which we shall soon turn. Having been on an imaginative journey to this land of plenty, Austin offers herself as our guide there.

Like Austin, the "Indian Messiah" borrowed images from two bodies of mythology and blended them into a new syncretic form, which he then employed to demonstrate the magical or miraculous powers central to his mission. One incident in particular shows Wovoka's synthesis of traditional (Paiute) powers and the symbolism of Christian ritual. Michael Hittman terms the incident "The Miracle (or Prophecy) of the Block of Ice" and cites the following story as told by Ed Dyer, a white store owner who grew up with Wovoka and was an eyewitness to the event. The Paiutes had become aware that some event concerning the prophet was going to take place at the Walker River. As the people began gathering there, Wilson was sitting on a large blanket under a cottonwood tree at the river's edge. "Suddenly a great outcry came from the group around Wilson. Every one rushed over to see what had happened. There in the center of the blanket lay a big block of ice some 25 or 30 pounds in weight. Wilson had caused it to come from the sky. . . . [N]ot being of my suspicious nature, Indians accepted the miracle in full faith." The Paiutes then performed a kind of revised communion and baptism by "ceremoniously" drinking the water melted from the ice block and, at Wilson's order, stripping off their clothes and plunging into the river.[32]

Such stories and mythological allusions show the inherent interconnections among water, power, and the act of storytelling. Water and story intertwine in a web that connects all beings to each other and to their environment, in a flow of power from place to plant, animal, and rock, and from those beings to humans and back again. Such a flow is captured in memory and transmitted through story. Jay Miller explains that "[f]or all of native America, the ultimate source of power is the mind of the focal being involved in creation, most especially the process of memory, which is crucial for imparting immortality. . . . Memory is the basis for transmitting knowledge . . . [of] family, community, and tribal traditions, [a knowledge] best encapsulated in mythology and rituals."[33] In this sense, then, the storyteller, the "focal being" involved in the creation (or transmission) of the story, becomes a conduit for the flow of power.

Austin's allusions to Joseph, Moses, and Jesus in the context of her figurative arrival at the spring Hassaympa, the source of life, has set the context in the book for a journey to a spiritual source or Promised Land that is foretold in both native and Christian traditions. Thus, both the narrator's allusion to the journey in the first chapter and her retelling of Winnenap's vision of it in **"Shoshone Land"** set the stage for a prophetic recounting and ritual reenactment of that journey in the remainder of the book.[34]

THE PROPHET WARNS THE PEOPLE AND SACRALIZES THE LAND

The prophet, as Abraham Heschel has observed, moves between the extremes created by compassion for the people and the realization that their ways are not God's ways. For this reason, he is both sympathetic and demanding, exhortatory and condemning, sad and outraged. He is positioned between the human and God, thus making necessary a strategy that is indirect. Heschel explains the process as follows: "His view is oblique. God is the focal point of his thought, and the world is seen as reflected in God. Indeed, the main task of prophetic thinking is to bring the world into divine focus. This, then, explains his way of thinking. He does not take a direct approach to things. It is not a straight line, spanning subject and object, but rather a triangle—through God to the object."[35]

In the chapter that follows **"Shoshone Land,"** Austin positions herself in a "prophetic" way. She shifts away not only from the "we" of her collaboration with Winnenap but also from the single "I" (eye) of the earlier chapters, who seems simply to be recording what goes on in this "land of lost borders." She adopts a new "we," aligning herself with the residents of Jimville while at the same time retaining the sense of her separate existence as a unique "I." She has thus situated herself strategically in a borderland—she is at once insider and outsider. This liminal narrative position is a

powerful one, as John O'Grady imaginatively explores in his analysis of Austin's journal writing, whether that position is constituted in the more secular terms of wilderness/civilization or in specifically spiritual terms. Indeed, Austin positions herself as narrator here just as she previously situated Winnenap, who is not only a Shoshone adopted into Paiute culture but also, and more important, a native doctor for whom liminality is central to the exercise of power.[36]

In **"Jimville,"** this narrative positioning involves the juxtaposition of the town's history with the narrator's own history as a resident there. Though the journey to Jimville is "of such interminable monotony as induces forgetfulness of all previous states of existence," the town itself is a "cove of reminder." The story of how the town got its name, which follows shortly after these clues, suggests that it is the history of the town's origins that is so easily forgotten. Since the story she tells involves two Jims, and since the town itself is called "Jimville," we might speculate that *this* name, in contrast to the Indian names Austin typically prefers, originates "in the poor human desire for perpetuity," something she has decried in the preface.[37] As with all the names used by Austin, however, this one serves a purpose, here carried out by filling in the history the name obscures.

The regional history of easterners taking the wealth and abandoning the land is mirrored in the local history, in which a white easterner takes an Indian wife, produces a child, and promptly abandons both. The child must be taken under the protection of white society, as represented by the "rough-handed folks of that place." The story implies that, like the child, the town is the offspring of a mixed-race union in which the white father abandons the Indian mother after striking it rich. Despite Austin's claim that she is "a mere recorder," the observations that preface the story make it clear that she is weaving a more complex sort of history here and that the town is a cipher for the history of the desert West. Taken together, the facts that "[t]he road to Jimville is the *happy hunting ground* of old stage-coaches," that "[t]he town looks to have spilled out of *Squaw Gulch*," and that its one street is "paved with *bone-white* cobbles" imply that the town is literally built on the bones of the displaced and dead Indian. Since myth by its very nature often obscures the literal facts of history even as it enshrines in the tale itself a different sort of historical reality, we might see the story as Austin's attempt to defeat this tendency—to be historically accurate even though not literally correct. The chapter thus not only serves as a sort of parable but also implicates the narrator, as a resident of Jimville, in the history of race relations that has been enacted there.[38]

Understanding this narrative position is crucial to understanding the chapter that follows **"Jimville."** In **"My Neighbor's Field,"** Austin brings us to the very site where she writes and issues a stern prophetic warning, a warning once again delivered by juxtaposing biblical and Paiute stories. The ancient Hebrews' arrival in the Promised Land was delayed—and sometimes their very survival was threatened—by their propensity to transgress and their repeated failure to abide by Yahweh's law and to have faith in him, despite the repeated warnings of his prophets. In **"My Neighbor's Field,"** Austin warns her contemporaries, and does so specifically by aligning herself with the prophets Elijah and Ezekiel, who, according to Mooney's account, were also two of Wovoka's primary biblical exemplars.

"My Neighbor's Field" opens with an assertion that this field "is one of those places God must have meant for a field from all time." Austin then goes on to situate the neighbor's field, and thus the narrator and her own house, which lies adjacent to the field, in the middle of "the land of little rain": It is fenced on the north and south "by low old glacial ridges," on the east by orchards and gardens, with the village street "break[ing] off abruptly at the edge of [it] in a footpath that goes up the streamside, beyond it, to the source of waters" in the Sierra Nevada immediately to the west.[39] This field, though "not greatly esteemed of the town," represents to the narrator the possibility of a synthesis of the wild and the civilized. Thus the chapter and the field are central both literally and symbolically: as the seventh of fourteen chapters, **"My Neighbor's Field"** is structurally central to the book and geographically central to the land described therein; as the site of the author's immediate present—the site where she is writing the book—it is temporally central; finally, as a symbol of the region's history of race relations, it is socioculturally central.

The succession of the field's owners enacts in microcosm the flow of power in the region. The Paiutes were the original inhabitants and "owners" of the field, followed by the shepherds and the cattlemen. The field then came to her neighbor, whom Austin calls Naboth because she "env[ies] his possession" of it. Austin's narrative stance puts her in the role of King Ahab, who, with the help of his wife, Jezebel, condemned Naboth to death and took possession of the field, only to repent later when the Lord's prophet, Elijah, foretold disaster for him and his sons.[40] Austin's narrator thus aligns herself with the culprits in the Indians' displacement from the field, and simultaneously evokes the prophecy that the children of the dispossessors will pay the price for the sins of their fathers. Registering both the spiritual emptiness of her fellow Euro-Americans and the consequent material impoverishment of her Native American contemporaries, her act of disappropriation signifies the ultimate "drought," or lack, to which the prophet must call attention, thereby announcing an end to the seven-year famine and the beginning of a similar period of plenty.

Austin's invocation of the biblical story of Naboth's vineyard turns this chapter into a parable and invites comparison between Elijah and Wovoka, and in turn between the narrator and those two prophets. Mooney's comparison of Wovoka and Elijah derives from eyewitness accounts of the Paiute prophet's power to control the weather and raise the dead, as Elijah had done. According to the biblical story preceding the Naboth episode, Elijah came to have influence with King Ahab precisely because he declared that for three years there would be no rain or even dew unless Yahweh ordained it and he foretold it. Wovoka likewise initially rose to prominence as a rain-maker and a "Great Weather Prophet" when he used his power to end the severe drought of 1887-88 and thereby gained considerable influence in the local farming economy, which prospered and declined according to the weather.[41] Like Elijah and Wovoka, Austin narratively exercises her powers of foretelling and controlling the weather by here figuring the end to her contemporaries' spiritual drought, and later (in **"Nurslings of the Sky"**) by making it rain and thereby initiating a season of plenty.

In Austin's "land of little rain," such natural power exercised over the elements has been replaced by political power exercised over people. Austin not only mirrors this change in the progression of plants that dominate the field, reflecting its past occupancy and ownership, but also addresses it directly in her prophetic message. The native plants—a "single shrub of 'hoopee'" and "three low rakish trees of hackberry," which, she notes, the Paiutes prized as items of food and trade—stand "[b]y the south corner, where the campoodie stood" and are "maintaining [themselves] hardly among alien shrubs." The Paiutes themselves were likewise crowded out of the field, which now holds only their memory in the form of obsidian chips, "kitchen middens, and the pits of old sweathouses." Next came the shepherds, represented by "a single clump of mesquite of the variety called 'screw bean,'" which is found "[b]y the fork of the creek where the shepherds camp" and which "must have shaken there from some sheep's coat."[42] Now, neighbor Naboth has put a fence around the field, trying, it would seem, to keep out not only the intruding (originally native) plants, but also the Indians and shepherds, who still gather and live along its borders.

That the field lies precisely between the mesa and the town, the habitations of the Indians and the Euro-American settlers, respectively, and that the stream that nourishes the field "runs up to the source of waters" suggest that while the two cultures are indeed far apart, they are yet connected along an axis of power that has a single source. The allusion to the Paiute myth that follows at this point shows just how the *moral* power flows in a direction exactly opposite to that of the *legal* power: "A mile up from the water gate that turns the creek into supply pipes for the town, begins a row of long-leaved pines . . . that puzzle the local botanist . . . [because they are] unrelated to other conifers of the Sierra slope; the same pines of which the Indians relate a legend mixed of brotherliness and the retribution of God."[43]

The legend she refers to, the tale of Winnedumah, is well known in the region; it is an etiological myth explaining the presence of a huge rock monolith atop the Inyo Range and of some unusual pines along Independence Creek. Winnedumah and his brother Tinnemaha, mythic forebears of the Paiutes, are engaged in a war with one of the Sierra tribes to the west. They are strategically fleeing their opponents, heading east toward the Owens Valley and their own territory, when Tinnemaha, who is trailing his brother, is shot with an arrow. When Winnedumah, who has vowed that he will always remain faithful to his brother, reaches the top of the Inyo Range, he looks back over his shoulder at his pursuers and sees that Tinnemaha has been shot. Immediately he becomes the monolith that still testifies to his faithfulness; his pursuers are simultaneously turned into the long-leaved pines along Independence Creek, which Austin calls "Pine Creek."[44]

If, as in **"Shoshone Land,"** trees are people, then the personification of trees in the passage that follows the story encodes the same politically charged message of native resurgence:

> Once the pines possessed the field . . . and it would seem their secret purpose to regain their old footing. . . . Since I came to live by the field one of these has tiptoed above the gully of the creek, beckoning the procession from the hills, as if in fact they would make back toward that skyward-pointing finger of granite on the opposite range from which, according to the legend, when they were bad Indians and it a great chief, they ran away. This year the summer floods brought the round, brown fruitful cones to my very door, and I look, if I live long enough, to see them come up greenly in my neighbor's field.[45]

That plants represent people is reemphasized as the narrator goes on to describe the wild plants retaking the field; she notes in particular that the clematis and the wild almond—plants later linked with Paiute and white cultures, respectively—will not come inside the fence.[46] More important, the references by which they are linked convey a religious theme—the power conferred by names—and reinscribe the motif of the journey to the Promised Land. The connection between the wild almond and white culture becomes apparent in a digression about how the trees' sudden blooming might explain the story in Exodus about Moses' encounter with the burning bush; the connection of the clematis to Paiute culture becomes clear two chapters later, where, in profiling Seyavi, the narrator quotes the Paiute basket maker as singing, "I am the white flower of twinn-

ing," which Austin parenthetically glosses as "clematis." In the biblical story, God's appearance in the burning bush is designed to inspire the awe necessary to convince Moses to lead the Israelites out of Egypt to the Promised Land. When Moses hesitates, asking what name he should give the Israelites to establish his authority, Yahweh responds, "I AM WHO I AM. This is what you are to say to the Israelites. I AM has sent me to you."[47] Austin's reference here thus reinvokes the context of the journey to a Promised Land.

Likewise, Seyavi's self-identification with clematis has a spiritual element because it ties into the traditional Paiute practice of naming girls after flowers.[48] To the extent that during such ritual naming ceremonies girls took on some of the power of the flower for which they were named, and since the acquisition of power (*puha*) is seen as the central enterprise of Great Basin religions, the naming has a religious significance analogous to that in the biblical story, conferring an authority to be exercised not *over* but *within* a particular community.

Symbolically, then, the exclusion of these two particular plants from the field implies whites' unwillingness to mingle and live with the Indians and their disregard for the "common ground" shared by the two cultures and the source of their mutual nourishment. In contrast, just outside the fence, the wild almond mixes freely with native plants such as the lupine:

> Plants are so unobtrusive in their material processes, and always at the significant moment some other bloom has reached its perfect hour. One can never fix the precise moment when the rosy tint the field has from the wild almond passes into the inspiring blue of lupines. . . . Go and stand by any crown of bloom and the tall stalks do but rock a little as for drowsiness, but look off across the field, and on the stillest days there is always a trepidation in the purple patches."[49]

It is interesting that the colors of the flowers are not said to blend; rather, an awareness of one leads, sometimes imperceptibly, into an awareness of the other, and each has "its perfect hour." Further, such awareness leads, as one backs up to take a wider view, to a perception of movement, almost as if God himself were walking along the border of the field among the wild plants. The biblical metaphor of the wind as the breath of God in addition to Yahweh's reminder to Moses in the Exodus passage that "the place whereon thou standest is holy ground" both serve in this context to imply what Austin laments.[50] By erecting a fence that alters the field's natural mix of native and introduced species, Naboth (representing Euro-American culture) has created an artificial boundary that effectively excludes God from the field. The explicit warning given throughout the book of the consequences of not paying attention to "natural law" is turned in this chapter into the implicit warning that, by dispossessing the Indians, Euro-American civilization will ultimately suffer consequences—and is even now, although only the prophet can see it, morally imperiled.

Further, Austin's warning shades over into prophetic exhortation in the chapter's more oblique evocations of the later prophet, Ezekiel, giving to her message a deeper layer of meaning. The first hints of Ezekiel are in the opening line and paragraphs, which begin with the assertion "It is one of those places God must have meant for a field from all time," and continue with a description of what borders the field in each of the four cardinal directions. Ezekiel 39-44 not only deals in great detail with "one of those places God must have meant for a field from all time" but also offers a plot and themes that have parallels in **"My Neighbor's Field."** In Ezekiel, Yahweh denounces Gog with a warning: "And I will smite thy bow out of thy left hand, and will cause thine arrows to fall out of thy right hand. Thou shalt fall upon the mountains of Israel. . . . Thou shalt fall upon the open field." After this denunciation, Yahweh leads Ezekiel up to the holy mountain to see the site of the new temple, gives him precise directions for its construction, and instructs him in the rules that are to govern the division and use of the land. These rules stipulate that in the midst of the temple area there is to be a field set aside for use by the priests. Yahweh in effect reveals to Ezekiel directions for the consecration of the place that he "meant for a field from all time." Yahweh offers these directions to Ezekiel through a man whose appearance is like bronze and who provides a precise description of the gates that bound the sacred area in all directions.[51]

Austin's chapter contains the same elements. The Paiute tale of Winnedumah mirrors in basic plot the situation described in Ezekiel—the images there reminiscent of the Paiute myth's depictions of the fate of the combatants. More important, however, her description of the field contains several thematic parallels to the biblical passage.[52] Austin's manipulation of the two tales serves not only to explain a geophysical feature and to remind listeners of the importance of loyalty but additionally serves as a warning. Recall as well that at this point in the book Austin's narrator has only recently returned from a journey to Shoshone Land, with a "bronze man," Winnenap, as her guide.

The bronze man directs Ezekiel to describe the temple to the people of Israel, "that they may be ashamed of their iniquities," and to make known to them its design, its regulations, and its laws: "Write it in their sight. . . . This is the law of the house; Upon the top of the mountain the whole limit thereof round about shall be most holy."[53] Remembering that one of Austin's first moves in the book is to replace the law of Yahweh with the law of the Land, we can venture to say that Austin is

decreeing by virtue of this law that the field and "all the surrounding area on top of the mountain" are sacred. Indeed, in *The Land of Little Rain* Austin seems to be following the very directions Yahweh gave to Ezekiel: she offers a description of a sacred land, its design and regulations, written down so that followers can be faithful to its requirements. In doing so, Austin is consecrating the land around the neighbor's field. Whereas in Ezekiel the temple and the adjacent field are the most sacred sites, in Austin the land *around* the field is most sacred—because by fencing the field Naboth has disregarded the Land's decrees. The fact that Austin, like the author of Ezekiel, images God as coming from the east—the direction of Shoshone Land—further reinforces the centrality of Winnenap's vision to Austin's prophetic project. And when she later notes that the entrances to all Paiute wickiups face eastward, she not only reinforces this point but also portrays how, in contrast to Naboth and her fellow townspeople, the Indians' spirituality is fully integrated into their daily lives.[54]

The most striking parallel to Ezekiel, however, is in Austin's adaptation of the mandate that the native and the nonnative must mix peaceably with each other. This is not only the theme at the heart of **"My Neighbor's Field"** but also a distinguishing feature of Wovoka's revelation within the Native American tradition of prophecy. Ezekiel is told to deliver this message: "[D]ivide this land unto you according to the tribes of Israel. And it shall come to pass that ye shall divide it by lot for an inheritance unto you, and to the strangers that sojourn among you; and they shall be unto you as born in the country among the children of Israel; they shall have inheritance with you among the tribes of Israel." After he is told how the remainder is to be divided and that the holy portion in the middle is to be reserved for the priests, Ezekiel is then given the specific injunction that those "who went astray when the children of Israel went astray"—that is, those who "went astray away from [the Lord] after their idol" and who must therefore "bear their iniquity"—must "not sell of it, [nor] exchange" any land allotted to them, because "it is holy unto the LORD."[55]

"My Neighbor's Field" likewise begins with the history of the field's occupancy and ownership and ends with a discussion of plans to divide it. Furthermore, the field, with Austin's house across from it, is situated at the center of an area whose dimensions correspond roughly to the land set aside in Ezekiel as the portion to be offered to the Lord, within which "will be the sanctuary and the most holy place."[56] In the Bible this area is approximately seven miles long and three miles wide. Maps of the Owens Valley reveal that Austin describes an area with roughly the same dimensions in her opening paragraph. The area lies between the lowermost flank of the Sierra Nevada and the town of Independence on the west and east, respectively, and between the field and Pine Creek (now called Independence Creek) on the south, and the next source of water to the north (Oak Creek). Before its dispossession, Naboth's field would have corresponded to the "most holy place" in Ezekiel. Austin's house, then, corresponds to the temple, and Austin herself to the priest who recalls the people to right living according to the law.

The warning to the "princes of Israel" in Ezekiel to "remove violence and spoil, and execute judgment and justice, [and] take away your exactions from my people" is mirrored not only in the beginning and conclusion of **"My Neighbor's Field"** but also in the juxtaposition of myths in its body, which together constitute an analogous warning to Austin's fellow residents to stop the transgression implicit in their dispossession of the Indians from the field. Through the sanctuary in Ezekiel's vision flows a river that produces food enough for all.[57] This river is reminiscent of rivers in Eden, and, indeed, the temple itself is meant to be a reincarnation of Eden. Austin's depiction likewise features the stream, which "goes on up to the source of waters," as a significant feature. For her, the river is significant as a material resource, but it is also laden with symbolic moral implications. Recall, for instance, that in Winnenap's paradisiacal vision, the scanty waters supply plentiful food for the Shoshones; the actual historical situation, however, is far different, as Austin will remind us two chapters later when she discusses the deprivations visited on Seyavi and the Paiutes by the soldiers stationed at Fort Independence.

Austin's adaptation of Ezekiel shows a shrewd manipulation of the terms of race. While indicting her Euro-American contemporaries' emphasis on the profit the land can bring, she finesses the native-born/alien distinction found in Ezekiel. In the biblical passage, the injunction that the alien is to be considered native-born seeks to render the Self/Other dichotomy instrumentally impotent by substituting a political designation for what the Israelites would consider a biological one. Yahweh's law insists that the Israelites accord full political rights—rights of property ownership—regardless of biology (race). Of course, the move toward a unifying national identity also has potentially negative political implications, in particular if the "alien" is forced to choose between national and ethnic identities.

In turn-of-the-century America, at least in the imagination of the many Euro-Americans who saw themselves as the chosen people of God, the native had become the alien, and the negative potentialities of that substitution had been inscribed in the law in effect at the time. With the passage of the Indian Homestead Act on March 3, 1875, Indians were granted the right to gain patent on up to 160 acres of land—but only if they abandoned all tribal relations. Even before the passage of the act, Joseph Diaz, a Paiute, was allotted land that he had been farming in the Owens Valley, but only after he forswore his tribal relations. Newspaper accounts show that at least one Land Office official in the Owens Valley effectively skirted the Indian Homestead Act by decreeing that tribal relations could not be forsworn by an individual but only by the tribe as a whole and that such an arrangement had to be affirmed by the federal government. This unofficial practice made it difficult, oftentimes impossible, for Indians to own land.[58]

Austin's manipulation of the myths shows that she, like Ezekiel, is insisting that the Indians be accorded full political rights, but *without* being required to forswear tribal relations as a prerequisite. She implicates her contemporaries through the figure of Naboth, who erected the fence in disregard of nature's law. And it is this fence that serves as the instrument making aliens (intruders) out of the Indians. By calling attention to the ways in which the erection of the fence runs counter to the law, Austin condemns the perspective that undergirds local discriminatory practices. This is the first phase in her strategy.

At the end of the chapter, Austin initiates phase two through a subversive act of rhetorical monkey-wrenching. She reverses the terms of race and thereby reinforces the symbolic instrumentality of the fence only in order to rhetorically disable it. In the chapter's last paragraph the narrator tells us that Naboth hopes to sell the field for town lots and thereby to make his fortune. This not only serves as a pointed reminder that the naturalness of the material processes along the field's borders offers a marked contrast to the artificiality of the economic materialism that propels it from owner to owner, but, more important, shows that it is *Naboth's* idol—money—that has led him away from the law and rendered him blind to the qualities dear to the narrator. Of all the townspeople, she alone sees that the field is "admirably compounded for variety and pleasantness,—a little sand, a little loam, a grassy plot, a stony rise or two, a full brown stream, a little touch of humanness, a footpath trodden out by moccasins."[59] Rhetorically, Naboth is thus transformed into a representative of the "alien" with his "idol," and the designation of "native" is reinscribed for the Indians, figuratively rendering *them* as the possessors of moral (if not political) power.

A summary of my argument to this point may be useful. The stage has been set in the opening chapter for a journey to a Promised Land that, as it is foretold in both biblical and native traditions, is available to whites and Indians alike. **"Shoshone Land"** shows the power of a native paradisiacal vision such as Winnenap's (or Wovoka's) to guide believers in their daily lives. By contrast, the events described in the biblical stories alluded to in **"My Neighbor's Field"** occur as a result of Euro-Americans' failure to live by God's law as outlined in his prophets' visions, a failure that in Austin's universe is the same as the failure to abide by the law the Land imposes. By disregarding nature's dictate regarding the intermingling of native and introduced species/races, Euro-American society has turned its collective back on both its God and its Indian neighbors. The Paiute tale of Winnedumah provides the contrasting example of one (and, by extension, an entire race) who kept faith with his brother, a faith to which the land itself testifies in the form of the monolith atop the Inyo Range. While the chapter's overt allusions to the story of Naboth place the _narrator_ in the role of Ahab and thus implicate her as one of the dispossessors of the native inhabitants of the field, the story's placement in the book as well as the juxtaposition of mythical allusions within the chapter put the _author_ in the role of the prophets Elijah and Ezekiel, the first foretelling tragedy to the descendants of the dispossessors, the second exhorting the people to stop such moral transgressions and recalling them to a reverence for the sacred nature of the land.

Austin's narrative stance in this chapter moves between the two poles outlined by Heschel: identification with the people and sympathy for God's (the Land's) purposes, which the people have forgotten. Read in this way, the chapter is crucial to understanding the unique nature of the book's prophetic project. It does more than just reinforce the point that the new inhabitants of the land must adapt their habits and attitudes to nature's dictates, a point made overtly throughout the book; more important, it stipulates that those dictates are best perceived through an adaptation of our guiding mythologies, an adaptation analogous to a new religious understanding such as that offered by Wovoka.

Furthermore, the narrative trajectory in the book to this point re-creates the outlines of Wovoka's Great Revelation. In so doing, it creates a world of literal and figurative drought and lack that must be brought back to a state of plenty via the prophetic process—thus reversing the cycle foretold in Joseph's prophecy but maintaining his vision of a Promised Land. Like the world of peace and plenty envisioned by Wovoka, the narrator's destination, Hassaympa, is a syncretically constructed Promised Land. Just as Wovoka must "die" (enter into a trance state) in order to receive this vision, so too must Austin's narrator experience both Winnenap's death (albeit vicariously) and his forevision of the sacred place to which he travels. Both literal and imaginative, that place is an idealized copy of Winnenap's homeland, a world of peace and plenty accessible to all. Like Wovoka admonishing believers to stop stealing, lying, and drinking and to work peaceably with whites, Austin admonishes her fellow townspeople to stop their sins of stealing from and lying to the Indians, transgressions heretofore countenanced in the dispossession of the Indians from their homeland.

THE TRAIL TO THE LOST GARDEN

From the sites of Winnenap's paradisiacal vision and the prophet's warning, we travel by way of the "Mesa Trail" to encounter Seyavi, a figure who is simultaneously native elder, biblical prophet, and, more important in the light of the author's gender, a woman. **"The Mesa Trail"** threads through the three central chapters of _The Land of Little Rain_ not only literally but also symbolically, connecting the Paiute encampment in Naboth's field to the one along George's Creek outside Lone Pine, where Seyavi lives. "The mesa trail begins in the campoodie at the corner of Naboth's field," Austin tells us in the first line of that chapter, and goes past the foot of Mount Kearsarge approximately fifteen miles from Independence to Lone Pine (where Austin lived when she first settled in the Owens Valley in 1892), and "on toward the twilight hills and the borders of Shoshone Land."[60] The Paiute encampment, Naboth's field, Shoshone Land: since she has told us she lives directly across from Naboth's field, the narrator has situated herself directly between the two tribes historically inhabiting "the land of little rain." She has also balanced herself on the brink of the present as she experiences it while writing the book in her home in Independence.

That the narrator's route follows an Indian trail is made all the more significant by the importance Basin peoples traditionally placed on trails, which were seen simultaneously as routes of travel and as sacred pathways connecting modern people with their ancestors.[61] Thus, Austin follows an established route along which power is known to flow. She depicts this flow as a cultural continuity not only between ancient and modern but also between two modern cultures—the white and the Indian. By way of this trail, Austin literally and symbolically leads us back into another world—a world in which the pasts of Seyavi and her people are united with Austin's own past and, as the comparison with Deborah indicates, with that of _her_ people.[62]

"The Basket Maker" is crucial to the book's prophetic project, for it is here that Austin links the prophetic tradition with women's art, and specifically with her own art form, writing. Austin explicitly constructs Seyavi as a "natural" blend of Indian figure and biblical prophet. She compares the Paiute woman in her prime with the biblical figure of Deborah: both were "deep bosomed, broad in the hips, quick in counsel, slow of speech, esteemed of [their] people." Not only does Austin compare Seyavi and Deborah, she describes both in the same terms that she later uses to describe the desert itself, the well-known desert-as-woman passage from _Lost Borders_ [_Stories from the Country of Lost Borders_], which begins: "If the desert were a woman, I know well what like she would be: deep-breasted, broad in the hips, tawny, with tawny hair, great masses of it lying smooth along her perfect curves." Marjorie Pryse has pointed out that "tawny" and other descriptors are reminiscent of Austin's self-depiction in *Earth Horizon,* and draws the conclusion that "[t]he desert [thus] becomes a mirror in which Austin explores 'her own desires.'" I would extend the analogy of the mirror and reinsert the presence of the biblical figure. The link Austin forges between herself, a native woman artist, *and* a biblical prophet points to one of the "various natures" of her book: it is simultaneously art and prophecy, and both are indebted simultaneously to Euro- and Native American traditions.[63]

We know that Seyavi and other Paiute basket weavers were the models for Austin-the-artist.[64] But we can also place Austin's comment about Seyavi having "come through [a] period of unfaith in the lore of [her] clan with a fine appreciation of its beauty and significance" in the context of the multiple reflections suggested in the comparison with Deborah and thus reveal how Seyavi might be seen as a model for Austin-the-prophet as well.[65] That Austin places the emphasis in this passage on the lore's "beauty and significance," as opposed to its *truth,* sets up reverberations with her own personal history: though read out of the Methodist church for teaching the "Higher Criticism," Austin nevertheless maintained a lifelong interest in Christian history and mythology.[66] It is after her visit with the prophet/artist Seyavi, after demonstrating that women are crucial links in the prophetic tradition in both cultures, that Austin takes to the trail again to lead us into the future. That the trail on which she travels "begins at the campoodie," a line the narrator repeats, suggests that the Indians have shown her the path connecting past to present to future—the trail on which she now leads us toward a vision of a Promised Land.

In an unpublished work she titled "The Lost Garden," Austin traverses the same actual and mythological trail and covers the same terrain she travels in *The Land of Little Rain.* Beyond Naboth's field, she says, lies Hassaympa,

> the place of springs. It lies at the end of the mesa where the trail runs between strange unfinished shapes of ancient rocks. . . . The springs are in the unfilled hollow between the rim of the mesa and the leaning cliffs of Oppopago, in a swale opening toward the great Bitter lake. They break out along the edge of the hollow and spread downward with greenness. From their sources one looks off toward the Coso hills and the clouded sapphire of the lake with the faint citron tinge of the pickleweed on the salt marshes. Here betimes the moon comes walking across Shoshone Land, on the flushed opalescent trail of the day. . . .
>
> I saw the Dreams walking. . . . Although there was no wind, the flitting of them among the irises kept up a continuous hint of motion. If you walked among them stilly, touching the blossom tops[,] the Dreams walked too and touched fingers with you.[67]

This description—nearly identical with her account in *The Land of Little Rain* of what happens outside Naboth's field[68]—is followed by her tale of being in an Indian burial ground, an area marked by "scattered blue beads which the Indians strewed there" and by "an altar to the god of Uninhabited Places" that she made of twelve stones, perhaps following the Yokut custom of marking places of power with rock cairns.[69] There she could commune with "those I wished to have come to me," which presumably includes the dead—her mother, Winnenap, and Seyavi among them. She then continues, "At this time I do not recall very clearly how I passed from the place of springs to the Garden, but I think it was oftenest by way of the Twilight Hills." Since the Twilight Hills that are here said to be the way to the Garden are depicted in **"The Mesa Trail"** as leading toward Shoshone Land, Austin's "Lost Garden" stands as another name for Shoshone Land.[70] Both, moreover, bear a striking resemblance to the Paiute Land of the Dead, where in his Great Revelation Wovoka traveled, talked to God, and saw "all the dead people," Indian and white alike, dancing in harmony.

Throughout the Bible, in both Old and New Testaments, the lost garden of Genesis is re-created in the prophetic vision of the city on a hill. Analogously, Austin's narrator, following the mesa trail, re-creates the past by refashioning the stories through which Euro- and Native Americans arrived at the present state of racial disharmony, and then forges on to recast the future. Narratively traveling to her own version of the mythical city by way of "streets of the mountains" that "lead to the citadel," she eventually arrives at "the little town of the Grape Vines," a city on a hill in which she finds a vision of peace and plenty like that found in both the Bible and Wovoka's Ghost Dance.[71]

Just as the spring in Shoshone Land is an incarnation of the fabled Hassaympa, so, too, is the vision offered in Austin's book an incarnation of Winnenap's vision. That this vision is delivered in a form modeled on the art of the basket maker Seyavi shows the nature of the book to be both syncretic art and syncretic prophecy. Just as she opens her book with an invitation to her readers to stop by for "news," so she closes with an invitation to "come away" to this paradise.[72] This final invitation is addressed directly to those who "have got nothing [they] did not sweat for," a characterization evoking the moment when God casts Adam and Eve out of the garden and tells them that henceforth they will have to work by the sweat of their brows. Entrance back into this lost garden, according to Christian faith, has been purchased by Jesus. Just as she transforms her conversion experience on Cottonwood Creek into an apparent reversal of the "Christianizing" of an Indian, so her reentry into a lost garden reinscribes the "Indianizing" of Christian belief as embodied in Wovoka's Great Revelation, which depicts the reunion of the living and the dead occurring on a regenerated earth.

At once syncretic and prophetic, Austin's mythic vision thus immortalizes its Paiute and Shoshone roots, not only in the form of individual people but also in the form of its telling. Austin translates their stories by imitating the native storyteller who makes sacred not only places but individual elders and their visions as well. But she is also translating *for* an audience whose minds are accustomed to the patterns and figures of biblical stories. The question of Austin's stance and method as translator is therefore inseparable from a consideration of her positionality and technique as prophet. She does not efface the Native American subject any more than the Hebrew prophet effaces the prophets preceding him: all seek to remind the people of the law, whether one conceives of that law as coming from Yahweh or from the Land.

These three chapters, then, form the crux of Austin's syncretic vision. Like Seyavi twining her baskets, Austin patterns her story after the land, fashioning it directly from material provided by the land and by the cultures it sustains. It is a story that seeks both to expose the history of white dealings with the Indians and at the same time to join the experience of Austin's own people with that of the native people and the land itself. Just as **"Shoshone Land"** immortalizes Winnenap's syncretic vision, **"The Basket Maker"** immortalizes Seyavi's artistic vision by utilizing the power of memory through storytelling. The chapter between them, **"My Neighbor's Field,"** shows Austin's own prophetic and syncretic art, her way of attempting through story to connect two seemingly irreconcilable worlds in a mythic vision that, while based on the pattern of the literal landscape, does not ignore but instead self-consciously revises actual historical conditions in order to suggest what is possible.

For Austin, Wovoka's Ghost Dance both epitomizes the magnitude of those historical conditions and embodies the path toward actualizing that vision. Like Moses carrying Joseph's memory in the bones of the dead prophet on the Hebrews' journey to the Promised Land, like Wovoka calling on the spirits of the dead ancestors, Austin carries the bones and spirits of Seyavi and Winnenap, of Wovoka and the biblical prophets, with her toward a new Promised Land.

Notes

1. The quotation in the chapter title is from Abraham J. Heschel, *The Prophets* (New York: Harper, 1962): "[T]he main task of prophetic thinking is to bring the world into divine focus" (24).

2. See, e.g., Pryse, introduction to *Stories,* xiv-xvii.

3. James C. Work, "The Moral in Mary Austin's *The Land of Little Rain,*" in *Women and Western American Literature,* ed. Helen Winter Stauffer and Susan J. Rosowski (Troy, N.Y.: Whitston, 1982), 297-99; Graulich, introduction to *Western Trails;* Pryse, introduction to *Stories;* Esther Lanigan Stineman, *Mary Austin: Song of a Maverick* (New Haven: Yale University Press, 1989); William J. Scheick, *The Ethos of Romance at the Turn of the Century* (Austin: University of Texas Press, 1994).

4. Shelley Armitage, "Mary Austin: Writing Nature," in *Wind's Trail: The Early Life of Mary Austin,* by Peggy Pond Church, ed. Shelley Armitage (Santa Fe: Museum of New Mexico Press, 1990), 28; Mary Austin, *The Land of Journey's Ending* (1924; reprint, Tucson: University of Arizona Press, 1983), xxvii-xxviii. In "The Feel of the Purposeful Earth: Mary Austin's Prophecy," Henry Smith discusses several of Austin's works, including *The Land of Little Rain,* as prophecy, which he defines simply as "insight into the state of [the author's] tribe, . . . out of [which he] speaks thoughts needful to he heard by his fellows"; see Henry Smith, "The Feel of the Purposeful Earth: Mary Austin's Prophecy," *New Mexico Quarterly* 1 (February 1931): 27-28. Smith goes on to discuss Austin's creation of a new mythology and that mythology's ties to the environment. Other critics—most notably Graulich—have highlighted the prophetic voice in Austin's writing, focusing on Austin's efforts as a pioneering woman writer to create "strong, prophetic women artists." My treatment of these issues differs from those of Smith and other critics in that I trace in depth the specific sources for that prophecy and mythology and add a distinctly religious dimension to their nature. In doing so, I am perhaps following in the footsteps of Mary Hallock Foote, an important western writer of Austin's time. In a personal letter written after reading Austin's sketches, Foote registered her sense that the young author had succeeded in writing "the unwritable" and telling "the untellable" (Graulich, introduction to *Western Trails,* 3, 26).

5. Austin, *EH* [*Earth Horizon*], 267; AU [Mary (Hunter) Austin Collection, Huntington Library, San Marino, California. Hereafter, items from the Austin Collection are designated AU followed by the item number.] 754-55; Mooney, *The Ghost Dance Religion,* 928 ff.

6. Mary Austin, *The Land of Little Rain,* in *Stories from the Country of Lost Borders,* ed. and intro. Marjorie Pryse (New Brunswick: Rutgers University Press, 1987), 3, 9. All subsequent references are from this edition and are abbreviated *LLR.*

7. Acts 9:3; AU box 124. All biblical verses, unless otherwise noted, are from the King James Bible. This is the version that Austin, brought up as an Illinois Methodist, probably knew best, although an inventory of her library at her home in Santa Fe after her death turned up several other versions (AU box 122, folder 10).

8. AU 267 (emphasis added).

9. Murray, *Forked Tongues,* 127.

10. The tenets of deep ecology I am thinking of here are (1) that humans live according to the bounds set by the ecosystem rather than, say, those dictated by national political and international economic systems; and (2) that humans act according to a principle of "biological egalitarianism," by which they make decisions according to the effects on the ecosystem rather than for their own convenience or desires. For a discussion of deep ecology, see George Sessions and Bill Duvall, *Deep Ecology* (Salt Lake City: Peregrine Smith, 1985).

11. *LLR,* 17.

12. J. Miller, "Basin Theology," 81.

13. Austin, *Stories,* 266.

14. *Strong's Exhaustive Concordance of the Bible* (Iowa Falls: Riverside Book and Bible House, n.d.), 910-12.

15. Genesis 49:22, 50:24. I use the wording of the New International Version here because it more boldly highlights the parallel I am drawing. The King James Version gives "bough" and "well" for "vine" and "spring," respectively.

16. Though her first story, "The Mother of Felipe," was published in the *Overland Monthly* in 1892, Austin was not regularly published until after she moved to Independence, beginning in 1897 with "The Conversion of Ah Lew Sing" and "The Wooing of the Señorita" in the *Overland Monthly.* See Mary Austin, "The Mother of Felipe," *Overland Monthly* 20 (November 1892): 534-38; idem, "The Conversion of Ah Lew Sing," *Overland Monthly* 30 (October 1897): 307-12; idem, "The Wooing of the Señorita," *Overland Monthly* 29 (March 1897): 258-63.

17. In "Mary Austin's Disfigurement of the Southwest in *The Land of Little Rain,*" *Western American Literature* 27 (1992): 37-46, William Scheick sees Austin's habit of using Indian names as concomitant with her "rhetorical disfigurement" of the land, both of which Scheick sees as evidence of her colonizing instinct. Scheick's use of "disfigurement," however, seems to imply a standard of literal accuracy in description, a standard that misconstrues the mythologizing impetus central to Austin's project. An important element of oral traditions, moreover, is the storyteller's adaptation of already existing stories. I would argue that this is the tradition in which Austin is participating, rather than that of a colonizing metanarrative legitimating Euro-American subjugation of the land and, with it, the Indian.

18. Austin, *Christ in Italy,* 71, x-xi, 66, 42-43.

19. Austin, *California: The Land of the Sun,* 3-4; Mooney, in Hittman, *Wovoka and the Ghost Dance,* 89.

20. Hittman, *Wovoka and the Ghost Dance,* 30-31.

21. Michael, "'At the Plow,'" 55.

22. Austin, *LLR,* 56, 55. It is interesting also to note here that, according to one anthropologist, the Dieguено believed man was first created in the desert to the east (cited in Applegate, "Native," 118).

23. In J. Miller, "Basin Theology," 81. According to Gilbert Natches, the same kind of association is captured in Northern Paiute words containing the common root *su: su-na-mi* (to think), *su-na-ha* (to breathe), *su-na-pe* (breath, spirit), and *su-ma-ye* (to remember); see Gilbert Natches, "Northern Paiute Verbs," *University of California Publications in American Anthropology and Ethnology* 20 (December 1923): 252.

24. "Becoming Indian Doctor," in Frederick Hulse, sera-Inyo: Owens Valley Fieldnotes (1935), Ethnological Documents Collection, University Archives, Bancroft Library, University of California, Berkeley, cu-23.1/152.4.

25. Austin, *LLR,* 57.

26. AU 359-60; Austin, *LLR,* 58.

27. Austin, *LLR,* 57.

28. Quoted in Mooney, *The Ghost Dance Religion,* 1055.

29. Austin, *LLR,* 60-61; E. Johnson, *Walker River Paiutes,* 45-46; Mooney, *The Ghost Dance Religion,* 765.

30. William Chalfant, "Medicine Men of the Eastern Mono," *Masterkey* 5 (July-August 1931): 53-54.

31. Austin, *LLR,* 61.

32. Hittman, *Wovoka and the Ghost Dance,* 75-77. Hittman goes on to comment on the political overtones of the event in the light of one source's observation that it took place on July 4: "Not only did Wovoka with his divinely-revealed weather

control powers implicitly gain control over all aspects of ranching and farming in the Walker River regional economy, the prophecy that ice would fall from the skies on that most important of all American holiday [*sic*] suggests a nascent attempt on this prophet's part to introduce a parallel ceremonial calendar." Such hidden political implications of Wovoka's syncretic religion are important in the context of this study in that Austin's syncretic vision likewise has an implicit political agenda concerning Native Americans.

33. J. Miller, "Basin Theology," 78.

34. Austin reinforces the allusion to the Exodus and the Hebrews' journey to Canaan throughout her book—e.g., by calling Owens Lake the "bitter lake," thereby evoking Marah (bitter), the Israelites' first source of water in the desert of Shur after crossing through the Red Sea; the bitter waters must be miraculously transformed before they can be drunk (Exod. 15:22-23). Austin may have chosen the name "bitter lake" because it was the site of an infamous battle in which nearly a whole Paiute village was killed, a battle she alludes to in her profile of Seyavi (*LLR*, 93).

35. Heschel, *The Prophets*, 24.

36. Although O'Grady and I differ in the contexts in which we place Austin—he focuses on liminality in terms of the shamanistic process as described by anthropologist Victor Turner—we agree fundamentally in our insistence that Austin be read in terms of spiritual autobiography. See John P. O'Grady, *Pilgrims to the Wild* (Salt Lake City: University of Utah Press, 1993); see also Victor Turner, *The Ritual Process: Structure and Anti-Structure* (Chicago: Aldine, 1969). Austin likewise positions several of the narrators and characters in her later works. To cite but a few examples, she features women dressed as men, or vice versa, in *The Basket Woman* and *Isidro,* and the Chisera in *The Arrow-Maker* lives apart and feels alienated from the rest of the tribe. In Austin's works, such characters always have special gifts or talents, and a struggle often takes place between the use of those gifts for the good of the tribe or group and the characters' individual need or desire for inclusion within the group.

37. Austin, *LLR*, 3.

38. Ibid., 65-68 (emphasis added). Scheick uses Austin's claim of being "a mere recorder" to support his argument that she "disfigures" the landscape and rhetorically colonizes it, which, in my opinion, again misses the mythologizing impetus central to the work. I do grant, however, that Austin seems to be creatively rearranging the geography

of the Owens Valley to suit her purposes. A "Squaw Mountain" can be found, at least on modern maps, in the White Mountains north of Cerro Gordo, the model for Jimville, but there is no site with that name in the vicinity of Cerro Gordo itself. There is, however, an unnamed gulch above Cerro Gordo that, to my eye, at least, looks as though it could have "spilled" the town into place. William Michael, Owens Valley historian and director of the Eastern California Museum in Independence, knows of no mining activity historically occurring in the area of the current Squaw Mountain (personal communication).

39. Austin, *LLR*, 75.

40. I Kings 21:29.

41. I Kings 17:1; Hittman, *Wovoka and the Ghost Dance,* 67-68.

42. Austin, *LLR*, 76.

43. Ibid., 77.

44. There are many versions of the myth; the one I summarize here appears in Julian Steward, "Myths of the Owens Valley Paiutes," *University of California Publications in American Anthropology and Ethnography* 34 (1934-36): 355-440. Although some of the other versions diverge in interesting ways from Steward's, most share the basic plot outlines recounted here.

45. Austin, *LLR*, 77.

46. Austin's "wild almond" is most probably *Prunus fasciculata,* commonly called "desert almond." My thanks to John O'Grady for making this identification.

47. Austin, *LLR*, 78, 96; Exodus 3:13-14.

48. See, e.g., Lalla Scott, *Karnee: A Paiute Narrative* (Reno: University of Nevada Press, 1966), 79, which says that the Paiutes "like to name their girls for flowers"; and Sarah Winnemucca Hopkins, *Life among the Piutes: Their Wrongs and Claims* (1883; reprint, Bishop, Calif.: Chalfant, 1969), 46 ff., which also discusses this practice.

49. Austin, *LLR*, 78.

50. Exodus 3:5.

51. Austin, *LLR*, 75; Ezekiel 39:3-5, 40:2 ff.

52. I might also note here that the destruction of Magog by fire, the fate told to Ezekiel in the verses immediately following those from chapter 39 (cited above), is the very kind of apocalyptic prophecy made by Wovoka. In Paiute Ghost Dance songs, the whirlwind is the usual cleansing agent, although fire and flood appear in some versions of the prophecy.

53. Ezekiel 43:10-12

54. Austin, *LLR,* 94.

55. Ezekiel 47:21-22, 44:10, 48:11-14.

56. Ezekiel 45:1-3.

57. Ezekiel 45:9, 47 ff.

58. See the *Inyo Independent* editions of April 18, 1874, May 1, 1875, and May 27, 1876. Diaz and several other Paiutes were eventually able to secure legal title to their small allotments before 1900.

59. Austin, *LLR,* 80.

60. Ibid., 83.

61. J. Miller, "Basin Theology," 81.

62. Melody Graulich suggests that Austin's "trail metaphors always stress connections between places, people, cultures" (introduction to *Western Trails,* 4). In "Mesa Trail," *San Jose Studies* 21 (1995): 44-57, David Robertson provides valuable insight, leavened with humor, into the function and significance of the trail in *The Land of Little Rain,* extending his observations into Austin's potential significance as a figure within the environmentalist community.

63. Austin, *LLR,* 98; Austin, *Lost Borders,* in *Stories,* 160 (all subsequent references are to this edition and are abbreviated *LB*); Pryse, introduction to *Stories,* xxix; Austin, *LLR,* 3.

64. Austin, *EH,* 289.

65. Austin, *LLR,* 97. In her introduction to *Western Trails,* Melody Graulich traces the many women, native and white, who are models for Austin's women prophets, focusing primarily on Austin's literary representation of them.

66. Austin, *EH,* 286-87.

67. This excerpt from "The Lost Garden" comes from the Austin Collection (AU 318) and is reproduced by permission of the Huntington Library, San Marino, California.

68. Austin, *LLR,* 78.

69. Campbell Grant, *The Rock Paintings of the Chumash* (Berkeley: University of California Press, 1966), 67-68.

70. Austin, *LLR,* 83.

71. Ibid., 103.

72. Ibid., 4, 149.

Works Cited

Applegate, Richard. "Native California Concepts of the Afterlife." In *Flowers of the Wind: Papers on Ritual, Myth, and Symbolism in California and the Southwest,* ed. Thomas C. Blackburn, 105-19. Socorro, N.M.: Ballena Press, 1977.

Armitage, Shelley. "Mary Austin: Writing Nature." In *Wind's Trail: The Early Life of Mary Austin,* by Peggy Pond Church. Ed. Shelley Armitage, 3-31. Santa Fe: Museum of New Mexico Press, 1990.

Austin, Mary. *The Arrow-Maker.* Rev. ed. 1911. Boston: Houghton, 1915.

———. *The Basket Woman: A Book of Indian Tales for Children.* 1904. Reprint. Boston: Houghton, 1910.

———. *California: The Land of the Sun.* New York: Macmillan, 1914.

———. *Christ in Italy.* New York: Duffield, 1912.

———. "The Conversion of Ah Lew Sing." *Overland Monthly* 30 (October 1897): 307-12.

———. "The Divorcing of Sina." *Sunset* 40 (January-June 1918): 26.

———. *Earth Horizon.* New York: Literary Guild, 1932.

———. *Isidro.* Boston: Houghton, 1904.

———. *The Land of Journey's Ending.* 1924. Reprint. Tucson: University of Arizona Press, 1983.

———. "The Mother of Felipe." *Overland Monthly* 20 (November 1892): 534-38.

———. *Stories from the Country of Lost Borders.* Ed. and intro. Marjorie Pryse. New Brunswick: Rutgers University Press, 1987.

———. *Western Trails.* Ed. Melody Graulich. Reno: University of Nevada Press, 1987.

———. "The Wooing of the Señorita." *Overland Monthly* 29 (March 1897): 258-63.

Austin, Mary (Hunter), Collection. Huntington Library, San Marino, California.

Chalfant, William. "Medicine Men of the Eastern Mono." *Masterkey* 5 (July-August 1931): 50-54.

Grant, Campbell. *The Rock Paintings of the Chumash.* Berkeley: University of California Press, 1966.

Graulich, Melody. Introduction to *Western Trails,* by Mary Austin, 1-28. Reno: University of Nevada Press, 1987.

Heschel, Abraham J. *The Prophets.* New York: Harper, 1962.

Hittman, Michael. *Wovoka and the Ghost Dance.* Carson City: Grace Dangberg Foundation, 1990.

Hopkins, Sarah Winnemucca. *Life among the Piutes: Their Wrongs and Claims.* 1883. Reprint. Bishop, Calif.: Chalfant, 1969.

Hulse, Frederick. SERA-Inyo: Owens Valley Fieldnotes (1935). Ethnological Documents Collection, University Archives, Bancroft Library, University of California, Berkeley. CU-23.1, nos. 88-98, 104, 149-55.

Johnson, Edward. *Walker River Paiutes: A Tribal History*. Schurz, Nev.: Walker River Paiute Tribe, 1975.

Michael, William H. "'At the Plow and in the Harvest Field': Indian Conflict and Accommodation in the Owens Valley 1860-1880." Master's thesis, University of Oklahoma, 1993.

Miller, Jay. "Basin Theology and Religion: A Comparative Study of Power (*Puha*)." *Journal of California and Great Basin Anthropology* 5 (1983): 66-86.

Mooney, James. *The Ghost Dance Religion and the Sioux Outbreak of 1890*. Fourteenth Annual Report (Part 2) of the Bureau of American Ethnology to the Smithsonian Institution, 1892-1893. Washington, D.C.: Government Printing Office, 1896.

Murray, David. *Forked Tongues: Speech, Writing, and Representation in North American Indian Texts*. London: Pinter, 1991.

Natches, Gilbert. "Northern Paiute Verbs." *University of California Publications in American Anthropology and Ethnology* 20 (December 1923): 245-59.

O'Grady, John P. *Pilgrims to the Wild*. Salt Lake City: University of Utah Press, 1993.

"Osakie Legend of the Ghost Dance." *Journal of American Folklore* 12 (1899): 284-86.

Pryse, Marjorie. Introduction to *Stories from the Country of Lost Borders,* by Mary Austin, vii-xxxv. New Brunswick: Rutgers University Press, 1987.

Robertson, David. "Mesa Trail." *San Jose Studies* 21 (1995): 44-57.

Scheick, William J. *The Ethos of Romance at the Turn of the Century*. Austin: University of Texas Press, 1994.

——. "Mary Austin's Disfigurement of the Southwest in *The Land of Little Rain*." *Western American Literature* 27 (1992): 37-46.

Scott, Lalla, *Karnee: A Paiute Narrative*. Reno: University of Nevada Press, 1966.

"Self Defense." *Inyo Independent,* December 5, 1890, 3.

Sessions, George, and Bill Duvall. *Deep Ecology*. Salt Lake City: Peregrine Smith, 1985.

Smith, Henry. "The Feel of the Purposeful Earth: Mary Austin's Prophecy." *New Mexico Quarterly* 1 (February 1931): 17-33.

Steward, Julian. "Myths of the Owens Valley Paiutes." *University of California Publications in American Anthropology and Ethnography* 34 (1934-36): 355-440.

Stineman, Esther Lanigan. *Mary Austin: Song of a Maverick*. New Haven: Yale University Press, 1989.

Strong's Exhaustive Concordance of the Bible. Iowa Falls: Riverside Book and Bible House, n.d.

Turner, Victor. *The Ritual Process: Structure and Anti-Structure*. Chicago: Aldine, 1969.

Work, James C. "The Moral in Mary Austin's *The Land of Little Rain*." In *Women and Western American Literature,* ed. Helen Winter Stauffer and Susan J. Rosowski, 297-309. Troy, N.Y.: Whitston, 1982.

Anna Carew-Miller (essay date 1998)

SOURCE: Carew-Miller, Anna. "Mary Austin's Nature: Refiguring Tradition through the Voices of Identity." In *Reading the Earth: New Directions in the Study of Literature and Environment,* edited by Michael P. Branch, Rochelle Johnson, Daniel Patterson, and Scott Slovic, pp. 79-95. Moscow, Idaho: University of Idaho Press, 1998.

[*In the following essay, Carew-Miller focuses on the "narrative voice" Austin created and employed in her work, in an effort to understand, not "her struggles as a woman writer at the turn of the century," as many previous critics have done, but "how her representations of nature reveal her sense of place within the natural world."*]

Mary Austin's notoriety died with her in 1934, and her writings, well known during her lifetime, remained relatively obscure until recent years. Much of Austin scholarship has focused on her significant contribution to a women's tradition of nature writing and, in particular, on her proto-feminist characterizations of the natural world. Austin's life has received as much attention as her work; many critics read her work as a revelation of her struggles as a woman writer at the turn of the century.[1] Biographical criticism of this sort purports to look for the *real* Mary Austin, the truth about her life. However, I believe richer readings of Austin's work can be attained through persona criticism, which is concerned not so much with biography as with reading the literary self-constructions of the persona, or voice, a writer uses to narrate his or her work.[2] The persona or narrative voice is created by a writer's psychology and history but doesn't add up to a historical figure. Rather than read Austin's work for information about her struggles as a woman or for insight into her contributions to the field of nature writing, I propose to read Austin's narrative voice in order to arrive at a clearer understanding of how her representations of nature reveal her sense of place within the natural world. I want to explore how her narrative voice reflects her experience of nonhuman nature.

Austin scholars have frequently made the connection between Austin's writing and her relationship with her mother, finding it to be a damper on her creativity.[3] I will argue instead that Austin's struggle to define herself against her mother and the standards of femininity her mother represented gave Austin's writing its power and purpose, giving her narrative voice the idiosyncratic subjectivity that readers have found so compelling and unusual in the genre of nature writing. Rather than attempt to psychoanalyze Austin with details from her biography, we can use her biographical information to examine the inflections in Austin's narrative voice—to see, on the one hand, how the pain in Austin's life wrote through her and, on the other hand, how she used her life experiences to textually represent nature in a new way. Only by understanding how Austin's life shaped her literary methodology will we begin to understand her innovations in the genre of nature writing.

What most interests me in Austin's nature writing is the tension that is produced by the dichotomy in Austin's narrative voice. Austin's voice can be read as *two* voices, one that confidently overturns tradition and believes in her intuitive connection to nature, and one—which Austin works at rejecting—that feels trapped by traditions of Victorian womanhood and fears the natural world. What gives her writing its power is the pull between these two narrative voices. In her autobiography, *Earth Horizon* (1932), Austin labeled these voices "I-Mary" and "Mary-by-herself," respectively. I-Mary is Austin's voice of public performance, confidently narrating most of her published work. Mary-by-herself is the private voice of Austin's journals, poetry, and letters, which also appears as a shadow in her published works. Mary-by-herself speaks for Austin's fearfulness, and I-Mary speaks for her complicated desires. With I-Mary's voice, Austin successfully feminizes the masculine genre of nature writing by claiming that intuition is as valid a means of understanding the natural world as observation, by turning the tropes of "Mother Nature" into powerful goddesses, and by inventing a female character who embodies an ideal relationship to the natural world. However, I-Mary's voice is shadowed by that of Mary-by-herself, and through reading this voice, we are led to the source of her creative energy: her painful relationship with her mother.

Austin's mother, Susannah Hunter, kept her emotional distance; she was critical of her daughter's attempts to be a wife and mother and made little effort to support Austin's career as a writer.[4] During her mother's lifetime, Austin's fear of rejection by her mother appears to have had an enervating effect, limiting her creativity and ambition. This fear is transcribed by the voice of Mary-by-herself into ominous representations of a female nature, which are found most often in her private papers. The fear of some nameless threat, a brooding presence that Mary-by-herself experiences over and over again, mimics Austin's own fear of repeated rejection by her mother. Moreover, just as Austin returned

again and again to her mother, hoping her mother's response to her would change, Mary-by-herself repeatedly returns to nature, in spite of her fear. However, throughout Austin's writing career, her longing for connection with her mother, so tied to her fear of rejection, is slowly transformed into I-Mary's desire for communion with nature.

Austin pushed the voice of Mary-by-herself to the periphery of her writing as she put more distance between her own life and the world of her mother. With her marriage in 1891 and birth of her daughter in 1892, Austin seems to have separated herself from her mother enough to begin writing. Her first published story, **"The Mother of Felipe,"** appeared in *The Overland Monthly* in 1892. Austin recalled her early work in the later *Earth Horizon*: "It was as I-Mary walking a log over the creek, that Mary-by-herself could not have managed, that I wrote two slender little sketches" (231). Simultaneously, she grew in confidence as a writer as she became more successful, and the voice of I-Mary pulled more strongly against the fears of Mary-by-herself. Austin produced her most powerful nature writing during the period between Susannah Hunter's death and Austin's own relocation from the foothills of the Sierra Nevada to Carmel, California—roughly 1896 to 1906. This writing is marked by the tension between the energies of the newly liberated voice of I-Mary and the nearly vanquished doubts of Mary-by-herself.

During this period, Austin transformed her fear into desire and used it as a creative force; seven years after her mother's death, her first book, *The Land of Little Rain,* was published. We can hear I-Mary as the knowledgeable voice in *The Land of Little Rain,* the voice of union with the landscape, of collectivity and creativity, the voice of desire for connection. Desire, for I-Mary, is not predicated on emptiness and hunger, but on abundant creative energy and appetite for connection. "Far from being detached," she writes in *Everyman's Genius,* "I have so excellent an appetite for life that if there are any experiences that a woman, remaining within the law and a reasonable margin of respectability, might have, I am still hopeful of being able to compass them" (184). This is the authentic voice of the woman unbound by social restrictions, the voice of subjective authority, hungry for experience and privileged knowledge.

In this first book, *The Land of Little Rain* (1903), Austin crafted a textual persona much different from those typically found in nature writing texts; I-Mary speaks in a highly personal voice and shares an extremely subjective vision of the desert landscape. This voice also narrates several of Austin's later works, including *Lost Borders* (1909) and *The Flock* (1906). In these later works, Austin continued to develop an alternative woman's tradition of nature writing by transforming the conventional metaphors for a female nature.[5] She replaces the conventional tropes—the bounteous mother earth and seductive nymph—with a wilder goddess, frequently representing the landscape of the desert as a lioness. In Austin's writing, this version of a female nature is powerful and dangerous. Only women who have rejected Victorian codes of conduct for ladies can live unmolested by this lioness because their relationship to nature is one of connection and communion. Austin created a character that embodied these ideals, the chisera, who provides Austin with a model for herself as a woman writer. The chisera has an intuitive knowledge of nature and a constant desire for fulfillment through close interaction with the natural world.

Austin could not always successfully shed her identity as a Victorian lady in order to become her more idealized self in the desert, particularly as a young woman who hadn't yet become a successful writer. But before examining Austin's transformative refigurations of the wild, we should listen to the voice of Mary-by-herself, through which we can hear fear in Austin's response to the wild. Mary-by-herself is diminished by the land, rendered helpless by her terrors. Melody Graulich observes: "Mary-by-herself is partially the poignant offspring of Austin's conflicted relationship with her mother, partially the outcast from social constructions of femininity that left her feeling as if she failed as a woman" (379). Perhaps this is the voice that feels the restrictions of Victorian ladyhood most severely. Austin recalls in her unpublished essay, "The Friend in the Wood": "Looking back, I realize that those years in which fear hung on the fringes of my consciousness and occasionally became a factor in all outdoor experience, coincided with the years in which I had lived most actively in my life as a woman" (194). These were her years in the land of little rain, in which she negotiated the end of her painful relationship with her mother, as well as a troubled marriage and her own trying experiences as the mother of a mentally disabled child.[6]

We first hear the fear this version of a fierce nature evoked in the journals—now called the *Tejon Notebook*—that she kept during the first few years when she lived with her mother and brother in Kern County. There she wrote of the land as sometimes having a Gothic severity and grim quality: "There are times when everything seems to have a sinister kind of life. It shows its teeth to me. At other times, it is merely beautiful and gentle." This image begins to be more clearly fleshed out in later writing. Austin's fear of the wild emerges when we hear Mary-by-herself revealing that her longing for connection and communion to the land is met by a lioness whose indifference and ferocity frighten her. Her unpublished poem "Inyo" includes a fierce rendition of the lioness, in which the "untamed and barren" valley is "Like some great lioness beside the river

/ With furies flaming in her half-shut eyes." In Austin's work, the lioness appears only in connection to this particular landscape—the high desert and mountains, where Austin lived during the era that the voice of Mary-by-herself was strongest.

Because Austin worked to control her fear while living in the mountains and desert of California, finding evidence of Mary-by-herself is difficult. Speaking as I-Mary, she suppresses the voice of Mary-by-herself when she describes her first encounter with the desert that was to become her home. In the third person voice of *Earth Horizon,* she writes: "All that long stretch between Salt Lake and Sacramento Pass, the realization of presence which the desert was ever after to have for her, grew upon her mind, not only the warm tingling presence of wooded hills and winding creeks, but something brooding and aloof, charged with dire indifference, of which she was never afraid for an instant" (182). I-Mary's voice in *Earth Horizon* can describe what might be frightening, but cannot admit to being afraid. Only privately could she recall these early experiences with the voice of Mary-by-herself. In **"The Friend in the Wood"** (intended to be a private autobiography of her relationship with nature), she describes her introduction to the desert and mountains while also admitting to her fear:

> There was one special time of its coming that stands as the type of all terror. That was after I had left the pleasant middle-western wood where I began, and had come to the desert outposts of the eastern slope of the high Sierras. There, astonishingly, with cold sickness fear had come to me in flashes. Walking or riding, out of utter desuetude, instantly the land would bare its teeth at me, crouch, tighten for the spring, and before the sweat of terror was dried, fall into desuetude again.
>
> (190)

Recalling her young womanhood in this essay, Austin allows the voice of Mary-by-herself to reveal her terrified reaction to a natural world she found threatening.

Less typically, this sense of fear intrudes on a public text in a description of the Sierra Madre mountains in *California: Land of the Sun*:

> [T]he land rested. And all in the falling of a leaf, in the scuttle of a horned toad, in the dust of the roadway, it lifted into eerie life. It bared its teeth; the veil of the mountain was rent. Nothing changed, nothing stirred or glimmered, but the land had spoken. As if it had taken a step forward, as if a hand were raised, the mountain [Sierra Madre] stood over us. And then it sank again. . . . Shall not the mother of the land do what she will with it?
>
> (39-40)

The lioness broods and suddenly turns, repeating the image of bared teeth. Significantly, this is the Madre (mother) mountain, unpredictable and unyielding, who in her beauty might nonetheless turn and bite. As articulated by Mary-by-herself, nature threatens violence on her human children. Intruding on an otherwise serene recollection of the beauties of the California landscape, the voice of Mary-by-herself reveals its still-potent fear of nature and its feelings of helplessness and passivity.[7]

With the voice of I-Mary, Austin consciously turned her back on a rational, science-based knowledge of nature in exchange for knowledge based on intuitive readings of the natural world. In *Earth Horizon,* Austin rejects what she called the "male ritual of rationalization in favor of a more direct intuitional attack" (15). This rejection reveals Austin's own feelings of connection to the natural world. In **"The Friend in the Wood,"** she tries to explain how she was umbilically connected to the land:

> Even stick and stone, as well as bush and weed, are discovered to be charged with an intense secret life of their own; the sap courses, the stones vibrate with ion-shaking rhythms of energy, as I too shake inwardly to the reverberating tread of life and time. . . . Now and again I have that sharp impress of virtue in a plant or beauty in a flower, of which the Indians say, "It speaks to me . . . I begin to be aware of the soundless orchestration of activities beyond the ordinary reach of sense, the delicate unclasping of leaves of grass, the lapsing of dry petals into dust, the dust itself impregnate [sic] by the farthest star.
>
> (196)

Rather than being a mere objective observer of the natural world, I-Mary claims that she is part of this world, and that what she writes is shaped by her intimacy with it. Being subjective, for Austin, does not delegitimize her nature writing, as some critics have claimed, but instead serves as the very quality which gives her writing both authority and authenticity.[8]

How the land affects her, how she personally responds to the land: these, Austin claims, are the legitimate sources of her knowledge of the land about which she writes. Looking back on her career in her autobiography, Austin complains about how her approach has been misunderstood: "All the public expects of the experience of practicing Naturists is the appearance, the habits, the incidents of the wild; when the Naturist reports upon himself, it is mistaken for poeticizing" (*Earth Horizon* 188). She insists that she is not "poeticizing," that is, using nature to inspire her expression of emotion. This is a fairly radical departure from the literary status quo, as Austin began writing in the age of realism and naturalism, when nature writing began to be taken to task for its scientific inaccuracies.[9] Austin claims that she gives her readers an authentic version of the natural world because she uses the experiences of her body and emotions as the filter through which the natural world is distilled.

As I-Mary, Austin separates herself not only from the largely male tradition of nature writing, but also from most other women in her ability to connect with the natural world. In **"The Friend in the Wood,"** she explains, "Women, I suspect, withdraw themselves from the appeal of the Wild because it distracts them from that compacted rounding of themselves which is indispensable to the feminine achievement" (187). Women, according to Austin, are frequently too caught up with the business of being an ornament to male culture to pay much attention to nature. In *Lost Borders,* she elaborates on those kind of women: "Women, unless they have very large and simple souls, need cover; clothes, you know, and furniture, social observances to screen them, conventions to get behind; life when it leaps upon them, large and naked, shocks them into disorder" (165). For Austin, Mary-by-herself belongs to this category.

Elsewhere, Austin has labeled such women bound by convention "ladies," finding them inferior to authentic women—women with "large and simple souls"—who live free from social restrictions and enjoy a powerful connection to nature. In an unpublished article entitled "If Women Did," she explains her belief that there exists for every woman, underneath her construction as a lady, a distant memory of her power as a woman. Austin asserts this power as a kind of primal source that connects women to the spirit of the earth:

> Among millions of modern women the cosmos still works, the *wokonda* [spirit] of the earth is a felt activity. But among other millions these influences have been cut off by the intervention of the falsely flattering persuasion of their ladyhood. Around the natural activities of women has been erected a series of reactions and inhibitions based upon the exemptions of their preciousness, of a commendable fragility and withdrawal.

Authentic women who reject the limitations and protections of "ladyhood" are not afraid to absorb the wild through their skin, to feel its rhythms. I-Mary is this kind of authentic woman, connected to the spirit of the earth through the experiences of her body and emotions.

With I-Mary, Austin abandoned her mother, rejecting her mother's choices and persisting in becoming a writer. In the *Tejon Notebook,* Austin puts her mother in the category of "ladyhood" but places herself in her category of natural woman: "I think the openness of everything scares mother. She has always lived in towns. And it frets her that I am not homesick. I can not make her understand that I am never homesick out of doors." Unlike her mother, I-Mary needs no shelter but the sky, nor any of the accessories of ladyhood in order to be at home there.

Models for I-Mary, women with "large and simple souls," can be found in the characters of Walking Woman in *Lost Borders* and Seyavi in *The Land of*

Little Rain. More than fictional characters, these were women Austin knew in Kern County who became the basis for Austin's chisera figure—a wise woman, or prophet, who appears throughout Austin's work.[10] Austin describes this type of character in *The Flock* as someone who had made some "acknowledgment of the power of the Wild to effect a social divorcement without sensible dislocation" (261). Both Seyavi and Walking Woman had separated themselves from the Victorian world which confined women, but they were not lost; they were free to explore their desire.

The Walking Woman is free from the social constraints that normally bind women. Faith Jaycox writes that this figure is "the precise opposite of a confined woman: the endless mobility . . . is a powerful symbolic challenge to the enforced physical restriction of women at a moment in history when they had only recently worn clothes designed to suggest that they 'glided' rather than walked on two feet" (9). Austin explains how her character shed the conventions of ladyhood to become a woman: "She had walked off all sense of society-made values, and, knowing the best when the best came to her, was able to take it" (*Lost Borders* 261). The Walking Woman's freedom is not based on sexual neutrality; she has had the experiences of female sexuality and knows her body as a woman through love and motherhood, but has rejected the constraints of ladyhood. Yet the Walking Woman acquires her freedom only in the loss of her man and child, what David Wyatt calls an "erotic loss" that she replaces with desire; her walking marks her physical relationship with the female earth (90). She connects to the landscape by resituating her human desires within the geography inscribed by her footsteps. By walking, she has been "sobered and healed . . . by the large soundness of nature" (257). For Austin, the Walking Woman possesses a utopian relationship with nature, in which desire makes possible communion with the landscape.

Like the Walking Woman, Seyavi, the Paiute basket maker, is self-sufficient and has reduced her needs and wants without eliminating desire.[11] While the Walking Woman provides Austin with a model for the ideal intuitive relationship to nature, Seyavi takes Austin a step further and provides her with an intuitive form of creativity, of art, and for I-Mary, of writing. Seyavi's creativity comes not from the mind, but the body: "Every Indian woman is an artist,—sees, feels, creates, but does not philosophize about her processes. Seyavi's bowls are wonders of technical precision, inside and out, the palm finds no fault with them, but the subtlest appeal is in the sense that warns of humanness in the way the design spreads into the flare of the bowl" (*Land* [*The Land of Little Rain*] 106). Seyavi transforms the impersonal geometry of design by weaving into her baskets her experiences of loss and love. Austin believes that rather than "philosophizing" about her cre-

ativity, Seyavi is connected to a tribal consciousness and her own unconscious, which invigorates her work—a work that moves according to the rhythms of her body and the rhythms of the desert landscape.[12]

Seyavi achieves what Austin desires for herself as an artist: to be so connected to the spirit of the land (the *wokonda*) that she can write through her body, not her mind. Only then will experience supersede analysis in her understanding and representation of the natural. Desire, Austin reveals, enables Seyavi's communion with the life of the land and her creativity. Authentic art must be created by body and emotion because, according to Austin, we create art in order to satisfy desire: "Seyavi made baskets for the satisfaction of desire,—for that is a house-bred theory of art that makes anything more of it" (*Land* 107). In Austin's "natural" theory of art (as opposed to "house-bred" theories), creativity is motivated by the complex matrix of emotion and body that creates desire, at once erotic, primal, and innocent. I-Mary is modeled on Seyavi; her creative power, in which the body and emotion are more important than the intellect, is driven by desire.

Not surprisingly, the emotion that dominates I-Mary's voice is desire, the craving for fulfillment of body and soul through connection to the land. In *Lost Borders,* she admits: "Only Heaven, who made my Heart, knows why it should have become a pit, bottomless and insatiable" (174). For example, in *The Land of Little Rain,* I-Mary's voice admits to desire, to needing more, to longing to satisfy her "keen hunger," to wanting to know her way into the secret heart of the unresponsive desert (108). This becomes clearest in the passage about her desire to learn the "secrets of plant powers": "I remember very well when I first came upon a wet meadow of *yerba mansa,* not knowing its name or use. It *looked* potent; the cool, shiny leaves, the succulent pink stems and fruity bloom. A little touch, a hint, a word, and I should have known what use to put them to. So I felt, unwilling to leave it until we had come to an understanding" (144).[13] For Austin, such knowledge is not acquired through study but through her desire for "an understanding," for some sort of intuitive connection.

I-Mary's desire for connection appears in various depictions of nature, some of which make clear that this nature is female. At times, such metaphorical transformations border on the homoerotic, as in this passage from *California: Land of the Sun* (1914):

> A pomegranate is the one thing that makes me understand what a pretty woman is to some men. . . . The flower of the pomegranate has the crumpled scarlet of lips that find their excuse in simply being scarlet and folded like the petals of a flower; and then the fruit, warm from the sunny wall, faintly odorous, dusky flushed! It is so tempting when broken open . . . the

rich heart colour, and the pleasant, uncloying, sweet, sub-acid taste.

(90)

Here, I-Mary evokes the seductive power of women in a highly eroticized image of female genitalia and claims to understand women's power of seduction as a man would, with physical hunger for a taste of beauty.[14] Rarely does I-Mary's desire take on such an erotic form. More frequent in Austin's writing are passages which blend mildly sensual images of the landscape with a sense of loss. Speaking of the "musky and sweet" gilia blooming on her path in her unpublished story, "The Lost Garden," she writes: "Some scents there are that come to us so freighted with a sense of remembered beauty as sets the mind agrope for a warrant for it . . . sweet with the pressage [sic] of satisfaction" (2).[15] In this image, beauty and desire come together in nostalgia and longing. John O'Grady explains: "Desire in Austin's work is always predicated upon loss—lost borders, lost loves, lost lives" (129). At the same time, the gilia represents not simply a yearning for remembered beauty, but a living beauty that foretells the coming fulfillment of desire. In these eroticized images, I-Mary's desire for a connection with a feminized nature is made possible.

I-Mary also transforms Mary-by-herself's lioness from a representation of nature as frightening into a figure of desire, like the pomegranate and gilia. This transformation suggests I-Mary's desire not only for connection to the feminine in nature, but also for completion of herself as a woman: mythical, powerful, fulfilled. Perhaps the best known rendition of the lioness appears merged with an image of Austin's idealized self early on in *Lost Borders*:

> If the desert were a woman, I know well what she would be like: deep-breasted, broad in the hips, tawny, with tawny hair, great masses of it lying smooth along her perfect curves, full lipped like a sphynx, but not heavy-lidded like one, eyes sane and steady as the polished jewel of her skies, such a countenance as should make men serve without desiring, such a largeness to her mind as should make their sins of no account, passionate, but not necessitous, patient—and you could not move her, no, not if you had all the earth to give, so much as one tawny hair's-breadth beyond her own desires.

(160)

As photos of Austin reveal, this goddess even looks like Austin, sharing her thick tawny hair and full lips. Now a sphynx, this lioness represents female strength, passion, and self-assuredness. Both seductive and indifferent, this goddess is powerfully compelling.

In relation to men, I-Mary's lioness is far different than the one that confronts Mary-by-herself. Gone are the images of bared teeth; instead of an aggressor, the sphynx-lioness is seductive but not a seductress; she is basically indifferent to the male desire to possess her. This version of the lioness powerfully toys with the men who want to control her and finally rejects them. She seduces the male sojourning in the desert; in the short story, **"The Hoodoo of the Minnietta,"** a man is described as caught in her power: "[T]he desert had him, cat-like, between her paws" (*Lost* [*Lost Borders*] 164). In *The Flock*, she awaits the emotional disintegration of the man faced with her indifference: "But over the faces of the men whose life is out of doors . . . comes the curious expression which is chiefly the want of all expressiveness. . . . It is as if one saw the tawny land above them couched, lion-natured, lapping, lapping" (256). Men clearly have no control of this creature. In her novella, *Cactus Thorn*, she explains the hypnotic power of the desert wild over men: "[O]ne perceives the lure of the desert to be the secret lure of fire, to which in rare moments men have given themselves as to a goddess" (8). This goddess is the sphynx-lioness who embodies desire.

With the lioness, Austin not only represents her own fears and desires, but she also uses this metaphor to critique the traditional (male) relationship to nature as a power struggle through which men try to control nature. Austin observes that rather than a love of the land, men have "the love of mastery, which for the most part moves men into new lands" (*Lost* 192). For Austin, this is not only the "mastery" of dams and fences, but also the scientific approach to the natural world that tries to diminish its power by dissecting it intellectually. For men, the desire that the land stirs is for possession and control; the result, according to Austin, is eternal damnation, for the men who face the lioness are destroyed by their unsatisfied longing. For authentic women, the desire that the land stirs is for connection. Austin's ideal women come to know the land through intuition and the experiences of their bodies—think of the Walking Woman's footsteps, Seyavi's baskets, or the written image of I-Mary's pomegranate. Their desire is fulfilled not through an actual embrace of the female body by the land, but through the creative processes this feminized nature stimulates in women.[16] When Austin merges the sphynx with I-Mary, she is merging the voices of desire and creativity, and placing both out of men's grasp.

Austin's desire for a connection to this feminized land is her desire for both the creative fulfillment of self as well as a connection with the maternal, which reenacts her relationship with her mother—whose approval she could never win, whose affection seemed so tentative. In her autobiography, Austin explains that she was an unwanted child, who "was not desired, not, in fact, welcome" (*Earth Horizon* 32). Austin's experience of her mother was one of longing: a hunger for a portion of herself, a reflection of herself in her mother's love and reassurance. Austin depicts her mother as a woman who demanded her free-spirited daughter's conformity to the restrictions of Victorian femininity and judged her harshly when she failed to meet this standard. This experience created Mary-by-herself.

For Mary-by-herself, union with the maternal is a ferocious devouring of the child by the mother. I-Mary replaces longing for the union with the mother with a desire for an umbilical connection with a female-gendered nature that will animate her own creative processes. Elizabeth Ammons observes: "As Austin's language suggests . . . her need for art to be physical, to hold the body as well as the spirit, contains powerful erotic longing. Particularly, her need suggests the ferocious hunger of the infant, in this case the daughter, for the unconditional and intensely physical love of the mother" (90). Austin seems to have experienced her own mother as either a brooding presence that motivated her fear, or an absence that stimulated her desire. Austin herself recognized that desire is stimulated by absence and that hunger for connection creates art. Commenting in *Everyman's Genius* on how many artists are unwanted children, Austin writes, "this craving for communication, this tormenting desire to tell, is merely the emotional register of the inward drive which is indispensible to all creative success" (111). Therefore, I-Mary's creativity and desire for connection depend on Mary-by-herself's longing and fear of abandonment.

We can see that Austin's efforts to write nature emerge from a complex matrix, and her desire to write is complicated by the tension between being the woman she wanted to be and bearing the burden of ladyhood that her mother had passed on to her. Divided by the fetters of convention and her own desires for communion with the female embrace of the land, her narrative voice is fueled by the tension this division creates. Austin takes as the touchstone of her work her own experience of the desert and mountains. In this landscape so indifferent to human concerns, Austin replaces the tropes of the nymph and earth mother with the lioness, transforming the notion of nature's female power into something fierce and passionate. Austin's dual response to these qualities marks her narrative voice, refiguring the desert and mountains of the Southwest as well as the shape of the natural history essay. Austin's writing looks forward to the subjective visions found in the work of Annie Dillard, Barry Lopez, and others, who also narrate their relationships to the natural world through a web of unnamed private experience and history.

Notes

1. See Ammons, Fink, Graulich, Langlois, Lanigan, Morrow, and Pryse.

2. Cheryl Walker has identified a useful term for the critical method I will employ: "persona criticism," which she defines as "a critical practice that both expands and limits the role of the author . . . finding in the text an author-persona but relating this functionary to psychological, historical, and literary intersections quite beyond the scope of any scriptor's intentions, either conscious or unconscious. The persona functions more like a form of sensibility in the text than a directional marker pointing back toward some monolithic authorial presence" (114).

3. See Wyatt in particular. Also, Karen Langlois's article on Austin shares this point of view.

4. For a more complete discussion of Austin's relationship with her mother, Susannah Hunter, see Lanigan Stineman's biography of Austin.

5. Other critics of Austin have observed this figurative strategy as well; Shelley Armitage writes: "Seeking to awaken this society to truths visible in its own landscape, yet ignored, commercialized, or managed without stewardship for profits, she often characterizes the land as feminine, applying the Native American concept of Mother Earth. . . . The land is nurturing, spiritual, and resilient" (21).

6. Mary Hunter married Stafford Wallace Austin in 1891 and soon found her husband's inability to make a living a burden. They were often separated, even after the birth of their daughter, Ruth, in 1892. Austin was frequently left alone to support herself and her disabled daughter, which she did through teaching and, eventually, writing. She left her husband permanently in 1904 (although they did not divorce until 1914) and made the difficult decision to institutionalize her daughter a year later.

7. I can only speculate what brought about the return of Mary-by-herself in a piece of Austin's published work, as Austin had only permitted this voice to be exposed in letters and poems. After the publication of *The Land of Little Rain,* Mary-by-herself is often heard in Austin's private papers when Austin discusses illness, professional discouragement, and problems with relationships. It is interesting to note that Austin finally obtained a divorce from her husband in 1914, the same year *California: Land of the Sun* was published.

8. See Blend and Scheick.

9. In 1895, naturalist John Burrough's wrote "the literary naturalist does not take liberties with facts; facts are the flora upon which he lives. . . . To interpret Nature is not to improve on her: it is to draw her out" (quoted in Lutts 9).

10. See Graulich.

11. Vera Norwood comments that "Seyavi provides Austin with a human incarnation of the spirit of the feminine southwest land and since for Austin,

under the best circumstances, land culture and human culture are one, the best human method for living on that land" (14).

12. See especially *The American Rhythm* (1923) for Austin's theories about Native American creative processes and the tribal consciousness which enables their art.

13. Austin is referring to *la yerba del manso,* a Hispanic folk cure for burns, sores, colic, and dysentary.

14. Paula Bennett identifies what has been called "the Language of Flowers" as a language "through which women's body and . . . women's genitals have been represented and inscribed" (240).

15. Austin writes on the cover page to this manuscript: "This is the original sketch rewritten in 1906 from note[s] made in 1902. In 1912 it was again rewritten and slightly revised in 1928 for Albert Bender."

16. In a very different reading, Ammons believes that Austin's search to recover the mother—"the Mother Earth, the mother artist, the mother tongue of the land" is "gentle and earthbound," and "her experimental prose rocks and caresses" the reader, rather than challenges the reader, as I believe Austin's work does (97).

Works Cited

AMMONS, ELIZABETH. *Conflicting Stories: American Women Writers at the Turn into the Twentieth Century.* New York: Oxford UP, 1991.

ARMITAGE, SHELLY, ED. "Writing Nature." Introduction to *Wind's Trail: The Early Life of Mary Austin.* Santa Fe: Museum of New Mexico P, 1990.

AUSTIN, MARY HUNTER. *The American Rhythm.* 1923. New York: AMS, 1970.

———. *Cactus Thorn.* Ed. Melody Graulich. Reno: U of Nevada P, 1988.

———. *California: Land of the Sun.* New York: Macmillan, 1914.

———. *Earth Horizon: An Autobiography.* 1932. Albuquerque: U of New Mexico P, 1991.

———. *The Flock.* Boston: Houghton Mifflin, 1906.

———. *Everyman's Genius.* Indianapolis: Bobbs-Merrill, 1923.

———. "The Friend in the Wood." In *Wind's Trail: The Early Life of Mary Austin.* Ed. Shelley Armitage. Santa Fe: Museum of New Mexico P, 1990: 183-98.

———. "If Women Did" [1918<>1934]. Ts. AU 232. Austin papers. Huntington Library, San Marino, CA. N. pag.

———. *Inyo* [1899]. Ts. AU 261. Austin papers. Huntington Library, San Marino, CA.

———. *The Land of Little Rain.* 1903. Albuquerque: U of New Mexico P, 1974.

———. *Lost Borders. Stories from the Country of the Lost Borders.* Ed. Marjorie Pryse. New Brunswick, NJ: Rutgers UP, 1987. 151-263.

———. "The Lost Garden" [1906]. Ts. AU 318. Austin papers. Huntington Library, San Marino, CA.

———. *Tejon Notebook* [1889?]. Ms. AU 267. Austin papers. Huntington Library, San Marino, CA. N. pag.

BENNETT, PAULA. "Critical Clitoradectomy." *Signs* 18.2 (Winter 1993): 1-27.

BLEND, BENAY. "Women Writers and the Desert: Mary Austin, Iza Sizer Cassidy, and Alice Corbin." Ph.D. diss., U of New Mexico, 1988.

FINK, AUGUSTA. *I-Mary: A Biography of Mary Austin.* Tucson: U of Arizona P, 1983.

FLAX, JANE. "Mother-Daughter Relationships: Psychodynamics, Politics, and Philosophy." *The Future of Difference.* Ed. Hester Eisenstein and Alice Jardine. 1980. New Brunswick, NJ: Rutgers UP, 1988: 20-40.

GRAULICH, MELODY. Afterword. *Earth Horizon: An Autobiography.* By Mary Austin. Albuquerque: U of New Mexico P, 1991.

JAYCOX, FAITH. "Regeneration through Liberation: Mary Austin's 'The Walking Woman' and Western Narrative Formula." *Legacy: A Journal of Nineteenth-Century American Women Writers* 6.1 (Spring 1989): 5-12.

LANGLOIS, KAREN. "Mary Austin's *A Woman of Genius*: The Text, the Novel, and the Problem of Male Publishers and Critics and Female Authors." *Journal of American Culture* 15.2 (Summer 1992): 79-86.

LUTTS, RALPH H. *The Nature Fakers: Wildlife, Science, and Sentiment.* Golden, CO: Fulcrum, 1990.

MORROW, NANCY. "The Artist as Heroine and Anti-Heroine in Mary Austin's *A Woman of Genius* and Anne Douglas Sedgewick's *Tante.*" *American Literary Realism, 1870-1910* 22.2 (Winter 1990): 17-29.

NORWOOD, VERA. "The Photographer and the Naturalist: Laura Gilpin and Mary Austin in the Southwest." *Working Paper #6.* Tuscon: Southwest Institute for Research on Women, 1981.

O'GRADY, JOHN P. *Pilgrims to the Wild: Everett Ruess, Henry David Thoreau, John Muir, Clarence King, Mary Austin.* Salt Lake City: U of Utah P, 1993.

FRYSE, MARJORIE. Introduction. *Stories from the Country of Lost Borders.* By Mary Austin. New Brunswick, NJ: Rutgers UP, 1987: vii-xxxviii.

SCHEICK, WILLIAM J. "Mary Austin's Disfigurement of the Southwest in *The Land of Little Rain*." *Western American Literature* 27.1 (Spring 1992): 37-46.

STINEMAN, ESTHER LANIGAN. *Mary Austin: Song of a Maverick.* New Haven: Yale UP, 1989.

WALKER, CHERYL. "Persona Criticism and the Death of the Author." *Contesting the Subject: Essays in the Postmodern Theory and Practice of Biography and Biographical Criticism.* Ed. William Epstein. West Layfayette, IN: Purdue UP, 1991: 113-19.

WYATT, DAVID. "Mary Austin: Nature and Nurturance." *The Fall into Eden: Landscape and Imagination in California.* Cambridge: Cambridge UP, 1986: 68-94.

Beverly A. Hume (essay date fall 1999)

SOURCE: Hume, Beverly A. "'Inextricable disordered ranges': Mary Austin's Ecofeminist Explorations in Lost Borders." *Studies in Short Fiction* 36, no. 4 (fall 1999): 401-15.

[*In the following essay, Hume maintains that Austin's "environmentalist perspective" offered in her collection* Lost Borders *defines her as an "ecofeminist" pioneer, claiming that the stories in this work both expose patriarchal systems of domination and explore essential connections between women and nature.*]

Although Mary Austin has generally come to be perceived as a writer who, as Patrick Murphy summarizes, "gives primacy to nature as a dynamic interactive system in which people can participate if they follow the lead of the land" (67), recent critical reevaluations of her writings have provoked critical debates about the relation of her quasi-sentimental mysticism and tendencies toward feminist or cultural essentialism to her more compellingly detailed descriptions of the desert and her early championing and felt indignation regarding the status of women and Native cultures in the early twentieth century.[1] In one of her earliest short story collections, *Lost Borders* [*Stories from the Country of Lost Borders*] (1909), Austin uses her tales to establish the parameters of this debate through her creation of characters who mirror the "inextricable disordered ranges" that frame their borderlands (156), simultaneously revealing their narrator (an unnamed storyteller, a thinly-disguised narrative voice for Austin) to be neither strictly feminist nor environmentalist, but rather a combination of the two—that is, an early ecofeminist. Although individual tales in *Lost Borders* have been discussed and anthologized in recent years, their collective impact, as the following reading argues, clarifies Austin's environmentalist perspective—a perspective that suggests that most "civilized" men and women remain unable to understand the "inextricable," if not inscrutable, "disorder" of the natural landscape of the desert, even though their spiritual growth and general well-being, in terms of these sketches, depends upon it. In these sketches, characters are continually challenged to awaken and explore this landscape. As the poetic versification that frames this collection suggests, the narrator remains hopeful that such explorations for a "Word" that has "never" been "printed in a page" will "wake" in this region of lost borders "with the wind that wakes the morning on a thousand miles of sage" (154).

In *Lost Borders,* Austin, as storyteller, consciously engages in a reexamination of this "Word"—which is voiceless and seems, as it did for earlier romantic nature writers such as Thoreau or Muir, both connected to and beyond human experience. Unlike these authors, however, Austin becomes engaged in this short story collection with what it means to be human in relation to a civilization (whether European and American) that remains asleep to its own "feminine" potential. In Austin's desert borderlands, "lost" civilized wanderers—typically men—have only barely begun to comprehend what she calls the "Power" of "desertness," a "Power" that she specifically links not only to women but also to indigenous Native cultures. Such a perspective makes Austin an ecofeminist insofar as ecofeminism, as Karen Warren summarizes, not only refers to a "variety of multicultural perspectives on the nature of the connections within social systems of domination" between women and "nonhuman nature," but also has a "twofold commitment to the recognition and elimination of male-gender bias wherever and whenever it occurs . . . ." (1). Although the term "ecofeminist" was not coined until the 1970s,[2] Austin is best understood as one of its pioneers, particularly in *Lost Borders,* where Austin's storytelling exposes, in Warren's words, "social systems of domination," explores connections between women and "nonhuman nature," and reveals an implicit commitment to the "recognition and elimination of male-gender bias. . . ."

In *Lost Borders,* Austin's desert is not only depicted as "real" but also as metaphoric for the "lost" borders of westward expansion—borders that Austin links to the expanding parameters of gender self-consciousness in her early twentieth-century America. In this collection, Austin offers a curious blending of mysticism, realistic detailing, and personal belief about gender and culture to suggest (1) that the desert, as a wilderness that bears a complex relation to the universe, is eternal and self-sustaining; (2) that the "feminine" qualities of the desert both define and limit the true "borders" of westward expansion; and (3) that indigenous or Native cultures who have learned to live in relation to the "inextricable disordered ranges" of the desert have, like the land, been devalued by civilized people who are too obtuse or blind in their understanding of both.

Austin feminizes the "primitive" desert borderlands in this short story collection not only to mirror a latent power in all humans, but also to call attention to the encroachment of what she classifies as civilized "maleness." Increasingly, and in later non-fictional writings, Austin associates such encroachment with the "male" approach to living on the Earth; further, she links "maleness" in the abstract not only to civilized "assaults" of the natural world, but also to "Nations" and to the "State," which, according to Austin, "Man invented . . . in the key of maleness, with combat for its major occupation, profit the spur, and power the prize" (Austin, **"Sex Emancipation"** 54). Although such rhetoric is essentialist in its declarations about inherent gender qualities, it is ecofeminist insofar as it claims that power structures identified as "male" or "patriarchal" have played a significant role in creating such problems; and it is this abstract sense of "maleness" and "femaleness"—that is, of gender in relation to "civilized" and "primitive" cultures—that, Austin, as storyteller, explores in *Lost Borders.*

In *Lost Borders,* Austin asserts not only that the desert (and, by extension, wilderness or nature) is more powerful than *all* humans, but that the historical notion of the progressive nature of westward expansion is antithetical to an understanding of these infinitely more complex western regions. For Austin, part of this understanding is related to her religious mysticism—a mysticism that appears to be a synthesis of Judeo-Christian heritage and pantheistic primitivism;[3] of her sympathies for Native cultures and religions; and of her own felt experiences in Western regions as a woman. "If the desert were a woman," she writes in her introductory sketch to *Lost Borders,* "I know well what like she would be: deep-breasted, broad in the hips, tawny, with tawny hair, great masses of it lying smooth along her perfect curves, full lipped like a sphinx . . ." (160). Although Austin's feminization of the desert is anthropomorphic, her qualifying "If" also suggests a certain hesitation regarding an understanding of "desertness," since in the desert, "the borders of conscience break down" and "Nature herself" seems to have "obscured the medium . . . in her secret operations" (156). The desert is, for this narrator, feminine, but not to be directly associated with human females, or even to be particularly reflective of a human female's singular potential—unless that female discovers the same uncivilized power and wildness that this feminized other, this desert sphinx, represents. Both civilized women and men, Austin implies, need to become like the "wild creatures" she describes in her earlier non-fictional *Land of Little Rain*; that is, creatures who not only live in a kind of complex interdependence but, unlike humans, remain "cognizant of the affairs of their own kind" (37).

In *The Land of Little Rain,* for example, Austin asserts that the Shoshone know how to adapt more successfully to desert regions than "white" civilized humans, since the "primitive" Shoshones have come to realize that the "manner of the country makes the usage of life there, and the land will not be lived in except in its own fashion" (57). Such an understanding does not rise strictly from gender or cultural experience, but rather from experiencing these regions in a certain way. For example, in *The Land of Little Rain,* Winnenap, a Shoshone who is a Paiute captive, "lived gingerly among the Paiutes and in his heart despised them" (55). Winnenap serves as a medicine-man to the Paiutes, but as a Shoshone youth, he learns in the desert "what civilized children never learn, to be still and to keep on being still, at the first hint of danger or strangeness" (58). As a Paiute captive, however, he learns, in his brief visits back to the Shoshone lands, the true nature and beauty of these lands. For Austin, thus, there is "never any but Winnenap who could tell and make it worth telling about Shoshone Land" (59). The Paiutes with whom Winnenap lives do not, in this story, seem to share this medicine man's understanding of or passion for Shoshone Land—and Austin cites Winnenap not so much as a generic "Native American" but rather as a member of the Shoshone tribe, an individual man with a specific and enhanced capacity for appreciating the full mystery, complexity, and beauty of desert wilderness. The same situation proves true for Seyavi, the Paiute basket maker in *The Land of Little Rain.* Seyavi, despite her similarities to other Paiute women who make baskets, is singled our for the storyteller's praise as an artist who has, among other things, "gone beyond learning to do for her son" and has created baskets that are not only "wonders of technical precision" but retain a subtle "appeal . . . in the sense that warns us of humanness" in their designs (95).

In her fictional portraits in *Lost Borders,* Austin also depicts Native people—most often women—not in relation to the land, but to the civilized inhabitants of these desert borderlands. The most clearly oppressive characters in *Lost Borders* are, in fact, civilized "white" males who attempt to dominate women, particularly Native women. In her first sketch, **"The Land,"** Austin observes that "law runs with the boundary, not beyond it," whereas "most [civilized] men make law for the comfortable feel of it, defining them to themselves." Such men, she angrily continues, "shoulder along like blindworms, rearing against restrictions," often having to "pinch themselves with regulations to make sure of being sentient, and organize within organizations" (156). Yet, such civilized men are perpetually drawn into, if not seduced by, this "feminine" desert, and even though several of them appear in these sketches as the "crawling" and limited creatures described in **"The Land,"** their civilized female counterparts are treated no more sympathetically. In **"The Hoodoo of the Minietta,"** for example, Austin recounts a tale of a mining operation—the Minietta Mining and Milling Company—cursed by its formation through the greed, betrayal, and murderous actions of its founders against the land and each other. Eventually, this operation collapses and is taken over by one of the miners, Mr. McKenna, who does not stay for the money, but rather "because the desert had him, cat-like, between her paws" (164). Into this trap, he brings his new wife, identified simply as "Mrs. McKenna," a woman who detests the desert because she is civilized, and, therefore, conventional. Women, Austin observes, "unless they have very large and simple souls, need cover; clothes, you know, and furniture, social observances to screen them, social conventions to get behind; life when it leaps upon them, large and naked, shocks them into disorder" (165). Mrs. McKenna becomes one of these shocked women, and, predictably, abandons her desert-locked husband to return to civilization with another man.

Many of the civilized settlers in *Lost Borders* are variations on Mr. and Mrs. McKenna—though the desert proves harsher to the men "she" seduces than to the women "she" drives away and, like Austin, appears to be more angered by male gender bias. In three interrelated stories that literally "introduce" each other (**"A Case of Conscience," "The Ploughed Land,"** and **"The Return of Mr. Wills"**), Austin, as storyteller, elaborates on this perspective with a disorderly narrative that increasingly indicts "civilized" men for their self-destructive passions and calls for "civilized" women to awaken to the "Power" in the desert and in themselves.

In **"A Case of Conscience,"** the reader is immediately confronted with gender and cultural conflict between Saunders, "an average Englishman with a lung complaint," and Turwhase, the Shoshone woman who falls in love with him and bears his child. This relationship creates difficulties for Saunder's proper English conscience, which is plagued by "the old obstinate Anglo-Saxon prejudice that makes a man responsible for his offspring" (169); by his realization that his English mother (and family) would be prejudiced toward such a child; and by his own racial prejudices and general discomfort at telling Turwhase that he feels morally obligated to take their child (but not her) back to England. Saunder's "moral dilemma," as Austin calls it, is resolved for him when Turwhase takes the child from him, "fiercely" declaring the child hers. He tries to pay her for the child, she laughs at him, refuses, and "began to walk desertward" (173). After Saunders later informs Austin (as storyteller) that his plan to take the child back to England "really wouldn't have done" (174), she observes that he looked "very English, smug and freshly shaven" and sardonically concludes, "I believe he thought he had come to that conclusion by himself" (174).

Although this tale depicts Turwhase's partial triumph, Austin chooses to tack on a conclusion with an ethno-centric and unflattering digression about the fact that all Indian women "talk together" since they are "great gossips" about "children, marriage, and the ways of the whites"—with the last appearing "as a sort of pageant, which, though it is much of sheer foolishness, is yet charged with a mysterious and compelling portent" (175). Further, Austin continues, "all" women like to discuss "the conduct of men" in "relation to women"—even in the "great spaces [of the desert that is] disinterested of men" (175). After displaying a certain contempt for the chatter of *all* women, Austin concludes that "where the Borders run out, through all the talk of the women, white women, too," there is gained "no better understanding of the thing they witness to," no true comprehension that "through the thin web of their lives moves the vast impersonal rivalry of desertness"—a rivalry best described as a "Power moving nakedly in the room" (175).

In the next story, **"The Ploughed Land,"** Austin elaborates on this inhuman "Power" in her description of the relationship between Tiawa, another Native woman, and another civilized man, Gavin. In this story, Gavin is led by Tiawa from her desert wilderness back to the "ploughed land" of his civilization. This civilization, like Saunders's, abruptly forces the termination of a relationship in which Tiawa (like other Native women) had erroneously assumed that she has "the right to love unasked and unashamed" without the "snigger of the sophisticated male" (177). After this relationship is "shamed" by the standards of Gavin's civilized (or "ploughed") lands into dissolution (179), Gavin, like Saunders, goes "back to his own kind" and Tiawa "married a Paiute and grew fat, for mostly in encounter with the primal forces woman gets the worst of it" (180). A woman, Austin adds, can sometimes come out ahead in such an encounter "when there are children in question" since she then "becomes a primal force herself" (180). Such "primal force" motherhood appears biologic and essentialist, particularly since it is immediately juxtaposed against Austin's gender-biased insinuation that "great souls" (such as "Buddha, Mahomet, and the Galilean") who go up against the primal force of desertness become "saints and prophets—declaring unutterable things" (179). That is, a maternal desert appears here to be aligned against women generally, while only extraordinary male saints and prophets can gain insights (unutterable as they might be) into these phenomenal primal forces.

Austin, however, has not finished her exploration of the impact of desertness upon the gendered and acculturated imaginations of her civilized men and women in **Lost Borders.** As she announces at the end of **"The Ploughed Land,"** she intends to examine further the "sort of chemist's cup" that the "open country" has for "resolving [gender] obligations," and does so in her final story of this triptych, **"The Return of Mr. Wills."**

Here, Austin recounts the transformation of Mrs. Wills from a civilized woman who depends upon "the tradition that a husband is a natural provider" to one who realizes "that she not only did not need Mr. Wills, but got on better without him" (184). In the beginning, Mrs. Wills depends upon Mr. Wills, a man who is a "sort of man bred up in close communities" (particularly in the "East") and is like a "cask, to whom the church, public opinion, [and] the social note" are a "sort of hoop hold him in serviceable shape" (182). When such men move West, this "hoop" collapses—and these men go "to pieces," or, in Mr. Wills's case, to "Lost Mines," to wandering around the desert, a "long Wilderness" that "lies brooding, imperturbable," while filling "her" victims with glittering illusions of becoming "amazingly rich" (182).

Like Gavin in **"The Ploughed Lands"** and Saunders in **"A Case of Conscience,"** Mr. Wills gets "lost" in this deceptive and feminized desert (which, unlike the Native women, "keeps" him). Predictably, all "the hoops" fall off, and he deserts his wife by wandering off to find lost treasure, as his mind fades "out at the edges like the desert horizon . . ." (184). Unlike Gavin and Saunders, however, Mr. Wills wanders back and attempts to settle on his wife and family "like a blight"—not only bringing "the desert with him on his back," but creating a domestic atmosphere in which the "power of the wilderness lay like a wasting sickness on the home" (186). Although Mrs. Wills tolerates his intrusion, she no longer has any expectations of him; indeed, she has learned in his absence that she can be self-sufficient since "nature never makes the mistake of neglecting to make the child-bearer competent to provide" (184). Thus "when" Mr. Wills wanders off into the desert again, Austin observes, it will be final—not because of his choice but hers since "this time, if I know Mrs. Wills, he will not come back" (187). In the context of the other two interlinked stories, Mrs. Wills has, in Austin's terms, awakened to her potential as an independent woman. Although she is still too passive, the narrator "knows," or at least trusts, that if Mr. Wills again feels compelled to, like a "blindworm" (156), be seduced by the desert, Mrs. Wills will prevent his return. Mrs. Wills could do this, Austin implies, by aligning herself with the inhuman but feminine "Powers" of "desertness" and against those cultural or gender "obligations" that have previously constrained her.

If, on the other hand, a civilized man comes finally to understand (rather than be sickened by) the true "Power" of Austin's feminized desert wilderness, he can emerge, like Winnenap in Austin's *Land of Little Rain,* an heroic figure—as does Little Pete, who appears in the next tale, **"The Last Antelope."** Little Pete is a Basque shepherd who has learned to live in harmony with wilderness in a hollow called Ciserno that is carved out in the desert hills, and he, according to Aus-

tin, is clearly more akin to wild creatures than to man. "He loved his dogs as brothers; he was near akin to the wild things; he communed with the huddled hills, and held intercourse with the stars . . ." (188). Learning to "respect . . . signs and seasons" and all living creatures and even "differentiating the natures and dispositions of inanimate things," Little Pete is a man who, like the narrator, feels "small respect" for other men and has "no time" for civilized women. Instead, his "heart warmed toward the juniper-tree" that held a solitary post in the hills and "the antelope was the noblest thing he had ever loved" (193). The antelope, in particular, is "loved" by Little Pete not only because it is a wild creature, but also because he begins to "perceive a reciprocal friendliness" in this creature. Little Pete feels an unspoken intimacy with this antelope, one intensified when the creature defends the shepherd's herd against coyotes. When the antelope is finally hunted and killed by a homesteader, Little Pete, writes Austin, "suffered the torture" of coming up against the "inevitable"; he had been "breathed upon by that spirit which goes before cities like an exhalation and dries up the gossamer and the dew" (195)—and "from that day the heart had gone out of" the land for Little Pete. Little Pete, one of Austin's two tragic heroes in *Lost Borders,* mourns the loss of the antelope and the symbolic death of this wilderness region, eventually passing out of that part of the country, which does indeed seem to "die" when the last "juniper-tree" is cut down by a homesteader for firewood (195).

Austin's other tragic hero in this collection is an indigenous woman who appears in the next sketch, **"Agua Dulce."** Austin introduces this sketch at the end of **"The Last Antelope"** as the story of an event that stands in stark contrast to "all the obvious mechanism of modern burial" (196). In this tale, the reader is again given a story about the intimate feelings a "white" civilized man (the stagecoach driver) feels for a woman, Catameneda, whom he simply describes as an "Indian woman." Despite the driver's racial self-consciousness and uneasiness about having a relationship with this "Indian woman," the emphasis of his tale is on his struggle for survival in the wilderness and on Catameneda's heroic self-sacrifice. His simple narration remains compelling because of his sometimes faltering but frankly astonished depiction of Catameneda's struggle to save him from the forces of wilderness—in this case a three-day windstorm near Agua Dulce that threatens to prevent them from finding a waterhole (200). When the driver survives and realizes the full extent of Catameneda's strength, her knowledge of the desert, and her self-sacrifice, he tells the storyteller (who accepts without question the truth of his perception) that Catameneda's impassioned selflessness is deathless, eternal: "But I don't suppose anybody knows . . . how it is that I don't think of her dead any more, nor any of that hard time we had . . . only sometimes when it's spring like this, and I smell sage-brush burning . . . it reminds me . . . of some loving way she had out there . . . at Agua Dulce" (202). In both **"The Last Antelope"** and **"Agua Dulce,"** civilized men are arguably touched by or awakened to the "Power" of wilderness—something that, for Austin, appears intimately connected not only to understanding and loving women or at least the "feminine" aspect of the natural world, but also to a mystical apprehension of a transcendent cosmic force.

Similarly, the female title characters of two other sketches, **"The Woman of the Eighteen-Mile House"** and **"Walking Woman,"** possess a "vitality that had nothing, absolutely nothing, but the blank occasionless life of the desert to sustain it," and are counted among "the very few people . . . able to keep a soul alive and glowing in the wilderness" (205). Both of these women, former civilized women, have been reshaped, according to Austin, by their existence on the frontier (or borderlands) of desert wilderness. They have discovered its truths, its beauty, its power. The Woman of the Eighteen-Mile House, through an adulterous affair, learns, according to Austin, not only that "Love is Life's own way of reducing the clash of human contacts in order that the pair may turn a more opposing front to the adversary, the Wilderness," but also that human passion, in its essential primitiveness, "cannot yet square with Respectability, with the Church and Property," particularly not "here in the Borders, where the warp runs loose and wide" (210). Eros thus becomes not only the means by which humans might begin to understand the true distance between themselves, as civilized humans, and their "adversary, the Wilderness," but also the means by which civilized women, in particular, might begin to discover, as Rudnick suggests, the "spiritual and aesthetic resources" to develop into "independent and creative" persons (16).

This theme is reiterated in Austin's more well-known **"Walking Woman,"** the final story of *Lost Borders*. During a storm, a previously-civilized woman helps a Basque shepherd, Filon, save his sheep and herself. She does this by working "with a man" and not feeling the need to be submissive or apologize for her abilities (259). This new form of "working together" with a man awakens the Walking Woman (who has discarded her civilized name) to self-understanding and self-respect that, in turn leads to respect, understanding, affection, and sexual passion for Filon—and, finally, to a child, though it does not lead to respectability, social convention, or marriage. The Walking Woman is unconcerned with such respectability since "she had walked off all sense of society-made values, and, knowing the best when the best came to her, was able to take it" (260). This "best"—for both the Walking Woman and, it would seem, for Austin—includes not only working and loving as a co-equal with a man and bearing a child, but

something more; "it was the naked thing the Walking Woman grasped, not dressed and tricked out, for instance, by prejudices in favor of certain occupations." The Walking Woman here seems to "grasp" the same naked "Power" that the narrator describes earlier in **"A Case of Conscience."** It is a "Power" that teaches her, despite her civilized training, to embrace sexual passion and the birth of an illegitimate child without "obligation of permanency" and without guilt (262). More, it remains an inhuman "Power" that stimulates her feelings of self-dependency and self-sufficiency. In making the claim, however, that a "child; any way you get it, a child is good to have, say nature and the Walking Woman," Austin's last tale again flirts with the essentialist idea that "nature" and **"Walking Woman"** are maternal; that is, that women can draw their personal power from this fundamental biologic fact. As Catriona Sandilands summarizes, contemporary ecofeminists who depend upon such "facts" open up the "real possibility of a kind of biological reductionism and essentialism that any feminism . . . ought to spend much of its time debunking" (4). Although Austin's failure to address the implications of such essentialism is a weakness in this story, the remaining stories in *Lost Borders* do, in part, address it.

"The House of Offense" (which immediately precedes **"The Walking Woman"**) deals ironically and unsentimentally with the nature of motherhood—in this case, with the childless Mrs. Henby's fluctuating perceptions about Hard Mag, the local Madam (and unlikely mother). If Mrs. Henby had a child, the narrator observes, "she would have been perfectly happy" and would have had "no time to trouble" about her next-door neighbor, Hard Mag, and what was occurring at Mag's "House" (248). Although Mrs. Henby eventually agrees to adopt Hard Mag's daughter, Marietta (who does not know that her mother is a prostitute) and is willing to get a child, in Walking Woman's terms, "any way" she can, the primary impetus of the story is on Mrs. Henby's conflicting perceptions about Hard Mag's maternal conduct. Although Mrs. Henby fails to appreciate the social implications of the life Hard Mag leads, she determines to adopt Marietta after she senses that Hard Mag represents a maternal "quagmire of unwarned water-holes where cattle sink and flounder" (251); that is, after she realizes that Hard Mag has kept her daughter away not because she wanted to protect her from a life of prostitution but because it would be bad for business.

Hard Mag may feel vaguely maternal—insofar as she takes some responsibility for the welfare of her daughter, but she has no desire either to change herself or to nurture Marietta (249). Hard Mag's negative maternal presence raises questions not only about the "primal force" power of motherhood, but also about whether the desire to be a mother is social or biologic since

Mrs. Henby, a socially respectable woman, is childless but almost too desperately wants to be a mother. Hard Mag's character also raises questions about the social double standard that decrees, as Hard Mag recognizes, that men can frequent a House of Offense but "go away to raise a family" (253), while prostitutes like her are condemned to a hopeless existence of an "ineradicable baseness" by both "respectable" men and women (like the "maternal" Mrs. Henby). When Hard Mag departs on the night of her daughter's arrival (to start a new business elsewhere), she is "helped" by the "coarse laughter" of the "creatures" (the respectable men) she has "preyed upon." Mag is also arguably "helped" in a similarly coarse fashion by Mrs. Henby, who can only feel relieved that she won't have to "put to any great strain of inventiveness to account for the little girl she had decided to adopt" since the child's arrival is "overshadowed" not only by Mag's harried departure but also by the accidental fire that is indifferently allowed to burn the House of Offense to the ground since "none of the townspeople had any interest in it and no property was endangered" (254).

The four remaining tales in *Lost Borders* continue to examine, through indirection, essentialist issues raised in this "Country of Lost Borders" (159). In **"The Bitterness of Women,"** Austin describes a female bitterness felt by women who, because of their physical appearance, feel sexually marginalized by men—women who do not "look" feminine and, "lacking the spark of a glance, the turn of an ankle, the treasures of tenderness in them wither unfulfilled" (245). Austin's purpose in this sketch, however, is not to focus on the nature of such socially-conditioned bitterness, but to make Louis Chabot, her male protagonist (and former handsome seducer among woman) *feel* such bitterness. After being physically mutilated by a bear (245), Chabot comes to understand this bitterness—perhaps even more so than the "commonplace," "fat," and homely Marguerita (246) whom he marries once he has become a "maimed and twisted thing" of a man (245). After marrying the mutilated Chabot, whom she desperately loves, Marguerita can have her bitterness transformed "with one kiss of his crooked mouth" (246), whereas he, says the narrator, can "never" again feel "the lift, the exultation, the exquisite, unmatched wonder of the world" that is created by great passion, by great love. The "bitterness" of women, in this context, is not only related to homeliness but also to the failure of men like Chabot to move beyond physical appearances—though in this disconcerting fable, Chabot's confrontation with wildness, with the bear, does not awaken him to an empathetic understanding of this bitterness but only compels him to condemn himself to an even more bitter, if not permanent, state of emotional suffering and despair.

In **"The Fakir,"** an equally dark story, Austin, as an even more involved narrating storyteller, uneasily ac-

knowledges not only her "sense of detached helplessness" toward women in her community and "the strained, meticulous inadequacy of my own soul," but also the way in which she participates, as a spiritual "fakir" (220), with the "horribly fascinating" (212) Franklin Challoner in the deception of his adulterous lover, Netta Saybrick (216). What is seductive about Challoner, according to Austin, "is the sort of talk many women would have called beautiful" (217) and a strange "Look" in which Austin claims to see Netta's "soul rising rehabilitated, astonished, and on the instant, out there beyond the man and the woman, between the thin fiery lines of the rails, leading back to the horizon, the tall, robed Figure writing in the sand" (219). Despite the fact that she knows this is an "hallucination" (219) and that Challoner is a spiritual fraud, Austin is, like Netta, seduced by Challoner's "Look"—a "Look" that she appears to associate, however vaguely, with the same supernatural "Power" of the desert that she has described in earlier sketches. Because of Challoner's strange, quasi-mystical abilities at seducing women, Austin not only claims to be able to "forgive" Netta for her "sin" (of adultery) and herself for assisting him, but ironically concludes that "the most I . . . learned of the efficient exercise of forgiveness was from the worst man I had ever known"—a man whose sexual force she likens to spiritual violation (221).

This tale breaks down with Austin's uncertainty about her role as storyteller and about the "religion" of the desert, which "had," she reflects, "a reputation in times past for the making of religious leaders," but which is also "no field for converts" (222). She then begins to reflect on the meaning of the tale of **"The Pocket Hunter,"** a tale that she says also challenges any "conventional, pew-fed religion" (222), such as the one she says she was raised on. This tale expands Austin's critique of civilized male "fakirs" to suggest that they may be driven by irrational, brutish passions to own, conquer, and possess not only the land but other humans. The male protagonists in this Pocket-Hunter's "hair-lifting horror" story (223) are simultaneously obsessed with owning mines, with owning an unnamed "Indian woman" (who both men regard as potential property, though neither values her as a human), with irrational rage and hatred toward any man who challenges their "claims," and, finally, even with supernaturally possessing the physical body of another man in order to sustain that rage and hatred from beyond the grave. Although Austin allows the Pocket-Hunter to narrate his supernatural tale without editorial comment, later in her career, she explicitly denounced in non-fictional writings (and in generalized, gender-biased terms) what she calls the "intrinsic male weaknesses" that embraces "the greed of exclusive possessions, the mastery of the seas, the control of world finance" (**"Sex Emancipation"** 55).

Spiritual fakery and supernaturalism also appear in **"The Readjustment,"** a ghost story in which a dead wife, Emma Jeffries, now a "Presence," hears from her husband, Sim—a man of "insuperable commonness" who has as little in common with her as he does "the benumbing spirit" of the desert regions in which he lives (233). Sim tells the Presence not only "all the stuff of his life," but also confesses his feelings of guilt about having "begotten a cripple[d]" child upon his wife (236-37). In fact, Sim is more honest with Emma as a dead "Presence" than he ever was with her as a living woman. However, this relationship is brought to an abruptly ironic conclusion after Emma's "Presence" is given the pragmatic advice by a neighboring woman that it would be a "mistake" to continue listening to Sim since "in a little while, if you stay, it will be as bad as it always was" since Sim is a "common man" and it's better to "go . . . while there's understanding between you" (238). "Understanding" between men and women becomes, in this context, a deeply ironic enterprise in *Lost Borders,* one that may even be related, as the confessing narrator of **"The Fakir"** implies, to Austin's, own well-documented domestic disorders or often-expressed cultural marginalization as a woman and writer.[4]

Despite its relative critical neglect, Mary Austin's *Lost Borders* remains a compelling early collection. Close readings of these sketches suggest that Austin is often conflicted in her narrative explorations of gender limitations and possibilities in her characters' "borders of conscience" (156). At times "feminine," at others, powerfully non-human and even supernatural, Austin's desert wilderness sets the "boundaries" for her struggling "civilized" characters who, she continually suggests, must deal with their culturally biased perceptions in a desert environment where the "boundary of soul and sense is as faint as a trail in a sand-storm" (156). Because they are awakened to the "Word" or "Power" of Austin's desert, some of these civilized characters walk away from their culture—to become walking women or antelope or desert-loving men. Sometimes, this estrangement leads to self-destruction, to death, but in these sketches it more often leads to spiritual insight, emotional health, self-reliance, and a self-appreciation that can be likened to that manifest in Native women such as Tiawa, Turwhase, or Catameneda. Conversely, other "lost border" characters such as Mr. and Mrs. McKenna, Saunders, Mr. Wills, Louis Chabot, Hard Mag, or the hateful men of **"The Pocket-Hunter Story"** do not awaken, instead remaining blind to what they might, if they saw more deeply and clearly, learn from these desert regions. As such, they become the true "lost" borderers in Austin's fictive desert realms, since they are capable of living only in unstable, denigrated relations to their own species or of attempting to foolishly and blindly possess, civilize, control, dominate, plough, or otherwise contain or categorize narrowly defined social and natural environments. Critics have aptly classified Mary Austin as a romantic, one who attempts, as the poetic verse that concludes this collection reveals, to put her own personal (and "feminine") perceptions of the "Word" or "Power" of the desert to "its sweetest use/In the moonlit sandy reaches when the desert wind is loose" (261). Despite occasional lapses into essentialist rhetoric and thought, Austin does reveal in *Lost Borders* an early and admirable sense of the need to awaken her early twentieth-century readers not only to their own gender and cultural biases, but also to an awareness of the significance of the natural or non-human environment to their self-understanding, well-being, and even, arguably, survival.

Notes

1. Even a brief survey of recent critical evaluations of Austin's writings reveals interpretive difficulties her "feminist" strategies have posed for her critics. She has, for example, been credited with attempting to revise "traditional Anglo male perceptions of the West" (Rudnick 10); with integrating mystical ideas into her work, "nearly all of which are connected . . . with American Indian experience" (Ruppert 250); with offering feminist perspectives on man's "inhumanity to women" (Lanigan 74); and with creating narrative contradictions in her "feminist vision," which might "prove" her "not to have been feminist at all" (Stout 96). See also Vera Norwood's "Heroines of Nature: Four Women Respond to the American Landscape" and Anna Carew-Miller's "Mary Austin's Nature: Refiguring Tradition through the Voices of Identity" for recent studies that reach differing conclusions about Austin's feminization of the natural world.

2. Greta Gaard and Patrick Murphy include information on the historical use of this term in their recent collection of essays on ecofeminist literary theory, noting that the "majority of ecofeminist literary criticism" is "being practiced by younger academics who have received their degrees since 1990 and doctoral students who are building on the wealth of materials" (5). I use it in relation to Austin to suggest a new way of understanding both the eccentricities, difficulties, and complexities of her feminist paradigms, which have frequently been noted by her critics.

3. See James Ruppert's essay, "Discovering America: Austin and Imagism," on Austin and Native American religious and literary traditions for a general summary regarding these influences; for additional information on this subject, see Linda Karrell's "Lost Borders and Blurred Boundaries," which discusses the influence of Native American storytelling traditions on Austin's fictional sketches

in *Lost Borders* and Mark Hoyer's recent book, *Dancing Ghosts,* a comparative study of Native American and Christian religions.

4. Pryse summarizes Austin's well-known and documented personal difficulties, including her unhappy childhood, her unsuccessful marriage, the difficulties she endured as the mother of a "mentally retarded daughter, possibly a genetic inheritance from her husband's family," and her "disappointing love affair with Lincoln Steffens" (xiii-xiv).

Works Cited

Austin, Mary Hunter. *Stories from the Country of Lost Borders.* Ed. Marjorie Pryse. New Brunswick: Rutgers UP, 1987.

———. "Sex Emancipation." *Beyond Borders: The Selected Essays of Mary Austin.* Ed. Reuben J. Ellis. Carbondale: Southern Illinois UP, 1996. 43-55.

Carew-Miller, Anna. "Mary Austin's Nature: Refiguring Tradition and Voices of Identity." *Reading the Earth: New Directions in the Study of Literature and Environment.* Ed. Michael Branch et al. Moscow: U of Idaho P, 1998. 79-95.

Gaard, Greta and Patrick Murphy. "Introduction." *Ecofeminist Literary Criticism: Theory, Interpretation, Pedagogy.* Urbana: U of Illinois P, 1998. 1-13.

Hoyer, Mark T. *Dancing Ghosts: Native American and Christian Syncretism in Mary Austin's Work.* Reno: U of Nevada P, 1998.

Karell, Linda K. "Lost Borders and Blurred Boundaries: Mary Austin as Storyteller." *American Women Short Story Writers.* Ed. Julie Brown. New York: Garland, 1995.

Lanigan, Esther. *A Mary Austin Reader.* Tucson: U of Arizona P, 1996.

Norwood, Vera. "Heroines of Nature: Four Women Respond to the American Landscape." *The Ecocriticism Reader: Landmarks in Literary Ecology.* Athens: U of Georgia P, 1996. 34-56.

Murphy, Patrick D. "Voicing Another Nature." *A Dialogue of Voices: Feminist Literary Theory and Bakhtin.* Ed. Karen Hogne and Helen Wussow. Minneapolis: U of Minnesota P, 1991. 59-82.

Oelschlaeger, Max. *The Idea of Wilderness: From Prehistory to the Age of Ecology.* New Haven: Yale UP, 1991.

Pryse, Marjorie. "Introduction." Austin, *Stories* vii-xxxv.

Rudnick, Lois. "Re-Naming the Land: Anglo-Expatriate Women in the Southwest." *The Desert is No Lady: Southwestern Landscapes in Women's Writing and Art.* Ed. Vera Norwood and Janice Monk. New Haven: Yale UP, 1987. 10-26.

Ruppert, James. "Discovering America: Mary Austin and Imagism." *Studies in American Indian Literature.* Ed. Paula Gunn Allen. New York: MLA, 1983. 243-58.

Scheick, William. "Mary Austin's Disfigurement of the Southwest in *The Land of Little Rain.*" *Western American Literature* 27 (1992): 37-46.

Sandilands, Catriona. *The Good-Natured Feminist: Ecofeminism and the Quest for Democracy.* Minneapolis: U of Minnesota P, 1999.

Stineman, Esther Lanigan. *Mary Austin: Song of a Maverick.* New Haven: Yale UP, 1989.

Stout, Janis P. "Mary Austin's Feminism: A Reassessment." *Studies in the Novel* 30 (1998): 77-101.

Warren, Karen J. "Introduction." *Ecological Feminism.* Ed. Karen J. Warren. London: Routledge, 1994. 1-13.

Nicole Tonkovich (essay date 1999)

SOURCE: Tonkovich, Nicole. "At Cross Purposes: Church, State, and Sex in Mary Austin's *Isidro.*" In *Exploring Lost Borders: Critical Essays on Mary Austin,* edited by Melody Graulich and Elizabeth Klimasmith, pp. 1-20. Reno, Nev.: University of Nevada Press, 1999.

[*In the following essay, Tonkovich highlights the central trope of "border crossings" in Austin's first novel,* Isidro, *equating this idea with that of "cross-dressing" or gender-crossing in the work and contending that the novel "demonstrates that identities are fluid, existing within a network of roles proffered by church and state, family and peers, and are always able to be crossed."*]

When critics notice Mary Austin's first novel at all, they generally slight it. Recently it has been called a book with a "prosaic setting" wherein a "conventional hero" is saved by a "chum" in classic dime-novel style. The only "new twist" *Isidro* gives to the dime novel is to make the chum a "woman in disguise who accomplishes heroic feats."[1] An early Austin biographer, T. M. Pearce, considers *Isidro* to be "one of [her] fine achievements in the long narrative form";[2] nevertheless he faults the novel because it only hints at the social and political stakes at issue in the secularization of the California missions. Thus, Pearce dismisses it as a novel with "only an inkling of social consciousness."[3]

Regrettably, such dismissive evaluations have consigned *Isidro* to the status of mere biographical curiosity—a precursor, at best, to Austin's later narratives that show a mature feminism, a grounded and textured sense of locale and history. Yet the intricacies of *Isidro*'s plot conceal a profound and complex social consciousness. In fact, the seemingly gratuitous or formulaic plot elements find coherence in Austin's pervasive use of the figure of crossing,[4] a trope that indicates the overlapping interests of church and state in 1830s colonial California, where *Isidro* is set; in the early twentieth century, when it was written; and in the present moment. Moreover, such a reading suggests new dimensions to Austin's work. Scholars already appreciate Austin as a regionalist who explored the mystic potential of the southwestern landscape. *Isidro* establishes her as a novelist aware of wider national, social, and political issues as well.

A novel set in the exotic world of the Southwest missions, remote to eastern readers in space and time, that includes murder, romance, intrigue, several chase scenes, robbery, two kidnappings, an Indian uprising, an incipient revolution, and a forest fire in its 425 pages may justly be said to have a dime-novel plot. It is likely, in fact, that these elements are precisely what made the novel attractive to its first readers, easterners who had shown a great appetite for "historical novels set in picturesque locales," Helen Hunt Jackson's *Ramona* (1884) chief among them.[5] *Isidro* was, in fact, one of Austin's most widely circulated novels. First serialized in the *Atlantic Monthly,* this "fascinating Old California romance" found instant approval among that magazine's readers.[6] In 1905, Houghton Mifflin printed 11,770 copies of the novel's first edition, nearly twice as many copies as it published of any other Austin work.[7]

Yet plot is not the book's central concern, if plot be understood as merely how the novel comes out. In fact, the denouement is revealed in the first sentence: "It was the year of our Lord 18—, and the spring coming on lustily, when the younger son of Antonio Escobar rode out to seek his fortune, . . . as if it were no great matter for a man with good Castilian blood in him, and his youth at high tide, to become a priest; rode merrily, in fact, as if he already saw the end of all that coil of mischief and murder and love, as if he saw Padre Saavedra appeased, Mascado dead, and himself happy in his own chimney corner, no priest, but the head of a great house."[8] This sentence deflects the reader's attention from *whether* Isidro will become a priest to *how* he escapes the obligation and *why* his path to the priesthood will be crisscrossed with four hundred pages of distractions. It also summarizes the substance of those distractions—"mischief and murder and love." These three "coiled" elements name the categories of crossings the book contains. "Mischief," an element grammatically equated with "Padre Saavedra appeased" in the following clause, signals the thematic treatments of the double-dealings of and with the church in the face of imminent seizure of its lands and monies by the new Mexican republic. "Murder," or "Mascado dead," introduces the theme of patricide, a sin that results from cross-breeding, mistaken parenthood, and parental default, whether of families, churches, or nations.[9] Nor

does "love," which eventually enshrines Isidro in a domestic rather than a Catholic "house," proceed in a straightforward fashion, for it begins in the affection of a patrician gentleman for a "slim, dark lad" (33). The book's plot is driven by the necessity of sorting out these and similar double crosses, which produce convoluted chases across religious, political, and sexual boundaries—differences just beginning to be erased in colonial California, and so completely effaced by Austin's day that California had indeed become a "country of lost borders."

"A Priest Is a Shepherd in Some Sort"
(Religion in Colonial California)

Isidro is a novel written under the sign of the cross. The first edition bears the image of the Mission San Carlos Borromeo at Carmel on its cover, and the novel opens: "It was the year *of our Lord*" (1; emphasis added). The first two chapters introduce a trope of shepherding and immediately establish a rough equivalence between the crosier of the cleric and the crook of his secular counterpart, the shepherd. Before events intervene to keep him from his priestly obligations, Isidro Escobar proves that he need not be a priest in order to be a good shepherd when he rescues two dumb creatures—a fox and an Indian—from predators ("Priest's work," he tells himself [6, 12]) and, aided by a young shepherd lad, tries to restore a flock of sheep to its owner.

As the novel progresses, it becomes evident that Isidro represents the future of both church and state in post-1830 Mexico. His secular shepherding proves far superior to the church's. Isidro protects his adopted flock from predators; by contrast, the padres of Carmel *are* predators, punishing their neophyte Indian slaves for stealing food to keep from starving. Whereas Isidro tries to return lost sheep to their owner and takes care to ensure that the flock does not become dispersed nor intermingle promiscuously with others' sheep, the padres lose track of their flock. Most seriously, they have lost a lamb of pure lineage and the best breeding stock. Their attempts to recover this lost lamb set in motion a plot whose resolution demonstrates the stakes in power, land, and inheritance incipient in the realignment of church and state in the new Mexican republic. The new state, heady with rhetoric and posturing, proves to be as ephemeral as Valentin Delgado's fashionable clothing. The church's interests will best be served by pure-blooded gentlemen like Isidro who father secular dynasties and practice their religion independent of the promises rendered to—and the supervision of—the Mother Church.

The action begins when Valentin Delgado, a foppish fortune hunter sympathetic to the new republic, is given the task of identifying and locating sixteen-year-old Jacinta Concepcion Castro, daughter of the comandante of the Presidio of Carmel. Jacinta stands to inherit "a considerable estate," and if Delgado succeeds in finding her, he will win her hand in marriage. If he fails, or if Jacinta's pure bloodline cannot be established, her fortune "reverts to the church" (52). One of the reasons this particular ewe cannot be found is that she is dressed in wolves' clothing, as it were. Delgado is looking for a young woman, but he is doomed to fail because the young woman he seeks is dressed as and behaving like a young man. In fact, she is Zarzo/the Briar, the "lad" who has helped Isidro rescue the flocks of the murdered shepherd Ruiz.

In *Isidro,* cross-dressing is not simply a sensationalistic or dime-novel device. Rather, the gender instability manifest in cross-dressing suggests an accompanying political instability. Like other families of pure blood and privilege in the novel, the Castro and Ramirez families stand to lose their patrimony because their lines of genealogical inheritance, which depend on documentable heterosexual reproduction, are crossed. Jacinta has been abandoned by her mother and father and left to the care of an Indian woman who dresses her as a boy because "she fancied [the child] was safer so" (232). Isidro, potentially a fine breeder himself, has been promised to the church, where he will be expected to dress in skirts and obey laws of sexual abstinence. That this will not happen is reinforced in an early conversation between Isidro and Zarzo. Trying to discover the state of his new friend's soul, Isidro asks whether Zarzo has ever seen a priest. Zarzo replies, "One. He was fat, and had small hair, and wore a dress like a woman's. You look not like such a one" (77).

The friars' "dresses" echo Zarzo's improper attire and suggest political, rather than familial, instability. Their robes, and the clothing of most of the novel's supporting cast, are "essentially uniforms: garments denoting the one form or single shape to which each individual's life [is] confined by birth, by circumstance, by custom, by decree."[10] The priests' feminized attire is a source of amusement to the soldiers of the Mexican state and to renegade Indians, whose uniforms and ceremonial garb signify manly bravery. Both groups believe that a colony ruled by men who wear women's clothing, but who own all the arable land and control all the cheap labor, is a world upside down, a world ripe for revolution.

Confusion and mayhem dominate this world of petticoat government and bad shepherding. It is a world of double crosses and substitutions. Isidro is on his way to become a priest not of his own volition, but because his mother, who "had vowed herself to Holy Church and the Sisterhood of the Sacred Heart," had been drawn back from her novitiate to become the bride of the "hothearted" Antonio Escobar, Isidro's father. Her family

was thus "obliged to surrender a good lump of her dowry to Holy Church, with the further promise, not certified to, but spiritually binding, to give back of her issue as much as in herself [the family] had taken away" (3). Like his maternal grandparents, Isidro doublecrosses the church—doubly. He repeats his mother's defection, and for the same carnal reasons. Worse, he easily locates and promptly marries Jacinta Concepcion, thus cheating the church of both the Escobar and Ramirez fortunes.

In a world ruled by men who dress like women, where novices desert the church for passionate love, where wives run away from their husbands and heiresses dress like men, the lines of power and inheritance become crossed. The novel is generally populated by mongrels, "men of no blood" (14), whose faculties of reason are poor, who can sign their legal papers only with "a cross" (161). These crossbreeds, although would-be rebels, are not, the narrator assures us, "the stuff of which new civilizations are made" (336). They "wished not to live always in one place, wear clothes, marry one wife and stay by her. . . . They missed the excitement of tribal feasts and dances, feuds and border wars" (336, 337). Nomadism, improper dress, and impure breeding, this declaration implies, inevitably produce fathers who are not fathers, sons who are not loyal sons.

In such a topsy-turvy world, revolution and patricide go hand in hand. *Isidro*'s first murder is committed by a drunken shepherd who, hearing his mother's reputation sullied, unwittingly murders the man who is his father. Patricide is in turn a figure for other social and political disruptions that result when genealogical inheritance and fraternal obligation are disregarded. Indians who run away from the missions foment rebellion against the father-priests—an act again associated with a form of atavistic cross-dressing. When Isidro expresses doubt that Indians who had been raised in the missions, "made Christians, [and] taught to save their souls from hell," would turn against the church, his guide ironically replies, "Manuel . . . was a Christian. I remember an Easter when he served the mass. That was he you saw last night, with the rattle of ram's horn and a bear's teeth grinning on his shoulders" (284, 285). Manuel's reversion is doubly dangerous: not only does he dance "out of season"—suggesting that he has become estranged from his indigenous tribal culture—but he is also engaged in the "Devil's work," participating in a war dance preparatory to raiding the mission (275-76).

Most seriously, in rebelling against Spain, Mexico is attempting patricide. The revolutionary ideas on which the rebellion is based are laid at the feet of unruly and unfaithful women who have exceeded appropriate social roles. For its part, Spain blames Mexico's insurrection on the church. As the narrator ironically remarks, "Liberty in the figure of a female finds easy worship among a people who count a woman chief among the Holy Family" (123). The implication here is that loyalty and respect to the state are undermined by the church's inappropriate Mariolatry. Similarly, however, the church, which stands to lose its real estate if the Mexican rebellion succeeds, figures Mexico as "the strumpet Republic [contriving] evil against the Brothers of St. Francis" (45).

The dime-novel plot of *Isidro,* then, entails a number of different crossings: cross-dressing implies the confusion of apparently unproblematic sexual identity; chases and pursuits involve the physical crossing of territory; disputed state boundaries are soon to be obscured by other modes of political organization, whether because of the impending revolt of the Indian tribes or because of revolution in the south. Padres and shepherds exchange functions: the best shepherds are generally also the best fathers; careless shepherds are also impotent, disposable, absent, or despicable fathers. Highbred women and their sons renege on their promises to the Holy Church. Daughters forsake proper reticence to dress as men, ride horses, herd sheep, and pursue lovers. Parents are unwilling to stay put to raise their children; mothers abandon or are abandoned by their children's fathers, leaving their mongrel children with no natural loyalty to family or nation. All these unruly subjects threaten the authority of the church, the spiritual and political center of colonial California. Only by extricating Isidro from his vow to this doomed system can an orderly line of familial inheritance be maintained. Thus the novel's purpose, of showing how and why Isidro breaks his promise, is closely related to its social, political, temporal, and geographic settings.

"I Wish to Do a Man's Work More"

(Isidro's *Resonances in Fin-de-Siècle America*)

Although T. M. Pearce faults *Isidro* for lacking consciousness of the social issues confronting colonial California, at least his evaluation indicates his thoughtful measure of the novel. Virtually no Austin scholar, however, has considered how *Isidro* spoke to the social and political issues of Austin's own day.[11] Yet its success in the *Atlantic* and Houghton Mifflin's large press run suggest that it was positively received. Certainly this success was the result of the novel's treatment of issues still coiled around church, state, and sex, exacerbated by pressures of immigration, labor unrest, and women's increasing agitation for a more liberal share in the intellectual and political issues current in the first decade of the twentieth century.

Isidro joined a flood of other nostalgic works about the romantic West and Southwest. Eastern editors, publishers, writers, and readers had had their appetites for this material whetted by such popular tales as Jackson's *Ramona* and Wister's *The Virginian,* as well as by the illustrations of Russell and Remington that appeared regularly in the periodical press. In southern California, antiquarians, artists, and writers actively courted the interest of eastern readers, both by contributing to eastern periodicals and by seeking to establish their own version of an authentic regional culture. According to Kevin Starr, a "consolidated myth of Southern California" emerged beginning in the 1880s, using the nostalgic appeal of mission times as the myth around which to tout the restorative benefits of Southwest living.[12] Chief among the promoters of this myth was Austin's friend and mentor Charles Lummis. Lummis, a former editor of the *Los Angeles Times,* housed the Museum of the Southwest at El Alisal, his Los Angeles estate. Devoted to saving the California missions, Lummis used funds from the Landmarks Club to begin "reroofing California missions and preserving other historical landmarks."[13] During his years of acquaintance with Austin, he took over the editorship of *Land of Sunshine,* a magazine promoting regional interests, and fashioned it into an important venue for literature of the Southwest. Austin herself shared these interests, seeking with her writing to insist that "American" history and literature recognize the importance of the southwestern Indian and Hispanic cultures.[14]

Isidro's mission-days setting, characters, and theme exceed the period's fascination with things southwestern, however. Austin's chronicling of church history in *Isidro* also speaks to the uneasy truce between church and state in turn-of-the-century United States. The novel measures quite accurately the paradoxical fascination of contemporary Protestant readers with things Catholic.[15] The United States had only recently emerged from an era of rabid anti-Catholicism marked by the formation, in 1887, of the American Protective Association, a secret anti-Catholic order whose prejudices were fueled by a second wave of immigration from Catholic Europe; by rumors that major American cities—San Francisco among them—were under Catholic control; and by the church's support of labor union agitators.[16] Membership in the APA peaked in 1893, but declined rapidly thereafter. By the 1896 presidential election, both major political parties had turned their attention to other issues—notably free silver. By 1899, H. D. Sedgwick Jr. could write in the *Atlantic Monthly*: "old feuds between Protestant and Catholic have ceased to be as important as their united battles against moral decay."[17]

Isidro captures the essence of the nation's fascination—both negative and positive—with Catholicism. In its detailing of the moral laxity, economic opportunism, racial oppression, and ineffective civic leadership of the friars of San Carlos Borromeo, the book virtually endorses what many Americans thought they already knew about the church. In Isidro, however, readers found a hero who could be a model of acceptable Catholic American citizenship. Isidro respects the Mother Church while resisting the "unnatural" chastity of the priesthood; he demonstrates a characteristic American independence of thought and action by refusing to honor earlier generations' thralldom to the church; he chooses to be "a man": to father children and pursue economic opportunity and political independence; and, above all, he knows how to handle his woman, allowing her independent ways—indeed, even finding them attractive—but also harnessing her independence to the ends of pure breeding.

By "The End of the Trail," the novel's final chapter, turn-of-the-century readers would have had any lingering doubts about the Catholic threat completely assuaged. Isidro's assertion that he will not be bound by a promise made before he was born, and "therefore hardly within [his] power of agreeing or disagreeing" (411), is an effective assurance that second-generation Catholic immigrants might naturally reject their parents' unquestioning support of and obedience to church policy. The perception of monastic life as unnatural and demeaning to men, depriving them of their inherent masculinity as expressed in the qualities of action and sexuality, is simultaneously endorsed and forestalled in Isidro's reply to Father Saavedra's query about whether he wishes "not to do the work of Our Father Christ?" Isidro answers: "It is not that I do not wish it, but I wish to do a man's work more" (412). By the novel's end, readers are informed that Isidro has fathered children, taken over the Ramirez estates, and obtained "political preferment" (422). In an implicit address to readers convinced that the power of monastic politics had not declined over the intervening fifty years,[18] Isidro confesses an enlightened doubt "in regard to the foundation of the Franciscans—the Missions" (413), a doubt engendered, the narrator claims, by "all that Jacintha [*sic*] had taught him, all that he had learned from Mascado in the hills, all the eager young straining after ideals of liberty which fomented in the heart of Mexico" (414). In fine, Isidro embodies the ideal new turn-of-the-century American Catholic: respectful of the church and its traditions, aware of its failings, and independent of its dictates. In the best (Pan-) American tradition, he and his wife leave a land where religion has become corrupt to establish a "great house" in a new land of liberty (1).

For readers not embroiled in anti-Catholic sentiment, the book addresses, at least by implication, a number of other political and social issues. Southern Californians certainly would have been aware of Austin's implicit comparison of the "strumpet Republic's" wish to dismantle the mission system as an obstacle to economic development to the then-current arguments from developers in the Los Angeles area who saw the water claims of Owens Valley farmers as hindering the city's economic growth. Readers across the United States could not have overlooked the similarities between the Mexican struggle for independence from Spain in 1830 and the currently escalating border tensions under Mexican president Díaz, the recently resolved Spanish-American War, the ongoing negotiations over the Panama Canal, and the debates over Philippine independence. As Austin's fiction repeatedly demonstrates, "knowing the real estate history is one way of tracing the trail of a particular piece of land."[19]

The entanglement of politics with gender is foundational to the personal tensions Austin and other intellectual women like her suffered during the period in which *Isidro* was written. In the novel, the genealogy of real estate is paralleled by a concern over the personal genealogical entitlement manifested in heritable physical traits, as well as in more overtly political matters such as property inheritance and political enfranchisement. Here, family—like race and gender—is a mutable concept, one whose meaning far exceeds the "natural" bonds between parents and children. *Isidro* has no mothers, a theme that echoes Austin's own distance from her mother, a troubled relationship that remained unresolved at her mother's death in 1896, as well as the distance of this generation of New Women from their mothers. In 1905-6, as *Isidro* was reaching publication, Austin made the difficult decision to institutionalize her handicapped daughter, Ruth, an act she saw as effectively reproducing the maternal abandonment she herself had suffered and that she figured as "losing" her daughter.[20] By placing Jacinta/Zarzo under the foster care of a half-breed Indian woman and her French sheepherder common-law husband, Austin fictionally explores what might happen to a child bereft of her natural family. Both the artificial family of *Isidro* and the institution into which Ruth was placed are marginal to the dominant social/class system and are therefore more forgiving of deviance from the norm. Jacinta is allowed to grow and dress as a young man because it is natural and proper within her environment. Austin can thus believe that Ruth's institutional family will tailor her care to the child's "natural" behaviors as well. Austin, then, would be free to attend to supporting herself and pursuing her artistic dream in a society unforgiving of such unnatural maternal decisions.

Just before the novel was published, Austin received information that led her to attribute Ruth's mental deficiencies to heritable characteristics from her husband's side of the family.[21] Her attention in the novel to the supposed links between pure blood, miscegenation, and "natural" (or genetically linked) traits are evidence of her struggle with this issue. *Isidro* seems to assert that mixed blood leads almost inevitably to subaltern status. For example, the novel's villains are invariably characterized as being of mixed race. Mascado is "comely in a dark, low-browed sort, and look[s] to have some foreign blood in him" (12).[22] Mariano is a "man of no blood" (14), while his murderer, Ruiz, who is also his illegitimate and unacknowledged son, is "a mongrel as to breed" (15). The perquisites of "pure blood," on the other hand, cannot be denied. The novel emphasizes Isidro's "white" lineage: he is "of good Castilian blood" (1), with a "touch of Saxon ruddiness that he had from some far-off strain of his mother's" (9). And while Zarzo initially appears to be an ill-bred and wild young man, the narrator also stresses that "he" possesses inward traits of grace and inherent privilege: "The lad had seen only Indians, vaqueros, and some such wayfarer as Escobar. It had been a rough life, but he showed no roughness; he had been servilely bred, but used no servility" (88).

Austin's concerns over this issue were entirely consistent with those of her contemporaries. In the wake of Reconstruction and with floods of immigrants entering the country from both coasts, white Americans had become obsessed with the purity of their Anglo-Saxon heritage, seeking to equate whiteness with Americanness. When, by century's end, it had become apparent that race could not be guaranteed by surface signifiers of skin color, shape of skull, or alignment of facial features, white Americans sought to prove their entitlement by other means. Genealogy, earlier used to establish class privilege, now was pursued to document racial purity.[23] Genealogically based societies such as the Daughters of the American Revolution effected a rapprochement between whites North and South through establishing their common patriotic identity in ancestral Revolutionary patriotism, at the same time effectively barring recent immigrants from a claim to that identity. In California, the Native Sons of the Golden West echoed those policies on a local scale. Founded in 1875, the group was created to "function as a living, self-perpetuating monument in memory of [the pioneer] forebears of the gold rush era."[24] Membership was "limited to white males born in California on or after July 7, 1846," a date selected "because it marked the raising by Commodore Sloat of the Stars and Stripes at Monterey and proclaimed California under American rule."[25]

Such organizations reinforced gender roles as well, usually by designating the men's group as the main organization and then establishing women's "auxiliary" organizations. (The Native Daughters of the Golden West was founded in 1886.) The popular press urged women of Austin's generation to trace the heritable traits of their children through regular photographs, measurements, and written estimations of their health, accomplishments, and talents. Thus personal and nostalgic artifacts collected in albums and baby books, buttressed by documentary records, became ad hoc claims to citizenship and its entitlements.[26]

Despite her exacerbated personal concerns over these troubling and divisive issues of genetic inheritance, however, Austin also demonstrated a passionate commitment to challenging the dangerous race hatred such obsessions could fuel. Her obvious admiration for the Indian and Hispanic women with whom she associated led her to resist actively the deplorable practice of "*mahala* chasing," sexual violence against and abduction of women of color in Austin's own community.[27] (This practice offers an interesting parallel to Austin's decision to explain how Jacinta's assumption of masculine disguise has kept her safe in a dangerous world.) And while *Isidro*'s mixed-breed men are more or less amiable and amoral weaklings, all the novel's women, regardless of racial descent, are admirable, strong, principled, affectionate, self-reliant, intelligent, and brave.

"The Whole Art of Putting Yourself into Your Appearance"

(Isidro's *Relevance to the Twentieth-Century Reader*)

Clearly the crossings of *Isidro* have social relevance to the circumstances, personal and political, under which it was composed. The book's address to social issues of our own time centers on the novel's resolution, which might be seen as problematic for readers eager to establish Austin's feminism. In her afterword to *A Woman of Genius,* Nancy Porter calls Austin an "overlooked classic of feminism" and a "significant contributor to feminist analysis."[28] While such evaluations may be true of *A Woman of Genius,* they are harder to see as relevant to *Isidro,* especially to the novel's ending, in which Jacinta is properly married and reproducing children who will receive and pass on the Escobar and Ramirez inheritances. Sadly, it would seem, Jacinta Concepcion, who is much more interesting to contemporary readers—as well as to her would-be lover—when she is dressed as a man, is exposed. She is dressed in women's clothing and given a married woman as a dueña to teach her "the mysteries of the toilet and needlework, of which she knew nothing at all" (318). Worse, because she dressed in men's clothing, accompanied Isidro and slept by his side, and was kidnapped by a renegade Indian, it is assumed that "hands have been laid on her" (268), and Isidro must marry her to save her honor.

The novel's obsession with crossings "saves" this star-crossed marriage for feminism, however. The first, improperly contracted, marriage of Isidro and Jacinta/Zarzito stands not at the end of the novel but at its midpoint (237), suggesting that it is yet another double cross. It does not produce a comedic, happily-ever-after resolution because the couple was married for the wrong reasons: he has no romantic interest in her, nor she in him. Having rushed Jacinta to the altar to save her reputation, Isidro immediately abandons her to return to his father and defend himself against charges that he besmirched her virtue. Jacinta, for her part, is left to mull over this unforeseen and thoroughly unpleasant change in her circumstances. Thus their initial alliance threatens to reproduce the loveless marriage of Jacinta's parents (and Austin's own marriage as well). Only after Isidro is kidnapped by Mascado and Jacinta resumes mannish garb to search for him do they realize their love for each other. The narrator insists that "[a]s often as he thought of the Briar his heart warmed toward the lad,—always the lad,—never the cold, still girl" (267).

The novel's narration provides both a puzzle and a clue to an interpretation more comfortable to contemporary feminism. The puzzle is that even after it has been revealed that Jacinta is a woman, the narrator on occasion refers to her as Zarzo. This duplicity suggests that the narrator does not insist on Jacinta/Zarzo's essential identity as either woman or man, but seeks to emphasize the connection of gendered behavior to social and political context. Demonstrating in small how contingent the seemingly self-evident matter of dress may be is this short interchange between Jacinta and Marta, one of her surrogate mothers. Having again donned masculine clothing so that she can pursue her husband, Jacinta confesses to Marta, "I doubt I shall ever grow to like skirts." Marta replies, "I see no use in them myself. . . . It was not so in my mother's time, but is a custom of the Missions. No doubt it is an offense to God to look on a priest or a woman and know that they have two legs" (354). The answer to the puzzling inconsistency in narration lies in this interchange. When constrained by mission society, Jacinta dresses and acts as a woman; in the borderlands, as well as in the private sexually charged interchanges, dressed in trousers and doing men's deeds, she becomes Zarzo.

When abducted by Mascado, Zarzo foils the half-breed's sexual designs simply by refusing to play the woman: "Mascado saw he had still to deal with Peter Lebecque's graceless boy. Many a time in the last year at the hut of the Grapevine he had tried to betray her into some consciousness of himself as a lover through her consciousness of herself as a maid, and had been beaten back by the incorrigible boyishness of her behavior" (182). Yet he persists in his fantasy, imagining her as womanly against all odds. In the novel's climactic scene, as Zarzo enters the rebel compound, Mascado looks at her "in her boy's dress" and sees "the same slim lad . . . rounded and ripened to the woman of his dreams" (365). (Admittedly, at the time Mascado is suffering some delirium from a serious wound.)

Only moments later, Isidro, who is "thinking homesickly of El Zarzo," sees an entirely different person: "She stood beyond him in the shadow . . . the *erect* young figure and the level, unfrightened gaze. . . . 'Lad, lad,' he whispered. 'Señor,' she breathed" (372, emphasis added). In fact, the novel emphasizes that "lad" "was always after a word of supreme endearment between them" (402). This term implies that even after their marriage, Isidro considers Zarzo his companion rather than his property. That Doña Jacinta, who is, the

novel assures us, "kept at home with her young children" (422), will retain a measure of independence is forecast by her choice to ride to the couple's second, church-sanctioned wedding "as the custom was . . . not [on] her father's splendid mount as would any girl in her senses, but [on] the same kicking pinto" she had ridden when in the mountains with Isidro (420). She dominates the willful animal conventionally associated with male sexuality, effectively incorporating and reversing the symbolism of this custom. Thus marriage affords the best of all possible worlds for Jacinta/Zarzito and Isidro. She need not be a conventional woman within her home, since her husband (who was once satisfied to enter a celibate fraternity) still prefers to think of her as a lad. Just as important, Zarzo need not be merely a serving boy or an asexual companion to Isidro. Rather, s/he assumes, to use Sandra Gilbert's terms, a "third sex beyond gender,"[29] an identity that places her outside the traditional subordination of women. Because Jacinta has name, blood, and inheritance but lacks social conditioning as a woman, she knows that masculine as well as feminine behavior can be taught and learned, and, like clothing, may be assumed and discarded as the situation warrants.

Furthermore, a refusal to have Isidro and Jacinta marry would not only violate dime-novel sensibilities, but also would be unthinkably false to history and politics. Throughout the novel, Austin foregrounds her determination to keep her characters' actions and perceptions consistent with historical fact, frequently prefacing descriptions and actions with the explanatory phrase "as any one of that time must have done" (292). She occasionally addresses the reader overtly as well:

> These are the pipes of history, the breadth of whose diapason sets many small figures going to various measures like midges in the sun. They go merrily or strenuously, with no notion of how they are blown upon; but let the great note of history be stilled, and they fall flat and flaccid out of the tune of time. If you would know how . . . Isidro and Mascado, Peter Lebecque and his foster child, called the Briar, played out their measure, you must know so much of the note of their time.
>
> (288)

Emphasizing historical accuracy, Austin thus withholds her own judgment of her characters' actions. *Isidro*'s historical and geographical setting offers no alternative model for Jacinta's life; its women are either respectable señoras; déclassé mixed-breed unmarried mothers, such as Marta; or promiscuous and slightly ridiculous public gossips such as Delfina. Equally important, marriage keeps Jacinta's inheritance, Isidro's good character, and the Escobar money from the grasp of a compromised and doomed Catholicism. Other alternatives are unthinkable. If Jacinta and Isidro do not marry, she and her money will become the property of the fortune-hunting revolutionary gigolo, Valentin Delgado. If her true identity is not revealed, her fortune will revert to the church.

The contemporary reader wishing to claim Mary Austin as a feminist foremother must bear in mind the novel's contexts. Not only is the novel true to the gendered norms for behavior predominant in colonial California, it also respects a code of reality for Austin's own day. Although Austin and others of her generation of "New Women" successfully challenged many of the norms that hindered the fictional Jacinta, they were nevertheless not entirely free of stereotypical presumptions about their own behavior. Like her friend Charlotte Perkins Gilman, Austin left her husband and child, but not without consequences. Both Gilman and Austin may have explored new ways of thinking and writing, and may even have pushed at the boundaries of acceptable sexual behavior, but their success was limited to their immediately personal behavior and had limited effect on the masculine enclaves of art, religion, and politics. An example from Austin's life illustrates this contention. After separating from her husband, she bought land in Carmel and began to associate with the artists' colony there. The homosexual dalliances among several of this mostly male group—notably George Sterling, Jack London, and Ambrose Bierce—as well as their disdain for the formalities of marriage vows led Austin to assume that she, too, was free to explore her own desires. She soon discovered, however, that "the official logic of the Carmelites claimed grand passions necessary to the poetic inspiration of the male" but not the female.[30]

In her short story **"Frustrate"** (1912), Austin comments directly on the double standard that prevailed even among the supposedly enlightened intelligentsia in the early twentieth century, granting men a degree of sexual license while presuming that women's sexuality was—and should be—containable. In this autobiographical fiction, a gifted woman learns that men, despite their bohemian pretensions, prefer women who are attractive, self-effacing, and charming; these same men read the writer's own eagerness as unattractive aggression. A woman friend comforts her with these words: "It is the whole art . . . of putting yourself into your appearance. . . . I have too much waist for that sort of thing. I have my own game."[31] "Frustrate" appeared in *Century* magazine in January 1912 but, according to Melody Graulich, was never reprinted because Austin "may well have felt the story was too autobiographical, revealing too much about her own disappointments."[32] Thus Austin's biography and autobiographical fictions are echoed in *Isidro.* The novel works because most of the male characters persist in not seeing what is in front of them. Assuming that men dress and act in predetermined ways, they eat, sleep, ride, work, and travel with Zarzo for weeks on end, never suspecting the truth. Yet

Delfina, who does not share these limited perceptions, discovers the Briar's secret within moments. Delfina plays such a minor part in the novel, in fact, that one suspects she has been inserted into the plot at this moment precisely to emphasize Austin's ironic point about the differential privileges of gender.

Although many readers may be interested in finding a place for *Isidro* in a feminist tradition of U.S. fiction, others may assume this to be a nonissue in a scholarly world supposedly enlightened by a quarter century of feminist politics. Regrettably, however, binary thinking and gendered language persist, even in the most careful scholarship. For example, Eldon G. Ernst summarizes the Spanish/Catholic impact on colonial California in these words: "At best some Indians benefited from Franciscan spirituality and European technology; at worst many Indians died from imported diseases; overall, much of the Indians' cultural heritage was *emasculated.*"[33] While some might argue that this is merely a figure of speech, it seems clear that the traditional associations of religion with feminized weakness still pervade the thinking about this period. Ernst's language is a symptom of a larger problem facing scholars wishing to account for religion's role in U.S. history as well, particularly in the matter of racial politics. Just as gender is presumed to be binary and stable, so is it apparent that church, state, and ethnicity are separate concerns, at least in popular histories. For example, a scholar wishing to learn about the history of Catholicism in California will discover a relative paucity of survey sources that consider religion after the secularization of the missions in the 1830s. One seeking such information must consult specialized regional and religious histories.

Literary history repeats the assumption that church and state remain separate concerns in scholarship and in biography. Scholars, for example, agree on the importance of understanding Austin's immersion in and devotion to Native American mystical, spiritual, and religious practices; yet her biographers only briefly acknowledge her fascination with the mystical practices of Catholicism. Nancy Porter is relatively straightforward in asserting that Austin "credited" "Catholic mystical practices" "with her recovery from the cancer she was certain she had developed back in Carmel,"[34] although her short essay does not allow Porter space to elaborate on Austin's experience. Only Augusta Fink treats Austin's friendship with Cardinal Merry delVal, who had an interest in the mission at Carmel and its pivotal role in Austin's novel. In turn, delVal introduced Austin to other scholarly practicing Catholics who instructed her in church history and in the practice of prayer. Yet Fink, whose biographical intent is to emphasize mysticism, devotes only a page to Austin's experiences in Rome while giving an entire fifteen-page chapter to the writer's first contact with Native American mysticism in the Owens Valley days. As well, Fink deflects attention from Austin's contact with Catholicism by asserting that she was interested in how the "rites of the early Christian church resembled the approach she had learned from the Paiute Indians."[35] Esther Stineman, otherwise an impeccable source, scants Austin's Italian sojourn, only summarizing her transcendent experience in conquering breast cancer: "In Italy, even with 'pronounced' symptoms of breast cancer, Austin 'evaded' it by praying, by which she did 'not mean the practice of petition, but the studied attitude of the spirit of transaction with the creative attitude working within.'"[36] Admittedly, Austin's account of her association with Catholicism in **Earth Horizon** is also brief, but neither Fink nor Steinman honors the tone of awe that pervades her account of the experience;[37] nor do they probe for the details of mysticism, details that cannot be subsumed to Austin's interest in the supposedly quaint practices of ethnic groups.

Thus *Isidro* emerges as a novel of great potential interest to a generation of scholars who study performances of gender as well as those interested in Austin and the West. Those pursuing gender studies, particularly of transvestism and the performance of gendered identity,[38] should find in Austin a fascinating use of the trope of cross-dressing to address not only the politics of gender and race, but also the relationship of church and state, a political alliance rarely considered in scholarly discourse. Scholars whose interests center on Austin's corpus and its development will see in *Isidro* a breadth of social concern, present even in her earliest works, that exceeds the regionalism by which she is most traditionally classified. A literary community interested in the political issues surrounding national and postnational identities will find that the novel makes clear the links between crossing land and crossing gender, and between crossing gender and crossing national identities.[39] Finally, a political society still convulsed with the issues of gender hierarchies and racial/ethnic identities will be challenged by a novel that demonstrates that identities are fluid, existing within a network of roles proffered by church and state, family and peers, and are always able to be crossed.

Notes

1. Shelley Armitage, "Mary Austin: Writing Nature," in *Wind's Trail: The Early Life of Mary Austin,* by Peggy Pond Church, ed. Shelley Armitage (Santa Fe: Museum of New Mexico Press, 1990), 28.

2. T. M. Pearce, *Mary Hunter Austin* (New York: Twayne, 1956), 89.

3. Ibid., 91.

4. I am indebted to Ona Russell for several discussions in which our mutual understandings of this figure have been clarified. Her dissertation, "Dis-

courses of Crossing: Reconceptualizing Representation in the Nineteenth-Century United States, 1840-1890" (Ph.D. diss., University of California, San Diego, 1998), offers a study of the trope of crossing in U.S. literatures in figures ranging from Henry David Thoreau to Calamity Jane.

5. Karen S. Langlois, "Mary Austin and Houghton Mifflin Company: A Case Study in the Marketing of a Western Writer," *Western American Literature* 23.1 (1988): 34.

6. *Atlantic Monthly,* January 1905.

7. Langlois, "Mary Austin," 41.

8. Mary Austin, *Isidro* (Boston: Houghton Mifflin, 1905), 1. All subsequent parenthetical citations in the text refer to this edition.

9. Francis F. Guest presents a valuable analysis of the theological bases of the Franciscans' treatment of the Indian populations of California. According to Guest, under Spanish law, priests became "legal guardians" of their converts, which gave them binding responsibilities as parents (Francis F. Guest, "The Franciscan WorldView," in *New Directions in California History: A Book of Readings,* ed. James J. Rawls [New York: McGraw-Hill, 1988], 27, 30). Father Junípero Serra, for example, wrote to the military commander of the Alta California presidios: "I state to you that those wayward sheep [fugitive neophytes] are my burden, and I am responsible for them not at the treasury in Mexico but at a much higher tribunal than that" (qtd. in Guest, 31).

10. Sandra M. Gilbert, "Costumes of the Mind: Transvestism as Metaphor in Modern Literature," *Critical Inquiry* 7.2 (1980): 392.

11. Esther Lanigan Stineman suggests that *Isidro*'s plot offers parallels to Austin's biography, but she does not relate the novel to a larger cultural and historical context. See Stineman, *Mary Austin: Song of a Maverick* (New Haven: Yale University Press, 1989), 68.

12. Kevin Starr, "A Myth for Southern California," in Rawls, ed., *New Directions in California History,* 205.

13. Stineman, *Song,* 63.

14. Vera Norwood, "Mary Austin 1868-1934," in *Heath Anthology of American Literature,* 2d ed., ed. Paul Lauter et al. (Lexington, Mass.: D. C. Heath), 2:917.

15. For the interest of southern California Protestants in mission-period Catholicism, see Kevin Starr's *Inventing the Dream: California through the Pro-*

gressive Era (New York: Oxford University Press, 1985), 86-89. Starr characterizes northern California at the turn of the century as predominantly populated by "foreign-born Roman Catholics," while in southern California "the dominant population was Midwestern native-born Protestant" (238). According to Starr, "the mission myth was an essentially Protestant creation for an essentially Protestant Southern California. . . . For all its luxuriant imagery, the mission myth fundamentally celebrated the Protestant virtues of order, acquisition, and the work ethic" (89).

16. In San Francisco, for example, the church appointed Peter C.Yorke as a priest in 1891. In 1894, Yorke, an impressive rhetor, took on the de facto assignment of defending the church's interests against attacks from the American Protective Association. Father Yorke so successfully mobilized Catholic voters that, according to Mary E. Lyons, "in the [San Francisco] city elections of 1896 even the mere suggestion that a candidate shared some allegiance with the APA could and did sway the large Catholic vote" (Lyons, "Peter C.Yorke: Advocate of the Irish from the Pulpit to the Podium," in *Religion and Society in the American West: Historical Essays,* ed. Carl Guarneri and David Alvarez [Lanham, Md.: University Press of America, 1987], 402-3). Encouraged by this success, Yorke went on to support Irish dock workers in their waterfront strike in 1901, invoking the 1891 papal encyclical *Rerum novarum* as the basis for his position (Lyons, 404; Eldon G. Ernst, "American Religious History from a Pacific Coast Perspective," in Guarneri and Alvarez, 17).

17. Arthur M. Schlesinger Sr., "A Critical Period in American Religion, 1875-1900," in *Religion in American History: Interpretive Essays,* ed. John M. Mulder and John F. Wilson (Englewood Cliffs, N.J.: Prentice-Hall, 1978), 314, 317 n. 48.

18. For example, in 1893, rumors circulated concerning a spurious papal encyclical "ordering the faithful to 'exterminate all heretics' at the time of the feast of Ignatius Loyola" and of Catholics stockpiling weapons in the basements of church buildings (Schlesinger, "A Critical Period," 313).

19. Marjorie Pryse, introduction to *Stories from the Country of Lost Borders,* by Mary Austin, ed. Marjorie Pryse (New Brunswick: Rutgers University Press, 1987), xxvi.

20. Stineman, *Song,* 54.

21. Ibid., 227 n. 43.

22. In this case, the implication is that Mascado's comeliness is the result of foreign blood, Indian breeding being considered the lowest of the low in colonial California.

23. By 1900, at least seventy organizations in the United States based their membership on hereditary privilege. Thirty-five of them were founded in the 1890s. See Donald K. Pickens, *Eugenics and the Progressives* (Nashville: Vanderbilt University Press, 1968), 16.

24. Peter Thomas Conmy, *The Origin and Purposes of the Native Sons and Native Daughters of the Golden West* (San Francisco: Dolores Press, 1956), 5.

25. Ibid., 9.

26. Shawn Smith's "Superficial Depths: Visions of Identity in the Age of Mechanical Reproduction" (Ph.D. diss., University of California, San Diego, 1994) offers a brilliant analysis of the relation of technologies of photography, genealogy, and domestic documentation to the discourses of white supremacy in the United States in the late nineteenth century.

27. Augusta Fink, *I-Mary: A Biography of Mary Austin* (Tucson: University of Arizona Press, 1983), 84.

28. Nancy Porter, afterword to *A Woman of Genius,* by Mary Austin (Old Westbury, N.Y.: Feminist Press, 1985), 297.

29. Gilbert, "Costumes," 416.

30. Porter, afterword, 301.

31. Austin, "Frustrate," in *Western Trails: A Collection of Short Stories by Mary Austin,* ed. Melody Graulich (Reno: University of Nevada Press, 1987), 234.

32. Ibid., 228.

33. Eldon G. Ernst, "American Religious History from a Pacific Coast Perspective," in Guarneri and Alvarez, eds., *Religion and Society in the American West,* 4; emphasis added.

34. Porter, afterword, 302.

35. Fink, *I-Mary,* 144.

36. Stineman, *Song,* 105.

37. Mary Austin, *Earth Horizon: An Autobiography* (New York: Literary Guild, 1932), 103.

38. Marjorie Garber, *Vested Interests: Cross-Dressing and Cultural Anxiety* (New York: Routledge, 1992); Judith Butler, *Gender Trouble: Feminism and the Subversion of Identity* (New York: Routledge, 1990).

39. George L. Mosse, *Nationalism and Sexuality: Respectability and Abnormal Sexuality in Modern Europe* (New York: H. Fertig, 1985); Andrew Parker et al., eds., *Nationalisms and Sexualities* (New York: Routledge, 1992).

Works Cited

Armitage, Shelley. "Mary Austin: Writing Nature." In *Wind's Trail: The Early Life of Mary Austin,* by Peggy Pond Church. Ed. Shelley Armitage. Santa Fe: Museum of New Mexico Press, 1990.

Austin, Mary Hunter. "The American Form of the Novel." 1922. In *Beyond Borders: The Selected Essays of Mary Austin.* Ed. Reuben J. Ellis, 84-88. Carbondale: Southern Illinois University Press, 1996.

———. *Earth Horizon: Autobiography.* 1932. Reprint. Albuquerque: University of New Mexico Press, 1991.

———. "Frustrate." In *Western Trails: A Collection of Stories by Mary Austin.* Ed. Melody Graulich, 228-35. Reno: University of Nevada Press, 1987.

———. *Isidro.* Boston: Houghton Mifflin, 1905.

———. *Stories from the Country of Lost Borders.* Ed. Marjorie Pryse. New Brunswick: Rutgers University Press, 1987.

———. *Western Trails: A Collection of Stories by Mary Austin.* Ed. Melody Graulich. Reno: University of Nevada Press, 1987.

———. *A Woman of Genius.* New York: Doubleday, Page, 1912. Reprint. Old Westbury, N.Y.: Feminist Press, 1985.

Butler, Judith. *Gender Trouble: Feminism and the Subversion of Identity.* New York: Routledge, 1990.

Church, Peggy Pond. *Wind's Trail: The Early Life of Mary Austin.* Santa Fe: Museum of New Mexico, 1990.

Ernst, Eldon G. "American Religious History from a Pacific Coast Perspective." In *Religion and Society in the American West: Historical Essays,* ed. Carl Guarneri and David Alvarez, 3-39. New York: University Press of America, 1987.

Fink, Augusta. *I-Mary: A Biography of Mary Austin.* Tucson: University of Arizona Press, 1983.

Garber, Marjorie. *Vested Interests: Cross-Dressing and Cultural Anxiety.* New York: Routledge, 1992.

Gilbert, Sandra M. "Costumes of the Mind: Transvestism as Metaphor in Modern Literature." *Critical Inquiry* (Winter 1980): 391-417.

Guarneri, Carl, and David Alvarez, eds. *Religion and Society in the American West: Historical Essays.* Lanham, Md.: University Press of America, 1987.

Guest, Francis F. "The Franciscan World View." In *New Directions in California History: A Book of Readings,* ed. James J. Rawls, 26-33. New York: McGraw-Hill, 1988.

Langlois, Karen. "Mary Austin and Houghton Mifflin Company: A Case Study in the Marketing of a Western Writer." *Western American Literature* 23.1 (1988): 31-42.

Lyons, Mary E. "Peter C. Yorke: Advocate of the Irish from the Pulpit to the Podium." In *Religion and Society in the American West: Historical Essays,* ed. Carl Guarneri and David Alvarez, 401-22. Lanham, Md.: University Press of America, 1987.

Mosse, George L. *Nationalism and Sexuality: Respectability and Abnormal Sexuality in Modern Europe.* New York: Fertig, 1985.

Norwood, Vera. "Mary Austin 1868-1934." In *Heath Anthology of American Literature II.* 2d ed., ed. Paul Lauter et al., 916-18. Lexington, Mass.: D. C. Heath, 1994.

Parker, Andrew, et al., eds. *Nationalisms and Sexualities.* New York: Routledge, 1992.

Pearce, T. M. *Mary Hunter Austin.* New York: Twayne, 1965.

Pickens, Donald K. *Eugenics and the Progressives.* Nashville: Vanderbilt University Press, 1968.

Porter, Nancy. Afterword to *A Woman of Genius,* by Mary Austin, 296-321. Old Westbury, N.Y.: Feminist Press, 1985.

Pryse, Marjorie, ed. Introduction to *Stories from the Country of Lost Borders,* by Mary Austin, vii-xxxv. New Brunswick: Rutgers University Press, 1987.

Rawls, James J., ed. *New Directions in California History: A Book of Readings.* New York: McGraw-Hill, 1988.

Schlesinger, Arthur M., Sr. "A Critical Period in American Religion, 1875-1900." In *Religion in American History: Interpretive Essays,* ed. John M. Mulder and John F. Wilson, 302-17. Englewood Cliffs, N.J.: Prentice-Hall, 1978.

Smith, Shawn. "Superficial Depths: Visions of Identity in the Age of Mechanical Reproduction, 1839-1900." Ph.D. diss., University of California San Diego, 1994.

Starr, Kevin. *Inventing the Dream: California through the Progressive Era.* New York: Oxford University Press, 1985.

———. "A Myth for Southern California." In *New Directions in California History: A Book of Readings,* ed. James J. Rawls, 205-12. New York: McGraw-Hill, 1988.

Stineman, Esther Lanigan. *Mary Austin: Song of a Maverick.* New Haven: Yale University Press, 1989.

Anne Raine (essay date 1999)

SOURCE: Raine, Anne. "'The Man at the Sources': Gender, Capital, and the Conservationist Landscape in Mary Austin's *The Ford.*" In *Exploring Lost Borders:*

Critical Essays on Mary Austin, edited by Melody Graulich and Elizabeth Klimasmith, pp. 243-66. Reno, Nev.: University of Nevada Press, 1999.

[*In the following essay, Raine emphasizes Austin's treatment of the environment in her novel* The Ford, *arguing that whereas her best-known work,* The Land of Little Rain, *champions "the desert's sublime indifference to human agency and selfhood," her later novel seeks "a viable relationship between the acute ecological sensitivity of* The Land of Little Rain*" and the "equally acute awareness of the need for nonurban space to be recognized and reimagined as part of the landscape of capitalist modernity."*]

In her 1922 essay **"The American Form of the Novel,"** Mary Austin alludes rather ominously to the "scores of novels, eyeless and amorphic, kept moving on the submerged social levels by the thousands of readers who never come any nearer the surface of the present than perhaps to be occasionally chilled by it."[1] For Austin, the mass circulation of second-rate novels participates in but fails to reflect on the vast flow of social forces that constitutes modernity. In contrast to the naturalist view of modernity, the novel of "prophetic form" should reconstruct the present not simply as a flow of inscrutable subterranean forces, but as a lucidly reflecting surface whose shrewd revelations of "place, relationship and solidarity" may be chilling, but enable the recognition and cultivation of "the green bough of constructive change." For Austin, in other words, the modern novel's formal success depends on its progressive potential. Successful novels, she writes, "will eventually be found to lie along in the direction of the growing tip of collective consciousness" because they "deal with patterns that . . . have a constructive relation to the society in which we live." And to develop such a "constructive relation," the novelist cannot adopt the authorial pose of a "superior being standing about with his hands in his pockets, 'passing remarks,'" but instead must "be inside his novel," and "see himself as he is seen by the people with whom he does business" (85-87). By positioning herself within the social relations of modern capitalism, Austin's American novelist can render "the color, the intensity and solidarity of experience *while it is passing*" and at the same time "fix upon the prophetic trend of happenings" (86).

Austin proposes a modernist vision that is simultaneously aesthetic, pragmatic, and prophetic; like Emerson's "The Young American" and Frank Norris's portrait of the railroad magnate as the epic poet of industrial capitalism, her progressivist model of cultural production posits modern art and modern business as intertwined or coterminous rather than inevitably opposed.[2] Shifting between commercial and organic images of national community, she echoes Emerson's argument that literary form, like government, "has been a

fossil; it should be a plant"; and that given the fact of modernity, "our part is plainly not to throw ourselves across the track, to block improvement and sit till we are stone, but to watch the uprise of successive mornings and to conspire with the new works of new days."[3] Like Emerson, Austin views the land and the commercial-industrial system as two crucial factors in American social and spiritual progress.[4] But while Emerson sees social evolution as inseparable from natural processes because both manifest the same spiritual laws, Austin argues more concretely that cultural practice is embedded in the ecological as well as the social environment: not in universal Nature, but in particular material landscapes.[5]

Despite her valorization of "the quality of experience called Folk, and the frame of behavior known as Mystical," Austin's work as a political and environmental activist argues that attentiveness to the land is as much scientific and practical as aesthetic and mystical, and in fact is essential to good business sense.[6] As Reuben J. Ellis observes, Austin's interest in environment and adaptation paralleled then-current theories of evolutionary biology, process psychology, and pragmatic philosophy, and her use of "close observation and inductive exposition" to describe and interpret western landscapes and indigenous peoples "speak[s] to the liberal faith in 'facts' and the scientific method as debunkers of superstition and agents of progress."[7] A 1925 letter opposing the proposed Boulder Dam affirms Austin's earlier "prophecy" that if urban developers "resist the deep-seated factors of cultural evolution" such as the land's aridity and the farmers' water needs, "presently the land itself [will] speak." She insists that intuiting socio-ecological consequences is "not poetry," or "even prophecy in the sense that it proceeds from any supernormal or hifalutin faculty," but "plain deduction from known facts and measured forces."[8] In place of Emerson's poet's eye that "can integrate all the parts" of the landscape, Austin posits a pragmatic and prophetic "structural capacity" that her modern novelist shares with the social psychologist, the ecologist, and those able "to pronounce the word capitalism without a hiss."[9] The range of her professional and political work suggests that the "green bough of constructive change" depends as much on these modern forms of knowledge as on any purely aesthetic or mystical vision.

Austin's view of cultural practice as "prophetic pragmatism" is central to her 1917 novel ***The Ford,***[10] whose stark contrast to her better-known desert writings is important because it demonstrates the provocative complexity of Austin's "environmental imagination," to borrow a phrase from Lawrence Buell. In contrast to ***The Land of Little Rain***'s lyrical evocations of sublime "desertness," where "not the law, but the land sets the limit," ***The Ford*** constructs a conservationist fictional space in which it is no longer possible to perceive the nonurban landscape as a remote, resistant, and elusive "country of lost borders." Relations between human beings and the physical landscape are inextricable from social and economic structures: even the open range beyond the ranch fences is not wilderness, but "government land" fragmented by "invisibly divided squares" of private property (*Ford,* 55). The river delta is not a wild space teeming with nonhuman life, but a "glittering hieroglyphic" signifying the river's unfulfilled desire to "tur[n] mills or whirring dynamos," to "wate[r] fields and nurs[e] orchards"; the "watery waste," in other words, is a negative sign of the river's productive potential within the human regional economy (*Ford,* 34).[11] Several of the characters are lovingly attentive to the "intimate properties of the earth" and its plant and animal life (*Ford,* 414), but their relations with the local landscape take place within a systematically surveyed terrain traversed by flows of information and capital as well as of natural resources. The oil pipeline and the controversial aqueduct that would redistribute water from rural farms to city reservoirs are only part of the modern communication and distribution networks, which also include railroads, telegraph and telephone lines, and the U.S. Postal Service. In *The Ford,* both urban and rural spaces are structured not only by ecological relationships, but by systems of governmental, technological, and corporate power that also form part of the landscape with which, and within which, individuals must come to terms.

Admirers of Austin's desert writings are likely to be ill at ease in the systematized modern landscape of *The Ford,* and those who read Austin as an exemplary ecocentric writer may be disturbed by the novel's overt anthropocentrism. In *The Land of Little Rain,* Austin responds to the desert's sublime indifference to human agency and selfhood by decentering the individual human subject and imaginatively unsettling the boundaries between self and other, human and nonhuman, organism and environment, structure and process.[12] If that text represents Austin writing, as she asserts, "directly, in her own character,"[13] this "character" only "fleetingly gives [itself] a shape and a history," and more often registers its distinctive presence precisely through its permeability, both to "other people's stories" and to "diffuse perceptual centers" through which the speaker "imagine[s] the desert as it might look through the eyes of birds and animals."[14] In contrast, *The Ford* replaces this diffusion of narrative persona with a narrative form based on the bildungsroman, a genre centrally concerned with establishing the distinct "shape and history" of its male protagonist in relation to his social environment.[15] Austin's novel subverts the bildungsroman's anthropocentric and androcentric conventions not with experiments in ecocentric perception, but by redefining environment as simultaneously social, economic, and ecological, and by ironically juxtaposing Kenneth Brent's narrative of self-construction with his sister

Anne's less histrionic and more efficient progress toward individual agency.

Rather than examining the intrinsic value or affective power of desert ecology, *The Ford* explores how different relations to landscape produce or enable differing configurations of social and economic power. It considers the relation between gender identity and socioecological practice, and projects the possibility of ameliorating regional and individual economic disparities by irrigating "desertness" into farmland. Precisely for this reason, the book's recent reissue by the University of California Press is timely: Austin's feminist, conservationist novel anticipates the concerns of many 1990s environmental activists, historians, and cultural critics for whom the dialectical relation between nature and culture is inseparable from the sociospatial relations of gender, race, and class.[16] Less convincing but no less important than her better-known desert writings, *The Ford* is Austin's provocative attempt to articulate a viable relationship between the acute ecological sensitivity of *The Land of Little Rain* and her equally acute awareness of the need for nonurban space to be recognized and reimagined as part of the landscape of capitalist modernity.

The Ford is a fictionalized account of the 1905 controversy over water rights in Owens Valley, California, where Austin and her husband were active in an unsuccessful struggle to prevent the Owens River water from being diverted from local irrigation projects to the Los Angeles city water supply.[17] The novel traces the coming of age of Anne and Kenneth Brent and their childhood friends Frank, the son of local capitalist and land baron T. Rickart, and Virginia, the daughter of Rickart's ranch manager. Anne and Kenneth spend their childhood on their parents' ranch, but when drought strikes the valley, their father sells Las Palomitas and tries to restore his fortunes and satisfy his wife's social ambitions by investing in oil development with other local farmers. A born rancher who dreams of revitalizing the valley through irrigation, Steven Brent is a poor businessman. The farmers strike oil but are unable to store and transport it when Rickart unexpectedly gains control of the oil pipeline, causing their financial ruin and precipitating the death of Mrs. Brent, who dies after aborting an unwanted pregnancy. After this tragedy, Anne refuses to marry; she becomes a successful real estate agent and eventually buys back the ranch for her father. Meanwhile, Kenneth becomes an apprentice in Rickart's San Francisco law office, flirts with the bohemian socialism to which Virginia introduces him through her career as a labor agitator and would-be actress, and tries to heal the psychic wounds of his father's failure and his mother's death by defining his own vocation and the larger problems of gender and socioeconomic inequality. Kenneth eventually resolves his confusion by returning to the valley, reaffirming his affective and spiritual bond with the land, and trying to rally the farmers against the water-diversion project engineered by Elwood, a San Francisco booster, and against Rickart's bid for control of the valley's water rights. While the novel endorses Kenneth's utopian coming of age, its ironic treatment of his sexist assumptions and his limitations as a businessman and political strategist casts considerable doubt on his potential to revitalize the rural community. Austin describes his agonized wrestling with the "angels" of capitalism, socialism, feminism, and the land with alternating sympathy, amused tolerance, and exasperation, and proposes the practical and "long-sighted" feminist real estate developer Anne Brent as a far more promising protagonist for the modern novel of "constructive change."[18]

The Ford frames the problem of incompatible water-use proposals as part of a larger question about competing forms of foresight: the valley's social, economic, and ecological future depends on competing readings of the land and its potential, and the futures of individuals depend on their ability to envision and establish a "constructive relation" to a social and material landscape already incorporated into modern capitalist sociospatial relations. Austin's complex view of the rural landscape in *The Ford* differs dramatically from that of John Muir and other wilderness preservation advocates who launched an influential campaign to prevent the Hetch-Hetchy Valley from becoming a reservoir for San Francisco. The Hetch-Hetchy activists saw their campaign as a sacred mission to protect the natural landscape's intrinsic aesthetic and spiritual value from contamination by urban and technological expansion and the hegemony of exchange value.[19] In a famous statement, Muir called the proponents of the dam project "temple destroyers, devotees of raging commercialism," who "have a perfect contempt for Nature, and, instead of lifting their eyes to the God of the mountains, lift them to the Almighty Dollar. Dam Hetch Hetchy! As well dam for water-tanks the people's cathedrals and churches, for no holier temple has ever been consecrated by the heart of man."[20]

In contrast, Austin foresaw the impending desolation of Owens Valley not as the destruction of sacred wilderness, but as "the *return* of a great acreage of orchard and alfalfa to desertness," which would support urban development while "wiping out . . . the best of the few remaining chances for people of limited means to obtain homes on Government land."[21] [**"The Owens River Water Project"**] For Austin, the farmers and businesspeople living and working in Owens Valley complicated the preservationist binary between crassly commercial urban space and pristine, nonurban Nature. Like other conservationists, she recognized that the borders between human economies and natural ecosystems could not be so neatly drawn,[22] and she defined the issue at stake as "how far it is well to destroy the agricultural

interests of the commonwealth to the advantage of the vast aggregations of cities."[23] Like other conservationists, Austin believed that the best alternative to urban expansion and its attendant social and ecological problems was not wilderness preservation but regional development.

Originally a doctrine of scientific management of surplus water and public pastureland, conservationism by 1910 had become a broad-ranging "moral crusade" concerned, among other things, with the revitalization of rural life.[24] As William Kahrl notes in his study of the Owens Valley Project, both the conservationist principle of efficient use of "waste waters" and the ideal of the family farm were integral to the irrigation movement in California, where the expansion of irrigated agriculture seemed "the driving wheel of social and spiritual progress" as well as of economic development.[25] Supported by legislation such as the 1902 Reclamation Act, irrigation was to "extend opportunities for settlement and self-reliance to the common people by creating a whole new class of lands which would be made habitable through irrigation." Class conflict over land use would be eliminated, not by "breaking up the holdings of western corporate interests and redistributing their properties among a new class of resident farmers," but by scientifically restructuring rural space to accommodate both corporate interests and a revitalized agrarian individualism.[26] This model of regional development addressed widespread concern about the fate of the individual farmers who remained, in Austin's phrase, "producers rather than players of the game" (*Ford,* 289) in the era of urbanization, big business, and expanding managerial and distributive networks. It appealed to popular images of an idealized rural past in its attempt to reconstruct, through modern scientific management, family farm-based modes of production and social life that were becoming obsolete in the "age of incorporation."[27] Yet it also posited the nonurban landscape as a legitimate and progressive site of modernity, distinct from but no less modern than the spaces of the city. Combining Progressive Era social interventionism with scientific knowledge disseminated through national agencies such as the Reclamation Service and the Association of Agricultural Colleges and Experiment Stations, the conservation and rural revitalization movements sought to modernize the rural landscape and to insist, as Austin does in *The Ford,* that the landscape of modernity does not end at the city limits.

If the national system of railroads gave nineteenth-century progressives an exhilarating image of the technological annihilation of space and time that would modernize and Americanize the landscape, water conservation offered an alternative metaphor for progressive regional and national integration as a system of rationalized distribution, not of citizens and commodities, but of natural resources. This utopian image resonated even in texts not directly concerned with the problem of food production in arid regions: Edward Bellamy's decidedly urban novel *Looking Backward,* for example, uses irrigation as a figure for centralized distribution of social wealth, imagining human labor as a "fertilizing stream which alone render[s] earth habitable" and must be "regulated by a system which expend[s] every drop to the best advantage" to prevent "some fields [from being] flooded while others [are] parched, and half the water [runs] wholly to waste."[28] As Austin observes, water companies rivaled the railroads in "play[ing] the part of Providence" in western settlement and economic development; while the railroad companies pioneered what would become standard managerial methods in modern business, irrigation projects were central to the development of twentieth-century resource management and regional planning.[29] But if the need for irrigation figured "the complete helplessness of the individual in the arid West" without "an available water supply, organizing capacity, and that commodity known as capital," the water companies made production possible, and so seemed more intrinsically benevolent than the monopoly-controlled railroad system described in *The Octopus* as "the ironhearted monster of steel and steam, implacable, insatiable, huge—its entrails gorged with the lifeblood that it sucked from an entire commonwealth."[30] Norris's naturalistic image of the railroad as a monstrous organism evokes anxiety about the "miscegenation of the natural and the cultural" in the landscape of modernity.[31] But like Frederick Jackson Turner's description of commercial expansion as "an ever richer tide" pouring through "the arteries made by geology . . . until at last the slender paths of aboriginal intercourse have been broadened and interwoven into the complex mazes of modern commercial lines," the conservationist image of irrigation made the expansion of capitalist industrial technology seem reassuringly, rather than threateningly, continuous with the networks and flows of natural forces.[32]

Biologist and agricultural educator Liberty Hyde Bailey was one influential rural revitalization advocate who used conservationist imagery to reinvent the American farmer as both gifted producer and successful manager.[33] Bailey's book *The State and the Farmer* (1908) critiques popular nostalgic distress over the spectacle of the "abandoned farm," arguing that empty farm buildings indicate not the decline of American agriculture, but rather its changing practices. Small farms, Bailey says, have become larger agricultural enterprises that complement tilled fields with pastures, fallow lands, and timber stands, and augment working knowledge of local ecology with technological innovation, rationalized production and distribution methods, and systematic knowledge of changing urban and global markets. While some fail, many farmers have proved that the "fittest" can indeed survive—and expand their power and property holdings—by combining hands-on experi-

ence with a "rational outlook" and "respect for ideas in print," and by adopting new, scientific approaches to the business of farming. Like *The Ford*'s "long-sighted" capitalists, Bailey's modern farmer occupies a strategic position within a "ganglionic" network of canals, railroads, telegraph lines, mail order services, newspapers, agricultural periodicals, educational outreach programs, and banking systems.[34] Similarly, the farmer's vital importance to society lies in his unique position as "the man who stands at the sources": He is both the producer of nourishment and wealth, and the "natural conservator of the native resources of the earth," who manages flows of crops, soil, and water as shrewdly as he manages flows of information and capital.[35] By constructing agriculture as conservation, Bailey both naturalizes farming and rationalizes natural processes; his heroic vision of the farmer-as-conservationist conflates natural with economic flows, production with distribution, and the farmer-as-producer with the farmer-as-businessman, and so invests farming with the cultural capital of modern science and commerce, and agribusiness with the moral capital of traditional agrarian values.

Yet while attributing modern agricultural success to rural values and local knowledge, Bailey insists that rural life can be revitalized only through federal and state government agency. Echoing Emerson's assertion that "[g]overnment must educate the poor man" and that the very landscape "seems to crave government," Bailey argues that while the ganglionic networks are now primarily "concentrative or centripetal . . . piling up wealth in small cities and towns," progressive governments must expand their "distributive or centrifugal" capacity to transfer wealth from cities back to rural producers and disseminate vital medical, sociological, and agricultural knowledge into "the open country."[36] "It is not only important to farming," Bailey writes, "but absolutely essential to the nation that the man at the sources be reached": local agricultural societies must be "assembled, solidified, and educationalized" into a centralized hierarchy for national progress toward "definite social ends."[37] Bailey's obsession with systematizing rural space, like the California movement to restructure rural space through irrigation, suggests that behind his utopian rhetoric lay an anxiety about the ability of "the man at the sources" to survive in the modern capitalist landscape without being either consumed by "the organized interests of the business world" or subsumed into a rural mass movement that too closely resembled organizations of "the labor-union kind."[38]

In the modern landscape of both *The State and the Farmer* and *The Ford,* the individual farmer "born to wrestle with the earth" is a compelling yet deeply problematic figure (*Ford,* 228). Austin shared Bailey's concern for the farmers' economic prospects, and in opposing the Owens Valley Project she supported the "profounder moral right" of rural producers to conserve water for irrigation over the claims of an urban society she considered economically parasitic and culturally barren.[39] ["**The Future of the Southwest**"] But in *The Ford,* she is highly skeptical of the farmers' ability to read the modern landscape in a viable way. In the landscape of modernity, the characters who succeed are those, like Bailey's farmer-conservator and Austin's American novelist, who have pragmatic and prophetic insight into how the landscape has changed. Unlike the homesteaders, Timothy Rickart and Anne Brent are able to see the landscape not as an object of manual labor and conjugal desire, but as a map of socioeconomic relationships and of real estate and resource claims to be measured, managed, and sold. Unlike John Muir, and contrary to the expectations of most late twentieth-century environmentalist and ecofeminist readers, Austin does not suggest that the managerial and entrepreneurial gaze is automatically a desecration of the land. In both *The Ford* and her autobiography, she presents it simply as the "structural capacity" that allows her enterprising capitalists to "arrive directly without noticeable fumbling at the structural features of any situation," to "maintain within the main structures an immense amount of detail which was inherent in the situation itself," and so to see farther ahead than those still deluded by an obsolete pastoral imaginary.[40] Kenneth and others are struck by the "likenesses of method" with which Anne and Rickart benefit from the "noticing disposition" that allows them to intuit connections between apparently "inconsiderable items" (*Ford,* 274); locating themselves strategically within the modern distributive and communicative networks, they access and manage the flows of information, capital, and resources to secure for themselves, and perhaps for their communities, "an especial privilege in futures" (*Ford,* 227).

Unlike Bailey, who conflates production and distribution to posit "the man at the sources" as the successful manager of both, Austin suggests that production and management are fundamentally incompatible: the farmers' inability to outmaneuver Rickart and Elwood is caused by "the very elements which made them good farmers, producers rather than players of the game" (*Ford,* 289). While the rural landscape offers developers like Elwood and even ineffectual visionaries like Steven Brent "a clear call to realization" that speaks of "canals, highways, towns" or of "water and power [and] farms," the homesteaders find the land's voice "compelling" but "inarticulate" and productive of a kind of "enslavement" (*Ford,* 273, 361). Bound to the land by affection and physical labor, they respond to both drought and capitalist expansion by continuing to "tu[g] at the dry breast of the valley" rather than by imagining in any practical way how to transform their environment with development projects that serve local needs rather than urban growth or corporate profits (*Ford,* 225). The inauspiciously named Homestead Development Company is defeated less by lack of capital or by Rickart's or Elwood's machinations than by its own narrowness of vision, by the "invincible rurality" that binds the farmers to their own plots of land and makes them fear any enterprise that might "grow beyond their individual capacity to deal with it" (*Ford,* 221). Faithful to "the partial gods of their own boundaries," they lack organizing or "structural capacity," and so remain "completely out of the game," immobile as the stone "figures in the group of the Laocoön . . . serpent-wrapped, their mouths open and no cry to issue from it," trapped in the coils of the "octopus" of modern capital rather than assuming a strategic managerial position within its ganglionic system (*Ford,* 409, 368).

In her compelling description of the farmers' defeat, Austin draws on the imagery of American literary naturalism to conflate nature and capital, not as manageable systems and flows, but as vast, impersonal, and only partly apprehended forces whose power manifests itself in the homesteaders' invincibly rural temperament. The farmers become iconic figures paradoxically dwarfed, defeated, subsumed, and ennobled by monumental forces both within and external to themselves: the discrepancy between their reading of the modern landscape and that of the successful capitalists gives their inevitable defeat "the quality of ancient tragedy; the tragedy of men defeated, not squalidly by other men, but by forces within themselves which had the form and dignity of gods" (*Ford,* 290). Invoking what Mark Seltzer calls "a miscegenation of the natural and the cultural: the erosion of the boundaries that divide persons and things, labor and nature, what counts as an agent and what doesn't,"[41] Austin's powerful language dissolves the preservationist binary between nature and commerce into a naturalist landscape of mysterious forces and flows beyond human comprehension or control.

But if *The Ford* constructs a naturalist "melodrama of uncertain agency" in its compelling portrayal of the farmers' predicament, it also lucidly critiques the different forms of agency by representing them as complementary forms of partial blindness. The farmers labor in the "half-blind social struggle" represented by the one-eyed socialist organizer who is the "temperamental Pioneer of social revolution" (*Ford,* 191-92); the capitalists, meanwhile, engage in the half-blind pursuit of profit embodied in the unscrupulous prospector Jevens, whose one cast eye has "a separate intelligence of its own" (*Ford,* 8). With their eyes "far fixed upon the ultimate triumph," rural producers and bohemian socialists suffer "incredible immediate defeat" because they misinterpret the relationship between labor and capital "in the terms of personal conflict" (*Ford,* 191, 204). Meanwhile, the "half-gods whose divinity is conferred by dollars" succeed not by scheming against them, but by "taking the shortest distance between two points, ignoring the human element" altogether (*Ford,* 287, 385). For Rickart, laws are "not human institutions at the making of which men prayed and sweated, but so many hazards and hurdles of the game": "The most that he knew of mortgages, overdue installments, foreclosures, were their legal limitations; he did not know that men are warped by these things and that women died of them. It was as if a huge bite had been taken out of the round of his capacity, and left him forever and profitably unaware of the human remainder" (*Ford,* 176). Through this analysis of both failures of foresight, *The Ford* critiques naturalism's limitations as a model for constructive socioecological relations. While attributing both forms of "half-blindness" to innate temperamental differences, Austin nonetheless insists that the landscape of modernity is not intrinsically unmanageable, and that human agents possess the capacity and the social responsibility to propagate the "green bough of constructive change."

When he returns to the valley after his apprenticeship as a corporate lawyer, Kenneth Brent disrupts the naturalist tableau of the "half-gods of capital" and the "temperamental, the incurable pioneer[s]." He rides into the breach between "the kind of a man T. Rickart had become and the sort that was fleeced by him" (*Ford,* 386, 87, 295). Like Bailey's "man who stands at the sources," Kenneth embodies the spirit of rural revitalization, combining business and legal expertise with traditional rural values and intimate working knowledge of soil and stream. While claiming to be "done with business" because he is now a producer, he aspires to "produce an irrigation canal and a farming district" as well as alfalfa and mutton, and eventually becomes both a farmer and the president of a new water conservation company (*Ford,* 406). Kenneth's dual capacities are prefigured in his childhood "double consciousness" of both "public, boyish interest in the activities of the oil fields" and "absorbed, contemplative pleasure in which the piercing of the sod by the first faint spears of the brodea marked an epoch, and the finding of the first meadow-lark's nest a momentous discovery" (*Ford,* 90-91). Wavering between filial respect for Rickart's inhuman but impressive "structural capacity" and desire for the "maternal breast" of the rural landscape, he sympathizes with the farmers' vulnerability to both capitalism and the land, and shares Steven Brent's "desire to cover their lack with his own larger outlook" (*Ford,* 294).

Despite his good intentions, however, Kenneth's return as "Brent of Palomitas" resolves neither the novel's plot nor its central problem of "constructive relation." The plot continues for sixty more pages of revelations, setbacks, resolutions, and deliberations, during which the female characters critique the way Kenneth's rural revitalization project is circumscribed by his relentless personal project of masculine identity formation. Kenneth's renewed association with "the grazing flocks, the ribbed hills, the steady fall of the valley seaward" inspires him to argue that "it wasn't any feeling for the System that had got him, it was a feeling for the land," and that "the biggest fact in [his] existence" is that he is "Brent of Palomitas." Virginia objects that "you can't stop with just getting after the individual" because "it all comes back to the Cap[italist System]" (*Ford,* 404), but the novel's own sensitivity to landscape and satirical treatment of Virginia's fashionable socialist phrases undermine the force of this otherwise quite plausible critique.[42] Anne, however, is no less impatient with the homesteaders and her brother for what she considers their lack of "structural capacity" and myopic preoccupation with their own individual relationships to the land, and her dual status as a skilled and respected businesswoman and the novel's real heroine lends considerable weight to her liberal feminist critique of Kenneth's romantic agrarianism.

Succeeding at real estate "the same way other people are musicians and writers," because she likes it, Anne bases her own relationship to land on managerial rather than manual labor, and on a theory of property in which the market and legal systems overrule labor in determining value and ownership (*Ford,* 199). Like another successful female capitalist, Alexandra Bergson in Willa Cather's *O Pioneers!,* Anne disregards her brother's agrarian conviction that "the earth was the right and property of those who worked it, and that its values should accrue to them if to anybody" (*Ford,* 436). Like Alexandra, who prospers by emulating "the shrewd ones" who buy up "other people's land [and] don't try to farm it,"[43] Anne possesses what Austin calls "the gift of detachment": she can "buy land without wanting to work it . . . with the distinct intention of unloading it on somebody else who believed himself elected to work it and was willing to pay handsomely for the privilege" (*Ford,* 178). Anne's and Alexandra's investment skills depend on detachment from their brothers' Lockean view of property, in which, as Howard Horwitz writes, "property is created by mixing with nature one's labor, an inalienable part of the self," and so figures as "an analogue to subjectivity . . . a structure of representation and reproduction in which self is experienced."[44] Although Alexandra is also a producer who sets her face toward the land "with love and yearning" and "expresses herself" in the soil, she ultimately "loves the land not for its service but for its resistance to human will." For her, longing and personhood are not "absolute, or absolutely individuated" but only "for a little while."[45] As Horwitz argues, Cather's narrative of sublimely impersonal love for the land challenges natural-rights assumptions about the inalienability of both property and selfhood by disentangling "love from yearning, from identificatory desire, from viewing possessions as monuments to the self."[46]

Austin furthers this critique of natural-rights theory by pointing out how men's impulse to produce both property and selfhood by "mixing with nature their labor" feminizes the land as object of conjugal desire. In *Earth Horizon,* she describes the "spell of the land over all the men who had in any degree given themselves to it, a spell of its lofty and intricate charm, which worked on men like the beauty of women" to "set up in men the desire to master and make it fruitful."[47] Looking at "the almost untouched valley as a man might look at his young wife, seeing her in his mind's eye in full matronly perfection with all her children about her," men like Steven Brent view the land's "potential fecundity" as both "invitation and the advertisement of man's inadequacy" (*Ford,* 35, 225), while women like his wife and daughter "look at one another with sharp—or weary—implications of exasperated resignation."[48] But unlike some later ecofeminists, Austin objects not to the men's desire to own and develop the land, but to the lack of "organizing capacity" that prevents them from doing so effectively. In *The Ford,* the river itself wants to "tur[n] mills or whirring dynamos," to "wate[r] fields and nurs[e] orchards," but is "discouraged at last by the long neglect of man." The land "doesn't mean crops" to Anne as it does to Steven and Kenneth, but it does mean "people—people who want land and are fitted for land, and the land wants—how it wants them!" (*Ford,* 34, 199). While Rickart uses his entrepreneurial skills to accumulate capital for himself and his son, Anne uses hers to make real estate a profitable *and* progressive "liberal profession" and scientific managerial practice that she claims will ensure socioecological harmony: "Say a certain piece of land will grow prunes or potatoes; then you've got to have prune people or potato people. . . . I can make a Socialist out of a prune man . . . by keeping him six years on a piece of ground that was only meant to grow potatoes" (*Ford,* 234). Like Emerson's "true lords, *land-lords,* who understand the land and its uses and the applicabilities of men" and "mediat[e] between want and supply," Anne is "an agent for the land," using scientific analysis of "soil constituents and subsoil and drainage" to identify the land's intrinsic use values, and then selling it to the person best suited to realize its productive potential.[49] Alexandra Bergson ultimately argues, with John Muir, that the land "belongs" only to "the people who love it and understand it," suggesting the insignificance of both labor-based and legal property claims in the face of nature's transcendence.[50] Anne, however, argues that "you can absolutely find out what land is good for, and . . . it only belongs to the people who can do those things." Like Bailey's, her practice affirms the natural-rights bond between property and persons as based on inalienable qualities inherent in both, yet denaturalizes this bond by pointing out its dependence on and mediation by an expanding network of scientific, legal, and business institutions (*Ford,* 234).

Like his more enterprising daughter, Steven Brent recognizes that the arid western landscape undermines the masculine myth of "absolute and absolutely individuated" selfhood inherent in property, since "a man cannot simply appropriate individual holdings" of land and "make any quarter-section of it bear."[51] But like the other farmers, he lacks the capital and "organizing capacity" to sublimate his love for the land into a system of resource management that would nurture its potential fecundity. Enamored of "the promise of the land," the "residue of the romantic mining experience [and] allure of the desertness," men like Brent "spen[d] their lives going around and around in it," feeling themselves "enchanted by its longer eye-reach, its rainbow horizons; but in fact it [is] the *timeless space* that [holds] them."[52] Their form of foresight fails to be truly "prophetic" (that is, historically progressive) because it remains a contemplative, individualized desire for conjugal relation with the feminized landscape rather than a participatory attentiveness to socioecological structures and processes that is "true for the observer and successful in the outcome" because it is "related to the main structure as the twig is to the branch and the leaf to the twig."[53]

Anne, therefore, desires for her brother a *bildung* that will unsettle his devotion to the "partial gods of his own boundaries" (*Ford,* 409) and make him, as Alexandra Bergson hopes for her brother Emil, "fit to cope with the world" by developing in him "a personality apart from the soil."[54] Before Anne "wake[s] Kenneth to a sense of the future," he labors in "the snare of that strange, intimate delight, the mastery over his own body": the "satiny, smooth feeling of his skin and the taut muscles shor[e] him up against the sense of family defeat" and his father's subsequent "slackness of . . . surfaces" (*Ford,* 163, 161). Kenneth's "wholly pagan revelations of identity" focus on the boundaries of his own body rather than on the plots of land that ensnare the homesteaders. But the disciplining of his own body helps him to lift the traumatic question of the reasons for his father's failure and his mother's death "out of the obscure region of his feelings about them" to become "events merely, hard, reasonless features of the landscape in which he [is] to find his way about," though he does "not yet think of any way out and beyond them" (*Ford,* 162). This link between affirming the boundaries of individual selfhood and finding one's way in the socio-ecological environment also characterizes Kenneth's attitude in the struggle to revitalize the valley: "at the moment nothing mattered so much to young Brent as that he should take his own measure. Whatever he was up against,—laws, institutions, the passions and prejudices of other men,—he must know once and for all its nature and its name" (*Ford,* 398). And for him, the question of social agency in the landscape of modernity is inseparable from his own identificatory desire for the land. Having proposed his plan to put all the farmers' land and water claims in escrow to keep Rickart from buying them up and selling them out, "Brent of Palomitas" becomes literally "the man who stands at the sources" as he camps out and works on his own water-rights claim; his contact with the maternal landscape supplies "the need he stood in of healing and reassurance," and he grows "brown and leaner and at ease with himself, a kind of ease . . . inexplicable to Anne almost to the point of irritation" (*Ford,* 414).

While she shares her father and brother's "feeling for the land," which binds "them to it through the nurture of common experience," Anne's vocation is social rather than ecological. Her attentiveness to the land is instrumental rather than affective, focused on use values rather than aesthetic or ecological ones (*Ford,* 403, 361). Once she has "learned all that [is] necessary to the construction of the work in hand," she loses patience with Kenneth and Ellis's affectionate absorption in the details of local ecology (*Ford,* 414). And unlike Kenneth, Anne believes that "taking one's own measure" only counts if it is "successful in the outcome." While recognizing its valuable masculinizing function for her brother, she views his solitary retreat into physical labor on his claim as "a sort of sublimated mudpie making" that doesn't "settle anything," but merely allows him to ignore the reality that his Thoreauvian return to nature will only last "until she or Rickart or somebody of the same stripe [comes] along and [takes] it away from him" (*Ford,* 414, 431). By constructing his relation to the land as a matter of individual identity and labor rather than social or corporate power, Kenneth makes another shortsighted misreading of the landscape of modernity. Rather than establishing a "constructive relation," he merely "escape[s] the necessity of settling anything, of having to decide things that are important to be decided" (*Ford,* 430).

Anne's impatience with Virginia suggests her agreement with Emerson that "our young people have thought and written much on labor and reform, and for all that they have written, neither the world nor themselves have got on a step"; and her impatience with Kenneth echoes Emerson's assertion that "[s]o many things are unsettled which it is of the first importance to settle,—and, pending their settlement, we will do as we do."[55] But if Austin agrees with Emerson that progressive socioecological evolution emerges out of "muscular activity" rather than mere "intellectual tasting of life," her conception of "settlement" unsettles the opposition between intellectual and material production. For her, "settlement" refers both to the intellectual process of decision making *and* to the materially productive human settlement of the landscape that her real estate practice will bring about.[56] But through Anne's ironic critique of Kenneth's masculine quest for identity through working the land, Austin also insists that "muscular activity" is no more progressive than the "eyeless

and amorphic" novels she deplores, as long as both are directed toward individual self-production rather than toward "the structural features of any situation" and the "growing tip of *collective* consciousness."[57]

Retelling the Owens Valley events in her autobiography, Austin writes, "All this Mary business is a nuisance; having to stop and tell why she did things and what she thought about them" in the face of "affairs of the utmost constructive importance to the commonwealth, to which her status was that of a short person at a circus parade."[58] This wry remark suggests why Kenneth remains the "hero" of *The Ford* when Anne is clearly its working model of constructive practice. Virginia's dramatic but ineffectual narrative of "finding herself" as the "Friend of Labor," "Spirit of the West," and "woman of genius" suggests that rewriting the male bildungsroman as a female "Development of the Ego" has limited progressive potential. Instead, Austin ironizes both narratives of self-construction by contrasting them with Ellis's and Anne's less introspective outlook (*Ford,* 242, 307). Ellis surprises Kenneth by asking "a thousand questions of the land and the trail and the new life that came crowding to her quick, excited notice" rather than seeming "in the least interested" in him or in herself. And in contrast to the meticulous narration of Kenneth's every thought and emotion, Anne's development is more indirectly marked in the admiring but condescending comments of the men she outwits, and in Kenneth's belated realization that his sister has "views" (*Ford,* 296, 170). Anne is blunt and forceful in promoting her own practice of real estate as socioecological engineering, but her monumental stature as *The Ford*'s model of progressive womanhood and conservationist practice is announced not by a self-description like Kenneth's "I'm Brent of Palomitas," but by Kenneth's revelation that while he had "accepted for his sister, as most men had for all women, the necessity that one or the other thing in her should waste," "he saw now that it wasn't necessary, but simply stupid. It wasn't in the least that a woman couldn't be both as big as Anne was, and as womanly, but that men weren't big enough to afford her both within the scope of their lives" (*Ford,* 372-73).

Anne, who like Ellis is of a "noticing disposition," returns to Palomitas not to reconstruct her mother's house and garden in her own image, but to make it a center of operations from which one can see "full from the veranda the perspective of the valley" as far as "the line of the Caliente fence and the breach in the Coast Range, curving seaward"; or, if one chooses, take in "nothing at all but the banks of red geraniums, the new-planted beds, and the red rambler working close under the waves, with here and there a lifted, inquiring streamer" (*Ford,* 393). Through this "inconsiderable" image, Austin unobtrusively delineates the relational capacity that is central to Anne's success precisely by decentering her personal identity, by drawing attention away from herself and toward what she sees. In its graceful affiliation of intimacy and distance, Anne's perspective quietly overlooks the boundaries of property and identity in which Kenneth and the homesteaders are so intensely invested, and suggests a mode of vision that is neither "half-blind" nor torn, as in Kenneth's "double consciousness," between two conflicting views. Through the exquisite impersonality of this image, Austin suggests an affinity between Anne's disturbingly instrumental "structural capacity" and Ellis's more stereotypically feminine gift for intuiting and nurturing personal and ecological relations, which at first glance appears far more compatible with the perspectives of later twentieth-century ecofeminism. In the context of Anne's successful practice, the view from the veranda suggests a mode of vision that can operate simultaneously at multiple scales. Such a vision depends not only on "the estheticization of a particular place-bound relation to nature," which in the case of men like Kenneth ends up "fetishizing the human body [and] the Self," but on a more abstract structural understanding of "broader socioecological processes occurring at scales that cannot be directly experienced and which are therefore outside of phenomenological reach."[59] The subtlety of Austin's methods and "views" is perhaps easier to discern in *The Land of Little Rain,* in which her anti-androcentric deconstruction of individual narrative voice asserts itself more directly; but in *The Ford,* her critique registers its presence in, against, and around the edges of the narrative of self-construction, to be noticed by readers, like *Earth Horizon*'s Mary, who have "edged in," "scrooged and peeked between the elbows," and "judge[d] many times what was going on from what taller people said."[60]

Late twentieth-century readers whose environmental imaginations have been shaped more by John Muir's preservationism than by Liberty Hyde Bailey's conservationism will be disturbed by the extent to which Anne's "gift of detachment" obstructs her "feeling for the land." From our perspective, her conservationist faith in modern progress, capitalist entrepreneurship, and privatized social engineering makes her an unlikely candidate for an ecofeminist heroine. Yet *The Ford*'s pragmatic and prophetic insistence that nonurban space is inescapably part of the landscape of modern capitalism lends considerable weight to Anne's mode of foresight, and provides an important complement to the individual affective relations with the nonhuman landscape that make *The Land of Little Rain* so luminous with attention and desire. If, as Tara Hart argues elsewhere in this volume, the textual strategies of Austin's less anthropocentric desert writings "keep possibility alive" by constructing a "conditional female occupation of a suspended space" and a relation to landscape that is perpetually unsettled, *The Ford*'s commitment to the human beings who make their living in the landscape

insists on the centrality of "settlement" to the construction of a viable *working* relation between human and natural economies. In *The Organic Machine,* Richard White observes that "[e]nvironmentalists, for all their love of nature, tend to distance humans from it" by stressing "the eye over the hand, the contemplative over the active, the supposedly undisturbed over the connected," and argues for an understanding of natural and human economies as a single system of energy and labor.[61] Underlying Bailey's and Austin's vision of conservationist regional development is a similar argument that a pragmatic and prophetic relation to the landscape *in which we live* must accommodate a reading of human work on and in the natural environment as not always and automatically a desecration. There are naturalist moments in *The Ford* when the plight of the farmers and the ugliness of the oilfields stand as dystopian images of "that mysterious quality taken on by the works of man, power ungoverned by sensibility"; but the Brent family's collaborative rural revitalization project shows that both sensibility and power are necessary for effective resistance to male dominance and capitalist instrumentality (*Ford,* 145). For Austin, constructive socioecological practice requires both compassion and a more impersonal awareness that "the structural features of any situation" encompass self and other, culture and nature, human and nonhuman landscapes. When the young Kenneth Brent imagines even the oil derricks as "tall, iron trees—for does not iron come up out of the earth even as oak and pine?" this unsettling novel leaves the question open (*Ford,* 92).

Notes

1. Mary Austin, "The American Form of the Novel" (1922), in *Beyond Borders: The Selected Essays of Mary Austin,* ed. Reuben J. Ellis (Carbondale: Southern Illinois University Press, 1996), 84-88, 85.

2. See Clare Eby's lucid argument that Shelgrim the industrialist rather than Presley the writer is the epic poet of *The Octopus,* and that Norris's novel celebrates rather than opposes the epic project of capitalist expansion embodied in the railroad. Clare Virginia Eby, "*The Octopus*: Big Business as Art," *American Literary Realism* 26 (1994): 33-51.

3. Ralph Waldo Emerson, "The Young American" (1844), in *Collected Works,* vol. 2 (Boston: Houghton Mifflin, 1921), 379.

4. "I think we must regard the *land* as a commanding and increasing power on the citizen, the sanative and Americanizing influence, which promises to disclose new virtues for ages to come. . . . [T]he uprise and culmination of the new and antifeudal power of Commerce is the political fact of most significance to the American at this hour" (ibid., 370).

5. In *The American Rhythm*, Austin argues that poetry originates in affective motor responses to the experience of "rhythmic forms" in the natural environment, and that adaptation to the American landscape produces an affinity between Native American and modernist poetry. While valorizing "folk" and "mystical" relations to landscape, she suggests that subjectivity and culture are rooted both in the land *and* in the commercial-industrial system whose "new attacks on the mastery of time and space" transform the landscape and the "whole new scale of motor impulses . . . built into the subconscious structure of the individual" (Mary Austin, *The American Rhythm: Studies and Reexpressions of Amerindian Songs* [1923; rev. ed., Boston: Houghton Mifflin, 1930], 9).

6. Mary Austin, *Earth Horizon* (1932; reprint, Albuquerque: University of New Mexico Press, 1991), vii.

7. Reuben J. Ellis, introduction to *Beyond Borders*, 18.

8. Austin, "The Future of the Southwest," *New Republic*, 8 April 1925, 186.

9. Austin, *Earth Horizon*, 205.

10. Austin's conception of the "prophetic" resonates with Cornell West's term for the intellectual tradition of American pragmatism, and her model of socioecological practice prefigures West's view of "prophetic pragmatism" as a form of "left romanticism" that "tempers its utopian impulse with a profound sense of the tragic character of life and history": "Prophetic pragmatism is a form of tragic thought in that it confronts candidly individual and collective experiences of evil in individuals and institutions—with little expectation of ridding the world of *all* evil. Yet it is a kind of romanticism in that it holds many experiences of evil to be neither inevitable nor necessary but rather the results of human agency, i.e., choices and actions" (Cornell West, "Prophetic Pragmatism," in *Pragmatism: A Reader*, ed. Louis Menand [New York: Vintage-Random House, 1997], 406). Mary Austin, *The Ford* (1917; reprint, Berkeley: University of California Press, 1997). All subsequent parenthetical notations refer to this edition.

11. Even in *The Land of Little Rain*, "[i]t is the proper destiny of every considerable stream in the west to become an irrigating ditch," and "it would seem that the streams are willing" (Mary Austin, *The Land of Little Rain* [1903; reprint, New York: Penguin Books, 1988], 85).

12. As Kathryn DeZur points out in her essay in this volume, these unsettled boundaries are racial and cultural as well.

13. Austin, *Earth Horizon*, 189.

14. Lawrence Buell, *The Environmental Imagination: Thoreau, Nature Writing, and the Formation of American Culture* (Cambridge: Harvard University Press, 1995), 176-77.

15. See Elizabeth Abel, Marianne Hirsch, and Elizabeth Langland, eds., *The Voyage In: Fictions of Female Development* (Hanover: University Press of New England, 1983).

16. I have in mind the social ecology and environmental justice movements and some forms of ecofeminism that complicate mainstream environmentalism's emphasis on nature preservation by pointing out how the category of "nature" is defined and used to support various forms of socioeconomic oppression or to override the claims of indigenous peoples or those who live and work "in nature"—subsistence farmers and loggers, for instance—to participate in decisions about land use. See the essays in *Ecology*, ed. Carolyn Merchant (Atlantic Highlands, N.J.: Humanities Press, 1994); and *Uncommon Ground: Rethinking the Human Place in Nature*, ed. William Cronon (New York: Norton, 1996). See also, for example, the work of Howard Horwitz in American studies, Donna Haraway in feminist science studies, William Cronon and Richard White in environmental history, and David Harvey in geography.

17. See William L. Kahrl, *Water and Power: The Conflict over Los Angeles' Water Supply in the Owens Valley* (Berkeley: University of California Press, 1982).

18. The biblical image of Jacob wrestling with the angel is central to *The Ford*. In *Earth Horizon*, Austin writes that while for John Muir "the spirits of the wild were angels, who bore him on their wings through perilous places," for her the spirit of the desert was an elusive and terribly beautiful woman whose "dreadful, never-to-be appeased desire" inspired her answering desire to come back, as Kenneth does in *The Ford*, "to wrestle with the Spirit of the Arroyos" (188).

19. The Hetch-Hetchy campaign failed as well, but its premises were much more influential on the mandates and conceptual boundaries of mainstream environmental groups such as the Sierra Club, which, ironically, have often been forced to follow Muir's lead in preserving nature by marketing "wilderness" as a profitable tourist attraction.

20. John Muir, *The Yosemite* (1912; reprint, Garden City, N.Y.: Anchor-Doubleday, 1962), 202.

21. Austin, "The Owens River Water Project," *San Francisco Chronicle*, 3 September 1905, 19; emphasis added.

22. William Cronon similarly critiques the boundary between Chicago's urban history and the natural history of its hinterland: "Nature's Metropolis and the Great West are in fact different labels for a single region and the relationships that defined it" (Cronon, *Nature's Metropolis: Chicago and the Great West* [New York: Norton, 1991], 19).

23. Austin, "Owens River Water Project."

24. See Samuel P. Hays, *Conservation and the Gospel of Efficiency: The Progressive Conservation Movement, 1890-1920* (Cambridge: Harvard University Press, 1959).

25. Kahrl, *Water and Power,* 30.

26. Ibid., 32.

27. See Alfred D. Chandler, *The Visible Hand: The Managerial Revolution in American Business* (Cambridge: Harvard University Press, 1977), on the "managerial revolution" in American business. Also see the influential discussions of Gilded Age economics in literary and cultural history in Walter Benn Michaels, *The Gold Standard and the Logic of Naturalism: American Literature at the Turn of the Century* (Berkeley: University of California Press, 1987); and in Alan Trachtenberg, *The Incorporation of America: Culture and Society in the Gilded Age* (New York: Hill and Wang, 1982).

28. Edward Bellamy, *Looking Backward* (1887; reprint, New York: Penguin Books, 1982), 228-29.

29. See Chandler, *The Visible Hand*; Hays, *Conservation.*

30. Austin, *Earth Horizon,* 199, 271; Frank Norris, *The Octopus* (1901; reprint, New York: Airmont, 1969), 224.

31. Mark Seltzer, *Bodies and Machines* (New York: Routledge, 1992), 21.

32. Frederick Jackson Turner, "The Significance of the Frontier in American History" (1893), in *The Turner Thesis: Concerning the Role of the Frontier in American History,* ed. George Rogers Taylor (Boston: D. C. Heath, 1949), 7.

33. For a useful discussion of the nineteenth-century roots of Bailey's position, see Alan I. Marcus, *Agricultural Science and the Quest for Legitimacy: Farmers, Agricultural Colleges, and Experiment Stations, 1870-1890* (Ames: Iowa State University Press, 1985). Marcus argues that the development, promotion, and institutionalization of agricultural science enforced a distinction between "agriculturists" and "scientific professionals" and so implied that "farmers properly belonged within the business community" (219).

34. Liberty Hyde Bailey, *The State and the Farmer* (New York: Macmillan, 1908), 14, 16.

35. Ibid., 56-57.

36. Emerson, "Young American," 384; Bailey, *The State and the Farmer,* 125.

37. Bailey, *The State and the Farmer,* 115-16.

38. Ibid., 120, 122. The nineteenth-century Populist movement clearly underlies this anxiety about rural mass politics, even though organized labor generally did not support the Populists because they addressed the interests of "*employing* farmers" rather than wage-earning farm workers (Trachtenberg, *Incorporation,* 176). As Marcus points out in *Agricultural Science and the Quest for Legitimacy,* Populist revolt was partly motivated by ambivalence toward the kind of institutionalized agricultural science that Bailey represented and promoted as president of the Association of American Agricultural Colleges and Experiment Stations.

39. Austin, "Future," 186.

40. Austin, *Earth Horizon,* 205. In this section of her autobiography, Austin is describing Henry Miller, a San Joaquin capitalist and land baron whom she admired and used as the model for Rickart in *The Ford.*

41. Seltzer, *Bodies and Machines,* 21.

42. Here, Kenneth and Virginia rehearse two "half-blind" perspectives that still obstruct dialogue between some forms of ecological and Marxist theory. See David Harvey, *Justice, Nature and the Geography of Difference* (Cambridge, Mass.: Blackwell, 1996); and Merchant, ed., *Ecology.*

43. Willa Cather, *O Pioneers!* (1913; reprint, New York: Penguin Books, 1989), 68.

44. Howard Horwitz, *By the Law of Nature: Form and Value in Nineteenth-Century America* (New York: Oxford University Press, 1991), 222-23.

45. Cather, *O Pioneers!,* 65, 84, 308; Horwitz, *By the Law of Nature,* 223, 235.

46. Horwitz, *By The Law of Nature,* 235.

47. Austin, *Earth Horizon,* 270.

48. Ibid., 271.

49. Emerson, "Young American," 384; Austin, *Ford,* 200.

50. Cather *O Pioneers,* 308.

51. Austin, *Earth Horizon,* 270-71.

52. Ibid., 284-85; emphasis added.

53. Ibid., 205.

54. Cather, *O Pioneers,* 213.

55. Emerson, "Experience" (1844), in *The Oxford Authors: Ralph Waldo Emerson,* ed. Richard Poirier (Oxford: Oxford University Press, 1990), 222, 225.

56. Ibid., 222.

57. Austin, *Earth Horizon,* 205; Austin, "American Form of the Novel," 85, 86 (emphasis added).

58. Austin, *Earth Horizon,* 205.

59. Harvey, *Geography of Difference,* 303-4.

60. Austin, *Earth Horizon,* 204.

61. Richard White, *The Organic Machine* (New York: Hill and Wang, 1995), x.

Works Cited

Abel, Elizabeth, Marianne Hirsch, and Elizabeth Langland, eds. *The Voyage In: Fictions of Female Development.* Hanover: University Press of New England, 1983.

Austin, Mary Hunter. "The American Form of the Novel." 1922. In *Beyond Borders: The Selected Essays of Mary Austin.* Ed. Reuben J. Ellis, 84-88. Carbondale: Southern Illinois University Press, 1996.

———. *The American Rhythm.* New York: Harcourt, Brace, 1923.

———. *The American Rhythm: Studies and Reexpressions of Amerindian Songs.* Boston: Houghton Mifflin, 1930.

———. *Beyond Borders: The Selected Essays of Mary Austin.* Ed. Reuben J. Ellis. Carbondale: Southern Illinois University, 1996.

———. *Earth Horizon: Autobiography.* 1932. Reprint. Albuquerque: University of New Mexico Press, 1991.

———. *The Ford.* Boston: Houghton Mifflin, 1917. Reprint. Berkeley: University of California Press, 1997.

———. "The Future of the Southwest." *New Republic,* 8 April 1925, 186.

———. *The Land of Little Rain.* 1903. Reprint. Albuquerque: University of New Mexico Press, 1974; New York: Penguin Books, 1988.

———. *The Land of Little Rain.* 1903. In *Stories from the Country of Lost Borders.* Ed. Marjorie Pryse. New Brunswick: Rutgers University Press, 1987.

———. "The Owens River Water Project." *San Francisco Chronicle,* 3 September 1905, 19.

Bailey, Liberty Hyde. *The State and the Farmer.* New York: Macmillan, 1908.

Bellamy, Edward. *Looking Backward.* 1887. Reprint. New York: Penguin Books, 1982.

Buell, Lawrence. *The Environmental Imagination: Thoreau, Nature Writing, and the Formation of American Culture.* Cambridge: Harvard University Press, 1995.

Cather, Willa. *O Pioneers!* 1913. Reprint. New York: Penguin Books, 1989.

Chandler, Alfred D. *The Visible Hand: The Managerial Revolution in American Business.* Cambridge: Harvard University Press, 1977.

Cronon, William. *Nature's Metropolis: Chicago and the Great West.* New York: Norton, 1991.

———, ed. *Uncommon Ground: Rethinking the Human Place in Nature.* New York: Norton, 1996.

Eby, Clare Virginia. "*The Octopus*: Big Business as Art." *American Literary Realism* 26 (1994): 33-51.

Ellis, Reuben J. Introduction to *Beyond Borders: The Selected Essays of Mary Austin,* 1-21. Carbondale: Southern Illinois University Press, 1996.

Emerson, Ralph Waldo. "Experience." 1844. In *The Oxford Authors: Ralph Waldo Emerson.* Ed. Richard Poirier, 216-34. Oxford: Oxford University Press, 1990.

———. "The Young American." 1844. In *Collected Works,* 2:363-95. Boston: Houghton Mifflin, 1921.

Haraway, Donna. *Simians, Cyborgs, and Women: The Reinvention of Nature.* New York: Routledge, 1991.

Harvey, David. *Justice, Nature and the Geography of Difference.* Cambridge, Mass.: Blackwell, 1996.

Hays, Samuel P. *Conservation and the Gospel of Efficiency: The Progressive Conservation Movement, 1890-1920.* Cambridge: Harvard University Press, 1959.

Horwitz, Howard. *By the Law of Nature: Form and Value in Nineteenth-Century America.* New York: Oxford University Press, 1991.

Kahrl, William L. *Water and Power: The Conflict over Los Angeles' Water Supply in the Owens Valley.* Berkeley: University of California Press, 1982.

Marcus, Alan I. *Agricultural Science and the Quest for Legitimacy: Farmers, Agricultural Colleges, and Experiment Stations, 1870-1890.* Ames: Iowa State University Press, 1985.

Merchant, Carolyn, ed. *Ecology.* Atlantic Highlands, N.J.: Humanities Press, 1994.

Michaels, Walter Benn. *The Gold Standard and the Logic of Naturalism: American Literature at the Turn of the Century.* Berkeley: University of California Press, 1987.

The Yosemite. 1912. Reprint. Garden City, N.Y.: Anchor-Doubleday, 1962.

Norris, Frank. *The Octopus.* 1901. Reprint. New York: Signet, 1964; New York: Airmont, 1969.

Seltzer, Mark. *Bodies and Machines.* New York: Routledge, 1992.

Trachtenberg, Alan. *The Incorporation of America: Culture and Society in the Gilded Age.* New York: Hill and Wang, 1982.

Turner, Frederick Jackson. "The Significance of the Frontier in American History." 1893. In *The Turner Thesis: Concerning the Role of the Frontier in American History,* ed. George Rogers Taylor, 1-18. Boston: D. C. Heath, 1949.

West, Cornell. "Prophetic Pragmatism." 1989. In *Pragmatism: A Reader,* ed. Louis Menand, 403-16. New York: Vintage-Random House, 1997.

White, Richard. "'Are You an Environmentalist or Do You Work for a Living?': Work and Nature." In *Uncommon Ground: Rethinking the Human Place in Nature,* ed. William Cronon, 171-85. New York: Norton, 1996.

―――. *The Organic Machine.* New York: Hill and Wang, 1995.

Betsy Klimasmith (essay date 2003)

SOURCE: Klimasmith, Betsy. "'I have seen America emerging': Mary Austin's Regionalism." In *A Companion to the Regional Literatures of America,* edited by Charles L. Crow, pp. 532-50. Malden, Mass.: Blackwell Publishing, 2003.

[*In the following essay, Klimasmith discusses Austin's development of her theories of regionalism, especially her stress on the writer's intimate expression of "the specificity of place," and traces her application of these ideas throughout her career, from her first published essay to her late novels,* The Ford *and* Cactus Thorn.]

As a child, Mary Austin recalls, she foresaw her artistic future: "it was clear that I would write imaginatively, not only of people, but of the scene, the totality which is called Nature" (1991: vii). From 1900 until her death in 1934, Mary Hunter Austin published prolifically, authoring more than 30 books in genres including drama, poetry, fiction, literary theory, and nonfiction, as well as over 250 periodical pieces on topics ranging from irrigation to Indians to gender to genius. A century later, we can see that Austin's prophesied "totality" describes her versatility and productivity as a writer. Yet Austin understands her "totality" in terms of place. Toward the end of her autobiography she writes: "my books were always of the West, which was little known; and always a little in advance of the current notion of it. They were

never what is known as 'Westerns' . . . I wrote what I lived, what I had observed and understood. Then I stopped" (Austin 1991: 320). Austin's generative connection to the Western landscape is reinforced by the enduring popularity of *The Land of Little Rain* (1903), an episodic, largely nonfictional account of California's Owens Valley. Although Austin wrote perceptively of the various places she inhabited, including Illinois, New York, and California, readers and critics persistently link her work and personality with the arid landscape of the desert West. Identifying Austin with any single geography, however, obscures a theory of environment visible throughout her work.

Austin's focus on the meaning of place, honed by her experiences living in and writing from the southwestern United States, defines a brand of regionalism—and a theory of environment—that surface throughout her œuvre, connecting her widely varied texts and integrating her conception of region with her narrative practice. Austin left a textual legacy including her excellent naturist books *Little Rain* and *Lost Borders* [*Stories from the Country of Lost Borders*] (1909), as well as a theory of regionalism that considers environment more broadly. Her theory of regionalism makes visible the importance of place in all of her work, from the naturist texts to her fantasy, domestic and conservationist novels, to her autobiography.

Before exploring Austin's theory and tracing her practice of regional writing, it is useful to distinguish between her notions of place and environment. Place, considered both as object and as subject, is at the center of Austin's texts. In order to convey the meaning of a place, she believed, a writer needed to reveal its distinguishing qualities. Austin's texts, particularly her naturist works, are characterized by attentive and thorough descriptions of setting that lend an experiential quality to her work. This commitment to place reflected and helped to define the meaning of environment in her day. Austin's persistent grappling with "the land and its meaning" arose from and reinforced a commonly held Progressive Era belief that environments inevitably shaped people, who embodied the places they inhabited. Extending this argument, Austin claimed that a particular landscape should produce its own brand of narrative. Melody Graulich notes that Austin "believed that the desert landscape, the western storytellers and drifters, and the Indians helped her develop her voice, her way of seeing, and her art" (Afterword, in Austin 1991: 384). Austin applied the desert's lessons widely. Living out an inheritance of mobility, Austin followed a trajectory through geography and genre extending that of her pioneer foremothers as she moved from Midwest to West to East to Europe, finally returning to the desert in Santa Fe, New Mexico, where she returned as well to the naturist writing that had initiated her career.

IN RETROSPECT: A THEORY OF REGIONALISM

In 1932, living in Santa Fe, writing of the West, and engaged in political activism on behalf of Native Americans, Austin explicated her theory of regional writing in
an article titled **"Regionalism in American Fiction."**
She opens by noting the centrality of environment to
the human experience and to artistic creativity:

> Art . . . is the response [people] make in various me-
> diums to the impact that the totality of their experience
> makes upon them, and there is no sort of experience
> that works so constantly and subtly upon man as his re-
> gional environment. . . . It is the thing always before
> his eye, always at his ear, always underfoot. Slowly or
> sharply it forces upon him behavior patterns such as
> earliest become the habit of his blood, the unconscious
> factor of adjustment in all his mechanisms.
>
> (Austin 1932: 97)

Like many of her contemporaries, Austin believed that
environments inevitably shaped individuals and cultures; in her work, she constructs "the physical environment as the primary reality which must shape human
thoughts and choices" (Buell 1995: 81). Working
through the senses and intellect, an environment,
whether urban, small-town, or rural, exerts itself upon
the body and mind. Physical and emotional responses
to particular environments produce the genuine regionalism Austin admires. Regional writing is therefore intensely personal; it must "come up through the land,
shaped by the author's own adjustments to it"; it is
"deep-rooted" and "intensively experienced" (Austin
1932: 101).

Because intensive experience is the wellspring of "true"
regional writing, only a faithful representation of that
experience's particularity can convey the nuances of the
region. Austin derives her notion of particularity from a
variety of literary sources including Hawthorne's *The
House of the Seven Gables* and Cather's *My Antonia*;
children's literature offered another powerful model for
regional particularity. Labeling children "the most confirmed regionalists," she recalls that in her own childhood, "the best of everything appeared in *St. Nicholas*;
and the best was always explicitly localized, dealt with
particular birds and beasts, trees and growing things"
(Austin 1932: 102). This "explicitly localized" specificity asserts itself throughout Austin's work. Her narrators emphasize the importance, in coming to know
place, of time and patience, asserting that in order to
understand (and certainly to represent) a region one
must experience it both consciously and conscientiously.
She notes, "It is not in the nature of mankind to be all
of one pattern . . . any more than it is in the nature of
the earth to be all plain, all seashore, or all mountains.
Regionalism, since it is of the very nature and constitution of the planet, becomes at last part of the nature and
constitution of the men who live on it" (Austin 1932:

98). For Austin, regional specificity and variety constitute the core of personal, cultural, and literary experience.

Austin offers several criteria to help readers recognize
the type of writing that emerges from such careful attention to the specificity of place. In addition to being
of rather than *about* the place, she notes, a regionalist
narrative will feature the environment as more than
backdrop: "The region must enter constructively into
the story, as another character, as an instigator of plot"
(Austin 1932: 105). Today, readers note her success: "It
is a mark of the maturity of her vision . . . that her
protagonist is the land" (Buell 1995: 80). Her short stories and novels offer abundant examples of active environments, from the untamed California landscape that
produces the cross-dressing rebel heroine in *Isidro*
(1905), to the small town that acts as the "villain" in *A
Woman of Genius* (1912), to Dulcie Adelaid's personification of the Southwestern desert in *Cactus Thorn* (c.
1927, published posthumously in 1988). Whether it produces people in its image, forces people to adapt to its
conditions, or destroys people who resist or ignore its
demands, the environment acts powerfully, even in texts
which are not of the "West" with which Austin remains
most frequently associated.

In insisting on the particularity of different regions,
Austin emphasizes the heterogeneity of the nation and
claims that any national literature must reflect this diversity. Alluding to the "long disappointed expectation
of the 'Great American Novel,'" she asserts that an alternative vision of national literature is already at work
in the United States, a "genuine" regionalism emanating
not from politics or language, but from the "'guts,' the
seat of life and breath and heartbeats, of loving and hat-
ing and fearing" (Austin 1932: 98). As the source "from
which the only sound patriotism springs," a mosaic of
texts derived from increasingly particular regions—"the
Far West has split into the Southwest, the Northwest,
the California Coast and the Movie West"—most accurately reflects the nation's vastly varied geographies (p.
104). Austin's vision of nation, not surprisingly, is "not
one vast, pale figure of America, but several Americas,
in many subtle and significant characterizations" (p.
98).

While Austin defined regional writing as national writing, the tension between region and nation repeatedly
asserted itself as she tried to bring her work to a national audience. Given her readers' insistence on Austin's Western-ness, the bid for national recognition was
difficult, a fact emphasized by the caustic tone of her
article **"New York: The Dictator of American Criticism."** In this essay, Austin writes that, according to literary taste-makers, the nation is "centered in New York,
with a small New England ell in the rear and a rustic
gazebo in Chicago; the rest of it is magnificently predi-

cated through a car window" (Austin 1996a: 58). Reuben Ellis remarks that "ironically Austin, the western regionalist, at times felt herself embattled with a smug Northeastern narrow-mindedness that represented to her the worst of what a regional perspective could be" (Austin 1996a: 55). It is fitting, then, that Austin published both **"Regionalism"** [**"Regionalism in American Fiction"**] and **"New York"** in national periodicals. Although they did not pay well—always a concern for the self-supporting Austin—these periodicals allowed her to engage with a national audience.[1]

Aiming to reach that national audience, Austin offered regional writing as an alternative to the homogenizing forces of modernity. What she called an "automobile eye view" represented a force that privileged homogeneity over specificity, overlooking history and culture as it sped by (Austin 1932: 100). Austin notes, for instance, that the "world of American Indian lore," while literally quite accessible, is almost completely overlooked as an element of regional—and thus national—environment. "This world begins in the dooryard of every American child; it can be fully entered at the edge of every American town, it can be looked out upon from every train window and crossed by every automobile" (p. 104). Paradoxically, the technology that opened new regional worlds to Americans helps to close off the cultural history of place, region, and nation from the careful observation Austin advocates. In regional writing:

> Time is the essence of the undertaking, time to live into the land and absorb it; still more time to cure the reading public of its preference for something less than the proverbial bird's-eye view of the American scene, what you might call an automobile eye view, something slithering and blurred, nothing so sharply discriminated that it arrests the speed-numbed mind to understand, characters like garish gas stations picked out with electric lights.
>
> (Austin 1932: 107)

Austin's mission is clear: to identify and perpetuate a national literature made up of intensely regional work that, like the nation it reflects, can be understood only as a collective. Reciprocally, such a literary mosaic will help to produce for the nation a heightened consciousness of history, environment, and self. Investing the time necessary to know a region improves the individual—and thus the nation. Austin notes, "Whoever has lived deeply and experientially into his own environment" may develop the "nimble wit and . . . considerable capacity for traveling in one's mind" required of the regionalist (1932: 105). Self-knowledge and imaginative power serve as antidotes to the blurred vision and decentered self of high modernism.

Austin's vision of environment was not entirely deterministic; in her life and in her writing she asserted that people could escape from difficult or unsympathetic environments and seek out places to which they were better suited. In Austin's case, the desert landscapes of California and New Mexico provided the environment she sought as alternative to the frustrations of her Illinois childhood and the New York of her thirties. With "a mind made to the desert's order," John Farrar stated in a 1923 profile, "Mary Austin went into the southwest and the desert made her life articulate. It has never failed her since, nor freed her" (Farrar 1923: 47). Though Austin chafed at being constrained by her regionalism, she found in the Western landscape inspiration and structure for almost all of her published work.

ENCOUNTERING THE DESERT: *"ONE HUNDRED MILES ON HORSEBACK"*

Mary Austin's efforts to distance her writing about the West from "Westerns" surface even in her earliest work. In 1889, aged 21, Austin published **"One Hundred Miles on Horseback,"** a travelogue of the final leg of her journey from Carlinville, Illinois to the desert near Bakersfield, California, where her family planned to homestead. Although she was traveling with her mother and brother, here Austin narrates an individual journey in a voice reminiscent of such nineteenth-century diarists and letter-writers as Caroline Kirkland (*A New Home—Who'll Follow?*) and Mary Hallock Foote, whose encounters with Western landscapes were published nationally. Austin shares Kirkland and Foote's task of interpreting an alien region; like them, she is quite literally writing home. **"One Hundred Miles"** was published in *The Blackburnian,* the literary journal of Austin's alma mater. Although Austin had earlier rejected her mother's advice to become an English major, rebelliously choosing biology instead, she rebelled within the safety of a tiny Presbyterian college in her home town. Blackburn College was an extension of Austin's domestic reality, firmly affiliated with the religious values and moralistic perspective she would later reject. The familiar, epistolary style both recalls domestic narrative forms and presages her observant, descriptive naturist texts. She would later note in her largely third-person autobiography *Earth Horizon* (1932) that when she wrote **"One Hundred Miles,"** "all the derived and imitative influence of academic training fell away, and she wrote for the first time directly, in her own character, much as she did in **'The Land of Little Rain'**" (Austin 1991: 189). But the transformation was not quite so sudden, as the essay's content shows.

While Austin would sharpen her precise observations of landscape in her later work, she came to scorn most of the textual reference points she uses in **"One Hundred Miles"** to orient her Illinois audience to the desert environment. Having arrived in California knowing "nothing except what she read in Bret Harte and Helen Hunt Jackson," Austin uses the Bible, Jackson's *Ramona,* and Harte's Western stories—some of the very texts she would later decry as warping the nation's sense of region—to describe the structures, people, and scenery she encounters (Austin 1991: 177). In her later work Austin would convey the sense that the more deeply one knew the West, the more one could sense its unknowability. Here, however, her narrative voice has the naïve authority of the novice that Austin would later critique and complicate.

Echoing some of her literary sources, Austin's travelogue exoticizes and denigrates the people who make up part of the region. Though in much of her subsequent theory and practice of region Austin was careful, thorough, and generally respectful of the region's people, in **"One Hundred Miles"** her early textual training in how to frame her encounter with the West is apparent. Unlike the landscape, Westerners neither possess beauty nor inspire awe. She remarks upon the "outlandish-" and "fierce-looking Mexican shepherds," and the "dirty but picturesque children" (1996b: 26-8). This othering depiction of the desert's human and animal inhabitants would almost disappear from Austin's later work as her narrators increasingly integrated themselves into the landscapes they produced. We can see inklings of this heterarchical stance when Austin turns her attention to the domestic spaces of the West.

A vocabulary and perspective more closely linked to her later work surfaces briefly in **"One Hundred Miles"** when Austin discusses houses and begins to imagine the desert as home: "In each [canyon a] Mexican or Indian has built his hut of adobe or tule, planted his grapevine and set up his hive of bees" (Austin 1996b: 28). Like her contemporary Edith Wharton, Austin was raised to be attentive to the details of domestic space, and here that intimate understanding brings an imaginative identification otherwise absent from her initial encounter with the landscape. We begin to see how she would imagine her way into the people, animals, and even plants that make up the environment as she focused on the Owens Valley and began to develop her eye for landscape.

THE LAND OF LITTLE RAIN: WRITING OF THE REGION

Throughout her career, Mary Austin claimed that knowing a region required an intimate knowledge of its particularities. By 1903, when she published *The Land of Little Rain,* she had developed her practice of specificity. Her best-known and most widely available work, the text is a composite of fiction and nonfiction episodes—what Carl Bredahl (1989) terms a "divided narrative"—describing animal, plant, and human life in and around the Owens Valley. Significantly, the narrator does not attempt to speak about or for the West considered broadly, but attends instead to truths evoked by particular places. Only through the effort of intimacy,

she implies, can a person begin to see and eventually comprehend a place. She notes, for example, that while the casual visitor may never find a buzzard's nest, the diligent observer will be rewarded: "by making a business of it one may come upon them in wide, quiet canyons or on the lookouts of lonely, tabletop mountains" (Austin 1950: 19). Significantly, this effort at intimacy is not merely visual; the narrator "hunger[s] . . . for bits of lore and 'fool talk'" that will limn the cultural and historical complexities of the landscape (p. 63). Through intimate experience, region is figured on a human scale.

The Land of Little Rain mirrors Austin's efforts to understand the landscape that she had rendered alien in **"One Hundred Miles."** Austin integrated herself into the landscape in a variety of ways. She remembers ceaselessly observing her new surroundings. At night she would sit and watch "the frisking forms of field mouse and kangaroo rat, the noiseless passage of the red fox and the flitting of the elf owls at their mating. By day she would follow a bobcat to its lair in the bank of the Wash, and, lying before its den, the two would contemplate each other wordlessly for long times" (Austin 1991: 194). Here the facility and vibrancy that characterize Austin's regionalism in *Little Rain* [*The Land of Little Rain*] are visible. Further, she notes in her autobiography that she possessed "the scientist's itch to understand by getting inside the material in which he works" (1991: 159). As Austin explored the region, her training in rhetoric and botany led her to see in particular elements of her surroundings the chance for the landscape to "explain itself": "Mary was spellbound in an effort not to miss any animal behavior, any birdmarking, any weather signal, any signature of tree or flower" (1991: 195). Together, these elements become part of the complex system that Austin believed a regionalist must experience personally in order to represent her subject.

As practiced in *Little Rain,* Austin's regionalism integrates both people and nonhuman elements into the place. This literary move was foreshadowed by Austin's own encounters with the people of the Tejon Pass and Owens Valley. Biographer Esther Lanigan calls attention to Austin's productive relationships with older male mentors such as General Edward Beale, who guided Austin's understanding of the Tejon Pass, taking her to Indian villages, telling stories of his long and illustrious past in the region, introducing her to "sheepherders, Indians, and tall Mexican vaqueros," and securing "Government documents, military explorations, agricultural reports . . . [and] geological and botanical surveys" (1997: 197). All of these sources are woven into *Little Rain,* filtered (as Austin's own knowledge was) through the fabric of personal relationships. Similarly, in *Earth Horizon* Austin stresses women's roles in helping her to develop an ear for the stories the place had to tell.

Later, when they moved to the Owens Valley, Austin and her husband boarded for three months with a Mrs. Dodge, who "had knocked about the mining country for thirty years and loved talking. Dodge was an old-timer whose every word was interlarded with the quaintest blasphemies, between priceless idioms of the camp. By this time Mary had come to realize that blasphemies were a sort of poetizing" (Austin 1991: 237). Mexican and Indian women, too, live the stories that become the foundation for Austin's knowledge and the material for her representations of the landscape.[2]

In *Little Rain,* environment emerges as a complex system that must be understood both objectively and subjectively. *Little Rain* thus begins the argument that Austin would develop in works like *Lost Borders* and *The Land of Journey's Ending* for the complexity and connectedness of place. These naturist texts attend to connections among animals, plants, geological features, weather, and human culture in the isolated region. Coyotes make the same trails that Austin imagines "very intelligent men" would make (Austin 1950: 11). Animals and people use the water trails that were marked by ancient tribes (p. 16). The environment "breeds in the men, as in the plants, a certain well-roundedness and sufficiency" (p. 33). People learn "direct from the tutelage of the earth" (p. 94). Characterized by connection, the landscape asserts again and again that it can be understood only in all its complexity, a notion Austin emphasizes through her narrative technique.

Although she clearly writes from her own experience, in *Little Rain* Austin rejects the epistolary narration of **"One Hundred Miles,"** diffusing her personal voice. At least three narrative voices are present in *Little Rain*—Austin chooses among an ungendered third-person narrator, a male narrator, and a female narrator given to addressing her audience directly—each helping to initiate the reader into a personal, if textual, experience of the region. This narrative multiplicity implicitly allows narrators to occupy several subject positions at once, a strategy that underpins Austin's conjoined claims in *Little Rain*: first, that the desert landscape can be understood only if it is known intimately, and second, that an intimate knowledge might best be achieved by imaginatively entering into and observing from the perspectives of other desert-dwellers.

While claiming that place knowledge can only develop with time, Austin both offers and denies this knowledge to her readers by manipulating time in the narratives that comprise *Little Rain.* As she notes in **"The Basket Maker,"** "To understand the fashion of any life, one must know the land it is lived in and the procession of the year" (Austin 1950: 59). In **"The Streets of the Mountains,"** the narrator cautions the reader: "Never believe what you are told, that midsummer is the best time to go up the streets of the mountain—well—perhaps for the merely idle or sportsmanly or scientific; but for seeing and understanding the best time is when you have the longest leave to stay" (p. 67).

Here, Austin integrates her readers into her project, assuming either that they come to her text with the same eye she brings to the landscape, or that her text will help them develop this vision. Though she claims that only extended time will allow visitors to understand the mountains, her text immediately sets out to imitate and perhaps offer an alternative to extended experience. Austin plays with time, expanding and contracting it in order to allow her readers an experience of place accessible only via narrative.

> The drone of bees, the chatter of jays, the hurry and stir of squirrels, is incessant; the air is odorous and hot. The roar of the stream fills up the morning and evening intervals, and at night the deer feed in the buckthorn thickets. It is worth watching the year round in the purlieus of the long-leafed pines. One month or another you get sight of the trails of most roving mountain dwellers as they follow the limit of forboding snows, and more bloom than you can properly appreciate.
>
> (Austin 1950: 68)

Although the narrator begins watching the mountains during the tourist-approved summer season, the text quickly moves readers into seasons available only to more committed individuals. This "diffusion of narrative angle" allows Austin to manipulate space and time using a technique comparable to time-lapse photography (Buell 1995: 176). The text, then, begins to approximate through narrative the experience of prolonged watching Austin advocates.

Time changes the way in which environment operates in the narrator's mind, shifting memory, altering perception, and precluding the text from replacing—or even fully representing—the experience of intimacy with the landscape. One narrator acknowledges when she sees a place through "a rosy mist of reminiscence" that she "must always see it with a sense of intimacy in the light that never was" (Austin 1950: 31). Lanigan notes, "Her search for the authentic permits her to suspend ordinary consciousness in favor of the nonordinary or heightened consciousness . . . and by so doing, to enter into the spirit of the tale she tells" (1997: 79). Yet Austin is careful to call attention to the positions from which her narrators speak, reminding the reader of the text's constructedness. The meaning of place can be shaped only in reference to experience; if that experience is gained second-hand, through narrative, the meaning of place can never be separated from the narrator's construction.

Like time, intimacy brings with it an emotional attachment that shades the way in which the narrative is produced. When Austin writes, for instance, that "none other than this long brown land lays such a hold on the affections," or that "one finds butterflies, too, about these high, sharp regions which might be called desolate, but will not by me that love them," she reminds the reader of her subjective presence (1950: 6, 75). Austin's technique might be termed relational in that the narrator always writes from—and emphasizes—a personal relationship to the environment he or she describes. This relational quality extends from the land to animals to the people who together comprise the region.

If her narrators emphasize their own feelings about the landscapes they encounter, Austin also effaces the narrators' presence. Narrative is often positioned as hearsay, narrators as interpreters of others' stories. Austin's narrators gain access to the places and people that make up the region through careful observation and perceptive listening. In **"The Pocket Hunter,"** for example, the narrator notes, "I think he said the best indication of small pockets was an iron stain, but I never could get the run of miner's talk . . ." (Austin 1950: 25). Similarly, in **"Shoshone Land,"** Austin undermines her narrator's power when she reminds us that "there was never any but Winnenap' who could tell and make it worth telling about Shoshone Land" (p. 36). This alternate emphasis on and effacement of the narrator's role in constructing the narrative allows Austin to convey the complexity of environment; she would utilize this technique frequently as she began to publish in different genres.

NARRATIVE MULTIPLICITY IN *LITTLE RAIN* AND *LOST BORDERS*

When writing *Little Rain,* Austin notes, her authorial breakthrough came when she used the rhythms of the environment to structure her work: "She found it at last in the rhythm of the twenty-mule teams that creaked in and out of the borax works, the rhythm of lonely lives blown across the trails" (1991: 296). Graulich notes that for Austin "language and style originate from an understanding of what she would have called the 'landscape line'" (Austin 1991: 384). Austin linked the development of her distinctive style, form, and narration to the particular environments that had shaped her, including the Midwestern landscape that had molded her early life and the various landscapes she moved among as an adult. Given the variety and particularity of place Austin encountered even within a given region, it is fitting that she began her fictional explorations of region with short stories. In those short stories, especially in the collection of linked tales titled *Stories from the Country of Lost Borders* (1909), Austin evokes the particularity and complexity of place using some of the narrative strategies she initiated in *Little Rain.*

In *Lost Borders,* stories are overheard, gleaned from gossip, partially told or retold, recollected from the past. Any narrator's reliability is always open to ques-

tion; this is just as true of the main narrator as of the desert inhabitants whose stories she relates. Here, the "narrator acts as a filter of the tales related to her by and about the desert's inhabitants" (Lanigan 1997: 107). When we recall Austin's dictum that regional writing considers people as a part of the place, the stories told in this manner have the effect of emerging from the land itself via people who experience the land individually and know the land intimately. Another of Austin's observations in "Regionalism in American Fiction," that the land should be an active element in the narrative, is reflected in way the land acts: "The desert 'herself' enters every story in *Lost Borders* as a character and serves to unify and motivate each one" (Austin 1987: xxx).

We see here the development of a narrative style that takes its cues from the land itself, a strategy introduced in *Little Rain,* where

> Austin allows the book to be taken over by other peoples' stories and her speaker to imagine the desert as it might look through the eyes of birds and animals. In this diffusion of centers of consciousness, and her refusal to maintain an executive control over the perceptual center except at the level of the prescriptive aphorism, Austin adheres to what she sees as the ethic dictated by the place: "Not the law, but the land sets the limit."
>
> (Buell 1995: 176)

Austin's narrator plays with the notion of narrative omniscience here, sometimes revealing more than she has promised, remarking on the parts of stories she will never reveal, sharing her frustration when gripping stories refuse to be told. In some stories, like **"The Woman at the Eighteen Mile,"** she does all three. When she hears the woman's story, the narrator recalls: "I sat within the shallow shadow of the eaves experiencing the full-throated satisfaction of old field prospectors over the feel of pay dirt, rubbing it between the thumb and palm, swearing over it softly below the breath. It was as good as that. And I was never to have it" (Austin 1987: 207).

Later, she does learn the details of the woman's story, and while she promises never to reveal what she has learned, she later decides that this pledge "should not mean beyond the term of her life" (Austin 1987: 210). This pattern is repeated and varied throughout the text, and thus, "*Lost Borders,* enmeshing the reader in its web of fact and fiction, of gossip, speculation, and concrete detail, involves the reader in a collaboration with the narrator" (Lanigan 1997: 112). This collaboration gives the narrator a certain freedom and allows Austin to construct for her readers a sense of the region that echoes her own.

In *Earth Horizon,* Austin recalls that stories structured her early experience of the region: "Pete Miller's bear stories, Jerke Johnson's horse stories, sheepherders' tales, deeply touched with a far derived pagan lore, Basque, Mexican, Old French" (1991: 215). It is clear that Austin's West, as critics note of the region today, is a place where many cultures meet.[3] The water trails that interlace through the arid landscape in *Little Rain* become the narrative that webs the region in *Lost Borders.* Stories come and go; told through many mouths, they disperse, change, and return to their initiators in a participatory process that the text both explains and reflects. Austin would return to this form later in her life with *The Land of Journey's Ending* (1924) and *One Smoke Stories* (1934), in which she returns to the practice of writing *of* a region—the New Southwest—by knowing it intimately.

Her narrative strategies in *Little Rain* and *Lost Borders* also allow Austin to undermine and subtly critique conventions of gender. Using a male or gender-neutral narrator let her claim a more culturally powerful voice and distance herself from the nineteenth-century women writers who wrote about their personal encounters with nature (Lanigan 1997: 40). As she notes in *Earth Horizon,* Rudyard Kipling's tales were an early model: "with their slightly mocking detachment, their air of completely disengaging the author from any responsibility for the moral implications of the scene and the people of whom he wrote, [they] had at least pointed the way for a use of the sort of material of which I found myself possessed" (Austin 1991: 230).

Because Austin does not explicitly identify the narrator as herself, she gains the ability to cross boundaries of genre, geography, and gentility more easily than the earlier women writers whose narratives called attention to and were confined by cultural limits. No such limitations seem to be imposed upon Austin's narrator, who is equally comfortable in (and gains apparently unfettered access to) spaces ranging from mining towns to stormy mountain ranges to Mexican villages to Indian campoodies. Intimacy is afforded to a narrator who has become a part of the region.

While we can read Austin's disidentification with the narrator as a rejection of the domestic voice present in **"One Hundred Miles,"** it is perhaps more fruitful to see her narration as an outgrowth of domesticity's intimacy that enables her to convey a deeper sense of place, especially when we note the shift to a consistently female (if still somewhat effaced) narrator in *Lost Borders.* Lois Rudnick claims that "Austin is the first feminist critic to have argued for the importance of what she called the 'homecentric novel.' It was 'stupid and inexcusable,' she told a primarily male audience of critics, to ignore the centrality of women's fiction to an understanding of the development of American culture" (Rudnick 1987: 22, emphasis added).

In making the desert her home, Austin opens domestic modes of perception and communication, such as gos-

sip and the letter, to a broader audience. She uses these forms to redefine both domesticity and the West. Later, Austin would explicitly critique Midwestern domesticity's constraints, particularly in *Earth Horizon* and her largely autobiographical novel *A Woman of Genius.* In her desert texts, however, Austin offers a model for how the ideals and ethics of the home, such as intimate knowledge, sympathetic understanding, acceptance of the unusual, emotional connection, and imaginative identification are the very values that might lead to, or perhaps already characterize, a vibrant national literature.

As Austin's career progressed, *Little Rain*'s blend of place-centered fiction and nonfiction was refracted into the novels, plays, poems, stories, and journalism that comprise her varied œuvre. Because her regionalism aims to encompass both place and people, in much of her work, particularly her more realistic novels, place becomes one factor among many that shape narrative. In her most successful texts, she achieves what she would later term "the first of the indispensable conditions" of regionalism, incorporating environment "constructively into the story, as another character, as an instigator of plot" (Austin 1932: 105). In attempting to render the settings of her fiction recognizable to the inhabitants of that region, whether the region was the California West, New Mexico, or the Midwestern "Ohianna" with which she evoked her Illinois upbringing, Austin does more than account for the visuality of place with which a more touristic eye might be content. Rather, she engages actively with the complex elements that combine to form a particular landscape: its economics, its social and political culture, and its history, along with the physical environment.

REGION AS FANTASY: *ISIDRO* AND *OUTLAND*

Austin even applies her theory and practice of regionalism to her fantasy novels. She explains: "the countries down the rabbit hole and behind the looking glass never depart for an instant from fidelity to the topsy-turviness of the land of dreams" (1932: 103). Here Austin is describing children's books; but fantasy worlds structure two of her earliest sustained narratives, the novels *Isidro* (1905) and *Outland* (1910, co-written with George Sterling). Straddling two genres, the dime novels Austin read as a child and the utopian fantasies that were a part of the Progressive Era's zeitgeist, these often bizarre texts read as early attempts to translate her practice of regional writing into novels, a form more readily consumed than her less classifiable naturist work (Austin 1991: 63). As she would later write to H. G. Wells, "I agree with you that I can't write novels, but publishers will have them" (Pearce 1979: 107). In addition to their marketability, novels could serve as vehicles for social commentary. The sustained, authoritative narration inappropriate to her desert texts could proclaim that social problems like those she explored in her naturist works should not be dismissed as merely local issues.

Just as exploring and writing from the desert offered Austin a way to rewrite her domestic and narrative inheritance, in her fantasy novels the environment offers alternatives to conventional domesticity. In *Isidro,* for instance, the colonial California setting produces El Zarzo, a slim, heroic lad who becomes Isidro's buddy and partner in adventure until it becomes clear that the lad is in fact a gal. And while the two must marry, as Nicole Tonkovich explains, "she need not be a conventional woman within her home, since her husband (who was once satisfied to enter a celibate fraternity) still prefers to think of her as a lad" (Graulich and Klimasmith, eds. 1999: 14).

If Austin's critique of the constraints of traditional marriage and gender roles is (barely) concealed and (ironically) abandoned in *Isidro,* it is far more obvious in *Outland,* a fantasy novel of warring Indian tribes who live unseen by white people in the forests, mountains, and deserts near the California coast. *Outland* begins with an adult version of the tumble down the rabbit hole: Mona, a professor turned writer, and Herman, her sociologist suitor, follow a woodland trail into the forest realm of the Outlander tribe. As in *Isidro, Outland*'s environment has produced a culture that offers alternatives to conventional bourgeois love and marriage. When Mona rejects Herman's marriage proposal at the novel's beginning, she sets the stage for the reader's encounter with Trastevera, the female prophet or *chisera* figure present in stories such as **"The Walking Woman"** and dramas like *The Arrow Maker* and *Fire.*[4] As the visionary Trastevera charts the course for this unconventional society's survival outside of Anglo political and economic relationships with the land, she maintains an unconventional marriage to a younger man and enforces the tribe's commitment to rituals that require certain attractive young women to postpone marrying for seven years while they serve the tribe as wards. Significant here, as in *Isidro,* is Austin's implicit claim that the pre-Anglo conquest environment has produced female roles much more powerful than those condoned within bourgeois culture. The flip side of this environmental theory of gender surfaces in the novels that move back into more conventional domestic settings.

MODERNITY AND REGION: CONSIDERING THE
CITY

The intimacy with place Austin developed in her naturist texts also structures her novels set in more urban cultural, social, and physical environments. Upon moving to New York in 1910, Austin approached the city much as she had approached the desert. In her effort to "know New York," Austin explored different regions of the city, moving frequently, posing as a typist, working at artificial flowers, and selling pencils and shoelaces (Austin 1991: 352). She writes: "what I was looking for was the web of city life, the cross-ties and interweavings which brought all classes into coalition, made the city unit. . . . I had it in mind that I would make a fiction of my findings, which would do what nobody was doing in fiction for New York, presenting a closely woven section of the life of the city" (1991: 352). Austin lived in New York for 13 years, but "as a matter of fact," she confesses, "I never found it" (p. 352). While Austin tries to use the tools and practice of environmental intimacy in her new surroundings, the urban landscape eludes representation. Yet her efforts at representing urban landscapes again show how she channels her perceptive practice of experiencing place to criticize and offer alternatives to bourgeois domesticity.

Regionalist theory and practice link Austin's urban domestic novels *Santa Lucia* (1908), *A Woman of Genius* (1912), and *No. 26 Jayne Street* (1920) to her naturist work. First, in all of these texts the environment operates as a force that confronts and shapes the novels' characters, rewarding people who fit it and destroying those who misunderstand it. This role is made explicit in *A Woman of Genius,* the strongest novel of the three; the narrator describes the story as "the struggle between a Genius for Tragic acting and the daughter of a County Clerk, with the social ideal of Taylorville, Ohianna, [the protagonist's home town] for the villain" (Austin 1912: 5). In *Santa Lucia,* a fiction that combines the Western adventure genre (knife fights, ambushes) with the novel of manners (three versions of the marriage plot), Austin exposes the small town's cruelty when the vibrant Julia Stairs, unable to reconcile her passionate nature to the brand of femininity demanded by the college town's moral surveillance, commits suicide. *Jayne Street* tells the story of an idealistic young woman's doomed affair with a womanizing reformer. Here, high-minded political discourse is no match for the moral degradation produced by modernity's urban environment.

In these texts, Austin's treatment of bourgeois domesticity and gender roles reads as an outgrowth of the critiques embedded in *Lost Borders*' stories of cavalier men and the women who suffer them but survive (Lanigan 1997: 108). In *Lost Borders,* the desert becomes an alternative home, where morality is always considered in relation to setting and circumstances. Similarly, in her urban novels Austin imagines alternative homes for her heroines. The stage (*Woman of Genius*), the wilderness (*Santa Lucia*), and Europe (*No. 26 Jayne Street*) all serve as spaces where women may find new homes free from traditional domesticity's constraints. Significantly, both these alternative spaces and the repressive spaces they replace are described with the detail that characterizes Austin's attention to the land in her naturist works.

Although city novels are not usually considered regionalist, in **"Regionalism in American Fiction"** Austin allows for this possibility. For instance, Austin notes that Edith Wharton's *The House of Mirth* "fulfills the regional test of not being possible to have happened elsewhere" (1932: 100). Austin's urban novels echo *The House of Mirth* in criticizing social realities by describing them explicitly. In addition, the novels allow Austin to maintain her commitment to writing *of* place while fighting one risk of regionalism—that in focusing on the particularities of place, social commentary will be defused and dismissed as anomaly.

REGION AND THE CONSERVATIONIST NOVELS

Austin's regionalism is not limited to the aesthetics or visuality of place; region is never divorced from economics or culture, as her conservationist texts emphasize. *The Flock* (1906), *The Ford* (1917), and *Cactus Thorn* (c.1927) differently construct the forces of people, animals, natural resources, and economics in relation to environment. In these texts, as Anne Raine notes of *The Ford*, Austin's "commitment to the human beings who make their living in the landscape insists on the . . . construction of a viable *working* relationship between human and natural economies" (Graulich and Klimasmith eds. 1999: 262). *The Flock* and *Cactus Thorn* present different extremes of the conservationist viewpoint. *The Flock,* a novel describing the lives of sheep and sheepherders, asserts that the people who work the land are its best stewards, and only obliquely criticizes the national forces (here national parks) that contend for rights to the land. In *Cactus Thorn,* however, Grant Arliss, representing an exploitative national politics, is knifed to death by his erstwhile lover Dulcie Adelaid, who strikes on the desert's behalf. *The Ford's* vision of region falls in between. While these texts may not be completely in tune with equations of "environment" to "wilderness," they persuasively reveal Austin's regionalist commitment to landscape's specificity.

The Ford reads as a revisionist Western romance with a subplot focused on natural resources in an arid California climate. Exploring the issue of how rural communities can negotiate the future in relationship to an increasingly urban economy, the novel asks what constitutes a natural connection with the land and considers how to translate this connection into political, educational, agricultural, or commercial action. *The Ford* traces the economic history of a rural California town increasingly connected to the city by train, car, and telephone, and correspondingly evolving as the city's resource-rich hinterland. Austin's attention to detail leads her to show how modernity reshapes the space

of region. The novel's valley-dwellers cling to an idealized vision of the land's power and possibility, despite their lived knowledge of its harshness and vicissitudes. "It had come out so naturally for the bucolic imagination that, as Elwood had lived with the land, he had become possessed of a sense of its possibilities; its voice, so compelling and to them so inarticulate, had spoken to him in terms of canals, highways, towns . . ." (Austin 1997: 272). Though they are able neither to envision nor to mastermind the rural West's transformation, Austin's rural people want development, modernization, and especially the capital that new development may bring. Austin's optimistic attitude in *The Ford* toward modernity and development stems from her version of environmental determinism: that is, that the land determines what is best for it.

In portraying a family learning to read, coming to terms with, and eventually prospering from the particularities of place, *The Ford* articulates a regionalism grounded in realism and emphasizing progress. Both Brent children, the novel's most highly valorized characters, experience the attractions of San Francisco but decide to remain at their family ranch, forestalling the rural community's demise. Of course, the forces of modernity have linked the ranch to the city, offering Kenneth and Anne many more choices than their parents had. When Anne's doomed mother says, "Though I do live in the country, I don't have to be country," we see not only that the previous generation marked sharp delineations between rural and urban, but that ignoring the land's force is fundamentally destructive (Austin 1997: 52). As the boundaries between urban and rural break down, Austin suggests, so do many of the gender restrictions associated with the pioneer generation. Thus, Anne Brent is free not just to choose a successful career as a real estate agent and reject marriage, but to create the terms upon which she relates to the land that is her home. As in her domestic novels, in her conservationist texts Austin writes *of* place in order to re-imagine modernity and home.

REPRESENTING THE WEST

Austin's regionalism demanded a thorough and specific knowledge of place accessible only through sustained experience; yet by focusing persistently on particular places she risked both marginalization and limited understanding by the audiences and publishers for whom the regions she described were foreign. Writing in the third person, Austin recalls this difficulty in *Earth Horizon*:

> Mary wrote one of the earliest accounts of it, which in the East nobody would publish until it had long been an old story, seen by a sufficient number of Easterners for an account of it to have credibility in the printed page. That was how it was with a great many things Mary wanted to write about. When they were new and

fresh to her, Eastern editors wouldn't believe them, and by the time the East had become aware, Mary had moved on to something new and unauthenticated by New York.

(Austin 1991: 213)

Frustrated by this dynamic, Austin would abandon the novel after 1920 and return to the mosaic narrative form she had derived from the Western landscape.[5] Ultimately, it is *Earth Horizon* that brings together her theory and practice of environment, allowing her to say something "new and unauthenticated" about the different environments that had shaped her own life and work.

In *Earth Horizon,* Austin adopts the form of autobiography to depict herself as an embodiment of her theory of environment. She explores the different places that produced her: Illinois, California's Tejon Pass and Owens Valley and Carmel, New York, and New Mexico, showing how and why she committed herself to the settings that best represented who she was and offered what she needed at the time. *Earth Horizon* also details Austin's activity to represent—perhaps even to embody—the West through performance, lectures, and activism, as well as her profound ambivalence about the professional and material consequences of doing so.

Thus, Austin's career underlines how double-edged is the regionalist project. At stake are the pleasure of deep knowledge and the risk of marginalization. Yet her powerful attraction to place—"the land always"—was ultimately stronger than her considerable drive for professional success and recognition. She represents as inescapably visceral her engagement with landscape:

> And still, whenever, out of a car window, over the wall of a rich man's garden, about which I am being proudly shown by the proprietor I get sight of any not utterly ruined corner of it, I am torn in my vitals. This is the way a Naturist is taken with the land, with the spirit trying to be evoked out of it. . . . It is time somebody gave a true report.
>
> (Austin 1991: 188)

The powerful, painful nature of engagement with place is present throughout Austin's œuvre, yet only through this intense relation to place, she states at the close of *Earth Horizon,* had she "seen America emerging" (1991: 368). Writing of the subjective experience of the self in environment and seeing beyond the automobile-eye view of the landscape proved irresistible for Austin. The particularity, detail, and multiplicity she saw around her, which she constructed by revising domestic narrative strategies, allowed her to represent place, environment, region, and nation with the complexity and depth she knew they deserved.

Notes

1. Perhaps this tension between "nation" and "region" led Austin to assert a vision of modernism that ran counter to the high modernism of her peers such as H. D. and Ezra Pound. Dale Metcalfe claims that Austin rejected what she termed the "maimed voices" of modernism, and offered as an alternative a healing modernism arising from the landscape (see Mary Austin, "Fig Leaves," quoted in Dale Metcalfe, "Singing Like the Indians Do: Mary Austin's Poetry" in Graulich and Klimasmith, eds. 1999; see also Graulich's introduction.). As Lois Rudnick notes, like other South-westerners Austin sought to "heal what T. S. Eliot called *the* disease of modernity: 'the dissociation of sensibility'" (1996: 27). Austin aimed to re-inject sensibility into modern US culture by privileging the particularities of place.

2. See Metcalfe, "Singing Like the Indians Do," and Klimasmith 1995.

3. For recent perspectives on the West as a zone of intercultural contact, see Comer 1999; Lape 2000.

4. For discussion of the *chisera* figure in Austin's plays, see Mark Hoyer, "Ritual drama/dramatic ritual: Austin's Indian plays," in Graulich and Klimasmith, eds. 1999.

5. Austin did write a novella, *Cactus Thorn,* around 1927, but it remained unpublished until 1988.

References

Austin, Mary (1905). *Isidro.* Boston and New York: Houghton Mifflin.

Austin, Mary (1906). *The Flock.* Boston and New York: Houghton Mifflin.

Austin, Mary (1908). *Santa Lucia.* New York: Harper & Bros.

Austin, Mary (1912). *A Woman of Genius.* New York: Doubleday Page.

Austin, Mary (1919). *Outland.* New York: Boni and Liverwright. (First publ. 1910.)

Austin, Mary (1920). *No. 26 Jayne Street.* Boston: Houghton Mifflin.

Austin, Mary (1932). "Regionalism in American Fiction." *English Journal* 21, 97-107.

Austin, Mary (1950). *The Land of Little Rain.* Boston: Houghton Mifflin. (First publ. 1903.)

Austin, Mary (1987). *Stories from the Country of Lost Borders.* New Brunswick: Rutgers University Press, intr. Marjorie Pryse. (First publ. 1909.)

Austin, Mary (1988). *Cactus Thorn.* Reno: University of Nevada Press.

Austin, Mary (1991). *Earth Horizon: the Autobiography of Mary Austin.* Albuquerque: University of New Mexico Press. (First publ. 1932.)

Austin, Mary (1996a). "New York: The Dictator of American Criticism." In *Beyond Borders: The Selected Essays of Mary Austin,* ed. Reuben J. Ellis. Carbondale and Edwardsville: Southern Illinois University Press. (First publ. 1920.)

Austin, Mary (1996b). "One Hundred Miles on Horseback." In *Beyond Borders: The Selected Essays of Mary Austin,* ed. Reuben J. Ellis. Carbondale and Edwardsville: Southern Illinois University Press. (First publ. 1889.)

Austin, Mary (1997). *The Ford.* Berkeley: University of California Press. (First publ. 1917.)

Bredahl, Carl (1989). *New Ground: Western American Narrative and the Literary Canon.* Chapel Hill: University of North Carolina Press.

Buell, Lawrence (1995). *The Environmental Imagination.* Cambridge, Mass.: Harvard University Press.

Comer, Krista (1999). *Landscapes of the New West: Gender and Geography in Contemporary Women's Writing.* Chapel Hill: University of North Carolina Press.

Farrar, John (1923). "The Literary Spotlight; 22: Mary Austin." *Bookman* 53, 47-52.

Graulich, Melody, and Klimasmith, Elizabeth, eds. (1999). *Exploring Lost Borders: Critical Essays on Mary Austin.* Reno: University of Nevada Press.

Klimasmith, Betsy (1995). "Storytellers, Story Sellers: Artists, Muses, and Exploitation in the Work of Mary Austin." *Southwestern American Literature* 20: 2, 21-33.

Lanigan, Esther (1997). *The Song of a Maverick.* Tucson: Arizona University Press. (first publ. 1989.)

Lape, Noreen Groover (2000). *West of the Border: The Multicultural Literature of the Western Frontiers.* Athens, Ohio: Ohio University Press.

Pearce, T. M., ed. (1979). *Literary America 1903-1934: The Mary Austin Letters.* Westport: Greenwood.

Raine, Anne (1999). "'The Man at the Sources': Gender, Capital, and the Conservationist Landscape in Mary Austin's *The Ford.*" In Melody Graulich and Elizabeth Klimasmith, eds., *Exploring Lost Borders: Critical Essays on Mary Austin.* Reno: University of Nevada Press.

Rudnick, Lois (1987). "Re-naming the Land: Anglo Expatriate Women in the Southwest." In Vera Norwood and Janice Monk (eds.), *The Desert is No Lady.* New Haven: Yale University Press.

Rudnick, Lois (1996). *Utopian Vistas.* Albuquerque: University of New Mexico Press.

Tonkovich, Nicole (1999). "At Cross Purposes: Church, State, and Sex in Mary Austin's *Isidro.*" In Melody Graulich and Elizabeth Klimasmith, eds., *Exploring Lost Borders: Critical Essays on Mary Austin.* Reno: University of Nevada Press.

Heike Schaefer (essay date 2004)

SOURCE: Schaefer, Heike. "'The Land Sets the Limit': Austin's Concept of Regionalism." In *Mary Austin's Regionalism: Reflections on Gender, Genre, and Geography,* pp. 19-52. Charlottesville, Va.: University of Virginia Press, 2004.

[*In the following essay, Schaefer explores Austin's "theory and practice of regionalism" as demonstrated in a number of her texts, both fiction and nonfiction, maintaining that her "regionalist project is not an attempt to conceptualize and formulate a new synthesis of human and nonhuman, of environment and society, of self and other," but instead repudiates such "dualistic preconceptions" and reminds her readers "that nature and culture overlap in significant ways."*]

REGIONAL IDENTITY FORMATION AND COMMUNITY BUILDING

For Mary Austin regional differentiation represented a universal fact of life. She believed with William Carlos Williams that "[t]he locale is the only thing that's universal."[1] In her essay **"Regionalism in American Fiction"** (1932), Austin argues that regionalism is one of the general principles governing life on earth. "Regionalism, since it is of the very nature and constitution of the planet, becomes at last part of the nature and constitution of the men who live on it" (98). Human identity is necessarily regional, Austin reasons, because "there is no sort of experience that works so constantly and subtly on man as his regional environment" (97). Austin was convinced that the natural environment exerted a significant influence both on the shape of individual lives and on the collective makeup of society.

Her belief that human identity to a large extent is environmentally determined can be traced to her earliest publications. "Not the law, but the land sets the limit," the narrator of **The Land of Little Rain** (1903) declares categorically (3). "For law runs with the boundary, not beyond it," the narrator of **Lost Borders** (1909) specifies in explaining the name of her region (2). Since human existence in the arid regions depends on the population's ability to adapt to the land, regional ways of life develop in response to environmental conditions. Grounded in their environment, they cannot be comprehended apart from their nonhuman matrix. As the narrator points out: "To understand the fashion of any life, one must know the land it is lived in and the procession of the year" (*LLR* [*The Land of Little Rain*] 164).

Austin further elaborated the argument in later works such as **The American Rhythm** (1923, 1930) and in the numerous regionalist essays she published in the twenties and thirties. In her article **"Regional Culture in the Southwest"** (1929), she gives the following definition of regional identity: "A regional culture is the sum, expressed in ways of living and thinking, of the mutual adaptations of a land and a *people*: In the long run, the land wins" (474). While the development of regional cultures is said to involve a reciprocal relationship between the human population and its natural environment, the basic character of these "mutual adaptations" is determined by the land. Considered from a long-term perspective, the environment is seen to control the outcome of the adaptive process. "In the long run, the land wins."

Since the land manifests "immutable forces" (*LB* [*Lost Borders*] 80) that remain unaffected by human presence, human survival depends on competent adjustment to environmental conditions. The fatal consequences of a refusal to acquire the necessary environmental knowledge are dramatized in many of Austin's stories. Men go astray and die of thirst in the desert, and towns are destroyed by floods. A population reluctant to "adapt itself willingly and efficiently" is doomed, Austin prophesizes in **"Regional Culture in the Southwest"** (475). The "land destroys it and makes room for another tribe." Intent on provoking her predominantly white readership into reimagining the relation between their culture and its land base, Austin applies the trope of the vanishing American to European American settlers. In her work the land defines the limits of human existence. The environment determines the possibilities of regional development and by extension also the future of the nation.

REGIONAL IDENTITY FORMATION

How does Austin conceive of this process of geographical determination, of "the mutual adaptations of a land and a people"? Through which acts and responses is human identity environmentally determined? In **"Regionalism in American Fiction"** Austin describes the process through which people are molded by their environment as a transformation that involves all aspects of their lives. For any person, Austin tells us, the regional environment "is the thing always before his eye, always at his ear, always underfoot. Slowly or sharply it forces upon him behavior patterns such as earliest become the habit of his blood, the unconscious factor of adjustment in all his mechanisms. Of all the responses of his psyche, none pass so soon and surely into the field of consciousness from which all invention and creative effort of every sort proceed" (97). In Austin's account, our natural surroundings profoundly affect our sense of identity and agency in the world. Through our corporeal experience of our environment, we acquire behavioral patterns and bodily habits that govern both our inner processes and outer actions. Even if we are not consciously aware of this interaction, our response to the land and "the particular region called home" (98) is the component that coordinates the biological and social dimensions of our existence.

A similar analysis of the relation of self and world is developed by John Dewey in *Art as Experience* (1934). Dewey points out that our ties to our surroundings provide us with the sense that our inner lives and outer world cohere. "Whenever the bond that binds the living creature to his environment is broken, there is nothing that holds together the various factors and phases of the self. Thought, emotions, sense, purpose, impulsion fall apart. . . . For their unity is found in the coöperative rôles they play in active and receptive relations to the environment" (252). In order to integrate the different aspects of our existence, we need to acknowledge that our individual lives evolve out of and into our human surroundings and the natural world at large. In a way, our mental stability and our ability to act purposefully depend on a relational and reciprocal mode of being—and so does our culture. As Dewey reminds us, "culture is the product not of efforts of men put forth in a void or just upon themselves, but of prolonged and culmulative interaction with environment" (28).

The understanding that nature and culture constitute interrelated rather than mutually exclusive spheres also provides Austin with the basis for developing her theory and practice of regionalism. Her regionalist project is not an attempt to conceptualize and formulate a new synthesis of human and nonhuman, of environment and society, of self and other, then; rather, it is an effort to demonstrate that these elements are already interwoven on the level of lived experience. Austin's regionalist texts repudiate dualistic preconceptions, reminding the readers that nature and culture overlap in significant ways.[2]

Austin's and Dewey's argument that our interactions with the environment play a significant role in the ongoing formation of our sense of selfhood is supported both by phenomenological explanations of perception and by feminist concepts of relational identity. Both accounts of subjectivity assert that it is a basic human need to engage with a world outside ourselves. To conceptualize how our sense of identity depends on the physical experience of social and natural environments, it is helpful to think, as David Abram proposes, "of the sensing body as a kind of open circuit that completes itself only in things, and in the world."[3] The phenomenological understanding of human existence as fundamentally open to the world acknowledges that our senses cannot operate without a world surrounding us. It reminds us that our different senses converge in the perception of a world external to us. Hence, as Abram points out, it allows for the realization that "it is primarily through my engagement with what is *not* me that I effect the integration of my senses, and thereby experience my own unity and coherence" (125).

The phenomenological proposition that we do not live in a "night of identity"[4] explains on the sensory level of perception a phenomenon that also occurs on the psychological level, as feminist inquiries into the dynamics of subject formation have suggested. The experience of difference is integral to the development of identity. Feminist concepts of relational identity, such as the notion of ecological selfhood that Val Plumwood develops in *Feminism and the Mastery of Nature,* acknowledge that our psychological constitution requires us to encounter unmerged others in order to arrive at any sense of being a differentiated self. Plumwood explains, "The reciprocity and mutuality which form such a self are not only compatible with but actually *require* the existence of others who are distinct and not merged . . . union and contact [occur] in active exchange with an other who contributes enough difference to create a boundary to the self" (156). Unlike the stable, self-contained subject of Western Enlightenment discourse, the ecological self is seen as being shaped in dynamic relations of interdependence. Our sense of selfhood develops through the exchange with human and nonhuman others. The contact with whom and what we are not is integral to the development of our sense of self.

AUSTIN'S VISION OF ENVIRONMENTAL SELFHOOD IN CACTUS THORN

In her literary and critical writing, Austin argues that the development of individuals and their communities depends on their ongoing engagement with an environing world. Similar to the way in which firsthand experiences of place affect the personal sense of self, regional culture develops out of the collective encounter with the land. According to Austin, individual subject formation and cultural history always involve an interplay of social, cultural, biological, and geographical relations. Narrative dramatizations of this regionalist stance abound in Austin's work. A representative example is the rural heroine of Austin's novella **Cactus Thorn.**[5] Dulcie Adelaid expresses the author's regionalist philosophy. She observes that her nonbuilt environment, the California desert, exists in its own right, while human survival depends on a successful adaptation to environmental conditions. Despite this apparent imbalance of power, Austin's protagonist regards the land and its human population not as antagonistic but as imbricated elements of a regional world. They are organized according to a common principle, which she indeterminately names "It." Convinced that human orientation is predicated on an embodied experience of place, Dulcie suggests that the development of regional culture should be directed toward realigning society with the organizational pattern of its environment. She explains the necessity of recognizing the nonhuman matrix of human life to her urban lover.

> "It is something you learn in a place like this. There is something here." She waved her arm over the wild disorder of the ranges. "It goes on by itself, doing things that you don't see either the beginning of, or the end, except that It has very little to do with men. It can use

> men, It *will* use them, but It can get on without them. They have to make themselves worth using.

> "You remember what happened when you went walking by yourself? You were just thinking and thinking, weren't you? And suddenly you were lost. That was because you got away from—It. And then you were scared. But if you had waited, just held still and waited, It would have come back. You would have found yourself."

> "There were things like that in the city to me. The people had gone off by themselves, and they were beginning to run around and shout to one another that this was the way, and this. But if they would keep still, the way would have come forth like a wild thing and shown itself."

> (**CT** [*Cactus Thorn*] 47)

Because human life unfolds within a larger-than-human world, Austin's heroine explains, individual and collective self-definitions would benefit from a recognition of the nonhuman factors that enter into the formation of personal and collective identities. For Dulcie a culture that does not acknowledge its continuity with the natural environment is bound to remain confused about its place and purpose in the world. Blind to its nonhuman support system, it ignores an important condition of its existence. Having dissolved "the bond that binds the living creature to his environment," society resembles a terrified person who has lost his or her way. In Dulcie's eyes such a society is reduced to a hub of random motion and undirected activity. It makes its members run around without getting anywhere—except maybe farther away from one another.

Since Dulcie explains her regionalist ethic as the representative of western rural life to a visiting East Coast urbanite, it may seem as if she merely restates in regionalized terms the familiar opposition between wilderness appreciation and cosmopolitanism. The West is identified as the site of direct contact with wild nature, the East as the locus of urbanization and civilized culture. The West enables wholesome experiences of tranquility and a benignly ordered world; the East provokes confusion, self-aggrandizement, and senseless activity. Yet Dulcie neither returns with her argument to the wilderness cult prevalent at the turn of the nineteenth century nor does she advocate a nostalgia steeped version of regionalism.[6] She recommends neither a sojourn in the wilderness nor an antimodernist fantasy of a preindustrial golden age as an antidote to the complications of modern life. She acknowledges that the decidedly non-human appearance of her region's "wild disorder" is as alien to her visitor as the bustle of eastern urban life is to her. Comparing her friend's to her own regional experience, Dulcie asserts that cityscape and desertscape offer the same possibility for realigning human life with the environing world. The "way" is present in both desert and city.[7] Since "It" is the fundamental structure or pattern of the world, it can be perceived in all places—provided that one has acquired the necessary calmness, patience, and attentiveness.

Dulcie's argument that it is the manner of engaging with one's surroundings that makes the difference between being lost and finding oneself modifies the romantic belief in the integrative and healing function of encounters with the natural world. She extends it to include modern manmade environments. In this way her reasoning eschews the regressive tendencies that contemporaneous critics of regionalist literature found fault with. As Henry Nash Smith sums up in "The Feel of the Purposeful Earth" the critical climate at the time when Austin wrote **Cactus Thorn,** to "a New Humanist or to a Young Intellectual . . . talk of regional cultures sounds either Rousseauistic (and therefore evil) or naïve (and therefore ridiculous)" (31). What matters according to Austin's heroine are not the relative merits of different types of spaces but the particular mode of a person's or culture's engagement with place. Keeping with Austin's call for the development of plural regional cultures, Dulcie asserts the value of any sense of place, rural or urban, that involves the recognition that human life evolves out of and into a larger-than-human world.

CORPOREAL CONVERSATIONS

For Dulcie this realization is best facilitated by an embodied engagement with one's environment in a calm and alert state of mind. As she reminds her friend, human orientation is predicated on a somatic awareness of one's physical situation. He got lost on his walk, she says, because he was absorbed in his thoughts. Preoccupied with the workings of his mind, "just thinking and thinking, weren't you?" he isolated himself from the outside world. As a result, he "got away from—It" and lost his way. By valorizing the corporeal conversation between self and world, Dulcie affirms the environmental situatedness of human life.

In this respect Dulcie's account reads like a modern echo of Thoreauvian, rather than Emersonian, transcendentalism. Austin's words call up the epiphany that Henry David Thoreau describes in the "Monday" chapter of *A Week on the Concord and Merrimack Rivers* (1849). Sleeping in the open during a storm, his back pressed into the grass and attentively listening to the passing thunder, the speaker looks up at the night sky; he feels related to the stars and is elated by the feeling "that IT was well" (213). He is physically aware of a universal order, principle, or God operating in the natural world. "I see, smell, taste, hear, feel, that everlasting Something to which we are allied, at once our maker, our abode, our destiny, our very Selves; the one historic truth, the most remarkable fact which can become the distinct and uninvited subject of our thought, the actual glory of the universe; the only fact which a human being cannot avoid recognizing, or in some way forget or dispense with" (213). An effect of his embodied awareness of his surroundings, the epiphany itself is a somatic experience that involves all his senses.

Austin's and Thoreau's narratives suggest that the contemplation of human embodiedness provides an ideal starting point for reflections on the value of an environmentally grounded sense of identity. Inquiring what it means to be human in a larger-than-human world, both Austin and Thoreau focus on embodied experiences. The body indeed is an excellent case in point for assertions of the continuity of self and world. Our existence as bodies, who eat, breathe, grow, and decompose in social and natural environments, renders highly instable any dichotomy we may construct between nature and culture. Since bodies are to a certain extent pliable, they are shaped by and are shaping the matrix they live in, as feminist theorists such as Judith Butler, Elizabeth Grosz, and Donna Haraway recently have argued. The body always belongs to both realms, it is culturally molded and biologically given, and it acts in social contexts as well as in ecological systems. The transitions and overlaps between natural and cultural dimensions are an integral property of our bodies.

According to Austin, an embodied sense of place allows people to align the biological and cultural dimensions of their lives. It enables them to exchange a preoccupation with human concerns—the unproductive and hectic state of having "gone off by themselves" and the concept of culture, in Dewey's words, as something "men put forth in a void or just upon themselves"—for an attentive engagement with external realities that include but are not limited to human affairs. Paying attention to what lies outside the merely human ken, whether this is natural or supernatural, the encounter with what is other returns us to ourselves with a clearer sense of self. The "everlasting Something" now is recognized as "our very Selves." In other words, the experience of difference issues into an experience of continuity that deepens the understanding of our subjectivity. Dulcie describes to her friend this paradoxical movement in which the focus on the other leads to a heightened comprehension of the self. "But if you had waited, just held still and waited, It would have come back. You would have found yourself" (**CT** 47).

AUSTIN'S CONCEPT OF GEOGRAPHICAL DETERMINATION

Austin's idea of geographical determination has been admired as radical and utopian and dismissed as naïve and reactionary. B. A. Botkin attributed "cosmic grandeur" to her insights, whereas Mark Van Doren was more skeptical, finding that Austin's work "is impressive, and though it is not convincing it is great."[8] While most regionalists of Austin's time as well as contemporary bioregionalists and cultural geographers would agree with Austin's notion that cultural identity represents an interplay of social and geographical forces, the extent to which the nonhuman environment factors into the formation of regional culture was and still is open to debate. As Jared Diamond notes, "the notion that environmental geography and biogeography influenced societal development is an old idea. Nowadays, though, the view is not held in esteem by historians; it is considered wrong or simplistic, or it is caricatured as environmental determinism and dismissed. . . . Yet geography obviously has *some* effect on history; the open question concerns how much effect, and whether geography can account for history's broad pattern."[9]

The question to which degree place exerts an influence on the development of regional and by extension national society is central to Austin's work. Since many of her texts assert that nonhuman environmental conditions take precedence over human engineered factors— "not the law, but the land sets the limit"—it seems as if Austin advocated a strong form of geographical determination. Her narratives and essays frequently maintain that geography designs "history's broad pattern."

Yet while Austin was certainly convinced that the land should affect the pattern of regional cultures and that regional cultures in turn should determine the character of national culture, her texts also tend to acknowledge that regional identity formation is not a natural occurrence but requires directed effort and thus represents cultural work. As Austin contends in her lecture "What Is a Native Culture?" the colonization of the American continent demonstrates "that merely to be born in a given spot does not make a man native to that place" (1).[10] She argues that one becomes native to the place one inhabits solely by allowing one's natural and social environment to dominate one's habitus, outlook, and behavior. For Austin the determining factors are the climate and unbuilt environment; the mode of economy; and moral, religious, and philosophical values and systems of belief (1-2). Once these new influences are greater than the disposition acquired in previous environments, Austin concludes, "we have a native culture" (2).

Austin's inclusion of social processes, such as "the forming and reforming of new social patterns" and "the conflicts of racial temperaments," in her list of forces that direct the development of place-based cultures makes her concept of regionalism relevant to modern life in (post)industrialized Western societies, where the majority of the population leads urbanized lives in predominantly human built environments.[11] ["**Artist Life in the United States**"] Austin's awareness of both social and natural influences is particularly important to note in light of the suspicions current critics have voiced, that regionalism represents just one more essen-

tialism trap. While Austin's style, choice of words, and logic are bound to elicit nervous responses from contemporary readers, she usually does not present sociohistorical change as a natural process, directed entirely by nonhuman forces. She seeks not to exalt a preindustrial rural American nation but to conceptualize human identity and "the formation of a democratic society out of such diverse human materials as America has to work with" as bound to both a social and an environmental matrix.[12]

But if Austin did not regard the processes of adaptation an automated response to environmental factors, why did she routinely insist that human identity was geographically determined? Austin plausibly overstated her point for strategic reasons as she sought to convince her readers of the necessity of developing sustainable relations to their land base. For her it was a development into which a complicated web of human and nonhuman forces entered. If one wanted to expand on Austin's regionalist credo, one could say that the land sets the limit, but it does not dictate the process.

THE SIGNIFICANCE OF THE ENVIRONMENT IN DEFINITIONS OF AMERICAN IDENTITY

Austin's emphasis on the environment as a factor in the formation of cultural identity links her concept of regionalism to a long tradition of arguments about the nation's possibilities for developing a uniquely American culture. Since Americans tended to see the assimilation of new immigrants as dependent not only on their political allegiance to the republican ideology and on their acquisition of a common language but also on their contact with the land, the environment traditionally held a prominent place in definitions of American national characteristics. A famous expression of this position is Frederick Jackson Turner's essay "The Significance of the Frontier in American History" (1893), in which he argues that the development of American society could only be explained in terms of the westward movement of the settlements and the consequent colonization of the wilderness. Turner's dictum that the "frontier is the line of most rapid and effective Americanization" because the "wilderness masters the colonist" and forces him or her to either "accept the conditions which it furnishes, or perish" (3-4) testifies to the widespread belief in the assimilatory powers of the immigrant's encounter with the environment. While Austin did not subscribe to a Turnerian view of American history, her work echoes the established rhetoric that "the land will not be lived in except in its own fashion" (*LLR* 88) or that the "really astonishing thing would have been to find the American people as a whole resisting the influence of natural environment in favor of the lesser influences of a shared language and a common political arrangement" ("**Regionalism in American Fiction**" 98).

Generally speaking, the colonization of the American continent was envisioned as a process in which nature was transformed into culture, as far as the agricultural development of the land was concerned, and in which culture was transformed into nature—in regard to the settlers. For the Americanization of the immigrant population was supposed to effect not only the cultural and social assimilation of the first generation into the American citizenry but also to culminate in the evolution of a new, distinctly American race. An exemplary description of this passage from a culturally to a biologically defined concept of national identity is offered by Hector Saint Jean de Crèvecoeur in his *Letters from an American Farmer* (1782): "He becomes an American by being received into the broad lap of our great *Alma Mater.* Here individuals of all nations are melted into a new race of men" (561). Although concepts of race changed considerably from Crèvecoeur's to Austin's times, a fundamental idea remained intact: Americanization involved a magical transformation of the newly acquired political, social, and geographical aspects of the immigrants' lives into biological reality.

This aspect is also present in Austin's work. In *The American Rhythm* (1923), Austin speculates on the influence of environmental factors on "the becoming race of Americans" (14). She describes the colonization of the American continent as an adaptive process that results in the physical transformation of the recently immigrated settlers. Austin's account lends a mythical quality to American history. "There was hunger in man for free flung mountain ridges, untrimmed forests, evidence of structure and growth. Life set itself to new processions of seed time and harvest, the skin newly tuned to seasonal variations, the very blood humming to new altitudes" (14).

Austin pictures the creation of the new "race of Americans" not as a singular event, however, but as an ongoing process that repeats itself with significant variations in each generation. In the course of our lives, Austin proposes, our experiential alignment with the rhythms of our natural surroundings becomes so ingrained that it begins to function analogous to our instincts. For Austin instinct is but another term for the "coördinations achieved as a result of habitual experiential adjustments to environment" (*AR* [*The American Rhythm*] 149). Since our acquired regional identity is part of our physical makeup, Austin reasons, it can become hereditary. It can be passed on biologically "from the parent to the offspring," although, Austin kids, not as easily or intact as the family jewels (7, 150).

Since Austin embraces Lamarckian concepts of cultural evolution to predict the emergence of an American race in central works such as *The American Rhythm,* it is helpful to briefly consider her logic in the context of nativist discourse. Historically, the Lamarckian belief that cultural components passed into the pool of transmittable biological traits had fostered a conceptualiza-

tion of assimilation as a natural process that followed its own laws and did not have to be enforced. Since assimilation was supposed to occur regardless of the national origins of the immigrants, it might seem as if the idea of the geographical determination of American national character would posit a fundamental challenge to "the principle of racial consistency."[13] For if the contact with a common environment is seen to effect the evolution of a new race, the different races participating in this process cannot be defined as given immutable elements of identity. Yet, despite its stated universal applicability, the environmental definition of American nationality from its inception was a racialized concept since it excluded nonwhite people, in particular African Americans and Native Americans, on the basis of their racial identity.

Austin's argument, however, departs from this nativist logic. First, in her account, the process does apply to all races. Native Americans are presented to European Americans as role models in adaptation due to their longstanding experience and expertise in inhabiting American environments. Second, Austin argues that the process does not simply occur but requires cultural work and cross-cultural negotiations and the balancing of regional and national interests. Instead of making a nativist argument, then, Austin defines *ethnicity* as a positionality that shares with other components of human identity a genesis in sociocultural processes that are specifically concerned with relating the human to the nonhuman, with negotiating the conditions of human life within an ecological matrix. Both the social and environmental dimensions of human life thus become transparent; their interrelatedness, their continuities and discontinuities, are the subject of Austin's inquiry.

Austin's discussion of ethnicity as a factor in the formation of regional culture in her 1929 essay **"Regional Culture in the Southwest"** is a case in point. With the article Austin contributed to a symposium on the question of whether the Southwest could develop a unique culture "more satisfying and profound" than the imported dominant European American culture (474). In a familiar mode she argues that the region offers the environment and the Native American and Hispanic traditions to do so. She adds that the quality of a regional culture depends not only on the population's willingness to adapt but also on its racial profile. Only a "particularly good stock" will produce a "high" regional culture (475). Among the characteristics that determine the regional potential of a "stock," however, Austin enlists again the instinctual response to the environment that the process of experiential alignment with the environment facilitates. The "White elements," she concludes, still have not committed themselves sufficiently to a local way of life. Lacking the "cultural disposition

. . . to understand and develop the country upon which it lives," the European American population is bent on "imposing its derived notions" on the environment (475).

Closing the circle by reasoning that regional identity is influenced by the ethnicity of the population engaged in the process of adaptation and that this ethnicity is not a naturally given component of identity but a result of the cultural practices that a group engages in as it tries to or refuses to adapt to its environment, Austin presents region and nation building as a response to biological and cultural as well as human and nonhuman conditions. Instead of naturalizing concepts of regional and national identity through a recourse to nativist views on the conditions and consequences of adaptation to the American continent, Austin's argument grounds biology in cultural work. When Austin asks, "[W]hat is race but a pattern of response common to a group of people who have lived together under a given environment long enough to take a recognizable pattern?" she suggests that race to a certain extent is a product of cultural practices and that cultural practices inflect human biology.[14]

The major achievement of Austin's theoretical regionalist writings, it seems to me, are those argumentative instances in which she elucidates the interrelatedness of the natural and cultural aspects of human identity and describes the perpetual transformation of one into the other, without reducing one to the other. Austin's cross-translation neither relegates all of biology to the cultural realm nor does it completely naturalize the cultural. It amounts to an argument that human identity is both culturally conditioned and naturally given. For Austin regional and ethnic identities are neither entirely determined by the nonhuman environment nor are they an entirely intrahuman concern.

In sum, Austin contended that the regional encounter with the land constituted the native origin of national character. For her, "the processes of regional culture" were the source "from which the only sound patriotism springs" (**"Regionalism in American Fiction"** 104). In shifting the balance of power from nation to region, Austin's argument exhibits one of the prime characteristics of the American regionalism of the twenties and thirties. As Robert L. Dorman demonstrates in his seminal study *Revolt of the Provinces,* the regionalists of the interwar years routinely questioned national self-definitions to dissolve centripetal distributions of power. Donald Davidson, for instance, proposes in his essay "Regionalism and Nationalism in American Literature" that "Regionalism is a name for a condition under which the national American literature exists as a literature: that is, its constant tendency to decentralize rather than to centralize; or to correct overcentralization by conscious decentralization" (53). By defining regional culture and diversity as the ground for the development of national identity, Austin can argue that the leveling of regional difference impoverishes national culture while the flourishing of a multiplicity of regional cultures contributes to the nation's prosperity and progress. Her assertion that regional interests serve national interests since regional identity fortifies national identity allows Austin to counter contemporaneous critiques of the regionalist project as a post-Civil War retrieval of agrarian sectionalism and lends authority to her rejection of a homogenized national culture. Austin can now legitimately criticize the "vast, pale figure of America" and call for the acknowledgement of "several Americas, in many subtle and significant characterizations."[15]

REGIONALIST LITERATURE: THE RELATIONS AMONG ENVIRONMENTS, WRITERS, READERS, AND TEXTS

Austin conceived of regionalism, as we have seen, as a place-based mode of identity formation and cultural development that followed an environmentalist and pluralist agenda and aimed at the reimagination of regional and national society. This section asks how Austin's sociopolitical stance informed her concept and practice of regionalist literature. How can we conceive of literature as a response to experiences of place and as an expression of cultural practices grounded in specific geographies? What exactly is regional literature?

AUSTIN'S DEPARTURE FROM LOCAL COLOR AESTHETICS

In the essay **"Regionalism in American Fiction"** Austin argues that an American literary masterpiece has to "come up through the land, shaped by the author's own adjustments to it" (101). She emphasizes that it is only through firsthand experience that authors can acquire a solid understanding of the region they are writing about. "The regionally interpretive book must not only be about the country, it must be of it" (106).[16] This requirement may seem so obvious as to be redundant; yet it is a crucial criterion that helps to differentiate Austin's concept of regionalist literature from other forms of regional writing. When we think, for instance, of a certain kind of local color fiction—fiction written about a region by outsiders for the amusement of an outside audience—the requirement may seem less superfluous.[17]

Austin repeatedly sought to distinguish her version of regionalism from local color literature, which she thought offered merely "an automobile eye view" of a particular region, "something slithered and blurred, nothing so sharply discriminated that it arrests the speed-numbed mind to understand" (**"Regionalism in American Fiction"** 107). The distinction informs her early collections, including *The Land of Little Rain* and *Lost Borders,* whose narrators over and again distance themselves from local color fiction. They mock the local color tradition in stories such as **"Jimville—A Bret Harte Town,"** identifying it as a male-dominated field of literary production, written by short-term visitors to a region for the amusement of a disaffected readership.[18]

The suggestion that the perspectives and objectives of local color and regionalist writers are incompatible also provides a fitting conclusion for the *Lost Borders* story **"The Last Antelope."**[19] The story addresses the environmental degradation of California's arid regions by describing the death of the region's last wild antelope. The animal dies at the hands of a European American settler, who epitomizes the destructive "love of mastery, which for the most part moves men into new lands" (74). At the end of the emblematic story about the death of the last antelope, the narrator contrasts her understanding of regional reality with the perceptions of a local color writer. "There was a man once who skidded through Lost Borders in an automobile with a balloon silk tent and a folding tin bath-tub, who wrote some cheerful tales about that country, mostly untrue, about rattlesnakes coiling under men's blankets at night, to afford heroic occasions in the morning, of which circumstance seventeen years' residence failed to furnish a single instance" (80).

The nonresident writer, unwilling to adapt to local customs, is trapped in his romantic preconceptions of western life and gains only superficial impressions of the places he visits. Cut off from the physical and emotional experience of the region by a buffer of modern comforts, his insight into local ways of life remains as shallow as his engagement with the fundamental questions that his stories potentially could raise. Unable to "slough off and swallow [his] acquired prejudices as a lizard does his skin" (*LLR* 113), he writes "cheerful tales" that contrast sharply with the narrator's sad story about the environmental degradation of her region. As a resident writer, the narrator defines her responsibilities primarily in regard to her local community. She is more concerned with the preservation of her environment than with the entertainment of an outside readership. Her regional sense of identity allows her to explore the political, emotional, and spiritual significance of the events she reimagines, in contrast to the local color writer whose limited imagination adheres to pre-established story patterns. The text thus presents the narrator's experiential engagement with place as a source of environmental and communal ethics as well as the basis of original rather than imitative art.

AUSTIN'S EXPERIENTIAL CONCEPT OF REALIST LITERATURE

Austin's experiential concept of literary and critical practice distinguishes her regionalist version of realism not only from local color writing but also from the Howellsian tradition of realism. Austin contended that William Dean Howells initiated "the thinning out of American fiction by a deliberate choice of the most usual, the most widely distributed of American story incidents, rather than the most intensively experienced."[20] She considered Howells and Sinclair Lewis representative of a trend among American novelists to eschew regional subject matter and to withdraw "from the soil, undertaken on the part of Howells in a devout pilgrim spirit, bent on the exploration of the social expression of democracy, and on the part of Lewis with a fine scorn and a hurt indignation for the poor simp."[21] As an advocate of regional diversity and an experiential concept of culture, Austin suspected that certain forms of realism served to homogenize the American literary imagination. She saw them as offering generalized, ready-made images of American realities rather than inviting readers to participate in the creation of detailed, regionally specific fictional worlds. Therefore, Austin argued, they could not involve their readers in an imaginative process that would heighten their awareness of their present living conditions and expand their understanding of other parts of the country. Austin blamed both realist writers and the reading public for this situation. For her, the "insistence on fiction shallow enough to be common to all regions, so that no special knowledge of other environments than one's own is necessary to appreciation of it, has pulled down the whole level of American fiction" (**"Regionalism in American Fiction"** 99). In her work Austin sought to develop a regionalist form of realist writing that on one hand would allow her to describe in a spirit of detached sympathy and personal involvement the specifics of everyday life in the arid regions and that on the other hand would encourage her readers to reflect self-critically on their own ways of living in place.

A fuller portrait of the experiential concept of literature at the core of Austin's regionalist aesthetic emerges in *The Land of Little Rain.* Its self-referential narrator realizes Austin's ideal of a regionally committed writer. The narrator is cast as a long-term resident of the region of which she writes. She considers it her task to represent regional realities accurately, "to keep faith with the land" (ix). For Austin, to render the land faithfully does not mean to practice a form of mimetic realism, however, as the formulation may suggest. Austin's narrator makes no pretensions of offering an exhaustive objective description of the desert and its climate, flora, and fauna. Instead, she reflects on the basis and context of her observations and comments on the psychological, sociopolitical, and ecological implications of her narrative practices. She regularly addresses her readers to remind them that their perceptions and representations of the natural world are subjective and culturally mediated.

The preface to *The Land of Little Rain* offers a representative example of Austin's regionalist realism. In it the narrator discusses the options she has for selecting or inventing appropriate names for the places she describes. She prefers Native American to English place names because she considers the supposedly "Indian fashion of name-giving" to have the greater propensity for capturing regional particularities (vii). She uses names such as Oppapago, "The Weeper," for a mountain with "streams that run down from it continually like tears," while she dismisses established geographical names that fail to provide adequate characterizations of the land.[22] To qualify her preference she contrasts European American and Native American customs of naming. "For if I love a lake known by the name of the man who discovered it, which endears itself by reason of the close-locked pines it nourishes about its borders, you may look in my account to find it so described. But if the Indians have been there before me, you shall have their name, which is always beautifully fit and does not originate in the poor human desire for perpetuity" (vii-viii).[23]

The narrator thinks that her European American cultural heritage interferes with her attempt to give a personal and specific account of the land. She seeks to render the land in a way which would express her personal relation to the region—the lake, after all, is said to "endear itself" and she renames it to express her impression of the lakeshore's vegetation—without erasing the features of the land that caused her to respond. She adopts a flexible practice of naming in recognition of "a fluid world where identities are relational and communal rather than tied to a single fixed image."[24]

As an environmentally committed regionalist writer, the narrator is wary of literary conventions that would foster in her readers a disaffected stance toward the natural world. She directly addresses her audience: "And I am in no mind to direct you to delectable places toward which you will hold yourself less tenderly than I. So by this fashion of naming I keep faith with the land" (*LLR* ix). The narrator asks her readers to engage as she does in an environmental learning process. On this condition, they "shall have such news of the land, of its trails and what is astir in them, as one lover of it can give to another" (xi). The narrator's self-reflexive comments thus draw the reader's attention to the ongoing negotiations between self and world in which any writer would have to engage to fulfill the "two indispensable conditions" that Austin identifies in **"Regionalism in American Fiction"** as the prerequisites for regional writing. "The environment entering constructively into the story, and the story reflecting in some fashion the essential qualities of the land" (106).

THE RELATIONS AMONG ENVIRONMENT, AUTHOR, AND TEXT

But how can the biophysical environment enter a text? And how can a text reflect an unconstructed reality? At least in the contemporary critical climate, attempts to establish causal relations between the environment and literary practice as well as assertions that there may be such a thing as unbuilt reality tend to trigger the objections of poststructurally inclined critics. They ask, for instance, as does Peter Quigley in his essay "Rethinking Resistance," "If our 'reading' of the world is thoroughly constructed and if reference to a base is illusory, then what is it that we could possibly be faithful to, and how would we measure such faithfulness?" (304). The inquiry certainly is relevant for both Austin's theory and practice of regionalism and for ecocritical approaches to literary studies. This becomes even clearer when we consider the recent remarks of another irritated critic, Dana Phillips, which seem diametrically opposed to Austin's understanding of literature. "Poetry is not a 'manifestation' of anything, apart from the conscious decisions and unconscious motivations of poets, and the structural and aesthetic effects of the genres and languages in which they write. To suppose otherwise is occult" (581). Yet the concept of textuality that underlies this statement is not as incompatible with the idea of geographical influence as the exasperated tone would suggest. One could, for instance, rephrase the initial questions as follows: How does the experience of place enter into "the conscious decisions and unconscious motivations of poets"? How does it affect their textual practice and thus eventually enter the text? Rather than posit any direct or organic relation between text and environment, I propose with Austin that we produce our "thoroughly constructed" readings of the world in response to both sociocultural and environmental realities. Since the subjective, embodied experience of our environments is an integral element of our lives, it can also inflect our critical and literary practice.

"To keep faith with the land," in this sense, means to keep faith with our culturally and personally mediated experiences or embodied readings of the land. The base of reference shifts from the nonhuman environment to our experience of our surroundings; this experience, however—and this is the crux—is not an entirely human affair but a conversation between ourselves and the world that transforms and to a certain extent thus also produces self and other. As SueEllen Campbell reasons in "The Land and Language of Desire," our choices "depend on the shape of our lives—where we live, how we spend our days, how we've been taught—and especially on the role the land itself has played in what we might call the writing of our textuality" (209). To conceive of human identity and agency as an interplay of social and environmental factors allows us to reject the limited either/or logic of the determinism versus constructionism debates. Literature and criticism are neither organic manifestations of natural forces nor disembodied effects of cultural dynamics.

What assumptions, then, does Austin's regionalist aesthetic make about the relation between the environment, its perception and investment with meaning by human subjects, and the literary communication of these conceptualizations of the natural world? Austin was convinced that prediscursive, nonhuman systems of meaning existed—ecological and spiritual principles of organization, for example, that would function independent of human readers. The guiding universal principle or "way" that underlies the regionalist ethic of *Cactus Thorn,* as examined in the introduction to this study, is a representative instance of this perspective. Yet although Austin believed in a nonhuman world of consequence and significance, her theoretical proposition on the intersections of environment and text in regionalist literature—the "environment entering constructively into the story, and the story reflecting in some fashion the essential qualities of the land"—is misleading. For the assertion that the text needs to reflect an apparently already existing and essential reality suggests that Austin naïvely conceives of language as an instrument to mirror a prediscursive world and that she reduces the author to a passive recipient of sensory data, to a portal through which the environment can enter the narrative. Although Austin certainly was not an early believer in what we today would call radical constructionism, she also did not think of the author as a mere medium through which impressions of the object world passed unaltered into the realm of textuality. Instead, as the above discussion of the preface to *The Land of Little Rain* as regionalist realist writing demonstrates, Austin was keenly aware of the conceptual and textual conventions that come into play when literary attempts are made to communicate the mediated experience of being, or imagining oneself to be, out in nature.

Convinced that our human, sociocultural, and personal perspectives enable and delimit our access to the natural world, Austin insisted that nature writers had to include their personal response to the environment in their accounts. In *Earth Horizon* she states provocatively, "It is time somebody gave a true report. All the public expects of the experiences of practicing Naturists is the appearance, the habits, the incidents of the wild; when the Naturist reports upon himself, it is mistaken for poeticizing" (188). Since the personal experiences and sociohistorical situation of writers inevitably inform their descriptions, Austin reasons, the writer's subjectivity and his or her relation to the place under consideration should be recognized as an essential component of nature writing. Given the situatedness of our perceptions, a "true report" for Austin has to be self-reflexive; it has to strike "the authentic note of confession" (188). If an account limits itself to the presentation of factual information and does not comment on the conditions under which the presented knowledge was acquired, the observations are falsified and the report in its entirety cannot be considered accurate.

Accordingly, Austin includes in her natural history writing meta-narrative comments and self-critically reflects on her textual practice. Through the persona of the narrator, she offers us, for instance in *The Land of Little Rain,* both a fictional record of regional identity formation and a discussion of how the experience of a particular place can be communicated in writing. Although the narrator wishes to present herself as a "mere recorder" of regional life and reality (*LLR* 112), she is aware that her experiences are subjective. Therefore, she encourages her readers to "blow out this bubble from your own breath" (113). Instead of making claims to neutral observation, she marks in her account the experiential basis for her writing. She interpolates her descriptions of the desert ecosystem and its inhabitants with general discussions of the relations between language, self, other, and world.

In this way Austin attributes in her stories and essays a fundamentally reciprocal character to the relations between regionalist authors, including nature writers, and their environments. She suggests that the world inscribes itself in the subject while the subject inscribes itself in the world and that both are changed through their interaction. Thus Austin defines the authors' experiential negotiations between their sense of self and sense of place as the basis of environmental literature.

THE AESTHETIC EXPERIENCE OF ENVIRONMENTAL RESISTANCE

Austin's regionalist aesthetic and her experiential concept of literature at times seem to anticipate the theory of art that John Dewey developed in *Art as Experience.* Austin shared with Dewey the conviction that the innovative force of a work of art rested on its aptitude to express the rhythms of the embodied conversation between self and world. In *Art as Experience* Dewey describes experience as a process of communication between self and environment in which the subject is neither entirely distinct from nor completely merged with but participant in the world. As Dewey puts it, "Experience is the result, the sign, and the reward of that interaction of organism and environment which, when it is carried to the full, is a transformation of interaction into participation and communication" (22). Both quotidian experiences and their intensified aesthetic renderings—art in Dewey's sense as "the clarified and intensified development of traits that belong to every normally complete experience" (46)—represent the result of ongoing exchanges with and readjustments to the world. For Dewey an experience always entails that self and world, step-by-step, are bound together as shapeshifting yet nonidentical entities. Therefore, Dewey points out, the "factor of resistance is worth especial notice at this point. Without internal tension there would be a fluid rush to a straightaway mark; there would be nothing that could be called development and fulfillment" (138).

Dewey's notion that participatory experience represents a cumulative response to resisting environmental forces reminds us that self and world, as well as the inner and outer realities of our lives, are mutually constitutive, interconnected, and yet disparate modes of reality. We create our experiences in a reciprocal process that originates in our encounter with forces that invite yet resist us and that builds in dialogue with these forces as we try to synchronize them with our way of being. "In an experience," Dewey explains, "things and events belonging to the world, physical and social, are transformed through the human context they enter, while the live creature is changed and developed through its intercourse with things previously external to it" (246). In other words, experiences can be considered relational processes into which the person enters not as a self-contained agent or "carrier of an experience" but as a communicating agency, as "a factor absorbed in what is produced" (250). Dewey's notion of environmental resistance, aesthetic tension, and experience as cumulative process can help us understand how the relations between embodied subjects and their surroundings give rise to experiences that reveal and express the continuity of self and world without denying that the encountered others also have an existence outside the formed relations.

Austin gives a representative account of this process in her portrait of her first encounter with southern California. "There was something else there besides what you find in the books" (**EH [Earth Horizon]** 187), Austin writes of her initial impressions of the San Joaquin Valley, through which she traveled with her family on their way from Los Angeles to their new homestead in Tejon country in 1888.[25] In the unfamiliar landscape, Austin perceives a quality that arrests her attention. She phenomenologically describes it as "a lurking, evasive Something, wistful, cruel, ardent; something that rustled and ran, that hung half-remotely, insistent on being noticed, fled from pursuit, and when you turned from it, leaped suddenly and fastened on your vitals" (187). It is a presence that escapes her intellectual awareness but that encroaches upon her when she diverts her conscious attention. It provokes an "insistent experiential pang" and a desire to capture the sensation in language (187). Yet this "Beauty-in-the wild, yearning to be made human" resists easy acquaintance (187). Although Austin perceives it as inviting her to transform it into something human, her experience of this dimension of the landscape first requires her to change in response to her environment. The success of her effort to observe and describe the "evasive Something" is predicated, she feels, on her capacity to give "herself up wholly to the mystery of the arroyos" and to "be alone with it for uninterrupted occasions, in which they might come to terms" (187). In other words, as Austin physically experiences and perceptually makes sense of her surroundings, she changes in relation to the world while she also

transforms the reality that she encounters. She seeks to understand and describe that which is not her, which is not human, and which she cannot readily assimilate by reconfiguring her subjective world. This process includes a negotiation of self and world, a mutual coming to terms, that is not innately harmonious but also marked by tensions. Despite her "kindred yearning," the "wistful, cruel, ardent" land escapes her grasp (187). To bring her fleeting sensations and her response to what she perceives as the spirit of the place, its genius loci, into concrete verbal form, she first has to adopt a flexible sense of self that allows her to continually realign herself in relation to her environment. In Austin's words, she has "to wrestle with the Spirit of the Arroyos" (188).

AUSTIN'S AESTHETICS, ECOCRITICAL PRACTICE, AND ENVIRONMENTAL ETHICS

Austin insisted that human perceptions of the natural world are situated and that the biophysical environment nonetheless should not be subsumed under the human world of linguistically mediated reality. Her ideas predate current ecological thought and ecocritical approaches to literary studies. Since "we do not create the land itself or its other inhabitants," as SueEllen Campbell writes ("The Land and Language of Desire" 205), the land matters beyond our readings of it. For an ecological understanding of reality the ability to distinguish, for instance, between a specific river as a thing in itself and the human construction of particular images of this river is pertinent. From an ecological perspective the respective components are both separate and converging. They are interrelated, Holmes Rolston points out in *Philosophy Gone Wild,* in that for "every landscape, there is an inscape; mental and environmental horizons reciprocate" (24). In studying the relations between literary, cultural, and social practices and the environment, ecocritics, therefore, tend to think of categories such as perception and representation or empirical reality and social construction as polarities in a continuum of interrelated processes rather than as mutually exclusive spheres. They draw on a concept of textuality that grants that reality is intersubjectively produced but also insists there are nonhuman texts that are not dependent on human readers. Lawrence Buell, for instance, argues in *The Environmental Imagination* "that reported contacts with particular settings are intertextually, intersocially constructed" and "that the nonbuilt environment is one of the variables that influence culture, text, and personality" (13). This understanding, Buell points out, avoids "reductionism at the level of formal representation, such as to compel us to believe either that the text replicates the object-world or that it creates an entirely distinct linguistic world" (13). Instead of following such a dichotomizing logic, an ecocritical reading, as delineated above, can interpret literary renderings of nature as aesthetic enactments of imaginary and actual encounters with the natural world within both a social and an ecological context.

For a brief illustration of an ecocritical perspective on the relations among the object world, human mindscapes, and their literary renderings—a perspective that helps to understand the implications of Austin's regionalist aesthetic—I return to the example of the river. The empirical reality of the river and the human inscapes and representations of it can be considered separate, because the particular river exists whether we look at it or ignore it, name it "river" or "ditch," or write about it as part of a watershed or a recreational area or as a local symbol for the Acheron. In short, the river exists within its own environmental context and natural history. It evolved at some point out of geological changes, and it has since changed its course, meandering, eroding the banks, and providing a habitat for an also changing vegetation and wildlife. Just as clearly, however, the components are not separate but interrelated both on a pragmatic and a conceptual level. First of all, it is likely that human history and river history have mutually influenced each other. On one hand, the river course may have been altered by human intervention or the water and the riverbed may be polluted; on the other hand, the river may have entered human history by providing fishing grounds or a trade route—any port city is evidence of this. But even if the river and its banks were a wilderness uninhabited by humans and unaffected by human-induced changes in other regions, when we speak of human contact with the natural world, it is difficult to disentangle nonhuman nature as such from the human perception of it. Our vision and experiences are mediated through multiple filters, including our sense of selfhood, prior experiences, preceding encounters with the nonhuman world, intentions, and the linguistic organization of our patterns of thought. The river has a different meaning for and plausibly looks different to a farmer on the neighboring fields, for a commuter driving by on the freeway, and for an ecologist studying the impact of the freeway on the river's wildlife habitats. Also, identifying the stretch of water that we may see from the riverbank as part of the larger entity "river" already constitutes an act of interpretation. Our general concept of "riverness" and its distinction from other bodies of water and entities come to bear on our experience, as does our acquaintance with symbolical readings of rivers and water, in which they may denote life or, conversely, the transitoriness of existence.

While many ecologically minded critics would agree with poststructural theorists that reality is intertextually constructed, their concepts of intertextuality diverge when applied to the relations between humans and nonhuman nature. While ecocritics tend to acknowledge that our readings inevitably produce culturally mediated environmental "texts," they also will maintain that the world cannot be reduced to these human-authored texts.[26]

As SueEllen Campbell convincingly argues in "The Land and Language of Desire," poststructuralists have extended Ferdinand de Saussure's analysis of the relational and arbitrary character of linguistic signs to a conceptualization both of language and of empirical reality as a network of intertexts dependent on human readers, while ecologists have emphasized that the nonhuman world also has an existence apart from human signifying systems. Environmentally committed critics tend to insist, as Austin did, that human nonhuman interactions are reciprocal and that the nonhuman environment not only invites and provokes human readings but also escapes, resists, and exceeds the comprehension of human readers. As Donna J. Haraway points out in *Simians, Cyborgs, and Women,* "Accounts of a 'real' world do not, then, depend on a logic of 'discovery,' but on a power-charged social relation of 'conversation.' The world neither speaks itself nor disappears in favor of a master decoder. The codes of the world are not still, waiting only to be read. The world is not raw material for humanization" (198). While we may know and speak of the nonhuman only from a human perspective, this perspective is defined in relation to what we are not; it cannot claim to encompass a natural world that extends beyond the human, including our interpretations of it.

The articulation of this critical position is often motivated by environmentalist concerns. In contrast to the poststructuralist valorization that our readings of reality are situated and that we "always change what we study," environmentalists tend to perceive this complicity "not as liberating but as a call to caution," SueEllen Campbell explains (205). "A 'misread' text and a depleted acquifer present quite different practical problems and raise quite different moral and ethical questions" (206). Ecocritics frequently assert that in order to realign human life with its nonhuman matrix, in order to turn from viewing nature as a resource infinitely available for human use and consumption, we have to recognize its self-organizing existence. The acknowledgement that the nonhuman exists in its own right and on its own terms while it also influences human history is meant to facilitate a more acute comprehension of the limits that natural systems impose on human agency.

This understanding provides a possible basis for environmental ethics—as the concept of regionalist nature writing exemplifies that Austin develops in the previously quoted account of her first journey through southern California. Austin presents environmental literature as the product of an interaction between self and world, as an expression of a writer's subjective encounter with the natural world that is informed by the author's sense of self, by her mode of engagement with the environment, by the natural features and processes that attract her attention, and by the degree of resistance that the environment offers to human observation and participation. Austin reveals and emphasizes the environmentalist motivation of her critical stance by ending her autobiographical portrait of "the way a Naturist is taken with the land, with the spirit trying to be evoked out of it" with an expression of the "frustration" and "deep resentment" she feels in light of the environmental degradation of southern California (*EH* 188). Austin's attempts to experience and describe its *genius loci* have remained an "incomplete adventure," she asserts, because human development has severely altered if not destroyed the regional environment (188). The "place of the mystery was eaten up, it was made into building lots, cannery sites; it receded before the preëmptions of rock crushers and city dumps" (187-88). By contrasting her initial enchantment with her later aversion to southern California, Austin uses her autobiographical recollections for environmentalist purposes. She ends her discussion of the necessary psychological and physical adjustment of regionalist writers to the place they wish to describe with a blend of mysticism and environmental advocacy. She insists on the self-organizing existence of the nonhuman and indicts dominant society for the region's environmental degradation. In a place "slavered over with the impudicity of a purely material culture," Austin's **"Spirit of the Arroyos"** remains "wistful with long refusals" (189).

Austin's theoretical and literary explorations of the options writers have for keeping "faith with the land" thus seem to have anticipated the current ecocritical inquiry whether and to which extent reality can be perceived and rendered in human language from a nonanthropocentric perspective. In thinking about the factors that enter into the production and reception of regional and environmental literature, Austin persistently asked which possibilities textual practices have to mark the intersections between unconstructed reality and mediated human experiences of it. For her the question of how the environment could enter literary texts allowed for polemics but not for easy answers. Instead, it provoked a "yearning" (*EH* 187) and a narrative practice that suggests the porousness and mutability of categories such as subject and object, self and other, and environment and identity.

To return to her earlier definition of regionalist literature, Austin may have realized that the land's prediscursive "essential qualities" could only be experienced subjectively and rendered discursively. Yet she insisted that environmental writing has to alert its readers to the inevitable mismatch between human readings and environmental actualities through meta-narrative comments, because paradoxically this self-referentiality—through its explication of what the text is and its simultaneous reference to what it cannot be—provides a way for the author to remain faithful to both the phenomenological reality of human encounters with the nonhuman world as an unmerged other and to the self-organizing existence of natural systems. Austin recognized the importance that our conversations with the nonhuman world hold for our sanity and survival. Hence, she simultaneously could consider it the writer's task to "give in human terms the meaning of that country in which the action of the story takes place" (**"Regionalism in American Fiction"** 105) and define the author's obligation in environmentalist terms as an accountability to nonhuman others.

THE SPIRITUAL AND DEMOCRATIC FUNCTION OF LITERATURE

Literary, epistemological, and sociopolitical (environmentalist, feminist, and pluralist) concerns converge in Austin's regionalist work, as we have seen. The different aspects of her regionalist aesthetic cohere because they derive from one common source. They result from Austin's conviction that it should be the primary function of art to help people integrate the intellectual, emotional, corporeal, and spiritual dimensions of their lives and to align themselves with their community, environment, and the universal "Something" present in all of these. Literature, Austin believed, has to be environmentally grounded and has to validate the ordinary processes of life because these qualities make it most affective on a personal, social, and spiritual level.

Austin's most extensive comment on the social and religious purpose of art is **"The American Rhythm,"** the introductory essay to her poetry collection of the same title, *The American Rhythm*.[27] In the essay she seeks to develop a place-based, democratic, and spiritual poetics out of her study of the aesthetic, ritual, and social functions of Native American oral traditions. According to Austin, poetry is an essentially rhythmic and somatic form of aesthetic expression, and as such it is prone to be affected by the factors that enter into the human experience of rhythm, namely the rhythms of our bodies—heartbeat, breath, biochemical, neurological, and energetic changes (*AR* [*The American Rhythm*] 5)—and the variations that these corporeal rhythms undergo as they are affected by environmental conditions and experiential knowledge (3), by emotional states (13), and by modes of work and transportation (12-13). Made of words but molded by experience, poetry in Austin's sense is not primarily concerned with language or ideas but with relating the poet and his or her audience to the social, ecological, and spiritual matrix of their lives. For Austin the source and objective of poetry are collective and religious (21-22). She cites Native American oral traditions and ritual practices as evidence that poetry originally served no "other purpose than that of producing and sustaining collective states" (23), "those happy states of reconciliation with the Allness through group communion" (54). In other words, what interests Austin most about poetry is its spiritual and democratic potential.[28]

Again, Austin's regionalist aesthetic brings Dewey's experiential concept of art to mind. Dewey argues in *Art as Experience* that aesthetic perception presents us with a heightened recognition of the embeddedness of our daily lives in a world that extends beyond the human. Because it facilitates experiences of the subject's wholeness and the interrelatedness of the different dimensions of our lives and the world at large, Dewey reasons, art serves both a psychologically sustaining and a cosmological function. Through aesthetic perception, accompanied at times by "religious feeling," we are

> introduced into a world beyond this world which is nevertheless the deeper reality of the world in which we live in our ordinary experiences. We are carried out beyond ourselves to find ourselves. . . . art operates to deepen and to raise to great clarity that sense of an enveloping undefined whole that accompanies every normal experience. . . . Where egotism is not made the measure of reality and value, we are citizens of this vast world beyond ourselves, and any intense realization of its presence with and in us brings a peculiarly satisfying sense of unity in itself and with ourselves.

> (195)

Dewey describes the potential of art to spiritually intensify and clarify the reality of our daily lives. Similarly, Austin argues in her regionalist work for the fundamentally integrative nature of art and validates the ordinary processes of life as the basis for the creation of literature. In *The American Rhythm* she asserts, as said, that the objective of poetry is to make us simultaneously feel personally integrated, part of our community, and aligned with our environment and the universal principles inherent in all these aspects of the world.

Certainly the notion that art is a modern effort to achieve "reconciliation with the Allness," as Austin says, or a modern attempt to preserve an interpretation of the world as "an enveloping undefined whole," in Dewey's words, is not a new insight. The rise of landscape perception in the history of Western art, for instance, is generally seen as contingent on the modern decline of the *theoria,* the philosophical tradition of interpreting the natural world as an all-encompassing divine whole.[29] In Western history the cosmological conception of nature in the sense of the *theoria* was increasingly replaced by conceptualizations based on empirical and rationalist studies. Industrialization intensified the split between society and the environment, since the human dependence on the nonhuman world ceased to determine the collective experience to the extent it had in preindustrial agrarian societies.

The experience of the unity of humankind and nature was not fully suppressed, however, but remained accessible for individuals in the aesthetic perception of nature as landscape. In this sense the development of landscape perception can be considered a modern attempt to preserve an interpretation of the world as a harmoniously ordered cosmos. Since it presupposes a distanced attitude of the observer to the environment, the conceptualization of nature as landscape can only facilitate the aesthetic experience of nature in the sense of the *theoria* if the vision of the observing subject has been adequately conditioned. Only when the observer has learned to assemble and integrate the components of a particular section of the respective scenery into a unified and coherent image and to invest it with subjective meaning does a "landscape" come into existence. In other words, the landscape does not exist outside the culturally trained mind and imagination of the observer, but it constitutes a subjective prospect, composed by means of a discerning individual vision from a single viewpoint. The historical evolution of Western landscape perception and representation demonstrates that the subjective processes involved in mentally organizing our biochemical vision into coherent aesthetic images are in themselves results of sociocultural developments.

While this line of reasoning helps to remind us that our perception of the environment is a cultural artifact, it unfortunately also relegates holistic aesthetic experiences of the kind described by Austin and Dewey to an isolated field of art. Aesthetic experiences are seen to serve primarily to compensate the observer's culturally conditioned mind and imagination for the lack of integration prevalent in his or her daily life. Austin's and Dewey's experiential theories of art, by contrast, refuse to base modern aesthetics on a fundamentally distanced relation between observer and world and writer and environment. Instead, they focus on our elemental connectedness with the world around us, on the experiences we undergo as environmentally bound "live creatures," irrespective of whether we are aware of this level of our existence. As Dewey contends in *Art as Experience,* "the uniquely distinguishing feature of esthetic experience is exactly the fact that no such distinction of self and object exists in it, since it is esthetic in the degree in which the organism and environment cooperate to institute an experience in which the two are so fully integrated that each disappears" (249). Rather than emphasize the potential of aesthetic experience to overcome dualistic conceptions of nature and culture, subject and object, Dewey and Austin insist that these aspects of reality are always already fundamentally interrelated at the level of our lived experience and creative processes.

REGIONALIST LITERATURE AND NATIONAL CULTURE

On the basis of her experiential regionalist poetics, Austin argues in *The American Rhythm* that American poetry can be considered distinctly American to the degree that it represents an aesthetic response to the peculiar rhythms of American environments. She asserts, for instance, that it is the contact with the "new earth" and "a new experiential adaptation of social mechanisms" that makes European American poetry distinctly American (*AR* 9). In answer to her query, "How much of the character called national in any literature is owed to the influences taken in through the senses?" Austin grants a predominant influence to present living conditions rather than to cultural heritage.[30] She proposes that the encounter with particular places and ways of living may provoke similar responses from poets of different cultural backgrounds. For her, similarities between traditional indigenous and modern European American poetry prove that American culture to a significant extent is environmentally determined. "That scene is immensely more potent than race is testified by the independent emergence of similar verse patterns among the poets of the race amalgam, taking its name from the scene, called American" (*AU* 11). As the contact with a common environment can level the cultural difference among diverse groups inhabiting one region, Austin suggests, so the contact with one continent can unify the different segments of the American population.

Yet the American continent and American society are heterogeneous environments that can hardly be expected to provoke a singular response. How could such a kaleidoscope of diverse forms and processes issue into a single American rhythm, as the title of Austin's study suggests? Austin's simultaneous advocacy of regionalized, and thus plural, American cultures and of a singular national character seems contradictory.[31] Her attempt to extend her concept of geographical determination from the sphere of regional society to the plane of the nation renders her argument problematic. For Austin here posits not only that specific environments influence particular people but that the common quality supposedly shared by the variety of built and natural environments on the American continent shapes American history and the process of nation building. Even if we would assume that a common regional orientation could unite an otherwise diverse group of people, it seems arbitrary to define the limits of such a union in national terms.

Austin's search for the common denominator of the various rhythms that she considered particular to American environments and cultures seems to have been motivated by a patriotic attachment to the idea of a unified American nation. Her interest "in an Americanization program" considerably weakens her argument, however, as Lewis Mumford observes in his review "The American Rhythm" (24). To prove her point that the diverse American rhythms issue into a single national rhythm, Austin deliberately conflates, for instance, the differences among poets such as Amy Lowell, Vachel Lindsay, Edgar Lee Masters, and Carl Sandburg as well as between their work and Native American poetry to prove a common environmental influence (*AR* 46).[32] Although Austin angrily rejected the suggestion that her argument had nationalistic tendencies, Mumford's comment is justified in so far as Austin argues in *The American Rhythm* not only that environmental rhythms exert an influence on the production and reception of art but also that the environmental and social conditions prevalent on the American continent result in a distinctly national literature.[33]

The larger project that Austin pursues in regionalist works such as *The American Rhythm,* through her theory of geographical determination and her presentation of Native American culture as a role model for European American acculturation, is the creation of a national myth of origin. The definition of a common national origin is key to Austin's argument since the assertion of a shared foundation lends coherence to the diverse indigenous, imported, and hybrid American cultures. Equally important, the supposition of new particularly American sources of experience, thought, and identity makes it possible to value American culture on its own terms—an established line of thought since the declarations of cultural independence that dominated the field of American literature during the mid-nineteenth century. As Austin reasons in "What Is a Native Culture?": "For i[f] we are only a lot of mongrelized Europeans in the western continent, we are n[o]thing, but as the American People we are of first rank" (*AU* 625, 3).

Austin seeks to contribute with her work to the creation of a national mythology that would help Americans home into their regional environments. From *The Land of Little Rain* to *The American Rhythm,* from *The Land of Journey's Ending* to *One-Smoke Stories,* she casts the place-based southwestern cultures as the prototypes of an environmentally grounded, democratic future American society. For her, the Native American and Hispanic regional cultures anticipate the desired regionalization and democratization of dominant American society. Austin proposes that the "general adoption of native symbols for experiences intimate and peculiar to the land" will accelerate the cultural development of the nation because the "cultural evolution" of any society depends on its adaptation to its land base (*LJE* [*The Land of Journey's Ending*] 440). Accordingly, Austin adopts narrative practices and concepts of authorship and democratic culture gleaned from Native American oral traditions and Hispanic and white folk cultures. Appealing to the self-interest of her predominantly white audience, she argues that the subjugation of Native Americans and Hispanics and the eradication of their cultural heritages not only has a devastating effect on their communities but also harms the development of dominant American society, as it slows down European American acculturation. In **"Cults of the Pueblos,"** Austin warns her readers, for instance, "we cannot put our weight on the left hand of God and not ourselves go down with it" (35). For Austin the definition of national identity represents not a purely political enterprise but also a mythical and spiritual task.

Austin's contemporaries appreciated her speculative talent and her mythological project of nation building. "She has issued a challenge which will make every honest American poet stop to examine himself. And that is an excellent thing," reckoned Mark Van Doren ("The American Rhythm" 472). Austin's intentions were clearly discerned by Henry Nash Smith, who had profited as a young regionalist and editor of the *Southwest Review* from his elder's expertise. In "The Feel of the Purposeful Earth," Smith notes, "Mrs. Austin is trying to do for the American race what myths did for the Greeks and for other European peoples. Modern skepticism makes this task hard; she has explored the mythology and the folk-lore of the Indians and the early Spanish settlers, but she has been forced in the end to express her meaning in philosophical terms and through the traditional form of nature-writing. Of course she has not been able to create an American mythology—it takes generations to do that. But she has seen the problem, and made it clear" (30). While Smith regarded it as Austin's achievement that she managed to "impose upon Americans the task of becoming a tribe, of building a civilization" (32), other critics found the implied criticism of the status quo as objectionable as the idea of cross-cultural learning. Anglo-Saxonism and racial prejudice against Native Americans fueled opposition to Austin's ideal of an "Amerindian" society.[34]

From a contemporary perspective, Mary Austin's focus on the dynamics of intercultural communication and her emphasis on the social, ecological, and psychological benefits of a place-based culture seem innovative. In works such as **The American Rhythm** she takes up the challenge of her precursors to create a distinctly American culture and develops a poetics that can be understood as a regionalist update of their romantic utopia of cultural autonomy. The historical continuity is readily apparent, and Austin was not the first regionalist to take up the romantic lead.[35] She certainly agreed with Emerson's dictum that "America is a poem in our eyes; its ample geography dazzles the imagination, and it will not wait long for metres" ("The Poet" 997). For Austin, however, the American poets had already arrived and were flourishing both within and outside European American society. Further cultural development now depended, Austin proposed, on a cross-cultural dialogue on the diverse experiences of place. In formulating the ideal of a place-based democratic American society that would emerge out of cross-cultural negotiations and the sustainable inhabitation of the American continent, Austin went beyond the romantic conceptions of her predecessors.[36] Her environmentalist awareness and sensitivity to social imbalances of power—for instance, along the lines of regional and educational backgrounds and ethnic, class, and gender differences—allowed Austin to contribute an innovative regionalist vision to American literary history.

Notes

1. Williams, *A Novelette and Other Prose, 1921-31* (Toulon: To Publishers, 1931) 185, qtd. in Bracher, "California's Literary Regionalism" 276.

2. Dualism has been thoroughly critiqued by feminist theorists as the conceptual framework that "interlocking systems of domination" share (hooks, *Talking Black* 22). For a comprehensive definition of dualism, see Plumwood, *Feminism and the Mastery of Nature*. "A dualism is more than a relation of dichotomy, difference, or non-identity, and more than a simple hierarchical relationship. . . . Dualism is a relation of separation and domination inscribed and naturalised in culture and characterised by radical exclusion, distancing and opposition between orders construed as systematically higher and lower, as inferior and superior, as ruler and ruled, which treats the division as part of the natures of beings construed not merely as different but as belonging to radically different orders or kinds, and hence as not open to change" (47-48). Dualistic paradigms, in other words, require and effect distortions of difference that serve to legitimize the colonization of human and nonhuman others by a "master subject"; see Haraway, *Simians, Cyborgs, and Women* 177.

3. Abram, *The Spell of the Sensuous* 125.

4. Merleau-Ponty, *The Visible and the Invisible* 58.

5. Although it was plausibly written in 1927, *Cactus Thorn* was not published until 1988, as a result of Graulich's research (Foreword, *CT* viii). The novella is also analyzed in chapter 4 of this study.

6. In the chapter "The Wilderness Cult" in his study *Wilderness and the American Mind,* Nash points out that increasing urbanization and industrialization resulted in a positive reevaluation of the concept of wilderness at the turn of the century (141-60). For a history of the idea of wilderness from prehistory to present times, see Oelschlaeger, *The Idea of Wilderness*. A recent anthology that offers a variety of revisionary perspectives on concepts of wilderness and preservation is *Uncommon Ground,* ed. Cronon. Austin's feminist revisions of the wilderness cult are examined in chapter 4 of this study.

7. While the choice of words suggests that Austin was conversant with Eastern religions, especially Taoism, I have found no evidence in her published or private writings that she ever undertook any extensive studies of Asian philosophy.

8. Botkin, "Mary Austin" 64; M. Van Doren, "The American Rhythm" 472. Austin did not appreciate general dismissals of her work, no matter how galantly presented. She wanted to be taken seriously and not merely flattered. For her, Mark Van Doren's review was "the usual New York thing. Extremely complimentary in a vague large way and more or less irritated by the necessity for admitting that anybody who lives outside of New York and does not admire it, can have anything really vital to say" (Letter to Daniel Trembly MacDougal, 12 Oct. 1923, AU 1192).

9. Diamond, *Guns, Germs, and Steel* 25-26; also qtd. in Love, "Ecocriticism and Science" 568.

10. AU 625. Her audience at times chose to ignore this point and misread her argument on behalf of a self-conscious regional inhabitation of the American continent as an unqualified assertion of patriotism. A reviewer of a lecture Austin delivered in Carmel on the topic reports her as having said that "the greatest human achievements" were "the national roots which bind us to our own native soil" and that the "most essential fact of life, says Mrs. Austin, is our feeling for the land where we were born" (A. Burroughs, "Mary Austin's Ideas of American Patterns" 6). However, Austin's regionalist texts define as essential not one's place of birth but one's mode of inhabiting the place one chooses to live in. For a recent collection of essays on "becoming native," see *At Home on the Earth,* ed. Barnhill.

11. Austin, "Artist Life in the United States" 151.

12. Austin, *The American Rhythm* (1923) 153.

13. Harper, *The Course of the Melting Pot Idea* 253-54. The faith that assimilation simply occurred is reflected in the title of William C. Smith's 1939 social science work, *Americans in the Making: The Natural History of the Assimilation of Immigrants,* qtd. in Gleason, "American Identity and Americanization" 47.

14. Austin, "Regionalism in American Fiction" 97. Austin's concept of race is further analyzed in chapter 5 of this study.

15. Austin, "Regionalism in American Fiction" 98. It is important to note that Austin promoted the development of plural regional cultures rather than privileged one particular regional identity over others. Although the potential links between regionalism and xenophobic or nativist attitudes merit discussion, it is reductionist to interpret any assertion of regional identity as a value-hierarchical statement. To consider a particular place home is not necessarily to deny that other places are home to other people, nor does it inevitably imply that one's home is better than others or that it is even exclusively one's own. It is plausibly apparent to most people who feel intimately connected with one particular place that this place does not exist in a vacuum but is situated in and continuous with the larger world. The general refutation of the regional environment as a positive source of identity is in itself problematic because it establishes a one-directional relation between our ethical commitments and our lives, reducing our lived experience to pliable raw material that is passively shaped by preestablished norms and exterior structures.

16. Austin saw this ideal realized, for instance, "in the way that *Huckleberry Finn* is of the great river, taking its movement and rhythm, its structure and intention, or lack of it, from the scene" ("Regionalism in American Fiction" 106). By contrast, Austin did not consider novels such as Stowe's *Uncle Tom's Cabin* (106) or Cather's *Death Comes for the Archbishop* regional literature, since these works did not represent the outlook of the regional population they described (105-6).

17. The distinction between local color and regionalist literature is discussed in more detail in chapter 6 of the study.

18. Significantly, the narrator of *The Land of Little Rain* for the first time identifies herself explicitly as a woman writer in her criticism of Bret Harte and local color fiction (113).

19. First published in 1903, "The Last Antelope" was reprinted in *Lost Borders* and also included in *One-Smoke Stories* (1934), the last collection of stories that Austin published. In the 1934 version, as in the original, the story ends with the tale of the last antelope, eliding the self-reflective passages. Austin plausibly edited the reprinted version to fit the short short story format of the anthology, which features, as its title indicates, mostly brief narratives that could be read within the duration of a single smoke.

20. Austin thought *Silas Lapham* Howells's best work because she considered it regional of Boston ("Regionalism in American Fiction" 101).

21. Austin, "Regionalism in American Fiction" 102. A convincing argument that the satiric form and social concern of Austin's work exerted a crucial influence on her friend Sinclair Lewis is developed in Witschi, "Sinclair Lewis, the Voice of Satire, and Mary Austin's Revolt from the Village."

22. Austin, *LLR* 194, 261; Austin, *The Basket Woman: A Book of Indian Tales for Children* 221. Oppapago lies in the vicinity of the highest mountain

in the continental United States, Mount Whitney, which was named after Josiah D. Whitney, the leader of the California State Geological Survey. Frederick Turner points out in *Beyond Geography* that the European conquest of the Americas involved from its beginning the replacement of names attributed to the land by the native population with new names registering the cultural identity of the colonizers (131). A joke of the 1990s captures the relation between the naming and colonization of the "New World": "Why are the Indians called Indians? 'Cause a white man got lost."

23. In *The Land of Little Rain* Austin generally presents Native American cultures, especially Paiute culture, as a learning model for the European American development of a sustainable place-based society. While in this work she avoids for the most part stereotypical notions about "the Indian," she does fall into essentialist arguments at other times, especially in her critical essays. The complications of Austin's cross-cultural work are examined in chapter 5 of this study. See also Hoyer, *Dancing Ghosts*.

24. Bredahl, *New Ground* 54.

25. Austin also described this journey in "One Hundred Miles on Horseback," her first significant publication. Originally published in the journal of Austin's alma mater, *Blackburnian*, the essay was reprinted in *One Hundred Miles on Horseback*, ed. Ringler.

26. An "intertext" may well be nonhuman; see S. Campbell, "The Land and Language of Desire." "A deer, for instance, has no being apart from things like the presence or absence of wolves, the kind of forage in its environment, the temperature and snowfall of any given winter, the other animals competing for the available food, the number of hunters with licenses, the bacteria in its intestines that either keep it healthy or make it sick" (208).

27. Although the essay formally introduces the collection, it is an independent piece of speculative critical writing rather than a foreword (*AR* 3-65). Its status is already indicated by its length. The essay takes up almost half of the first edition of *The American Rhythm*. The other half of this 1923 edition consists of two sections of roughly equal length: The first presents Austin's "reëxpressions" of Native American poems under the title "Amerindian Songs," the second contains her own poems or "Songs in the American Manner." The second, 1930 edition of *The American Rhythm* substitutes for Austin's original poetry and for the poems that communicate her general understanding of Native American thought more translated material. With its two new sections on "Magic Formulas" and "Tribal Lays," the enlarged edition includes significantly more translations and reexpressions of Native American poetry and legends than the first edition.

Reëxpression is Austin's term for her method of cross-cultural composition. The process of reexpression entailed that, in a first step, Austin would either listen to Native American poems and stories as they were performed and translated for her or she would work with the material collected and translated by white ethnologists. Her subjective experience of the particular poem and of the respective Native American culture and its regional land base, then, would provide her with the inspiration to write a poem that she hoped would express the essential qualities of the original poem or chant (*AR* 38). To check the accuracy of her interpretation, she ideally would read her rendition back to a Native American storyteller (*AR* 55).

While Austin considered herself a weak poet, the reviewers of the first edition of *The American Rhythm* frequently praised Austin's poems while they criticized the argument of the introduction. "Mary Austin's poetry was better than her theories" is representative in this respect (Wynn, "A Critical Study" 235). Wynn offers a comparison of Austin's method of reexpression and the work of contemporaneous translators (383-90). Helpful recent analyses that situate Austin's poetry within the American literary field of the early twentieth century are Ruppert, "Discovering America"; and Metcalfe, "Singing Like the Indians Do." On Austin's view of Native American poetry, see also Castro, "Early Translators of American Poetry"; Drinnon, "The American Rhythm"; and Zolla, "Mary Austin, Essayist and Student of Rhythm."

28. Judging from the recorded observations of her contemporaries, Austin's lectures on poetic rhythm must have been vivid performances. Austin danced, chanted, and acted to illustrate her theories. She performed, for instance, a Greek dance accompanied by a tambourine while reciting Shelley's "Ode to a Skylark" to prove that the origins of English meter were Greek (Major, "Mary Austin in Fort Worth" 307). Audiences seem to have been particularly impressed by Austin's rendition of the "Gettysburg Address," which she recited while she mimed chopping wood to demonstrate its supposed underlying rhythm. One reviewer enthusiastically recalls the "dazzling splendor" of Austin's performance (Worthington, "American Patterns Skillfully Woven in Austin Lecture" 7); an anonymous reviewer is taken by the "utmost realism" of Austin's delivery ("Creative Worker in Literature Gave Interesting Lecture" 1). This ac-

count of Austin's "Aboriginal Poetry" talk at Mills College in February 1928 reveals more interesting details that are suggestive of the lecture hall atmosphere during Austin's readings. The writer reports: "The lecturer gave a very dramatic and tense rendition of an Indian prayer for rain accompanying herself on the drum. She then requested President Reinhardt to help her, and Mrs. Austin beat the drum while the president read the poem . . . by Carl Sandburg, and a selection from Walt Whitman" ("Creative Worker" 4). While this scenario may seem bewildering to contemporary readers, the audience did not consider Austin's performance eccentric. At least the reviewer gained the general impression that Austin "speaks in a calm, unimpassioned tone of voice, and her lecture was delightfully punctuated with bits of dry humor" (4).

29. Studies that agree on this point include Tuan, *Topophilia*; Merchant, *The Death of Nature*; Jauß, "Aisthesis und Naturerfahrung"; Piepmeier, "Das Ende der ästhetischen Kategorie 'Landschaft'"; and Ritter, "Landschaft."

30. Austin, untitled draft version of "The American Rhythm" AU 11.

31. In a private letter to Arthur David Ficke, Austin concedes "that the book would have been more truly called 'American Rhythms'" and attributes the choice of title to her publisher (Letter to Ficke, 27 Mar. 1930, AU 1096).

32. Jones, "Indian Rhythms" 647. Cf. the criticism of Austin's argumentative inconsistencies in Wynn, "A Critical Study" 216. Austin overstates her case in *The American Rhythm* in several respects. She establishes simplistic connections between physical experience and aesthetic expression, claiming, for example, that she can determine the type of environment that a given poet inhabits by listening to his poetry, even when it is in Native American languages unknown to her (*AR* 19).

33. Austin certainly was aware that the formation of national culture was an ongoing process, involving an array of changing factors, that was too complex and extensive to make its course entirely controllable or predictable. In her refutation of Mumford's criticism, she points out, "the whole conclusion of my argument" is that these processes "*can not be controlled by program*" (AU 24, emphasis in original). Still, Austin was interested in the development of a distinct national identity. Her concern with the issue of Americanization was not chauvinistic, however, as implied by Mumford. Her use of the term *American* is variable. Sometimes it refers specifically to citizens of the United States, at other times to all inhabitants

of the American continent. In the second edition of *The American Rhythm,* for instance, Austin recommends Mexican culture as a genuinely American role model to her European American readers, particularly to her critics (*AR* 1930, 84).

34. Mumford, for instance, proceeds in his review "The American Rhythm" from the assumption that "Mrs. Austin's latest work will not get the attention that it deserves" because the general reading public has "an a priori objection to the belief that a sophisticated culture can tie up with a primitive culture when it is planted in the same geographic environment" (23).

35. Sundquist notes, for instance, that Hamlin Garland's veritism follows Whitman's call for a democratic culture rooted in local realities ("Realism and Regionalism" 518).

36. Cf. Ruppert, "Mary Austin's Landscape Line in Native American Literature" 389-90; Ford, "*The American Rhythm*" 3.

Bibliography

A NOTE ON THE MANUSCRIPT SOURCE

The principle collection of Austin's manuscripts, drafts, documents, correspondence, journals, notes, and files is held by the Huntington Library, San Marino, California. Referenced material from the Mary Hunter Austin Collection is cited in the notes as AU [, followed by the archival number of the respective item. If the Huntington Library did not include an item number, the box number is provided instead]; individual pieces are not listed in the bibliography. Material from the Mary Hunter Austin Collection is reproduced by permission of the Huntington Library.

A SELECTION OF PUBLISHED WORKS BY MARY AUSTIN

BOOKS

The American Rhythm. New York: Harcourt, Brace, 1923. *The American Rhythm: Studies and Reëxpressions of Amerindian Songs.* Rev. ed. Boston: Houghton, 1930.

The Basket Woman: A Book of Indian Tales for Children. Boston: Houghton, 1904.

Cactus Thorn. Reno: U of Nevada P, 1988.

Earth Horizon: An Autobiography. Boston: Houghton, 1932.

The Land of Journey's Ending. New York: Century, 1924.

The Land of Little Rain. Boston: Houghton, 1903.

Lost Borders. New York: Harper, 1909.

One Hundred Miles on Horseback. 1889. Ed. Donald P. Ringler. Los Angeles: Dawson's, 1963.

One-Smoke Stories. Boston: Houghton, 1934.

ESSAYS AND CRITICISM

"Artist Life in the United States." *Nation* 120 (11 Feb. 1925): 151-52.

"Cults of the Pueblos: An Interpretation of Some Native Ceremonials." *Century* 109 (Nov. 1924): 28-35.

"Regional Culture in the Southwest." *Southwest Review* 14 (July 1929): 474-77.

"Regionalism in American Fiction." *English Journal* 21 (Feb. 1932): 97-107.

SECONDARY WORKS

Abram, David. *The Spell of the Sensuous: Perception and Language in a More-Than-Human World.* New York: Vintage, 1997.

Anonymous. "Creative Worker in Literature Gave Interesting Lecture in Lisser Hall: Mary Austin Discussed Aboriginal Poetry before Mills Audience." *Mills College Weekly* 18 (22 Feb. 1928): 1, 4.

Barnhill, David Landis, ed. *At Home on the Earth: Becoming Native to Our Place. A Multicultural Anthology.* Berkeley: U of California P, 1999.

Botkin, B.A. "Mary Austin." *Space* (Sept. 1934): 64.

Bracher, Frederick. "California's Literary Regionalism." *American Quarterly* 7.3 (1955): 275-84.

Bredahl, Carl A. *New Ground: Western American Narrative and the Literary Canon.* Chapel Hill: U of North Carolina P, 1989.

Buell, Lawrence. *The Environmental Imagination: Thoreau, Nature Writing, and the Formation of American Culture.* Cambridge: Harvard UP, 1995.

Burroughs, Ann. "Mary Austin's Ideas of American Patterns." *Carmel Pine Cone* (17 Aug. 1922): 6.

Campbell, SueEllen. "The Land and Language of Desire: Where Deep Ecology and Post-Structuralism Meet." *Western American Literature* 24 (fall 1989): 199-211.

Castro, Michael. "Early Translators of American Poetry." *Interpreting the Indian: Twentieth-Century Poets and the Native American.* Albuquerque: U of New Mexico P, 1983. 3-42.

Crèvecoeur, Hector Saint Jean de. "Letter III: What is an American?" *Letters from an American Farmer.* 1782. *The Norton Anthology of Literature.* Ed. Nina Baym et al. 3rd ed. Vol. 1. New York: Norton, 1989. 558-68. 2 vols.

Cronon, William, ed. *Uncommon Ground: Rethinking the Human Place in Nature.* New York: Norton, 1995.

Davidson, Donald. "Regionalism and Nationalism in American Literature." *American Review* 5 (Apr. 1935): 48-61.

Dewey, John. *Art as Experience.* 1934. New York: Perigee Books, 1980.

Diamond, Jared. *Guns, Germs, and Steel: The Fates of Human Societies.* New York: Norton, 1997.

Dorman, Robert L. *Revolt of the Provinces: The Regionalist Movement in America, 1920-1945.* Chapel Hill: U of North Carolina P, 1993.

Drinnon, Richard. "The American Rhythm: Mary Austin." *Facing West: The Metaphysics of Indian-Hating and Empire-Building.* Minneapolis: U of Minnesota P, 1980. 219-31.

Emerson, Ralph Waldo. "The Poet" (1844). *The Norton Anthology of Literature.* Ed. Nina Baym et al. 3rd ed. Vol. 1. New York: Norton, 1989. 984-99. 2 vols.

Ford, Thomas W. "*The American Rhythm*: Mary Austin's Poetic Principle." *Western American Literature* 5 (spring 1970): 3-14.

Gleason, Philip. "American Identity and Americanization." *Harvard Encyclopedia of American Ethnic Groups.* Ed. Stephan Thernstrom. Cambridge: Harvard UP, 1980. 31-58.

Graulich, Melody. Foreword. Afterword. *Cactus Thorn.* By Mary Austin. Reno: U of Nevada P, 1988. vii-ix. 101-22.

Haraway, Donna J. *Simians, Cyborgs, and Women: The Reinvention of Nature.* New York: Routledge, 1991.

Harper, Richard Conant. *The Course of the Melting Pot Idea to 1910.* Diss. Columbia U, 1967. New York: Arno, 1980.

hooks, bell. *Talking Black: Thinking Feminist, Thinking Black.* Boston: South End, 1989.

Hoyer, Mark T. *Dancing Ghosts: Native American and Christian Synchretism in Mary Austin's Work.* Reno: U of Nevada P, 1998.

Jauß, Hans Robert. "Aisthesis und Naturerfahrung." *Das Naturbild des Menschen.* Ed. Jörg Zimmermann. München: Wilhelm Fink, 1982. 155-82.

Jones, Llewellyn. "Indian Rhythms." *Bookman* 57 (Aug. 1923): 647-48.

Love, Glen A. "Ecocriticism and Science: Toward Consilience?" *NLH* [*New Literary History*] 30.3 (1999): 561-76.

Major, Mabel. "Mary Austin in Fort Worth." *New Mexico Quarterly* 4 (Nov. 1934): 307-10.

Merchant, Carolyn. *The Death of Nature: Women, Ecology and the Scientific Revolution.* London: Wildwood, 1982.

Merleau-Ponty, Maurice. *The Visible and the Invisible.* 1948. Ed. Claude Lefort. Trans. Alphonso Lingis. Evanston: Northwestern UP, 1968.

Metcalfe, Dale. "Singing Like the Indians Do: Mary Austin's Poetry." Graulich and Klimasmith 65-85.

Mumford, Lewis. "The American Rhythm." *New Republic* 35 (30 May 1923): 23-24.

———. *The Golden Day: A Study in American Experience and Culture.* New York: Boni, 1926.

Nash, Roderick Frazier. *Wilderness and the American Mind.* 1967. 3rd ed. New Haven: Yale UP, 1982.

Oelschlaeger, Max. *The Idea of Wilderness: From Prehistory to the Age of Ecology.* New Haven: Yale UP, 1991.

Phillips, Dana. "Ecocriticism, Literary Theory, and the Truth of Ecology." *NLH* 30.3 (1999): 577-602.

Piepmeier, Rainer. "Das Ende der ästhetischen Kategorie 'Landschaft.' Zu einem Aspekt neuzeitlichen Naturverhältnisses." *Westfälische Forschungen* 30 (1980): 8-46.

Plumwood, Val. *Feminism and the Mastery of Nature.* London: Routledge, 1993.

Quigley, Peter. "Rethinking Resistance: Environmentalism, Literature, and Poststructural Theory." *Environmental Ethics* 14 (winter 1992): 291-306.

Ritter, Joachim. "Landschaft: Zur Funktion des Ästhetischen in der Modernen Gesellschaft." *Subjektivität. Sechs Aufsätze.* Frankfurt/M.: Suhrkamp, 1989. 141-90.

Rolston, Holmes. *Philosophy Gone Wild: Essays in Environmental Ethics.* Buffalo: Prometheus, 1986.

Ruppert, James. "Discovering America: Mary Austin and Imagism." Allen 243-58.

———. "Mary Austin's Landscape Line in Native American Literature." *Southwest Review* 68 (autumn 1983): 376-90.

Smith, Henry Nash. "The Feel of the Purposeful Earth: Mary Austin's Prophecy." *New Mexico Quarterly* 1 (Feb. 1931): 17-33.

Sundquist, Eric J. "Realism and Regionalism." *Columbia Literary History* 501-24.

Thoreau, Henry David. *A Week on the Concord and Merrimakc Rivers.* 1849. New Orleans: Parnassus, 1987.

Tuan, Yi Fu. *Topophilia.* Englewood Cliffs: Prentice Hall, 1974.

Turner, Frederick. *Beyond Geography: The Western Spirit against the Wilderness.* 1980. New Brunswick: Rutgers UP, 1986.

Turner, Frederick Jackson. "The Significance of the Frontier in American History." 1893. *The Frontier in American History.* New York: Holt, 1953. 1-38.

Van Doren, Carl. "American Rhythm." *Century* 107 (Nov. 1923): 151-56.

Van Doren, Mark. "The American Rhythm." *Nation* 116 (18 Apr. 1923): 472.

Witschi, Nicholas. "Sinclair Lewis, the Voice of Satire, and Mary Austin's Revolt from the Village." *American Literary Realism* 30.1 (1998): 75-90.

Worthington, James. "American Patterns Skillfully Woven in Austin Lecture." *Carmel Pine Cone* (17 Aug. 1922): 7.

Wynn, Dudley Taylor. "A Critical Study of the Writings of Mary Hunter Austin (1868-1934)." Diss. New York U, 1939.

Zolla, Elémire. "Mary Austin, Essayist and Student of Rhythm." *The Writer and the Shaman: A Morphology of the American Indian.* Trans. Raymond Rosenthal. New York: Harcourt, 1973. 187-97.

LIST OF ABBREVIATIONS

AR	*The American Rhythm* (first edition, 1923)
AR 1930	*The American Rhythm* (revised edition)
CT	*Cactus Thorn*
EH	*Earth Horizon*
LB	*Lost Borders*
LJE	*The Land of Journey's Ending*
LLR	*The Land of Little Rain*

Corey Lee Lewis (essay date 2005)

SOURCE: Lewis, Corey Lee. "Mary Austin in the Land of Little Rain." In *Reading the Trail: Exploring the Literature and Natural History of the California Crest*, pp. 47-68. Reno, Nev.: University of Nevada Press, 2005.

[*In the following essay, Lewis stresses the precise knowledge of the California desert Austin demonstrated in her work, but notes as well her recognition of "the limits of linguistic representation" and her self-confessed difficulties in finding the right language to convey her experiences of the desert. Lewis then traces a number of narrative techniques Austin employed in her writings, both her fiction and nonfiction, to confront these "problems of representation and authority."*]

There was something else there besides what you find in the books; a lurking, evasive Something, wistful, cruel, ardent; something that rustled and ran, that hung half-remotely, insistent on being noticed, fled from pursuit, and when you turned from it, leaped suddenly and fastened on your vitals. This is no mere figure of speech, but the true movement of experience.

Mary Austin. *Earth Horizon*

My wife and I have been hiking through the heat all afternoon, across the sagebrush flats and past the few pinyon pines that dot the hillsides. We rise above the Owens Valley along a stretch of the southern Sierra Nevada, the great range standing to the north and west of us, while the wide arid lands of the Great Basin and Mojave deserts disappear into the distant horizon to the east. The sun pounds down from above, burning, incessant, and merciless. No clouds. Barely a breath of wind. Nothing it seems but an overpowering golden glow emanating from an endless pale-blue sky to rule over this burned land. I am reminded of Mary Austin's fitting descriptions of living in this land, where "the air breathes like cotton wool" (1997, 31).

Water is sucked out of our pores as we hike, the sweat drying on the skin so quickly that I begin to believe that dehydration could become an audible exercise here, in this land of little rain. Yet one feels strangely calm here; a serene silence lies over the land, settling slowly as we walk on the soul. Mary Austin must have felt it, too, on her journeys through this haunting and beautiful country. In *The Land of Little Rain,* she notes that this is "[a] land of lost rivers, with little in it to love; yet a land that once visited must be come back to inevitably" (5). Yesterday, we had to hike an extra four miles just to find water, since the seasonal stream we had planned to camp at was dry. There are no guarantees in this wide simmering land, I reminded myself, marking another of Austin's "lost rivers" on my map along with the time of the season during which it had leaped its banks and vanished into the sky. Here one can lose rivers and springs in a maze of both space and time.

The search for water, an endlessly repeated quest in such a place, tutors us as we strive to become literate in reading the landscape. The land continues to give us cryptic signs of the sweet liquid life we seek: a game trail, a distant shade of green, or the flocking of birds. Signs. They point the way to water; if we read them correctly and have the patience to keep reading and walking, we know we will get there—not soon, but eventually—to the blessed banks of some secret spring, or the tasty trickle of a sweet-water creek, or even, perhaps, the full-bodied roar of a river like the Kern.

As we explore the country and reread passages from Austin's work, I am amazed by the accuracy of her descriptions, the fidelity of her representations of experience to my own experiences, and the uncanny manner in which her prose seems to capture the unique character of this wild and strange land. Although a century

has passed since Austin lived and wrote in this rugged region, many of the things she describes in her fiction can be found in the desert today. In **"Lost Borders,"** she instructs her readers in the realities of desert travel: "[W]here you find cattle dropped, skeleton or skin dried, the heads almost invariably will be turned toward the places where water-holes should be" (1987, 43). Almost one hundred years later, trekking with a group of students through the Silver Peak Wilderness Study Area in the central Great Basin, I was haunted by the accuracy of Austin's description as we stumbled upon a mummified cow carcass. Complete with a plastic ear tag, white grinning skull, and sun-dried hide, the cow's remains appeared as if they had literally jumped off the pages of Austin's book and taken shape on the ground before us. In order to test her knowledge of the desert further, I took a bearing off the cow's exposed skeletal nose and began searching for the spring that Austin assured me must be there. A little more than a mile later, I came upon a small mud-bottomed spring, surrounded by willow and wild rose, just as she had promised.

Mary Austin's unique ability to accurately represent the land, people, and wildlife of the southern California region has been widely acknowledged. Marjorie Pryse notes that Austin always "remains faithful to literal accuracy in her natural description" (1987, xiv). Austin's fidelity to the manner of life and quality of experience endemic to the American Southwest represents one of the most important aspects of her fiction as well as one of the most consistent preoccupations of her writing life. As she laments in **"Lost Borders,"** "I was sore then about not getting myself believed in some elementary matters, such as that horned toads are not poisonous, and that Indians really have the bowels of compassion" (1987, 158). Austin's anger at not being believed about things she had experienced herself caused her to strive for an extraordinary degree of authenticity in her writing. She complains in **"Regionalism in American Fiction"** that "[o]ur Southwest, though actually the longest-lived-in section of the country, has not yet achieved its authentic literary expression in English" (1996b, 134). The resolution of this problem became one of Austin's most persistent ambitions and perhaps one of her greatest accomplishments.

Austin's descriptions of the rugged lands, sparse wildlife, and colorful characters of the Southwest often focus upon the phenomenological, attempting to put into words the actual experience of the thing described rather than the rational explanation of it. In her description of the extremely effective camouflaging techniques of horned lizards, for example, Austin relates her observations as they are experienced by one who has just witnessed the uncanny ability with her own eyes: "Now and then a palm's breadth of the trail gathers itself together and scurries off with a little rustle under the brush, to resolve itself into sand again. This is pure witchcraft. If you succeed in catching it in transit, it loses its power and becomes a flat, horned, toad-like creature, horrid looking and harmless, of the color of the soil" (1997, 98). Rather than begin her description with the intellectual rationalization of the event—the ability of horned lizards to blend in with the sand—Austin relates the event as it is experienced by the senses. As we explored Austin's country, we came across a number of horned lizards and other similarly camouflaged reptiles. Each time one scurried from its hiding place in the sand, even though our previous experience had taught us the truth behind the illusion, we were caught momentarily by the inexplicable experience of actually "seeing" the sand animate itself, slide across the trail, and then slowly resolve into the recognizable shape of *Phrynosoma platyrhinos.*

In other descriptions of the region, Austin's detailed knowledge of the habits of local plant and animal species adds both a factual accuracy to her observations and an immediacy of significance that could save one's life. In the opening passage of the chapter **"The Mesa Trail,"** Austin describes the trail's route by noting that "[i]t strikes diagonally across the foot of the hill-slope from the field until it reaches larkspur level" (92). Such a description, for someone knowledgeable about the botany of the area, is as accurate as giving the trail's precise elevation, a very common method used by modern-day guidebooks to aid reader-travelers in navigation. Tall larkspur, or *Delphinium glaucum,* a three- to six-foot-tall brilliantly blue and purple, easily distinguishable flower is limited to an elevation range of five thousand to ten thousand feet. The trail Austin describes begins at Naboth's field at an approximate elevation of forty-one hundred feet. It then climbs nine hundred feet in elevation in a southwesterly direction until it reaches the five thousand-foot mark and turns directly south, neither losing nor gaining elevation for quite some time. Without the aid of modern altimeters and GPS units, Austin is able to use her own intimate knowledge of the flora and fauna of the region to provide just as precise directions as any contemporary guidebook could.

Likewise, Austin's descriptions of desert plants are as accurate as those within any contemporary field guide. She describes one of the most common plants of her region—one that is easy to overlook because of its uniformity across the landscape—with the precision of a professional botanist and the lyricism of a poet:

> Sagebrush, the silvery pubescent *Artemisia tridentata,* is no sage, nor yet brushy as are the spined and brittle members of the chaparral. It has a twisty woody base and herbaceous tops, well feathered with gray-green velvet leafage, and grass-like tips of self-colored, aromatic seed. "Tridentata" it is called because of the three-lobed leaves, and "Artemisia," being sacred to

> young Artemis, hung up in her temple in votive wreaths. Always there is about sagebrush that virginal suggestion, shy-colored, fresh-smelling, sufficient to itself.

> (1927, 171)

One who is familiar with this common and aromatic shrub of the West will instantly recognize the aptness of both Austin's objective observations and subjective associations. Additionally, Austin employs almost every conceivable rhetorical strategy here to convey the fullest description of the plant possible. She describes it in both negative and positive terms (that is, what it is not like as well as what it is like); records finely shaded details in color, shape, and smell; and offers less objective but perhaps equally useful subjective associations commonly attributed to the plant.

In a similar manner, Austin displays a close knowledge of animal behavior and the ability to read wildlife signs correctly in her description of the water trails of the Ceriso. She notes that "[b]y the end of the dry season the water trails of the Ceriso are worn to a white ribbon in the leaning grass, spread out faint and fanwise toward the homes of gopher and ground rat and squirrel" (1997, 17). She then admonishes readers to get "down to the eye level of rat and squirrel kind" if they are to perceive the trails in detail. The "fanwise" description, easily passed over by those without a close knowledge of arid regions, relates an exceedingly important detail about both animal trails and the availability of water in the desert. Although animals forage, rest, and den in a wide variety of manners and places, they all (at least the animals that need it) water at the same spots, which are usually limited in number and widely dispersed in desert regions. From a bird's-eye view, the web of criss-crossing trails made by different species converges on the same sources of water. Thus, whenever two trails meet, the diverging prongs of the fork almost always face away from water, whereas the bottom of the V points toward the nearest water source like an arrow. As Austin well knows, such forms of precise place-based knowledge can mean the difference between life and death for the desert traveler. A few paragraphs later, she warns readers: "Venture to look for some seldom-touched water-hole, and so long as the trails run with your general direction make sure you are right, but if they begin to cross yours at never so slight an angle, to converge toward a point left or right of your objective, no matter what the maps say, or your memory, trust them; they *know*" (19; emphasis in original). As Austin demonstrates, knowing in the desert entails relearning what our culture has let us forget and finding mentors in the movements of animals and teachers in the habits of trees.

Such descriptions are easy for the literary scholar, working in an air-conditioned office and drinking coffee, to ignore; however, after spending a ten-mile day on the trail and coming upon a dry creek bed where one planned to find water, these textual passages become much more significant. The quest for water, in Austin country, underlies everything that one does and sees. It dictates the types and numbers of native plant life, directs the pattern of game trails, and haunts the thoughts of every desert traveler. Whether one is reduced to relying on a few precious mouthfuls of water trapped in a *tinaja* or is lucky enough to find a bubbling spring of sweet water seeping out of the ground, the presence or absence of water can mean the difference between life and death. Even today, with topographic maps, maintained trail systems, and developed springs for backcountry travelers, it is still as Austin described it: "Not the law, but the land sets the limit" (3).

Even at a developed Bureau of Land Management (BLM) spring used by PCT hikers, for example, I was reminded of the paradoxical nature of the desert so often described in Austin's writing, where both life and death are so often present together. At the same time that we were filling our bottles with life-giving water, I could not help but wonder about Giardia, E. coli bacteria, and a host of other contaminants that might be living in that spring. At the time, I was recovering from a bout of Giardia contracted on another field-studies expedition, and although I was aided by a modern-day water filter, my recent illness made me even more conscious of the very real and ever present dangers that must have faced Austin and other desert travelers during her time. Such dangers, although now mitigated by a web of roads and trails, developed springs, and technologically advanced camping gear, still exist over much of the Southwest. They serve to remind the ecocritical field scholar that Austin's representations of the natural world—along with their associated questions of accuracy—retain a significance that goes well beyond the artistic and linguistic. Maintaining the accuracy of her descriptions was not only an artistic principle for Austin, but also a practical necessity.

THE PROBLEMATICS OF LITERARY REPRESENTATION

Although Austin's descriptions of the Southwest display a remarkable degree of accuracy, we cannot assume, as poststructuralists often point out, an unproblematic mimesis between the text and the place it is meant to represent. No matter how accurate the picture painted in words, it still fails to replace or re-create the experience of actually "being there," simply because words can describe only things; they are not the things themselves. This distancing effect of language was not unforeseen by Austin, however. Like many other nature writers, Austin was self-consciously—almost painfully—aware of the limits of linguistic representation and often emphasized them in her work.

Austin is often quite direct in discussing the difficulties involved in trying to accurately express her observations of, and experiences in, the southern California region in words. She prefaces *The Land of Little Rain* by stating, "[T]here are certain peaks, cañons, and clear meadow spaces which are above all compassing of words," and warns readers directly that "if you do not find it all as I write, think me not less dependable nor yourself less clever" (xvi). Austin clearly recognizes the limits of her ability to re-present the reality of the desert Southwest in a book. However, because she is engaged in an attempt to translate some semblance of her experiences there for readers, she simply confronts the problem directly and honestly so that readers become aware of it as well. By emphasizing the limits of language, Austin destroys its usual transparency for readers, forcing them to recognize that what they are experiencing is not the desert itself, but a textual representation of it.

In **"The Friend in the Wood,"** Austin admits the distance between her experiences of the desert and her literary expressions of those experiences, while also emphasizing the craft she puts into those "inadequate" literary representations. She confesses, "By this time I had realized that the illuminations which came from those silent sessions in the wild were the sort of which set in motion the search for words, for nice distinctions of definition, for intricate unfoldings of smooth-pointed buds of suggestion" (1990, 196). Even as she foregrounds the literary craft and choices involved in the linguistic representation of her home region, Austin admits that as careful as those choices are, as accurate as she tries to make her descriptions, they are still merely "suggestions" of meaning.

Austin's initial experiences in the region helped her to understand the limits of language and to recognize the importance of exposing those limits to her readers. As Shelley Armitage notes, "Initially, [Austin] felt the rigors and bleakness of the desert denied her a vocabulary and her mysticism: This was a 'wordless wilderness' for which her reading of Hugh Miller, Emerson, Tennyson, and the Romantic poets hardly prepared her" (1990, 8).

As she notes in her autobiography, Austin, the newly transplanted emigrant and nature writer, was in desperate need of what she called "a vocabulary expressive of experience" (1932, 265). Such a vocabulary was to be found not in the annals of literature but in the land itself. In *Earth Horizon,* Austin catalogs a variety of things in the region upon which she kept "voluminous notes" as she began to learn how to write about the West. Her attention to detail, concern for accuracy, and emphasis on language are evidenced as she writes, "Along with these things, there were collections of colloquial phrases, Spanish folklore, intensively pondered adjectives for the color and form of natural things, the exact word for a mule's cry—'maimed noises'—the difference between the sound of ripe figs dropping and the patter of olives shaken down by the wind; single lines of verse imprisoning these things" (228). Although Austin's use of the word *imprison* to describe how her language manages to capture, embody, or represent the reality of the desert might strike the poststructuralist critic as evidencing too great a faith in the accuracy of linguistic representation, it does suggest a second recognition about language that accords with poststructural theory: the power of language to colonize.

As poststructuralists and postcolonial theorists have thoroughly demonstrated, conquest, whether over people or nature, begins with the act of naming or linguistically "claiming" the "other." The act of naming, especially in one's own native tongue or after oneself, establishes a proprietary relationship over the thing being named, assumes the ability to "know" the thing named, and, whether violence follows the naming or not, exacts a kind of ideological violence over the "other's" identity. The first act of explorers in the New World, for example, regardless of their country of origin, was to name the (already occupied) lands they encountered in their native language and claim that place in the name of their king or country.

Austin recognizes this colonizing power of language in much of her work, writing in **Lands of the Sun**: "The name *Sequoia* is one of the few cheering notes among our habitual botanical stupidities; an attempt to express quality as it is humanly measured in a name" (1927, 203). Austin then proceeds to relate the history behind the name: that it was taken from a Cherokee chief, Sequoyah, who invented an alphabet, migrated west, and settled in the Upper Kern River area. She also notes the importance of attempting, in poststructuralist terms, to match the expression of the signifier (the tree's and chief's names) with the quality of the signified (the idea of the tree and the story of the chief) and the quality of the referent (the tree and the chief themselves). Austin observes reproachfully of the name: "At least no botanist with his nose in a book has usurped it" (204).

In **The Land of Little Rain,** Austin once again discusses the power and quality of naming, opening her preface by writing, "I confess to a great liking for the Indian fashion of name-giving: every man known by that phrase which best expresses him to whoso [*sic*] names him." Interestingly, this form of name giving embodies another tenet of poststructuralism that posits a kind of multiple subjectivity to describe the fact that we all experience the world—the same objects, events, people, and places—differently based upon our own individual subject position, or perspective. Austin asserts: "No other fashion [of name giving], I think, sets so well with the various natures that inhabit us, and if you agree with me you will understand why so few names are written here as they appear in the geography" (1997, xv). Here, of course, she is alluding to the fact that the majority of the names found in "geography" are the im-

ported and imposed names of colonization, exploitation, and domination rather than the native names of habitation.

In **"Lost Borders,"** Austin offers a second justification for her use of native names, arguing, in a manner that unites poststructuralist and postcolonial theories, that there is less distance among the signifier, signified, and referent in native names than in foreign ones: "[Y]ou can always trust Indian names to express to you the largest truth about any district in the shortest phrases" (1987, 156). Rather than offering a racist or culturally biased remark, Austin is simply referring here to the native practice of naming places with descriptive phrases. Although there are a number of exceptions in both Euro-American and Native American languages, as a general rule we tend to find fewer places named after people and more based upon descriptions of the physical landscape or a particular event that occurred there in indigenous cultures than in colonizing ones. Recognizing these tendencies exposes both an anthropocentric bias and a greater detachment from the natural world in colonizing cultures and their naming practices.

Austin resists this tradition on the grounds that it is both more exploitative of nature and less accurate in its representations of the natural world. She asserts that this "is a country where names mean something. Ubehebe, Pharanagat, Resting Springs, Dead Man's Gulch, Funeral Mountains. . . . There is always a tang of reality about them like the smart of wood smoke to the eyes, that warns of neighboring fires" (156). Austin adopts the traditional ecocritical position that names (at least some of them) can "mean something," or can adequately refer to or represent the natural world, yet she maintains a protopoststructuralist position that recognizes that they do not directly re-present or re-create that reality but point to it suggestively, just as surely as smoke points to fire.

AUSTIN, REPRESENTATION, AND FIELD EXPERIENCE

The particular strength of Austin's recognitions about the limits of literary representation is that they were founded on her own experiences living in the region while simultaneously writing about it for audiences who had never been there. Although Austin's first encounters left her grasping for the ideas and language necessary to express herself in a "wordless wilderness," her thirst for experiencing the region and learning from its inhabitants eventually led her to find a language so suitable, so fitted to the terrain, that her work still stands among the best desert literature in the English language.

As she records in her autobiography and many scholars have noted, Austin spent an extraordinary amount of time exploring the rugged and sparsely populated deserts of southern California and Nevada. She went on extensive camping trips with her husband, angled the snow-fed streams dropping down out of the Sierra Nevada, spent a great deal of time out on the Beale Ranch in the Tejon Region, and enjoyed riding atop the Mojave stage, swapping stories with the driver and perusing the landscape. In addition, she collected stories, information, insights, perceptions, ideas, and language from almost everyone she came into contact with, including the Paiute and Shoshone still living in the area, Mexican and Basque sheep-herders, miners, stagecoach drivers, faro dealers, "bawdy girls," and children. Austin's experiences in the region form the foundation of her work, informing its literary style, prose rhythms, visual imagery, and ethical stance, as well as animating it with colorful characters, rugged landscapes, and interesting events. In short, both the form and content of Austin's fiction are derived directly from the southern California bioregions.

Melody Graulich notes the significance of Austin's personal experiences on her work: "Austin's Tejon notebooks show that she had been collecting stories and experimenting with form and style since arriving in California. . . . But it would take almost ten years for her stylistic experiments to pay off and for her understanding of her subject matter to mature" (1987, 10). Nowhere is this evidenced more clearly than in a comparison of Austin's literary representations of the region in **"One Hundred Miles on Horseback"** (1889) and *The Land of Little Rain* (1903). During the fourteen years separating these works, Austin's perceptions of the desert changed as her knowledge and experience grew, until the land dictated not only *what* she wrote about but also *how* she wrote about it.

In order to see clearly how Austin's perceptions evolved between the two works, I will examine her representations of the region's weather, landscape, native species, and local inhabitants. In **"One Hundred Miles on Horseback,"** Austin describes "the pleasure of a journey on horseback through the most picturesque part of California," yet she evidences a variety of culturally determined notions that distance her from appreciating, experiencing, and accurately describing the region. She confesses, "A drizzling rain, forerunner of the rainy season, compelled me to abandon my equestrian ambitions and make an inglorious retreat to the canvas shelter of the wagon" for the rest of "the afternoon journey" (1996a, 25).

Fourteen years later, in *The Land of Little Rain,* she praises the pocket hunter because "he had gotten to that point where he knew no bad weather, and all places were equally happy so long as they were out of doors." Although Austin herself has not developed the "kind of weather shell" of the pocket hunter and the indigenes of the region, her attitude toward inclement weather has

changed: "I do not know just how long it takes to become saturated with the elements so that one takes no account of them. Myself can never get past the glow and exhilaration of a storm, the wrestle of long dust-heavy winds, the play of live thunder on the rocks, nor past the keen fret of fatigue when the storm outlasts physical endurance" (1997, 47).

After ten years of living and traveling in the deserts and mountains of the Owens Valley area, Austin has developed a much more favorable view of the region's weather and an ability to distinguish between the characteristics of different types of storms. Whereas rain "drizzles" in her early representations, in the latter text storms "glow," "wrestle," and "play." In addition, she no longer alienates herself physically from such storms but has experienced at least some of them without mediation. The final line implies that Austin has actually felt "the keen fret of fatigue" caused by remaining out in such weather until the body reaches its physical limits.

Austin's perceptions of the desert itself have also changed, evolving from her preconceived and culturally biased notions of environmental aesthetics to a perspective that allows her to appreciate the region for its own inherent beauty and character. On her first journey into the region's arid lands she laments, "An autumn landscape in California is strangely devoid of color, and this silent succumbing to a process of nature made us homesick for the glory of the October hills of Illinois" (1996a, 25). Here, Austin imports culturally determined notions of fall "color" from a completely different bioregion and thus is incapable of "seeing" the desert as it truly is.

After having lived in the desert for more than a decade, however, she lauds its beauty, stating that "[n]one other than this long brown land lays such a hold on the affections. The rainbow hills, the tender bluish mists, the luminous radiance of spring, have the lotus charm" (1997, 11). By this point in her life Austin is able to recognize, and represent in literature, the desert's own colors, its own beauty and charm. Austin no longer has to mediate her representations through the filter of transplanted culture but is capable of representing the desert's inherent aesthetic value as it is. She has also recognized that her earlier aesthetic revulsion was not due to any quality inherent in the desert itself but was imposed upon it by the expectations of culture. "And yet—and yet—is it not perhaps to satisfy expectation that one falls into the tragic key in writing of desertness?" she asks her readers in an effort to make them aware of the same tendency in themselves (12).

Austin's love for the southwestern landscape extended to its inhabitants as well, as she demonstrates in her evolving representations of the region's wildlife and local residents. She complains, for example, in **"One Hundred Miles on Horseback"**: "During that night coyotes came close up to the camp and howled, and growled, and barked, and shrieked like so many demons. There seems to be no limit to the hideous noises the animals can produce" (1996a, 28). The demonization of predators and the desert are traditional biblical themes, just as Austin's description of the "Mexican shepherds with their flocks and faithful dogs recalled vividly well-known scriptural scenes" (26). In addition, Austin applies such adjectives as *hideous* and descriptive verbs like *shrieked* to the yipping and howling of the coyotes, exhibiting a stark contrast to her later representation of them in *The Land of Little Rain,* where she describes a lone coyote signaling his pack "in a long-drawn, dolorous whine" (1997, 19).

Like Austin, I can recall the first time I heard the cacophony of yips, barks, and howls of a pack of coyotes close by camp in the darkness of night. I was about ten at the time and camping alone, and I did, indeed, find it an unnerving experience. However, as soon as I recognized that they were no threat to me and began to listen to the quality of their voices, without allowing any culturally induced nightmares of werewolves to distort the experience, the rising symphonic, multivoiced sound of their chorus was both haunting and beautiful. I sat up in the darkness listening to their singing for quite some time. And as the last of their voices dropped off and faded into the night, I found myself wishing fervently that they might come back and serenade me once again.

Similarly, as soon as we divest ourselves of our culturally induced prejudices against such predators—formed primarily by an ill-informed livestock industry—the intelligent nature and beneficial ecosystemic role of the coyote becomes apparent. As Austin notes in *The Land of Little Rain,* the coyote is intelligent, resourceful, and can actually aid other creatures in their survival: "The coyote is your true water-witch, one who snuffs and paws, snuffs and paws again at the smallest spot of moisture-scented earth until he has freed the blind water from the soil. Many water-holes are no more than this detected by the lean hobo of the hills where not even an Indian would look for it" (18). Although her description does anthropomorphize the coyote, calling it both witch and hobo, it is also extremely accurate about coyote behavior, recognizes their inherent intelligence, and is based upon personal experience.

As she admits later, she has often trailed a coyote "and found his track such as a man, a very intelligent man accustomed to hill-country, and a little cautious, would make to the same point. . . . [I]t is usually the best way,—and making his point with the greatest economy" (20). Here, Austin relates the coyote's intelligence in navigation not only to that of men, but also to that of a "very intelligent man" who is "accustomed to hill-

country." As she states later in *The Land of Little Rain,* "The coyote is your real lord of the mesa" (96). In the intervening years between the composition of her first serious nature essay about the region and *The Land of Little Rain,* Austin has been able to observe, learn about, and come to appreciate the coyote on its own terms, in its own land.

Finally, Austin's representations of the human inhabitants of the country of lost borders change as well. Her first impressions of the Mexican shepherds of the region is that they are "outlandish," their houses "overflowing with dogs and children in dirty but picturesque confusion" (1996a, 26, 28). "Occasionally," she continues, "somewhat back from the house a little white wooden cross gleaming over a mound of earth made pathetically human a scene that might otherwise have been disgusting or merely amusing" (28). Here Austin's own ethnocentric prejudices are evident as she, the white colonizer, views the "disgusting," "dirty," and "amusing" colonized other who is only made "pathetically human" by the presence of death, signified by the cross, another sign of the dominant, colonizing hegemony.

By the time Austin wrote *The Land of Little Rain,* however, she had lived among both the Paiute and the Mexican inhabitants of the Owens Valley, made lasting friendships, and successfully dropped her culturally inherited prejudices so that she could finally see them as they were. She opens **"The Little Town of the Grapevines"** by saying, "There are still some places in the west where the quails cry '*cuidado*'; where all the speech is soft, all the manners gentle; where all the dishes have *chile* in them, and they make more of the Sixteenth of September than they do of the Fourth of July" (1997, 163). Though this representation does smack of romanticism, in many ways it is the representation of an insider to the culture, rather than that of a colonizer with cultural blinders on. The term *cuidado* needs no explanation, nor does the "Sixteenth of September," just as throughout the chapter the town is called by its Spanish name, El Pueblo de Las Uvas.

Austin's descriptions of the residents of the pueblo contrast markedly from her earlier descriptions of the "outlandish" or "pathetically human" occupants; in fact, while noting some of the town's problems, she elevates most of its inhabitants to an admirable level of humanity, decency, and compassion. She ends the chapter and the book by addressing her readers directly: "Come away, you who are obsessed with your own importance in the scheme of things, and have got nothing you did not sweat for, come away by the brown valleys and full bosomed hills to the even-breathing days, to the kindliness, earthiness, ease of El Pueblo de Las Uvas" (171).

Austin's ability to see and appreciate the desert and its inhabitants on their own terms evolved over the years due to her own experiences on the land and with its residents. By describing the land and its inhabitants accurately and sympathetically, Austin hopes to offer readers a vicarious experience similar to the physical and imaginative experiences that she enjoyed in the region.

READING AUSTIN IN THE FIELD

As many scholars have noted, Austin's fiction contains a fair amount of autobiography; it is primarily derived from her own experiences or those of others she met in the rugged deserts and mountains of the Southwest. In "Mary Austin's Nature: Refiguring Tradition Through the Voices of Identity," Anna Carew-Miller notes that Austin's "narrative voice reflects her experience of non-human nature" and that this experience is the primary factor informing her fiction (1998, 79). Comparing the development of Austin's narrative voices in her fiction and her partly fictional autobiography, *Earth Horizon,* with those of her rooted female characters, such as Seyavi and Walking Woman, Carew-Miller contends that as an author, Austin strove to become so connected to the land that she could "write through her body, not her mind. Only then will experience supersede analysis in her understanding and representation of the natural" (88).

Unlike Austin, however, many Austin scholars have had little opportunity to study and explore the lands she writes about in a sustained manner and thus lack the experience Austin advocates. As John P. O'Grady notes in *Pilgrims to the Wild,* one of the consistent themes in Austin's work is "her insistence on the *experiential quality* of the wild. Although she knew that words were not up to the task of conveying such experience, she nevertheless continued to attempt its articulation" (1993, 127). Yet this attempt at articulating physical experiences in the natural landscape has been largely ignored by ecocritics. Because of our methodological constraints, we seem to be voluntarily ignoring one of the most salient features of Austin's work and, by extension, one of the most important elements affecting all environmental texts, namely, their environment.

Such omissions may necessarily limit our knowledge of environmental texts and their relationships with American ecocultural regions simply by delimiting what we can include within our field of inquiry. Likewise, they also threaten us with critical and interpretive inaccuracy, as we remain largely ignorant of the very real physical, historical, and environmental influences operating in a given text.

Austin recognizes that many of her readers, lacking their own experience of the desert, may have difficulty understanding and appreciating it as she has. Therefore, she consistently adopts the second person, addressing her readers directly in order to encourage them to experience the arid Southwest themselves. In **"Jimville"**—a town Austin likens to a desert tortoise—she explicitly informs her readers that, like her, they will have to drop their culturally received ideas of the desert if they wish to truly see it. "You could never get into any proper relation to Jimville unless you could slough off and swallow your acquired prejudices as a lizard does his skin" (1997, 73). The best way to shed such prejudices, according to Austin, is through direct experience of the land. However, for those readers who are unable to gain these experiences physically, Austin at least provides them imaginatively by placing readers in the country of lost borders through the use of second-person prose.

Austin uses the second person to emphasize the importance of direct experience as well as to resist the mediated nature of linguistic representation. Writing in the second person also functions rhetorically to minimize the distance between the reader and the referent. For Austin, it is a conscious and deliberate strategy to overcome the inevitable mediation of language—the representative distance that exists among the signifier, signified, and referent. Placing the reader in the desert rhetorically through the use of second-person prose is the closest Austin can come to placing the reader there physically. She advises readers, "[F]or seeing and understanding [the land], the best time is when you have the longest leave to stay. And here is a hint if you would attempt the stateliest approaches; travel light, and as much as possible live off the land" (117). She encourages readers to gain as intimate an experience with the land as possible, not only traveling through the region but also living off whatever it provides, foraging for edible plants and hunting wild game. This type of interaction places one in much closer contact with the landscape and forces one to study its native species and their characteristics and habits very closely.

Direct experience of the land was exceedingly important to Austin, not only for understanding it, but also for understanding the literature written about it. In her notable work on American literature, *The American Rhythm,* Austin details a theory of "geographic determinism," arguing that the most important influence on American literature is the natural and geographical region from which it is produced. She argues that as American literary culture matures, we will find an increasing correspondence between its rhythms and those of the regional landscapes that produce that culture. Thomas W. Ford notes in *"The American Rhythm*: Mary Austin's Poetic Principle," "Mrs. Austin argues that rhythm is an *experience,* and as such is distinct from our intellectual perception of that experience. . . . The stimuli come from the environment, from the land, and a sense of well-being occurs in the human organism when the rhythms are coordinated" (1970, 4). Without our own experience in that land and with its rhythms, it will be difficult for us to fully understand or recognize the rhythms of its literature. Similarly, James Ruppert observes, "Austin saw movement, both the movements of necessary social labor in the environment and the movements of personal response, as playing an important role in the transmission of the rhythms of the land into the rhythms of the dance-drama and, ultimately song/poetry" (1983, 379). If we accept Austin's assertions about her own writing, we must be able to study both the rhythms of the landscapes she wrote about as well as the rhythms of her prose; thus, we must incorporate some manner of direct experience of, and movement in, those landscapes into our scholarly practice.

In **"Lost Borders,"** for example, Austin asserts, "Every story of that country is colored by the fashion of life there, breaking up in swift, passionate intervals between long, dun stretches, like the land that out of hot sinks of desolation heaves up great bulks of granite ranges with opal shadows playing in their shining, snow-piled curves" (1987, 157). In addition to explicitly arguing that the land shapes the story, Austin illustrates her concept of geographic determinism in the long, slow, jumbled rhythm of her prose that mirrors the vast spaces and long silences of the broken and rugged basin and range. As is often the case in her work, Austin's prose is subtly onomatopoeic here. Instead of merely describing the elements of her southwestern landscape, she attempts to embody the rhythms and characteristics of the land in her prose, thereby resisting the mediated nature and distancing effects of linguistic representation. This careful attention to rhythm—this attempt to close the gap in signification between word and world—represents a conscious and concerted effort on Austin's part. In her autobiography Austin explains this correspondence between text and terrain in the third person, stating, "She had been trying to hit upon the key for it [*The Land of Little Rain*] for a year or more, and found it at last in the rhythm of the twenty-mule teams that creaked in and out of the borax works, the rhythm of the lonely lives blown across the trails" (1932, 296).

For Austin, the land not only informs the content of her work but shapes its formal structures as well. As William Scheick points out, "Austin particularly appreciates the minimalism of the desert" (1992, 38). One of the region's greatest values, and most distinguishing characteristics, for Austin, is its sparsely populated nature. Whether one is talking about the desert's native flora and fauna or native and immigrant human populations, a clear pattern emerges: space, silence, and scarcity dominate the landscape and define its inhabitants. In *The Land of Little Rain,* Austin celebrates this quality of desert flora: "There is neither poverty of soil nor species to account for the sparseness of desert growth, but simply that each plant requires more room. So much earth must be preempted to extract so much moisture" (1997, 8).

In her prose, Austin attempts to embody these minimalistic qualities of the desert by populating her stories with very few characters, allowing them very little speech, and spacing out both descriptions of their actions and instances of dialogue with long narrative sections of philosophical reflection, commentary, or descriptions of the surrounding landscape. In addition, she often attempts to infuse her prose with silence by leaving much unsaid and suggesting or merely hinting at her central point. She describes the ever present danger of dehydration, death, and mummification, for example, by euphemistically stating, "To underestimate one's thirst, to pass a given landmark to the right or left, to find a dry spring where one looked for running water—there is no help for any of these things" (6). The result of not finding water in the desert, in Austin's linguistic representation, is a nonaction, a nonevent. Instead of describing a flurry of frenzied activity, trying to find or obtain water, or detailing the slow, painful process of dying of thirst, Austin silences her prose. Instead of describing a presence—in this case death or the actions to prevent it—she posits an absence: the absence of help. As Austin asserts in **"Regionalism in American Fiction"** and embodies in this example, "The regionally interpretive book must not only be about the country, it must be of it, flower of its stalk and root" (Ellis 1996, 139).

AUSTIN'S MULTIPLE PERSPECTIVES

A final strategy Austin adopts for confronting problems of representation and authority is to adopt a number of different subject positions from which to observe the world. Rather than assuming the traditional stance of objective observer who holds authority over whatever he or she describes, Austin writes from a variety of perspectives. In *Earth Horizon,* Austin's autobiography, this practice of developing multiple personae or perspectives is significantly foregrounded. She writes of "I-Mary" in the first person and "Mary-by-herself" in the third person, alternating between describing her own actions and thoughts as those of one or the other of the two personae.

These two personae are quite different. As Linda K. Karrell observes, the "self-confident 'I-Mary' . . . is associated with writing, creativity, and . . . requires little emotional nurturance." On the other hand, "Mary-by-herself" is "much more uncertain, lonely, and achingly vulnerable to rejection" (1997, 269). Austin illustrates the poststructural recognition that pure objectivity is never possible because we are always already perceiving the world from within a particular perspective—a perspective that varies from person to person, as well as varying within the same individual from time to time or place to place.

In her fiction Austin extends her use of multiple-subject perspectives to adopt ecocentric points of view that stand in direct opposition to the traditional authority of the human observer. They provide readers with a variety of perspectives from which to view the desert country, and by adopting the point of view of particular animal species, places, and processes Austin encourages readers to drop their inherent anthropocentric perspectives. In *The Land of Little Rain,* for example, she adopts an explicitly coyote-centric point of view and forces readers not only to see the world, but also to see themselves from the coyote's perspective. Addressing readers in the second person, Austin observes, "[H]e makes sure you are armed with no long black instrument to spit your teeth into his vitals at a thousand yards" (1997, 96). In this passage Austin describes a rifle as she imagines a coyote might perceive it—a "long black instrument" for spitting "teeth" at prey. Although Austin must anthropomorphize a bit here, this description represents a concerted effort to make readers aware of the subjective positions of other desert inhabitants. Simultaneously, she encourages readers to recognize that their own way of seeing the world is not objective, or authoritative, but merely one of an infinite number of subjective perceptions. This destroys the transparency and assumed authority of the human observer's gaze and successfully resists its colonizing nature.

In addition to the artistic implications of these passages, they also introduce an element of realism (always a concern for Austin). As a longtime hunter, wildlife observer, and outdoor recreationalist, I support Austin's claim that animals like coyotes are intelligent enough to distinguish between a hunter and a hiker and even to tell the difference between the same person engaged in each activity. I have often known coyotes and rabbits to allow me to approach them very closely, and to even demonstrate curiosity toward me when I have been empty-handed, but to avoid my approach and run at first clear sight of me when I have had either my bow or rifle in hand. I can even recall one curious coyote who, after we watched each other for quite some time, disappeared in a flash as soon as I picked up my bow. Many hunters and hikers have had the uncanny experience of seeing a multitude of different wild creatures when hiking for pleasure or scouting terrain without a gun but not seeing a single animal in the same area when carrying their hunting tools.

As Austin describes in her chapter **"The Scavengers,"** the desert dwellers in her country observe each other's behavior, listen to the calls and warning signals of other species, and demonstrate an intelligent awareness of the habits of others and what they signify. "Probably we never fully credit the interdependence of wild creatures, and their cognizance of the affairs of their own kind" (36). By adopting the perspective of these wild creatures, Austin is better able to demonstrate this "cognizance" and aids readers in dropping their culturally limited perceptions of the desert and its non-human inhabitants.

Austin pushes her experiments with perspective even further in the chapter **"My Neighbor's Field,"** explaining, "Naboth expects to make town lots of it and his fortune in one and the same day; but when I take the trail to talk with old Seyavi at the campoodie, it occurs to me that though the field may serve good turn in those days it will hardly be the happier. No, certainly not the happier" (88). The "happiness" or "unhappiness" of the field implies a kind of sentience on its part. In this final passage of the chapter, Austin asks readers to adopt the perspective of Naboth's field, a place that up until now she has so far been observing, describing, and representing from the human point of view. She nudges readers subtly toward this "field-centric" perspective by admitting that it "occurs to me" that the field "will hardly be the happier." Then she repeats this idea in a short sentence fragment that acts as the final word of the chapter on the subject of Naboth's field: "No, certainly not the happier." The brevity of the sentence, its grammatical division from the preceding sentences, its repetition of the earlier field-centric recognition, and its placement at the end of the chapter all serve to emphasize the significance of the field's subjective experience and perception.

As Austin asserts in **"The Friend in the Wood,"** "Even stick and stone, as well as bush and weed, are discovered to be charged with an intense secret life of their own; the sap courses, the stones vibrate with ion-shaking rhythms of energy, as I too shake inwardly to the reverberating tread of life and time; they are each in its sphere as important to themselves as I to me" (1990, 196). Austin not only posits that plants, animals, and inanimate natural objects have a type of sentience, but also that they have, and are aware of, their own inherent value, a value equal to that which we assign to ourselves.

By adopting these varied perspectives, or subject positions, Austin is able to resist the distancing effects of language while encouraging readers to see the natural world from an ecocentric perspective. In addition, by embodying these multiple-subject positions, she is able to more accurately describe the various features, details, and experiences of the deserts and mountains of the southern California ecoregion. The Owens Valley area Austin writes about covers a number of distinct ecosystems and ecotones, ranging from desert lakes to playas and mesquite-covered basins, from arroyos and sagebrush steppes to the pinyon and juniper forests of the desert ranges and the Jeffrey and ponderosa pine of the southern Sierra Nevada.

This wide variety of both ecosystems and experiences was emphasized to me on the last day of an early spring backpacking trip my wife and I took on the Pacific Crest Trail just west of Austin's home in Independence, California. After camping on the Kern and spending several crisp spring days exploring the "Streets of the Mountains," as Austin calls them, we began climbing over a high pass in order to leave the trail and drop down the eastern face of the Sierra Nevada, ultimately coming out at Naboth's field and Austin's home. As we climbed toward the pass, we soon found ourselves confronted by six-foot-deep drifts of snow. A blanket of hard, crusty snow covered the entire area, leaving no way to circle the drifts and forcing us to hike over. In some areas the surface of the snowpack had melted and refrozen enough times to support our weight; in others we broke through, postholing with each step. With forty-pound packs on and no snowshoes, we struggled forward, thinking light thoughts and stepping as gingerly as possible across the icy drifts, only to break through with every few steps. The icy edges of the hard crust cut and clawed at our bare calves and shins, punishing us severely for each misplaced step. Within a few hours we were dropping rapidly down the face of what Austin called "the Sierra Wall" and could see the Owens Valley below us. We followed an old cattle trail down through the pines and into the lower elevation oaks and finally out into the sagebrush scrub. As we hiked through the now palpitating desert heat, the blood on my shins and calves dried and crusted over with absorbed layers of dust and sand. We wiped our sweaty brows, drained the last drops from our water bottles, and moved on through the sage, bitterbrush, and mesquite. Once again, I was reminded of the wonderful variety of landscapes in this region, a country of lost borders to be sure, but a country full of amazing diversity and starkly contrasting places.

In **"Regionalism in American Fiction,"** Austin explains what is required to get to know her beloved land of little rain:

> Time is the essence of the undertaking, time to live into the land and absorb it; still more time to cure the reading public of its preference for something less than the proverbial bird's-eye view of the American scene, what you might call an automobile eye view, something slithering and blurred, nothing so sharply discriminated that it arrests the speed-numbed mind to understand.

(1996b, 140)

Works Cited

Armitage, Shelley. 1990. "Mary Austin: Writing Nature." In *Winds Trail: The Early Life of Mary Austin,* ed. Peggy Pond Church and Shelley Armitage, 3-31. Santa Fe: Museum of New Mexico Press.

Austin, Mary. 1927. *Lands of the Sun.* Boston: Houghton Mifflin.

———. 1932. *Earth Horizon.* Boston: Houghton Mifflin.

———. 1987. "Lost Borders." In *Western Trails: A Collection of Short Stories by Mary Austin,* ed. Melody Graulich, 39-99. Reno: University of Nevada Press.

———. 1990. "The Friend in the Wood." In *Winds Trail: The Early Life of Mary Austin,* ed. Peggy Pond Church and Shelley Armitage, 183-98. Santa Fe: Museum of New Mexico Press.

———. 1996a. "One Hundred Miles on Horseback." In *Beyond Borders: The Selected Essays of Mary Austin,* ed. Reuben J. Ellis, 24-30. Carbondale: Southern Illinois University Press.

———. 1996b. "Regionalism in American Fiction." In *Beyond Borders: The Selected Essays of Mary Austin,* ed. Reuben J. Ellis, 129-40. Carbondale: Southern Illinois University Press.

———. 1997. *The Land of Little Rain.* 1903. Reprint, Albuquerque: University of New Mexico Press.

Branch, Michael P., Rochelle Johnson, Daniel Patterson, and Scott Slovic, eds. 1998. Introduction to *Reading the Earth: New Directions in the Study of Literature and the Environment.* Moscow: University of Idaho Press.

Carew-Miller, Anna. 1998. "Mary Austin's Nature: Refiguring the Voice of Tradition Through the Voices of Identity." In *Reading the Earth: New Directions in the Study of Literature and the Environment,* ed. Michael P. Branch, Rochelle Johnson, Daniel Patterson, and Scott Slovic, 79-95. Moscow: University of Idaho Press.

Ellis, Reuben J. 1996. *Beyond Borders: The Selected Essays of Mary Austin.* Carbondale: Southern Illinois University Press, 1996.

Ford, Thomas W. 1970. "*The American Rhythm*: Mary Austin's Poetic Principle." *Western American Literature* 5, no. 1 (spring): 3-14.

Graulich, Melody. 1987. *Western Trails: A Collection of Short Stories by Mary Austin.* Reno: University of Nevada Press.

Karrell, Linda K. 1997. "The Immanent Pattern: Recovering the Self in Mary Austin's *Earth Horizon.*" *Auto/Biography Studies* 12, no. 2 (fall): 261-75.

O'Grady, John P. 1993. *Pilgrims to the Wild: Everett Ruess, Henry David Thoreau, John Muir, Clarence King, Mary Austin.* Salt Lake City: University of Utah Press.

Ruppert, James. 1983. "Mary Austin's Landscape Line in Native American Literature." *Southwest Review* 68, no. 4 (autumn): 376-90.

Scheick, William. 1992. "Mary Austin's Disfigurement of the Southwest in *The Land of Little Rain.*" *Western American Literature* 27, no. 1 (spring): 37-46.

FURTHER READING

Criticism

Brooks, Van Wyck. "The Southwest." In *The Confident Years: 1885-1915,* pp. 353-70. New York: E. P. Dutton & Co., Inc., 1952.

> Highlights the influence of the American southwest and Native American culture on Austin's writings, though he concludes that the author "could never establish a real relation with the world beyond the desert," and that her work "was always abortive when she left this world."

Dickson, Carol E. "Sense, Nonsense, and Sensibility: Teaching the 'Truth' of Nature in John Burroughs and Mary Austin." In *Sharp Eyes: John Burroughs and American Nature Writing,* edited by Charlotte Zoë Walker, pp. 220-31. Syracuse, N.Y.: Syracuse University Press, 2000.

> Studies John Burroughs's nature writings within the context of Austin's work, claiming that the narratives of both writers reflect an "acute awareness of the difficulties inherent in the act of placing the natural world within a human, narrative framework."

———. "'Recounting' the Land: The Nature of Narrative in Mary Austin's Narratives of Nature." In *Such News of the Land: U.S. Women Nature Writers,* edited by Thomas S. Edwards and Elizabeth A. De Wolfe, pp. 47-55. Hanover, N.H.: University Press of New England, 2001.

> Challenges the tendency of scholars to group Austin with other nature writers and conservationists that flourished during the first decades of the twentieth century, such as John Muir and Ernest Thompson Seton, maintaining that she was unique in questioning "the nature of linguistic representation" of the natural landscape and in emphasizing "the inadequacy of narrative to represent fully the nonhuman world," a position which the critic states is most clearly expressed in her best-known work, *The Land of Little Rain.*

DuBois, Arthur E. "Mary Hunter Austin: 1868-1934." *Southwest Review* 20, no. 3 (April 1935): 231-64.

> Describes Austin's character as "epical" and claims that through her writings, she "came to be identical with types or sets of being larger than herself," reflecting "in her own person" the "needs, experiences, and aspirations . . . of the human race at large or of the middle-western American."

Graulich, Melody. "Creating Great Women: Mary Austin and Charlotte Perkins Gilman." In *Charlotte Perkins Gilman and Her Contemporaries: Literary and Intellec-* tual Contexts, edited by Cynthia J. Davis and Denise D. Knight, pp. 139-54. Tuscaloosa, Ala.: The University of Alabama Press, 2004.

> Compares Austin's and Charlotte Perkins Gilman's writings and feminist ideas, maintaining that the two authors "developed parallel feminist analyses that they expressed in social critiques, fiction, and other genres, with considerable bravery and defiance."

Howard, Helen Addison. "Mary Hunter Austin (1868-1934)." In *American Indian Poetry,* pp. 67-87. Boston: Twayne Publishers, 1979.

> Surveys Austin's translations and "re-expressions" of Native American songs and poems published in her collection *The American Rhythm,* praising the author as "one of the early pioneers who investigated the aesthetic principles underlying indigenous motifs of Indian poetry."

Inness, Sherrie A. "Looking Westward: Geographical Distinctions in the Regional Short Fiction of Mary Foote and Mary Austin." *Studies in Short Fiction* 35, no. 4 (fall 1998): 319-30.

> Examines Austin's story "The Return of Mr. Wills" as well as two additional stories by Mary Hallock Foote to demonstrate "the ways that regional fiction created a textual space in which western women writers could explore and critique the division between East and West."

Jaycox, Faith. "Regeneration Through Liberation: Mary Austin's 'The Walking Woman' and Western Narrative Formula." *Legacy* 6, no. 1 (spring 1989): 5-12.

> Interprets Austin's short story "The Walking Woman," focusing on "the conventions it shares with other Western narratives" but arguing, as well, that the story offers an "alternative vision" of the American West and uses "Western conventions to give voice, deliberately and positively, to feminist issues."

Langlois, Karen S. "Mary Austin and Lincoln Steffens." *The Huntington Library Quarterly* 49, no. 4 (autumn 1986): 357-83.

> Based on letters from Austin to the poet Lincoln Steffens, attempts to determine the nature of the relationship of the two writers and, more specifically, to assess the effect the relationship had on Austin's life in New York City, from 1910 to 1920, and her work during this period.

———. "Mary Austin and Houghton Mifflin Company: A Case Study in the Marketing of a Western Writer." *Western American Literature* 23, no. 1 (spring 1988): 31-42.

> Examines Austin's relationship with her primary publisher, Houghton Mifflin, in order to "enhance our understanding of her literary career and our

knowledge of how the work of a western writer was perceived and marketed by the eastern publishing industry in the early decades of this century."

———. "Mary Austin and the New Theatre: The 1911 Production of *The Arrow Maker.*" *Theatre History Studies* 8 (1988): 71-87.

Recounts the details and events surrounding the 1911 production of Austin's "Indian drama," *The Arrow-Maker,* at the New Theatre in New York City, maintaining that "this curious theatrical venture deserves our attention" because of the insights it provides into "aspects of early twentieth century American drama."

———. "A Fresh Voice from the West: Mary Austin, California, and American Literary Magazines, 1892-1910." *California History* 69, no. 1 (spring 1990): 22-34.

Traces Austin's development as a writer of short stories and regional articles for literary magazines on both the east and west coasts of America, between 1892 and 1910.

———. "Mary Austin's *A Woman of Genius*: The Text, the Novel and the Problem of Male Publishers and Critics and Female Authors." *Journal of American Culture* 15, no. 2 (summer 1992): 79-86.

Focuses on the feminist themes and issues at the center of Austin's novel *A Woman of Genius* and discusses, in particular, the manner in which the work was interpreted and promoted by its original publisher, Doubleday, Page and Company, and how it was received by the "male-dominated" critical establishment at the time.

Lyday, Jo W. *Mary Austin: The Southwest Works,* Austin, Tex.: Steck-Vaughn Company, 1968, 40 p.

Short monograph that provides a biography of Austin and surveys her work as a nature writer, novelist, poet, and short story writer, claiming that "her place in literature" rests on her nonfiction writings that depict the environment of the southwest, as well as on "her contribution to the preservation of Indian lore."

Nelson, Barney. "Hoofed Locusts or Wild Eco-Sheep." In *The Wild and the Domestic: Animal Representation, Ecocriticism, and Western American Literature,* pp. 74-91. Reno, Nev.: University of Nevada Press, 2000.

Compares Austin's *The Flock* and John Muir's writings on the Sierra range in California, such as *My First Summer in the Sierra,* in order to illuminate the "strongly opposing ecological perspectives" of these two authors, especially with regard to their views on the growing population of sheep in the state.

Paes de Barros, Deborah. "Reclaiming the Territory: Mary Austin and Other (Un)Natural Girls." In *Fast Cars and Bad Girls: Nomadic Subjects and Women's Road Stories,* pp. 57-88. New York: Peter Lang, 2004.

Argues that Austin, along with such contemporary writers as Diane Smith, Pam Huston, and Annie Proulix, subverts the romantic and masculine view of nature as sublime and feminine, depicting a vision of the American southwest that is "blighted and nearly demonic," a "geography populated by irresponsible and dominating men, and by nameless mobile women, women without fixed identity, who must negotiate this unmapped space."

Richards, Penny L. "Bad Blood and Lost Borders: Eugenic Ambivalence in Mary Austin's Short Fiction." In *Evolution and Eugenics in American Literature and Culture, 1880-1940: Essays on Ideological Conflict and Complicity,* edited by Lois A. Cuddy and Claire M. Roche, pp. 148-63. Lewisburg, Pa.: Bucknell University Press, 2003.

Emphasizes the importance of eugenics in Austin's life and traces the appearance of "eugenic themes and language" in her stories collected in *Lost Borders* and published in various magazines during her career.

Ruppert, James. "Discovering America: Mary Austin and Imagism." In *Studies in American Indian Literature: Critical Essays and Course Designs,* edited by Paula Gunn Allen, pp. 243-58. New York: The Modern Language Association of America, 1983.

Places Austin in the context of the "renewal" of American poetry during the early decades of the twentieth century and describes her as "a pivotal figure in understanding the relation between American Indian literature and modern American literature."

Scheick, William J. "The Art of Maternal Nurture in Mary Austin's *The Basket Woman.*" In *Literature and the Child: Romantic Continuations, Postmodern Contestations,* edited by James Holt McGavran, pp. 211-32. Iowa City, Iowa: University of Iowa Press, 1999.

Maintains that Austin's often-overlooked book of children's tales and Indian stories, *The Basket Woman,* "deserves reconsideration not only for its . . . clever use of Paiute myth and ritual" but also for its indication of the author's "adroit adaptation of the Victorian construction of childhood in Romantic terms."

Wild, Peter. "The Dangers of Mary Austin's *The Land of Little Rain.*" *North Dakota Quarterly* 56, no. 3 (summer 1988): 119-27.

Comments on the ways in which Austin's writings about the California desert, specifically her book *The Land of Little Rain,* "dovetailed with a wave of popular sentiment for nature that is still swelling in America," and for this reason he cautions that read-

ers should not accept the author's "genuine romanticism" as an accurate picture of desert life.

Additional coverage of Austin's life and career is contained in the following sources published by Gale: *American Nature Writers*; *Contemporary Authors,* Vols. 109, 178; *Dictionary of Literary Biography,* Vols. 9, 78, 206, 221, 275; *Feminist Writers*; *Gale Contextual Encyclopedia of American Literature*; *Literature Resource Center*; *Short Story Criticism,* Vol. 104; *Twentieth-Century Literary Criticism,* Vol. 25; **and** *Twentieth-Century Western Writers,* **Eds. 1, 2.**

James K. Baxter
1926-1972

(Full name James Keir Baxter) New Zealand poet, play-wright, critic, and essayist.

The following entry provides an overview of Baxter's life and works. For additional information on his career, see *CLC,* Volume 14.

INTRODUCTION

Baxter is considered one of New Zealand's leading twentieth-century authors, whose works, perhaps more than any other writer, delineated the New Zealand mind, culture, and landscape. A playwright, literary critic, and social commentator, Baxter is best known for his poetry, collected in such volumes as *Pig Island Letters* (1966), *Jerusalem Sonnets* (1970), and *Autumn Testament* (1972), which offer his observations on the relationship between humanity and the natural world and emphasize the contradictions and failings of modern society. In these and other works, the author employed classical mythology and Christian imagery in his depiction of contemporary culture and addressed themes related to death, regeneration, community, and love, while promoting anti-materialist ideals and Christian values. A controversial writer and social activist, noted for his nonconformist lifestyle, Baxter remains one of the central figures in New Zealand's literature after World War II, respected for his craftsmanship, poetic mastery, and unique understanding of modern life. Trevor James, who praised Baxter's intuitive "grasp of the bonds between flesh and spirit," remarked that "throughout his poetry there is a consistent thread of thought which connects one poem with another," reflecting "his sense of a shaping order in the world which enabled him to believe that life was intelligible, however painful, that this was cosmos and not chaos."

BIOGRAPHICAL INFORMATION

Baxter was born June 29, 1926, in Brighton, Otago, New Zealand. At the young age of seven, he decided to pursue a career in poetry. In 1937, Baxter's family moved to England, and the author was sent to a Quaker school in the Cotswolds. Two years later, they returned to New Zealand, and Baxter continued his secondary education at King's High School in Dunedin. Throughout this period, the author wrote poems regularly. At the end of 1943, he left high school and enrolled at Otago University as an arts student, but he dropped out after little more than a year. His first book, *Beyond the Palisade,* was published in 1944. At the age of nineteen, he began working in a rolling mill at Green Island in Dunedin but moved to Christchurch in 1948, where he met two prominent literary figures, Denis Glover, a poet and printer, and Allen Curnow, a poet-journalist and influential critic. During this time, Baxter also published a second collection of poetry, *Blow, Wind of Fruitfulness* (1948), and married Jacqueline Sturm, whom he had met in Dunedin. Soon after, the author moved to Wellington and took a job at the meat-freezing works. He also enrolled in several classes at Victoria University College, eventually earning a Bachelor of Arts degree in 1952. Throughout the 1950s, Baxter lived in Wellington and worked as a mail carrier and teacher, before serving as an editor in the School Publications branch of the Education Department. He also suffered from alcoholism during this time, before becoming an active member of Alcoholics Anonymous, and continued to write poetry and criticism, as well as his first play, *Jack Winter's Dream* (1956).

During the late 1950s, Baxter developed a growing interest in Roman Catholicism and was formally converted in 1958. He became a spokesman for the church in New Zealand and became increasingly active in social causes. In 1962, Baxter left his job at the Education Department and returned to the post office, where he remained until 1965, when he was awarded a Robert Burns Fellowship, which took him back to the University of Otago. During this time, he published another important volume of poetry, *Pig Island Letters,* and wrote several more plays, including *The Devil and Mr. Mulcahy* (1967), which helped establish his reputation as a playwright. In the late 1960s, Baxter suffered what scholars have described as an "identity crisis," leaving his family in Wellington and taking up residence in a small Maori village on the Wanganui River, called Jerusalem. Living alone at first, he later attracted a group of social drop-outs and refugees, who treated him as a "patriarch" of the "family." He took a vow of poverty, grew his own food, and became known as "Hemi," the Maori equivalent of James, but he also continued to write, producing various volumes of poetry and prose, including *Jerusalem Sonnets* and *Jerusalem Daybook* (1971). Pressure from Maori landowners, as well as the Wanganui County Council, who had concerns regarding sanitation at Jerusalem, resulted in the dissolution of

Baxter's commune in 1971, after which the author returned to his family at Wellington. *Autumn Testament,* written during the last months of his life, was published in 1972. Although Baxter had some hopes of returning to Jerusalem with a smaller "family" of followers, he died on October 22, 1972, before his plans could be realized.

MAJOR WORKS

Baxter's first collection of poetry, *Beyond the Palisade,* focuses on the New Zealand landscape and uses animistic terms to describe nature, which is mostly presented as savage and brooding, as demonstrated by the poem "The Mountains." Baxter relies on surrealistic imagery throughout the collection and offers a deterministic view of the relationship between humanity and the natural world. The impossibility of human freedom in an indifferent and sometimes hostile environment is another important theme in the collection. Another pivotal work from Baxter's oeuvre, *Howrah Bridge and Other Poems* (1961), includes poems inspired by the author's trip to India in the late 1950s. The volume features verses about Madras, Delhi, and Elphanta, as well as urban Indian culture. In the words of Vincent O'Sullivan, however, "the point to which each poem pressed was to the basic response of pity, and the loneliness of pain." Scholars have noted that the collection signals a shift in Baxter's poetic voice, to one of greater maturity, as evidenced in such poems as "This Indian Morning," while other verses, including "A Clapper to Keep off Crows," "Night in Delhi," and "She who is like the moon," reflect the romantic virtuosity of his earlier work. In his next volume of poetry, *Pig Island Letters,* Baxter adopted an informal tone, characterized by a rougher and more natural voice than that employed in previous volumes. Most of the poems in the collection are unrhymed and presented in first person, often without a formal stanza pattern. In this work, Baxter presents a dark view of himself and humanity, but as C. K. Stead observed, "not without flashes of humour." While some poems in the collection, such as "Easter Testament" and "A Wish for Berries," provide a wry commentary on modern life and suburbia, others, such as "Waipatiki Beach," address the presence of death and its ordering effect on the chaos of life.

For some scholars, Baxter's later volumes of poetry represent his finest literary achievements. Comprised of thirty-nine sonnets, *Jerusalem Sonnets* maintains a consistent setting, voice, and theme, and may also be read as one long poem. Many of the poems portray the speaker's experience as he seeks to live in harmony with nature. While grounded in the natural world, the speaker also searches for communion with a greater creative force. In the opening sonnet of the sequence,

he presents himself as a "madman, a nobody, a raconteur," playfully joking with God, whose "silent laugh still shakes the hills at dawn." In *Jerusalem Daybook,* Baxter emphasizes what Charles Doyle described as an "all-consuming desire for community." As in *Jerusalem Sonnets,* the author promotes Christian values of love, humility, and a rejection of material wealth. *Autumn Testament* treats similar themes and is comprised of prose and verse. One long poem, "He Waiata Mo Te Kare," is addressed to the author's wife, while a section titled "Autumn Testament" is comprised of forty-eight sonnets, similar in style and theme to the poetry of *Jerusalem Sonnets.* The collection also incorporates elements of Maori culture and promotes ideas related to community and compassion for others, as in the last poem, "Te Whiori O Te Kuri," in which the speaker declares "A Man's body is a meeting house,/Ribs, arms, for the tribe to gather under,/And the heart must be their spring of water."

Although best known for his poetry, Baxter also produced a significant number of plays during his literary career, including *Jack Winter's Dream,* a drama that demonstrates the influence of the Welsh poet and playwright Dylan Thomas, as well as *The Wide Open Cage* (1959), *Three Women and the Sea* (1961), and *The Devil and Mr. Mulcahy.* As in his poetic works, Baxter often employed Christian imagery and classical mythology to represent contemporary New Zealand life in his plays, and addressed similar themes of community, love, death, and religion, as well as free will, drunkenness, bureaucracy, and what he called the "lost garden." Though generally considered less polished than his meticulously crafted poetry, Baxter's plays have garnered increasing respect in recent years. Howard McNaughton, writing in 1982, observed that "the uniqueness of Baxter's drama derives partly from the lack of any authoritative local tradition: it presents a poet evolving for himself a medium to express material that was not tractable in poetic form."

CRITICAL RECEPTION

Baxter first achieved critical acclaim in 1944, with the appearance of his debut work, *Beyond the Palisade,* which established the author as an emerging young talent in New Zealand poetry. His stature increased after he became a member of the so-called Wellington Group of writers during this time, which included Louis Johnson, W. H. Oliver, and Alistair Campbell. Baxter continued to attract attention during the 1940s and early 1950s, with the publication of such poetic works as *Blow, Wind of Fruitfulness* and *The Iron Breadboard* (1957), as well as the critical study *The Fire and the Anvil* (1955), but he also gained popularity as a playwright, particularly for the drama *Jack Winter's Dream,* first broadcast as a radio play in 1956. As his literary career progressed, however, the author's personal life, marked by alcoholism, ribaldry, social activism, and conversion to Catholicism, increasingly overshadowed his literary accomplishments. After taking a vow of poverty and moving to the isolated Jerusalem commune in 1968—a time when he produced some of his most memorable works as a poet—Baxter was recognized as much for his anti-materialist, anti-war, and Christian activities as for his many literary accomplishments. At the time of his death in 1972, he had reached legendary status in his country and was generally considered one of New Zealand's greatest modern poets.

In the years immediately following his death, Baxter continued to draw critical attention, particularly for his later literary works. In his 1973 tribute to the author, C. K. Stead praised *Jerusalem Sonnets* as "the most impressive yet written by a New Zealander," while Charles Doyle argued that Baxter's lifelong quest for "an ideal community" culminates in the "Christian vision" of his final three collections. Although studies of Baxter's work diminished during the 1980s and 1990s, essays by Trevor James and Vincent O'Sullivan, as well as new collected editions of the author's plays and poetry and Frank McKay's book-length biography, kept Baxter in the public eye. In recent years, scholars have turned again to the author's poetry, focusing especially on the predominant themes and influences in his verse. In his introduction to a 2001 edition of Baxter's poems, Paul Millar highlighted the paradoxes in the author's life, what he called the "'gap' between the selves," as an essential condition of his poetic writing, which he claimed resulted in some of the greatest poems written in the English language. Writing in 2005, John Dennison studied Baxter's representation of Maori and Pakeha cultures in his verse and argued that "the model of cross-cultural relationship" that he articulated "remains remarkable for its movement beyond the timorous antagonism and entrenched indolence of cultural division." Dougal McNeill, on the other hand, stressed the influence of the Scottish poet Robert Burns on Baxter's poetry, stating that the "poetic relations" of the two writers structures "each aspect of [Baxter's] poetic career." Although critics continue to assess the full significance of Baxter's writings, they generally agree that he deserves his position as one of New Zealand's leading writers, as well as a significant figure of contemporary English literature. Millar maintained that while "New Zealand lies at the heart of his poems, the best of which constitutes an unparalleled, intensely personal engagement with the country, its people, and society," Baxter is "more than a New Zealand poet," but rather belongs "among the major poets of the twentieth century."

PRINCIPAL WORKS

Beyond the Palisade (poetry) 1944
Blow, Wind of Fruitfulness (poetry) 1948
Recent Trends in New Zealand Poetry (criticism) 1951
The Fallen House (poetry) 1953
The Fire and the Anvil (criticism) 1955; revised edition, 1960
Jack Winter's Dream (radio play) 1956
The Iron Breadboard (poetry) 1957
In Fires of No Return (poetry) 1958
The Wide Open Cage (play) 1959
Howrah Bridge and Other Poems (poetry) 1961
The Silver Plate (play) 1961
Three Women and the Sea (play) 1961
The Spots on the Leopard (play) 1962
The First Wife (play) 1966
Mr. Brandywine Chooses a Gravestone (play) 1966
Pig Island Letters (poetry) 1966
Aspects of Poetry in New Zealand (criticism) 1967
The Band Rotunda (play) 1967
The Bureaucrat (play) 1967
The Devil and Mr. Mulcahy (play) 1967
The Lion Skin (poetry) 1967
The Man on the Horse (lectures) 1967
Mr. O'Dwyer's Dancing Party (play) 1967
The Sore-Footed Man (play) 1967
The Starlight in Your Eyes (play) 1967
The Day Flanagan Died (play) 1968
The Temptations of Oedipus (play) 1968
The Flowering Cross (prose) 1969
The Rock Woman (poetry) 1969
Who Killed Sebastian (play) 1969
Jerusalem Sonnets (poetry) 1970
The Junkies and the Fuzz (poetry) 1970
Jerusalem Daybook (poetry and prose) 1971
Autumn Testament (poetry and prose) 1972
Letter to Peter Olds (poetry) 1972
Ode to Auckland and Other Poems (poetry) 1972
Runes (poetry) 1973
The Tree House (poetry) 1973
The Labyrinth (poetry) 1974
Collected Poems (poetry) 1979
Collected Plays (plays) 1982
New Selected Poems (poetry) 2001

CRITICISM

J. E. Weir (essay date 1970)

SOURCE: Weir, J. E. "The Search for Order in Nature." In *The Poetry of James K. Baxter,* pp. 21-33. Wellington, New Zealand: Oxford University Press, 1970.

[*In the following essay, Weir traces Baxter's evolving "attitude to Nature" as expressed in his poetry—from his "conception of a malignant natural world" in his first volumes of verse to a growing affinity with nature in his later works.*]

It is scarcely surprising that Baxter's first published poems should be concerned with the natural world, for poetic practice in New Zealand at that time was greatly involved with the predicament of Man Alone near the shores and mountains of this 'cold threshold-land'.

Allen Curnow, the most significant poet and critic then active on our literary scene, has formulated this sense of the alienation of Man in a hostile natural environment in terms of a metaphysic: 'The idea that . . . our presence in these islands is accidental, irrelevant; that we are interlopers on an indifferent or hostile scene; that idea, or misgiving, occurs so variously and so often, and in the work of New Zealand poets otherwise so different, that it suggests some common problem of the imagination[1]. . . .'

Curnow viewed this association with islands, the isolation of Man in time and place, as generating a fundamental significance for New Zealand verse: 'Whether open or implicit, it is this vital discovery of self in country and country in self, which gives the best New Zealand verse its character[2]. . . .'

The prevailing literary current undoubtedly had some effect on Baxter's attitudes at this highly impressionable stage of his literary development, but it is possible to exaggerate the extent of his debt to the tradition. The basis of his sense of alienation was really found in his own relationship with society. The hostile universe was a projection of a hostile society, and its disorder was a reflection of his own psychological state. Such an expression of alienation, then, is significantly different from that which Curnow discerned in Baxter's early writing: 'Taking up the theme of our failure to apprehend, imaginatively, the physical realities of land and latitude, Baxter began by interrogating the Otago scene[3]. . . .' The critic has misinterpreted the cause of those morose verses.

As a child Baxter had delighted in the Otago landscape; as an adolescent he had retreated into the earth's sheltering womb to find again that peace which eluded him:

> *. . . Again and again I came*
> *And was healed of the daftness, the demon in the head*
> *And the black knot in the thighs, by a silence that*
> *Accepted all[4]. . . .*
>
> ([**"The Hollow Place"**])

The well-loved, comforting natural world that Baxter then knew receded as the pressures of living threatened to overwhelm him.

It should be noted that his attitudes were reinforced by those of the Romantic poets whose verse his father so greatly admired. Their themes exerted a pressure which swung open the gate of Baxter's mind and allowed penetration from the New Zealand environment.

Such was the accumulation of influences that led to those early descriptions of the natural world. Nature, as presented in **Beyond the Palisade,** is the unintelligible goddess, her features foreboding and her ways inimical to human kind. '**The Mountains**' illustrates this dark poetic vision:

> . . . .
>
> *The mountains crouch like tigers—or await*
> *As women wait. The mountains have no age.*
>
> *But O the heart leaps to behold them loom:*
>
> *A sense as of vast fate rings in the blood; no refuge,*
> *No refuge is there from the flame that reaches*
>
> *Among familiar things and makes them seem*
> *Trivial, vain. O spirit walks on the peaks;*
> *Eye glances across a gorge to further crags.*
> *There is no desire: but the stream, but the avalanche*
>   *speaks*
> *And their word is louder than freedom, the mountain*
>   *embrace*
> *Were a death dearer than freedom or freedom's*
>   *flags.. . .*

Nature, the savage goddess, entices Man, but he who follows the call 'leaves home, leaves kindred. . . .' In this elemental world there is no room for human freedom, the will is overwhelmed and 'the seeking eyes grow blind. . . .' so that man and nature become one in a meaningless shared existence. The child who once wandered at peace with Nature, the bland nurse, is now trapped in the grasp of the torturer; the fertile garden is distorted into a 'surrealist nightmare' where a 'vast fate' looms.

The poem has Freudian connotations. In his manuscript book Baxter has written 'Mountains are mothers' alongside the poem. The mountains are kindly since their embrace brings 'a death dearer than freedom. . . .'—a final release from the sufferings of adolescence.

It is probably not fanciful to suggest that this animistic conception of the New Zealand landscape also has its roots in the songs of the skalds of the Scandinavian tradition. As a child Baxter had been greatly impressed by his reading of northern mythology. He had, in fact, written a poem which described 'cold Niflheim', world of clouds and shadows, lying in the regions north of the Abyss, and the fountain Hvergelmir, source of the twelve glacial rivers. The transition from this to the Otago scene where 'giant wings brood over loftily and near. . . .' is readily made.

In the course of this volume Baxter insists on the malignity of nature in these 'lands seen in the light of an inhuman dawn. . . .', in this

> *. . . immense*
> *And hump-backed planet [which] has cast the slough*
> *Of human habitation[5]. . . .*
>
> ([**"Death of a Man"**])

The philosophy which lies behind these reflections is sometimes nihilistic, always deterministic—his dialogue with nature is commonly an argument about human freedom. The imagery he uses is often strained and surrealistic.

Blow, Wind of Fruitfulness was published in February, 1948, when Baxter was twenty-one. Some traces of an animistic conception of the universe remain, but the dominant tone of the collection is lyrical and contrasts markedly with the ponderous verse-forms and doom-laden pronouncements of the poems in ***Beyond the Palisade.***

At first glance the general shift in this second collection appears to be towards a theistic interpretation of the universe. **'O Wind Blowing'** seems to celebrate this change:

> *O wind blowing from the grave of stars*
> *Wind of dissolution, wind of creation*
> *O breath life-instinct from the lips of God*
> *I am overwhelmed by a truth clear as water*
> *A truth eternal as life is eternal . . .*

It is probable, however, that Baxter is using Jungian concepts rather than Christian ones, that in poems such as this he was entertaining an imaginative conception of the natural world and there encountering something of the divine.

Nature itself or the force, perhaps, behind Nature (the reader faces problems similar to those set by Wordsworth) can bring comfort and tranquillity to the solitary man. This is the theme of that frequently anthologised lyric **'High Country Weather'**:

> *Alone we are born*
> *And die alone;*
> *Yet see the red-gold cirrus*
> *Over snow-mountain shine.*
>
> *Upon the upland road*
> *Ride easy, stranger:*
> *Surrender to the sky*
> *Your heart of anger.*

Once again, as in childhood, Baxter considers the natural world as the source of peace and order. Whoever contemplates it long enough will share its tranquillity:

> *. . . . .*
> *Lie still: let thunder beat upon the brain*
> *Sun clothe the naked shoulders like a grave—*
> *Till air and earth and sea revive again*

> *The mountains and the dark imagined plain*
> *The wild lost city of a mother's love.[6]*
>
> ([**"Earth Does at Length"**])

The 'mother' of the last line is Mother Earth, Gea, the mythological figure whom Baxter has celebrated so often in his latest work. She alone can console the natural man.

This last conviction, dating, in all probability, from adolescence, when he used to withdraw into 'the hollow place' to be healed 'by a silence that / Accepted all . . .', has been the foundation of much of Baxter's best verse, verse securely founded in the natural world. **'The Cave'** is such a poem:

> *In a hollow of the fields, where one would least expect*
> *it,*
> *Stark and suddenly this limestone buttress:*
> *A tree whose roots are bound about the stones,*
> *Broad-leaved, hides well that crevice at the base*
> *That leads, one guesses, to the sunless kingdom*
> *Where souls endure the ache of Proserpine.*
> *. . . . .*
> *The whole weight of the hill hung over me;*
> *Gladly I would have stayed there and been hidden*
> *From every beast that moves beneath the sun,*
> *From age's enmity and love's contagion. . . .*

The lines describe a retreat from a reality which had become too hard to handle. If Baxter had succumbed to the temptation he must surely have formulated a considerable body of exquisite nature verse, so sharp was his ear for the rhythms of earth, but at this very stage his poetry was moving in another direction. **'Haast Pass'** can be read on one level as a poem enshrining the myth of isolation in an indifferent universe:

> *In the dense bush all leaves and bark exude*
> *The odour of mortality; for plants*
> *Accept their death like stones*
> *Rooted for ever in time's torrent bed.*
>
> *Return from here. We have nothing to learn*
> *From the dank falling of fern spores*
> *Or the pure glacier blaze that melts*
> *Down mountains, flowing to the Tasman.*
>
> *This earth was never ours. Remember*
> *Rather the tired faces in the pub*
> *The children who have never grown. Return*
> *To the near death, the loves like garden flowers.*

Curnow interpreted it in that manner. It does seem, however, that Baxter is announcing a new theme, and that his concern from now on will be Man.

In his first volume Baxter had provided a clue to the likelihood of just such a change. In **'The Mountains'** he had written:

> *. . . . .*
> *I will go to the coast-line and mingle with men.*
> *These mountain buttresses build beyond the horizon;*

They call: but he whom they lay their spell upon
Leaves home, leaves kindred. . . .

This was one of the points he subsequently made explicit in his critical study **Recent Trends in New Zealand Poetry** (1951). There he referred to the 'dangerous split between the moral and aesthetic factors in art', and noted that the position of the Romantic inclined more nearly to that of the pure aesthete. Of the artist's role he remarked:

> *If he breaks with society and departs into the*
> *Wilderness in customary Romantic style, then he*
> *loses brotherhood with all but similar outcasts.*
> *What Justice demands is something more*
> *difficult—that he should remain as a cell of*
> *good living in a corrupt society, and in this*
> *situation by writing and example attempt to*
> *change it. He will thus and only thus escape*
> *the isolation of the Romantic*[7] *. . .*

In **'Haast Pass'** Baxter was warning himself of the dangers of Romantic isolation and calling his own attention to 'the tired faces in the pub. . . .' Two other poems in this collection, **'Farmhand'** and **'Returned Soldier',** indicate the new direction, and a third, **'Sea Noon',** contrasts the pleasure arising from the company of men with the menacing countenance of the Nature Goddess.

There is a further change in Baxter's attitude to Nature at this time which is of the first importance. Three poems, **'Let Time Be Still', 'The Track'** and **'Tunnel Beach',** illustrate a new conviction—that a positive order can be found throughout nature by way of human sexuality.

The Fallen House contains some of Baxter's best-known poems. **'Virginia Lake'** is one of these. It views the natural world with the fresh romanticising gaze of a child, and is, in fact, a poem about the lost innocence of childhood:

> *The lake lies blind and glinting in the sun.*
> *Among the reeds the red billed native birds*
> *Step high like dancers. I have found*
> *A tongue to praise them, who was dumb;*
> *And from the deaf morass one word*
> *Breaks with the voices of the numberless*
>   *drowned. . . .*

This is the world where, as a child, Baxter wove his 'mythology of weeds and shells', the real world of a childhood vision—'the leaves' treasure house, the brown ducks riding / Over the water face. . . .' The beauty of that lost world of nature in childhood, that place of order and delight emblematic of innocence, is contrasted with the poet's later state—the legacy of a disordered adolescence, alcoholism and spiritual destitution generally. Such is the grief of the child-man,

> *. . . . .*
> *Who now lies dumb, the black tongue dry*
> *And the eyes weighed with coins.*
> *O out of this rock tomb*
> *Of labyrinthine grief, I start and cry*
> *Toward his real day—the undestroyed*
> *Fantastic Eden of a waking dream.*

One is reminded of Wordsworth's celebration of that primitive world in the **'Immortality Ode'** when the universe was apparelled in 'the glory and the freshness of a dream . . .', and of the same writer's sense of loss:

> *Wither is fled the visionary gleam?*
> *Where is it now, the glory and the dream?*

The theme of Wordsworth's great Ode is the key to much of Baxter's writing, for he, too, is concerned with the immortal nature of the human spirit, intuitively known by the child, neglected by the growing man, but recognised again in maturity through intense experience of mind and body.

The third part of **In Fires of No Return** indicates a shift from the Romanticism of the earlier collections towards what can be called the position of the Realist-Romantic. Some of these poems are confused, obsessive, the result of private stresses. Such a confusion exists only in the subjective area of his experience; the outward scene is depicted with a new realistic naturalism.

Baxter's reading of Lawrence Durrell's verse hastened the shift towards realism. This is made clear by the sequence of poems he wrote during his visit to India in 1958, some of which were republished in *Howrah Bridge*. **'Elephanta'** shows the new spareness:

> *. . . . .*
> *Great hawks like monoplanes*
> *Above the bony tamarind,*
>
> *Above the quarried rock sail high, high,*
> *And Shiva like a business uncle watches*
>
> *The village girls with cans to fill*
> *File through the temple to a covered cistern. . . .*

It seems likely that Baxter had come to recognise the dangers of an excessive rhetoric and had determined to pare his verses to the bone.

If the style of these poems was changing, the themes remain much the same. **'The Carvers'** describes in a foreign setting the therapeutic effect of nature on human lives:

> *. . . . .*
> *Look. The wasp has built her nest*
> *Of brown daubed clay below the cornice.*

Crabs clinging to the level blocks
With each new shoving wave.
They, the patient carvers
Whose massive music blossomed here
From hewn cloud and blown water,
Ignored the guide's grey chatter
And taught us what to be. . . .

The 'silence of the daimon' of this poem is demonstrably 'the hollow place', and the voice of earth which 'taught us what to be' is the same as that which spoke at an earlier time, enjoining the high country traveller to 'Surrender to the sky / Your heart of anger.'

Pig Island Letters uses elements of natural description in varying ways. In the tenth section of the title poem Baxter formulates an antidote for old age—a tribal existence spent close to nature,

> *While cloud and green tree like sisters keep*
> *The last door for the natural man. . . .*

Of all the poems in the collection, **'Waipatiki Beach'** comes closest to being a nature poem. It contains many of the elements that are best in his later work, a bareness and assurance of form and language, a positive contemplative philosophy, and a strength based on perspectives held in tension—the mythological and the everyday:

> *Under rough kingly walls the black-and-white*
> *Sandpiper treads on stilts the edges*
>
> *Of the lagoon, whose cry is like*
> *A creaking door. We came across the ridges*
>
> *By a bad road, banging in second gear,*
> *Into the only world I love. . . .*

There was a time when physical love transformed the natural world and helped 'to cap and seal my joy', but now 'bare earth, bare sea' teach a more lasting lesson, that closer than the union of physical love is that of death, when flesh, bone and the probing earth and wave mingle and unite.

A 'lip of sand' left at the gully mouth gives entrance to the haven of the Earth Mother 'to whom my poems go / Like ladders down. . . .', bridging the gap between life and death, bringing order where it did not previously exist. There is an oblique reference here to the tree of Ygdrasil, to whose roots Odin descended in search of life-giving waters. The journey does not end there: the protagonist walks in the company of his son beyond the creek under its 'froth of floating sticks', beyond the 'hundred-headed cabbage-tree / At the end of the beach . . .' to 'a bay too small to have a name. . . .' Only then does he find

> *Her lion face, the skull-brown Hekate*
> *Ruling my blood since I was born. . . .*

Having penetrated outwards in space and inwards in time, Baxter has completed the mythological presentation of the event, so that what we are left with is not so much a nature poem as a parable of life and death. What Baxter found in the natural scene of Waipatiki Beach was an unmistakable sign of the presence of death, that event which brings a final order to the chaos of living.

The natural scene of Baxter's late poems is clearly the kind of generous wilderness which allows the growth of the natural man and a tranquil movement towards death. In his poem **'At Day's Bay'**, as in **'Waipatiki Beach'**, Baxter codifies nature as the Mother Goddess. The earth is 'Gea's breast, the broad nurse / Who bears with me. . . .' In her lies the harmony of all creation, an aspect of the search for the Lost Eden, since the peace of the natural world reflects that of man in his unfallen state.

Behind this late attitude to nature lies a marked transition from a conception of a malignant natural world to a belief that sexual love can provide an order throughout nature, and finally to the conception of death as the fundamental biological experience. Mother Earth both gives reminders of death and yet provides solace for those journeying towards it. In her care one can rest, as **'The Waves'** puts it,

> *Accepted here, here only,*
> *For what one is, not the chalk mask,*
> *Gentility of a robot or a clown,*
> *But the sad mandrake torn*
> *From earth, getting no likely truce*[8] *. . . .*
>
> ([*The Rock Woman*])

What seems to have happened is that Baxter first found a metaphysic which brought order into his own life; subsequently he projected this into his conception of the natural world. Reason, not emotion, has led to the change:

> *. . . The river*
> *is foul weed and sludge*
> *narrower*
> *than I had supposed, fed by*
>
> *a thousand drains: thus*
> *the heart is twisted free*
> *by thought's knife*[9]*. . . .*
>
> (["The River"])

The spare style of this last poem indicates a new and authentic direction in Baxter's writing and a new sense of detachment towards nature:

> *. . . the creek*
> *runs to sea*
> *finding its way without us.*

Notes

1. *A Book of New Zealand Verse 1923-45*; Caxton (1945) p. 52.

2. Introduction to the *Penguin Book of New Zealand Verse*; [(Edited by Allen Curnow; 1960)] p 21.

3. ibid. p. 62.

4. 'The Hollow Place'; *Pig Island Letters*; p. 31.

5. 'Death of a Man'; *Beyond the Palisade*; p. 15.

6. 'Earth Does at Length'; *Blow, Wind of Fruitfulness*; p. 21.

7. *Recent Trends in New Zealand Poetry*; p. 18.

8. *The Rock Woman*; p. 83.

9. 'The River'; New Zealand *Listener*; 14 October 1966.

Publications by James K. Baxter

Beyond the Palisade (poems); Caxton Press, Christchurch; 1944.

Blow, Wind of Fruitfulness (poems); Caxton; 1948.

Recent Trends in New Zealand Poetry (criticism); Caxton; 1951.

Poems Unpleasant (with Louis Johnson and Anton Vogt); Pegasus Press, Christchurch; 1952.

The Fallen House (poems); Caxton; 1953.

In Fires of No Return (selected poems); Oxford University Press; 1958.

Pig Island Letters (poems); Oxford; 1966.

The Rock Woman (selected poems); Oxford; 1969.

C. K. Stead (essay date autumn 1973)

SOURCE: Stead, C. K. "James K. Baxter: Towards Jerusalem." In *Kin of Place: Essays on 20 New Zealand Writers*, pp. 306-19. Auckland, New Zealand: Auckland University Press, 2002.

[*In the following essay, originally published in the autumn 1973 issue of the journal* Islands, *Stead praises Baxter's late collection,* Jerusalem Sonnets, *connecting the work to the poet's earlier volumes and calling it "the most impressive yet written by a New Zealander."*]

I hadn't intended to write any kind of a 'survey' of James K. Baxter's poetry—only something about his *Jerusalem Sonnets,* because I admired them as much as or more than anything else of his, and I didn't seem able to find more than one or two whose opinion I could

take seriously who took *them* seriously. Now Baxter is dead and already a posthumous book, *Autumn Testament,* in proof before his death, offers (together with some prose pieces) his most recent poems. I write in London, in a hurry, with a number of Baxter books at hand but not all I would like. I have, too, a copy of my last article on Baxter, written thirteen years ago, also in London—a review of his Oxford book, *In Fires of No Return* (1958). It has weighed on me since (though I don't think I have re-read it until now) because of a certain sourness of tone. I took to task what were then Baxter's most recent poems, and took them apart. I found the worst of them 'diffuse', 'hysterical', 'melodramatic', full of 'pickings off the scrapheap of poetry'—and I offered ample evidence. My word-counting wasn't forgotten (I had used the same method earlier on the poetry of Alistair Campbell) and Baxter cited it with as much bitterness as he could muster (which wasn't much) in several radio talks.

His next book, *Howrah Bridge* (1961), somehow passed me by. Then came *Pig Island Letters* (1966). It won me over so completely I felt my 1959 review must have been wrong—that my motives must have been mixed and impure. Some poems in *London Magazine* round about 1967, and then the *Jerusalem Sonnets* completed the process. It seemed to me there were no New Zealand poems I wanted so much to read and re-read.

Of course I had always admired Baxter. (That, perhaps, is what was wrong with my 1959 review—that I neglected to say so.) In the early fifties when I was a student poems like **'Rocket Show', 'Wild Bees', 'Letter to Noel Ginn II',** and one I don't have a copy of now but was called, I think, **'Venetian Blinds'**—these and others were as important a part of my intellectual landscape as the poems of Donne and Eliot, Curnow and Fairburn. They had in common a personal, informal, verse-letter tone, a formal, well-managed stanzaic pattern, and a more or less contrived movement through varieties of sensuous experience towards moral statements. These poems of Baxter's more than any others probably lie behind my own 'Night Watch in the Tararuas'; and I suppose my present discontent with that poem comes precisely from its forced march to a moral conclusion. Those orotund Baxterian roundings-off—

> But loss is a precious stone to me, a nectar
> Distilled in time, preaching the truth of winter
> To the fallen heart that does not cease to fall.
>
> (**"Wild Bees"**)

or

> I thought of our strange lives, the grinding cycle
> Of death and renewal come to full circle;
> And of man's heart, that blind Rosetta stone,
> Mad as the polar moon, decipherable by none.
>
> (**"Rocket Show"**)

—they came naturally enough to him; but if I accepted them it can only have been as a concluding seal at the bottom of the parchment, a stylistic habit like the ending of a Beethoven symphony, not as statements of particular value in themselves. What brought me back to the poems was not their quality as statements but their creation of a personality in balance against its surroundings—people, places, scenes, events—in which everything quivered with a symbolic resonance, a heightened sense of life. They were poems of the twentieth century in the romantic tradition as it passes through late Yeats to early Auden; but they were distinctly our own experience. No poetry moved me in quite the same way, at so profound a level, as our own, not just because the sensuous world it recreated was the one I knew from day to day, but because the Eden we are all cast out from is that of the world fresh to our awakening senses. For me one of the most important functions of poetry was to take us back there, and Baxter was one of the magicians who knew the way.

I think I need not have felt too badly about that 1959 review. It was more brutal in finding fault than I would ever wish to be now; but it praised where praise was due, and it looked forward accurately enough to what Baxter's future development might be. No doubt I have become more open-minded; but for me the present discovery is that I do not (as I supposed I would) need to conclude either that I was emphatically wrong in my judgement of the earlier book, or that I have since grown soft in the head. Baxter's poetry improved dramatically during the last twelve years of his life. All the enormous promise apparent in those first two boyish books of the forties, a promise which seemed perhaps not quite to be fulfilling itself in the fifties, blazes forth in the best poems of the sixties. I doubt whether this is widely recognized. A haze of undiscriminating feeling surrounds Baxter, which his death may only serve to thicken. To many older writers he is the marvellous boy they welcomed on to the scene who gracelessly turned his back on them, first to play out the melodrama of the doomed, boozing, fornicating Calvinist, and latterly the farce of the Catholic hippie. To the young, on the other hand, he has become a culture hero, and if his poems were much less remarkable than they are I suspect his youthful disciples would not know it and would admire them quite as much.

* * *

If you have to write about poetry or lecture on it two things may make the task easier; if the poems are bad, or if they are good but obscure. In the first instance you can show where and why they fail; in the second you can show what they mean. But what is there to be said of successful poems whose meaning is plain except 'Behold!'? That seems to me the case with *Jerusalem Sonnets*—either you see their merits or you don't—and

I knew when I resolved to write about them I would have difficulties. Why are they good? How do I demonstrate to someone who hasn't felt it the superiority I believe they have? Why do they seem to me, taken together as a single long poem, perhaps the most impressive yet written by a New Zealander?

There is no easy answer to these questions. But now that I have sat down and read all the Baxter I could get my hands on, in sequence, I feel a little nearer to an answer—because I can see the qualities slowly emerging that are given their fullest expression in the sonnets.

Towards the end of *Howrah Bridge* (1961) a new voice begins to be heard which for lack of another word I will call that of the mature Baxter. It is a relaxed, matter-of-fact note, sometimes, in its first appearances, juxtaposed with more conventional, high-toned lines.

> Eagles have bathed their wings at the ocean streams.
> In a cold taxi coming from the mass
> With Bertha in her blue silk dress
> I think of money.
>
> **("This Indian Morning")**

There is something expansive in those lines. In their connected-disconnected way they have the 'feel' of actual experience. A younger Baxter might have written one poem about the eagles and another about Bertha; he could hardly have succeeded in casually yoking them together in a stanza whose ostensible subject was his own return from mass. Here, as in **'Election 1960', 'A Dentist's Window', 'The Sixties',** and others, Baxter is coming down off his high romantic stilts—not a stylistic event, not the result of a decision to write differently, but a development in the man's confidence, in his belief that he can be seen to exist without trappings.

Yet at the same time that this is occurring (if, as I suppose, all the poems of part II of *Howrah Bridge* belong to one period) Baxter also returns to those stilts for the last time and performs more remarkably on them than ever before. **'A Clapper to Keep off Crows',** the last stanza of **'Night in Delhi',** and three love poems, **'The Apple Tree', 'She who is like the moon',** and **'On the death of her body',** in their romantic virtuosity remind me of Fairburn at his most fluent.

> Beauty you possess, time's daughter,
> Lamp of my life, O hidden one,
> You who are the song you sing,
>
> Silently, silently,
> From faithful pillows on a night of love
> Pouring in my heart's gulf
>
> Your light, your song, your cataract of beauty.
>
> **("She who is like the moon")**

With *Pig Island Letters* (1966) the informal tone predominates. The voice becomes rougher, more natural, though the poems are quite as well made. They are mostly in the first person, often without rhyme and sometimes without a formal stanza pattern. The physical background, the scene, is strongly evoked. But at the centre is the rough, grating, resonant voice and personality of Jim the Catholic family man chafing with wry self-knowledge against work and suburbia.

> but smoking one small cigar
> confess Christ, as the bones creak
>
> this excellent Friday, not
> expecting martyrdom—thus
> I hang my balls and car-coat
> at the church door, and go up
> to swap saliva on those
> metal feet that touch the lip . . .
>
> ("**Easter Testament**")

> 'Pity all things'—Do the tough
> kids need pity who wrestle
> under the bathing shed wall?
> or the girls whose broad muscles
> slide in bermuda shorts, all
> intent on a thunder-proof
>
> world of knowledge? I cannot
> pity what is; but look up
> at the karaka tree . . .
>
> ("**A Wish for Berries**")

The development I am describing is not dramatic or sudden but it is distinct enough and occurs in a matter of a few years. Already those lines are a long way from those last beautiful flings of romanticism in *Howrah Bridge.* Compare them, for example, with

> I saw where in a wilderness did lie
> The royal spirits of our burdened age.
> Some slept; some roared, and shook the walls in rage;
> Crowned beasts in cages open to the sky . . .
>
> ("**Night in Delhi**")

and so on—lines which wouldn't look out of place, or out of countenance, anywhere in the works of Shelley.

The full effect of the change can't be felt in one or two poems because it is partly an effect of personality—the strong, uncompromising personality whose vision of himself and of all men is dour as it always was but not sour; dark, but not without flashes of humour. The poems are not all equally successful. In '**Ballad of One Tree Hill**' feeling runs away with the writing, inflating it, and some of the old, bad, self-pitying melodrama slips in. The sequence which gives the book its title has weaker moments too. But for most of the book the tone is level, confident, moving easily from present scene to reminiscence to moral observation and back to the present with a total effect richer than anything Baxter had achieved before.

> About twilight we came to the whitewashed pub
> On a knuckle of land above the bay
>
> Where a log was riding and the slow
> Bird-winged breakers cast up spray.
>
> ("**East Coast Journey**")

The skill in lines like these is in how little is needed to call up a whole scene: twilight, the whitewashed pub standing out above the bay, and then that detail of the log and its movement in breakers—so particular you feel it as something experienced. You cannot 'see' that log without seeing more than is literally in the words of the poem. The same is true of the lines which follow:

> One of the drinkers round packing cases had
> The worn face of a kumara god,
>
> Or so it struck me. . . .

We are directed to look at one man but those casual 'packing cases' bring with them the whole scene. And don't the 'bird-winged breakers' seem now to join with the face of the kumara god to suggest something hidden below the casual surface? Some revelation is at hand.

> . . . Later on
> Lying awake in the veranda bedroom
>
> In great dryness of mind I heard the voice of the sea
> Reverberating. . . .

That image of the log still rolls in the mind, like a body in the surf. The poet is seeking intensity of life in the knowledge of death:

> . . . As a man
>
> Grows older he does not want beer, bread, or the
>   prancing flesh,
> But the arms of the eater of life, Hine-nui-te-po. . . .

Out of such hard-gained evocations of particular places, events, people, Baxter is continually wringing something which I think can properly be called wisdom—a wisdom richer than any available to him in conversation or in prose where, for all his colour and horse sense, he was also rambling and partial. In the best of these poems, in fact in all but a few which are weak, that prose Baxter yields precedence to the deep implacable will of the artist to discover the real and the true. I suspect it was the prose Baxter who had followers, the Baxter of '**Elegy for Boyle Crescent**', for example (*Islands* 1), which has been recommended to me more than once as a moving document but which seems to me a shabby exercise in rhetoric, a giving in to the sentimental self that rises most readily when we believe we have a just cause. Then policemen are 'the fuzz' and 'the pigs', our culture is a 'death-ship' with 'burnt-out eyes and broken ear-drums', while 'junkies' become heroes and martyrs ('I never met a junkie who was incapable of love.').

Against that prose Baxter I set what I call the wisdom of the poet:

>   . . . Shall Marx and Christ
> Share beds this side of Jordan? I set now
> Unwillingly these words down:
>
> *Political action in its source is pure,*
> *Human, direct, but in its civil function*
> *Becomes the jail it laboured to destroy.*
>
> **("Pig Island Letters 8")**

Or this, which contains all that is true in **'Elegy for Boyle Crescent'** quite as memorably and with none of the falseness and overstatement:

> This love that heals like a crooked limb
> In each of us, source of our grief,
> Could tell us if we cared to listen, why
> Sons by mayhem, daughters by harlotry
> Pluck down the sky's rage on settled houses. . . .
>
> **("Pig Island Letters 7")**

The Rock Woman, published in 1969, is a selection (not a good one) from the whole range of Baxter's poetry. It includes only a few poems written after the publication of *Pig Island Letters,* but at about this time the transformation was occurring in which Jim the Catholic family man became Hemi the prophet. I can now see *Jerusalem Sonnets* (1970) as a development out of all that had gone before; but it is probably true that it needed the personal upheaval of his leaving home and of his wandering between the Jerusalem commune and the 'junkie' houses of Auckland, to shake the new poems out of him. The freshness of seeing that poetry requires doesn't come readily out of a settled suburban life. Nor did it come best to Baxter out of living in cities, which encouraged him in his darkest, broadest, and least convincing generalizations. If there were periods of boredom and irritation in Jerusalem it's clear there was much more, in the pace of life there and in the proximity of living things, to help than to hinder his writing. In his own way Baxter did what Fairburn (in 'To a Friend in the Wilderness') only talked about.

Jerusalem Sonnets may be read as thirty-nine sonnets or as a single poem in thirty-nine stanzas. It has one setting, one voice, one theme (stated on the title page). The sonnet form chosen has fourteen lines, spaced out in pairs but not 'paired' in any sense other than that, with no rhyming pattern. It is loose, but not as loose as it looks. The lack of a rhyme scheme means that no aura of appropriateness will be lent to any word by the form: only the statement being made will justify the words chosen. That statement must be (as in any sonnet) single, unified, the expression of one idea, not because the rule book says so but because that is all fourteen lines will carry. The difficulty is always that if you write economically fourteen lines is rather a lot for one idea, and too little for more than one. With the conventional sonnet, however, you have some leeway. For example you may complete your statement in twelve lines and simply recapitulate in a final couplet. In Baxter's sonnet every line must carry its weight of relevant meaning or look empty and irrelevant. To have said all you have to say in thirteen and a half lines is fatal. You have not filled the form, yet any additional words will seem weightless; they will clutter and obscure the effect. To put this point in a less technical way: I find it impossible to believe that anyone who had not Baxter's skill in handling rhymed stanzas could manage the 'freedom' of this sonnet form as well as he does.

But of course the achievement is not primarily formal; or the formal qualities are not distinct from the achievement as a whole, which I still find very difficult to pin down. Let me approach it obliquely in the following way: when I write letters I write them usually as fast as I can make pen or typewriter move across the page. When I write a piece of criticism (such as this present one) the writing inches along painfully with probably a third of the manuscript scored out and written over. Yet if I read my letter over before posting it it doesn't seem a worse piece of writing than the critical article. Why, then (I sometimes ask myself) shouldn't I be able to dash down critical articles as fast as letters? I suppose the answer is that in critical writing I am trying to say more difficult things—I am labouring to achieve clarity. In letters you don't normally try to define anything but simply to be yourself, and whatever a letter lacks in clarity of definition will usually be made up in that way. It's not easy to 'be yourself' even in letters, but you don't overcome the difficulty by 'trying hard'—whereas with expository prose you do: by trying hard you can achieve greater clarity. Poetry of any kind, but especially poetry of the kind Baxter wrote, is much nearer to a letter than to expository prose. The great aim is to give the fullest possible expression to all that the sensibility is capable of. More often than not poets fail—or rather their success is limited; that is why the sin of being more interested in the poet than in the poems is pardonable—because most poets, even those whose work endures, are more brilliantly charged with promise than with achievement. Would we admire Keats quite as much as we do if he hadn't also written those extraordinary letters? Weren't even the best of the early Baxter poems rather pale by comparison with the drunk in the gaberdine raincoat and galoshes who wrote them? Wasn't it possible to feel, because Fairburn was so much weightier than his funny poems and so much less solemn than his serious ones, that only half the man had gone into each?

What Baxter has managed in *Jerusalem Sonnets* (as in the best of *Pig Island Letters*) is to get something like the whole range of the personality into the poetry—but (this being poetry) it is a personality heightened and simplified. Here is the opening poem:

> The small grey cloudy louse that nests in my beard
> Is not, as some have called it, 'a pearl of God'—
>
> No, it is a fiery tormentor
> Waking me at two a.m.
>
> Or thereabouts, when the lights are still on
> In the houses in the pa, to go across thick grass
>
> Wet with rain, feet cold, to kneel
> For an hour or two in front of the red flickering
>
> Tabernacle light—what He sees inside
> My meandering mind I can only guess—
>
> A madman, a nobody, a raconteur
> Whom He can joke with—'Lord', I ask Him,
>
> 'Do You or don't You expect me to put up with lice?'
> His silent laugh still shakes the hills at dawn.

The beauty of these poems is subtle; even, for all the rough candour of the voice, delicate. I suppose 'the small grey cloudy louse' is accurate description but it is more than that, almost affectionate. The word 'cloudy' seems in its context beautiful enough to render the louse inoffensive, 'a pearl of God' despite the denial; and if we are invited in line three to see it as a 'fiery tormentor', in that role too it seems God's instrument, driving the poet out (and here we begin to experience the physical setting, as in all these poems) across the marae to the church and the 'red flickering / Tabernacle light'. A whole tradition of Christian asceticism has been tactfully evoked. Has Baxter the right to place himself in that tradition? He doesn't know. He knows himself as 'a madman, a nobody, a raconteur'—and we are left with the question he puts to God: is he or isn't he to put up with lice?—and with God's answer, a 'silent laugh' that 'still shakes the hills at dawn'. The humour is quiet, rich, an extension of the sense of life the poem imparts, not a belittling of it.

Depending on such qualities, the sonnets lend weight to one another and need to be read in sequence if their full effect is to be felt. Here is the second:

> The bees that have been hiving above the church porch
> Are some of them killed by the rain—
>
> I see their dark bodies on the step
> As I go in—but later on I hear
>
> Plenty of them singing with what seems a virile joy
> In the apple tree whose reddish blossoms fall
>
> At the centre of the paddock—there's an old spring-cart,
> Or at least two wheels and the shafts, upended
>
> Below the tree—Elijah's chariot it could be, Colin,
> Because my mind takes fire a little there
>
> Thinking of the woman who is like a tree
> Whom I need not name—clumsily gripping my beads,
>
> While the bees drum overhead and the bouncing calves look at
> A leather-jacketed madman set on fire by the wind.

This is again a case of revealing enough to set the mind of the reader unconsciously at work so that it 'sees' more than it is shown—a derelict church, insufficiently secure against the elements to protect from rain the bees that hive in its porch; a field in which an old spring-cart has been left to fall to pieces under an apple tree. . . . Yet the mood is not of decay but of regeneration. This is a spring poem. The surviving bees sing with a 'virile joy'; the apple tree sheds blossom; the calves are bouncing; and the poet, thinking of a woman 'who is like a tree', becomes for a moment 'a leather-jacketed madman set on fire by the wind' (again that subtle rhetorical force gathered up in the last line). The man and the world about him are brought into harmony. It is a moment of affirmation rare in a poet whose vision has been consistently dark.

But to go on dealing particularly with poems of this kind may be an evasion of a more general question which I now put to myself: 'Doesn't a set of doctrines and beliefs which you yourself find at least false and possibly repugnant lie behind these poems? In your enjoyment of the poems aren't you ignoring an essential part of their meaning?'

My answer to this is that I'm not concerned with what lies behind the poems but with what is *in* them. I ignore nothing that is there and I find nothing untrue or repugnant. They are not poems of doctrine but poems of experience. Our experiences as human beings differ very little. What differs is the interpretation we put on them. These poems present rather than interpret—and where there are elements of interpretation they come usually in the form of the poet's dialogue with himself in which there is conflict and contradiction rather than settled doctrine:

> If Ngati-Hiruharama turns out to be no more than
> A child's dream in the night—well then,
>
> I have a garden, a bed to lie on,
> And various company—some clattering pigeons roost
>
> At my back door, and when I meditate in the paddock
> Under the apple tree two healthy dung-smeared pigs
>
> Strike up a conversation, imagining, I think,
> I am their benefactor—that should be quite enough

To keep the bowels moving and the mind thankful;
Yet when the sun rises my delusion hears him shout

Above the river fog—'This is the hill fort
Of our God; it is called Hiruharama!

The goat and the opossum will find a home
Among the rocks, and the river of joy will flow from
    it.'

                                              (**Sonnet 30**)

Is his faith that he is achieving Hiruharama (Jerusalem)
a delusion? The poem says so but the faith is given the
last word. There is contradiction and no final answer.
These poems are deeply grounded in the natural world;
if they aspire beyond it that too is 'natural'.

* * *

I have not had *Autumn Testament* long enough, nor is
there time now, to write about it. It consists of a long
poem, **'He Waiata Mo Te Kare',** addressed to Baxter's
wife, to which six pages of notes are attached; then
'Autumn Testament', forty-eight sonnets in the Jerusalem Sonnet form; a further eight pages of prose, **'Letter to Colin';** and a final seven sonnets, **'Te Whiori o
Te Kuri'.** The poetry seems all to be drawing off the
same vein as the earlier sonnet sequence and with undi-
minished power and richness. In particular the Maori
elements seem here to have become a deep and genuine
part of Baxter's intellectual and emotional life—something new in Pakeha writing. The prose sections leave
me unsatisfied. The 'brief tribute' by Frank McKay
seems to me unfortunate and something of an obstacle
at the front of the book.

* * *

On Frank Sargeson's wall, up above the fireplace, there
used to be (perhaps there still is) a wooden cross. I
think he told me it was the start of what a friend had
intended to be a wooden doll or puppet and Sargeson
had hung it up as a sign of respectability to catch the
eye of any policeman who might call on him. One day
I found among cards and pictures on the shelf above
the fireplace a photograph of the young Baxter in his
alcoholic raincoat. I climbed up and pinned the photograph on the cross where it remained for years curling
at the edges and gathering dust.

When someone dies there are always things left unsaid
which we regret. They are usually kind things, but in
Baxter's case I find myself troubled by the fact that on
the few occasions when we talked at length I listened
so patiently to his monologues and didn't interrupt and
question and contradict. I'm not sure why I was so
obliging. It seems a kind of insincerity for which I am
now punished by being stuck with it. We have, how-

ever, our conversations with the dead, and in mine I
now interrupt him, usually with the statement 'Jim, you
know as well as I do that there's no God.'

When I think of Baxter the man and the poet my first
thought is always of the strengths he had which I lack.
He would never have sat through a monologue half of
which he didn't agree with, simply to be agreeable.
Keats's idea of the poet—that he has no character because he is forever becoming, or at least adjusting to,
the object of his contemplation—is true only of some
poets (Keats, for example). It doesn't fit Baxter, who
had a Wordsworthian ruggedness and certainty, never
cared much about money or status or what the neighbours might think, and went resolutely his own way.

But there is another part of my dialogue with the dead
Baxter. In it I interrupt him not to tell him there is no
God but to ask him why he talks so much. He replies
(and I can hear it in exactly his voice): 'The walls are
caving in, brother. When I stop shovelling I'll be
buried.' Or he says, 'Why does a man cling to his coat?
Because he feels the cold.'

I think Baxter knew perfectly well what it meant to say
'There is no God.' But our needs are more powerful
than our sense of probabilities and Baxter could not live
without postulating an Authority, against which he then
threw himself with all his force in order to be sure of
his own existence. He became a Catholic in order to be
a better rebel; and on the rare occasions when he tried
to be a 'good' Catholic, as in some of the essays in *The
Man on the Horse,* he sounded false and insincere.

It seems to me he died at the height of his powers and
with a great deal yet to say. I think he was a major
poet, and if I believed in his God I would say in my
prayers: 'If You had looked on us with half an eye,
Lord, You would have seen that our need of him was
greater than Yours.'

Charles Doyle (essay date July 1974)

SOURCE: Doyle, Charles. "James K. Baxter: In Quest
of the Just City." *Ariel* 5, no. 3 (July 1974): 81-98.

[*In the following essay, Doyle highlights Baxter's quest
for an "ideal of community" and, conversely, his social
protest against the "state secularism" of his native New
Zealand as central motivating forces in his poetry,
which culminates, according to the critic, in the "Christian vision" of his three final collections:* Jerusalem
Sonnets, Jerusalem Daybook, *and* Autumn Testament.]

It is possible without obvious absurdity for our politicians to call our country a Happy Island, in some degree a just one. But poets are different from politi-

cians. . . . I believe that our island is in fact an unjust, unhappy one, where human activity is becoming progressively more meaningless.[1]

The last years of Baxter's foreshortened life were spent in active communitarian efforts to overcome the human injustices and false "realities" of New Zealand society as he experienced it. From his activities at the Jerusalem commune and among the derelicts of the cities, some of his finest writing was also produced. The present essay, which addresses itself to a consideration of Baxter's view of man in society, will however focus chiefly on his work and experience before that final, triumphant, period.

From very early in his career Baxter believed that the link between artist and society is close, and necessary. He suggested that, "The analogy between the processes of art and the ritual of tribal magic is an exact one. Both enable catharsis by discovering shape in history, thus relieving the isolation of the individual" (*Trends* [*Recent Trends in New Zealand Poetry*], p. 5) He saw the artist as "a cell of good living in a corrupt society" (*Trends,* p. 18) and could never have agreed with that New Critical shibboleth which holds that an artist's life bears no relevance to the evaluation of his work. Rather, and the final shape of his own life seems to bear it out, he held the Keatsian view that "a man's life of any worth is a continual allegory" and once said of himself, "What happens is either meaningless to me, or else it is mythology,"[2] adding that he mythologized his own life. Throughout his career, and centrally for most of it, he believed that the poet's life and work are inextricably bound together and that poetry, indeed all art, has the function of speaking to man's condition and alleviating that condition.

Much of his work suggests that his human world is experienced as chaos, for which his repeated image is "the lion's den"—thus, in *Pig Island Letters*[3] a poem is "A plank laid over the lion's den." Man's struggle is to reduce chaos to life-giving order, though Baxter does not finally make clear whether, as he sees it, the individual imposes order or simply discovers an order already inherent in nature. Whatever the case, he began by seeing poetry both as the means of individuation and the expression of the journey towards individuation.

A poet of varied moods, modes and approaches, Baxter by and large is subjective, expressionist; but he is not merely confessional, even though at one stage in his career he admired, and learnt from, Robert Lowell. A seminal experience was his early reading of Jung's *Modern Man in Search of a Soul* which confirmed his sense that day-to-day experience has much more than its surface significance, hence his lifelong habit of parable-making and his declaration that consciousness itself can only assimilate "the crises, violations and rec-

onciliations of the spiritual life in mythical form" (*Man on the Horse,* p. 23). Beyond this, he had some sense of himself as part of the flux, process. In *The Fire and the Anvil* (1955), he observed that, "nearly all poetry is dramatic in character. The catharsis which a reader experiences could not occur if he felt the self that the poem expresses to be entirely actual; rather, the self is a projection of complex associations in the poet's mind, and the poem enables the reader to make the same projection."[4] Given the generally Jungian tendency of his mind, I believe that Baxter here is not adverting to the problem of aesthetic distance, but acknowledging his sense of collectivity. He is not "confessional" if only because he sees himself as typical or paradigm, as well as individual. In some part, too, his mythologizing is exploratory, an attempt to locate and clarify his own archetypes.

II

Another part is his effort to locate himself in the world. When still very young, he concluded that in searching for the true self, the discovery of a home in nature, identification with a place and a past, are vitally necessary. For the *pakeha*[5] New Zealander, peculiar problems arose from the historical fact that *pakeha* society was a transplant from Britain, grafted with incomplete success onto an already existing native society in the islands of Ao-Tea-Roa. Although the graft was virtually to consume the original plant, the attempt to transport the soil from which it had originally grown was doomed to failure. The artist in such a strangely nurtured "society," which lacked "even the shadow of a folk culture" (*Trends,* p. 8) was forced into the isolation of unreality.

Still a long way from that all-embracing sensitivity to the Maoris which characterised his last years, Baxter in his mid-twenties was already very conscious of the Maori "presence" in New Zealand, but saw it only as antithetical to the pioneers' intrusion. The Maoris "had their gods to shield them—we have none."[6] For the original settlers, "the first forgotten," fate is the "life that knows not life," and "unPolynesian, our deaths are near. / From the hills no dream but death / frowns." Yet, curiously, the earliest *pakeha* were to an extent forced to re-enact the nomadic stage of establishing a culture, and many artists have attested to the importance in New Zealand consciousness of "the comfortless semi-nomadic existence of the swagger and rabbiter and worker on gold dredges" (*Trends,* p. 5), not to mention the whaling-men and early missionaries. What intervenes between these early pioneers and present-day New Zealand society is the almost craven emulation of British custom and British education, which continues to exist in "the schizophrenia of the New Zealander who cannot distinguish himself from his grandfather" (*Trends,* p. 9) and to be part of the consciousness of every New Zealander. Without any show of flag-waving nationalism, Baxter fought this cultural dependence constantly, his method at first being to locate the bad spots in his society and fulminate against them, and later to minister to those who had become victims of the society.

Much of his first book, **Beyond the Palisade,** published when he was eighteen, concerns the natural New Zealand environment, the *pakeha* ancestors failing to make a home there, the land remaining a "cold threshold land" still overshadowed by "the weight of an earlier and prehistoric isolation." Brooding nature is felt as indifferent, or hostile, ground of man's suffering and defeat. This passive oppressive sense of it continues in **Blow, Winds of Fruitfulness** (1948),[7] but the landscape is more peopled and there are more localized, specifically human experiences. By 1951 Baxter felt clearly that animism is essential to the artist's view of the world, his greatest contribution being the linking of "submerged animism with our immediate affairs." A few years later, in **The Fire and the Anvil,** he declared it the poet's task to lay bare "the animistic pattern which underlies civilized activity" (p. 61).

Animism he took to be characteristic of the child and the primitive, and believed that poetry's vital force derived from rediscovering and revaluing childhood experience, which was at one with nature in "the paradise of childhood," Eden, the lost garden. In contrast, New Zealand's natural environment was experienced by the *pakeha* intruder as remote, impersonal, indifferent, an obstacle to his material possession of the land. As Charles Brasch once put it, "To New Zealanders, however, nature remains above all the enemy to be subjected by force,"[8] concluding that, "It is less nature than we ourselves, suffering from a form of *hubris* almost world-wide today, who have to be subdued and given a proper sense of our place in the scheme of things." This was Baxter's view also. He, more than any other New Zealand artist, in both his work and his life, laboured to achieve that "proper sense."

What brings about the change from the child's animism to adult *hubris* and anti-naturism? As Baxter sees it, there are two very different kinds of adult in modern society. These are *natural man* and *bourgeois man,* and each is incomplete. I do not know whether Baxter ever read Hesse, but the distinction he makes is similar to the Steppenwolf/Harry Haller division, although Baxter's "natural man" is a roisterer from the start. Most adults are bourgeois, conscious of a lost freedom, but not nearly conscious enough. Some passages of **The Fire and the Anvil** concern a third category, the intermediate stage between child and man, the adolescent, who "recognizes then for the first and often the last time that he is an individual, a free agent" (p. 52). His "huge discovery" is that freedom is our present condition. Most find the discovery too burdensome and

choose instead conformity, but for the few who do not the intermediate stage between child and man becomes a seed-time of creativity. Most turn away from "His flawed mirror," the natural world:

> hiding our souls' dullness
> From that too blinding glass: turn to the gentle
> dark of our human daydream, child and wife,
> Patience of stone and soil, the lawful city
> Where man may live and no wild trespass
> Of what's eternal shake his grave of time.[9]

Baxter is not totally unsympathetic to this retreat, but it would be a self-betrayal for the artist, or creative man, the one who has embraced his "huge discovery." His role is to provide a health-giving element of rebellion.

Natural man and bourgeois man is each a "half-man," and "the poet as family man" experiences a double portion of Original Sin, conscious of himself participating in each half, involved in a hopeless struggle to integrate the two halves, though he is instinctively nearer to natural man whom, in the fictitious guise of Timothy Harold Glass, Baxter describes as "the fallen Adam, who remembers, as if in a dream, his first state" (**Man on the Horse,** p. 20).

For the young Baxter a valued experience in this struggle, an embryonic hint of community, is that of friendship, in his own case with Denis Glover, Louis Johnson, Colin McCahon (painter of profound New Zealand "landscapes"), Bob Lowry, the Auckland printer—"Opening his heart like a great door / To poets, lovers, and the houseless poor"—or Fitz, the barman at the National Hotel, Wellington, subject of Baxter's great ballad, **"Lament for Barney Flanagan":**

> Flanagan got up on a Saturday morning,
> Pulled on his pants while the coffee was warming;
> He didn't remember the doctor's warning,
>   'Your heart's too big, Mr. Flanagan.'
>
> Barney Flanagan, sprung like a frog
> From a wet root in an Irish bog—
> May his soul escape from the tooth of the dog!
>   God have mercy on Flanagan.
>
> Barney Flanagan R.I.P.
> Rode to his grave on Hennessey's
> Like a bottle-cork boat in the Irish Sea.
>   The bell-boy rings for Flanagan.
>
> Barney Flanagan, ripe for a coffin,
> Eighteen stone and brandy-rotten,
> Patted the housemaid's velvet bottom—
>   'Oh, is it you, Mr. Flanagan?'
>
> The sky was bright as a new milk token.
> Bill the Bookie and Shellshock Hogan
> Waited outside for the pub to open—
>   'Good day, Mr. Flanagan.'

At noon he was drinking in the lounge bar corner
With a sergeant of police and a racehorse owner
When the Angel of Death looked over his shoulder—
   'Could you spare a moment, Flanagan?'

Oh the deck was cut; the bets were laid;
But the very last card that Barney played
Was the Deadman's Trump, the bullet of Spades—
   'Would you like more air, Mr. Flanagan?'

The priest came running but the priest came late
For Barney was banging at the Pearly Gate.
St. Peter said, 'Quiet! You'll have to wait
   For a hundred masses, Flanagan.'

The regular boys and the loud accountants
Left their nips and their seven-ounces
As chickens fly when the buzzard pounces—
   'Have you heard about old Flanagan?'

Cold in the parlour Flanagan lay
Like a bride at the end of her marriage day.
The Waterside Workers' Band will play
   A brass goodbye to Flanagan.

While publicans drink their profits still,
While lawyers flock to be in at the kill,
While Aussie barmen milk the till
   We will remember Flanagan.

For Barney had a send-off and no mistake.
He died like a man for his country's sake;
And the Governor-General came to his wake.
   Drink again to Flanagan!

Despise not, O Lord, the work of Thine own hands
And let light perpetual shine upon him.

III
The hope of the body was coherent love
As if the water sighing on the shores
Would penetrate the hardening muscle, loosen
Whatever had condemned itself in us:
Not the brown flagon, not the lips
Anonymously pressed in the dim light,
But a belief in bodily truth rising
From fountains of Bohemia and the night,

The truth behind the lie behind the truth
That Fairburn told us, gaunt
As the great moa, throwing the twisted blunt
Darts in a pub this side of Puhoi—'No
Words make up for what we had in youth.'
For what we did not have: that hunger caught
Each of us, and left us burnt,
Split open, grit-dry, sifting the ash of thought.

          (*Pig Island Letters,* p. 10)

Memory of Eden gives the natural man his consciousness of himself as manbeast, and his drive to rebel against the society which otherwise encourages all that is basest in humanity, particularly inertia and indifference. Acedia is the dread affliction to be fought. Baxter states the dichtomy in many poems, such as **"At Aramoana":**

    I turn also
to my dream, in nooks below
the sandhill cone, where Gea
speaks in parables of rock,

wordless, unconnected with
the acedia of a tribe
never *once* happy, never
at peace . . .

          (*Man on the Horse,* p. 24)

Bill Pearson, in a valedictory note just after Baxter's death, recalls a period of friendship in the late 1940s, when the two saw a great deal of each other: "We remembered *Darkness at Noon,* and read Graham Greene, talking in terms no longer in vogue of natural man and original sin and of eros and agape and caritas and the sin of sloth or despair to which he felt especially prone and called by its mediaeval name *accidie.*"[10] Since they name the central concerns of his life the terms never became unfashionable for Baxter. In his **"Prose Poems"** of 1952 we find him petitioning, "Acedia, my mother, when shall I be born? / A thousand times I have lain down in your black swamp, desireless;"[11] many years later he will declare, "it is worth remembering that the devil of acedia is the most subtle as well as the most brutle of the masters of Hell" (**Man on the Horse,** pp. 15-16).

Closely related to "custom," acedia is both cause and symptom of the individual's lack of a tribe. Always deeply conscious of the sufferings of the poor and all kinds of social derelicts, Baxter was yet highly sceptical of socialism and the welfare state as tribal matrixes. In answer to the question, "How does this acedia affect the fabric of our society and how does it perpetuate itself?" he would have replied that since New Zealand society (a variation of Western society) is materialistic, secular and hostile, the individual is without a tribe and consequently lacks life-sustaining *aroha* (love), but that the socialist state could not be the ultimate answer.

To Yevtushenko, Baxter wrote:

    Reading you
I remember our own strangled Revolution:
1935. The body of our Adam was dismembered
By statisticians.[12]

          ([*The Rock Woman*])

He grew up and came to maturity during a period when the New Zealand Labour Party first had clear Governmental power (1935-1949). To many, that period still seems the finest in New Zealand's brief history. Baxter's father, who has his own respected place in New Zealand consciousness as the country's best-known and most courageous pacifist, was a socialist sympathizer. Baxter himself, influenced deeply by his father, was yet sceptical of the socialists. They, as much as the National Party, in power for most of Baxter's adult life, seemed responsible for the fact that New Zealand society was in his eyes "an unjust, unhappy one where human activity is becoming progressively more meaningless" (*Trends,* p. 16).

This failure to implement the pioneering dream of establishing a Just City Baxter attributed chiefly to the "spirit of secularism" which he felt led to sterility and joylessness. In an unpublished passage of a lecture on "Poetry and Education" he defines the secular spirit as one which:

> has its own pseudo-sacred canons, derived in the main from the social sciences; which, though deeply hominist, is impatient of individual intuition, fantasy or eccentricity; which adheres vaguely to a notion of inevitable moral progress among mankind; which relies for its evidence on numerical calculations; which regards art as decoration or adornment for the museums and cemeteries of public culture; which regards the State, or agencies of the State, as an ultimate authority superior to tribes, families, religious organisations, or the individual conscience. Belief in it excludes belief in anything beyond it.[13]

Such a matrix led inevitably to sterility and joylessness and in such circumstances the poet's commitment is to speak out against centralization, depersonalization and mass conformity. Social criticism began to occupy a central place in Baxter's poetry in the mid-1950s; from that time on he employed the poem as a weapon in dealing with a variety of social problems.

Among his earliest socio-critical poems are those based on the *persona* of Harry Fat, a group in which he makes fine use of enviable skills as a balladist. One, **"A Rope for Harry Fat,"** is the most effective poem I have seen pleading for the abolition of capital punishment. Another, **"The Private Conference of Harry Fat,"** epitomizes the "virtues" of the secular welfare state—material possessions, anti-intellectualism, hidebound insularity, mindless patriotism and pseudo-democracy:

> Said Harry Fat, "I've read about
>   A doll who liked to sing,
> And when you tapped his wooden head
>   His little bell would ring.
> I like the kind of country where
>   The little man is king."
>
> "I quite agree," said Holyoake,
> "It is a splendid thing."
>
> Said Harry Fat, "I've heard it said
>   The Civil Service needs
> Protection from the Communists
>   Who sow rebellious seeds.
> The right man in the right place
>   Will pluck them out like weeds."
>
> "We must keep watch," said Holyoake,
> "On any man who reads."[14]

Sympathizing as he did with socialist attitudes to welfare economics, Baxter nonetheless felt strongly that state organization and administration of man's affairs led to dehumanization. Before him he had the example of individual protest by his father and brother, each of whom had been a conscientious objector (one in each of the World Wars). Archibald Baxter, the father, had been physically tortured:

> But he is old now in his apple garden
> And we have seen our strong Antaeus die
> In the glass castle of the bureaucracies
> Robbing our bread of salt. Shall Marx and Christ
> Share beds this side of Jordan? I set now
> Unwillingly these words down:
>
> *Political action in its source is pure,*
> *Human, direct, but in its civil function*
> *Becomes the jail it laboured to destroy.*

> (*Pig Island Letters,* p. 10)

Life in the land of "Rev. Fraser" and "Seddon and Savage, the socialist father" is a "civil calm" which "breeds inward poverty / That chafes for change." The crude impoverished texture of daily existence in the welfare state, is wittily, scorchingly captured in **"The Ballad of Calvary Street,"**

> Where two old souls go slowly mad,
> National Mum and Labour Dad.[15]

> ([*Howrah Bridge and Other Poems*])

having raised their typical family into the same environment, of bored habit and neurotic possibility which has nurtured them.

State secularism had removed even the need for surface religious observance, but it had failed to remove a restrictive puritan outlook which always seemed to Baxter the main enemy of community. Aspiring writers wishing for social success, he advised, had best ignore, "the doctrine of Original Sin, offensive to a society whose wealth and culture is founded on clean refrigeration."[16] In **"Elegy at the Year's End"** (and many other poems) secular puritanism is perceived as the force behind "what men hold in common, / The cross of custom, the marriage bed of knives":

> Spirit and flesh are sundered
> In the kingdom of no love. Our stunted passions bend
> To serve again familiar social devils.
>
> Brief is the visiting angel. In corridors of hunger
> Our lives entwined suffer the common ill:
> Living and dying, breathing and begetting,
> Meanwhile on maimed gravestones under the towering fennel
> Moves the bright lizard, sunloved, basking in
> The moment of animal joy.[17]

> ([*In Fires of No Return*])

Baxter's portrayals of "the kingdom of no love," many and penetrating as they are, range from the direct social consciousness of the early **"Mill Girl"** to such middle pieces as **"A Takapuna Businessman Considers his Son's Death in Korea,"** from the bawdy, cloacal wit of **"Ballad of Calvary Street"** (where "yin and yang will never meet") to the all-consuming desire for community in late works such as *Jerusalem Daybook*. At eighteen he had experienced "A sense of being at / The absolute unmoving hub," the cold hub of nothingness, in a country of emptiness, where (as he put it later in *The Fire and the Anvil*):

> Our pioneer fathers while laying waste the bushland wiped out also the spiritual flora and fauna of Polynesian animism, and replaced it, not, as we might think, with the highest humanist values and the seasonal ritual of the Church, but with Douglas Social Credit and the Women's Christian Temperance Union. In our arts and institutions we have cultivated a narrow ground—political loyalty; business acumen; an admiration (via the Tourist Bureau) of large scenery; the community of the hotel bar and playing field; the Puritan virtues, with their accompanying vices . . . but outside the cultivated area remain unexplored the creative powers of man.
>
> (pp. 30-31)

IV

Among institutions, the education system was most frequent butt of Baxter's sardonic wit. His work abounds in portraits of frustrated schoolmistresses, mad or malevolent headmasters, and the desolate prison-like atmosphere of schoolrooms or country schoolhouses. In a late poem, addressed to a child, he wrote:

> These poor words are my track to Heaven
> Because they are a gift of sorts
> And may blow in among your thoughts
> Like a fresh wind, where you lie bound
> In that grim dungeon underground,
> The spidery crypt our time has made
> To prove no shovel is a spade,—
> I mean, that graveyard of the nation,
> The oubliette of Education,
> Where God's voice calling finds no daughter
> And charity grows thin as water.[18]
>
> (["Letter to Eugene O'Sullivan"])

Autobiographical passages of *The Man on the Horse* reveal that from the first Baxter resisted formal education, intuitively realising that it is destructive of individual vital force, and that it interferes with "the discovery of a sacred pattern in natural events" (p. 132), replacing it with "the lens of abstract thought." This process reaches its culmination in universities with their chimerical exponents of "lean / Philosophies of When and If."

Baxter repeatedly excoriated the education system because it did not answer to the deepest needs of the individual, on the contrary tending to denature him. In ad-

dition, the system works to perpetuate New Zealand's subservient status, even to the extent of having the children sit in classrooms where "murals represented the English seasons, with lambs and green fields in April" (*Trends,* p. 6). In this ambience young New Zealanders are indoctrinated in "the Calvinist ethos," taught to subscribe to the work ethic, to distrust sex as evil and all kinds of pleasure as debilitating, and to be career-minded and goal-oriented. A typical parable in **"Notes on the Education of a New Zealand Poet,"** relates an encounter between an Education Department official and an old country Maori. Looking for the right road, coming to a fork, the official asks the old man the right direction.

"I don't know, boss," said the Maori, "Over the hill somewhere." Becoming exasperated, the official says:

> "Look . . . if I don't get to Auckland today I'll miss the beginning of a very important conference . . . This country needs education, and they need me to make the right plans for it . . . What's wrong with you, anyway? You're more lost than I am."
>
> "No, I'm not lost, boss. You see, I'm not going anywhere."
>
> (*Man on the Horse,* pp. 128-29)

Presumably the old Maori's "core of primitive experience" had never been threatened by the education system, a system from which people need to be rescued (Baxter admired A. S. Neill because he felt that Neill's approach was to allow children scope to de-educate, and thus free themselves). "What kind of education would I have preferred?" he asks. "Perhaps—till ten years old, on a farm in the South Island mountains or the Urewera country, learning to handle a horse or a dog or a gun; then, for a year or two, during puberty, in a Maori *pa*;[19] then perhaps on the coastal boats . . . But our firms and departments require literate peons for their dreary empires of economic liberalism. So we have universal and compulsory education" (*Man on the Horse,* p. 137).

V

Part of the inward poverty of New Zealand life is an uneasy awareness of "overseas." For perhaps the first hundred years of his country's existence as an independent state, the New Zealander thought of Britain as "Home." Since the generation of the 1930s writers have tried to alter this and have succeeded, but partly at the expense of feeding a neurotic insularity. When Allen Curnow resented and fulminated against "overseas experts" he had in mind Britain and, in particular, the tendency of British visitors to New Zealand to offer lofty advice; but throughout the 1950s and 1960s the fabric of New Zealand's daily life (not exempt from the fate of the rest of the Western world, in spite of its isolation) became progressively more Americanized. In particular, the intervention of the U.S.A. in Asian affairs doubly impinged on New Zealand where consciousness grows that Asia is not, after all, "the Far East," but is the Near North.

Baxter, who spent a period at school in Britain just before the Second World War and visited India at the end of the 1950s, saw himself positively as a New Zealander, committed fully to life in "Pig Island," but he always refused to be merely nationalistic or to pretend that the fate of New Zealand was somehow different from that of other small, relatively uninfluential Western countries.

The substratum of anti-American feeling which has existed in New Zealand throughout the post-1945 period, was given impetus by New Zealand's direct involvement in the Vietnam War. Particularly from early 1965 on, various writers such as Barry Mitcalfe, Hone Tuwhare and Baxter became immediately and directly involved in anti-war protest at a time when most of the population seemed to be in favour of troops being sent to Vietnam and when street protest was a very uncomfortable business. Baxter issued a number of anti-war ballads, such as **"A Bucket of Blood for a Dollar," "a death song for mr mouldybroke"** and **"The Green Beret."** While these poems are not among his best work they were the most effective *writer's* contribution to the campaign against New Zealand involvement and they show Baxter as an active "cell of good living" in the period just before his final total commitment to the ideal of community. At the time he said, "The economic liberal Caesar and the communist Caesar, for complex public reasons, are tearing the world apart; in order to die differently, I listen instead to the voice that speaks to me out of the ground. I will never take up arms for any Caesar" (*Man on the Horse,* p. 30). Throughout his career he many times characterized the poet's vocation as listening to the voice of the earth. His voice told him, increasingly, to act.

Baxter's New Zealandness was no simple thing. No isolationist, he rejected the 1930s mystique of Allen Curnow and M. H. Holcroft who had seen the country as an Island in Time. Baxter was committed to New Zealand first because he happened to be born there and to live there. He felt New Zealand's uniqueness, but was also aware that it shared most of its social problems with other Western countries. What, we may ask even so, of the particular sense of "being a New Zealander" manifested in the poetry? In one sense this is answered by the whole work, in another by his particular conception of "Pig Island"—realm of limited expectations, with its covenant of sheep, farm gear and sale day drink, always within the sound of the vast seas, reminder of human littleness in the scale of nature. "Love is not valued much in Pig Island," but rather

its domestic simulacrum—captive demanding wife, husband puzzled as to the origin of his vague frustrations, son and daughter growing in their parents' stunted image; yet for Baxter New Zealand was "the only world I love: / This wilderness." As he saw it, a large part of his vocation was to restore wilderness freedom to the Unjust City of contemporary society.

Throughout the years Baxter's social concern involved many aspects of life in society: drugs, sex, pornography and censorship, the submerged class system, bourgeois conformity. For most of his life there was nothing exceptional in his views on these matters. They were, if one may put it so, conventionally "open" and "liberal." The final years, however, witnessed a notable change, a deepening, which we may sum up with a statement from the concluding essay of his *Six Faces of Love*: "To love means in the long run to die for one's friends. There are no exceptions to that rule."[20] Baxter lived up to this discovery in his work at the Jerusalem Commune which he founded deep in the New Zealand country side, and in the doss-houses in Auckland and Wellington.

So far three collections of writing have come from this last period, *Jerusalem Sonnets* (1970),[21] *Jerusalem Daybook* (1971)[22] and *Autumn Testament* (1972).[23] The chief qualities manifest in these works are Christian destitution (poverty) and love. The work is totally possessed by Christian vision. Back at the beginning of his career, particularly when he was in his twenties, Baxter wrote poem after poem which displayed the rich rhetoric, the incandescence of a writer possessed by the word. His work had a bejewelled density which occasionally got the better of him and became windily splendiferous. *The Fallen Horse* (1953) is perhaps the finest early work, full of memorable images and a palpable sense of the human situation, but *Pig Island Letters* (1966) is a finer book because the rhetoric is under control, in the service of a vision, though a dour one, of a paradisal land ruined by grubbing materialism, stony lack-love and life-choking senseless puritanism.

In the last works, this world's harshness and suffering are acknowledged, accepted, included in a kind of amplitude Baxter had never before achieved. The self-indulgences of the early work are fully put away, and so is the neurotic note of *Pig Island Letters.* We receive instead a man at peace with himself, humble and yet sure. Poverty, hunger, hard-grubbing physical labour, loss of privacy, loss of almost all the "civilized" amenities, but the founding, and finding, of a community based on Christian love, The Word beyond the word—this was Baxter's final experience and ultimate achievement. The poems of that period come together as one masterly, flowing work from a whole spirit, a work from which it is difficult to excerpt, but perhaps the quality may be gauged from the last lines of **"Te**

Whiori O Te Kuri" ("The Dog's Tail"), which end
Autumn Testament:

> To go forward like a man in the dark
> Is the meaning of this dark vocation;
>
> So simple, tree, star, the bare cup of the hills,
> The lifelong grave of waiting
>
> As indeed it has to be. To ask for Jacob's ladder
> Would be to mistake oneself and the dark Master,
>
> Yet at times the road comes down to a place
> Where water runs and horses gallop
>
> Behind a hedge. There it is possible to sit,
> Light a cigarette, and rub
>
> Your bruised heels on the cold grass. Always because
> A man's body is a meeting house,
>
> Ribs, arms, for the tribe to gather under,
> And the heart must be their spring of water.
>
> (p. 52)

Notes

Although the bibliographical information in these notes is far from exhaustive, I have made them fairly extensive as a means of providing information about Baxter's work. Since he is one of the finest poets from any Commonwealth country, his work should be much better known. Its absence, for example, from the recent *Norton Anthology of Modern Poetry* edited by Ellman and O'clair is distressing, especially considering the dullness of much that is included.

1. James K. Baxter, *Recent Trends in New Zealand Poetry* (Christchurch: The Caxton Press, 1951), p. 16. Further page references to *Recent Trends* will be made parenthetically.

2. James K. Baxter, *The Man on the Horse* (Dunedin: University of Otago Press, 1967), p. 122. Further page references to *The Man on the Horse* will be made parenthetically.

3. James K. Baxter, *Pig Island Letters* (London: Oxford University Press, 1966). Further page references to *Pig Island Letters* will be made parenthetically.

4. James K. Baxter, *The Fire and the Anvil* (Wellington: New Zealand University Press, 1955), p. 48. Further page references to *The Fire and the Anvil* will be made parenthetically.

5. *pakeha* (Maori word), white New Zealander.

6. James K. Baxter, *Beyond the Palisade* (Christchurch: The Caxton Press, 1944), p. 7.

7. James K. Baxter, *Blow Winds of Fruitfulness* (Christchurch: The Caxton Press, 1948).

8. Charles Brasch, "Notes," *Landfall,* 4, No. 3 (September 1950), 186-87.

9. James K. Baxter, *The Fallen Horse* (Christchurch: The Caxton Press, 1953), p. 35.

10. Bill Pearson, "Two Personal Memories of James K. Baxter: I," *Islands,* 2, No. 1 (Autumn 1973), 3.

11. James K. Baxter, "Prose Poems," *Salient Literary Issue* (Wellington: Victoria University College, July 1952), p. 5.

12. James K. Baxter, *The Rock Woman* (London: Oxford University Press, 1970), p. 81.

13. Baxter papers, Hocken Library, Dunedin, New Zealand.

14. *New Zealand Poetry Yearbook: 1956-57,* 6 (Christchurch: The Pegasus Press, 1958), pp. 18-19.

15. James K. Baxter, *Howrah Bridge and Other Poems* (London: Oxford University Press, 1961), p. 53.

16. *New Zealand Poetry Year Book: 1954,* 4 (Christchurch: The Pegasus Press, 1955), p. 24.

17. James K. Baxter, *In Fires of No Return* (London: Oxford University Press, 1958), p. 39.

18. James K. Baxter, "Letter to Eugene O'Sullivan," *Poetry New Zealand,* 1 (Christchurch: The Pegasus Press, 1971), p. 26.

19. *pa* (Maori word), Maori village.

20. James K. Baxter, *Six Faces of Love* (New Zealand: Futuna Press, 1972), n.p.

21. James K. Baxter, *Jerusalem Sonnets* (Dunedin: University of Otago Bibliography Room, 1970).

22. James K. Baxter, *Jerusalem Daybook* (Wellington: Price Milburn, 1971).

23. James K. Baxter, *Autumn Testament* (Wellington: Price Milburn, 1972). Further page references to *Autumn Testament* will be made parenthetically.

Howard McNaughton (essay date June 1982)

SOURCE: McNaughton, Howard. Introduction to *Collected Plays of James K. Baxter,* by James K. Baxter, edited by Howard McNaughton, pp. vii-xvi. Auckland, New Zealand: Oxford University Press, 1982.

[*In the following essay, published as his introduction to the* Collected Plays of James K. Baxter *and dated June 1982, McNaughton discusses key themes in Baxter's plays, stating that the "uniqueness of Baxter's drama derives partly from the lack of any authoritative local tradition: it presents a poet evolving for himself a medium to express material that was not tractable in poetic form."*]

In 1948 the twenty-two-year-old James K. Baxter made his first public appearance as an actor in a minor role in Sartre's *The Flies* in Christchurch; Ngaio Marsh had initiated the production, but was overseas by the time it opened. In the same year Baxter attended the première of Allen Curnow's *The Axe,* a verse play on a Polynesian historical subject, and he promptly wrote to his mother that he had started his own first play. Eight years, however, passed before the completion of *Jack Winter's Dream,* a play for radio, and eleven years before his emergence as a stage playwright with *The Wide Open Cage* in 1959. During the following ten years he wrote more than twenty plays, and then he abruptly stopped: from the start of his period at Jerusalem on the Wanganui River in 1969 until his death in 1972, he showed little interest in revising his plays for publication or for professional production in the new community theatres which were appearing throughout the country. Wanganui, just down the river from Jerusalem, had a resident professional theatre from 1970; but Baxter wrote in *Jerusalem Sonnets* that 'The bright coat of art He has taken away from me. . . .'[1] [*Collected Poems*]

The journalistic descriptions of Baxter's final years of Franciscan poverty and solitude at Jerusalem overlooked the very similar circumstances of Baxter's boyhood at Brighton, a coastal township twelve miles south of Dunedin. The minimal community life offered by Brighton's school, post office, and four shops fell far short of anything approaching theatrical activity; adults had to travel almost to Dunedin to find a pub, and the schoolboy Baxter was similarly isolated from the city's cultural and recreational life, such as it then was. The solitude of Brighton stimulated introspective poetry, and retarded Baxter's discovery of the process of artistic collaboration that is fundamental to theatre.

As a playwright, as in other aspects of his life, Baxter was an individualist. He did not participate in the movement towards the new community theatres, just as, at the start of his writing career, he praised—but did not contribute to—the highly literary theatre of Ngaio Marsh and Allen Curnow. However, as a negative example, Curnow's *The Axe* preoccupied Baxter in the years before the completion of his own first play, and ultimately led to the consolidation of his own dramaturgic theories. A 1967 radio talk reasserted opinions which Baxter had been voicing since the early 1950s:

> I recall how in my early twenties I attended a Christchurch performance of Allen Curnow's verse drama, *The Axe.* To hear the poetry spoken was in itself an absorbing experience. I was sitting at the back with Denis Glover and had the advantage of being somewhat drunk. There were occasions when it seemed that spirits might indeed ascend from the floorboards or descend from the ceiling; yet, taking into full account the nobility of Curnow's conception and the intricate skill of his verse, I still had a mainly subconscious nagging feeling—'this is fine, but it's not quite drama; something has got clogged in the works. . . .' There are several factors (other than my drunkenness) which may have accounted for this negative impression. The first factor is . . . the tendency of poets to conceive of a given speech as a total poem, not, as it were, as a single unit in the total dramatic poem which is the play.[2]

([**"Some Possibilities for New Zealand Drama"**])

Baxter often spoke of his poetry in dramatic terms. In a late interview with J. E. Weir, he emphasized that 'the "I" of the poem is not the autobiographical "I", it is a dramatic "I". The poem is a dramatic device which one uses.' Agreeing with Weir that there might be 'ten voices' within the same poem, he said that some of his poems reflect 'the rather multiple world of experience. Of course there are contradictions—that is the drama. Men just live in contradictions—that's the nature of man.'[3]

Some of Baxter's most successful plays are simple formalizations of this principle. *The Day that Flanagan Died* (1967) is the most obvious example, projecting the ballad **'Lament for Barney Flanagan'** by giving each element of the 'multiple world of experience' a discrete voice. Hal Smith has astutely pointed out the ritualistic folk ballad element in *The Devil and Mr Mulcahy* (1967).[4] Of *The Band Rotunda* (1967) Baxter insisted that 'I am not Concrete Grady, though Concrete Grady is one of my secret selves',[5] and he had already developed the character in **'The Ballad of Grady's Dream'** and other poems. He credited Patric Carey with showing him (during his period at Dunedin's Globe Theatre, 1966-68) that a play was 'a metaphoric structure in which the multiple statements of the characters corresponded to the accumulated images of a poem',[6] but even his first play *Jack Winter's Dream* (1956) had expanded a ballad structure in a similar way.[7] Baxter believed that his first stage play, *The Wide Open Cage* (1959), was impeded by the same defect as Curnow's *The Axe* because the priest articulated an authorial viewpoint: 'Thus the play was stalled nearly ever time the priest spoke. At best I had tried to give him poems to speak.'[8] The play's production history has proved him wrong, but the perils of self-consciously 'poetic' drama continued to haunt him. His only attempt at verse drama was the brief and unproduced *Requiem for Sebastian,* and he once admitted that 'being by habit a poet, I have often wished one could write good plays in verse. Yet verse seems to be a dead language in our theatre. . . . The later plays of T. S. Eliot may seem an exception; but I suggest that they contain in fact no language of poetry, but a rhythmical bureaucratic prose set out as verse.'[9] [**"Some Notes on Drama"**]

Baxter never attempted historical drama, and this in itself is indicative of his disinclination towards autonomous characterization. His need to see his characters as simplified elements of his own identity explains why his female characters are rarely developed much beyond crude stereotypes; he told Weir that in one poem the figure of Mother Mary Joseph Aubert 'would represent part of my own mind—perhaps the rather housewife figure of the Church'. Richard Campion, directing a notable revival of *The Wide Open Cage* at Unity Theatre, Wellington, in 1973, prefaced the play with a silent, dimly-lit scene in which the naked girl moved round Jack Skully's bedroom; one effect of this was frankly to establish the character as little more than a sexual trophy from the start.

Though there is no evidence of direct influence, such interplay of secret selves is close to the technique of hallucinatory dramaturgy outlined by Strindberg in his preface to *A Dream Play* (1901). **The First Wife** (1966) shows its simplest form: the authorial central character is jolted out of comfortable domestic realism into a dream world in which fragments of his own identity are in conflict. Since these fragments are loosely autobiographical, they occasionally also appear in Baxter's poems and prose writings: the Ancestor of the play is familiar from the essay **'Conversation with an Ancestor',**[10] [*The Man on the Horse*] and the whole action of the play is parallelled in the poetic sequence **'The Waves',** also set at Brighton Bay. The same hallucinatory method is given a further degree of complication in **Jack Winter's Dream** where the ancestral figure is in turn fragmented into a period melodrama, and the alcoholic dreamer is annihilated by the intensity of his vision. Such plays inevitably end with a suggestion of the narrative energy arbitrarily exhausting itself; the same was the case with Strindberg's dream plays.

For the poet who has little contact with the local theatre, radio is a dramatic medium with obvious attractions. The action need not be fully realized in concrete terms, there is accommodation for the Protean view of characterization which Baxter favoured, and the dream may be gently dissolved into music. However, the translation of these methods on to the stage was problematic; the première of **The Wide Open Cage** at Unity Theatre in 1959 was widely greeted as a major event in the history of the New Zealand stage, but several literary critics had strong reservations about the script. Though mistakenly viewing the play in realist terms, J. G. A. Pocock offered a cogent analysis:

> The trouble, it seems to me, lies in the fact that these are for the most part solitary vices, sins committed against oneself. . . . Their effect is to isolate human beings in the solitariness of their guilt, and if a play is written in the realist and not the poetic convention, it has to be about the web of relationships formed by a number of human beings acting on each other. Mr Bax-

ter's play seems to me deficient in its web of relationships. He has not written it about a number of people isolated by their guilts and struggling to reach one another; his characters are much too vital and articulate for that, and bed and bottle bring them together fast enough. But their very vitality seems to underline the very limited extent to which he has related them to one another, and for this his limited and rather melodramatically conceived range of sins appears to me responsible. These people, one feels, should be capable of hurting and helping each other in a greater variety of ways. . . . Guilt and grace, consequently, operate a little mechanically, rather irrespectively of who and what the people are.[11]

James Bertram, writing about the production, admitted that he was offended by the presentation of a Catholic confession on stage, but conceded that the play 'has the disturbing and perhaps valuable quality of exposing areas of experience most New Zealanders prefer to conceal, if they cannot evade them'. It was customary for premières of New Zealand plays at Unity Theatre to be followed by formal critical discussion in the theatre. Bertram has given an account of his own reaction:

> I suggested that the play lacked unity of action: the plot was episodic, there was not enough inevitability about its tragic outcome. While some of the characters were really interesting, Skully . . . did not develop, and did not act but was acted upon; Hogan was pasteboard. . . . The language had eloquence; but since the basic speech was New Zealand colloquial, deliberately lowered in tone, the injection of poetry in a number of carefully calculated images had a somewhat artificial effect. . . . Above all, for a tragi-comic 'slice of life' of this kind, one was never made aware of any social or accumulated pressure behind the situation: all the tension and conflict had to be built up from within the characters themselves, in their casual relationships. . . . Mr Baxter himself indicated that he had rejected the idea of a neat plot in favour of a scheme—satisfying to him poetically—of the eclipse of the forces of light by the forces of darkness; that his approach was psychological rather than sociological. . . .[12]

Though voicing scorn for his critics,[13] Baxter did attempt a more socially complex web of relationships in his next play, **Three Women and the Sea** (1961); it was an unmitigated failure, and from it he moved into the farcical revue of **The Spots of the Leopard,** written in 1962 but unproduced until 1967 when, surprisingly in view of its frivolous nature, it was premièred almost simultaneously in Wellington and New York. Nevertheless, both Pocock and Bertram had focused on issues which were to be important to Baxter's development as a dramatist: the treatment of 'solitary vices' and the use of 'deliberately lowered' colloquial language.

In an almost literal sense, 'sins committed against oneself' meant alcoholism to Baxter, and the inevitable 'solitariness' of this 'guilt' is frankly acknowledged in the title metaphor of **The Wide Open Cage**. Baxter stopped drinking in 1958, and, with a few notable exceptions, his later poems make few references to his period of dependence. In his plays, however, drunkenness is a theme that is continually insistent: Winter, Skully, Brandywine, Flanagan, and the inhabitants of the band rotunda are all alcoholics, the figure of Dionysus dominates *Mr O'Dwyer's Dancing Party* (1969), and there are numerous drunks in the other plays. As a dramaturgic determinant, alcoholism illustrates particularly clearly the process of autobiographical self-dissection in Baxter's plays and, in the theatre, serves as a catalyst for the interplay of secret selves. The process is not glamorized, it achieves no overt moment of truth, and its only end is solipsism; yet the value that is to be placed on the experience is ambiguous. George Steiner's famous assertion that 'In tragedy, there are no temporal remedies'[14] is pertinent here: although Baxter believed that only divine intervention could relieve the alcoholic, audiences might nevertheless prefer to believe in temporal remedies, and the tone of the plays in production has often allowed this attitude to be indulged. Baxter certainly saw some conditions, such as whoredom, as ugly; the 'human gumboot' self-image is one of the most poignant details in *The Wide Open Cage.* In production, a similar ugliness must surround the theme of alcoholism if enough fear or pity is to be generated to make sense of a central dilemma such as Jack Skully's. Directors have often neglected this repulsive facet of the theme in favour of a more positive quality, the garrulousness that comes with drunkenness. In the pastoral writings which Baxter contributed to the Catholic magazine *New Zealand Tablet* in 1968, he wrote that 'The imagination of nearly all alcoholics is over-active' and that the effect of treating 'the chronically over-sensitive alcoholic' as a 'moral idiot' is 'invariably to drive him deeper into himself'.[15] [*The Flowering Cross*] This is precisely the situation between Snowy Lindsay and the Salvationist at the end of the first act of *The Band Rotunda*; the formulaic preaching of 'vigorous folk Christianity' is totally intolerant of Snowy's heterodoxy, but so too is an audience which ignores the moral urgency latent in the alcoholic rhetoric. The death of Jock Ballantyne, trapped between conflicting biological and moral imperatives, has a complexity similar to that of Ibsen's Osvald Alving. There is no obvious remedy because of the complexity of the characters' needs; moral over-sensitivity, rather than moral idiocy, leads to the solitude of Baxter's alcoholic characters.

Bertram's observation of Baxter's use of 'deliberately lowered' language suggests that Baxter was avoiding 'poetic' abstruseness and seeking a vehicle for the ugliness of his subject-matter. In this, he might have been guided by Artaud's plea for an anti-literary 'theatre of cruelty' in his essay 'No More Masterpieces'.[16] In 1967, Baxter outlined his own principles of theatre language in *Act* magazine:

the two poles of modern literary language are the deadpan banalities of our bureaucracies (invaluable for satiric use) and the explosive language of the street and pubs and the farms and the wharves. Together they can make a dramatic idiom; but that idiom will necessarily be prose. . . . If the state of our language is as I suppose, then there are two corollaries that follow from it. The first would be that any dramatist who tries seriously to work within the conventions of radio and television . . . will imprison himself within the straitjacket of bureaucratic language; and when he tries to construct a 'poetic' or metaphoric alternative, he will find that his images are like cut flowers, that he is constructing only a bogus poetry—that is, unless his theme is death and the void itself, when he may achieve a razor-edge metaphysical sharpness in the manner of the script of a Hitchcock film. The aesthetics of bureaucracy are the aesthetics of nihilism. Words, like people, are told what to do by the State. The second corollary would be that the theatre should and must offer its stages to playwrights who use street language, and put aside its remnants of middle-class decorum. . . .[17]

Artaud, in blaming 'the idolatry of fixed masterpieces which is one of the aspects of bourgeois conformism', had asserted that 'it is not upon the stage that the true is to be sought nowadays, but in the street; and if the crowd in the street is offered an occasion to show its human dignity, it will always do so'.[18] Baxter, independently reaching a similar conclusion, should not have been surprised that the New Zealand community theatres, largely dependent on middle-class audiences, should be slow to act on his suggestion. Various movements towards a New Zealand working-class or street theatre in the 1970s had no lasting success, and Baxter's own defeat of 'middle-class decorum' was achieved not in the theatre but at Jerusalem.

Whereas Baxter's alcoholic plays are mainly written in street language, the language of the bureaucracies is generally mobilized only incidentally in other plays, for satire or caricature. Inevitably, some aspects of his dramaturgy remained undeveloped. While he learned subtleties of tragic structure and the techniques of ideological conflict in drama, his sense of comic strategy often seemed crude, and the influence of student revue slapstick may be detected even in his last plays. The *naiveté* of vaudeville was symptomatic of the wider New Zealand theatre in the 1960s, when even Wellington's Downstage Theatre (founded 1964), the first 'community theatre', often resorted to semi-improvised revue methods just to ensure that the vitality at the core of the theatre did not lapse. Baxter's most sustained revue writing, in *The Spots of the Leopard* (1962) and *The Runaway Wife* (1967), is omitted from this collection, but the style recurs in *The Bureaucrat* (1967), in which an adaptation of the Prometheus story serves as an energetic satire on the School Publications branch of the Department of Education. Baxter reasserted his opinions on dramatic language in his introduction to *The Band Rotunda,* but it is in his treatment of Theseus, the Commissar, in *The Temptations of Oedipus* that the language of the bureaucracies is most effectively deployed; beneath the veneer of myth, readers may detect in Theseus the figure of Mouldybroke, familiar from several of Baxter's poems as well as from *The Runaway Wife.*

The sporadic nature of Baxter's dramatic output was largely because of his intermittent contact with Richard Campion, Patric Carey, and the N.Z.B.C. producers: 'My relation to the theatre has been a sporadic liaison rather than a marriage. I had felt that to know "everything" about the theatre . . . might lead me into a world of mirrors.'[19] Patric Carey and the Globe Theatre environment taught Baxter the refinement of Greek principles of dramaturgy, Richard Campion's workshop approach to *The Wide Open Cage* in Wellington in 1959 led to the social plays set in an alcoholic microcosm, and the N.Z.B.C. educated him in radio techniques, eliciting the very personal dream plays which in places may accommodate poetry. Without question, Baxter was fortunate in the directors and producers he worked with; in the period of his dramatic writing, between 1956 and 1969, the New Zealand theatre was in a state of depression, and Campion and Carey heroically mounted his plays while fighting formidable campaigns on both artistic and economic fronts.

The uniqueness of Baxter's drama derives partly from the lack of any authoritative local tradition: it presents a poet evolving for himself a medium to express material that was not tractable in poetic form. It has become almost customary to regret that Baxter's relatively unpolished plays bear little stylistic affinity to his meticulously crafted poetry: rather than revise a play for revival, he generally preferred to draft a new play. But Baxter never stopped being a poet; he wrote poetry while he was working on plays, and seems never to have hesitated about the choice of genre. When the same character occurs in both poetry and drama, quite different facets of that character are generally explored; Vincent O'Sullivan's explication of the Concrete Grady of the poems reveals a very different figure from the play.[20] Baxter's view of the discrete territories of poetry and drama is clearly established in two quotations. In *Pig Island Letters* (1966), he wrote: 'The poem is / A plank laid over the lion's den.'[21] In his 1967 radio talk, **'Some Possibilities for New Zealand Drama'**, he said:

> Human stupidity, not divine illumination, is the communal foundation of dramatic art. If man's intellect were not partially blinded, he would reject the spectacle of the theatre, since no illusion could satisfy a mind already in possession of the truth; if man's will were not weak and his passions disordered, the main material of the dramatist would be lacking. It is precisely the element of doubt and possibility, both moral and intellectual, which enables the dramatist to 'corrupt' his audience with illusions which they find more satisfying than a void reality.[22]

Baxter's plays take their audiences into the lion's den itself, often with no obvious 'plank' for escape. The situation is realized almost literally in his dramatic reshaping of the Old Testament story of Daniel, *Mr Brandywine Chooses a Gravestone* (1966), but the chaotic den of self-dissection is the arena for most of his major plays. Baxter's characters are all functions of 'human stupidity', which may imply the bewildered stupor of a victim of society to whom all action seems pointless. In his last plays, such as *The Temptations of Oedipus* and *The Starlight in Your Eyes,* the central characters are blind or crippled, creating in production an extraordinarily intense atmosphere of a tactile world on stage; Patric Carey's design methods at the Globe Theatre exploited this dimension particularly well, and Baxter's mimes, used as preludes to the plays, served as logical complements to them, heightening sensory awareness by a process of privation.[23] Even Baxter's ostensibly astute Greek characters are revealed as groping clumsily towards an imagined truth, as dependent on the cage of their rationalization as Jack Skully is in *The Wide Open Cage*; Odysseus might speak for all of Baxter's characters, Greeks and drunks, when at the end of *The Sore-Footed Man* he says, 'But I didn't know, and that's the knife blade I walk on; darkness on each side of me and a blade of fear in the centre.' He is, of course, reiterating Baxter's assertion that in the theatre 'man's intellect' is 'partially blinded', but the main theatrical impact comes not from his verbalization but from his physical behaviour; he has just illustrated the 'stupidity' principle by risking all his strategic advantage in turning his back on the bow of Hercules and walking off stage away from the unseen weapon.

There can be little doubt that Baxter would have been ill at ease in the relatively sophisticated New Zealand community theatres of the 1970s, when Campion and Carey, his most sympathetic directors, moved into semi-retirement. Baxter's defiance of everything that he recognized as élitist meant that his commitment to a pioneering theatre waned once that theatre became institutionalized. His plays epitomize what Australian drama nostalgically recalls as its 'larrikin' phase.

This volume contains all of Baxter's plays which have been successfully produced, and a few shorter pieces which have been undeservedly neglected. The omissions are few and easily justified. Baxter was quick to recognize that the abortive realism of *Three Women and the Sea* was a mistake, and critics were unanimous in condemning the shapeless vaudeville of *The Spots of the Leopard* and *The Runaway Wife,* both of them justifiably rejected by Patric Carey. A few shorter pieces from the early 1960s are omitted because Baxter later incorporated elements from them in longer plays.

Baxter's plays were first drafted in longhand in quarto exercise books, now held in the Hocken Library, Dunedin; the only plays for which no such manuscripts have been sighted are *Jack Winter's Dream, The Wide Open Cage* and *Requiem for Sebastian.* Up to five further drafts were then typed; at least some of these were typed not by Baxter but by production assistants, with Baxter's idiosyncratic handwriting clearly discernible in corrections. Generally, the dialogue shows little variation from the first draft, with the bulk of revision being concentrated on stage directions, no doubt often on the advice of directors. As well as the mimes, six of Baxter's plays have been previously published: *Jack Winter's Dream, The Wide Open Cage, The Devil and Mr Mulcahy, The Band Rotunda, The Sore-Footed Man* and *The Temptations of Oedipus.* Since Baxter himself supervised their publication, they are here reprinted with only obvious mistakes corrected. The only text presenting substantial problems is *The Day that Flanagan Died*: it is uncertain whether Baxter preferred the ballad proper to come at the beginning (as in his manuscript) or at the end (as in the Globe version), or, possibly, in both positions (as indicated in this text).

Baxter's approval for my research on his plays was given shortly before his death, and Mrs Jacquie Baxter has subsequently given great encouragement, allowing unrestricted access to the manuscripts. Patric Carey (formerly of the Globe Theatre, Dunedin) and Michael Hitchings (of the Hocken Library, Dunedin) were both generous in their assistance. Father John Weir gave stimulus to the work, and the University Grants Committee supported the early research financially. In checking, collating, and general advice, my wife Rosemary McNaughton has given invaluable assistance.

Notes

For criticism within a broader perspective, see *James K. Baxter* by Charles Doyle (Boston: Twayne, 1976), and *New Zealand Drama* by Howard McNaughton (Boston: Twayne, 1981). The standard bibliographical checklist is *A Preliminary Bibliography of Works by and Works about James K. Baxter* by J. E. Weir and Barbara A. Lyon (Christchurch: University of Canterbury, 1979).

1. Baxter, *Collected Poems* (Wellington: Oxford, 1979), p. 473.

2. 'Some Possibilities for New Zealand Drama'. Typescript in Hocken Library, Dunedin, extracts in *James K. Baxter as Critic* ed. Frank McKay (Auckland: Heinemann, 1978).

3. *Landfall* 28.3 (1974), pp. 241-50.

4. 'Baxter's Theatre, a critical appraisal,' by Hal Smith, programme note at the James K. Baxter Play Festival at Victoria University, Wellington, in June 1973. An earlier interpretation is contained in 'James K. Baxter: the Poet as Playwright,' by Harold Smith, *Landfall* 22.1 (1968), pp. 56-62.

5. 'Some Possibilities for New Zealand Drama', p. 11.

6. Baxter's Introduction to *The Sore-Footed Man* and *The Temptations of Oedipus* (Auckland: Heinemann, 1971), p. vii.

7. 'From Animism to Expressionism in the Early James K. Baxter' by Howard McNaughton, *Kunapipi* (1980) argues a source for *Jack Winter's Dream* in Alistair Campbell's poem 'Hut near Desolated Pines'.

8. 'Some Possibilites for New Zealand Drama', p. 3.

9. Baxter, 'Some Notes on Drama', *Act* 3 (1967), p. 20.

10. Baxter, *The Man on the Horse* (Dunedin: University of Otago Press, 1967) pp. 11-35.

11. J. G. A. Pocock, review of *Two Plays, Landfall* 14.2 (1960), p. 199.

12. James Bertram, 'The Wide Open Cage', *Landfall* 14.1 (1960), p. 84.

13. The opinion is reiterated vehemently in 'Some Possibilities for New Zealand Drama'.

14. George Steiner, *The Death of Tragedy* (London: Faber, 1961), p. 291.

15. Baxter, *The Flowering Cross* (Dunedin: *New Zealand Tablet,* 1969), pp. 20-21.

16. Artaud, *The Theatre and Its Double* (New York: Grove Press, 1958), pp. 74-83.

17. Baxter, 'Some Notes on Drama', *Act* 3 (1967), pp. 20-21.

18. Artaud, *The Theatre and Its Double,* p. 76.

19. Baxter, 'Some Notes on Drama', *Act* 3 (1967), p. 21.

20. Vincent O'Sullivan, *James K. Baxter* (Wellington: Oxford, 1976), pp. 46-8.

21. Baxter, *Collected Poems,* p. 282.

22. 'Some Possibilities for New Zealand Drama', p. 11.

23. Alternative interpretations are in 'Three Mimes,' by Marilyn Parker, *Landfall* 22.1 (1968), pp. 63-65, and in 'Oedipus at Dunedin,' by O. E. Middleton, *Landfall* 24.2 (1970), pp. 171-73.

Trevor James (essay date autumn 1983)

SOURCE: James, Trevor. "Poetry in the Labyrinth: The Poetry of James K. Baxter." *World Literature Written in English* 22, no. 2 (autumn 1983): 342-51.

[*In the following essay, James argues that all of Baxter's work is informed by a "symmetrical" and "consistent" pattern, based on "the imagery of the circle and its centre," which the critic claims shaped his sense of "order in the world" and actually preceded his use of myth in his writings.*]

There is an extraordinary quality about James K. Baxter's poetry which has always fascinated me. I can think of no other poet—except perhaps for John Donne—who has so intuitive a grasp of the bonds between flesh and spirit, so strong a sense of a symmetry to the sum, if not the parts, of reality. Throughout his poetry there is a consistent thread of thought which connects one poem with another although they may be, and usually are, quite independent creations. The evolution of this symmetrical image in his poetry reflects his sense of a shaping order in the world which enabled him to believe that life was intelligible, however painful, that this was cosmos and not chaos.

The use of versions of a symmetrical pattern to suggest what was most real occurs everywhere in Baxter's work. The cluster of images that relate to this pattern is so pervasive that I think it forms a fundamental concept which underlies all Baxter's work. Much has been made of Baxter's use of myth and of his sense of the Fall and the Incarnation, but all such techniques and concepts are anteceded by his intuitive sense of a shape to reality which encompassed everything. I think it was subsequently that he found myths and doctrines which, by their very nature, expressed aspects of this very primitive concept, and he used or adapted them accordingly.

Before tracing the evolving sophistication of a consistent pattern, a few examples can show how the threads of an idea were woven together. In 1965, Baxter concluded some observations on his poetry with these remarks:

> There is a spot in the arena to which the fighting bull returns (a different spot for each bull) and from which he comes out more assured and formidable. For me it was once the beaches of the place I grew up in; then the pub; and latterly perhaps the hour of death which one looks forward to. If this spot is correctly located one can generally go on writing.[1]

Certainly Baxter uses the image of the bullfighter in at least one poem, but the symmetry of the arena and the spot to which the bull returns belong to the imagery of the circle and its centre. The bond between this imagery and the images and concerns of the quest of Theseus in the labyrinth for the Minotaur at its centre is quite obvious. What is important is the way the sense of symmetrical form and a centre of absolute reality is common to both.

In 1946, C. Day Lewis concluded the Clark Lectures on poetry at Trinity College, Cambridge, with a stirring call to those poets who were yet to fulfil their vocation. In the course of that final lecture, he described the process of poetic creation through a memorable image:

> . . . had I the ear of wombèd poets, I would say to them something like this. You will step more confidently perhaps through a region that was dark and difficult to us. But as you explore deeper into the labyrinth of man's mind, do not lose hold of the clue which will lead you back to light. Every poem is created by a journey through darkness and a return to light, the journey from light back to light which cannot be made except through darkness, and the finished poem is the image of that journey. In the poem, you are reborn; it is a re-creation, a resurrection of the body in which your experience is given blood and flesh and bone: and no man, touched by that poem, will be quite the same man thereafter, so infectious, so satisfactory are the joys that spring from the poem's operative truth. But, because a poem can so work upon men's hearts, you have an obligation to men and to the humankind within yourself. You may sing to yourself alone, but you cannot sing for yourself alone. The poet is the only child of solitude. He should guard and cultivate his solitude. But, as he goes about his business there, he must not forget his other obligation: as he explores the labyrinth, he must not lose hold of the clue.[2]

The lectures were published and widely available in 1947. While I have no positive evidence, I am almost certain that Baxter read these words soon after their publication and that they made a deep and lasting impression at the formative stage in his development as a poet. Each of the four principal aspects of C. Day Lewis' remarks have a special relevance to Baxter's work. First, the labyrinth and its centre: the labyrinth guards a centre of ultimate reality, and the journey through it involves hardships during which the questor may get lost or be destroyed. Second, the rebirth image for the poetic process: it is a symmetrical process that is vivid and entirely positive in this context, but as a pattern in another context it is a closed cycle which does not allow for progress. Third, the way through the labyrinth involves using clues, and here the principal aid is the skein of thread given to Theseus by Ariadne. To refer to the skein or a related image evokes the labyrinth and the journey to a centre. Finally, C. Day Lewis demands the poet exercise a social responsibility, but I don't intend to consider this last feature, although Baxter would have been fully in agreement.

To see how eagerly Baxter appropriated—or developed—a cyclical view of the poet's task one needs to read **"The Cave,"** which was written in 1948, the year after the Clark Lectures were published.

> In a hollow of the fields, where one would least expect it,
> Stark and suddenly this limestone buttress;
> A tree whose roots are bound about the stones,
> Broad-leaved, hides well that crevice at the base
> That leads, one guesses, to the sunless kingdom
> Where souls endure the ache of Proserpine.
>
> Entering where no man it seemed
> Had come before, I found a rivulet

Beyond the rock door running in the dark.
Where it sprang from in the heart of the hill
No one could tell: alone
It ran like Time there in the dank silence.

I spoke once and my voice resounded
Among the many pillars. Further in
Were bones of sheep that strayed and died
In nether darkness, brown and water-worn.
The smell of earth was like a secret language
That dead men speak and we have long forgotten.

The whole weight of the hill hung over me.
Gladly I would have stayed there and been hidden
From every beast that moves beneath the sun,
From age's enmity and love's contagion:
But turned and climbed back to the barrier,
Pressed through and came to dazzling daylight out.[3]

([*Collected Poems*])

Certainly there is nothing slavishly derivative in this; the ideas are well assimilated. The idea of the labyrinth is not developed, but the symmetry of the poet's journey is precisely as C. Day Lewis had described it. The whole movement of the poem is from light to light through the darkness of the cave, which is the place of the word-birth where the poet learns an archaic wisdom, "a secret language / That dead men speak and we have long forgotten." The symmetry imposed upon the poet's journey is obvious, and this poem provides the first published evidence within Baxter's poetry of an attempt to image the process of making a poem.

Baxter's earliest poems reflect the desire for symmetry. When he was about sixteen, he composed **"Song of the Sea-Nymphs at the Death of Icarus,"** in which Icarus denotes a melancholic adolescent view of "youth / Forever living and forever slain" (p. 6). The following year, in **"O wind blowing,"** he attempted to unite himself with the patterns of the creation, ebb and flow, the movement of the seasons, death and rebirth. Yet the claim of that poem, "No barren cycle is this" (p. 10) rings a little hollow. Baxter seems to have quickly sensed that the cycle is deficient, that despite an attractive symmetry it allows for no substantial progress. From 1943 onwards, the various images of cyclical repetition express what is wrong with man's condition: "the wheel of custom," "the mill of gossip," "a cage, a treadmill motion," "a Persian wheel." In **"Rocket Show,"** Baxter plainly establishes the connection between his view of life and the force of a cyclical pattern: "I thought of our strange lives, the grinding cycle / Of death and renewal come to full circle" (p. 81). The much anthologized poem **"The Homecoming"** domesticates this image of bondage with appalling economy— "the quiet maelstrom spinning / In the circle of their days" (p. 121).

If C. Day Lewis helped Baxter to find in the image of the labyrinth a symmetry with a purposeful movement, it would explain how Baxter's use of the image evolved.

Before 1948, Baxter had only used the maze or labyrinth as a variation on the bondage of the cycle: the tenor of each was concerned with being trapped or lost. In the very early poems, there was a tendency for the maze to be implied rather than overt—as in **"Christmas Poem"**:

Pray for the children lost
Within a haunted forest
No path for turning back.

(p. 37)

The finely structured poem **"The Bay"** echoes the idea of the maze with the lament for "How many roads we take that lead to Nowhere" (p. 44). But when Baxter correlates specific images with the motifs of classical mythology, he gives substance to the idea, and for this we need the later poems. In **"A Rented Room,"** he suggests the illusory goals of the young adult are signs of loss and not of gain:

Indeed he seemed to lie
Masterless at length at the good centre
Of nineteen years' maze, the green boy come of age—
Not seeing the handsized cloud in the clear sky
And the door ajar to let the Furies enter.

(p. 94)

By 1959, this habit of thought had so become habitual and direct that, almost instinctively, he compressed the sense of an awful symmetry in man's existence by mythologizing it. **"The Indian morning"** provides a concise example: "the Cretan labyrinth / Of money, conscience, work, glum dreams" (p. 198).

It was only after 1948 that the symmetry of the labyrinth acquired an alternative interpretation. Although the maze continued to express estrangement, from then onwards it was also used to image the search for a centre of ultimate reality. It is almost uncanny how closely Baxter's evolving imagination conforms to the patterns that Mircea Eliade has noted in his studies of religious symbols. Concerning the search for the "centre," Eliade observes that ". . . the thing that symbolizes absolute reality, sacred power and immortality, is hard of access. Symbols of this sort are situated in a 'centre.'"[4] In the 1948 **"Poem by the Clock Tower, Sumner,"** Baxter sees childhood endowed with access to a centre denied to adults. While he mourns loss of access, the centre still remains, and that is a considerable advance in the application of the image.

And for them rises yet
From earth's still centre the heaven-bearing
Immortal Tree.

(p. 73)

Although in **"To God the Son"** he gives the centre a specific identity—"all roads lead it seems / To that great tree planted upon a skull" (p. 151)—he is not always so definite. In a late love poem, the centre upon which human love is founded revolves about the idea of creation and the innocent wonder of the first lovers: "We met in that strange garden at / The centre of the world" (**"Grass and Night Wind,"** p. 421). The clearest statement about the centre is **"The Cold Hub,"** where Baxter recalls and interprets the painful searching of his youth that lead him to a basic reality:

> And something bust inside me, like a winter clod
> Cracked open by the frost. A sense of being at
> The absolute unmoving hub
> From which, to which, the intricate roads went.
> Like Hemingway, I call it *nada*:
> *Nada*, the Spanish word for nothing.
>
> *Nada*; the belly of the whale; *nada*;
> *Nada*; the little hub of the great wheel;
> *Nada*; the house on Cold Mountain
> Where the east and the west wall bang together;
> *Nada*; the drink inside the empty bottle.
> You can't get there unless you are there.
> The hole in my pants where the money falls out,
> That's the beginning of knowledge; *nada*.
>
> (pp. 256-57)

For Baxter to use "nada" inevitably involves associations that are central to Christian asceticism, since St. John of the Cross and his mystical way involved a method of negation that led to him being called *el doctor de la nada*.

The idea of the labyrinth is evoked by Baxter's recurring metaphorical allusions to the thread Theseus used, and it suggests the symmetrical unwinding towards a centre. Just as the labyrinth can image being lost or the journey to the centre, so, too, the skein can suggest a sense of absence of direction - it depends whether it is tangled or untangled. For example: "To tie all threads in a knot of disillusion (**"Venetian Blinds,"** p. 84); ". . . skein of peace untangled" (**"Sestina,"** p. 78); ". . . tangled days" (**"Host and Stranger,"** p. 150); ". . . the great skein cannot be unwound" (**"[Because the flax blades],"** p. 422). Sustained over many years, such consistent imagery reflects the steady concentration of Baxter's imagination within an evolving symmetrical pattern which could be almost infinitely variable.

One purposeful evolution from the labyrinth image was the wheel that created or sharpened. Just as the labyrinth was the means to the centre, so a grindstone had a similar purposefulness. The symmetrical image metamorphosed to suggest a cutting to the centre or by the centre, and the labyrinth became the wheel, its darkness replaced by the abrading stone "From which it is death to be unbound" (**"Pig Island Letters,** 12," p. 284). This particular image does not seem to begin before 1963, when **"The Axe-blade"** is composed. The poem begins with Baxter "Watching my father sharpen a notched axe-blade / On the lurching grindstone" (p. 269), and ends with him reflecting on his youthful ignorance of the process whereby ". . . year by year the lurching world would abrade / Nerve, heart, mind, flesh, bone" (p. 270). The interest of the metaphor is how it so precisely conforms to the purpose of the labyrinth and its symmetry. The image of the onion skin extends the concentric honing process, especially in **"Easter Testament"**:

> This Easter
> another skin has peeled off
> the onion—heart, head, either
> useless—leaving me just one
> ploy, to let the hair shirt chafe
> till the earth speaks through the man.
>
> (p. 320)

The function of the grindstone and its abrading symmetry in relation to Baxter is recalled in the **"Iron Scythe Song,"** where Baxter compares himself to the much abraded "iron scythe"

> That hangs out of the rain,
> By sharpener and by wrath
> Worn down to its backbone,
> My life has the shape
> That it will keep.
>
> (p. 381)

Inevitably, this concern for form recalls Baxter's use of the bullring and the spot to which the bull returns, while the shape he finds is itself symmetrical like the wheel and worn like the scythe.

In the same year, **"The Victim"** brings together the sense of the centre and a painful means of access to it.

> my uncle (who is now dead) bending in the shade
> Of a ngaio hedge, turning the uneven wheel
> Of a grindstone, pouring water, sharpening an axe,
> While the thud of the wheel kept saying:
> "The body dies;
> The soul is not yet born." This I understand.
>
> (p. 412)

The aim of the process is recognizably that of Christian asceticism—and in **"Poem Against Comfort,"** this is combined with the grindstone and the journey to the centre in unequivocal terms:

> We have to strip
> To the bone and beyond before the gate can open
> And our silence be united both to what we leave
> And to the dark centre of the sun.
>
> (p. 422)

A poem written for John Weir in Jerusalem in 1970, **"The Labyrinth,"** is a conspectus of the evolving symmetrical imagery of the preceding years. Written at a time when Baxter was trying to live out his poetry, it defines the centre through the Theseus myth, but for the first time the Minotaur is Christ.

> So many corridors—so many lurches
> On the uneven filthy floor
> Daedalus made and then forgot,—"What *right*
> Have you to be here?" the demons thick as roaches
> Whispering . . .
>   Mind fixed on the Minotaur
> I plugged onward like a camel that first night,
> Thinking—"Not long, brother, not long now!"—
> But now so many nights have passed
> The problem is to think of him at all
> And not of, say, the fact that I am lost
> Or the spark of light that fell upon my brow
> From some high vault,—I sit down like a little girl
> To play with my dolls,—sword, wallet and the god's
>   great amulet
> My father gave me.
>   In the bullfights it was easy
> (Though heroic no doubt) because their eyes, their
>   eyes held me
> To the agile task. Now I am a child
> Frightened by falling water, by each nerve-pricking
>   memory
> Of things ill done,—but I do not forget
> One thing, the thread, the invisible silk I hold
> And shall hold till I die.
>   I tell you, brother,
> When I throw my arms around the Minotaur
> Our silence will be pure as gold.

                    (pp. 488-89)

The work is full of echoes from the earlier poems. The "lurches" of the floor recall the lurching world and grindstone of **"The Axe-blade"**; the "camel" echoes the "blind camel" on the Persian wheel in **"Words and Money."** The difficulties that deter anyone from attaining the centre, from being fulfilled, are strewn throughout Baxter's works, and there are many nuances of the problem of

> Thinking of Christ—Christ, who is all men
> Yet has to be discovered
> By each on his own—. . .

            ("The Flame," pp. 400-01)

In the poem, Baxter locates himself in the labyrinth of the world where he must press through the concentric rings that hinder but, as he expressed the idea in the **"Ballad of One Tree Hill,"**

>   it takes a giant's will
> In the house of the black bull
> To live and breathe at all.

                   (p. 295)

Yet in **"The Labyrinth,"** Baxter has advanced far beyond the earlier poems. There is no strident assertion, just a plugging away in the dark, holding a tenuous thread of hope as if his life depends upon it—as indeed

it does. The labyrinth is a painful process, the Minotaur at the centre will not be reached until death takes Baxter to the end of the skein. The Minotaur remains hidden, seen only in the mind, and this provides a tremendous pathos and urgency to the journey. Baxter admits to having lost any autonomy—he is "like a little girl" or a frightened child, conscious of weakness and uncertainty—and yet is still drawn on.

The process that we are being made aware of is a steady denudation of the self that has been foreshadowed in many of the earlier poems. As Baxter is drawn to the centre, like Theseus, so he is cut down to an elemental simplicity—that of the child—as on a grindstone. This latter image recalls the cycle of spiritual rebirth required in the gospel for entry into the kingdom of heaven. Here Baxter is linking a number of New Testament images: the story of Nicodemus in John (3: 1-3), and the various sayings of the kingdom—probably from Luke (18: 15-30). In this context, the camel earlier in the poem brings to mind Jesus's observation on how "it is easier for a camel to go through the eye of a needle than for a rich man to enter the kingdom of God" (Luke 18: 25). This process, which images the "self-emptying" of the Jerusalem poems, means that encounter with the Minotaur—beyond the grave—will be in terms that a child could understand. The emotional weight of the last three lines resides in that embrace and silence.

The kenosis or "self-emptying" of Christian theology is the process which Baxter based his life upon in Jerusalem as he subjected himself to discipline and contemplation. The grindstone and the onion skin presaged this development. In **"Autumn Testament 4,"** the centre becomes the void—"Wahi Ngaro."

> Wahi Ngaro, the gap from which our prayers
> Fall back like the toi-toi arrows
>
> Children shoot upwards—Wahi Ngaro,
> The limitless, the silent, the black night sky
>
> From which the church huddles like a woman
> On her hillock of ground—into your wide arms
>
> Travelling, I forget the name of God,
> Yet I can hear the flies roam through the rooms
>
> Now at midday, feel the wind that flutters
> The hippie goddess picture somebody painted
>
> On an old blind and nailed on the wall. I can see
> The orange flowers withering in a milk bottle,
>
> Taste my tobacco phlegm, touch, if I like, the great
>   bronze Christ
> Theodore put up, on the poles of a cross he cut and
>   bound himself.

                   (p. 542)

In the earlier poems, the labyrinth has always been the world through which Baxter must make his way to

God—it has been a hindrance. Now it is still present but with a different emphasis: Baxter reaches towards the centre by means of the world. There is no certainty, no vision, but while "Travelling, I forget the name of God," it is the world that secures him as he presses towards God, the Minotaur, here as "Wahi Ngaro." The senses, the capacity to hear, taste, touch, feel and see, give the finite and particular an immense significance. They are the thread through the labyrinth to the centre.

There are many images and symbols of the way to God, but Baxter's consistent preference for the indirect and dark way is impressive. In the last poem of the *Autumn Testament* series, **"Autumn Testament 7,"** Baxter rejects the ease of a "Jacob's ladder" and returns to language that is reminiscent of the labyrinth—and perhaps even of **"The Cave."** The symmetrical pattern is present but only obliquely, embedded in the description of going "forward like a man in the dark."

> To go forward like a man in the dark
> Is the meaning of this dark vocation;
>
> So simple, tree, star, the bare cup of the hills,
> The lifelong grave of waiting
>
> As indeed it has to be. To ask for Jacob's ladder
> Would be to mistake oneself and the dark Master,
>
> Yet at times the road comes down to a place
> Where water runs and horses gallop
>
> Behind a hedge. There it is possible to sit,
> Light a cigarette, and rub
>
> Your bruised heels on the cold grass. Always because
> A man's body is a meeting house,
>
> Ribs, arms, for the tribe to gather under,
> And the heart must be their spring of water.
>
> (p. 568)

That Baxter should have concluded his finest collection with the pattern that runs through all his poetry is typical of the symmetry he found in the world and sought in his life and work. His need of a pattern that could comprehend flesh and spirit, world and God, evil and good, echoed John Donne's, whom Baxter used to demonstrate a critical point and unintentionally epitomized his own search and, perhaps, our own.

> . . . an art form can state the human situation in something like its entirety, when the voice of the flesh and spirit are bound in one. In John Donne's words—
>
> As the first Adam's sweat surrounds my face
> May the last Adam's blood my soul embrace.[5]

Notes

1. F. McKay, *James K. Baxter as Critic* (Auckland: Heinemann, 1978), p. 210.

2. C. Day Lewis, *The Poetic Image* (London: Jonathan Cape, 1947), pp. 154-55.

3. *Collected Poems,* ed. J.E. Weir (Oxford: Oxford Univ. Press, 1981), p. 69. Further references are incorporated in the text.

4. M. Eliade, *Patterns in Comparative Religion,* trans. Rosemary Sheed (London: Sheed and Ward, 1958), pp. 380-81.

5. McKay, p. 186.

Vincent O'Sullivan (essay date 1987)

SOURCE: O'Sullivan, Vincent. "Urgently Creating a Past: Remarks on James K. Baxter." In *The Writer's Sense of the Past: Essays on Southeast Asian and Australasian Literature,* edited by Kirpal Singh, pp. 94-101. Kent Ridge, Singapore: Singapore University Press, 1987.

[*In the following essay, O'Sullivan identifies two tendencies that Baxter expressed in all his work: his "feeling for a past that has been betrayed" and "a disposition to look at life in terms of loss, and a suspicion of most of what he looked on."*]

One of the first and most celebrated statements of a new literature author looking at what he has, and what he hasn't, is in Hawthorne's Preface to his last novel, a novel in fact so weighted down with the past that it quite cracks under the strain. But before showing us what it is like to have Rome on your back, he tells us what it feels like to be a writer who is a second or third generation European in a recently colonised country. "No author," he says, "can conceive of the difficulty of writing a romance about a country where there is no shadow, no antiquity, no mystery, no picturesque and gloomy wrong, nor anything but a commonplace prosperity, in broad and simple daylight, as is happily the case in my dear native land".[1] Hawthorne as so often is foxing, but for the moment let it stand. Thirty years later Henry James, in his most ironical vein, converted those sentences into an equally famous paragraph of his own. Fancy, James says in effect, not being able to dress up for the races; not being able to put your boy down for Eton; not being able to drop into a cathedral and praying like an Englishman.[2] He deliberately side-steps the "New Literature" problem much as Pearl avoided it at the end of *The Scarlet Letter*—by running for cover in the past that has been left behind. Her mother may have been stuck forever with that dreadful "A" that meant America quite as much as it did Adultery. But as an alternative to going native, as it were, Hawthorne has Pearl go ancestral, marry an English nobleman, and so make herself eligible for a Jamesian role.

Well, it is the international sophisticate who is the more dated of the two authors, at least on that point. Even most of Mrs Thatcher's supporters would not offer much from Henry James' list of sheer necessities. But hundreds of writers would respond at once to what Hawthorne was talking about—how to cope with a present that may seem comparatively thin? How to relate to a past that our forebears chose—or were selected—to relinquish? Can we adequately claim a present unless we have certain assumptions about a past?

In speaking about the New Zealand poet James K. Baxter, who died in 1973 at the age of 46, I use the title "Urgently Creating a Past" for two reasons. Everything that Baxter wrote has about it a strong sense of the *necessary* in psychological terms; and because so much of his comparatively short but vastly prolific life was a deliberately fabricated performance. Another paper on myth, say, could demonstrate with ample detail his aligning his own mind, and his own experience, with a dozen major European myths, or if one prefers, with as many Freudian and Jungian positions: from the lost Eden and the Gorgon mother, through the tripartite goddess of sexual experience, various *rites du passage,* the role of outcast and prophet and scapegoat, to the final years where his notions of election, and his attitudes to suffering, coincide in both social and poetic acts.[3] Social, in that he became a national figure with his unkempt beard, his bare feet, his cast-off clothes, his public statements on morality and political affairs; poetic, in that this *role* was accompanied by poems that are a fairly astonishing display of how a man thought and felt seeing himself as the deliberate enemy of normal bourgeois New Zealand life. An enemy to the extent that he could identify with Christ in the job they believed themselves chosen to do: castigate the demons of materialism, and offer all there is finally for any man to offer, pity and love.

But to Baxter's own inherited past. Although he was connected on his mother's side to a solid English academic tradition, what he preferred to emphasise was a group of ancestors, a Scottish Gaelic-speaking tribe, who were driven from their land after the breakdown of Culloden in 1745. For it is the tribal spirit that gives a man his centre. The Maori word *whenua,* as Baxter well knew, means both one's tribal land and the umbilical cord. It is this spirit that any highly-centralised state labours to destroy: "the regional mind is anathema to Caesar. Wherever a tribe is left, he feels it itching like a flea, and will rub till he kills it." He was speaking there in 1966, and his words applied to Asia as much as they did to Scotland or to his own country, where the Maoris had experienced pretty much what the Scots had. As he said specifically of Vietnam, "The face of the war god, turned in our direction, is honourable and smiling; but to the man of the tribe it is instead a bloody and tormented skull, the face of nihilism."[4] [*The Man on the Horse*] It didn't matter much to Baxter whether Caesar was dressed as a capitalist or a communist. Either way, the tribe would go down.

In Baxter's case, the tribe in which he would have liked to locate himself was quite gone before he was born. All that his forebears brought to New Zealand was their Presbyterian faith, a language which soon was lost, and a gift for hard work that crushed almost everything else from life. But this sense of tribal loss carried immense force in Baxter's mind. It was inseparable from a sense of personal isolation, "the sense," as he said, "of having been pounded all over with a club by invisible adversaries is generally with me, and has been with me as long as I remember".[5] [**"Notes on the Education of a New Zealand Poet"**] I don't believe these two things are easily separable in Baxter, that feeling for a past that has been betrayed, and what in a necessarily loose way we must call "temperament"—a disposition to look at life in terms of loss, and a suspicion of most of what he looked on. And so his poetry will throw up hundreds of lines like these, as he considers the country he was born in:

> If there is any culture here
> It comes from the black south wind
> Howling above the factories
> A handsbreadth from Antarctica.

("On Possessing the Burns Fellowship 1966")

To make the kind of jump that only limited time excuses, I go from this inherited and temperamental ground of so much in Baxter, towards what I think is the turning point towards the rather extraordinary life, and the equally extraordinary poems, of his later years. This is his visit to India for six months in 1958. His recent conversion to Catholicism offered a Franciscan tradition that validated poverty, but it was India that showed him something rather more vividly than merely reading about it—the possibility of a community living at peace with itself, quite outside our western capitalist expectations. Now this is a view of India that won't be shared by everyone, and quite clearly he based it on village rather than city. "The village communities are each autonomous, each a small republic as it were. Despite their evident poverty, the villagers convey an impression of relaxation and well-being, which springs no doubt from a life lived in deep accordance with natural law."[6] [**"Kilokery and Kalechan, a study of Indian village life"**] Over-simplified, surely. But the question is not whether Baxter saw India accurately, but how it brought home to him the possibilities of a society totally different to the one he had grown up in. As his wife later wrote, "I myself am quite convinced that India was a sort of crossroads, and Jim, being the kind of person he was, had no choice but to turn in the direction of a new and then unknown destination—Jerusalem. . . . It didn't shake him *to* his foundations . . .

but *from* his foundations. And it took nearly 10 years to find himself again in a new relation to God and man."[7]

Baxter's first volume after India was called *Howrah Bridge.* He wrote poems about Madras and Delhi and Elephanta, about local artisans and urban prostitutes. The point to which each poem pressed was to the basic response of pity, and the loneliness of pain. For Baxter saw not much hope in what he called "the Marxist cage". These are not among his best poems. They are important more as weather-vanes indicating how he will look at his own country when he returns. Just before he left for India, he had written a poem that said this about New Zealand:

> Consider this barbarian coast,
> Traveller. . . . It has never made
> Anything out of anything.
> Drink at these bitter springs.
>
> **("At Akitio")**

The affluent and secular society he came back to repelled him more than ever, a social fabric that he found shabby and morally indifferent:

> I walked forth gladly to find the angry poor
> Who are my nation; discovered instead
> The glutton seagulls squabbling over crusts
> And policies made and broken behind locked doors.
>
> **("Pig Island Letters 8")**

Life became increasingly oppressive in a society, as he said, that "murders by triviality"; where it is no longer possible to relate action and value. In a poem called **"Words and Money"** then:

> Words divided from things, money divided from
>   things,
> Have made a gap between us and the world
> And in that gap our intellects are crucified.

These constant jeremiads against the society he lived in were partly balanced by a handful of fine love lyrics, and ballads that began to focus his affection for the drunks and dead-beats who were the refuse of society. These figures are set into a kind of religious frieze. God's holy fire, as Yeats would have put it, becomes something like this in Baxter, in a poem in which Concrete Grady, one of his Irish drunks, is given shock treatment in an asylum:

> The Trinity inside my head
> Is blacked out when they pull the switch.
> I met Bill Diamond in the yard
> And asked him for a match.
> There's fire in Heaven. Through the bars
> I see burnt patches in the wheat fields of the stars.
>
> **("Grady Under Shock Treatment")**

Behind his more public accusation or laments, there is Baxter's continuing scrutiny of his own spiritual shifts. I say "shifts" because there is no question of there being a straight line in his spiritual odyssey. What one finds are diverse responses that alternate, jostle, and unsettle critics who like a neat graph. But by the early 1960s there was *always* the sense that life, seen simply in humanistic terms, was a massive let-down. Taking a Maori myth that Jung had so admired, the woman who can be read as both life and death, light and darkness, sexual desire and sexual destruction, Baxter wrote:

> In great dryness of mind I heard the voice of the sea
> Reverberating, and thought: As a man
>
> Grows older he does not want beer, bread, or the
>   prancing flesh,
> But the arms of the eater of life, Hine-nui-te-po,
>
> With teeth of obsidian and hair like kelp
> Flashing and glimmering at the edge of the horizon.
>
> **("East Coast Journey")**

Or as he put this perception more starkly in one of his plays: "Hunger, dark, and cold: the three ugly sisters. They stand above the cradle; they go to bed with every soul; they hammer down the coffin lid."[8] [*The Wide Open Cage*]

A grim view, certainly, if it is one's only view. But New Zealand society did offer Baxter one area where he would not feel quite that sense of *angst*. That was Maori life. For all the official self-congratulation on our integrated and classless society, Maoris comprise over seventy per cent of prison population; they are in the lowest income brackets; their educational levels are lower. In other words, it is fairly much the story of any defeated native people anywhere in the world. But what has survived is a strong tribal identity. Most Maoris know who they are, in a way that far fewer European New Zealanders do. As I've noted in writing about Maori fiction, "the measure of degradation is the distance travelled from the tribal centre".[9] Knowing that matters to them in important ways. Perhaps this can be best illustrated from a short story by Witi Ihimaera, called "The Gathering of the Whakapapa". An old man puts off dying until he has completed the ancestral tree. When he is asked does the *whakapapa* really matter, "Oh yes," he says. "Because it gives me unison with the universe. It tells me that I am not alone or ever will be. It weaves me into a pattern of life that began at world's creation and will be there at world's end. . . . Although I die, the pattern will not be broken."[10]

Baxter deliberately set himself to earn a place in that pattern. He had married a Maori woman and always had Maori friends. But after his time in India, he begins to see Maori life as the only life that offers the chance at least of humane behaviour. The Maori concept of *aroha* becomes the centre of his thought—"the appearance or reality of group love, a merging of the collective warmth of the tribe . . . the proper natural base of divine charity".[11] [**"The Man on the Horse"**]

It was a long haul over more than a decade, as Baxter dug himself out from what he regarded as the European mire, and plaited this new certainty into his Catholicism. He managed to give offence on several fronts. A certain kind of New Zealand *litterateur,* like a certain kind of Christian, is still as comfortable with him as with an electric fence.

Part of the problem—assuming that there is one—lies in Baxter's dramatic sense. There is no easy way to divide the public figure from the private man, the utterance from the personality. That should hardly surprise us in a man who declared that "Without the dramatic role, life tends to be experienced as chaos."[12] [*The Sore-Footed Man* and *The Temptations of Oedipus*] Or who said on another occasion, "What happens is either meaningless to me, or else it is mythology."[13] [**"Notes on the Education of a New Zealand Poet"**]

Baxter's final and self-imposed role was to assume the voice of a new tribe—to create, if you like, a dramatic present that verified his relationship with a living past. For three diverse elements came together in 1968, when he was instructed in a dream to set up a community at Hiruharama, the old Maori mission village of Jerusalem. Maori and Catholic were brought sharply into alignment. And that sympathy he had always had for the outcast and the drop-out and the addict, was to find its logical end in "nga mokai", a phrase that originally meant pet animals, or the youngest members of a family, but which Baxter appropriated to mean "the fatherless ones", his own tribe.

That sense of drama I spoke of had about it a dash of enormous effrontery. It is one thing, I suppose, to speak of

> . . . my hungry wandering children
> Who drink at the springs of the marae
> And find a Maori ladder to clamber
> Up to the light. . . .

> (**"The Dark Welcome"**)

But it is another to write this:

> They say it is best
>
> To break a rotten egg in the creek
> To get eels—I think I am that egg
>
> And Te Ariki must crack me open
> If the fish are to be drawn in at all

> (**"Jerusalem Sonnets, 35"**)

One doesn't envy the biographer who has to untangle role from posturing, seriousness from solemnity, text from voice. But it is not the social contours of Baxter's last years that are most interesting. It is the way he is driving his language back so hard that he himself spoke

of "losing the coat of art". The confluence of Maori, Catholic, and radical views brought a new energy to his poetry, a new bareness to a writer who had always found it too easy, if anything, to come by rhetoric and the sonorous. Again, a quite different paper could be given on precisely that, as though in Roland Barthes' words about what Sartre called "l'ecriture blanche", Baxter "could no longer find purity but in the absence of all signs . . . the last episode of a Passion of writing, which recounts stage by stage the disintegration of bourgeois consciousness".[14]

The other aspect which interests me as much, is how Baxter takes traditional Christian concepts, and runs them with others from pre-Christian Maori thought. In the Maori cosmogony, there was a supreme being, Io, and the evil force Te Whiro, who sought always to destroy the souls of men. These fit easily enough across the Christian patterns of God and Satan, and Baxter at times employs them in that way. Common adjectives used of Io were "the faceless one", "the concealed one", in much the sense that Baxter speaks of "the dark master", John of the Cross of the masked lover, or *The Cloud of Unknowing* of the God who can be loved but never revealed. But there are other concepts that took him beyond traditional Christian thought. How much he manages to draw under the nomenclature of Te Whaea, the Source of all things, and also the Mother of God. In the poems of his last year or so, she can still be seen as Mary, *mater misericordiae*; but there are times when she takes on aspects of something approaching the Aztec Coatlicue, the snake-skirted, skull-decorated *Madre de la Vida.* There can be few Christian poets who have talked about the Virgin Mary as

> . . . not the blue and white
> Lady of our adoration,
>
> But a woman built like a tank (both senses of the word)
> Who swears in English at the . . . truckdriver.

> (**"The Moon and the Chestnut Tree"**)

There is another Maori concept, Wahi Ngaro. This is the primordial emptiness referred to in ancient creation chants, the Void that can accrue modern associations of the Gulf, *Le Neant,* or the pressure towards the existential leap that Kierkegaard wrote of.

> Wahi Ngaro,
> The limitless, the silent, the black night sky
>
> From which the church huddles like a woman
> On her hillock of ground—into your wide arms
>
> Travelling, I forget the name of God.

> (*Autumn Testament,* 4)

I will end with a poem where Te Whaea and Wahi Ngaro, the Source and the absence of all things, the

Mother of God and the darkness of God, are brought together in a step that quite goes beyond usual theological limits.

It is a point he has arrived at, I believe, only through that urgency I spoke of; a present that makes sense only through a choice that was made among possible pasts.

Hard, heavy, slow, dark,
Or so I find them, the hands of Te Whaea

Teaching me to die. Some lightness will come later
When the heart has lost its unjust hope

For special treatment. Today I go with a bucket
Over the paddocks of young grass,

So delicate like fronds of maidenhair,
Looking for mushrooms, I find twelve of them,

Most of them little, and some eaten by maggots,
But they'll do to add to the soup. It's a long time now

Since the great ikons fell down,
God, Mary, home, sex, poetry,

Whatever one uses as a bridge
To cross the river that only has one beach,

And even one's name is a way of saying—
'This gap inside a coat'—the darkness I call God,

The darkness I call Te Whaea, how can they translate
The blue calm evening sky that a plane tunnels
 through

Like a little wasp, or the bucket in my hand,
Into something else? I go on looking

For mushrooms in the field, and the fist of longing
Punches my heart, until it is too dark to see.

(***The Ikons***)

Notes

1. Preface to *The Marble Faun,* 1860.

2. *Hawthorne,* 1879. Edition cited, edited by Tony Tanner, Macmillan, 1967, p. 55.

3. This is discussed in greater detail in my *James K. Baxter,* Oxford University Press, 1976.

4. "Conversation with an Ancestor", *The Man on the Horse,* University of Otago Press, 1967, pp. 29, 30.

5. "Notes on the Education of a New Zealand Poet", *The Man on the Horse,* p. 121.

6. Kilokery and Kalechan, a study of Indian village life", *Education* 9, no. 1 (February 1960): 21-24. In view of Baxter's later attitudes in establishing a community at Jerusalem, it is interesting that he visited Santiniken, the rural university established

by Tagore, and wrote warmly about it. See "Rabindranath Tagore: An Appreciation in his centenary year", *Education* 1, no. 8 (September 1961): 237-42.

7. The quotation kindly provided by Dr Frank McKay, who at present is working on the official biography of Baxter.

8. *The Wide Open Cage,* in *Two Plays,* Capricorn Press, 1959, p. 6.

9. Introduction, *New Zealand Writing Since 1945,* edited by MacD.P. Jackson and Vincent O'Sullivan, Oxford University Press, 1983, p. xxv.

10. Witi Ihimaera, *A New Net Goes Fishing,* Heinemann, 1977.

11. "The Man on the Horse", *The Man on the Horse,* pp. 105, 120.

12. *The Sore-Footed Man, The Temptations of Oedipus,* Heinemann, 1971, p. ix.

13. "Notes on the Education of a New Zealand Poet", *The Man on the Horse,* p. 122.

14. Roland Barthes, *Writing Degree Zero,* 1953, translated by Annette Lavers and Colin Smith, 1967, Hill and Wang, p. 5.

Paul Millar (essay date 2001)

SOURCE: Millar, Paul. Introduction to *New Selected Poems,* by James K. Baxter, pp. xiii-xvii. Auckland, New Zealand: Oxford University Press, 2001.

[*In the following essay, published as his introduction to a 2001 collection of Baxter's selected poems, Millar comments on the "paradoxes" in Baxter's life and the tension this created in his poetry, but he adds that this "'gap' between the selves" was an essential condition for the poet's writing, resulting in some of the greatest poems produced in the English language.*]

The poems in this selection place James K. Baxter among the major poets of the twentieth century. They show him emphatically as being more than a New Zealand poet. Yet New Zealand lies at the heart of his poems, the best of which constitutes an unparalleled, intensely personal engagement with the country, its people, and society.

As has often been the case with major literary figures in New Zealand and elsewhere, Baxter's reputation at home has waxed and waned since his death in 1972. Following a period of near beatification in the early 1970s, a climate of calculated scholarly indifference developed in New Zealand during the 1980s that continued in the 1990s, even while his work was being chosen for international anthologies and cementing its place as representing the finest among world literatures written in English. From the mid-1990s, however, new publications and original creative works in film, theatre, dance, and music have tapped a powerful and growing interest in Baxter. Usually the spotlight has been on the poet's colourful life, and only secondarily on his writing. This selection intends to place the focus back on Baxter's essential achievement: his poetry.

It has become something of a habit among critics to regard Baxter as a writer of great lines or phrases, rather than a writer of great poems. His prolific output contributed to the idea that poems came too easily and were not sufficiently polished; that his work habits were as scruffy as his later appearance. But the care Baxter lavished on his manuscripts, the reworking of numerous poems, often over a period of years, and the way successive versions of his final Jerusalem books were meticulously drafted, attest to the attention he paid to his craft and the high skill he attained. Few poets have approached their profession with such dedication or served so long an apprenticeship. Baxter read prodigiously and practised assiduously, experimenting with language and style, and developing a wide-ranging repertoire of technical tricks from which an entirely original type of poetry would ultimately develop.

The poetry covers a range of forms. Love lyrics like **'Let Time be Still'**; ballads and songs like **'Lament for Barney Flanagan'**—the dramatic situations of which explain his interest in writing for the stage; and poems of protest like **'A Rope for Harry Fat'** represent only a handful of the genres in which he wrote successfully. The largest single group of his poems are letters. Many of these are long verse letters personally addressing Noel Ginn, Sam Hunt, or Max Harris. Others are in series, like the *Pig Island Letters* to Maurice Shadbolt or the *Jerusalem Sonnets: Poems for Colin Durning*; then there is a range of intensely personal letters to his wife and family members. Devotional poems, like **'Song to the Lord God'**—which relates Baxter to a long and rich tradition of devotional poetry in English—and some more generally addressed, like **'Ode to Auckland',** also fall into this category. Just as often, Baxter's poems are letters to himself, many of them entries in a spiritual verse diary, or building blocks of a grand testamentary poem carefully crafted to connect backwards and forwards through metaphor and imagery.

It is in the best of the letter poems, when the language seems most natural and colloquial, the verse least structured, and the ideas fresh off the top of the mind, that Baxter's genius is most apparent. It is remarkable how exact and apt his use of language is, how carefully metaphor is used or extended, and how subtly a complex idea can be expressed through the barest articulation of a concept or experience.

To appreciate Baxter's poetry from a twenty-first-century perspective, the controversial aspects of both his life and his writing must be placed in some sort of context. These often put him at odds with a society unable to stomach its disturbing reflection in his work. Indifference was not something Baxter generated. His various manifestations—pacifist, poet, alcoholic, Catholic, commune leader, to name a few—elicited strong reactions, attracting devotees and provoking antagonists. His deficiencies have been extensively catalogued: he left a trail of broken friendships and relationships, his attitudes to women were problematic, his infidelities were legendary, his depictions of the middle classes were offensive to them, and his challenges to conventional morality were disturbing. How could the author of the deeply devotional **'Song to the Lord God'** write at around the same time the scabrous **'Truth Song'** from **'Ballad of Fire Trap Castle'**? He became, by his own description, 'the nuns' devil and a bad smell in the noses of good churchgoing people'.

Baxter classed as his most successful poems those containing a 'kernel of actual experiential knowledge', and emphasised the intimate connection between his life experiences and his verse: 'I know only a little about the world; and most of it is somewhere in the poems I have written.' But when biographical elements occur in the poems they are generally projected through a mythic lens. He once described each of his poems as 'part of a large subconscious corpus of personal myth, like an island above the sea, but joined underwater to other islands', and elsewhere commented that what 'happens is either meaningless to me, or else it is mythology'. The elements Baxter the poet valued in his own and others' lives were those that connect individuals to a wider mythical landscape of human experience. In the majority of his verse there are no individuals, only archetypes like the **'National Mum and Labour Dad'** of the **'Ballad of Calvary Street'**.

Baxter's unusual ability to move between worlds, saying one thing while apparently doing another, was disconcerting, and has often been taken as evidence of personal duplicity for which the poetry must be held to account. Yet he never regarded himself as part of mainstream New Zealand society, and his poetry is written consistently from that position of principled self-marginalisation. From his teenage years as the son of pacifists in a world at war, he was a deliberate nonconformist who relished his description of the poet as the 'sore thumb of the tribe'. In practice he was the sore thumb of the dominant social order: the respectable citizens conforming to the dictates of a passionless central government that he characterises in **'The Bureaucrats'** as 'Caesar'. In Wellington, where he had done it 'hard/Carving stones in Caesar's graveyard' (**'Ballad of Nine Jobs'**), he was happy to leave his office desk to become a postman. To many in 1963 such a move would have seemed a retrograde step, but it was totally in keeping with his resistance to what he saw as a corrupting 'Calvinist ethos which underlies our determinedly secular culture like the bones of a dinosaur buried in a suburban garden plot'. Resistance to this ethos was his way of being a 'cell of good living in a corrupt society'.

Baxter was by nature tribal. He affiliated with small, tightly knit groups, whose cohesion was generally a function of persecution and alienation, and identified with various tribal manifestations. They ranged from the oppressed Highland clans of his Scottish forbears through pacifists, poets, alcoholics, and Catholics—a minority group in New Zealand—to the tribes of the Wanganui settlement called Jerusalem (where he ended his short life): the local Maori iwi, and Baxter's own commune, which he called Nga Mokai—the fatherless.

One of Baxter's intentions during the Jerusalem period was to present to other pakeha an entirely new way of relating to the tangata whenua—the people of the land. This aim, reflected in both his life and his writing, was the outcome of a steadily intensifying identification, over a number of years, with Maori culture, tradition, and spirituality. Through marriage to the Maori poet J. C. Sturm he had been drawn into participating in her activities among her own people. He also experienced the racial prejudice that she encountered. But she believed that not until his time in India in the late 1950s, and the experience of being the single white face in a throng of brown, did he truly understand her sense of alienation in the predominantly pakeha world they inhabited. It is an understanding that lies at the heart of poems like **'The Maori Jesus'** and 'Tangi'. At his death Baxter received the rare honour for a pakeha of being buried in the urupa at Jerusalem following a full tangi arranged by the elders of the local tribe, Ngati Hau.

For most of his life Baxter followed a double track, oscillating between the demands of correct society—where he played many roles—and his attraction to alienated tribes. This led to one of the key tensions in his life. The 'family man, teetotal, moderately pious, not offensive to sight or smell, able to say the right thing in a drawing room', was ever at odds with the clannish, anarchic other self, 'my collaborator, my schizophrenic twin, who has always provided me with poems'.

The paradoxes that are so evident, and to some so problematic, in Baxter's life produced a tension that assisted his creative process. During his teenage years he developed an enduring conception of the poetic self as a composite of opposites, dwelling within in a state of perpetual poem-producing tension. As he once explained, a 'kind of tension of belief often lies behind the poems, and it leads to a certain edge'. That type of tension would be for many years a necessary condition for producing poetry. Always at the locus of tension was some version of the 'gap' between the selves, a contradictory place where nothing existed but from which poems originated. Notions of this 'gap' are ubiquitous in Baxter's writing, but it is not a fixed symbol. It may be a paradoxical site of absence within which to discover the true self, or a place of stillness where the mind is silenced and God is experienced. In the later poetry it becomes 'Wahi Ngaro: the void out of which all things come. That is my point of beginning. That is where I find my peace.'

In the final decade of his life Baxter began exploring ways of practising the things he had been writing about. At first this occurred subtly in the plays he wrote in the 1960s, where the concerns of his verse were translated into the more externally dynamic medium of the stage. But ultimately the life became the poem. In the Jerusalem period, acting out beliefs on the importance of communality, poverty, and sacrifice, Baxter would come to describe himself as the man whose 'name is a way of saying—"This gap inside a coat"'.

There is not, as many have implied, any significant contradiction between Baxter's early and later years. Jerusalem was less a deviation than a natural progression. Baxter's poetry was the product of strong influences— parents, pacifism, war, and adolescence—that saw him break out in words. He began by reading the English poetic canon and writing in that tradition before gradually moving away from it. At around the same time as he was consciously deciding that he was a New Zealander rather than an Englishman (see 'Under the Dank Leaves',) his verse made its first concrete moves away from imitation and towards authenticity. Despite various attempts throughout his life to conform to the world around him, he remained outside the mainstream and its depersonalised way of living. Over time, impelled by recovery from alcoholism, conversion to Catholicism, and a life-changing few months in Asia, Baxter's conviction grew that simply writing about his beliefs was insufficient. Deprivation, which was little more than theoretical in New Zealand, was painfully real in India. He was forever changed by these experiences and moved inexorably towards Jerusalem and 'the Lord on his axe-chopped cross'.

Eventually Baxter's art and life coalesced, and his move to Jerusalem was a way of actualising what he had until then only written about. Poetry, for so long the mainspring of his life, became his own cross. One of the features of Baxter's decision to abandon his old life so ostentatiously was his commitment to stop writing poetry, an activity that now seemed at odds with his new vocation of poverty. Yet he could no more stop writing than he could cease breathing. The Jerusalem period produced some of his most significant poetry and something entirely new. Whereas the earlier verse might, with ponderous metre and latinate diction, move towards a final grand, sonorous phrase, now unrhymed run-on couplets (increasingly the unit of choice in his later work) create a tone both direct and personal, moving closer to a synthesis of Baxter's various selves that had for so long operated in tension.

If, at times, Baxter appears to evaluate New Zealand society harshly, his judgments are always from the perspective of one intimately involved in the social process. His criticisms of national life and his ultimate decision to step out of the mainstream seemed to develop naturally from the preoccupations of a lifetime of verse. Yet these preoccupations were, as a rule, neither negative nor despairing. Rather, the deliberately mythological cast of mind that underpinned his poetry sought to place the individual (and the nation) within a wider frame by directing attention towards universal elements of human experience. The Baxter who, writing shortly before his death, found the Medusa's head of present-day urban global civilisation—with its 'depersonalisation, centralisation, [and] desacralisation'—intolerable could still find reason for hope 'in the hearts of people'.

John Dennison (essay date 2005)

SOURCE: Dennison, John. "Ko te Pakeha te teina: Baxter's Cross-Cultural Poetry." *Journal of New Zealand Literature* 23, no. 2 (2005): 36-46.

[*In the following essay, Dennison attempts "to articulate" the significance of Baxter's "cross-cultural poetry" of his so-called Hiruharama period, from 1969 to 1972, asserting that while his verse draws from and is inspired by Maori culture and religion, it "retains an inescapable cultural specificity that ties it to te ao Pakeha," or to the poet's identity as a white, European settler in New Zeland.*]

WHAT TO DO WITH HEMI?

Like it or not, Baxter remains, like a battered beacon, deeply anchored in the midst of the muddy stream of New Zealand poetry, still 'issuing noisy instructions.'[1] While his is a voice doubtless monotonous and overbearing in its pronouncements at times, the fact that much of Baxter's later verse is increasingly cross-cultural in character is surely worth more than a cursory hearing, given all that has transpired in the way of cultural relations over the last three decades. Intriguing then—disturbing even—to discover that thorough consideration of Baxter's engagement in his poetry with te ao Maori is conspicuous by its near absence. As a re-

sult, while the Baxter oeuvre continues to be well thumbed for its literary, and, more recently, its theological profundities,[2] the potential of Baxter's engagement to inform a radical understanding of Pakeha identity has not been fully appreciated.

In part, this critical blind spot is symptomatic of the dominant coordinates of cultural discourse: for both the nationalism of Baxter's day, and subsequent contemporary criticism typically dominated by the either/or imperatives of cultural difference, such distinctive articulations of Pakeha identity, grounded in personal engagements with te ao Maori, pose the problem of how to approach this unsettling literature.[3] Distinguished by its origin, language and attitude from 'bi-cultural' or 'bi-lingual' writing, this *cross*-cultural poetry is inescapably defined by *movement* and the unfulfilled tensions of *reaching out* while never arriving.[4] While drawing from te ao Maori, such writing retains an inescapable cultural specificity that ties it to te ao Pakeha. The tension between these two coordinates of origin—the vertical of the cross-cultural moment and the horizontal that begins in Pakeha culture—can result in a profound reflexive effect: even as the poetry reaches into, and draws from, te ao Maori, it is given the capacity to say new things about Pakeha culture and identity. Just such a movement is evident in the poetry of Baxter's Hiruharama period (roughly, 1969-72), immensely significant for the way in which it models the necessary corrective of Pakeha as teina to Maori as tuakana.

The other significant factor in this brief diagnosis of Baxter criticism is the considerable legacy of critics contemporaneous with Baxter, who have tended to treat his later poems primarily as literary objects, the embedded religious, cultural, and political agendas of which are firmly dumbed down. While the safety fences of the new-critical formalist framework—a 'hermeneutically sealed' approach, as it were—have given way to the acknowledgement of wider contexts of discourse, the anaemia of Baxter criticism has yet to be fully addressed. C.K. Stead comes closest to the mark when, in writing about **Autumn Testament** in 1973, he comments that 'the Maori elements seem here to have become a deep and genuine part of Baxter's intellectual and emotional life—something new in Pakeha writing.'[5] It is an intuition never fully pursued. John Newton rightly points out that the failure of Stead and others to reflect on the implications of that 'something new' for Pakeha writing—and it also follows, identity—is due in no small part to the critical framework within which they were operating.[6] So helpful in other ways, Vincent O'Sullivan's *James K. Baxter* (1976) makes little of the cross-cultural aspects of the poetry, interpreting them as an affected idiosyncrasy of Baxter's religious conviction: 'In these poems "Maori" is the synonym for spontaneous, traditional, close to God; "pakeha" for self-centred and spiritually dead'.[7] They entail merely the superimposition of a Maori-Pakeha cultural dichotomy over the social and spiritual landscape of Aotearoa/New Zealand. There is certainly a deep connection between Baxter's theological and cultural convictions, often expressed through such a subversive dichotomy. The overall effect of O'Sullivan's approach is, however, to ultimately explain away religious and cultural agendas as symptomatic of basic existential concerns. By association, the cross-cultural elements of Baxter's poetry are duly overlooked, and any possibility of understanding the theological and cultural kaupapa of the poetry is foregone.

What follows is an attempt to articulate something of the substance of that 'something new in Pakeha writing' that emerges in Baxter's Hiruharama period. More specifically, what I hope to delineate here is the kaupapa—the foundation, or rationale—of this cross-cultural poetry and its significance for understanding the historical construal of Pakeha identity in New Zealand poetry in English: Baxter's later poetry is significant not only for poetic function but for purposive kaupapa, occupying a key transition point within the wider cultural discourse.

A MAORI JESUS? THE DISLOCATION OF PAKEHA NATIONALISM

Evident in the earliest published example of Baxter's cross-cultural poetry, **'Regret at Being a Pakeha'** (1963), the ubiquitous and often simplistically rendered cultural duality that pervades the poetry of the Hiruharama period entails an insistence on cultural particularity over and against assimilationist nationalism, and a subversive comparison with te ao Maori in which Pakeha culture is laid bare in the light of te ao Maori.[8] As O'Sullivan has noted, this basic cultural dualism does not abate during the later poetry but accrues explicit spiritual significance. Grounded in a bald analysis of socio-political inequality, it functions as a prophetic, if simplistic, inversion of the dominant cultural power dynamic.[9] The stark contrast here is, however, not simply a cultural gloss for a disparity that is basically spiritual: for Baxter, cultural and spiritual aspects in Aotearoa/New Zealand are deeply aligned, setting the material and spiritual conditions of Maori and Pakeha in inverse relation. The dispossessed, not the possessors, are blessed.[10] Moreover, te ao Maori had retained its spiritual and communal vision of the world. Thus the reformational and liberating kaupapa that informs Baxter's cross-cultural poetry involves a congruence and revisioning of Maori spiritual concepts and Catholic theology, made specific to Aotearoa/New Zealand.

A thorough subversion of the Eurocentric Christ, the Maori Jesus is central to Baxter's critique of Pakeha culture. As a resonant trans-cultural symbol with dual cultural currency, the Maori Jesus is a typically arche-typal focal point for the prophetical critique and revisioning of the later poetry (O'Sullivan, 6). 'The Maori Jesus' fleshes out Baxter's dislocation of Pakeha culture's easy adaptation of Christianity.[11] He walks Wellington harbour, his dungarees and degenerate hairdo overturning middle-class sensibilities. The fleshly, earthy details—the kai moana on his breath; his cosmic flatulence—totally dislocate Christ from the puritanical society that Baxter continually railed against. Where in **'Poem For Colin—17'** Baxter berates the image of Pakeha nationalism, the 'cloudgazing pakeha Christ/With His heart in His hand, well felted against the weather—', the Maori Jesus actively refuses to fulfil the expectations of the majority.[12] The anarchy presented by the inebriating laughter of the Maori Jesus threatens Pakeha culture specifically.

This is, nevertheless, an orthodox re-visioning of Christ for Aotearoa/New Zealand: as with the Nazarene, the Maori Jesus chooses disciples from among the marginalised and dispossessed victims of society; he bears in his own body the suffering and evil systematic in society, a passion substantiating and dignifying Maori suffering in terms that resonate deeply within the western cultural legacy. The function of the Maori Jesus is thus not wholly negative, but shaped by the need to articulate the belief that Christ is irreducibly as much Maori as he is Pakeha, a distinction Baxter insisted upon as 'necessary for this country'; a cultural specification with soteriological consequence.[13] [*Thoughts about the Holy Spirit*] He further insists, 'the Risen Christ is a spectrum of all races and all cultures', a spectrum reflected throughout the later poetry:

> The crucifix my friend Milton carved
>
> With its garments made of wood shavings
> And a faceless face, Maori or pakeha either
>
> As the light catches it
>
> (Jerusalem Sonnets, 43)

This blank visage is no defacement, but an acknowledgement of the full play of cultural difference found in Christ. As a focal point of Baxter's cultural re-visioning, the Maori Jesus de-centers Pakeha identity and fleshes out a reconfigured basis for cross-cultural relationship. To embrace the Maori aspect of Christ and privilege it over the European face of Christ is to accept the belief that salvation for Pakeha culture lies in receiving the aroha—the Humanity of Christ—found in te ao Maori (McKay, 237). It is the point at which the antagonistic dichotomy deepens into the tuakana-teina relationship. Considering this conceptual dynamic is, therefore, essential to understanding Baxter's revisioning of Pakeha identity.

Ko te Pakeha te teina: necessary
CORRECTIVE

Central to the account of Baxter's call to go to Hiruharama is his assertion that 'the Maori is in this country
the Elder Brother in poverty and suffering and closeness to Our Lord—and it is suitable that the pakehas
should learn from him and not vice versa' (McKay,
237). Far from being an obsequious flourish, the designation 'Elder brother' points beyond the simplistic and
reductive dichotomy to the conceptual appropriation of
the tuakana-teina whanau dynamic, the most complete
and schematic model of cross-cultural relations present
in Baxter's work. For the most part, the model remains
only implicit, informing metaphors, language use and
structure; of those occasions where Baxter does expli-
cate the concept in systematic prose, few are published.
Nevertheless, as accounts of his 1968 vision indicate,
the tuakana-teina model was central to Baxter's thinking, and recognition of this aspect of the poems' kaupapa reveals just how radical, and hopeful, Baxter's
take on cross-cultural relationship and Pakeha identity
is.

The hierarchical dynamic of the tuakana or older sibling over the teina or younger sibling is a firmly established aspect of the Tikanga Maori understanding
through which relationships within the whanau are ordered and mana is allocated.[14] The hierarchical distinctions on the basis of birth nonetheless entail interdependence in mutually defining relationship, and these
elements—hierarchy and interdependence—are present
in Baxter's conceptualisation of cross-cultural relationship. The adoption of the tuakana-teina dynamic provided Baxter with a conceptual paradigm, focusing his
long-standing criticism of Pakeha culture's vacuity and
self-satisfied materialism. Recalling his sermon at the
Christchurch Cathedral, Baxter quotes a whakatauki-
style proverb probably of his own coinage: 'Ko te Maori
te tuakana. Ko te Pakeha te teina'.[15] ["**In My View
. . .**"] In a neat parallelism, the two cultures are not
only made distinct, but are drawn in hierarchical relationship, a necessary correction of cross-cultural relations in Aotearoa/New Zealand, eschatological in its inversion of an unjust social order. Through this fusion of
Christian theology and Tikanga Maori the dichotomised
representation of Pakeha and Maori cultures finds reconciliatory substance in the tuakana-teina relationship:
hope for cross-cultural relations in Aotearoa/New
Zealand lies in the acceptance by Pakeha of te ao Maori
as the tuakana in whom the aroha of Christ is found.

Such cross-cultural relationship is modelled in **'For
Hone'**, one of the few instances where Baxter directly
uses the Tikanga Maori terms in verse: 'Tuakana, I am
a hard stone' (**Collected Poems**, 439). The Pakeha teina
is passive, 'a hard stone/Thrown from a heavy sling',
an identity half dead in a dead world, 'a stone man

walking'. It is an existence lamented in the repeated
question 'Ko wai koe?'—who are you? The centrality
of aroha to this tuakana-teina relationship is substantiated by the coat of the Maori tuakana that 'will keep
me warm when I lie down' (an image typically an expression of aroha in the later poetry),[16] a demonstration
of transformative love through which 'the cigarette burn
on the left side of it' becomes 'better than a pocket full
of money'. This is the symbolic hope offered by Baxter's conceptualisation of the tuakana-teina pattern as a
model for race relations, constituting a necessary corrective for inequality and ongoing injustice between
Maori and Pakeha and giving the pervasive dichotomy
reconciliatory substance. Pakeha identity is reconfigured
with te ao Maori in the same conceptual whanau in a
relationship of deferential love.

While manifest even within the structures of the poems,
the modeling of the reciprocal and restorative tuakana-
teina relationship is conveyed most strongly through the
metaphors of the Hiruharama period, which epitomise
the cross-cultural movement of the poetry, enabling a
reconciliatory critique and reconfiguration of being Pakeha.[17] In **'He Waiata mo taku Tangi'** Baxter takes up
the image of the opossum to profess cultural dispossess-
sion, conveying the necessarily deferential stance of the
Pakeha teina towards Maoritanga:

> My soul has long since grown
> blind as an old opossum
> in the roof of the Maori church.

> (**Collected Poems,** 506)

Blindness conveys well the stupidity and lack of self-
awareness attributed elsewhere to Pakeha culture as a
whole; but the image nonetheless expresses the hope
that Pakeha will find sanctuary in relationship with
Maori. The metaphor of the introduced species is also
taken up in the climactic eschatological statement of
Jerusalem Sonnets:

> . . . 'This is the hill fort
> Of our God; it is called Hiruharama!
>
> The goat and the opossum will find a home
> Among the rocks, and the river of joy will flow from
> it!'

> (38)

While made in a declaration of hope for restored community, the image is not flattering: as alien species the
goat and opossum have so overrun their new environment as to become pests. To be given shelter is a mercy
granted, not a right claimed, contingent upon Pakeha
acceptance of God's love as revealed in te ao Maori. As
with that expressed in the Maori Jesus, this judgement
is restorative, imagining Maori and Pakeha as tuakana
and teina in aroha. Such metaphors constitute vital re-

configurations of Pakeha identity in reciprocal relation-ship with Maoritanga, critiquing and reforming the one while restoring and elevating the other.

Far from being merely an idiosyncrasy of his later pe-riod, the 'Maori elements' of Baxter's later poetry—the use of te reo Maori, and references to te ao Maori—are grounded in a revisionist kaupapa in which Pakeha iden-tity is subjected to the necessary corrective of the tuakana-teina model. The dichotomy that pervades Bax-ter's representation of Pakeha and Maori cultures, and which is most often a simplistic inversion of Pakeha na-tionalism, finds reconciliatory substance in this concep-tual appropriation of the tuakana-teina relationship. His-torically speaking, in doing so Baxter anticipated the radical shift in the dominant frame of reference for Pa-keha identity brought on by the Maori renaissance. Moreover, the model of cross-cultural relationship ar-ticulated throughout the later poetry remains remarkable for its movement beyond the timorous antagonism and entrenched indolence of cultural division, suggesting in-stead a necessary corrective of ordered family love.

Notes

1. The image is Gregory O'Brien's. *After Bathing at Baxter's: Essays and Notebooks* (Wellington: Vic-toria University Press, 2002), p. 27.

2. See Mike Riddell, 'Funding Contextual Theology in Aotearoa/New Zealand: The Theological Con-tribution of James K. Baxter' (doctoral thesis, Uni-versity of Otago, 2003). Also *Stimulus: The New Zealand Journal of Christian Thought and Prac-tice* 11.1 (February 2003).

3. The issue is by no means confined to Baxter. Glenn Colquhoun is the latest in a slender yet sig-nificant strand of Pakeha poets who, since the late 1960s, have moved beyond the sentimentalism and tokenism of earlier generations to write what is best described as *cross-cultural* Pakeha poetry. Such writers include: Barry Mitcalfe, Warren Dibble, Graham Lindsay, Bernard Gadd, Berna-dette Hall, Kathleen Gallagher, Simon Williamson, and Anna Jackson.

4. Keri Hulme uses 'bi-cultural' to describe 'Writers of double beginning, inhabiting both *Te Ao Maori* and *Te Ao Pakeha,* but writing for *Te Ao Hou*'. 'Mauri: An Introduction to Bicultural Poetry in New Zealand' in *Only Connect: Literary Perspec-tives East and West,* ed. by G. Amirthanayagam, and S.C. Harrax (Adelaide: Centre for Research in the New Literatures in English, 1981), p. 296. The concern here, however, is with writing by Pakeha who begin in, and move reflexively back into, te ao Pakeha. 'Bi-lingual', used for example by Ian Wedde to explain Hulme's work, is similarly inac-curate as a description of such an approach, as in

most instances the use of te reo Maori is not to an extent that might properly be called bi-lingual. See Wedde's Introduction, *The Penguin Book of New Zealand Verse* (Auckland: Penguin, 1985), p. 51.

5. C.K. Stead, 'James K. Baxter: Towards Jerusalem,' *Kin of Place* (Auckland: Auckland University Press, 2002), p. 318 (first publ. in *Islands* 3 (Autumn 1973).

6. John Newton, 'The Death Throes of Nationalism,' *Landfall* 205 (May 2003), 90-101 (p. 99).

7. Vincent O'Sullivan, *James K. Baxter* (Wellington: Oxford University Press, 1976), p. 52.

8. James K. Baxter, *Listener,* 13 December 1963, p. 12.

9. The final lines of 'The Moon and the Chestnut Tree' contrast a world of light and aroha with one of darkness and oppressive legalistic moralism. *Jerusalem Daybook* (Wellington: Price Milburn, 1971), p. 18.

10. This notion is evident in accounts of the 'minor revelation' in 1968 that led him to Hiruharama. See Frank McKay, *The Life of James K. Baxter* (Auckland: Oxford University Press, 1990), p. 237.

11. *Collected Poems* (Auckland: Oxford University Press, 1995), pp. 347-8.

12. *Jerusalem Sonnets* (Wellington: Price Milburn, 1970), p. 25.

13. *Thoughts about the Holy Spirit* (Wellington: Fu-tuna Press, 1973), p. 5.

14. Arahi Mahuru explains: 'Ko te tuakana te kai-pupiri i te mana, ko te teina te kai-whakatinana. The tuakana is the one who holds the mana of the whanau, the teina is the one who gives it sub-stance, that is, the doer. The teina must always re-spect his tuakana; whatever he does, he must seek his permission before or his approval afterwards if it is to have mana'. In Joan Metge, *New Growth From Old: The Whanau in the Modern World* (Wellington: Victoria University Press, 1995), p. 89.

15. 'In My View . . .' *Listener,* 24 January 1969, p. 10.

16. See for example *Jerusalem Daybook* (Wellington: Price Milburn, 1971), p. 19.

17. The pattern of capitalisation throughout the Hiru-harama period reinforces the shift towards the pri-macy of te ao Maori as tuakana, consistently ren-dering Pakeha in the lower case. Similarly, where

there is explicit translation within the text te reo Maori is most often given preeminence over English, manifesting the deliberate inversion of the reigning power dynamic. Cf. 'Poem to Colin—34' *Jerusalem Sonnets*, p. 42; Sonnet 6, 'Te Whiori O Te Kuri' *Autumn Testament* (Wellington: Price Milburn, 1972), p. 51. Concerning metaphor, Paul Millar makes no overstatement when he affirms it as 'the key to *Jerusalem Sonnets, Jerusalem Daybook* and *Autumn Testament*'. Introduction, *Autumn Testament* by James K. Baxter. New ed. (Auckland: Oxford University Press, 1997), p. xxi.

Dougal McNeill (essay date September 2009)

SOURCE: McNeill, Dougal. "Baxter's Burns." *ka mate ka ora* 8 (September 2009): http://www.nzepc.auckland.ac.nz/kmko/08/ka_mate08_mcneill.asp.

[*In the following essay, taken from the New Zealand Electronic Poetry Centre's online journal,* ka mate ka ora, *McNeill explores the importance of the Scottish poet Robert Burns to Baxter's development as a writer, saying that "Baxter's poetic relations to Burns . . . structure each aspect of his poetic career, and can be heard in unexpected places, most particularly as an unspoken companion to the poetry of the Jerusalem period."*]

There has never been any doubt about the importance of Robert Burns for James K. Baxter: the Scottish poet's ancestral, poetic, political and sexual inspirations and provocations appear everywhere across the range of Baxter's writing and it is a critical commonplace to note affinity and identification. At the same time it is curious to note how this debt is so often acknowledged and then passed over. Family connections are noted, Scottish heritage acknowledged perhaps: but what of *poetics*? What did Baxter *do* with his Burns? There is so much at work in the Baxter oeuvre—so much to pick and so few to do the picking—that to list some of the work still in front of us gives a sense of the enormity of Baxter's range and reach: Baxter and Burns sits as an undeveloped topic alongside Baxter and Lawson, Baxter and Blake, Baxter and Dylan Thomas, Baxter and Lawrence Durrell, to say nothing of that work already done on Baxter and Lowell or Baxter and ballads. Baxter's poetic relations to Burns, I will argue here, structure each aspect of his poetic career, and can be heard in unexpected places, most particularly as an unspoken companion to the poetry of the Jerusalem period.

Baxter, who as a pre-schooler grew up with his father 'quoting Burns and Byron' (*Poems* [*Collected Poems*] 66), was open about his debts to Burns and reflected on them regularly. 'The modern poet,' Baxter wrote in 1945, 'is not a species distinct, and may be taught by Burns as readily as by Eliot.' (McKay 90) This teaching involved a poetic stance or attitude as much as anything else, and in 1943 Baxter wrote to Noel Ginn that 'one who cannot appreciate Burns because he is on the whole traditional and sentimental is in my eyes a literary lost soul.' Indeed, as Ginn learnt a year or two later, it would be 'better to err with Burns and Byron than fall in line with Brasch;' and the young Baxter aspired to 'eventually gain something of the standpoint of Burns.' (Millar, *Spark* 242, 405, 406) This aspiration stayed with Baxter all through his life—he would write of 'the god of Robbie Burns' in a late poem, **'Letter to Max Harris'** (*Poems* 451)—and forms, I will argue here, a central and abiding concern in his poetics and poetic project. Baxter's Burns was more than a poetic ancestor to be acknowledged; he was a point of reference and, via the statue of the Bard in Dunedin's Octagon, a piece of poetic occasion Baxter positioned and re-positioned himself around. Alistair Paterson remembers Baxter reciting Burns' poems in Wellington pubs in the early 1950s, and *The Merry Muses of Caledonia* was one of the few books on Baxter's shelf when he was Burns Fellow at Otago (Drummond 25; McKay 209). At each stage of his poetic development Baxter had Burns as a point of reference. The Bard was a constant presence in his imaginative life. We can hear, if we listen closely enough, echoes of Burns at each moment of Baxter's own development and by the time of the last poems he found 'something of the standpoint of Burns,' not in the dull mannerisms of imitation but in a shared *stance,* an adapted poetics. Most of the evidence for this modelling has been hiding in plain sight, and can, if we linger a little longer over it, help us hear continuities and conversations at work across Baxter's verse.

LITERARY RELATIONS

Baxter's relations to Burns have, in most criticism, been cast as forms of ancestral imagining, with Burns standing in for a wider Scottish inheritance. 'The affinity Baxter wished to assert' with Burns, Alan Riach suggests, was 'a tribal relation rather than a merely literary one.' (120) 'Throughout his life,' Riach argues, 'Baxter chose deliberately and selectively to privilege certain aspects of social identity which could be described as tribal' (112), and this led him to highlight his paternal links with Scotland and Scottish culture over his mother's more genteel, English and academic family connections. This selection had political consequences. 'Baxter's *choice* of tribal alternatives was often intended to be seen as a criticism of the normative Western bourgeois liberal social structures.' Riach continues:

> Privileging the tribal aspect of his family history over the academic, making so much more of his Scottish Gaelic-speaking ancestors than he did of the solid aca-

demic tradition that adhered to his mother's side of the family, was a means by which Baxter could affirm a precedent for his adoption of Māori tribalism.

(118)[1]

A *merely literary* relation: the diminished status Riach accords literary relations strikes me as odd, especially in the discussion of a poet of such passionate and wide-ranging debts and influences. Literary relations—the anxiety and thrill of influence, the conversation with ancestors—are surely central to any serious poet's sense of their own work and project, and the acoustic aspect of these relations—what sounds and phrases linger in the ear, what echoes occur—has been the occasion for much self-reflection and poetic production. Allen Curnow's poem 'An Abominable Temper' significantly *fuses* literary and ancestral relations, noting that 'Allen will get the Bible and the *Poems*' of Burns as part of his ancestral inheritance. (152) With Baxter, a poet for whom ancestry and tribe are such important subjects, literary relations and ancestral relations are more likely blurred than kept separate. Vincent O'Sullivan observes an 'affinity':

> Baxter, to begin with, always felt an affinity with Robert Burns. He admired that poet of his own race who could turn from lyrical delicacy to full-blooded attack when the moment asked for it.

(32)

This has the advantage of drawing our attention to poetic strategy and to the kind of options and vocal range Burns opened up for the young Baxter; but I will argue in this essay that O'Sullivan doesn't take his own case far enough. The clouds of sentimentality and slack mythology that still surround Burns for so many readers— the biscuit-tin reading, perhaps—can distract us from attending to the deep affinities between Baxter and Burns, and from the quite startling measure of Burns' own success. Growing up with the poet and adjusting his reading of him at each new stage in his own career, Baxter's Burns appears as an example of so many of the poetic types Baxter will aspire to become. Burns was a bi-cultural poet, writing with an ear to both his own Lowland Scottish, to the Anglicised culture of his education and to the newly-forming British identity the Union had produced (see Robert Crawford, *Devolving* 88-110). Baxter would in his later work attempt similar sorts of bi-cultural imagination. Burns' poetry is deliberately mixed and 'impure,' shifting between high and low registers, mixing local words and obscenities with philosophical sophistication and exalted vocabulary. It is also bi-lingual, as he produced poems both in Scottish and, albeit less successfully, in English. Baxter's work was always similarly 'impure' and linguistically athletic, and if the red book 'from which [he] should learn Māori' stayed shut (*Poems* 460), a Māori-English linguistic reimagining of Pākehā culture is a clear ambi-

tion of the late poems. These parallels and affinities suggest richly complex literary relations between Baxter and Burns.

WINDS OF FRUITFULNESS: IDENTIFYING POETRY

In his 1963 **'Letter to Robert Burns'** Baxter raises 'a brother's horn' to the other poet (*Poems* 289), suggesting a relation more horizontal, equal and imaginative-collaborative than vertical, ancestral or patriarchal-tribal. Baxter's reading of Burns went deeper than admiration or affinity and was characterised throughout his career by a much more thorough-going process of assimilation and adaptation. Lines, sounds and forms from Burns echo all through Baxter's work. From the use of the difficult Standard Habbie stanza form (sometimes called the 'Burns Stanza') in **'The Thistle'** through the Scottish words and subject-matter of **'The Debt'** to the frequent use of verse letters and quotations within poems, Baxter's poetic tool kit was fitted out with Burnsian innovations. There are plenty of direct allusions too, including 'for all that and all that' in **'A Ballad for the Men of Holy Cross'**—an echo of Burns' famous 'for a' that, an' a' that' in 'A Man's A Man for a' That'—and a hint of Burns' 'blow, blow ye winds!' in the early 'blow wind of fruitfulness.' (*Poems* 337, 41; *Canongate Burns* 494, 512) Burns' passions and obsessions with the natural world, with mortality and death are so often Baxter's, and Baxter's excoriation of 'Pig Island' sexual hypocrisy and bourgeois deceit sounds echoes from Burns' mocking the 'unco guid's' 'better art o' hidin.' (192) Others have made these connections but then passed on: more needs to be made of them.

Robert Crawford's term 'identifying poets' offers a particularly useful frame for viewing the poetic relations between Baxter and Burns. Identifying poets, for Crawford, are 'poets who have made for themselves identities which let them be identified with, re-state and even renovate the identity of a particular territory,' and often they develop this identity 'with and for their own cultures through a fructifying engagement with another culture and literatures.' The identifying poet, as Crawford develops the term, produces work which is concerned with the task of identifying and its problems. Identifying poetry works to create accounts of land and location that can bring it into connection with a culture and a history. This task requires engagement, and the engagement is a source of literary and imaginative energy: 'it is only by remaining dynamic, by evolving, that a culture or a literary tradition continues to live. It is its loopholes, its openness to the "other" or "others" which allows it to re-view and develop itself.' (*Identifying* 1, 13) The advantage of thinking about the activity of 'identifying' as against the status of 'identity' is that it draws our attention to the *process* involved in the task, its status as an incomplete project requiring negotiation and self-reflection. Such focus is doubly useful in the context of Pākehā literature where the quest for 'the identity of a particular territory' takes place against the historical legacy of colonisation and alongside pre-existing Māori narratives and identities.[2]

It is obvious how Baxter, writing for 'the tribe that is not a tribe' (*Poems* 494), fits Crawford's model of the 'identifying poet.' Burns is also, Crawford suggests, 'one of the archetypal modern poets in his formation of a multiple self or selves' (*Identifying* 4), and the two poets share this shape-shifting, identity-constructing quality as their work negotiates dual languages, cultures and contested historical and geographical sites. The use of multiple names to indicate this shape-shifting—Baxter's development from Jim to Hemi, from Jum to Jimmy to James Q Oxter, Burns' punningly allusive signatures as Robert Ruisseaux or Rab the Ranter—indicate another affinity. Baxter took from Burns a sense of the poet's vocation and sources. Burns found his inspiration on the land and, in society, from the edges, writing to a correspondent: 'I have often coveted the acquaintance of that part of mankind commonly known by the ordinary phrase of Blackguards, sometimes farther than was consistent with the safety of my character' (Thomas Crawford, 'Burns' 190) and he attributed a good deal of his inspiration to this company. Baxter generalises this Romantic stance:

> Art [. . .] is not bred by culture but by its opposite: that level of hardship or awareness of moral chaos where the soul is too destitute to be able to lie to itself.
>
> (Isichei 246)

From this shared vantage point, Burns' and Baxter's work circles around a surprisingly similar set of themes: the land, cultural identity, especially the possibilities of the bi-cultural and bi-lingual poetic form. Tracing Baxter's Burns, the Burns that emerges from his work and the relations they produce can offer us a guide to shifts in Baxter's own poetics. What starts out as an ancestral figure develops in the writing into a poetic model. Baxter's Burns turns, to use Robert Crawford's phrase, from a piece of the poet's identity into a poetic occasion for *identifying*. The shift affects each stage in Baxter's career.

The Taieri: 'As tartan clans'

'I would glorify / Innumerable men in whose breasts my heart once beat, / Is beating' (*Poems* 31): Baxter's earliest poems set out to honour a particular account of his family past and of Scottish settlement in Otago. The land, in these early poems, is bound up with European ancestry, and the imperative, unusual in his oeuvre, is deployed: 'Forget not those whom Scotland bred / Above whose bones our cities stand.' (*Poems* 32) The young man had a father who 'used to sit him on his knee and read him Burns, whose poems were almost his Bible' (McKay 26), and in these early poems he turns his reading out to describe the world around him.

'The Thistle' uses natural imagery to represent Scottish settlement and heritage and to make some sly observations on the trick of standing upright here. Baxter writes Standard Habbie—the verse form Burns perfected and made his own—with an ease all the more astonishing when one remembers the author was not yet twenty:[3]

> Their seeds within an alien land
> Cast heedful from a Scottish hand
> Have flowered a hundred years, to stand
>   In their own right,
> Their gossamer by breezes fanned
>   Airy as sunlight.
>
> I have forgiven, nor upbraid
> That they so ruinous invade
> Valley and homestead, green arrayed
>   As tartan clans—
> Full arrogant with ready blade
>   On all that's Man's.
>
> ("The Thistle," *Poems* 50)

These early conversations with Burns, though, for all their metrical dexterity are for the most part relatively unsophisticated meditations: Baxter's identification with the 'tartan clans' is clear and uncomplicated. In 1951 he restated in prose some of the arguments he had made in the 1944 verse:

> a hundred years is long enough for our society to have acquired a shape of its own. And not always by a complete break with the situation of our ancestors. The peasant clansmen of the Western Highlands of Scotland became the clannish farmers of Otago. The Otago hills and sea coast are not unlike the hills and sea coast of Argyllshire. So I have been fortunate enough to find the readymade myth of longbearded Gaelic-speaking giants distilling whisky among the flax from time immemorial. The ancestral face is very familiar to me.
>
> (*Recent Trends* [*Recent Trends in New Zealand Poetry*] 7)

This initial immersion in Burns helps explain Baxter's astonishing lyrical self-confidence and ready mythologising stance. The 'readymade myth' he makes for himself in these early works is not enough to carry the weight of his later ambitions but it allows him to bypass then-prevalent 'never a soul at home' anxieties. The audacity of Baxter's first act of 'identifying poetry' involves him transplanting Burns and Burns' context and insisting that they are familiar to Otago. Compare this familiarity and the standing 'in their own right' of Baxter's Standard Habbie with Curnow's more strained account of Dunedin's relationship to Scotland in 'Dunedin—for James K. Baxter':

> There, none wills
> Redress or dreams it, or pondering some lapse

Out of a dream strays back into that town
A mirage of the cracked antarctic stole,
Or stumbles on the original dazed stone
Pitched out of Scotland to the opposite Pole.

(Curnow 200)

Baxter is much too sure-footed to stumble 'among these hills' (*Poems* 32) and where Curnow reads dislocation and confusion in the Scottish-Otago juxtaposition ('dazed stone' and 'straying' dreams) Baxter's is a self-confident image of a 'shape of its own.' Whatever the ethical and imaginative inadequacy in this initial identifying act, it offered Baxter a confident and clear starting-point for his later, more complex work.

Occasional notes of anxiety break through—'And Scotland was my spiritual home, / Or so it seemed' runs a line in the **'Letter to Noel Ginn'** (*Poems* 29)—but the earliest of Baxter's engagements with Burns and Burns' context are generally happy to remain at the level of identification rather than engagement. We can read the suggestion that the Otago hills are 'not unlike' Argyll metonymically for what the later verse will reject as an example of spiritual and cultural sickness: Pākehā refusal to recognise Aotearoa's distinctive history and the indigenous claims and relations to land that pre-date Pākehā ones.

All that comes later though, and the first development in Baxter's dialogue with Burns must be a more limited, negative and seemingly anti-Romantic one. In 1951 Baxter outlines poetry's apparent exhaustion and impossibility in a deftly dialectical verse, and at the same time positions himself to take up Burns' role, this time as a consciously worked inheritance. **'The Immortals':**

Less than the wind's rant now
Red Hugh, Little John
Too handy with a gun;
Clods cover the randy
Bullnecked Ayrshireman
Who sent cannon to the French—
And who'll fill their bench?

Could I with pentagon, candle,
Gather ghost, limb,
As they stood in manhood's prime,
We'd drink till Truth glimmered
Over the glass's rim;
And at cockcrow's judgement
Count the night well spent.

But truth's out of fashion.
Why should a man beat
His brain for rhymes, and sweat?
Add shilling to shilling
And walk the flat street:
Keep door and window sealed
When the wind's wild.

(*Poems* 99)

By alluding to Burns as the man who 'sent cannon to the French' and thus drawing attention to Burns' politi-cal activity, Baxter brings him into a more immediate relation with the present as an example of political daring and potential poetic and political radicalism (see Thomas Crawford, *Burns*, cn. 7). He was also showing himself to be some decades in advance of most Burns scholarship, which has only in the last few decades fully acknowledged the extent of Burns' radical democratic political engagement.[4] Baxter's family background and literary upbringing provided him with the raw materials to build his own work but his relationship to Burns needed to be worked over before he could use it fully in his own poetic projects. **'The Immortals'** begins this process by casting Burns as an example that contemporary poetry fails to follow ('truth's out of fashion') and by setting himself up as an inheritor of the tradition: the rhetorical question 'who'll fill their bench?' may be answered negatively by the rest of the poem but the very context of articulation in a poem and the act of questioning lead the reader to see Baxter as pursuing what he feigns to refuse. If the poetry of the 1940s positions Burns as one of the ancestors then this poem of the 1950s draws on him for poetry's contemporary demands. It will take a realisation in the 1960s—that 'the Māori owned the land' (*Poems* 279)—and with it an abandonment of imagery of Scottish-New Zealand *identity* for these two parts of Baxter's Burns to be integrated and for him to be able to put his poetic 'brother' to use.

THE LEITH: 'A TRIBESMAN CUT OFF FROM HIS
TRIBE'

For anyone associated with Dunedin, Robert Burns is not just an imaginary relation but also a very physical one. His statue in the Octagon marks the city's distinctive relationship with Victorian Scotland[5] and several times in the 1960s Baxter uses the Burns statue to renegotiate his own connections to Burns and Burns' place in his imaginative world. When a student at Otago University Baxter would often 'look to the statue of Burns, with his back to the big cathedral and his face to the Oban Hotel, for approval and consolation.' (*The Man* [*The Man on the Horse*] 93) Two poems of the 1960s—**'Letter to Robert Burns'** (1963) and **'A Small Ode on Mixed Flatting'** (1967)—address the statue directly and in doing so allow Baxter the chance to reposition himself and his poetry as part of a conversation with his model identifying poet.

Pig Island Letters made more explicit than before Baxter's conviction that 'a poet is / The sore thumb of the tribe' (*Poems* 268), and **'Letter to Robert Burns'** identifies Burns as a fellow dissident, another outsider figure. This is the poem where Baxter is closest in his *poetic* (rather than ancestral) identification with Burns. The two poet 'brothers' share as outsiders the restrictions of self and society: 'King Robert with the horn of stone! / Perhaps your handcuffs were my own.' Baxter imagines Burns' romantic and alcoholic dilemmas:

If, lying in the pub latrine,
You muttered, 'Take me back to Jean,'
The reason for your mandrake groans
Is wrapped like wire around my bones.

(*Poems* 290-91)

Baxter's Romantic anti-academic stance—'Biology, mythology, / Go underground when the bookmen preach'
(*Poems* 291)—matches some moods of Burns:

What's a' your jargon o' your Schools,
Your Latin names for horns an' stools?
If honest nature made you *fools*
          What sairs your Grammers?
Ye'd better taen up *spades* and *shools*
Or *knappin-hammers.*

(*Canongate Burns* 135)

What is significant about the **'Letter'** [**"Letter to Robert Burns"**] is the way that Baxter for the first time
combines ideological and poetic identification with a
recognition of cultural distance. When in 1944 he saw
flowers 'from a Scottish hand' standing 'in their own
right,' by 1963 he places himself as a 'stranger' in
Burns' Scottish cultural context:

Robert, only a heart I bring,
No gold of words to grace a king,
Nor can a stranger lift that flail
That cracked the wall of Calvin's jail
And earned you the lead garland of
A people's moralising love,
Till any Scotsman with the shakes
Can pile on your head his mistakes
And petrify a boozaroo
Reciting *Tam O'Shanter* through

(*Poems* 290)

Baxter asserts his poetic authority to read Burns against
the 'lead garland' of moralising and misreading—indeed, three years on from this poem's composition he
will offer his own reading of 'Tam O'Shanter' and
through it map out his political vision—but unlike his
youthful work the **'Letter'** marks a clear distance between the poet 'stranger' and the 'Scotsman with the
shakes' as they relate to the Scottish poet. The distance
this brings between poet and subject matter, one of
Crawford's 'loopholes' for the 'identifying poet', allows
Baxter to sound ideas and positions off Burns, to set
Burns up as a model Baxter. Opposing knowledge to
the 'iron boot of education,' identifying a 'snake-haired
Muse' connected to poetry, sexuality and wild otherness
against respectability, and opposing these to 'Calvin's
jail' and Puritanism the **'Letter'** rehearses what will become familiar Baxterian themes and rehearses them
against the example of Burns. When the **"Letter"** announces that 'Biology, mythology, / Go underground
when the bookmen preach' Baxter also introduces two
elements from what will become for him a poetic keyword: tribe.

Before 1960 the word 'tribe' appears only once in Baxter's published writing and in a context where it is not
referring to Pākehā. In 1963 it appears for the first time
as a word to be applied to Pākehā in **'The Dragon
Mask.'** After that it appears by my count thirty-two
times, twenty-three of them after 1968. By contrast the
word 'clan' appears three times—twice in work of the
1940s, once in a poem of 1951—and appears nowhere
in Baxter's poetry after 1951.⁶ This shift in vocabulary
has clear political and cultural connotations. Clan, according to the *OED* derives from Scottish Gaelic and
has traditionally been used to describe groups related
by ancestry or marriage; in New Zealand English it is
used to refer to non-Māori societies. Tribe, at least before iwi and hāpu became common terms in English usage, usually describes Māori society or what Pākehā
understand of Māori society.⁷ 'Tribe' became the great
connotative keyword in Baxter's late imagining of Pākehā identity: 'The founding of a tribe,' 'the tribe of
nga mokai,' 'the roll call of the tribe,' 'the drunks are
my own tribe' (*Poems* 468, 507, 509, 510). Time and
again in the late poems the word 'tribe' is at the centre
of a poem's imaginative order and carries the utopian
energy and charge of Baxter's new 'identifying poetry'
of potential Pākehā location and place. This word, carrying a heavy ideological and spiritual burden in the
imaginative schemes of the later poems, first appears as
part of Baxter's conversation with Burns.

In 1951 Baxter told the New Zealand Writers' Conference that he had 'readymade myths' from the 'clansmen
of the Western Highlands.' By 1967, in lectures delivered in his role as Burns Fellow, both the word 'clan'
and the sense of unproblematic identification with Scottish myths have been replaced by a more troubled tone
and by a more complex and rewarding 'tribal' identification that recognises its own problems and the contested national and historical legacy it is operating
within. There is a well-nigh Brechtian alienation effect
occurring in these lectures as a Pākehā writer uses in
place of the familiar term (clan) with all its denotative
certainties a term (tribe) used to that point almost exclusively to denote Māori and for most of his audience
carrying connotations of Māori life. Riach's comment
about tribal and literary relations misses the poetic complexity in the 1967 context of a Pākehā writer using the
term tribe. The word is out ahead of the concept, making it new. The more complex Jerusalem-era images of
cultural relations find their gestation in these meditations on Burns and Scottishness. Discussing his ancestors in 1967 Baxter described an artist as 'a tribesman
cut off from his tribe [. . .] I stand then as a tribesman
left over from the dissolution of a tribe.' (*The Man* 12)
Accepting that the tribe has been dissolved and that the
'readymade myths' cannot be sustained, Baxter faces
the dilemma: 'what can a tribesman do when he has no
tribe?'

For me it is not death itself but the knowledge of death that makes me reach out to *the tribe that no longer exists*. As I have done time and again in imagination, looking for some fragment of the lost unity on which to build a poem, but now for a different reason, I go along the river track towards that gully where the clan built their houses.

(**The Man** 28; my emphasis)

Baxter's slippage from tribe to clan here reveals the strain and the full linguistic and ideological strangeness and originality of his own re-imagining. As part of this re-imagining Burns, whose work Baxter tells his audience he has 'loved' all his life, is presented both as an alternative poetic resource to Englishness and as a part of a tribal connection: 'he is much nearer to me than Shakespeare [. . .] a tribal gift, the book by which I could communicate with the dead.' (**The Man** 91) For all its talk of ancestry, these passages from **The Man on the Horse** point towards new *poetic* connections: what, after all, will be the radical impulse of the *Jerusalem Sonnets* and *Autumn Testament* but to imagine what sort of poetic 'tribal gifts' could produce cross-cultural relations of the kind captured in the image of 'a faceless face, Māori or Pākehā either // As the light catches it' (*Poems* 472)? Many critics have read these lectures for the insights they offer to Baxter's poetics and social vision: it deepens our understanding of this vision if we remember that his points are made not in a generalising or explicitly polemical context but as part of his ongoing conversation with Burns.

The shift from 'clan' to 'tribe' is one indication of a shift in Baxter's use of Burns, and after the negative work of de- or re-mythologising in **'The Immortals'** and **'Letter to Robert Burns'** the 1967 lectures allowed Baxter the chance to position Burns in a poetic relation to the more explicitly social programmatic task his own later verse would set itself. 'Tam O'Shanter,' he told his audience, 'has lain at the bottom of my mind for thirty years, a fable of Everyman brought from the mind of the tribe by a great poet.' (**The Man** 119) Setting Burns up as a great poet able to summon fables from 'the mind of the tribe' places him in an active and identifying relation to the present, and in the 1967 writings Baxter is able to start this sort of strategic deployment of Burns. Having sharpened his poetic relations through early negative dialectic ('Clods cover the randy / Bullnecked Ayrshireman'), Baxter can now put Burns to present use. At a 1966 rally against the Vietnam War, 'Baxter assured the crowd of some four hundred that had Burns been alive, he would have been on their side.' (McKay 212) The 1967 lecture **'The Man on the Horse'** is given over to an analysis of Burns' great poem 'Tam O'Shanter':

Care, mad to see a man sae happy,
E'en drown'd himsel amang the nappy;
As bees flee ham wi' lades o' treasure,

The minutes wing'd their way wi' pleasure:
Kings may be blest, but *Tam* was glorious,
O'er a' the ills o' life victorious!

(*Canongate Burns* 397)

It soon becomes obvious that Baxter's analysis is not a reading of Burns at all but a reading of Burns' poetics in the light of Baxter's own developments and plans. He is, as so often in his work, sounding off Burns the better to hear his own thoughts:

'a' the ills o' life' [. . .] a cold pressure never absent from the adult mind; and this burden is cast off for a moment, not just by intoxication, but by what it stands for—the Roman *fraternitas*, the Māori *aroha*, the appearance or reality of group love, a merging in the collective warmth of the tribe.

(*The Man* 104-05)

The value of love or aroha as 'the collective warmth of the tribe' will become a dominant note in Baxter's verse and social commentary: it first emerges as part of a meditation on Burns. Burns is produced as a 'great poet' able to bring this fable of love 'from the mind of the tribe': again he is placed in an active and identifying relationship. That Baxter's reading of 'Tam O'Shanter' is hardly convincing as Burns criticism is beside the point. What matters in these lectures is the way Baxter uses a great Burns poem as an occasion for his own poetic re-positioning. **'A Small Ode on Mixed Flatting'** from the same year as the important lecture deploys Burns in a similarly programmatic fashion:

But Robert Burns, that sad old rip
From whom I got my Fellowship
Will grunt upon his rain-washed stone
Above the empty Octagon,
And say—'O that I had the strength
To slip yon lassie half a length!
Apollo! Venus! Bless my ballocks!
Where are the games, the hugs, the frolics?
Are all you bastards melancholics?
Have you forgotten that your city
Was founded well in bastardry
And half your elders (God be thankit)
Were born the wrong side of the blanket?
You scholars, throw away your books
And learn your songs from lasses' looks
As I did once'—Ah, well; it's grim;
But I will have to censor him.
He liked to call a spade a spade
And toss among the glum and staid
A poem like a hand grenade—

(*Poems* 397)

This poem involves a complex ventriloquism in its mixing of familiar and new themes and emphases. There is also a careful vagueness or double-meaning to games, hugs and frolics, a vagueness of a kind that will be developed in the poetry of the Jerusalem era: **'A Small Ode on Mixed Flatting'** manages to be at once about sex and ostensibly about non-sexual physicality and affection. The sexual energy and its opposition to the hypocrisy of the authorities draws on both Burns and Baxter's earlier work, as does the confidence in the poet's social vocation, to toss 'a poem like a hand grenade' amongst the complacency or indifference of the social world. At the same time Baxter has Burns voice two new themes that will dominate the next stage of his own work. His plea for scholars to throw away their books is more emphatic and absolute than earlier anti-academic moments and anticipates his soon to be announced plan for a place 'where the people, both Māori and Pākehā, would try to live without money or books, worship God and work on the land.' (McKay 237) Baxter's Burns poses a question—'where are the games, the hugs, the frolics?'—that expands a long-standing critique of social coldness and Puritanism. Earlier poems had attacked that legacy; the Burns statue's ventriloquised call for games, hugs and frolics anticipates a very visible part of the social project of Baxter's last years. McKay:

> One public expression of aroha was the celebrated Jerusalem hug. Baxter would bear down on people and envelop them in his arms. Outside Jerusalem the hairy guru he had become caused physical consternation to those uncomfortable with physical contact. Hugging was part of the hippie culture.
>
> (263)

In 1967 **'A Small Ode on Mixed Flatting'** and lecture **'The Man on the Horse'** both use Burns, then, to indicate new directions. By the end of 1968 it was clear that these new directions could not be pursued in Dunedin: 'My dreams do not go South.' (**'Valediction,'** *Poems* 432) Baxter's final, more indirect though more thoroughly integrated engagement with Burns, I want to finish by suggesting, is to be found in his own most self-consciously 'identifying' poetry.

THE WHANGANUI: 'FOUNDING A TRIBE'

What is the distinctive tone of the poetry of the Jerusalem era? A number of descriptive terms have been suggested—demotic, folk, plain language, writing coming down off 'its high romantic stilts' (Stead 10)—and whatever the aspect identified most accounts of these works see in them breaks with past practice. This poetic break has wider implications. As John Newton notes: 'the Baxter of the Jerusalem era achieved what for a New Zealand poet remains unrivalled celebrity. And in this re-invention he discovered a path, if not precisely *in* his poetry then *through* it, to the public vocation to which he had always aspired. The poet emerges as social activist.' ('The Baxter Effect' 11) This social activist stance is amongst other things an integration of his long-standing poetic relations with Burns. After a passing reference in **'Letter to Max Harris'** (1969) to 'the god of Robert Burns' (*Poems* 455) there are no more explicit references to the Bard in Baxter's work, but his example—especially when we remember Baxter's frequent testimonies to his life-long engagement with Burns—can be heard everywhere.

Consider the first of the *Jerusalem Sonnets*:

> The small grey cloudy louse that nests in my beard
> Is not, as some have called it, 'a pearl of God'—
>
> No, it is a fiery tormentor
> Waking me at two a.m.
>
> Or thereabouts, when the lights are still on
> In the houses in the pa, to go across thick grass
>
> Wet with rain, feet cold, to kneel
> For an hour or two in front of the red flickering
>
> Tabernacle light—what He sees inside
> My meandering mind I can only guess—
>
> A madman, a nobody, a raconteur
> Whom He can joke with—'Lord,' I ask Him,
>
> 'Do You or don't You expect me to put up with lice?'
> His silent laugh still shakes the hills at dawn.
>
> (*Poems* 455)

This is not usually the poetry we reach for when we think of examples of Baxter's relations with Burns' inheritance. But in many ways these lines mark a deep re-imaging of the Burns role and the Burns stance for the oppositional needs the Jerusalem era demanded.

We can hear across the Jerusalem-era poetry what we in the twenty-first century have come to call an ecological vision, something Baxter and Burns both share. 'The simple bard, rough at the rustic plough' (*Canongate Burns* 177) stands behind the ecological imagery of the *Jerusalem Sonnets*: 'Many many think it out of date / That I should bend my back in a field' (*Poems* 458). The spirituality of the sonnets is connected to their presentation of a particular relationship to land and labour:

> Yesterday I planted garlic,
> Today, sunflowers—'the non-essentials first'
>
> Is a good motto
>
> (*Poems* 463)

Which in turn echoes Burns' complexly formed connections between Christianity, nature and learning:

> Give me a spark o' Nature's fire,
> That's a' the learning I desire;
> Then, tho' I drudge thro' drab an' mire
> At pleugh or cart,
> My Muse, tho' hamely in attire,
> May touch the heart.
>
> (*Canongate Burns* 132)

The 'small grey cloudy louse' in Baxter's beard echoes another louse, the 'ugly, creepan, blasted wonner' of Burns' 'To a Louse.' Lice are for both poets images of the waywardness and physicality of existence, and both use lice to develop an ideal of a Christianity based on honesty, in opposition to hypocrisy and social cant, and based on self-knowledge and love. Spotting the 'crowlan ferlie' leads Burns to wonder:

> O wad some Power the giftie gie us
> To *see oursels as others see us*!
> It wad frae monie a blunder free us,
>   An' foolish notion:
> What airs in dress an' gait wad lea'e us,
>   An' ev'n Devotion!
>
> ('To a Louse,' *Canongate* 132)

The informality of this image has both a thematic importance and a role in creating what Newton calls the 'conversational' mode of address in the later work. ('The Baxter Effect' 13) Baxter favoured the verse letter from the beginning of his career but it becomes a much more prominent form in the last years, and again the modelling from Burns becomes clear in comparison. Burns used his interlocutors—his verse Epistles and Epitaphs, and his extensive correspondence with various supporters, friends, and lovers—to create for himself a world of poetic civility and equality where his ideas and poems could find community, in verse versions of eighteenth-century clubs and societies, something hard to come by for their author in the politically constricted world of Hanoverian Scotland. Baxter borrows the move for similar political ends. In addressing Colin Durning, Sam Hunt, Frank McKay, Peter Olds, Eugene O'Sullivan, John Weir and others, Baxter created for himself a world of informal company where ideas and utopian impulses could circulate, providing the poetry with both the immediacy and directness of friendly communication and the social civility of friendship. Like Burns', Baxter's was a notably masculine (and masculinist) verse community; for all the other pressures from the times that the Jerusalem era poems register, they are remarkably untouched by the upheaval in gender relations and battles for women's liberation. Like Burns also, it is notable that the bulk of Baxter's late writing did not appear until after his death. Part of the private posture of a verse letter is, to be sure, posturing, as the poem reaches a wider audience, but part of it in both poets was genuine, and many of Baxter's later poems were sent to friends with little formal thought as to their publishing destiny (see Millar, Introd. to *Autumn Testament*).

These echoes and similarities are important but, more than any stylistic instance of affinity, it is in the cultural and poetic *modelling* of the late poems that Burns' presence can be most clearly felt. I mentioned Burns' bilingualism and bi-culturalism above, and while it would be absurd to suggest these as major motivating factors in Baxter's own poetic direction, it is surely important for his last works' shaping that he had grown up as a poet in constant contact with bi-lingual and bi-cultural poetry of this kind. The Māori words in *Jerusalem Sonnets* are hardly an example of bi-lingual poetry[8] but that is where their utopian impulse and energies point, and they have a poetic relation to the complexly bilingual Scottish and English poems of Burns. The language of Baxter's last poems struggles to find a location for its own authenticity, placing words in Māori, youth slang ('he kept his cool, man' *Poems* 446), religious devotion and proper names against the official language of bureaucracy and 'mainstream' Pākehā culture:

> I am only half sane
> But the sane half tells me that newspapers were made
>
> For wiping arses and covering tables,
> Not for reading—now, man, I have a table cloth.
>
> (*Poems* 462)

In wiping his arse with the language of official culture Baxter asks where the location of authentic culture is to be found. He engages in what Robert Crawford, discussing Burns, calls 'vernacular negotiations with cultural authority.' (*Burns and Cultural Authority* x)

What has been the impact of these negotiations? For Ian Wedde, Baxter's work:

> has done more than anything else in our literature to bring into balance, for us and in us, that precariously alert yet instinctive sense of internal relation between *who* and *where,* between language and location: the culture of what *is.*
>
> (44)

That Baxter may have learnt at least part of this sense through years of close reading and attention to a poet for whom 'language and location' were abiding concerns adds an extra dimension to our understanding of his own poetic lineage. Burns was striving for an adequate balance between the *who* of poetic self-fashioning and the *where* of a repressively anti-democratic and kirk-dominated Ayrshire, working at the relations between the uncertain *who* of Scottishness and the newly organised *where* of post-Union Britain between the languages of English and Scottish and the locations of Ayr, Edinburgh and Dumfries. This was a lucky inheritance for a Pākehā poet trying to re-imagine the ethics, poetics and politics of his own spirituality, language and location.

'AND WHEN THE RIVER FOG RISES'

My aim in this essay has been more analytical than evaluative and I have tried to show some of the details of the literary relations between Baxter and Robert

Burns. There has been implicit in my organisation a teleological scheme, as Baxter's writing around Burns proceeds from the identification of the early work through the de-mythologising and distancing complexities of the poems of the 1960s and comes to a conclusion in the fully integrated local voice of the Jerusalem era. To illustrate this movement in the poems does not tell us anything though, about their *success*. Did Baxter's writing around with 'the culture of what *is*' achieve this success? *Does it work?*

> But Mousie, thou art no thy lane,
> In proving *foresight* may be vain:
> The best-laid schemes o' *Mice* an' *Men*
>   Gang aft agley,
> An' leave us nought but grief an' pain,
>   For promised joy!

('To a Mouse,' Canongate 96)

A full assessment of the ethical and spiritual 'schemes' of the Jerusalem era falls outside the scope of an essay like this. The difficulties they pose for us as contemporary readers though may stand as a final affinity between Baxter and Burns. Edwin Muir, writing in 1949, declared that 'for a Scotsman to see Burns simply as a poet is almost impossible.' (57) Reading and thinking about Burns is always, whatever the wishes of even the most formalist or New Critical of readers, at the same time reading and thinking about Scottish culture in general, about the status of the Scottish language, about the place of the Bard in the national mythology. In a similar manner, for a Pākehā to see Baxter simply as a poet is almost impossible because the obsessions of his work—to do with Pākehā recognition of Māori, unresolved questions of land and ownership and identity and possession—are obsessions with a cultural and political charge still quite active today. Baxter, like Burns, is a culturally contested figure.

If in some moods his poetry strikes the contemporary reader as too casual in its assumptions of how easily Pākehā may approach the Māori world (**'Sestina of the River Road'** asks of God to 'grant me a hut in the Māori paddock' **Poems** 590); at other moments there is in Baxter a recognition that the sort of relations the poems envisage are *anticipatory,* requiring the labour of time, negotiation and the imaginative leaps of identifying poetry:

>   I must go, my friends,
> Into the dark, the cold, the first beginning
> Where the ribs of the ancestors are the rafters
> Of a meeting house—windows broken
> And the floor white with bird dung—in there
> The ghosts gather who will instruct me
> And when the river fog rises
> Te ra rite tonu te Atua—
> The sun who is like the Lord
> Will warm my bones, and his arrows

> Will pierce to the centre of the shapeless clay of the mind.

("A Pair of Sandals," Poems 600-01)

There are windows to be fixed, bird dung to be swept away: there is in other words work to be done, labour requiring the properly de-colonised relations the earlier poems promised. But there is waiting to be done too, for the river fog to rise, for the sun to shine. The political and ethical obligations Baxter's poems imply need to be assessed with this anticipation in mind, and in a different register to how we would think through the pamphlet or the manifesto. Writing about 'Burns' art speech,' Seamus Heaney observes:

> We can prefigure a future by re-imagining our pasts. In poetry, however, this prefiguring is venturesome and suggestive, more like a melodic promise than a social programme. It is not like a blueprint for a better world which might spring from the mind of a social engineer. Rather, it arises from the cravings of the spirit as expressed in language, in all of those patiences and impatiences which language embodies.

(383)

'A melodic promise' to end with, then. Not Baxter's Burns, but to stretch the word a little, Baxter's *burns,* Baxter's rivers, and the promise they hold for re-imagining the Pākehā past and working toward the impatient demands for recognition in the present:

> only the voice of rivers,
> Rakaia, Rangitata,
> Ohau, Clutha,
> and now the Wanganui
> who washes my body
> before its burial

("He Waiata mo taku Tangi," Poems 508)

Notes

1. I am not convinced that Baxter did anything as simple as 'adopt Māori tribalism.' Such a view would need rethinking in the light of John Newton's *The Double Rainbow: James K. Baxter, Ngāti Hau and the Jerusalem Commune.*

2. These are far from merely historical questions. Michael Laws' championing of Wanganui against Whanganui, while hardly poetic, shows why what might seem like the excessive care or self-consciousness in Crawford's phrasing is politically vital.

3. On the Standard Habbie see Dunn.

4. It is worth noting also that the important Burns scholar Thomas Crawford taught at Auckland University during part of Baxter's life, and chapters 5 and 6 of his *Burns: A Study of the Poems and Songs* first appeared in *Landfall,* so we can as-

sume that Baxter had at least seen them. Crawford also reviewed Baxter's *Howrah Bridge* in *Landfall* 64. Paul Millar suggests that 'it's quite likely Tom Crawford met Baxter on a number of occasions. Crawford and Bill Pearson were close friends, and Pearson was extremely close to Baxter and they'd often meet and drink together in Auckland—drinking sessions Crawford would attend.' (Personal communication)

5. This is a distinctive relationship more vexed than the City Council's promotional imagery always lets on, and if there is an 'Antipodean Antisyzygy' it is represented by the images of the two Burns statues: one a statue of a great democrat, libertine and sensualist, the other a tribute to the fanatically Puritanical Rev. Dr Burns of First Church, who found 'the name he bore was odious' and who claimed he would 'spend the rest of his days in repudiating the connection' between himself and his uncle (Alexander Duffield, *Recollections of Travels Abroad,* 1889, quoted in Dougherty 40). Thomas Burns was also honoured in 1892 with a statue in the Octagon; his uncle's remains but his own was taken down in 1949.

6. For 'clan' see *Poems* 31, 50, 114. For 'tribe' or 'tribal' in 1957, 181 (once), 1962, 250 (once), 1963, 268, 289 (twice), 1965, 318 (once), 1966, 336 (once), 1967, 394 (once), 1968, 425, 428 (twice), 1969, 458, 468, 471 (three times), 1971, 507, 510, 510, 509, 531, 531, (six times), 1972, 538, 550, 554, 560, 564, 568, 574, 574, 575, 581, 590, 592 (thirteen times).

7. So, to confine my example to New Zealand works printed around the time Baxter was Burns Fellow, compare John Kidd, *The Sutherland Clan* (1969; Hocken Library Pamphlet OCO9K) and C R Willis and M Bathgate, *Genealogical Table of Anderson Branch of the Calder Clan* (1969; Hocken Library Pamphlet 090983711) with Matine Kereama, *The Tail of the Fish: Māori Memories of the Far North* (1968; Hocken Library Pamphlet KPP, WMK), noted as 'a collection of legends of the Aupouri tribe' or Best, *Tuhoe: The Children of the Mist.* For a contemporary use of 'clan' see Hunter.

8. I am using the terms bi-lingual and bi-cultural rather loosely, subordinate as they are here to 'identifying' poetry, which is always at work as a process and never at rest as an achieved state. But see Dennison.

Works Cited

Baxter, James K. *Collected Poems.* Ed. John Weir. Melbourne: Oxford UP, 2004.

———. *The Man on the Horse.* Dunedin: Otago UP, 1967.

———. *Recent Trends in New Zealand Poetry.* Christchurch: Caxton, 1951.

Best, Elsdon. *Tuhoe: The Children of the Mist. A Sketch of the Origin, History, Myths and Beliefs of the Tuhoe Tribe.* 1925. Wellington: Reed, 1972.

Burns, Robert. *The Canongate Burns: The Complete Poems and Songs.* Ed. Andrew Noble and Patrick Scott Hogg. Edinburgh: Canongate, 2001.

Crawford, Robert. *Devolving English Literature.* Oxford: Clarendon, 1992.

———. *Identifying Poets: Self and Territory in Twentieth-Century Poetry.* Edinburgh: Edinburgh UP, 1993.

———, ed. *Robert Burns and Cultural Authority.* Iowa City: U of Iowa P, 1997.

Crawford, Thomas. *Burns: A Study of the Poems and Songs.* Edinburgh: Oliver and Boyd; Stanford, CA: Stanford UP, 1960.

———. 'Burns, Love, and Liberty.' In *Society and the Lyric: A Study of the Song Culture of Eighteenth-Century Scotland.* Edinburgh: Scottish Academic Press, 1979. 185-212.

Curnow, Allen. *Early Days Yet: New and Collected Poems 1941-1997.* Auckland: Auckland UP, 1997.

Dennison, John. 'Ko Te Pākehā Te Teina: Baxter's Cross-Cultural Poetry.' *Journal of New Zealand Literature* 23.2 (2005): 36-46.

Dougherty, Ian. *As Others See Us: Dunedin through Visitors' Eyes.* Dunedin: Saddle Hill, 2009.

Drummond, Wilhelmina J. 'Insights into James K. Baxters' Personality and the New Zealand Cultural Environment 1950s to 1970s.' *Journal of New Zealand Literature* 13 (1995): 23-38.

Dunn, Douglas. 'A Very Scottish Kind of Music: Burns' Native Metric.' In Robert Crawford, ed. *Robert Burns and Cultural Authority.* 58-85.

Heaney, Seamus. 'Burns' Art Speech.' *Finders Keepers: Selected Prose 1971-2001.* New York: Farrar, Straus, Giroux, 2002. 378-95.

Hunter, James. *Scottish Exodus: Travels Among a Worldwide Clan* Edinburgh: Mainstream, 2005.

Isichei, Elizabeth. 'James K. Baxter: Religious Sensibility and a Changing Church.' *Journal of New Zealand Literature* 13 (1995). 235-56.

McKay, Frank. *The Life of James K. Baxter.* Auckland: Oxford UP, 1990.

Millar, Paul. Introd. and ed. *Autumn Testament.* By James K. Baxter. Auckland: Oxford UP, 1997.

————, ed. *Spark to a Waiting Fuse: James K. Baxter's Correspondence with Noel Ginn.* Wellington: Victoria UP, 2001.

————. Personal communication with the author. July 2009.

Muir, Edwin. *Essays in Literature and Society.* London: Hogarth, 1949.

Newton, John. *The Double Rainbow: James K. Baxter, Ngāti Hau and the Jerusalem Commune.* Wellington: Victoria UP, 2009.

————. '"By Writing and example": The Baxter Effect.; *Ka Mate Ka Ora* 1 (2005). 11-33.

O'Sullivan, Vincent. *James K. Baxter.* Wellington: Oxford UP, 1976.

Riach, Alan. 'James K. Baxter and the Dialect of the Tribe.' In *Opening the Book: New Essays on New Zealand Writing.* Ed. Mark Williams and Michele Leggott. Auckland: Auckland UP, 1995. 105-22.

Stead, C.K. 'Towards Jerusalem: The Later Poetry of James K. Baxter.' *Islands* 3 (1973). 7-18.

Wedde, Ian. Introduction. *The Penguin Book of New Zealand Verse.* Ed. Ian Wedde and Harvey McQueen. Auckland: Penguin, 1985. 23-52.

FURTHER READING

Biographies

McKay, Frank. *The Life of James K. Baxter,* Auckland, New Zealand: Oxford University Press, 1990, 320 p.
  Book-length biography of Baxter that places the author within his "historical context" and whose aim is to present his life "as lived despite all the shifting lights that play over such an undertaking."

Oliver, W. H. *James K. Baxter: A Portrait,* Sydney: George Allen & Unwin, 1983, 160 p.
  Biography of Baxter that includes numerous photographs documenting his life and work.

Shadbolt, Maurice. "James K. Baxter." In *Love and Legend: Some 20th Century New Zealanders,* pp. 167-79. Auckland, New Zealand: Hodder and Stoughton, 1976.
  Provides a brief biography of Baxter, whom he refers to as "one of the most extraordinary men [New Zealand] has known."

Weir, J. E. Introduction to *Collected Poems,* by James K. Baxter, edited by J. E. Weir, pp. xxi-xxvii. Wellington, New Zealand: Oxford University Press, 1980.
  Introduction to the Oxford University Press's 1980 edition of Baxter's collected poems, in which the critic offers a brief biography of the poet and discusses the criteria that he employed in selecting the poems for this collection.

Criticism

Alcock, Peter. "James K. Baxter and the Terror of History: The De-colonisation of a New Zealander." In *Awakened Conscience: Studies in Commonwealth Literature,* edited by C. D. Narasimhaiah, pp. 92-110. New Delhi, India: Sterling Publishers, 1978.
  Disputes the view that Baxter's poetry repeats a "compulsive pattern," or "monomyth," consisting of a "separation-experience-return" formula, suggesting instead that the poet should be judged by his final "Jerusalem" works, where his focus is a "concern for society," for its "colonial alienations and structures," and "thus for the processes of history in our time."

Doyle, Charles. *James K. Baxter,* Boston: Twayne Publishers, 1976, 189 p.
  First full-length treatment of Baxter's life and writings, which seeks "to offer a coherent introduction to his published work as a whole" and to demonstrate that he was "both an engaging writer and an important one."

Doyle, Mike. "James K. Baxter: The Jerusalem Writings." *The Literary Half-Yearly* 18, no. 1 (January 1977): 100-16.
  Examines the three volumes of poetry and prose that derived from Baxter's final years at the Jerusalem settlement, namely, *Jerusalem Sonnets, Jerusalem Daybook,* and *Autumn Testament,* noting the scarcity of style and rhetoric in these works and stressing their central themes of "poverty of self," "comfort in God," and "the rare moment always possible of love shared."

Moody, David. "For James K. Baxter." *Meanjin Quarterly* 32, no. 2 (June 1973): 219-24.
  Assessment of Baxter's work as a poet and critic that emphasizes "two dominant impressions": one, that his "genius . . . was a real and lasting power"; the other, that he constantly sought to develop his skills and attempt new techniques in his writings.

O'Sullivan, Vincent. *James K. Baxter,* Wellington, New Zealand: Oxford University Press, 1976, 64 p.
  Monograph on Baxter that includes a brief biography of the author and discusses key themes and issues in his poetry, such as the wilderness, "his notion of the tribe," and human sexuality, among other concerns.

————. "James K. Baxter." In *Poetry of the Pacific Region: Proceedings of the CRNLE/SPACLALS Confer-*

ence, edited by Paul Sharrad, pp. 9-18. Adelaide, Australia: Centre for Research in the New Literatures in English, 1984.

> Describes Baxter as "a religious writer" and highlights the fundamental importance of myth in his work and life, saying, "Baxter could no more *not* think mythically than he could stop talking, or believe that his life was not being acted out on a cosmic stage."

Simpson, Peter. "'The Trick of Standing Upright': Allen Curnow and James K. Baxter." *World Literature Written in English* 26, no. 2 (autumn 1986): 369-78.

> Examines the developing relationship of Baxter and his fellow New Zealand poet and critic Allen Curnow, noting the ways in which the different phases of their relationship are reflected in their respective aesthetics and views on poetry.

Additional coverage of Baxter's life and career is contained in the following sources published by Gale: *Contemporary Authors,* **Vol. 77-80;** *Contemporary Literary Criticism,* **Vol. 14;** *Contemporary Poets,* **Ed. 1;** *Encyclopedia of World Literature in the 20th Century,* **Ed. 3; and** *Literature Resource Center.*

Uwe Johnson
1934-1984

German novelist, short story writer, and essayist.

The following entry provides an overview of Johnson's life and works. For additional information on his career, see *CLC,* Volumes 5, 10, 15, and 40.

INTRODUCTION

Uwe Johnson is a significant German novelist of the latter half of the twentieth century. Best known for writing complex and formally experimental novels, including *Mutmaßungen über Jakob* (1959; *Speculations about Jakob*) and the multivolume *Jahrestage: Aus dem Leben von Gesine Cresspahl* (1970-83; *Anniversaries: From the Life of Gesine Cresspahl*), Johnson was one of the first writers of the post-World War II era to address social and political themes related to the division between East and West Germany. Throughout his career, he focused on a number of recurring issues, such as the psychological effects of division and borders on the individual; the disparity between truth and appearance, or human perception; and the relationship between language and reality. These themes were underscored by the author's innovative style, precise use of language, and complex narrative strategies. Although not as well known in the West as some of his contemporaries, such as Christa Wolf and Günter Grass, Johnson is considered one of the most original writers of postwar Germany and a significant figure of that country's literature. Robert Detweiler described Johnson as a "novelist of honesty and integrity" and "an excellent craftsman," who "caught better than any other writer the language, mood, and tone of the cold war impasse."

BIOGRAPHICAL INFORMATION

Johnson was born July 20, 1934, in Cammin in the province of Pomerania, to Erna Sträde and Erich Johnson, a farmer, but spent his early years in the town of Anklam an der Peene. After primary school, Johnson was chosen to attend a National Socialist "Deutsche Heimschule," or German home school, in Koscian, in what is now Poland. After the war, Johnson's father was interned and died in a camp in Belorussia in the late 1940s. The remaining members of the family settled in a village in Mecklenburg, where Johnson's mother found work as a train conductor. In 1946, Johnson began attending the John Brinkman-Oberschule in Güstrow and developed an interest in writing and literature. After completing an exit exam, he enrolled in classes at the University of Rostock in 1952 but was briefly expelled the following year after defending the activities of the Christian youth organization, Junge Gemeinde, which the government accused of sabotage and espionage. Once he was able, Johnson resumed his studies in Leipzig and began working his Rostock experiences into his first novel, *Ingrid Babendererde: Reifeprüfung 1953* (1985). As a result of political tensions, the author was unable to find a publisher for the work in East Germany, and it remained unpublished until after his death. In his final months of study at Leipzig, Johnson continued to suffer as a result of the political climate. Both his thesis and his controversial final exam were rejected, and after finally receiving his diploma in 1956, he had difficulties finding employment. He supported himself with odd jobs and editorial work during this time and began writing *Speculations about Jakob.* After the novel appeared in 1959, Johnson moved to West Berlin.

Following the success of his first published novel, Johnson traveled throughout Europe and the United States for lectures, public readings, and visits to universities. During this time, he began work on his next major work, *Das dritte Buch über Achim* (1961; *The Third Book about Achim*). In 1962, Johnson married Elisabeth Schmidt, whom he had met in Leipzig, and a year later they had a daughter, Katherina. Over the next few years, Johnson continued to write, publishing a collection of short fiction and the novel *Zwei Ansichten* (1965; *Two Views*). In 1966, the author and his family moved to New York, where Johnson immersed himself in American culture and worked with the publisher Harcourt, Brace and World to produce an anthology of contemporary German literary texts. He remained for two years and began writing *Anniversaries: From the Life of Gesine Cresspahl,* a four-volume work that dominated the latter years of Johnson's literary career. During the 1970s, Johnson suffered personal and professional setbacks, including the dissolution of his marriage in 1977. He incorporated these experiences into the novella *Skizze eines Verunglückten,* which was published in 1982. During the last years of his life, Johnson became increasingly isolated and suffered from poor health. Although he had hoped to return to the United States in 1984, his plans were never realized. In late February of that year, Johnson died of heart failure in Sheerness, England.

MAJOR WORKS

Johnson's first publication, *Speculations about Jakob,* remains one of the author's most respected achievements. The central character of the novel is the recently-deceased Jakob Abs, a Dresden train dispatcher, who is struck and killed by a train on his way to work. Featuring multiple perspectives of various characters, the story is written in a complex narrative style, which includes fragments of conversation and three stream-of-consciousness monologues, as well as a third-person narrative. The often-conflicting stories force the reader to draw conclusions and become an active participant in the process of discovering the truth concerning Jakob's last days and death. While it is unclear if his death is suicide, murder, or an accident, it is known that Jakob is a man of integrity, who experiences political and personal pressure after becoming embroiled in a plot that involves his mother and a woman named Gesine Cresspahl, an ex-GDR citizen. The novel also offers linguistic challenges for the reader, as it utilizes unusual syntax, compound words, and punctuation, as well as a mixture of English, Russian, and Mecklenburg dialects. While the book offers insight into the division between East and West Germany, and examines the conflict between the individual and the political collective, it also demonstrates the subjective nature and unreliability of human perception. In his next novel, *The Third Book about Achim,* Johnson explores themes similar to those that dominate *Speculations about Jakob,* including questions of identity, the effects of political pressure, and the relationship between language and reality. In the work, the protagonist, a West German journalist named Karsch, recounts his failed attempt to write the biography of Achim T., a cyclist and national sports hero. As he begins to research his subject, Karsch has difficulties reconciling Achim's background with his current political role as a sports celebrity. While the journalist finds the discrepancies in Achim's life essential to his biography, the publisher of the book discounts these events, wanting only to focus on the cyclist's current position in East Germany. Ultimately, the project is aborted when evidence surfaces that Achim participated in the 1953 uprising at Leipzig against the Stalinist GDR government. The novel also features reflections on life in the GDR, especially the division between the East and West, and raises questions regarding truth and appearance. Although less formally experimental than Johnson's previous novels, *Two Views* treats similar themes, particularly the problems associated with borders, distance, and division, and the disparity between reality and appearance. The novel examines the rela-

tionship between B. and D., a West German photographer and a nurse from East Germany, respectively, whose brief and casual affair escalates after the construction of the Berlin Wall. Eventually reunited, they discover that the reality of their relationship bears little semblance to the expectations they harbored during their separation. As the title indicates, the story is told alternately from the perspective of each of the two characters.

Johnson's multivolume work, *Anniversaries: From the Life of Gesine Cresspahl,* treats the predominant themes of his literary career and, for many scholars, represents the author's most ambitious and successful literary achievement. Written in diary form, the novel presents daily entries, beginning on August 21, 1967, and ending August 20, 1968, documenting a year in the life of Gesine Cresspahl, a character first introduced in *Speculations about Jakob.* Gesine's contemporary life in Manhattan is recounted, as well as events from her past, including her birth in Germany during the Third Reich and education under the Nazis, her flight from East Germany in the 1950s, and her eventual move to the United States in the 1960s. The question of identity is an important theme in the collection, as well as Gesine's struggle to maintain her ideals when confronted with a world very different from her own socialist vision. Near the conclusion of the novel, she is increasingly inspired by the reforms of the Prague Spring in Czechoslovakia and begins to hope that she might witness the establishment of a vital socialist state free from Soviet control. The final entry of the diary, however, marks the Soviet Union's violent suppression of the revolution, and the novel ends ambiguously with regard to Gesine's reaction to the devastating events.

CRITICAL RECEPTION

Johnson attracted serious critical attention with the appearance of his first published novel, *Speculations about Jakob,* in 1959. Although some reviewers were disturbed by the novel's complex narrative style and unorthodox use of language, there was general admiration and enthusiasm for the debut work, which demonstrated not only the author's skill as a literary craftsman but also his willingness to address a heretofore neglected theme—the division of Germany following World War II. As a result of the novel's success, Johnson quickly emerged as an important new voice in German letters and received various honors, including the Fontane Prize of the City of West Berlin in 1960. His next novel, *The Third Book about Achim,* was also well received, although some detractors complained of Johnson's "ugly" prose and raised questions about his skeptical treatment of language. Among his supporters, however, Johnson became known as "the poet of both Germanies," a term that the author rejected because he refused to accept the political and ideological implications of the title. During the 1960s, Johnson continued to attract attention and was awarded the International Publisher's Prize in 1962 for *The Third Book about Achim.* Johnson's insistence on linguistic precision and his refusal to adopt prescribed polemical rhetoric in public discussions of East and West German politics at times resulted in unfavorable publicity and misrepresentations of his political views. His career was further stymied by the lukewarm reception of *Two Views,* published in 1965, which represented, for some scholars, a regression to a more conventional literary style. Johnson's career recovered during the 1970s, however, with the appearance of *Anniversaries.* While the first volume elicited a mixed response, the second and third volumes, published in 1971 and 1973, drew increasing admiration from critics, many of whom praised Johnson's mastery and complex evocation of the delicate relationship between the past and present. With the publication of the final volume in 1983, the novel was declared one of the most remarkable achievements of twentieth-century literature, and was compared to the literary accomplishments of James Joyce and Marcel Proust.

In the decades following his death, Johnson has continued to draw critical attention. The posthumous publication of his first written novel, *Ingrid Babendererde,* generated a new debate about the author's career and contributions as a writer. Scholars, such as Robert K. Shirer and Gary L. Baker, attempted to place the early work within the context of Johnson's complete oeuvre. Critics also continued to assess the author's formal strategies, his complex narrative techniques, and his original treatment of events in a postwar divided Germany. Kurt Fickert, writing in 1987, studied Johnson's use of newspaper articles in *Anniversaries,* stating that the device enabled him to explore "the dark side of political and socioeconomic events in 1967-68" and "pursue his theme of the individual in confrontation with the forces of history in his era" in an unbiased manner. Noting formal and thematic limitations in *Anniversaries,* Sara Lennox questioned Johnson's representation of history, however, arguing that by "oversimplifying the complexities of a crisis period in recent history, Johnson has made his novel a much less substantial inquiry into the turbulent historical period than it might have initially seemed." Although he remains as controversial today as he was at the beginning of his career, Johnson continues to draw respect for his groundbreaking examination of the major issues of postwar Europe and his ability, through his art and language, to provoke readers to re-examine their notions of personal identity and contemporary history. In the words of Gary L. Baker, Johnson offered "one of the most fascinating—some would say perplexing—styles in German litera-

ture," and his works, particularly *Speculations about Jakob* and *Anniversaries,* remain among the most celebrated achievements of postwar German writing.

PRINCIPAL WORKS

Mutmaßungen über Jakob [*Speculations about Jakob*] (novel) 1959

Das dritte Buch über Achim [*The Third Book about Achim*] (novel) 1961

Karsch und andere Prosa (short stories and novella) 1964

Zwei Ansichten [*Two Views*] (novel) 1965

An Absence (novella) 1969

Jahrestage: Aus dem Leben von Gesine Cresspahl. 4 vols. [*Anniversaries: From the Life of Gesine Cresspahl*] (novel) 1970-83

Eine Reise nach Klagenfurt (nonfiction) 1974

Berliner Sachen (essays) 1975

Begleitumstände: Frankfurter Vorlesungen (lectures) 1980

Skizze eines Verunglückten (novella) 1982

Ingrid Babendererde: Reifeprüfung 1953 (novel) 1985

*This work includes the story "Eine Reise wegwohin," which was translated and published as the novella *An Absence* in 1969.

CRITICISM

Robert Detweiler (essay date November 1968)

SOURCE: Detweiler, Robert. "The Achievement of Uwe Johnson." *South Atlantic Bulletin* 33, no. 4 (November 1968): 22-4.

[*In the following essay, Detweiler assesses Johnson's literary achievements, maintaining that he is a "novelist of honesty and integrity" and an "excellent craftsman," who caught "the language, mood, and tone of the cold war impasse" better than any other writer.*]

It is extremely tempting to approach Uwe Johnson as if he were a political novelist—as in fact he has been handled and mishandled by the book reviewers. From this perspective the border between the two German states becomes Johnson's focal image, the conflict between East and West structures the action of his three novels, and his characters assume credibility in the tension of antagonistic ideologies, of propaganda, and underground maneuverings. It is, I say, a tempting approach, for Johnson does invite and excite one to geopolitical considerations, but it is also too limiting, since it does not take into account the radical nature of his experimentalism. The other seductive angle of analysis is the one that treats Johnson as a displaced relative of Robbe-Grillet, as a neo-realist who might be excused for his refusal forthrightly to condemn his abandoned East German homeland because he is, after all, avantgarde, and avant-gardism could have little in common with the "fuddy-duddy" Ulbricht regime.

But Johnson will not behave like a grateful political refuge from the East nor write like a Parisian new novelist on a cultural mission to the Germans, and his career as a *chosisme* author must be a mild embarrassment to East and West. Both must worry, for contrasting reasons, how he has developed his vision and technique under an originally communist influence. For the Easterner it would mean, "If a man such as this can emerge from among us, our system must have holes," whereas the Westerner would ponder, "How can a man such as this emerge without the benefit of our system?"

How can he indeed? Ironically, Johnson is a product of dialectical materialism that the Russians would not package and the Americans would not buy, and I mean this in a quite elementary sense. It is a dialectic first, which, unlike the Marxist use of the Hegelian opposites to fuse a political reality, begins with the conflicting political realities and employs them to search for a transcendent and suprapolitical truth. But his art remains materialistic in its dedication to a language of detachment and of surface objectivity, a language almost neoclassic in its disavowal of symbolic qualities, yet that manages finally to insinuate much more than the sum of its syntax. More explicitly, Johnson uses dialectical materialism as a working paradigm to articulate an ideal freedom; his language hides much but at once reveals essential truths about humanity that are neither communist nor democratically inspired.

The political and experimental literary aspects of Johnson's fiction do coalesce in his *Deutsch-sein*—his "Germanity"—and in his sense of responsibility as a novelist. In an address delivered some years ago at Wayne State University (on his first trip to the United States), Johnson remarked that Berlin, the two Berlins, are in a literal sense the focal point of the modern world, for there is the borderline between the two dominant ideologies of the world. At the border, further, the atmosphere is neither East nor West, neither communist nor democratic, but an obscure new something that cannot be understood or interpreted according to the old vocabulary and concepts. "A border in this spot creates a new literary form," Johnson says. "It requires adapting technique and language to an extraordinary situation." Johnson's career as a novelist is his attempt at such an adaptation, and his progress can be marked in the three novels he has published to date.

Behind *Speculations about Jakob,* published in 1959, is Uwe Johnson the traveler from the East who has arrived at the far side—our side—of the Berlin border. Johnson wrote the novel in East Germany, refused to make the changes demanded of him for publication there, and moved to West Berlin just before the book was issued in that city. *Speculations about Jakob* is a justification of Johnson's "change of address," as he calls it (he would not label it a defection), but it is not an apology. He is not embodied in the protagonist Jakob Abs, the young Dresdener railroad dispatcher who is killed by a train and the circumstances of whose death form the vague basis of the novel's speculations. Rather, Johnson as author seems to be a disinterested reporter who gathers information on the events surrounding Jakob's death, no matter how trivial and contradictory such information may appear. Fragments of overheard conversation, communist political slogans, American Forces Network jargon, tortured interior monologues by intelligence agents, descriptions of locomotives, Jakob's own thoughts and speeches—these and more, presented in an intentionally confusing time sequence, form the puzzle of the book. The story is a kind of anti-narrative, and nothing is finally solved: not the mystery of Jakob's death (whether it was assassination, suicide, or accident), not the nature of his involvement with East and West intelligence operations, not even why he chose not to remain in West Berlin with his NATO-employed girl friend when he had the chance.

How then is the novel a justification of Johnson's own decision to leave the East? At this point, what I called his involvement with dialectic becomes instructive. First, it becomes apparent quite soon that Johnson does not subscribe to the Marxist theory of dialectic and much less to its Soviet modifications. His characters from the East are doubters, for the most part; although they may maintain a loyalty to the state, they have little faith in an ultimate historical vindication of the system. They laugh at the vision of a workers' paradise; they are cynical about the official "truths" fed them by the state propaganda machine, and, being Germans, they react by turning markedly nonpolitical and concentrating upon hard work, skill, and discipline in their various vocations. Why don't they flee? Because there may be nothing to flee to. Johnson rejects also the internationalist stance and its dialectical possibilities. One does not necessarily flee to freedom when one defects to the West because, for the Easterner at least, capitalism and Western democracy are also rigid systems that impose strictures of thought and act upon the individual. But more than that, the conflict between East and West, between thesis and antithesis, does not show promise of creating a new synthesis. True, a political and economic coexistence may be possible, but the genuine, unbiased truth of reality is lost in the mechanics and maneuvering of it all. Johnson uses dialectic to show the failure of dialectic, and the failure of dialectic seems to be his rationale for leaving the East. Assuredly, the other side will not be any better for the truth-seeker, but it *is* the other side, and one must know both sides, both poles of the dialectic, in order to overcome and transcend them. The speculations about Jakob, therefore, remain just that: speculations—*Mutmassungen,* in the German title—because it is an author's job not to invent truth but to report imaginatively on as many facets of a given situation as one can see. As Johnson himself said, "It is too early to worry about the truth of the incident, what matters at this point is how it is going to be used." For Johnson, that consideration results in the determination to write fiction that cannot be exploited for its propaganda value by either side.

Johnson may be attempting the impossible. His effort to write a fiction that rejects established points of view may result in no point of view at all, and a recent reviewer, following that logic, asserted that Johnson is above all a novelist of the impasse. He meant to portray Johnson as a commentator on the political impasse, but I think one could say also that Johnson leads one to an epistemological impasse as well. The honest artist desires to write the truth, but he can write fiction only in terms of concrete situations that do not embody the truth or that at best carry political implications that are one-sided and therefore only partial truths. Johnson is aware of the dilemma. He writes, "Where does the author stand in relation to his text? Attitudes of omniscience are suspicious. . . . How can the author who first has to invent and assemble his text squat on a stool high above the field like a referee during a tennis match, how can he know all the rules, all the players, and unerringly observe them besides, intervene supremely at any time he chooses and even change places with his characters and look into their hearts as he rarely manages to look into his own? The author ought to admit that he has invented what he tells, that his information is incomplete and imprecise."

The dilemma leads Johnson, as it has many other contemporary artists, into a deeper level of self-awareness. His second work, entitled *The Third Book about Achim* (1961), is a novel about writing a novel, something like Fellini's *Eight and One Half,* a movie about making a movie. The results are similar. As Fellini's director in *Eight and One Half* must finally admit that he cannot make the movie because the complexity of life and truth has become so overwhelming, so Karsch the journalist in Johnson's second work discovers that he cannot write the novel. Karsch is a West German who has become intrigued with the personality of Achim, an East German bicycle racing champion and a cultural hero. Two official state-endorsed biographies of Achim have already been written, but Karsch feels they do not tell the truth. Karsch travels to a nameless East German city (that seems to be Leipzig) to interview Achim and learns details in Achim's past that do not jibe with his

present reputation. Achim was in the front ranks of the protesters in the workers' rebellion of 1953, yet now he is a sports hero and an emerging politician. Can he explain the change? No, he cannot, or at least he will not. Karsch cannot comprehend and returns to the West without his story. Again the impasse: concrete situations that reveal only half-truths.

And what about Johnson, the author on the East-West border? Can one write fiction about the impossibility of writing fiction? Johnson tries, and if the results, like Fellini's, are inevitably autobiographical, it is because the modern artist is forced to project metaphors of himself more than ever before, since he no longer visualizes dialectically viable or universally applicable situations. One writes personal fiction because of the epistemological embarrassment. One knows for certain only the difficulty of creating, and that becomes the subject of the creation. "Je me vois voyant," "I see myself seeing," Robbe-Grillet has said, and Johnson has the same introspective view.

Why then continue to write fiction at all? Robbe-Grillet has also argued that the modern novelist not only has nothing to say but that he should not have anything to say. The impasse, therefore, is intentional and welcome, and the curiosity is that a German, one of a nation that has had considerable to say, should adopt this aspect of the neorealist position. A writer whose political interest is intense and most personal rejects the traditional modes of narration, refuses to tell stories and create myths, and commits himself to pure form. Perhaps I should have begun this study with an analysis of Johnson's experimental techniques and worked toward an inductive application of them to the meaning of his fiction. But even that approach is outmoded in the light of the esthetic and moral premises behind Johnson's work. For Johnson the distinction between reality and fiction has disappeared as the relativity and partiality of truth impresses itself upon him, and a critique of his work that stresses technique errs in presuming a dichotomy of form and message that he denies. The use of dialectic to destroy dialectic extends this far, that it forces artist and critic to abandon content-oriented language and structure-oriented language as well. What is left? *Chosisme.* "Thingness." Not *Sachlichkeit* but *Sachheit.* Each thing is itself and only that. Fiction tries to become nonrepresentational; the revenge upon idealism and symbolism begins at last. In France, *chosisme* flourishes as a wayward child of Sartre's phenomenology. For Johnson, it grows more naturally out of Eastern materialism, and its significance can be seen most clearly in his third novel, *Two Views,* published in 1965.

Two Views deals with objects as much as with characters. Unlike the first two books, it also develops a narrative of temporal-spatial continuity. Dietbert, a young Schleswig-Holstein photographer, attempts to bring

Beate, an East Berlin nurse, across the border to begin a new life with him in the Federal Republic. He succeeds, through no personal courage or integrity of his own, and Beate, without much conviction or enthusiasm, starts life in the West. The story line exists, it seems, to demonstrate the futility of attempting to write truth through conventional narration. Dietbert and Beate are both less than admirable people, and Johnson does not try to create sympathy for them. Their love affair is superficial, their motives are selfish, and one has the feeling that they are not worth the attention paid them by the Berlin underground. The vital, determinative factors in the novel are Dietbert's sports cars, the Berlin Wall, the bars, the intracity train, and especially the anonymous, impersonal group that smuggles people across the border with mechanical efficiency. These are the material realities conducive to the search for truth. It is not that Johnson wishes to dehumanize existence. It is dehumanized already through Eastern and Western materialism and the ideologies used to perpetrate the materialism, and Johnson's effort, in his concentration on "thingness," is to find a way back to an authentic, humane mode of living.

In the second novel, ***The Third Book about Achim,*** the italicized voice that speaks from time to time says at one point, "After all, a bicycle is a bicycle." By the same logic, in ***Two Views*** one could say, "After all, the border is the border," and "The wall is the wall." When things are seen as themselves, they lose some of their *mana,* some of their mystical power to terrify. If dialectic is used to destroy itself, materialism is also utilized to demythologize its own content. In the search for truth, Johnson does not retreat into total subjectivity but turns to things, to objects, but then, instead of allowing things to dehumanize still further, he voids them of their autonomy and puts them back in their proper place, as the servants of mankind. The art of fiction, correspondingly, instead of producing finished objects that can be used (as the state wishes to use Achim's biography), becomes a continuing act of perception. In the process Johnson is overcoming the impasse and moving toward a strategy of paradox. If the poles of the dialectic do not merge, as Johnson insists they cannot, they must result in contradiction, and contradiction can be resolved into formal paradox. And in the frustration of logic and ideology that paradox produces is a favorable atmosphere for responsible action. Is it not paradoxical, for example, that the Berlin Wall, an instrument of separation and isolation, becomes the object that unites people? Is it not paradoxical that the people whose lives are most crucially molded by the wall and the border, that anonymous, impersonal, mechanically-functioning group of smugglers, become the instruments of human compassion? They help, no questions asked, because the existence of the wall creates a new view, a new kind of truth that must be acted upon. And is it not paradoxical, finally, that fiction which works

very hard to say nothing, in Robbe-Grillet's sense, says at last much more than one could articulate in any other way?

What is the achievement of Uwe Johnson? He is a novelist of honesty and integrity who is passionately concerned with the political and moral destiny of his country—his countries, perhaps—but who will not misuse the novel form for pet or pat solutions. He is an excellent craftsman who has caught better than any other writer the language, mood, and tone of the cold war impasse and who by the radical innovation of his fictive form offers imaginative directions out of the impasse. In his commitment to art as process and perception, he demonstrates the nature of truth as process and perception. Truth emerges in Johnson's fiction as a kind of montage. The "thingness" of individual objects and situations is stressed, so that they retain their identities, but the result of the total composition is a new kind of reality, an ideal freedom that East and West may not yet fathom but toward which they can strive.

Mark Boulby (essay date May 1974)

SOURCE: Boulby, Mark. "Surmises on Love and Family Life in the Work of Uwe Johnson." *Seminar* 10, no. 2 (May 1974): 131-41.

[*In the following essay, Boulby stresses the importance of the "family material" in Johnson's* Anniversaries: From the Life of Gesine Cresspahl, *asserting that the governing feature of the work is the interrelationship between "family and erotic conflicts" and "ideological and existential" crises.*]

Critical analysis of the works of Uwe Johnson has tended to follow consistent and in some respects rather self-evident directions. What was striking about his books in the first place—on the one hand their unusual and highly pertinent political content, and on the other their structural and syntactical experimentation—inevitably established guidelines for much of the commentary of the past decade. Most critics have taken account of the connection between these two principal aspects of his work. The praise bestowed on Johnson, at the very outset of his career, for the emphatic manner in which he handled the almost untouched subject matter of the division of Germany has generally been accompanied by the recognition that some of his success is due to his readiness to confront technical difficulties ignored by other writers. His achievement has been widely seen to lie not so much, or not merely, in the innovations of his subject matter and style, but more deeply in his desire to resist the ideological contamination of language and in his struggle with the innate political cliché as a dominant feature of the literature of both the Federal Republic and the GDR. In contending with the formidable difficulties of narrative description, elucidated in his essay **'Berliner Stadtbahn,'** Johnson made his first two novels, at any rate, exercises in the pursuit of truth ('Wahrheitsfindung'), and in this light critical attention has centred upon the terms of his social commentary, upon the ideological problems and ideological balance of his novels, and upon his reflection of a type of human experience which to some has seemed politicized to the bone. It has, of course, not gone unnoticed that the issues raised by this author—those of engagement, of choice and self-recognition, of role-playing, of authenticity and personal coherence—do seem to transcend the immediacy of the sociopolitical milieu in the direction of existential and universal questions; although even commentators sensitive to these dimensions have tended, or so it seems to me, to find and accept the implication that for Johnson, as for Sartre, it is by and large in the encounter with the external demands of political action and decision that the most essential inner problems of human experience need to be presented, and can only be resolved.

There is certainly a good deal of validity in this view. To depart too far from it must surely lead to distortion. Thus the recent attempt by W.J. Radke, in his exceedingly painstaking and learned dissertation,[1] to demonstrate that *Mutmassungen über Jakob* is a complex allegory of the search for God, and that Jakob Abs himself is no less than a personification of the Logos, remains unconvincing. Were these things really the case, then this novel would be a much weaker book than it in fact is, for a great deal of its strength surely lies precisely in its convincing actuality. But this is not to say that this writer's works do not contain a great deal of material which has little to do with political, ideological, or even social questions in the narrower sense. If from time to time this fact has indeed been noted, it can now be seen in a fresh light if we begin with the observation that there are certain analogies between Johnson's novels and what may for convenience be called the realist-naturalist tradition which originated in the nineteenth century, especially the genre of the 'Familienroman.' The similarity, for instance, between the figure of Heinrich Cresspahl (in *Mutmassungen* rather than in *Jahrestage*) and the petit-bourgeois master craftsman often found idealized as a symbol of integrity in nineteenth-century fiction (for example, in *Zwischen Himmel und Erde*) is not difficult to see. It is interesting to come across Günter Blöcker, when he discusses the important motif of personal integrity and authenticity in Johnson's books, using the somewhat baneful term 'das Eigentliche,' and thus slipping into that jargon so criticized by Adorno but perhaps indeed not wholly irrelevant to our appreciation of Johnson.

In his essay of 1966 'Deutsche Gesellschaft in deutschen Romanen'[2] Reinhard Baumgart draws attention to what he believes to be parallels between Grass, Böll, and Johnson: all of these writers, he finds, may, if their work be closely inspected, be seen to use traditional characters; all exploit a 'Stamm-Milieu'; all reflect what is at bottom an almost Biedermeier parochialism; and Johnson's petit-bourgeois personages, for instance, display the persistence of old-fashioned moral attitudes in a crumbling world. Moreover it is precisely such prominent representatives of this ethos as Cresspahl or Achim's father who have Johnson's fullest sympathy. Quite frankly, Baumgart's remarks seem to me to be half truths at best. The point about the 'Stamm-Milieu' may perhaps have looked better in 1966 than it does now, after the publication of *Jahrestage*. And where Johnson's sympathies lie is often problematical. But clearly the analogies with the 'Familienroman' have more than a little substance. Frank Trommler, moreover, has noted the importance of the tradition of the novel of bourgeois realism specifically for the literature of the GDR, while making the crucial point that Johnson's work can only be properly understood if full account is taken of his emergence as a writer within the East German environment and in response to and reaction against those influences (largely Soviet) which had shaped the East German novel of the fifties.

That Johnson has always had it in him to write a 'Familienroman' can easily be discerned from a perusal of his earliest work; it has now surely been proved beyond doubt with the appearance of the first two volumes of *Jahrestage* (1970; 1971; at the time of writing the third volume is still to appear[3]), a novel in which a framework of experience in contemporary New York encapsulates an elaborate tale of family life in Mecklenburg in the 1930s. Important fresh surmises about Johnson's work may be made if critical attention is drawn to the specific pattern of family and erotic conflict which may be discovered in *Jahrestage* and also in the earlier novels. Tentative conjectures will remain in order rather than firm conclusions, but the evidence for the existence of a significant substratum in Johnson needing this kind of analysis should at least be convincing. The patterns in question may be observed in some degree in all Johnson's novels but most clearly and importantly in his first and his latest books. Here again a remark by Baumgart may be relevant, if only in that it seems to invite refutation. 'Ganz allgemein fällt,' he tells us, 'an Johnsons ersten Büchern der warme vertraute Umgang aller Figuren untereinander auf. Die Liebe zwischen den jungen Leuten hat sich dort in der gleichen Scheu, Reinheit und ungebrochenen Verbindlichkeit erhalten wie bei Böll. Der private Bereich, soweit er sich eben noch privat halten kann, scheint durchaus unproblematisch geblieben.'[4] Baumgart moreover regards such a warm and indeed idyllic 'Vertraulichkeit' as a natural social consequence of life in a society like that of the GDR.

To notice only this highly qualified aspect of the relationship between, say, Jakob and Gesine is misleading. It also suggests that the interpreter is concerned with human connections chiefly as a function of the politically centred action of the novel. A very different angle of vision is offered by a French critic, apparently the only commentator who has perceived the nature of some of the material with which I am now going to deal, and who has done so, moreover, without the very considerable assistance provided by *Jahrestage*. This material is, *pace* Baumgart, by no means 'durchaus unproblematisch'—quite the reverse. Jean Baudrillard, writing in *Les Temps Modernes* (1962), speaks of the hero of *Mutmassungen über Jakob* in the following terms: 'Jakob sans père ni mère réels, entre un père d'adoption, celui de Gesine, et l'autre, Rohlfs, tuteur politique, une sœur d'adoption elle aussi, et qu'il aime d'amour . . . Jakob se retrouve seul au milieu de rapports gravement déplacés où l'affectivité œdipienne se mêle curieusement aux nouvelles exigences de la collectivité politique de l'Etat.'[5] It is at the very least suggestive that the family structure in *Mutmassungen über Jakob* is so fragmented and that the erotic links are so complex and ambiguous. This is a type of subject matter, as Baudrillard remarks, which mingles oddly with the ideological and political material, but it is not dependent upon it and it has its own autochthonous existence. It may even be primary, and the existential problems with which Johnson is principally concerned may possibly be conditioned in substantial measure by the tension underlying the character relationships. In a real degree Johnson's depiction of the structures which bind the individual to the community and the state reflects a deeper pattern of family and erotic bonds and conflicts. Certainly if these had not been present the power of *Mutmassungen über Jakob* as a work of art, drawing its energy from unconscious as well as conscious sources, would be much depleted.

The importance of the 'family' material in this novel can be gathered in the first place from the frequency of certain circumlocutions in the text: Gesine, for instance, is often referred to cumbersomely as 'Cresspahls Tochter'[6] instead of by her name, while her father's residence, in a stock phrase carrying the biblical allusion so common in *Mutmassungen,* is called 'meines Vaters Haus.'[7] Plurals of generality—'die Liebe der Väter zu ihren Töchtern,' 'die Brüder von Mädchen'—point further to this concern with basic familial structures.[8] The most important of these is the father motif. This goes to the heart of this novel, and indeed of all of Johnson's work. We learn nothing about Jakob's own father, except that he was killed in the war, and that he had returned to Germany because of home-sickness just before it broke out (a significant point). Jakob has an adoptive father, Cresspahl, who, as we have noted, seems to represent a certain traditional and nearly Biedermeier integrity, practically to the point of stereotype.

These traits are naturally important in the economy of the novel, and Gesine's first monologue evokes her father poetically in just this light: 'Mein Vater war achtundsechzig Jahre alt in diesem Herbst und lebte allein in dem Wind, der grau und rauh vom Meer ins Land einfiel hinweg über ihn und sein Haus.'[9] The strong bond between Gesine and her father is made quite clear. Jakob's relationship with Cresspahl, however, is somewhat obliquely handled. Nevertheless there is an indication that the relationship has always been open and positive; for Cresspahl Jakob means 'eine Wirklichkeit von Lächeln und Antworten und Spaß und Leben überhaupt.'[10]

Another passage compares this connection with that between Jonas Blach and his Ordinarius, and in doing so makes a meaningful point: both relationships are founded *mutatis mutandis* upon filial respect, a search for strength—'mein Vater ist ein Turm mit kurzen grauen Haaren'[11]—and also upon the search for some symbol of resistance. Both Cresspahl and the old Ordinarius gave a good account of themselves during the Nazi period and may be relied upon to resist ideological pressure now. At the very least they will act as a counterbalance, appropriately enough in the aesthetic economy of *Mutmassungen über Jakob,* since Jonas and Jakob both have another filial relationship to cope with, that with their state. Herr Rohlfs, the security agent, is, in Baudrillard's phrase, Jakob's 'tuteur politique,' and also the representative of the collective. He is himself a father in the ordinary sense—Rohlfs's feelings for his little daughter and his commitment to his family life are no doubt stressed because Johnson wishes always to balance the personal and private against the collective and to avoid an aesthetic disequilibrium. Typical qualities of a father-image cluster around Rohlfs—his dignity, his authority (indeed authoritarianism), his omniscience, his function as the arm of Justice. Justice is the essence of his faith—in himself, in his ideology and his state, and in Jakob. The ironic allusion he makes to his police colleagues in Jerichow as 'unsere lieben Verwandten'[12] supports the other indications of the predominance of the family analogy in the individual's experience of state and collective, as do occasional personifications: 'Was sind das für Zeiten, in denen die Staatsmacht verkleidet sich schleichen muß in ihre eigenen Häuser!'[13]

Two surrogate fathers, one representing the ideological challenge and one its evasion or refusal, seem to be supplied to Jakob Abs. In between them stands Gesine, pursued by the one for ideological and policy reasons, protected by the other out of natural affection, and in love, as it now dawns on her, with the person she had regarded for years as her brother. The third volume of *Jahrestage* will probably explain the reason for her dangerous return to Jerichow in the fall of 1956.[14] Popp interprets it generally as a search for the past, in a life which has now become rootless and gravely impaired.[15] In the first volume of *Jahrestage* Gesine complains that her 'family'—Cresspahl, Jakob, and also Jonas—treated her on this occasion 'wie eine Wahnsinnige.'[16] The change of relationship with her adoptive brother—'es hat sich etwas verändert'[17]—certainly seems to have taken her by surprise. But actually her previous correspondence with Jakob appears to have been connected indirectly with the end of his friendship with Sabine and thus the dissolution of one of the triangular situations built into the novel. The other triangle—Jonas, Gesine, Jakob—comes to an end because Jonas finally sees that Gesine is in love with Jakob. This gives him less reason to leave the GDR for the West. In Jakob's case, however, it strengthens the case for departure, and might be the real motive for his journey. Johnson goes out of his way at any rate to indicate that the excuse of a visit to his mother, Frau Abs, then in a refugee camp, is a half truth. Though the passage which recounts the episode is somewhat oblique, it is evident that, while Jakob is in the Rhineland, he and Gesine become lovers. But then Jakob returns to the East; his reactions to the Federal Republic and its way of life have been distinctly negative; his feelings for Gesine are not powerful enough, one must suppose, to overcome his social revulsion and his sense of duty. His mother he leaves in Gesine's charge, he returns to the realm of the father, and there he dies. And this dense web of psychic conflict is further complicated, though perhaps illuminated, when we notice the penultimate sentence of the novel, a thought of Herr Rohlfs when Gesine enters the bar in which they have agreed to meet in West Berlin: 'Ich wäre froh eine Schwester zu haben.'[18] The only possible meaning of this unexpected sentiment on the part of Rohlfs is surely that he puts himself in the place of Jakob, who had been Gesine's 'brother.' As Rohlfs' own amanuensis in the pursuit of 'die Taube auf dem Dach,' as in a way Rohlfs' spiritual son Jakob was torn between duty to the paternal authority, the collective, which is austere and 'pure,' and a deep preoccupation with the assertion of private identity which issues in the end inevitably in erotic love. Rohlfs, in wishing to have Gesine for a sister, revokes for himself at least that triumph of personal feeling of which he could only disapprove, and restores a more just equilibrium with the collective.

It is after all the erotic relationship which forms the link between the two Germanies in Johnson's muffled allegories. As B. loves D., in *Zwei Ansichten,* so Bundesrepublik loves, or maybe loathes, the Demokratische Republik. Moreover the frontier which lies between East and West is complemented by that which divides person from citizen, self from collective self. As Baudrillard remarks both of *Mutmassungen über Jakob* and of *Das Dritte Buch über Achim*: 'Dans les deux romans, la femme est le signe contradictoire de cette double frontière.'[19] In the triangle she forms with Karsch and Achim Karin links compromise with criticism, simulation of integrity with search for authenticity, and engagement with a subjective personalism. In *Zwei Ansichten* the motif of the erotic bond across the border is handled almost comically, but again it is the woman in whom integrity and the will to self-determination have real roots. Evidently, however, the woman is not always, as Karin shows, linked with the West. That Gesine is so associated in the first novel facilitates the presentation of the fundamental œdipal situation with its curious political and social parallels. The term œdipal does not seem to me to be inappropriate or exaggerated. Though we may not clearly detect that jealous hostility toward one parent which is a feature of the Oedipus complex (this appears in *Jahrestage*), Jakob clearly contests with Rohlfs for Gesine, and love for the sister can replace that for the mother very easily (*vide* Otto Rank). Furthermore Jakob is at the outset deprived of both his parents (since his mother soon flees to the corrupt West where his sister and lover-to-be has already elected to live) and he has only his adoptive father, Cresspahl, to adhere to. When Rohlfs in his imagination replaces Jakob as Gesine's brother he purifies a relationship which for him has become sullied and in effect restores Jakob posthumously to the condition in which he needs to have him. Such moral severity, albeit *ex post facto,* in the rejection of sex is an essential part of the Oedipus material.

What is missing in Johnson's early novels is obviously a significant mother figure, for Frau Abs can scarcely count as such. As Gesine's adoptive mother she does little more than draw attention to the absence of the true mother. It is the appearance of the true mother—Lisbeth Papenbrock in *Jahrestage*—which provides a key, if a slightly bent one, to the psychic conflicts of the earlier novels and, I hope, some further justification for all these surmises. In *Jahrestage,* as before, certain phrases, allusions, and comparisons persistently stress the importance of family relationships. 'Cresspahls Tochter' is here 'Vaters Tochter,'[20] recounting to her uncommonly precocious daughter (who is really more like a sister) that past which for her is symbolized by the three graves in Jerichow (Cresspahl, Lisbeth, and Jacob) and the one in Hannover (Frau Abs), for all of which she still meticulously cares. Families are of the essence; Karsch visits America to study them too—though these are Mafia 'families.'

In the long and tedious attacks upon 'die Tochter Stalins,' leading to the implied analogy between the suicide of Svetlana's mother and that of Lisbeth, we find one of those eccentric and maybe deliberately ill-fitting parallels which perhaps clarify, perhaps muddy the whole work. Lisbeth Papenbrock is significant first of all as her father's daughter and as Heinrich Cresspahl's wife. A principal theme in *Jahrestage* is the manner in which she forces her husband to abandon his business in Richmond, England, and return to Germany in 1933. She does this apparently because of her attachment to family and homeland, but the result is that husband and child are subjected unnecessarily to all the rigours of life under the Nazi regime. Once more there is a contest for the prize of a woman, in which one contestant is the lover (and husband) and the other the 'father,' in this case old Papenbrock himself, his wife Louise, who in some respects dominates the family, and of course 'Germany.' To this family, this Germany, Cresspahl is the outsider, the emigré, known in Jerichow as 'der Engländer.' In being forced back to Germany he loses the contest, his marriage becomes one in name only, and his wife, repelled by sexual relations, turns towards the church under the influence of her mother Louise's false piety which she takes seriously. She feels that she has already made 'das größere Opfer' in going to England in the first place. She tells her husband that he is welcome to import his English mistress, Mrs Trowbridge, and install her in the neighbourhood. She does not wish to bear a second child, and it is noteworthy that on the day the first, Gesine, is christened, Cresspahl has to leave to attend the funeral of his aged mother in another part of Mecklenburg. Purity for Lisbeth supposedly resides in the home with the father. She accepts old Papenbrock's authority, although when she was a girl she had seen through him and even exposed him once to the community as a liar. The irony is, of course, that the father figure is not pure in this novel at all, neither Papenbrock, nor his wife and family (brother Horst is in the SA and brother Robert becomes a senior party official), nor *a fortiori* Germany. Hitler's state is not the GDR; it has no connections, however remote, with a putative just society. Becoming aware of the injustice around her, Lisbeth also feels the lack of justice in her treatment of her husband. Her overbred conscience is but one consequence of her disastrously neurotic relationship with her parents. As Marie, Gesine's daughter, observes, grandmother in present-day New York would have quickly ended up with a psychiatrist ('Schädelschrumpfer'). Her obsessive sense of guilt embraces and confuses her own sins of omission and commission, those of her family, and those of her nation. The first sentence of the following quotation is especially striking: 'Ihre Schuld hatte dann viel Verwandtschaft bekommen. Sie war nicht nur zurückgegangen zu der vielfältigen Schuld ihres Vaters, der verarmten Leuten Darlehen gab und als Rückzahlung ihre Häuser forderte . . . Sie hatte dann bleiben wollen in einem Land, dessen neue Regierung die Kirche bedrängte, bei einer Familie, der man weiterhin Verdienst an der neuen Herrschaft nachsagen konnte und dem eigenen Bruder einen Totschlag . . .'[21]

Lisbeth Papenbrock's behaviour soon begins to show psychotic characteristics. She practically causes, or permits, the death of her child in a water butt; later she nearly starves her to death. Either she wishes to save her from a guilt like her own, or else she seeks some deeper form of expiation. Three times she tries to commit suicide and finally succeeds, immolating herself in the burning of Cresspahl's workshop. This deed is immediately provoked, quite significantly, by her being witness to an anti-semitic atrocity carried out by the SA. She therefore expiates her own, her family's, and her nation's guilt in a single act with psychotic features, expiates above all the previous triumph of that father principle, now recognized as corrupt, on which her life has been founded. In the light of all this it is perhaps no wonder that Marie would like to be, as the novel puts it, 'gefeit gegen Verwandtschaft,' because there are certain unresolved consequences of these matters which may mould or threaten her life too.

When we recall how the returning Cresspahl is ensnared and how his life is brutally damaged by the 'Clytemnestra-like' combination of Lisbeth and Louise, we cannot be surprised at Gesine Cresspahl's pronounced Electra complex. In *Jahrestage* Gesine harbours an intense resentment against her mother. Her complete devotion to her father involves a kind of resolution of the conflict between the two father figures in favour of the figure of resistance, but the whole contest has been displaced by the shifting of the framework narrative to New York in the late sixties and the evocation of another political environment and a fresh type of generation conflict. Gesine's inclination to find a satisfying political ideal in the 'socialism with a human face' of the Prague spring means that she is still building her life on her own father image, as her mother did. This image, by the way, is seriously challenged by Marie. The defeat of Herr Rohlfs in *Mutmassungen* does not tell us what he might have made of his victory, but in *Jahrestage,* certainly, Stalinism at least has been left behind. However the 'impurity' of the family in Mecklenburg finds its American equivalent in Gesine's resistance to the marriage offer she receives from Erichson, the emigré Mecklenburger who works for the Pentagon and whose mother, not accidentally, she confuses when delirious with Louise Papenbrock. Idealizing her father, Gesine is afraid of committing his error once again and marrying into the 'family' of the corrupt United States. But like Cresspahl, she does not openly resist the policies of a government she dislikes; like Cresspahl, she puts the security of her family first.

The message of *Jahrestage* may conceivably be a 'plus ça change, plus c'est la même chose,' but it is delivered in a voice which lacks complete conviction. For the political and psychoanalytic parallels are impressive and yet inexact. We may surmise, at least in the light of the first two volumes of *Jahrestage,* that the battle for the allegiance of the woman is always the core of Johnson's work. In retrospect Jakob Abs in *Mutmassungen über Jakob* seems almost an interloper, a fourth term intruding itself for accidental reasons into what is basically a triadic situation. This pattern of three is essentially consistent throughout the novels, as is also the theme of the broken or troubled family. We look almost in vain in these books for an example of a happy family. We find only the lovable Paepckes (in *Jahrestage*), but they seem to represent happiness at the price of comic ineffectiveness and irresponsibility, and their end is a peculiarly dismal one—Alexander disappears in Russia, while Hilde and the children are killed by a low-flying Russian plane during their flight from Pomerania. And we look entirely without success for an example of a happy community which can be more than a dream. Neither the GDR, nor the FRG, nor, of course, the USA constitutes one. The end of Dubcek's Czechoslovakia is perhaps the last bitter draught of disillusionment. And since there is consistency of conflict and disappointment on these two levels, it seems reasonable to enquire whether conceivably the substratum does not determine the surface problematics of Johnson's novels in a substantial degree. Evidently Johnson cannot write about the one unless he also writes about the other; and it is a fair guess that he will never envision utopia until he puts together the pieces of his psychological puzzle too. This is surely the governing feature of his work as a novelist. Hence in his books, unless the family and erotic conflicts can be resolved, there will be no solution to the ideological and existential crisis either.

Notes

1. 'Untersuchungen zu Uwe Johnsons Roman *Mutmassungen über Jakob*,' dissertation Stanford, 1970.

2. In *Literatur für Zeitgenossen* (Frankfurt: Suhrkamp, 1966).

3. Volume 3 appeared while this essay was in press but, contrary to previous indications, does not conclude the work.

4. Baumgart, p. 50.

5. 'Uwe Johnson: La Frontière,' *Les Temps Modernes,* 18 (1962), 1101.

6. *Mutmassungen über Jakob* (Frankfurt: Fischer Bücherei, 1962), pp. 79, 106, 119, 165, 171, 175.

7. *Mutmassungen,* pp. 127 and 132; cf also 'deines Vaters Haus' (pp. 130 and 142).

8. *Mutmassungen,* pp. 41 and 60.

9. *Mutmassungen,* p. 6.

10. *Mutmassungen,* p. 112.

11. *Mutmassungen,* p. 88.

12. *Mutmassungen,* p. 106.

13. *Mutmassungen,* p. 79.

14. See n. 3.

15. See Hansjürgen Popp, 'Einführung in "Mutmassungen über Jakob,"' *Über Uwe Johnson,* hrsg. Reinhard Baumgart (Frankfurt: Suhrkamp, 1970), pp. 55-6.

16. *Jahrestage* (Frankfurt: Suhrkamp, 1970 and 1971), p. 386.

17. *Mutmassungen,* p. 128.

18. *Mutmassungen,* p. 202.

19. Baudrillard, p. 1102.

20. *Jahrestage,* p. 619.

21. *Jahrestage,* p. 511.

Mark Boulby (essay date 1974)

SOURCE: Boulby, Mark. "An Old Fashioned Tale: *Two Views.*" In *Uwe Johnson,* pp. 67-93. New York: Frederick Ungar Publishing Co., 1974.

[*In the following essay, Boulby comments on the themes and use of irony in Johnson's short stories "An Absence" and "A Tavern Vanishes," as well as in the longer work* Two Views, *which he describes as the "most purely ironic" and "most widely underestimated" of the author's works.*]

Uwe Johnson's story **"Eine Reise wegwohin, 1960,"** translated into English as **"An Absence,"** is an excellently written supplement to **The Third Book about Achim.** The relative simplicity of the technique in comparison with that of the two novels already discussed is nonetheless associated with a most effective satirical manner. First published in 1964, the novella relates a journey made in the year before the building of the Wall, in fact Karsch's journey. Like most of Johnson's (relatively few) short stories and fragments, **"An Absence"** is fully comprehensible only if read in conjunction with the novel with which it is connected, in this case **The Third Book.** Briefly, it retells the story of Karsch's visit to the East but from a quite different standpoint; and since no longer Achim but now Karsch is at the center of the picture, Johnson is enabled to deal also with the after-effects of Karsch's trip, what happens on his return to Hamburg. Johnson made no changes in his original plot, he merely freshly illuminated it and elaborated upon it. Numerous details were added, in some cases episodes parallel to but not identical with those already narrated in the novel—for instance Karsch is ordered off a café floor because of the American style of his ballroom dancing. Other incidents, such as his final expulsion from the GDR over the affair of the hitchhiker, are simply recounted once more in summary form.

The ironic dimension to Johnson's work, which, though present in *Speculations about Jacob,* had grown more prominent in his second novel, is still important here, although the figure of Karsch himself is not treated with the lucid and detached irony we might expect, nor is his moral decision, and this is no doubt a weakness in the novella. But apart from this, the satiric note is strong. Sardonic turns of phrase abound; sharply edged sketches of people, objects, and events proliferate. There is for example the head waiter (a true link with the past like all his kind) whose "glance and bitter nod" at Karsch's order reflect his chagrin at having to sneak across the street to get the breakfast sausage (not usually provided these days in his hotel except for spoiled West German palates). There is the four-year-old boy who plays at soldiers and distinguishes already between "naughty panzer attacks and nice ones." There are beautifully judged, deadpan phrases, such as, "the dignity of the state frontiers," or, "how exactly he once again failed to understand." A marvelous sting-in-tail effect savagely pillories the obnoxious aspects of Achim's supposed "influence": "He was said to be powerful and honest, as though he could intercede for innocent people who had been arrested, for justice in general, proof not being required."

Johnson also indulges a penchant for politically insurgent puns, one of the best being "Staat machen" (usually "to show off," but here also in the sense of "showing the face and authority of the state"), as a description of the attitude of some East German bureaucrats toward the public. Time and again the unusual detail is seized and neatly exploited. What could be more telling, for instance, than the description of the old ladies in their black, struggling in the direction of the S-Bahn steps, "who with slanted heads and blinking eyes got out of the way of any kind of uniform as though they smelled it coming"? Objects are as acutely seen as ever, like the raincoat in the cupboard, which "lolled with its shoulders askew." And who but Johnson would have caught the awkwardness and embarrassment, when Karsch visits some long-lost relatives in Thuringia, by the comment: "with them he did not have enough family connection as was needed to fill out the lengthy pauses between the sips of coffee"? As Günter Blöcker has succinctly put it, Johnson's stylistic originality depends above all on the millimeter shift of vision that transforms the familiar into the new and strange.

Those readers who were disappointed by **"An Absence,"** such as Johnson's former admirer Marcel Reich-Ranicki, seem to have rather overlooked these virtues. They tended to notice only that the complex technique of the first two novels had been radically modified, and that this appeared to go hand in hand with the elimination of the previous creative ambiguity, and thus to subtract from the quality of the work. Instead of speculations, complains Reich-Ranicki, all we have in this story are "certainties"—moreover, certainties that he and many others found difficult to swallow, that is to say naively based political disparagement of West Germany. Of course, this rebuke does have some validity. The last section of the novella does indeed present the West German diplomatic and political position in a rather slanted manner, and that of the GDR somewhat uncritically. The issues are the diplomatic recognition of the East by the West, a subsequent possible reunification, and the question who is to blame that these things, in the early 1960s, still seem so far away.

Karsch, who at first is embarrassed when Achim tells him how much he admires him as a western journalist fighting against the "warmongering" government of the Federal Republic, becomes by the end of the story a voluntary exile who leaves Hamburg in utter disgust, to live in Milan (scene of Johnson's public rejection of the standardized West German political stance). Karsch comes back from the East as an "eye witness," as one of his colleagues on the paper says. But *Eye witness* is for Karsch first of all the title of an East German magazine; and though he has certainly seen something, it is not quite what he, with his western eyes, was supposed to have seen. In the GDR there may be many wrong or disagreeable things, but Karsch has at least been convinced that it really is a state. Justice (the burning hidden theme of Johnson's books) demands that recognition be granted it. Reason supports this: "East Germany showed the classic features of a state . . . what a state needs in the eyes of science." Feeling certainly pleads for it too. That mysterious land, "East German land" as Johnson calls it, all but evoking, for a purpose fortunately new, that sorry catchword of the National Socialist yesteryear, "East-land" (*Ostland*), and indeed allowing its poetry to speak again: "The whole East German land, forgotten, still living, lost from the proximity of our times"—what justice can there be in shutting this reality off and up in ideological clichés?

It is the case, however, that **"An Absence"** cannot simply be written off as a seriously biased work. The critique of communist society is hardly less severe than before. The comparison, for example, between the two refugee camps, that in the West for those from the East and that in the East for those from the West, does not fail to notice points that tell against the GDR, such as the fact that practically all the "refugees" the GDR receives are either its own former citizens who have found the going in the West too rough, or those in flight from the police, or else, even more commonly, those hoping to escape their families. As usual, motives are multiple, obscure, but practically never truly idealistic and/or ideological as they are discerned by Johnson. People do ideologically and politically significant things for naively personal reasons. Basic impulses, fear, sex, property, and kith and kin, originate pseudoexistential choices. And in the GDR there is above all that grave defect uncovered in *The Third Book*—the inhabitants live double lives. As they travel into Berlin from East Germany proper they give false destinations, always in the eastern sector of the city, to fool the police, and "as harmless citizens placed themselves alongside and in front of the people they really were with their actual lives, which up till now and in this spot had ducked away before the inventive expectations of state authority." Karsch sees this conduct as typically East German and is astonished to discover that he himself, when in the GDR, behaves likewise. The Federal Republic, he thinks, is totally different. After, however, he recommends recognition of the GDR while participating in a Hamburg TV show, he finds himself hounded. He is abused by obscene phone calls, and finally his apartment is searched by police while he is away and some of his files are confiscated. He is evidently suspected of being a communist agent. So West Germany also is not a free society. The tyranny of the right is quite as menacing as that of the left and just as insidious. Karsch therefore leaves his homeland for good, a thoroughly alienated man.

It is this characteristic, what we may choose to call his alienation, increasingly developed through the story, that has completely transformed the figure of Karsch, as he appears in **"An Absence."** Nothing of this sort was suggested in *The Third Book about Achim,* in which, as has been noted, Karsch functions more as a pure observer, his mind a kind of screen across which the curiosities of East German life transiently flicker, his project and its failure a kind of plumbing of the moral reality of the GDR. The first line of the novella draws attention to the fact that Karsch, when he receives the wholly unexpected telephoned invitation, is quite a sick man. Divorced, isolated, with an unsatisfactory relationship to his child whom he rarely sees, he is exhausted, insomniac, and plagued by headaches. He has doubts about the profession of journalism. In politics he is more or less a neutral, certainly no keen advocate of western positions, but his behavior throughout seems less the result of clear political choice and conviction and more a response to the pressures of neurosis. Perhaps indeed his "feeling of betweenness" (*Empfindung von Dazwischen*) is little but a manifestation of this. A touch of ambiguity attaches to the eventual choice, this near act of engagement involved in the decision to speak up for the diplomatic recognition of the GDR. His fresh insight and its result, his emigration, do in fact appear to some of his Hamburg colleagues as neurotic reactions, "signs of senility." Certainly Karsch is as uncomfortable on his return to West Germany as ever he was in the East.

The details of his more than three months' stay in the latter richly supplement, with vignettes and obiter dicta, the picture of life in the GDR found in *The Third Book.*

Johnson devotes particular attention to the problem of language, central for him, the creative writer, as it is for Karsch the journalist, in whom we may with fair confidence discern some features of a self-portrait. The peculiar terminology of much GDR German, incomprehensible in the West as Karsch discovers when he tries out some of these expressions on his return, is illuminated by various examples. The matter of adjustment to life in communist society is gone into once more, as it was in *The Third Book,* but the tone is again rather more personal and less ironically detached. The confrontation of the two ways of life is described this time in a more involved and intimately concerned fashion. Of Achim and Karin, the reader learns very little more, although the problem of biography is reexamined. Karsch's interest in writing such a work is accounted for in part as a predilection for those insights this task can give to an author interested in the history of social conditions. The biographer's amazement at Achim's ruthless censorship is recounted again, and specifically spelled out is his realization that "it wasn't a question of typical problems of biography here." But what further light **"An Absence"** sheds on Karsch's behavior in the East is largely the suggestion that he was held there, at least partially, by sheer sluggishness and neurasthenic apathy.

On the whole, then, **"An Absence"** makes of Karsch a less elusive, shadowy figure than he is in *The Third Book about Achim.* The obscurity of motivation that is so universal a feature of Johnson's characterization, and which may be understood in itself as a kind of philosophical commentary upon social existence, is mitigated in this story. But not entirely. Though we may see a little more of Karsch's conscious motives than we did before, the presence of a possibly determinant unconscious element is now more openly implied. For the first time Johnson portrays an individual whose social behavior is conditioned by, or expresses itself in, an alienation interpretable as neurotic. We have noticed, in *The Third Book,* how Karsch may be regarded as representative of the West in the unflattering sense that his individualism, his apparent freedom, is actually perhaps a lack of moral and social coherence and a sign of degeneration. In **"An Absence"** the somewhat unconvincing nature of his reaction to what goes on in Hamburg, his insistence that his report must be published in his own paper when it would certainly be possible for it to appear somewhere else, actually strengthens the impression of lack of balance, although such was clearly not Johnson's intention.

In fact, the intemperance of Karsch in **"An Absence,"** and other features, brings him close to the alienated heroes found in some of the works of Heinrich Böll and Alfred Andersch. His exodus resembles both the inner emigration of Böll's clown Schneer and the external one of Andersch's journalist Efraim. Put another way, this means that **"An Absence"** is, in its turning toward psychological problematics and the matter of the outsider, more run-of-the-mill, more hackneyed, than Johnson's previous works. The situation is changed again, however, for the better in **Two Views,** the most widely underestimated of Johnson's books, in which the detachment in some measure surrendered in **"An Absence"** is so far restored as to produce a novel that is not only ironic but perhaps truly comic. The psychiatric material still, however, surges in the background, and in due course this increasing concern with aspects of psychopathology was to come into its own in the massive undertaking of **Anniversaries.**

A DEATH-MARKED LOVE

Two Views (1965) is Uwe Johnson's *Romeo and Juliet,* as he himself once remarked. To Mike S. Schoelmann's suggestion that such a subject was outdated and exhausted, he replied: "I agree, with the one reservation: in time of peace. In a country like ours examples of so very old-fashioned a tale occur every day. . . ." The events that nowadays, in Germany, have unfortunately separated numerous Romeos from their Juliets may even be regarded, Johnson continues, in the light of certain traditional motifs: the family feud, that of two households, has become a quarrel of states; understanding between them is so flawed and defective that an allusion to the false news Romeo received in Alexandria is not out of place; and the possibility of permanent separation through death is potentially present in the situation. As Johnson points out, however, certain features of his version of the story are new. The "love" between his Romeo and Juliet "develops only after the separation and is really brought about by this," turning into (to use Johnson's words again) "a more and more extravagant idea of belonging and obligation which cannot be tested," but yet not strong enough to make the lovers ready to accept a life together no matter where—Johnson's Romeo, this much is quite clear, has no intention whatever of going to live behind the Wall, which protects Juliet's household! New also (and an important source of Johnson's interest in this rather paltry affair) is the fact that the protagonists have enough luck to obtain a special kind of outside help. All in all, then, it is not surprising that the end of this sardonic tale does not resemble previous treatments of the theme.

It needs to be added here that Johnson's whimsical analogy in some respects disguises the truth about his novel by overlooking its deeper ironies, and is also misleading in other ways. **Two Views** is the most purely ironic of all his works, not so much because the traditional romance of star-crossed lovers is modernized in a setting that deprives it of all poetry while emphasizing its all too immediate actuality, but because the detached and sarcastic treatment goes so far that that love which supposedly binds (however "extravagantly") Herr B. to

Nurse D. has practically no foundation whatsoever in real feeling. Not only is this love not strong enough to persuade Herr B. to cross over and settle down in the GDR—it is simply not love at all. All pathos and even the faintest note of potential tragedy are therefore expelled, and the characters (at any rate Herr B.) slide distinctly in the direction of caricature. The "ordinary people," who, as Johnson claims, offer the most significant examples of conditions of life in our day, and whose tragedy it is that, unlike the rich and the powerful, they have to endure the worst consequences of political changes within their own narrow and inescapable circumstances, these people are certainly aware what love and separation can be and are simply not well represented by the West German photographer and his East German nurse.

So Johnson has perhaps made of his novel more of an ironic comedy than he either intended or maybe even realized, despite the rather conscious deliberation with which the book was clearly put together. Its title seems to have a number of implications: two opinions, two (physical) standpoints, and also, conceivably, the sense of a paramount uncertainty—everything in German life can, since the country is divided as it is, be seen in two ways, subserves the purposes of two ideologies, and has therefore no firm and final truth to it. The novel is built up in a series of chapters presenting alternately the consciousness of the two lovers, Herr B. of the Federal Republic and Nurse D. of the GDR. The straight narrative technique that Johnson opted for in **"An Absence"** is retained; only a minor ploy at the very end of the book when the story teller suddenly materializes as a participant in the action, helping to take Herr B. to hospital after his accident and listening to Nurse D.'s confidences after her escape from the GDR, playfully disrupts the sense of a conventional narrator who is omniscient. This conventionality, according to Johnson, is quite appropriate, since the book is, in his own words, "a fairly simple story largely suited to the traditional procedure for describing the development of emotions."

It is at this point, however, that queries perhaps ought to be raised, since it is evident that the ironic mode Johnson has selected here largely precludes any impressive concentration upon the psychology of feelings. While it is not true, as some reviewers have claimed, that the principal characters are without significant feelings, the style in which their portraits are drawn circumscribes these emotions to such a degree and so deprives them of status that they become little more than reactions; these emotions are responses to stimuli in an environment to which they are entirely subordinate. As the reflection of this environment—and as little else—the personalities of these people have been formed. At the same time, while the technical means used to portray these two hardly varies from the one to the other, the result is still different in each case. This is because of the satirical emphases of the novel and specifically because each of them is in substantial measure the representative of his or her society but in a totally different way.

Briefly, Herr B. is much less sympathetically depicted than is Nurse D. He is particularly Pavlovian, that is to say, nothing but responses. In him especially we see that kind of typological characterization in which the writer aims less at psychological coherence and individual credibility and more at the isolation of certain features of behavior and attitude that represent the governing tendencies in a given social group. Characters handled in this way are found widely, for example, in the modern theater, especially in the works of playwrights such as Brecht, Dürrenmatt, and Frisch. These dramatis personae may be vividly representative, but when we look at them coldly we notice that they have no real life. Perhaps Herr B. might be usefully compared with such a figure as Herr Biedermann in Frisch's play *The Firebugs,* although the conclusion would probably then be that Johnson's character is appreciably less allegorical and less of a caricature.

Both Herr B. and Nurse D., therefore, typify a certain kind of response to the society in which each of them lives, but since these two responses are utterly different the satirical treatment varies too. Herr B. is seen almost entirely negatively. He is a free-lance photographer, and we have already picked up a few hints, in **The Third Book about Achim,** as to what this may imply. Certainly, he represents the small-time capitalist entrepreneur and opportunist interested solely in success and in appearances, that is to say, in money and status. The bright red sportscar he acquires at the beginning of the novel, which is then stolen on a visit to West Berlin, is expressive of his goals in life. His sense of values is laconically conveyed by the information that he is willing to pay the organizers of his girlfriend's escape from the East "the tenth part of the sum a medium car cost at that time." On the very day her long-awaited, and highly dangerous, flight is set in motion, Herr B. goes off to Stuttgart to take delivery of a new automobile, having first purchased "a pair of Karlsbad gloves, which are leather on the inside but wool on the back outside, for wiping misted windshields."

Herr B.'s feelings, such as they are, are in the first place very much attached to material things—the theft of his car brings him close to tears, which the separation from his loved one fails to do. Then, his moral principles are quite secondary; to make a sale of his photographs, he is prepared to suppress those that may embarrass the local authorities in his little town (he lives in Holstein). Comically, his sense of guilt then leads him for days to turn his head away whenever he meets his own eyes in the shaving mirror. An individual of little sophistication and insignificant skills, Herr B.

combines empty-headedness with living by his wits—which is perhaps why he is not very successful. Impractical, he is also easily tricked, for instance by a West Berlin taxi driver. A natural snob, he is equally the obvious provincial, and the petty bourgeois quickly intimidated by those who have more wealth and style than he. When he tries to emulate them, he makes a fool of himself, and the gulf between his romantic pretensions (for example his desire to appear the worldly air traveler) and the reality (his terror and air sickness) yawns wide. Arrogant, often aggressive where this is uncalled for, he is sometimes craven, especially when it comes to taking risks on the other side of the Wall. He much prefers just photographing it for money, the supposedly typical West German who considers the GDR a dangerous insanity best viewed cosily from afar. "Her state," as the narrator refers to it, intimidates him, it seems overpowering, and when he does feel obliged to offer assistance to someone in the East, he is secretly pleased to have this declined: "He took his leave, in his whole bearing an example of West German solidarity, ready to give any help and thoroughly relieved that this was not appropriate."

Sharp comments of this kind illustrate Johnson's careful aim as a satirist. But there are subtler aspects to the portrait. The compensation for Herr B.'s marked inferiority complex (which has, the inference is, social roots—i.e., the competitive society and the class system) is his "ideal of a Herr B.," and this involves some sense of the need to assume obligations and adopt a moral stance. His separation, through the building of the Wall, from Nurse D., in whom his interest—like that in his various other conquests—is essentially transient and trivial, thwarts him thoroughly for about the first time in his life. This is one reason for his decision to help her flee to the West. The other impulse comes from his sense of duty and his notion of love.

The important point, however, is that both of these are inauthentic. They are spurious because they are entirely the superficial product of a trivialized and conventional social awareness. "Education through his school friends and through films had led him to regard a promise of love as binding, until the two people quarreled." To this nonsense he adds the argument that, though he and D. did indeed quarrel, since subsequently he wrote her a love letter, his obligation to her is reestablished. The fatuity of this attitude is paralleled by his vacuous sense of honor, again wholly soaked up from the meretricious culture with its pompous but sham values of which he is the conspicuous agent. Though Herr B. does have feelings, they are merely those validated by the popular weeklies. He exemplifies the western conviction that the "real self" lies within—"like the illustrated magazines he regarded the inner life of a person as the essential"—and at the same time he shows this belief up for the decadent and dishonest evasion Marxist thinkers have declared it to be. In the figure of Herr B., Johnson presents an acid indictment of a self-deluded and inauthentic society, founded upon commercialism and cheapness of feeling and cut off from any genuine commitment or the possibility of that kind of natural human encounter that might make moral experience and social justice more than mere words.

Disorganized and often panic-stricken, Herr B. is usually a creature of impulses. His several flights back and forth between Hamburg and West Berlin often take place on the spur of the moment, so that he hardly knows why he is in the plane. His final disaster, being run down by a truck on a Berlin street, is a tragicomical pointer to the self-destructive nature of his sort and his world. His conflicts over the matter of aiding Nurse D. do not represent a serious moral theme, and of course he makes no clearcut moral choices. Even in the decision to help her escape he is responding to his conditioning. The difference between him and his girl is really a function of the distinction between the two "households." His own is confused and anarchic, there is no meaningful authority, and Herr B., whose family is never referred to, may be regarded as a classic instance of a weak person adrift, finally ruined by permissiveness. It is not, of course, in Johnsonian terms real freedom that B. enjoys, only the illusion thereof. For since there is no moral authority in his state, there is no justice and so in fact no true liberty.

D.'s case seems near enough the opposite in that her state is highly authoritarian (or is so presented). There is therefore no disorder and also no sham freedom in it. But Johnson is not a Stalinist author. Thus he notes that the presence of an authority claiming to represent an ideal is in itself not the slightest guarantee of justice or of liberty for anyone. In the GDR there is another—perhaps worse—kind of spuriousness, namely, the organized simulation of a just social system. The critical difference lies exactly in this: while Herr B. gives expression to his chaotic society as its typical protagonist, Nurse D. reacts against her totalitarian one as its typical (because rather ordinary) antagonist. The presence of an authority, especially an unjust one, at least offers people the possibility of a moral existence, for it forces them to discriminate between the true and the false, and to discern the need for, and the feasible extent of, a personal moral autonomy. As Jacob Abs, in his confrontation with Rohlfs, feels a harsh challenge to his identity, so Nurse D., limited and superficial as she is, reacts to this again. The family feud between Montagues and Capulets has indeed been replaced by that between ideologies and states, perhaps these days the only external power that can still separate lovers. On another level, the allegorical one, as B. loves D., so *B*undesrepublik loves, or perhaps detests, *D*eutsche Demokratische Re-

publik. And on yet a third, the level of the psyche, the patterns of archetypal conflict important in all Johnson's novels may once more be noticed.

It is noteworthy that D. owes some of the difficulties of her situation to the alleged misdeeds of her family, in particular the fact that her father was a general under Hitler. In the GDR the sin of class is visited upon subsequent generations: "Later she was excluded from the upper grades in school and from higher education because the state regarded her as the daughter of a criminal, in accordance with the military rank of her father, dead though he was." Her youngest brother flees to the West; as a result she is investigated and loses her private apartment in East Berlin, which she had acquired without the proper residence permit. Like Cresspahl and his "family," in *Speculations about Jacob,* but unlike the Papenbrocks in *Anniversaries,* the family of Nurse D. is not at all identified with the paternal authority of the state, and represents a rudimentary form of resistance to it. The apartment is an important motif, it might almost be called symbolic, were it not that Johnson's style in *Two Views* is so contained, so sober, so factual that it seems hardly permissible to speak of symbolism. At all events the pursuit of physical privacy is for Nurse D. her modest variant upon the yearning for individuality and freedom that is expressed by earlier characters. Obtaining her own room at all, away from the hospital, is a triumphant feat: "For quite some time, when she closed the door, behind which no one knew she was, she used to feel almost proud. She had something to defend, she had stood up and resisted, and successfully."

The chapters that deal with Nurse D. explore the development of her reluctant decision to leave for the West, the nature of her interest in B. and his contribution to this choice. In some respects she may be compared with him fairly closely. She too seems to live in the shallower waters of the personality, her urges and responses restricted to everyday things to the extent that one hesitates to speak of her possessing an autonomous individuality, or any kind of depth or originality of feeling. For her as well, the encounter with B. was a triviality—"an affair, a flirtation, a week, a relationship, a beginning. She didn't know what it was, nor why." She expects neither its continuation nor any emotional consequences from it. He irritates her, for example when he calls her up at the hospital, thus putting her in danger, and she exclaims: "That idiot!" At the same time, she sometimes feels vaguely guilty about him, thinking for instance that on one occasion she may have stood him up. It is surely not love that persuades her to accept the help, arranged by B., that will get her to the West, though love—or at least the idea of it—may be somewhere in her mind. In her imagination she warns him: "You're telling yourself fibs, it won't be sufficient for a whole life, it's far from being sufficient just for coming over." When, at the very last moment, she discovers from her false passport that he has forgotten, or never even noticed, the color of her eyes, she has suddenly had enough of him and of the whole enterprise. When she finally arrives in West Berlin, he is not there to meet her. Afterward she refuses to see him, but eventually visits him in the hospital. Then however she turns back to herself, to her private affairs, for "she wanted to look for a room."

Nurse D. is an interesting case of a character whose motives are mixed and certainly not completely clear. It is not ultimately evident just why she loses interest in B.—there are after all moments in the novel when she seems to think seriously of him and to excuse the difficulty she has in visualizing his face by the fact that they have not met for some time. Perhaps the error in the color of her eyes changes her view of him, perhaps it is the fact that he has chosen the time of her escape to go to Stuttgart for his new car. It is more likely that her "love" for him was always as insubstantial as his for her, a few nights' diversion and little more, and that just as his conviction that he must aid her springs not from real affection but from concern for appearances and from a spurious sense of honor, so her decision to go to the West has quite different determinants, which conceal themselves behind the supposed sexual bond. Hans Erich Nossack's remarkable phrase "private life as camouflage" may be relevant here, and elsewhere in Johnson's work. The erotic link across the frontier, sexual love or its memory (Karsch), as the motive for crossing—all this may be a disguise for the struggle of conscience, the painfully ambivalent feelings involved in the confrontation with the other society, the alternative moral reality.

The search for freedom and for privacy in Johnson's work may well go deeper than the search for love. Not one single character, neither Jacob nor Gesine nor Jonas Blach, neither Karsch nor Karin, neither Nurse D. nor Herr B., is really prepared to change his residence, his "household," to surrender his social and moral identity, for the sake of *love*. The tragic dimension in *Anniversaries* derives, as we shall see, from the belated revelation that Heinrich Cresspahl did do just this, and its consequences turned out to be horrendous. But in *Two Views,* Nurse D., who appears to be about to perform this act of reunification, nevertheless nullifies it immediately on arrival and makes clear that this was not what it really was. It is of course true that there are several immediate precipitants of her decision to leave—she has lost her apartment, she is in trouble because her youngest brother has fled the country, she has been unfairly treated at the hospital where she works. This last incident may be the straw that breaks the camel's back, but it is not the explanation of her departure. There is of course no single explanation, and no clear moment of choice. When contacted by the student organization that arranges the escape she merely tells them she is willing to go. Her choice emerges from her life, and it does at least contain a moral element.

The essential context for this choice is of course the construction of the Wall. Each of Johnson's first three novels is intimately related to crucial events on the plane of political history—*Speculations* [*Speculations about Jacob*] to the Hungary and Suez crises, *The Third Book* to the 1953 workers' revolt in the GDR, and *Two Views* to the Wall. For the first time, in August 1961, the German Democratic Republic became entirely cut off from the West, as far as the movement of its ordinary citizens was concerned. Nurse D. is bitterly angered by this act on the part of her government. If she is capable of passion, then it is over this. For she feels "solidarity" with her fellow inhabitants. But we should remember that, educated as she has been in the ideology of her country, a "worker" herself and suspicious of intellectuals, she has up to this moment accepted a good deal of standard doctrine, except where it encroaches upon her family (especially her attitude to her father). She has accepted that the West (delightful though window shopping in West Berlin may be) is corrupt and will one day collapse; it is certainly no place to live. As she says to herself, watching refugees leaving the train on the forbidden platform: "The worst is still before you." She even understands the reason for the official prohibition on travel to West Berlin (unenforceable of course before the Wall), she merely does not recognize it as applying to her. She has learned to erect the facade Karsch noticed in everyone in the East: "To accommodate herself to things as they were, she had given up translating her actions out of her own language into that of her state; she had learned, with people connected with the power and authority of the state, to pretend to be someone else. . . ." She does not appear to have any moral qualms about such behavior.

Insofar, on the other hand, as she is prepared to serve the state, it is just by doing her job as a nurse and no more. She has, after all, caught her state in the act of telling lies. But lest we imagine that this provides D. with a fundamental motive for moral resistance, the narrator craftily adds: "besides this she was indifferent to politics, besides this in the afternoons there was no school and she had younger brothers. . . ." When the Wall goes up, certainly, D.'s anger is intense, for she feels she has lost her right to choose: "She had lived under this state as though in her own country, at home, trusting to an open future and the right to choose the other country. Locked up in the one she felt cheated, deceived, lied to. . . ." To the soldiers who guard the masons building the Wall she says: "How can you have the nerve?" Of all the faults of the regime this alone fills her "with cold rage as the spiteful breach of a promise did when she was a child." Choice becomes all important to those who are deprived of it.

In the case of Nurse D., then, Johnson gives us the context of the choice, but no insight into the actual moment of decision itself, if such a moment is to be presumed. The act of choice is, as usual in Johnson's writings, not described, and all the reader can do is to make tentative inferences on the matter. In her resentment over the Wall, be it noted, Nurse D. is a representative figure, she stands for the typical reaction of the ordinary citizen to what has just been done. This sort of response was generally, as Johnson points out, a rather short-lived thing. Less transient, much more deeply formative in her case, is the relationship with the family, with her dead father (a man "to be despised, yet not despicable") and with her youngest brother, for whom she feels a maternal kind of responsibility. From the psychic substance of her family relationships emerges something intimately connected with her urge to have a private life, to achieve autonomy. Relevant in this regard is the account of D.'s dreams, shortly before her flight, though the stylistic harmony and unity of the novel is possibly somewhat impaired by the introduction of such material. These dreams reflect the tensions of the risky undertaking, but also the pressures of personal conflicts. She dreams, for instance, of someone dead behind a door, and this appears first of all to be B. but then turns into her brother, "as she knew all along."

In the development of Johnson's work, the use of these dreams, with their depth-psychological implications, represents an important departure. *Two Views* remains, however, in spite of this innovation a concise social satire first and foremost, in which the barbs are directed on one side of the Wall at a character, Herr B., and through him at a society, and on the other side directly at a regime and its policies. Nurse D. herself is spared the ironic lash, she is even allowed to arouse the reader's sympathy as a heroine. Only a harsh and skeptical critic could surmise that once in West Berlin she might well lose her rudimentary but real moral center and soon become another B. For *Two Views* is not a cynical book, although the vignettes and the marginalia are often biting—the wealthy Berliners who have their property photographed so that they may claim full compensation from the Bonn government if the communists should one day seize West Berlin, or the beds in D.'s hospital containing patients who have suffered nervous collapse as the result of the East German government's resolve to protect "the dignity" of its frontiers, or the communist managerial intellectuals who use western soaps and toiletries anyway and who then, happening to be in the West when the Wall goes up, choose to remain there.

The satirist finds that neither of these societies is a just one. The ideal has to be sought elsewhere. In *Two Views* it is found especially in the young people, students who band together to operate in Scarlet Pimpernel fashion an escape network from the East. Connected with a particular tavern in West Berlin, this group survives only a short time, in the autumn of 1961. Its representative figure is the barmaid (Anita), self-assured, efficient, and kind-hearted, and she perhaps, rather than Herr B., is Nurse D.'s true equivalent in the West. Nurse D. has to defend her right to her own individuality against the encroachments of a monolithic collective, and has to seek to realize her privacy and freedom by the act of crossing the border into the other sphere. But once there, though the nature of the menace will be different, the challenge may be equally severe. Karsch's collision with West German authority and reaction in **"An Absence"** merely brings out an aspect that, though crude, is at first not very obvious. More subtle and dangerous still is the subversion of identity and liberty in the West by the commercialism of capitalist affluence and the sheer absence of a moral structure in social life, for these factors, though fairly obvious in themselves, are generally underestimated.

The answer to being confronted by an impossible pair of alternatives can only be some third way, the possibility of which is suggested in the kind of commitment that the students for a short time seem to find. The cynicism of the Western pseudocommitment, the indifference of the "photographic" attitude, is transcended by what these young people do, is replaced by a wholly admirable (if in the long run quixotic) form of direct action. But it must not be overlooked that the necessity of engagement, if this is taken to mean acceptance of an ideology, is precisely not Johnson's message. It is hard to imagine Johnson endorsing the kind of solution dangled before the reader in Sartre's *Les chemins de la liberté*. On this issue he commented as follows: "Indeed not engagement; en-gagement would have to have two sides, not just carrying out the work, but receiving the commission for it, and the honorarium."[1] His novel, therefore, in his own words, which as usual seem designed more to preclude misinterpretation than to offer a firm basis for understanding, is "simply my experience, life and times in the two German states, and the conviction that their difference is significant enough for us to be destroyed by it." The ironic demise, not of Johnson's Romeo and Juliet but of their love instead, stands the old tale on its head. Their very failure to come together leaves the feud between "two households, both alike in dignity" as a real threat of national ruin.

SUPPLEMENTS AND FRAGMENTS

The short story **"A Tavern Vanishes"** (**"Eine Kneipe geht verloren"**), published in 1965 (*Kursbuch*, No. 1) bears a similar relationship to its parent novel, *Two Views,* as **"An Absence"** does to *The Third Book about Achim.* Switching the angle of vision, it focuses on an element only marginally treated in the novel, though in this instance one that may well have been an important factor in the genesis of the main work. This is the existence of the student group organizing escapes from East Berlin, the account of which is based on fact. The story explains something of the origin of this activity, which has as its headquarters a West Berlin tavern. At the center stands the barmaid, a student, running the establishment for her aunt, who merely sits in a vacant stupor. In an exact, neatly edged prose Johnson sketches in the circumstances leading to the barmaid's decision to involve herself in these perilous matters, gives some account of their actual machinery, and finally describes the factors (chiefly economic) that eventually result in the end of the enterprise and the closing down of the bar. As in the case of **"An Absence,"** it cannot be said that this story breaks any really new ground; what it does do is provide supplemental examples of Johnson's techniques and his primary concerns at this point in his career.

Johnson's technical capacity comes through forcefully once more in the acute precision of many of the descriptions. For instance, the voice with which the barmaid answers the phone, reflecting her tension, is described as "very slightly hemmed in and hard." The trick of the devastating gloss, so well developed by now, continues to be displayed: the GDR requires a "securely disposable population," it has a government characterized by "the diligence of a collector"; a homosexual is called not that but rather "a despiser of the female genitals." The changed perspective allows Herr B. and Nurse D. to be mentioned once more, the former with a critical, the latter a favorable reference, and there is a hint that the woman does indeed wish to escape in order to get married, but not evidently to "that man from Holstein." (It is as though Johnson gave the reader a glimpse of some of the material out of which the intrigue of *Two Views* was to be made, before his imagination had recomposed it in a thoroughly fictional pattern). The barmaid has to make a choice, to engage herself in fact, and her motivation at the crucial moment is made clear enough—she does not want to be thought a coward. There is really no enigma here, although there is again the insight that the personal, subjective factor is always preeminent in such "political" decisions.

Particularly interesting and informative is the stress upon the actual mechanics of the illegal operations, in which we may note once more Johnson's preoccupation with the technical problems involved in the crossing of frontiers that are often supposedly closed, with the organized outwitting of governments, with intelligence and indeed espionage work. The gun that Gesine Cresspahl carries in *Speculations about Jacob,* the false identities (and passports) used by characters in *Two Views,* in **"A Tavern Vanishes,"** and later in *Anniversaries,* attest to one kind of subject matter that may have a certain symbolic usefulness although it properly belongs to the world of the spy story. In Johnson's work it provides plot material that dovetails rather nicely with the ideological, social, and existential issues the books try to present.

Probably the most interesting passage in **"A Tavern Vanishes"** is a longish commentary upon the nature of the risks taken in these operations, the motivation of those involved, and the implications of what occurs:

> the couriers who were imprisoned for life, their own, in the jails of the East German environment for the sake of having one passport too many, for the sake of that fallacy which had falsified, out of assistance to neighbors for private reasons personal to them, a citizen's duty based on public grounds . . . punished for what they had done, with the silence of their own community, with the prison regulations of the East German authorities, with the transvaluation, before courts like these, of the individual motive into a political one.

A deep-seated skepticism toward any kind of "public grounds" seems to find expression here. The individual, personal motivation is justifiable and sane, Johnson appears to be saying, the general and political one dangerous, thankless, and usually misled. It is, perhaps, a sad message, probably not the ultimate one. It is a fairly substantial elucidation, maybe modification, of the mood of *Two Views.*

In this respect the story tells us more than Johnson's other slighter pieces do, these being on the whole of little importance. A number of short anecdotes from this period or a little earlier, published in the same volume as **"An Absence,"** are of interest only in that they show some further development of the saga of Gesine Cresspahl. In one, **"Unsolicited Gift"** (**"Geschenksendung, keine Handelsware"**), the reader learns for his pains that the heroine of *Speculations about Jacob* has a child. Subsequently, Johnson published in *Kursbuch* one or two items in which he turns his attention to quite a new theme, namely the United States and its war in Vietnam. His position, naturally, is severely critical. His experience of America, a two-year stay in New York (1966-1968), is the essential background for *Anniversaries,* which he seems to have begun writing in 1967. One phrase in **"Letter from New York"** (**"Ein Brief aus New York,"** *Kursbuch,* No. 10) tells the reader that what he is writing is "a letter about what is otherwise here about a difference." Remembering the aim of *The Third Book*—which was to evoke "the frontier: the distance: the difference"—we may well expect that, though there will no doubt be a radically changed locale in *Anniversaries,* the symbolic geography will not be so much transformed as merely displaced.

Notes

1. Johnson is playing here with the literal sense of "engagement," i.e. "entering into a contract for

which there is a reward" (compare French: "être aux gages de quelqu'un").

Bibliography

I. WORKS BY UWE JOHNSON

Mutmaßungen über Jacob, novel, (Frankfurt: Suhrkamp, 1959).

(*Speculations about Jacob,* New York, Grove, 1963).

Das dritte Buch über Achim, novel, (Frankfurt: Suhrkamp, 1961).

(*The Third Book about Achim,* New York: Harcourt, Brace, 1967).

Karsch und andere Prosa, (Frankfurt: Suhrkamp, 1964) Includes: "Osterwasser," "Beihilfe zum Umzug," "Geschenksendung, keine Handelsware," "Eine Reise wegwohin, 1960" ("An Absence," London: Cape, 1969), "Jonas zum Beispiel."

"Eine Kneipe geht verloren," story, *Kursbuch,* No. 1, 1965, pp. 47-72.

Zwei Ansichten, novel, (Frankfurt: Suhrkamp, 1965) (*Two Views,* New York: Harcourt, Brace, 1966).

"Ein Brief aus New York," essay, *Kursbuch,* No. 10, 1967, pp. 189-92.

Jahrestage, volume I, novel (Frankfurt: Suhrkamp, 1970).

Jahrestage, volume II, (Frankfurt: Suhrkamp, 1971).

Marianne Hirsch (essay date 1981)

SOURCE: Hirsch, Marianne. "*Speculations about Jakob*: 'Truthfinding'." In *Beyond the Single Vision: Henry James, Michel Butor, Uwe Johnson,* pp. 82-110. York, S. C.: French Literature Publications Company, 1981.

[*In the following essay, Hirsch explores Johnson's use of multiple narrative perspectives in* Speculations about Jakob *and asserts that the novel is not only an "effort to reconstruct" the life of the character Jakob but also "an effort to restore to Germany its common history, its common language and tradition."*]

In *The Golden Bowl,* the ethics of American capitalist-imperialism, translated onto an aesthetic plane with the character of Maggie Verver, threatens to taint any possibility of human community. Manipulation, dominance and possession become the instruments of knowledge and understanding as well as the agents of Maggie's marriage. And yet, the novel's open-ended biphonic structure sets up the possibility of a type of community through the participation of a third consciousness, that

of the implied reader, a reader aware of the threats of manipulation and willing to resist them. If there is a possible community in *The Golden Bowl,* it is extremely tenuous and it takes place outside the confines of the novel. The fictional process is itself too seriously implicated in the power structures that define the cultural interaction. But with the consciousness of the implied reader there also emerges a fourth consciousness, that of the manipulative implied author; the triangle becomes a square and the power struggle remains central.

This political consciousness, translated onto a formal level within the novel, links *The Golden Bowl* to Johnson's **Speculations about Jakob.** Johnson begins with the silence with which James ends, with the consciousness of the limits of fiction as an epistemological tool and an instrument of community. Johnson's silence comes out of a feeling of paralysis brought about by the political division of Germany and the linguistic contamination it produces. Johnson's short 1961 text **"Berliner Stadtbahn,"** one of his few quasi=theoretical statements, outlines the dilemma of the writer in the politically defined world of the divided Germany.

"Berliner Stadtbahn" begins with a nucleus of a potentially dramatic situation, one which Johnson intended to incorporate as a vignette into one of his novels, but which he found impossible to write. It was to concern a young East German man who gets off the train in a West Berlin subway stop, crosses the platform and walks toward the street.[1] In view of the political situation of Berlin at that time, this seemingly simple story is full of ambiguities involving the young man's motivations—is he going to the West for a visit, is he moving there, or should one say he is fleeing the East?—his expectations and fears, the reality of the life he leaves behind and of the one to which he can look forward. To talk about the young man's simple outward action is to consider not only motives, desires, and feelings but a complex social and political situation that has invaded all areas of individual existence. In **"Berliner Stadtbahn"** the initial fictional kernel is overgrown with the writer's doubts, questions, insecurities. Writing any human story in the context of a divided country involves a battle with the clichés of thought and language of two opposite political and ideological systems, what Johnson calls "alternative realities." Doing justice to both without getting trapped by either one seems impossible. The writer feels paralyzed by this dilemma. Not a single area is neutral in the particular context in which Johnson writes; even facts and statistics are loaded.

> He can consider the single universal. He can call the private typical. He can wish to recognize a law, where there appears a mere statistical accumulation. He is in the constant danger of trying to make something true that is merely factual.[2]

The writer's inability to describe either the behavior or the motivation of an individual, or the scene in which he lives, is due in part to the corruption of the language available to him as a tool. The linguistic conventions and structures that arise out of different political systems require an extreme caution on the writer's part if he tries to stay out of their propagandistic influences. Despite the acknowledged difficulties, Johnson's goal remains to find "a language . . . that can get a handle on both regions and can also be trans-regionally understood."[3]

The significance of Johnson's dilemma is not restricted to the particular situation in post-war Germany, however; as the essay clearly demonstrates, most of the factors that paralyze Johnson are merely intensified versions of those that hover over modern literature in general. The general breakdown of the modern writer's capacity to uncover and communicate an external reality makes any third scheme that Johnson might want to oppose to the two politically tainted schemata that usurp his character's story equally partial and suspect. The modern writer is limited in his single point of view and his unreliable personal experience. He cannot generalize on the basis of his own vision. Language itself is contaminated by ideology. In a politically defined world, the form of the word is evaluative and no neutral words external to the ideological system can exist. This Roland Barthes point out in *Writing Degree Zero*:

> In the Stalinist world, in which *definition,* that is to say the separation between Good and Evil, becomes the sole content of all language, there are no more words without values attached to them, so that finally the function of writing is to cut out one stage of a process: there is no more lapse of time between naming and judging, and the closed character of language is perfected, since it is a value which is given as explanation of another value.[4]

Here Barthes speaks of Marxist and Stalinist literature but the problem is naturally aggravated when two separate value systems exist next to and against each other as they do in Germany: "Both Berlin cities call themselves free and each other not free, themselves democratic and each other undemocratic, themselves peaceful, each other aggressive, etc."[5]

For all these reasons, the author's and the reader's position in the literary text is a problematic one and demands constant redefinition; the author's freedom is in need of severe limitation:

> If the author first has to invent and put together his text, how can he then sit on the high chair above the playing field like the umpire in tennis, know all the rules, how can he both know the characters and observe them impeccably, interfere at any time he chooses and even change places with one of his characters and know them as he can hardly ever know himself. The author should admit that he invented what he presents, he should not disguise the fact that his information is partial and precise.[6]

"Erfindung" for Johnson is not the free invention of an independent imaginary realm but the only possibility for a writer whose insight into himself and his world is limited, to gain at least some form of knowledge: "With my writing I would like to find out the truth. With my characters I am trying to reach the actual life."[7] Paradoxically, Johnson has to invent a fictional world to find out the truth about reality. With knowledge as the stated goal of Johnson's writing, the direction of his fictional invention is delimited not by the richness of his imagination but by the astuteness of observation, the accuracy of information, and their responsible rendition.

Johnson's statement is reminiscent of James' credo about the observed life which forms the substance of the artist's creation; the metaphors of the umpire in the great arena describe the author's relation to his work in strikingly similar ways. In contrast to James, however, Johnson allows the artist little freedom to alter and embellish the meager observations he might have been able to gather; piecing the fragments together is his job: "Precision is demanded of him."[8] James claims exactly that privilege that Johnson denies the author: to move at will between his place as arbiter of the great game and in the middle of the arena itself. James' privilege protects, just as Johnson's limitation exposes the author.

In the divided condition of Germany, the reader's role becomes more problematic as well. The reader is called upon to shed his assumptions, taking nothing for granted, and to participate in the arduous search for the truth which alone can preoccupy the conscientious writer. The novelistic form that arises out of the dilemma described in **"Berliner Stadtbahn"** is a collaborative and self-conscious, often tortuous, effort:

> He can admit this by demonstrating explicity the difficult search for the truth, by comparing and relativising his conception of the events with his characters, by omitting what he cannot know, by not exposing as pure fiction what amounts to a kind of truthfinding.[9]

Johnson's "truthfinding" is quite different from James' reign of an imagination which, at every point, threatens to lose contact with the real. This form to which **"Berliner Stadtbahn"** itself conforms enables the writer to avoid at least some of the pitfalls the text describes and to approach the goal of honesty. The structure of this short text is symptomatic for Johnson's other works; not a story but the negation of a story emerges. Its final sentence suggests the compensations such a form can offer the reader who is cheated out of the tale whose impossibility it recounts: "I hope nevertheless to have described the difficulties with the subway in such a way that you can imagine it somewhat." Thus the story emerges out of the account of its impossibility and through the imaginative investment of the reader. **"Ber-**

liner Stadtbahn" gives us the material of a potential fictional situation; if it were to tell us a "story" it would be partial at best, utterly false at worst. Johnson's questions about the possibilities of fiction and his efforts to broaden its capacities are his response to division, his effort to understand it and thus to investigate the possibility of a reunification.

The political situation of Germany—its confrontation of two "alternate realities"—exacerbates the individual's limited capacities of knowledge and the possibility of perception emphasized by James. To write an individual story is also to describe the political, historical, geographical and economic forces that shape behavior and character. To do so, Johnson finds that he must redefine the fictional forms he has inherited: "Of a writer we expect information about the situation, should he describe it with means which it has long surpassed? . . . [He tries] constantly to change the aesthetic instruments with the constant changes of reality."[10] Like Butor, Johnson finds that to be a realist he must be an experimentalist. The solutions he suggests in **"Berliner Stadtbahn"** do not solve the writer's dilemma but present him with a medium in which it is feasible to continue writing: fiction as "truthfinding," as both a search for truth and the depiction of that search. It is a collaborative process all of whose materials are laid bare; it is unfinished, imperfect, in demand of constant revision.

The central intelligence in James' fiction, in its attempt to exercise control amidst the competing individual realities and to impose, through manipulation and force, one of those realities over the others, demonstrates the moral dangers of authority, the dubiousness of authorship. In Johnson's work, the break-up of fictional authority is a response to political authoritarianism. The authoritarianism of the East German state, the assumption of absolute power by a small number of strong individuals in the name of a supra-individual cause, is an extreme manifestation of the strong individualism which is at the basis of James' aesthetic. The details of Rohlfs' investigation in *Speculations about Jakob* are but a political, an official version of the prying questions, the suppositions and speculations, of the secretive dialogues of the Assinghams, for example, the difference being that here they are *official* facts, backed up by political power:

> The eyes had no scruples and avidly seized upon each detail solely for the sake of finding out (as a lover might pursue a mistress he has never met) yet this was an assignment, and the hirelings the wage slaves . . . forgot what they saw, derived neither benefit nor experience from it for their own lives. Thus, reports and speculations grew out of meetings and neighborliness and telephone conversations and indifferent glances exchange in city conveyances, and took shape on tape recorders and typewriters and in the intimate atmosphere of whispers and were sorted out and bundled and

stapled together and stored . . . for a man who gave a different name to everyone he met, who therefore, even nominally, could not muster anything but a general and public concern for Jakob's well-being.

(p. 23)[11]

> Der Einblick war bedenkenlos und ergriff gierig jede Einzelheit nur um sie zu wissen (wie einer nachlaufen kann einer unbekannten Geliebten), doch war er beauftragt, und die Bediensteten die Lohndiener . . . vergassen was sie wahrnahmen und zogen aus dem nicht Vorteil noch Belehrung für das eigene Leben. So aus Begegnungen und Nachbarschaften und telephonischen Gesprächen und gleichgültigem Blick wechsel in den Fahrzeugen des städtischen Verkehrs ergaben sich Berichte und Vermutungen, die nahmen Gestalt an in laufenden Tonbändern und schreibenden Maschinen und in der innigen Atmosphäre des Flüsterns und wurden sortiert und gebündelt und geheftet und . . . aufbewahrt für einen Mann, der seinen Namen austauschte vor jedem Gegenüber und also schon dem Namen nach keine andere Teilnahme an Jakobs Ergehen verwalten konnte als eine allgemeine und öffentliche.

(pp. 18-19)

In this passage, it is not only the growth of a story out of small fragments and suggestions that is reminiscent of James' novels, but also the lack of real commitment to the subjects of the speculations. James' observers are motivated by curiosity, Johnson's by an assignment. Rohlfs' political plots correspond to the manipulative plots of Maggie and Fanny and by extension to the fictional plots of the traditional omniscient author that Johnson attacks.

Johnson's aesthetic, the dialectical juxtaposition of multiple narrative perspectives, is devised in reaction to such a central controlling power as that of the state and has as its goal the restoration of the individual's voice. The extensive search for a truth in which a multiplicity of voices can participate is contrasted to the imposed control of a power that admits only single answers and interpretations. Offering an alternative to the fictional structures of the past, Johnson's novels point out the connection between fictional and political structures and respond to political authoritarianism with fictional openness. The fragmentary style and structure of Johnson's fictions dramatize the division of a country that was once one, as well as the alienation of the individual in a system which he can neither fully understand nor identify with. In their openness and their suggestion of new structural possibilities, the novels are experiments in reconstruction. They are formal representations of the perspectivism of value and meaning that results from the political division of a country, of the modern world into two camps, East and West. The unbiased inclusion of many voices is an attempt to develop an idiom that could include both camps, to create a common ground on which they could meet. With conjecture and speculation as the cognitive mode, Johnson's works are formal images of the elusiveness of human motive, of the individual's growing inability to recognize a proper place within the warring systems that control his life.

While James' attempted fusion of cultures is a desire for enrichment and enlargement, Johnson's represents the necessity of reuniting that which was severed. Culture, for Johnson, is defined neither by history nor geography, neither by moral nor by intellectual values. It is politics that has severed the country and has divided its cities, its language, objects, and people. For Johnson, then, the question is not to reach a "sublime consensus of the educated," but to survive in a country that has been forcefully divided.

Speculations about Jakob, published in West Germany in 1958, is about the effects of the division: "This situation has altered considerably the life of so many people, and my life as well, often negatively," says Johnson. "And we will die from it—or end up well."[12] When Johnson says that the differences between the two German states are serious enough to kill us, he is not using a figure of speech. The novel deals not with the interaction between two people but with the fragments of one victim of the division—the dead Jakob Abs. The effort to reconstruct his life is at the same time an effort to restore to Germany its common history, its common language and tradition; it is, one could say, an effort to transcend the political differences through the revived consciousness of what is common.

The novel has the form of an investigation; a number of people connected with Jakob's life get the chance to express their thoughts and feelings about him, either through the mediation of a third-person narrator, through direct dialogues or through interior monologues. The novel has two levels: the speculations about Jakob which take place after his death and the reconstructed story that emerges from them. Johnson's approach to his subject is perspectivistic; he illuminates it from as many angles as possible so as to have the best chance of arriving at the truth. Among Johnson's work, *Speculations [Speculations about Jakob]* uses the technique of multiple perspectives in the fullest way.

The fact of Jakob's death reduces the narrators of his life to conjecture and speculation and is responsible for the inordinate complexity of this story. There are in the novel several emblems for these perceptual hardships: the attempt to distinguish the figure of Jakob through the thick morning fog, the difficulty of reading Rohlf's old map of the Jerichow region in which water, flatland and mountain are all indicated by the same color, the effort of the philologist to reconstruct old speech patterns from fragmentary and incomplete evidence: in each of the cases, conjecture is the only possible cognitive mode.

The novel's reader has to rely on conjecture as well to integrate versions and interpretations, piece together a variety of small independent details, weigh often contradictory evidence with very little guidance. Enmeshed in dialogues and monologues whose speakers remain, until the last scene of the novel, unidentified, the reader, in trying to deduce their identity and their relationships from the context, becomes a participant in the speculations about Jakob rather than the recipient of a story.[13]

Most facts are known; it is their motivations, their psychological background which remain a mystery. This is so because of the complex interrelations between individual actions and the supra-individual context in which that action occurs. Thus, even though the suppositions of Johnson's characters have a firm basis in fact and although concrete detail and minute description form the substance of a great deal of this novel, the individual seeker is exposed to a world where nothing is certain, nothing clearly knowable, no one trustworthy.

Skepticism about the accuracy of observation and conviction of the subjective nature of perception make even observable facts questionable. The numerous mechanical aids to perception, such as photographs, tapes, movies, and official documents, do not alleviate the mystery; they can all be quite misleading. The picture taken in the car by Gesine shocks Jakob because of its failure to represent the people clearly and objectively: "I don't think one ought to . . . use a camera that way,' he said. 'Everything looks alike, you understand? As though Rohlfs might just as well be working for *your* secret service?'" (p. 227). ["Ich glaube es ist nicht richtig . . . so zu fotografieren . . ." sagte er. "Es sieht aus als wär alles eins, verstehst du: als könnt Rohlfs auch bei Eurem Geheimdienst sein?" (p. 191)] Not only must facts be pieced together from units of perception reported at different times, and objects from their separate facets, but the usefulness of these factual details is increasingly called into question. When Cresspahl gets on the train with two suitcases, does that mean that he is leaving the country? Not necessarily. The narrators gain an increasing conviction that the truth does not lie in the factual realm. It is a conviction that the reader quickly comes to share. We can determine the exact time of every event in the novel, as we can reconstruct the appearance of Cresspahl's house and the layout of the control tower, but that does not bring us closer to Jakob's truth. In spite of the novel's organizational complexity, we can piece together a comprehensible plot, as well, a plot of mystery, detectives, spies, the police, and secret arrests, similar in its nature to the "feature" film in which Gesine is sometimes aware of playing a part. Neither the novel's focus, nor the story of Jakob lie in this adventure-filled plot, however, and the precision of the novel's details culminates in the elusiveness of the whole.

Supposition and speculation are the cognitive mode and the narrative method of James' novels, as well. Here too we are concerned with a truth that is hidden and perhaps unreachable. The same technique is applied quite differently in the two writers, however. The success of James' style depends on a certain amount of concealment, on a rich surface that suggests multiple depths without actually revealing them. There is, then, an aesthetic justification for vagueness and mystery that is absent from Johnson. His ellipses are due to the incapacity to disclose the truth. There is in the intricate conjectures of the Assinghams or those of Strether and Maria an element of game and pleasure, the pleasure of invention that is not weighed down by the attempted fidelity to fact. Without Johnson's factual basis, the speculation of James' characters is often a totally imaginative activity. Whereas in James, mystery is necessary to the success of the story, and the central narrator exercises a certain amount of control over concealment and revelation, mystery has become the condition for the writer who reveals as much as he knows. Mystery is never intentional mystification in Johnson's work.

Not only the congitive but also the linguistic tools have become insufficient, as the old linguistics professor demonstrates in his lecture. In order to speak at all, he must surpass syntactical and lexical rules:

> . . . words were not enough too polished threadbare to express the giant maze of proved and assumed facts, tirelessly he'd add to his sentences, break them off ruthlessly as soon as they led to something new.
>
> (p. 211)

> . . . die Worte reichten ihm vor lauter Abgeschliffenheit und Dürftigkeit nicht aus für die übermässige Verschränktheit der bewiesenen und der vermutharen Tatsachen, unermüdlich erweiterte er die begonnenen Sätze und brach sie rücksichtslos ab, wenn sie ihn einmal an einen brauchbaren Nebenansatz gebracht hatten.
>
> (p. 177)

The professor tries to extend the potentials of the language and creates a disorderly pattern that is more and more difficult to follow, yet is better able to render complexity and multiplicity.

Johnson's style, as well as the structure of the novel and its narrative technique, represents a movement away from imposed authorial control toward openness and variety. Johnson's stylistic devices are interesting, not only in themselves, but also as manifestations of his larger aesthetic. For example, the frequently criticized habit of using a row of adjectives to modify each noun is a manifestation of Johnson's general effort at precision and individualization. His punctuation is also quite unusual. He omits commas almost consistently, suggesting perhaps that the several adjectives which modify a noun are not additional to each other but are to be understood as alternatives. The frequently used colon has the function of pointing to that which follows, thus creating a choppy rhythm, separating the different parts of

the sentence from one another. The parenthesis, another mark of Johnson's style, permits the inclusion of grammatically unrelated parts within a sentence. All of these syntactic devices are aimed at enlarging the complexity of traditional syntax, so as to render different relationships that traditional syntax is unable to render. The thrust of Johnson's epistemological search is to define the evershifting relationships between private and public, individual and collective, personal and impersonal. The sentence thus reflects the structure of the entire work and of the world that the work represents; relations between syntactic units can indicate relationships between elements of that universe.[14]

Parataxis, the formal juxtaposition of the parts of a sentence indicates, the precise logical relationships between its different parts; in a paratactic sentence there is no subordination. Instead, each unit is autonomous and asserts its individual importance. Again, this syntactic principle can be extended to the novel as a whole. The structure of the entire novel is characterized by the disjunction of separate autonomous elements whose relationships are to a large extent left up to the interpretation of the participating reader.

There is, on every level of the novel, a tension between the subordinate function of various fictional elements and their desire for self-assertion. Initially, the different narrators, as we shall soon see in more detail, are mere vehicles to Jakob's story and define themselves only in relation to Jakob. As their involvement progresses, however, they increasingly assert their own personality to the point where it becomes a distorting filter greatly affecting the evocation of Jakob. Jöche and Jonas, the two characters least personally tied to Jakob and to each other are the dialogue speakers of the first two chapters, whereas Jonas and Gesine who are in a complex triangle relationship with Jakob speak in the third chapter, and the deeply involved Gesine and Rohlfs virtually fight for Jakob's soul in the fourth chapter.

Such autonomy is granted neither to James' characters not to any of his syntactic or structural units. James' syntax is also additive, as modifier is piled upon modifier, suggestion upon suggestion, layer upon layer. Its different elements stand in a fixed relationship to each other, however. The effect of vagueness is due to the effort at multiple suggestion which sometimes resembles mystification. James' language is less concerned with a correspondence to a certain vision of reality than how much it can suggest, so as to contribute to the richness of the imaginative structure that is being raised like a gilded pagoda. In his admirable essay on the first paragraph of *The Ambassadors,* Ian Watt[16] names as the prevalent characteristics of James' style the delayed specification of referents, his preference for nontransitive verbs, the frequent use of abstract nouns, of elegant variations that avoid using "he," "his," "him," and of many negative constructions, as well as his preference for reported rather than direct speech. James' is an abstract style that situates the action in a mental setting removed from time and space; he passes through the filter of a literary intelligence with aims at the most suggestive expression possible. When Cresspahl analyzes Jonas' manner of using words to complicate reality, he could be speaking about Henry James:

> How reckless he was in his handling of words. Easily, fluently, they poured from his mouth, sometimes Cresspahl had the impression of sorcery: as though someone were constantly drawing nasty cartoons of the world—an accurately calculated world, in spite of all the exaggerations and condensations, with nothing omitted; its truth looked unfamiliar . . . he sacrificed all customary means of communication with his twisted, triple-meaning insinuations.
>
> (pp. 135-137)

> Nun hatte er eine gewissenlose Weise im Umgang mit Worten. Sie gingen ihm leicht und ohne Zögern vom Munde, so dass Cresspahl manchmal einen Anschein von Zauberei wahrnahm: als bringe jemand ohne Aufhören immer neue boshafte Zeichnungen von der Welt zustande, und darin sei bei aller Übertreibung und Gedankenverkürzung doch genau gerechnet worden und nichts unterschlagen; die Richtigkeit sah fremd aus . . . er gab mit seinen dreideutig verknoteten Wortbezüglichkeiten die herkömmliche Weise von Verständigung auf.
>
> (pp. 113-114)

At the close of these reflections Cresspahl expresses a requirement or a wish: ". . . a thing should be crystal-clear and handy. You'd like that, wouldn't you?" (p. 137). [. . . die Dinge sollten klar sein und handlich. Ja, das möchtest du wohl. (p. 114)] Whether the last sentence is his own self-deprecating exclamation or the author's ironic reminder that things just are not clear, Johnson takes Cresspahl's requirement seriously. The small components of his story are as straightforward as possible, only their relations are hazy and ambiguous.

Yet James' style is no less a response to complexity than is Johnson's. Watt speaks of the relationship of character and narrator as a relationship which indicates that behind every individual circumstance there ramifies an endless network of general moral, social and historical relations. James' style, Watts says, "can be seen as a supremely civilized effort to relate every event and every moment of life to the full complexity of its circumambient conditions."[17] This is the effort of Butor and Johnson as well; although, through Jacques Revel, Butor also demonstrates its absurdity. Johnson expands on the two voices whose interplay suggests those complex relations in James, by creating a forum in which a multiplicity of voices are heard. Similarly, he allows one individual syntactic unit to assume more than one function.

Lexically, as well, Johnson's style is marked by a concern for directness and precision. Rejecting the worn-out phrases of traditional usage as well as the politically contaminated expressions of the divided country, Johnson dramatizes the tension between automatic unreflected responses that are no longer communicative and the spontaneous individual form of expression that is so hard to achieve. It is to clarify this distinction that Johnson intersperses his text with a number of alien codes such as Russian propaganda slogans, common English idioms, Italian and American advertising slogans, expressions in Pommeranian dialect, popular songs and children's riddles, as well as echoes of Lutheran German. Most of these are formulae, instinctive responses triggered off by one word or thought, representing the first unreflected reaction to a particular situation. The false sense of community that such forms of "communication" engender is demonstrated by the music in the train compartment: the travelers who listen to popular songs throughout the journey suddenly begin to speak in the first person plural. The unreflective nature of these responses is illustrated by Gesine's talk in her sleep: "Jakob, how broad you've grown!" (p. 168). The famous line from "Little Red Riding Hood" that is an analogue for Gesine's concern with the changes she finds in Jakob, just as the biblical "Es ist meine Seele die liebet Jakob," expresses her love for him. This choice of expressions points to Gesine's distance from her own feelings about whose legitimacy she has doubts.

Different from these automatic forms of expression is the Pommeranian dialect. Standing in sharp contrast to the stilted high German used by Rohlfs and other party officials, this private idiom is the most direct and the most vivid. It can still be communicative because, as an archaic form, it is protected from both political and commercial corruption. Dialect is less vulnerable to distortion than the official language used by media, press and political propaganda. It is a language shared by a limited number of people and excluding all others.

The narrators of Jakob's story interact in different ways within the novel's three narrative media: interior monologue, dialogue, and narration. James used the multiple perspective form to present two different perspectives one after the other; the narrative remains within the mind of each and they interact only in a few ritualized dialogue passages. For this reason they need a mediator, a third who might effect a meeting between them. Johnson, in contrast, attempts to use this form not only to present several points of view but to demonstrate their interaction. It is a vehicle for sorting out individual and supra-individual impulses, private and public motivations. It could be the medium through which the gap between the personal and the collective might be bridged, where disparate perceptual grids might be integrated to bring about a consensus. Such a consensus is the necessary basis for a community that would supersede deeply ingrained differences of outlook and ideology.

The interest and involvement of each narrator demonstrates the danger of authorship, the violation inherent in the process of "truthfinding." As these different perspectives are juxtaposed, we recognize the limiting perceptual grids of each individual, the necessity of collaboration and its difficulty. The conglomeration of viewpoints suggests the possibility of transcending single and superior authorship.

Jakob's story unfolds from the narrations and discussions of Jonas, Jöche, Gesine, Rohlfs and an impersonal narrator; it does not exist independently of these filters. Similarly these main characters are defined primarily through their connection to Jakob, either on the past level of the novel, by their personal relation to him, or on the present level, in their function as narrators of his story, their service to his memory. There is, as I have mentioned, a continuing tension between the subordinate function of these figures and their desire to assert their own individuality. At first, they are no more than anonymous voices whose identity cannot be determined; gradually they become recognizable as their language, their interests and their narrative methods become more and more differentiated. Speculation is never disinterested and the image of Jakob is shaped by the narrators' needs and dreams. The effort of discovering the truth about Jakob is frustrated by the distortions of their own interest in the outcome of the common investigations. Yet only their deep involvement can make Jakob as strongly present as he comes to be. Only the strongly affective quality of the reminiscences can suggest the pain of his loss. Unlike the missing voices in James, those of Adam Verver, Charlotte and even Mme. de Vionnet and Amerigo, Jakob is the focus of the story, the locus for everyone's imaginative investment, the force that brings them together in the effort to understand him. Like the fog in which Jakob and Gesine walk, the narrator's mediation both shields and reveals.

Jonas is a linguist and a humanist. His language is clearly that of an intellectual, "he was talking—to no one in particular, sure of himself, practiced, breezy" (p. 79). [[er] sprach . . . sicher geübt respektlos vor sich hin. (p. 66)] In spite of his careless use of language in his dialogue with others, Jonas' thoughts are filled with his concern for words and his consciousness of their insufficiency in the face of a real person like Jakob. "*If I remember correctly, I immediately began searching for words. Which I discarded again, one after the other, they all described a characteristic, this mn didn't seem to have any*" (p. 59). [*Wenn ich mich recht erinnere, begann ich sogleich nach Worten zu suchen. Das Nächste war dass ich ein Wort nach dem andern wegwarf, sie meinten sämtlich Eigenschaften, dieser schien keine zu*

haben. (p. 49)] Jonas feels that by describing Jakob through words he would rob him of everything that is personal and unique, and Jakob's individuality is of primary importance to Jonas. His criticism of the East German government concerns their lack of respect for the integrity and self-determination of the individual, an attitude exemplified in their distortion of literature and of the past:

> Language lives in the community that speaks it and perishes with it; whereas literature preserves for us one individual's relationship to the world, should one pay exclusive attention to the individual . . . and the linguistic means it used to come to terms with and overcome the world? . . . Whereas, on the other hand, if history is a history of class struggles and literature a tangible illustration of Marxist theories, the benefit is undeniable . . . And if one fine day each word that has been written with literary intention finds itself twisted around and around . . .
>
> (p. 81)

> Die Sprache lebt mit der Gemeinschaft, von der sie gesprochen wird, und vergeht mit ihr; in der Literatur aber ist erhalten das Weltverhältnis eines einzelnen Subjekts . . . und welcher sprachlichen Mittel es sich bedient zur Erfassung und Bewältigung der Welt? . . . Andererseits, hingegen, wenn die Geschichte eine ist von Klassenkämpfen, die Literatur als anschauliche Illustration zu den Lehren des Marxismus. . . . Und wenn nun eines Tages jedes in literarischer Absicht hingeschriebene Wort um und um gedreht ist . . .
>
> (pp. 67-68)

For Jonas, Jakob is still the kind of person who, unlike Jonas himself, could form the subject of literature. Jonas is determined to salvage the individual from the manipulation of the Marxist regime and Jakob is for him the example of autonomy.

As an intellectual, Jonas feels removed from the immediacy of experience and the directness of response of which Jakob and Gesine are capable. Jonas' relationship with Cresspahl's cat, described at great length, is an effort to achieve an intuitive, non-cerebral form of experience: ". . . but could life be found in a text? he had the impression it was passing him by" (p. 85). [. . . war aber das Leben in einem Text? er kam sich vor als versäume er es. (p. 71)] When he visits Jakob at his job, he suddenly feels the desire to participate in a similarly concrete form of work: "These were tangible durable objects, boxcars, locomotives, coaches; . . . every occurrence in Jakob's head corresponded to a reality, something really did happen" (p. 192). [Hier handelte es sich um feste dauerhafte Dinge, Wagen, Zugmaschinen, Apparate . . . aber was in Jakobs Kopf vorfiel und geschah, das hatte eine wirkliche Entsprechung, da fiel in der Tat etwas vor. (p. 161)] Jakob is all that Jonas is not, unquestionably committed to communism and fulfilled by important and necessary manual labor. For the unselfconscious and reflective Jakob, freedom is no more than the strength of his unquestioning attitude; the meaning of the state has become second nature for him. For Jonas he is "the reasonable practical justifiable side of life" (p. 191)." [das vernünftige, verantwortbare, praktische Leben. (p. 160)] How different is Jonas from this image of Jakob, Jonas whose life is marked by the effort to define freedom, to reflect, understand, and explain.

As a narrator, Jonas shows a great deal of empathy and intuitive understanding even while being painfully aware of the limitations imposed on his ability to perceive the truth about others. That Jonas is suspicious of the distortions a narrator's imagination can inflict is apparent in his wonderfully evocative description of Gesine:

> She was in his memory like a feeling of an inexchangeable way of looking at one, of climbing stairs, of startled halts: details could be dismissed, because the inexchangeability stemmed from all this being real in itself, independent from any spectator or listener or someone who was, strangely enough, sitting in the Jerichow Rathskeller thinking about her. In the end, one could merely express one's gladness that such things existed in the world . . . without reservations.
>
> (p. 144)

> Sie war erinnerlich als das Gefühl einer unverwechselbaren Weise von Augenzuwenden und Treppensteigen und Erschrecken und Stillstehen: da konnte man von den Einzelheiten absehen, denn das Unverwechselbare hing daran dass dies alles für sich selbst wirklich war unabhängig von einem Betrachter und Zuhörer und einem, der sonderbarer Weise im Jerichower Krug sass und sich ihrer erinnerte. Am Ende war nur zu sagen man sei zufrieden dass es dies gebe in der Welt, es war nichts zu bedenken.
>
> (p. 120)

This is one of the few times that Jonas shows complete confidence in his perceptions. He is so convinced that he has gotten at the very essence of Gesine in this observation that he does not hesitate to represent a feeling as a reality that exists independently of himself as observer. Willing to efface himself in his function as narrator, Jonas expresses a vision of Gesine unmediated by his own interests and discovers an intuitive form of understanding that is based on trust rather than on analysis or narrative. This unique form of knowledge represents the only kind of certainty in this novel, because it is a knowledge that respects the individual's integrity.

Both his aloof intellectualism and his desire not to impose himself allow Jonas to continue entertaining several different interpretations of Jakob's death. He is convinced, however, that, whether his death is accident, suicide, or murder, Jakob could be the one person able to elude the pressures of the state. As the ideal communist citizen, Jakob thus continues to justify Jonas' efforts to reform the system. Thus Jonas simply cannot avoid imposing on Jakob his own vested interest: the success of a communist ideology independent of the present regime.

Unlike Jonas who, in spite of his dissatisfaction, remains in the East and attempts to change it, Gesine leaves out of a compulsion. The move turns out to be less satisfactory than expected; working for NATO in a reaction to the East, Gesine is still full of sympathy for communism and cannot commit herself to the West. The division of her life into two irreconcilable parts has severe repercussions on Gesine's state of mind. In her life and work in the West she feels disillusioned, fragmented and isolated to the point of abandoning even the hope for companionship, in the East there remain mere childhood memories, not the hope of a future.

Gesine needs Jakob as the symbol of her unspoiled past, as the solution to her present discomfort. Eager to re-establish a link with her own childhood, Gesine is the only one to offer us an insight into Jakob's childhood and youth. Perhaps her desire to emphasize Jakob's wholeness and integrity which makes him so much like her father and so unlike herself makes her vision too rigid. She is loath to admit any changes in him. Their somewhat incestuous relationship can be seen in Gesine's flight back into childhood and away from the conflicts of the divided country. In her concern for Jakob's integrity, Gesine refuses to believe that Jakob ever intended to stay in the West. She despairs at the lack of a place where they could live together so as to reunify their severed lives.

In spite of the importance she has for all the other characters in the novel, Gesine remains a mysterious figure. The nature of her trip to the East—she comes with a gun and a miniature camera—is never elucidated. Her feelings of guilt and responsibility for Jakob's death undoubtedly color her memories of him: "As long as nobody can get up and say: This is how it was and no other way. It's this one's, it's that one's fault. What if it were your fault, Jonas?" (p. 132) [Ich möchte nur wahrhaben dass keiner sich hinstellen kann und sagen: So war es und nicht anders. Die Schuld hat der und der. Wenn du sie nun hättest Jonas. (p. 110)] Gesine's frequent use of Lutheran German or of English idiomatic expressions when she speaks of all that is closest to her reveals her unwillingness to face her own feelings. Although she has known Jakob the longest, her relationship to him is the most conflicted and undefined at the time of his death. Her ability to convey the strength of Jakob's personality, his warmth and tenderness, is offset by the interested nature of her reminiscences. Gesine best conveys the impact Jakob could have on others, and, as the person closest to him, she also reveals his ultimate unknowability.

As a representative of the East German state who takes personal responsibility for the regime, Rohlfs is the most dogmatic of all the narrators. Unlike the representatives of the official position in Johnson's other novels, Rohlfs is a complex and full figure with dreams and ideals. He is eager to stress the difference between himself and the policemen he calls "dogcatchers." Rohlf's loyalty to the state is a complicated phenomenon. He will go so far as to relinquish his personality to serve the state. He is initially presented as a faceless shadow, a mere instrument of the government investigation: his numerous names attest to a similar willingness to efface himself for his mission.

Insight into Rohlfs' reflections discloses his desperate spiritual dependence on the rightness of the communist regime. Unlike Gesine, who values wholeness to the point of accepting the responsibility for the ugliness of the German past, Rohlfs sacrifices his youth and his parents to the communist present: "the same stubbornness that considered half of his life an error: in order to make the present look right" (p. 145) [. . . [der] Eigensinn, der die Hälfte seines Lebens für einen Irrtum ansah: damit das Gegenwärtige das Rechte blieb. (p. 121)] His willful rejection of all doubts and questions makes Rohlfs' perspective terribly narrow. He will accept, for example, only one view of the nocturnal landscape around Jerichow, thereby revealing the precarious security of his position:

> The regular shimmering structure of the castle that rises from the forest in the night and draws the onlooker's eyes along the lanes of its park is not architecture or petrified history, but a memorial to exploitation. Whoever is not for us is against us, and unjust with regard to progress. Who is for us: will be the question; and not: how do you like the night with the dark villages between the curves of the soil under the huge cloudy sky.
>
> (p. 147)

> Der schimmernde ebenmässige Bau des Schlosses, der aufsteigt aus dem nächtlichen Wald und den Blick des Betrachters an sich zieht durch die Alleen des Parks, ist nicht Architektur und stehengebliebene Geschichte sondern ein Denkmal der Ausbeutung. Wer nicht für uns ist ist gegen uns und ungerecht im Sinne des Fortschritts. Es wird gefragt werden wer ist für uns und nicht wie gefällt die die Nacht mit den dunklen Dörfern zwischen den Falten des Bodens unter dem mächtug bewölkten Himmel.
>
> (p. 123)

In this interpretation of the landscape Rohlfs places himself in opposition to his father whose old map he is using. He demonstrates that the communist ideology can only impose itself by displacing all other meanings and interests, whether they be geographical, historical, geological or simply the enjoyment of a beautiful night. it needs to co-opt entirely the mind of the individual.

As a government agent instructed to win the services of Gesine for the East, Rohlfs should have no personal commitment to Jakob's story. As he gains insight into Jakob's life, however, Rohlfs comes to see him as the ideal communist, totally fulfilled by his work and his service to the state. He believes that Jakob shares his strongest convictions. Although he denies this personal affinity, Jakob treats Rohlfs as a friend. Their mutual sympathy turns out to be less powerful than their disparate social positions, however.

Using Jakob as a test for the rightness of communism, Rohlfs becomes humanly involved with him and with the interpretation of his death. In their conversation, Rohlfs and Gesine virtually for Jakob's soul; Rohlfs has to believe that Jakob hated and condemned the West, that he returned out of conviction and that his death was death was an accident. Thinking of a scene that Gesine mentions from Jakob's trip to the West, Rohlfs vividly imagines Jakob's ardent defense of communism and his condemnation of the West German revival of Nazism. To Gesine's different picture he says, "But I can't listen to you without prejudice or else I mislay Jakob. I can no longer fit him into my memory" (pp. 221-22), [Aber ich kann Ihnen nicht zuhören ohne Vorurteil, denn dann gerät Jakob mir in Verust, dann passt er nicht mehr zu meiner Erinnerung." (p. 186)] evoking her reproach: "What do you do with facts you don't like? . . . But can't you see that you are belittling reality?" (pp. 222-24). ["Was machen Sie eigentlich mit solchen Tatsachen, die Ihnen nicht gefallen? . . . Aber sehen Sie denn nicht dass Sie die Wirklichkeit verarmen?" (pp. 187-188)]

In his function as narrator, Rohlfs appears as a compulsive figure reminiscent of Faulkner's Jason or Beckett's Moran. His observations are primarily factual; with all the technical aids available to him, the lives of Jakob, Gesine, and Jonas are totally open to him. He notes down every detail about their lives, but soon realizes that even his knowledge is only minimal. His interior monologues are marked by paranoia and nervousness as well as by selfconsciousness and hastiness. His hate and fear of others dictates his perceptions. Rohlfs' feelings of inferiority are due to his crippled hand and foot, injuries inflicted accidentally by a comrade during the war. His concern for his small daughter who often appears in his thoughts, as well as his touching desire for her respect, reveal the vulnerable side of Rohlfs' personal character.

The power Rohlfs gains from his official status and from the detective apparatus that facilitates his investigation gives him a virtually authorial control over the lives of the other figures. Yet his advantage becomes less and less real. Rohlfs' one-sided interpretations continually clash with others that are at least as valid. In spite of the wealth of information available to him, Rohlfs also experiences the precariousness of all knowledge.

In his goal of influencing other people by convincing them of the rightness of his own vision, Rohlfs resembles Maggie Verver. Like Maggie, he derives his authority from a supra-personal source; Maggie represents her civilization, Rohlfs the communist regime. It is his failure to be totally authoritarian that is Rohlfs' mistake as well as his humane substance. Admitting that "compulsory decisions are no decisions" (p. 229), [Erpresste Entscheidungen sind keine. (p. 192)] he gives his subjects a choice, lets them reflect and compare, waits for them to respond. Thereby Rohlfs relinquishes the advantage his detective apparatus gives him, one he finds useless anyway. He makes himself vulnerable by offering Jakob his friendship: ". . . this is my face, take a look at it, Jakob" (p. 228). [. . . so sehe ich aus, sich es dir an Jakob. (p. 192)] In this offer, he endangers both his own position and Jakob's: ". . . he spoke to him as the State: personally" (p. 129). [. . . da redete er mit ihm als Staatsmacht: persönlich. (p. 107)] Such a relationship is a contradiction and a failure. Rohlfs rightly suspects that he might have done better with "dogcatcher" methods. His insistence that Jakob embrace communist ideology out of conviction and not out of unreflective necessity endangers Jakob's security and constitutes a plausible cause of his death.

Unlike Maggie, Rohlfs is not aware of taking risks; the strength of his conviction makes him utterly blind: "*I thought there was only one answer. And I expected it from people who don't have my interests at heart. Conversation is an error. 'Perhaps you'd have done better to refrain from this democratic fraternizing'*" (p. 229). [*Ich habe gedacht es gibt nur eine Antwort. Und habe sie erwartet von Leuten, die es nicht absehen auf meine Sache. Gespräch ist ein Fehler. "Hätten Sie doch lieber verzichtet auf diese demokratischen Brüderlichkeiten."* (pp. 192-193)] While Maggie's entire existence depends on the Prince's answer, Rohlfs easily survives a failure that has devasting effects on the lives of Jakob, Jonas, Gesine, and Frau Abs. He is the only one able to walk away: ". . . he thought of tomorrow, that the sun would rise anew, that they'd be somewhere else, nothing but files would be left of today and of the day before" (p. 238). [. . . [er] dachte . . . an den folgenden Tag und dass dann wieder die Sonne aufgehen wurde und dass sie die Zeit auch verbringen würden an einem anderen Ort und dass von Heute und Gestern nur Aktennotizen übrigsein würden. (p. 201)]

The relation of Jakob's story by such different individuals dramatizes not so much the unreliability of single narrators as the different perceptual grids that delimit our apprehensions. Rohlfs' optic is reductively political,

just as Gesine's is lyrically personal and Jonas' narrowly intellectual: "Cresspahl would say: most of them were probably there, but each saw a different house burn down. And houses never look alike anyway" (p. 53). [Cresspahl würde sagen: anwesend seien wohl die mehreren gewesen, aber da habe jeder ein anderes Haus brennen sehen. Häuser seien sich ohnehin nicht gleich. (p. 44)] The question that is raised here is what we see when we see and what influence our personal and ideological outlook has on our perceptions.

More than Rohlfs, the narrator is privileged in having an overview and in being able to supplement substantially the dialogues and monologues of the other narrators. He introduces, for example, the accounts of Jonas' secretary and Jakob's assistant. Moreover, he has the function of providing the voices of those characters who lack the verbal ability of Rohlfs, Jonas and Gesine and who prefer silence, Cresspahl and Jakob especially. Although a conversation between Cresspahl and Jonas is announced in the last chapter, its content is never revealed. Cresspahl remains a closed and silent figure, representing a certain type of integrity that Johnson opposes to the intellectualism of Jonas or the garrulity of Rohlfs. As Peter Demetz says, Johnson's "narrative cards are stacked against quick thinkers and articulate intellectuals who do not work with their hands but merely with paper and words: and Johnson's explicit sympathies are with the inarticulate craftsman who putters around with old furniture [Cresspahl]; the near-silent dispatcher who cherishes his systematic work."[18] Such figures can be brought to the fictional surface only through the mediation of a narrator able to make his vision present without compromising his natural reticence and silence.

In spite of the material available to him, the narrator does not reach the truth about Jakob more easily than the other characters. Although he is able to assess evidence from various sources and to provide a consensus and although he is not weighed down by a personal involvement with Jakob, on many occasions he is forced to resort to conjecture in his interpretation of the facts, providing that narration cannot help but be interpretive. When he relates the occasion on which Jakob gives Cresspahl Gesine's gun, he is unable to choose between two possible versions and so presents both. The reader must decide which is the more truthful. Thus the narrator conforms to the requirements of **"Berliner Stadtbahn"**; he admits the limits of his knowledge.

The narrator's tone is polemical; he addresses the reader as a partner in a dialogue and invites him to participate in the speculations about Jakob and even to become personally involved in the story: "But Jakob always cut straight across the tracks" (p. 7); "But if someone should happen to ask you" (p. 12); "And she didn't look as though she had been crying; that's a point we do want to make" (p. 240). ["Aber Jakob ist immer quer über die Gleise gegangen" (p. 5); "Aber wenn einer Sie mal fragen sollte" (p. 9); "Und sie sah nicht aus wie eine, die geweint hat; das wollen wir doch mal sagen" (p. 202).] The impartial reader is perhaps in the best position to attempt a clear vision of Jakob's life and his mysterious death. While the novel's characters see each other only from the outside and are unable, even through great efforts at empathy, to penetrate each other's thoughts, the reader is privileged to their interior monologues in addition to external observations, and so has a greater overview even than Rohlfs. The difficulties are great nevertheless. Rather than gaining a clear insight into the person Jakob, as we do with Lambert Strether or Maggie Verver, we experience in a very real way the difficulties of the process Johnson calls "truthfinding." In its language and structure, the novel acts out the ambiguity and complexity faced by the actual "readers" of Jakob and the reader's experience parallels their.

Jakob's story violates all our preconceptions about fiction. Rather than unfolding, it demands to be painfully recomposed out of disjointed fragments. It thwarts our need for order and plot and forces us to deal with fragmentation and disjunction. An agent of "truthfinding," the reader must recognize and attempt to avoid its inherent exploitative impulse.

The complex structure of third-person narration, interior monologue, and dialogue presents serious problems of orientation for the reader. While monologues are indicated by italics and dialogues by hyphens, the respective speakers are hardly ever identified. [The English translator has supplied the speakers' names in the italic passages; they are not given in the original text.] Not only must the reader learn to identify the different speakers as he becomes more familiar with them, but he must also keep track of the sudden transitions from one mode to another, transitions which often involve changes in time from the scene of the dialogues after Jakob's death to the remembered weeks leading up to it presented in the other two modes. While it is often possible to identify the speakers of the monologues from the context, the dialogue scenes are not set up until the fifth chapter. Jöche and Jonas, for example, speak from page 7 (p. 5) on, but are not introduced as characters on the inner level of the story until pages 46 (p. 38) and 57 (p. 48), respectively. The scene of their conversation on page 7 (p. 5) is not described until page 237 (p. 200). The reader, then, not only joins the other narrators in their speculations about Jakob, but is forced to speculate about every scene presented to him. Sometimes it is impossible to determine the source of a comment or a thought, since the three modes are often mixed:

And Jakob was holding his hand out to her from the other side of the brook so she wouldn't skid on the smooth slimy gnarled logs and she said, so, on her toes bent forward for balance and, no, Jakob said. Even if they had seen something, it couldn't be told.

(p. 150)

Und Jakob auf dem andern Ufer hielt ihr die Hand entgegen dass sie nicht ausrutschen sollte auf dem schmierig glatten knorrigen Baumstamm und sie sagte so auf den Zehenspitzen vorwärtsgebeugt im Gleichgewicht nein Jakob sagte. Selbst wenn da etwas in Sicht gekommen wäre liesse es sich nicht erzählen.

(pp. 125-126)

These sentences are part of an interior monologue of Jonas. From his narration it is unclear whether it was Gesine or Jakob who said no. Moreover, as Jonas is telling a story that was reported to him, it is unclear whether the last sentence of the quote is a reflection of his own effort to retell their experiences, or whether it is a comment made by Gesine when she told Jonas of the scene.

Through the immersion into almost entirely anonymous thoughts and reminiscences, the reader experiences a great emotive immediacy. He gets the emotion before being able to situate it intellectually. Becoming involved with Jakob and experiencing the depth of his loss through all the mediating narrators, the reader feels compelled to penetrate his mystery. The affective power of Johnson's style and the elusive absence of Jakob himself substitutes for the suspense of traditional narrative.

The structural principle of the novel and its syntactical property, the conglomeration of unconnected fragments, attributes to the reader the important role of arranging and compiling. The material resists the reader's impulses, however; it resists what Johnson calls his "curiosity for stories." [Neugier nach Geschichten.] It is in **The Third Book about Achim** that the tension between the writer's and the reader's impulse to shape a life into a unified and harmonious form and the resistance of that life to such manipulation is most vividly dramatized. In **Jakob** [**Mutmassungen über Jakob**] the "feature" Gesine speaks of, the romantic love story, stands in contrast to the shapeless fragments of Jakob's story. Jakob is protected from the assault and manipulation of his "readers" not only by the fact of his death but also by his inherent mystery, elusiveness, silence. His entire mode of being is non-verbal and opaque. We know what he means to his friends and how they see him, we know what he looked like and how he lived, but we never find out what he felt and why he dies. His love for a mechanical job, the efficiency with which he lets the Russian military train pass through are factors which are hard to reconcile with the positive picture the narrators draw of him. The essence of Jakob's character, his deepest feelings about the East, the West, about Sabine and Gesine are forever unknowable. Ironically, his integrity lies in his mystery.

The other characters' usurpation of Jakob's life and character for individual purposes, their greed to know, violate his privacy and constitute a comment on the moral ambiguity of the reader's position.

The interior monologues are similar to James' method, in that they demonstrate the great difference between the various outlooks—in the two accounts of Jonas' and Gesine's first meeting, for example—and the isolation of the helpless single mind faced with a complex reality. The narrator's passages combine different viewpoints and provide the scene for arguments. Even though he is uninvolved, he is a filter and can provide only the chance for a meeting, and a mediated one at that. The dialogues are the most original of Johnson's experiments. Here people get together to search for the truth about Jakob, to confront and challenge each other's opinions and join in remembering and imagining different scenes. When Rohlfs and Gesine imagine Jonas' arrival at the control tower, they literally piece the incident together in a wonderful example of communal storytelling. Those two most contrary of the characters establish a relation of mutual sympathy in their conversations about Jakob, even if they cannot ultimately develop a common vision.

In these dialogues it is the dead Jakob who becomes the potential vehicle for a meeting of his different friends. He is continually being used for their individual needs. People's appraisal of each other is subject to a self-interest and greed that resembles that of Jamesian characters. Jakob becomes their puppet, as they are each other's. The literary act, the process of narration as well as reading, is revealed as tainted by self-interest. The desire to know is greedy and can have destructive effects; Rohlfs' direct questions to Frau Abs are an example, but are they so different from Jonas' "avid excitement" as he watches Jakob on the train?

The artistic process becomes doubly guilty of violating the individual's integrity in its connection to the social and political institutions of East and West Germany, institutions which demand the submission of the individual to the community. Interest in the mysterious Jakob is charged with a nostalgia that the characters as well as the reader feel for the "central" individual, the "central" intelligence celebrated in the work of Henry James, now lost, absorbed by the community. The elusive Jakob defies this absorption, but is unable to survive.

Convinced that had he lived several years earlier, he would have learned how to kill Jews too, Joche denies the individual's power to delineate his supposedly unique personality:

> But this—let's call it: personal uniqueness needs its opportunities, shows up only in exterior things; in what

you do and not in how you feel. And the possibilities to do are only those that you find in the light of the world, what the know-betters, your educators, offer you.

(p. 77)

> Diese wir können ja sagen: persönliche Eigenart braucht aber Gelegenheiten, wird ja nur in Äusserlichkeiten sichtbar; in dem was du tust und nicht in dem wie du dich fühlst. Und Möglichkeiten zu tun gibt es nur was du vorfindest im Licht der Welt und was die Besserwisser: deine Erzieher dir anbieten.

(pp. 64-65)

Although this novel focuses on the constraints imposed by the East German state, it dramatizes the fact that any social system demands the conformity of its inhabitants. The hotel clerk in the West German city puts, in a sense, as much pressure on Jakob to behave according to set standards as Rohlfs does. Moreover, in any society the individual's actions are so intimately tied up with those of others that the chance for self-expression is severely limited. Jakob is convinced that the shame of the German past is incompatible with the present German pride and he refuses to participate in it, though he may not personally have contributed to the ugly past. Gesine's job as an interpreter is the emblem of lack of self-expression in our world; the words she says are not her own: "I do nothing but talk from morning to night, just think if I had to answer for all those words" (p. 30). [Ich rede von morgens his abends, bedenk mal wenn ich das alles verantworten sollte. (p. 24)] The individual must fit his meaning into impersonal shapes whose meaning is inflexible, not only incapable of expressing uniqueness, but also controlled by prevailing ideologies.

The characters of the novel are caught between two crucial political events which determine their lives but over which they have no control: the Hungarian Revolution, on the one hand, the Suez Crisis, on the other. Jakob's refusal to stop the Russian military train to Hungary is his resigned and cynical comment on the individual's impotence in the face of political events. It is one of the most powerful scenes in the novel and one of the most pessimistic. Jakob dismisses Jonas' suggestion of personal resistance as "playing stupid just for the fun of it." The only form of protest Gesine can envision against the British bombing of Egypt is to leave her job at NATO. Jonas' scientific response to political events is judged equally weak and insufficient.

The supra-personal power, the cultural force that in James was still defined by the individual, in Butor by other than human factors, is circumscribed by the political reality in Johnson's world. His book investigates the individual's freedom in the context of a given ideological system. More than just the general social and political factors named above, however, Johnson examines the specific position of the individual in the East

German state. According to its own propaganda, the communist state belongs to the people and represents the personal needs and desires of each. In return for total subjugation, the limited existence of each citizen is glorified in the service to a greater goal: "'Can a man waste himself on a purpose?' . . . 'Yes,' Herr Rohlfs said gruffly" (p. 124). ["Soll einer sich selbst versäumen über einem Zweck," . . . "Ja," sagte Herr Rohlfs grob. (p. 103)] Those who have done so, like Herr Rohlfs, transfer their own greed and self-interest to the state which thereby becomes like an allpowerful individual. The identity of every individual no longer depends totally on the rightness of the state; the individual has ceased to be responsible for itself. The state's destructive power is even greater than that of a single Maggie Verver. It coopts the lives and minds of its citizens, robs them of their power to think and speak. Rohlfs is not satisfied with Jakob's unquestioning devotion; he wants more. Jonas' description of the march is reminiscent of Revel's depiction of the effects of the Bleston wind on its inhabitants; here is the government instead of the city which molds people after a faceless pattern. Cresspahl alone is able to lead a public life defined by his own private essence; he remains in the remote Mecklenburg village as an artisan, continuing his previous existence, unafraid of even the powerful functionaries of the East German regime. Cresspahl, like the cat, embodies what we sense as the reality of freedom from all ideological systems. Cresspahl is connected to the wind and the sea, to Jerichow and *Plattdeutsch,* to his manual work, to the old Germany that so wonderfully rises out of the old map and that represents the setting for Gesine's dreams of freedom and fulfillment. It is a past which Rohlfs and the new regime must reject, but which persists not only in the names of the villages whose suffix *hagen* harks back to forests that disappeared thousands of years before, but also in the dreams and memories of Johnson's characters. Gesine and Jakob's own childhood merges with the undivided childhood of the country. As they dream of flying kites on the beautiful mountains around Jerichow, they express a desire that in its simplicity defines all that is missing in both East and West Germany: "*I'd like to be up there on those clouds* (p. 231)" [. . . *ich möchte auf die Wolken.* (p. 194)]

It is clear that characters with such dreams are not the cripples of Beckett nor the crushed and impotent human beings of Butor; neither, however, are they the allpowerful individuals of James. Although the story of Johnson's characters is so deeply connected to the forces that govern their lives that it is no longer a psychological story, and although he dramatizes the fact that the traditional analysis of character can no longer lead to the perception of his essence, he does allow for a kind of insight that pierces through the protective barrier of the individual without violation and bridges the gap between these lonely beings. Only one form of perception grants the individual's integrity. He assumes the effacement of the perceiver's personal interest and is exemplified in Jonas' reminiscence of Gesine, quoted above, or in Cresspahl's evocation of Jakob, the most suggestive of the whole novel:

> The thought of Jakob made Cresspahl smile, he felt so present. Jakob never froze into an image of departure, he stayed in one's memory as a reality of smiles and answers and fun and life as a whole: like a gesture.
>
> (p. 135)

> Als Cresspahl sich an Jakob erinnerte, lächelte er vor lauter Gegenwärtigkeit, denn Jakob erstarrte nicht in den Bildern des Abschieds sondern blieb im Gedächtnis als soeine Wirklichkeit von Lächeln und Antworten und Spass und Leben überhaupt: wie eine Gebärde.
>
> (p. 112)

These epiphanic moments of insight are very rare in the novel but they form perhaps the basis for a new form of community which would replace the alienating societies in which we live now, the basis for a reunification on an individual and supra-individual level. Nonintellectual and non-narrative experiences of recognition, they suggest a new form of reading, as well, one free from greed and exploitation.

These fleeting moments of contact between Jonas and Gesine, between Cresspahl and Jakob are tenuous, brief, yet they still point to the possibility of overcoming the self-interest of authority and of preserving, in the process of knowing and reading, the integrity of the object of one's quest. For Cresspahl, Jakob is a gesture, an expression that would only be impoverished if analyzed. He wants to remember him, not possess him. For Rohlfs, Jakob is the dove on the roof, someone to be captured, understood, controlled. It is clearly Cresspahl's knowledge that Johnson values and that even Rohlfs would have liked to experience: "That Jakob would have understood. Not with words, in a brief casual silence, just looking at each other" (p. 240). [Dass er mit Jakob darüber sich hätte verständigen konnen. Wortlos, in einem kurzen unauffälligen Schweigen und Blickwechseln. (p. 202)] In its qualifications about both language and "truthfinding" in general and in its elevation of a non-verbal, non-narrative epistemology, Johnson's novel questions profoundly its own premises as a novel. Horst Kruger's description of the emotional background of *Two Views* applies to all of Johnson's works: "This book emerges from the depths of a woundedness that has not healed . . . the toothgrinding protest of a wounded silent man." Johnson speaks because he has no choice.

Jakob resists any form of reading; he resists the exploitative interests of Rohlfs and Jonas, the loving violation of Gesine. The novel's epistemological failure is at the same time the triumph of an unassailable individual integrity. Johnson offers his reader an insight into the moral dubiousness of an activity that, in capitalizing on the lives of others in the effort to uncover all their mystery, is related to the activities of the authoritarian state. To see only plots, whether literary or political, is an act of violation. It is not redeemed by the thirst for knowledge or the cause of communism. James also found the fictional process morally reprehensible, but he redeemed it, at least in part, by the exhilaration of knowledge and power that makes the reader into the potential vehicle of a cultural fusion. In *Jakob,* the reader must learn to accept his own humility in the face of a largely unknowable reality.

Each of the novel's characters emerges as an individual struggling against violation and absorption by the system; Jakob, Cresspahl, and the cat, however, escape all the grids; they are impenetrable and inviolable. What the reader learns here is to overcome an appetite for that Other that is enticing and attractive because it is foreign and mysterious. Through his difficulties, through his inability to penetrate some figures, he learns how to approach his object without endangering that mystery and integrity that made it initially attractive. Learning this is a lesson in humility. Jakob himself demonstrates the insurmountable difficulties of that lesson. He may escape the observers' various grids but is unable to escape death. In his life, he may attempt to maintain the greatest possible integrity, but ultimately he cannot escape the assault of the state and also survive.

Notes

1. The S-Bahn runs through both East and West Berlin. Before the wall was built, it was possible to get off at any stop and most people leaving the East chose this route.

2. *Merkur,* 15 (August 1961): 728.

3. *Ibid.,* p. 732.

4. *Writing Degree Zero and Elements of Semiology* (Boston: Beacon Press, 1967), p. 24.

5. Johnson, *loc. cit.*

6. *Ibid.,* p. 733.

7. Quoted by Wilhelm Johannes Schwarz, *Der Erzähler Uwe Johnson* (Bern: Francke Verlag, 1970), p. 93.

8. Johnson, *loc. cit.*

9. *Loc. cit.*

10. *Loc. cit.*

11. Page number in parentheses refer to *Speculations about Jakob,* trans. by Ursule Molinaro (New York: Harcourt Brace Jovanovich, 1963); the German references are to *Mutmassungen über Jakob* (Frankfurt: Fischer, 1962).

12. Quoted by Reinhard Baumgart, *Über Uwe Johnson* (Frankfurt: Suhrkamp, 1970), p. 132.

13. For a discussion of the reader's role, see Manfred Durzak, *Der deutsche Roman der Gegenwart* (Stuttgart: Kohlhammer, 1971), p. 184.

14. In her interesting essay, "Johnsons Darstellungsmittel und der Kubismus," in Baumgart, Ingrid Riedel gives us a useful framework in which to speak about the structural characteristics of Johnson's novels. Fragmentation, disjunction and recomposition, multiple angles, foregrounding, montage and collage are all devices that link Johnson to the cubist movement. Both in his work and in cubist painting these devices serve an impulse toward an accurate, "realistic" portrayal of modern reality.

15. For an excellent discussion of this syntatic device, see Herbert Kolb, "Rückfall in die Parataxe," *Neue deutsche Hefte,* 10 (1963): 42-74.

16. "The First Paragraph of *The Ambassadors*: An Explication," rpt. in Rosenbaum, pp. 465-484.

17. *Ibid.,* p. 475.

18. "Uwe Johnson: A Critical Portrait," *Ventures,* 10, 1 (1970): 53.

A Selected Bibliography

I. By Henry James

The Ambassadors. Ed. L. Edel. Cambridge, Mass.: Riverside, 1960.

The Ambassadors. Ed. S.P. Rosenbaum. New York: Norton, 1964.

The Golden Bowl. Ed. J. Halperin. New York: Meridian, 1972.

V. By Uwe Johnson

"Berliner Stadtbahn." *Merkur* 15 (August 1961): 722-733.

Jahrestage: Aus dem Leben von Gesine Cresspahl. Frankfurt: Suhrkamp. Vol. 1, 1970. Vol. 2, 1971. Vol. 3, 1973. Volumes 1 and part of 2 transl. as *Anniversaries* by Leila Vennewitz. New York: Harcourt, Brace, Jonanovich, 1975.

Mutmassungen über Jakob. Frankfurt: Fischer, 1962. Transl. as *Speculations about Jakob* by Ursule Molinaro. New York: Harcourt, Brace, Jovanovich, 1963.

Zwei Ansichten. Frankfurt: Rowohlt, 1968.

VI. About Uwe Johnson

Baumgart, Reinhart. *Über Uwe Johnson.* Frankfurt: Suhrkamp, 1970.

Demetz, Peter. "Uwe Johnson: A Critical Portrait." *Ventures* X, 1 (1970): 48-53.

Durzak, Manfred. *Der deutsche Roman der Gegenwart.* Stuttgart: Kohlhammer, 1971.

Kolb, Herbert. "Rückfall in die Parataxe." *Neue Deutsche Hefte* 10 (1963): 42-74.

Schwarz, Wilhelm Johannes. *Der Erzähler Uwe Johnson.* Bern: Francke Verlag, 1970.

VII. GENERAL

Barthes, Roland. *Le Degré zéro de l'écriture.* Paris: Seuil, 1953.

Kurt Fickert (essay date 1987)

SOURCE: Fickert, Kurt. "Documenting the Novel: Uwe Johnson's Novel *Jahrestage.*" *Germanic Notes* 18, no. 1-2 (1987): 13-16.

[*In the following essay, Fickert traces instances in which "documentation is affixed to the narrative" of Johnson's novel* Anniversaries: From the Life of Gesine Cresspahl, *arguing that in using this device, the author is able to explore "the dark side of political and socio-economic events in 1967-68" in an unbiased manner, and also to "pursue his theme of the individual in confrontation with the forces of history in his era."*]

Uwe Johnson's novel *Jahrestage* (1970ff.) must be considered an important contribution to twentieth century literature. Indeed, it is included in a list of the one hundred great books in world literature, compiled by the weekly *Die Zeit*.[1] The high regard this work has achieved stems both from the significance of the goal Johnson has set for himself in writing it and the intricacy of the means he has used in reaching his objective. In telling the story of his protagonist's perception of life in Germany in the thirties, forties, and fifties in the latter instance, largely from an East German vantage point Johnson has adopted as one of his literary devices the procedure of providing the events of the novel with a framework which is in itself a story. He follows in this regard the tradition established and maintained by writers of the German *Novelle,* notably by Heinrich von Kleist and Theodor Storm. In *Jahrestage,* however, the narrative element in which the novel proper is embedded has several functions in addition to those of introducing and bringing the story to a close.[2] The events in Germany forming the core of the narrative are depicted as they occur in the memory and in the imagination of the principal character, Gesine Cresspahl, who has set for herself the task of making a record of the days of one year from August 20, 1967 to August 20, 1968 during her life in exile in New York. Gesine's account of

the daily life of a bank secretary concerned with transactions in foreign languages and also as the mother of an eleven-year-old daughter concerned with the problems of bringing up a fatherless child is interwoven with the episodes from her past and from her family's past. Thus the fictionalized journal becomes a novel of overwhelming proportions, consisting of about two thousand pages, published in four separate volumes.

Contributing to the girth and weightiness in the sense of depth of *Jahrestage* is Johnson's use of the literary device of documenting the days of Gesine's year, that is, anchoring the imaginative events securely in the history of the times in which they occur, by citing articles from the New York *Times* (in translation), either in the form of a precis or in their entirety. The obvious function of these quotations and summaries, the undergirding of a sense of authenticity which is meant to pervade the realistic novel,[3] does not seem to have been Johnson's sole objective, however. The material from the *Times,* he has insisted, has been chosen for inclusion in *Jahrestage* not by its author, but by its protagonist; in the transcription of a series of lectures on his own work, published as *Begleitumstände,* Johnson has emphasized that the excisions from the *Times* have been selected "subjectively, with the eyes of Mrs. Cresspahl" (p.413, my translation). Thus, in addition to their function of providing a background of realistic detail depicting the political, socioeconomic, and extra-legal aspects of New York life, the excerpts from the newspaper represent the confrontation between Gesine and the society which surrounds her and thereby assume symbolic significance.

In their simplest form, suggestive of headlines or a quick perusal of them, they have as their subject matter a broad spectrum of events, of both local and national interest. The way of life they describe has its counterpart in every metropolis throughout the world. A typical entry of news items from the *Times,* made by Gesine during Thanksgiving week, includes mention of the forming of a new political party in Germany, of an ambassador's statement that the public does not understand the war in Vietnam, of a robbery and rape in an apartment in the Bronx.[4] Gesine summarizes these articles without comment and turns her attention so abruptly to the past "Aber in Richmond war es Juli" (p.375) that any attempt to relate happenings in 1967 to the thirties in Europe is forestalled. This pattern of the juxtaposition of random newsworthy occurrences and precipitous transition to Gesine's recreation of life in Germany in the eras of Hitler, the war, and its aftermath recurs throughout *Jahrestage*; so, for example, a rather wry remark about war casualties: "Für die amtlich in Viet Nam Getöteten aus der new yorker Gegend nimmt die Times heute nicht mehr die normale, sondern die allerkleinste Type" is followed by an episode out of the past which is completely unrelated to any aspect of the aforegoing material: "Sein Kind hatte Cresspahl zu den Paepckes gebracht" (p.827).

The longer selections, translations of copyrighted articles, have a more sophisticated relationship to Gesine's accounts of past events culled from her memory or reconstructed in her imagination. There are about sixteen of these lengthy passages from the *Times*; the topics are diverse, but they are unified in that they reflect Gesine's preoccupation and thereby the major themes of Johnson's novel. Several deal with political figures and with some who are political only by dint of circumstance. One of the latter is an inconspicuous shopkeeper in New York, the survivor of a concentration camp who becomes a victim again, when he is assaulted and killed during a robbery. Gesine has chosen to preserve his story because she feels a kinship with him; against their will both have become embroiled in political and socioeconomic currents beyond their control. Gesine has had no part in and no knowledge of the persecution of the Jews in Germany, and yet she finds herself unable to establish a life for herself in either of the two Germanies because of the lack of conscience which characterizes their governments in their domestic and foreign policies. An article about the death of Cardinal Spellman of New York, who, by way of contrast to the Jewish merchant, is a famous person, conveys the same messages of the helplessness of even the powerful when they are compelled, despite their dedication to peace, to become an agency for the perpetuation of violence in the political sphere.

An even more trenchant example one in which no trace of irony appears occurs in the case of the *Times'* account of the assassination of Martin Luther King. In this instance, a religious figure, a minister, has deliberately taken on a political role, and Gesine, who on a number of occasions has avoided making political commitments even as an admitted advocate of socialism and peace, mourns the death of someone who had the courage or foolhardiness to take nonviolent action in behalf of a cause in which he believed. There ist also a personal element in her pain over the loss of Dr. King. The suicide (it must be assumed) of her mother who suffocated in a locked room in which a fire had been set, was, as she and the author of *Jahrestage* have inferred, the result of the religious conviction that atonement must follow sin; in her mother's situation the transgression had been both personal and communal the fault lay both within her and within her fellow Germans, whose persecution of the Jews she had witnessed at close hand.

The analogy between the treatment of the Jews by the Nazis and the consequences of the institution of slavery in the United States—the abuse heaped on the blacks by the white community in America—plays a part in another article copyrighted by the *Times* and translated and included by Johnson in his novel. Gesine[5] has excised material from the *Times* relating to the arrest of the black writer LeRoi Jones as a result of his participation in the rioting which took place in the to a large extent segregated sections of several cities in the United States in 1967. One can but assume that Gesine is in accord with the general tone of the article which allows one to deplore the riots and the writer's presence among the rioters while condoning actions on the part of blacks to improve their lot. Gesine accepts this dichotomous attitude on the part of the newspaper because the stance of the *Times* is somewhat similar to her own. Johnson has to a limited extent depicted the relationship between Gesine and the *Times* in responding to questions put to him by Manfred Durzak and published in his book *Gespräche über den Roman*; in it Johnson characterizes the contents of Gesine's journal as representing the consciousness (Bewußtsein) on an individual, her self-awareness and the moral judgements—*wie man leben sollte*—she makes about the world in which she lives.[6] In the novel itself Johnson has called the *Times* "das Bewußtsein des Tages" (p.68), that is, the perceptions and standards of a much larger agency, a consensus, rather than those of an individual conscience. For this group Johnson uses the symbol of the pragmatic maiden aunt, strict in regard to matters of good conduct and yet understanding. This figure, as Johnson has proposed (*Jahrestage,* p.15), is a kind of invented character whom Gesine respects as she would all her elders but does not necessarily agree with. By juxtaposing a private world and a public one, the morality of the individual beside the amorality or the conventions of society the collective, Johnson tries to achieve the goal which he believes is the objective of all literature: the greater awareness on the part of the readers of themselves and their situation in the world. In *Gespräche über den Roman* Johnson has stated his purpose in writing *Jahrestage*: "Es handelt sich um einen Anruf zu moralischer Genauigkeit in der Gegenwart" (p.477). In an article Heinz D. Osterle has rephrased this statement of intent in terms of its relevance to life in the United States: "By asking the right questions about a democracy in disarray and upheaval, the reader may overcome national prejudices and rise to an international point of view with new possibilites for insight into the state of the world."[7]

Another German writer, Johnson's contemporary, figures in the documentation which Johnson has added to *Jahrestage*. Hans Magnus Enzensberger and his demeanor during a sojourn in the United States received a great deal of newspaper coverage. Having been funded by Wesleyan University in Connecticut, Enzensberger returned his grant because of his outrage over American participation in the conflict in Vietnam. Enzensberger's preference for life in Cuba under a communistic regime to life in the warmongering and capitalistic United States troubled Johnson because it indicated to him the lack of insight which plagues the writer who places subservience to a cause above reliance on his conscience. In a similar fashion an article excised from the *Times* which concerns the publication of Che Guevara's memoirs gives Johnson occasion to decry the situation of the committed writer; in Johnson's view he or she has replaced the individual's code of morality with a political creed. Additional documentary material in Gesine's journal is related to the theme of the priority of conscience over religious legalism and political pragmatism only indirectly: In concert with Gesine Johnson snips from the *Times* an item which deals with North Vietnamese soldiers chained to their machine guns, a fitting symbol for people caught in a war not of their making, and another item of similar import which depicts the pitiful lot of Vietnamese refugees after the siege of Hue.

The *Times'* description of a German-American parade in New York City, its lengthy list of American casualties in Vietnam, and its exposition of crime at Kennedy airport seem to support Johnson's assertion that the documentary and novelistic parts of *Jahrestage* do not overlap, that there are no direct parallels between the fictitious and actual events; "ich will das nicht erreichen," he is quoted as saying in *Gespräche über den Roman* (p.438); consequently he points out that the situation he describes in New York should not mistakenly be equated with the situation in West Berlin. However, Johnson has permitted himself to make a few analogies in the course of the novel itself. These comments are stated as generalizations: "Viet Nam ist das Spanien unserer Generation," he alleges at one point (p.801), but specific references to the Spanish Civil War are relatively few in *Jahrestage.* On another occasion (p.800) he proposes: "Sowie in den USA heutzutage war es in den mittleren dreißiger Jahren in Deutschland." A hasty conclusion might be drawn that this casually interjected analogy is a statement of the author's theme; more probably it would represent a logical assumption made by Gesine in the course of her ruminations.

The device by means of which documentation is affixed to the narrative in *Jahrestage,* the inclusion of newspaper accounts and general information, is not Johnson's invention; at least two prominent models in novellistic prose preceded *Jahrestage* in this regard. Alfred Döblin's *Berlin Alexanderplatz,* which gave new directions to the German novel in the twentieth century, would necessarily have had an effect on Johnson's work, especially so in the case of *Jahrestage,* since both books are "city" novels. Just as Berlin is a character, that is, a strongly felt presence in Döblin's book, given form by the inclusion of data and other informative material about the metropolis, so does New York appear in Johnson's novel, depicted by items culled from the *Times.* In the case of the *Times,* however, Johnson distinguishes between the content of the articles themselves, which describe a troubled city, and the paper's editorial stance, which he equates with that of a maiden aunt, critical and tolerant at the same time. Picturing this proper lady from an aristocratic family (not at all like Gesine's) with whom Gesine engages in subtle but non-argumentative conversation, Johnson pictures "our good, old aunt just, helpful, our ethical guardian (*Gallionsfigur*)" (p.609, my translation). In enlarging the scope of his novel by including a great deal of material directly from the *Times* in such a way that he can take into account the dark side of political and socio-economic events in 1967-68 while remaining non-judgemental about them, Johnson is able deftly to pursue his theme of the individual in confrontation with the forces of history in his era.

This pattern of dealing alternately with the lives of characters and the actual social phenomena of their time predominates stylistically in the other novel (or series of novels) which undoubtedly served as a model for *Jahrestage*: John Dos Passos' *U.S.A.* trilogy *The 49th Parallel, 1919,* and *The Big Money.* In *Begleitumstände* Johnson refers to his predilection for the three-volume novel without mentioning *U.S.A.*; in *Jahrestage* itself there is, however, a casual mention of Dos Passos (p.207). With reference to the device of using newspaper headlines and stories as an integral part of the text the books by Dos Passos are much more a predecessor to *Jahrestage* than *Berlin Alexanderplatz* is. The function that Dos Passos has assigned this material is, pointedly, descriptive rather than related to the persons in his narrative; he also makes equal use of two other devices, the interior monologue for recording a character's impressions and the short, free-verse biography to include in his panorama portraits of the leading figures of his age. Therefore, Johnson's "borrowings" became an amalgamation of the stylistic features of both *U.S.A.* and *Berlin Alexanderplatz,* to which Johnson has added an element of his own, his projection of the individual conscience against the background of the moral neutrality of public events. As a result of this juxtaposition, Johnson' protagonist is closer to the goal she has set for herself and her daughter at the end of the novel's two thousand pages, the successful conclusion of the search which each individual must undertake for his or her "moral Switzerland," that symbolic place where the public good and private morality meet in harmony. Gesine has arrived at the border of the socialist state of Czechoslovakia on the final pages of *Jahrestage,* but since August 20, 1968, is the date of the invasion of this country, trying desperately to remain independent, by Russian troops, readers who mave managed to reach this point in the novel must conclude that at least in Johnson's philosophy the principle of hope prevails over political reality.

Notes

1. See Heinz D. Osterle, "The Lost Utopia: The Images of America in German Literature," *The German Quarterly,* 54:4 (Nov.1981), 438.

2. Johnson himself has indicated that he intended to provide a sense of the inter relationship between the beginning and the end of the novel: "Die Erzählung [sollte] aus einem Bewußtsein zu mindest des Jahres 1920 voranschreiten bis zu dem gegenwärtigen Jahr und Tag in New York, so daß hier einmal einer Katze es gelingen sollte, den eigenen Schwanz zu fangen," Uwe Johnson *Begleitumstände* (Frankfurt am Main: Suhrkamp, 1980), 416.

3. In *Begleitumstände* Johnson has pointed out that in *Jahrestage* (and by inference in his other novels) he has striven to be realistic: "es habe eben zu dem ge meinsamen Plan gehört, die Wirklichekit jenes Jahres 1967/68 in diese Auswahl aus dem Leben von Gesine Cresspahl aufzunehmenn . . . (.448). See also Bernd Neumann, *Utopie und Mimesis* (Kronberg/Ts.: Athenäum, 1978), p.294f.: "Die naturalistische Detail-Genauigkeit soll die realistische 'Wahrheit' des Ganzen gewährleisten - dies das Haupt-Prinzip der Jahrestage.'"

4. Uwe Johnson, *Jahrestage* (Frankfurt am Main: Suhrkamp, 1983), 375. Pagination from this edition given hereafter in the text.

5. Johnson has deliberately obscured the matter of the relationship between the author and his protagonist. Although he has pointed out that the selection of the articles has been undertaken by the character, their inclusion in *Jahrestage* is nonetheless his work; see the dialog between Gesine and Johnson recorded on page 256: "Wer erzählt hier eigentlich, Gesine. Wir beide. Das hörst du doch, Johnson."

6. Manfred Durzak, *Gespräche über den Roman* (Frankfurt am Main: Suhrkamp, 1976), 478.

7. Heinz D. Osterle, "The Lost Utopia: New Images of America in German Literature," *The German Quarterly,* 54:4 (Nov. 1981), 441.

Robert K. Shirer (essay date 1988)

SOURCE: Shirer, Robert K. "Uses and Misuses of Language: Uwe Johnson's *Ingrid Babendererde* as a GDR Novel." *Colloquia Germanica* 21, no. 1 (1988): 77-84.

[*In the following essay, Shirer examines Johnson's first novel,* Ingrid Babendererde, *contending that it "represents a remarkable and virtually unique attempt to ponder the contradictions of language, ideology, and reality" of the German Democratic Republic.*]

Uwe Johnson is seldom discussed as a GDR author, for it was not until after his 1959 decision «to relocate,»[1] ["**Vita**"] as he put it, to the West that Johnson became established as a literary force. Literary historians often mention Johnson along with Günther Grass and Martin Walser when they discuss the important novelists that burst onto the literary scene in West Germany at the end of the 1950's. But Johnson's work—from *Mutmaßunmgen über Jakob* to *Jahrestage*—is unthinkable without his education and experiences in the Soviet Occupation Zone and the GDR. With the posthumous publication of his first novel *Ingrid Babendererde. Reifeprüfung 1953* we have the opportunity to examine how the young Johnson strove to portray and to come to terms with the society he ultimately chose to leave.[2]

In one of the earliest reviews of the novel Gert Ueding in the *Frankfurter Allgemeine Zeitung* wonders why the novel was not published by Suhrkamp when it was submitted in late 1956, and he compares it favorably with other notable publications of the same year, novels by Nossack, Andersch, Frisch, and Walser.[3] I have no quarrel with this comparison, but it is curious that no mention is made of contemporary publications in the East. After all, *Ingrid Babendererde* portrays the situation in a small Mecklenburg city in 1953, was written by a student in Rostock, who revised it in Leipzig in 1956, and who did not leave the GDR for West Berlin until 1959. Before Johnson submitted the manuscript to Suhrkamp in the West, it had been the rounds of the best literary publishers in the GDR, from whom the young author received compliments on his promise as a writer and assurances that his manuscript was politically impossible.[4]

If one, then, reads *Ingrid Babendererde* as an example of GDR prose of the fifties, it becomes more than a good, if unaccountably unpublished, first novel. It represents a remarkable and virtually unique attempt to ponder the contradictions of language, ideology, and reality in the fledgling socialist state. Many GDR novels of the time did not examine the present, but instead looked back to the war and to the anti-facist struggle. Those that did look to the present—*Produktions*—or *Aufbau* novels like Hans Marschwitzas *Roheisen* of Rudolf Fischer's *Martin Hoop IV*—tend to portray the efforts of workers to come to terms with the new system, to accept and grasp the logic of socialism. Nowhere in these novels is there an effort to examine the relationship between the rhetoric of the new ideology and reality of the new system—one was ultimately either for the new system and accepted its terms, or one did not support it, and represented, consciously or not, a throwback to the old.

Uwe Johnson, by his own account in the *Frankfurter Vorlesungen,* took an interest in precisely this relationship between public language and the reality such language sought to describe, the relationship other novelists of the period had left unexamined. He explains that his study of literature provided him with «eine Vorliebe für das Konkrete . . . , eine geradezu parteiische Aufmerksamkeit für das, was man vorzeigen, nachweisen, erzählen kann» (**BU** [*Begleitumstände*], p. 23). He points out that, because his childhood and adolescence were dominated by the values of Hitler and Stalin, symbolized by the pictures that hung in virtually every public and private place, he had had ample opportunity to observe how language can be used and abused. Johnson details numerous examples of duplicitous language usage, first by the Nazis and then by the Stalinists, and concludes his first lecture by conceding that he might appear to have a psychological fixation on the two leaders. He believes, however, that their pervasive influence had provided him with an essential insight: «Allerdings meint er, vornehmlich sie hätten ihm vorgeführt, wie man Sprache falsch benutzen kann, sogar mit dem Vorsatz zu betrügen» (**BU,** p. 54).

One of Johnson's examples of languages abuse in the Soviet Occupation Zone and in the early GDR brings us to the language problem Johnson examines in *Ingrid Babendererde*—the impossibility of saying precisely what one means without running afoul of predetermined, ideologically acceptable, versions of reality. He speaks of the contradictions between what school children could observe and what their teachers told them.

> Andere Lehrer wissen, daß der Schüler lügt beim Aufsagen von Lügen, die er von Niemandem weiß als von ihnen selber, und eine Eins schreiben sie ihm an, und der Schüler sieht ihnen zu dabei.
>
> (**BU,** p. 49)

The central problem of *Ingrid Babendererde* concerns just such a contradiction between observable reality and the prescribed truth of the party. The novel covers five days in late spring of 1953 in a small city, the five days prior to the beginning of the written *Abitur*. The protagonists—the title character Ingrid, her boyfriend Klaus Niebuhr (who in *Jahrestage* turns out to be Gesine Cresspahl's cousin), and their friend Jürgen Petersen, a leader of the *Freie Deutsche Jugend*—find themselves affected by the GDR-wide compaign to discredit the Christian youth organisation *Die junge Gemeinde. Die junge Gemeinde* has been accused of complicity with Western sabotage and espionage activities, and there is pressure to denounce the Christian organization and its members. At the local level, within the school Ingrid, Klaus, and Jürgen attend, the campaign is patently ridiculous, and the students know it. When Klaus discusses the local leader of the *Junge Gemeinde* with Jürgen, he suggests,

> Aber versucht mal erst mit ihm zu reden: sagte Klaus: Peter Beetz sei nicht die kapitalistische Klasse sondern jemand mit einem Irrtum.
>
> (**IB** [*Ingrid Babendererde*], p. 107)

Jürgen, despite his deep commitment to the party, does not need to be told that. He understands the necessity for dialogue and believes his party organization and his Christian fellow students capable of it. As he listens to the local party leader, the school director Robert Siebmann, whom the students refer to as Pius, denounce the Christians, Jürgen finds himself in a dilemma. He would like to accept and respect what his party leader has to say, but his own experience refutes what he is hearing.

> Irgend wo hatte Pius recht: dachte Jürgen: Aber das war nicht in seinem Reden. Sicherlich hatten die von der Jungen Gemeinde sich etwas gedacht bei der Schrift in ihrem Schaukasten Liebet eure Feinde unter Umständen hatten sie damit wirklich den Klassenkampf behindern wollen. Warum nahm Pius das ernst? Unter ihnen hatte wahrlich niemand Anlaß das kapitalistische Ausland zu lieben: nicht einmal Marianne. Die wäre dort nie bis in die Abiturklasse einer Oberschule gekommen. Man konnte doch mit ihr reden, man konnte auch mit Peter Beetz reden. Jürgen konnte das. Mochten die doch verhandeln an ihren Mittwochabenden über den Bund Christi mit der Welt; die Welt würde Peter Beetz das Studium bezahlen und am Ende mochte der ohnehin gemerkt haben worauf erstens zu achten war. Ach ja: Pius hatte irgend wo recht. Aber das war nicht in seinem Reden.
>
> (91)

Indeed, Jürgen's initial response to the problem of the *Junge Gemeinde* is conciliatory. Under Jürgen, the party youth organization is a group where policy is born of discussion and argument, where the dialectic process is at work: «Sie redeten durcheinander, rauchten, waren betriebsam, hatten Einfälle, kamen gut vorwärts» (**IB,** p. 55). When Ingrid's mother asks Klaus, «So wie Jürgen ist—ist das die Partei?», Klaus responds: «Wir wollen ihm das wünschen» (**IB,** p. 61).

The party, however, is not always like Jürgen. When a school assembly is called for the purpose of expelling the young Christians, it falls to Jürgen, in his role as leader of the *FDJ,* to advocate the party line. Johnson's laconic description of Jürgen's speech and the probable further proceedings of the meeting underscores the main language problem—the relationship between what one sees and what one says—and identifies a number of corallary problems.

> Er (Jürgen) sagte aber dieses: Peter Beetz sei ein Böses Kind; und jenes war: daß Peter Beetz nun mit vorgeschobener Unterlippe würde nach Stuttgart reisen müssen oder nach Hamburg. So sagte Pius dieses und die ihn anhörten fürchteten daß er jenes wollte. Sie konnten seit langem die Bedeutung der Worte nicht mehr übersehen, sie waren also bedacht wenig gesagt zu haben. Aber nächstens würden sie sagen müssen, als Gute Kinder: der neben mir sitzt ist ein Böses Kind, und er soll nicht neben mir sitzen; und das Böse Kind würde zu jenem gezwungen sein. Und sie würden die Hände heben zum Zeichen ihres einmütigen Willens, und in-

dem sie dieses taten, würden sie hoffen jenes nicht gemeint zu haben.

(**IB**, p. 145)

Not only must Jürgen say what he does not believe to be true, but he must also say things that have implications far beyond their surface meanings. By identifying Peter Beetz as «ein böses Kind,» the party casts him from the school, negates the possibility that he will ultimately be integrated into GDR society, and leaves him little choice but to go to the West.

This dangerous connection between what is said and its implications discourages meaningful speech altogether. The students «konnten seit langem die Bedeutung der Wörter nicht übersehen,» and, as a consequence, they prefer to say as little as possible. Dialogue, the discussion Jürgen had hoped would occur with the *Junge Gemeinde,* simply isn't possible under these circumstances.

Jürgen's behavior illustrates one response to these problems. Convinced as he is of the ultimate legitimacy of the party's aspirations and ideology, he accepts the decisions of his superiors in the party. (Although, as we shall see, there are limits to how far he will go.) Jürgen's two closest friends—Klaus Niebuhr and Ingrid Bebendererde—offer two other possible responses. If we return to Jürgen's speech, we can observe first Klaus's reaction and then Ingrid's.

> Also beobachtete Klaus den redenden Jürgen wie etwas Belustigendes und Seltsames, er lag zurückgelehnt und lächelte dann und wann besonders.

(**IB**, p. 145)

Klaus is the first in the line of intelligent, capable, and laconic North German men that populate Johnson's novels—most notably Klaus's uncles Heinrich Cresspahl and Martin Niebuhr and his cousin Gesine Cresspahl's friend and lover Jakob Abs. Klaus, in addition to his natural Mecklenburg taciturnity, has good reason for being skeptical of how language is used. His parents were executed by the Nazis because of their resistance activities, and their deaths were explained as having been caused by heart attack. When Klaus is confronted with situations where the autorities say one thing and mean another, he either withdraws and observes with detached and rather bitter amusement—as he does during Jürgen's speech—, or he adds his own measure of unreliability to the conversation:

> Die Erzieherpersönlichkeit sagte: so sei es, und sei da keine andere Weise die Dinge zu betrachten. Dabei jedoch ließ sie außer Acht daß frühere Erzieherpersönlichkeiten von Herzschlag gesprochen hatte; es war dann aber etwas anderes gewesen. Als der Schüler Niebuhr nun abermals eine Schule besuchte, so also achtete er darauf daß die Erzieherpersönlichkeit nicht abermals dieses für ein anderes sagte; andernfalls würde der

Schüler Niebuhr sich erlauben dieses zu sagen und ein anderes zu meinen auch. So waren Klauses Worte unzuverlässig geworden wie die von Pius, er hatte gelernt daß es etwas auf sich hatte mit den Namen für die Dinge, er hatte gelernt daß dies alles seine Notwendigkeit besaß, und gewisser Maßen machte es ihm nicht viel Freude.

(**IB**, p. 170)

In the days before, upon the arrival of Pius, the school took on a pervasive party influence, Klaus had been a leader in the school chapter of the *Freie Deutsche Jugend.* However, even during his *FDJ* days his disinclination to use ideological language had been problematic for him:

> Unangenehm war ihm die Notwendigkeit vielen Redens; vieles und der Sparsamkeit seines Ausdrucks war Verteidigung gegen den Nebensinn, der in allzu kennzeichnenden Worten wie «bürgerlicher Klassenfeind» und «Führer der Völker» enthalten war.

(**IB**, p. 156)

Klaus refuses to attend the second session of the meeting called to denounce the *Junge Gemeinde.* He knows that open disagreement with the party's decision to expell the church group will result in one's own expulsion, and although he is disgusted with the performances and speeches he has witnessed, he will stay away and go sailing. He urges Ingrid to go with him

> Hörst du . . . hast du nicht die Lehrerbank gesehen? Diese Leute, die nichts weiter haben als was Lehrbefähigung genannt wird und großkarierte Psychologie, Alleswissende, Vertrauenspersonen—; denen nichts einfällt als daß sie ihr Brot nicht verlieren wollen; sollte mich angehen, geht mich aber gar nicht, finde ich ekelhaft verstehst du! . . . Und dieser alberne Betrieb von Parlament und Verfassungsbruch. Liebe Ingrid komm mit segeln. Da ist doch Wind, das riechst du doch, riechst du das nicht?

(**IB**, p. 149)

Ingrid cannot share Klaus's bitter amusement or his withdrawal. Her observation of Jürgen's speech is very different from Klaus's.

> Vor ihm (Klaus) saß sehr aufgerichtet Ingrid und sah von jedem Worte Jürgens wie er es aussprach. . . . sie beobachtee mit ihrer unheimlichen Aufmerksamkeit wie Jürgen nach seiner Rede sich auf den leeren Stuhl in der Mitte des Präsidiums setzte . . .

(**IB**, p. 145)

Ingrid feels ashamed to be part of a group that will accept the abuses of language she has just witnessed. She reminds Klaus of the behavior of their teachers and fellow classmates after the first session of the meeting—going about their business, as though what had just happened hat been normal—, and she refuses to be like that.

Ich will das nicht mehr, ich will nicht auf dem Oberen
See liegen als wenn ich da nie gesessen hätte!

(148)

The idea of going back into school to prepare for the
Abitur, to recite high-sounding ideals, to memorize more
formulas has become repulsive to Ingrid in the face of
the absurd charade she feels she has observed. She feels
she must witness the completion of what has begun,
and she will not go with Klaus.

. . . es sei nicht gut so und sie könne dies nicht leiden,
es sei einfach nicht gut so, sie rieche unter solchen
Umständen überhaupt nichts von Wind!

(**IB,** p. 150)

Ingrid returns to the afternoon session of the assembly.
She had been asked to make a statement about «*Die
Junge Gemeinde* and the rights of the church,*»* in support of the party's denunciation of the group. She refused, but when criticized by the school director for a
lack of social responsibility, she takes the floor and
makes a very curious speech. After rejecting the topic
she has been asked to speak about because she lacks
the competence to do so intelligently, Ingrid begins to
talk about her classmate Eva Mau's slacks. These had
created quite a stir when Eva had worn them to school,
because it was clear that they had been purchased in the
West. The school director had forbidden her to wear
them. Ingrid uses this episode to denounce the intolerance and the hypocrisy of Pius, the school director, in
particular, and of the party in general.

. . . In dieser Zeit führen alle Wege zum Kommunis-
mus: sagte Herr Direktor Siebmann, und wir haben das
wohl begriffen. Herr Direktor Siebmann soll aber be-
denken woher wir kommen. Warum will er wohl daß
wir einen Umweg über Stuttgart oder Hamburg machen, nur weil wir uns noch nicht gewöhnt haben, nur
weil wir nach sieben Jahren noch in anderen Büchern
lesen? Wir sagen dabei nichts gegen Pius' Bücher, Peter Beetz hat nie etwas gegen Pius' Bücher gesagt. Wir
tragen nur noch nicht den Anzug von Herrn Direktor
Siebmann. Und was geht es Dieter Seevken (a FDJ
functionary) an daß Eva Mau neulich in der Großen
Straße ging mit verbotenen Hosen?

(**IB,** pp. 174-5)

As a result of her speech, Ingrid is also expelled from
the school.

Klaus returns the next day and withdraws from school.
He cites the violation of several articles of the GDR
constitution as his reason for doing so. Jürgen, who
voted as one of only 17 students out of 306 against Ingrid's expulsion, is disciplined by the party and explains his behavior to the furious party leader, in terms
almost identical to what Klaus had said in his withdrawal letter:

Jürgens persönliche Gründe seien diese: er sehe zwischen den Artikeln der Verfassung 41 42 43 und dem
Vorgehen der Partei einen Unterschied, dessentwegen
und in Erachtung der Artikel 9 12 habe er gegen den
Ausschluß von Fräulein Babendererde gestimmt. Ich
bin nämlich der Meinung sie hat recht, verstehen Sie?
fragte er Pius' hilflos empörtes Gesicht. Er meine daß
die benutzten Argumente Vorwände seien, die das Ver-
bot einer anderen Meinung rechtfertigen sollten. An-
statt darüber zu diskutieren. Das halte er sowohl für der
Partei schädlich als er das auch überhaupt nicht leiden
möge.

(**IB,** p. 226)

The following day Ingrid finds herself under surveillance by state security agents. She and Klaus conclude
that their situation is untenable, and, with Jürgen's help,
they obtain documents that allow them to reach West
Berlin. Their decision is by no means a symbolic em-
bracing of Western ideology of anti-Communism. It is a
criticism of the misuse of Socialist ideology and of the
type of language such abuse spawns, not of the ideology itself. In five passages that begin each section of
the book we observe Klaus and Ingrid briefly in West
Berlin, where, as Johnson later put it in his *Frankfurter
Vorlesungen,* «sie umsteigen in jene Lebensweise, die
sie ansehen für das falsche . . . » (**BU,** p. 87). Ingrid's
and Klaus's decision is like Uwe Johnson's six years
later, a decision he always characterized as a prudent
decision to relocate.

The difficulty of this decision becomes clear through a
further use of language in the novel. Johnson, as he was
later to do with far greater facility in *Jahrestage,* contrasts the direct and economical use of *Plattdeutsch* by
his protagonists and their families, with the inflated and
frequently duplicitous standard speech of public discourse. In a particularly telling passage, Ingrid and
Klaus walk together beyond the city wall, pursued by
the state-security agent following Ingrid. They walk
around the city, within sight of the lakes that are such
an integral part of the Mecklenburg landscape they love.
In dialect they share the anecdote, «Pete hett eis Melk
to s-tadt füet . . . ,» alternating speeches, jumping in at
a pause, in perfect harmony with each other. They have,
for a moment, excluded the power that they cannot accept and asserted their place in their surroundings.

—Secht hei! sagte Ingrid lachend. Ihre Schultern legte
sie erschüttert zurück und sie lachte, es ging nicht so
einfach und von vornherein, es war nun allerhand mit
ihrem Lachen; aber sie blieb dabei und lachte sehr, sie
konnte gar nicht davon abkommen zu lachen in ihrem
Hals und Klaus sah es alles an mit Petes Gesicht und
sie lachte noch mehr. Es war ungewöhnlich erfreulich
sie lachen zu sehen und zu hören in dieser unmäßigen
Weise von Heiterkeit.

An den Koppeldrähten vor dem Kleinen Eichholz pfiff
der Wind andächtig durch den Vormittag, der untere
See lief klatschend auf am Ufer; die Pferde kamen ihnen von weitem entgegen.

Öwe Pete un de Jung, mit eern Waogn, de füen wire.
Und sie sahen sich nicht um nach ihrer rückwärtigen
Begleitung.

                                        (**IB,** p. 231)

By leaving Mecklenburg, Klaus and Ingrid will lose the
context for this alternative means of communication,
this link to their *Heimat.* This loss of language, and the
loss of *Heimat* it represents, plays an extraordinarily
important role in Johnson's subsesequent work.

There are a number of areas for further investigation
suggested by this study. It would be, I believe, instructive to compare the skeptical attitude toward language
in this novel to that of other, later evocations of this period in GDR history; Kant's *Die Aula* and Christa
Wolf's *Nachdenken über Christa T.* come to mind immediately. It should also be productive to look at this
novel in comparison with other, later GDR works that
examine disaffected youth, like Volker Brauns *Unvollendete Geschichte* or Plenzdorff's *Neue Leiden des jungen W.* Such investigations, unfortunately, would take
us far beyond the scope of the present study.

It is ironic and rather sad that Johnson was unable to
add his enormously talented voice to the literature of
the GDR, a literature which, a decade or so later, in
works like those just mentioned, began to confront some
of the questions he had raised in this, his first literary
effort.

Notes

1. Uwe Johnson, «Vita,» in *über Uwe Johnson,* ed.
   Reinhard Baumgart (Frankfurt/Main: Suhrkamp,
   1970), p. 175.

2. Uwe Johnson, *Ingrid Babendererde: Reifeprüfung
   1953* (Frankfurt/Main: Suhrkamp, 1985). Subsequently referred to as IB.

3. Gert Ueding, «Uwe Johnsons Reifeprüfung. 'Ingrid Babendererde' - sein früher Roman in einer
   späten Edition,» review of *Ingrid Babendererde:
   Reifeprüfung»,* in *Frankfurter Allgemeine Zeitung,*
   18 May, 1985.

4. Uwe Johnson, *Begleitumstände: Frankfurter Vorlesungen* (Frankfurt/Main: Suhrkamp, 1980), pp.
   88-96. Subsequently referred to as BU.

Sara Lennox (essay date winter 1989)

SOURCE: Lennox, Sara. "History in Uwe Johnson's
Jahrestage." *The Germanic Review* 64, no. 1 (winter
1989): 31-41.

[*In the following essay, Lennox questions the unity and
integrity of Johnson's four-volume work,* Anniversaries:
From the Life of Gesine Cresspahl, *and observes limitations, derived from both form and content, within its
presentation of history. She adds that by "oversimplifying the complexities of a crisis period in recent history,
Johnson has made his novel a much less substantial inquiry into the turbulent historical period than it might
have initially seemed."*]

Geschichte ist ein Entwurf," remarks Gesine's aged English teacher on the next-to-last page of the last volume
of Uwe Johnson's *Jahrestage.*[1] That observation resonates with meaning for the entirety of Johnson's novel.
Speaking through one of his work's respected and authoritative figures, Johnson here proposes that any his-
toriographical account is *one* story that some other author might have told quite differently. There is no
history "wie es eigentlich gewesen," that statement indicates; history, like other stories, is a narrative behind
which stands an author who determines criteria of selection and significance, makes judgments, and comes
to conclusions. History is a major theme of *Jahrestage,*
for Johnson's final novel, like his other works, revolves
around and is structured by important public events of
twentieth-century politics, "politische Schlüsselereign-
isse"[2] or "zeitgeschichtliche Schlüsseldaten,"[3] as
Johnson scholars have termed them. Johnson himself
often invited his readers to compare the world of his
novels with their own: "Es ist eine Welt, gegen die Welt
zu halten. Sie sind eingeladen, diese Version der Wirklichkeit zu vergleichen, mit jener, die Sie unterhalten und
pflegen."[4] [**"Vorschläge zur Prüfung eines Romans"**]
Since history is central to the world of *Jahrestage,* we
must assess Johnson's own historical *Entwurf,* measur-
ing it against our own understanding of the historical
periods he treats, in order to evaluate his novel properly.

In this essay, I would like to suggest that, in contrast to
what most Johnson critics and scholars have maintained,
the image of a piece of history presented in *Jahrestage*
is a very partial and tendentious one, made convincing
only via a number of narrative decisions on Johnson's
part that prevent readers from seeing what Johnson had
determined not to include. As I will show, the limitations of *Jahrestage* derive from both its form and its
content, which interact to misrepresent both events and
possibilities of the times of which Johnson wrote. Those
limitations reveal themselves in at least three aspects of
the novel: in the structure which shapes the presentation
of the novel's events; in Johnson's choice of the central
consciousness whose memories, perceptions and experiences *Jahrestage* details; and in the very eccentric use
of documentary material selected mostly from the *New
York Times* to represent contemporary American reality.
For reasons of both form and content, Johnson's story
leads his readers, with some inevitability, to draw certain conclusions about history, to conclude, more precisely, that individuals are at history's mercy, powerless
to change it. (Thus Fritz Raddatz maintains, for in-

stance: "Das ist das Thema des gesamten Roman-Zyklus, eine einzige Paraphrase über Politik und Verbrechen, über den Versuch der Menschen, sich zu befreien und über die Vergeblichkeit dieses Versuchs . . ."[5]) But those conclusions must be drawn because Johnson has stacked the cards of *Jahrestage* against human agency in history, an extraordinary sleight of hand to perform on a year, 1967-68, which has now come to represent the revolutionary hopes and expectations of an entire epoch. Such limitations, I will argue, were present in Johnson's conception of his novel from the beginning, but they are greatly exacerbated in the novel's fourth volume, which Johnson finally succeeded in publishing in 1983, ten years after volume three. Thus I will conclude by asserting that not only do the four volumes of *Jahrestage not* form the unity that many critics have claimed to find there, but that the fourth volume so modifies the concerns of the novel that the very integrity of Johnson's project is placed in question.

As most everyone knows by now, *Jahrestage* presents a daily account of Gesine Cresspahl's experiences mainly in New York City from August 20, 1967, to August 20, 1968, the day of the Soviet invasion of Czechoslovakia. Many days of *Jahrestage* begin with citations or summaries of events reported in the *New York Times,* of which Gesine is an avid, even obsessive, reader, and she recalls and recounts, for her daughter Marie as well, her own and her family's history in Jerichow, a small village in Mecklenburg, from the early Weimar Republic through National Socialism to Gesine's decision to leave the GDR for the Federal Republic in 1953. When the first volume of *Jahrestage* appeared in 1970, it was clear to readers and critics that the point of Johnson's novel lay in the implied parallels and contrasts his novel drew between Nazi Germany and the contemporary United States, waging the Vietnam war abroad while subduing racial unrest at home. (A now almost forgotten model for Johnson's novel was Reinhard Lettau's *Der tägliche Faschismus,* a collection of articles drawn from local U.S. newspapers in the mid-sixties.) But as the actuality of 1968 has faded, attention to the U.S. portions of *Jahrestage* has faded as well, and, beguiled or dazzled (perhaps in the afterglow of the television film *Heimat*) by the story of Gesine's German past, most critics and scholars now concentrate, with evident relief, on Johnson's gripping tales of the Cresspahls in Mecklenburg.[6] But in doing so they have rewritten Johnson's novel and obscured its structuring principles, which are most obviously responsible for the kinds of conclusions *Jahrestage*'s readers must draw about history.

Johnson's treatment of the past, the present, and the future, the democratic socialism in Czechoslovakia for which Gesine hopes, is roughly dialectical (or, as Norbert Mecklenburg has put it, *Jahrestage* employs "das metaphysische Schema" of the occidental novel, "der Dreischnitt Heimat—Fremde—Heimat," with "Sozialismus als Synonym für Heimat" à la Ernst Bloch).[7] The past Gesine recalls, the Old World of Europe, is, Johnson shows in detail, both good and bad. It is good because Jerichow represents a smaller world of *Geborgenheit,* one where individuals still count and where moral action, if ultimately futile, is still possible and significant, even tragic, as evidenced most clearly in the moving account of Gesine's mother's suicide after Reichskristallnacht. It is of course bad because Jerichow acceded or succumbed to National Socialism, particularly to its anti-Semitism. Nonetheless, as Bernd Neumann has observed, Jerichow is portrayed as a non-alienated origin, home, or paradise from which the characters of the present are now exiled: "Die Natur Mecklenburgs, die See, die Bäume, der Regen und selbst noch der Tod geraten zum ursprünglich-ungeschichtlichen, mythischen Gegenpol zur Verdrängung und Zerstörung von Natur und Natürlichkeit durch die kapitalistische Gesellschaftlichkeit der USA."[8] As well, whatever its failures, the past of Jerichow as recounted by Gesine to Marie is a story of experiences that can still be told, satisfying Benjamin's criteria for an archaic art of story-telling now lost to us: "Der Erzähler nimmt, was er erzählt, aus der Erfahrung, aus der eigenen oder der berichteten, und er macht es wiederum zur Erfahrung derer, die seiner Geschichte zuhören."[9] Jerichow is depicted nostalgically and lovingly as a "world we have lost," a past which, as in one meaning of the novel's title, can still be celebrated, "Feiertage," Benjamin called them, to commemorate "die Stellen des Eingedenkens."[10]

In contrast, the present, the New World, is bad in most regards. Though Johnson is careful to distinguish between National Socialism and U.S. racism and imperialism in 1967-68, the novel's obvious parallels between Nazi Germany and the United States of the sixties suggest that many evils of the past continue in the present. But the virtues of the past have vanished in the Manhattan of the present, in Brechtian terms "das schlechte Neue."[11] As Reinhard Baumgart had already discerned in 1964, Johnson from his earliest works onward contrasted the comfortable but fast disappearing world of the German petty bourgeoisie to the heartless social arrangements of East German socialism, portrayed as a particular representation of rationalized modernity: "Die abgeschirmte Stube, in der seine Figuren noch hausen und intim miteinander umgehen, sie stimmt nicht mehr zu der äußeren Arbeitswelt, über die der sozialistische Staat entscheidet. Gegen Cresspahls Intarsienwerkstatt, gegen die Gartenlaube von Achims Vater stehen das Stellwerk und die Radrennbahn. Gegen die würdigen Kleinbürger treten die neuen Funktionäre auf."[12] In *Jahrestage,* Johnson's New York City stands for the summation and furthest development of such tendencies of Western society, as he suggested in a communication to Theo Buck: ". . . daß ich beim Studium einer Zusammenfassung des Westens, in New York, ein neues Buch fand und leider immer noch daran sitze."[13] His depiction of life in New York is mostly negative,[14] manifesting a rootless racial and ethnic heterogeneity, unpredictable criminality, and social and physical disintegration—"Diese Stadt hält sich nicht mehr lange," says Gesine. The extended family of Jerichow is reduced to the family's most elemental form, mother and child, Marie "verläßlich mit niemand auf der Welt verwandt" (259); Gesine's intimate relations are carried on with figures from the Mecklenburg past, and (with a few partial exceptions) she has no friends in New York, only acquaintances, who appear and disappear at apparent random. The possibilities of the work world, an arena of fulfillment and self-realization for Gesine's father, an artisan, or even for Jakob, a railway dispatcher in the GDR, are also reduced for Gesine. She works as a translator in a bank in central Manhattan, at the heart of international capitalism, operating within two systems of equivalencies, money and language. Hers is a job best performed (at least until she receives her Czechoslovakian assignment) if she seeks no personal self-expression at all, serving instead as a transparent medium to facilitate the exchange of commodities.

The changed quality of life of the present is manifest not only in the brutality and violence of the city and Gesine's reduced possibilities there, but also in Johnson's narrative treatment of contemporary life in New York. No closed and coherent story can be told about the present, which is ordered according to the empty time of the calendar, the days of the year which are the second meaning of this novel's title. In Benjamin's terms, New York confronts Gesine as a series of "Chockerlebnisse," as characters appear and disappear and crime strikes at random; Gesine's access to the present is through the modern newspaper, whose very intention is, according to Benjamin, to prevent occurrences from becoming *Erfahrung*: "[Ihre Absicht] besteht darin, die Ereignisse gegen den Bereich abzudichten, in dem sie die Erfahrung des Lesers betreffen könnten. Die Grundsätze journalistischer Information (Neuigkeit, Kürze, Verständlichkeit und vor allem Zusammenhanglosigkeit der einzelnen Nachrichten untereinander) tragen zu diesem Erfolge genauso bei wie der Umbruch und wie die Sprachgebarung."[15] The shattering political events of 1967-68 on which the *Times* reports appear as irrational, inexplicable, and unavoidable as the natural catastrophes which it also features, and Gesine regards herself as helpless to intervene in any way against them: "Ich könnte einen Leserbrief an die New York Times schreiben; ich könnte fürs Leben ins Zuchthaus gehen wegen eines erfolglosen Attentats auf den Präsidenten Johnson; ich könnte mich öffentlich verbrennen. Mit Nichts könnte ich die Maschine des Krieges aufhalten um einen Cent, um einen Soldaten; mit Nichts" (894). As Walter Schmitz has observed, the model of history that emerges from

Johnson's account of Gesine's life in New York is thus one that shows human beings overwhelmed by events they are powerless to affect or control: "Übermächtig stürzt die Fülle der Ereignisse über das unmittelbar erlebende, nicht das denkend ordnende, räsonierende und reflektierende Bewußtsein herein, und eingepaßt in hochrationale, präzis verwickelte Funktionsketten steht es mitten im Ablauf naturwüchsiger Katastrophen. Außerhalb des Schutzraums der privaten Geschichte herrscht, im Jahrhundert der großen Kriege, das Geschichtsmodell der Apokalypse."[16]

Before examining the third term of *Jahrestage,* the socialist future, it is worth asking whether the versions of the past and present Johnson offers are really adequate or accurate as exemplars of the particular developments they are intended to represent. Many of the Jerichow sections are narrated in the grand nineteenth-century manner, but that narrative form was already an anachronism before the Second World War: Benjamin's essay lamenting the loss of the storyteller appeared in 1936, and the aesthetic innovations Johnson draws upon elsewhere in his works were developed mainly in the period around the First World War (that is, before the Jerichow section begins) in response to the social and cultural dislocations of the time. Moreover, if Johnson intends an exemplary account of the period, it seems necessary again to ask questions posed both in the Brecht-Lukács debate and in the discussion regarding the television film *Heimat*: can "an account of life on the fringes of history," to employ Michael Geisler's phrase,[17] really explain what it is significant to understand about the causes and the consequences of National Socialism? And, as Ernst Ottwalt (representing a Brechtian position) asked long ago, can any realistic depiction of the course of individual lives adequately come to terms with the complexity of life in the twentieth century?[18] These larger literary questions aside, Jerichow alone is a highly problematic portrayal of the quality of German life in the twenties and thirties: in fact, it was the *erosion* of such comforting models of *Gemeinschaft* (never so idyllic as they seemed in retrospect), occasioned both by the consequences of Germany's defeat in World War I and the rapid economic and social change of the Weimar Republic, that made the Nazis' promised return to Germanic tradition seem so attractive. The economic, social, and personal disruptions of a major German city like Berlin in the twenties and thirties, not so totally different from New York in the sixties, as well as the threat and allure Berlin represented for Germans outside of the cities, are equally part of the German reality of this period and probably reveal more about the reasons for the appeal of National Socialism to the German people than the description of provincial villages, however accurately they are treated.

In Johnson's portrayal of the present there is also a failure to take nonsynchronicity into account, which means that his account of 1967-68 is incomplete as well. The United States consists not only of the *Chockerlebnisse* of New York, but also, say, of villages of 1,000 people like Fairbank, Iowa, where my father grew up, in the twenties and thirties probably not so different from Jerichow or from Schabbach, and of medium-sized cities like South Bend, Indiana, my home town. One of the reasons for the country's swing to the right in the latter half of 1968 (a development which might have been, but is not, addressed in the novel's fourth volume), culminating in the election of Richard Nixon in November, is the Republican appeal to a "Middle America" which deeply feared particularly the racial threat that Black uprisings in the city represented. Johnson's insistence on an apocalyptic present and his determination to restrict his portrayal of the United States to New York City alone (and to only particular dimensions of life there) mean that he can give no hint of how the American crisis management of the late sixties and seventies was able to succeed. His images of both past and present are too one-dimensional to represent either period's complexity.

The third term of Johnson's dialectical structure, the future toward which the whole novel moves, a future that would reconcile and redeem the past and the present, is the potential for democratic socialism in Czechoslovakia, represented in the accounts of the Prague Spring, the fulfillment of what Gesine and her friend Anita term socialism, "unsere Kinderwünsche" (990). It is striking that the model Johnson establishes literally demands a return home, to a socialism in Central Europe (a "Sozialismus mit 'Heimat'-Qualität," Norbert Mecklenburg terms it),[19] an ironic reversal of the New World as redeemer of the Old. The vision is thus not one of worldwide socialism, hopes for which might have been symbolized via support for the struggle of the North Vietnamese against U.S. imperialism, also a common topos of the time, and in fact Gesine is explicitly depicted as failing to understand why student radicals in Berlin chant "Ho-Ho-Ho-Tschi-Minh" (988-989). Real hopes for liberalization in Czechoslovakia aside, most non-aligned Marxists would recoil at the portrayal of "socialism in one country" as the Golden Age or the reconciliation of contradictions, and the Eurocentrism of Johnson's construction is another indication that he failed to understand sufficiently the period about which he wrote or what would really be necessary to change the world into one he would find satisfactory. But what is most significant about this dialectical structure is of course the irony with which Johnson advances it—for *readers* know from the very beginning of the novel that it will end with the Russian invasion of Czechoslovakia, dashing all Gesine's hopes for that better world, that home at the end of history. (Perhaps, as Johnson maintained, it was in fact by chance that he decided,

before the invasion, to begin his year of days on August 20, 1967, but he did not need to hold to that plan after the invasion, and indeed was urged not to.)[20] History, Johnson thus suggests, is neither designed or destined to satisfy human desires or meet human needs, and all human efforts to achieve that better world will be futile. But of course Johnson's narrative here is an overly schematic one. In fact, history rarely takes place so neatly or so melodramatically, and people's lives—and their histories—continue on the day after the catastrophe, too. A whole variety of other versions of the same time period could be and have been written which would cause us to come to quite different conclusions about the meaning of this period of history.

Gesine Cresspahl herself serves as another vehicle for Johnson's tendentious *Geschichtsbild*. Johnson staunchly insisted throughout his life that his task in *Jahrestage* had been merely to register the contents of Gesine Cresspahl's consciousness through 1967-68.[21] But, though she appears to be a representative figure, a woman like ourselves, whose perspective on the panorama of German and American history readers could compare with their own, Gesine in fact is shaped by her class location and occupation, nationality and personal predispositions in ways which incline her to take a very particular view of that course of events. Gesine's class, nationality, and temperament influence both the novel's content and, perhaps even more importantly, its form, the way Gesine tells her story, the shape given to the account of the past and the present as allegedly filtered through Gesine's consciousness. In this year of political activism, Johnson must take special measures to make his character's lack of political involvement credible, especially given her strong political convictions. By creating Gesine as the character that she is, Johnson assures for two sets of reasons that we will both agree and sympathize with her adamant insistence that any political action on her part (with the exception of her job-related effort to arrange bank credits for Czechoslovakia) will be futile.

First, as Bernd Neumann has perceptively observed, Gesine's consciousness corresponds to her class location: she is a white-collar office worker, an *Angestellte*,[22] and a fairly straightforward Marxist analysis can explain why she thinks and acts as she does. Gesine's romantic-anticapitalist nostalgia for a vanished past, her lively and fully developed character in the present, and her quest for enlightenment and moral integrity can be regarded as the bourgeois (or perhaps petty bourgeois) qualities of consciousness of a nineteenth-century *Mittelstand* for which no social location exists in the second half of the twentieth century. Her present-day politics, her lament in *Jahrestage* that effective political intervention into history is impossible, derives also from that class location and corresponds to the "objective" situation of a political stratum unable to locate a political standpoint or develop a political consciousness that, at least according to Marxist theory, would enable them to struggle for their collective interest. A Marxist might maintain that Gesine's insistence that effective political action is impossible derives, not from her (or Johnson's) particular personal limitations, but from the political limitations of an entire social stratum. Her consciousness is what Georg Lukács in *History and Class Consciousness* (like Marx before him) termed "contemplative," and from that perspective she cannot bridge the gap between her own subjectivity and an object world over which she has no control. To use the language of Marx's eleventh thesis on Feuerbach, Gesine may struggle to understand the world, but, at least in part because her class location precludes it, she is incapable of determining a way to *change* it.

A Marxist analysis of this sort can help to understand Gesine's character formation but does not altogether justify her political quiescence during a period of political activism like 1967-68, when a great many people with class backgrounds like Gesine's believed, and thought they could demonstrate, that their own collective political efforts were changing the course of history. Johnson must thus take extra pains to create a character whose lack of political engagement will seem convincing. He reinforces the point that Gesine is without ties to a community or collectivity that could engage in effective political activity by endowing her in addition with qualities which isolate her even more. By choosing a German national more or less in exile in New York (and one whose response to difficulty in every land in which she has lived has always been flight), Johnson assures that she will neither understand nor perhaps even know about those here-and-now struggles in which she might realistically engage: when, for instance, a young man appears at the Cresspahl's door campaigning for Eugene McCarthy, one of the anti-war candidates in the 1968 Democratic Presidential primary, Gesine listens politely but laments privately: "Daß wir doch das Land verstünden, in dem wir leben wollen! nach sieben Jahren" (1128). Her promotion within the bank early in the novel removes her from contact with other (non-unionized) clerical workers in the bank with whom she might have discussed or acted upon job-related complaints during a period when a significant amount of union organization and political activity took place among white-collar workers. Because her daughter attends a private school, Gesine can ignore the tumultuous confrontations of the period regarding parent control of New York public schools. As well, Gesine's isolation in New York, where she is almost without friends and prefers even for her acquaintances European immigrants like herself, means that she is without an affective community with whom she might choose to act in concert or about whose issues she would care passionately.[23] Of course a great many Americans, not just workers, or students, or political radicals, engaged

in a wide range of political activities in 1967-68 (as the most casual reading of the *New York Times* from that year reveals), and any American citizen, white-collar or otherwise, with Gesine's strong political beliefs could scarcely have refrained from some variety of political involvement. Yet within the world of the novel as Johnson presents it and Gesine experiences it, there really seems to be nothing political for her to do, as one of Johnson's most sympathetic readers, Ingeborg Gerlach, has noted:

> Johnsons Wahrheit ist konkret, sie ist eine des hic und nunc: An seinem Platz soll jeder tun, was in seinen konkreten Möglichkeiten liegt. Kleine Schritte in der unmittelbaren Umgebung werden empfohlen statt weltumfassender Theorien ohne Praxisbezug. Doch selbst dieses Minimum setzt höchst konkrete Ansatzmöglichkeiten voraus; aber wo könnte beispielsweise die Angestellte Cresspahl tätig werden (sieht man von ihrem tschechischen Spezialauftrag einmal ab)?[24]

To the limitations that derive from Gesine's class location Johnson thus adds anomalous qualities she does not share with most of *Jahrestage*'s readers, her situation of voluntary exile and isolation to make her status of mere observer, of non-combatant, believable.[25]

Gesine's a priori determination that political practice is purposeless has many consequences for the content of *Jahrestage,* what readers are allowed to learn about political activities in the United States and Europe during 1967-68. Gesine is often scathing in her denunciation of most New Leftists and anti-war activists, her critiques directed, for instance, at Hans Magnus Enzensberger (795-803), the march on the Pentagon in October 1967 (206-210), the anti-Springer demonstrations in Berlin in April 1968 (988-991), and the student occupation of Columbia University in May 1968 (1092-1096). She also advances a wide range of reasons, from the futility of the action to the faultiness of the protesters' reasoning to their use of marijuana or guerrilla theater, to explain why she herself will not participate in such demonstrations, often arguing with internal voices or with her daughter. With respect to the novel's claim to be a representative treatment of 1967-68, what is most important is what *isn't* presented in *Jahrestage*: with the exception of poor Annie Fleury, whose opposition to the Vietnam war derives in good part from her anger toward her husband, no characters from Gesine's circle of acquaintances take part in political activity at all. Thus, because Gesine keeps her distance from activism, readers also aren't given an alternative to Gesine's position, no characters who could explain the rationale for a particular political action, justify the strategy and tactics employed, or detail the resulting political triumphs or defeats. This omission is particularly striking in the case of Black political protest; though 1967-68 was a year of Black struggle and victory, a wide range of Black activists emerging both from the Black middle class and less privileged strata, the only significant Black character presented in *Jahrestage* is a helpless victim, ten-year-old Francine from the Harlem slums who can't properly use silverware, can't master her school lessons, steals the Cresspahl's loose change, and finally disappears into the jungles of the New York City welfare system. Though her situation is extreme, Francine is not untypical for the characters of the New York present in *Jahrestage*: characters do not exercise human agency, but are in one way or another passive victims of history.

Gesine's contemplative attitude toward history has even more important consequences for the presentation of the history of the present and past in *Jahrestage,* the form given to the story, In response to the internal voices who challenge her lack of engagement, Gesine concedes early on in the novel that she is content to allow her relationship to events of the novel to remain a passive one:

> Und es genügt dir, daß du die Vorfälle bei den gestrigen Demonstrationen hier und in der Welt erfährst aus der Zeitung? Damit läßt sich leben, statt mit Anwesenheit, Mitmachen, Eingreifen, Aktion?
>
> Es ist was mir übriggeblieben ist: Bescheid zu lernen. Wenigstens mit Kenntnis zu leben.

> (209-210)

That Gesine experiences the events of the present through the eyes of the "Tante Times" has not only the consequence that those events can not become *Erfahrung* for her, as Benjamin argued, but also that they must literally be contemplated, experienced by Gesine and by us readers as "out there," as divorced from the affairs that really matter to us and as already finished and preformed through the mode of their presentation— "wie im Kino," as Christa Wolf remarked in another context.[26] What is remarkable, in addition, is Gesine's (and Johnson's) uncritical acceptance of the *Time*'s information as sufficient—despite Gesine's own (affectionate) recognition of limitations in the perspectives of Tante Times, despite the recognition expressed elsewhere in the novel that editorial policies of national news publications are established in order to earn profits for their owners. Never does Gesine compare information from the *Times* with that from, say, *Der Spiegel,* of which she is also a regular reader; never does she consult an alternative American publication for its version of events—*Time* or the *Washington Post* or *Daily Worker* (mentioned on page 1071) or *Ramparts, Monthly Review, The Progressive,* or even the *National Enquirer,* or any of the many underground newspapers, leaflets, and flyers so ubiquitous in the sixties; never does this alert and educated woman undertake to research a matter herself when she is not satisfied with the information the *Times* presents. Also in areas where Gesine would not be obliged to contaminate herself by associa-

tion with actions she cannot wholeheartedly support, Gesine's attitude remains contemplative and passive; in spite of her declared intention to live "mit Kenntnis," she is not willing to assume an attitude that is active and critical even with respect to her acquisition of knowledge. Thus despite the abundance of information presented via the use of the *Times, Jahrestage* deals with public affairs in 1967-68 the same way most traditional novels treat them: they are the backdrop against which the really important activities of human life, the intimate concerns of human subjectivity, are examined. The presentation of contemporary politics only through the *Times* thus forces us readers to take the same contemplative attitude toward the present as Gesine herself.

That contemplative attitude toward history also shapes Gesine's telling of the story of Jerichow, producing an account of National Socialism and its consequences that is finally deeply problematic. In this regard *Jahrestage* can be productively compared to Christa Wolf's *Kindheitsmuster,* which Wolf may arguably have intended as a reply to Johnson's novel. Like *Jahrestage, Kindheitsmuster* recalls the central figure's youth under National Socialism, and Wolf's novel is also told from the perspective of a present-time in the United States, reporting from that standpoint the dismaying events of world history. What concerns Wolf in this novel, however, is the "Subjektwerden" of her central figure and the impact of National Socialism on the person she became. Wolf recognizes that there can be no objective history separated from the process of its recollection and writing, as she insists in her novel's first paragraph: "Das Vergangene ist nicht tot; es ist nicht einmal vergangen. Wir trennen es von uns ab und stellen es fremd."[27] Instead, she shows that past and present produce each other in dialectical interrelationship. No closed narrative of the past can exist, Wolf insists: "Muß nicht der Berichterstatter zögern, eine Vergangenheit von sich abzutrennen, die in ihm selbst noch arbeiten mag, die noch nicht fertig ist, daher nicht beherrschbar?"[28] In contrast to Johnson, Wolf maintains that both the past she recalls and the past she forgets, "um funktionsfähig zu bleiben,"[29] are shaped and conditioned by the values she holds in the present. Thus *Kindheitsmuster* is, on the one hand, an endeavor to explore how history constitutes the human being, a process of becoming which is falsified by a narrative that does not show how our construction of the past is affected by and affects the present, as is the case in *Jahrestage.* Simultaneously *Kindheitsmuster* is an attempt at "Vergangenheitsbewältigung," an effort of the human subject to come to grips with history instead of yielding to its power. For Wolf, no meaning inheres in human history which points it inevitably in the direction of human freedom or self-realization. As she argued in her essay "Lesen und Schreiben," meaning is constructed through human effort, of which writing can form a part: "Ist es denn wirklich der Sinn der Welt, daß sie uns unser eigenes

Wesen enthüllt? Natürlich nicht. Die Welt hat keinen Sinn. Ihr einen zu geben—gerade diesen—ist unser freier Entschluß."[30] In contrast to *Jahrestage, Kindheitsmuster* is intended as a dialectical intervention into history that can help to bring history under human control.

But, though the narrative pretext for the Jerichow sections of *Jahrestage* is similar to that of *Kindheitsmuster,* Gesine's past is separate from her life in the present, closed, and finished; though she recalls it almost obsessively, nothing in her present life modifies her recollection of the past. Moreover, though in a 1961 essay, **"Berliner Stadtbahn,"** Johnson had maintained, "Die Manieren der Allwissenheit sind verdächtig. . . . Der Verfasser sollte zugeben, daß er erfunden hat, was er vorbringt, er sollte nicht verschweigen, daß seine Informationen lückenhaft sind und ungenau."[31] [*Berliner Sachen*] Though his earlier novels had examined the difficulties of writing the truth and the perspectival nature of particular individuals' truth, *Jahrestage* is content to present a version of events in Jerichow that is almost totally omniscient, able to record the moment-by-moment thoughts and perceptions of long-dead characters. ("[Es] läßt sich eine ihre erzählerische Kompetenz offensichtlich überschreitende Erzählerin ausmachen," Peter Pokay has remarked in his useful study of *Jahrestage*'s narrative structure.[32]) Though Gesine maintains that, of her family, "ich war die erste von uns, die das Vergessen fürchtete" (937), she in fact rarely forgets, rarely is troubled by gaps in her own memory or the problem of missing information. Even on the few occasions where she claims to be inventing (for instance, the details of her father's wartime collaboration with the British, p. 811), her inventions are rarely problematized (like, say, the narrator's in *Nachdenken über Christa T.*), but instead also take on the status of truth for readers, as her friend D. E. tells her, "ich glaube es dir aufs Wort, als eine Wahrheit, mit der du dich durchs Leben bringst; oft als Warhheit" (817). As well, though historians of National Socialism are far from agreeing on how various manifestations of Nazism and its postwar consequences are to be understood, Gesine is mostly untroubled by such problems of interpretation. For readers, Gesine's historiography produces a narrative of National Socialism and East German socialism which is pre-packaged and "erledigt," over, once and for all, demanding no active effort from us, a history we also, like Gesine, can only comtemplate with horror and dismay. Perhaps most importantly, the presentation of this omniscient narrative as something detached from Gesine's present means that no work of "Vergangenheitsbewältigung" or mourning can take place for her. Because she does not work with the past to come to terms with it, her relationship to the past remains traumatic, rather than a relationship she can master and move beyond. The question this novel is able to avoid via its distanced presentation of the Nazi past is in what regards a childhood under fascism might produce character deformations that continue into the present, might also produce the attitudes of the present, might even be responsible for Gesine's belief that she is the victim of a history over whose course she has no power.

It might be tempting to postulate that *Jahrestage* could be intended as a mammoth critique of the limitations of Gesine's consciousness—though perhaps so subtle a critique that most readers have failed to notice it. Johnson's error would thus not be his portrayal of Gesine's consciousness, but his failure to differentiate his own narrative position from hers. Neumann suggests something of this sort when he maintains, "Die Problematik eines in solcher Weise 'objektiven' Verfahrens liegt also nicht darin, daß der Roman der 'Angestellten Cresspahl' das beschriebene Politik-Verständnis zuordnet. Sie liegt vielmehr darin, daß der Autor der 'Jahrestage' kraft Identifikation mit seiner Medial-Figur Gesine deren Welt- und Politikverständnis zur literarischen Struktur des Textes selber werden läßt."[33] However, there is not much indication that Johnson in fact took issue with his character's politics. It is not just Gesine who believes herself helpless in the face of history; as Ingeborg Gerlach has observed, almost all of Johnson's characters are victims of history: "Der Leser . . . gewinnt den Eindruck eines dichten Netzes von sozialen Beziehungen; die dargestellten Fälle ließen sich beliebig vermehren zum Totalgemälde einer Geschichte, die keinen Sieger kennt. Am glücklichsten sind diejenigen, die ihre Positionen bewahren konnten— und dies zumeist auf Kosten der anderen. 'Verloren' haben die meisten; es gibt kaum ein hoffnungsvolles Leben, das nicht dem Druck der Verhältnisse zum Opfer fiel."[34] Gesine's position on practice also seems to correspond roughly to Johnson's own, who in a famous passage from his Büchner Prize speech of 1971 quoted Büchner to argue that the present offered no opportunities for effective political intervention: "Wenn der Verfasser an vergangenen oder künftigen Ansätzen taktischer Politik keinen Teil nahm oder wenig teilnehmen wird, so geschieht es weder aus Mißbilligung noch Furcht, sondern weil er im gegenwärtigen Zeitpunkt jede revolutionäre Bewegung als eine vergebliche Unternehmung betrachtet . . ."[35] [**"Nachforschungen in New York"**] And even before the disappointments of 1968 Johnson issued a scathing denunciation (originally published in a 1967 *Kursbuch*) of what he considered to be the revolutionary posturing of the antiwar movement, maintaining that "die guten Leute" should restrict their activities to arenas of life over which they have some control:

> Auch diese guten Leute werden demnächst ihre Proteste gegen diesen Krieg verlegen bezeichnen als ihre jugendliche Periode, wie die guten Leute vor ihnen jetzt sprechen über Hiroshima und Demokratie und Cuba. Die guten Leute sollen das Maul halten. Sollen

sie gut sein zu ihren Kindern, auch fremden, zu ihren Katzen, auch fremden; sollen sie aufhören zu reden von einem Gutsein, zu dessen Unmöglichkeit sie beitragen.[36]

([**"Über eine Haltung des Protestierens"**])

Johnson's often-voiced sympathy for his character, his failure to differentiate himself narratively from her, and the profound irony he directs at her hopes for change suggest that his historical pessimism is even greater than her own.

The final series of narrative decisions buttressing the view of history Johnson presents in *Jahrestage* involves the daily news items Johnson extracts from the *New York Times* to frame the days of his year. By including material that is documentary in character (sometimes even with *New York Times* copyright attached), Johnson seems to be making a special claim for the veracity and authenticity of his novel: though the *Times* is an "alte Tante," the material that appears there is true in a way that fiction never claims to be. The cumulative effect of the *Times* articles thus makes the case that this, indeed, was the way it was in 1967-68. Remarkably, almost all scholars have taken at face value *Jahrestage*'s apparent claim to present a documentary account of 1967-68 without questioning Johnson's criteria of inclusion or comparing his selection with all the news actually printed in the *Times*. The results of such an examination are quite remarkable: a day-by-day comparison of Johnson's selection of news items with the actual contents of the *Times* shows that Johnson's choice of material is so eccentric and unrepresentative as perhaps even to raise ethical questions about the use to which he has put documentary material.

Every news item Johnson claims to have found in the *Times* is really there, and almost always where he said it was; but what is startling, day after day, is what Johnson chooses to leave out. (Johnson's insistence that he bore no responsibility for the contents of *Jahrestage*, since he only recorded what Gesine perceived, particularly tries scholarly patience in this case, since it is simply not credible that his character could have failed to notice events that produced articles of multiple-column length on the *Times*' front page for weeks or ignored articles, also on topics of concern to her, in columns adjacent to articles included in the novel.) What Johnson excises from the *Times* is the *good* news, the accounts of human agency, especially the activities of ordinary people (with Black political protest particularly slighted), the victories achieved, and the accounts of the small steps it takes to bring victories about. Ree Post-Adams' observation, "Aber mindestens einen Fortschritt der Neger auf dem Weg zu sozialer Gerechtigkeit hat Gesine übersehen: Am 7. November 1967 haben sich bei den Bürgermeisterwahlen in zwei wichtigen Städten des mittleren Westens schwarze Kandidaten durch-

gesetzt: In Gary, Indiana und in Cleveland, Ohio"[37] is only the tip of the iceberg. Johnson's inclination to omit articles on activism increases as the novel progresses and as the activism of that period itself accelerates. By the third volume, dealing with April 20 to June 19, 1968, a period that has come to symbolize the aspirations of that epoch, Johnson seems determined to record only the bad or banal news. Thus not only does Johnson present a version of events that no veteran of 1968 in the United States, Germany, or France could accept; he wilfully omits, day after day, the major news stories of the times.

An examination of several quite representative days from volume three can show what Johnson chooses to leave out. On April 21, 1968, for instance, the second day of volume three, Johnson cites from page three of the first section of the Sunday *Times* an article on the West German celebration of the fiftieth anniversary of Baron von Richthofen's death and a report on the beatings to death of mentally disturbed prisoners in the Klingelpütz prison in Cologne. "In so ein Land willst du nun zurück, Gesine," says Marie (1026). But what neither Gesine nor Johnson reports about West Germany is a two-column essay on p. 6B of "The Week in Review," "Revolt of the Students is the Bursting of a Dam," analyzing with balance and accuracy the growth of German SDS, the nature and quality of the grievances of the German student movement, and the kinds of activities the extraparlamentary opposition had engaged in since the SPD joined the Grand Coalition and "the fatal shooting of a young student at a demonstration last June by a West German policeman." With regard to the United States, Johnson reports on the same day that many New Yorkers ("throngs," according to the *Times* in its article on page forty-seven [!]) visited the NATO flotilla parked in New York harbor, an apparent documentation of American enthusiasm for militarism. But he does not tell us what the *Times* also reported that Sunday about Black struggles in the three weeks since Martin Luther King's death ("Black Power Unit Stirs Florida City," "Negroes to Seek More in Memphis"); white response to Black unrest ("City U. May Start 2 Special Schools to Serve Harlem," "Suburbanites Come to City and Help Clean Up Slums" (both articles on page one), "Lindsay, at Harvard, Accuses Democrats of Inaction in [Racial] Crisis"); the three-way race for the Democratic presidential candidacy, their debates revolving around the Vietnam War ("McCarthy Scorns Nixon on Vietnam"); or the growing antiwar movement to the left of the Democratic Party ("Kennedy, McCarthy Chided by Dr. Spock;" "War Foes Rally Barred on Coast: California Residents Forbid a 'Vietnam Commencement.'"

Johnson's treatment of the *Times* on May 12 similarly exemplifies the distortion the news undergoes at Johnson's hands in *Jahrestage*. On that day the *Times* reported on its front page "Parents Aim to Bar 19 Ousted Teachers," an account of a drawn-out struggle by Black parents in Brooklyn to control community schools; "Striking Students At Columbia Ask to See Trustees," the latest on the student occupation of Columbia University; four columns on Paris, including "Paving-Stone Barricades Mark the Scenes of Student Rioting in Paris" and "Students Backed By French Unions"; "Procedures Set for Paris Talks; 2 Sides Pleased," regarding the U.S.-North Vietnamese peace negotiations; "Kennedy Favors Basic Tax on Rich," "City Easing Rules On Admitting Poor To Public Housing," and "Prague Twits Bloc on Moscow Parley." On page two the *Times* reported from the Federal Republic, "30,000 Marchers Assail Bonn Bill, Oppose Broad Emergency Power of Government." Confronted with these accounts of activism around the world, Johnson chose three selections from the *New York Times* to characterize the day for readers of *Jahrestage,* the quote of the day: "Wir haben dreimal versucht, eine Straße hinunterzukommen, und bisher haben wir fünf Tote und siebzehn Verwundete in meiner Kompanie. Ich pfeif drauf, wer heute Geburtstag hat, wir gehen wieder vor und räuchern sie aus.—Stabsfeldwebel Herman Strader in Saigon, wo gestern der 2,512. Geburtstag Buddhas gefeiert wurde" (1151); an article from the front page, "Airlines Unable to Halt Crime Flourishing at Kennedy Airport," translated in almost its entirety as "Das Verbrechen blüht auf dem Flughafen Kennedy, Polizeibehörden und Luftlinien sind hilflos" and extending over five pages of *Jahrestage* (1151-1155); and a classified ad: "EINEN GLÜCKLICHEN MUTTERTAG wünschen Sylvia, der besten Mutter in der Welt, ihre Kinder Ellen, Peter Frank und Amy" (1155).

Johnson's omissions in his treatment of May 1968 are even more striking. There is no mention at all of the revolutionary exuberance of that month and the international connections it forged among young people throughout the West, no citation of the report on page one of the *Times* on May 7: "'This is our Berlin,' boasted one student leader, alluding to leftist student riots that swept West Germany last month. An American Negro student, who was a bystander, added, 'This isn't Berlin, this is Watts,'" or the report from page two of the Week in Review on May 12: "'The Americans have had their Berkeley, the Germans have had their Berlin,' commented one student as he dug up paving stones on the Boulevard St. Germain, his eyes streaming from the pall of tear gas. 'And now,' he declared triumphantly, 'you can add Paris to the list.'" The events of May 1968 dominated the *Times*' front page for over two weeks. But *Jahrestage* mentions Paris only four times. On May 4 Johnson remarks sarcastically, "Zum Frühstück also hauen die pariser Studenten sich mit ihrer Polizei, weil einige von ihnen den Lehrbetrieb kontrollieren möchten und die Einrichtung des Kapitalismus umstürzen, den Boulevard St. Michel entlang, zum

Beispiel" (1106-1107). On May 13: "In Paris hingegen verstehen die Arbeiter, was die Studenten sprechen und wollen ihnen gegen die Regierung helfen mit einem Generalstreik für einen Tag und eine Nacht" (1155). On May 20: "Charles de Gaulle hat sein Wort zum französischen Generalstreik nun gefunden: Reformen, Ja, ins Bett machen, Nein. Chienlit. Der große alte Mann" (1191). On May 21, a day when the three-column *Times* headline read "France is Near Paralysis as Millions Join Strike; Reds Press for Coalition," Johnson observes, "Erst haben die französischen Kommunisten den Generalstreik weder kommen sehen noch unterstützt, nun wollen sie gleich ein Bündnis der gesamten Linken, ein wahrhaft republikanisches Regime, und auf dem Weg zum Sozialismus sehen sie es auch" (1199). Not content merely to shape his fiction in such a way as to preclude human beings from taking action to change the conditions of their lives, Johnson also excludes from the documentary sections of his novel the evidence that real people have done so. When readers compare Johnson's version of reality in 1967-68 with their own, on the basis of the facts alone, as reported in the public source of information on which he himself drew, his view of history in *Jahrestage* is again revealed to be partial, distorted, and tendentious.

By 1983, when volume four appeared, Johnson seemed to have lost much of his interest in the contemporary United States, perhaps as a consequence of the personal difficulties he recounted in *Begleitumstände,* also responsible in part for delaying the final volume's appearance for a decade. In volume four, Johnson's use of *Times* articles, except those dealing with the growing crisis in Czechoslovakia, subsides markedly. Though, as I have argued, Johnson's attention to the news of the *Times* in the novel was neither fair nor representative of what actually took place, his presentation of contemporary life was both mostly internally consistent and compelling, evidence for the qualities that constitute his "Bad New World," the second term of his novel's dialectical structure. From the first volume onward, apparently random details from the present are in fact carefully selected to produce an effect of general social disintegration framing Gesine's daily life and her memories. In volume one Johnson had quickly set the context: Gesine's world is one of racial unrest, military assaults and body counts in Vietnam (mentioned on many days of the first volume), random and violent crime in New York, the growth of neo-Nazism in both the United States and the Federal Republic, and continued repression in the GDR and the Soviet Union (on which Johnson frequently comments sardonically, as evidenced, for instance, by his somewhat excessive attention to the defection of Stalin's daughter). In early volumes, violence, unrest, and repression are also worldwide phenomena—no place on earth remains unscathed, and no "moralische Schweiz" (382) exists to which Gesine could escape. The very first news item mentioned in *Jahrestage* is itself significant in this regard: after Johnson swiftly establishes German and U.S. anti-Semitism as a major concern of his novel, he notes: "An der israelisch-jordanischen Front ist wieder geschossen worden" (9).

But in the fourth volume that same concern with the New York and world context greatly diminishes. In contrast to earlier volumes, Johnson does not deal with the Third World at all in volume four, though problems of course continue there, including tensions in the Middle East after the 1967 Israeli invasion, the cultural revolution in China, famine in Biafra, and student unrest in Mexico and South America. As well, Johnson leaves out most of the national news about U.S. political activities during the summer of 1968: the Poor People's Campaign and march on Washington, continued student and antiwar activism across the country, the political jockeying leading up to the Democratic and Republican party conventions as well as the New Left plans for demonstrations at the Democratic convention, Black protest and white concessions. Some areas of contemporary U.S. affairs addressed in earlier volumes appear again in volume four: the effects of the war on Vietnam, crime and police violence in New York (as well as its July heat wave), residues of National Socialism in the Federal Republic. Yet in contrast to earlier volumes, those topics are so infrequently (and often so perfunctorily) invoked in volume four that the texture of Gesine's life in the bad present, so omnipresent a backdrop in the first three volumes, almost disappears from view in the fourth.

This shift of emphasis in volume four affects a number of the thematic and formal concerns that had both structured the first three volumes of his novel and had been responsible for much of *Jahrestage*'s interest and profundity. One of the most essential structuring principles of earlier volumes, the contrasts and parallels of the American present and German past, similar and yet very different in their racism and violence, has disappeared. The diminished attention to the bad present, New York in 1967-68, also means that a central theme that had informed Johnson's work since *Mutmaßungen über Jakob,* the damage modernity wreaks upon community and subjectivity, vanishes also. The powerful formal contrast of the chaotic and random *Chockerlebnisse* of the present, events from a hostile external world violently imposing themselves upon Gesine's consciousness, and the *Erfahrung* still possible in her German past, is lost as well. Instead, volume four's bitter account of past Communist abuses during the GDR's *Aufbau* years (uncomfortably Cold War in tone) flows easily into its daily reports from the *Times* of present Soviet pressure on the Dubček regime in Czechoslovakia. Events in Czechoslovakia are also so constant a subjective concern of Gesine's that her life, in previous volumes divided between an elaborate internal life, filled with memories and recollections, and an indifferent and barren outside world, also now appears to be of a single piece, the present as *erzählbar,* as Benjamin might have termed it, as the past. All those qualities that had preserved *Jahrestage*'s first volumes from being merely nostalgic evocations of a vanished epoch are much less clearly visible in volume four. *Jahrestage*'s concluding volume turns Johnson's novel into a more conventional, less thematically and formally interesting, and politically even more problematic work than his previous three volumes had seemed to predict.

As well, Johnson's changes of course in the fourth volume seriously draw the unity of his tetralogy into question. By volume four the structure that had previously sustained his massive undertaking is much less clearly in evidence. If readers take seriously the project that Johnson initiated in *Jahrestage*'s first volume, the *contrast* of the past and the present and the hopes for the future resolution that arise from that contrast, it becomes impossible to argue, as many critics have wished to do, that "Der vierte Band . . . führt bruchlos und beeindruckend zu Ende, was die vorhergehenden Jahrestage-Werke exponiert hatten"[38]—for that contrast is of much less central concern in the fourth volume. Only those readers who disregard Johnson's treatment of the present and attend only to his narrative of the Mecklenburg past will find it possible to maintain that the four volumes of *Jahrestage* form a unity. His abandonment of any serious treatment of the problems of 1967-68 in the fourth volume of the novel instead raises doubts both about the integrity of his novel and the quality of the achievement that *Jahrestage* represents.

Since the publication of *Jahrestage*'s first volume, critics and scholars have debated the question of Johnson's "resignation," whether he had reconciled himself to a bad reality by resigning himself to the impossibility of changing it. Perhaps surprisingly, no one has ever really examined the narrative decisions that shape the "Version der Wirklichkeit" that Johnson presents in *Jahrestage,* particularly the portions dealing with New York City in 1967-68, to discover why *Jahrestage* might convey that impression of authorial resignation. Such an examination shows that, despite its apparently documentary claims, the reality of *Jahrestage* is in many regards different from and often much bleaker than the reality experienced by others who lived through that period in the United States. By oversimplifying the complexities of a crisis period in recent history, Johnson has made his novel a much less substantial inquiry into that turbulent historical period than it might initially have seemed. His novel is diminished because of it, and the choices Johnson made in *Jahrestage* may also cast their shadows over the rest of his work, raising troubling questions about his assessment as a novelist altogether.

Notes

1. Uwe Johnson, *Jahrestage* (Frankfurt am Main: Suhrkamp Verlag, 1970-1983), vol. 4, p. 1891. All references to *Jahrestage* hereafter cited within the text.

2. Michael Bengel, "Johnsons Jahrestage und einige ihrer Voraussetzungen," in *Johnsons 'Jahrestage,'* ed. Michael Bengel (Frankfurt am Main: Suhrkamp Verlag, 1985), p. 320.

3. Walter Schmitz, *Uwe Johnson* (Munich: Verlag C. H. Beck/Verlag edition text + kritik, 1984), p. 42.

4. Uwe Johnson, "Vorschläge zur Prüfung eines Romans," in *Romantheorie: Dokumentation ihrer Geschichte in Deutschland seit 1880,* ed. Eberhard Lämmert (Cologne: Kiepenheuer & Witsch, 1975), pp. 402-403.

5. Fritz Raddatz, "Ein Märchen aus Geschichte und Geschichten," in Bengel, p. 179.

6. Thus Joachim Kaiser speaks of "die im Band IV Gott sei Dank nicht mehr so dominierende 'New York Times'" (Kaiser, "Für wenn wir tot sind," in Bengel, p. 175), and Norbert Mecklenburg, "Das Buch ist ja nicht nur ein Provinzroman, sondern auch gleichzeitig, *worauf nicht einzugehen ist,* ein Großstadtroman von Rang" (Mecklenburg, "Ein Stück Herkunft, kenntlich gemacht. Realismus und Regionalismus in Uwe Johnsons *Jahrestagen,*" in Bengel, p. 245, my emphasis). Cf. also the remarks of one of the interlocutors in Mecklenburg's 1980 essay: "Dieses Zusammengeschnibbelte in jedem Kapitel hat mich beim Lesen derart irritiert und ungeduldig gemacht, daß ich mir nach den ersten Hundert Seiten die Jerichow-Abschnitte durch den ganzen ersten Band hindurch mit einem roten Markierungsstrich am Rand herausgesucht und dann, ohne den New Yorker Tagebuchballast, in einem Zug durchgelesen habe" in *text + kritik: Uwe Johnson,* nos. 65/66 (January 1980), p. 52.

7. Mecklenburg, "Leseerfahrungen," p. 62.

8. Bernd Neumann, *Utopie und Mimesis: Zum Verhältnis von Ästhetik, Gesellschaftsphilosophie und Politik in den Romanen Uwe Johnsons* (Kronberg/Ts.: Athenäum, 1978), p. 298.

9. Walter Benjamin, *Gesammelte Schriften* (Frankfurt am Main: Suhrkamp Verlag, 1980), II, 2, 443.

10. Ibid., I, 2, 643.

11. See Bertolt Brecht, "Die Essays von Georg Lukács," in *Marxismus und Literatur: Eine Dokumentation in drei Bänden,* ed. Fritz J. Raddatz (Hamburg; Rowohlt, 1969), II, 88.

12. Reinhard Baumgart, *Literatur für Zeitgenossen* (Frankfurt am Main: Suhrkamp Verlag, 1970), pp. 50-51.

13. Theo Buck, "Uwe Johnson," in *Kritisches Lexikon zur deutschsprachigen Gegenwartsliteratur,* ed. Heinz Ludwig Arnold (Munich: edition text + kritik, 9. Nachlieferung (Stand 1.9.1981), p. 1.

14. As Sigrid Bauschinger has observed, the topics in the *Times* of interest to Gesine, hence reported in Johnson's novel, "gibt gerade im Hinblick auf New York einen recht beschränkten Katalog von Nachrichten. Gesine scheint sich vor allem zu interessieren für die Mafia, Banküberfälle, Morde und Vergewaltigungen, Demonstrationen und brutale Vorbeugungsmaßnahmen dagegen . . . Wie bei der Zeitungslektüre große Teile des täglichen Lebens der Stadt ausgespart bleiben, so auch in Johnsons Manhattan überhaupt. Es ist eine merkwürdig farblose Stadt, unmusikalisch, amusisch. Der Rhythmus, der die Stadt durchpulst, ihre Lieder, ihre Tänze, all das felht" (Sigrid Bauschinger, "Mythos Manhattan: Die Faszination einer Stadt," in *Amerika in der deutschen Literatur: Neue Welt—Nordamerika—USA,* ed. Sigrid Bauschinger, Horst Denkler, and Wilfried Malsch (Stuttgart: Philipp Reclam jun., 1975), pp. 390-391.

15. Benjamin, 1, 2, 610-611. For further discussion of this point, see Sara Lennox, "Die *New York Times* in Johnsons *Jahrestagen,*" in *Die USA und Deutschland,* ed. Wolfgang Paulsen (Bern: Francke Verlag, 1976), pp. 106-109.

16. Walter Schmitz, "Grenzreisen: Der hermeneutische Realismus Uwe Johnsons," *text + kritik,* p. 43.

17. Michael Geisler, "'Heimat' and the German Left: The Anamnesis of a Trauma," *New German Critique,* no. 36 (Fall 1985), p. 27.

18. See Ernst Ottwalt, "'Tatsachenroman' und Formexperiment: Eine Entgegnung von Georg Lukács," in *Marxismus und Literatur,* ed. Raddatz, pp. 159-165.

19. Mecklenburg, in Bengel, p. 239.

20. See Uwe Johnson, *Begleitumstände: Frankfurter Vorlesungen* (Frankfurt am Main: Suhrkamp Verlag, 1980), pp. 447-451.

21. Johnson maintained for instance in a 1971 interview: "Begonnen hat das Buch ja als ein Versuch, dieses Bewußtsein Gesine Cresspahl darzustellen—was es alles enthält an Vergangenheit und Gegenwart" (Dieter E. Zimmer, "Eine Bewußtseinsinventur: Das Gespräch mit dem Autor: Uwe Johnson," *Die Zeit,* 26 November 1971, p. LIT 39), and in a 1972 interview: "Ich habe von einer fiktiven Person den Auftrag bekommen, für sie das Bewußtsein von heute und gestern ja nach Tagen aufzuschreiben" (Martin Meyer/Wolfgang

Strehlow, "'Das sagt mir auch mein Friseur:' Film- und Fernsehäußerungen von Uwe Johnson," *Sprache im technischen Zeitalter,* no. 95 [1985], p. 175). Cf. also Johnson's repeated protestations in this regard in one of the last interviews of his life in Heinz D. Osterle, "Dokumentation: Uwe Johnson: Todesgedanken? Gespräch mit Heinz D. Osterle über die *Jahrestage,*" *German Quarterly,* 58, no. 4 (Fall 1985): 576-584. Those assertions are of course contradicted by the famous exchange between Gesine and her "Genosse Schriftsteller," in volume one of *Jahrestage*:

> Wer erzählt hier eigentlich, Gesine.
>
> Wir beide. Das hörst du doch, Johnson.
>
> (256)

22. Neumann, pp. 290-295.

23. Gesine of course discusses many major issues of the day with her daughter Marie, her primary conversation partner: the Vietnam war, the assassination of King and Kennedy, the student occupation of Columbia University. But for the most part Marie's opinions and allegiances do not differ much from those of her mother. She displays "eine Hinneigung . . . zur Parteinahme, zur fast moralischen Solidarisierung mit Unterlegenen in geschichtlichen Vorgängen" (313), but "sie [trug] die Plakette GEHT RAUS AUS VIET NAM nur so lange angesteckt . . . , wie die Mode in ihrer Klasse sich hielt. Sie ist so unaufrichtig, wie ich [Gesine] sie erzogen habe" (493). Johnson uses the discussions with Marie as a way to elaborate Gesine's political opinions, but, despite some disagreements with her mother's assessments, Marie never poses any sort of fundamental challenge to Gesine's beliefs.

24. Ingeborg Gerlach, *Auf der Suche nach der verlorenen Identität: Studien zu Uwe Johnsons "Jahrestagen,"* Monographien Literaturwissenschaft 47 (Königstein/Ts.: Scriptor Verlag, 1980), p. 107.

25. One might note in passing that in New York in 1967-68 the opportunity also existed for Gesine to join in a struggle not just for other people's causes but on her own behalf—for by that time the first consciousness-raising groups of the second wave of feminism had begun to form, though Gesine would not have read about them in the *New York Times.* (For an account of feminism's origins in this period, see Sara Evans, *Personal Politics: The Roots of Women's Liberation in the Civil Rights Movement and the New Left* [New York: Vintage Books, 1979], especially chapters eight and nine.) That the very prospect of Gesine in a consciousness-raising group seems ludicrous tells us something, I think, not just about Gesine's politics but about Johnson's success in portraying his

female protagonist. As a character, Gesine seems both sex- and genderless, for Johnson seems to have invested remarkably little energy in imagining himself into a consciousness which is authentically female. (For counter examples in works also written in the seventies, one might examine Volker Braun's Karin in "Unvollendete Geschichte," which, if not free from stereotypes, at least takes a female protagonist's gender-specificity seriously, or Nadine Gordimer's Rosa Burger in *Burger's Daughter,* who combines a deep concern with history and politics with attention to her particular situation as a woman.) When pressed on the issue of distinctions between himself and his figure Gesine by Heinz Osterle, Johnson maintained that Gesine's experiences were shaped by her gender in a way that his could not have been: "Sehen Sie, meine Erfahrungen wären, wenn sie bloß so gezeigt würden, nicht geeignet für diese Gesine. Es ist zum Beispiel ganz unterschiedlich, wie man in den Schuhgeschäften behandelt wird. Gesine ist einmal von einem jungen Mann bedient worden. Der hat den Verkaufsvorgang unterbrochen und hat sie gebeten, eine Weile weggehen zu dürfen und eine zu rauchen. Er sei schrecklich sexuell erregt. Das ist ihr passiert, kann ihr passieren, aber nie mir" (Osterle, p. 577). So bizarre and somewhat grotesque an anecdote does not inspire confidence in Johnson's understanding of the conditions for women in New York City during 1967-68, or of the much more fundamental ways in which women of his generation differ from himself. Instead, Gesine seems to be one more example of a male author's use of a female figure to explore the conflict between subjectivity and society. (On that topic, see Myra Jehlen, "Archimedes and the Paradox of Feminist Criticism, *Signs,* 6, no. 4 [Summer 1981]: 575-601, esp. 596-597). Almost twenty years of feminist scholarship have made it impossible not to recognize that historical experience is profoundly gender-specific, and Johnson's failure adequately to portray his character's femininity must be regarded as another disappointing and inaccurate aspect of *Jahrestage.*

26. Christa Wolf, "Selbstversuch," in *Unter den Linden: Drei unwahrscheinliche Geschichten* (Darmstadt: Luchterhand, 1974), p. 167.

27. Christa Wolf, *Kindheitsmuster* (Darmstadt: Luchterhand, 1979), p. 9. I am indebted to Sandra Frieden, "'In eigener Sache:' Christa Wolf's *Kindheitsmuster,*" *German Quarterly,* 54, no. 4 (November 1981): 473-487, for some of the ideas expressed here.

28. Ibid., p. 90.

29. Ibid., p. 358.

30. Christa Wolf, *Lesen und Schreiben: Neue Sammlung* (Darmstadt: Luchterhand, 1980), p. 45.

31. Uwe Johnson, *Berliner Sachen: Aufsätze* (Frankfurt am Main: Suhrkamp Verlag, 1975), p. 20. Johnson described this essay as "veraltet" in this edition of his essays; however, according to Ingeborg Hoesterey, Johnson told her that that designation referred to his description of Berlin and not to the essay's literary-theoretical assertions (Ingeborg Hoesterey, "Die Erzählsituation als Roman: Uwe Johnsons *Jahrestage*," *Colloquia Germanica*, 16, no. 1 [1983]: 25).

32. Peter Pokay, "Die Erzählsituation der *Jahrestage*," in Bengel, p. 294.

33. Neumann, p. 294.

34. Gerlach, p. 83.

35. Uwe Johnson, "Nachforschungen in New York: Rede bei der Entgegennahme des Georg-Büchner-Preises," *SZ am Wochenende: Feuilleton* (30/31 Oktober/1 November 1971), p. 1.

36. Uwe Johnson, "Über eine Haltung des Protestierens," in *Berliner Sachen*, pp. 95-96.

37. Ree Post-Adams, "Von Mecklenburg bis Manhattan: Amerikabilder in den 'Jahrestagen,'" *text + kritik*, p. 89.

38. Joachim Kaiser, "Für wenn wir tot sind: Zum Abschluß von Uwe Johnsons großer 'Jahrestage'-Tetralogie," in Bengel, p. 168.

D. G. Bond (essay date 1993)

SOURCE: Bond, D. G. "Identity." In *German History and German Identity: Uwe Johnson's* Jahrestage, pp. 164-96. Amsterdam: Rodopi, 1993.

[*In the following essay, Bond details the theme of German historical identity in Johnson's novels* Anniversaries: From the Life of Gesine Cresspahl *and* Skizze eines Verunglückten, *maintaining that the latter work is both an "antithesis" and "complimentary" to the former work. The critic adds that the value of* Skizze eines Verunglückten *lies in its complexity as an autobiographical text and "in its reflection . . . on the relationship between enlightenment and repression, reason and violence."*]

Es ist nicht die Zeit für Ich-Geschichten.

Max Frisch[1]

I. GERMAN IDENTITY

In his treatment of the Cap Arcona disaster in *Jahrestage* Johnson emphasizes that the Germans in Lübeck must have known very well what was going on; he thus suggests that they are implicated in the massacre, or even accomplices to it due to their passivity. Moreover, his use of his historical source is characterized by generalization of responsibility, for, as I have shown, Johnson writes of the Germans where Goguel uses the term Nazis. This generalization has considerable implications for the view of German history encountered in *Jahrestage* and in Johnson's other works of the 1970s and 1980s. A few further examples should illustrate what is meant.

In *Eine Reise nach Klagenfurt* Johnson ingeniously turns the equation round: whereas for Lübeck he wrote about the Germans, for Austria he uses the term Nazis. Here again Johnson is working from a particular historical source and adapting it in a way which may appear to make it more exact and which is also revealing when it comes to considering his view of the Third Reich. Here again it is important to note Johnson's creative use of document, in what is probably his most documentary text. He quotes the results of the Austrian plebiscite of 10 April 1938, which followed the 'Anschluß':

> Stimmberechtigt waren 4,484,000 Österreicher
>
> Für Hitler stimmten 4,453,000 Nazis
>
> Ungültig stimmten 5,776 Österreicher
>
> Gegen das Reich stimmten 11,929 Österreicher

(p. 41)

It is easy to miss what Johnson has done here, and a quick reading of *Eine Reise nach Klagenfurt* will fail to note the significance of the vocabulary. Johnson's source, which he himself names, is Gerhard Tomkowitz and Dieter Wagner's book *'Ein Volk, ein Reich, ein Führer!' Der 'Anschluß' Österreichs 1938*. There the election results are rendered as follows:

> Am 10. April gaben von den 4,484 Millionen stimmberechtigten Österreichern 4,453 Millionen ihr 'Ja' bei Hitlers Volksabstimmung ab. Das waren 97,73 Prozent. 5776 Zettel waren ungültig. 11 929 Österreicher stimmten mit 'Nein'.[2]

Johnson's figures are impeccable, but he has none the less fundamentally altered his source. By calling all the Austrians who voted for Hitler 'Nazis' and the few who did not 'Austrians' Johnson not only pays respect to those few who refused to swim with the tide but also provocatively demonstrates that the majority expressed their approval of the 'Anschluß'. The point made is exactly that which Johnson's use of the word 'Germans' in *Jahrestage* intends: in both cases it should be quite clear to what extent the great majority supported Hitler and the Third Reich.

There is undoubtedly a proximity to theories of collective guilt here, with which Johnson would most likely not have wished to be associated, due to the tendencies inherent in such theories to relieve the individual of particular guilt and the obvious danger of likening the perpetrator in an obvious position of power to the passive, 'ordinary' citizen. Johnson is not interested in offering possibilities to relativize guilt, but rather in forcing reflection on the magnitude of that guilt. This is a national and collective problem, but it is also one which, Johnson argues, each individual must come to terms with for him or herself.

It might be said that harsh judgements such as that which calls all the Austrians who voted 'yes' Nazis are based on a considerable lack of empathy for the historical experience of the 1930s and that Johnson's moral interpretation owes a lot to the advantage of his youth, even to the 'Gnade der späten Geburt'. In his collaboration with Margret Boveri on her autobiography *Verzweigungen,* published in 1977, Johnson's questioning of his elderly friend is at times aggressive, and particularly so when the issue of emigration is raised. Just as Gesine in *Jahrestage* is interested in why Cresspahl returned to Germany, Johnson wants to know why Boveri did not leave for good, but continued to work for the *Berliner Tageblatt.* He quotes a report about 'Rassenschande' from this newspaper and then quizzes Boveri on her own responsibility for the state of Germany in the 1930s: '*Sie haben durch Verbleiben in Deutschland und durch Berichten für Deutschland sich sowohl für Rassenschande-Urteile wie die Intervention in Spanien erklärt, in Form einer Stellungnahme.*'[3] This is certainly a provocative way of challenging Boveri and it forces her to think hard about her past; it is also a method with which Boveri herself agreed. Yet Johnson's comments do often verge on moral condemnation which appears not to appreciate the complexities of the personal and political motives behind Boveri's decision to stay. Johnson dismisses Boveri's discussion of her conviction at the time that she was not a supporter of the Nazis and that, within the limits imposed, she was able to retain integrity:

> *Das Deutschland, dem Sie sich zugehörig fühlten, war nicht das, in dem Sie aufgewachsen sind. Sie haben sich eine Lebensmöglichkeit geschaffen, in der Sie rundum sich zu umgeben trachteten mit einer Atmosphäre guter Taten, guter Freunde. Sie haben sich kleine Alibis verschafft durch eingeschmuggelte Adjektive oder Nebensätze. Im Zentrum immer Frau Boveri, die ihre nicht genau durchdachten, aber vorhandenen Bedürfnisse in dieser Art befriedigte. Das nenne ich amoralisch.*
>
> (p. 294)

Johnson is clearly aiming at a critique of the notion of 'innere Emigration', a critique which Boveri herself accepts (p. 292), although she also points out that perceptions of history have changed, that 'ein Bewußtsein von öffentlichem Gewissen' was not widespread at the time, whereas the younger generation, now faced with the

Vietnam war, has a much stronger sense of responsibility (p. 294). Thus Boveri indirectly identifies Johnson's own position as someone examining the Third Reich with a moral code of a later generation. Some reviewers of *Verzweigungen* reacted strongly against this, and defended the respected *grande dame* of German journalism against the young upstart. Christa Rotzoll's review is entitled programmatically, 'Margret Boveris Mut', and begins by saying that only readers who remember history from their own experience can appreciate Boveri's courage. Johnson is portrayed as a younger, left-wing interrogator who is determined to catch Boveri out from the outset.[4] Joachim Günther was more forthright, likening Johnson to an 'Entnazifizierungskomitee' and writing of 'Zwischenreden des Herausgebers von quälender Pedanterie'.[5] Margret Boveri may not have shared these criticisms herself; judging by Johnson's documentation of their collaboration in his afterword to *Verzweigungen* Boveri was challenged by Uwe and Elisabeth Johnson's questions, and sometimes disturbed by them, yet she also gained from these sessions (pp. 354-56). Boveri, it seems, was more willing to accept the moral interrogation of a representative of the next generation than were reviewers of *Verzweigungen*; both Rotzoll and Günter fail to take up the challenge and thus attempt to preserve the view of a noble and untarnished career in journalism.

Moreover, Boveri probably appreciated Uwe Johnson's position and character very exactly. He had approached her in 1968 when searching for information about the Third Reich for *Jahrestage,* about, as he writes, 'Ereignisse, die vorgefallen waren, lange bevor er [Johnson] sie sehen oder begreifen konnte' (p. 351). Gradually the Johnsons persuaded Boveri to write her autobiography, and in September 1970, when the work on *Verzweigungen* was well progressed, Boveri reviewed *Jahrestage* 1. Her comments were not only complimentary, praising the importance of the issue of political and individual conscience in *Jahrestage,* but also revealed aspects of her own experience with Johnson. She characterizes the author himself as 'ein Moralist, aber kein Eiferer'.[6]

Between Uwe Johnson and Margret Boveri respect was mutual.[7] [**"Besuch im Krankenhaus"**] Whereas he helped her to write her autobiography and spared her no pain in the process, she was a source of inspiration for his work on *Jahrestage.* For, although Johnson's questions in *Verzweigungen* do sometimes appear to represent preconceived moral judgements, he himself writes that all he wanted was to learn from her: 'Wir wollten es ganz einfach wissen' (*Verzweigungen*, p. 356). What he learnt was the value of experience, which precedes all moral judgement. In his afterword he cites a letter from Margret Boveri of 10 November 1970:

> Nur eins weiß ich, und das ist entscheidend und verändert alles: das Leben. Wir haben gelebt. Das war

das Stärkste, wenn wir, wenn ich es vielleicht auch im Augenblick mir nicht bewußt gemacht habe, wenn ich auch zuerst, 1933, gedacht habe: 'es ist alles aus, es gibt nur noch dagegen sein'. Es wurde wieder ein Leben und daraus dann das, was Sie als Nutznießertum ansehen—Sie haben allerdings das Wort nicht gebraucht. Wenn Sie Jerichow in den dreißiger Jahren beschreiben, wissen Sie, was ich meine, da ist das Leben, und die öffentlichen Verhältnisse, das Verhalten zu ihnen, ist nur ein Bruchteil davon.

(p. 355)

In *Jahrestage* the questions which appear to be central to Johnson's interest in the life of Margret Boveri recur, but they are not put as simply as they are in *Verzweigungen*. Rather here Johnson has done justice to the complexity of motivation, has taken into account what Boveri calls 'das Leben'. The prime example is Cresspahl, who returns to Germany as the Nazis are taking over power. The answer to the question why he did so is never formulated, but the narrative still answers it, as simply as could be imagined. In order to understand Cresspahl it is necessary to note that the question itself originates only after the event, when the history is known, and thus to appreciate that it may not be entirely appropriate: Cresspahl was returning to Germany and also to wife and daughter, and then to his own way of coming to terms with the political situation. The answer to the question why might just as well be: 'why not?'

The pattern Johnson-Boveri is also that which determines Gesine's relationship to the past in *Jahrestage*. It takes the form of the younger generation caught between an attempt to understand the past fairly and the instinct to pass moral judgement. The truth has to be somewhere between the two extremes: absolute understanding is absolute forgiveness, absolute (pre)judgement is blindness. This is a pattern which is constituted by a difference in age, and it would be unfair to talk of the 'Gnade der späten Geburt' in this respect, since it is perfectly legitimate that Johnson writes about the experience of his own generation, of the children who had to come to terms with their parents' history in their own way. Whenever Johnson's treatment of 'the Germans' appears absolute, be this is in *Jahrestage* or toward Margret Boveri, then this is because he is writing of his own experience too, as a German.

In his Frankfurt lectures, *Begleitumstände,* Johnson begins on poetics, as this lecture series envisaged, but quickly turns to his own experience of German history, with which virtually the whole of the book is concerned. In fact it appears that Johnson is here indirectly defining his poetics in terms of the relationship of his writing to German history and politics. He mentions that he was born in 1934 and then jumps eleven years, to the key year of 1945:

Mithin war ich fast elf Jahre alt, als ich meinem Staatsoberhaupt Adolf Hitler zum letzten Mal begegnete in einem mecklenburgischen Dorf. Vertrauensvoll und gerissen blickte er da in eine Gute Stube, als stünden keine Sowjets vor seinem Bunker, als sei der Reichssender Hamburg immer noch in grossdeutschen Händen statt in denen der Angelsachsen. Dann gilt als Kindermund die Frage, ob dieser Wandschmuck auch rechtzeitig abgehängt werde.

Die Antwort lautete: Das hat äe nich vedient, mein Kint.

(pp. 25-26)

Ironically Johnson refers to Hitler as his own head of state, and thus suggests that the child assumes the responsibility for something which was quite out of his own control. The child's perspective is merged with the adult's later knowledge of what was really going on, with the result that the adults of the older generation, who knew at the time what was happening, appear in a particularly unpleasant light. Whereas the child Johnson sensed that the picture of Hitler would have to go, his elders clung to their illusions right up to the last minute, and beyond. Johnson describes the situation whereby it was still a capital crime to remove pictures of Hitler up to the very moment when the Soviets marched in. Suddenly the picture is removed, its shadow covered by an innocuous print, and children are said to be far too young to understand why (p. 28). Yet Johnson suggests that as a boy his instinctive understanding of history was far better than that of his elders. The defeat of Germany could be seen in different ways:

[Die Erwachsenen nennen es:] Zusammenbruch, wohingegen Kinder schon beim Indianer- wie beim Geländespiel gelernt haben, dass es verloren heisst, und verloren bleibt. Die Erwachsenen sprechen von der völkerrechtlichen Pflicht der Besatzungsmächte, Deutschland zu erhalten in den Grenzen von 1937. Sie sind in den Krieg gezogen, haben für den Krieg gearbeitet, ohne seine erste Regel zu kennen: das Eroberte wird behalten. Die Ukraine als eine deutsche Provinz, sie wäre ihnen eben recht gewesen, aber die Sowjets, mit ihnen die Ukrainer, sollen ihnen Schlesien wiedergeben und Pommern und Westpreussen und Danzig und Ostpreussen. Auch ihre Zeitrechnung ist falsch. Sie sagen: Nach dem Zusammenbruch. Die Kinder wissen: Seit dem Ende des Bombens. Seit wir den Krieg verloren haben.

(p. 30)

The older generation, responsible for the Second World War, is still bound by egocentric, even narcissistic thinking. As Johnson implies, it will, in general, be up to the children to break radically with the past. Johnson may again seem harsh, for he offers these 'Erwachsenen' no room to make excuses, but he is so because of his own experience of history.

In the early schools of the Soviet zone of occupation Johnson was then provided with a further crucial experience, as the education included details of the Nazi extermination camps. He cites in *Begleitumstände* the report of the Nürnberg war crimes trials, at a point when details of Treblinka camp are being reviewed (pp. 43-47). The conclusion is that to be German is to be aware of guilt:

> Hinweise auf Bedenken beim Umgang mit der deutschen Sprache, leicht verständlich.
>
> Die Vorbereitung auf das Bild der Deutschen, das sie erwartet in der Welt, war gründlich und verlässlich.
>
> (p. 47)

This can be seen as the crux to Johnson's *oeuvre* from *Jahrestage* onwards, and it is only fair to say that, if as a result Johnson's interrogation of the older generation of Germans was inexorable, then his uncompromising manner was no less true of the standards by which he judged himself. Johnson was a German, and relentlessly aware of what that meant. In the apparently minor text **'Ach! Sie sind ein Deutscher'**, first published in 1978, Johnson puts it in a nutshell. A stranger visits Sheerness-on-Sea, and, because he is a German he is afraid to open his mouth: 'Dieser Deutsche war damals ein Kind [. . .]; er bleibt ein Deutscher, einer von den Feinden.'[8] To his great surprise he is treated kindly.

Johnson is not only hard on the older generation, he is also hard on himself, taking on the task that should have been theirs of facing German identity in the light of the Third Reich. His cameo appearance in *Jahrestage* should be seen in this light, for its significance as a comment on German identity is perhaps even greater than what it has to say about the narrative form of the novel. Johnson speaks before the Jewish American Congress in New York and tries to explain present West German insensitivity, as shown by such matters as appointments of former Nazis to governmental positions and the success of the extreme right-wing Nationaldemokratische Partei Deutschlands. This is not meant as a deliberate insult to the victims, but is simply forgetful, Johnson argues: 'Es mangele lediglich an Verständnis dafür, daß jede deutsche Regierung dieses Jahrhunderts gemessen werde an ihrer Distanz zum Establishment der Nazis' (p. 255).[9] The assembly before him reacts by openly recalling how their families died in the extermination camps, and Johnson, the younger German who cannot be held responsible, is none the less associated with German guilt.[10]

Gesine is in the audience when Johnson makes a fool of himself, and the chapter is narrated as if she were telling the story of his mistake. Thus it is here that the famous exchange concerning the narration of the novel occurs. I have considered this in my section on narrative form above (pp. 89-90), but it is none the less worth quoting again:

> *Wer erzählt hier eigentlich, Gesine.*

> *Wir beide. Das hörst du doch, Johnson.*
>
> (p. 256)

I take the 'wir beide' here to signify more than just the narrative fiction of the contract between author and character. On another level it also indicates the common identity of Johnson and Gesine as Germans. At this point Gesine is in charge and Johnson is in the hot seat; Gesine is given a break, as it were, from her task of representing the Germans for the rest of the world. She may well be pleased to see Johnson squirm, for he is just as hard on her as he is on himself: Gesine's identity in *Jahrestage* is determined by her nationality. It is Gesine who is confronted with Jewish exiles in New York, Gesine who is asked by friends and colleagues to explain the sometimes peculiar behaviour of Germans such as Hans Magnus Enzensberger or the insensitivity of contemporary German politicians, Gesine who prefers to speak English rather than German in public.

Johnson always denied that *Jahrestage* was in any way autobiographical—he had to do so in order to ensure the consistency of his convictions as to the independence of his characters. Yet the manner in which Johnson made this point is revealing. Whenever he was asked if Gesine was not also in some way a medium for his own experience, his arguments against this always centred on questions of detail: he got to know the Baltic Sea later than she did or his New York experiences are different from hers because she is a woman.[11] Asked whether Gesine is a 'Denk- und Spielfigur, hinter der sich Uwe Johnson verbirgt', Johnson replied as follows:

> Dieses Mißverständnis würde voraussetzen, daß ich eine von mir erfundene Person, der ich durch meine Erfindung Lebensmöglichkeit verschaffen wollte, verkrüppele und durch meine eigene Idee verändere. Dazu wäre ich nicht imstande. Ich würde mich jedenfalls darauf verlassen wollen, daß man Personen in einem Roman ebenso aufmerksam gegenübertritt wie Personen hier in einem Hotel, so daß man sie also nicht verwechselt mit Leuten, die ein anderes Geburtsjahr haben, die auf völlig andere Schulen gegangen sind, in völlig anderen Landschaften aufwuchsen.[12]

While Johnson may be justified in objecting to such formulations as 'Denk- und Spielfigur', his answer avoids addressing the real issue of an autobiographical dimension in *Jahrestage*. This misleading citation of the differences between himself and Gesine is even more conspicuous in *Begleitumstände*, in which Johnson addresses the 'Vorwurf des Autobiographischen' (p. 441), which, Johnson argues, disregards the reality ('Wirklichkeit') and the facts ('Tatsachen') of Gesine's life and his own, which he then lists (pp. 441-43). This backfires, however, for what it makes apparent are the similarities in these two biographies, rather than the differences in matters of detail. Gesine was born in North Germany in 1933, Johnson in 1934, their education was by no means completely different; both left the GDR, spent some time in West Germany or West Berlin and then in New York.[13] *Jahrestage* is an autobiographical work, but not in any simplistic sense, for Johnson is not telling the true story of his own life. Gesine's biography is, however, one way for Johnson to address a theme which is important in his own biography: that of German identity.

Christa Bürger has argued a similar point in her essay on Uwe Johnson, in which she quite rightly compares *Jahrestage* with Peter Weiss's *Die Ästhetik des Widerstands* in this respect. Bürger sees the fundamental experience of a generation which experienced the end of National Socialism as children as being one of loss and the disruption of biography: 'Gesine/Johnson und Peter Weiss/Roman-Ich der *Ästhetik des Widerstands* müssen schreibend erst sich eine Biographie schaffen, weil das, was sie gelebt haben, für sie keine Kontinuität ergibt.'[14] The reconstruction of the past which these novels undertake is thus both the fictional story of the principal character and also the exploratory autobiography, or, as Weiss put it, a 'Wunschautobiographie' of the author.[15] These novels are not straightforward autobiography because the integrated sense of identity which is the precondition for that is lacking. But they are autobiographical in that they explore this loss of identity and attempt to reconstruct an identity of what it is to be a German after the Third Reich.[16]

II. SKIZZE EINES VERUNGLÜCKTEN

In March 1991 the Israeli intellectual Yoram Kaniuk and Günter Grass publicly discussed German history, politics and the 1991 Gulf War in Berlin. The core of their disagreement was caused by Grass's critique of the war, which Kaniuk took as an indication of a poor consciousness of German responsibility towards Jews and the state of Israel. Kaniuk accused Grass of having failed to write about Jews in the context of German history:

> Fast die gesamte deutsche Nachkriegsliteratur der Schriftsteller, die selbst noch Juden gekannt oder mit Juden gelebt haben, ist judenrein; ich habe darauf hingewiesen, und das hat Grass geärgert. Obwohl er wußte, daß ich recht habe, berief er sich zum Beweis auf zwei Juden in seinen Büchern.[17]

The accusation may not be entirely fair, and the use of the word 'judenrein' even less so. There are non-Jewish post-war German writers who have written about Jews during the Third Reich, amongst them Günter Grass, although it cannot be denied that their images of Jews are not always unproblematical.[18]

It is certainly not possible to accuse Uwe Johnson of not having confronted German-Jewish history. From the time he began to deal in earnest with the theme of the

Third Reich he also began to write about Jewish characters. Johnson was provoked to do so by the experience of living in New York in 1967 and 1968, where he was able to observe the Jewish exile community, and sharpen his awareness of what it is to be German in the process. The first results of this process are visible in 'Ein Teil Von New York', in which Johnson notes the presence of the community of Jewish exiles (pp. 37-38, p. 50). He includes a portrait of a woman who is a model for Mrs. Ferwalter in *Jahrestage,* for both miss the taste of the bread of their former home in Carlsbad or Budweis (*Jahrestage,* p. 47; 'Ein Teil von New York', p. 38). Hannah Arendt was perhaps also influential at the time, as Johnson indicates in his obituary for his friend. He relates his memory of walking through a Jewish quarter with Arendt, who informed him of the professions and former places of residence in Germany of passers-by.[19] The result in *Jahrestage* is not only the Jewish characters Semig and the Tannebaums in Jerichow, but also the prominence of a discourse about the extermination camps, and a number of significant Jewish characters in the New York present. Kreslil, Mrs. Ferwalter, Mrs. Blumenroth and Dr. Rydz are the most important of these, whose life histories are told.[20] Jews in New York are so central to the novel and to Gesine's consciousness that Jewish public holidays are recorded in the chapter headings of the calendar of the days of the year 1967-68. Johnson also outlines what each festival symbolizes, so that this becomes a kind of history lesson for the German reader: the Jewish holidays in New York were once those of everyday German life too.[21]

In *Jahrestage* there is one minor character whose importance is only recognizable in the context of this complex of Jewish themes and through a number of cross-references in Johnson's *oeuvre.* Johnson's various uses of this character relate to his thematization of German history and also to the question of identity and autobiography in his later work. All of these issues are concentrated in a problematical late text, *Skizze eines Verunglückten,* first published in 1981 in a *Festschrift* for Max Frisch's seventieth birthday, and then as a slim book in 1982. I shall interpret this text in the following as a kind of antithesis and yet also complementary work to *Jahrestage.* In order to do so it is necessary to begin with some detective work, by tracing the origins of *Skizze eines Verunglückten* in the appearances of its principal character, the German Jew Joe Hinterhand, in *Jahrestage* 1 and 4 and in Johnson's important Büchner Prize address of 1971. I shall then continue by reviewing existing criticism on *Skizze eines Verunglückten* and the importance of the autobiographical dimension to this text, before finally offering my own reading.

In *Jahrestage* 1 Johnson describes the lives of old Jewish exiles on Broadway, their loneliness and their poverty: 'Ihnen ist nicht gelungen, Besitz aus Europa vor den Nazis zu retten' (p. 98). Their social contact is limited to sitting alone in cafés, and even this is precarious, since these cafés change hands when the lease runs out, and the old Jews are left with only the security of park benches. One of these old customers is described in more detail a little later on:

> Von dem alten Herrn, der uns durchs Fenster der Cafeteria zunickt, wissen wir nur, daß er uns regelmäßig anruft mit: Na Liebling! Er ist sehr sorgfältig gekleidet in seine verjährten Sachen, und im Jackenspalt ist zu sehen, daß ihm der Hosenbund bis dicht unter die Brustwarzen reicht. Sein Blick über die erhobene Tasse weg ist ganz leer gewesen, von einer anderen Ansicht gefüllt.
>
> (pp. 175-76)

Both these passages belong in the **'Ein Teil von New York'** complex of *Jahrestage,* since both follow on from the text which is lifted from that sociological essay. Thus it is possible to note again the significance of Johnson's own personal confrontation with Jewish exiles in New York. In terms of the fictional story of Gesine Cresspahl in *Jahrestage,* into which this confrontation has been incorporated, such Jewish exiles also represent Gesine again facing up to German history, for Gesine knows that these old exiles have remained victims of that history right up to the present. Gesine is, like Johnson in 1967 and 1968, a German in New York.

It is in the context of his discussion of the challenge that New York's Jewish population represents to a German in his Büchner Prize address of 1971 that Johnson again describes an old man. The date 1971 is important, for Johnson's own New York experience was still fresh, and work on *Jahrestage* was in full swing. In fact the Büchner Prize address can be seen as Johnson's most important statement about his stay in New York and about the major novel which that stay produced. Johnson discusses Gesine's relationship to German history, notes 'daß sie an den Verbrechen der Deutschen gegen die Juden noch beteiligt ist, und sei es als Angehörige der Kindgeneration nach der schuldigen'.[22] For Gesine, to whom the effects of German crimes are visible every day in New York, there is 'weiterhin eine jüdische Frage deutscher Art' (p. 59). This is the case for Johnson too, and he introduces his thumb-nail sketch of a Jew in New York by suggesting that he himself met this man:

> Es kann ihr [Gesine] geschehen wie dem Verfasser [Johnson], daß sie eines Abends am Broadway essen geht [. . .]. In den hunderter Straßen geht ein alter Mann abends in sein Restaurant. Es war mal seines. Jetzt ist es von Puertorikanern geführt; er hat sich von der Räumlichkeit nicht trennen können, reinlich und gut beleuchtet wie sie ist. Die Neuen haben von ihm gelernt, daß er abends immer nur Kaffee und Toast bestellt, aber sie antworten nicht richtig. Überhaupt ist es nicht richtig. Er hat seinen Stammplatz! mit dem

Rücken zum Straßenfenster. Sie wissen es; sie halten ihm den Platz nicht frei. [. . .] Wenn man wenig sagen kann den ganzen Tag über, sieht man am Abend krank aus. [. . .] Unterhält sich mit Toten. Deutsche dürfen die Toten allerdings nicht sein. [. . .] 1941, bei der Zeremonie zur Einbürgerung, haben die amerikanischen Beamten ihn davor gewarnt, die deutsche Staatsbürgerschaft abzulegen. Es könne sein, daß er Heimweh bekomme nach dem Ende des Kriegs. Heimweh.

> Bei solchen Zusammentreffen läßt Mrs. C. den größeren Teil ihres Essens stehen.
>
> (p. 59)

This anonymous man provides a further and here particularly convincing example of Johnson's and Gesine's sensitivity to the effects of the Third Reich. The character in the Büchner Prize address is almost certainly the same figure in *Jahrestage* 1, and if he is not then these are two men in very similar situations as exiles in New York, whose function of provoking a consciousness of German guilt is exactly alike.

A decade later, in 1981, Johnson devoted an independent text to the old man from the Büchner Prize address, *Skizze eines Verunglückten,* which begins with that earlier Büchner Prize sketch of a victim, dated '1971' and almost identical to the earlier text (p. 7).[23] His name is Joachim de Catt, and his pen-name and pseudonym Joe Hinterhand. Hinterhand appears by name in *Jahrestage* 4 also, as a local writer from Gneez, who was forced into exile by the Nazis (p. 1670, p. 1775). In a letter to Anita Gantlik of 13 July 1968 Gesine shows that she knows the essentials of Hinterhand's biography. He is introduced exactly as was the old man in *Jahrestage* 1 and in the Büchner Prize address: Gesine tells Anita that she went into a restaurant (Charlies Gutes EßGeschäft) on Broadway. She reads in the *New York Times* about kosher food, and thus this chapter of *Jahrestage* raises the Jewish theme before it tells Hinterhand's story. Then Gesine sees the Jew Joe Hinterhand:

> Damit ich doch keineswegs vergesse, in was für einer Stadt wir versuchen durchzukommen. Damit ich es mir hinfürder einpräge, rutschte mein Blick vom Rand der Zeitung auf den Nachbarn, vom Sehen wohlbekannt. Ein alter Mann, ein Augenwegwender, ein Beiseitetreter, den Nacken hält er immer wie eben geschlagen. Einer von denen, die sie . . . dachte ich: A victim. [. . .] [Ich ging gleich] hoch vom Hocker und tat für Charlie, seiner Gastlichkeit zuliebe, als habe unverhofft ein Übelbefinden mich überkommen.
>
> (pp. 1545-46)

Faced with this old man Gesine is unable to eat, exactly the reaction to the old Jew in a restaurant which Johnson had described as his own and Gesine's twelve years earlier in his Büchner Prize address.[24] A little later Gesine relates to Anita how the cause of Hinterhand's misery came up in conversation with D.E. and Marie. Gesine is asked (it is not clear whether by D.E. or Marie, although the wording sounds more like the latter): 'Haben die Deutschen den . . . fertig gemacht?' She answers: 'Das war eine Deutsche' and some lines later identifies Hinterhand: 'Lebt bloß noch so. Ehemals Deutscher. [. . .] de Catt mit Namen' (p. 1548).

These lines from *Jahrestage* tell the plot of *Skizze eines Verunglückten in nuce*: Hinterhand has a German-Jewish background and his misery is caused by his discovery of his wife's unfaithfulness. He murders her, spends many years in prison and then waits to die in New York. Because Joe Hinterhand is the character from the Büchner Prize address this later story of a broken marriage and of violence originates, in a sense, in the theme of Jewish exiles provoking reflections on German history. This is the theme which Johnson first raised in **'Ein Teil von New York'**, made a fundamental part of *Jahrestage,* and then most strongly outlined in the Büchner Prize address. Whether Joe Hinterhand and the old exile Gesine sees in a café in *Jahrestage* 1 are intended to be identical or not is irrelevant, for the connection to the thematic complex of German-Jewish exiles in New York is made through the Büchner Prize address, a passage from which Johnson puts on the first page of *Skizze eines Verunglückten.*[25] Hinterhand is Johnson's most intensely drawn German-Jewish character, and *Skizze eines Verunglückten* by dint of this a complex and contradictory text. For, like *Jahrestage,* this work is autobiographical, though in a completely different sense.

Peter Bürger wrote of the creative use of autobiography in modernist literature, whereby autobiographical elements of particular works are not a matter of simple correspondence between the fiction and the life of the author. In *Skizze eines Verunglückten* Johnson comes very close to such simple correspondence, and yet retains that element of invention: this is Johnson's 'Wunschautobiographie', or, as Bernd Neumann has put it, his 'fiktive (und doch wieder auch partiell eingelöste) Schreckens-Biographie'.[26] In 1975 Johnson suffered a heart attack, with the result that his work on *Jahrestage* was halted by writer's block for several years. In 1979 he concluded his Frankfurt lectures by explaining what had happened. He revealed that his wife, Elisabeth, had had a liaison with a member of the Czechoslovakian secret service, which began in 1961 and lasted almost fifteen years (*Begleitumstände,* pp. 451-53). Johnson says that his heart attack and the writer's block were a result of discovering this in 1975. The important Czechoslovakian element of *Jahrestage,* which Elisabeth Johnson had helped to research and write, was disrupted, for the betrayal was not just sexual, but political, since Johnson's work on Czechoslovakia was called into question by this connection with the enemy.[27] Johnson did not stop working altogether, since he did publish his edition of Philipp Otto Runge's *Von dem Fischer un*

syner Frau in 1976 (surely a comment on his own situation), *Verzweigungen* in 1977 and numerous minor texts during these years. His major work had ceased, however, and it was only with the Frankfurt lectures in 1979 that Johnson's return to that work began. Even then it was a slow process: Johnson needed almost as long to finish the final volume of *Jahrestage* as he had to write the first three.

That there is autobiography in *Skizze eines Verunglückten* cannot be denied; that it is only autobiography is too simple. Siegfried Unseld, Johnson's publisher and friend, has attempted to explain the break in the work on *Jahrestage* and Johnson's early death very much in Johnson's own terms, as caused by his broken marriage. He describes his own attempts to help Johnson out of his deep depression by encouraging him to write again. Unseld persuaded Johnson to lecture in Frankfurt, and he was also influential in getting Johnson to write *Skizze eines Verunglückten,* arguing with Johnson that he should attempt to overcome his problem by writing about it, because 'der Schriftsteller eine Person sei, die ihr Leben nicht anders als schreibend zu bestehen vermöge'.[28] Yet Unseld confuses Johnson's biography and his literature when he quotes from *Skizze eines Verunglückten* as if he were repeating Johnson's own words, and without even noting the source in the literary work, in which the speaker is Joe Hinterhand.[29] Other critics have made the same simplistic use of this text, none more unsatisfactorily than Tilman Jens in his book about Johnson's life and death in Sheerness, in which Johnson's works are all viewed as no more than material for a biography.[30]

Because of Johnson's own public pronouncement in *Begleitumstände* most critical writing—there is not a great deal—on *Skizze eines Verunglückten* has concentrated on debating its autobiographical content and thus almost entirely on its thematization of broken marriage. Reviewers in *Der Spiegel* and *Die Zeit* (Fritz J. Raddatz) did little to avoid giving the impression that this text is Johnson's confession; the former wrote of 'Johnson-Hinterhand', the latter that Johnson has survived the crisis and produced a masterful story as a result.[31] Johnson himself objected to this direct reduction of *Skizze eines Verunglückten* to the story of his own life, although he was partially responsible for it through the manner in which he concluded his Frankfurt lectures. None the less he heavily criticizes 'der klatschselige Raddatz' and lists the reasons why this text is not autobiographical. Amongst these are the fact that it was written for Max Frisch, which I shall return to in some detail below: for now it suffices to note that this work certainly makes a different impression in its original surroundings, along with many other tributes to Frisch. Johnson also cites the fact that the text is written largely in the subjunctive as evidence against a simple autobiographical reading, and the origin of the story of Hinterhand in the Büchner Prize address.[32] This is one matter which Johnson criticism has ignored, preferring instead to continue discussing the autobiographical aspect of the failed marriage. Theo Buck attempted to draw attention away from the autobiography and towards the form of the text, when he—as the first commentator to do so—appealed for the prominent role of the subjunctive mood in *Skizze eines Verunglückten* to be recognized.[33] Bernd Neumann promptly dismissed this as an argument with no more substance than the 'Charme der Treuherzigkeit', and insisted that *Skizze eines Verunglückten* was an autobiography.[34] Michael Bengel discussed *Skizze eines Verunglückten* in his article on Johnson's poetics, arguing for the distance between the real world and literature. Even in this seemingly most confessional of texts, that distance must be recognized.[35] Marlis Becher has provided the most detailed list of the points of comparison between the life of Uwe Johnson and the fictional biography of Joe Hinterhand, without, however, arguing that *Skizze eines Verunglückten* is pure autobiography. Important stages in the lives of Johnson and Hinterhand can be compared to each other, the main difference being that for Hinterhand these take place a generation (twenty-eight years) earlier.[36] Yet the complex form of *Skizze eines Verunglückten,* to which Becher's study is devoted, belies the autobiographical elements, and demands that the interplay of different voices in the text be acknowledged. Kurt Fickert's more recent essay on *Skizze eines Verunglückten* argues far more simplistically that Johnson's text is autobiographical:

> Obgleich das verräterische Wort 'ich' außer Sicht bleibt, handelt es sich ganz offensichtlich in der *Skizze eines Verunglückten* um autobiographische Bekenntnisse aus Johnsons Leben und literarischem Schaffen.[37]

These 'Bekenntnisse', according to Fickert, show that Johnson's experience with adultery caused him to lose his confidence as a man and as an author. Fickert goes on to claim that Johnson's achievement in *Skizze eines Verunglückten* is to have written a text in which questions of individual identity are central, and autobiography and fiction are redefined. Here Johnson and Frisch are both following a trend in contemporary writing, the 'Tendenz [. . .], die Seele [. . .] in die Mitte des Weltalls zu rücken oder die Wahrheit der Existenz durch eine Verinnerlichung des Weltalls zu ergründen' (p. 50). This sort of pretentious and meaningless comment is what transpires when the critic fails to examine critically the writer's investigation of subjectivity.

The readings of *Skizze eines Verunglückten* offered by Johnson scholarship are characterized by an utter lack of critical imagination.[38] (I exclude Becher here, whose aim is not to interpret, but to illuminate linguistic form.) It is otiose to continue arguing whether or not the text is an autobiographical story of a broken marriage and

writer's block. Of course the text is autobiographical in this sense, and it does not require much intelligence to realize that: the name Joachim Catt was a pseudonym which Johnson almost used in 1959 for *Mutmassungen über Jakob.*[39] Johnson felt doubly betrayed because his wife's—alleged—adultery was with a Czech enemy; in Hinterhand's case it is an Italian fascist who fulfils this role of the enemy. But noting the autobiographical element can only be the first step towards interpretation, for which it is necessary to accept the text in its own right, if the danger of being banal is to be avoided. For there can be no more banal register in literary criticism than that which reduces the text to an argument about the author's life, thus ignoring aspects which may otherwise challenge the reader. An interpretation of *Skizze eines Verunglückten* would have to take into account aspects which transcend the simplistic autobiographical level. In my analysis I wish to concentrate on two: this text's thematization of German history and its presentation of a humanist project. Both these issues are also autobiographical in that they are the great concerns of Johnson in *Jahrestage,* as I have argued in this thesis, but they are no longer dependent on a discourse on autobiography which is forever uncomfortably close to gossip and indiscretion.

German history becomes a theme in *Skizze eines Verunglückten,* because, like all of Johnson's later major texts, it tells the biography of a German in the twentieth century. This biography is introduced as 'Berichtigungen, Ausführungen, Auskünfte und Nachträge' (p. 9) to the sketch of a broken old man given in the Büchner Prize address of 1971. The text proper begins by explaining how Hinterhand came to settle in New York after coming out of prison in 1957, but it does not say why he was in prison. It then continues with the story of his life from early childhood, and the theme of German history is introduced via a discussion of Hinterhand's uncertain Jewish background: 'Was Judentum oder Jüdisches angehe, so verübe jene erste Skizze an ihm wohl eher einen Augenschein nach Hörensagen' (p. 12). 'Jene erste Skizze' is the text of 1971, in which the old man is certainly Jewish. Hinterhand believes, however, that in his youth he cast off any Jewish identity 'in religiöser und behördlicher Hinsicht' (p. 12), so that the question was never relevant. It is not even certain that Hinterhand was born Jewish, for he was left outside an orphanage at the age of two months, with a sign naming him Jochim de Catt, was then given a protestant baptism and the less Jewish sounding name Joachim and received no Jewish education whatsoever. But de Catt grows up with that element of doubt: the nurses at the orphanage suspected that he might be Jewish, he tells his future wife that this may be the case, and in 1931 he publishes a book under a pseudonym which furthers his Jewish reputation. He chose the name Joe Hinterhand, which the Nazi press falsely takes to be Jewish; his books are heavily criticized as the products of a seditious Jewish intellectual, and in 1933 he is forced to emigrate. Here the first of many Max Frisch themes in *Skizze eines Verunglückten* is raised: Hinterhand becomes the victim of the image which others make of him, the image of a Jew, which no longer requires a grounding in truth to justify the persecution which it entails. As Frisch had demonstrated in his parable *Andorra*, every potential victim is a potential Jew: Andri is, like de Catt, taken to be an orphan and a Jew, and gradually incorporates the anti-Semitic images of Jews into his own identity. A similar motif also occurs in Günter Grass's *Aus dem Tagebuch einer Schnecke*, in which the teacher Zweifel is himself not Jewish, but, because of the help he gives to Danzig's Jews, has associated himself with the Jews to the point of identifying with them, and has to spend the war years in hiding.

Hinterhand, therefore, is another character in Johnson's *oeuvre* whose biography has been destroyed by the Nazis: he spends years of exile in England and then in the United States, where he concentrates on campaigning against the Third Reich and getting American support for this cause. The text thus begins with the theme of German history, due to the inclusion of the sketch from the Büchner Prize address which deals with a German-Jewish exile, and in its following narration of Hinterhand's life to 1933. It does not reveal the reason for his imprisonment until much later on, in section 7 (pp. 50-57). The reader acquainted with Johnson's work and without prior knowledge of the plot of *Skizze eines Verunglückten* might expect this text to continue to develop the historical theme as told through the biography of a victim. Instead the plot takes an unexpected turn, or at least one which could have been unexpected if Johnson and his critics had not drawn so much attention to the autobiographical story of adultery. For what now follows is a story about intersexual relations which is both familiar and yet unusual in Johnson's *oeuvre*.

All of Johnson's novels tell love stories: those of Ingrid and Klaus (and Jürgen) in *Ingrid Babendererde*, of Gesine and Jakob (and Jonas Blach) in *Mutmassungen über Jakob*, of Karin and Achim (and Karsch) in *Das dritte Buch über Achim*, of B. and D. (and the German Democratic Republic) in *Zwei Ansichten* and of Gesine and Jakob (and D.E.) in *Jahrestage*. In *Zwei Ansichten* the 'love' story is that of a false love, and the novel therefore devotes so much space to portraying the lies and illusions of the major characters; in *Das dritte Buch über Achim* relationships have lost any love that may once have been present, and thus the theme is hardly developed. In the other three novels love is a major theme and plays a crucial role in the lives of the characters, with the characteristic threesome of desired woman, preferred man and potentially jealous man prominent in each case.[40] This unhappy triad is repeated in *Skizze eines Verunglückten*, with Hinterhand, his

wife and her Italian lover, whose names we never discover. The difference lies in the way in which this story of love and jealousy is told, and in the way in which the jealous man deals with his problem. The first two novels portray an ideal situation, where the jealousy is never spoken, the love needs no words, and the characters can retain their integrity and mutual respect. Similar respect and integrity are essential components of the characters' discourse on love and desire in *Jahrestage*. In these works the essential words on love are situated between the lines, or told in brief and chaste moments of truth. In *Skizze eines Verunglückten* Johnson has developed the theme of jealousy which was his own from the beginning, and written of a very different reaction to it from the stoicism of which Jürgen Petersen or Jonas Blach were capable. In so doing he has written a work which is based on the confessional form, and which is replete with outspoken definitions of what an ideal love should be, producing a quite uncharacteristic protracted discourse on intersexual relations. In the terms of the Max Frisch connection, it is not only the themes of jealousy and of murder motivated by jealousy, dealt with in *Stiller, Mein Name sei Gantenbein* or *Biographie. Ein Spiel*, which Johnson draws on, but also the form of a confession. Joe Hinterhand is similar to one of Frisch's first-person narrators, and the confession he gives to the narrator of *Skizze eines Verunglückten* can be likened to that of the narrator of Frisch's *Montauk*, a text which Johnson admired for its mixture of autobiography and fiction.[41]

The discourse about love in *Skizze eines Verunglückten* comprises—at first sight at least—entirely Joe Hinterhand's views and experiences. He tells of his marriage and of the betrayal, and he tells what his ideal love should be like. His childhood experiences were crucial:

> Siebzehn Jahre lang als Pflegekind unterwegs in wechselnden Haushalten, Zeuge der Verletzungen, die ein Mann und eine Frau einander antun können, habe er eine Vorstellung vom Leben in einer Ehe für sich selbst noch einmal erfinden müssen, eine anachronistische in einer Zeit, da der Ehebruch zum bürgerlichen Schwank verkommen sei.

> (p. 20)

Hinterhand's anachronistic ideal of marriage contains a number of absolutes: absolute fidelity and honesty, absolute support and symbiosis. In his wife he believes he has met the 'counterpart soul' of which Plato writes in his *Symposion*, and not just the 'other half' of meaningless vernacular (p. 21). Thus Hinterhand the orphan derives his identity from this relationship:

> Mit der Summe seines Lebenslaufs aber habe er ihr ausgeliefert, was in seiner Person die Mitte zusammengesetzt habe, jenen Ort im Bewußtsein, von dem aus und in dem der einzelne Mensch das Wort Ich zu

denken wagt, das Geheimnis des Individuums, die einzig unersetzliche und unheilbare Stelle in ihm, wofür man früher das Wort Seele gebraucht habe [. . .]. Und es sei ihm diese Mitteilung vorgekommen weder als Opfer noch als Verlust, im Gegenteil, als sichere Bewahrung.

(pp. 24-25)

In the light of this faith Hinterhand's identity as an antifascist campaigner, even as a German 'Jew', means very little: what really holds him together is his wife. Thus when he discovers her betrayal he interprets this as an attack on his public persona too, since her adultery was with an Italian fascist (pp. 50-51). He murders her because his entire identity is threatened, including that as a writer: this lie that he has unwittingly been living makes of his wife 'die Drohung, die Gültigkeit der Worte abzuschaffen' (p. 56), and makes all his memories of the past '*Unwahr. Falsch. Vergiftet. Entwertet. Ungültig*' (p. 68).[42] From the time of his release from prison Hinterhand never regains any positive identity, but has invented his own form of death penalty, 'abzuleisten durch Ableben' (p. 76).

Peter von Matt is one writer on *Skizze eines Verunglückten* who has offered a convincing interpretation of the text as text rather than as information about Uwe Johnson's marriage, and it is probably symptomatic that he comes from outside the realms of established Johnson research. In the final chapters of his book *Liebesverrat. Die Treulosen in der Literatur* von Matt discusses Tolstoy's 'The Kreutzer Sonata', Max Frisch's texts 'Skizze eines Unglücks' and 'Glück' and Johnson's *Skizze eines Verunglückten,* all tales of jealous men murdering women. For von Matt they all testify to the divide between the various possible explanations for these violent acts, be these psychological or legal, and the experience of the subject who commits them. The individual is forced to invent his own norms at a time when traditional values are breaking down: Joe Hinterhand defines his own terms of marriage 'ganz allein gegen alle Welt'.[43] When these subjective norms are violated he murders his wife, and is quite immune to the court of law which tries him, for his real punishment is his loss of identity. Von Matt notes that the autobiographical content of *Skizze eines Verunglückten* is liable to draw attention away from its real significance, which does not lie in its value as a document about the life of Uwe Johnson, but, along with Tolstoy's and Frisch's texts, as a story illuminating the isolation of the modern individual forced to invent his own morality: 'Die Geschichten von Trostlosigkeit, Verrat und Rache [. . .] sind [. . .] dramatische Untersuchungen über die Einsamkeit des moralischen Subjekts in der Moderne' (p. 419).

Von Matt's interpretation of *Skizze eines Verunglückten* is certainly acceptable within the terms of his investigation, and yet also incomplete in a number of respects. He does not consider the concrete historical setting of *Skizze eines Verunglückten* in pre-Nazi Germany and post-Nazi exile. Nor does he view Hinterhand's self-avowedly anachronistic project of marriage critically. Von Matt accepts Hinterhand's norms as subjective and thus beyond criticism, and, apart from reading murder as an expression of isolation, he has nothing to say about the fact that this is a story of violence. A more critical view of Hinterhand's values is essential to an understanding of this text, which itself provides a number of hints that Hinterhand's words should not be accepted lightly. It is one of the major faults of Johnson criticism to fail to assess properly the causes of Hinterhand's identity crisis, because this is also seen as Johnson's own, and it is also stunning that no one has taken seriously the violence of the act of murder. The problem is reminiscent of a much older and now classical one concerning literature and autobiography: Goethe wrote the story of an unrequited love and suicide in *Die Leiden des jungen Werther,* but he did not commit suicide himself. To see *Werther* as only autobiographical would be to ignore the crucial act of violence which marks the difference between autobiography and fiction. The same weaknesses are encountered in Johnson criticism: Johnson did not murder his wife, whereas his fictional character Joe Hinterhand did, and yet critics still manage to ignore the violence. Von Matt's commentary, although he argues against reducing *Skizze eines Verunglückten* to autobiography, displays a similar weakness when he fails to look behind the violent act.

Skizze eines Verunglückten offers the means to gain distance from Hinterhand in its complex narrative form, and thus also the means to go beyond a simplistic autobiographical reading. Even if there are elements of Johnson's own experience in the story of Hinterhand these are presented at a distance, and so it would only be fair to say that Johnson himself must have been able to see his own crisis critically. Hinterhand's confession, which is the basis for the text, is not permitted to stand alone: he may provide most of the information, but he does not provide the form in which this is conveyed. Much of the text consists of Hinterhand's version of events as reported in the subjunctive by a narrator, so that there are two major voices collaborating in the production or even competing for control of the text. The result is that Hinterhand's words are never without a second relativizing and perhaps doubting voice. Within these two major voices are countless others, including the opening sketch of 1971, the Nazi view of Hinterhand, the brief utterances of friends and neighbours during Hinterhand's life, the voice of the court of law, and the voices of the many writers whom Hinterhand quotes on the subject of marriage. This polyphonic text contains a myriad of different views of Hinterhand, all contained within what deceptively appears to be just his own narrative. Acknowledging this is to begin to refuse to accept what Hinterhand has to say.

A critique of Hinterhand's anachronistic view of marriage, or, in von Matt's terms, of the moral code which he has had to reinvent for himself, need not originate in images from outside the text, although these will obviously always have some influence. The text itself provides enough material: Hinterhand draws on a number of witnesses from intellectual history, from Plato to Ernst Bloch, whose comments he keeps close at hand on index cards. They should serve to support his image of the ideal marriage and of his own predicament. The texts which he uses reveal exactly what is anachronistic about his ideals: Bloch is used to prove that the woman ('das Weib') desires only to have her existence justified through the successful creative production of the man (pp. 25-26); Kandinsky demonstrates that he has become dependent on his wife knowing everything about him (p. 43); Marie Luise Kaschnitz proves that the writer's wife is his only 'Verbindung mit der Welt' (p. 44). It is the weakness of male identity which is crucial in these quotations, and thus Johnson is following a theme of Max Frisch's here too. Without his wife Hinterhand has no identity, and yet the image he has of her is also an utter illusion, even to the extent that the son he thought his own was probably begotten by her lover (p. 64). Hinterhand's wife is his connection to the world in more ways than one: she helped him revise his first book (p. 25), and she is also indispensable as someone who can type up his manuscripts, as the voices of their Folkestone neighbours note: 'Im Grunde beide Schriftsteller; er mit der Hand, sie für ihn an der Maschine. Wären alle Ehen so' (p. 37). The last sentence is ambivalent: it may signify admiration for what seems a perfect match, yet it may also be an expression of incomprehension at the dangerous way in which the Hinterhands seem to run their affairs. In *Jahrestage* Johnson had already written about a marriage with similar division of labour, at least as far as the work of writing is concerned. The critical view in *Jahrestage* of the way in which Frederick Fleury misuses his wife Annie, so that she eventually leaves him for a long period (pp. 153-56 and pp. 564-67), is a useful subtext for Hinterhand's uncritical resumé of his own marriage and his behaviour towards his wife in *Skizze eines Verunglückten.* One might even argue that, like the Fleurys, the Hinterhands are a negative model pair. It would certainly be difficult to imagine a woman like Gesine Cresspahl putting up with a man like Joe Hinterhand.

Skizze eines Verunglückten gives virtually no voice to Hinterhand's unnamed wife. This has to be seen as symptomatic of the crisis: Hinterhand wishes to eradicate her from his consciousness and thus cannot speak her name, let alone see the past from her point of view. Yet an attempt to reconstruct the marriage before the disaster from the sparse evidence given indicates the extent of Hinterhand's illusion: in order to secure identity for himself he creates an image of his wife which derives more from his reading of the classics than from reality. She, it seems, is not entirely at ease with the situation, is not keen to hurry into following Hinterhand to Britain and then America, and is often on her own in Europe. It is only possible to surmise what her image of an ideal marriage might be: at any rate it would allow her independence, and perhaps, as Max Frisch's ideal would have it, not imprison her in any particular image. In one of the few moments when she is permitted to speak (indirectly), this is exactly her criticism of her husband, and it becomes a criticism of his violent act: 'Des weiteren sei er überzeugt, Mrs. Hinterhand habe die Tat gewünscht, indem sie ihm vorhielt, er selbst trage die Verantwortung für das Bild, das sie ihm von sich selbst gemacht habe' (p. 54). Hinterhand created the image of his wife which he needed, and she did her best not to destroy his illusion. When that illusion was finally destroyed, then this was reason enough for Hinterhand to murder his wife. To attempt to see the matter from her point of view would be to acknowledge Hinterhand's own guilt: the image he made of her clearly offered her little room for own experience. This intolerance is latent in most of the views of the classics which Hinterhand cites, and one further reference to a great writer of the past makes the point absolutely clear. Hinterhand punishes himself by looking at photographs of his former life, in order to remain forever aware of the false image he held of his wife. One such photograph shows her returning from the post office in Folkestone, where she has arranged to collect the post so that her husband's work is not disturbed by the postman. Now Hinterhand knows the real reason for her concern about the post: it was so that she was able to receive letters from her lover, which she hid in a secret place in her desk (p. 62). The later discovery of hidden love letters is a motif from Fontane's *Effi Briest,* itself a classic story of jealousy and violence.[44] Hinterhand himself refers to *Effi Briest* during his trial, to explain why he murdered his wife and why he did so some time after he had known of her adultery, when the affair became public. The result of publicity was 'das Innstetten-Syndrom' and 'Buchstabieren des Namen Wüllersdorf' (p. 53). Wüllersdorf is Innstetten's second in the duel with Effi's lover Crampas, and he is also the character with whom Innstetten discusses the pros and cons of the duel. They decide that a duel is unavoidable because honour must be upheld. In the same way Hinterhand explains his violence as a defence of his honour once his wife's affair has been made public. Here Hinterhand again uses a motif from the classics to justify his behaviour, and again this backfires and works against him. For in the terms of this comparison Hinterhand is Innstetten and his wife Effi: clearly neither Innstetten nor the sort of relationship he controls can be a plausible ideal for marriage. Thus the text here hints at a level beyond Hinterhand's consciousness, and there is perhaps a sense in which Hinterhand is very like Innstetten, since neither of them seem to have any awareness of nor interest in the experience of their wives.

The marital norms which Hinterhand reinvents for himself are more than just anachronistic: they are those of a male relic. Peter von Matt has discussed these in terms of the isolation of the moral subject in modernism, yet without considering the sexual roles in question. It is quite possible and justifiable to interpret *Skizze eines Verunglückten* and Frisch's 'Skizze eines Unglücks' and 'Glück' as texts which reflect not on the abstract issue of the destruction of binding values in the modern age, but on the disintegration of male control over women. The male reaction is violence, and thus *Skizze eines Verunglückten* becomes a study of male violence. No critic has faced this issue to date, simply because it would be impossible to do so if the text is seen only for its autobiographical value. Johnson did not murder his wife, and I do not know whether he was violent in any way or not. That is not the issue at stake here either: what is important is that Johnson chose to write about his own autobiographical experience of a failed marriage by writing a fictional text about murder. This decision, which again places *Skizze eines Verunglückten* in dialogue with works by Max Frisch, takes Johnson's text well beyond autobiography.

One of the greatest problems which Hinterhand's violent act poses is that of how to relate it to his stand against fascism, which can be seen as the epitome of all violent oppression. Moreover Hinterhand is himself a victim of that oppression, as a 'Jewish' exile. Hildegard Baumgart has included comment on *Skizze eines Verunglückten* in her psychological study of jealousy, and she rightly notes the paradox of Hinterhand's action:

> Welche Gewalttätigkeit eines Menschen, der sein Leben dem Kampf gegen die faschistische Gewalt verschrieben hat, welche ungeheure Anmaßung eines, der bewußt nichts weiter will, als sich dienend einer als richtig erkannten Sache unterordnen. Jemand, der sich der Wahrheit verschrieben hat, kann auf fremde Wahrheit nur antworten: Weil du anders bist, mußt du sterben.[45]

Later in her study Baumgart offers a psychological explanation of the phenomenon. Hinterhand is an orphan and has not undergone the oedipal experience of accommodating the loss of the hope of realizing a desire for the mother. The result is that he expects illusory absolutes and cannot see the real woman (pp. 194-95). This interpretation can be supported by Hinterhand's own comments that the Oedipus conflict is unreal for him, since he was brought up by a series of foster parents (pp. 70-71). Whilst it may be possible to explain Hinterhand's violence psychologically, and it is certainly valid to note that simply being against fascism does not make anyone immune to violence themselves, this sort of explanation does not define the whole challenge of the text. That challenge can be identified as the way in which *Skizze eines Verunglückten* deals with the reverse side of a humanist project.

The humanism in question is Hinterhand's anti-fascism, and also his attempt to construct the ideal marriage, drawing, as he does, on a number of important humanist thinkers in this endeavour. The insight which *Skizze eines Verunglückten* seems to offer is that this project runs according to the dialectics of the Enlightenment. It is repressive, allowing no room for the irrational and the violent within the individual, who is thus himself a victim of his own ideals. He is also forced to repress that which does not fit into the plan, in this case a woman. Heiner Müller interprets Louis Althusser's murder of his wife in a similar way: the contemporary critical intellectual is faced with the increasing irrelevance of his system of thought to the realm of action. Under these circumstances, Müller suggests, violence is action: 'Das erste Ereignis im Leben von Althusser war die Ermordung seiner Frau. Das spricht allerdings gegen seine Biographie als Denker.'[46] The murder is the reverse side of the humanist project, or the backlash of enlightenment.

This formula can be found at a prominent place on the penultimate pages of *Skizze eines Verunglückten.* It is the most important of all the references to Max Frisch, a quotation from *Mein Name sei Gantenbein,* which Johnson had already put at the end of his anthology of excerpts from Frisch in 1975:

> Er [Hinterhand] halte sich an einen Befund, den MAX FRISCH vor elf Jahren veröffentlicht habe: es sei nicht die Zeit für Ich-Geschichten. Auch er habe einmal sich bemüht, einzelne Personen nur zu zeigen in ihrem Zusammenhang mit mehreren, in der Einrichtung der Gesellschaft, und sei Geschichten aus dem Wege gegangen, wenn sie ihm befangen schienen in nur einem Menschen, oder zweien, müßig, unverantwortlich, unstatthaft. Und doch, so die Antithese, vollziehe das menschliche Leben sich am einzelnen Ich, oder verfehle sich daran. Nirgends sonst.
>
> (pp. 74-75)[47]

This is Hinterhand's own bitter experience: thinking that his personal identity was secure by dint of his wife's love and support, he devoted his energies to social and political issues, only to find neglected personal concerns strike back with a vengeance. Thus Hinterhand is forced to experience the dilemma of enlightenment at first hand, and it should not be forgotten that it is his wife who bears the consequences.

It is also legitimate to see this quotation from Frisch as a comment made by Uwe Johnson on his own situation, and on his own literary work. In his foreword to *Stich-Worte* Johnson wrote how he read and admired *Stiller* in 1957:

> Das ist jemand [Johnson], der im Jahre 1957 zum ersten Mal ein Buch von ihm, *Stiller,* in die Hand bekommen hat und mit Neid feststellte, daß ein Mann der westlichen deutschsprachigen Literatur sich beschäftigen darf mit den Schwierigkeiten subjektiver Identität.
>
> (p. 7)

Here Johnson is referring to the dominant parameters of GDR literature and literary politics of the 1950s, and alluding to the fact that such a subjective slant as in *Stiller* was not possible in the GDR, where he himself was still trying to write and publish. Yet this comment has a further significance with regard to Johnson's *oeuvre,* for even when he moved West and began to publish novels, Johnson did not turn to the theme of subjective identity. On the contrary, he remained true to the first half of the equation in the important quotation from *Mein Name sei Gantenbein,* always relating the subject to his or her social environment, concentrating on political and historical themes and on political and historical identity. Johnson's main interest was that which he gave to the writer Karsch in the project of writing a biography in *Das dritte Buch über Achim,* and in **"Eine Reise wegwohin, 1960"**, to find out 'wie viel eine Person enthielt an Geschichte der gesellschaftlichen Verhältnisse, der Kampfmethoden, des Anstands, an Mitlebenden' (*Karsch, und andere Prosa,* p. 45). This is the case with all of Johnson's major works, including the most important of them all, *Jahrestage,* in which Gesine's identity is that of a German after the Third Reich.[48] As I have argued above this is the most pressing issue for Johnson in *Jahrestage* and the associated works, and it dominated his literary production from the late 1960s onwards: until, perhaps, the 'Ich-Geschichte' raised its head in 1975, Johnson suffered a heart attack, and the break in his work set in. The insight from *Mein Name sei Gantenbein* is thus both a comment on the state of Johnson's work from 1975, and on his own personal crisis.

With *Begleitumstände* Johnson began his return to his own literary work, and he did so by writing his own autobiography. Yet this is an autobiographical text which relates the subject to his historical environment throughout, having begun with the warning that: 'Das Subjekt wird hier lediglich vorkommen als das Medium der Arbeit, als das Mittel einer Produktion./ Damit ist Ihnen garantiert, dass private Mitteilungen zur Person entfallen werden' (pp. 24-25). Johnson almost keeps this promise, concentrating on a political history of his times. He thereby nearly edges the identity of the subject out of *Begleitumstände* completely, repeatedly turning to a documentary and historical style in which the subject is no more than an ordering consciousness.

Nothing is left to chance, and everything concerning the subject relates to history and politics. It is thus possible to compare the history in *Begleitumstände* to Johnson's historical novels in this respect. At the end of *Begleitumstände* Johnson suddenly turns the tables and reveals the repressed other side, the 'Ich-Geschichte' which has been the cause of four years without work on *Jahrestage.* In *Skizze eines Verunglückten* the same pattern can be observed, although the proportions of text which deal with the historical and the private are rather different.

As I have indicated above, *Skizze eines Verunglückten* begins as a story about the individual's place in German history. It would appear that the text is to discuss Johnson's main theme of the 1970s, that of German historical identity, for it even opens with an excerpt from the Büchner Prize address about a Jewish victim. It continues by telling of Hinterhand's 'Jewishness' and of his life up to and during his exile from the Nazis. The text soon adds the theme of marriage to this historical subject, then allows the theme of betrayal to eradicate the history completely: just as Hinterhand's obsession has destroyed his public career, so it has robbed *Skizze eines Verunglückten* of the theme of German history. Unlike those of all of the exiles in *Jahrestage* Hinterhand's misery and poverty are not a result of German history, but of a personal crisis.

This is why it is possible to read *Skizze eines Verunglückten* as an antithesis and as complementary to *Jahrestage.* It is as if Johnson has written of the other side to the humanist equation which his project of considering German historical identity in *Jahrestage* could not accommodate. Yet in writing this 'Ich-Geschichte' Johnson has produced a text with a fundamental and disturbing contradiction.

This contradiction arises from the fact that Johnson chose to write his 'Ich-Geschichte' about a 'Jewish' victim of the Third Reich. If *Skizze eines Verunglückten* is taken to be autobiographical on a simplisitic level, then possible criticisms are obvious. What right does Johnson have to identify himself with a Jewish victim, transferring his own personal crisis on to the character from the Büchner Prize address? This surely negates everything that Johnson had said and written about his and Gesine Cresspahl's German identity, which is characterized by an awareness of belonging to the nation that was responsible for persecution. To identify with the victim under those terms was always to recognize one's own guilt, and Gesine is made to suffer this complex again and again in *Jahrestage.* Identifying with the victim in *Skizze eines Verunglückten* is a very different affair indeed, lacking all consciousness of one's own guilt, and may be seen to amount to misuse. On a more tolerant and less directly autobiographical level the question should still be asked: why did Johnson choose to write about betrayal and murder in marriage by writing about a Jewish character taken from his Büchner Prize address? Why did he choose the theme of a Jewish victim of the Third Reich if his text was meant to be no more than a playful tribute to Max Frisch, full of clever quotation and allusion?[49] By picking a character from his past *oeuvre* Johnson may well have intended to suggest that *Skizze eines Verunglückten* was not autobiographical, but a story he had invented before his crisis, yet the choice of the old man from the Broadway restaurant is hardly fortunate. Even taking *Skizze eines Verunglückten* as a work in its own right, ignoring the context of the sketch in the Büchner Prize address and the *Jahrestage* connection, does not resolve the problem, for Johnson has worked the Jewish theme into the text of *Skizze eines Verunglückten* itself. The treatment of the relationship to the victim in *Skizze eines Verunglückten* is the exact opposite to that which Johnson had demonstrated in his own personal appearance in *Jahrestage*. In the earlier text Johnson had shown that, as a German, he cannot escape national guilt, and had himself treated unfairly by a Jewish audience to make the point. In the later text he identifies with the victim but eradicates the sense of the historical causes of Hinterhand's misery and thus also of German guilt.[50] This is not to say that Johnson's *Skizze eines Verunglückten* is a worthless text, nor that it can only be seen as of interest as a striking alternative work in Johnson's *oeuvre*, or even as Johnson's own complex 'Wunschautobiographie'. On the contrary, its value lies in its very complexity: as a creative autobiographical text, in its thematization of a radically personal crisis, as a study of male violence, in its reflection on the failure of a humanist project and on the relationship between enlightenment and repression, reason and violence. In a sense *Skizze eines Verunglückten* does reflect on the Jewish question after all, but only because of the relationship of the attempted genocide of the Jews to the belief in reason and progress: horrific history remains the real subtext to these humanist aspirations.

Notes

1. *Mein Name sei Gantenbein* (Frankfurt/Main: Suhrkamp, 1964), p. 103.

2. Gerhard Tomkowitz and Dieter Wagner, *'Ein Volk, ein Reich, ein Führer!' Der 'Anschluß' Österreichs 1938,* 2nd edn (Munich and Zurich: Piper, 1988), p. 363. First edition 1968. The inconsistencies in the punctuation of these figures derive from their source.

3. Margret Boveri, *Verzweigungen. Eine Autobiographie,* ed. by Uwe Johnson (Munich: Piper, 1977), p. 291. Johnson's questions and comments are italicized. Further references in the text.

4. Christa Rotzoll, 'Margret Boveris Mut. Die Autobiographie *Verzweigungen*—ein vollendetes

Bruchstück', *Frankfurter Allgemeine Zeitung,* 19 November 1977, Beilage.

5. 'Margret Boveri: *Verzweigungen*', *Neue Deutsche Hefte,* 25 (1978), 157-60 (p. 158 and p. 160). Johnson was quite aware of how precarious his questioning of Boveri might seem. In a letter of 27 July 1977 to Helen Wolff he wrote: 'Wir sitzen an den Memoiren Frau Boveris. [. . .] Das ist eine knifflige Sache, denn der zweite Teil des Buches besteht aus unseren Tonbandgesprächen mit ihr, da sind wir nicht gerade glimpflich umgegangen bei der Frage, warum sie nicht emigriert ist [. . .]. Im Sprechen geht sowas an, aber im Druck sehen wir aus wie eine Inquisition.' Cited by Eberhard Fahlke in his chronicle of Uwe Johnson's 'Leben und Werk', *du. Die Zeitschrift der Kultur* (1992), 10, pp. 72-81 (p. 79).

6. Margret Boveri, 'Dollpunkt Gewissen', *Frankfurter Allgemeine Zeitung,* 22 September 1970, Literaturblatt, p. 2.

7. Johnson's obituary for Margret Boveri, whom he last visited in hospital the day before she died, is a testimony of his respect, and a remarkable obituary too. See 'Besuch im Krankenhaus. Erinnerung an Margret Boveri', in *Porträts und Erinnerungen,* pp. 63-66.

8. *Die Zeit,* 6 February 1978, p. 38.

9. Compare Johnson's 'Rede anläßlich der Entgegennahme des Georg-Büchner-Preises 1971', in Bengel, *Johnsons 'Jahrestage',* pp. 53-72: 'Sie [Gesine] hat durch das Leben im Ausland annehmen müssen, daß die Deutschen noch auf Dekaden hinaus in den Augen der anderen Völker gemessen werden auf ihre Distanz zum versuchten Genozid an den Juden, und der Verfasser [Johnson] hält diese ihre Einsicht für eine, die er unter die Leute zu bringen hat' (p. 58).

10. Again and again *Jahrestage* shows that there is no 'Gnade der späten Geburt', whenever Gesine and in this case Johnson are confronted with the victims. In this respect a comparison to Gert Heidenreich's story 'Die Gnade der späten Geburt', in which a young man is driven mad by meeting a survivor of the concentration camps, is perfectly valid: in *Die Gnade der späten Geburt. Sechs Erzählungen* (Munich and Zurich: Piper, 1986), pp. 7-70.

11. Interview with Prangel, 'Gespräch mit Uwe Johnson', p. 267; interview with Osterle, 'Todesgedanken?', p. 146.

12. Barbara Bronnen, '"Beauftragt, Eindrücke festzustellen." Ein Gespräch mit dem Schriftsteller und Büchner-Preisträger Uwe Johnson', in Johnson, *Gespräch,* pp. 257-62 (pp. 260-61).

13. This story of the differences between himself and Gesine is just one of a number of 'texts' which Johnson had prepared, with minor variations, for public statements. Johnson was highly aware of the need to preserve a strategic public image, and Barbara Bronnen, for one, found this irritating: 'Wie kommt es, daß ich das Gefühl habe jede Ihrer Antworten sei vorfabriziertes Material?' (interview with Bronnen, '"Beauftragt, Eindrucke festzustellen"', p. 261).

14. 'Uwe Johnson: Der Erzähler', p. 374. Weiss was no longer a child in 1945, but this does not detract from Bürger's argument. As a Jewish exile his relationship to Germany was entirely destroyed for many years, and in *Die Ästhetik des Widerstands* he writes against that destruction.

15. '"Es ist eine Wunschautobiographie". Peter Weiss im Gespräch mit Rolf Michaelis über seinen politischen Gleichnisroman', in *Peter Weiss im Gespräch,* ed. by Rainer Gerlach and Matthias Richter (Frankfurt/Main: Suhrkamp, 1986), pp. 216-23 (p. 217).

16. Peter Bürger's formulation of an autobiographical feature of the modern novel may put Johnson in unusual company, but it makes the point nicely: 'Von Proust und Kafka über Musil, Céline und Sartre bis hin zu Peter Weiss und Uwe Johnson ist der moderne Roman nicht abtrennbar von autobiographischer Erfahrung, mit der er wiederum nicht zusammenfällt' (*Prosa der Moderne,* p. 399). Note also that Lukács wrote of the autobiographical nature of the *Erziehungsroman* (see above, p. 39).

17. Yoram Kaniuk, 'Dreieinhalb Stunden und fünfzig Jahre mit Günter Grass in Berlin', *Die Zeit,* 21 June 1991, pp. 53-54 (p. 53).

18. This is an issue which I cannot discuss here. For introductory essays on the subject see Christiane Schmelzkopf, 'Zur Gestaltung jüdischer Figuren in der deutschsprachigen Literatur nach 1945' and Hans Dieter Zimmermann, 'Spielzeughändler Markus, Lehrer Zweifel und die Vogelscheuchen. Die Verfolgung der Juden im Werk von Günter Grass', both in *Juden und Judentum in der Literatur,* ed. by Herbert A. Strauss and Christhard Hoffmann (Munich: dtv, 1985), pp. 273-94 and pp. 295-306. Also Manfred Karniuk, 'Die größere Hoffnung. Über jüdisches "Schicksal" in deutscher Nachkriegsliteratur', in *Juden in der deutschen Literatur. Ein deutsch-israelisches Symposium,* ed. by Stephané Moses and Albrecht Schöne (Frankfurt/Main: Suhrkamp, 1986), pp. 366-85. In none of these works is Johnson mentioned.

19. '"Mir bleibt nur, ihr zu danken." Zum Tode von Hannah Arendt', in *Porträts und Erinnerungen,* pp. 74-77 (pp. 76-77).

20. The important passages are: Mrs Ferwalter: pp. 45-48; pp. 789-94; pp. 1165-69; pp. 1785-89; Mrs Blumenroth: pp. 1708-10; Dr. Rydz: pp. 593-95. I have considered Kreslil in Chapter Three.

21. '4. Oktober, 1967 Mittwoch/ Heute mit dem Sonnenuntergang beginnt das jüdische Neujahrsfest, Rosch Ha-Scha'nah' (p. 140); '13. Oktober, 1967 Freitag; Yom Kippur, Bußtag der Juden' (p. 169); '18. Oktober, 1967 Mittwoch/ Heute mit dem Sonnenuntergang beginnen die Juden das Fest der Laubhütten, Sukkoth' (p. 187); on 23 December details of the Chanukah festival (p. 501); '13. März, 1968 Mittwoch Purim/ Seit die Sonne unten ist, lesen die Juden in ihren Synagogen und Tempeln die Geschichte von der Königin Esther' (p. 862); '12. April, 1968 Karfreitag [. . .] Für die Juden beginnt an diesem Abend die Feier zur Erinnerung an den Auszug aus Ägypten vor mehr als 2000 Jahren' (pp. 980-81); kosher food, p. 1545 and chapter for 11 August 1968, in which details of kosher food are linked with Mrs. Ferwalter's story of her experience in Auschwitz (pp. 1785-89).

22. 'Rede anläßlich der Entgegennahme des Georg-Büchner-Preises 1971', p. 58.

23. There are two diferences between the passage in the Büchner Prize address and that in *Skizze: Skizze* line 9 has an additional comma, line 19 shows that Johnson has improved his German, substituting 'sich selbst' for the 'sich selber' of the original.

24. This is also exactly the reaction to the dead of Gesine and Marie elsewhere in *Jahrestage* and of Johnson himself in *Begleitumstände*. See above p. 134 and p. 155.

25. Michaelis's *Adreßbuch,* which does not take the Büchner Prize address into account, gives references for Joe Hinterhand only in *Skizze eines Verunglückten* and in *Jahrestage* 4, and thus ignores the figure in *Jahrestage* 1, whom it does not list under 'Namenslose' or 'Anonyme' either (see pp. 125-27 and pp. 275-78).

26. '"Heimweh ist eine schlimme Tugend"', p. 273.

27. I am unable and unwilling to comment on whether these accusations are true or not: the result of whatever happened in Sheerness in 1975 was a heart attack and the end of work on *Jahrestage*. It should be noted that Elisabeth Johnson has always denied the story (see below, p. 182, note 38).

28. 'Uwe Johnson: "Für wenn ich tot bin"', in Siegfried Unseld/ Eberhard Fahlke, *Uwe Johnson: 'Für wenn ich tot bin'* (Frankfurt/Main: Suhrkamp, 1991), pp. 9-71 (p. 40). Compare Unseld's earlier

essay, in which he also supports Johnson's own explanation of the crisis: 'Uwe Johnson als Partner seiner Figuren. Anmerkungen zur Poetologie', in *Poetik. Essays über Ingeborg Bachmann . . . und andere Beiträge zu den Frankfurter Poetik-Vorlesungen,* ed. by Hans Dieter Schlosser and Hans Dieter Zimmermann (Frankfurt/Main: Athenäum, 1988), pp. 81-92.

29. 'Uwe Johnson: "Für wenn ich tot bin"', p. 13.

30. *Unterwegs an den Ort, wo die Toten sind. Auf der Suche nach Uwe Johnson in Sheerness* (Munich and Zurich: Piper; 1984), pp. 54-56 on *Skizze.* If, as Jens writes (p. 77), his intended title, 'Für wenn ich tot bin', was disallowed by the Suhrkamp Verlag, then Unseld's own use of this seems peculiar. Vorsicht Einsturzgefahr! (The quote 'Für wenn ich tot bin' comes from *Jahrestage,* p. 151.)

31. *Der Spiegel* (anon.), 'Hinterhands Unglück. Ein Schriftsteller erfährt vom Ehebruch seiner Frau und erleidet eine Schreibhemmung. Thema einer neuen Erzählung von Uwe Johnson', *Der Spiegel,* 8 November 1982, p. 237 and pp. 241-42 (p. 241). Fritz J. Raddatz, 'Das verratene Herz. Uwe Johnson: *Skizze eines Verunglückten*', *Die Zeit,* 12 November 1982, Literatur, p. 1. See also Raddatz's review of *Begleitumstände,* in which he challenges Johnson to back up his claim about his wife with evidence, and his review of *Jahrestage* 4, in which he repeats this critique of Johnson's accusations and calls *Skizze eines Verunglückten* 'die grausige Camouflage seiner Denunziation von Elisabeth Johnson als Ost-Agentin': 'Lesebücher deutscher Not und deutscher Schande. Uwe Johnsons "Frankfurter Vorlesungen" und Stephan Hermlins "Aufsätze und Reden"', *Die Zeit,* 10 October 1980, Literatur, pp. 7-8 (p. 8); 'Ein Märchen aus Geschichte und Geschichten. Uwe Johnson: *Jahrestage* 4. Zum Abschlußband eines großen Romanwerks', in Bengel, *Johnsons 'Jahrestage',* pp. 177-87 (p. 183).

32. Michael Bengel, 'Gespräch mit Uwe Johnson', in Bengel, *Johnsons 'Jahrestage',* pp. 120-28. On *Skizze* pp. 125-27 (p. 127 on Raddatz).

33. 'Uwe Johnson', in *Kritisches Lexikon zur Gegenwartsliteratur,* ed. by Heinz Ludwig Arnold (Munich: Edition Text und Kritik), no date, p. 15. This was published in summer 1984.

34. '"Heimweh ist eine schlimme Tugend"', pp. 273-75 (p. 275 contra Buck).

35. 'Johnsons *Jahrestage* und einige ihrer Voraussetzungen', in Bengel, *Johnsons 'Jahrestage',* pp. 303-39 (pp. 314-15).

36. Marlis Becher, *Der Konjunktiv der indirekten Redewiedergabe. Eine linguistische Analyse der 'Skizze eines Verunglückten' von Uwe Johnson*

(Hildesheim, Zurich, New York: Georg Olms, 1989), pp. 12-14. The points of comparison are quite stunning.

37. 'Zwei gemeinsame Ansichten: Zu Max Frischs *Montauk* und Uwe Johnsons "Skizze eines Verunglückten"', in Jurgensen, pp. 41-52 (p. 48).

38. For the sake of completeness I mention Walter Schmitz, who does not read *Skizze* as autobiography. His interpretation is not without insight, but is brief and uncritical also. He sees *Skizze* as a story about the breakdown of identity and the failure of (political) commitment. Schmitz also notes numerous parallels to the work of Max Frisch (*Uwe Johnson,* pp. 102-06). Sigrun Storz-Sahl argues that *Skizze* should not be reduced to autobiography, pointing out that, whereas de Catt's breakdown is complete, Johnson managed to return to writing. Yet she has no interpretation of *Skizze* to offer (*Erinnerung und Erfahrung,* pp. 291-95). Colin Riordan sees *Skizze* only as Johnson's fictional working-out of a personal crisis (*The Ethics of Narration,* p. 67 and p. 218). A recent article on Johnson in *Der Spiegel* has again popularized the break up of Johnson's marriage and noted that *Skizze* is Johnson's scarcely disguised own story. See *Der Spiegel* (anon.), '"Autor braucht Gehirnwäsche"', *Der Spiegel,* 6 January 1992, pp. 128-34 (p. 130). Elisabeth Johnson protested in a letter to *Der Spiegel,* saying that practically everything about herself in the article was false. See 'Richtiger Satz', *Der Spiegel,* 20 January 1992, p. 10.

39. See Eberhard Fahlke, '"Erinnerung umgesetzt in Wissen." Spurensuche im Uwe Johnson-Archiv', in Unseld/Fahlke, *Für wenn ich tot bin,* pp. 73-143 (p. 85). See also Eberhard Fahlke, '"Ach, Sie sind ein Deutscher?" Uwe Johnson im Gespräch', in Johnson, *Gespräch,* pp. 7-48 (pp. 19-20). Here Fahlke notes that Johnson also nearly used the name Joachim de Catt for an excerpt from *Mutmassungen* published in *Akzente* in 1959.

40. Two critics have commented on the triangle in *Ingrid Babendererde*: Norbert Mecklenburg, 'Zeitroman oder Heimatroman?', p. 180; and Bernd Neumann, 'Ingrid Babendererde als Ingeborg Holm', pp. 223-24.

41. 'Zu *Montauk*', in *Über Max Frisch II,* ed. by Walter Schmitz (Frankfurt/Main: Suhrkamp, 1976), pp. 448-50. Apparently Johnson's unfinished *Marthas Ferien* was also to be a tale of adultery and broken marriage, and it would have gone into the sort of detail found in *Skizze.* In the fragment which survives motifs from *Skizze* can be identified: the significance of the year 1926 as that in which the lovers meet, photographs as memen-

tos of former, happier times, the independent woman resisting the man's ideas as to how the relationship should be organized. In *Skizze* there is a reference to Martha's adultery (p. 38). See also Norbert Mecklenburg's 'Nachwort' to *Versuch, einen Vater zu finden. Marthas Ferien,* pp. 71-96 (pp. 94-96).

42. Johnson's italics. This line is cited by both Tilman Jens and Siegfried Unseld as if it were Johnson's own confession and without reference to *Skizze eines Verunglückten* (*Unterwegs,* p. 56 and 'Für wenn ich tot bin', p. 13). This is both indiscrete and a misuse of the literary text.

43. Von Matt, *Liebesverrat. Die Treulosen in der Literatur* (Munich and Vienna: Hanser, 1989), p. 413.

44. Love letters hidden in a desk are also important in Flaubert's *Madame Bovary,* but, due to the references to Fontane in *Skizze eines Verunglückten* and to Johnson's great interest in Fontane in general, the *Effi Briest* connection is more relevant here.

45. *Eifersucht. Erfahrungen und Lösungsversuche im Beziehungsdreieck* (Reinbek bei Hamburg: Rowohlt, 1985), p. 71. Baumgart's comments on *Skizze* are on pp. 69-72 and pp. 194-95.

46. '"Mich interessiert der Fall Althusser . . ." Gesprächsprotokoll', in *Heiner Müller Material. Texte und Kommentare,* ed. by Frank Hörnigk, 2nd edn (Leipzig: Reclam, 1989), pp. 25-29 (p. 29).

47. See also Max Frisch, *Stich-Worte. Ausgesucht von Uwe Johnson* (Frankfurt/Main: Suhrkamp), p. 249, where Johnson quotes the entire relevant passage from *Mein Name sei Gantenbein* (p. 103).

48. The socially critical impulse to all of Johnson's novels represents the traditional core to an *oeuvre* which critics have often taken to be radically modern. Moreover, the continuous interest in the individual from a social viewpoint in *Jahrestage* has been identified by recent critics who have noted just how without a particular feminine identity Gesine Cresspahl is. That she is a woman does indeed seem to be secondary to her role as a German reflecting on German guilt. See Fries, *Uwe Johnsons 'Jahrestage',* pp. 127-42 (p. 136); Frauke Meyer-Gosau, 'Weibliche Perspektive des männlichen Erzählers? Uwe Johnsons *Jahrestage* der Gesine Cresspahl', in Jurgensen, pp. 121-39. The argument can be traced back to an earlier essay by Sigrid Bauschinger, in which a lack of sensuality in Gesine's New York life is noted: 'Mythos Manhattan. Die Faszination einer Stadt', in *Amerika in der deutschen Literatur. Neue Welt - Nordamerika - USA,* ed. by Sigrid Bauschinger and others (Stuttgart: Reclam, 1975), pp. 382-97.

49. I find this idea echoed in Andreas Isenschmid's review of a book by Felix Philipp Ingold. The reviewer is perturbed by the seemingly redundant German-Jewish theme in a story otherwise characterized by a mass of literary allusions: 'Ein Jude im Dritten Reich als Kleiderständer für literarische Zitatspielchen, in der Tat ein Zeichen aparten Geschmacks.' See 'Mensch, Zitat. Felix Philipp Ingolds problematische Erzählung *Ewiges Leben*', *Die Zeit,* 8 November 1991, Literatur, p. 11.

50. Kurt Fickert is the *only* critic who bothers to discuss in detail the Jewish theme in *Skizze eines Verunglückten,* yet his comments make little sense, and I mean this literally. His conclusion is simply baffling: 'Johnson scheint sich hier mit der Judenverfolgung im Dritten Reich zu beschäftigen und mit der von ihm und vielen anderen gezeigten Unempfindlichkeit diesbezüglich abzufinden' ('Zwei gemeinsame Ansichten', p. 48). Does this mean what it seems to mean: that Johnson himself showed insensitivity to the persecution of the Jews and accepts that insensitivity, in which case it is slanderous? Or does Fickert mean that Johnson has revealed the insensitivity of others and attempts to come to terms with it critically, in which case he should have used different verbs ('aufzeigen' and 'abrechnen' perhaps)? In any case his comment says nothing about the Jewish theme in *Skizze eines Verunglückten.* Bernd Neumann writes of the importance of Hannan Arendt in sharpening Johnson's consciousness of Jewish issues, and suggests that Johnson's 'Selbstidentifikation mit dem Juden de Catt' derives from his friendship with Arendt. He does not, however, reflect on the implications of this 'Selbstidentifikation'. See 'Korrespondenzen. Uwe Johnson und Hannah Arendt', p. 62. Another critic who discusses at least the Büchner Prize address connection manages not to notice the Jewish theme, and suggests instead that this connection may be evidence for the autobiography in Hinterhand's crisis. See Michael Bengel, 'Voraussetzungen', pp. 314-15. *Skizze* was clearly successful in smothering its Jewish theme: no critic has paid serious attention to it, and most seem to have missed it completely.

Bibliography

I Works by Uwe Johnson

i. Books

Mutmassungen über Jakob (Frankfurt/Main: Suhrkamp, 1959)

Das dritte Buch über Achim (Frankfurt/Main: Suhrkamp, 1961) Also '*Das dritte Buch über Achim. Ein*

Roman von Uwe Johnson', *Süddeutsche Zeitung*, 26/27 August 1961, Feuilleton, and then each weekend until 28/29 October 1961

Karsch, und andere Prosa (Frankfurt/Main: Suhrkamp, 1964).

Zwei Ansichten (Frankfurt/Main: Suhrkamp, 1965)

Jahrestage. Aus dem Leben von Gesine Cresspahl, 4 vols (Frankfurt/Main: Suhrkamp, 1970, 1971, 1973, 1983)

Eine Reise nach Klagenfurt (Frankfurt/Main: Suhrkamp, 1974)

Begleitumstände. Frankfurter Vorlesungen (Frankfurt/Main: Suhrkamp, 1980)

Skizze eines Verunglückten (Frankfurt/Main: Suhrkamp, 1982) First published in *Begegnungen. Eine Festschrift für Max Frisch zum 70. Geburtstag*, ed. by Siegfried Unseld (Frankfurt/Main: Suhrkamp, 1981), pp. 69-107

Ingrid Babendererde. Reifeprüfung 1953 (Frankfurt/Main: Suhrkamp, 1985)

'Ich überlege mir die Geschichte . . .' Uwe Johnson im Gespräch, ed. by Eberhard Fahlke (Frankfurt/Main: Suhrkamp, 1988)

Porträts und Erinnerungen, ed. by Eberhard Fahlke (Frankfurt/Main: Suhrkamp, 1988)

II. TRANSLATION AND EDITORIAL WORK

Philipp Otto Runge, *Von dem Fischer un syner Frau. Ein Märchen nach Philipp Otto Runge mit sieben Bildern von Marcus Behmer, einer Nacherzählung und mit einem Nachwort von Uwe Johnson* (Frankfurt/Main: Insel, 1976)

Margret Boveri, *Verzweigungen. Eine Autobiographie*, ed. by Uwe Johnson (Munich: Piper, 1977)

III. OTHER TEXTS (ESSAYS, ARTICLES ETC.)

'Ein Teil von New York', in *Johnsons 'Jahrestage'*, ed. by Michael Bengel, pp. 35-52. First published in *Die Neue Rundschau*, 80 (1969), 261-74

'Rede anläßlich der Entgegennahme des Georg-Büchner-Preises 1971', in *Johnsons 'Jahrestage'*, ed. by Michael Bengel, pp. 53-72. Also in *Büchner-Preis-Reden 1951-1971*, ed. by Ernst Johann (Stuttgart: Reclam, 1972), pp. 217-40

'"Für wen schreibt der eigentlich?" Antwort auf eine Umfrage von Manfred Bosch und Klaus von Konjetzky, 1973', in Uwe Johnson, *'Ich überlege mir die Geschichte . . .' Uwe Johnson im Gespräch*, p. 154

'Besuch im Krankenhaus. Erinnerung an Margret Boveri', in Uwe Johnson, *Porträts und Erinnerungen*, pp. 63-66. First published in *Die Zeit*, 15 August 1975, p. 32

'"Mir bleibt nur, ihr zu danken." Zum Tode von Hannah Arendt', in Uwe Johnson, *Porträts und Erinnerungen*, pp. 74-77. First published as 'Ich habe zu danken', *Frankfurter Allgemeine Zeitung*, 8 December 1975, p. 19

'Vorwort', in Max Frisch, *Stich-Worte. Ausgesucht von Uwe Johnson*, pp. 7-11

'Zu *Montauk*', in *Über Max Frisch II*, ed. by Walter Schmitz (Frankfurt/Main: Suhrkamp, 1976), pp. 448-50

'Nachwort', in Margret Boveri, *Verzweigungen. Eine Autobiographie*, pp. 351-409

'Ach! Sie sind ein Deutscher?', *Die Zeit*, 6 February 1978, p. 38. Reprinted in *BRD heute. Westberlin heute. Ein Lesebuch*, ed. by Christlieb Hirte and others (Berlin: Volk und Welt, 1982), pp. 209-10. Also in Uwe Johnson, *Eine Reise wegwohin und andere kurze Prosa*, pp. 287-89

IV. INTERVIEWS WITH UWE JOHNSON

Bronnen, Barbara, '"Beauftragt, Eindrücke festzustellen." Ein Gespräch mit dem Schriftsteller und Büchner-Preisträger Uwe Johnson' (1971), in Uwe Johnson, *'Ich überlege mir die Geschichte . . .' Uwe Johnson im Gespräch*, pp. 257-62

Osterle, Heinz D.,'Todesgedanken? Gespräch mit Uwe Johnson über die *Jahrestage*' (1983), in *Internationales Uwe-Johnson-Forum*, 1 (1989), ed. by Nicolai Riedel, pp. 137-68. Shorter version first in *The German Quarterly*, 58 (1985), 576-84

Prangel, Matthias, 'Gespräch mit Uwe Johnson' (1974), in Uwe Johnson, *'Ich überlege mir die Geschichte . . .' Uwe Johnson im Gespräch*, pp. 263-67

II SECONDARY LITERATURE ON JOHNSON AND OTHER WORKS

Arnold, Heinz Ludwig, ed., *Text & Kritik*, 65/66: *Uwe Johnson* (Munich: Edition Text & Kritik, 1980)

Baumgart, Hildegard, *Eifersucht. Erfahrungen und Lösungsversuche im Beziehungsdreieck* (Reinbek bei Hamburg: Rowohlt, 1985)

Bauschinger, Sigrid, 'Mythos Mannhattan. Die Faszination einer Stadt', in *Amerika in der deutschen Literatur. Neue Welt - Nordamerika - USA*, ed. by Sigrid Bauschinger and others (Stuttgart: Reclam, 1975), pp. 382-97

Becher, Marlis, *Der Konjunktiv der indirekten Redewiedergabe. Eine linguistische Analyse der 'Skizze eines Verunglückten' von Uwe Johnson* (Hildesheim, Zurich, New York: Georg Olms, 1989)

Bengel, Michael, ed., *Johnsons 'Jahrestage'* (Frankfurt/Main: Suhrkamp, 1985)

———'Johnsons *Jahrestage* und einige ihrer Voraussetzungen', in *Johnsons 'Jahrestage'*, ed. by Michael Bengel, pp. 303-39

Boveri, Margret, 'Dollpunkt Gewissen', *Frankfurter Allgemeine Zeitung,* 22 September 1970, Literaturblatt, p. 2

————*Verzweigungen. Eine Autobiographie,* ed. by Uwe Johnson (Munich: Piper, 1977)

Buck, Theo, 'Uwe Johnson', in *Kritisches Lexikon zur Gegenwartsliteratur,* ed. by Heinz Ludwig Arnold (Munich: Edition Text und Kritik)

Bürger, Christa, Uwe Johnson: Der Erzähler', in Peter Bürger and Christa Bürger, *Prosa der Moderne* (Frankfurt/Main: Suhrkamp, 1988), pp. 353-82

Bürger, Peter and Christa Bürger, *Prosa der Moderne* (Frankfurt/Main: Suhrkamp, 1988)

Fahlke, Eberhard, '"Ach, Sie sind ein Deutscher?" Uwe Johnson im Gespräch', in Uwe Johnson, *'Ich überlege mir die Geschichte . . .' Uwe Johnson im Gespräch,* ed. by Eberhard Fahlke (Frankfurt/Main: Suhrkamp, 1988), pp. 7-48

————'"Erinnerung umgesetzt in Wissen". Spurensuche im Uwe Johnson-Archiv', in Siegfried Unseld/ Eberhard Fahlke, *Uwe Johnson: 'Für wenn ich tot bin'* (Frankfurt/Main: Suhrkamp, 1991), pp. 73-143

————'Leben und Werk', du. Die Zeitschrift der Kultur (1992), 10, pp. 72-81 (p. 79).

Fickert, Kurt, 'Zwei gemeinsame Ansichten: Zu Max Frischs *Montauk* und Uwe Johnsons 'Skizze eines Verunglückten', in *Johnson. Ansichten - Einsichten - Aussichten,* ed. by Manfred Jurgensen, pp. 41-52

Fontane, Theodor, *Effi Briest,* in *Werke,* ed. by Hans Josef Mundt (Munich: Kurt Desch, 1954), pp. 661-894

Fries, Ulrich, *Uwe Johnsons 'Jahrestage'. Erzählstruktur und politische Subjektivität* (Göttingen: Vandenhoeck und Ruprecht, 1990)

Frisch, Max, *Stiller* (Frankfurt/Main: Suhrkamp, 1954)

————*Andorra. Stück in zwölf Bildern* (Frankfurt/Main: Suhrkamp, 1961)

————*Mein Name sei Gantenbein* (Frankfurt/Main: Suhrkamp, 1964)

————*Biografie. Ein Spiel* (Frankfurt/Main: Suhrkamp, 1967)

————'Skizze eines Unglücks', in *Tagebuch 1966-1971* (Frankfurt/Main: Suhrkamp, 1972), pp. 229-52

————'Glück', in *Tagebuch 1966-1971,* pp. 357-64

————*Montauk* (Frankfurt/Main: Suhrkamp, 1975)

————*Stich-Worte. Ausgesucht von Uwe Johnson* (Frankfurt/Main: Suhrkamp, 1975)

Grass, Günter, *Aus dem Tagebuch einer Schnecke,* in *Werkausgabe in zehn Bänden,* ed. by Volker Neuhaus (Darmstadt and Neuwied: Luchterhand, 1987), IV, ed. by Volker Neuhaus, pp. 265-567

Heidenreich, Gert, 'Die Gnade der späten Geburt', in *Die Gnade der späten Geburt. Sechs Erzählungen* (Munich and Zurich: Piper, 1986), pp. 7-70

Isenschmid, Andreas, 'Mensch, Zitat. Felix Philipp Ingolds problematische Erzählung *Ewiges Leben*', *Die Zeit,* 8 November 1991, Literatur, p. 11

Jens, Tilman, *Unterwegs an den Ort, wo die Toten sind. Auf der Suche nach Uwe Johnson in Sheerness* (Munich and Zurich: Piper, 1984)

Johnson, Elisabeth, 'Richtiger Satz', letter to *Der Speigel,* 20 January 1992, p. 10

Jurgensen, Manfred, *Das fiktionale Ich. Untersuchungen zum Tagebuch* (Berne and Munich: Francke, 1979)

————ed., *Johnson. Ansichten - Einsichten - Aussichten* (Berne and Stuttgart: Francke, 1989)

Kaniuk, Yoram, 'Dreieinhalb Stunden und fünfzig Jahre mit Günter Grass in Berlin', *Die Zeit,* 21 June 1991, pp. 53-54

Karniuk, Manfred, 'Die größere Hoffnung. Über jüdisches "Schicksal" in deutscher Nachkriegsliteratur', in *Juden in der deutschen Literatur. Ein deutsch-israelisches Symposium,* ed. by Stephané Moses and Albrecht Schöne (Frankfurt/Main: Suhrkamp, 1986), pp. 366-85

Lukács, Georg, *Die Theorie des Romans. Ein geschichtsphilosophischer Versuch über die Form der großen Epik,* 12th edn (Frankfurt/Main: Luchterhand, 1989)

————*Der historische Roman,* in *Werke,* VI: *Probleme des Realismus III* (1965), pp. 15-429

von Matt, Peter, *Liebesverrat. Die Treulosen in der Literatur* (Munich and Vienna: Hanser, 1989)

Mecklenburg, Norbert, 'Zeitroman oder Heimatroman? Uwe Johnsons *Ingrid Babendererde*', *Wirkendes Wort,* 36 (1986), 172-89

————'Nachwort' in Uwe Johnson, *Versuch, einen Vater zu finden. Marthas Ferien,* ed. by Norbert Mecklenburg (Frankfurt/Main: Suhrkamp, 1988), pp. 71-96

Meyer-Gosau, Frauke, 'Weibliche Perspektive des männlichen Erzählers? Uwe Johnsons *Jahrestage* der Gesine Cresspahl', in *Johnson. Ansichten - Einsichten - Aussichten,* ed. by Manfred Jurgensen, pp. 121-39

Michaelis, Rolf, ed., *Kleines Adreßbuch für Jerichow und New York. Ein Register zu Uwe Johnsons Roman 'Jahrestage'. Angelegt mit Namen, Orten, Zitaten und Verweisen von Rolf Michaelis* (Frankfurt/Main: Suhrkamp, 1983)

Müller, Heiner, '"Mich interessiert der Fall Althusser . . ." Gesprächsprotokoll', in *Heiner Müller Material. Texte und Kommentare,* ed. by Frank Hörnigk (Leipzig: Reclam, 1989), pp. 25-29

Neumann, Bernd, '"Heimweh ist eine schlimme Tugend." Über Uwe Johnsons Gedächtnisroman *Jahrestage. Aus dem Leben von Gesine Cresspahl,* von seinem vierten Band her gesehen', in *Johnsons 'Jahrestage',* ed. by Michael Bengel, pp. 263-80

————'Ingrid Babendererde als Ingeborg Holm. Über Uwe Johnsons ersten Roman', *Germanisch-Romanische Monatsschrift,* 37 (1987), 218-26

————'Korrespondenzen: Uwe Johnson und Hannah Arendt', *du. Die Zeitschrift der Kultur* (1992), 10, pp. 62-66

Raddatz, Fritz J., 'Lesebücher deutscher Not und deutscher Schande. Uwe Johnsons "Frankfurter Vorlesungen" und Stephan Hermlins "Aufsätze und Reden", *Die Zeit,* 10 October 1980, Literatur, pp. 7-8

————'Das verratene Herz. Uwe Johnson: *Skizze eines Verunglückten', Die Zeit,* 12 November 1982, Literatur, p. 1

Riordan, Colin, *The Ethics of Narration. Uwe Johnson's Novels from 'Ingrid Babendererde' to 'Jahrestage'* (London: The Modern Humanities Research Association for the Institute of Germanic Studies, 1989)

Rotzoll, Christa, 'Margret Boveris Mut. Die Autobiographie *Verzweigungen* - ein vollendetes Bruchstück', *Frankfurter Allgemeine Zeitung,* 19 November 1977, Beilage

Schmelzkopf, Christiane, 'Zur Gestaltung jüdischer Figuren in der deutschsprachigen Literatur nach 1945', in *Juden und Judentum in der Literatur,* ed. by Herbert A. Strauss and Christhard Hoffmann (Munich: dtv, 1985), pp. 273-94

Schmitz, Walter, *Uwe Johnson* (Munich: Beck/Edition Text & Kritik, 1984)

Der Spiegel, 'Hinterhands Unglück. Ein Schriftsteller erfährt vom Ehebruch seiner Frau und erleidet eine Schreibhemmung. Thema einer neuen Erzählung von Uwe Johnson', *Der Spiegel,* 8 November 1982, p. 237 and pp. 241-42

Der Spiegel, "Autor braucht Gehirnwäsche", *Der Spiegel,* 6 January 1992, pp. 128-34

Steinert, Hajo, 'Alles zu spät. Chronik der laufenden Versäumnisse', *Die Zeit,* 9 March 1990, Literatur, p. 11.

Storz-Sahl, Sigrun, *Erinnerung und Erfahrung. Geschichtsphilosophische und ästhetische Erfahrung in Uwe Johnsons 'Jahrestagen'* (Frankfurt/Main, Berne, New York, Paris: Peter Lang, 1988)

Tolstoy, Lyof N., 'The Kreutzer Sonata', in *Master and Man. The Kreutzer Sonata. Dramas* (New York: Thomas Y. Crowell, 1899), pp. 58-154

Tomkowitz, Gerhard and Dieter Wagner, *'Ein Volk, ein Reich, ein Führer!' Der 'Anschluß' Österreichs 1938,* 2nd edn (Munich and Zurich: Piper, 1988)

Unseld, Siegfried, 'Die Prüfung der Reife im Jahre 1953', in Uwe Johnson, *Ingrid Babendererde* (Frankfurt/Main: Suhrkamp, 1985), pp. 249-64

————'Uwe Johnson als Partner seiner Figuren. Anmerkungen zur Poetologie', in *Poetik. Essays über Ingeborg Bachmann . . . und andere Beiträge zu den Frankfurter Poetik-Vorlesungen,* ed. by Hans Dieter Schlosser and Hans Dieter Zimmermann (Frankfurt/Main: Athenäum, 1988), pp. 81-92

————'Uwe Johnson: "Für wenn ich tot bin"', in Siegfried Unseld/Eberhard Fahlke, *Uwe Johnson: 'Für wenn ich tot bin'* (Frankfurt/Main: Suhrkamp, 1991)

Weiss, Peter, *Die Ästhetik des Widerstands,* 3 vols (Frankfurt/Main: Suhrkamp, 1975, 1979, 1981)

————'"Es ist eine Wunschautobiographie." Peter Weiss im Gespräch mit Rolf Michaelis über seinen politischen Gleichnisroman' (1975), in *Peter Weiss im Gespräch,* ed. by Rainer Gerlach and Matthias Richter (Frankfurt/Main: Suhrkamp, 1986), pp. 216-23

Die Zeit, 18 November 1988, pp. 1-7

Zimmermann, Hans Dieter, 'Spielzeughändler Markus, Lehrer Zweifel und die Vogelscheuchen. Die Verfolgung der Juden im Werk von Günter Grass', in *Juden und Judentum in der Literatur,* ed. by Herbert A. Strauss and Christhard Hoffmann (Munich: dtv, 1985), pp. 295-306

Gary L. Baker (essay date 1999)

SOURCE: Baker, Gary L. "*Ingrid Babendererde*: Political Maturation." In *Understanding Uwe Johnson,* pp. 25-46. Columbia, S.C.: University of South Carolina Press, 1999.

[*In the following essay, Baker surveys the formal strategies and themes of Johnson's first novel,* Ingrid Babendererde, *noting that "many of the themes and experiences that lie at the root of Johnson's later stories are present in this text."*]

Even though **Ingrid Babendererde** was Uwe Johnson's first novel, it was published posthumously in 1985. Its publication one year after his death conflates, in a curious way, the fact of Johnson's life and death with a structural principle of many of his works. The story-laden moment as the point from which the story evolves reveals itself with the novel **Ingrid Babendererde** as a literary moment for Johnson's life as a writer. Thus, the germinating elements of his literary production revealed themselves to the reading public in this novel published after his death. Only in such books as this study of

Johnson's life and work can *Ingrid Babendererde* sit at the beginning of Johnson's literary production, where it offers a sense of linearity in Johnson's development as an author, a linearity that Johnson never sanctioned in his stories. Many of the themes and experiences that lie at the root of Johnson's later stories are present in this text, initially conceived by a youth of nineteen years. In 1970, Wilhelm Schwarz said of Johnson's feelings about his first novel, "Today Johnson is glad that this work never appeared, because he considers it to be an immature product of a young man."[1] However, in 1956, the possible publication of this text meant a lot to Johnson, who wrote to Aufbau Verlag, one of the most well-known publishers in East Germany, "It is important to me that the pages that lie before you will become a book in the Democratic Republic."[2] [**"Ein Briefwechsel mit dem Aufbau-Verlag"**] After those years in which this novel was written, 1953-56, Johnson's writing style evolved dramatically to become one of the most fascinating—some would say perplexing—styles in German literature. Thematically, however, Johnson remained consistent from this first literary attempt up to his final opus, *Anniversaries.*

It is important to keep in mind that Johnson intended for *Ingrid Babendererde* to be published in the GDR and to be accessible to readers in that country. Johnson wrote about the party slogans written on bright red banners, the public newspaper displays, the Freie Deutsche Jugend (Free German Youth), the Junge Gemeinde (Young Congregation), and the dreaded Stasi, which together comprised the prevalent novelistic trappings familiar to an East German reading public. Johnson hoped to join in a discussion about life in the first socialist republic on German soil with a sincere desire to improve it through the publication of a critical novel about life there. In *Ingrid Babendererde* the characters, although they enter into conflict with representatives of the state, do not question the principles on which GDR society was based. Although the mornings in school are "boring"[3] and the atmosphere of the newly established republic offers little excitement to these young people, the novel's earnest and constructive critical stance is built on an implicit belief that the socialist society of the GDR can be ameliorated. This novel generally concerns uprightness in government, a commitment to democratic socialism, the misuse of education as ideological conditioning, the importance of friendship in the face of adversity, and the unfortunate historical development of the GDR as a Stalinist-inspired dictatorship. Stagnating dogmatism faces off against youthful energy and hopeful anticipation while a Mecklenburg community comes to terms with or attempts to adapt to another authoritarian political leadership. Against this backdrop Johnson casts the story of a love triangle similar to those in his later novels, *Speculations about Jakob* and *The Third Book about Achim.* Thus, *Ingrid Babendererde* is also a love story about two young men vying for the same

woman, but they do so in a strangely noncompetitive, undramatic manner typical of Johnson's stories. As in much of his work, the Mecklenburg landscape plays an important role in the description of homeland. In other words, readers come to understand that the mere topography of the land is a deeply significant element that somehow connects to the emotional makeup of his main characters. The novel ends with two young people crossing the border to the West, thus irretrievably losing the landscape, the dialect, and the people with which they grew up.

If this novel had appeared in 1957 in the GDR, as Johnson had intended, it would have, due to its candid depiction of life there, transformed the East German literary scene and probably would have brought international attention to East German literature much earlier. As it turned out, that transformation came after the Berlin Wall was erected in 1961 with the appearance of novels such as Christa Wolf's *Der Geteilte Himmel* (*Divided Heaven*) and Erwin Strittmatter's *Ole Bienkopp* (*Old Bienkopp*) in 1963 and Erik Neutsch's *Spur der Steine* (*Trace of Stones*) in 1964. All of these books, though legitimizing in the end, depicted life in the GDR from an undeniably critical posture. *Ingrid Babendererde* was, in light of these other novels, a manuscript that came before its time in East Germany as well as West Germany, where the Peter Suhrkamp publishing house turned it down.

Because it was rejected in both the East and the West, the publication history of *Ingrid Babendererde* elucidates, to a certain extent, the political and cultural nature of its contents. The novel was conceived, before its final published version, in three other versions. The first version of ninety pages, mentioned by Johnson in *Begleitumstände,* is lost (**BU** [*Begleitumstände*] 73). The other manuscripts are stored in the Uwe Johnson Archive at the J. W. Goethe University in Frankfurt am Main. Johnson began writing in the spring of 1953 at the age of nineteen and reworked the manuscript to be less critical of East German political functionaries and altered the narrative structure before he finally submitted it for publication.[4] Soviet leader Nikita Khrushchev made a speech to his country's leadership denouncing the way Stalin dealt with national affairs. This speech was only intended for the rulers of the Soviet Union, but it was somehow leaked to the Western press. On hearing that the Soviet leadership had admitted to mistakes made in the past—in other words, due to a perceived thawing of relations between the Soviet government and the peoples it ruled—Johnson believed the time was right to publish his manuscript (**BU** 88). In July 1956 he submitted his novel to four different East German publishers in the cities of East Berlin, Leipzig, Rostock, and Halle. But the liberalizing tone of political discourse was not as extensive as Johnson believed. Although the editors recognized Johnson's talent as a writer, all of them rejected the manuscript because of the political potency of its critical contents. An internal memorandum from one East German publishing house dated 18 July 1956 and published in *Der Spiegel* in 1992 concluded about Johnson, "Author needs a brain-washing."[5] The unpublished manuscript drew attention to him as an unreliable citizen much more than it served to affirm (as he would have hoped) his sincere desire to contribute to a constructive conversation about improving life in the GDR. In the West, Suhrkamp turned the manuscript down at the behest of Siegfried Unseld, one of his chief editors and eventual successor. Unseld's main criticism was that the author demonstrated "too little worldliness."[6] (Johnson was, after all, only twenty-two years old and had never been out of the GDR when he submitted the final version to Suhrkamp.) Unseld's afterword to *Ingrid Babendererde* is one of those rare and enheartening instances in which a powerful and influential man admits that he was guilty of gross misjudgment years earlier. He reveals in his candid discussion of *Ingrid Babendererde* other possible reasons for having advised Suhrkamp against publishing the manuscript. Unseld intimates that he used metaliterary criteria to form a negative opinion about the text. Those criteria include the social context in which the story takes place: the socialist concerns of the author, the provincial north German town, the use of Mecklenburg dialect, and the pervasive naïveté of the school pupils. These reasons plus the party loyalty shown by the author to the East German communists all "cut off" Unseld's "access" to the text.[7] Furthermore, Unseld was apparently uncomfortable with the ubiquitous descriptions of landscape and nature that placed the novel, in his mind, too close to the "blood and soil" novels of the fascist years.[8] ["**'Schicksalhaft' war es nicht**"] Interestingly, in 1957's anticommunist atmosphere, Unseld perceived too much communist loyalty in the text, while the East German publishers found the novel too critical of GDR functionaries. This interesting set of circumstances brings Colin Riordan to conclude, "Johnson's self-censorship may thus have left him with a novel which confirmed neither side's image of the other sufficiently to allow publication."[9] As Johnson later discovered, like his manuscript and the truth, he was at home neither in the East nor the West.

HISTORICAL SITUATION AND PLOT

As with most of Johnson's major novels, the story in *Ingrid Babendererde* was inspired by historical developments in the newly established GDR. Soon after the Second World War, the Communist Party in the Soviet occupation zone founded a youth organization called the Free German Youth (FDJ). When the GDR came into existence in 1949, the Socialist Unity Party, derived from the fusion of the Communist Party and the East German Social Democratic Party, became the state's leading political party. The party's youth group

enjoyed special privileges from the government, because the government wanted to position the FDJ to exercise the greatest influence on the youth in East Germany. The FDJ was rivaled in popularity and influence only by the Christian youth organization known as the Young Congregation. As far as social issues are concerned, one can see how a Christian group and a communist group might share some common cause. Moreover, with the exception of Jews, Christian faithful and committed communists were the most persecuted people under Nazi rule and formed, in this way, a genuine antifascist alliance. But after the war their differing world views became cause for animosity, especially on the part of the Socialist Unity Party. The official atheism of the FDJ was a direct affront to the teachings of the Bible that formed the backbone of the Young Congregation. As the Socialist Unity Party positioned itself to establish its dominant role in the lives of the GDR's people, it tolerated no challenges to its power. It effectively negated all political opposition, took control of the media and industries, and attempted to curtail the church's influence. The government exercised coercive powers through its youth organization, its State Security Service (the Stasi or SSD), and its political apparatus to contain and eventually eliminate the Young Congregation's role in the lives of East German youth. The aggressive and overtly implemented negative campaign against the Young Congregation lasted from 1950 to 1953. In June 1953 there was a violent and spontaneous reaction to the pressures put on the population by policies of the Socialist Unity Party. Although the uprising was mainly a protest against food shortages and higher production quotas, it was also a reaction to the attacks on the church and its youth group as well as offensive tactics exercised against the other political parties allowed by the GDR's constitution. The communist government then rescinded its aggressive campaign, but many people had already been arrested or fled.

The plot of *Ingrid Babendererde* describes an incident of coercion and thus serves as a small-scale example of how the East German state's campaign against the Young Congregation took shape. The novel also portrays the population's reaction to the Socialist Unity Party's aggression against its own citizens as two intelligent and promising young people reluctantly turn their backs on their homeland to live in the West. The plot centers around a confrontation similar to one that Johnson experienced as a young man. At the University of Rostock, where he was a leading FDJ functionary, Johnson was to give a speech accusing members of the Young Congregation of attacking a Red Army recruit with a knife. The incident was fabricated, which Johnson pointed out in his talk. He also drew attention to the fact that the GDR's government was contravening its own constitution in its attempt to eliminate the

Young Congregation. Indeed, Article 41 of the East German constitution guaranteed religious freedom. Ironically, while Johnson had little to do with the Young Congregation, his defense of the organization ruined his future in the GDR. Johnson was expelled from the university for his candid speech breaking with the party line, and he was only allowed to return to university studies after the popular uprisings in June 1953 (**BU** 63-66).

The altered, autobiographical story in *Ingrid Babendererde* revolves around high school class 12A, whose members are preparing for the *Abitur,* a rigorous German high school graduation examination also referred to as a *Reifeprüfung,* or test of maturation, from which the subtitle of the book comes. The exams at the Gustav Adolf-Oberschule are scheduled for May 1953, one month before the country will erupt in rebellion. The narrative focuses on three friends, Klaus Niebuhr, Jürgen Petersen, and Ingrid Babendererde, who are preparing for these exams and enjoying the favorable spring weather to engage in all manner of water sports as a welcome diversion from studying. Klaus lives with his brother, Günter, and their Uncle Martin and Aunt Gertrud in a house by one of the many locks in Mecklenburg's waterways. Martin is a foreman for the *Wasserstraßenamt* (Department of Water Transportation) in that province. Klaus and Günter live with their aunt and uncle because their parents were murdered by the Nazis on 4 August 1944 (**IB** [*Ingrid Babendererde*] 169). Jürgen is a party loyalist and sincere believer in the socialist ideals that have been introduced into their lives. His father is absent from the scene as well, having been arrested and taken away after the war for his association with the Nazi party. Klaus and Jürgen's friendship is truly remarkable because they have two reasons to be antagonistic toward each other—not only were their parents on opposing sides during the war, but both young men are in love with Ingrid. She is an intelligent, beautiful young woman who is a popular and highly respected person in the school and community. The narrator describes how Klaus, Ingrid, and Jürgen nurture their friendship and interact with their families, their community, their classmates, and their teachers as well as cope with the school's negative political climate. This friendship becomes novelistic by virtue of the irreversible life choices that these young people are forced to make at the story's end.

Klaus, Ingrid, and Jürgen feel compelled to decide for or against the GDR because of another member of their class, Elisabeth Rehfelde, who belongs to both the Young Congregation and the Free German Youth. When pressured one day by the head of the FDJ to choose between the two supposedly irreconcilable organizations, Elisabeth, in a gesture of defiance, tosses her FDJ membership booklet at his feet. The school director and party loyalist, Pius Siebmann, politicizes the incident,

which is merely an immediate emotional response to an unfairly imposed constraint. The party organization uses this incident as a pretext to intensify a demonization process aimed at the entire Young Congregation organization. Jürgen attempts diplomatically to defuse the situation by approaching Elisabeth to admit to her that a mistake had been made and to return her membership booklet. But the party line represented by Pius prevails. Eventually Ingrid is appointed to speak to the assembled pupils, denouncing the Young Congregation as a spy organization financed and controlled by the enemy in the West. As Ingrid takes the stand before a full auditorium, she changes the subject to the importance of individuality for the development of a socialist society. She also takes the opportunity to point out indirectly that the representatives of the GDR's ruling party should have more respect for the republic's written law. As a result of this courageous speech, Ingrid is expelled from school and ejected from the FDJ, Klaus withdraws voluntarily from school, and Jürgen is reprimanded by the party because he shares Ingrid's views and will not renounce his friendship with Klaus or Ingrid. While Jürgen decides to remain in the GDR, the closing scene of the novel describes a police motorboat speeding off to a larger town, where Ingrid and Klaus will catch a direct train to Berlin and then cross the border into the West.

Narrative Structure

Ingrid Babendererde is by far the least prismatic of Johnson's novels—that is, the organization of the narrative is relatively straightforward compared to his subsequent works. Little is known about the first version of the novel, but one of the later versions possesses an identifiable witness named Dietrich Erichson who narrates the story (**BU** 77). (Erichson, or D. E., appears again as Gesine Cresspahl's friend and lover in *Anniversaries.*) Johnson abandoned the idea of the identifiable witness for an almost omniscient narrator in the final, published version. The narrator is only almost omniscient because there remain vestiges of the book's earlier conception as a narrative of a specific, this time unnamed, witness who speaks with the reader: "there you can see" (**IB** 109) and "but look there" (**IB** 208) serve to show that another person is telling the story.[10] The most obvious sign of a knowledgeable but not all-knowing narrating witness reveals itself when Klaus, Ingrid, and Jürgen are out for their last sailing tour together. Only the three friends are in the boat, so Johnson's "unnamed witness" can only offer the perspective from land: "But (as far as can be judged from land) they were doing well" (**IB** 239).[11] Otherwise the narrative approach is straightforward.

Still, the narrative does not begin in a conventional manner with the initiating event of the story. Instead, Johnson commences with the adverbial construction "on the other hand" (**IB** 9), thereby creating what Bernd

Neumann refers to as an "ironic reversal of dialectical causal thinking."[12] In other words, Johnson shows the reader first the result of the combination of events that make up the story. Effect comes before cause as two pages later the words "on the one hand" (**IB** 11) introduce the story of how the flight of the youths presented on pages 9 and 10 comes to be. In no other book does Johnson make so explicit the story-laden moment around which he weaves his narrative. The four larger sections of the book each open with a two-page description of the progress of the youths' emigration: section 1 alludes to the train ride to Berlin; section 2 shows Klaus and Ingrid resting in West Berlin; section 3 alludes to a stopover in an acquaintance's apartment; and section 4 describes them boarding a plane to West Germany. At the end of section 4 the narrative catches up with itself where the final page (**IB** 248) describes the midnight boat ride that chronologically leads back into the first page, their train travel to Berlin. The descriptions of the emigration are not included as part of the numbered chapters and they are printed in italics; their separation from the main body of the text is augmented by the vagueness of the descriptions, which represent allusions to events more than being part of any concrete plot structure. This trenchant separation of the result from the cause focuses the reader's attention on the issue of why the emigration takes place. The story behind the flight, however, remains intact in its linearity and causality, clearly laid out in sixty-one short chapters.

The prime number sixty-one possesses its own significance as an indication of Johnson's resigned agreement with Walter Benjamin, one of his principal philosophical and literary inspirations. Benjamin claims in the last of his thirteen theses for the writer that in the end, "the work is the death mask of the conception."[13] The death mask is a metaphor for the form and printed words that become the work when it is finished. The primordial inspiration, the experience of the lived moment, the authenticity of the narrative instant, and the initial idea of the work all disappear when the work comes to stand on its own in textual form (**BU** 88). Its original conception has flowed from it, and the shell that is left is, from that point on, open to any conception that readers supply. The life that the work subsequently receives comes from readers as they read the text and, in doing so, once again bring it to meaning. As Johnson admits, "One cannot help a book that is offered to people and read by some people. Whatever effect occurs is completely withdrawn from the control and the supervision of the author."[14] In his discussion of thesis thirteen, Johnson is either recreating his youthful disappointment at discovering such a notion or demonstrating a measure of ambivalence about Benjamin's thought. Johnson refers to this thesis as the fatal one and yet advocates similar ideas in his essay **"Vorschläge zur Prüfung eines Romans,"** where he says that readers can and should claim authority over published texts. Despite the

"fatality" of thesis thirteen, ironically, it is the condition on which the text can gain new life in reading, for the text sheds its Benjaminian death mask momentarily with each new reading. In this manner, the total number of chapters equaling the prime number sixty-one represents a disheartened acknowledgment of Benjamin's thesis written after the prime number thirteen (**BU** 88). Johnson recognizes the reality of Benjamin's thesis thirteen, however, for all the rest of his work and as an underlying principle of all narrative production.

THE INDIVIDUAL AND THE STATE

In remaining with his dialectical treatment of the subject matter, Johnson sets up certain oppositions in *Ingrid Babendererde* that serve to elucidate the antagonisms of the plot. The dissonance between individual desires and the interests of the state take their place as the fundamental opposition of the entire novel. In fact, this basic opposition would later represent the thematic focus of much of East German literature. As such, Johnson's *Ingrid Babendererde* could have been the first work in an East German literary tradition that would make as its central theme the individual's problematic relationship to the collective. In practice, the state creates an atmosphere and social order in which individual desires must clash with the state's ideologically justified interests. Ingrid's speech to the school addresses this problem as she throws open for debate the state's intrusive appropriation of individuals who believe and think differently from the state. Those who do not comply are summarily rejected and/or harassed by the state's institutions and denied access to the fruits of society, such as an education or a meaningful profession. The crux of Ingrid's speech is that the contradiction perceived by the state between individual desires and state interests is unproductive and senseless. The simple example of a pair of pants worn one day by her classmate, Eva Mau, suffices to make a point of political and sociological gravity. Eva purchased the pants in West Berlin, the territory of the capitalist enemy. The school director, Pius Siebmann, orders Eva to never wear the pants to school again, and she complies. Ingrid too has been the target of such constraints. She owns and still wears a "scandalous dress" (**IB** 24)—scandalous because it comes from the capitalist West. Ingrid shows that the state's control has reached absurd levels that alienate individuals from the state's goal of a socialist society more than convince or persuade them of its moral superiority.

A figure for whom the invention of qualifiers such as "Ingridbeauty" (**IB** 40), "Ingridirony" (**IB** 53), and "Ingridcountenance" (**IB** 42) is warranted is most suitable for addressing the importance of the individual within the collective. Unseld found these constructions *unangenehm* [unpleasant] when he initially read the manuscript.[15] In actuality, these annoying or awkward creations constitute the author's attempt to make his champion of individuality in a society that set the interests of the state, in the guise of class interests, above the interests and constitutional rights of the individual. Even her last name possesses significance for Ingrid's role as the champion of individuality. In Low German, Babendererde means "on the earth" (**BU** 98); thus, Ingrid conducts herself in a concrete, grounded, and basic manner that shows that the individual must possess some autonomy to become an active agent for a socialist society. The individual separated into private and collective selves represents an analogy to the prevalent Marxist theory of society, which holds that the economic base has a cultural superstructure. In other words, party functionaries who curtail and scorn expressions of individuality are unquestionably familiar with a premise for thinking in terms of dichotomous positions (base and superstructure) that form and shape each other. However, the application of such dialectical thinking does not transfer in government representatives' minds to the distinction between the private self and the collective self. Ingrid's rhetorical speech questions whether it is more important that young people support the party doctrines in a genuine manner or that they stoically submit to the party's heavy-handed tactics. In this respect her speech is not confrontational but is a plea for understanding and prioritizing with the needs of individuality in mind yet on behalf of the state's goals to establish a socialist society.

Ingrid does not defend individual self-determination in direct defiance of the dogmatic and all-powerful school director. In fact, she attempts to remind the assembly of the words of the director himself, ostensibly by quoting him—"In this time all ways lead to communism" (**IB** 174)—and implicitly by expressing her opinion candidly, taking Pius at his word that they live in a truly democratic order with the freedom of expression as one of its social and political pillars: "Pius had spoken for some time about the right of democratic expression of opinion" (**IB** 173). Ingrid does not argue against the validity of Pius's "books" for their education, but she defends Eva's right to wear any pair of pants she wishes while expressing that Peter Beetz has the constitutionally guaranteed right to belong to and wear the badge of the Young Congregation. In her speech, Ingrid goes from the benign and insignificant to the lofty and ethereal elements of being an individual, from a decision of what to wear to school on a given day to a principled belief system by which to guide one's practices in life. She shifts the focus of the discussion from the putative incompatibility of the communist and Christian world views to the value of the individual in the collective, which for her is a more basic and immediately pressing issue. She implies that socialist society will only establish itself after individuals can know themselves, which requires a type of fundamental freedom that the state is apparently not willing to grant. Ingrid suggests that

communism can evolve only from the basic starting point of the self-assured and free-thinking individual.

The discrepancy between the state's words and its actions exposes the fact that it does not take its own words seriously or demonstrate any trust in its people. If the state is really only interested in the blind submission of its people and superficial compliance with party doctrine, then the legacy of socialist ideals will never be passed down in any genuine manner to future generations. Jürgen intimates as much when he accuses an especially ambitious and militant fellow pupil and party loyalist of having "the wrong way of going about persuading" (**IB** 114). Just as the Marxist base determines the views and institutions of the superstructure, so the quality of an individual's private life will create the public person who is an agent for the good of the collective. Johnson's precocious young people quickly ascertain that the Socialist Unity Party does not believe in its own idealistic notions. Klaus, Ingrid, and Jürgen are constrained to create among themselves a sort of resistance movement in the face of this dogmatism.

However, modifiers such as *heroic, brave, intrepid,* and so on are too flamboyant and superficial to suit Johnson's manner of positioning his characters against the state's ideological imperatives. The ethos of resistance in ***Ingrid Babendererde*** is captured in two prevalent words that only occur in conjunction with characters in the community who either maintain a resistant association to the dominant power or come into open conflict with it. Thus these modifiers, *überlegsam* and *höflich,* apply only to characters who possess a decidedly distanced relationship to the state. *Überlegsam* is an especially curious neologism whose meaning is difficult to discern. However, taking the meanings of *überlegen* in its various forms together with the suffix *-sam* results in a working definition of "reflexive in a superior manner." *Höflich* means "polite"—that is, to be conscious of or recognize the relative position of and demonstrate respect for (an)other person(s). Politeness involves everything a community requires to be human and civil in its demeanor, a sense of the word that comes through in ***Speculations about Jakob*** and ***Anniversaries*** as well. Both adjectives describe a communal attitude that is set against the aggressive, self-promoting, and unreflective power represented by the school director. These modifiers take the segmenting and decentering competitiveness out of the community's political existence. They slow down the political tempo and confuse the antagonistic atmosphere that the party seeks to create, while the *überlegsame* and *höfliche* person exercises an annulling effect on confrontational action. Only an individual of true independence can be "superiorly reflective" because only an individual can think about self and other simultaneously. Klaus, Ingrid, and Jürgen see the many sides of the issue at hand. These adjectives or adverbs are badges of integrity that, no matter how superior in a moralistic way, still cannot win against the political power of the party. Of course, *höflich* and *überlegsam* are modifiers that signal to readers a character of solid inner spiritual and personal strength. Thus, as words that describe persons in a state of passive resistance, it is not possible to say with complete conviction that the Socialist Unity Party ever really wins, despite the fact that its policies and tactics force Klaus and Ingrid to leave the country. Many who opposed the regime in a similar fashion did not leave. Nonetheless, history shows that the Socialist Unity Party never truly established itself as a legitimate political authority: in 1990, East Germans voted for a rapid unification with West Germany, demonstrating that relatively few citizens had been convinced that the socialist system in the form familiar to the population was worth reforming.

Johnson employs a musical motif to further distinguish between stagnant party discourse and youthful exuberance—that is, he accentuates with music the difference between expected uniformity and the desire for self-expression. Nothing fluidizes the humors more readily than music; listening to jazz thus offers a refreshing respite to these pupils from the quiescent and oppressive atmosphere of school. Jazz, however, signifies something greater than just another venue of escape and self-determination for Klaus, Ingrid, and Jürgen. For Johnson the spirit of the individual does not live only in his characters but also exists authentically and suggestively in this music. The jazz motif comes through with consistency in the text and represents a musical discourse in line with these young people's struggle to claim and defend their individuality. Born out of the African American musical tradition, jazz has often served as a music of resistance, a function that it performs in Johnson's novel as well. Listening to jazz, something Johnson himself often did, is a political risk for Klaus, Ingrid, and Jürgen. It is a genre not officially sanctioned by the East German government and is available only via the American Forces Network, the enemy's radio station in West Berlin. For Johnson jazz codifies the dynamic relationship of the individual to the socialist society depicted in ***Ingrid Babendererde.*** Johnson places the students' love of jazz in sharp contrast to Pius Siebmann's speech patterns, which are "almost singing" (**IB** 87), "melodic" (**IB** 221), or like a "song" (**IB** 226). Thus, jazz music stands in marked contrast to the singsong fluency with which Pius expresses the party doctrine to his pupils. Often the words in Pius's oratorical barrages are spelled together to stress their monotonous flow and their total uniformity, something he expects of his pupils. Here the spontaneous and joyful improvisations of jazz explode the repressive and mindless submission to party doctrine expected by the state. In jazz, although there is one overriding harmonic structure to which the musicians adhere, individual players improvise their own varia-

tions and unique musical statements within that framework. Thus, in its resistance to rigidity, its structure of organized disorder, and its unifying harmonic framework, jazz entirely harmonizes with the attitude of the three friends (especially Klaus). Jazz codifies in the novel an ideal fusion of the private and the public, the individual and the collective, a social dynamic in which there is room for expression of the self within the broader collective. It is music that is part of a world of escape but also a metaphorical affirmation to how circumstances could be different, for jazz music creates an analogy to a society in which flight to the West would not be necessary.

The experiences of Klaus, Ingrid, and Jürgen in their water environment and in school represent yet another opposition that gives balance and proportion to the narrative as well as creates a revealing dichotomy in the text. Norbert Mecklenburg refers to the morning hours of school as wasted life, as opposed to the afternoon hours of the love story and a successful, fulfilling life.[16] The natural surroundings of Mecklenburg are the locales for the bonding of these young friends; their love, trust, and respect for each other resonate with the wind, the water, and the reeds of the familiar landscape. In school they are bored and forced to make a stand in their relationship to a regime that accepts nothing less than absolute loyalty and obedience to the party line. It is in their altercations with the state that the potential for weakness in their bonds of friendship become apparent. The results of the assembly to which Ingrid delivers her talk turn out to be nothing more or less than an ideological litmus test as Pius discovers who is for and who is against the party. The fustian charade of the assembly stands in marked contrast to the honest and open assessment of the political atmosphere outlined by Ingrid in the assembly and later by Jürgen in private consultation with Pius. Symbolic of their potential division in the face of political confrontation, the friends find themselves in three distinctly separate spaces as each person copes differently with the climactic event. Klaus, in a gesture of individualism, avoids the conflict completely and goes sailing by himself. Jürgen, seated in the auditorium, remains quiet throughout the meeting but is one of the seventeen dissenting votes against the 289 who vote to expel Ingrid from school and the FDJ. Ingrid—and this is the reason the novel carries her name as its title—counters the injustice done to her classmates honestly, unreservedly, directly, and with her integrity fully intact at the podium in front of those who will judge her. The last year of school forces the three characters through an unpleasant maturation process that they do not wish to face. In the natural environment of the Mecklenburg landscape there is no necessity to grow up, while the approaching final examinations and political expectations of school and society represent the vacuous, hypocritical world that awaits them as adults.

Since Jürgen has voted against Ingrid's shunning, he creates yet another opposition in his stance against Pius's dogmatic and ineffectual pedagogical style. If Ingrid champions the individual in a socialist society, then Jürgen is the champion of a humanistic, pluralistic, and democratic socialism: "He felt that the arguments used were pretexts that were supposed to justify the prohibition of another opinion instead of discussing it" (**IB** 226). Jürgen lists the articles of the constitution that were breached in Pius's action against the Young Congregation and those who refused to join the attack on the group. Pius and Jürgen obviously disagree on the fundamental issue of the function of the constitution. Jürgen views the document as a broadly based consensual agreement on the ultimate value and inalienability of certain human rights. For Pius and the party apparatus, it apparently has no function in politics save for its use to advance particularistic party goals. In other words, whenever the establishment of its unquestioned power is at stake, the party recognizes no mistakes or contradictions in its actions. This particular party stance underscores Pius's otherwise inexplicable name: "Nobody knew why Pius was called Pius. Popes were called such, and indeed Pius was at the head of the school and its party organization with such authority" (**IB** 86). The authority and infallibility of Pius, like those of the Pope, manifest themselves in his actions and reflect an expected ideological premise of the time expressed in a poem and popular song of the period in which a line reads "Die Partei hat immer recht" (the party is always right). Standing independently, Jürgen engages the dogmatism of the school director, admits that he voted against the party line, and suffers a reprimand, which he rejects on both moral and legal grounds. The blemish of a party admonition on his record, however, leaves little doubt that Jürgen will have difficulties advancing or obtaining meaningful work opportunities in that society. He has revealed himself to be "politically unreliable," a label used in the former GDR by the party to mark and stigmatize undesirable citizens. His personal traits of honesty, sincerity, and fairness as well as his dedication to a humanistic altruism where the constitution is concerned point more to tragic flaws than to useful values that are rewarded in the context of the GDR's existing socialist society.

Test of Maturation

The novel does not dwell on the emigration of Klaus and Ingrid to the West or Jürgen's adversity with the Socialist Unity Party. The fact that their lives have been negatively affected by party politics is the result of a greater issue that involves the lack of a consensus concerning the ideals on which their society purportedly bases itself. Johnson creates in Klaus, Ingrid, and Jürgen three people who should feel quite at home in the new socialist order. Johnson provides each character a basis on which he or she could feel a sense of solidarity with the socialist regime. Klaus's parents perished at the hands of the same fascist government that sent many communists and Social Democrats to the concentration camps. On this account he should be a preferred child of the regime. Ingrid has wealthy relatives in the capitalist West, in Lübeck, but expresses personal difficulty in her relationship with them and their money. She could have chosen to live with them years ago but desires to remain with the community in which she feels comfortable. She possesses an innate sense of social fairness for the distribution of wealth, one that is in line with party doctrine. As Johnson intimates elsewhere, Klaus and Ingrid leave for the West, to a way of life that they consider wrong (**BU** 87). Jürgen, whose father was a Nazi, is especially drawn to the new ideals of the fledgling socialist society despite his origins in the propertied middle class (his mother owns a lawn and garden shop). He believes in socialism because of what Johnson has referred to as the "two moral roots" of GDR society: the antifascist stance and its social achievements.[17] [**"Versuch, eine mentalität zu erklären"**] Johnson wrote this novel with a presupposition about the psychological and emotional development of these seventeen-, eighteen-, and nineteen-year-olds. He claimed that like most people their age, they want to accept the social order in which they live: these young people "of course" try to live according to the socialist principles they learn in school.[18] Thus, any system caught in a falsehood or acting in contradiction to its stated values and guiding principles, "can get eighteen- and nineteen-year-olds riled up and cause them to doubt the wisdom of the State."[19] The tragedy of the story is that the government, as represented in this Mecklenburg community, is not able to prove to these young people that socialism represents a system morally superior to the previous regime or to the Western alternative, as the government continually states to be the case. The implementation of socialist ideals through arbitrary intimidation, coercion, falsehoods, and demonization of certain communal elements smacks of fascist strategies. The party obviously seeks to annihilate all opposition to consolidate its dominant role in the lives of the population. In an unpublished version of the novel, Johnson likened the Stasi of the Socialist Unity Party to the Gestapo of the Nazi party.[20] The manner in which the regime, represented by Pius Siebmann, treats the young people of the school as they attempt to defend the socialist and democratic ideals from abuse by the very regime that propounds them leads to Klaus and Ingrid's disillusionment and ultimate flight to the West. Only the optimist Jürgen is prepared to stay and see what will come of the principles in which he sincerely believes.

Johnson's novelistic conflict ostensibly revolves around a genuine political issue, the antagonism between the worldviews of the Young Congregation and the FDJ. However, as is often the case with Johnson's work, the circuitous poignancy of this text is located in revealing the corruption of greater values of trust, steadfastness, and consistency in upholding stated ideals. These are the deeper issues that resonate in the action of the story. After all, none of the main characters who forfeit their futures in the GDR by defending the right of the Young Congregation to undertake its activities freely is actually a member of that group. Viewed this way, the subtitle of the novel as a test of maturity takes on its full significance. Indeed, the young friends face dire circumstances in their coming of age, but the GDR government is also measured in its political maturity throughout the story.[21] The outcome of the many-leveled conflict of the novel proves that the state fails miserably to demonstrate the integrity of its goals, while the youngsters represent a level of mature and courageous conduct that reaches beyond any measure of development that the state can hope to achieve. Klaus, Jürgen, and Ingrid realize that they must stand by their convictions or commit themselves to an existence of falsehood or voicelessness. As Walter Schmitz explains, "The choice between the 'truthfulness' of a direct perception of reality and the 'realistic' adaptation to the power creation of the party signifies in Johnson's novel the actual 'test of maturity.'"[22] Even though the three friends are not involved in the particulars of the incident, none of them can stand by and allow principles in which they believe, emotionally invest themselves, and have adopted as their own to be marred by shortsighted, particularistic, political dogmatism. Their authentic sign of maturity is manifested in the fact that the pupils do not lose sight of their higher principles in the commotion of political altercation. They do not allow themselves to be forced to think oppositionally about their own self-interest as the state pursues its interests. Their attention remains fixed on the principles at issue while the party loses its vision for anything higher than the immediate, self-interested assertion of its power.

But Johnson's story concludes with some major questions unanswered and remains despairingly open-ended in this respect. Although maturity indicates a completion of a developmental process, the *Reifeprüfung* ("test of maturity") is unfinal and remains untreated in this novel. The perfection or completion in development that the term *maturity* implies is not attained because these young people make decisions for whose mastery they do not possess the emotional capacity. This is especially the case with Klaus and Ingrid, whose emigration implies that they believe they can live in the West in a less contradictory and more honest manner. In reality, new tests of maturity await them there, because the same premises that allowed them to relate to the East German state—the death of Klaus's parents at the hands of the Nazis and Ingrid's alienating relationship to her wealthy relatives—will return to loom up at them as they live with the disproportionate distribution of wealth and witness the freedom of ex-Nazis to exist in peace in the West. Jürgen's decision to stay is equally naive

since humanistic socialism is as impossible in the East as it would be in the West. Although humanistic socialism is potentially realizable, his party comrades do not possess the courage or imagination to see their own errors and thereby to pursue socialism's grander possibilities. Thus, the reader can imagine a subsequent life for Jürgen that will offer him only frustration until he compromises his beliefs, leaves the GDR, or is imprisoned.

POLITICS AND THE COMMUNITY

Ingrid Babendererde possesses an abundance of motifs and issues that speak to young people facing transitions in their lives and to the diversions that allow them to forget those anxiety-ridden changes. The friendship among Klaus, Ingrid, and Jürgen revolves around sun, water, boating, camping, swimming, studying, examinations, and social life. All three enjoy a harmonious life in the community before the party, in the person of Pius Siebmann, plays a more intrusive role in their lives. Politics, in this respect, becomes an unnatural addition to the communal experience of the three main characters. What the party views as the evils of society are, in actuality, vital aspects of the harmony and homeostasis of the small community. Herr Wollenberg and Jürgen's mother are both, by definition, "capitalists" since each makes a living selling wares (jewelry and garden supplies, respectively) for profit. Since Jürgen is a member of the party, he maintains a rather difficult relationship to his mother, who feels threatened that the party that wants to dispossess her of her property is now, in a sense, living in her house. Herr Wollenberg is a kind old man who sells to Klaus (at a discount) a token of love to present to Ingrid. Neither Jürgen's mother nor Herr Wollenberg represents an enemy of the working class, although readers fear that they will end up like the farmer mentioned at the beginning (**IB** 13)—in the West with their property confiscated by the state. The Christian faithful in town are also viewed as enemies of a state that instructs its citizens to "purge vigilantly and inexorably our ranks of the enemies of our democratic order" (**IB** 140). Of course Herr Wollenberg and Frau Petersen are not industrialists who have millions in capital surplus at their disposal while they exploit thousands of workers; nor are the Christians, such as Elisabeth Rehfelde and Peter Beetz, Western agents working for the demise of the East German republic. Thus, the attacks on the putative enemies of the fledgling socialist republic immediately amount to attacks on friends and upstanding citizens.

The community in which the three main characters reside possesses a distinct common heritage and culture expressed in its common Low German language. The political aims pursued by Pius are interests of the Socialist Unity Party, putative class interests that are not shared by the members of the community. He expresses them only in High German, which has an alienating and distancing effect on the community. Johnson elucidates Pius's lack of compromise and a certain arrogance by never putting a Low German word in his mouth. But his lack of any Low German phrases is one more proof that his politicking is an unwanted external phenomenon lacking any real connection to the community. Jürgen is the only bona fide member of the community who has joined the party and adopted party doctrine as his own belief system. But even he does not see a "class struggle," as the party doctrine stipulates (**IB** 167). For Jürgen, politics comes from the foreign, unfamiliar outside as expressed in the time when discord reigns among the three friends; as Ingrid's mother explains, "It was nothing between you but something outside of you: something political" (**IB** 190). The local police, too, guard their fellow citizens against the intrusions of the state security apparatus as, one morning, one of its members trails Ingrid on her walk through town (**IB** 211). The police normally worked along with state security in pursuit of citizens it deemed suspicious, but here the policeman realizes that the political directive that motivates the hated Stasi is misguided. He knows this based on his familiarity with the person, with Ingrid. Thus, Heini Holtz's interference on behalf of Ingrid, ironically against the state that he is supposed to defend, only accentuates Ingrid's direct, natural, and unproblematic relationship to the community. It is an unfeigned, ingenuous relationship that neither Jürgen nor Pius can establish (**IB** 110). The schoolteachers themselves, supposed disseminators of ideological material in a dictatorship, cannot relate in any effective manner to the information that they must pass on to their students. Klaus realizes that his teacher cares as little as Klaus himself does about the material to be imparted: "Up there stood this well-bred and educated and thoroughly honorable gentleman . . . , he said things that were really unpleasant for him to say, because he certainly felt they were degrading and uncivil . . . things, moreover, that none of his listeners cared about (with one exception)" (**IB** 17-18). The political agenda of the Socialist Unity Party is unconvincing in its urgency and demonstrates itself to be, in its present form, an unnatural addition to the existence of this small Mecklenburg town whose houses stand with "discretion and reliability" and whose people speak "deliberately in an ironic friendly manner" (**IB** 36). The local imperviousness to ideological sway makes the 289 votes against Ingrid all the more a sign of necessitated and pragmatic collaboration rather than genuine conviction.

In their interaction with the dominant political doctrine, Klaus, Ingrid, and even Jürgen turn out to be distinct representatives of their community, Klaus and Ingrid because they reject outright the socialist society in its real form and Jürgen because he, in a true communal and democratic spirit, "seeks political discussion" within the newly established socialist order.[23] In a sense Johnson continues writing about Klaus, Ingrid, and Jür-

gen in his future works because their postures reflect those of many other characters. Ingrid and Klaus represent precursors of Gesine Cresspahl (*Speculations about Jakob* and *Anniversaries*), Karin F. (*The Third Book about Achim*), and Beate Dusenschön (*Two Views*), all of whom retreat or run away from the contradictions inherent in the socialist system. Jürgen possesses even more "epic twins"[24] such as Jonas Blach (*Speculations about Jakob*); Achim T. (*The Third Book about Achim*); and Dieter Lockenvitz, Pius Pagenkopf, and Gerd Schumann (*Anniversaries*)—figures who are, on some level, aware of the system's flaws and either placidly accept them or openly challenge the system in a bid to improve it. They all pay a high price for their close association with the state, either through imprisonment or societal alienation.

To distance themselves from the political arena in which Pius Siebmann has established his rule and his rules, if only superficially, the three go sailing together one final time. Here, while the other members of their class take their final exams, they lick the wounds dealt them in the assembly while silently reaffirming their friendship and loyalty to each other. Political confrontations are affairs that take place outside the comfort zone of their togetherness, which becomes most apparent when the three sailors encounter a storm. The shrillness of Pius's party rhetoric, the drone of the schoolteachers, and the complacency of fellow citizens toward the social order of the ruling party make the silent communication of these young people in the face of the storm all the more poignant: "It was important there that they could completely and quickly understand each other merely with glances" (**IB** 239). Despite the din of the wind and rain, each friend communicates with the other two; each knows his or her task; each understands what the other is doing; yet none speaks a word. In this highly symbolic scene the three of them operate the boat through the tempest in a silent team effort; like their friendship, their boat does not capsize (**IB** 240). Their relationship is based on such a high degree of trust and dedication that it prevails in the direst of circumstances. This scene establishes a metonymic connection with the community at large. It is one of Johnson's key images, one in which the quiet communication between members of a community or family creates a hermetic realm of seclusion to which the state possesses no access. The citizens of Jerichow in *Speculations about Jakob* and *Anniversaries* communicate constantly in this manner, merely with meaningful looks, glances, nods, and smiles. Beate Dusenschön in *Two Views* communicates in this manner with those who will help her across the border. Furthermore, Achim T. in *The Third Book about Achim* utilizes this type of communication with his team to win bicycle races for the state. The relationship of the three friends to each other and the school administration parallels, in effect, that of members of Johnson's invented communities to the superimposed political order of the Socialist Unity Party. Johnson offers literary examples of what later came to be known as the "niche society," described by the West German diplomat Günter Gaus as a private place in which East Germans found refuge from their overly politicized surroundings. It is a phenomenon that grew out of the necessity of GDR citizens to withdraw into "realms free from the ruling doctrine."[25] In this respect the water and the boat mean much more than mere recreation to this group of young people. Like the moat of a fortress, the water offers protection from the onslaught of the enemy trying to divide them.

POLITICAL EDUCATION

When the students of the Gustav Adolf-Oberschule enter the school, they walk past quotations from Goethe and Marx. Above Goethe's name the pupils read, "May humans be noble, helpful, and good," while Marx reminds them, "Work is the source of all culture" (**IB** 24). These quotations represent a direct response to the terror regime that held Germany in its grip from 1933 to 1945. Goethe creates a connection to an earlier humanistic tradition in Germany whose national culture had been defiled by twelve years of fascist rule. The reconstruction of Germany necessitated a more positive cultural legacy, which ministers of culture and education found in classic German literature. Here Goethe sets a tone for a society that values and respects all individuals in the community and emphasizes the nobler character of which humankind is capable. Goethe writes in celebration of the innate, divine goodness in people. He addresses the entirety of humankind with his assumption that human beings are noble, helpful, and good, thus setting certain premises for societal norms. The quotation from Marx echoes his base-and-superstructure model of society. Work, as an aspect of the base, belongs to the economic structure in which women and men work and produce. According to Marx, culture and its institutions grow out of the economic base; thus, they appear according to and appropriate to the economic structure. The Marxist subtext here tells the pupils that their work in and for a morally superior socialism will lead to a morally superior culture. The socialist economic base, then, through the individual's work, will create suitable political, educational, and judicial institutions as well as shape philosophical, artistic, and cultural views in accordance with them. Furthermore, work promotes individual development while it creates a basis on which members of society can relate to each other. Thus, work helps to integrate the individual with the larger socialist community.

These short but meaningful utterances at the entrance to the school expose the students to an entire humanistic and socialist belief system that is meant to guide the school and the society in which they live. The conflict arises when the students see these noble beliefs on dis-play every day as slogans but do not see them confirmed by the government that placed them there. Goethe and Marx are systematically ignored. The gap between the ideal and the real becomes too great to be tolerable for these idealistic young people, so they reject the falsehood that intimidates them.

In a school in which "Friendship!" has become an obligatory greeting, Friedrich Schiller's (1759-1805) poem "Die Bürgschaft" ("The Hostage") offers an obverse view on the story of Klaus, Ingrid, and Jürgen, and the friendship dictated by political authority that stresses the subversiveness of true friendship in the face of authoritarian rule. Schiller's poem is about a rebel who is caught in his attempt to assassinate a tyrannical king. The king arranges for an immediate execution, but the rebel asks for time to return home to marry off his sister. In other words, he must fulfill another obligation at home before paying his debt to the king. The king grants the request because the rebel's friend has agreed to remain in his stead and be executed should the rebel fail to return in three days. The rebel makes it safely home and marries off his sister but encounters floods, robbers, and extreme heat that hinder his speedy return. The rebel, however, perseveres and at the last moment bursts onto the scene to save his friend's life. The king is so touched by the loyalty of the two friends that he spares their lives and asks to be included in their exemplary friendship. By the sheer emotion of the moment and fine example of these two friends, he is converted from a tyrant to a friend.

In the subtly subversive stance he often displays, Klaus offers to read "Die Bürgschaft" for the German class conducted by an unpopular teacher whom the students refer to as the "Blond Poison." He does not read the original version by Schiller but a poetic study of Schiller's poem by Bertolt Brecht (**IB** 98-99).[26] Thus, Klaus presents the heritage of German classic literature with a Marxist twist. Brecht's version only alludes to the story of Schiller's poem and instead accentuates the themes of trust and loyalty as they pertain to contractual agreements and financial arrangements. Brecht implies that this example of trust maintains the capitalist system that counts on goods being delivered, contracted work being completed, and financial arrangements being honored. Brecht shows that noble principles such as trust, honor, and loyalty are, in actuality, based on self-interest. This reading ostensibly makes the poem acceptable in the Blond Poison's classroom, but the students evoke Schiller's subtext, in Brecht's version, about the power of goodness and steadfastness in the face of the tyrannical ruler. One student, in the many spontaneous reactions that erupt, shouts out, "What would the leader of all peoples say to that?" (**IB** 99). The "leader of all peoples" is the Soviet dictator, Joseph Stalin (1879-1953), who at the time of the novel has been dead for two months. He along with his miniature, Pius Siebmann, obviously represent, for Klaus and the entire 12A high school class, the tyrant in Brecht's and Schiller's poems. Klaus seeks to evoke that message with the poem, which in its own way touches on the major themes of the novel. He explains to his teacher that he possesses an "indirect" relationship to the classics. Thus reading Schiller through Brecht in the voice of a newscaster ironizes his use of eighteenth-century poetry to speak about twentieth-century life to such an extent that his innate criticism establishes a spiritual allegiance to his classmates while excluding the teacher. The immediate application of the poem's message for the students in their own grappling with political issues resonates more with Schiller's version. Klaus and his classmates understand the poem's subversive nature in the context of the antagonism between the FDJ and the Young Congregation as well as the value of real friendship in the face of the inappropriate and ungenuine friendship dictated by the party.

Thus Schiller's and Brecht's poems possess significance for **Ingrid Babendererde**'s plot on two levels. If trust, loyalty, love, and friendship are the qualities on which contracts and agreements can be made, then the ruling Socialist Unity Party proves that it contains none of these traits with regard to honoring the GDR's constitution. Its aggressive pursuit of the members of the Young Congregation is a blatant breach of its own contract with the people. Thus, the pupils involved with the conflict all understand that the constitution should be an objective document from which societal norms and rights are derived. It should stand as a promise above which no one can act. The integrity of the constitution is in jeopardy when political norms can be opened to the whim and arbitrary application of the ruling party. In a more private manner, the poem speaks to the possibility of transforming tyrants through an appeal to any humanistic feelings they may harbor. The poem foreshadows the negative outcome of the novel. The trust, loyalty, and love among Jürgen, Ingrid, and Klaus will remain strong, as in the poem, but the affirmation of their friendship in the face of the tyrant will have no affect on the miniature Stalin, Pius. Ingrid has a less idealistic reading of the poem as she realizes that tyrants do not possess the capacity to transform, which she acknowledges in a discussion of Schiller's version of the poem with the Blond Poison. Ingrid comes to this realization with a "start" (**IB** 101). As the thematic guide of the novel, Ingrid signals that readers should also know that tyrants are not predisposed to reform. This foreknowledge of the futility of their situation, the realization that they can neither reform nor conform, moves Ingrid and Klaus to leave their homeland. For these students Schiller's idealism does not become reality in their struggle with the tyrant.

Notes

1. Schwarz, *Der Erzähler Uwe Johnson,* 8.

2. Uwe Johnson, "Ein Briefwechsel mit dem Aufbau-Verlag," in *Über Uwe Johnson,* ed. Raimund Fellinger (Frankfurt am Main: Suhrkamp, 1992), 11.

3. Uwe Johnson, *Ingrid Babendererde: Reifeprüfung 1953* (Frankfurt am Main: Suhrkamp, 1985), 19. Hereafter cited in the text as IB.

4. Colin Riordan, "Reifeprüfung 1961: Uwe Johnson and the Cold War," in *German Writers and the Cold War, 1945-1961,* ed. Rhys W. Williams, Stephen Parker, and Colin Riordan (Manchester: Manchester University Press, 1992), 206.

5. "Autor braucht Gehirnwäsche," *Der Spiegel,* 6 January 1992, 132.

6. Siegfried Unseld, "Die Prüfung der Reife 1953," in *Ingrid Babendererde,* by Johnson, 258.

7. Ibid., 258-59.

8. Uwe Johnson, "'Schicksalhaft' war es nicht," in *Porträts und Erinnerungen,* ed. Eberhard Fahlke (Frankfurt am Main: Suhrkamp, 1988), 7.

9. Riordan, "Reifeprüfung 1961," 210.

10. Baumgart, "Uwe Johnson Im Gespräch," 226.

11. Norbert Mecklenburg, "Zeitroman oder Heimatroman? Uwe Johnsons 'Ingrid Babendererde,'" in *Literatur und Provinz: Das Konzept "Heimat" in der neueren Literatur,* ed. Hans-Georg Pott (Paderborn: Schöningh, 1986), 52.

12. Bernd Neumann, "Ingrid Babendererde als Ingeborg Holm: Über Uwe Johnsons ersten Roman," *Germanisch-Romanische Monatshefte* 37 (1987): 220.

13. Walter Benjamin, "ANKLEBEN VERBOTEN! Die Technik des Schriftstellers in dreizehn Thesen," in *Schriften,* ed. Theodor W. Adorno and Gretel Adorno (Frankfurt am Main: Suhrkamp, 1955), 1:538.

14. Neusüß, "Über die Schwierigkeiten beim Schreiben der Wahrheit," in *Uwe Johnson,* ed. Gerlach and Richter, 47.

15. Unseld, "Die Prüfung der Reife 1953," in *Ingrid Babendererde,* by Johnson, 298.

16. Mecklenburg, "Zeitroman oder Heimatroman?" 45.

17. Uwe Johnson, "Versuch, eine Mentalität zu erklären," in *Ich bin Bürger der DDR und lebe in der Bundesrepublik,* ed. Barbara Grunert-Bronnen (Munich: Piper, 1970), 121.

18. Baumgart, "Uwe Johnson im Gespräch," [in *"Ich überlege mir die Geschichte . . ."*: *Uwe Johnson im Gespräch,* ed. Eberhard Fahlke (Frankfurt am Main: Suhrkamp, 1988), 222.

19. Willson, "Interview," 403.

20. Riordan, "Reifeprüfung 1961," 209-10.

21. Mecklenburg, "Zeitroman oder Heimatroman?" 46.

22. Walter Schmitz, "Die Entstehung der 'immanenten Poetik' Uwe Johnsons: Ein Fassungsvergleich zu *Ingrid Babendererde: Reifeprüfung 1953,*" in *Johnson. Ansichten. Einsichten. Aussichten,* ed. Manfred Jurgensen (Bern: Francke, 1989), 154.

23. Volker Bohn, "'In der anständigsten Art, die sich dafür denken läßt': Uwe Johnsons Erstlingsroman *Ingrid Babendererde,*" in *Über Uwe Johnson,* ed. Fellinger, 29.

24. Mecklenburg, "Zeitroman oder Heimatroman?" 43.

25. Günter Gaus, *Wo Deutschland liegt: Eine Ortsbestimmung,* (Munich: Deutscher Taschenbuch Verlag, 1986), 115.

26. Bertolt Brecht, "Über Schillers Gedicht 'Die Bürgschaft,'" in *Gedichte* (Frankfurt am Main: Suhrkamp, 1961), 4:166.

Bibliography

Works by Uwe Johnson in order of Publication

Mutassungen über Jakob. Frankfurt am Main: Suhrkamp, 1959. Translated by Ursule Molinaro as *Speculations about Jakob.* New York: Grove Press, 1963.

Das dritte Buch über Achim. Frankfurt am Main: Suhrkamp, 1961. Translated as *The Third Book about Achim.* New York: Harcourt, Brace, and World, 1967.

Zwei Ansichten. Frankfurt am Main: Suhrkamp, 1965. Translated by Richard and Clara Winston as *Two Views.* New York: Harcourt, Brace, and World, 1966.

"Versuch, eine Mentalität zu erklären." In *Ich bin Bürger der DDR und lebe in der Bundesrepublik,* ed. Barbara Grunert-Bronnen, 119-29. Serie Piper 3. Munich: Piper, 1970.

Jahrestage: Aus dem Leben von Gesine Cresspahl. 4 vols. Frankfurt am Main: Suhrkamp, 1970-83. Translated by Leila Vennewitz as *Anniversaries: From the Life of Gesine Cresspahl.* New York: Harcourt Brace Jovanovich, 1975. The second volume is *Anniversaries II: From the Life of Gesine Cresspahl.* Translated by Leila Vennewitz and Walter Arndt. New York: Harcourt Brace Jovanovich, 1987. Vol. 1 of the translation covers the first six months of *Jahrestage,* and vol. 2 finishes the year.

Begleitumstände. Frankfurt am Main: Suhrkamp, 1980. A series of autobiographical essays on Johnson's development as a writer.

Ingrid Babendererde: Reifeprüfung 1953. Afterword by Siegfried Unseld. Frankfurt am Main: Suhrkamp, 1985.

Porträts und Erinnerungen. Ed. Eberhard Fahlke. Frankfurt am Main: Suhrkamp, 1988. This volume contains letters and speeches about Johnson's friends and colleagues.

Critical Works on Uwe Johnson

Monographs

Schwarz, Wilhelm Johannes. *Der Erzähler Uwe Johnson.* Bern: Francke Verlag, 1970. This monograph is an interesting study of Johnson's work up to the appearance of *Jahrestage.* The most informative part of this book is the author's interview with Johnson, who appears to have been in an uncharacteristically talkative mood. This is the first text that offers insights into the first of Johnson's novels, *Ingrid Babendererde.*

Books

Brecht, Bertolt. *Gedichte.* Frankfurt am Main: Suhrkamp, 1961.

Gaus, Günter. *Wo Deutschland liegt: Eine Ortsbestimmung.* Munich: Deutscher Taschenbuch Verlag, 1986.

Collections of Articles, Interviews, Conference Proceedings, and Yearbooks

Baumgart, Reinhard, ed. *Über Uwe Johnson.* Frankfurt am Main: Suhrkamp, 1970. The first collection of secondary literature on Uwe Johnson, this volume includes reviews and articles on Johnson's first four publications. There is also a short vita and afterword by Baumgart.

Fellinger, Raimund, ed. *Über Uwe Johnson.* Frankfurt am Main: Suhrkamp, 1992. The advantage of the Fellinger collection over other Suhrkamp products on Johnson is that it includes items from the archive and deals with Johnson's entire opus. *Ingrid Babendererde* is included here, along with some East German views of Johnson.

Gerlach, Rainer, and Matthias Richter, eds. *Uwe Johnson.* Frankfurt am Main: Suhrkamp, 1984. All of Johnson's major works are addressed in this volume that contains reviews, articles, interviews, and Johnson's treatise "Vorschläge zur Prüfung eines Romans."

Jurgensen, Manfred, ed. *Johnson. Ansichten. Einsichten. Aussichten.* Bern: Francke, 1989. This volume addresses many of Johnson's works and contains two important articles on *Ingrid Babendererde.*

SELECTED ARTICLES AND CHAPTERS IN BOOKS

Benjamin, Walter. "ANKLEBEN VERBOTEN! Die Technik des Schriftstellers in dreizehn Thesen." In *Schriften,* ed. Theodor W. Adorno and Gretel Adorno, 1:536-38. Frankfurt am Main: Suhrkamp, 1955.

Mecklenburg, Norbert. "Zeitroman oder Heimatroman? Uwe Johnson's 'Ingrid Babendererde.'" In *Literatur und Provinz: Das Konzept "Heimat" in der neueren Literatur,* ed. Hans-Georg Pott, 39-59. Paderborn: Schöningh, 1986.

Neumann, Bernd. "Ingrid Babendererde als Ingeborg Holm: Über Uwe Johnsons ersten Roman." *Germanisch-Romanische Monatshefte* 37 (1987): 218-26.

Riordin, Colin. "Reifeprüfung 1961: Uwe Johnson and the Cold War." In *German Writers and the Cold War, 1945-1961,* ed. Rhys W. Williams, Stephen Parker, and Colin Riordin, 203-20. Manchester: Manchester University Press, 1992.

Willson, A. Leslie. "An Interview with Uwe Johnson: 'An Unacknowledged Humorist.'" *Dimension* 15 (1982): 401-13.

A NOTE ON TRANSLATIONS

Unless otherwise indicated, all translations from the German are my own. Any other special circumstances involving the translation of Johnson's texts are explained in the notes.

FURTHER READING

Criticism

Baker, Gary Lee. "The Outsider Experience and Narrative Strategy in Uwe Johnson's *Jahrestage.*" *Colloquia Germanica* 24, no. 2 (1991): 83-120.

Discusses the "melancholic outsider existence" of the character Gesine Cresspahl in Johnson's *Anniversaries: From the Life of Gesine Cresspahl,* suggesting that since this "main ego of the text is represented simultaneously as subject and object, romantic irony becomes an intrinsic aspect of the narrative strategy" in the novel.

———. "(Anti-)Utopian Elements in Uwe Johnson's *Jahrestage*: Traces of Ernst Bloch." *The Germanic Review* 68, no. 1 (winter 1993): 32-45.

Addresses connections between Johnson's novel *Anniversaries: From the Life of Gesine Cresspahl* and Ernst Bloch's ideas of utopia, noting that "Bloch's double-edged future is the jeremiadic future portrayed" in Johnson's work.

———. "The Influence of Walter Benjamin's Notion of Allegory on Uwe Johnson's *Jahrestage*: Form and Approach to History." *The German Quarterly* 66, no. 3 (summer 1993): 318-29.

Contends that Walter Benjamin's ideas regarding allegory were influential in Johnson's depiction of history in *Anniversaries: From the Life of Gesine Cresspahl* and that, "due to the significance of death in the novel," the work "presents a non-teleological depiction of history" by "offering readers an allegorical representation of it."

Bond, Greg. "'Der Brunnen der Vergangenheit': Historical Narration in Uwe Johnson's *Heute neunzig Jahr* and Thomas Mann's *Joseph und seine Brüder.*" *German Life and Letters* 52 n.s., no. 1 (January 1999): 68-84.

Draws comparisons between Thomas Mann's novel *Joseph and His Brother* and Johnson's unfinished, posthumous work, *Heute neunzig Jahr,* asserting that despite disparities between the two works, there remains a "common poetical ground in terms of their status as historical novels."

Botheroyd, Paul F. "Johnson: *Das dritte Buch über Achim.*" In *Ich und Er: First and Third Person Self-Reference and Problems of Identity in Three Contemporary German-Language Novels,* pp. 62-94. The Hague, The Netherlands: Mouton, 1976.

Treats the narrative form of Johnson's *The Third Book about Achim* and asserts that the "multi-layered structure" of Karsch's narrative allows both the characters of Karsch and Achim "ambivalent expression of their personalities," and thus facilitates the "re-integration" of Karsch's personality.

Cock, Mary E. "Uwe Johnson: An Interpretation of Two Novels." *The Modern Language Review* 69, no. 2 (April 1974): 348-58.

Focuses on the often overlooked, "carefully evolved structure" of Johnson's novels *Speculations about Jakob* and *The Third Book about Achim,* concluding that the "value of the individual" is Johnson's "major concern in these two novels," which is expressed "through the inventive structure" of each work.

Fickert, Kurt J. "The Theme of a Separate Peace in Uwe Johnson's *Zwei Ansichten.*" *The International Fiction Review* 10, no. 2 (summer 1983): 104-07.

Draws parallels between Johnson's novel *Two Views* and *A Farewell to Arms* by Ernest Hemingway, particularly noting both authors' treatment of the concept of "a separate peace," or the idea that "in an age of intense interpersonal and societal conflicts the individual might be compelled to withdraw" to "maintain his integrity."

———. "Autobiography as Fiction: Uwe Johnson's *Skizze eines Verunglückten.*" *The International Fiction Review* 14, no. 2 (summer 1987): 63-7.

Examines Johnson's short work, *Skizze eines Verunglückten,* arguing that by "combining the autobiographical, first-person narrative with a fictitious framework," the author was able to give his "self-examination" both political and mythical dimensions, and thus describe not only his own "shattered world" but that "of the intellectual and writer in the latter decades of the twentieth century."

———. "Truth in Fiction: Uwe Johnson's *The Third Book About Achim.*" *The International Fiction Review* 17, no. 1 (winter 1990): 20-4.

Analyzes *The Third Book about Achim* with respect to Johnson's pursuit of truth, claiming that in this work the author describes "the failure of the standard form of biography due to the collapse of honesty or morality" and proposes that fiction, "in its imaginative recreation of life," replaces it "as a medium for expressing what is true to life."

———. "The Protean Narrator in Uwe Johnson's *Speculations about Jakob.*" *The International Fiction Review* 20, no. 2 (1993): 89-94.

Explores the formal narrative strategies of Johnson's "modern, multilayered" novel, *Speculations about Jakob,* maintaining that the author "speaks from within that group of twentieth-century writers who hold that authorial omniscience" as a narrative strategy endangers the "truthfulness" and "effectiveness" of a story.

———. "The 'Fictitious' Uwe Johnson in *Jahrestage.*" *Seminar* 30, no. 1 (February 1994): 32-43.

Highlights the narrative strategies and the undisguised authorial presence of Johnson in his novel *Anniversaries: From the Life of Gesine Cresspahl,* asserting that by "using multiple points of view" in this work, the author "freed himself from the restrictions" of writing history and created the opportunity to write "a happening," in his pursuit of artistic truth.

———. *Dialogue With the Reader: The Narrative Stance in Uwe Johnson's Fiction,* Columbia, S.C.: Camden House, 1996, 151 p.

Book-length study of Johnson's major writings that focuses on the "singular form" the author chose for each work. Fickert argues that by employing a num-

ber of modernist narrative devices, the author "was making his contribution to the dramatization of the novel and to the inclusion of the reader in the process of amalgamating the elements of the text."

———. "Names and Themes in Uwe Johnson's *Jahrestage.*" *The International Fiction Review* 26, no. 1-2 (1999): 74-81.

Demonstrates the significance of names in Johnson's *Anniversaries: From the Life of Gesine Cresspahl,* remarking that their true value "lies in their association with the novel's themes" and that together, they "form a thread of narrative that characterizes a generation" that is "victimized by a fascist government and a brutal war."

Gaines, Jeremy. "Richmond in Literature: On Three Themes in Uwe Johnson's *Jahrestage.*" *German Life and Letters* 45 n.s., no. 1 (January 1992): 74-93.

Emphasizes Johnson's choice of Richmond as a setting for the novel *Anniversaries: From the Life of Gesine Cresspahl,* stating that the author outlines the "psychology and background" of the character, Lisbeth Cresspahl, by "building a Richmond" that reflects her, and draws "on the three themes of foreignness, class status and religion."

Good, Colin H. "Uwe Johnson's Treatment of the Narrative in *Mutmassungen über Jakob.*" *German Life and Letters* 24 n.s., no. 4 (July 1971): 358-70.

Discusses the "narrative-component" of Johnson's *Speculations about Jakob* and argues that the multiple narrative voices in the novel become "synonymous and identical with one another," serving both "formally" and "in content" as "speculations."

Honold, Alexander. "Working on German Memory: Peter Weiss and Uwe Johnson." In *German Studies in the Post-Holocaust Age: The Politics of Memory, Identity, and Ethnicity,* edited by Adrian del Caro and Janet Ward, pp. 206-13. Boulder, Colo.: University Press of Colorado, 2000.

Contrasts the writings of Johnson and German writer Peter Weiss, noting differences in the "internal aesthetic conditions of their two projects" and asserting that while Weiss's narrative "shows the manner of its own construction," Johnson's writing "manages to link the level of historical reflection with the experience of everyday life."

Kenosian, David. "The Death of the Collective Subject in Uwe Johnson's *Mutmassungen über Jakob.*" *Orbis Litterarum* 58 (2003): 452-65.

Concentrates on Johnson's critique of a core Marxist concept, namely "the collective subject," in the novel *Speculations about Jakob,* stating that the "ensemble of voices" in the book "anticipates the polyphonic model of representing history" in Johnson's later work, *Anniversaries: From the Life of Gesine Cresspahl.*

Koepnick, Lutz. "Zapping Channels: Uwe Johnson, Margarethe von Trotta, and the Televisual Aesthetics of *Jahrestage.*" *Gegenwarts Literatur* 1 (2002): 175-90.

> Studies Johnson's *Anniversaries: From the Life of Gesine Cresspahl* and Margarethe von Trotta's televised version of the novel, suggesting that von Trotta's work is "neither about the textures of German history nor the textualities of Uwe Johnson's novel," but rather about "public television itself."

Lennox, Sara. "Yoknapatawpha to Jerichow: Uwe Johnson's Appropriation of William Faulkner." *Arcadia* 14 (1979): 160-76.

> Probes formal and thematic connections between the writings of Johnson and William Faulkner, observing that all of Johnson's novels can be viewed as "a protest against the atomized and impersonal industrialized society," and that the author "discovered in Faulkner" the "formal means of representing the implications for human perception of the loss" of our social community.

Martin-Mendonça, Brigitte. "Technology and Symbolism in Uwe Johnson's *Mutmassungen über Jakob.*" *Forum for Modern Language Studies* 25, no. 2 (April 1989): 139-46.

> Argues that Johnson employs lengthy descriptions of technical and mechanical objects in his novel *Speculations about Jakob* "in order to add a symbolic level to the text" that facilitates the identification and classification of characters in the narrative, "especially in respect to their motivations and interests."

Miller, Leslie L. "Uwe Johnson's *Jahrestage*: The Choice of Alternatives." *Seminar* 10, no. 1 (February 1974): 50-70.

> Notes differences between *Anniversaries: From the Life of Gesine Cresspahl* and Johnson's earlier novels, but suggests that a thematic unity links these works, namely, that characters placed in a totalitarian society are confronted with a difficult "choice of alternatives."

O'Neill, Patrick. "The System in Question: Story and Discourse in Uwe Johnson's *Zwei Ansichten.*" *The German Quarterly* 64, no. 4 (fall 1991): 531-43.

> Assesses the "textual" and narrative strategies of Johnson's novel *Two Views,* claiming that the work is "an intriguingly complex text" that is concerned "with the ways in which narrative is produced and the ways in which it is received," which invites the

reader to become "an active fellow participant in the production of the narrative instead of remaining a passive consumer."

Riordan, Colin. "Reifeprüfung 1961: Uwe Johnson and the Cold War." In *German Writers and the Cold War: 1945-1961,* edited by Rhys W. Williams, Stephen Parker, and Colin Riordan, pp. 203-20. Manchester, England: Manchester University Press, 1992.

> Traces the publication history and reception of Johnson's first novel, *Ingrid Babendererde,* exploring the ways in which the author's work was "exploited for political capital on either side" of the border between East and West Germany.

Shirer, Robert K. *Difficulties of Saying 'I': The Narrator as Protagonist in Christa Wolf's* Kindheitsmuster *and Uwe Johnson's* Jahrestage, New York: Peter Lang, 1988, 274 p.

> Book-length examination of the complex role of the narrator in Christa Wolf's *Kindheitsmuster* and Johnson's *Anniversaries: From the Life of Gesine Cresspahl,* which focuses on the "interplay between past and present" in both novels and the methods by which both narrators provoke readers into sharing their "reflections, their increased self-knowledge, and, ultimately, their hope."

Stewart, Mary E. "A Dialogic Reality: Uwe Johnson, *Mutmaßungen über Jakob.*" In *The German Novel in the Twentieth Century: Beyond Realism,* edited by David Midgley, pp. 164-78. Edinburgh: Edinburgh University Press, 1993.

> Investigates Johnson's novel *Speculations about Jakob* and asserts that "the complex modes of narration" are an "essential and positive aspect of the text, generating rather than obscuring possibilities of meaning."

Taberner, Stuart. "Uwe Johnson's Gesine Cresspahl: The Exemplary Intellectual." In *Distorted Reflections: The Public and Private Uses of the Author in the Work of Uwe Johnson, Günther Grass and Martin Walser, 1965-1975,* pp. 37-63. Amsterdam: Rodopi, 1998.

> Describes Johnson's Gesine Cresspahl as the "exemplary 1960s intellectual," who is "plagued by doubt" and self-consciously aware of her own "impotence," arguing that the conflict between her "nostalgia for realism" and "modernist sensitivities" results in paralysis.

Thomas, R. Hinton and Wilfried van der Will. "Uwe Johnson." In *The German Novel and the Affluent Society,* pp. 112-34. Toronto: University of Toronto Press, 1968.

> Studies Johnson's fiction, particularly the novel *Speculations about Jakob,* and concludes that "Johnson alone has shaped the division of Germany

into a theme of foremost literary significance," by "freeing the treatment of it from the limitations of merely political discussion" and instead addressing the question of identity.

Additional coverage of Johnson's life and career is contained in the following sources published by Gale: *Concise Dictionary of World Literary Biography,* **Vol. 2;** *Contemporary Authors,* **Vols. 1-4R, 112;** *Contemporary Authors New Revision Series,* **Vols. 1, 39;** *Contemporary Literary Criticism,* **Vols. 5, 10, 15, 40;** *Dictionary of Literary Biography,* **Vol. 75;** *Encyclopedia of World Literature in the 20th Century,* **Ed. 3;** *Literature Resource Center*; *Major 20th-Century Writers,* **Ed. 1; and** *Reference Guide to World Literature,* **Eds. 2, 3.**

How to Use This Index

The main references

> **Calvino, Italo**
> 1923-1985 .... CLC 5, 8, 11, 22, 33, 39,
> 73; SSC 3, 48

list all author entries in the following Gale Literary Criticism series:

AAL = Asian American Literature
BG = The Beat Generation: A Gale Critical Companion
BLC = Black Literature Criticism
BLCS = Black Literature Criticism Supplement
CLC = Contemporary Literary Criticism
CLR = Children's Literature Review
CMLC = Classical and Medieval Literature Criticism
DC = Drama Criticism
FL = Feminism in Literature: A Gale Critical Companion
GL = Gothic Literature: A Gale Critical Companion
HLC = Hispanic Literature Criticism
HLCS = Hispanic Literature Criticism Supplement
HR = Harlem Renaissance: A Gale Critical Companion
LC = Literature Criticism from 1400 to 1800
NCLC = Nineteenth-Century Literature Criticism
NNAL = Native North American Literature
PC = Poetry Criticism
SSC = Short Story Criticism
TCLC = Twentieth-Century Literary Criticism
WLC = World Literature Criticism, 1500 to the Present
WLCS = World Literature Criticism Supplement

The cross-references

> See also CA 85-88, 116; CANR 23, 61;
> DAM NOV; DLB 196; EW 13; MTCW 1, 2;
> RGSF 2; RGWL 2; SFW 4; SSFS 12

list all author entries in the following Gale biographical and literary sources:

AAYA = Authors & Artists for Young Adults
AFAW = African American Writers
AFW = African Writers
AITN = Authors in the News
AMW = American Writers
AMWR = American Writers Retrospective Supplement
AMWS = American Writers Supplement
ANW = American Nature Writers
AW = Ancient Writers
BEST = Bestsellers
BPFB = Beacham's Encyclopedia of Popular Fiction: Biography and Resources
BRW = British Writers
BRWS = British Writers Supplement
BW = Black Writers
BYA = Beacham's Guide to Literature for Young Adults
CA = Contemporary Authors
CAAS = Contemporary Authors Autobiography Series
CABS = Contemporary Authors Bibliographical Series
CAD = Contemporary American Dramatists
CANR = Contemporary Authors New Revision Series
CAP = Contemporary Authors Permanent Series
CBD = Contemporary British Dramatists
CCA = Contemporary Canadian Authors
CD = Contemporary Dramatists
CDALB = Concise Dictionary of American Literary Biography

CDALBS = *Concise Dictionary of American Literary Biography Supplement*
CDBLB = *Concise Dictionary of British Literary Biography*
CMW = *St. James Guide to Crime & Mystery Writers*
CN = *Contemporary Novelists*
CP = *Contemporary Poets*
CPW = *Contemporary Popular Writers*
CSW = *Contemporary Southern Writers*
CWD = *Contemporary Women Dramatists*
CWP = *Contemporary Women Poets*
CWRI = *St. James Guide to Children's Writers*
CWW = *Contemporary World Writers*
DA = *DISCovering Authors*
DA3 = *DISCovering Authors 3.0*
DAB = *DISCovering Authors: British Edition*
DAC = *DISCovering Authors: Canadian Edition*
DAM = *DISCovering Authors: Modules*
    DRAM: *Dramatists Module;* **MST:** *Most-studied Authors Module;*
    MULT: *Multicultural Authors Module;* **NOV:** *Novelists Module;*
    POET: *Poets Module;* **POP:** *Popular Fiction and Genre Authors Module*
DFS = *Drama for Students*
DLB = *Dictionary of Literary Biography*
DLBD = *Dictionary of Literary Biography Documentary Series*
DLBY = *Dictionary of Literary Biography Yearbook*
DNFS = *Literature of Developing Nations for Students*
EFS = *Epics for Students*
EW = *European Writers*
EWL = *Encyclopedia of World Literature in the 20th Century*
EXPN = *Exploring Novels*
EXPP = *Exploring Poetry*
EXPS = *Exploring Short Stories*
FANT = *St. James Guide to Fantasy Writers*
FW = *Feminist Writers*
GFL = *Guide to French Literature,* Beginnings to 1789, 1798 to the Present
GLL = *Gay and Lesbian Literature*
HGG = *St. James Guide to Horror, Ghost & Gothic Writers*
HW = *Hispanic Writers*
IDFW = *International Dictionary of Films and Filmmakers: Writers and Production Artists*
IDTP = *International Dictionary of Theatre: Playwrights*
LAIT = *Literature and Its Times*
LAW = *Latin American Writers*
JRDA = *Junior DISCovering Authors*
MAICYA = *Major Authors and Illustrators for Children and Young Adults*
MAICYAS = *Major Authors and Illustrators for Children and Young Adults Supplement*
MAWW = *Modern American Women Writers*
MJW = *Modern Japanese Writers*
MTCW = *Major 20th-Century Writers*
NCFS = *Nonfiction Classics for Students*
NFS = *Novels for Students*
PAB = *Poets: American and British*
PFS = *Poetry for Students*
RGAL = *Reference Guide to American Literature*
RGEL = *Reference Guide to English Literature*
RGSF = *Reference Guide to Short Fiction*
RGWL = *Reference Guide to World Literature*
RHW = *Twentieth-Century Romance and Historical Writers*
SAAS = *Something about the Author Autobiography Series*
SATA = *Something about the Author*
SFW = *St. James Guide to Science Fiction Writers*
SSFS = *Short Stories for Students*
TCWW = *Twentieth-Century Western Writers*
WLIT = *World Literature and Its Times*
WP = *World Poets*
YABC = *Yesterday's Authors of Books for Children*
YAW = *St. James Guide to Young Adult Writers*

Literary Criticism Series
Cumulative Author Index

Ambler, Eric 1909-1998 .... **CLC 4, 6, 9**
  See also BRWS 4; CA 9-12R; 171; CANR
  7, 38, 74; CMW 4; CN 1, 2, 3, 4, 5, 6;
  DLB 77; MSW; MTCW 1, 2; TEA

Ambrose c. 339-c. 397 .... **CMLC 103**

Ambrose, Stephen E. 1936-2002 .... **CLC 145**
  See also AAYA 44; CA 1-4R; 209; CANR
  3, 43, 57, 83, 105; MTFW 2005; NCFS 2;
  SATA 40, 138

Amichai, Yehudah 1924-2000 .. **CLC 9, 22, 57,**
  116; PC 38
  See also CA 85-88; 189; CANR 46, 60, 99,
  132; CWW 2; EWL 3; MTCW 1, 2;
  MTFW 2005; PFS 24; RGHL; WLIT 6

Amichai, Yehudah
  See Amichai, Yehuda

Amiel, Henri Frederic 1821-1881 .... **NCLC 4**
  See also DLB 217

Amis, Kingsley 1922-1995 . **CLC 1, 2, 3, 5, 8,**
  13, 40, 44, 129
  See also AAYA 77; AITN 2; BPFB 1;
  BRWS 2; CA 9-12R; 150; CANR 8, 28,
  54; CDBLB 1945-1960; CN 1, 2, 3, 4, 5,
  6; CP 1, 2, 3, 4; DA; DA3; DAB; DAC;
  DAM MST, NOV; DLB 15, 27, 100, 139,
  326, 352; DLBY 1996; EWL 3; HGG;
  INT CANR-8; MTCW 1, 2; MTFW 2005;
  RGEL 2; RGSF 2; SFW 4

Amis, Martin 1949- ... **CLC 4, 9, 38, 62, 101,**
  213; SSC 112
  See also BEST 90:3; BRWS 4; CA 65-68;
  CANR 8, 27, 54, 73, 95, 132, 166, 208;
  CN 5, 6, 7; DA3; DLB 14, 194; EWL 3;
  INT CANR-27; MTCW 1; MTFW 2005

Amis, Martin Louis
  See Amis, Martin

Ammianus Marcellinus c. 330-c.
  395 .... **CMLC 60**
  See also AW 2; DLB 211

Ammons, A.R. 1926-2001 .. **CLC 2, 3, 5, 8, 9,**
  25, 57, 108; PC 16
  See also AITN 1; AMWS 7; CA 9-12R;
  193; CANR 6, 36, 51, 73, 107, 156; CP 1,
  2, 3, 4, 5, 6, 7; CSW; DAM POET; DLB
  5, 165, 342; EWL 3; MAL 5; MTCW 1,
  2; PFS 19; RGAL 4; TCLE 1:1

Ammons, Archie Randolph
  See Ammons, A.R.

Amo, Tauraatua i
  See Adams, Henry

Amory, Thomas 1691(?)-1788 .... **LC 48**
  See also DLB 39

Anand, Mulk Raj 1905-2004 ..... **CLC 23, 93,**
  237
  See also CA 65-68; 231; CANR 32, 64; CN
  1, 2, 3, 4, 5, 6, 7; DAM NOV; DLB 323;
  EWL 3; MTCW 1, 2; MTFW 2005; RGSF
  2

Anatol
  See Schnitzler, Arthur

Anaximander c. 611B.C.-c.
  546B.C. .... **CMLC 22**

Anaya, Rudolfo 1937- ...... **CLC 23, 148, 255;**
  HLC 1
  See also AAYA 20; BYA 13; CA 45-48;
  CAAS 4; CANR 1, 32, 51, 124, 169; CLR
  129; CN 4, 5, 6, 7; DAM MULT, NOV;
  DLB 82, 206, 278; HW 1; LAIT 4; LLW;
  MAL 5; MTCW 1, 2; MTFW 2005; NFS
  12; RGAL 4; RGSF 2; TCWW 2; WLIT
  1

Anaya, Rudolfo A.
  See Anaya, Rudolfo

Anaya, Rudolpho Alfonso
  See Anaya, Rudolfo

Andersen, Hans Christian
  1805-1875 ...... **NCLC 7, 79, 214; SSC 6,**
  56; WLC 1
  See also AAYA 57; CLR 6, 113; DA; DA3;
  DAB; DAC; DAM MST, POP; EW 6;
  MAICYA 1, 2; RGSF 2; RGWL 2, 3;
  SATA 100; TWA; WCH; YABC 1

Anderson, C. Farley
  See Mencken, H. L.; Nathan, George Jean

Anderson, Jessica (Margaret) Queale
  1916- .... **CLC 37**
  See also CA 9-12R; CANR 4, 62; CN 4, 5,
  6, 7; DLB 325

Anderson, Jon (Victor) 1940- .... **CLC 9**
  See also CA 25-28R; CANR 20; CP 1, 3, 4,
  5; DAM POET

Anderson, Lindsay (Gordon)
  1923-1994 .... **CLC 20**
  See also CA 125; 128; 146; CANR 77

Anderson, Maxwell 1888-1959 .... **TCLC 2,**
  144
  See also CA 105; 152; DAM DRAM; DFS
  16, 20; DLB 7, 228; MAL 5; MTCW 2;
  MTFW 2005; RGAL 4

Anderson, Poul 1926-2001 .... **CLC 15**
  See also AAYA 5, 34; BPFB 1; BYA 6, 8,
  9; CA 1-4R; 181; 199; CAAE 181; CAAS
  2; CANR 2, 15, 34, 64, 110; CLR 58;
  DLB 8; FANT; INT CANR-15; MTCW 1,
  2; MTFW 2005; SATA 90; SATA-Brief
  39; SATA-Essay 106; SCFW 1, 2; SFW
  4; SUFW 1, 2

Anderson, R. W.
  See Anderson, Robert

Anderson, Robert 1917-2009 .... **CLC 23**
  See also AITN 1; CA 21-24R; 283; CANR
  32; CD 6; DAM DRAM; DLB 7; LAIT 5

Anderson, Robert W.
  See Anderson, Robert

Anderson, Robert Woodruff
  See Anderson, Robert

Anderson, Roberta Joan
  See Mitchell, Joni

Anderson, Sherwood 1876-1941 ... **SSC 1, 46,**
  91, 142; TCLC 1, 10, 24, 123; WLC 1
  See also AAYA 30; AMW; AMWC 2; BPFB
  1; CA 104; 121; CANR 61; CDALB
  1917-1929; DA; DA3; DAB; DAC; DAM
  MST, NOV; DLB 4, 9, 86; DLBD 1; EWL
  3; EXPS; GLL 2; MAL 5; MTCW 1, 2;
  MTFW 2005; NFS 4; RGAL 4; RGSF 2;
  SSFS 4, 10, 11; TUS

Anderson, Wes 1969- .... **CLC 227**
  See also CA 214

Andier, Pierre
  See Desnos, Robert

Andouard
  See Giraudoux, Jean

Andrade, Carlos Drummond de
  See Drummond de Andrade, Carlos

Andrade, Mario de
  See de Andrade, Mario

Andreae, Johann V(alentin)
  1586-1654 .... **LC 32**
  See also DLB 164

Andreas Capellanus fl. c. 1185- .... **CMLC 45**
  See also DLB 208

Andreas-Salome, Lou 1861-1937 ... **TCLC 56**
  See also CA 178; DLB 66

Andreev, Leonid
  See Andreyev, Leonid

Andress, Lesley
  See Sanders, Lawrence

Andrew, Joseph Maree
  See Occomy, Marita (Odette) Bonner

Andrewes, Lancelot 1555-1626 .... **LC 5**
  See also DLB 151, 172

Andrews, Cicily Fairfield
  See West, Rebecca

Andrews, Elton V.
  See Pohl, Frederik

Andrews, Peter
  See Soderbergh, Steven

Andrews, Raymond 1934-1991 .... **BLC 2:1**
  See also BW 2; CA 81-84; 136; CANR 15,
  42

Andreyev, Leonid 1871-1919 ... **TCLC 3, 221**
  See also CA 104; 185; DLB 295; EWL 3

Andreyev, Leonid Nikolaevich
  See Andreyev, Leonid

Andrezel, Pierre
  See Blixen, Karen

Andric, Ivo 1892-1975 .... **CLC 8; SSC 36;**
  TCLC 135
  See also CA 81-84; 57-60; CANR 43, 60;
  CDWLB 4; DLB 147, 329; EW 11; EWL
  3; MTCW 1; RGSF 2; RGWL 2, 3

Androvar
  See Prado (Calvo), Pedro

Angela of Foligno 1248(?)-1309 .... **CMLC 76**

Angelique, Pierre
  See Bataille, Georges

Angell, Judie
  See Angell, Judie

Angell, Judie 1937- .... **CLC 30**
  See also AAYA 11, 71; BYA 6; CA 77-80;
  CANR 49; CLR 33; JRDA; SATA 22, 78;
  WYA; YAW

Angell, Roger 1920- .... **CLC 26**
  See also CA 57-60; CANR 13, 44, 70, 144;
  DLB 171, 185

Angelou, Maya 1928- ...... **BLC 1:1; CLC 12,**
  35, 64, 77, 155; PC 32; WLCS
  See also AAYA 7, 20; AMWS 4; BPFB 1;
  BW 2, 3; BYA 2; CA 65-68; CANR 19,
  42, 65, 111, 133, 204; CDALBS; CLR 53;
  CP 4, 5, 6, 7; CPW; CSW; CWP; DA;
  DA3; DAB; DAC; DAM MST, MULT,
  POET, POP; DLB 38; EWL 3; EXPN;
  EXPP; FL 1:5; LAIT 4; MAICYA 2; MAI-
  CYAS 1; MAL 5; MBL; MTCW 1, 2;
  MTFW 2005; NCFS 2; NFS 2; PFS 2, 3,
  33, 38; RGAL 4; SATA 49, 136; TCLE
  1:1; WYA; YAW

Angouleme, Marguerite d'
  See de Navarre, Marguerite

Anna Comnena 1083-1153 .... **CMLC 25**

Annensky, Innokentii Fedorovich
  See Annensky, Innokenty (Fyodorovich)

Annensky, Innokenty (Fyodorovich)
  1856-1909 .... **TCLC 14**
  See also CA 110; 155; DLB 295; EWL 3

Annunzio, Gabriele d'
  See D'Annunzio, Gabriele

Anodos
  See Coleridge, Mary E(lizabeth)

Anon, Charles Robert
  See Pessoa, Fernando

Anouilh, Jean 1910-1987 ..... **CLC 1, 3, 8, 13,**
  40, 50; DC 8, 21; TCLC 195
  See also AAYA 67; CA 17-20R; 123; CANR
  32; DAM DRAM; DFS 9, 10, 19; DLB
  321; EW 13; EWL 3; GFL 1789 to the
  Present; MTCW 1, 2; MTFW 2005;
  RGWL 2, 3; TWA

Anouilh, Jean Marie Lucien Pierre
  See Anouilh, Jean

Ansa, Tina McElroy 1949- .... **BLC 2:1**
  See also BW 2; CA 142; CANR 143; CSW

Anselm of Canterbury
  1033(?)-1109 .... **CMLC 67**
  See also DLB 115

Anthony, Florence
  See Ai

Anthony, John
  See Ciardi, John (Anthony)

Anthony, Peter
  See Shaffer, Anthony; Shaffer, Peter

Anthony, Piers 1934- .... **CLC 35**
  See also AAYA 11, 48; BYA 7; CA 200;
  CAAE 200; CANR 28, 56, 73, 102, 133,
  202; CLR 118; CPW; DAM POP; DLB 8;

FANT; MAICYA 2; MAICYAS 1; MTCW
1, 2; MTFW 2005; SAAS 22; SATA 84,
129; SATA-Essay 129; SFW 4; SUFW 1,
2; YAW

Anthony, Susan B(rownell)
1820-1906 .... **TCLC 84**
See also CA 211; FW

Antin, Mary 1881-1949 .... **TCLC 247**
See also AMWS 20; CA 118; 181; DLB
221; DLBY 1984

Antiphon c. 480B.C.-c. 411B.C. .... **CMLC 55**

Antoine, Marc
See Proust, Marcel

Antoninus, Brother
See Everson, William

Antonioni, Michelangelo
1912-2007 .... **CLC 20, 144, 259**
See also CA 73-76; 262; CANR 45, 77

Antschel, Paul
See Celan, Paul

Anwar, Chairil 1922-1949 .... **TCLC 22**
See also CA 121; 219; EWL 3; RGWL 3

Anyidoho, Kofi 1947- .... **BLC 2:1**
See also BW 3; CA 178; CP 5, 6, 7; DLB
157; EWL 3

Anzaldua, Gloria (Evanjelina)
1942-2004 .... **CLC 200; HLCS 1**
See also CA 175; 227; CSW; CWP; DLB
122; FW; LLW; RGAL 4; SATA-Obit 154

Apess, William 1798-1839(?) .... **NCLC 73;
NNAL**
See also DAM MULT; DLB 175, 243

Apollinaire, Guillaume 1880-1918 .... **PC 7;
TCLC 3, 8, 51**
See also CA 104; 152; DAM POET; DLB
258, 321; EW 9; EWL 3; GFL 1789 to
the Present; MTCW 2; PFS 24; RGWL 2,
3; TWA; WP

Apollonius of Rhodes
See Apollonius Rhodius

Apollonius Rhodius c. 300B.C.-c.
220B.C. .... **CMLC 28**
See also AW 1; DLB 176; RGWL 2, 3

Appelfeld, Aharon 1932- ... **CLC 23, 47; SSC
42**
See also CA 112; 133; CANR 86, 160, 207;
CWW 2; DLB 299; EWL 3; RGHL;
RGSF 2; WLIT 6

Appelfeld, Aron
See Appelfeld, Aharon

Apple, Max 1941- .... **CLC 9, 33; SSC 50**
See also AMWS 17; CA 81-84; CANR 19,
54, 214; DLB 130

Apple, Max Isaac
See Apple, Max

Appleman, Philip (Dean) 1926- .... **CLC 51**
See also CA 13-16R; CAAS 18; CANR 6,
29, 56

Appleton, Lawrence
See Lovecraft, H. P.

Apteryx
See Eliot, T. S.

Apuleius, (Lucius Madaurensis) c. 125-c.
164 .... **CMLC 1, 84**
See also AW 2; CDWLB 1; DLB 211;
RGWL 2, 3; SUFW; WLIT 8

Aquin, Hubert 1929-1977 .... **CLC 15**
See also CA 105; DLB 53; EWL 3

Aquinas, Thomas 1224(?)-1274 ...... **CMLC 33**
See also DLB 115; EW 1; TWA

Aragon, Louis 1897-1982 .... **CLC 3, 22;
TCLC 123**
See also CA 69-72; 108; CANR 28, 71;
DAM NOV, POET; DLB 72, 258; EW 11;
EWL 3; GFL 1789 to the Present; GLL 2;
LMFS 2; MTCW 1, 2; RGWL 2, 3

Arany, Janos 1817-1882 .... **NCLC 34**

Aranyos, Kakay 1847-1910
See Mikszath, Kalman

Aratus of Soli c. 315B.C.-c.
240B.C. .... **CMLC 64, 114**
See also DLB 176

Arbuthnot, John 1667-1735 .... **LC 1**
See also BRWS 16; DLB 101

Archer, Herbert Winslow
See Mencken, H. L.

Archer, Jeffrey 1940- .... **CLC 28**
See also AAYA 16; BEST 89:3; BPFB 1;
CA 77-80; CANR 22, 52, 95, 136, 209;
CPW; DA3; DAM POP; INT CANR-22;
MTFW 2005

Archer, Jeffrey Howard
See Archer, Jeffrey

Archer, Jules 1915- .... **CLC 12**
See also CA 9-12R; CANR 6, 69; SAAS 5;
SATA 4, 85

Archer, Lee
See Ellison, Harlan

Archilochus c. 7th cent. B.C.- .... **CMLC 44**
See also DLB 176

Ard, William
See Jakes, John

Arden, John 1930- .... **CLC 6, 13, 15**
See also BRWS 2; CA 13-16R; CAAS 4;
CANR 31, 65, 67, 124; CBD; CD 5, 6;
DAM DRAM; DFS 9; DLB 13, 245;
EWL 3; MTCW 1

Arenas, Reinaldo 1943-1990 .. **CLC 41; HLC
1; TCLC 191**
See also CA 124; 128; 133; CANR 73, 106;
DAM MULT; DLB 145; EWL 3; GLL 2;
HW 1; LAW; LAWS 1; MTCW 2; MTFW
2005; RGSF 2; RGWL 3; WLIT 1

Arendt, Hannah 1906-1975 .... **CLC 66, 98;
TCLC 193**
See also CA 17-20R; 61-64; CANR 26, 60,
172; DLB 242; MTCW 1, 2

Aretino, Pietro 1492-1556 .... **LC 12, 165**
See also RGWL 2, 3

Arghezi, Tudor
See Theodorescu, Ion N.

Arguedas, Jose Maria 1911-1969 .... **CLC 10,
18; HLCS 1; TCLC 147**
See also CA 89-92; CANR 73; DLB 113;
EWL 3; HW 1; LAW; RGWL 2, 3; WLIT
1

Argueta, Manlio 1936- .... **CLC 31**
See also CA 131; CANR 73; CWW 2; DLB
145; EWL 3; HW 1; RGWL 3

Arias, Ron 1941- .... **HLC 1**
See also CA 131; CANR 81, 136; DAM
MULT; DLB 82; HW 1, 2; MTCW 2;
MTFW 2005

Ariosto, Lodovico
See Ariosto, Ludovico

Ariosto, Ludovico 1474-1533 ... **LC 6, 87; PC
42**
See also EW 2; RGWL 2, 3; WLIT 7

Aristides
See Epstein, Joseph

Aristides Quintilianus fl. c. 100-fl. c.
400 .... **CMLC 122**

Aristophanes 450B.C.-385B.C. .... **CMLC 4,
51; DC 2; WLCS**
See also AW 1; CDWLB 1; DA; DA3;
DAB; DAC; DAM DRAM, MST; DFS
10; DLB 176; LMFS 1; RGWL 2, 3;
TWA; WLIT 8

Aristotle 384B.C.-322B.C. .... **CMLC 31, 123;
WLCS**
See also AW 1; CDWLB 1; DA; DA3;
DAB; DAC; DAM MST; DLB 176;
RGWL 2, 3; TWA; WLIT 8

Arlt, Roberto 1900-1942 .. **HLC 1; TCLC 29**
See also CA 123; 131; CANR 67; DAM
MULT; DLB 305; EWL 3; HW 1, 2;
IDTP; LAW

Arlt, Roberto Godofredo Christophersen
See Arlt, Roberto

Armah, Ayi Kwei 1939- . **BLC 1:1, 2:1; CLC
5, 33, 136**
See also AFW; BRWS 10; BW 1; CA 61-
64; CANR 21, 64; CDWLB 3; CN 1, 2,
3, 4, 5, 6, 7; DAM MULT, POET; DLB
117; EWL 3; MTCW 1; WLIT 2

Armatrading, Joan 1950- .... **CLC 17**
See also CA 114; 186

Armin, Robert 1568(?)-1615(?) .... **LC 120**

Armitage, Frank
See Carpenter, John

Armstrong, Jeannette (C.) 1948- .... **NNAL**
See also CA 149; CCA 1; CN 6, 7; DAC;
DLB 334; SATA 102

Arnauld, Antoine 1612-1694 .... **LC 169**
See also DLB 268

Arnette, Robert
See Silverberg, Robert

**Arnim, Achim von (Ludwig Joachim von
Arnim)** 1781-1831 .. **NCLC 5, 159; SSC
29**
See also DLB 90

Arnim, Bettina von 1785-1859 ...... **NCLC 38,
123**
See also DLB 90; RGWL 2, 3

Arnold, Matthew 1822-1888 ..... **NCLC 6, 29,
89, 126, 218; PC 5, 94; WLC 1**
See also BRW 5; CDBLB 1832-1890; DA;
DAB; DAC; DAM MST, POET; DLB 32,
57; EXPP; PAB; PFS 2; TEA; WP

Arnold, Thomas 1795-1842 .... **NCLC 18**
See also DLB 55

Arnow, Harriette (Louisa) Simpson
1908-1986 ...... **CLC 2, 7, 18; TCLC 196**
See also BPFB 1; CA 9-12R; 118; CANR
14; CN 2, 3, 4; DLB 6; FW; MTCW 1, 2;
RHW; SATA 42; SATA-Obit 47

Arouet, Francois-Marie
See Voltaire

Arp, Hans
See Arp, Jean

Arp, Jean 1887-1966 .... **CLC 5; TCLC 115**
See also CA 81-84; 25-28R; CANR 42, 77;
EW 10

Arrabal
See Arrabal, Fernando

Arrabal, Fernando 1932- .. **CLC 2, 9, 18, 58;
DC 35**
See also CA 9-12R; CANR 15; CWW 2;
DLB 321; EWL 3; LMFS 2

Arrabal Teran, Fernando
See Arrabal, Fernando

Arreola, Juan Jose 1918-2001 .... **CLC 147;
HLC 1; SSC 38**
See also CA 113; 131; 200; CANR 81;
CWW 2; DAM MULT; DLB 113; DNFS
2; EWL 3; HW 1, 2; LAW; RGSF 2

Arrian c. 89(?)-c. 155(?) .... **CMLC 43**
See also DLB 176

Arrick, Fran
See Angell, Judie

Arrley, Richmond
See Delany, Samuel R., Jr.

Artaud, Antonin 1896-1948 ... **DC 14; TCLC
3, 36**
See also CA 104; 149; DA3; DAM DRAM;
DFS 22; DLB 258, 321; EW 11; EWL 3;
GFL 1789 to the Present; MTCW 2;
MTFW 2005; RGWL 2, 3

Artaud, Antonin Marie Joseph
See Artaud, Antonin

Artemidorus fl. 2nd cent. - .... **CMLC 129**

Arthur, Ruth M(abel) 1905-1979 ..... **CLC 12**
See also CA 9-12R; 85-88; CANR 4; CWRI
5; SATA 7, 26

Azuela, Mariano 1873-1952 .. **HLC 1; TCLC 3, 145, 217**
See also CA 104; 131; CANR 81; DAM MULT; EWL 3; HW 1, 2; LAW; MTCW 1, 2; MTFW 2005

Ba, Mariama 1929-1981 ...... **BLC 2:1; BLCS**
See also AFW; BW 2; CA 141; CANR 87; DLB 360; DNFS 2; WLIT 2

Baastad, Babbis Friis
See Friis-Baastad, Babbis Ellinor

Bab
See Gilbert, W(illiam) S(chwenck)

Babbis, Eleanor
See Friis-Baastad, Babbis Ellinor

Babel, Isaac
See Babel, Isaak (Emmanuilovich)

Babel, Isaak (Emmanuilovich)
1894-1941(?) . **SSC 16, 78; TCLC 2, 13, 171**
See also CA 104; 155; CANR 113; DLB 272; EW 11; EWL 3; MTCW 2; MTFW 2005; RGSF 2; RGWL 2, 3; SSFS 10; TWA

Babits, Mihaly 1883-1941 .... **TCLC 14**
See also CA 114; CDWLB 4; DLB 215; EWL 3

Babur 1483-1530 .... **LC 18**

Babylas
See Ghelderode, Michel de

Baca, Jimmy Santiago 1952- . **HLC 1; PC 41**
See also CA 131; CANR 81, 90, 146; CP 6, 7; DAM MULT; DLB 122; HW 1, 2; LLW; MAL 5

Baca, Jose Santiago
See Baca, Jimmy Santiago

Bacchelli, Riccardo 1891-1985 .... **CLC 19**
See also CA 29-32R; 117; DLB 264; EWL 3

Bacchylides c. 520B.C.-c.
452B.C. .... **CMLC 119**

Bach, Richard 1936- .... **CLC 14**
See also AITN 1; BEST 89:2; BPFB 1; BYA 5; CA 9-12R; CANR 18, 93, 151; CPW; DAM NOV, POP; FANT; MTCW 1; SATA 13

Bach, Richard David
See Bach, Richard

Bache, Benjamin Franklin
1769-1798 .... **LC 74**
See also DLB 43

Bachelard, Gaston 1884-1962 ...... **TCLC 128**
See also CA 97-100; 89-92; DLB 296; GFL 1789 to the Present

Bachman, Richard
See King, Stephen

Bachmann, Ingeborg 1926-1973 ..... **CLC 69; TCLC 192**
See also CA 93-96; 45-48; CANR 69; DLB 85; EWL 3; RGHL; RGWL 2, 3

Bacon, Francis 1561-1626 ..... **LC 18, 32, 131**
See also BRW 1; CDBLB Before 1660; DLB 151, 236, 252; RGEL 2; TEA

Bacon, Roger 1214(?)-1294 ... **CMLC 14, 108**
See also DLB 115

Bacovia, G.
See Bacovia, George

Bacovia, George 1881-1957 .... **TCLC 24**
See Bacovia, George
See also CA 123; 189; CDWLB 4; DLB 220; EWL 3

Badanes, Jerome 1937-1995 .... **CLC 59**
See also CA 234

Bage, Robert 1728-1801 .... **NCLC 182**
See also DLB 39; RGEL 2

Bagehot, Walter 1826-1877 .... **NCLC 10**
See also DLB 55

Bagnold, Enid 1889-1981 .... **CLC 25**
See also AAYA 75; BYA 2; CA 5-8R; 103; CANR 5, 40; CBD; CN 2; CWD; CWRI 5; DAM DRAM; DLB 13, 160, 191, 245; FW; MAICYA 1, 2; RGEL 2; SATA 1, 25

Bagritsky, Eduard
See Dzyubin, Eduard Georgievich

Bagritsky, Edvard
See Dzyubin, Eduard Georgievich

Bagrjana, Elisaveta
See Belcheva, Elisaveta Lyubomirova

Bagryana, Elisaveta
See Belcheva, Elisaveta Lyubomirova

Bailey, Paul 1937- .... **CLC 45**
See also CA 21-24R; CANR 16, 62, 124; CN 1, 2, 3, 4, 5, 6, 7; DLB 14, 271; GLL 2

Baillie, Joanna 1762-1851 ...... **NCLC 71, 151**
See also DLB 93, 344; GL 2; RGEL 2

Bainbridge, Beryl 1934-2010 ..... **CLC 4, 5, 8, 10, 14, 18, 22, 62, 130, 292**
See also BRWS 6; CA 21-24R; CANR 24, 55, 75, 88, 128; CN 2, 3, 4, 5, 6, 7; DAM NOV; DLB 14, 231; EWL 3; MTCW 1, 2; MTFW 2005

Baker, Carlos (Heard)
1909-1987 .... **TCLC 119**
See also CA 5-8R; 122; CANR 3, 63; DLB 103

Baker, Elliott 1922-2007 .... **CLC 8**
See also CA 45-48; 257; CANR 2, 63; CN 1, 2, 3, 4, 5, 6, 7

Baker, Elliott Joseph
See Baker, Elliott

Baker, Jean H.
See Russell, George William

Baker, Nicholson 1957- .... **CLC 61, 165**
See also AMWS 13; CA 135; CANR 63, 120, 138, 190; CN 6; CPW; DA3; DAM POP; DLB 227; MTFW 2005

Baker, Ray Stannard 1870-1946 .... **TCLC 47**
See also CA 118; DLB 345

Baker, Russell 1925- .... **CLC 31**
See also BEST 89:4; CA 57-60; CANR 11, 41, 59, 137; MTCW 1, 2; MTFW 2005

Baker, Russell Wayne
See Baker, Russell

Bakhtin, M.
See Bakhtin, Mikhail Mikhailovich

Bakhtin, M. M.
See Bakhtin, Mikhail Mikhailovich

Bakhtin, Mikhail
See Bakhtin, Mikhail Mikhailovich

Bakhtin, Mikhail Mikhailovich
1895-1975 .... **CLC 83; TCLC 160**
See Bakhtin, Mikhail Mikhailovich
See also CA 128; 113; DLB 242; EWL 3

Bakshi, Ralph 1938(?)- .... **CLC 26**
See also CA 112; 138; IDFW 3

Bakunin, Mikhail (Alexandrovich)
1814-1876 .... **NCLC 25, 58**
See also DLB 277

Bal, Mieke 1946- .... **CLC 252**
See also CA 156; CANR 99

Bal, Mieke Maria Gertrudis
See Bal, Mieke

Baldwin, James 1924-1987 ...... **BLC 1:1, 2:1; CLC 1, 2, 3, 4, 5, 8, 13, 15, 17, 42, 50, 67, 90, 127; DC 1; SSC 10, 33, 98, 134; TCLC 229; WLC 1**
See also AAYA 4, 34; AFAW 1, 2; AMWR 2; AMWS 1; BPFB 1; BW 1; CA 1-4R; 124; CABS 1; CAD; CANR 3, 24; CDALB 1941-1968; CN 1, 2, 3, 4; CPW; DA; DA3; DAB; DAC; DAM MST, MULT, NOV, POP; DFS 11, 15; DLB 2, 7, 33, 249, 278; DLBY 1987; EWL 3;

EXPS; LAIT 5; MAL 5; MTCW 1, 2; MTFW 2005; NCFS 4; NFS 4; RGAL 4; RGSF 2; SATA 9; SATA-Obit 54; SSFS 2, 18; TUS

Baldwin, William c. 1515-1563 .... **LC 113**
See also DLB 132

Bale, John 1495-1563 .... **LC 62**
See also DLB 132; RGEL 2; TEA

Ball, Hugo 1886-1927 .... **TCLC 104**

Ballard, James G.
See Ballard, J.G.

Ballard, James Graham
See Ballard, J.G.

Ballard, J.G. 1930-2009 ..... **CLC 3, 6, 14, 36, 137, 299; SSC 1, 53, 146**
See also AAYA 3, 52; BRWS 5; CA 5-8R; 285; CANR 15, 39, 65, 107, 133, 198; CN 1, 2, 3, 4, 5, 6, 7; DA3; DAM NOV, POP; DLB 14, 207, 261, 319; EWL 3; HGG; MTCW 1, 2; MTFW 2005; NFS 8; RGEL 2; RGSF 2; SATA 93; SATA-Obit 203; SCFW 1, 2; SFW 4

Ballard, Jim G.
See Ballard, J.G.

Balmont, Konstantin (Dmitriyevich)
1867-1943 .... **TCLC 11**
See also CA 109; 155; DLB 295; EWL 3

Baltausis, Vincas 1847-1910
See Mikszath, Kalman

Balzac, Guez de (?)-
See Balzac, Jean-Louis Guez de

Balzac, Honore de 1799-1850 ... **NCLC 5, 35, 53, 153; SSC 5, 59, 102; WLC 1**
See also DA; DA3; DAB; DAC; DAM MST, NOV; DLB 119; EW 5; GFL 1789 to the Present; LMFS 1; NFS 33; RGSF 2; RGWL 2, 3; SSFS 10; SUFW; TWA

Balzac, Jean-Louis Guez de
1597-1654 .... **LC 162**
See also DLB 268; GFL Beginnings to 1789

Bambara, Toni Cade 1939-1995 ..... **BLC 1:1, 2:1; CLC 19, 88; SSC 35, 107; TCLC 116; WLCS**
See also AAYA 5, 49; AFAW 2; AMWS 11; BW 2, 3; BYA 12, 14; CA 29-32R; 150; CANR 24, 49, 81; CDALBS; DA; DA3; DAC; DAM MST, MULT; DLB 38, 218; EXPS; MAL 5; MTCW 1, 2; MTFW 2005; RGAL 4; RGSF 2; SATA 112; SSFS 4, 7, 12, 21

Bamdad, A.
See Shamlu, Ahmad

Bamdad, Alef
See Shamlu, Ahmad

Banat, D. R.
See Bradbury, Ray

Bancroft, Laura
See Baum, L. Frank

Bandello, Matteo 1485-1561 .... **SSC 143**

Banim, John 1798-1842 .... **NCLC 13**
See also DLB 116, 158, 159; RGEL 2

Banim, Michael 1796-1874 .... **NCLC 13**
See also DLB 158, 159

Banjo, The
See Paterson, A(ndrew) B(arton)

Banks, Iain 1954- .... **CLC 34**
See also BRWS 11; CA 123; 128; CANR 61, 106, 180; DLB 194, 261; EWL 3; HGG; INT CA-128; MTFW 2005; SFW 4

Banks, Iain M.
See Banks, Iain

Banks, Iain Menzies
See Banks, Iain

Banks, Lynne Reid
See Reid Banks, Lynne

Bashkirtseff, Marie 1859-1884 .... **NCLC 27**

Basho, Matsuo
  See Matsuo Basho

Basil of Caesaria c. 330-379 .... **CMLC 35**

Basket, Raney
  See Edgerton, Clyde

Bass, Kingsley B., Jr.
  See Bullins, Ed

Bass, Rick 1958- . **CLC 79, 143, 286; SSC 60**
  See also AMWS 16; ANW; CA 126; CANR 53, 93, 145, 183; CSW; DLB 212, 275

Bassani, Giorgio 1916-2000 .... **CLC 9**
  See also CA 65-68; 190; CANR 33; CWW 2; DLB 128, 177, 299; EWL 3; MTCW 1; RGHL; RGWL 2, 3

Bassine, Helen
  See Yglesias, Helen

Bastian, Ann CLC 70

Bastos, Augusto Roa
  See Roa Bastos, Augusto

Bataille, Georges 1897-1962 .... **CLC 29; TCLC 155**
  See also CA 101; 89-92; EWL 3

Bates, H(erbert) E(rnest)
  1905-1974 .... **CLC 46; SSC 10**
  See also CA 93-96; 45-48; CANR 34; CN 1; DA3; DAB; DAM POP; DLB 162, 191; EWL 3; EXPS; MTCW 1, 2; RGSF 2; SSFS 7

Bauchart
  See Camus, Albert

Baudelaire, Charles 1821-1867 . **NCLC 6, 29, 55, 155; PC 1, 106; SSC 18; WLC 1**
  See also DA; DA3; DAB; DAC; DAM MST, POET; DLB 217; EW 7; GFL 1789 to the Present; LMFS 2; PFS 21, 38; RGWL 2, 3; TWA

Baudouin, Marcel
  See Peguy, Charles (Pierre)

Baudouin, Pierre
  See Peguy, Charles (Pierre)

Baudrillard, Jean 1929-2007 .... **CLC 60**
  See also CA 252; 258; DLB 296

Baum, L. Frank 1856-1919 ...... **TCLC 7, 132**
  See also AAYA 46; BYA 16; CA 108; 133; CLR 15, 107; CWRI 5; DLB 22; FANT; JRDA; MAICYA 1, 2; MTCW 1, 2; NFS 13; RGAL 4; SATA 18, 100; WCH

Baum, Louis F.
  See Baum, L. Frank

Baum, Lyman Frank
  See Baum, L. Frank

Baumbach, Jonathan 1933- .... **CLC 6, 23**
  See also CA 13-16R, 284; CAAE 284; CAAS 5; CANR 12, 66, 140; CN 3, 4, 5, 6, 7; DLBY 1980; INT CANR-12; MTCW 1

Bausch, Richard 1945- .... **CLC 51**
  See also AMWS 7; CA 101; CAAS 14; CANR 43, 61, 87, 164, 200; CN 7; CSW; DLB 130; MAL 5

Bausch, Richard Carl
  See Bausch, Richard

Baxter, Charles 1947- .... **CLC 45, 78**
  See also AMWS 17; CA 57-60; CANR 40, 64, 104, 133, 188; CPW; DAM POP; DLB 130; MAL 5; MTCW 2; MTFW 2005; TCLE 1:1

Baxter, Charles Morley
  See Baxter, Charles

Baxter, George Owen
  See Faust, Frederick

Baxter, James K(eir) 1926-1972 ...... **CLC 14; TCLC 249**
  See also CA 77-80; CP 1; EWL 3

Baxter, John
  See Hunt, E. Howard

Bayer, Sylvia
  See Glassco, John

Bayle, Pierre 1647-1706 .... **LC 126**
  See also DLB 268, 313; GFL Beginnings to 1789

Baynton, Barbara 1857-1929 . **TCLC 57, 211**
  See also DLB 230; RGSF 2

Beagle, Peter S. 1939- .... **CLC 7, 104**
  See also AAYA 47; BPFB 1; BYA 9, 10, 16; CA 9-12R; CANR 4, 51, 73, 110, 213; DA3; DLBY 1980; FANT; INT CANR-4; MTCW 2; MTFW 2005; SATA 60, 130; SUFW 1, 2; YAW

Beagle, Peter Soyer
  See Beagle, Peter S.

Bean, Normal
  See Burroughs, Edgar Rice

Beard, Charles A(ustin)
  1874-1948 .... **TCLC 15**
  See also CA 115; 189; DLB 17; SATA 18

Beardsley, Aubrey 1872-1898 .... **NCLC 6**

Beatrice of Nazareth 1200-1268 . **CMLC 124**

Beattie, Ann 1947- ..... **CLC 8, 13, 18, 40, 63, 146, 293; SSC 11, 130**
  See also AMWS 5; BEST 90:2; BPFB 1; CA 81-84; CANR 53, 73, 128; CN 4, 5, 6, 7; CPW; DA3; DAM NOV, POP; DLB 218, 278; DLBY 1982; EWL 3; MAL 5; MTCW 1, 2; MTFW 2005; RGAL 4; RGSF 2; SSFS 9; TUS

Beattie, James 1735-1803 .... **NCLC 25**
  See also DLB 109

Beauchamp, Katherine Mansfield
  See Mansfield, Katherine

Beaumarchais, Pierre-Augustin Caron de
  1732-1799 .... **DC 4; LC 61**
  See also DAM DRAM; DFS 14, 16; DLB 313; EW 4; GFL Beginnings to 1789; RGWL 2, 3

Beaumont, Francis 1584(?)-1616 .. **DC 6; LC 33**
  See also BRW 2; CDBLB Before 1660; DLB 58; TEA

Beauvoir, Simone de 1908-1986 .... **CLC 1, 2, 4, 8, 14, 31, 44, 50, 71, 124; SSC 35; TCLC 221; WLC 1**
  See also BPFB 1; CA 9-12R; 118; CANR 28, 61; DA; DA3; DAB; DAC; DAM MST, NOV; DLB 72; DLBY 1986; EW 12; EWL 3; FL 1:5; FW; GFL 1789 to the Present; LMFS 2; MTCW 1, 2; MTFW 2005; RGSF 2; RGWL 2, 3; TWA

Beauvoir, Simone Lucie Ernestine Marie Bertrand de
  See Beauvoir, Simone de

Becker, Carl (Lotus) 1873-1945 ..... **TCLC 63**
  See also CA 157; DLB 17

Becker, Jurek 1937-1997 .... **CLC 7, 19**
  See also CA 85-88; 157; CANR 60, 117; CWW 2; DLB 75, 299; EWL 3; RGHL

Becker, Walter 1950- .... **CLC 26**

Becket, Thomas a 1118(?)-1170 .... **CMLC 83**

Beckett, Samuel 1906-1989 ... **CLC 1, 2, 3, 4, 6, 9, 10, 11, 14, 18, 29, 57, 59, 83; DC 22; SSC 16, 74; TCLC 145; WLC 1**
  See also BRWC 2; BRWR 1; BRWS 1; CA 5-8R; 130; CANR 33, 61; CBD; CDBLB 1945-1960; CN 1, 2, 3, 4; CP 1, 2, 3, 4; DA; DA3; DAB; DAC; DAM DRAM, MST, NOV; DFS 2, 7, 18; DLB 13, 15, 233, 319, 321, 329; DLBY 1990; EWL 3; GFL 1789 to the Present; LATS 1:2; LMFS 2; MTCW 1, 2; MTFW 2005; RGSF 2; RGWL 2, 3; SSFS 15; TEA; WLIT 4

Beckett, Samuel Barclay
  See Beckett, Samuel

Beckford, William 1760-1844 .... **NCLC 16, 214**
  See also BRW 3; DLB 39, 213; GL 2; HGG; LMFS 1; SUFW

Beckham, Barry 1944- .... **BLC 1:1**
  See also BW 1; CA 29-32R; CANR 26, 62; CN 1, 2, 3, 4, 5, 6; DAM MULT; DLB 33

Beckman, Gunnel 1910- .... **CLC 26**
  See also CA 33-36R; CANR 15, 114; CLR 25; MAICYA 1, 2; SAAS 9; SATA 6

Becque, Henri 1837-1899 .... **DC 21; NCLC 3**
  See also DLB 192; GFL 1789 to the Present

Becquer, Gustavo Adolfo
  1836-1870 ...... **HLCS 1; NCLC 106; PC 113**
  See also DAM MULT

Beddoes, Thomas Lovell 1803-1849 .. **DC 15; NCLC 3, 154**
  See also BRWS 11; DLB 96

Bede c. 673-735 .... **CMLC 20, 130**
  See also DLB 146; TEA

Bedford, Denton R. 1907-(?) .... **NNAL**

Bedford, Donald F.
  See Fearing, Kenneth

Beecher, Catharine Esther
  1800-1878 .... **NCLC 30**
  See also DLB 1, 243

Beecher, John 1904-1980 .... **CLC 6**
  See also AITN 1; CA 5-8R; 105; CANR 8; CP 1, 2, 3

Beer, Johann 1655-1700 .... **LC 5**
  See also DLB 168

Beer, Patricia 1924- .... **CLC 58**
  See also BRWS 14; CA 61-64; 183; CANR 13, 46; CP 1, 2, 3, 4, 5, 6; CWP; DLB 40; FW

Beerbohm, Max
  See Beerbohm, (Henry) Max(imilian)

Beerbohm, (Henry) Max(imilian)
  1872-1956 .... **TCLC 1, 24**
  See also BRWS 2; CA 104; 154; CANR 79; DLB 34, 100; FANT; MTCW 2

Beer-Hofmann, Richard
  1866-1945 .... **TCLC 60**
  See also CA 160; DLB 81

Beethoven, Ludwig van
  1770(?)-1827 .... **NCLC 227**

Beg, Shemus
  See Stephens, James

Begiebing, Robert J(ohn) 1946- .... **CLC 70**
  See also CA 122; CANR 40, 88

Begley, Louis 1933- .... **CLC 197**
  See also CA 140; CANR 98, 176, 210; DLB 299; RGHL; TCLE 1:1

Behan, Brendan 1923-1964 ...... **CLC 1, 8, 11, 15, 79**
  See also BRWS 2; CA 73-76; CANR 33, 121; CBD; CDBLB 1945-1960; DAM DRAM; DFS 7; DLB 13, 233; EWL 3; MTCW 1, 2

Behan, Brendan Francis
  See Behan, Brendan

Behn, Aphra 1640(?)-1689 .. **DC 4; LC 1, 30, 42, 135; PC 13, 88; WLC 1**
  See also BRWR 3; BRWS 3; DA; DA3; DAB; DAC; DAM DRAM, MST, NOV, POET; DFS 16, 24; DLB 39, 80, 131; FW; NFS 35; TEA; WLIT 3

Behrman, S(amuel) N(athaniel)
  1893-1973 .... **CLC 40**
  See also CA 13-16; 45-48; CAD; CAP 1; DLB 7, 44; IDFW 3; MAL 5; RGAL 4

Bekederemo, J. P. Clark
  See Clark-Bekederemo, J. P.

Belasco, David 1853-1931 .... **TCLC 3**
  See also CA 104; 168; DLB 7; MAL 5; RGAL 4

Belben, Rosalind 1941- .... **CLC 280**
  See also CA 291

Belben, Rosalind Loveday
  See Belben, Rosalind

Beolco, Angelo 1496-1542 .... **LC 139**

Beranger, Pierre Jean de
1780-1857 .... **NCLC 34; PC 112**

Berdyaev, Nicolas
See Berdyaev, Nikolai (Aleksandrovich)

Berdyaev, Nikolai (Aleksandrovich)
1874-1948 .... **TCLC 67**
See also CA 120; 157

Berdyayev, Nikolai (Aleksandrovich)
See Berdyaev, Nikolai (Aleksandrovich)

Berendt, John 1939- .... **CLC 86**
See also CA 146; CANR 75, 83, 151

Berendt, John Lawrence
See Berendt, John

Berengar of Tours c. 1000-1088 .. **CMLC 124**

Beresford, J(ohn) D(avys)
1873-1947 .... **TCLC 81**
See also CA 112; 155; DLB 162, 178, 197;
SFW 4; SUFW 1

Bergelson, David (Rafailovich)
1884-1952 .... **TCLC 81**
See also CA 220; DLB 333; EWL 3

Bergelson, Dovid
See Bergelson, David (Rafailovich)

Berger, Colonel
See Malraux, Andre

Berger, John 1926- .... **CLC 2, 19**
See also BRWS 4; CA 81-84; CANR 51,
78, 117, 163, 200; CN 1, 2, 3, 4, 5, 6, 7;
DLB 14, 207, 319, 326

Berger, John Peter
See Berger, John

Berger, Melvin H. 1927- .... **CLC 12**
See also CA 5-8R; CANR 4, 142; CLR 32;
SAAS 2; SATA 5, 88, 158; SATA-Essay
124

Berger, Thomas 1924- .... **CLC 3, 5, 8, 11, 18,
38, 259**
See also BPFB 1; CA 1-4R; CANR 5, 28,
51, 128; CN 1, 2, 3, 4, 5, 6, 7; DAM
NOV; DLB 2; DLBY 1980; EWL 3;
FANT; INT CANR-28; MAL 5; MTCW
1, 2; MTFW 2005; RHW; TCLE 1:1;
TCWW 1, 2

Bergman, Ernst Ingmar
See Bergman, Ingmar

Bergman, Ingmar 1918-2007 ..... **CLC 16, 72,
210**
See also AAYA 61; CA 81-84; 262; CANR
33, 70; CWW 2; DLB 257; MTCW 2;
MTFW 2005

Bergson, Henri(-Louis) 1859-1941 . **TCLC 32**
See also CA 164; DLB 329; EW 8; EWL 3;
GFL 1789 to the Present

Bergstein, Eleanor 1938- .... **CLC 4**
See also CA 53-56; CANR 5

Berkeley, George 1685-1753 .... **LC 65**
See also DLB 31, 101, 252

Berkoff, Steven 1937- .... **CLC 56**
See also CA 104; CANR 72; CBD; CD 5, 6

Berlin, Isaiah 1909-1997 .... **TCLC 105**
See also CA 85-88; 162

Bermant, Chaim (Icyk) 1929-1998 ... **CLC 40**
See also CA 57-60; CANR 6, 31, 57, 105;
CN 2, 3, 4, 5, 6

Bern, Victoria
See Fisher, M(ary) F(rances) K(ennedy)

Bernanos, (Paul Louis) Georges
1888-1948 .... **TCLC 3**
See also CA 104; 130; CANR 94; DLB 72;
EWL 3; GFL 1789 to the Present; RGWL
2, 3

Bernard, April 1956- .... **CLC 59**
See also CA 131; CANR 144

Bernard, Mary Ann
See Soderbergh, Steven

Bernard of Clairvaux 1090-1153 .. **CMLC 71**
See also DLB 208

Bernard Silvestris fl. c. 1130-fl. c.
1160 .... **CMLC 87**
See also DLB 208

Bernart de Ventadorn c. 1130-c.
1190 .... **CMLC 98**

Berne, Victoria
See Fisher, M(ary) F(rances) K(ennedy)

Bernhard, Thomas 1931-1989 ..... **CLC 3, 32,
61; DC 14; TCLC 165**
See also CA 85-88; 127; CANR 32, 57; CD-
WLB 2; DLB 85, 124; EWL 3; MTCW 1;
RGHL; RGWL 2, 3

Bernhardt, Sarah (Henriette Rosine)
1844-1923 .... **TCLC 75**
See also CA 157

Bernstein, Charles 1950- .... **CLC 142,**
See also CA 129; CAAS 24; CANR 90; CP
4, 5, 6, 7; DLB 169

Bernstein, Ingrid
See Kirsch, Sarah

Beroul fl. c. 12th cent. - .... **CMLC 75**

Berriault, Gina 1926-1999 .... **CLC 54, 109;
SSC 30**
See also CA 116; 129; 185; CANR 66; DLB
130; SSFS 7,11

Berrigan, Daniel 1921- .... **CLC 4**
See also CA 33-36R, 187; CAAE 187;
CAAS 1; CANR 11, 43, 78; CP 1, 2, 3, 4,
5, 6, 7; DLB 5

Berrigan, Edmund Joseph Michael, Jr.
1934-1983 .... **CLC 37; PC 103**
See also CA 61-64; 110; CANR 14, 102;
CP 1, 2, 3; DLB 5, 169; WP

Berrigan, Ted
See Berrigan, Edmund Joseph Michael, Jr.

Berry, Charles Edward Anderson
1931- .... **CLC 17**
See also CA 115

Berry, Chuck
See Berry, Charles Edward Anderson

Berry, Jonas
See Ashbery, John

Berry, Wendell 1934- ..... **CLC 4, 6, 8, 27, 46,
279; PC 28**
See also AITN 1; AMWS 10; ANW; CA
73-76; CANR 50, 73, 101, 132, 174; CP
1, 2, 3, 4, 5, 6, 7; CSW; DAM POET;
DLB 5, 6, 234, 275, 342; MTCW 2;
MTFW 2005; PFS 30; TCLE 1:1

Berry, Wendell Erdman
See Berry, Wendell

Berryman, John 1914-1972 ... **CLC 1, 2, 3, 4,
6, 8, 10, 13, 25, 62; PC 64**
See also AMW; CA 13-16; 33-36R; CABS
2; CANR 35; CAP 1; CDALB 1941-1968;
CP 1; DAM POET; DLB 48; EWL 3;
MAL 5; MTCW 1, 2; MTFW 2005; PAB;
PFS 27; RGAL 4; WP

Berssenbrugge, Mei-mei 1947- .... **PC 115**
See also CA 104; DLB 312

Bertolucci, Bernardo 1940- ...... **CLC 16, 157**
See also CA 106; CANR 125

Berton, Pierre (Francis de Marigny)
1920-2004 .... **CLC 104**
See also CA 1-4R; 233; CANR 2, 56, 144;
CPW; DLB 68; SATA 99; SATA-Obit 158

Bertrand, Aloysius 1807-1841 .... **NCLC 31**
See also DLB 217

Bertrand, Louis oAloysiusc
See Bertrand, Aloysius

Bertran de Born c. 1140-1215 .... **CMLC 5**

Besant, Annie (Wood) 1847-1933 ..... **TCLC 9**
See also CA 105; 185

Bessie, Alvah 1904-1985 .... **CLC 23**
See also CA 5-8R; 116; CANR 2, 80; DLB
26

Bestuzhev, Aleksandr Aleksandrovich
1797-1837 .... **NCLC 131**
See also DLB 198

Bethlen, T.D.
See Silverberg, Robert

Beti, Mongo 1932-2001 .... **BLC 1:1; CLC 27**
See also AFW; BW 1, 3; CA 114; 124;
CANR 81; DA3; DAM MULT; DLB 360;
EWL 3; MTCW 1, 2

Betjeman, John 1906-1984 ...... **CLC 2, 6, 10,
34, 43; PC 75**
See also BRW 7; CA 9-12R; 112; CANR
33, 56; CDBLB 1945-1960; CP 1, 2, 3;
DA3; DAB; DAM MST, POET; DLB 20;
DLBY 1984; EWL 3; MTCW 1, 2

Bettelheim, Bruno 1903-1990 .... **CLC 79;
TCLC 143**
See also CA 81-84; 131; CANR 23, 61;
DA3; MTCW 1, 2; RGHL

Betti, Ugo 1892-1953 .... **TCLC 5**
See also CA 104; 155; EWL 3; RGWL 2, 3

Betts, Doris (Waugh) 1932- ..... **CLC 3, 6, 28,
275; SSC 45**
See also CA 13-16R; CANR 9, 66, 77; CN
6, 7; CSW; DLB 218; DLBY 1982; INT
CANR-9; RGAL 4

Bevan, Alistair
See Roberts, Keith (John Kingston)

Bey, Pilaff
See Douglas, (George) Norman

Beyala, Calixthe 1961- .... **BLC 2:1**
See also EWL 3

Beynon, John
See Harris, John (Wyndham Parkes Lucas)
Beynon

Bhabha, Homi K. 1949- .... **CLC 285**

Bialik, Chaim Nachman
1873-1934 .... **TCLC 25, 201**
See also CA 170; EWL 3; WLIT 6

Bialik, Hayyim Nahman
See Bialik, Chaim Nachman

Bickerstaff, Isaac
See Swift, Jonathan

Bidart, Frank 1939- .... **CLC 33**
See also AMWS 15; CA 140; CANR 106,
215; CP 5, 6, 7; PFS 26

Bienek, Horst 1930- .... **CLC 7, 11**
See also CA 73-76; DLB 75

Bierce, Ambrose 1842-1914(?) ...... **SSC 9, 72,
124; TCLC 1, 7, 44; WLC 1**
See also AAYA 55; AMW; BYA 11; CA
104; 139; CANR 78; CDALB 1865-1917;
DA; DA3; DAC; DAM MST; DLB 11,
12, 23, 71, 74, 186; EWL 3; EXPS; HGG;
LAIT 2; MAL 5; RGAL 4; RGSF 2; SSFS
9, 27; SUFW 1

Bierce, Ambrose Gwinett
See Bierce, Ambrose

Biggers, Earl Derr 1884-1933 .... **TCLC 65**
See also CA 108; 153; DLB 306

Bilek, Anton F. 1919-
See Rankin, Ian
See also CA 304

Billiken, Bud
See Motley, Willard (Francis)

Billings, Josh
See Shaw, Henry Wheeler

Billington, Lady Rachel Mary
See Billington, Rachel

Billington, Rachel 1942- .... **CLC 43**
See also AITN 2; CA 33-36R; CANR 44,
196; CN 4, 5, 6, 7

Binchy, Maeve 1940- .... **CLC 153**
See also BEST 90:1; BPFB 1; CA 127; 134;
CANR 50, 96, 134, 208; CN 5, 6, 7;
CPW; DA3; DAM POP; DLB 319; INT
CA-134; MTCW 2; MTFW 2005; RHW

Binyon, T(imothy) J(ohn)
1936-2004 .... **CLC 34**
See also CA 111; 232; CANR 28, 140

Bobette
See Simenon, Georges

Boccaccio, Giovanni 1313-1375 ... **CMLC 13, 57; SSC 10, 87**
See also EW 2; RGSF 2; RGWL 2, 3; SSFS 28; TWA; WLIT 7

Bochco, Steven 1943- .... **CLC 35**
See also AAYA 11, 71; CA 124; 138

Bock, Charles 1970- .... **CLC 299**
See also CA 274

Bode, Sigmund
See O'Doherty, Brian

Bodel, Jean 1167(?)-1210 .... **CMLC 28**

Bodenheim, Maxwell 1892-1954 .... **TCLC 44**
See also CA 110; 187; DLB 9, 45; MAL 5; RGAL 4

Bodenheimer, Maxwell
See Bodenheim, Maxwell

Bodker, Cecil
See Bodker, Cecil

Bodker, Cecil 1927- .... **CLC 21**
See also CA 73-76; CANR 13, 44, 111; CLR 23; MAICYA 1, 2; SATA 14, 133

Boell, Heinrich 1917-1985 ..... **CLC 2, 3, 6, 9, 11, 15, 27, 32, 72; SSC 23; TCLC 185; WLC 1**
See also BPFB 1; CA 21-24R; 116; CANR 24; CDWLB 2; DA; DA3; DAB; DAC; DAM MST, NOV; DLB 69, 329; DLBY 1985; EW 13; EWL 3; MTCW 1, 2; MTFW 2005; RGHL; RGSF 2; RGWL 2, 3; SSFS 20; TWA

Boell, Heinrich Theodor
See Boell, Heinrich

Boerne, Alfred
See Doeblin, Alfred

Boethius c. 480-c. 524 .... **CMLC 15**
See also DLB 115; RGWL 2, 3; WLIT 8

Boff, Leonardo (Genezio Darci)
1938- .... **CLC 70; HLC 1**
See also CA 150; DAM MULT; HW 2

Bogan, Louise 1897-1970 .... **CLC 4, 39, 46, 93; PC 12**
See also AMWS 3; CA 73-76; 25-28R; CANR 33, 82; CP 1; DAM POET; DLB 45, 169; EWL 3; MAL 5; MBL; MTCW 1, 2; PFS 21; RGAL 4

Bogarde, Dirk
See Van Den Bogarde, Derek Jules Gaspard Ulric Niven

Bogat, Shatan
See Kacew, Romain

Bogomolny, Robert L. 1938- .... **SSC 41; TCLC 11**
See also CA 121, 164; DLB 182; EWL 3; MJW; RGSF 2; RGWL 2, 3; TWA

Bogomolny, Robert Lee
See Bogomolny, Robert L.

Bogosian, Eric 1953- .... **CLC 45, 141**
See also CA 138; CAD; CANR 102, 148; CD 5, 6; DLB 341

Bograd, Larry 1953- .... **CLC 35**
See also CA 93-96; CANR 57; SAAS 21; SATA 33, 89; WYA

Bohme, Jakob 1575-1624 .... **LC 178**
See also DLB 164

Boiardo, Matteo Maria 1441-1494 .... **LC 6, 168**

Boileau-Despreaux, Nicolas
1636-1711 .... **LC 3, 164**
See also DLB 268; EW 3; GFL Beginnings to 1789; RGWL 2, 3

Boissard, Maurice
See Leautaud, Paul

Bojer, Johan 1872-1959 .... **TCLC 64**
See also CA 189; EWL 3

Bok, Edward W(illiam)
1863-1930 .... **TCLC 101**
See also CA 217; DLB 91; DLBD 16

Boker, George Henry 1823-1890 . **NCLC 125**
See also RGAL 4

Boland, Eavan 1944- ... **CLC 40, 67, 113; PC 58**
See also BRWS 5; CA 143, 207; CAAE 207; CANR 61, 180; CP 1, 6, 7; CWP; DAM POET; DLB 40; FW; MTCW 2; MTFW 2005; PFS 12, 22, 31

Boland, Eavan Aisling
See Boland, Eavan

Bolano, Roberto 1953-2003 .... **CLC 294**
See also CA 229; CANR 175

Bolingbroke, Viscount
See St. John, Henry

Boll, Heinrich
See Boell, Heinrich

Bolt, Lee
See Faust, Frederick

Bolt, Robert (Oxton) 1924-1995 ...... **CLC 14; TCLC 175**
See also CA 17-20R; 147; CANR 35, 67; CBD; DAM DRAM; DFS 2; DLB 13, 233; EWL 3; LAIT 1; MTCW 1

Bombal, Maria Luisa 1910-1980 .... **HLCS 1; SSC 37**
See also CA 127; CANR 72; EWL 3; HW 1; LAW; RGSF 2

Bombet, Louis-Alexandre-Cesar
See Stendhal

Bomkauf
See Kaufman, Bob (Garnell)

Bonaventura NCLC 35
See also DLB 90

Bonaventure 1217(?)-1274 .... **CMLC 79**
See also DLB 115; LMFS 1

Bond, Edward 1934- .... **CLC 4, 6, 13, 23**
See also AAYA 50; BRWS 1; CA 25-28R; CANR 38, 67, 106; CBD; CD 5, 6; DAM DRAM; DFS 3, 8; DLB 13, 310; EWL 3; MTCW 1

Bonham, Frank 1914-1989 .... **CLC 12**
See also AAYA 1, 70; BYA 1, 3; CA 9-12R; CANR 4, 36; JRDA; MAICYA 1, 2; SAAS 3; SATA 1, 49; SATA-Obit 62; TCWW 1, 2; YAW

Bonnefoy, Yves 1923- . **CLC 9, 15, 58; PC 58**
See also CA 85-88; CANR 33, 75, 97, 136; CWW 2; DAM MST, POET; DLB 258; EWL 3; GFL 1789 to the Present; MTCW 1, 2; MTFW 2005

Bonner, Marita
See Occomy, Marita (Odette) Bonner

Bonnin, Gertrude 1876-1938 .... **NNAL**
See also CA 150; DAM MULT; DLB 175

Bontemps, Arna 1902-1973 ... **BLC 1:1; CLC 1, 18; HR 1:2**
See also BW 1; CA 1-4R; 41-44R; CANR 4, 35; CLR 6; CP 1; CWRI 5; DA3; DAM MULT, NOV, POET; DLB 48, 51; JRDA; MAICYA 1, 2; MAL 5; MTCW 1, 2; PFS 32; SATA 2, 44; SATA-Obit 24; WCH; WP

Bontemps, Arnaud Wendell
See Bontemps, Arna

Boot, William
See Stoppard, Tom

Booth, Irwin
See Hoch, Edward D.

Booth, Martin 1944-2004 .... **CLC 13**
See also CA 93-96; 188; 223; CAAE 188; CAAS 2; CANR 92; CP 1, 2, 3, 4

Booth, Philip 1925-2007 .... **CLC 23**
See also CA 5-8R; 262; CANR 5, 88; CP 1, 2, 3, 4, 5, 6, 7; DLBY 1982

Booth, Philip Edmund
See Booth, Philip

Booth, Wayne C. 1921-2005 .... **CLC 24**
See also CA 1-4R; 244; CAAS 5; CANR 3, 43, 117; DLB 67

Booth, Wayne Clayson
See Booth, Wayne C.

Borchert, Wolfgang 1921-1947 .... **DC 42; TCLC 5**
See also CA 104; 188; DLB 69, 124; EWL 3

Borel, Petrus 1809-1859 .... **NCLC 41**
See also DLB 119; GFL 1789 to the Present

Borges, Jorge Luis 1899-1986 ... **CLC 1, 2, 3, 4, 6, 8, 9, 10, 13, 19, 44, 48, 83; HLC 1; PC 22, 32; SSC 4, 41, 100; TCLC 109; WLC 1**
See also AAYA 26; BPFB 1; CA 21-24R; CANR 19, 33, 75, 105, 133; CDWLB 3; DA; DA3; DAB; DAC; DAM MST, MULT; DLB 113, 283; DLBY 1986; DNFS 1, 2; EWL 3; HW 1, 2; LAW; LMFS 2; MSW; MTCW 1, 2; MTFW 2005; PFS 27; RGHL; RGSF 2; RGWL 2, 3; SFW 4; SSFS 17; TWA; WLIT 1

Borne, Ludwig 1786-1837 .... **NCLC 193**
See also DLB 90

Borowski, Tadeusz 1922-1951 .... **SSC 48; TCLC 9**
See also CA 106; 154; CDWLB 4; DLB 215; EWL 3; RGHL; RGSF 2; RGWL 3; SSFS 13

Borrow, George (Henry)
1803-1881 .... **NCLC 9**
See also BRWS 12; DLB 21, 55, 166

Bosch (Gavino), Juan 1909-2001 ..... **HLCS 1**
See also CA 151; 204; DAM MST, MULT; DLB 145; HW 1, 2

Bosman, Herman Charles
1905-1951 .... **TCLC 49**
See also CA 160; DLB 225; RGSF 2

Bosschere, Jean de 1878(?)-1953 ... **TCLC 19**
See also CA 115; 186

Boswell, James 1740-1795 ...... **LC 4, 50, 182; WLC 1**
See also BRW 3; CDBLB 1660-1789; DA; DAB; DAC; DAM MST; DLB 104, 142; TEA; WLIT 3

Boto, Eza
See Beti, Mongo

Bottomley, Gordon 1874-1948 ..... **TCLC 107**
See also CA 120; 192; DLB 10

Bottoms, David 1949- .... **CLC 53**
See also CA 105; CANR 22; CSW; DLB 120; DLBY 1983

Boucicault, Dion 1820-1890 .... **NCLC 41**
See also DLB 344

Boucolon, Maryse
See Conde, Maryse

Bourcicault, Dion
See Boucicault, Dion

Bourdieu, Pierre 1930-2002 .... **CLC 198, 296**
See also CA 130; 204

Bourget, Paul (Charles Joseph)
1852-1935 .... **TCLC 12**
See also CA 107; 196; DLB 123; GFL 1789 to the Present

Bourjaily, Vance 1922-2010 .... **CLC 8, 62**
See also CA 1-4R; CAAS 1; CANR 2, 72; CN 1, 2, 3, 4, 5, 6, 7; DLB 2, 143; MAL 5

Bourjaily, Vance Nye
See Bourjaily, Vance

Bourne, Randolph S(illiman)
1886-1918 .... **TCLC 16**
See also AMW; CA 117; 155; DLB 63; MAL 5

Boursiquot, Dionysius
See Boucicault, Dion

Bova, Ben 1932- .... **CLC 45**
See also AAYA 16; CA 5-8R; CAAS 18; CANR 11, 56, 94, 111, 157; CLR 3, 96; DLBY 1981; INT CANR-11; MAICYA 1, 2; MTCW 1; SATA 6, 68, 133; SFW 4

Brecht, Eugen Berthold Friedrich
See Brecht, Bertolt
Brecht, Eugen Bertolt Friedrich
See Brecht, Bertolt
Bremer, Fredrika 1801-1865 .... **NCLC 11**
See also DLB 254
Brennan, Christopher John
1870-1932 .... **TCLC 17**
See also CA 117; 188; DLB 230; EWL 3
Brennan, Maeve 1917-1993 ... **CLC 5; TCLC 124**
See also CA 81-84; CANR 72, 100
Brenner, Jozef 1887-1919 .... **TCLC 13**
See also CA 111; 240
Brent, Linda
See Jacobs, Harriet A.
Brentano, Clemens (Maria)
1778-1842 .... **NCLC 1, 191; SSC 115**
See also DLB 90; RGWL 2, 3
Brent of Bin Bin
See Franklin, (Stella Maria Sarah) Miles (Lampe)
Brenton, Howard 1942- .... **CLC 31**
See also CA 69-72; CANR 33, 67; CBD; CD 5, 6; DLB 13; MTCW 1
Breslin, James
See Breslin, Jimmy
Breslin, Jimmy 1930- .... **CLC 4, 43**
See also CA 73-76; CANR 31, 75, 139, 187; DAM NOV; DLB 185; MTCW 2; MTFW 2005
Bresson, Robert 1901(?)-1999 .... **CLC 16**
See also CA 110; 187; CANR 49
Breton, Andre 1896-1966 .. **CLC 2, 9, 15, 54; PC 15; TCLC 247**
See also CA 19-20; 25-28R; CANR 40, 60; CAP 2; DLB 65, 258; EW 11; EWL 3; GFL 1789 to the Present; LMFS 2; MTCW 1, 2; MTFW 2005; RGWL 2, 3; TWA; WP
Breton, Nicholas c. 1554-c. 1626 .... **LC 133**
See also DLB 136
Breytenbach, Breyten 1939(?)- .. **CLC 23, 37, 126**
See also CA 113; 129; CANR 61, 122, 202; CWW 2; DAM POET; DLB 225; EWL 3
Bridgers, Sue Ellen 1942- .... **CLC 26**
See also AAYA 8, 49; BYA 7, 8; CA 65-68; CANR 11, 36; CLR 18; DLB 52; JRDA; MAICYA 1, 2; SAAS 1; SATA 22, 90; SATA-Essay 109; WYA; YAW
Bridges, Robert (Seymour)
1844-1930 .... **PC 28; TCLC 1**
See also BRW 6; CA 104; 152; CDBLB 1890-1914; DAM POET; DLB 19, 98
Bridie, James
See Mavor, Osborne Henry
Brin, David 1950- .... **CLC 34**
See also AAYA 21; CA 102; CANR 24, 70, 125, 127; INT CANR-24; SATA 65; SCFW 2; SFW 4
Brink, Andre 1935- .... **CLC 18, 36, 106**
See also AFW; BRWS 6; CA 104; CANR 39, 62, 109, 133, 182; CN 4, 5, 6, 7; DLB 225; EWL 3; INT CA-103; LATS 1:2; MTCW 1, 2; MTFW 2005; WLIT 2
Brink, Andre Philippus
See Brink, Andre
Brinsmead, H. F(ay)
See Brinsmead, H(esba) F(ay)
Brinsmead, H. F.
See Brinsmead, H(esba) F(ay)
Brinsmead, H(esba) F(ay) 1922- ...... **CLC 21**
See also CA 21-24R; CANR 10; CLR 47; CWRI 5; MAICYA 1, 2; SAAS 5; SATA 18, 78

Brittain, Vera (Mary)
1893(?)-1970 .... **CLC 23; TCLC 228**
See also BRWS 10; CA 13-16; 25-28R; CANR 58; CAP 1; DLB 191; FW; MTCW 1, 2
Broch, Hermann 1886-1951 ... **TCLC 20, 204**
See also CA 117; 211; CDWLB 2; DLB 85, 124; EW 10; EWL 3; RGWL 2, 3
Brock, Rose
See Hansen, Joseph
Brod, Max 1884-1968 .... **TCLC 115**
See also CA 5-8R; 25-28R; CANR 7; DLB 81; EWL 3
Brodkey, Harold (Roy) 1930-1996 .. **CLC 56; TCLC 123**
See also CA 111; 151; CANR 71; CN 4, 5, 6; DLB 130
Brodskii, Iosif
See Brodsky, Joseph
Brodskii, Iosif Alexandrovich
See Brodsky, Joseph
Brodsky, Iosif Alexandrovich
See Brodsky, Joseph
Brodsky, Joseph 1940-1996 ..... **CLC 4, 6, 13, 36, 100; PC 9; TCLC 219**
See also AAYA 71; AITN 2; AMWS 8; CA 41-44R; 151; CANR 37, 106; CWW 2; DA3; DAM POET; DLB 285, 329; EWL 3; MTCW 1, 2; MTFW 2005; PFS 35; RGWL 2, 3
Brodsky, Michael 1948- .... **CLC 19**
See also CA 102; CANR 18, 41, 58, 147; DLB 244
Brodsky, Michael Mark
See Brodsky, Michael
Brodzki, Bella CLC 65
Brome, Richard 1590(?)-1652 .... **LC 61**
See also BRWS 10; DLB 58
Bromell, Henry 1947- .... **CLC 5**
See also CA 53-56; CANR 9, 115, 116
Bromfield, Louis (Brucker)
1896-1956 .... **TCLC 11**
See also CA 107; 155; DLB 4, 9, 86; RGAL 4; RHW
Broner, E. M. 1930- .... **CLC 19**
See also CA 17-20R; CANR 8, 25, 72, 216; CN 4, 5, 6; DLB 28
Broner, Esther Masserman
See Broner, E. M.
Bronk, William 1918-1999 .... **CLC 10**
See also AMWS 21; CA 89-92; 177; CANR 23; CP 3, 4, 5, 6, 7; DLB 165
Bronstein, Lev Davidovich
See Trotsky, Leon
Bronte, Anne
See Bronte, Anne
Bronte, Anne 1820-1849 .... **NCLC 4, 71, 102, 235**
See also BRW 5; BRWR 1; DA3; DLB 21, 199, 340; NFS 26; TEA
Bronte, (Patrick) Branwell
1817-1848 .... **NCLC 109**
See also DLB 340
Bronte, Charlotte
See Bronte, Charlotte
Bronte, Charlotte 1816-1855 ...... **NCLC 3, 8, 33, 58, 105, 155, 217, 229; WLC 1**
See also AAYA 17; BRW 5; BRWC 2; BRWR 1; BYA 2; CDBLB 1832-1890; DA; DA3; DAB; DAC; DAM MST, NOV; DLB 21, 159, 199, 340; EXPN; FL 1:2; GL 2; LAIT 2; NFS 4, 36; TEA; WLIT 4
Bronte, Emily
See Bronte, Emily
Bronte, Emily 1818-1848 .... **NCLC 16, 35, 165; PC 8; WLC 1**
See also AAYA 17; BPFB 1; BRW 5; BRWC 1; BRWR 1; BYA 3; CDBLB 1832-1890; DA; DA3; DAB; DAC; DAM

MST, NOV, POET; DLB 21, 32, 199, 340; EXPN; FL 1:2; GL 2; LAIT 1; NFS 2; PFS 33; TEA; WLIT 3
Bronte, Emily Jane
See Bronte, Emily
Brontes
See Bronte, Anne; Bronte, (Patrick) Branwell; Bronte, Charlotte; Bronte, Emily
Brooke, Frances 1724-1789 .... **LC 6, 48**
See also DLB 39, 99
Brooke, Henry 1703(?)-1783 .... **LC 1**
See also DLB 39
Brooke, Rupert 1887-1915 . **PC 24; TCLC 2, 7; WLC 1**
See also BRWS 3; CA 104; 132; CANR 61; CDBLB 1914-1945; DA; DAB; DAC; DAM MST, POET; DLB 19, 216; EXPP; GLL 2; MTCW 1, 2; MTFW 2005; PFS 7; TEA
Brooke, Rupert Chawner
See Brooke, Rupert
Brooke-Haven, P.
See Wodehouse, P. G.
Brooke-Rose, Christine 1923(?)- ..... **CLC 40, 184**
See also BRWS 4; CA 13-16R; CANR 58, 118, 183; CN 1, 2, 3, 4, 5, 6, 7; DLB 14, 231; EWL 3; SFW 4
Brookner, Anita 1928- . **CLC 32, 34, 51, 136, 237**
See also BRWS 4; CA 114; 120; CANR 37, 56, 87, 130, 212; CN 4, 5, 6, 7; CPW; DA3; DAB; DAM POP; DLB 194, 326; DLBY 1987; EWL 3; MTCW 1, 2; MTFW 2005; NFS 23; TEA
Brooks, Cleanth 1906-1994 . **CLC 24, 86, 110**
See also AMWS 14; CA 17-20R; 145; CANR 33, 35; CSW; DLB 63; DLBY 1994; EWL 3; INT CANR-35; MAL 5; MTCW 1, 2; MTFW 2005
Brooks, George
See Baum, L. Frank
Brooks, Gwendolyn 1917-2000 .... **BLC 1:1, 2:1; CLC 1, 2, 4, 5, 15, 49, 125; PC 7; WLC 1**
See also AAYA 20; AFAW 1, 2; AITN 1; AMWS 3; BW 2, 3; CA 1-4R; 190; CANR 1, 27, 52, 75, 132; CDALB 1941-1968; CLR 27; CP 1, 2, 3, 4, 5, 6, 7; CWP; DA; DA3; DAC; DAM MST, MULT, POET; DLB 5, 76, 165; EWL 3; EXPP; FL 1:5; MAL 5; MBL; MTCW 1, 2; MTFW 2005; PFS 1, 2, 4, 6, 32; RGAL 4; SATA 6; SATA-Obit 123; TUS; WP
Brooks, Gwendolyn Elizabeth
See Brooks, Gwendolyn
Brooks, Mel 1926- .... **CLC 12, 217**
See also AAYA 13, 48; CA 65-68; CANR 16; DFS 21; DLB 26
Brooks, Peter 1938- .... **CLC 34**
See also CA 45-48; CANR 1, 107, 182
Brooks, Peter Preston
See Brooks, Peter
Brooks, Van Wyck 1886-1963 .... **CLC 29**
See also AMW; CA 1-4R; CANR 6; DLB 45, 63, 103; MAL 5; TUS
Brophy, Brigid 1929-1995 ...... **CLC 6, 11, 29, 105**
See also CA 5-8R; 149; CAAS 4; CANR 25, 53; CBD; CN 1, 2, 3, 4, 5, 6; CWD; DA3; DLB 14, 271; EWL 3; MTCW 1, 2
Brophy, Brigid Antonia
See Brophy, Brigid
Brosman, Catharine Savage 1934- ..... **CLC 9**
See also CA 61-64; CANR 21, 46, 149
Brossard, Nicole 1943- .... **CLC 115, 169; PC 80**
See also CA 122; CAAS 16; CANR 140; CCA 1; CWP; CWW 2; DLB 53; EWL 3; FW; GLL 2; RGWL 3

Bufalino, Gesualdo 1920-1996 .... **CLC 74**
See also CA 209; CWW 2; DLB 196

Buffon, Georges-Louis Leclerc
1707-1788 .... **LC 186**
See also DLB 313; GFL Beginnings to 1789

Bugayev, Boris Nikolayevich
1880-1934 .... **PC 11; TCLC 7**
See also CA 104; 165; DLB 295; EW 9;
EWL 3; MTCW 2; MTFW 2005; RGWL
2, 3

Bukowski, Charles 1920-1994 ... **CLC 2, 5, 9,**
41, 82, 108; PC 18; SSC 45
See also CA 17-20R; 144; CANR 40, 62,
105, 180; CN 4, 5; CP 1, 2, 3, 4, 5; CPW;
DA3; DAM NOV, POET; DLB 5, 130,
169; EWL 3; MAL 5; MTCW 1, 2;
MTFW 2005; PFS 28

Bulgakov, Mikhail 1891-1940 .... **SSC 18;**
TCLC 2, 16, 159
See also AAYA 74; BPFB 1; CA 105; 152;
DAM DRAM, NOV; DLB 272; EWL 3;
MTCW 2; MTFW 2005; NFS 8; RGSF 2;
RGWL 2, 3; SFW 4; TWA

Bulgakov, Mikhail Afanasevich
See Bulgakov, Mikhail

Bulgya, Alexander Alexandrovich
1901-1956 .... **TCLC 53**
See also CA 117; 181; DLB 272; EWL 3

Bullins, Ed 1935- ...... **BLC 1:1; CLC 1, 5, 7;**
DC 6
See also BW 2, 3; CA 49-52; CAAS 16;
CAD; CANR 24, 46, 73, 134; CD 5, 6;
DAM DRAM, MULT; DLB 7, 38, 249;
EWL 3; MAL 5; MTCW 1, 2; MTFW
2005; RGAL 4

Bulosan, Carlos 1911-1956 .... **AAL**
See also CA 216; DLB 312; RGAL 4

Bulwer-Lytton, Edward
1803-1873 .... **NCLC 1, 45, 238**
See also DLB 21; RGEL 2; SATA 23; SFW
4; SUFW 1; TEA

Bulwer-Lytton, Edward George Earle
Lytton
See Bulwer-Lytton, Edward

Bunin, Ivan
See Bunin, Ivan Alexeyevich

Bunin, Ivan Alekseevich
See Bunin, Ivan Alexeyevich

Bunin, Ivan Alexeyevich 1870-1953 ... **SSC 5;**
TCLC 6
See also CA 104; DLB 317, 329; EWL 3;
RGSF 2; RGWL 2, 3; TWA

Bunting, Basil 1900-1985 ...... **CLC 10, 39, 47**
See also BRWS 7; CA 53-56; 115; CANR
7; CP 1, 2, 3, 4; DAM POET; DLB 20;
EWL 3; RGEL 2

Bunuel, Luis 1900-1983 ... **CLC 16, 80; HLC**
1
See also CA 101; 110; CANR 32, 77; DAM
MULT; HW 1

Bunyan, John 1628-1688 .... **LC 4, 69, 180;**
WLC 1
See also BRW 2; BYA 5; CDBLB 1660-
1789; CLR 124; DA; DAB; DAC; DAM
MST; DLB 39; NFS 32; RGEL 2; TEA;
WCH; WLIT 3

Buonarroti, Michelangelo
1568-1646 .... **PC 103**
See also DLB 339

Buravsky, Alexandr CLC 59

Burchill, Julie 1959- .... **CLC 238**
See also CA 135; CANR 115, 116, 207

Burckhardt, Jacob (Christoph)
1818-1897 .... **NCLC 49**
See also EW 6

Burford, Eleanor
See Hibbert, Eleanor Alice Burford

Burgess, Anthony 1917-1993 . **CLC 1, 2, 4, 5,**
8, 10, 13, 15, 22, 40, 62, 81, 94
See also AAYA 25; AITN 1; BRWS 1; CA
1-4R; 143; CANR 2, 46; CDBLB 1960 to
Present; CN 1, 2, 3, 4, 5; DA3; DAB;
DAC; DAM NOV; DLB 14, 194, 261;
DLBY 1998; EWL 3; MTCW 1, 2; MTFW
2005; NFS 15; RGEL 2; RHW; SFW 4;
TEA; YAW

Buridan, John c. 1295-c. 1358 ...... **CMLC 97**

Burke, Edmund 1729(?)-1797 .... **LC 7, 36,**
146; WLC 1
See also BRW 3; DA; DA3; DAB; DAC;
DAM MST; DLB 104, 252, 336; RGEL
2; TEA

Burke, Kenneth (Duva) 1897-1993 ... **CLC 2,**
24
See also AMW; CA 5-8R; 143; CANR 39,
74, 136; CN 1, 2; CP 1, 2, 3, 4, 5; DLB
45, 63; EWL 3; MAL 5; MTCW 1, 2;
MTFW 2005; RGAL 4

Burke, Leda
See Garnett, David

Burke, Ralph
See Silverberg, Robert

Burke, Thomas 1886-1945 .... **TCLC 63**
See also CA 113; 155; CMW 4; DLB 197

Burke, Valenza Pauline
See Marshall, Paule

Burney, Fanny 1752-1840 .... **NCLC 12, 54,**
107
See also BRWS 3; DLB 39; FL 1:2; NFS
16; RGEL 2; TEA

Burney, Frances
See Burney, Fanny

Burns, Robert 1759-1796 . **LC 3, 29, 40, 190;**
PC 6, 114; WLC 1
See also AAYA 51; BRW 3; CDBLB 1789-
1832; DA; DA3; DAB; DAC; DAM MST,
POET; DLB 109; EXPP; PAB; RGEL 2;
TEA; WP

Burns, Tex
See L'Amour, Louis

Burnshaw, Stanley 1906-2005 ..... **CLC 3, 13,**
44
See also CA 9-12R; 243; CP 1, 2, 3, 4, 5, 6,
7; DLB 48; DLBY 1997

Burr, Anne 1937- .... **CLC 6**
See also CA 25-28R

Burroughs, Augusten 1965- .... **CLC 277**
See also AAYA 73; CA 214; CANR 168

Burroughs, Edgar Rice 1875-1950 . **TCLC 2,**
32
See also AAYA 11; BPFB 1; BYA 4, 9; CA
104; 132; CANR 131; CLR 157; DA3;
DAM NOV; DLB 8; FANT; MTCW 1, 2;
MTFW 2005; RGAL 4; SATA 41; SCFW
1, 2; SFW 4; TCWW 1, 2; TUS; YAW

Burroughs, William S. 1914-1997 . **CLC 1, 2,**
5, 15, 22, 42, 75, 109; TCLC 121; WLC
1
See also AAYA 60; AITN 2; AMWS 3; BG
1:2; BPFB 1; CA 9-12R; 160; CANR 20,
52, 104; CN 1, 2, 3, 4, 5, 6; CPW; DA;
DA3; DAB; DAC; DAM MST, NOV,
POP; DLB 2, 8, 16, 152, 237; DLBY
1981, 1997; EWL 3; GLL 1; HGG; LMFS
2; MAL 5; MTCW 1, 2; MTFW 2005;
RGAL 4; SFW 4

Burroughs, William Seward
See Burroughs, William S.

Burton, Sir Richard F(rancis)
1821-1890 .... **NCLC 42**
See also DLB 55, 166, 184; SSFS 21

Burton, Robert 1577-1640 .... **LC 74**
See also DLB 151; RGEL 2

Buruma, Ian 1951- .... **CLC 163**
See also CA 128; CANR 65, 141, 195

Bury, Stephen
See Stephenson, Neal

Busch, Frederick 1941-2006 .. **CLC 7, 10, 18,**
47, 166
See also CA 33-36R; 248; CAAS 1; CANR
45, 73, 92, 157; CN 1, 2, 3, 4, 5, 6, 7;
DLB 6, 218

Busch, Frederick Matthew
See Busch, Frederick

Bush, Barney (Furman) 1946- .... **NNAL**
See also CA 145

Bush, Ronald 1946- .... **CLC 34**
See also CA 136

Busia, Abena, P. A. 1953- .... **BLC 2:1**

Bustos, Francisco
See Borges, Jorge Luis

Bustos Domecq, Honorio
See Bioy Casares, Adolfo; Borges, Jorge
Luis

Butler, Octavia 1947-2006 . **BLC 2:1; BLCS;**
CLC 38, 121, 230, 240
See also AAYA 18, 48; AFAW 2; AMWS
13; BPFB 1; BW 2, 3; CA 73-76; 248;
CANR 12, 24, 38, 73, 145, 240; CLR 65;
CN 7; CPW; DA3; DAM MULT, POP;
DLB 33; LATS 1:2; MTCW 1, 2; MTFW
2005; NFS 8, 21, 34; SATA 84; SCFW 2;
SFW 4; SSFS 6; TCLE 1:1; YAW

Butler, Octavia E.
See Butler, Octavia

Butler, Octavia Estelle
See Butler, Octavia

Butler, Robert Olen, Jr.
See Butler, Robert Olen

Butler, Robert Olen 1945- .... **CLC 81, 162;**
SSC 117
See also AMWS 12; BPFB 1; CA 112;
CANR 66, 138, 194; CN 7; CSW; DAM
POP; DLB 173, 335; INT CA-112; MAL
5; MTCW 2; MTFW 2005; SSFS 11, 22

Butler, Samuel 1612-1680 .... **LC 16, 43, 173;**
PC 94
See also DLB 101, 126; RGEL 2

Butler, Samuel 1835-1902 .... **TCLC 1, 33;**
WLC 1
See also BRWS 2; CA 143; CDBLB 1890-
1914; DA; DA3; DAB; DAC; DAM MST,
NOV; DLB 18, 57, 174; RGEL 2; SFW 4;
TEA

Butler, Walter C.
See Faust, Frederick

Butor, Michel (Marie Francois)
1926- .... **CLC 1, 3, 8, 11, 15, 161**
See also CA 9-12R; CANR 33, 66; CWW
2; DLB 83; EW 13; EWL 3; GFL 1789 to
the Present; MTCW 1, 2; MTFW 2005

Butts, Mary 1890(?)-1937 ... **SSC 124; TCLC**
77
See also CA 148; DLB 240

Buxton, Ralph
See Silverstein, Alvin; Silverstein, Virginia
B.

Buzo, Alex
See Buzo, Alex

Buzo, Alex 1944- .... **CLC 61**
See also CA 97-100; CANR 17, 39, 69; CD
5, 6; DLB 289

Buzo, Alexander John
See Buzo, Alex

Buzzati, Dino 1906-1972 .... **CLC 36**
See also CA 160; 33-36R; DLB 177; RGWL
2, 3; SFW 4

Byars, Betsy 1928- .... **CLC 35**
See also AAYA 19; BYA 3; CA 33-36R,
183; CAAE 183; CANR 18, 36, 57, 102,
148; CLR 1, 16, 72; DLB 52; INT CANR-
18; JRDA; MAICYA 1, 2; MAICYAS 1;
MTCW 1; SAAS 1; SATA 4, 46, 80, 163;
SATA-Essay 108; WYA; YAW

Clarke, Arthur C. 1917-2008 .. **CLC 1, 4, 13, 18, 35, 136; SSC 3**
See also AAYA 4, 33; BPFB 1; BYA 13; CA 1-4R; 270; CANR 2, 28, 55, 74, 130, 196; CLR 119; CN 1, 2, 3, 4, 5, 6, 7; CPW; DA3; DAM POP; DLB 261; JRDA; LAIT 5; MAICYA 1, 2; MTCW 1, 2; MTFW 2005; SATA 13, 70, 115; SATA-Obit 191; SCFW 1, 2; SFW 4; SSFS 4, 18, 29; TCLE 1:1; YAW

Clarke, Arthur Charles
See Clarke, Arthur C.

Clarke, Austin 1896-1974 .... **CLC 6, 9; PC 112**
See also BRWS 15; CA 29-32; 49-52; CAP 2; CP 1, 2; DAM POET; DLB 10, 20; EWL 3; RGEL 2

Clarke, Austin C. 1934- .... **BLC 1:1; CLC 8, 53; SSC 45, 116**
See also BW 1; CA 25-28R; CAAS 16; CANR 14, 32, 68, 140; CN 1, 2, 3, 4, 5, 6, 7; DAC; DAM MULT; DLB 53, 125; DNFS 2; MTCW 2; MTFW 2005; RGSF 2

Clarke, Gillian 1937- .... **CLC 61**
See also CA 106; CP 3, 4, 5, 6, 7; CWP; DLB 40

Clarke, Marcus (Andrew Hislop) 1846-1881 .... **NCLC 19; SSC 94**
See also DLB 230; RGEL 2; RGSF 2

Clarke, Shirley 1925-1997 .... **CLC 16**
See also CA 189

Clash, The
See Headon, (Nicky) Topper; Jones, Mick; Simonon, Paul; Strummer, Joe

Claudel, Paul (Louis Charles Marie) 1868-1955 .... **TCLC 2, 10**
See also CA 104; 165; DLB 192, 258, 321; EW 8; EWL 3; GFL 1789 to the Present; RGWL 2, 3; TWA

Claudian 370(?)-404(?) .... **CMLC 46**
See also RGWL 2, 3

Claudius, Matthias 1740-1815 .... **NCLC 75**
See also DLB 97

Clavell, James 1925-1994 .... **CLC 6, 25, 87**
See also BPFB 1; CA 25-28R; 146; CANR 26, 48; CN 5; CPW; DA3; DAM NOV, POP; MTCW 1, 2; MTFW 2005; NFS 10; RHW

Clayman, Gregory CLC 65

Cleage, Pearl 1948- .... **DC 32**
See also BW 2; CA 41-44R; CANR 27, 148, 177; DFS 14, 16; DLB 228; NFS 17

Cleage, Pearl Michelle
See Cleage, Pearl

Cleaver, (Leroy) Eldridge 1935-1998 .... **BLC 1:1; CLC 30, 119**
See also BW 1, 3; CA 21-24R; 167; CANR 16, 75; DA3; DAM MULT; MTCW 2; YAW

Cleese, John (Marwood) 1939- .... **CLC 21**
See also CA 112; 116; CANR 35; MTCW 1

Cleishbotham, Jebediah
See Scott, Sir Walter

Cleland, John 1710-1789 .... **LC 2, 48**
See also DLB 39; RGEL 2

Clemens, Samuel
See Twain, Mark

Clemens, Samuel Langhorne
See Twain, Mark

Clement of Alexandria 150(?)-215(?) .... **CMLC 41**

Cleophil
See Congreve, William

Clerihew, E.
See Bentley, E(dmund) C(lerihew)

Clerk, N. W.
See Lewis, C. S.

Cleveland, John 1613-1658 .... **LC 106**
See also DLB 126; RGEL 2

Cliff, Jimmy
See Chambers, James

Cliff, Michelle 1946- .... **BLCS; CLC 120**
See also BW 2; CA 116; CANR 39, 72; CD-WLB 3; DLB 157; FW; GLL 2

Clifford, Lady Anne 1590-1676 .... **LC 76**
See also DLB 151

Clifton, Lucille 1936-2010 .... **BLC 1:1, 2:1; CLC 19, 66, 162, 283; PC 17**
See also AFAW 2; BW 2, 3; CA 49-52; CANR 2, 24, 42, 76, 97, 138; CLR 5; CP 2, 3, 4, 5, 6, 7; CSW; CWP; CWRI 5; DA3; DAM MULT, POET; DLB 5, 41; EXPP; MAICYA 1, 2; MTCW 1, 2; MTFW 2005; PFS 1, 14, 29; SATA 20, 69, 128; WP

Clifton, Thelma Lucille
See Clifton, Lucille

Clinton, Dirk
See Silverberg, Robert

Clough, Arthur Hugh 1819-1861 .. **NCLC 27, 163; PC 103**
See also BRW 5; DLB 32; RGEL 2

Clutha, Janet Paterson Frame
See Frame, Janet

Clyne, Terence
See Blatty, William Peter

Cobalt, Martin
See Mayne, William

Cobb, Irvin S(hrewsbury) 1876-1944 .... **TCLC 77**
See also CA 175; DLB 11, 25, 86

Cobbett, William 1763-1835 .... **NCLC 49**
See also DLB 43, 107, 158; RGEL 2

Coben, Harlan 1962- .... **CLC 269**
See also AAYA 83; CA 164; CANR 162, 199

Coburn, D(onald) L(ee) 1938- .... **CLC 10**
See also CA 89-92; DFS 23

Cockburn, Catharine Trotter
See Trotter, Catharine

Cocteau, Jean 1889-1963 ... **CLC 1, 8, 15, 16, 43; DC 17; TCLC 119; WLC 2**
See also AAYA 74; CA 25-28; CANR 40; CAP 2; DA; DA3; DAB; DAC; DAM DRAM, MST, NOV; DFS 24; DLB 65, 258, 321; EW 10; EWL 3; GFL 1789 to the Present; MTCW 1, 2; RGWL 2, 3; TWA

Cocteau, Jean Maurice Eugene Clement
See Cocteau, Jean

Codrescu, Andrei 1946- .... **CLC 46, 121**
See also CA 33-36R; CAAS 19; CANR 13, 34, 53, 76, 125; CN 7; DA3; DAM POET; MAL 5; MTCW 2; MTFW 2005

Coe, Max
See Bourne, Randolph S(illiman)

Coe, Tucker
See Westlake, Donald E.

Coelho, Paulo 1947- .... **CLC 258**
See also CA 152; CANR 80, 93, 155, 194; NFS 29

Coen, Ethan 1957- .... **CLC 108, 267**
See also AAYA 54; CA 126; CANR 85

Coen, Joel 1954- .... **CLC 108, 267**
See also AAYA 54; CA 126; CANR 119

The Coen Brothers
See Coen, Ethan; Coen, Joel

Coetzee, J. M. 1940- ..... **CLC 23, 33, 66, 117, 161, 162**
See also AAYA 37; AFW; BRWS 6; CA 77-80; CANR 41, 54, 74, 114, 133, 180; CN 4, 5, 6, 7; DA3; DAM NOV; DLB 225, 326, 329; EWL 3; LMFS 2; MTCW 1, 2; MTFW 2005; NFS 21; WLIT 2; WWE 1

Coetzee, John Maxwell
See Coetzee, J. M.

Coffey, Brian
See Koontz, Dean

Coffin, Robert P. Tristram 1892-1955 .... **TCLC 95**
See also CA 123; 169; DLB 45

Coffin, Robert Peter Tristram
See Coffin, Robert P. Tristram

Cohan, George M. 1878-1942 .... **TCLC 60**
See also CA 157; DLB 249; RGAL 4

Cohan, George Michael
See Cohan, George M.

Cohen, Arthur A(llen) 1928-1986 ...... **CLC 7, 31**
See also CA 1-4R; 120; CANR 1, 17, 42; DLB 28; RGHL

Cohen, Leonard 1934- .. **CLC 3, 38, 260; PC 109**
See also CA 21-24R; CANR 14, 69; CN 1, 2, 3, 4, 5, 6; CP 1, 2, 3, 4, 5, 6, 7; DAC; DAM MST; DLB 53; EWL 3; MTCW 1

Cohen, Leonard Norman
See Cohen, Leonard

Cohen, Matt(hew) 1942-1999 .... **CLC 19**
See also CA 61-64; 187; CAAS 18; CANR 40; CN 1, 2, 3, 4, 5, 6; DAC; DLB 53

Cohen-Solal, Annie 1948- .... **CLC 50**
See also CA 239

Colegate, Isabel 1931- .... **CLC 36**
See also CA 17-20R; CANR 8, 22, 74; CN 4, 5, 6, 7; DLB 14, 231; INT CANR-22; MTCW 1

Coleman, Emmett
See Reed, Ishmael

Coleridge, Hartley 1796-1849 .... **NCLC 90**
See also DLB 96

Coleridge, M. E.
See Coleridge, Mary E(lizabeth)

Coleridge, Mary E(lizabeth) 1861-1907 .... **TCLC 73**
See also CA 116; 166; DLB 19, 98

Coleridge, Samuel Taylor 1772-1834 ..... **NCLC 9, 54, 99, 111, 177, 197, 231; PC 11, 39, 67, 100; WLC 2**
See also AAYA 66; BRW 4; BRWR 2; BYA 4; CDBLB 1789-1832; DA; DA3; DAB; DAC; DAM MST, POET; DLB 93, 107; EXPP; LATS 1:1; LMFS 1; PAB; PFS 4, 5; RGEL 2; TEA; WLIT 3; WP

Coleridge, Sara 1802-1852 .... **NCLC 31**
See also DLB 199

Coles, Don 1928- .... **CLC 46**
See also CA 115; CANR 38; CP 5, 6, 7

Coles, Robert (Martin) 1929- .... **CLC 108**
See also CA 45-48; CANR 3, 32, 66, 70, 135; INT CANR-32; SATA 23

Colette 1873-1954 ... **SSC 10, 93; TCLC 1, 5, 16**
See also CA 104; 131; DA3; DAM NOV; DLB 65; EW 9; EWL 3; GFL 1789 to the Present; GLL 1; MTCW 1, 2; MTFW 2005; RGWL 2, 3; TWA

Colette, Sidonie-Gabrielle
See Colette

Collett, (Jacobine) Camilla (Wergeland) 1813-1895 .... **NCLC 22**
See also DLB 354

Collier, Christopher 1930- .... **CLC 30**
See also AAYA 13; BYA 2; CA 33-36R; CANR 13, 33, 102; CLR 126; JRDA; MAICYA 1, 2; SATA 16, 70; WYA; YAW 1

Collier, James Lincoln 1928- .... **CLC 30**
See also AAYA 13; BYA 2; CA 9-12R; CANR 4, 33, 60, 102, 208; CLR 3, 126; DAM POP; JRDA; MAICYA 1, 2; SAAS 21; SATA 8, 70, 166; WYA; YAW 1

Collier, Jeremy 1650-1726 .... **LC 6, 157**
See also DLB 336

Coppola, Francis Ford 1939- ... **CLC 16, 126**
See also AAYA 39; CA 77-80; CANR 40, 78; DLB 44
Copway, George 1818-1869 .... **NNAL**
See also DAM MULT; DLB 175, 183
Corbiere, Tristan 1845-1875 .... **NCLC 43**
See also DLB 217; GFL 1789 to the Present
Corcoran, Barbara (Asenath)
1911-2003 .... **CLC 17**
See also AAYA 14; CA 21-24R, 191; CAAE 191; CAAS 2; CANR 11, 28, 48; CLR 50; DLB 52; JRDA; MAICYA 2; MAIC-YAS 1; RHW; SAAS 20; SATA 3, 77; SATA-Essay 125
Cordelier, Maurice
See Giraudoux, Jean
Cordier, Gilbert
See Rohmer, Eric
Corelli, Marie
See Mackay, Mary
Corinna c. 225B.C.-c. 305B.C. ...... **CMLC 72**
Corman, Cid 1924-2004 .... **CLC 9**
See also CA 85-88; 225; CAAS 2; CANR 44; CP 1, 2, 3, 4, 5, 6, 7; DAM POET; DLB 5, 193
Corman, Sidney
See Corman, Cid
Cormier, Robert 1925-2000 .... **CLC 12, 30**
See also AAYA 3, 19; BYA 1, 2, 6, 8, 9; CA 1-4R; CANR 5, 23, 76, 93; CDALB 1968-1988; CLR 12, 55; DA; DAB; DAC; DAM MST, NOV; DLB 52; EXPN; INT CANR-23; JRDA; LAIT 5; MAICYA 1, 2; MTCW 1, 2; MTFW 2005; NFS 2, 18; SATA 10, 45, 83; SATA-Obit 122; WYA; YAW
Cormier, Robert Edmund
See Cormier, Robert
Corn, Alfred (DeWitt III) 1943- .... **CLC 33**
See also CA 179; CAAE 179; CAAS 25; CANR 44; CP 3, 4, 5, 6, 7; CSW; DLB 120, 282; DLBY 1980
Corneille, Pierre 1606-1684 .. **DC 21; LC 28, 135**
See also DAB; DAM MST; DFS 21; DLB 268; EW 3; GFL Beginnings to 1789; RGWL 2, 3; TWA
Cornwell, David
See le Carre, John
Cornwell, David John Moore
See le Carre, John
Cornwell, Patricia 1956- .... **CLC 155**
See also AAYA 16, 56; BPFB 1; CA 134; CANR 53, 131, 195; CMW 4; CPW; CSW; DAM POP; DLB 306; MSW; MTCW 2; MTFW 2005
Cornwell, Patricia Daniels
See Cornwell, Patricia
Cornwell, Smith
See Smith, David (Jeddie)
Corso, Gregory 1930-2001 .... **CLC 1, 11; PC 33, 108**
See also AMWS 12; BG 1:2; CA 5-8R; 193; CANR 41, 76, 132; CP 1, 2, 3, 4, 5, 6, 7; DA3; DLB 5, 16, 237; LMFS 5; MTCW 1, 2; MTFW 2005; WP
Cortazar, Julio 1914-1984 ... **CLC 2, 3, 5, 10, 13, 15, 33, 34, 92; HLC 1; SSC 7, 76**
See also AAYA 85; BPFB 1; CA 21-24R; CANR 12, 32, 81; CDWLB 3; DA3; DAM MULT, NOV; DLB 113; EWL 3; EXPS; HW 1, 2; LAW; MTCW 1, 2; MTFW 2005; RGSF 2; RGWL 2, 3; SSFS 3, 20, 28, 31; TWA; WLIT 1
Cortes, Hernan 1485-1547 .... **LC 31**
Cortez, Jayne 1936- .... **BLC 2:1**
See also BW 2, 3; CA 73-76; CANR 13, 31, 68, 126; CWP; DLB 41; EWL 3

Corvinus, Jakob
See Raabe, Wilhelm (Karl)
Corwin, Cecil
See Kornbluth, C(yril) M.
Cosic, Dobrica 1921- .... **CLC 14**
See also CA 122; 138; CDWLB 4; CWW 2; DLB 181; EWL 3
Costain, Thomas B(ertram)
1885-1965 .... **CLC 30**
See also BYA 3; CA 5-8R; 25-28R; DLB 9; RHW
Costantini, Humberto 1924(?)-1987 . **CLC 49**
See also CA 131; 122; EWL 3; HW 1
Costello, Elvis 1954(?)- .... **CLC 21**
See also CA 204
Costenoble, Philostene
See Ghelderode, Michel de
Cotes, Cecil V.
See Duncan, Sara Jeannette
Cotter, Joseph Seamon Sr.
1861-1949 .... **BLC 1:1; TCLC 28**
See also BW 1; CA 124; DAM MULT; DLB 50
Cotton, John 1584-1652 .... **LC 176**
See also DLB 24; TUS
Couch, Arthur Thomas Quiller
See Quiller-Couch, Sir Arthur (Thomas)
Coulton, James
See Hansen, Joseph
Couperus, Louis (Marie Anne)
1863-1923 .... **TCLC 15**
See also CA 115; EWL 3; RGWL 2, 3
Coupland, Douglas 1961- .... **CLC 85, 133**
See also AAYA 34; CA 142; CANR 57, 90, 130, 172, 213; CCA 1; CN 7; CPW; DAC; DAM POP; DLB 334
Coupland, Douglas Campbell
See Coupland, Douglas
Court, Wesli
See Turco, Lewis
Courtenay, Bryce 1933- .... **CLC 59**
See also CA 138; CPW; NFS 32
Courtney, Robert
See Ellison, Harlan
Cousteau, Jacques 1910-1997 .... **CLC 30**
See also CA 65-68; 159; CANR 15, 67, 201; MTCW 1; SATA 38, 98
Cousteau, Jacques-Yves
See Cousteau, Jacques
Coventry, Francis 1725-1754 .... **LC 46**
See also DLB 39
Coverdale, Miles c. 1487-1569 .... **LC 77**
See also DLB 167
Cowan, Peter (Walkinshaw)
1914-2002 .... **SSC 28**
See also CA 21-24R; CANR 9, 25, 50, 83; CN 1, 2, 3, 4, 5, 6, 7; DLB 260; RGSF 2
Coward, Noel 1899-1973 .... **CLC 1, 9, 29, 51**
See also AITN 1; BRWS 2; CA 17-18; 41-44R; CANR 35, 132, 190; CAP 2; CBD; CDBLB 1914-1945; DA3; DAM DRAM; DFS 3, 6; DLB 10, 245; EWL 3; IDFW 3, 4; MTCW 1, 2; MTFW 2005; RGEL 2; TEA
Coward, Noel Peirce
See Coward, Noel
Cowley, Abraham 1618-1667 .. **LC 43; PC 90**
See also BRW 2; DLB 131, 151; PAB; RGEL 2
Cowley, Malcolm 1898-1989 .... **CLC 39**
See also AMWS 2; CA 5-8R; 128; CANR 3, 55; CP 1, 2, 3, 4; DLB 4, 48; DLBY 1981, 1989; EWL 3; MAL 5; MTCW 1, 2; MTFW 2005
Cowper, William 1731-1800 ..... **NCLC 8, 94; PC 40**
See also BRW 3; BRWR 3; DA3; DAM POET; DLB 104, 109; RGEL 2

Cox, William Trevor
See Trevor, William
Coyle, William
See Keneally, Thomas
Coyne, P. J.
See Masters, Hilary
Cozzens, James Gould 1903-1978 . **CLC 1, 4, 11, 92**
See also AMW; BPFB 1; CA 9-12R; 81-84; CANR 19; CDALB 1941-1968; CN 1, 2; DLB 9, 294; DLBD 2; DLBY 1984, 1997; EWL 3; MAL 5; MTCW 1, 2; MTFW 2005; RGAL 4
Crabbe, George 1754-1832 ... **NCLC 26, 121; PC 97**
See also BRW 3; DLB 93; RGEL 2
Crace, Jim 1946- .... **CLC 157; SSC 61**
See also BRWS 14; CA 128; 135; CANR 55, 70, 123, 180; CN 5, 6, 7; DLB 231; INT CA-135
Craddock, Charles Egbert
See Murfree, Mary Noailles
Craig, A. A.
See Anderson, Poul
Craik, Mrs.
See Craik, Dinah Maria (Mulock)
Craik, Dinah Maria (Mulock)
1826-1887 .... **NCLC 38**
See also DLB 35, 163; MAICYA 1, 2; RGEL 2; SATA 34
Cram, Ralph Adams 1863-1942 ..... **TCLC 45**
See also CA 160
Cranch, Christopher Pearse
1813-1892 .... **NCLC 115**
See also DLB 1, 42, 243
Crane, Harold Hart
See Crane, Hart
Crane, Hart 1899-1932 ... **PC 3, 99; TCLC 2, 5, 80; WLC 2**
See also AAYA 81; AMW; AMWR 2; CA 104; 127; CDALB 1917-1929; DA; DA3; DAB; DAC; DAM MST, POET; DLB 4, 48; EWL 3; MAL 5; MTCW 1, 2; MTFW 2005; RGAL 4; TUS
Crane, R(onald) S(almon)
1886-1967 .... **CLC 27**
See also CA 85-88; DLB 63
Crane, Stephen 1871-1900 ... **PC 80; SSC 7, 56, 70, 129; TCLC 11, 17, 32, 216; WLC 2**
See also AAYA 21; AMW; AMWC 1; BPFB 1; BYA 3; CA 109; 140; CANR 84; CDALB 1865-1917; CLR 132; DA; DA3; DAB; DAC; DAM MST, NOV, POET; DLB 12, 54, 78, 357; EXPN; EXPS; LAIT 2; LMFS 2; MAL 5; NFS 4, 20; PFS 9; RGAL 4; RGSF 2; SSFS 4, 28; TUS; WYA; YABC 2
Crane, Stephen Townley
See Crane, Stephen
Cranmer, Thomas 1489-1556 .... **LC 95**
See also DLB 132, 213
Cranshaw, Stanley
See Fisher, Dorothy (Frances) Canfield
Crase, Douglas 1944- .... **CLC 58**
See also CA 106; CANR 204
Crashaw, Richard 1612(?)-1649 .. **LC 24; PC 84**
See also BRW 2; DLB 126; PAB; RGEL 2
Cratinus c. 519B.C.-c. 422B.C. ..... **CMLC 54**
See also LMFS 1
Craven, Margaret 1901-1980 .... **CLC 17**
See also BYA 2; CA 103; CCA 1; DAC; LAIT 5
Crawford, F(rancis) Marion
1854-1909 .... **TCLC 10**
See also CA 107; 168; DLB 71; HGG; RGAL 4; SUFW 1

Demby, William 1922- ...... **BLC 1:1; CLC 53**
    See also BW 1, 3; CA 81-84; CANR 81;
    DAM MULT; DLB 33

de Menton, Francisco
    See Chin, Frank

Demetrius of Phalerum c.
    307B.C.- .... **CMLC 34**

Demijohn, Thom
    See Disch, Thomas M.

De Mille, James 1833-1880 .... **NCLC 123**
    See also DLB 99, 251

Democritus c. 460B.C.-c. 370B.C. . **CMLC 47**

de Montaigne, Michel
    See Montaigne, Michel de

de Montherlant, Henry
    See Montherlant, Henry de

Demosthenes 384B.C.-322B.C. ...... **CMLC 13**
    See also AW 1; DLB 176; RGWL 2, 3;
    WLIT 8

de Musset, (Louis Charles) Alfred
    See Musset, Alfred de

de Natale, Francine
    See Malzberg, Barry N(athaniel)

de Navarre, Marguerite 1492-1549 .... **LC 61,**
    167; SSC 85
    See also DLB 327; GFL Beginnings to
    1789; RGWL 2, 3

Denby, Edwin (Orr) 1903-1983 .... **CLC 48**
    See also CA 138; 110; CP 1

de Nerval, Gerard
    See Nerval, Gerard de

Denham, John 1615-1669 .... **LC 73**
    See also DLB 58, 126; RGEL 2

Denis, Claire 1948- .... **CLC 286**
    See also CA 249

Denis, Julio
    See Cortazar, Julio

Denmark, Harrison
    See Zelazny, Roger

Dennis, John 1658-1734 .... **LC 11, 154**
    See also DLB 101; RGEL 2

Dennis, Nigel (Forbes) 1912-1989 ...... **CLC 8**
    See also CA 25-28R; 129; CN 1, 2, 3, 4;
    DLB 13, 15, 233; EWL 3; MTCW 1

Dent, Lester 1904-1959 .... **TCLC 72**
    See also CA 112; 161; CMW 4; DLB 306;
    SFW 4

Dentinger, Stephen
    See Hoch, Edward D.

De Palma, Brian 1940- .... **CLC 20, 247**
    See also CA 109

De Palma, Brian Russell
    See De Palma, Brian

de Pizan, Christine
    See Christine de Pizan

De Quincey, Thomas 1785-1859 ..... **NCLC 4,**
    87, 198
    See also BRW 4; CDBLB 1789-1832; DLB
    110, 144; RGEL 2

De Ray, Jill
    See Moore, Alan

Deren, Eleanora 1908(?)-1961 .. **CLC 16, 102**
    See also CA 192; 111

Deren, Maya
    See Deren, Eleanora

Derleth, August (William)
    1909-1971 .... **CLC 31**
    See also BPFB 1; BYA 9, 10; CA 1-4R; 29-
    32R; CANR 4; CMW 4; CN 1; DLB 9;
    DLBD 17; HGG; SATA 5; SUFW 1

Der Nister 1884-1950 .... **TCLC 56**
    See also DLB 333; EWL 3

de Routisie, Albert
    See Aragon, Louis

Derrida, Jacques 1930-2004 ...... **CLC 24, 87,**
    225
    See also CA 124; 127; 232; CANR 76, 98,
    133; DLB 242; EWL 3; LMFS 2; MTCW
    2; TWA

Derry Down Derry
    See Lear, Edward

Dershowitz, Alan M. 1938- .... **CLC 298**
    See also CA 25-28R; CANR 11, 44, 79, 159

Dershowitz, Alan Morton
    See Dershowitz, Alan M.

Dersonnes, Jacques
    See Simenon, Georges

Der Stricker c. 1190-c. 1250 .... **CMLC 75**
    See also DLB 138

Derzhavin, Gavriil Romanovich
    1743-1816 .... **NCLC 215**
    See also DLB 150

Desai, Anita 1937- . **CLC 19, 37, 97, 175, 271**
    See also AAYA 85; BRWS 5; CA 81-84;
    CANR 33, 53, 95, 133; CN 1, 2, 3, 4, 5,
    6, 7; CWRI 5; DA3; DAM NOV;
    DLB 271, 323; DNFS 2; EWL 3; FW;
    MTCW 1, 2; MTFW 2005; SATA 63, 126;
    SSFS 28, 31

Desai, Kiran 1971- .... **CLC 119**
    See also BRWS 15; BYA 16; CA 171;
    CANR 127; NFS 28

de Saint-Luc, Jean
    See Glassco, John

de Saint Roman, Arnaud
    See Aragon, Louis

Desbordes-Valmore, Marceline
    1786-1859 .... **NCLC 97**
    See also DLB 217

Descartes, Rene 1596-1650 .... **LC 20, 35, 150**
    See also DLB 268; EW 3; GFL Beginnings
    to 1789

Deschamps, Eustache 1340(?)-1404 .. **LC 103**
    See also DLB 208

De Sica, Vittorio 1901(?)-1974 .... **CLC 20**
    See also CA 117

Desnos, Robert 1900-1945 ...... **TCLC 22, 241**
    See also CA 121; 151; CANR 107; DLB
    258; EWL 3; LMFS 2

Destouches, Louis-Ferdinand
    See Celine, Louis-Ferdinand

De Teran, Lisa St. Aubin
    See St. Aubin de Teran, Lisa

de Teran, Lisa St. Aubin
    See St. Aubin de Teran, Lisa

de Tolignac, Gaston
    See Griffith, D.W.

Deutsch, Babette 1895-1982 .... **CLC 18**
    See also BYA 3; CA 1-4R; 108; CANR 4,
    79; CP 1, 2, 3; DLB 45; SATA 1; SATA-
    Obit 33

Devenant, William 1606-1649 .... **LC 13**

Devi, Mahasweta 1926- .... **CLC 290**

Deville, Rene
    See Kacew, Romain

Devkota, Laxmiprasad 1909-1959 . **TCLC 23**
    See also CA 123

De Voto, Bernard (Augustine)
    1897-1955 .... **TCLC 29**
    See also CA 113; 160; DLB 9, 256; MAL
    5; TCWW 1, 2

De Vries, Peter 1910-1993 ..... **CLC 1, 2, 3, 7,**
    10, 28, 46
    See also CA 17-20R; 142; CANR 41; CN
    1, 2, 3, 4, 5; DAM NOV; DLB 6; DLBY
    1982; MAL 5; MTCW 1, 2; MTFW 2005

Dewey, John 1859-1952 .... **TCLC 95**
    See also CA 114; 170; CANR 144; DLB
    246, 270; RGAL 4

Dexter, John
    See Bradley, Marion Zimmer

Dexter, Martin
    See Faust, Frederick

Dexter, Pete 1943- .... **CLC 34, 55**
    See also BEST 89:2; CA 127; 131; CANR
    129; CPW; DAM POP; INT CA-131;
    MAL 5; MTCW 1; MTFW 2005

Diamano, Silmang
    See Senghor, Leopold Sedar

Diamant, Anita 1951- .... **CLC 239**
    See also CA 145; CANR 126; NFS 36

Diamond, Neil 1941- .... **CLC 30**
    See also CA 108

Diaz, Junot 1968- .... **CLC 258; SSC 144**
    See also AAYA 83; BYA 12; CA 161;
    CANR 119, 183; LLW; NFS 36; SSFS 20

Diaz del Castillo, Bernal c.
    1496-1584 .... **HLCS 1; LC 31**
    See also DLB 318; LAW

di Bassetto, Corno
    See Shaw, George Bernard

Dick, Philip K. 1928-1982 ... **CLC 10, 30, 72;**
    SSC 57
    See also AAYA 24; BPFB 1; BYA 11; CA
    49-52; 106; CANR 2, 16, 132; CN 2, 3;
    CPW; DA3; DAM NOV, POP; DLB 8;
    MTCW 1, 2; MTFW 2005; NFS 5, 26;
    SCFW 1, 2; SFW 4

Dick, Philip Kindred
    See Dick, Philip K.

Dickens, Charles 1812-1870 . **NCLC 3, 8, 18,**
    26, 37, 50, 86, 105, 113, 161, 187, 203,
    206, 211, 217, 219, 230, 231; SSC 17,
    49, 88; WLC 2
    See also AAYA 23; BRW 5; BRWC 1, 2;
    BYA 1, 2, 3, 13, 14; CDBLB 1832-1890;
    CLR 95, 162; CMW 4; DA; DA3; DAB;
    DAC; DAM MST, NOV; DLB 21, 55, 70,
    159, 166; EXPN; GL 2; HGG; JRDA;
    LAIT 1, 2; LATS 1:1; LMFS 1; MAICYA
    1, 2; NFS 4, 5, 10, 14, 20, 25, 30, 33;
    RGEL 2; RGSF 2; SATA 15; SUFW 1;
    TEA; WCH; WLIT 4; WYA

Dickens, Charles John Huffam
    See Dickens, Charles

Dickey, James 1923-1997 .... **CLC 1, 2, 4, 7,**
    10, 15, 47, 109; PC 40; TCLC 151
    See also AAYA 50; AITN 1, 2; AMWS 4;
    BPFB 1; CA 9-12R; 156; CABS 2; CANR
    10, 48, 61, 105; CDALB 1968-1988; CP
    1, 2, 3, 4, 5, 6; CPW; CSW; DA3; DAM
    NOV, POET, POP; DLB 5, 193, 342;
    DLBD 7; DLBY 1982, 1993, 1996, 1997,
    1998; EWL 3; INT CANR-10; MAL 5;
    MTCW 1, 2; NFS 9; PFS 6, 11; RGAL 4;
    TUS

Dickey, James Lafayette
    See Dickey, James

Dickey, William 1928-1994 .... **CLC 3, 28**
    See also CA 9-12R; 145; CANR 24, 79; CP
    1, 2, 3, 4; DLB 5

Dickinson, Charles 1951- .... **CLC 49**
    See also CA 128; CANR 141

Dickinson, Emily 1830-1886 ... **NCLC 21, 77,**
    171; PC 1; WLC 2
    See also AAYA 22; AMW; AMWR 1;
    CDALB 1865-1917; DA; DA3; DAB;
    DAC; DAM MST, POET; DLB 1, 243;
    EXPP; FL 1:3; MBL; PAB; PFS 1, 2, 3,
    4, 5, 6, 8, 10, 11, 13, 16, 28, 32, 35;
    RGAL 4; SATA 29; TUS; WP; WYA

Dickinson, Emily Elizabeth
    See Dickinson, Emily

Dickinson, Mrs. Herbert Ward
    See Phelps, Elizabeth Stuart

Dickinson, Peter 1927- .... **CLC 12, 35**
    See also AAYA 9, 49; BYA 5; CA 41-44R;
    CANR 31, 58, 88, 134, 195; CLR 29, 125;
    CMW 4; DLB 87, 161, 276; JRDA; MAI-
    CYA 1, 2; SATA 5, 62, 95, 150; SFW 4;
    WYA; YAW

Dickinson, Peter Malcolm de Brissac
See Dickinson, Peter
Dickson, Carr
See Carr, John Dickson
Dickson, Carter
See Carr, John Dickson
Diderot, Denis 1713-1784 .... **LC 26, 126**
See also DLB 313; EW 4; GFL Beginnings
to 1789; LMFS 1; RGWL 2, 3
Didion, Joan 1934- . **CLC 1, 3, 8, 14, 32, 129**
See also AITN 1; AMWS 4; CA 5-8R;
CANR 14, 52, 76, 125, 174; CDALB
1968-1988; CN 2, 3, 4, 5, 6, 7; DA3;
DAM NOV; DLB 2, 173, 185; DLBY
1981, 1986; EWL 3; MAL 5; MBL;
MTCW 1, 2; MTFW 2005; NFS 3; RGAL
4; TCLE 1:1; TCWW 2; TUS
di Donato, Pietro 1911-1992 .... **TCLC 159**
See also AMWS 20; CA 101; 136; DLB 9
Dietrich, Robert
See Hunt, E. Howard
Difusa, Pati
See Almodovar, Pedro
di Lampedusa, Giuseppe Tomasi
See Lampedusa, Giuseppe di
Dillard, Annie 1945- ...... **CLC 9, 60, 115, 216**
See also AAYA 6, 43; AMWS 6; ANW; CA
49-52; CANR 3, 43, 62, 90, 125, 214;
DA3; DAM NOV; DLB 275, 278; DLBY
1980; LAIT 4, 5; MAL 5; MTCW 1, 2;
MTFW 2005; NCFS 1; RGAL 4; SATA
10, 140; TCLE 1:1; TUS
Dillard, R(ichard) H(enry) W(ilde)
1937- .... **CLC 5**
See also CA 21-24R; CAAS 7; CANR 10;
CP 2, 3, 4, 5, 6, 7; CSW; DLB 5, 244
Dillon, Eilis 1920-1994 .... **CLC 17**
See also CA 9-12R, 182; 147; CAAE 182;
CAAS 3; CANR 4, 38, 78; CLR 26; MAI-
CYA 1, 2; MAICYAS 1; SATA 2, 74;
SATA-Essay 105; SATA-Obit 83; YAW
Dimont, Penelope
See Mortimer, Penelope (Ruth)
Dinesen, Isak
See Blixen, Karen
Ding Ling
See Chiang, Pin-chin
Diodorus Siculus c. 90B.C.-c.
31B.C. .... **CMLC 88**
Dionysius of Halicarnassus c. 60B.C.-c.
7B.C. .... **CMLC 126**
Diphusa, Patty
See Almodovar, Pedro
Disch, Thomas M. 1940-2008 .... **CLC 7, 36**
See also AAYA 17; BPFB 1; CA 21-24R;
274; CAAS 4; CANR 17, 36, 54, 89; CLR
18; CP 5, 6, 7; DA3; DLB 8, 282; HGG;
MAICYA 1, 2; MTCW 1, 2; MTFW 2005;
SAAS 15; SATA 92; SATA-Obit 195;
SCFW 1, 2; SFW 4; SUFW 2
Disch, Thomas Michael
See Disch, Thomas M.
Disch, Tom
See Disch, Thomas M.
d'Isly, Georges
See Simenon, Georges
Disraeli, Benjamin 1804-1881 ... **NCLC 2, 39,
79**
See also BRW 4; DLB 21, 55; RGEL 2
D'Israeli, Isaac 1766-1848 .... **NCLC 217**
See also DLB 107
Ditcum, Steve
See Crumb, R.
Dixon, Paige
See Corcoran, Barbara (Asenath)
Dixon, Stephen 1936- .... **CLC 52; SSC 16**
See also AMWS 12; CA 89-92; CANR 17,
40, 54, 91, 175; CN 4, 5, 6, 7; DLB 130;
MAL 5

Dixon, Thomas, Jr. 1864-1946 ..... **TCLC 163**
See also RHW
Djebar, Assia 1936- .... **BLC 2:1; CLC 182,
296; SSC 114**
See also CA 188; CANR 169; DLB 346;
EWL 3; RGWL 3; WLIT 2
Doak, Annie
See Dillard, Annie
Dobell, Sydney Thompson
1824-1874 .... **NCLC 43; PC 100**
See also DLB 32; RGEL 2
Doblin, Alfred
See Doeblin, Alfred
Dobroliubov, Nikolai Aleksandrovich
See Dobrolyubov, Nikolai Alexandrovich
Dobrolyubov, Nikolai Alexandrovich
1836-1861 .... **NCLC 5**
See also DLB 277
Dobson, Austin 1840-1921 .... **TCLC 79**
See also DLB 35, 144
Dobyns, Stephen 1941- .... **CLC 37, 233**
See also AMWS 13; CA 45-48; CANR 2,
18, 99; CMW 4; CP 4, 5, 6, 7; PFS 23
Doctorow, Cory 1971- .... **CLC 273**
See also AAYA 84; CA 221; CANR 203
Doctorow, E. L. 1931- ...... **CLC 6, 11, 15, 18,
37, 44, 65, 113, 214**
See also AAYA 22; AITN 2; AMWS 4;
BEST 89:3; BPFB 1; CA 45-48; CANR
2, 33, 51, 76, 97, 133, 170; CDALB 1968-
1988; CN 3, 4, 5, 6, 7; CPW; DA3; DAM
NOV, POP; DLB 2, 28, 173; DLBY 1980;
EWL 3; LAIT 3; MAL 5; MTCW 1, 2;
MTFW 2005; NFS 6; RGAL 4; RGHL;
RHW; SSFS 27; TCLE 1:1; TCWW 1, 2;
TUS
Doctorow, Edgar Laurence
See Doctorow, E. L.
Dodgson, Charles Lutwidge
See Carroll, Lewis
Dodsley, Robert 1703-1764 .... **LC 97**
See also DLB 95; RGEL 2
Dodson, Owen (Vincent)
1914-1983 .... **BLC 1:1; CLC 79**
See also BW 1; CA 65-68; 110; CANR 24;
DAM MULT; DLB 76
Doeblin, Alfred 1878-1957 .... **TCLC 13**
See also CA 110; 141; CDWLB 2; DLB 66;
EWL 3; RGWL 2, 3
Doerr, Harriet 1910-2002 .... **CLC 34**
See also CA 117; 122; 213; CANR 47; INT
CA-122; LATS 1:2
Domecq, Honorio Bustos
See Bioy Casares, Adolfo; Borges, Jorge
Luis
Domini, Rey
See Lorde, Audre
Dominic, R. B.
See Hennissart, Martha
Dominique
See Proust, Marcel
Don, A
See Stephen, Sir Leslie
Donaldson, Stephen R. 1947- ... **CLC 46, 138**
See also AAYA 36; BPFB 1; CA 89-92;
CANR 13, 55, 99; CPW; DAM POP;
FANT; INT CANR-13; SATA 121; SFW
4; SUFW 1, 2
Donleavy, J(ames) P(atrick) 1926- .... **CLC 1,
4, 6, 10, 45**
See also AITN 2; BPFB 1; CA 9-12R;
CANR 24, 49, 62, 80, 124; CBD; CD 5,
6; CN 1, 2, 3, 4, 5, 6, 7; DLB 6, 173; INT
CANR-24; MAL 5; MTCW 1, 2; MTFW
2005; RGAL 4
Donnadieu, Marguerite
See Duras, Marguerite

Donne, John 1572-1631 ... **LC 10, 24, 91; PC
1, 43; WLC 2**
See also AAYA 67; BRW 1; BRWC 1;
BRWR 2; CDBLB Before 1660; DA;
DAB; DAC; DAM MST, POET; DLB
121, 151; EXPP; PAB; PFS 2, 11, 35;
RGEL 3; TEA; WLIT 3; WP
Donnell, David 1939(?)- .... **CLC 34**
See also CA 197
Donoghue, Denis 1928- .... **CLC 209**
See also CA 17-20R; CANR 16, 102, 206
Donoghue, Emma 1969- .... **CLC 239**
See also CA 155; CANR 103, 152, 196;
DLB 267; GLL 2; SATA 101
Donoghue, P.S.
See Hunt, E. Howard
Donoso, Jose 1924-1996 ..... **CLC 4, 8, 11, 32,
99; HLC 1; SSC 34; TCLC 133**
See also CA 81-84; 155; CANR 32, 73; CD-
WLB 3; CWW 2; DAM MULT; DLB 113;
EWL 3; HW 1, 2; LAW; LAWS 1; MTCW
1, 2; MTFW 2005; RGSF 2; WLIT 1
Donoso Yanez, Jose
See Donoso, Jose
Donovan, John 1928-1992 .... **CLC 35**
See also AAYA 20; CA 97-100; 137; CLR
3; MAICYA 1, 2; SATA 72; SATA-Brief
29; YAW
Don Roberto
See Cunninghame Graham, Robert Bontine
Doolittle, Hilda 1886-1961 . **CLC 3, 8, 14, 31,
34, 73; PC 5; WLC 3**
See also AAYA 66; AMWS 1; CA 97-100;
CANR 35, 131; DA; DAC; DAM MST,
POET; DLB 4, 45; EWL 3; FL 1:5; FW;
GLL 1; LMFS 2; MAL 5; MBL; MTCW
1, 2; MTFW 2005; PFS 6, 28; RGAL 4
Doppo
See Kunikida Doppo
Doppo, Kunikida
See Kunikida Doppo
Dorfman, Ariel 1942- .... **CLC 48, 77, 189;
HLC 1**
See also CA 124; 130; CANR 67, 70, 135;
CWW 2; DAM MULT; DFS 4; EWL 3;
HW 1, 2; INT CA-130; WLIT 1
Dorn, Edward 1929-1999 .... **CLC 10, 18; PC
115**
See also CA 93-96; 187; CANR 42, 79; CP
1, 2, 3, 4, 5, 6, 7; DLB 5; INT CA-93-96;
WP
Dorn, Edward Merton
See Dorn, Edward
Dor-Ner, Zvi CLC 70
Dorris, Michael 1945-1997 .... **CLC 109;
NNAL**
See also AAYA 20; BEST 90:1; BYA 12;
CA 102; 157; CANR 19, 46, 75; CLR 58;
DA3; DAM MULT, NOV; DLB 175;
LAIT 5; MTCW 2; MTFW 2005; NFS 3;
RGAL 4; SATA 75; SATA-Obit 94;
TCWW 2; YAW
Dorris, Michael A.
See Dorris, Michael
Dorris, Michael Anthony
See Dorris, Michael
Dorsan, Luc
See Simenon, Georges
Dorsange, Jean
See Simenon, Georges
Dorset
See Sackville, Thomas
Dos Passos, John 1896-1970 ...... **CLC 1, 4, 8,
11, 15, 25, 34, 82; WLC 2**
See also AMW; BPFB 1; CA 1-4R; 29-32R;
CANR 3; CDALB 1929-1941; DA; DA3;
DAB; DAC; DAM MST, NOV; DLB 4,

Eastaway, Edward
See Thomas, (Philip) Edward

Eastlake, William (Derry)
1917-1997 .... **CLC 8**
See also CA 5-8R; 158; CAAS 1; CANR 5,
63; CN 1, 2, 3, 4, 5, 6; DLB 6, 206; INT
CANR-5; MAL 5; TCWW 1, 2

Eastman, Charles A(lexander)
1858-1939 .... **NNAL; TCLC 55**
See also CA 179; CANR 91; DAM MULT;
DLB 175; YABC 1

Eaton, Edith Maude
1865-1914 .... **AAL; TCLC 232**
See also CA 154; DLB 221, 312; FW

Eaton, (Lillie) Winnifred 1875-1954 .... **AAL**
See also CA 217; DLB 221, 312; RGAL 4

Eberhart, Richard 1904-2005 ...... **CLC 3, 11,
19, 56; PC 76**
See also AMW; CA 1-4R; 240; CANR 2,
125; CDALB 1941-1968; CP 1, 2, 3, 4, 5,
6, 7; DAM POET; DLB 48; MAL 5;
MTCW 1; RGAL 4

Eberhart, Richard Ghormley
See Eberhart, Richard

Eberstadt, Fernanda 1960- .... **CLC 39**
See also CA 136; CANR 69, 128

Ebner, Margaret c. 1291-1351 ...... **CMLC 98**

**Echegaray (y Eizaguirre), Jose (Maria
Waldo)** 1832-1916 .... **HLCS 1; TCLC 4**
See also CA 104; CANR 32; DLB 329;
EWL 3; HW 1; MTCW 1

Echeverria, (Jose) Esteban (Antonino)
1805-1851 .... **NCLC 18**
See also LAW

Echo
See Proust, Marcel

Eckert, Allan W. 1931- .... **CLC 17**
See also AAYA 18; BYA 2; CA 13-16R;
CANR 14, 45; INT CANR-14; MAICYA
2; MAICYAS 1; SAAS 21; SATA 29, 91;
SATA-Brief 27

Eckhart, Meister 1260(?)-1327(?) .. **CMLC 9,
80**
See also DLB 115; LMFS 1

Eckmar, F. R.
See de Hartog, Jan

Eco, Umberto 1932- .... **CLC 28, 60, 142, 248**
See also BEST 90:1; BPFB 1; CA 77-80;
CANR 12, 33, 55, 110, 131, 195; CPW;
CWW 2; DA3; DAM NOV, POP; DLB
196, 242; EWL 3; MSW; MTCW 1, 2;
MTFW 2005; NFS 22; RGWL 3; WLIT 7

Eddison, E(ric) R(ucker)
1882-1945 .... **TCLC 15**
See also CA 109; 156; DLB 255; FANT;
SFW 4; SUFW 1

Eddy, Mary (Ann Morse) Baker
1821-1910 .... **TCLC 71**
See also CA 113; 174

Edel, (Joseph) Leon 1907-1997 .. **CLC 29, 34**
See also CA 1-4R; 161; CANR 1, 22, 112;
DLB 103; INT CANR-22

Eden, Emily 1797-1869 .... **NCLC 10**

Edgar, David 1948- .... **CLC 42**
See also CA 57-60; CANR 12, 61, 112;
CBD; CD 5, 6; DAM DRAM; DFS 15;
DLB 13, 233; MTCW 1

Edgerton, Clyde 1944- .... **CLC 39**
See also AAYA 17; CA 118; 134; CANR
64, 125, 195; CN 7; CSW; DLB 278; INT
CA-134; TCLE 1:1; YAW

Edgerton, Clyde Carlyle
See Edgerton, Clyde

Edgeworth, Maria 1768-1849 ... **NCLC 1, 51,
158; SSC 86**
See also BRWS 3; CLR 153; DLB 116, 159,
163; FL 1:3; FW; RGEL 2; SATA 21;
TEA; WLIT 3

Edmonds, Paul
See Kuttner, Henry

Edmonds, Walter D(umaux)
1903-1998 .... **CLC 35**
See also BYA 2; CA 5-8R; CANR 2; CWRI
5; DLB 9; LAIT 1; MAICYA 1, 2; MAL
5; RHW; SAAS 4; SATA 1, 27; SATA-
Obit 99

Edmondson, Wallace
See Ellison, Harlan

Edson, Margaret 1961- ...... **CLC 199; DC 24**
See also AMWS 18; CA 190; DFS 13; DLB
266

Edson, Russell 1935- .... **CLC 13**
See also CA 33-36R; CANR 115; CP 2, 3,
4, 5, 6, 7; DLB 244; WP

Edwards, Bronwen Elizabeth
See Rose, Wendy

Edwards, Eli
See McKay, Claude

Edwards, G(erald) B(asil)
1899-1976 .... **CLC 25**
See also CA 201; 110

Edwards, Gus 1939- .... **CLC 43**
See also CA 108; INT CA-108

Edwards, Jonathan 1703-1758 .... **LC 7, 54**
See also AMW; DA; DAC; DAM MST;
DLB 24, 270; RGAL 4; TUS

Edwards, Marilyn
See French, Marilyn

Edwards, Sarah Pierpont 1710-1758 .. **LC 87**
See also DLB 200

Efron, Marina Ivanovna Tsvetaeva
See Tsvetaeva, Marina

Egeria fl. 4th cent. - .... **CMLC 70**

Eggers, Dave 1970- .... **CLC 241**
See also AAYA 56; CA 198; CANR 138;
MTFW 2005

Egoyan, Atom 1960- .... **CLC 151, 291**
See also AAYA 63; CA 157; CANR 151

Ehle, John (Marsden, Jr.) 1925- ...... **CLC 27**
See also CA 9-12R; CSW

Ehrenbourg, Ilya
See Ehrenburg, Ilya

Ehrenburg, Ilya Grigoryevich
See Ehrenburg, Ilya

Ehrenburg, Ilya 1891-1967 ... **CLC 18, 34, 62**
See also CA 102; 25-28R; DLB 272; EWL
3

Ehrenburg, Ilya Grigoryevich
See Ehrenburg, Ilya

Ehrenburg, Ilyo
See Ehrenburg, Ilya

Ehrenburg, Ilyo Grigoryevich
See Ehrenburg, Ilya

Ehrenreich, Barbara 1941- ..... **CLC 110, 267**
See also BEST 90:4; CA 73-76; CANR 16,
37, 62, 117, 167, 208; DLB 246; FW;
LNFS 1; MTCW 1, 2; MTFW 2005

Ehrlich, Gretel 1946- .... **CLC 249**
See also ANW; CA 140; CANR 74, 146;
DLB 212, 275; TCWW 2

Eich, Gunter
See Eich, Gunter

Eich, Gunter 1907-1972 .... **CLC 15**
See also CA 111; 93-96; DLB 69, 124;
EWL 3; RGWL 2, 3

Eichendorff, Joseph 1788-1857 .... **NCLC 8,
225**
See also DLB 90; RGWL 2, 3

Eigner, Larry
See Eigner, Laurence (Joel)

Eigner, Laurence (Joel) 1927-1996 ..... **CLC 9**
See also CA 9-12R; 151; CAAS 23; CANR
6, 84; CP 1, 2, 3, 4, 5, 6, 7; DLB 5; WP

Eilhart von Oberge c. 1140-c.
1195 .... **CMLC 67**
See also DLB 148

Einhard c. 770-840 .... **CMLC 50**
See also DLB 148

Einstein, Albert 1879-1955 .... **TCLC 65**
See also CA 121; 133; MTCW 1, 2

Eiseley, Loren
See Eiseley, Loren Corey

Eiseley, Loren Corey 1907-1977 .... **CLC 7**
See also AAYA 5; ANW; CA 1-4R; 73-76;
CANR 6; DLB 275; DLBD 17

Eisenstadt, Jill 1963- .... **CLC 50**
See also CA 140

Eisenstein, Sergei (Mikhailovich)
1898-1948 .... **TCLC 57**
See also CA 114; 149

Eisler, Steve
See Holdstock, Robert

Eisner, Simon
See Kornbluth, C(yril) M.

Eisner, Will 1917-2005 .... **CLC 237**
See also AAYA 52; CA 108; 235; CANR
114, 140, 179; MTFW 2005; SATA 31,
165

Eisner, William Erwin
See Eisner, Will

Ekeloef, Bengt Gunnar
See Ekelof, Gunnar

Ekeloef, Gunnar
See Ekelof, Gunnar

Ekelof, Gunnar 1907-1968 ... **CLC 27; PC 23**
See also CA 123; 25-28R; DAM POET;
DLB 259; EW 12; EWL 3

Ekelund, Vilhelm 1880-1949 .... **TCLC 75**
See also CA 189; EWL 3

Ekman, Kerstin 1933- .... **CLC 279**
See also CA 154; CANR 124, 214; DLB
257; EWL 3

Ekman, Kerstin Lillemor
See Ekman, Kerstin

Ekwensi, C. O. D.
See Ekwensi, Cyprian

Ekwensi, Cyprian 1921-2007 .... **BLC 1:1;
CLC 4**
See also AFW; BW 2, 3; CA 29-32R;
CANR 18, 42, 74, 125; CDWLB 3; CN 1,
2, 3, 4, 5, 6; CWRI 5; DAM MULT; DLB
117; EWL 3; MTCW 1, 2; RGEL 2; SATA
66; WLIT 2

Ekwensi, Cyprian Odiatu Duaka
See Ekwensi, Cyprian

Elaine
See Leverson, Ada Esther

El Conde de Pepe
See Mihura, Miguel

El Crummo
See Crumb, R.

Elder, Lonne III 1931-1996 .. **BLC 1:1; DC 8**
See also BW 1, 3; CA 81-84; 152; CAD;
CANR 25; DAM MULT; DLB 7, 38, 44;
MAL 5

Eleanor of Aquitaine 1122-1204 ... **CMLC 39**

Elia
See Lamb, Charles

Eliade, Mircea 1907-1986 .... **CLC 19; TCLC
243**
See also CA 65-68; 119; CANR 30, 62; CD-
WLB 4; DLB 220; EWL 3; MTCW 1;
RGWL 3; SFW 4

Eliot, A. D.
See Jewett, Sarah Orne

Eliot, Alice
See Jewett, Sarah Orne

Eliot, Dan
See Silverberg, Robert

Ercilla y Zuniga, Don Alonso de
1533-1594 .... **LC 190**
See also LAW
Erdman, Paul E. 1932-2007 .... **CLC 25**
See also AITN 1; CA 61-64; 259; CANR
13, 43, 84
Erdman, Paul Emil
See Erdman, Paul E.
Erdrich, Karen Louise
See Erdrich, Louise
Erdrich, Louise 1954- .... **CLC 39, 54, 120,**
176; NNAL; PC 52; SSC 121
See also AAYA 10, 47; AMWS 4; BEST
89:1; BPFB 1; CA 114; CANR 41, 62,
118, 138, 190; CDALBS; CN 5, 6, 7; CP
6, 7; CPW; CWP; DA3; DAM MULT,
NOV, POP; DLB 152, 175, 206; EWL 3;
EXPP; FL 1:5; LAIT 5; LATS 1:2; MAL
5; MTCW 1, 2; MTFW 2005; NFS 5, 37;
PFS 14; RGAL 4; SATA 94, 141; SSFS
14, 22, 30; TCWW 2
Erenburg, Ilya
See Ehrenburg, Ilya
Erenburg, Ilya Grigoryevich
See Ehrenburg, Ilya
Erickson, Stephen Michael
See Erickson, Steve
Erickson, Steve 1950- .... **CLC 64**
See also CA 129; CANR 60, 68, 136, 195;
MTFW 2005; SFW 4; SUFW 2
Erickson, Walter
See Fast, Howard
Ericson, Walter
See Fast, Howard
Eriksson, Buntel
See Bergman, Ingmar
Eriugena, John Scottus c.
810-877 .... **CMLC 65**
See also DLB 115
Ernaux, Annie 1940- .... **CLC 88, 184**
See also CA 147; CANR 93, 208; MTFW
2005; NCFS 3, 5
Erskine, John 1879-1951 .... **TCLC 84**
See also CA 112; 159; DLB 9, 102; FANT
Erwin, Will
See Eisner, Will
Eschenbach, Wolfram von
See von Eschenbach, Wolfram
Eseki, Bruno
See Mphahlele, Es'kia
Esekie, Bruno
See Mphahlele, Es'kia
Esenin, S.A.
See Esenin, Sergei
Esenin, Sergei 1895-1925 .... **TCLC 4**
See also CA 104; EWL 3; RGWL 2, 3
Esenin, Sergei Aleksandrovich
See Esenin, Sergei
Eshleman, Clayton 1935- .... **CLC 7**
See also CA 33-36R; 212; CAAE 212;
CAAS 6; CANR 93; CP 1, 2, 3, 4, 5, 6,
7; DLB 5
Espada, Martin 1957- .... **PC 74**
See also CA 159; CANR 80; CP 7; EXPP;
LLW; MAL 5; PFS 13, 16
Espriella, Don Manuel Alvarez
See Southey, Robert
Espriu, Salvador 1913-1985 .... **CLC 9**
See also CA 154; 115; DLB 134; EWL 3
Espronceda, Jose de 1808-1842 ..... **NCLC 39**
Esquivel, Laura 1950- ..... **CLC 141; HLCS 1**
See also AAYA 29; CA 143; CANR 68, 113,
161; DA3; DNFS 2; LAIT 3; LMFS 2;
MTCW 2; MTFW 2005; NFS 5; WLIT 1
Esse, James
See Stephens, James
Esterbrook, Tom
See Hubbard, L. Ron

Esterhazy, Peter 1950- .... **CLC 251**
See also CA 140; CANR 137; CDWLB 4;
CWW 2; DLB 232; EWL 3; RGWL 3
Estleman, Loren D. 1952- .... **CLC 48**
See also AAYA 27; CA 85-88; CANR 27,
74, 139, 177; CMW 4; CPW; DA3; DAM
NOV, POP; DLB 226; INT CANR-27;
MTCW 1, 2; MTFW 2005; TCWW 1, 2
Etherege, Sir George 1636-1692 . **DC 23; LC**
78
See also BRW 2; DAM DRAM; DLB 80;
PAB; RGEL 2
Euclid 306B.C.-283B.C. .... **CMLC 25**
Eugenides, Jeffrey 1960- .... **CLC 81, 212**
See also AAYA 51; CA 144; CANR 120;
DLB 350; MTFW 2005; NFS 24
Euripides c. 484B.C.-406B.C. .... **CMLC 23,**
51; DC 4; WLCS
See also AW 1; CDWLB 1; DA; DA3;
DAB; DAC; DAM DRAM; DFS 1,
4, 6, 25, 27; DLB 176; LAIT 1; LMFS 1;
RGWL 2, 3; WLIT 8
Eusebius c. 263-c. 339 .... **CMLC 103**
Evan, Evin
See Faust, Frederick
Evans, Caradoc 1878-1945 ... **SSC 43; TCLC**
85
See also DLB 162
Evans, Evan
See Faust, Frederick
Evans, Marian
See Eliot, George
Evans, Mary Ann
See Eliot, George
Evarts, Esther
See Benson, Sally
Evelyn, John 1620-1706 .... **LC 144**
See also BRW 2; RGEL 2
Everett, Percival 1956- .... **CLC 57**
See also AMWS 18; BW 2; CA 129; CANR
94, 134, 179; CN 7; CSW; DLB 350;
MTFW 2005
Everett, Percival L.
See Everett, Percival
Everson, R(onald) G(ilmour)
1903-1992 .... **CLC 27**
See also CA 17-20R; CP 1, 2, 3, 4; DLB 88
Everson, William 1912-1994 .... **CLC 1, 5, 14**
See also BG 1:2; CA 9-12R; 145; CANR
20; CP 1; DLB 5, 16, 212; MTCW 1
Everson, William Oliver
See Everson, William
Evtushenko, Evgenii Aleksandrovich
See Yevtushenko, Yevgenyn
Ewart, Gavin (Buchanan)
1916-1995 .... **CLC 13, 46**
See also BRWS 7; CA 89-92; 150; CANR
17, 46; CP 1, 2, 3, 4, 5, 6; DLB 40;
MTCW 1
Ewers, Hanns Heinz 1871-1943 ..... **TCLC 12**
See also CA 109; 149
Ewing, Frederick R.
See Sturgeon, Theodore (Hamilton)
Exley, Frederick (Earl) 1929-1992 .... **CLC 6,**
11
See also AITN 2; BPFB 1; CA 81-84; 138;
CANR 117; DLB 143; DLBY 1981
Eynhardt, Guillermo
See Quiroga, Horacio (Sylvestre)
Ezekiel, Nissim (Moses) 1924-2004 .. **CLC 61**
See also CA 61-64; 223; CP 1, 2, 3, 4, 5, 6,
7; DLB 323; EWL 3
Ezekiel, Tish O'Dowd 1943- .... **CLC 34**
See also CA 129
Fadeev, Aleksandr Aleksandrovich
See Bulgya, Alexander Alexandrovich
Fadeev, Alexandr Alexandrovich
See Bulgya, Alexander Alexandrovich

Fadeyev, A.
See Bulgya, Alexander Alexandrovich
Fadeyev, Alexander
See Bulgya, Alexander Alexandrovich
Fagen, Donald 1948- .... **CLC 26**
Fainzil'berg, Il'ia Arnol'dovich
See Fainzilberg, Ilya Arnoldovich
Fainzilberg, Ilya Arnoldovich
1897-1937 .... **TCLC 21**
See also CA 120; 165; DLB 272; EWL 3
Fair, Ronald L. 1932- .... **CLC 18**
See also BW 1; CA 69-72; CANR 25; DLB
33
Fairbairn, Roger
See Carr, John Dickson
Fairbairns, Zoe (Ann) 1948- .... **CLC 32**
See also CA 103; CANR 21, 85; CN 4, 5,
6, 7
Fairfield, Flora
See Alcott, Louisa May
Falco, Gian
See Papini, Giovanni
Falconer, James
See Kirkup, James
Falconer, Kenneth
See Kornbluth, C(yril) M.
Falkland, Samuel
See Heijermans, Herman
Fallaci, Oriana 1930-2006 .... **CLC 11, 110**
See also CA 77-80; 253; CANR 15, 58, 134;
FW; MTCW 1
Faludi, Susan 1959- .... **CLC 140**
See also CA 138; CANR 126, 194; FW;
MTCW 2; MTFW 2005; NCFS 3
Faludy, George 1913- .... **CLC 42**
See also CA 21-24R
Faludy, Gyoergy
See Faludy, George
Fanon, Frantz 1925-1961 ...... **BLC 1:2; CLC**
74; TCLC 188
See also BW 1; CA 116; 89-92; DAM
MULT; DLB 296; LMFS 2; WLIT 2
Fanshawe, Ann 1625-1680 .... **LC 11**
Fante, John (Thomas) 1911-1983 .... **CLC 60;**
SSC 65
See also AMWS 11; CA 69-72; 109; CANR
23, 104; DLB 130; DLBY 1983
Far, Sui Sin
See Eaton, Edith Maude
Farah, Nuruddin 1945- .. **BLC 1:2, 2:2; CLC**
53, 137
See also AFW; BW 2, 3; CA 106; CANR
81, 148; CDWLB 3; CN 4, 5, 6, 7; DAM
MULT; DLB 125; EWL 3; WLIT 2
Fardusi
See Ferdowsi, Abu'l Qasem
Fargue, Leon-Paul 1876(?)-1947 .... **TCLC 11**
See also CA 109; CANR 107; DLB 258;
EWL 3
Farigoule, Louis
See Romains, Jules
Farina, Richard 1936(?)-1966 .... **CLC 9**
See also CA 81-84; 25-28R
Farley, Walter (Lorimer)
1915-1989 .... **CLC 17**
See also AAYA 58; BYA 14; CA 17-20R;
CANR 8, 29, 84; DLB 22; JRDA; MAI-
CYA 1, 2; SATA 2, 43, 132; YAW
Farmer, Philip Jose
See Farmer, Philip Jose
Farmer, Philip Jose 1918-2009 .... **CLC 1, 19,**
299
See also AAYA 28; BPFB 1; CA 1-4R; 283;
CANR 4, 35, 111; DLB 8; MTCW 1;
SATA 93; SATA-Obit 201; SCFW 1, 2;
SFW 4
Farmer, Philipe Jos
See Farmer, Philip Jose

Foote, Horton 1916-2009 .... **CLC 51, 91; DC 42**
See also AAYA 82; CA 73-76; 284; CAD; CANR 34, 51, 110; CD 5, 6; CSW; DA3; DAM DRAM; DFS 20; DLB 26, 266; EWL 3; INT CANR-34; MTFW 2005

Foote, Mary Hallock 1847-1938 ..... **SSC 150; TCLC 108**
See also DLB 186, 188, 202, 221; TCWW 2

Foote, Samuel 1721-1777 .... **LC 106**
See also DLB 89; RGEL 2

Foote, Shelby 1916-2005 .... **CLC 75, 224**
See also AAYA 40; CA 5-8R; 240; CANR 3, 45, 74, 131; CN 1, 2, 3, 4, 5, 6, 7; CPW; CSW; DA3; DAM NOV, POP; DLB 2, 17; MAL 5; MTCW 2; MTFW 2005; RHW

Forbes, Cosmo
See Lewton, Val

Forbes, Esther 1891-1967 .... **CLC 12**
See also AAYA 17; BYA 2; CA 13-14; 25-28R; CAP 1; CLR 27, 147; DLB 22; JRDA; MAICYA 1, 2; RHW; SATA 2, 100; YAW

Forche, Carolyn 1950- .. **CLC 25, 83, 86; PC 10**
See also CA 109; 117; CANR 50, 74, 138; CP 4, 5, 6, 7; CWP; DAM POET; DLB 5, 193; INT CA-117; MAL 5; MTCW 2; MTFW 2005; PFS 18; RGAL 4

Forche, Carolyn Louise
See Forche, Carolyn

Ford, Elbur
See Hibbert, Eleanor Alice Burford

Ford, Ford Madox 1873-1939 ... **TCLC 1, 15, 39, 57, 172**
See also BRW 6; CA 104; 132; CANR 74; CDBLB 1914-1945; DA3; DAM NOV; DLB 34, 98, 162; EWL 3; MTCW 1, 2; NFS 28; RGEL 2; RHW; TEA

Ford, Helen
See Garner, Helen

Ford, Henry 1863-1947 .... **TCLC 73**
See also CA 115; 148

Ford, Jack
See Ford, John

Ford, John 1586-1639 .... **DC 8; LC 68, 153**
See also BRW 2; CDBLB Before 1660; DA3; DAM DRAM; DFS 7; DLB 58; IDTP; RGEL 2

Ford, John 1895-1973 .... **CLC 16**
See also AAYA 75; CA 187; 45-48

Ford, Richard 1944- .. **CLC 46, 99, 205, 277; SSC 143**
See also AMWS 5; CA 69-72; CANR 11, 47, 86, 128, 164; CN 5, 6, 7; CSW; DLB 227; EWL 3; MAL 5; MTCW 2; MTFW 2005; NFS 25; RGAL 4; RGSF 2

Ford, Webster
See Masters, Edgar Lee

Foreman, Richard 1937- .... **CLC 50**
See also CA 65-68; CAD; CANR 32, 63, 143; CD 5, 6

Forester, C. S. 1899-1966 ..... **CLC 35; TCLC 152**
See also CA 73-76; 25-28R; CANR 83; DLB 191; RGEL 2; RHW; SATA 13

Forester, Cecil Scott
See Forester, C. S.

Forez
See Mauriac, Francois (Charles)

Forman, James
See Forman, James D.

Forman, James D. 1932-2009 .... **CLC 21**
See also AAYA 17; CA 9-12R; CANR 4, 19, 42; JRDA; MAICYA 1, 2; SATA 8, 70; YAW

Forman, James Douglas
See Forman, James D.

Forman, Milos 1932- .... **CLC 164**
See also AAYA 63; CA 109

Fornes, Maria Irene 1930- .... **CLC 39, 61, 187; DC 10; HLCS 1**
See also CA 25-28R; CAD; CANR 28, 81; CD 5, 6; CWD; DFS 25; DLB 7, 341; HW 1, 2; INT CANR-28; LLW; MAL 5; MTCW 1; RGAL 4

Forrest, Leon (Richard)
1937-1997 .... **BLCS; CLC 4**
See also AFAW 2; BW 2; CA 89-92; 162; CAAS 7; CANR 25, 52, 87; CN 4, 5, 6; DLB 33

Forster, E. M. 1879-1970 .. **CLC 1, 2, 3, 4, 9, 10, 13, 15, 22, 45, 77; SSC 27, 96; TCLC 125; WLC 2**
See also AAYA 2, 37; BRW 6; BRWR 2; BYA 12; CA 13-14; 25-28R; CANR 45; CAP 1; CDBLB 1914-1945; DA; DA3; DAB; DAC; DAM MST, NOV; DLB 34, 98, 162, 178, 195; DLBD 10; EWL 3; EXPN; LAIT 3; LMFS 1; MTCW 1, 2; MTFW 2005; NCFS 1; NFS 3, 10, 11; RGEL 2; RGSF 2; SATA 57; SUFW 1; TEA; WLIT 4

Forster, Edward Morgan
See Forster, E. M.

Forster, John 1812-1876 .... **NCLC 11**
See also DLB 144, 184

Forster, Margaret 1938- .... **CLC 149**
See also CA 133; CANR 62, 115, 175; CN 4, 5, 6, 7; DLB 155, 271

Forsyth, Frederick 1938- .... **CLC 2, 5, 36**
See also BEST 89:4; CA 85-88; CANR 38, 62, 115, 137, 183; CMW 4; CN 3, 4, 5, 6, 7; CPW; DAM NOV, POP; DLB 87; MTCW 1, 2; MTFW 2005

Fort, Paul
See Stockton, Francis Richard

Forten, Charlotte
See Grimke, Charlotte L. Forten

Forten, Charlotte L. 1837-1914
See Grimke, Charlotte L. Forten

Fortinbras
See Grieg, (Johan) Nordahl (Brun)

Foscolo, Ugo 1778-1827 .... **NCLC 8, 97**
See also EW 5; WLIT 7

Fosse, Bob 1927-1987 .... **CLC 20**
See also AAYA 82; CA 110; 123

Fosse, Robert L.
See Fosse, Bob

Foster, Hannah Webster
1758-1840 .... **NCLC 99**
See also DLB 37, 200; RGAL 4

Foster, Stephen Collins
1826-1864 .... **NCLC 26**
See also RGAL 4

Foucault, Michel 1926-1984 . **CLC 31, 34, 69**
See also CA 105; 113; CANR 34; DLB 242; EW 13; EWL 3; GFL 1789 to the Present; GLL 1; LMFS 2; MTCW 1, 2; TWA

Fouque, Friedrich (Heinrich Karl) de la Motte 1777-1843 .... **NCLC 2**
See also DLB 90; RGWL 2, 3; SUFW 1

Fourier, Charles 1772-1837 .... **NCLC 51**

Fournier, Henri-Alban 1886-1914 ... **TCLC 6**
See also CA 104; 179; DLB 65; EWL 3; GFL 1789 to the Present; RGWL 2, 3

Fournier, Pierre 1916-1997 .... **CLC 11**
See also CA 89-92; CANR 16, 40; EWL 3; RGHL

Fowles, John 1926-2005 .... **CLC 1, 2, 3, 4, 6, 9, 10, 15, 33, 87; SSC 33, 128**
See also BPFB 1; BRWS 1; CA 5-8R; 245; CANR 25, 71, 103; CDBLB 1960 to Present; CN 1, 2, 3, 4, 5, 6, 7; DA3; DAB; DAC; DAM MST; DLB 14, 139, 207;

EWL 3; HGG; MTCW 1, 2; MTFW 2005; NFS 21; RGEL 2; RHW; SATA 22; SATA-Obit 171; TEA; WLIT 4

Fowles, John Robert
See Fowles, John

Fox, Norma Diane
See Mazer, Norma Fox

Fox, Paula 1923- .... **CLC 2, 8, 121**
See also AAYA 3, 37; BYA 3, 8; CA 73-76; CANR 20, 36, 62, 105, 200; CLR 1, 44, 96; DLB 52; JRDA; MAICYA 1, 2; MTCW 1; NFS 12; SATA 17, 60, 120, 167; WYA; YAW

Fox, William Price, Jr.
See Fox, William Price

Fox, William Price 1926- .... **CLC 22**
See also CA 17-20R; CAAS 19; CANR 11, 142, 189; CSW; DLB 2; DLBY 1981

Foxe, John 1517(?)-1587 .... **LC 14, 166**
See also DLB 132

Frame, Janet 1924-2004 ...... **CLC 2, 3, 6, 22, 66, 96, 237; SSC 29, 127**
See also CA 1-4R; 224; CANR 2, 36, 76, 135, 216; CN 1, 2, 3, 4, 5, 6, 7; CP 2, 3, 4; CWP; EWL 3; MTCW 1,2; RGEL 2; RGSF 2; SATA 119; TWA

France, Anatole 1844-1924 .... **TCLC 9**
See also CA 106; 127; DA3; DAM NOV; DLB 123, 330; EWL 3; GFL 1789 to the Present; MTCW 1, 2; RGWL 2, 3; SUFW 1; TWA

Francis, Claude **CLC 50**
See also CA 192

Francis, Dick 1920-2010 . **CLC 2, 22, 42, 102**
See also AAYA 5, 21; BEST 89:3; BPFB 1; CA 5-8R; CANR 9, 42, 68, 100, 141, 179; CDBLB 1960 to Present; CMW 4; CN 2, 3, 4, 5, 6; DA3; DAM POP; DLB 87; INT CANR-9; MSW; MTCW 1, 2; MTFW 2005

Francis, Paula Marie
See Allen, Paula Gunn

Francis, Richard Stanley
See Francis, Dick

Francis, Robert (Churchill)
1901-1987 .... **CLC 15; PC 34**
See also AMWS 9; CA 1-4R; 123; CANR 1; CP 1, 2, 3, 4; EXPP; PFS 12; TCLE 1:1

Francis, Lord Jeffrey
See Jeffrey, Francis

Franco, Veronica 1546-1591 .... **LC 171**
See also WLIT 7

Frank, Anne 1929-1945 ... **TCLC 17; WLC 2**
See also AAYA 12; BYA 1; CA 113; 133; CANR 68; CLR 101; DA; DA3; DAB; DAC; DAM MST; LAIT 4; MAICYA 1, 2; MAICYAS 1; MTCW 1, 2; MTFW 2005; NCFS 2; RGHL; SATA 87; SATA-Brief 42; WYA; YAW

Frank, Annelies Marie
See Frank, Anne

Frank, Bruno 1887-1945 .... **TCLC 81**
See also CA 189; DLB 118; EWL 3

Frank, Elizabeth 1945- .... **CLC 39**
See also CA 121; 126; CANR 78, 150; INT CA-126

Frankl, Viktor E(mil) 1905-1997 ...... **CLC 93**
See also CA 65-68; 161; RGHL

Franklin, Benjamin
See Hasek, Jaroslav

Franklin, Benjamin 1706-1790 .. **LC 25, 134; WLCS**
See also AMW; CDALB 1640-1865; DA; DA3; DAB; DAC; DAM MST; DLB 24, 43, 73, 183; LAIT 1; RGAL 4; TUS

Franklin, Madeleine
See L'Engle, Madeleine

Franklin, Madeleine L'Engle
See L'Engle, Madeleine
Franklin, Madeleine L'Engle Camp
See L'Engle, Madeleine
Franklin, (Stella Maria Sarah) Miles
(Lampe) 1879-1954 .... **TCLC 7**
See also CA 104; 164; DLB 230; FW;
MTCW 2; RGEL 2; TWA
Franzen, Jonathan 1959- .... **CLC 202**
See also AAYA 65; AMWS 20; CA 129;
CANR 105, 166
Fraser, Antonia 1932- .... **CLC 32, 107**
See also AAYA 57; CA 85-88; CANR 44,
65, 119, 164; CMW; DLB 276; MTCW 1,
2; MTFW 2005; SATA-Brief 32
Fraser, George MacDonald
1925-2008 .... **CLC 7**
See also AAYA 48; CA 45-48, 180; 268;
CAAE 180; CANR 2, 48, 74, 192; DLB
352; MTCW 2; RHW
Fraser, Sylvia 1935- .... **CLC 64**
See also CA 45-48; CANR 1, 16, 60; CCA
1
Frater Perdurabo
See Crowley, Edward Alexander
Frayn, Michael 1933- .... **CLC 3, 7, 31, 47,**
176; DC 27
See also AAYA 69; BRWC 2; BRWS 7; CA
5-8R; CANR 30, 69, 114, 133, 166; CBD;
CD 5, 6; CN 1, 2, 3, 4, 5, 6, 7; DAM
DRAM, NOV; DFS 22, 28; DLB 13, 14,
194, 245; FANT; MTCW 1, 2; MTFW
2005; SFW 4
Fraze, Candida 1945- .... **CLC 50**
See also CA 126
Fraze, Candida Merrill
See Fraze, Candida
Frazer, Andrew
See Marlowe, Stephen
Frazer, J(ames) G(eorge)
1854-1941 .... **TCLC 32**
See also BRWS 3; CA 118; NCFS 5
Frazer, Robert Caine
See Creasey, John
Frazer, Sir James George
See Frazer, J(ames) G(eorge)
Frazier, Charles 1950- .... **CLC 109, 224**
See also AAYA 34; CA 161; CANR 126,
170; CSW; DLB 292; MTFW 2005; NFS
25
Frazier, Charles R.
See Frazier, Charles
Frazier, Charles Robinson
See Frazier, Charles
Frazier, Ian 1951- .... **CLC 46**
See also CA 130; CANR 54, 93, 193
Frederic, Harold 1856-1898 .... **NCLC 10, 175**
See also AMW; DLB 12, 23; DLBD 13;
MAL 5; NFS 22; RGAL 4
Frederick, John
See Faust, Frederick
Frederick the Great 1712-1786 .... **LC 14**
Fredro, Aleksander 1793-1876 .... **NCLC 8**
Freeling, Nicolas 1927-2003 .... **CLC 38**
See also CA 49-52; 218; CAAS 12; CANR
1, 17, 50, 84; CMW 4; CN 1, 2, 3, 4, 5,
6; DLB 87
Freeman, Douglas Southall
1886-1953 .... **TCLC 11**
See also CA 109; 195; DLB 17; DLBD 17
Freeman, Judith 1946- .... **CLC 55**
See also CA 148; CANR 120, 179; DLB
256
Freeman, Mary E(leanor) Wilkins
1852-1930 .... **SSC 1, 47, 113; TCLC 9**
See also CA 106; 177; DLB 12, 78, 221;
EXPS; FW; HGG; MBL; RGAL 4; RGSF
2; SSFS 4, 8, 26; SUFW 1; TUS

Freeman, R(ichard) Austin
1862-1943 .... **TCLC 21**
See also CA 113; CANR 84; CMW 4; DLB
70
French, Albert 1943- .... **CLC 86**
See also BW 3; CA 167
French, Antonia
See Kureishi, Hanif
French, Marilyn 1929-2009 . **CLC 10, 18, 60,**
177
See also BPFB 1; CA 69-72; 286; CANR 3,
31, 134, 163; CN 5, 6, 7; CPW; DAM
DRAM, NOV, POP; FL 1:5; FW; INT
CANR-31; MTCW 1, 2; MTFW 2005
French, Paul
See Asimov, Isaac
Freneau, Philip Morin 1752-1832 .. **NCLC 1,**
111
See also AMWS 2; DLB 37, 43; RGAL 4
Freud, Sigmund 1856-1939 .... **TCLC 52**
See also CA 115; 133; CANR 69; DLB 296;
EW 8; EWL 3; LATS 1:1; MTCW 1, 2;
MTFW 2005; NCFS 3; TWA
Freytag, Gustav 1816-1895 .... **NCLC 109**
See also DLB 129
Friedan, Betty 1921-2006 .... **CLC 74**
See also CA 65-68; 248; CANR 18, 45, 74;
DLB 246; FW; MTCW 1, 2; MTFW
2005; NCFS 5
Friedan, Betty Naomi
See Friedan, Betty
Friedlander, Saul
See Friedlander, Saul
Friedlander, Saul 1932- .... **CLC 90**
See also CA 117; 130; CANR 72, 214;
RGHL
Friedman, Bernard Harper
See Friedman, B.H.
Friedman, B.H. 1926-2011 .... **CLC 7**
See also CA 1-4R; CANR 3, 48
Friedman, Bruce Jay 1930- ...... **CLC 3, 5, 56**
See also CA 9-12R; CAD; CANR 25, 52,
101, 212; CD 5, 6; CN 1, 2, 3, 4, 5, 6, 7;
DLB 2, 28, 244; INT CANR-25; MAL 5;
SSFS 18
Friel, Brian 1929- .. **CLC 5, 42, 59, 115, 253;**
DC 8; SSC 76
See also BRWS 5; CA 21-24R; CANR 33,
69, 131; CBD; CD 5, 6; DFS 11; DLB
13, 319; EWL 3; MTCW 1; RGEL 2; TEA
Friis-Baastad, Babbis Ellinor
1921-1970 .... **CLC 12**
See also CA 17-20R; 134; SATA 7
Frisch, Max 1911-1991 ...... **CLC 3, 9, 14, 18,**
32, 44; TCLC 121
See also CA 85-88; 134; CANR 32, 74; CD-
WLB 2; DAM DRAM, NOV; DFS 25;
DLB 69, 124; EW 13; EWL 3; MTCW 1,
2; MTFW 2005; RGHL; RGWL 2, 3
Froehlich, Peter
See Gay, Peter
Fromentin, Eugene (Samuel Auguste)
1820-1876 .... **NCLC 10, 125**
See also DLB 123; GFL 1789 to the Present
Frost, Frederick
See Faust, Frederick
Frost, Robert 1874-1963 . **CLC 1, 3, 4, 9, 10,**
13, 15, 26, 34, 44; PC 1, 39, 71; TCLC
236; WLC 2
See also AAYA 21; AMW; AMWR 1; CA
89-92; CANR 33; CDALB 1917-1929;
CLR 67; DA; DA3; DAB; DAC; DAM
MST, POET; DLB 54, 284, 342; DLBD
7; EWL 3; EXPP; MAL 5; MTCW 1, 2;
MTFW 2005; PAB; PFS 1, 2, 3, 4, 5, 6,
7, 10, 13, 32, 35; RGAL 4; SATA 14;
TUS; WP; WYA
Frost, Robert Lee
See Frost, Robert

Froude, James Anthony
1818-1894 .... **NCLC 43**
See also DLB 18, 57, 144
Froy, Herald
See Waterhouse, Keith
Fry, Christopher 1907-2005 .. **CLC 2, 10, 14;**
DC 36
See also BRWS 3; CA 17-20R; 240; CAAS
23; CANR 9, 30, 74, 132; CBD; CD 5, 6;
CP 1, 2, 3, 4, 5, 6, 7; DAM DRAM; DLB
13; EWL 3; MTCW 1, 2; MTFW 2005;
RGEL 2; SATA 66; TEA
Frye, (Herman) Northrop
1912-1991 .... **CLC 24, 70; TCLC 165**
See also CA 5-8R; 133; CANR 8, 37; DLB
67, 68, 246; EWL 3; MTCW 1, 2; MTFW
2005; RGAL 4; TWA
Fuchs, Daniel 1909-1993 .... **CLC 8, 22**
See also CA 81-84; 142; CAAS 5; CANR
40; CN 1, 2, 3, 4, 5; DLB 9, 26, 28;
DLBY 1993; MAL 5
Fuchs, Daniel 1934- .... **CLC 34**
See also CA 37-40R; CANR 14, 48
Fuentes, Carlos 1928- .. **CLC 3, 8, 10, 13, 22,**
41, 60, 113, 288; HLC 1; SSC 24, 125;
WLC 2
See also AAYA 4, 45; AITN 2; BPFB 1;
CA 69-72; CANR 10, 32, 68, 104, 138,
197; CDWLB 3; CWW 2; DA; DA3;
DAB; DAC; DAM MST, MULT, NOV;
DLB 113; DNFS 2; EWL 3; HW 1, 2;
LAIT 3; LATS 1:2; LAW; LAWS 1;
LMFS 2; MTCW 1, 2; MTFW 2005; NFS
8; RGSF 2; RGWL 2, 3; TWA; WLIT 1
Fuentes, Gregorio Lopez y
See Lopez y Fuentes, Gregorio
Fuentes Macias, Carlos Manuel
See Fuentes, Carlos
Fuertes, Gloria 1918-1998 .... **PC 27**
See also CA 178; 180; DLB 108; HW 2;
SATA 115
Fugard, Athol 1932- .... **CLC 5, 9, 14, 25, 40,**
80, 211; DC 3
See also AAYA 17; AFW; BRWS 15; CA
85-88; CANR 32, 54, 118; CD 5, 6; DAM
DRAM; DFS 3, 6, 10, 24; DLB 225;
DNFS 1, 2; EWL 3; LATS 1:2; MTCW 1,
2; MTFW 2005; RGEL 2; WLIT 2
Fugard, Harold Athol
See Fugard, Athol
Fugard, Sheila 1932- .... **CLC 48**
See also CA 125
Fujiwara no Teika 1162-1241 .... **CMLC 73**
See also DLB 203
Fukuyama, Francis 1952- .... **CLC 131**
See also CA 140; CANR 72, 125, 170
Fuller, Charles (H.), (Jr.) 1939- ..... **BLC 1:2;**
CLC 25; DC 1
See also BW 2; CA 108; 112; CAD; CANR
87; CD 5, 6; DAM DRAM, MULT; DFS
8; DLB 38, 266; EWL 3; INT CA-112;
MAL 5; MTCW 1
Fuller, Henry Blake 1857-1929 .... **TCLC 103**
See also CA 108; 177; DLB 12; RGAL 4
Fuller, John (Leopold) 1937- .... **CLC 62**
See also CA 21-24R; CANR 9, 44; CP 1, 2,
3, 4, 5, 6, 7; DLB 40
Fuller, Margaret 1810-1850 ...... **NCLC 5, 50,**
211
See also AMWS 2; CDALB 1640-1865;
DLB 1, 59, 73, 183, 223, 239; FW; LMFS
1; SATA 25
Fuller, Roy (Broadbent) 1912-1991 ... **CLC 4,**
28
See also BRWS 7; CA 5-8R; 135; CAAS
10; CANR 53, 83; CN 1, 2, 3, 4, 5; CP 1,
2, 3, 4, 5; CWRI 5; DLB 15, 20; EWL 3;
RGEL 2; SATA 87
Fuller, Sarah Margaret
See Fuller, Margaret

Author Index

Haley, Alexander Murray Palmer
See Haley, Alex
Haliburton, Thomas Chandler
1796-1865 .... **NCLC 15, 149**
See also DLB 11, 99; RGEL 2; RGSF 2
Hall, Donald 1928- ... **CLC 1, 13, 37, 59, 151, 240; PC 70**
See also AAYA 63; CA 5-8R; CAAS 7; CANR 2, 44, 64, 106, 133, 196; CP 1, 2, 3, 4, 5, 6, 7; DAM POET; DLB 5, 342; MAL 5; MTCW 2; MTFW 2005; RGAL 4; SATA 23, 97
Hall, Donald Andrew, Jr.
See Hall, Donald
Hall, Frederic Sauser
See Sauser-Hall, Frederic
Hall, James
See Kuttner, Henry
Hall, James Norman 1887-1951 ..... **TCLC 23**
See also CA 123; 173; LAIT 1; RHW 1; SATA 21
Hall, Joseph 1574-1656 .... **LC 91**
See also DLB 121, 151; RGEL 2
Hall, Marguerite Radclyffe
See Hall, Radclyffe
Hall, Radclyffe 1880-1943 ...... **TCLC 12, 215**
See also BRWS 6; CA 110; 150; CANR 83; DLB 191; MTCW 2; MTFW 2005; RGEL 2; RHW
Hall, Rodney 1935- .... **CLC 51**
See also CA 109; CANR 69; CN 6, 7; CP 1, 2, 3, 4, 5, 6, 7; DLB 289
Hallam, Arthur Henry
1811-1833 .... **NCLC 110**
See also DLB 32
Halldor Laxness
See Gudjonsson, Halldor Kiljan
Halleck, Fitz-Greene 1790-1867 .... **NCLC 47**
See also DLB 3, 250; RGAL 4
Halliday, Michael
See Creasey, John
Halpern, Daniel 1945- .... **CLC 14**
See also CA 33-36R; CANR 93, 174; CP 3, 4, 5, 6, 7
Hamburger, Michael 1924-2007 ... **CLC 5, 14**
See also CA 5-8R, 196; 261; CAAE 196; CAAS 4; CANR 2, 47; CP 1, 2, 3, 4, 5, 6, 7; DLB 27
Hamburger, Michael Peter Leopold
See Hamburger, Michael
Hamill, Pete 1935- .... **CLC 10, 261**
See also CA 25-28R; CANR 18, 71, 127, 180
Hamill, William Peter
See Hamill, Pete
Hamilton, Alexander 1712-1756 .... **LC 150**
See also DLB 31
Hamilton, Alexander
1755(?)-1804 .... **NCLC 49**
See also DLB 37
Hamilton, Clive
See Lewis, C. S.
Hamilton, Edmond 1904-1977 .... **CLC 1**
See also CA 1-4R; CANR 3, 84; DLB 8; SATA 118; SFW 4
Hamilton, Elizabeth 1758-1816 ... **NCLC 153**
See also DLB 116, 158
Hamilton, Eugene (Jacob) Lee
See Lee-Hamilton, Eugene (Jacob)
Hamilton, Franklin
See Silverberg, Robert
Hamilton, Gail
See Corcoran, Barbara (Asenath)
Hamilton, (Robert) Ian 1938-2001 . **CLC 191**
See also CA 106; 203; CANR 41, 67; CP 1, 2, 3, 4, 5, 6, 7; DLB 40, 155

Hamilton, Jane 1957- .... **CLC 179**
See also CA 147; CANR 85, 128, 214; CN 7; DLB 350; MTFW 2005
Hamilton, Mollie
See Kaye, M.M.
Hamilton, Patrick 1904-1962 .... **CLC 51**
See also BRWS 16; CA 176; 113; DLB 10, 191
Hamilton, Virginia 1936-2002 .... **CLC 26**
See also AAYA 2, 21; BW 2, 3; BYA 1, 2, 8; CA 25-28R; 206; CANR 20, 37, 73, 126; CLR 1, 11, 40, 127; DAM MULT; DLB 33, 52; DLBY 2001; INT CANR-20; JRDA; LAIT 5; MAICYA 1, 2; MAICYAS 1; MTCW 1, 2; MTFW 2005; SATA 4, 56, 79, 123; SATA-Obit 132; WYA; YAW
Hamilton, Virginia Esther
See Hamilton, Virginia
Hammett, Dashiell 1894-1961 . **CLC 3, 5, 10, 19, 47; SSC 17; TCLC 187**
See also AAYA 59; AITN 1; AMWS 4; BPFB 2; CA 81-84; CANR 42; CDALB 1929-1941; CMW 4; DA3; DLB 226, 280; DLBD 6; DLBY 1996; EWL 3; LAIT 3; MAL 5; MSW; MTCW 1, 2; MTFW 2005; NFS 21; RGAL 4; RGSF 2; TUS
Hammett, Samuel Dashiell
See Hammett, Dashiell
Hammon, Jupiter 1720(?)-1800(?) . **BLC 1:2; NCLC 5; PC 16**
See also DAM MULT, POET; DLB 31, 50
Hammond, Keith
See Kuttner, Henry
Hamner, Earl (Henry), Jr. 1923- ...... **CLC 12**
See also AITN 2; CA 73-76; DLB 6
Hampton, Christopher 1946- .... **CLC 4**
See also CA 25-28R; CD 5, 6; DLB 13; MTCW 1
Hampton, Christopher James
See Hampton, Christopher
Hamsun, Knut
See Pedersen, Knut
Hamsund, Knut Pedersen
See Pedersen, Knut
Handke, Peter 1942- .... **CLC 5, 8, 10, 15, 38, 134; DC 17**
See also CA 77-80; CANR 33, 75, 104, 133, 180; CWW 2; DAM DRAM, NOV; DLB 85, 124; EWL 3; MTCW 1, 2; MTFW 2005; TWA
Handler, Chelsea 1976(?)- .... **CLC 269**
See also CA 243
Handy, W(illiam) C(hristopher)
1873-1958 .... **TCLC 97**
See also BW 3; CA 121; 167
Haneke, Michael 1942- .... **CLC 283**
Hanif, Mohammed 1965- .... **CLC 299**
See also CA 283
Hanley, James 1901-1985 ..... **CLC 3, 5, 8, 13**
See also CA 73-76; 117; CANR 36; CBD; CN 1, 2, 3; DLB 191; EWL 3; MTCW 1; RGEL 2
Hannah, Barry 1942-2010 ... **CLC 23, 38, 90, 270; SSC 94**
See also BPFB 2; CA 108; 110; CANR 43, 68, 113; CN 4, 5, 6, 7; CSW; DLB 6, 234; INT CA-110; MTCW 1; RGSF 2
Hannon, Ezra
See Hunter, Evan
Hanrahan, Barbara 1939-1991 .... **TCLC 219**
See also CA 121; 127; CN 4, 5; DLB 289
Hansberry, Lorraine 1930-1965 ..... **BLC 1:2, 2:2; CLC 17, 62; DC 2; TCLC 192**
See also AAYA 25; AFAW 1, 2; AMWS 4; BW 1, 3; CA 109; 25-28R; CABS 3; CAD; CANR 58; CDALB 1941-1968; CWD; DA; DA3; DAB; DAC; DAM

DRAM, MST, MULT; DFS 2; DLB 7, 38; EWL 3; FL 1:6; FW; LAIT 4; MAL 5; MTCW 1, 2; MTFW 2005; RGAL 4; TUS
Hansberry, Lorraine Vivian
See Hansberry, Lorraine
Hansen, Joseph 1923-2004 .... **CLC 38**
See also BPFB 2; CA 29-32R; 233; CAAS 17; CANR 16, 44, 66, 125; CMW 4; DLB 226; GLL 1; INT CANR-16
Hansen, Karen V. 1955- .... **CLC 65**
See also CA 149; CANR 102
Hansen, Martin A(lfred)
1909-1955 .... **TCLC 32**
See also CA 167; DLB 214; EWL 3
Hanson, Kenneth O. 1922- .... **CLC 13**
See also CA 53-56; CANR 7; CP 1, 2, 3, 4, 5
Hanson, Kenneth Ostlin
See Hanson, Kenneth O.
Han Yu 768-824 .... **CMLC 122**
Hardwick, Elizabeth 1916-2007 .... **CLC 13**
See also AMWS 3; CA 5-8R; 267; CANR 3, 32, 70, 100, 139; CN 4, 5, 6; CSW; DA3; DAM NOV; DLB 6; MBL; MTCW 1, 2; MTFW 2005; TCLE 1:1
Hardwick, Elizabeth Bruce
See Hardwick, Elizabeth
Hardy, Thomas 1840-1928 . **PC 8, 92; SSC 2, 60, 113; TCLC 4, 10, 18, 32, 48, 53, 72, 143, 153, 229; WLC 3**
See also AAYA 69; BRW 6; BRWC 1, 2; BRWR 1; CA 104; 123; CDBLB 1890-1914; DA; DA3; DAB; DAC; DAM MST, NOV, POET; DLB 18, 19, 135, 284; EWL 3; EXPN; EXPP; LAIT 2; MTCW 1, 2; MTFW 2005; NFS 3, 11, 15, 19, 30; PFS 3, 4, 18; RGEL 2; RGSF 2; TEA; WLIT 4
Hare, David 1947- . **CLC 29, 58, 136; DC 26**
See also BRWS 4; CA 97-100; CANR 39, 91; CBD; CD 5, 6; DFS 4, 7, 16; DLB 13, 310; MTCW 1; TEA
Harewood, John
See Van Druten, John (William)
Harford, Henry
See Hudson, W(illiam) H(enry)
Hargrave, Leonie
See Disch, Thomas M.
Hariri, Al- al-Qasim ibn 'Ali Abu Muhammad al-Basri
See al-Hariri, al-Qasim ibn 'Ali Abu Muhammad al-Basri
Harjo, Joy 1951- ..... **CLC 83; NNAL; PC 27**
See also AMWS 12; CA 114; CANR 35, 67, 91, 129; CP 6, 7; CWP; DAM MULT; DLB 120, 175, 342; EWL 3; MTCW 2; MTFW 2005; PFS 15, 32; RGAL 4
Harlan, Louis R. 1922-2010 .... **CLC 34**
See also CA 21-24R; CANR 25, 55, 80
Harlan, Louis Rudolph
See Harlan, Louis R.
Harlan, Louis Rudolph
See Harlan, Louis R.
Harling, Robert 1951(?)- .... **CLC 53**
See also CA 147
Harmon, William (Ruth) 1938- .... **CLC 38**
See also CA 33-36R; CANR 14, 32, 35; SATA 65
Harper, Edith Alice Mary
See Wickham, Anna
Harper, F. E. W.
See Harper, Frances Ellen Watkins
Harper, Frances E. W.
See Harper, Frances Ellen Watkins
Harper, Frances E. Watkins
See Harper, Frances Ellen Watkins
Harper, Frances Ellen
See Harper, Frances Ellen Watkins

Harper, Frances Ellen Watkins
1825-1911 . BLC 1:2; PC 21; TCLC 14, 217
See also AFAW 1, 2; BW 1, 3; CA 111; 125; CANR 79; DAM MULT, POET; DLB 50, 221; MBL; RGAL 4

Harper, Michael S. 1938- .. BLC 2:2; CLC 7, 22
See also AFAW 2; BW 1; CA 33-36R, 224; CAAE 224; CANR 24, 108, 212; CP 2, 3, 4, 5, 6, 7; DLB 41; RGAL 4; TCLE 1:1

Harper, Michael Steven
See Harper, Michael S.

Harper, Mrs. F. E. W.
See Harper, Frances Ellen Watkins

Harpur, Charles 1813-1868 .... NCLC 114
See also DLB 230; RGEL 2

Harris, Christie
See Harris, Christie (Lucy) Irwin

Harris, Christie (Lucy) Irwin
1907-2002 .... CLC 12
See also CA 5-8R; CANR 6, 83; CLR 47; DLB 88; JRDA; MAICYA 1, 2; SAAS 10; SATA 6, 74; SATA-Essay 116

Harris, E. Lynn 1955-2009 .... CLC 299
See also CA 164; 288; CANR 111, 163, 206; MTFW 2005

Harris, Everett Lynn
See Harris, E. Lynn

Harris, Everette Lynn
See Harris, E. Lynn

Harris, Frank 1856-1931 .... TCLC 24
See also CA 109; 150; CANR 80; DLB 156, 197; RGEL 2

Harris, George Washington
1814-1869 .... NCLC 23, 165
See also DLB 3, 11, 248; RGAL 4

Harris, Joel Chandler 1848-1908 ..... SSC 19, 103; TCLC 2
See also CA 104; 137; CANR 80; CLR 49, 128; DLB 11, 23, 42, 78, 91; LAIT 2; MAICYA 1, 2; RGSF 2; SATA 100; WCH; YABC 1

Harris, John (Wyndham Parkes Lucas)
Beynon 1903-1969 .... CLC 19
See also BRWS 13; CA 102; 89-92; CANR 84; DLB 255; SATA 118; SCFW 1, 2; SFW 4

Harris, MacDonald
See Heiney, Donald (William)

Harris, Mark 1922-2007 .... CLC 19
See also CA 5-8R; 260; CAAS 3; CANR 2, 55, 83; CN 1, 2, 3, 4, 5, 6, 7; DLB 2; DLBY 1980

Harris, Norman CLC 65

Harris, (Theodore) Wilson 1921- ... BLC 2:2; CLC 25, 159, 297
See also BRWS 5; BW 2, 3; CA 65-68; CAAS 16; CANR 11, 27, 69, 114; CDWLB 3; CN 1, 2, 3, 4, 5, 6, 7; CP 1, 2, 3, 4, 5, 6, 7; DLB 117; EWL 3; MTCW 1; RGEL 2

Harrison, Barbara Grizzuti
1934-2002 .... CLC 144
See also CA 77-80; 205; CANR 15, 48; INT CANR-15

Harrison, Elizabeth (Allen) Cavanna
1909-2001 .... CLC 12
See also CA 9-12R; 200; CANR 6, 27, 85, 104, 121; JRDA; MAICYA 1; SAAS 4; SATA 1, 30; YAW

Harrison, Harry 1925- .... CLC 42
See also CA 1-4R; CANR 5, 21, 84; DLB 8; SATA 4; SCFW 2; SFW 4

Harrison, Harry Max
See Harrison, Harry

Harrison, James
See Harrison, Jim

Harrison, James Thomas
See Harrison, Jim

Harrison, Jim 1937- .... CLC 6, 14, 33, 66, 143; SSC 19
See also AMWS 8; CA 13-16R; CANR 8, 51, 79, 142, 198; CN 5, 6; CP 1, 2, 3, 4, 5, 6; DLBY 1982; INT CANR-8; RGAL 4; TCWW 2; TUS

Harrison, Kathryn 1961- .... CLC 70, 151
See also CA 144; CANR 68, 122, 194

Harrison, Tony 1937- .... CLC 43, 129
See also BRWS 5; CA 65-68; CANR 44, 98; CBD; CD 5, 6; CP 2, 3, 4, 5, 6, 7; DLB 40, 245; MTCW 1; RGEL 2

Harriss, Will(ard Irvin) 1922- .... CLC 34
See also CA 111

Hart, Ellis
See Ellison, Harlan

Hart, Josephine 1942(?)- .... CLC 70
See also CA 138; CANR 70, 149; CPW; DAM POP

Hart, Moss 1904-1961 .... CLC 66
See also CA 109; 89-92; CANR 84; DAM DRAM; DFS 1; DLB 7, 266; RGAL 4

Harte, Bret 1836(?)-1902 .. SSC 8, 59; TCLC 1, 25; WLC 3
See also AMWS 2; CA 104; 140; CANR 80; CDALB 1865-1917; DA; DA3; DAC; DAM MST; DLB 12, 64, 74, 79, 186; EXPS; LAIT 2; RGAL 4; RGSF 2; SATA 26; SSFS 3; TUS

Harte, Francis Brett
See Harte, Bret

Hartley, L(eslie) P(oles) 1895-1972 ... CLC 2, 22; SSC 125
See also BRWS 7; CA 45-48; 37-40R; CANR 33; CN 1; DLB 15, 139; EWL 3; HGG; MTCW 1, 2; MTFW 2005; RGEL 2; RGSF 2; SUFW 1

Hartman, Geoffrey H. 1929- .... CLC 27
See also CA 117; 125; CANR 79, 214; DLB 67

Hartmann, Sadakichi 1869-1944 ... TCLC 73
See also CA 157; DLB 54

Hartmann von Aue c. 1170-c.
1210 .... CMLC 15
See also CDWLB 2; DLB 138; RGWL 2, 3

Hartog, Jan de
See de Hartog, Jan

Haruf, Kent 1943- .... CLC 34
See also AAYA 44; CA 149; CANR 91, 131

Harvey, Caroline
See Trollope, Joanna

Harvey, Gabriel 1550(?)-1631 .... LC 88
See also DLB 167, 213, 281

Harvey, Jack
See Rankin, Ian

Harwood, Ronald 1934- .... CLC 32
See also CA 1-4R; CANR 4, 55, 150; CBD; CD 5, 6; DAM DRAM, MST; DLB 13

Hasegawa Tatsunosuke
See Futabatei, Shimei

Hasek, Jaroslav 1883-1923 ... SSC 69; TCLC 4
See also CA 104; 129; CDWLB 4; DLB 215; EW 9; EWL 3; MTCW 1, 2; RGSF 2; RGWL 2, 3

Hasek, Jaroslav Matej Frantisek
See Hasek, Jaroslav

Hass, Robert 1941- ...... CLC 18, 39, 99, 287; PC 16
See also AMWS 6; CA 111; CANR 30, 50, 71, 187; CP 3, 4, 5, 6, 7; DLB 105, 206; EWL 3; MAL 5; MTFW 2005; PFS 37; RGAL 4; SATA 94; TCLE 1:1

Hassler, Jon 1933-2008 .... CLC 263
See also CA 73-76; 270; CANR 21, 80, 161; CN 6, 7; INT CANR-21; SATA 19; SATA-Obit 191

Hassler, Jon Francis
See Hassler, Jon

Hastings, Hudson
See Kuttner, Henry

Hastings, Selina CLC 44
See also CA 257

Hastings, Selina Shirley
See Hastings, Selina

Hastings, Victor
See Disch, Thomas M.

Hathorne, John 1641-1717 .... LC 38

Hatteras, Amelia
See Mencken, H. L.

Hatteras, Owen
See Mencken, H. L.; Nathan, George Jean

Hauff, Wilhelm 1802-1827 .... NCLC 185
See also CLR 155; DLB 90; SUFW 1

Hauptmann, Gerhart 1862-1946 .... DC 34; SSC 37; TCLC 4
See also CA 104; 153; CDWLB 2; DAM DRAM; DLB 66, 118, 330; EW 8; EWL 3; RGSF 2; RGWL 2, 3; TWA

Hauptmann, Gerhart Johann Robert
See Hauptmann, Gerhart

Havel, Vaclav 1936- ..... CLC 25, 58, 65, 123; DC 6
See also CA 104; CANR 36, 63, 124, 175; CDWLB 4; CWW 2; DA3; DAM DRAM; DFS 10; DLB 232; EWL 3; LMFS 2; MTCW 1, 2; MTFW 2005; RGWL 3

Haviaras, Stratis
See Chaviaras, Strates

Hawes, Stephen 1475(?)-1529(?) .... LC 17
See also DLB 132; RGEL 2

Hawk, Alex
See Kelton, Elmer

Hawkes, John 1925-1998 .. CLC 1, 2, 3, 4, 7, 9, 14, 15, 27, 49
See also BPFB 2; CA 1-4R; 167; CANR 2, 47, 64; CN 1, 2, 3, 4, 5, 6; DLB 2, 7, 227; DLBY 1980, 1998; EWL 3; MAL 5; MTCW 1, 2; MTFW 2005; RGAL 4

Hawking, S. W.
See Hawking, Stephen W.

Hawking, Stephen W. 1942- ..... CLC 63, 105
See also AAYA 13; BEST 89:1; CA 126; 129; CANR 48, 115; CPW; DA3; MTCW 2; MTFW 2005

Hawking, Stephen William
See Hawking, Stephen W.

Hawkins, Anthony Hope
See Hope, Anthony

Hawthorne, Julian 1846-1934 .... TCLC 25
See also CA 165; HGG

Hawthorne, Nathaniel 1804-1864 ... NCLC 2, 10, 17, 23, 39, 79, 95, 158, 171, 191, 226; SSC 3, 29, 39, 89, 130; WLC 3
See also AAYA 18; AMW; AMWC 1; AMWR 1; BPFB 2; BYA 3; CDALB 1640-1865; CLR 103; DA; DA3; DAB; DAC; DAM MST, NOV; DLB 1, 74, 183, 223, 269; EXPN; EXPS; GL 2; HGG; LAIT 1; NFS 1, 20; RGAL 4; RGSF 2; SSFS 1, 7, 11, 15, 30; SUFW 1; TUS; WCH; YABC 2

Hawthorne, Sophia Peabody
1809-1871 .... NCLC 150
See also DLB 183, 239

Haxton, Josephine Ayres 1921-
See Douglas, Ellen

Hayaseca y Eizaguirre, Jorge
See Echegaray (y Eizaguirre), Jose (Maria Waldo)

Hayashi, Fumiko 1904-1951 .... TCLC 27
See also CA 161; DLB 180; EWL 3

Hayashi Fumiko
See Hayashi, Fumiko

Haycraft, Anna 1932-2005 .... **CLC 40**
See also CA 122; 237; CANR 90, 141; CN
4, 5, 6; DLB 194; MTCW 2; MTFW 2005

Haycraft, Anna Margaret
See Haycraft, Anna

Hayden, Robert
See Hayden, Robert Earl

Hayden, Robert E.
See Hayden, Robert Earl

Hayden, Robert Earl 1913-1980 .... **BLC 1:2;
CLC 5, 9, 14, 37; PC 6**
See also AFAW 1, 2; AMWS 2; BW 1, 3;
CA 69-72; 97-100; CABS 2; CANR 24,
75, 82; CDALB 1941-1968; CP 1, 2, 3;
DA; DAC; DAM MST, MULT, POET;
DLB 5, 76; EWL 3; EXPP; MAL 5;
MTCW 1, 2; PFS 1, 31; RGAL 4; SATA
19; SATA-Obit 26; WP

Haydon, Benjamin Robert
1786-1846 .... **NCLC 146**
See also DLB 110

Hayek, F(riedrich) A(ugust von)
1899-1992 .... **TCLC 109**
See also CA 93-96; 137; CANR 20; MTCW
1, 2

Hayford, J(oseph) E(phraim) Casely
See Casely-Hayford, J(oseph) E(phraim)

Hayman, Ronald 1932- .... **CLC 44**
See also CA 25-28R; CANR 18, 50, 88; CD
5, 6; DLB 155

Hayne, Paul Hamilton 1830-1886 . **NCLC 94**
See also DLB 3, 64, 79, 248; RGAL 4

Hays, Mary 1760-1843 .... **NCLC 114**
See also DLB 142, 158; RGEL 2

Haywood, Eliza (Fowler)
1693(?)-1756 .... **LC 1, 44, 177**
See also BRWS 12; DLB 39; RGEL 2

Hazlitt, William 1778-1830 ...... **NCLC 29, 82**
See also BRW 4; DLB 110, 158; RGEL 2;
TEA

Hazzard, Shirley 1931- .... **CLC 18, 218**
See also CA 9-12R; CANR 4, 70, 127, 212;
CN 1, 2, 3, 4, 5, 6, 7; DLB 289; DLBY
1982; MTCW 1

Head, Bessie 1937-1986 . **BLC 1:2, 2:2; CLC
25, 67; SSC 52**
See also AFW; BW 2, 3; CA 29-32R; 119;
CANR 25, 82; CDWLB 3; CN 1, 2, 3, 4;
DA3; DAM MULT; DLB 117, 225; EWL
3; EXPS; FL 1:6; FW; MTCW 1, 2;
MTFW 2005; NFS 31; RGSF 2; SSFS 5,
13, 30, 33; WLIT 2; WWE 1

Headley, Elizabeth
See Harrison, Elizabeth (Allen) Cavanna

Headon, (Nicky) Topper 1956(?)- ..... **CLC 30**

Heaney, Seamus 1939- . **CLC 5, 7, 14, 25, 37,
74, 91, 171, 225; PC 18, 100; WLCS**
See also AAYA 61; BRWR 1; BRWS 2; CA
85-88; CANR 25, 48, 75, 91, 128, 184;
CDBLB 1960 to Present; CP 1, 2, 3, 4, 5,
6, 7; DA3; DAB; DAM POET; DLB 40,
330; DLBY 1995; EWL 3; EXPP; MTCW
1, 2; MTFW 2005; PAB; PFS 2, 5, 8, 17,
30; RGEL 2; TEA; WLIT 4

Heaney, Seamus Justin
See Heaney, Seamus

Hearn, Lafcadio 1850-1904 .... **TCLC 9**
See also AAYA 79; CA 105; 166; DLB 12,
78, 189; HGG; MAL 5; RGAL 4

Hearn, Patricio Lafcadio Tessima Carlos
See Hearn, Lafcadio

Hearne, Samuel 1745-1792 .... **LC 95**
See also DLB 99

Hearne, Vicki 1946-2001 .... **CLC 56**
See also CA 139; 201

Hearon, Shelby 1931- .... **CLC 63**
See also AITN 2; AMWS 8; CA 25-28R;
CAAS 11; CANR 18, 48, 103, 146; CSW

Heat-Moon, William Least 1939- ..... **CLC 29**
See also AAYA 9, 66; ANW; CA 115; 119;
CANR 47, 89, 206; CPW; INT CA-119

Hebbel, Friedrich 1813-1863 . **DC 21; NCLC
43**
See also CDWLB 2; DAM DRAM; DLB
129; EW 6; RGWL 2, 3

Hebert, Anne 1916-2000 . **CLC 4, 13, 29, 246**
See also CA 85-88; 187; CANR 69, 126;
CCA 1; CWP; CWW 2; DA3; DAC;
DAM MST, POET; DLB 68; EWL 3; GFL
1789 to the Present; MTCW 1, 2; MTFW
2005; PFS 20

Hecht, Anthony (Evan) 1923-2004 .... **CLC 8,
13, 19; PC 70**
See also AMWS 10; CA 9-12R; 232; CANR
6, 108; CP 1, 2, 3, 4, 5, 6, 7; DAM POET;
DLB 5, 169; EWL 3; PFS 6; WP

Hecht, Ben 1894-1964 ..... **CLC 8; TCLC 101**
See also CA 85-88; DFS 9; DLB 7, 9, 25,
26, 28, 86; FANT; IDFW 3, 4; RGAL 4

Hedayat, Sadeq 1903-1951 . **SSC 131; TCLC
21**
See also CA 120; EWL 3; RGSF 2

Hegel, Georg Wilhelm Friedrich
1770-1831 .... **NCLC 46, 151**
See also DLB 90; TWA

Heidegger, Martin 1889-1976 .... **CLC 24**
See also CA 81-84; 65-68; CANR 34; DLB
296; MTCW 1, 2; MTFW 2005

Heidenstam, (Carl Gustaf) Verner von
1859-1940 .... **TCLC 5**
See also CA 104; DLB 330

Heidi Louise
See Erdrich, Louise

Heifner, Jack 1946- .... **CLC 11**
See also CA 105; CANR 47

Heijermans, Herman 1864-1924 .... **TCLC 24**
See also CA 123; EWL 3

Heilbrun, Carolyn G. 1926-2003 ..... **CLC 25,
173, 303**
See also BPFB 1; CA 45-48; 220; CANR 1,
28, 58, 94; CMW; CPW; DLB 306; FW;
MSW

Heilbrun, Carolyn Gold
See Heilbrun, Carolyn G.

Hein, Christoph 1944- .... **CLC 154**
See also CA 158; CANR 108, 210; CDWLB
2; CWW 2; DLB 124

Heine, Heinrich 1797-1856 .... **NCLC 4, 54,
147; PC 25**
See also CDWLB 2; DLB 90; EW 5; PFS
37; RGWL 2, 3; TWA

Heinemann, Larry 1944- .... **CLC 50**
See also CA 110; CAAS 21; CANR 31, 81,
156; DLBD 9; INT CANR-31

Heinemann, Larry Curtiss
See Heinemann, Larry

Heiney, Donald (William) 1921-1993 . **CLC 9**
See also CA 1-4R; 142; CANR 3, 58; FANT

Heinlein, Robert A. 1907-1988 .. **CLC 1, 3, 8,
14, 26, 55; SSC 55**
See also AAYA 17; BPFB 2; BYA 4, 13;
CA 1-4R; 125; CANR 1, 20, 53; CLR 75;
CN 1, 2, 3, 4; CPW; DA3; DAM POP;
DLB 8; EXPS; JRDA; LAIT 5; LMFS 2;
MAICYA 1, 2; MTCW 1, 2; MTFW 2005;
RGAL 4; SATA 9, 69; SATA-Obit 56;
SCFW 1, 2; SFW 4; SSFS 7; YAW

Hejinian, Lyn 1941- .... **PC 108**
See also CA 153; CANR 85, 214; CP 4, 5,
6, 7; CWP; DLB 165; PFS 27; RGAL 4

Held, Peter
See Vance, Jack

Heldris of Cornwall fl. 13th cent.
- .... **CMLC 97**

Helforth, John
See Doolittle, Hilda

Heliodorus fl. 3rd cent. - .... **CMLC 52**
See also WLIT 8

Hellenhofferu, Vojtech Kapristian z
See Hasek, Jaroslav

Heller, Joseph 1923-1999 . **CLC 1, 3, 5, 8, 11,
36, 63; TCLC 131, 151; WLC 3**
See also AAYA 24; AITN 1; AMWS 4;
BPFB 2; BYA 1; CA 5-8R; 187; CABS 1;
CANR 8, 42, 66, 126; CN 1, 2, 3, 4, 5, 6;
CPW; DA; DA3; DAB; DAC; DAM MST,
NOV, POP; DLB 2, 28, 227; DLBY 1980,
2002; EWL 3; EXPN; INT CANR-8;
LAIT 4; MAL 5; MTCW 1, 2; MTFW
2005; NFS 1; RGAL 4; TUS; YAW

Hellman, Lillian 1905-1984 . **CLC 2, 4, 8, 14,
18, 34, 44, 52; DC 1; TCLC 119**
See also AAYA 47; AITN 1, 2; AMWS 1;
CA 13-16R; 112; CAD; CANR 33; CWD;
DA3; DAM DRAM; DFS 1, 3, 14; DLB
7, 228; DLBY 1984; EWL 3; FL 1:6; FW;
LAIT 3; MAL 5; MBL; MTCW 1, 2;
MTFW 2005; RGAL 4; TUS

Hellman, Lillian Florence
See Hellman, Lillian

Heloise c. 1095-c. 1164 .... **CMLC 122**

Helprin, Mark 1947- .... **CLC 7, 10, 22, 32**
See also CA 81-84; CANR 47, 64, 124;
CDALBS; CN 7; CPW; DA3; DAM NOV,
POP; DLB 335; DLBY 1985; FANT;
MAL 5; MTCW 1, 2; MTFW 2005; SSFS
25; SUFW 2

Helvetius, Claude-Adrien 1715-1771 .. **LC 26**
See also DLB 313

Helyar, Jane Penelope Josephine
1933- .... **CLC 17**
See also CA 21-24R; CANR 10, 26; CWRI
5; SAAS 2; SATA 5; SATA-Essay 138

Hemans, Felicia 1793-1835 ...... **NCLC 29, 71**
See also DLB 96; RGEL 2

Hemingway, Ernest 1899-1961 .. **CLC 1, 3, 6,
8, 10, 13, 19, 30, 34, 39, 41, 44, 50, 61,
80; SSC 1, 25, 36, 40, 63, 117, 137;
TCLC 115, 203; WLC 3**
See also AAYA 19; AMW; AMWC 1;
AMWR 1; BPFB 2; BYA 2, 3, 13, 15; CA
77-80; CANR 34; CDALB 1917-1929;
DA; DA3; DAB; DAC; DAM MST, NOV;
DLB 4, 9, 102, 210, 308, 316, 330; DLBD
1, 15, 16; DLBY 1981, 1987, 1996, 1998;
EWL 3; EXPN; EXPS; LAIT 3, 4; LATS
1:1; MAL 5; MTCW 1, 2; MTFW 2005;
NFS 1, 5, 6, 14; RGAL 4; RGSF 2; SSFS
17; TUS; WYA

Hemingway, Ernest Miller
See Hemingway, Ernest

Hempel, Amy 1951- .... **CLC 39**
See also AMWS 21; CA 118; 137; CANR
70, 166; DA3; DLB 218; EXPS; MTCW
2; MTFW 2005; SSFS 2

Henderson, F. C.
See Mencken, H. L.

Henderson, Mary
See Mavor, Osborne Henry

Henderson, Sylvia
See Ashton-Warner, Sylvia (Constance)

Henderson, Zenna (Chlarson)
1917-1983 .... **SSC 29**
See also CA 1-4R; 133; CANR 1, 84; DLB
8; SATA 5; SFW 4

Henkin, Joshua 1964- .... **CLC 119**
See also CA 161; CANR 186; DLB 350

Henley, Beth 1952- ... **CLC 23, 255; DC 6, 14**
See also AAYA 70; CA 107; CABS 3; CAD;
CANR 32, 73, 140; CD 5, 6; CSW; CWD;
DA3; DAM DRAM, MST; DFS 2, 21, 26;
DLBY 1986; FW; MTCW 1, 2; MTFW
2005

Henley, Elizabeth Becker
See Henley, Beth

Henley, William Ernest 1849-1903 .. **TCLC 8**
See also CA 105; 234; DLB 19; RGEL 2
Hennissart, Martha 1929- .... **CLC 2**
See also BPFB 2; CA 85-88; CANR 64;
CMW 4; DLB 306
Henry VIII 1491-1547 .... **LC 10**
See also DLB 132
Henry, O. 1862-1910 . **SSC 5, 49, 117; TCLC
1, 19; WLC 3**
See also AAYA 41; AMWS 2; CA 104; 131;
CDALB 1865-1917; DA; DA3; DAB;
DAC; DAM MST; DLB 12, 78, 79; EXPS;
MAL 5; MTCW 1, 2; MTFW 2005;
RGAL 4; RGSF 2; SSFS 2, 18, 27, 31;
TCWW 1, 2; TUS; YABC 2
Henry, Oliver
See Henry, O.
Henry, Patrick 1736-1799 .... **LC 25**
See also LAIT 1
Henryson, Robert 1430(?)-1506(?) ..... **LC 20,
110; PC 65**
See also BRWS 7; DLB 146; RGEL 2
Henschke, Alfred
See Klabund
Henson, Lance 1944- .... **NNAL**
See also CA 146; DLB 175
Hentoff, Nat(han Irving) 1925- .... **CLC 26**
See also AAYA 4, 42; BYA 6; CA 1-4R;
CAAS 6; CANR 5, 25, 77, 114; CLR 1,
52; DLB 345; INT CANR-25; JRDA;
MAICYA 1, 2; SATA 42, 69, 133; SATA-
Brief 27; WYA; YAW
Heppenstall, (John) Rayner
1911-1981 .... **CLC 10**
See also CA 1-4R; 103; CANR 29; CN 1,
2; CP 1, 2, 3; EWL 3
Heraclitus c. 540B.C.-c. 450B.C. ... **CMLC 22**
See also DLB 176
Herbert, Edward 1583-1648 .... **LC 177**
See also DLB 121, 151, 252; RGEL 2
Herbert, Frank 1920-1986 ... **CLC 12, 23, 35,
44, 85**
See also AAYA 21; BPFB 2; BYA 4, 14;
CA 53-56; 118; CANR 5, 43; CDALBS;
CPW; DAM POP; DLB 8; INT CANR-5;
LAIT 5; MTCW 1, 2; MTFW 2005; NFS
17, 31; SATA 9, 37; SATA-Obit 47;
SCFW 1, 2; SFW 4; YAW
Herbert, George 1593-1633 . **LC 24, 121; PC
4**
See also BRW 2; BRWR 2; CDBLB Before
1660; DAB; DAM POET; DLB 126;
EXPP; PFS 25; RGEL 2; TEA; WP
Herbert, Zbigniew 1924-1998 ..... **CLC 9, 43;
PC 50; TCLC 168**
See also CA 89-92; 169; CANR 36, 74, 177;
CDWLB 4; CWW 2; DAM POET; DLB
232; EWL 3; MTCW 1; PFS 22
Herbert of Cherbury, Lord
See Herbert, Edward
Herbst, Josephine (Frey)
1897-1969 .... **CLC 34; TCLC 243**
See also CA 5-8R; 25-28R; DLB 9
Herder, Johann Gottfried von
1744-1803 .... **NCLC 8, 186**
See also DLB 97; EW 4; TWA
Heredia, Jose Maria 1803-1839 ...... **HLCS 2;
NCLC 209**
See also LAW
Hergesheimer, Joseph 1880-1954 ... **TCLC 11**
See also CA 109; 194; DLB 102, 9; RGAL
4
Herlihy, James Leo 1927-1993 .... **CLC 6**
See also CA 1-4R; 143; CAD; CANR 2;
CN 1, 2, 3, 4, 5
Herman, William
See Bierce, Ambrose

Hermogenes fl. c. 175- .... **CMLC 6**
Hernandez, Jose 1834-1886 .... **NCLC 17**
See also LAW; RGWL 2, 3; WLIT 1
Herodotus c. 484B.C.-c. 420B.C. .. **CMLC 17**
See also AW 1; CDWLB 1; DLB 176;
RGWL 2, 3; TWA; WLIT 8
Herr, Michael 1940(?)- .... **CLC 231**
See also CA 89-92; CANR 68, 142; DLB
185; MTCW 1
Herrick, Robert 1591-1674 .. **LC 13, 145; PC
9**
See also BRW 2; BRWC 2; DA; DAB;
DAC; DAM MST, POP; DLB 126; EXPP;
PFS 13, 29; RGAL 4; RGEL 2; TEA; WP
Herring, Guilles
See Somerville, Edith Oenone
Herriot, James 1916-1995 .... **CLC 12**
See also AAYA 1, 54; BPFB 2; CA 77-80;
148; CANR 40; CLR 80; CPW; DAM
POP; LAIT 3; MAICYA 2; MAICYAS 1;
MTCW 2; SATA 86, 135; SATA-Brief 44;
TEA; YAW
Herris, Violet
See Hunt, Violet
Herrmann, Dorothy 1941- .... **CLC 44**
See also CA 107
Herrmann, Taffy
See Herrmann, Dorothy
Hersey, John 1914-1993 .. **CLC 1, 2, 7, 9, 40,
81, 97**
See also AAYA 29; BPFB 2; CA 17-20R;
140; CANR 33; CDALBS; CN 1, 2, 3, 4,
5; CPW; DAM POP; DLB 6, 185, 278,
299; MAL 5; MTCW 1, 2; MTFW 2005;
RGHL; SATA 25; SATA-Obit 76; TUS
Hersey, John Richard
See Hersey, John
Hervent, Maurice
See Grindel, Eugene
Herzen, Aleksandr Ivanovich
1812-1870 .... **NCLC 10, 61**
See also DLB 277
Herzen, Alexander
See Herzen, Aleksandr Ivanovich
Herzl, Theodor 1860-1904 .... **TCLC 36**
See also CA 168
Herzog, Werner 1942- .... **CLC 16, 236**
See also AAYA 85; CA 89-92; CANR 215
Hesiod fl. 8th cent. B.C.- .... **CMLC 5, 102**
See also AW 1; DLB 176; RGWL 2, 3;
WLIT 8
Hesse, Hermann 1877-1962 ... **CLC 1, 2, 3, 6,
11, 17, 25, 69; SSC 9, 49; TCLC 148,
196; WLC 3**
See also AAYA 43; BPFB 2; CA 17-18;
CAP 2; CDWLB 2; DA; DA3; DAB;
DAC; DAM MST, NOV; DLB 66, 330;
EW 9; EWL 3; EXPN; LAIT 1; MTCW
1, 2; MTFW 2005; NFS 6, 15, 24; RGWL
2, 3; SATA 50; TWA
Hewes, Cady
See De Voto, Bernard (Augustine)
Heyen, William 1940- .... **CLC 13, 18**
See also CA 33-36R; 220; CAAE 220;
CAAS 9; CANR 98, 188; CP 3, 4, 5, 6, 7;
DLB 5; RGHL
Heyerdahl, Thor 1914-2002 .... **CLC 26**
See also CA 5-8R; 207; CANR 5, 22, 66,
73; LAIT 4; MTCW 1, 2; MTFW 2005;
SATA 2, 52
Heym, Georg (Theodor Franz Arthur)
1887-1912 .... **TCLC 9**
See also CA 106; 181
Heym, Stefan 1913-2001 .... **CLC 41**
See also CA 9-12R; 203; CANR 4; CWW
2; DLB 69; EWL 3
Heyse, Paul (Johann Ludwig von)
1830-1914 .... **TCLC 8**
See also CA 104; 209; DLB 129, 330

Heyward, (Edwin) DuBose
1885-1940 .... **HR 1:2; TCLC 59**
See also CA 108; 157; DLB 7, 9, 45, 249;
MAL 5; SATA 21
Heywood, John 1497(?)-1580(?) .... **LC 65**
See also DLB 136; RGEL 2
Heywood, Thomas 1573(?)-1641 . **DC 29; LC
111**
See also DAM DRAM; DLB 62; LMFS 1;
RGEL 2; TEA
Hiaasen, Carl 1953- .... **CLC 238**
See also CA 105; CANR 22, 45, 65, 113,
133, 168; CMW 4; CPW; CSW; DA3;
DLB 292; LNFS 2, 3; MTCW 2; MTFW
2005; SATA 208
Hibbert, Eleanor Alice Burford
1906-1993 .... **CLC 7**
See also BEST 90:4; BPFB 2; CA 17-20R;
140; CANR 9, 28, 59; CMW 4; CPW;
DAM POP; MTCW 2; MTFW 2005;
RHW; SATA 2; SATA-Obit 74
Hichens, Robert (Smythe)
1864-1950 .... **TCLC 64**
See also CA 162; DLB 153; HGG; RHW;
SUFW
Higgins, Aidan 1927- .... **SSC 68**
See also CA 9-12R; CANR 70, 115, 148;
CN 1, 2, 3, 4, 5, 6, 7; DLB 14
Higgins, George V(incent)
1939-1999 .... **CLC 4, 7, 10, 18**
See also BPFB 2; CA 77-80; 186; CAAS 5;
CANR 17, 51, 89, 96; CMW 4; CN 2, 3,
4, 5, 6; DLB 2; DLBY 1981, 1998; INT
CANR-17; MSW; MTCW 1
Higginson, Thomas Wentworth
1823-1911 .... **TCLC 36**
See also CA 162; DLB 1, 64, 243
Higgonet, Margaret CLC 65
Highet, Helen
See MacInnes, Helen (Clark)
Highsmith, Mary Patricia
See Highsmith, Patricia
Highsmith, Patricia 1921-1995 ...... **CLC 2, 4,
14, 42, 102**
See also AAYA 48; BRWS 5; CA 1-4R; 147;
CANR 1, 20, 48, 62, 108; CMW 4; CN 1,
2, 3, 4, 5; CPW; DA3; DAM NOV, POP;
DLB 306; GLL 1; MSW; MTCW 1, 2;
MTFW 2005; NFS 27; SSFS 25
Highwater, Jamake (Mamake)
1942(?)-2001 .... **CLC 12**
See also AAYA 7, 69; BPFB 2; BYA 4; CA
65-68; 199; CAAS 7; CANR 10, 34, 84;
CLR 17; CWRI 5; DLB 52; DLBY 1985;
JRDA; MAICYA 1, 2; SATA 32, 69;
SATA-Brief 30
Highway, Tomson 1951- ..... **CLC 92; DC 33;
NNAL**
See also CA 151; CANR 75; CCA 1; CD 5,
6; CN 7; DAC; DAM MULT; DFS 2;
DLB 334; MTCW 2
Hijuelos, Oscar 1951- .... **CLC 65; HLC 1**
See also AAYA 25; AMWS 8; BEST 90:1;
CA 123; CANR 50, 75, 125, 205; CPW;
DA3; DAM MULT, POP; DLB 145; HW
1, 2; LLW; MAL 5; MTCW 2; MTFW
2005; NFS 17; RGAL 4; WLIT 1
Hikmet, Nazim 1902-1963 .... **CLC 40**
See also CA 141; 93-96; EWL 3; PFS 38;
WLIT 6
Hildegard von Bingen
1098-1179 .... **CMLC 20, 118**
See also DLB 148
Hildesheimer, Wolfgang 1916-1991 .. **CLC 49**
See also CA 101; 135; DLB 69, 124; EWL
3; RGHL
Hill, Aaron 1685-1750 .... **LC 148**
See also DLB 84; RGEL 2

Howard, Sidney (Coe) 1891-1939 .... **DC 42**
See also CA 198; DLB 7, 26, 249; IDFW 3,
4; MAL 5; RGAL 4

Howard, Warren F.
See Pohl, Frederik

Howe, Fanny 1940- .... **CLC 47**
See also CA 117, 187; CAAE 187; CAAS
27; CANR 70, 116, 184; CP 6, 7; CWP;
SATA-Brief 52

Howe, Fanny Quincy
See Howe, Fanny

Howe, Irving 1920-1993 .... **CLC 85**
See also AMWS 6; CA 9-12R; 141; CANR
21, 50; DLB 67; EWL 3; MAL 5; MTCW
1, 2; MTFW 2005

Howe, Julia Ward 1819-1910 . **PC 81; TCLC
21**
See also CA 117; 191; DLB 1, 189, 235;
FW

Howe, Susan 1937- .... **CLC 72, 152; PC 54**
See also AMWS 4; CA 160; CANR 209;
CP 5, 6, 7; CWP; DLB 120; FW; RGAL
4

Howe, Tina 1937- .... **CLC 48**
See also CA 109; CAD; CANR 125; CD 5,
6; CWD; DLB 341

Howell, James 1594(?)-1666 .... **LC 13**
See also DLB 151

Howells, W. D.
See Howells, William Dean

Howells, William D.
See Howells, William Dean

Howells, William Dean 1837-1920 ... **SSC 36;
TCLC 7, 17, 41**
See also AMW; CA 104; 134; CDALB
1865-1917; DLB 12, 64, 74, 79, 189;
LMFS 1; MAL 5; MTCW 2; RGAL 4;
TUS

Howes, Barbara 1914-1996 .... **CLC 15**
See also CA 9-12R; 151; CAAS 3; CANR
53; CP 1, 2, 3, 4, 5, 6; SATA 5; TCLE 1:1

Hrabal, Bohumil 1914-1997 ...... **CLC 13, 67;
TCLC 155**
See also CA 106; 156; CAAS 12; CANR
57; CWW 2; DLB 232; EWL 3; RGSF 2

Hrabanus Maurus 776(?)-856 .... **CMLC 78**
See also DLB 148

Hroswitha of Gandersheim
See Hrotsvit of Gandersheim

Hrotsvit of Gandersheim c. 935-c.
1000 .... **CMLC 29, 123**
See also DLB 148

Hsi, Chu 1130-1200 .... **CMLC 42**

Hsun, Lu
See Shu-Jen, Chou

Hubbard, L. Ron 1911-1986 .... **CLC 43**
See also AAYA 64; CA 77-80; 118; CANR
52; CPW; DA3; DAM POP; FANT;
MTCW 2; MTFW 2005; SFW 4

Hubbard, Lafayette Ronald
See Hubbard, L. Ron

Huch, Ricarda (Octavia)
1864-1947 .... **TCLC 13**
See also CA 111; 189; DLB 66; EWL 3

Huddle, David 1942- .... **CLC 49**
See also CA 57-60, 261; CAAS 20; CANR
89; DLB 130

Hudson, Jeffery
See Crichton, Michael

Hudson, Jeffrey
See Crichton, Michael

Hudson, W(illiam) H(enry)
1841-1922 .... **TCLC 29**
See also CA 115; 190; DLB 98, 153, 174;
RGEL 2; SATA 35

Hueffer, Ford Madox
See Ford, Ford Madox

Hughart, Barry 1934- .... **CLC 39**
See also CA 137; FANT; SFW 4; SUFW 2

Hughes, Colin
See Creasey, John

Hughes, David (John) 1930-2005 ..... **CLC 48**
See also CA 116; 129; 238; CN 4, 5, 6, 7;
DLB 14

Hughes, Edward James
See Hughes, Ted

Hughes, James Langston
See Hughes, Langston

Hughes, Langston 1902-1967 .... **BLC 1:2;
CLC 1, 5, 10, 15, 35, 44, 108; DC 3;
HR 1:2; PC 1, 53; SSC 6, 90; WLC 3**
See also AAYA 12; AFAW 1, 2; AMWR 1;
AMWS 1; BW 1, 3; CA 1-4R; 25-28R;
CANR 1, 34, 82; CDALB 1929-1941;
CLR 17; DA; DA3; DAB; DAC; DAM
DRAM, MST, MULT, POET; DFS 6, 18;
DLB 4, 7, 48, 51, 86, 228, 315; EWL 3;
EXPP; EXPS; JRDA; LAIT 3; LMFS 2;
MAICYA 1, 2; MAL 5; MTCW 1, 2;
MTFW 2005; NFS 21; PAB; PFS 1, 3, 6,
10, 15, 30, 38; RGAL 4; RGSF 2; SATA
4, 33; SSFS 4, 7, 29; TUS; WCH; WP;
YAW

Hughes, Richard (Arthur Warren)
1900-1976 .... **CLC 1, 11; TCLC 204**
See also CA 5-8R; 65-68; CANR 4; CN 1,
2; DAM NOV; DLB 15, 161; EWL 3;
MTCW 1; RGEL 2; SATA 8; SATA-Obit
25

Hughes, Ted 1930-1998 . **CLC 2, 4, 9, 14, 37,
119; PC 7, 89**
See also BRWC 2; BRWR 2; BRWS 1; CA
1-4R; 171; CANR 1, 33, 66, 108; CLR 3,
131; CP 1, 2, 3, 4, 5, 6; DA3; DAB; DAC;
DAM MST, POET; DLB 40, 161; EWL
3; EXPP; MAICYA 1, 2; MTCW 1, 2;
MTFW 2005; PAB; PFS 4, 19, 32; RGEL
2; SATA 49; SATA-Brief 27; SATA-Obit
107; TEA; YAW

Hughes, Thomas 1822-1896 .... **NCLC 207**
See also BYA 3; CLR 160; DLB 18, 163;
LAIT 2; RGEL 2; SATA 31

Hugo, Richard
See Huch, Ricarda (Octavia)

Hugo, Richard F(ranklin)
1923-1982 .... **CLC 6, 18, 32; PC 68**
See also AMWS 6; CA 49-52; 108; CANR
3; CP 1, 2, 3; DAM POET; DLB 5, 206;
EWL 3; MAL 5; PFS 17; RGAL 4

Hugo, Victor 1802-1885 ..... **DC 38; NCLC 3,
10, 21, 161, 189; PC 17; WLC 3**
See also AAYA 28; DA; DA3; DAB; DAC;
DAM DRAM, MST, NOV, POET; DLB
119, 192, 217; EFS 2; EW 6; EXPN; GFL
1789 to the Present; LAIT 1, 2; NFS 5,
20; RGWL 2, 3; SATA 47; TWA

Hugo, Victor Marie
See Hugo, Victor

Huidobro, Vicente
See Huidobro Fernandez, Vicente Garcia

Huidobro Fernandez, Vicente Garcia
1893-1948 .... **TCLC 31**
See also CA 131; DLB 283; EWL 3; HW 1;
LAW

Hulme, Keri 1947- .... **CLC 39, 130**
See also CA 125; CANR 69; CN 4, 5, 6, 7;
CP 6, 7; CWP; DLB 326; EWL 3; FW;
INT CA-125; NFS 24

Hulme, T(homas) E(rnest)
1883-1917 .... **TCLC 21**
See also BRWS 6; CA 117; 203; DLB 19

Humboldt, Alexander von
1769-1859 .... **NCLC 170**
See also DLB 90

Humboldt, Wilhelm von
1767-1835 .... **NCLC 134**
See also DLB 90

Hume, David 1711-1776 .. **LC 7, 56, 156, 157**
See also BRWS 3; DLB 104, 252, 336;
LMFS 1; TEA

Humphrey, William 1924-1997 .... **CLC 45**
See also AMWS 9; CA 77-80; 160; CANR
68; CN 1, 2, 3, 4, 5, 6; CSW; DLB 6, 212,
234, 278; TCWW 1, 2

Humphreys, Emyr Owen 1919- .... **CLC 47**
See also CA 5-8R; CANR 3, 24; CN 1, 2,
3, 4, 5, 6, 7; DLB 15

Humphreys, Josephine 1945- ..... **CLC 34, 57**
See also CA 121; 127; CANR 97; CSW;
DLB 292; INT CA-127

Huneker, James Gibbons
1860-1921 .... **TCLC 65**
See also CA 193; DLB 71; RGAL 4

Hungerford, Hesba Fay
See Brinsmead, H(esba) F(ay)

Hungerford, Pixie
See Brinsmead, H(esba) F(ay)

Hunt, E. Howard 1918-2007 .... **CLC 3**
See also AITN 1; CA 45-48; 256; CANR 2,
47, 103, 160; CMW 4

Hunt, Everette Howard, Jr.
See Hunt, E. Howard

Hunt, Francesca
See Holland, Isabelle (Christian)

Hunt, Howard
See Hunt, E. Howard

Hunt, Kyle
See Creasey, John

Hunt, (James Henry) Leigh
1784-1859 .... **NCLC 1, 70; PC 73**
See also DAM POET; DLB 96, 110, 144;
RGEL 2; TEA

Hunt, Marsha 1946- .... **CLC 70**
See also BW 2, 3; CA 143; CANR 79

Hunt, Violet 1866(?)-1942 .... **TCLC 53**
See also CA 184; DLB 162, 197

Hunter, E. Waldo
See Sturgeon, Theodore (Hamilton)

Hunter, Evan 1926-2005 .... **CLC 11, 31**
See also AAYA 39; BPFB 2; CA 5-8R; 241;
CANR 5, 38, 62, 97, 149; CMW 4; CN 1,
2, 3, 4, 5, 6, 7; CPW; DAM POP; DLB
306; DLBY 1982; INT CANR-5; MSW;
MTCW 1; SATA 25; SATA-Obit 167;
SFW 4

Hunter, Kristin
See Lattany, Kristin Hunter

Hunter, Mary
See Austin, Mary Hunter

Hunter, Mollie 1922- .... **CLC 21**
See also AAYA 13, 71; BYA 6; CANR 37,
78; CLR 25; DLB 161; JRDA; MAICYA
1, 2; SAAS 7; SATA 2, 54, 106, 139;
SATA-Essay 139; WYA; YAW

Hunter, Robert (?)-1734 .... **LC 7**

Hurston, Zora Neale 1891-1960 ..... **BLC 1:2;
CLC 7, 30, 61; DC 12; HR 1:2; SSC 4,
80; TCLC 121, 131; WLCS**
See also AAYA 15, 71; AFAW 1, 2; AMWS
6; BW 1, 3; BYA 12; CA 85-88; CANR
61; CDALBS; DA; DA3; DAC; DAM
MST, MULT, NOV; DFS 6; DLB 51, 86;
EWL 3; EXPN; EXPS; FL 1:6; FW; LAIT
3; LATS 1:1; LMFS 2; MAL 5; MBL;
MTCW 1, 2; MTFW 2005; NFS 3; RGAL
4; RGSF 2; SSFS 1, 6, 11, 19, 21; TUS;
YAW

Husserl, E. G.
See Husserl, Edmund (Gustav Albrecht)

Husserl, Edmund (Gustav Albrecht)
1859-1938 .... **TCLC 100**
See also CA 116; 133; DLB 296

Huston, John (Marcellus)
1906-1987 .... **CLC 20**
See also CA 73-76; 123; CANR 34; DLB
26

Kempis, Thomas a 1380-1471 .... **LC 11**

Kenan, Randall (G.) 1963- .... **BLC 2:2**
See also BW 2, 3; CA 142; CANR 86; CN 7; CSW; DLB 292; GLL 1

Kendall, Henry 1839-1882 .... **NCLC 12**
See also DLB 230

Keneally, Thomas 1935- .... **CLC 5, 8, 10, 14, 19, 27, 43, 117, 279**
See also BRWS 4; CA 85-88; CANR 10, 50, 74, 130, 165, 198; CN 1, 2, 3, 4, 5, 6, 7; CPW; DA3; DAM NOV; DLB 289, 299, 326; EWL 3; MTCW 1, 2; MTFW 2005; NFS 17; RGEL 2; RGHL; RHW

Keneally, Thomas Michael
See Keneally, Thomas

Keneally, Tom
See Keneally, Thomas

Kennedy, A. L. 1965- .... **CLC 188**
See also CA 168, 213; CAAE 213; CANR 108, 193; CD 5, 6; CN 6, 7; DLB 271; RGSF 2

Kennedy, Adrienne (Lita) 1931- .... **BLC 1:2; CLC 66; DC 5**
See also AFAW 2; BW 2, 3; CA 103; CAAS 20; CABS 3; CAD; CANR 26, 53, 82; CD 5, 6; DAM MULT; DFS 9, 28; DLB 38, 341; FW; MAL 5

Kennedy, Alison Louise
See Kennedy, A. L.

Kennedy, John Pendleton
1795-1870 .... **NCLC 2**
See also DLB 3, 248, 254; RGAL 4

Kennedy, Joseph Charles
See Kennedy, X. J.

Kennedy, William 1928- .. **CLC 6, 28, 34, 53, 239**
See also AAYA 1, 73; AMWS 7; BPFB 2; CA 85-88; CANR 14, 31, 76, 134; CN 4, 5, 6, 7; DA3; DAM NOV; DLB 143; DLBY 1985; EWL 3; INT CANR-31; MAL 5; MTCW 1, 2; MTFW 2005; SATA 57

Kennedy, William Joseph
See Kennedy, William

Kennedy, X. J. 1929- .... **CLC 8, 42; PC 93**
See also AMWS 15; CA 1-4R, 201; CAAE 201; CAAS 9; CANR 4, 30, 40, 214; CLR 27; CP 1, 2, 3, 4, 5, 6, 7; CWRI 5; DLB 5; MAICYA 2; MAICYAS 1; SAAS 22; SATA 14, 86, 130; SATA-Essay 130

Kenny, Maurice (Francis) 1929- ..... **CLC 87; NNAL**
See also CA 144; CAAS 22; CANR 143; DAM MULT; DLB 175

Kent, Kathleen CLC 280
See also CA 288

Kent, Kelvin
See Kuttner, Henry

Kent, Klark
See Copeland, Stewart

Kenton, Maxwell
See Southern, Terry

Kenyon, Jane 1947-1995 .... **PC 57**
See also AAYA 63; AMWS 7; CA 118; 148; CANR 44, 69, 172; CP 6, 7; CWP; DLB 120; PFS 9, 17; RGAL 4

Kenyon, Robert O.
See Kuttner, Henry

Kepler, Johannes 1571-1630 .... **LC 45**

Ker, Jill
See Conway, Jill K.

Kerkow, H. C.
See Lewton, Val

Kerouac, Jack 1922-1969 ...... **CLC 1, 2, 3, 5, 14, 61; TCLC 117; WLC**
See also AAYA 25; AITN 1; AMWC 1; AMWS 3; BG 3; BPFB 2; CA 5-8R; 25-28R; CANR 26, 54, 95, 184; CDALB 1941-1968; CP 1; CPW; DA; DA3; DAB;

DAC; DAM MST, NOV, POET, POP; DLB 2, 16, 237; DLBY 1995; EWL 3; GLL 1; LATS 1:2; LMFS 2; MAL 5; MTCW 1, 2; MTFW 2005; NFS 8; RGAL 4; TUS; WP

Kerouac, Jean-Louis le Brisde
See Kerouac, Jack

Kerouac, John
See Kerouac, Jack

Kerr, (Bridget) Jean (Collins)
1923(?)-2003 .... **CLC 22**
See also CA 5-8R; 212; CANR 7; INT CANR-7

Kerr, M. E.
See Meaker, Marijane

Kerr, Robert CLC 55

Kerrigan, (Thomas) Anthony 1918- .. **CLC 4, 6**
See also CA 49-52; CAAS 11; CANR 4

Kerry, Lois
See Duncan, Lois

Kesey, Ken 1935-2001 .... **CLC 1, 3, 6, 11, 46, 64, 184; WLC 3**
See also AAYA 25; BG 1:3; BPFB 2; CA 1-4R; 204; CANR 22, 38, 66, 124; CDALB 1968-1988; CN 1, 2, 3, 4, 5, 6, 7; CPW; DA; DA3; DAB; DAC; DAM MST, NOV, POP; DLB 2, 16, 206; EWL 3; EXPN; LAIT 4; MAL 5; MTCW 1, 2; MTFW 2005; NFS 2; RGAL 4; SATA 66; SATA-Obit 131; TUS; YAW

Kesselring, Joseph (Otto)
1902-1967 .... **CLC 45**
See also CA 150; DAM DRAM, MST; DFS 20

Kessler, Jascha (Frederick) 1929- ...... **CLC 4**
See also CA 17-20R; CANR 8, 48, 111; CP 1

Kettelkamp, Larry (Dale) 1933- .... **CLC 12**
See also CA 29-32R; CANR 16; SAAS 3; SATA 2

Key, Ellen (Karolina Sofia)
1849-1926 .... **TCLC 65**
See also DLB 259

Keyber, Conny
See Fielding, Henry

Keyes, Daniel 1927- .... **CLC 80**
See also AAYA 23; BYA 11; CA 17-20R, 181; CAAE 181; CANR 10, 26, 54, 74; DA; DA3; DAC; DAM MST, NOV; EXPN; LAIT 4; MTCW 2; MTFW 2005; NFS 2; SATA 37; SFW 4

Keynes, John Maynard
1883-1946 .... **TCLC 64**
See also CA 114; 162, 163; DLBD 10; MTCW 2; MTFW 2005

Khanshendel, Chiron
See Rose, Wendy

Khayyam, Omar 1048-1131 ... **CMLC 11; PC 8**
See also DA3; DAM POET; RGWL 2, 3; WLIT 6

Kherdian, David 1931- .... **CLC 6, 9**
See also AAYA 42; CA 21-24R, 192; CAAE 192; CAAS 2; CANR 39, 78; CLR 24; JRDA; LAIT 3; MAICYA 1, 2; SATA 16, 74; SATA-Essay 125

Khlebnikov, Velimir
See Khlebnikov, Viktor Vladimirovich

Khlebnikov, Viktor Vladimirovich
1885-1922 .... **TCLC 20**
See also CA 117; 217; DLB 295; EW 10; EWL 3; RGWL 2, 3

Khodasevich, V.F.
See Khodasevich, Vladislav

Khodasevich, Vladislav
1886-1939 .... **TCLC 15**
See also CA 115; DLB 317; EWL 3

Khodasevich, Vladislav Felitsianovich
See Khodasevich, Vladislav

Kiarostami, Abbas 1940- .... **CLC 295**
See also CA 204

Kidd, Sue Monk 1948- .... **CLC 267**
See also AAYA 72; CA 202; LNFS 1; MTFW 2005; NFS 27

Kielland, Alexander Lange
1849-1906 .... **TCLC 5**
See also CA 104; DLB 354

Kiely, Benedict 1919-2007 . **CLC 23, 43; SSC 58**
See also CA 1-4R; 257; CANR 2, 84; CN 1, 2, 3, 4, 5, 6, 7; DLB 15, 319; TCLE 1:1

Kienzle, William X. 1928-2001 .... **CLC 25**
See also CA 93-96; 203; CAAS 1; CANR 9, 31, 59, 111; CMW 4; DA3; DAM POP; INT CANR-31; MSW; MTCW 1, 2; MTFW 2005

Kierkegaard, Soren 1813-1855 ..... **NCLC 34, 78, 125**
See also DLB 300; EW 6; LMFS 2; RGWL 3; TWA

Kieslowski, Krzysztof 1941-1996 .... **CLC 120**
See also CA 147; 151

Killens, John Oliver 1916-1987 ...... **BLC 2:2; CLC 10**
See also BW 2; CA 77-80; 123; CAAS 2; CANR 26; CN 1, 2, 3, 4; DLB 33; EWL 3

Killigrew, Anne 1660-1685 .... **LC 4, 73**
See also DLB 131

Killigrew, Thomas 1612-1683 .... **LC 57**
See also DLB 58; RGEL 2

Kim
See Simenon, Georges

Kincaid, Jamaica 1949- . **BLC 1:2, 2:2; CLC 43, 68, 137, 234; SSC 72**
See also AAYA 13, 56; AFAW 2; AMWS 7; BRWS 7; BW 2, 3; CA 125; CANR 47, 59, 95, 133; CDALBS; CDWLB 3; CLR 63; CN 4, 5, 6, 7; DA3; DAM MULT, NOV; DLB 157, 227; DNFS 1; EWL 3; EXPS; FW; LATS 1:2; LMFS 2; MAL 5; MTCW 2; MTFW 2005; NCFS 3; NFS 3; SSFS 5, 7; TUS; WWE 1; YAW

King, Francis (Henry) 1923- .... **CLC 8, 53, 145**
See also CA 1-4R; CANR 1, 33, 86; CN 1, 2, 3, 4, 5, 6, 7; DAM NOV; DLB 15, 139; MTCW 1

King, Kennedy
See Brown, George Douglas

King, Martin Luther, Jr.
1929-1968 ... **BLC 1:2; CLC 83; WLCS**
See also BW 2, 3; CA 25-28; CANR 27, 44; CAP 2; DA; DA3; DAB; DAC; DAM MST, MULT; LAIT 5; LATS 1:2; MTCW 1, 2; MTFW 2005; SATA 14

King, Stephen 1947- .... **CLC 12, 26, 37, 61, 113, 228, 244; SSC 17, 55**
See also AAYA 1, 17, 82; AMWS 5; BEST 90:1; BPFB 2; CA 61-64; CANR 1, 30, 52, 76, 119, 134, 168; CLR 124; CN 7; CPW; DA3; DAM NOV, POP; DLB 143, 350; DLBY 1980; HGG; JRDA; LAIT 5; LNFS 1; MTCW 1, 2; MTFW 2005; RGAL 4; SATA 9, 55, 161; SSFS 30; SUFW 1, 2; WYAS 1; YAW

King, Stephen Edwin
See King, Stephen

King, Steve
See King, Stephen

King, Thomas 1943- .... **CLC 89, 171, 276; NNAL**
See also CA 144; CANR 95, 175; CCA 1; CN 6, 7; DAC; DAM MULT; DLB 175, 334; SATA 96

Komunyakaa, Yusef 1947- . **BLC 2:2; BLCS; CLC 86, 94, 207, 299; PC 51**
See also AFAW 2; AMWS 13; CA 147; CANR 83, 164, 211; CP 6, 7; CSW; DLB 120; EWL 3; PFS 5, 20, 30, 37; RGAL 4

Konigsberg, Alan Stewart
See Allen, Woody

Konrad, George
See Konrad, Gyorgy

Konrad, George
See Konrad, Gyorgy

Konrad, Gyorgy 1933- .... **CLC 4, 10, 73**
See also CA 85-88; CANR 97, 171; CD-WLB 4; CWW 2; DLB 232; EWL 3

Konwicki, Tadeusz 1926- .... **CLC 8, 28, 54, 117**
See also CA 101; CAAS 9; CANR 39, 59; CWW 2; DLB 232; EWL 3; IDFW 3; MTCW 1

Koontz, Dean 1945- .... **CLC 78, 206**
See also AAYA 9, 31; BEST 89:3, 90:2; CA 108; CANR 19, 36, 52, 95, 138, 176; CMW 4; CPW; DA3; DAM NOV, POP; DLB 292; HGG; MTCW 1; MTFW 2005; SATA 92, 165; SFW 4; SUFW 2; YAW

Koontz, Dean R.
See Koontz, Dean

Koontz, Dean Ray
See Koontz, Dean

Kopernik, Mikolaj
See Copernicus, Nicolaus

Kopit, Arthur 1937- ... **CLC 1, 18, 33; DC 37**
See also AITN 1; CA 81-84; CABS 3; CAD; CD 5, 6; DAM DRAM; DFS 7, 14, 24; DLB 7; MAL 5; MTCW 1; RGAL 4

Kopit, Arthur Lee
See Kopit, Arthur

Kopitar, Jernej (Bartholomaus) 1780-1844 .... **NCLC 117**

Kops, Bernard 1926- .... **CLC 4**
See also CA 5-8R; CANR 84, 159; CBD; CN 1, 2, 3, 4, 5, 6, 7; CP 1, 2, 3, 4, 5, 6, 7; DLB 13; RGHL

Kornbluth, C(yril) M. 1923-1958 .... **TCLC 8**
See also CA 105; 160; DLB 8; SCFW 1, 2; SFW 4

Korolenko, V.G.
See Korolenko, Vladimir G.

Korolenko, Vladimir
See Korolenko, Vladimir G.

Korolenko, Vladimir G. 1853-1921 .... **TCLC 22**
See also CA 121; DLB 277

Korolenko, Vladimir Galaktionovich
See Korolenko, Vladimir G.

Korzybski, Alfred (Habdank Skarbek) 1879-1950 .... **TCLC 61**
See also CA 123; 160

Kosinski, Jerzy 1933-1991 ..... **CLC 1, 2, 3, 6, 10, 15, 53, 70**
See also AMWS 7; BPFB 2; CA 17-20R; 134; CANR 9, 46; CN 1, 2, 3, 4; DA3; DAM NOV; DLB 2, 299; DLBY 1982; EWL 3; HGG; MAL 5; MTCW 1, 2; MTFW 2005; NFS 12; RGAL 4; RGHL; TUS

Kostelanetz, Richard 1940- .... **CLC 28**
See also CA 13-16R; CAAS 8; CANR 38, 77; CN 4, 5, 6; CP 2, 3, 4, 5, 6, 7

Kostelanetz, Richard Cory
See Kostelanetz, Richard

Kostrowitzki, Wilhelm Apollinaris de 1880-1918
See Apollinaire, Guillaume

Kotlowitz, Robert 1924- .... **CLC 4**
See also CA 33-36R; CANR 36

Kotzebue, August (Friedrich Ferdinand) von 1761-1819 .... **NCLC 25**
See also DLB 94

Kotzwinkle, William 1938- ..... **CLC 5, 14, 35**
See also BPFB 2; CA 45-48; CANR 3, 44, 84, 129; CLR 6; CN 7; DLB 173; FANT; MAICYA 1, 2; SATA 24, 70, 146; SFW 4; SUFW 2; YAW

Kowna, Stancy
See Szymborska, Wislawa

Kozol, Jonathan 1936- .... **CLC 17**
See also AAYA 46; CA 61-64; CANR 16, 45, 96, 178; MTFW 2005

Kozoll, Michael 1940(?)- .... **CLC 35**

Krakauer, Jon 1954- .... **CLC 248**
See also AAYA 24; AMWS 18; BYA 9; CA 153; CANR 131, 212; MTFW 2005; SATA 108

Kramer, Kathryn 19(?)- .... **CLC 34**

Kramer, Larry 1935- .... **CLC 42; DC 8**
See also CA 124; 126; CANR 60, 132; DAM POP; DLB 249; GLL 1

Krasicki, Ignacy 1735-1801 .... **NCLC 8**

Krasinski, Zygmunt 1812-1859 .... **NCLC 4**
See also RGWL 2, 3

Kraus, Karl 1874-1936 .... **TCLC 5**
See also CA 104; 216; DLB 118; EWL 3

Kraynay, Anton
See Gippius, Zinaida

Kreve (Mickevicius), Vincas 1882-1954 .... **TCLC 27**
See also CA 170; DLB 220; EWL 3

Kristeva, Julia 1941- .... **CLC 77, 140**
See also CA 154; CANR 99, 173; DLB 242; EWL 3; FW; LMFS 2

Kristofferson, Kris 1936- .... **CLC 26**
See also CA 104

Krizanc, John 1956- .... **CLC 57**
See also CA 187

Krleza, Miroslav 1893-1981 .... **CLC 8, 114**
See also CA 97-100; 105; CANR 50; CD-WLB 4; DLB 147; EW 11; RGWL 2, 3

Kroetsch, Robert (Paul) 1927- ... **CLC 5, 23, 57, 132, 286**
See also CA 17-20R; CANR 8, 38; CCA 1; CN 2, 3, 4, 5, 6, 7; CP 6, 7; DAC; DAM POET; DLB 53; MTCW 1

Kroetz, Franz
See Kroetz, Franz Xaver

Kroetz, Franz Xaver 1946- .... **CLC 41**
See also CA 130; CANR 142; CWW 2; EWL 3

Kroker, Arthur (W.) 1945- .... **CLC 77**
See also CA 161

Kroniuk, Lisa
See Berton, Pierre (Francis de Marigny)

Kropotkin, Peter 1842-1921 .... **TCLC 36**
See also CA 119; 219; DLB 277

Kropotkin, Peter Aleksieevich
See Kropotkin, Peter

Kropotkin, Petr Alekseevich
See Kropotkin, Peter

Krotkov, Yuri 1917-1981 .... **CLC 19**
See also CA 102

Krumb
See Crumb, R.

Krumgold, Joseph (Quincy) 1908-1980 .... **CLC 12**
See also BYA 1, 2; CA 9-12R; 101; CANR 7; MAICYA 1, 2; SATA 1, 48; SATA-Obit 23; YAW

Krumwitz
See Crumb, R.

Krutch, Joseph Wood 1893-1970 ..... **CLC 24**
See also ANW; CA 1-4R; 25-28R; CANR 4; DLB 63, 206, 275

Krutzch, Gus
See Eliot, T. S.

Krylov, Ivan Andreevich 1768(?)-1844 .... **NCLC 1**
See also DLB 150

Kubin, Alfred (Leopold Isidor) 1877-1959 .... **TCLC 23**
See also CA 112; 149; CANR 104; DLB 81

Kubrick, Stanley 1928-1999 .... **CLC 16; TCLC 112**
See also AAYA 30; CA 81-84; 177; CANR 33; DLB 26

Kueng, Hans
See Kung, Hans

Kumin, Maxine 1925- .... **CLC 5, 13, 28, 164; PC 15**
See also AITN 2; AMWS 4; ANW; CA 1-4R, 271; CAAE 271; CAAS 8; CANR 1, 21, 69, 115, 140; CP 2, 3, 4, 5, 6, 7; CWP; DA3; DAM POET; DLB 5; EWL 3; EXPP; MTCW 1, 2; MTFW 2005; PAB; PFS 18, 38; SATA 12

Kumin, Maxine Winokur
See Kumin, Maxine

Kundera, Milan 1929- . **CLC 4, 9, 19, 32, 68, 115, 135, 234; SSC 24**
See also AAYA 2, 62; BPFB 2; CA 85-88; CANR 19, 52, 74, 144; CDWLB 4; CWW 2; DA3; DAM NOV; DLB 232; EW 13; EWL 3; MTCW 1, 2; MTFW 2005; NFS 18, 27; RGSF 2; RGWL 3; SSFS 10

Kunene, Mazisi 1930-2006 .... **CLC 85**
See also BW 1, 3; CA 125; 252; CANR 81; CP 1, 6, 7; DLB 117

Kunene, Mazisi Raymond
See Kunene, Mazisi

Kunene, Mazisi Raymond Fakazi Mngoni
See Kunene, Mazisi

Kung, Hans
See Kung, Hans

Kung, Hans 1928- .... **CLC 130**
See also CA 53-56; CANR 66, 134; MTCW 1, 2; MTFW 2005

Kunikida, Tetsuo
See Kunikida Doppo

Kunikida Doppo 1869(?)-1908 .... **TCLC 99**
See also DLB 180; EWL 3

Kunikida Tetsuo
See Kunikida Doppo

Kunitz, Stanley 1905-2006 ..... **CLC 6, 11, 14, 148, 293; PC 19**
See also AMWS 3; CA 41-44R; 250; CANR 26, 57, 98; CP 1, 2, 3, 4, 5, 6, 7; DA3; DLB 48; INT CANR-26; MAL 5; MTCW 1, 2; MTFW 2005; PFS 11; RGAL 4

Kunitz, Stanley Jasspon
See Kunitz, Stanley

Kunt, Klerk
See Copeland, Stewart

Kunze, Reiner 1933- .... **CLC 10**
See also CA 93-96; CWW 2; DLB 75; EWL 3

Kuprin, Aleksander Ivanovich 1870-1938 .... **TCLC 5**
See also CA 104; 182; DLB 295; EWL 3

Kuprin, Aleksandr Ivanovich
See Kuprin, Aleksander Ivanovich

Kuprin, Alexandr Ivanovich
See Kuprin, Aleksander Ivanovich

Kureishi, Hanif 1954- ...... **CLC 64, 135, 284; DC 26**
See also BRWS 11; CA 139; CANR 113, 197; CBD; CD 5, 6; CN 6, 7; DLB 194, 245, 352; GLL 2; IDFW 4; WLIT 4; WWE 1

Kurosawa, Akira 1910-1998 ..... **CLC 16, 119**
See also AAYA 11, 64; CA 101; 170; CANR 46; DAM MULT

Kushner, Tony 1956- . **CLC 81, 203, 297; DC 10**
See also AAYA 61; AMWS 9; CA 144; CAD; CANR 74, 130; CD 5, 6; DA3; DAM DRAM; DFS 5; DLB 228; EWL 3; GLL 1; LAIT 5; MAL 5; MTCW 2; MTFW 2005; RGAL 4; RGHL; SATA 160

Larkin, Maia
See Wojciechowska, Maia (Teresa)
Larkin, Philip 1922-1985 .... **CLC 3, 5, 8, 9, 13, 18, 33, 39, 64; PC 21**
See also BRWR 3; BRWS 1; CA 5-8R; 117; CANR 24, 62; CDBLB 1960 to Present; CP 1, 2, 3, 4; DA3; DAB; DAM MST, POET; DLB 27; EWL 3; MTCW 1, 2; MTFW 2005; PFS 3, 4, 12; RGEL 2
Larkin, Philip Arthur
See Larkin, Philip
La Roche, Sophie von
1730-1807 .... **NCLC 121**
See also DLB 94
La Rochefoucauld, Francois
1613-1680 .... **LC 108, 172**
See also DLB 268; EW 3; GFL Beginnings to 1789; RGWL 2, 3
Larra (y Sanchez de Castro), Mariano Jose de 1809-1837 .... **NCLC 17, 130**
Larsen, Eric 1941- .... **CLC 55**
See also CA 132
Larsen, Nella 1893(?)-1963 ... **BLC 1:2; CLC 37; HR 1:3; TCLC 200**
See also AFAW 1, 2; AMWS 18; BW 1; CA 125; CANR 83; DAM MULT; DLB 51; FW; LATS 1:1; LMFS 2
Larson, Charles R(aymond) 1938- ... **CLC 31**
See also CA 53-56; CANR 4, 121
Larson, Jonathan 1960-1996 .... **CLC 99**
See also AAYA 28; CA 156; DFS 23; MTFW 2005
La Sale, Antoine de c. 1386-1460(?) . **LC 104**
See also DLB 208
Lasarus, B. B.
See Breytenbach, Breyten
Las Casas, Bartolome de
1474-1566 .... **HLCS; LC 31**
See also DLB 318; LAW; WLIT 1
Lasch, Christopher 1932-1994 .... **CLC 102**
See also CA 73-76; 144; CANR 25, 118; DLB 246; MTCW 1, 2; MTFW 2005
Lasker-Schueler, Else 1869-1945 ... **TCLC 57**
See also CA 183; DLB 66, 124; EWL 3
Lasker-Schuler, Else
See Lasker-Schueler, Else
Laski, Harold J(oseph) 1893-1950 . **TCLC 79**
See also CA 188
Latham, Jean Lee 1902-1995 .... **CLC 12**
See also AITN 1; BYA 1; CA 5-8R; CANR 7, 84; CLR 50; MAICYA 1, 2; SATA 2, 68; YAW
Latham, Mavis
See Clark, Mavis Thorpe
Lathen, Emma
See Hennissart, Martha
Lathrop, Francis
See Leiber, Fritz (Reuter, Jr.)
Lattany, Kristin
See Lattany, Kristin Hunter
Lattany, Kristin Elaine Eggleston Hunter
See Lattany, Kristin Hunter
Lattany, Kristin Hunter 1931-2008 . **CLC 35**
See also AITN 1; BW 1; BYA 3; CA 13-16R; CANR 13, 108; CLR 3; CN 1, 2, 3, 4, 5, 6; DLB 33; INT CANR-13; MAICYA 1, 2; SAAS 10; SATA 12, 132; YAW
Lattimore, Richmond (Alexander)
1906-1984 .... **CLC 3**
See also CA 1-4R; 112; CANR 1; CP 1, 2, 3; MAL 5
Laughlin, James 1914-1997 .... **CLC 49**
See also CA 21-24R; 162; CAAS 22; CANR 9, 47; CP 1, 2, 3, 4, 5, 6; DLB 48; DLBY 1996, 1997
Laurence, Jean Margaret Wemyss
See Laurence, Margaret

Laurence, Margaret 1926-1987 ..... **CLC 3, 6, 13, 50, 62; SSC 7**
See also BYA 13; CA 5-8R; 121; CANR 33; CN 1, 2, 3, 4; DAC; DAM MST; DLB 53; EWL 3; FW; MTCW 1, 2; MTFW 2005; NFS 11; RGEL 2; RGSF 2; SATA-Obit 50; TCWW 2
Laurent, Antoine 1952- .... **CLC 50**
Lauscher, Hermann
See Hesse, Hermann
Lautreamont 1846-1870 .... **NCLC 12, 194; SSC 14**
See also DLB 217; GFL 1789 to the Present; RGWL 2, 3
Lautreamont, Isidore Lucien Ducasse
See Lautreamont
Lavater, Johann Kaspar
1741-1801 .... **NCLC 142**
See also DLB 97
Laverty, Donald
See Blish, James
Lavin, Mary 1912-1996 . **CLC 4, 18, 99; SSC 4, 67, 137**
See also CA 9-12R; 151; CANR 33; CN 1, 2, 3, 4, 5, 6; DLB 15, 319; FW; MTCW 1; RGEL 2; RGSF 2; SSFS 23
Lavond, Paul Dennis
See Kornbluth, C(yril) M.; Pohl, Frederik
Lawes, Henry 1596-1662 .... **LC 113**
See also DLB 126
Lawler, Ray
See Lawler, Raymond Evenor
Lawler, Raymond Evenor 1922- .... **CLC 58**
See also CA 103; CD 5, 6; DLB 289; RGEL 2
Lawrence, D. H. 1885-1930 ... **PC 54; SSC 4, 19, 73, 149; TCLC 2, 9, 16, 33, 48, 61, 93; WLC 3**
See also BPFB 2; BRW 7; BRWR 2; CA 104; 121; CANR 131; CDBLB 1914-1945; DA; DA3; DAB; DAC; DAM MST, NOV, POET; DLB 10, 19, 36, 98, 162, 195; EWL 3; EXPP; EXPS; GLL 1; LAIT 2, 3; MTCW 1, 2; MTFW 2005; NFS 18, 26; PFS 6; RGEL 2; RGSF 2; SSFS 2, 6; TEA; WLIT 4; WP
Lawrence, David Herbert Richards
See Lawrence, D. H.
Lawrence, T. E. 1888-1935 ..... **TCLC 18, 204**
See also BRWS 2; CA 115; 167; DLB 195
Lawrence, Thomas Edward
See Lawrence, T. E.
Lawrence of Arabia
See Lawrence, T. E.
Lawson, Henry (Archibald Hertzberg)
1867-1922 .... **SSC 18; TCLC 27**
See also CA 120; 181; DLB 230; RGEL 2; RGSF 2
Lawton, Dennis
See Faust, Frederick
Laxness, Halldor (Kiljan)
See Gudjonsson, Halldor Kiljan
Layamon fl. c. 1200- .... **CMLC 10, 105**
See also DLB 146; RGEL 2
Laye, Camara 1928-1980 .. **BLC 1:2; CLC 4, 38**
See also AFW; BW 1; CA 85-88; 97-100; CANR 25; DAM MULT; DLB 360; EWL 3; MTCW 1, 2; WLIT 2
Layton, Irving 1912-2006 ..... **CLC 2, 15, 164**
See also CA 1-4R; 247; CANR 2, 33, 43, 66, 129; CP 1, 2, 3, 4, 5, 6, 7; DAC; DAM MST, POET; DLB 88; EWL 3; MTCW 1, 2; PFS 12; RGEL 2
Layton, Irving Peter
See Layton, Irving
Lazarus, Emma 1849-1887 ...... **NCLC 8, 109**
See also PFS 37

Lazarus, Felix
See Cable, George Washington
Lazarus, Henry
See Slavitt, David R.
Lea, Joan
See Neufeld, John (Arthur)
Leacock, Stephen (Butler)
1869-1944 .... **SSC 39; TCLC 2**
See also CA 104; 141; CANR 80; DAC; DAM MST; DLB 92; EWL 3; MTCW 2; MTFW 2005; RGEL 2; RGSF 2
Lead, Jane Ward 1623-1704 .... **LC 72**
See also DLB 131
Leapor, Mary 1722-1746 .... **LC 80; PC 85**
See also DLB 109
Lear, Edward 1812-1888 ..... **NCLC 3; PC 65**
See also AAYA 48; BRW 5; CLR 1, 75; DLB 32, 163, 166; MAICYA 1, 2; RGEL 2; SATA 18, 100; WCH; WP
Lear, Norman (Milton) 1922- .... **CLC 12**
See also CA 73-76
Least Heat-Moon, William
See Heat-Moon, William Least
Leautaud, Paul 1872-1956 .... **TCLC 83**
See also CA 203; DLB 65; GFL 1789 to the Present
Leavis, F(rank) R(aymond)
1895-1978 .... **CLC 24**
See also BRW 7; CA 21-24R; 77-80; CANR 44; DLB 242; EWL 3; MTCW 1, 2; RGEL 2
Leavitt, David 1961- .... **CLC 34**
See also CA 116; 122; CANR 50, 62, 101, 134, 177; CPW; DA3; DAM POP; DLB 130, 350; GLL 1; INT CA-122; MAL 5; MTCW 2; MTFW 2005
Leblanc, Maurice (Marie Emile)
1864-1941 .... **TCLC 49**
See also CA 110; CMW 4
Lebowitz, Fran 1951(?)- .... **CLC 11, 36**
See also CA 81-84; CANR 14, 60, 70; INT CANR-14; MTCW 1
Lebowitz, Frances Ann
See Lebowitz, Fran
Lebrecht, Peter
See Tieck, (Johann) Ludwig
le Cagat, Benat
See Whitaker, Rod
le Carre, John
See le Carre, John
le Carre, John 1931- .... **CLC 9, 15**
See also AAYA 42; BEST 89:4; BPFB 2; BRWR 3; BRWS 2; CA 5-8R; CANR 13, 33, 59, 107, 132, 172; CDBLB 1960 to Present; CMW 4; CN 1, 2, 3, 4, 5, 6, 7; CPW; DA3; DAM POP; DLB 87; EWL 3; MSW; MTCW 1, 2; MTFW 2005; RGEL 2; TEA
Le Clezio, J. M.G. 1940- . **CLC 31, 155, 280; SSC 122**
See also CA 116; 128; CANR 147; CWW 2; DLB 83; EWL 3; GFL 1789 to the Present; RGSF 2
Le Clezio, Jean Marie Gustave
See Le Clezio, J. M.G.
Leconte de Lisle, Charles-Marie-Rene
1818-1894 .... **NCLC 29**
See also DLB 217; EW 6; GFL 1789 to the Present
Le Coq, Monsieur
See Simenon, Georges
Leduc, Violette 1907-1972 .... **CLC 22**
See also CA 13-14; 33-36R; CANR 69; CAP 1; EWL 3; GFL 1789 to the Present; GLL 1
Ledwidge, Francis 1887(?)-1917 .... **TCLC 23**
See also CA 123; 203; DLB 20

Lermontov, Mikhail Iur'evich
See Lermontov, Mikhail Yuryevich
Lermontov, Mikhail Yuryevich
1814-1841 .... **NCLC 5, 47, 126; PC 18**
See also DLB 205; EW 6; RGWL 2, 3;
TWA
Leroux, Gaston 1868-1927 .... **TCLC 25**
See also CA 108; 136; CANR 69; CMW 4;
MTFW 2005; NFS 20; SATA 65
Lesage, Alain-Rene 1668-1747 .... **LC 2, 28**
See also DLB 313; EW 3; GFL Beginnings
to 1789; RGWL 2, 3
Leskov, N(ikolai) S(emenovich) 1831-1895
See Leskov, Nikolai (Semyonovich)
Leskov, Nikolai (Semyonovich)
1831-1895 ... **NCLC 25, 174; SSC 34, 96**
See also DLB 238
Leskov, Nikolai Semenovich
See Leskov, Nikolai (Semyonovich)
Lesser, Milton
See Marlowe, Stephen
Lessing, Doris 1919- .. **CLC 1, 2, 3, 6, 10, 15,
22, 40, 94, 170, 254; SSC 6, 61; WLCS**
See also AAYA 57; AFW; BRWS 1; CA
9-12R; CAAS 14; CANR 33, 54, 76, 122,
179; CBD; CD 5, 6; CDBLB 1960 to
Present; CN 1, 2, 3, 4, 5, 6, 7; CWD; DA;
DA3; DAB; DAC; DAM MST, NOV;
DFS 20; DLB 15, 139; DLBY 1985; EWL
3; EXPS; FL 1:6; FW; LAIT 4; MTCW 1,
2; MTFW 2005; NFS 27; RGEL 2; RGSF
2; SFW 4; SSFS 1, 12, 20, 26, 30; TEA;
WLIT 2, 4
Lessing, Doris May
See Lessing, Doris
Lessing, Gotthold Ephraim
1729-1781 .... **DC 26; LC 8, 124, 162**
See also CDWLB 2; DLB 97; EW 4; RGWL
2, 3
Lester, Julius 1939- .... **BLC 2:2**
See also AAYA 12, 51; BW 2; BYA 3, 9,
11, 12; CA 17-20R; CANR 8, 23, 43, 129,
174; CLR 2, 41; JRDA; MAICYA 1,
2; MAICYAS 1; MTFW 2005; SATA 12,
74, 112, 157; YAW
Lester, Richard 1932- .... **CLC 20**
Lethem, Jonathan 1964- .... **CLC 295**
See also AAYA 43; AMWS 18; CA 150;
CANR 80, 138, 165; CN 7; MTFW 2005;
SFW 4
Lethem, Jonathan Allen
See Lethem, Jonathan
Letts, Tracy 1965- .... **CLC 280**
See also CA 223; CANR 209
Levenson, Jay CLC 70
Lever, Charles (James)
1806-1872 .... **NCLC 23**
See also DLB 21; RGEL 2
Leverson, Ada Esther
1862(?)-1933(?) .... **TCLC 18**
See also CA 117; 202; DLB 153; RGEL 2
Levertov, Denise 1923-1997 .. **CLC 1, 2, 3, 5,
8, 15, 28, 66; PC 11**
See also AMWS 3; CA 1-4R, 178; 163;
CAAE 178; CAAS 19; CANR 3, 29, 50,
108; CDALBS; CP 1, 2, 3, 4, 5, 6; CWP;
DAM POET; DLB 5, 165, 342; EWL 3;
EXPP; FW; INT CANR-29; MAL 5;
MTCW 1, 2; PAB; PFS 7, 17, 31; RGAL
4; RGHL; TUS; WP
Levi, Carlo 1902-1975 .... **TCLC 125**
See also CA 65-68; 53-56; CANR 10; EWL
3; RGWL 2, 3
Levi, Jonathan CLC 76
See also CA 197
Levi, Peter (Chad Tigar)
1931-2000 .... **CLC 41**
See also CA 5-8R; 187; CANR 34, 80; CP
1, 2, 3, 4, 5, 6, 7; DLB 40

Levi, Primo 1919-1987 ...... **CLC 37, 50; SSC
12, 122; TCLC 109**
See also CA 13-16R; 122; CANR 12, 33,
61, 70, 132, 171; DLB 177, 299; EWL 3;
MTCW 1, 2; MTFW 2005; RGHL;
RGWL 2, 3; WLIT 7
Levin, Ira 1929-2007 .... **CLC 3, 6**
See also CA 21-24R; 266; CANR 17, 44,
74, 139; CMW 4; CN 1, 2, 3, 4, 5, 6, 7;
CPW; DA3; DAM POP; HGG; MTCW 1,
2; MTFW 2005; SATA 66; SATA-Obit
187; SFW 4
Levin, Ira Marvin
See Levin, Ira
Levin, Meyer 1905-1981 .... **CLC 7**
See also AITN 1; CA 9-12R; 104; CANR
15; CN 1, 2, 3; DAM POP; DLB 9, 28;
DLBY 1981; MAL 5; RGHL; SATA 21;
SATA-Obit 27
Levine, Albert Norman
See Levine, Norman
Levine, Norman 1923-2005 .... **CLC 54**
See also CA 73-76; 240; CAAS 23; CANR
14, 70; CN 1, 2, 3, 4, 5, 6, 7; CP 1; DLB
88
Levine, Norman Albert
See Levine, Norman
Levine, Philip 1928- .. **CLC 2, 4, 5, 9, 14, 33,
118; PC 22**
See also AMWS 5; CA 9-12R; CANR 9,
37, 52, 116, 156; CP 1, 2, 3, 4, 5, 6, 7;
DAM POET; DLB 5; EWL 3; MAL 5;
PFS 8
Levinson, Deirdre 1931- .... **CLC 49**
See also CA 73-76; CANR 70
Levi-Strauss, Claude 1908-2008 ...... **CLC 38,
302**
See also CA 1-4R; CANR 6, 32, 57; DLB
242; EWL 3; GFL 1789 to the Present;
MTCW 1, 2; TWA
Levitin, Sonia 1934- .... **CLC 17**
See also AAYA 13, 48; CA 29-32R; CANR
14, 32, 79, 182; CLR 53; JRDA; MAI-
CYA 1, 2; SAAS 2; SATA 4, 68, 119, 131,
192; SATA-Essay 131; YAW
Levon, O. U.
See Kesey, Ken
Levy, Amy 1861-1889 .... **NCLC 59, 203**
See also DLB 156, 240
Lewees, John
See Stockton, Francis Richard
Lewes, George Henry 1817-1878 .. **NCLC 25,
215**
See also DLB 55, 144
Lewis, Alun 1915-1944 .... **SSC 40; TCLC 3**
See also BRW 7; CA 104; 188; DLB 20,
162; PAB; RGEL 2
Lewis, C. Day
See Day Lewis, C.
Lewis, C. S. 1898-1963 .. **CLC 1, 3, 6, 14, 27,
124; WLC 4**
See also AAYA 3, 39; BPFB 2; BRWS 3;
BYA 15, 16; CA 81-84; CANR 33, 71,
132; CDBLB 1945-1960; CLR 3, 27, 109;
CWRI 5; DA; DA3; DAB; DAC; DAM
MST, NOV, POP; DLB 15, 100, 160, 255;
EWL 3; FANT; JRDA; LMFS 2; MAI-
CYA 1, 2; MTCW 1, 2; MTFW 2005;
NFS 24; RGEL 2; SATA 13, 100; SCFW
1, 2; SFW 4; SUFW 1; TEA; WCH;
WYA; YAW
Lewis, Cecil Day
See Day Lewis, C.
Lewis, Clive Staples
See Lewis, C. S.
Lewis, Harry Sinclair
See Lewis, Sinclair

Lewis, Janet 1899-1998 .... **CLC 41**
See also CA 9-12R; 172; CANR 29, 63;
CAP 1; CN 1, 2, 3, 4, 5, 6; DLBY 1987;
RHW; TCWW 2
Lewis, Matthew Gregory
1775-1818 .... **NCLC 11, 62**
See also DLB 39, 158, 178; GL 3; HGG;
LMFS 1; RGEL 2; SUFW
Lewis, Sinclair 1885-1951 ... **TCLC 4, 13, 23,
39, 215; WLC 4**
See also AMW; AMWC 1; BPFB 2; CA
104; 133; CANR 132; CDALB 1917-
1929; DA; DA3; DAB; DAC; DAM MST,
NOV; DLB 9, 102, 284, 331; DLBD 1;
EWL 3; LAIT 3; MAL 5; MTCW 1, 2;
MTFW 2005; NFS 15, 19, 22, 34; RGAL
4; TUS
Lewis, (Percy) Wyndham
1884(?)-1957 . **SSC 34; TCLC 2, 9, 104,
216**
See also AAYA 77; BRW 7; CA 104; 157;
DLB 15; EWL 3; FANT; MTCW 2;
MTFW 2005; RGEL 2
Lewisohn, Ludwig 1883-1955 .... **TCLC 19**
See also CA 107; 203; DLB 4, 9, 28, 102;
MAL 5
Lewton, Val 1904-1951 .... **TCLC 76**
See also CA 199; IDFW 3, 4
Leyner, Mark 1956- .... **CLC 92**
See also CA 110; CANR 28, 53; DA3; DLB
292; MTCW 2; MTFW 2005
Leyton, E.K.
See Campbell, Ramsey
Lezama Lima, Jose 1910-1976 .... **CLC 4, 10,
101; HLCS 2**
See also CA 77-80; CANR 71; DAM
MULT; DLB 113, 283; EWL 3; HW 1, 2;
LAW; RGWL 2, 3
L'Heureux, John (Clarke) 1934- ...... **CLC 52**
See also CA 13-16R; CANR 23, 45, 88; CP
1, 2, 3, 4; DLB 244
Li, Fei-kan
See Jin, Ba
Li Ch'ing-chao 1081(?)-1141(?) .... **CMLC 71**
Lichtenberg, Georg Christoph
1742-1799 .... **LC 162**
See also DLB 94
Liddell, C. H.
See Kuttner, Henry
Lie, Jonas (Lauritz Idemil)
1833-1908(?) .... **TCLC 5**
See also CA 115
Lieber, Joel 1937-1971 .... **CLC 6**
See also CA 73-76; 29-32R
Lieber, Stanley Martin
See Lee, Stan
Lieberman, Laurence (James)
1935- .... **CLC 4, 36**
See also CA 17-20R; CANR 8, 36, 89; CP
1, 2, 3, 4, 5, 6, 7
Lieh Tzu fl. 7th cent. B.C.-5th cent.
B.C. .... **CMLC 27**
Lieksman, Anders
See Haavikko, Paavo Juhani
Lifton, Robert Jay 1926- .... **CLC 67**
See also CA 17-20R; CANR 27, 78, 161;
INT CANR-27; SATA 66
Lightfoot, Gordon 1938- .... **CLC 26**
See also CA 109; 242
Lightfoot, Gordon Meredith
See Lightfoot, Gordon
Lightman, Alan P. 1948- .... **CLC 81**
See also CA 141; CANR 63, 105, 138, 178;
MTFW 2005; NFS 29
Lightman, Alan Paige
See Lightman, Alan P.
Ligotti, Thomas 1953- .... **CLC 44; SSC 16**
See also CA 123; CANR 49, 135; HGG;
SUFW 2

Luzi, Mario (Egidio Vincenzo)
1914-2005 .... **CLC 13**
See also CA 61-64; 236; CANR 9, 70;
CWW 2; DLB 128; EWL 3

L'vov, Arkady **CLC 59**

Lydgate, John c. 1370-1450(?) ..... **LC 81, 175**
See also BRW 1; DLB 146; RGEL 2

Lyly, John 1554(?)-1606 ... **DC 7; LC 41, 187**
See also BRW 1; DAM DRAM; DLB 62,
167; RGEL 2

L'Ymagier
See Gourmont, Remy(-Marie-Charles) de

Lynch, B. Suarez
See Borges, Jorge Luis

Lynch, David 1946- .... **CLC 66, 162**
See also AAYA 55; CA 124; 129; CANR
111

Lynch, David Keith
See Lynch, David

Lynch, James
See Andreyev, Leonid

Lyndsay, Sir David 1485-1555 .... **LC 20**
See also RGEL 2

Lynn, Kenneth S(chuyler)
1923-2001 .... **CLC 50**
See also CA 1-4R; 196; CANR 3, 27, 65

Lynx
See West, Rebecca

Lyons, Marcus
See Blish, James

Lyotard, Jean-Francois
1924-1998 .... **TCLC 103**
See also DLB 242; EWL 3

Lyre, Pinchbeck
See Sassoon, Siegfried

Lytle, Andrew (Nelson) 1902-1995 ... **CLC 22**
See also CA 9-12R; 150; CANR 70; CN 1,
2, 3, 4, 5, 6; CSW; DLB 6; DLBY 1995;
RGAL 4; RHW

Lyttelton, George 1709-1773 .... **LC 10**
See also RGEL 2

Lytton, Edward G.E.L. Bulwer-Lytton
Baron
See Bulwer-Lytton, Edward

Lytton of Knebworth, Baron
See Bulwer-Lytton, Edward

Maalouf, Amin 1949- .... **CLC 248**
See also CA 212; CANR 194; DLB 346

Maas, Peter 1929-2001 .... **CLC 29**
See also CA 93-96; 201; INT CA-93-96;
MTCW 2; MTFW 2005

Mac A'Ghobhainn, Iain
See Smith, Iain Crichton

Macaulay, Catharine 1731-1791 .... **LC 64**
See also BRWS 17; DLB 104, 336

Macaulay, (Emilie) Rose
1881(?)-1958 .... **TCLC 7, 44**
See also CA 104; DLB 36; EWL 3; RGEL
2; RHW

Macaulay, Thomas Babington
1800-1859 .... **NCLC 42, 231**
See also BRW 4; CDBLB 1832-1890; DLB
32, 55; RGEL 2

MacBeth, George (Mann)
1932-1992 .... **CLC 2, 5, 9**
See also CA 25-28R; 136; CANR 61, 66;
CP 1, 2, 3, 4, 5; DLB 40; MTCW 1; PFS
8; SATA 4; SATA-Obit 70

MacCaig, Norman (Alexander)
1910-1996 .... **CLC 36**
See also BRWS 6; CA 9-12R; CANR 3, 34;
CP 1, 2, 3, 4, 5, 6; DAB; DAM POET;
DLB 27; EWL 3; RGEL 2

MacCarthy, Sir (Charles Otto) Desmond
1877-1952 .... **TCLC 36**
See also CA 167

MacDiarmid, Hugh
See Grieve, C. M.

MacDonald, Anson
See Heinlein, Robert A.

Macdonald, Cynthia 1928- .... **CLC 13, 19**
See also CA 49-52; CANR 4, 44, 146; DLB
105

MacDonald, George 1824-1905 .... **TCLC 9,
113, 207**
See also AAYA 57; BYA 5; CA 106; 137;
CANR 80; CLR 67; DLB 18, 163, 178;
FANT; MAICYA 1, 2; RGEL 2; SATA 33,
100; SFW 4; SUFW; WCH

Macdonald, John
See Millar, Kenneth

MacDonald, John D. 1916-1986 .. **CLC 3, 27,
44**
See also BPFB 2; CA 1-4R; 121; CANR 1,
19, 60; CMW 4; CPW; DAM NOV, POP;
DLB 8, 306; DLBY 1986; MSW; MTCW
1, 2; MTFW 2005; SFW 4

Macdonald, John Ross
See Millar, Kenneth

Macdonald, Ross
See Millar, Kenneth

MacDonald Fraser, George
See Fraser, George MacDonald

MacDougal, John
See Blish, James

MacDowell, John
See Parks, Tim

MacEwen, Gwendolyn (Margaret)
1941-1987 .... **CLC 13, 55**
See also CA 9-12R; 124; CANR 7, 22; CP
1, 2, 3, 4; DLB 53, 251; SATA 50; SATA-
Obit 55

MacGreevy, Thomas 1893-1967 .... **PC 82**
See also CA 262

Macha, Karel Hynek 1810-1846 .... **NCLC 46**

Machado (y Ruiz), Antonio
1875-1939 .... **TCLC 3**
See also CA 104; 174; DLB 108; EW 9;
EWL 3; HW 2; PFS 23; RGWL 2, 3

Machado de Assis, Joaquim Maria
1839-1908 . **BLC 1:2; HLCS 2; SSC 24,
118; TCLC 10**
See also CA 107; 153; CANR 91; DLB 307;
LAW; RGSF 2; RGWL 2, 3; TWA; WLIT
1

Machaut, Guillaume de c.
1300-1377 .... **CMLC 64**
See also DLB 208

Machen, Arthur
See Jones, Arthur Llewellyn

Machen, Arthur Llewelyn Jones
See Jones, Arthur Llewellyn

Machiavelli, Niccolo 1469-1527 ... **DC 16; LC
8, 36, 140; WLCS**
See also AAYA 58; DA; DAB; DAC; DAM
MST; EW 2; LAIT 1; LMFS 1; NFS 9;
RGWL 2, 3; TWA; WLIT 7

MacInnes, Colin 1914-1976 .... **CLC 4, 23**
See also CA 69-72; 65-68; CANR 21; CN
1, 2; DLB 14; MTCW 1, 2; RGEL 2;
RHW

MacInnes, Helen (Clark)
1907-1985 .... **CLC 27, 39**
See also BPFB 2; CA 1-4R; 117; CANR 1,
28, 58; CMW 4; CN 1, 2; CPW; DAM
POP; DLB 87; MSW; MTCW 1, 2;
MTFW 2005; SATA 22; SATA-Obit 44

Mackay, Mary 1855-1924 .... **TCLC 51**
See also CA 118; 177; DLB 34, 156; FANT;
RGEL 2; RHW; SUFW 1

Mackay, Shena 1944- .... **CLC 195**
See also CA 104; CANR 88, 139, 207; DLB
231, 319; MTFW 2005

Mackenzie, Compton (Edward Montague)
1883-1972 .... **CLC 18; TCLC 116**
See also CA 21-22; 37-40R; CAP 2; CN 1;
DLB 34, 100; RGEL 2

Mackenzie, Henry 1745-1831 .... **NCLC 41**
See also DLB 39; RGEL 2

Mackey, Nathaniel 1947- .... **BLC 2:3; PC 49**
See also CA 153; CANR 114; CP 6, 7; DLB
169

Mackey, Nathaniel Ernest
See Mackey, Nathaniel

MacKinnon, Catharine
See MacKinnon, Catharine A.

MacKinnon, Catharine A. 1946- .... **CLC 181**
See also CA 128; 132; CANR 73, 140, 189;
FW; MTCW 2; MTFW 2005

Mackintosh, Elizabeth
1896(?)-1952 .... **TCLC 14**
See also CA 110; CMW 4; DLB 10, 77;
MSW

Macklin, Charles 1699-1797 .... **LC 132**
See also DLB 89; RGEL 2

MacLaren, James
See Grieve, C. M.

MacLaverty, Bernard 1942- ..... **CLC 31, 243**
See also CA 116; 118; CANR 43, 88, 168;
CN 5, 6, 7; DLB 267; INT CA-118; RGSF
2

MacLean, Alistair 1922(?)-1987 .. **CLC 3, 13,
50, 63**
See also CA 57-60; 121; CANR 28, 61;
CMW 4; CP 2, 3, 4, 5, 6, 7; CPW; DAM
POP; DLB 276; MTCW 1; SATA 23;
SATA-Obit 50; TCWW 2

MacLean, Alistair Stuart
See MacLean, Alistair

Maclean, Norman (Fitzroy)
1902-1990 .... **CLC 78; SSC 13, 136**
See also AMWS 14; CA 102; 132; CANR
49; CPW; DAM POP; DLB 206; TCWW
2

MacLeish, Archibald 1892-1982 ... **CLC 3, 8,
14, 68; PC 47**
See also AMW; CA 9-12R; 106; CAD;
CANR 33, 63; CDALBS; CP 1, 2; DAM
POET; DFS 15; DLB 4, 7, 45; DLBY
1982; EWL 3; EXPP; MAL 5; MTCW 1,
2; MTFW 2005; PAB; PFS 5; RGAL 4;
TUS

MacLennan, (John) Hugh
1907-1990 .... **CLC 2, 14, 92**
See also CA 5-8R; 142; CANR 33; CN 1,
2, 3, 4; DAC; DAM MST; DLB 68; EWL
3; MTCW 1, 2; MTFW 2005; RGEL 2;
TWA

MacLeod, Alistair 1936- .. **CLC 56, 165; SSC
90**
See also CA 123; CCA 1; DAC; DAM
MST; DLB 60; MTCW 2; MTFW 2005;
RGSF 2; TCLE 1:2

Macleod, Fiona
See Sharp, William

MacNeice, (Frederick) Louis
1907-1963 .... **CLC 1, 4, 10, 53; PC 61**
See also BRW 7; CA 85-88; CANR 61;
DAB; DAM POET; DLB 10, 20; EWL 3;
MTCW 1, 2; MTFW 2005; RGEL 2

MacNeill, Dand
See Fraser, George MacDonald

Macpherson, James 1736-1796 .... **CMLC 28;
LC 29; PC 97**
See also BRWS 8; DLB 109, 336; RGEL 2

Macpherson, (Jean) Jay 1931- .... **CLC 14**
See also CA 5-8R; CANR 90; CP 1, 2, 3, 4,
6, 7; CWP; DLB 53

Macrobius fl. 430- .... **CMLC 48**

MacShane, Frank 1927-1999 .... **CLC 39**
See also CA 9-12R; 186; CANR 3, 33; DLB
111

Macumber, Mari
See Sandoz, Mari(e Susette)

Madach, Imre 1823-1864 .... **NCLC 19**

Madden, (Jerry) David 1933- .... **CLC 5, 15**
See also CA 1-4R; CAAS 3; CANR 4, 45;
CN 3, 4, 5, 6, 7; CSW; DLB 6; MTCW 1

Maddern, Al(an)
See Ellison, Harlan

Madhubuti, Haki R. 1942- .... **BLC 1:2; CLC 2; PC 5**
See also BW 2, 3; CA 73-76; CANR 24,
51, 73, 139; CP 2, 3, 4, 5, 6, 7; CSW;
DAM MULT, POET; DLB 5, 41; DLBD
8; EWL 3; MAL 5; MTCW 2; MTFW
2005; RGAL 4

Madison, James 1751-1836 .... **NCLC 126**
See also DLB 37

Maepenn, Hugh
See Kuttner, Henry

Maepenn, K. H.
See Kuttner, Henry

Maeterlinck, Maurice 1862-1949 .... **DC 32; TCLC 3**
See also CA 104; 136; CANR 80; DAM
DRAM; DLB 192, 331; EW 8; EWL 3;
GFL 1789 to the Present; LMFS 2; RGWL
2, 3; SATA 66; TWA

Maginn, William 1794-1842 .... **NCLC 8**
See also DLB 110, 159

Mahapatra, Jayanta 1928- .... **CLC 33**
See also CA 73-76; CAAS 9; CANR 15,
33, 66, 87; CP 4, 5, 6, 7; DAM MULT;
DLB 323

Mahfouz, Nagib
See Mahfouz, Naguib

Mahfouz, Naguib 1911(?)-2006 . **CLC 52, 55, 153; SSC 66**
See also AAYA 49; AFW; BEST 89:2; CA
128; 253; CANR 55, 101; DA3; DAM
NOV; DLB 346; DLBY 1988; MTCW 1,
2; MTFW 2005; RGSF 2; RGWL 2, 3;
SSFS 9, 33; WLIT 2

Mahfouz, Naguib Abdel Aziz Al-Sabilgi
See Mahfouz, Naguib

Mahfouz, Najib
See Mahfouz, Naguib

Mahfuz, Najib
See Mahfouz, Naguib

Mahon, Derek 1941- .... **CLC 27; PC 60**
See also BRWS 6; CA 113; 128; CANR 88;
CP 1, 2, 3, 4, 5, 6, 7; DLB 40; EWL 3

Maiakovskii, Vladimir
See Mayakovski, Vladimir

Mailer, Norman 1923-2007 ... **CLC 1, 2, 3, 4, 5, 8, 11, 14, 28, 39, 74, 111, 234**
See also AAYA 31; AITN 2; AMW; AMWC
2; AMWR 2; BPFB 2; CA 9-12R; 266;
CABS 1; CANR 28, 74, 77, 130, 196;
CDALB 1968-1988; CN 1, 2, 3, 4, 5, 6,
7; CPW; DA; DA3; DAC; DAM
MST, NOV, POP; DLB 2, 16, 28, 185,
278; DLBD 3; DLBY 1980, 1983; EWL
3; MAL 5; MTCW 1, 2; MTFW 2005;
NFS 10; RGAL 4; TUS

Mailer, Norman Kingsley
See Mailer, Norman

Maillet, Antonine 1929- .... **CLC 54, 118**
See also CA 115; 120; CANR 46, 74, 77,
134; CCA 1; CWW 2; DAC; DLB 60;
INT CA-120; MTCW 2; MTFW 2005

Maimonides, Moses 1135-1204 ..... **CMLC 76**
See also DLB 115

Mais, Roger 1905-1955 .... **TCLC 8**
See also BW 1, 3; CA 105; 124; CANR 82;
CDWLB 3; DLB 125; EWL 3; MTCW 1;
RGEL 2

Maistre, Joseph 1753-1821 .... **NCLC 37**
See also GFL 1789 to the Present

Maitland, Frederic William
1850-1906 .... **TCLC 65**

Maitland, Sara (Louise) 1950- .... **CLC 49**
See also BRWS 11; CA 69-72; CANR 13,
59; DLB 271; FW

Major, Clarence 1936- ...... **BLC 1:2; CLC 3, 19, 48**
See also AFAW 2; BW 2, 3; CA 21-24R;
CAAS 6; CANR 13, 25, 53, 82; CN 3, 4,
5, 6, 7; CP 2, 3, 4, 5, 6, 7; CSW; DAM
MULT; DLB 33; EWL 3; MAL 5; MSW

Major, Kevin (Gerald) 1949- .... **CLC 26**
See also AAYA 16; CA 97-100; CANR 21,
38, 112; CLR 11; DAC; DLB 60; INT
CANR-21; JRDA; MAICYA 1, 2; MAIC-
YAS 1; SATA 32, 82, 134; WYA; YAW

Maki, James
See Ozu, Yasujiro

Makin, Bathsua 1600-1675(?) .... **LC 137**

Makine, Andrei
See Makine, Andrei

Makine, Andrei 1957- .... **CLC 198**
See also CA 176; CANR 103, 162; MTFW
2005

Malabaila, Damiano
See Levi, Primo

Malamud, Bernard 1914-1986 .. **CLC 1, 2, 3, 5, 8, 9, 11, 18, 27, 44, 78, 85; SSC 15, 147; TCLC 129, 184; WLC 4**
See also AAYA 16; AMWS 1; BPFB 2;
BYA 15; CA 5-8R; 118; CABS 1; CANR
28, 62, 114; CDALB 1941-1968; CN 1, 2,
3, 4; CPW; DA; DA3; DAB; DAC; DAM
MST, NOV, POP; DLB 2, 28, 152; DLBY
1980, 1986; EWL 3; EXPS; LAIT 4;
LATS 1:1; MAL 5; MTCW 1, 2; MTFW
2005; NFS 27; RGAL 4; RGHL; RGSF 2;
SSFS 8, 13, 16; TUS

Malan, Herman
See Bosman, Herman Charles; Bosman,
Herman Charles

Malaparte, Curzio 1898-1957 .... **TCLC 52**
See also DLB 264

Malcolm, Dan
See Silverberg, Robert

Malcolm, Janet 1934- .... **CLC 201**
See also CA 123; CANR 89, 199; NCFS 1

Malcolm X 1925-1965 ..... **BLC 1:2; CLC 82, 117; WLCS**
See also BW 1, 3; CA 125; 111; CANR 82;
DA; DA3; DAB; DAC; DAM MST,
MULT; LAIT 5; MTCW 1, 2; MTFW
2005; NCFS 3

Malebranche, Nicolas 1638-1715 .... **LC 133**
See also GFL Beginnings to 1789

Malherbe, Francois de 1555-1628 .... **LC 5**
See also DLB 327; GFL Beginnings to 1789

Mallarme, Stephane 1842-1898 ...... **NCLC 4, 41, 210; PC 4, 102**
See also DAM POET; DLB 217; EW 7;
GFL 1789 to the Present; LMFS 2; RGWL
2, 3; TWA

Mallet-Joris, Francoise 1930- .... **CLC 11**
See also CA 65-68; CANR 17; CWW 2;
DLB 83; EWL 3; GFL 1789 to the Present

Malley, Ern
See McAuley, James Phillip

Mallon, Thomas 1951- .... **CLC 172**
See also CA 110; CANR 29, 57, 92, 196;
DLB 350

Mallowan, Agatha Christie
See Christie, Agatha

Maloff, Saul 1922- .... **CLC 5**
See also CA 33-36R

Malone, Louis
See MacNeice, (Frederick) Louis

Malone, Michael 1942- .... **CLC 43**
See also CA 77-80; CANR 14, 32, 57, 114,
214

Malone, Michael Christopher
See Malone, Michael

Malory, Sir Thomas 1410(?)-1471(?) . **LC 11, 88; WLCS**
See also BRW 1; BRWR 2; CDBLB Before
1660; DA; DAB; DAC; DAM MST; DLB
146; EFS 2; RGEL 2; SATA 59; SATA-
Brief 33; TEA; WLIT 3

Malouf, David 1934- .... **CLC 28, 86, 245**
See also BRWS 12; CA 124; CANR 50, 76,
180; CN 3, 4, 5, 6, 7; CP 1, 3, 4, 5, 6, 7;
DLB 289; EWL 3; MTCW 2; MTFW
2005; SSFS 24

Malouf, George Joseph David
See Malouf, David

Malraux, Andre 1901-1976 . **CLC 1, 4, 9, 13, 15, 57; TCLC 209**
See also BPFB 2; CA 21-22; 69-72; CANR
34, 58; CAP 2; DA3; DAM NOV; DLB
72; EW 12; EWL 3; GFL 1789 to the
Present; MTCW 1, 2; MTFW 2005;
RGWL 2, 3; TWA

Malraux, Georges-Andre
See Malraux, Andre

Malthus, Thomas Robert
1766-1834 .... **NCLC 145**
See also DLB 107, 158; RGEL 2

Malzberg, Barry N(athaniel) 1939- ... **CLC 7**
See also CA 61-64; CAAS 4; CANR 16;
CMW 4; DLB 8; SFW 4

Mamet, David 1947- .. **CLC 9, 15, 34, 46, 91, 166; DC 4, 24**
See also AAYA 3, 60; AMWS 14; CA 81-
84; CABS 3; CAD; CANR 15, 41, 67, 72,
129, 172; CD 5, 6; DA3; DAM DRAM;
DFS 2, 3, 6, 12, 15; DLB 7; EWL 3;
IDFW 4; MAL 5; MTCW 1, 2; MTFW
2005; RGAL 4

Mamet, David Alan
See Mamet, David

Mamoulian, Rouben (Zachary)
1897-1987 .... **CLC 16**
See also CA 25-28R; 124; CANR 85

Mandelshtam, Osip
See Mandelstam, Osip

Mandel'shtam, Osip Emil'evich
See Mandelstam, Osip

Mandelstam, Osip 1891(?)-1943(?) .... **PC 14; TCLC 2, 6, 225**
See also CA 104; 150; DLB 295; EW 10;
EWL 3; MTCW 2; RGWL 2, 3; TWA

Mandelstam, Osip Emilievich
See Mandelstam, Osip

Mander, (Mary) Jane 1877-1949 ... **TCLC 31**
See also CA 162; RGEL 2

Mandeville, Bernard 1670-1733 .... **LC 82**
See also DLB 101

Mandeville, Sir John fl. 1350- ...... **CMLC 19**
See also DLB 146

Mandiargues, Andre Pieyre de
See Pieyre de Mandiargues, Andre

Mandrake, Ethel Belle
See Thurman, Wallace (Henry)

Mangan, James Clarence
1803-1849 .... **NCLC 27**
See also BRWS 13; RGEL 2

Maniere, J. E.
See Giraudoux, Jean

Mankell, Henning 1948- .... **CLC 292**
See also CA 187; CANR 163, 200

Mankiewicz, Herman (Jacob)
1897-1953 .... **TCLC 85**
See also CA 120; 169; DLB 26; IDFW 3, 4

Manley, (Mary) Delariviere
1672(?)-1724 .... **LC 1, 42**
See also DLB 39, 80; RGEL 2

Mann, Abel
See Creasey, John

McGuane, Thomas 1939- .. **CLC 3, 7, 18, 45, 127**
See also AITN 2; BPFB 2; CA 49-52; CANR 5, 24, 49, 94, 164; CN 2, 3, 4, 5, 6, 7; DLB 2, 212; DLBY 1980; EWL 3; INT CANR-24; MAL 5; MTCW 1; MTFW 2005; TCWW 1, 2

McGuane, Thomas Francis III
See McGuane, Thomas

McGuckian, Medbh 1950- .... **CLC 48, 174; PC 27**
See also BRWS 5; CA 143; CANR 206; CP 4, 5, 6, 7; CWP; DAM POET; DLB 40

McHale, Tom 1942(?)-1982 .... **CLC 3, 5**
See also AITN 1; CA 77-80; 106; CN 1, 2, 3

McHugh, Heather 1948- .... **PC 61**
See also CA 69-72; CANR 11, 28, 55, 92; CP 4, 5, 6, 7; CWP; PFS 24

McIlvanney, William 1936- .... **CLC 42**
See also CA 25-28R; CANR 61; CMW 4; DLB 14, 207

McIlwraith, Maureen Mollie Hunter
See Hunter, Mollie

McInerney, Jay 1955- .... **CLC 34, 112**
See also AAYA 18; BPFB 2; CA 116; 123; CANR 45, 68, 116, 176; CN 5, 6, 7; CPW; DA3; DAM POP; DLB 292; INT CA-123; MAL 5; MTCW 2; MTFW 2005

McIntyre, Vonda N. 1948- .... **CLC 18**
See also CA 81-84; CANR 17, 34, 69; MTCW 1; SFW 4; YAW

McIntyre, Vonda Neel
See McIntyre, Vonda N.

McKay, Claude 1889-1948 ...... **BLC 1:3; HR 1:3; PC 2; TCLC 7, 41; WLC 4**
See also AFAW 1, 2; AMWS 10; BW 1, 3; CA 104; 124; CANR 73; DA; DAB; DAC; DAM MST, MULT, NOV, POET; DLB 4, 45, 51, 117; EWL 3; EXPP; GLL 2; LAIT 3; LMFS 2; MAL 5; MTCW 1, 2; MTFW 2005; PAB; PFS 4; RGAL 4; TUS; WP

McKay, Festus Claudius
See McKay, Claude

McKuen, Rod 1933- .... **CLC 1, 3**
See also AITN 1; CA 41-44R; CANR 40; CP 1

McLoughlin, R. B.
See Mencken, H. L.

McLuhan, (Herbert) Marshall 1911-1980 .... **CLC 37, 83**
See also CA 9-12R; 102; CANR 12, 34, 61; DLB 88; INT CANR-12; MTCW 1, 2; MTFW 2005

McMahon, Pat
See Hoch, Edward D.

McManus, Declan Patrick Aloysius
See Costello, Elvis

McMillan, Terry 1951- .. **BLCS; CLC 50, 61, 112**
See also AAYA 21; AMWS 13; BPFB 2; BW 2, 3; CA 140; CANR 60, 104, 131; CN 7; CPW; DA3; DAM MULT, NOV, POP; MAL 5; MTCW 2; MTFW 2005; RGAL 4; YAW

McMillan, Terry L.
See McMillan, Terry

McMurtry, Larry 1936- .... **CLC 2, 3, 7, 11, 27, 44, 127, 250**
See also AAYA 83; AITN 2; AMWS 5; BEST 89:2; BPFB 2; CA 5-8R; CANR 19, 43, 64, 103, 170, 206; CDALB 1968-1988; CN 2, 3, 4, 5, 6, 7; CPW; CSW; DA3; DAM NOV, POP; DLB 2, 143, 256; DLBY 1980, 1987; EWL 3; MAL 5; MTCW 1, 2; MTFW 2005; RGAL 4; TCWW 1, 2

McMurtry, Larry Jeff
See McMurtry, Larry

McNally, Terrence 1939- ... **CLC 4, 7, 41, 91, 252; DC 27**
See also AAYA 62; AMWS 13; CA 45-48; CAD; CANR 2, 56, 116; CD 5, 6; DA3; DAM DRAM; DFS 16, 19; DLB 7, 249; EWL 3; GLL 1; MTCW 2; MTFW 2005

McNally, Thomas Michael
See McNally, T.M.

McNally, T.M. 1961- .... **CLC 82**
See also CA 246

McNamer, Deirdre 1950- .... **CLC 70**
See also CA 188; CANR 163, 200

McNeal, Tom CLC 119
See also CA 252; CANR 185; SATA 194

McNeile, Herman Cyril 1888-1937 .... **TCLC 44**
See also CA 184; CMW 4; DLB 77

McNickle, D'Arcy 1904-1977 .... **CLC 89; NNAL**
See also CA 9-12R; 85-88; CANR 5, 45; DAM MULT; DLB 175, 212; RGAL 4; SATA-Obit 22; TCWW 1, 2

McNickle, William D'Arcy
See McNickle, D'Arcy

McPhee, John 1931- .... **CLC 36**
See also AAYA 61; AMWS 3; ANW; BEST 90:1; CA 65-68; CANR 20, 46, 64, 69, 121, 165; CPW; DLB 185, 275; MTCW 1, 2; MTFW 2005; TUS

McPhee, John Angus
See McPhee, John

McPherson, James Alan, Jr.
See McPherson, James Alan

McPherson, James Alan 1943- . **BLCS; CLC 19, 77; SSC 95**
See also BW 1, 3; CA 25-28R; 273; CAAE 273; CAAS 17; CANR 24, 74, 140; CN 3, 4, 5, 6; CSW; DLB 38, 244; EWL 3; MTCW 1, 2; MTFW 2005; RGAL 4; RGSF 2; SSFS 23

McPherson, William (Alexander) 1933- .... **CLC 34**
See also CA 69-72; CANR 28; INT CANR-28

McTaggart, J. McT. Ellis
See McTaggart, John McTaggart Ellis

McTaggart, John McTaggart Ellis 1866-1925 .... **TCLC 105**
See also CA 120; DLB 262

Mda, Zakes 1948- .... **BLC 2:3; CLC 262**
See also BRWS 15; CA 205; CANR 151, 185; CD 5, 6; DLB 225

Mda, Zanemvula
See Mda, Zakes

Mda, Zanemvula Kizito Gatyeni
See Mda, Zakes

Mead, George Herbert 1863-1931 . **TCLC 89**
See also CA 212; DLB 270

Mead, Margaret 1901-1978 .... **CLC 37**
See also AITN 1; CA 1-4R; 81-84; CANR 4; DA3; FW; MTCW 1, 2; SATA-Obit 20

Meaker, M. J.
See Meaker, Marijane

Meaker, Marijane 1927- .... **CLC 12, 35**
See also AAYA 2, 23, 82; BYA 1, 7, 8; CA 107; CANR 37, 63, 145, 180; CLR 29; GLL 2; INT CA-107; JRDA; MAICYA 1, 2; MAICYAS 1; MTCW 1; SAAS 1; SATA 20, 61, 99, 160; SATA-Essay 111; WYA; YAW

Meaker, Marijane Agnes
See Meaker, Marijane

Mechthild von Magdeburg c. 1207-c. 1282 .... **CMLC 91**
See also DLB 138

Medoff, Mark (Howard) 1940- .... **CLC 6, 23**
See also AITN 1; CA 53-56; CAD; CANR 5; CD 5, 6; DAM DRAM; DFS 4; DLB 7; INT CANR-5

Medvedev, P. N.
See Bakhtin, Mikhail Mikhailovich

Meged, Aharon
See Megged, Aharon

Meged, Aron
See Megged, Aharon

Megged, Aharon 1920- .... **CLC 9**
See also CA 49-52; CAAS 13; CANR 1, 140; EWL 3; RGHL

Mehta, Deepa 1950- .... **CLC 208**

Mehta, Gita 1943- .... **CLC 179**
See also CA 225; CN 7; DNFS 2

Mehta, Ved 1934- .... **CLC 37**
See also CA 1-4R, 212; CAAE 212; CANR 2, 23, 69; DLB 323; MTCW 1; MTFW 2005

Melanchthon, Philipp 1497-1560 .... **LC 90**
See also DLB 179

Melanter
See Blackmore, R(ichard) D(oddridge)

Meleager c. 140B.C.-c. 70B.C. ...... **CMLC 53**

Melies, Georges 1861-1938 .... **TCLC 81**

Melikow, Loris
See Hofmannsthal, Hugo von

Melmoth, Sebastian
See Wilde, Oscar

Melo Neto, Joao Cabral de
See Cabral de Melo Neto, Joao

Meltzer, Milton 1915-2009 .... **CLC 26**
See also AAYA 8, 45; BYA 2, 6; CA 13-16R; 290; CANR 38, 92, 107, 192; CLR 13; DLB 61; JRDA; MAICYA 1, 2; SAAS 1; SATA 1, 50, 80, 128, 201; SATA-Essay 124; WYA; YAW

Melville, Herman 1819-1891 ..... **NCLC 3, 12, 29, 45, 49, 91, 93, 123, 157, 181, 193, 221, 234; PC 82; SSC 1, 17, 46, 95, 141; WLC 4**
See also AAYA 25; AMW; AMWR 1; CDALB 1640-1865; DA; DA3; DAB; DAC; DAM MST, NOV; DLB 3, 74, 250, 254, 349; EXPN; EXPS; GL 3; LAIT 1, 2; NFS 7, 9, 32; RGAL 4; RGSF 2; SATA 59; SSFS 3; TUS

Members, Mark
See Powell, Anthony

Membreno, Alejandro CLC 59

Menand, Louis 1952- .... **CLC 208**
See also CA 200

Menander c. 342B.C.-c. 293B.C. .... **CMLC 9, 51, 101; DC 3**
See also AW 1; CDWLB 1; DAM DRAM; DLB 176; LMFS 1; RGWL 2, 3

Menchu, Rigoberta 1959- .. **CLC 160; HLCS 2**
See also CA 175; CANR 135; DNFS 1; WLIT 1

Mencken, H. L. 1880-1956 .... **TCLC 13, 18**
See also AAYA 85; AMW; CA 105; 125; CDALB 1917-1929; DLB 11, 29, 63, 137, 222; EWL 3; MAL 5; MTCW 1, 2; MTFW 2005; NCFS 4; RGAL 4; TUS

Mencken, Henry Louis
See Mencken, H. L.

Mendelsohn, Jane 1965- .... **CLC 99**
See also CA 154; CANR 94

Mendelssohn, Moses 1729-1786 .... **LC 142**
See also DLB 97

Mendoza, Inigo Lopez de
See Santillana, Inigo Lopez de Mendoza, Marques de

Menton, Francisco de
See Chin, Frank

Mercer, David 1928-1980 .... **CLC 5**
See also CA 9-12R; 102; CANR 23; CBD; DAM DRAM; DLB 13, 310; MTCW 1; RGEL 2

Merchant, Paul
See Ellison, Harlan

Millhauser, Steven 1943- ... **CLC 21, 54, 109, 300; SSC 57**
See also AAYA 76; CA 110; 111; CANR 63, 114, 133, 189; CN 6, 7; DA3; DLB 2, 350; FANT; INT CA-111; MAL 5; MTCW 2; MTFW 2005

Millhauser, Steven Lewis
See Millhauser, Steven

Millin, Sarah Gertrude 1889-1968 ... **CLC 49**
See also CA 102; 93-96; DLB 225; EWL 3

Milne, A. A. 1882-1956 .... **TCLC 6, 88**
See also BRWS 5; CA 104; 133; CLR 1, 26, 108; CMW 4; CWRI 5; DA3; DAB; DAC; DAM MST; DLB 10, 77, 100, 160, 352; FANT; MAICYA 1, 2; MTCW 1, 2; MTFW 2005; RGEL 2; SATA 100; WCH; YABC 1

Milne, Alan Alexander
See Milne, A. A.

Milner, Ron(ald) 1938-2004 .. **BLC 1:3; CLC 56**
See also AITN 1; BW 1; CA 73-76; 230; CAD; CANR 24, 81; CD 5, 6; DAM MULT; DLB 38; MAL 5; MTCW 1

Milnes, Richard Monckton
1809-1885 .... **NCLC 61**
See also DLB 32, 184

Milosz, Czeslaw 1911-2004 .... **CLC 5, 11, 22, 31, 56, 82, 253; PC 8; WLCS**
See also AAYA 62; CA 81-84; 230; CANR 23, 51, 91, 126; CDWLB 4; CWW 2; DA3; DAM MST, POET; DLB 215, 331; EW 13; EWL 3; MTCW 1, 2; MTFW 2005; PFS 16, 29, 35; RGHL; RGWL 2, 3

Milton, John 1608-1674 ..... **LC 9, 43, 92; PC 19, 29; WLC 4**
See also AAYA 65; BRW 2; BRWR 2; CD-BLB 1660-1789; DA; DA3; DAB; DAC; DAM MST, POET; DLB 131, 151, 281; EFS 1; EXPP; LAIT 1; PAB; PFS 3, 17, 37; RGEL 2; TEA; WLIT 3; WP

Min, Anchee 1957- .... **CLC 86, 291**
See also CA 146; CANR 94, 137; MTFW 2005

Minehaha, Cornelius
See Wedekind, Frank

Miner, Valerie 1947- .... **CLC 40**
See also CA 97-100; CANR 59, 177; FW; GLL 2

Minimo, Duca
See D'Annunzio, Gabriele

Minot, Susan (Anderson) 1956- ...... **CLC 44, 159**
See also AMWS 6; CA 134; CANR 118; CN 6, 7

Minus, Ed 1938- .... **CLC 39**
See also CA 185

Mirabai 1498(?)-1550(?) .... **LC 143; PC 48**
See also PFS 24

Miranda, Javier
See Bioy Casares, Adolfo

Mirbeau, Octave 1848-1917 .... **TCLC 55**
See also CA 216; DLB 123, 192; GFL 1789 to the Present

Mirikitani, Janice 1942- .... **AAL**
See also CA 211; DLB 312; RGAL 4

Mirk, John (?)-c. 1414 .... **LC 105**
See also DLB 146

Miro (Ferrer), Gabriel (Francisco Victor)
1879-1930 .... **TCLC 5**
See also CA 104; 185; DLB 322; EWL 3

Misharin, Alexandr .... **CLC 59**

Mishima, Yukio
See Hiraoka, Kimitake

Mishima Yukio
See Hiraoka, Kimitake

Miss C. L. F.
See Grimke, Charlotte L. Forten

Mister X
See Hoch, Edward D.

Mistral, Frederic 1830-1914 .... **TCLC 51**
See also CA 122; 213; DLB 331; GFL 1789 to the Present

Mistral, Gabriela 1899-1957 .... **HLC 2; PC 32; TCLC 2**
See also BW 2; CA 104; 131; CANR 81; DAM MULT; DLB 283, 331; DNFS; EWL 3; HW 1, 2; LAW; MTCW 1, 2; MTFW 2005; PFS 37; RGWL 2, 3; WP

Mistry, Rohinton 1952- ... **CLC 71, 196, 281; SSC 73**
See also BRWS 10; CA 141; CANR 86, 114; CCA 1; CN 6, 7; DAC; DLB 334; SSFS 6

Mitchell, Clyde
See Ellison, Harlan; Silverberg, Robert

Mitchell, Emerson Blackhorse Barney
1945- .... **NNAL**
See also CA 45-48

Mitchell, James Leslie 1901-1935 .... **TCLC 4**
See also BRWS 14; CA 104; 188; DLB 15; RGEL 2

Mitchell, Joni 1943- .... **CLC 12**
See also CA 112; CCA 1

Mitchell, Joseph (Quincy)
1908-1996 .... **CLC 98**
See also CA 77-80; 152; CANR 69; CN 1, 2, 3, 4, 5, 6; CSW; DLB 185; DLBY 1996

Mitchell, Margaret 1900-1949 .... **TCLC 11, 170**
See also AAYA 23; BPFB 2; BYA 1; CA 109; 125; CANR 55, 94; CDALBS; DA3; DAM NOV, POP; DLB 9; LAIT 2; MAL 5; MTCW 1, 2; MTFW 2005; NFS 9; RGAL 4; RHW; TUS; WYAS 1; YAW

Mitchell, Margaret Munnerlyn
See Mitchell, Margaret

Mitchell, Peggy
See Mitchell, Margaret

Mitchell, S(ilas) Weir 1829-1914 .... **TCLC 36**
See also CA 165; DLB 202; RGAL 4

Mitchell, W(illiam) O(rmond)
1914-1998 .... **CLC 25**
See also CA 77-80; 165; CANR 15, 43; CN 1, 2, 3, 4, 5, 6; DAC; DAM MST; DLB 88; TCLE 1:2

Mitchell, William (Lendrum)
1879-1936 .... **TCLC 81**
See also CA 213

Mitford, Mary Russell 1787-1855 ... **NCLC 4**
See also DLB 110, 116; RGEL 2

Mitford, Nancy 1904-1973 .... **CLC 44**
See also BRWS 10; CA 9-12R; CN 1; DLB 191; RGEL 2

Miyamoto, (Chujo) Yuriko
1899-1951 .... **TCLC 37**
See also CA 170, 174; DLB 180

Miyamoto Yuriko
See Miyamoto, (Chujo) Yuriko

Miyazawa, Kenji 1896-1933 .... **TCLC 76**
See also CA 157; EWL 3; RGWL 3

Miyazawa Kenji
See Miyazawa, Kenji

Mizoguchi, Kenji 1898-1956 .... **TCLC 72**
See also CA 167

Mo, Timothy (Peter) 1950- .... **CLC 46, 134**
See also CA 117; CANR 128; CN 5, 6, 7; DLB 194; MTCW 1; WLIT 4; WWE 1

Mo, Yan
See Yan, Mo

Moberg, Carl Arthur
See Moberg, Vilhelm

Moberg, Vilhelm 1898-1973 .... **TCLC 224**
See also CA 97-100; 45-48; CANR 135; DLB 259; EW 11; EWL 3

Modarressi, Taghi (M.) 1931-1997 ... **CLC 44**
See also CA 121; 134; INT CA-134

Modiano, Patrick (Jean) 1945- .... **CLC 18, 218**
See also CA 85-88; CANR 17, 40, 115; CWW 2; DLB 83, 299; EWL 3; RGHL

Mofolo, Thomas 1875(?)-1948 .... **BLC 1:3; TCLC 22**
See also AFW; CA 121; 153; CANR 83; DAM MULT; DLB 225; EWL 3; MTCW 2; MTFW 2005; WLIT 2

Mofolo, Thomas Mokopu
See Mofolo, Thomas

Mohr, Nicholasa 1938- .... **CLC 12; HLC 2**
See also AAYA 8, 46; CA 49-52; CANR 1, 32, 64; CLR 22; DAM MULT; DLB 145; HW 1, 2; JRDA; LAIT 5; LLW; MAICYA 2; MAICYAS 1; RGAL 4; SAAS 8; SATA 8, 97; SATA-Essay 113; WYA; YAW

Moi, Toril 1953- .... **CLC 172**
See also CA 154; CANR 102; FW

Mojtabai, A(nn) G(race) 1938- ..... **CLC 5, 9, 15, 29**
See also CA 85-88; CANR 88

Moliere 1622-1673 ..... **DC 13; LC 10, 28, 64, 125, 127; WLC 4**
See also DA; DA3; DAB; DAC; DAM DRAM, MST; DFS 13, 18, 20; DLB 268; EW 3; GFL Beginnings to 1789; LATS 1:1; RGWL 2, 3; TWA

Molin, Charles
See Mayne, William

Molina, Antonio Munoz 1956- .... **CLC 289**
See also DLB 322

Molnar, Ferenc 1878-1952 .... **TCLC 20**
See also CA 109; 153; CANR 83; CDWLB 4; DAM DRAM; DLB 215; EWL 3; RGWL 2, 3

Momaday, N. Scott 1934- ...... **CLC 2, 19, 85, 95, 160; NNAL; PC 25; WLCS**
See also AAYA 11, 64; AMWS 4; ANW; BPFB 2; BYA 12; CA 25-28R; CANR 14, 34, 68, 134; CDALBS; CN 2, 3, 4, 5, 6, 7; CPW; DA; DA3; DAB; DAC; DAM MST, MULT, NOV, POP; DLB 143, 175, 256; EWL 3; EXPP; INT CANR-14; LAIT 4; LATS 1:2; MAL 5; MTCW 1, 2; MTFW 2005; NFS 10; PFS 2, 11, 37; RGAL 4; SATA 48; SATA-Brief 30; TCWW 1, 2; WP; YAW

Momaday, Navarre Scott
See Momaday, N. Scott

Momala, Ville i
See Moberg, Vilhelm

Monette, Paul 1945-1995 .... **CLC 82**
See also AMWS 10; CA 139; 147; CN 6; DLB 350; GLL 1

Monroe, Harriet 1860-1936 .... **TCLC 12**
See also CA 109; 204; DLB 54, 91

Monroe, Lyle
See Heinlein, Robert A.

Montagu, Elizabeth 1720-1800 .... **NCLC 7, 117**
See also DLB 356; FW

Montagu, Mary (Pierrepont) Wortley
1689-1762 .... **LC 9, 57; PC 16**
See also DLB 95, 101; FL 1:1; RGEL 2

Montagu, W. H.
See Coleridge, Samuel Taylor

Montague, John (Patrick) 1929- ..... **CLC 13, 46; PC 106**
See also BRWS 15; CA 9-12R; CANR 9, 69, 121; CP 1, 2, 3, 4, 5, 6, 7; DLB 40; EWL 3; MTCW 1; PFS 12; RGEL 2; TCLE 1:2

Montaigne, Michel de 1533-1592 .... **LC 8, 105; WLC 4**
See also DA; DAB; DAC; DAM MST; DLB 327; EW 2; GFL Beginnings to 1789; LMFS 1; RGWL 2, 3; TWA

Nelson, Alice Ruth Moore Dunbar
1875-1935 .... **HR 1:2; SSC 132**
See also BW 1, 3; CA 122; 124; CANR 82;
DLB 50; FW; MTCW 1

Nelson, Willie 1933- .... **CLC 17**
See also CA 107; CANR 114, 178

Nemerov, Howard 1920-1991 ... **CLC 2, 6, 9,
36; PC 24; TCLC 124**
See also AMW; CA 1-4R; 134; CABS 2;
CANR 1, 27, 53; CN 1, 2, 3; CP 1, 2, 3,
4, 5; DAM POET; DLB 5, 6; DLBY 1983;
EWL 3; INT CANR-27; MAL 5; MTCW
1, 2; MTFW 2005; PFS 10, 14; RGAL 4

Nemerov, Howard Stanley
See Nemerov, Howard

Nepos, Cornelius c. 99B.C.-c.
24B.C. .... **CMLC 89**
See also DLB 211

Neruda, Pablo 1904-1973 .. **CLC 1, 2, 5, 7, 9,
28, 62; HLC 2; PC 4, 64; WLC 4**
See also CA 19-20; 45-48; CANR 131; CAP
2; DA; DA3; DAB; DAC; DAM MST,
MULT, POET; DLB 283, 331; DNFS 2;
EWL 3; HW 1; LAW; MTCW 1, 2;
MTFW 2005; PFS 11, 28, 33, 35; RGWL
2, 3; TWA; WLIT 1; WP

Nerval, Gerard de 1808-1855 ... **NCLC 1, 67;
PC 13; SSC 18**
See also DLB 217; EW 6; GFL 1789 to the
Present; RGSF 2; RGWL 2, 3

Nervo, (Jose) Amado (Ruiz de)
1870-1919 .... **HLCS 2; TCLC 11**
See also CA 109; 131; DLB 290; EWL 3;
HW 1; LAW

Nesbit, Malcolm
See Chester, Alfred

Nessi, Pio Baroja y
See Baroja, Pio

Nestroy, Johann 1801-1862 .... **NCLC 42**
See also DLB 133; RGWL 2, 3

Netterville, Luke
See O'Grady, Standish (James)

Neufeld, John (Arthur) 1938- .... **CLC 17**
See also AAYA 11; CA 25-28R; CANR 11,
37, 56; CLR 52; MAICYA 1, 2; SAAS 3;
SATA 6, 81, 131; SATA-Essay 131; YAW

Neumann, Alfred 1895-1952 .... **TCLC 100**
See also CA 183; DLB 56

Neumann, Ferenc
See Molnar, Ferenc

Neville, Emily Cheney 1919- .... **CLC 12**
See also BYA 2; CA 5-8R; CANR 3, 37,
85; JRDA; MAICYA 1, 2; SAAS 2; SATA
1; YAW

Newbound, Bernard Slade 1930- .... **CLC 11,
46**
See also CA 81-84; CAAS 9; CANR 49;
CCA 1; CD 5, 6; DAM DRAM; DLB 53

Newby, P(ercy) H(oward)
1918-1997 .... **CLC 2, 13**
See also CA 5-8R; 161; CANR 32, 67; CN
1, 2, 3, 4, 5, 6; DAM NOV; DLB 15, 326;
MTCW 1; RGEL 2

Newcastle
See Cavendish, Margaret

Newlove, Donald 1928- .... **CLC 6**
See also CA 29-32R; CANR 25

Newlove, John (Herbert) 1938- .... **CLC 14**
See also CA 21-24R; CANR 9, 25; CP 1, 2,
3, 4, 5, 6, 7

Newman, Charles 1938-2006 .... **CLC 2, 8**
See also CA 21-24R; 249; CANR 84; CN
3, 4, 5, 6

Newman, Charles Hamilton
See Newman, Charles

Newman, Edwin 1919-2010 .... **CLC 14**
See also AITN 1; CA 69-72; CANR 5

Newman, Edwin Harold
See Newman, Edwin

Newman, John Henry 1801-1890 . **NCLC 38,
99**
See also BRWS 7; DLB 18, 32, 55; RGEL
2

Newton, (Sir) Isaac 1642-1727 ...... **LC 35, 53**
See also DLB 252

Newton, Suzanne 1936- .... **CLC 35**
See also BYA 7; CA 41-44R; CANR 14;
JRDA; SATA 5, 77

New York Dept. of Ed. CLC 70

Nexo, Martin Andersen
1869-1954 .... **TCLC 43**
See also CA 202; DLB 214; EWL 3; NFS
34

Nezval, Vitezslav 1900-1958 .... **TCLC 44**
See also CA 123; CDWLB 4; DLB 215;
EWL 3

Ng, Fae Myenne 1956- .... **CLC 81**
See also BYA 11; CA 146; CANR 191; NFS
37

Ngcobo, Lauretta 1931- .... **BLC 2:3**
See also CA 165

Ngema, Mbongeni 1955- .... **CLC 57**
See also BW 2; CA 143; CANR 84; CD 5,
6

Ngugi, James T.
See Ngugi wa Thiong'o

Ngugi, James Thiong'o
See Ngugi wa Thiong'o

Ngugi wa Thiong'o 1938- .... **BLC 1:3, 2:3;
CLC 3, 7, 13, 36, 182, 275**
See also AFW; BRWS 8; BW 2; CA 81-84;
CANR 27, 58, 164, 213; CD 3, 4, 5, 6, 7;
CDWLB 3; CN 1, 2; DAM MULT, NOV;
DLB 125; DNFS 2; EWL 3; MTCW 1, 2;
MTFW 2005; RGEL 2; WWE 1

Niatum, Duane 1938- .... **NNAL**
See also CA 41-44R; CANR 21, 45, 83;
DLB 175

Nichol, B(arrie) P(hillip) 1944-1988 . **CLC 18**
See also CA 53-56; CP 1, 2, 3, 4; DLB 53;
SATA 66

Nicholas of Autrecourt c.
1298-1369 .... **CMLC 108**

Nicholas of Cusa 1401-1464 .... **LC 80**
See also DLB 115

Nichols, John 1940- .... **CLC 38**
See also AMWS 13; CA 9-12R, 190; CAAE
190; CAAS 2; CANR 6, 70, 121, 185;
DLBY 1982; LATS 1:2; MTFW 2005;
TCWW 1, 2

Nichols, Leigh
See Koontz, Dean

Nichols, Peter (Richard) 1927- .... **CLC 5, 36,
65**
See also CA 104; CANR 33, 86; CBD; CD
5, 6; DLB 13, 245; MTCW 1

Nicholson, Linda CLC 65

Ni Chuilleanain, Eilean 1942- .... **PC 34**
See also CA 126; CANR 53, 83; CP 5, 6, 7;
CWP; DLB 40

Nicolas, F. R. E.
See Freeling, Nicolas

Niedecker, Lorine 1903-1970 ..... **CLC 10, 42;
PC 42**
See also CA 25-28; CAP 2; DAM POET;
DLB 48

Nietzsche, Friedrich 1844-1900 ..... **TCLC 10,
18, 55**
See also CA 107; 121; CDWLB 2; DLB
129; EW 7; RGWL 2, 3; TWA

Nietzsche, Friedrich Wilhelm
See Nietzsche, Friedrich

Nievo, Ippolito 1831-1861 .... **NCLC 22**

Nightingale, Anne Redmon 1943- .... **CLC 22**
See also CA 103; DLBY 1986

Nightingale, Florence 1820-1910 ... **TCLC 85**
See also CA 188; DLB 166

Nijo Yoshimoto 1320-1388 .... **CMLC 49**
See also DLB 203

Nik. T. O.
See Annensky, Innokenty (Fyodorovich)

Nin, Anais 1903-1977 ..... **CLC 1, 4, 8, 11, 14,
60, 127; SSC 10; TCLC 224**
See also AITN 2; AMWS 10; BPFB 2; CA
13-16R; 69-72; CANR 22, 53; CN 1, 2;
DAM NOV, POP; DLB 2, 4, 152; EWL
3; GLL 2; MAL 5; MBL; MTCW 1, 2;
MTFW 2005; RGAL 4; RGSF 2

Nisbet, Robert A(lexander)
1913-1996 .... **TCLC 117**
See also CA 25-28R; 153; CANR 17; INT
CANR-17

Nishida, Kitaro 1870-1945 .... **TCLC 83**

Nishiwaki, Junzaburo 1894-1982 .... **PC 15**
See also CA 194; 107; EWL 3; MJW;
RGWL 3

Nissenson, Hugh 1933- .... **CLC 4, 9**
See also CA 17-20R; CANR 27, 108, 151;
CN 5, 6; DLB 28, 335

Nister, Der
See Der Nister

Niven, Larry 1938- .... **CLC 8**
See also AAYA 27; BPFB 2; BYA 10; CA
21-24R, 207; CAAE 207; CAAS 12;
CANR 14, 44, 66, 113, 155, 206; CPW;
DAM POP; DLB 8; MTCW 1, 2; SATA
95, 171; SCFW 1, 2; SFW 4

Niven, Laurence Van Cott
See Niven, Larry

Niven, Laurence VanCott
See Niven, Larry

Nixon, Agnes Eckhardt 1927- .... **CLC 21**
See also CA 110

Nizan, Paul 1905-1940 .... **TCLC 40**
See also CA 161; DLB 72; EWL 3; GFL
1789 to the Present

Nkosi, Lewis 1936-2010 ... **BLC 1:3; CLC 45**
See also BW 1, 3; CA 65-68; CANR 27,
81; CBD; CD 5, 6; DAM MULT; DLB
157, 225; WWE 1

Nodier, (Jean) Charles (Emmanuel)
1780-1844 .... **NCLC 19**
See also DLB 119; GFL 1789 to the Present

Noguchi, Yone 1875-1947 .... **TCLC 80**

Nolan, Brian
See O Nuallain, Brian

Nolan, Christopher 1965-2009 .... **CLC 58**
See also CA 111; 283; CANR 88

Nolan, Christopher John
See Nolan, Christopher

Noon, Jeff 1957- .... **CLC 91**
See also CA 148; CANR 83; DLB 267;
SFW 4

Norden, Charles
See Durrell, Lawrence

Nordhoff, Charles Bernard
1887-1947 .... **TCLC 23**
See also CA 108; 211; DLB 9; LAIT 1;
RHW 1; SATA 23

Norfolk, Lawrence 1963- .... **CLC 76**
See also CA 144; CANR 85; CN 6, 7; DLB
267

Norman, Marsha (Williams) 1947- . **CLC 28,
186; DC 8**
See also CA 105; CABS 3; CAD; CANR
41, 131; CD 5, 6; CSW; CWD; DAM
DRAM; DFS 2; DLB 266; DLBY 1984;
FW; MAL 5

Normyx
See Douglas, (George) Norman

Norris, Benjamin Franklin, Jr.
See Norris, Frank

O'Hara, Frank 1926-1966 .... **CLC 2, 5, 13, 78; PC 45**
See also CA 9-12R; 25-28R; CANR 33; DA3; DAM POET; DLB 5, 16, 193; EWL 3; MAL 5; MTCW 1, 2; MTFW 2005; PFS 8, 12, 34, 38; RGAL 4; WP

O'Hara, John 1905-1970 . **CLC 1, 2, 3, 6, 11, 42; SSC 15**
See also AMW; BPFB 3; CA 5-8R; 25-28R; CANR 31, 60; CDALB 1929-1941; DAM NOV; DLB 9, 86, 324; DLBD 2; EWL 3; MAL 5; MTCW 1, 2; MTFW 2005; NFS 11; RGAL 4; RGSF 2

O'Hara, John Henry
See O'Hara, John

O'Hehir, Diana 1929- .... **CLC 41**
See also CA 245; CANR 177

O'Hehir, Diana F.
See O'Hehir, Diana

Ohiyesa
See Eastman, Charles A(lexander)

Okada, John 1923-1971 .... **AAL**
See also BYA 14; CA 212; DLB 312; NFS 25

O'Kelly, Seamus 1881(?)-1918 .... **SSC 136**

Okigbo, Christopher 1930-1967 ..... **BLC 1:3; CLC 25, 84; PC 7; TCLC 171**
See also AFW; BW 1, 3; CA 77-80; CANR 74; CDWLB 3; DAM MULT, POET; DLB 125; EWL 3; MTCW 1, 2; MTFW 2005; RGEL 2

Okigbo, Christopher Ifenayichukwu
See Okigbo, Christopher

Okri, Ben 1959- .... **BLC 2:3; CLC 87, 223; SSC 127**
See also AFW; BRWS 5; BW 2, 3; CA 130; 138; CANR 65, 128; CN 5, 6, 7; DLB 157, 231, 319, 326; EWL 3; INT CA-138; MTCW 2; MTFW 2005; RGSF 2; SSFS 20; WLIT 2; WWE 1

Old Boy
See Hughes, Thomas

Olds, Sharon 1942- .. **CLC 32, 39, 85; PC 22**
See also AMWS 10; CA 101; CANR 18, 41, 66, 98, 135, 211; CP 5, 6, 7; CPW; CWP; DAM POET; DLB 120; MAL 5; MTCW 2; MTFW 2005; PFS 17

Oldstyle, Jonathan
See Irving, Washington

Olesha, Iurii
See Olesha, Yuri (Karlovich)

Olesha, Iurii Karlovich
See Olesha, Yuri (Karlovich)

Olesha, Yuri (Karlovich) 1899-1960 . **CLC 8; SSC 69; TCLC 136**
See also CA 85-88; DLB 272; EW 11; EWL 3; RGWL 2, 3

Olesha, Yury Karlovich
See Olesha, Yuri (Karlovich)

Oliphant, Mrs.
See Oliphant, Margaret (Oliphant Wilson)

Oliphant, Laurence 1829(?)-1888 .. **NCLC 47**
See also DLB 18, 166

Oliphant, Margaret (Oliphant Wilson) 1828-1897 ... **NCLC 11, 61, 221; SSC 25**
See also BRWS 10; DLB 18, 159, 190; HGG; RGEL 2; RGSF 2; SUFW

Oliver, Mary 1935- ... **CLC 19, 34, 98; PC 75**
See also AMWS 7; CA 21-24R; CANR 9, 43, 84, 92, 138; CP 4, 5, 6, 7; CWP; DLB 5, 193, 342; EWL 3; MTFW 2005; PFS 15, 31

Olivi, Peter 1248-1298 .... **CMLC 114**

Olivier, Laurence (Kerr) 1907-1989 . **CLC 20**
See also CA 111; 150; 129

O.L.S.
See Russell, George William

Olsen, Tillie 1912-2007 .... **CLC 4, 13, 114; SSC 11, 103**
See also AAYA 51; AMWS 13; BYA 11; CA 1-4R; 256; CANR 1, 43, 74, 132; CDALBS; CN 2, 3, 4, 5, 6, 7; DA; DA3; DAB; DAC; DAM MST; DLB 28, 206; DLBY 1980; EWL 3; EXPS; FW; MAL 5; MTCW 1, 2; MTFW 2005; RGAL 4; RGSF 2; SSFS 1, 32; TCLE 1:2; TCWW 2; TUS

Olson, Charles 1910-1970 . **CLC 1, 2, 5, 6, 9, 11, 29; PC 19**
See also AMWS 2; CA 13-16; 25-28R; CABS 2; CANR 35, 61; CAP 1; CP 1; DAM POET; DLB 5, 16, 193; EWL 3; MAL 5; MTCW 1, 2; RGAL 4; WP

Olson, Charles John
See Olson, Charles

Olson, Merle Theodore
See Olson, Toby

Olson, Toby 1937- .... **CLC 28**
See also CA 65-68; CAAS 11; CANR 9, 31, 84, 175; CP 3, 4, 5, 6, 7

Olyesha, Yuri
See Olesha, Yuri (Karlovich)

Olympiodorus of Thebes c. 375-c. 430 .... **CMLC 59**

Omar Khayyam
See Khayyam, Omar

Ondaatje, Michael 1943- ..... **CLC 14, 29, 51, 76, 180, 258; PC 28**
See also AAYA 66; CA 77-80; CANR 42, 74, 109, 133, 172; CN 5, 6, 7; CP 1, 2, 3, 4, 5, 6, 7; DA3; DAB; DAC; DAM MST; DLB 60, 323, 326; EWL 3; LATS 1:2; LMFS 2; MTCW 2; MTFW 2005; NFS 23; PFS 8, 19; TCLE 1:2; TWA; WWE 1

Ondaatje, Philip Michael
See Ondaatje, Michael

Oneal, Elizabeth 1934- .... **CLC 30**
See also AAYA 5, 41; BYA 13; CA 106; CANR 28, 84; CLR 13; JRDA; MAICYA 1, 2; SATA 30, 82; WYA; YAW

Oneal, Zibby
See Oneal, Elizabeth

O'Neill, Eugene 1888-1953 ..... **DC 20; TCLC 1, 6, 27, 49, 225; WLC 4**
See also AAYA 54; AITN 1; AMW; AMWC 1; CA 110; 132; CAD; CANR 131; CDALB 1929-1941; DA; DA3; DAB; DAC; DAM DRAM, MST; DFS 2, 4, 5, 6, 9, 11, 12, 16, 20, 26, 27; DLB 7, 331; EWL 3; LAIT 3; LMFS 2; MAL 5; MTCW 1, 2; MTFW 2005; RGAL 4; TUS

O'Neill, Eugene Gladstone
See O'Neill, Eugene

Onetti, Juan Carlos 1909-1994 ... **CLC 7, 10; HLCS 2; SSC 23; TCLC 131**
See also CA 85-88; 145; CANR 32, 63; CDWLB 3; CWW 2; DAM MULT, NOV; DLB 113; EWL 3; HW 1, 2; LAW; MTCW 1, 2; MTFW 2005; RGSF 2

O'Nolan, Brian
See O Nuallain, Brian

O Nuallain, Brian 1911-1966 .... **CLC 1, 4, 5, 7, 10, 47**
See also BRWS 2; CA 21-22; 25-28R; CAP 2; DLB 231; EWL 3; FANT; RGEL 2; TEA

Ophuls, Max
See Ophuls, Max

Ophuls, Max 1902-1957 .... **TCLC 79**
See also CA 113

Opie, Amelia 1769-1853 .... **NCLC 65**
See also DLB 116, 159; RGEL 2

Oppen, George 1908-1984 ..... **CLC 7, 13, 34; PC 35; TCLC 107**
See also CA 13-16R; 113; CANR 8, 82; CP 1, 2, 3; DLB 5, 165

Oppenheim, E(dward) Phillips 1866-1946 .... **TCLC 45**
See also CA 111; 202; CMW 4; DLB 70

Oppenheimer, Max
See Ophuls, Max

Opuls, Max
See Ophuls, Max

Orage, A(lfred) R(ichard) 1873-1934 .... **TCLC 157**
See also CA 122

Origen c. 185-c. 254 .... **CMLC 19**

Orlovitz, Gil 1918-1973 .... **CLC 22**
See also CA 77-80; 45-48; CN 1; CP 1, 2; DLB 2, 5

Orosius c. 385-c. 420 .... **CMLC 100**

O'Rourke, Patrick Jake
See O'Rourke, P.J.

O'Rourke, P.J. 1947- .... **CLC 209**
See also CA 77-80; CANR 13, 41, 67, 111, 155; CPW; DAM POP; DLB 185

Orris
See Ingelow, Jean

Ortega y Gasset, Jose 1883-1955 ...... **HLC 2; TCLC 9**
See also CA 106; 130; DAM MULT; EW 9; EWL 3; HW 1, 2; MTCW 1, 2; MTFW 2005

Ortese, Anna Maria 1914-1998 .... **CLC 89**
See also DLB 177; EWL 3

Ortiz, Simon
See Ortiz, Simon J.

Ortiz, Simon J. 1941- . **CLC 45, 208; NNAL; PC 17**
See also AMWS 4; CA 134; CANR 69, 118, 164; CP 3, 4, 5, 6, 7; DAM MULT, POET; DLB 120, 175, 256, 342; EXPP; MAL 5; PFS 4, 16; RGAL 4; SSFS 22; TCWW 2

Ortiz, Simon Joseph
See Ortiz, Simon J.

Orton, Joe
See Orton, John Kingsley

Orton, John Kingsley 1933-1967 .... **CLC 4, 13, 43; DC 3; TCLC 157**
See also BRWS 5; CA 85-88; CANR 35, 66; CBD; CDBLB 1960 to Present; DAM DRAM; DFS 3, 6; DLB 13, 310; GLL 1; MTCW 1, 2; MTFW 2005; RGEL 2; TEA; WLIT 4

Orwell, George 1903-1950 .... **SSC 68; TCLC 2, 6, 15, 31, 51, 123, 128, 129; WLC 4**
See also BPFB 3; BRW 7; BYA 5; CA 104; 132; CDBLB 1945-1960; CLR 68; DA; DA3; DAB; DAC; DAM MST, NOV; DLB 15, 98, 195, 255; EWL 3; EXPN; LAIT 4, 5; LATS 1:1; MTCW 1, 2; MTFW 2005; NFS 3, 7; RGEL 2; SATA 29; SCFW 1, 2; SFW 4; SSFS 4; TEA; WLIT 4; YAW X

Osborne, David
See Silverberg, Robert

Osborne, Dorothy 1627-1695 .... **LC 141**

Osborne, George
See Silverberg, Robert

Osborne, John 1929-1994 .... **CLC 1, 2, 5, 11, 45; DC 38; TCLC 153; WLC 4**
See also BRWS 1; CA 13-16R; 147; CANR 21, 56; CBD; CDBLB 1945-1960; DA; DAB; DAC; DAM DRAM, MST; DFS 4, 19, 24; DLB 13; EWL 3; MTCW 1, 2; MTFW 2005; RGEL 2

Osborne, Lawrence 1958- .... **CLC 50**
See also CA 189; CANR 152

Osbourne, Lloyd 1868-1947 .... **TCLC 93**

Osceola
See Blixen, Karen

Osgood, Frances Sargent 1811-1850 .... **NCLC 141**
See also DLB 250

Park, Jordan
See Kornbluth, C(yril) M.; Pohl, Frederik
Park, Robert E(zra) 1864-1944 ..... **TCLC 73**
See also CA 122; 165
Parker, Bert
See Ellison, Harlan
Parker, Dorothy 1893-1967 .... **CLC 15, 68;**
DC 40; PC 28; SSC 2, 101; TCLC 143
See also AMWS 9; CA 19-20; 25-28R; CAP
2; DA3; DAM POET; DLB 11, 45, 86;
EXPP; FW; MAL 5; MBL; MTCW 1, 2;
MTFW 2005; PFS 18; RGAL 4; RGSF 2;
TUS
Parker, Dorothy Rothschild
See Parker, Dorothy
Parker, Robert B. 1932-2010 .... **CLC 27, 283**
See also AAYA 28; BEST 89:4; BPFB 3;
CA 49-52; CANR 1, 26, 52, 89, 128, 165,
200; CMW 4; CPW; DAM NOV, POP;
DLB 306; INT CANR-26; MSW; MTCW
1; MTFW 2005
Parker, Robert Brown
See Parker, Robert B.
Parker, Theodore 1810-1860 .... **NCLC 186**
See also DLB 1, 235
Parkes, Lucas
See Harris, John (Wyndham Parkes Lucas)
Beynon
Parkin, Frank 1940- .... **CLC 43**
See also CA 147
Parkman, Francis, Jr. 1823-1893 .. **NCLC 12**
See also AMWS 2; DLB 1, 30, 183, 186,
235; RGAL 4
Parks, Gordon 1912-2006 . **BLC 1:3; CLC 1,**
16
See also AAYA 36; AITN 2; BW 2, 3; CA
41-44R; 249; CANR 26, 66, 145; DA3;
DAM MULT; DLB 33; MTCW 2; MTFW
2005; NFS 32; SATA 8, 108; SATA-Obit
175
Parks, Gordon Roger Alexander
See Parks, Gordon
Parks, Suzan-Lori 1964(?)- ..... **BLC 2:3; DC**
23
See also AAYA 55; CA 201; CAD; CD 5,
6; CWD; DFS 22; DLB 341; RGAL 4
Parks, Tim 1954- .... **CLC 147**
See also CA 126; 131; CANR 77, 144, 202;
CN 7; DLB 231; INT CA-131
Parks, Timothy Harold
See Parks, Tim
Parmenides c. 515B.C.-c.
450B.C. .... **CMLC 22**
See also DLB 176
Parnell, Thomas 1679-1718 .... **LC 3**
See also DLB 95; RGEL 2
Parr, Catherine c. 1513(?)-1548 .... **LC 86**
See also DLB 136
Parra, Nicanor 1914- ... **CLC 2, 102; HLC 2;**
PC 39
See also CA 85-88; CANR 32; CWW 2;
DAM MULT; DLB 283; EWL 3; HW 1;
LAW; MTCW 1
Parra Sanojo, Ana Teresa de la 1890-1936
See de la Parra, Teresa
Parrish, Mary Frances
See Fisher, M(ary) F(rances) K(ennedy)
Parshchikov, Aleksei 1954- .... **CLC 59**
See also DLB 285
Parshchikov, Aleksei Maksimovich
See Parshchikov, Aleksei
Parson, Professor
See Coleridge, Samuel Taylor
Parson Lot
See Kingsley, Charles
Parton, Sara Payson Willis
1811-1872 .... **NCLC 86**
See also DLB 43, 74, 239

Partridge, Anthony
See Oppenheim, E(dward) Phillips
Pascal, Blaise 1623-1662 .... **LC 35**
See also DLB 268; EW 3; GFL Beginnings
to 1789; RGWL 2, 3; TWA
Pascoli, Giovanni 1855-1912 .... **TCLC 45**
See also CA 170; EW 7; EWL 3
Pasolini, Pier Paolo 1922-1975 .. **CLC 20, 37,**
106; PC 17
See also CA 93-96; 61-64; CANR 63; DLB
128, 177; EWL 3; MTCW 1; RGWL 2, 3
Pasquini
See Silone, Ignazio
Pastan, Linda (Olenik) 1932- .... **CLC 27**
See also CA 61-64; CANR 18, 40, 61, 113;
CP 3, 4, 5, 6, 7; CSW; CWP; DAM
POET; DLB 5; PFS 8, 25, 32
Pasternak, Boris 1890-1960 ... **CLC 7, 10, 18,**
63; PC 6; SSC 31; TCLC 188; WLC 4
See also BPFB 3; CA 127; 116; DA; DA3;
DAB; DAC; DAM MST, NOV, POET;
DLB 302, 331; EW 10; MTCW 1, 2;
MTFW 2005; NFS 26; RGSF 2; RGWL
2, 3; TWA; WP
Pasternak, Boris Leonidovich
See Pasternak, Boris
Patchen, Kenneth 1911-1972 .... **CLC 1, 2, 18**
See also BG 1:3; CA 1-4R; 33-36R; CANR
3, 35; CN 1; CP 1; DAM POET; DLB 16,
48; EWL 3; MAL 5; MTCW 1; RGAL 4
Patchett, Ann 1963- .... **CLC 244**
See also AAYA 69; AMWS 12; CA 139;
CANR 64, 110, 167, 200; DLB 350;
MTFW 2005; NFS 30
Pater, Walter (Horatio) 1839-1894 . **NCLC 7,**
90, 159
See also BRW 5; CDBLB 1832-1890; DLB
57, 156; RGEL 2; TEA
Paterson, A(ndrew) B(arton)
1864-1941 .... **TCLC 32**
See also CA 155; DLB 230; RGEL 2; SATA
97
Paterson, Banjo
See Paterson, A(ndrew) B(arton)
Paterson, Katherine 1932- .... **CLC 12, 30**
See also AAYA 1, 31; BYA 1, 2, 7; CA 21-
24R; CANR 28, 59, 111, 173, 196; CLR
7, 50, 127; CWRI 5; DLB 52; JRDA;
LAIT 4; MAICYA 1, 2; MAICYAS 1;
MTCW 1; SATA 13, 53, 92, 133, 204;
WYA; YAW
Paterson, Katherine Womeldorf
See Paterson, Katherine
Patmore, Coventry Kersey Dighton
1823-1896 .... **NCLC 9; PC 59**
See also DLB 35, 98; RGEL 2; TEA
Paton, Alan 1903-1988 ..... **CLC 4, 10, 25, 55,**
106; TCLC 165; WLC 4
See also AAYA 26; AFW; BPFB 3; BRWS
2; BYA 1; CA 13-16; 125; CANR 22;
CAP 1; CN 1, 2, 3, 4; DA; DA3; DAB;
DAC; DAM MST, NOV; DLB 225;
DLBD 17; EWL 3; EXPN; LAIT 4;
MTCW 1, 2; MTFW 2005; NFS 3, 12;
RGEL 2; SATA 11; SATA-Obit 56; SSFS
29; TWA; WLIT 2; WWE 1
Paton, Alan Stewart
See Paton, Alan
Paton Walsh, Gillian
See Paton Walsh, Jill
Paton Walsh, Jill 1937- .... **CLC 35**
See also AAYA 11, 47; BYA 1, 8; CA 262;
CAAE 262; CANR 38, 83, 158; CLR 2,
6, 128; DLB 161; JRDA; MAICYA 1, 2;
SAAS 3; SATA 4, 72, 109, 190; SATA-
Essay 190; WYA; YAW
Patsauq, Markoosie 1942- .... **NNAL**
See also CA 101; CLR 23; CWRI 5; DAM
MULT

Patterson, (Horace) Orlando (Lloyd)
1940- .... **BLCS**
See also CA 65-68; CANR 27, 84;
CN 1, 2, 3, 4, 5, 6
Patton, George S(mith), Jr.
1885-1945 .... **TCLC 79**
See also CA 189
Paulding, James Kirke 1778-1860 ... **NCLC 2**
See also DLB 3, 59, 74, 250; RGAL 4
Paulin, Thomas Neilson
See Paulin, Tom
Paulin, Tom 1949- .... **CLC 37, 177**
See also CA 123; 128; CANR 98; CP 3, 4,
5, 6, 7; DLB 40
Pausanias c. 1st cent. - .... **CMLC 36**
Paustovsky, Konstantin (Georgievich)
1892-1968 .... **CLC 40**
See also CA 93-96; 25-28R; DLB 272;
EWL 3
Pavese, Cesare 1908-1950 .... **PC 13; SSC 19;**
TCLC 3, 240
See also CA 104; 169; DLB 128, 177; EW
12; EWL 3; PFS 20; RGSF 2; RGWL 2,
3; TWA; WLIT 7
Pavic, Milorad 1929-2009 .... **CLC 60**
See also CA 136; CDWLB 4; CWW 2; DLB
181; EWL 3; RGWL 3
Pavlov, Ivan Petrovich 1849-1936 . **TCLC 91**
See also CA 118; 180
Pavlova, Karolina Karlovna
1807-1893 .... **NCLC 138**
See also DLB 205
Payne, Alan
See Jakes, John
Payne, Rachel Ann
See Jakes, John
Paz, Gil
See Lugones, Leopoldo
Paz, Octavio 1914-1998 . **CLC 3, 4, 6, 10, 19,**
51, 65, 119; HLC 2; PC 1, 48; TCLC
211; WLC 4
See also AAYA 50; CA 73-76; 165; CANR
32, 65, 104; CWW 2; DA; DA3; DAB;
DAC; DAM MST, MULT, POET; DLB
290, 331; DLBY 1990, 1998; DNFS 1;
EWL 3; HW 1, 2; LAW; LAWS 1; MTCW
1, 2; MTFW 2005; PFS 18, 30, 38; RGWL
2, 3; SSFS 13; TWA; WLIT 1
p'Bitek, Okot 1931-1982 . **BLC 1:3; CLC 96;**
TCLC 149
See also AFW; BW 2, 3; CA 124; 107;
CANR 82; CP 1, 2, 3; DAM MULT; DLB
125; EWL 3; MTCW 1, 2; MTFW 2005;
RGEL 2; WLIT 2
Peabody, Elizabeth Palmer
1804-1894 .... **NCLC 169**
See also DLB 1, 223
Peacham, Henry 1578-1644(?) .... **LC 119**
See also DLB 151
Peacock, Molly 1947- .... **CLC 60**
See also CA 103, 262; CAAE 262; CAAS
21; CANR 52, 84; CP 5, 6, 7; CWP; DLB
120, 282
Peacock, Thomas Love
1785-1866 .... **NCLC 22; PC 87**
See also BRW 4; DLB 96, 116; RGEL 2;
RGSF 2
Peake, Mervyn 1911-1968 .... **CLC 7, 54**
See also CA 5-8R; 25-28R; CANR 3; DLB
15, 160, 255; FANT; MTCW 1; RGEL 2;
SATA 23; SFW 4
Pearce, Ann Philippa
See Pearce, Philippa
Pearce, Philippa 1920-2006 .... **CLC 21**
See also BYA 5; CA 5-8R; 255; CANR 4,
109; CLR 9; CWRI 5; DLB 161; FANT;
MAICYA 1; SATA 1, 67, 129; SATA-Obit
179

Phillips, Caryl 1958- ..... **BLCS; CLC 96, 224**
See also BRWS 5; BW 2; CA 141; CANR 63, 104, 140, 195; CBD; CD 5, 6; CN 5, 6, 7; DA3; DAM MULT; DLB 157; EWL 3; MTCW 2; MTFW 2005; WLIT 4; WWE 1

Phillips, David Graham
1867-1911 .... **TCLC 44**
See also CA 108; 176; DLB 9, 12, 303; RGAL 4

Phillips, Jack
See Sandburg, Carl

Phillips, Jayne Anne 1952- .... **CLC 15, 33, 139, 296; SSC 16**
See also AAYA 57; BPFB 3; CA 101; CANR 24, 50, 96, 200; CN 4, 5, 6, 7; CSW; DLBY 1980; INT CANR-24; MTCW 1, 2; MTFW 2005; RGAL 4; RGSF 2; SSFS 4

Phillips, Richard
See Dick, Philip K.

Phillips, Robert (Schaeffer) 1938- .... **CLC 28**
See also CA 17-20R; CAAS 13; CANR 8; DLB 105

Phillips, Ward
See Lovecraft, H. P.

Philo c. 20B.C.-c. 50 .... **CMLC 100**
See also DLB 176

Philostratus, Flavius c. 179-c.
244 .... **CMLC 62**

Phiradausi
See Ferdowsi, Abu'l Qasem

Piccolo, Lucio 1901-1969 .... **CLC 13**
See also CA 97-100; DLB 114; EWL 3

Pickthall, Marjorie L(owry) C(hristie)
1883-1922 .... **TCLC 21**
See also CA 107; DLB 92

Pico della Mirandola, Giovanni
1463-1494 .... **LC 15**
See also LMFS 1

Piercy, Marge 1936- .... **CLC 3, 6, 14, 18, 27, 62, 128; PC 29**
See also BPFB 3; CA 21-24R, 187; CAAE 187; CAAS 1; CANR 13, 43, 66, 111; CN 3, 4, 5, 6, 7; CP 1, 2, 3, 4, 5, 6, 7; CWP; DLB 120, 227; EXPP; FW; MAL 5; MTCW 1, 2; MTFW 2005; PFS 9, 22, 32; SFW 4

Piers, Robert
See Anthony, Piers

Pieyre de Mandiargues, Andre
1909-1991 .... **CLC 41**
See also CA 103; 136; CANR 22, 82; DLB 83; EWL 3; GFL 1789 to the Present

Pil'niak, Boris
See Vogau, Boris Andreyevich

Pil'niak, Boris Andreevich
See Vogau, Boris Andreyevich

Pilnyak, Boris 1894-1938
See Vogau, Boris Andreyevich

Pinchback, Eugene
See Toomer, Jean

Pincherle, Alberto 1907-1990 .. **CLC 2, 7, 11, 27, 46; SSC 26**
See also CA 25-28R; 132; CANR 33, 63, 142; DAM NOV; DLB 127; EW 12; EWL 3; MTCW 2, 3; MTFW 2005; RGSF 2; RGWL 2, 3; WLIT 7

Pinckney, Darryl 1953- .... **CLC 76**
See also BW 2, 3; CA 143; CANR 79

Pindar 518(?)B.C.-438(?)B.C. .... **CMLC 12, 130; PC 19**
See also AW 1; CDWLB 1; DLB 176; RGWL 2

Pineda, Cecile 1942- .... **CLC 39**
See also CA 118; DLB 209

Pinero, Arthur Wing 1855-1934 .... **TCLC 32**
See also CA 110; 153; DAM DRAM; DLB 10, 344; RGEL 2

Pinero, Miguel (Antonio Gomez)
1946-1988 .... **CLC 4, 55**
See also CA 61-64; 125; CAD; CANR 29, 90; DLB 266; HW 1; LLW

Pinget, Robert 1919-1997 .... **CLC 7, 13, 37**
See also CA 85-88; 160; CWW 2; DLB 83; EWL 3; GFL 1789 to the Present

Pink Floyd
See Barrett, Syd; Gilmour, David; Mason, Nick; Waters, Roger; Wright, Rick

Pinkney, Edward 1802-1828 .... **NCLC 31**
See also DLB 248

Pinkwater, D. Manus
See Pinkwater, Daniel

Pinkwater, Daniel 1941- .... **CLC 35**
See also AAYA 1, 46; BYA 9; CA 29-32R; CANR 12, 38, 89, 143; CLR 4; CSW; FANT; JRDA; MAICYA 1, 2; SAAS 3; SATA 8, 46, 76, 114, 158, 210; SFW 4; YAW

Pinkwater, Daniel M.
See Pinkwater, Daniel

Pinkwater, Daniel Manus
See Pinkwater, Daniel

Pinkwater, Manus
See Pinkwater, Daniel

Pinsky, Robert 1940- .... **CLC 9, 19, 38, 94, 121, 216; PC 27**
See also AMWS 6; CA 29-32R; CAAS 4; CANR 58, 97, 138, 177; CP 3, 4, 5, 6, 7; DA3; DAM POET; DLBY 1982, 1998; MAL 5; MTCW 2; MTFW 2005; PFS 18; RGAL 4; TCLE 1:2

Pinta, Harold
See Pinter, Harold

Pinter, Harold 1930-2008 ...... **CLC 1, 3, 6, 9, 11, 15, 27, 58, 73, 199; DC 15; WLC 4**
See also BRWR 1; BRWS 1; CA 5-8R; 280; CANR 33, 65, 112, 145; CBD; CD 5, 6; CDBLB 1960 to Present; CP 1; DA; DA3; DAB; DAC; DAM DRAM, MST; DFS 3, 5, 7, 14, 25; DLB 13, 310, 331; EWL 3; IDFW 3, 4; LMFS 2; MTCW 1, 2; MTFW 2005; RGEL 2; RGHL; TEA

Piozzi, Hester Lynch (Thrale)
1741-1821 .... **NCLC 57**
See also DLB 104, 142

Pirandello, Luigi 1867-1936 .. **DC 5; SSC 22, 148; TCLC 4, 29, 172; WLC 4**
See also CA 104; 153; CANR 103; DA; DA3; DAB; DAC; DAM DRAM, MST; DFS 4, 9; DLB 264, 331; EW 8; EWL 3; MTCW 2; MTFW 2005; RGSF 2; RGWL 2, 3; SSFS 30, 33; WLIT 7

Pirdousi
See Ferdowsi, Abu'l Qasem

Pirdousi, Abu-l-Qasim
See Ferdowsi, Abu'l Qasem

Pirsig, Robert M(aynard) 1928- ... **CLC 4, 6, 73**
See also CA 53-56; CANR 42, 74; CPW 1; DA3; DAM POP; MTCW 1, 2; MTFW 2005; NFS 31; SATA 39

Pisan, Christine de
See Christine de Pizan

Pisarev, Dmitrii Ivanovich
See Pisarev, Dmitry Ivanovich

Pisarev, Dmitry Ivanovich
1840-1868 .... **NCLC 25**
See also DLB 277

Pix, Mary (Griffith) 1666-1709 ..... **LC 8, 149**
See also DLB 80

Pixerecourt, (Rene Charles) Guilbert de
1773-1844 .... **NCLC 39**
See also DLB 192; GFL 1789 to the Present

Plaatje, Sol(omon) T(shekisho)
1878-1932 .... **BLCS; TCLC 73**
See also BW 2, 3; CA 141; CANR 79; DLB 125, 225

Plaidy, Jean
See Hibbert, Eleanor Alice Burford

Planche, James Robinson
1796-1880 .... **NCLC 42**
See also RGEL 2

Plant, Robert 1948- .... **CLC 12**

Plante, David 1940- .... **CLC 7, 23, 38**
See also CA 37-40R; CANR 12, 36, 58, 82, 152, 191; CN 2, 3, 4, 5, 6, 7; DAM NOV; DLBY 1983; INT CANR-12; MTCW 1

Plante, David Robert
See Plante, David

Plath, Sylvia 1932-1963 ..... **CLC 1, 2, 3, 5, 9, 11, 14, 17, 50, 51, 62, 111; PC 1, 37; WLC 4**
See also AAYA 13; AMWR 2; AMWS 1; BPFB 3; CA 19-20; CANR 34, 101; CAP 2; CDALB 1941-1968; DA; DA3; DAB; DAC; DAM MST, POET; DLB 5, 6, 152; EWL 3; EXPN; EXPP; FL 1:6; FW; LAIT 4; MAL 5; MBL; MTCW 1, 2; MTFW 2005; NFS 1; PAB; PFS 1, 15, 28, 33; RGAL 4; SATA 96; TUS; WP; YAW

Plato c. 428B.C.-347B.C. .... **CMLC 8, 75, 98; WLCS**
See also AW 1; CDWLB 1; DA; DA3; DAB; DAC; DAM MST; DLB 176; LAIT 1; LATS 1:1; RGWL 2, 3; WLIT 8

Platonov, Andrei
See Klimentov, Andrei Platonovich

Platonov, Andrei Platonovich
See Klimentov, Andrei Platonovich

Platonov, Andrey Platonovich
See Klimentov, Andrei Platonovich

Platt, Kin 1911- .... **CLC 26**
See also AAYA 11; CA 17-20R; CANR 11; JRDA; SAAS 17; SATA 21, 86; WYA

Plautus c. 254B.C.-c. 184B.C. .... **CMLC 24, 92; DC 6**
See also AW 1; CDWLB 1; DLB 211; RGWL 2, 3; WLIT 8

Plick et Plock
See Simenon, Georges

Plieksans, Janis
See Rainis, Janis

Plimpton, George 1927-2003 .... **CLC 36**
See also AITN 1; AMWS 16; CA 21-24R; 224; CANR 32, 70, 103, 133; DLB 185, 241; MTCW 1, 2; MTFW 2005; SATA 10; SATA-Obit 150

Plimpton, George Ames
See Plimpton, George

Pliny the Elder c. 23-79 .... **CMLC 23**
See also DLB 211

Pliny the Younger c. 61-c. 112 ...... **CMLC 62**
See also AW 2; DLB 211

Plomer, William Charles Franklin
1903-1973 .... **CLC 4, 8**
See also AFW; BRWS 11; CA 21-22; CANR 34; CAP 2; CN 1; CP 1, 2; DLB 20, 162, 191, 225; EWL 3; MTCW 1; RGEL 2; RGSF 2; SATA 24

Plotinus 204-270 .... **CMLC 46**
See also CDWLB 1; DLB 176

Plowman, Piers
See Kavanagh, Patrick (Joseph)

Plum, J.
See Wodehouse, P. G.

Plumly, Stanley 1939- .... **CLC 33**
See also CA 108; 110; CANR 97, 185; CP 3, 4, 5, 6, 7; DLB 5, 193; INT CA-110

Plumly, Stanley Ross
See Plumly, Stanley

Plumpe, Friedrich Wilhelm
See Murnau, F.W.

Plutarch c. 46-c. 120 .... **CMLC 60**
See also AW 2; CDWLB 1; DLB 176; RGWL 2, 3; TWA; WLIT 8

Author Index

Pratchett, Terry 1948- .... **CLC 197**
See also AAYA 19, 54; BPFB 3; CA 143;
CANR 87, 126, 170; CLR 64; CN 6, 7;
CPW; CWRI 5; FANT; MTFW 2005;
SATA 82, 139, 185; SFW 4; SUFW 2
Pratolini, Vasco 1913-1991 .... **TCLC 124**
See also CA 211; DLB 177; EWL 3; RGWL
2, 3
Pratt, E(dwin) J(ohn) 1883(?)-1964 . **CLC 19**
See also CA 141; 93-96; CANR 77; DAC;
DAM POET; DLB 92; EWL 3; RGEL 2;
TWA
Premacanda
See Srivastava, Dhanpat Rai
Premchand
See Srivastava, Dhanpat Rai
Premchand, Munshi
See Srivastava, Dhanpat Rai
Prem Chand, Munshi
See Srivastava, Dhanpat Rai
Prescott, William Hickling
1796-1859 .... **NCLC 163**
See also DLB 1, 30, 59, 235
Preseren, France 1800-1849 .... **NCLC 127**
See also CDWLB 4; DLB 147
Preston, Thomas 1537-1598 .... **LC 189**
See also DLB 62
Preussler, Otfried 1923- .... **CLC 17**
See also CA 77-80; SATA 24
Prevert, Jacques 1900-1977 .... **CLC 15**
See also CA 77-80; 69-72; CANR 29, 61,
207; DLB 258; EWL 3; GFL 1789 to the
Present; IDFW 3, 4; MTCW 1; RGWL 2,
3; SATA-Obit 30
Prevert, Jacques Henri Marie
See Prevert, Jacques
Prevost, (Antoine Francois)
1697-1763 .... **LC 1, 174**
See also DLB 314; EW 4; GFL Beginnings
to 1789; RGWL 2, 3
Price, Edward Reynolds
See Price, Reynolds
Price, Reynolds 1933-2011 .... **CLC 3, 6, 13,
43, 50, 63, 212; SSC 22**
See also AMWS 6; CA 1-4R; CANR 1, 37,
57, 87, 128, 177; CN 1, 2, 3, 4, 5, 6, 7;
CSW; DAM NOV; DLB 2, 218, 278;
EWL 3; INT CANR-37; MAL 5; MTFW
2005; NFS 18
Price, Richard 1949- .... **CLC 6, 12, 299**
See also CA 49-52; CANR 3, 147, 190; CN
7; DLBY 1981
Prichard, Katharine Susannah
1883-1969 .... **CLC 46**
See also CA 11-12; CANR 33; CAP 1; DLB
260; MTCW 1; RGEL 2; RGSF 2; SATA
66
Priestley, J(ohn) B(oynton)
1894-1984 .... **CLC 2, 5, 9, 34**
See also BRW 7; CA 9-12R; 113; CANR
33; CDBLB 1914-1945; CN 1, 2, 3; DA3;
DAM DRAM, NOV; DLB 10, 34, 77,
100, 139; DLBY 1984; EWL 3; MTCW
1, 2; MTFW 2005; RGEL 2; SFW 4
Prince 1958- .... **CLC 35**
See also CA 213
Prince, F(rank) T(empleton)
1912-2003 .... **CLC 22**
See also CA 101; 219; CANR 43, 79; CP 1,
2, 3, 4, 5, 6, 7; DLB 20
Prince Kropotkin
See Kropotkin, Peter
Prior, Matthew 1664-1721 ...... **LC 4; PC 102**
See also DLB 95; RGEL 2
Prishvin, Mikhail 1873-1954 .... **TCLC 75**
See also DLB 272; EWL 3 !**
Prishvin, Mikhail Mikhailovich
See Prishvin, Mikhail

Pritchard, William H(arrison)
1932- .... **CLC 34**
See also CA 65-68; CANR 23, 95; DLB
111
Pritchett, V(ictor) S(awdon)
1900-1997 .. **CLC 5, 13, 15, 41; SSC 14,
126**
See also BPFB 3; BRWS 3; CA 61-64; 157;
CANR 31, 63; CN 1, 2, 3, 4, 5, 6; DA3;
DAM NOV; DLB 15, 139; EWL 3;
MTCW 1, 2; MTFW 2005; RGEL 2;
RGSF 2; TEA
Private 19022
See Manning, Frederic
Probst, Mark 1925- .... **CLC 59**
See also CA 130
Procaccino, Michael
See Cristofer, Michael
Proclus c. 412-c. 485 .... **CMLC 81**
Prokosch, Frederic 1908-1989 ...... **CLC 4, 48**
See also CA 73-76; 128; CANR 82; CN 1,
2, 3, 4; CP 1, 2, 3, 4; DLB 48; MTCW 2
Propertius, Sextus c. 50B.C.-c.
16B.C. .... **CMLC 32**
See also AW 2; CDWLB 1; DLB 211;
RGWL 2, 3; WLIT 8
Prophet, The
See Dreiser, Theodore
Prose, Francine 1947- .... **CLC 45, 231**
See also AMWS 16; CA 109; 112; CANR
46, 95, 132, 175; DLB 234; MTFW 2005;
SATA 101, 149, 198
Protagoras c. 490B.C.-420B.C. ...... **CMLC 85**
See also DLB 176
Proudhon
See Cunha, Euclides (Rodrigues Pimenta)
da
Proulx, Annie 1935- . **CLC 81, 158, 250; SSC
128**
See also AAYA 81; AMWS 7; BPFB 3; CA
145; CANR 65, 110, 206; CN 6, 7; CPW
1; DA3; DAM POP; DLB 335, 350; MAL
5; MTCW 2; MTFW 2005; SSFS 18, 23
Proulx, E. Annie
See Proulx, Annie
Proulx, Edna Annie
See Proulx, Annie
Proust, Marcel 1871-1922 ..... **SSC 75; TCLC
7, 13, 33, 220; WLC 5**
See also AAYA 58; BPFB 3; CA 104; 120;
CANR 110; DA; DA3; DAB; DAC; DAM
MST, NOV; DLB 65; EW 8; EWL 3; GFL
1789 to the Present; MTCW 1, 2; MTFW
2005; RGWL 2, 3; TWA
**Proust, Valentin-Louis-George-Eugene
Marcel**
See Proust, Marcel
Prowler, Harley
See Masters, Edgar Lee
Prudentius, Aurelius Clemens 348-c.
405 .... **CMLC 78**
See also EW 1; RGWL 2, 3
Prudhomme, Rene Francois Armand
See Sully Prudhomme, Rene-Francois-
Armand
Prus, Boleslaw 1845-1912 .... **TCLC 48**
See also RGWL 2, 3
Prynne, William 1600-1669 .... **LC 148**
Prynne, Xavier
See Hardwick, Elizabeth
Pryor, Aaron Richard
See Pryor, Richard
Pryor, Richard 1940-2005 .... **CLC 26**
See also CA 122; 152; 246
Pryor, Richard Franklin Lenox Thomas
See Pryor, Richard
Przybyszewski, Stanislaw
1868-1927 .... **TCLC 36**
See also CA 160; DLB 66; EWL 3

Pseudo-Dionysius the Areopagite fl. c. 5th
cent. - .... **CMLC 89**
See also DLB 115
Pteleon
See Grieve, C. M.
Puckett, Lute
See Masters, Edgar Lee
Puig, Manuel 1932-1990 .... **CLC 3, 5, 10, 28,
65, 133; HLC 2; TCLC 227**
See also BPFB 3; CA 45-48; CANR 2, 32,
63; CDWLB 3; DA3; DAM MULT; DLB
113; DNFS 1; EWL 3; GLL 1; HW 1, 2;
LAW; MTCW 1, 2; MTFW 2005; RGWL
2, 3; TWA; WLIT 1
Pulitzer, Joseph 1847-1911 .... **TCLC 76**
See also CA 114; DLB 23
Pullman, Philip 1946- .... **CLC 245**
See also AAYA 15, 41; BRWS 13; BYA 8,
13; CA 127; CANR 50, 77, 105, 134, 190;
CLR 20, 62, 84; JRDA; MAICYA 1, 2;
MAICYAS 1; MTFW 2005; SAAS 17;
SATA 65, 103, 150, 198; SUFW 2; WYAS
1; YAW
Purchas, Samuel 1577(?)-1626 .... **LC 70**
See also DLB 151
Purdy, A(lfred) W(ellington)
1918-2000 .... **CLC 3, 6, 14, 50**
See also CA 81-84; 189; CAAS 17; CANR
42, 66; CP 1, 2, 3, 4, 5, 6, 7; DAC; DAM
MST, POET; DLB 88; PFS 5; RGEL 2
Purdy, James 1914-2009 .... **CLC 2, 4, 10, 28,
52, 286**
See also AMWS 7; CA 33-36R; 284; CAAS
1; CANR 19, 51, 132; CN 1, 2, 3, 4, 5, 6,
7; DLB 2, 218; EWL 3; INT CANR-19;
MAL 5; MTCW 1; RGAL 4
Purdy, James Amos
See Purdy, James
Purdy, James Otis
See Purdy, James
Pure, Simon
See Swinnerton, Frank Arthur
Pushkin, Aleksandr Sergeevich
See Pushkin, Alexander
Pushkin, Alexander 1799-1837 . **NCLC 3, 27,
83; PC 10; SSC 27, 55, 99; WLC 5**
See also DA; DA3; DAB; DAC; DAM
DRAM, MST, POET; DLB 205; EW 5;
EXPS; PFS 28, 34; RGSF 2; RGWL 2, 3;
SATA 61; SSFS 9; TWA
Pushkin, Alexander Sergeyevich
See Pushkin, Alexander
P'u Sung-ling 1640-1715 .... **LC 49; SSC 31**
Putnam, Arthur Lee
See Alger, Horatio, Jr.
Puttenham, George 1529(?)-1590 ...... **LC 116**
See also DLB 281
Puzo, Mario 1920-1999 .... **CLC 1, 2, 6, 36,
107**
See also BPFB 3; CA 65-68; 185; CANR 4,
42, 65, 99, 131; CN 1, 2, 3, 4, 5, 6; CPW;
DA3; DAM NOV, POP; DLB 6; MTCW
1, 2; MTFW 2005; NFS 16; RGAL 4
Pygge, Edward
See Barnes, Julian
Pyle, Ernest Taylor
See Pyle, Ernie
Pyle, Ernie 1900-1945 .... **TCLC 75**
See also CA 115; 160; DLB 29; MTCW 2
Pyle, Howard 1853-1911 .... **TCLC 81**
See also AAYA 57; BYA 2, 4; CA 109; 137;
CLR 22, 117; DLB 42, 188; DLBD 13;
LAIT 1; MAICYA 1, 2; SATA 16, 100;
WCH; YAW
Pym, Barbara (Mary Crampton)
1913-1980 .... **CLC 13, 19, 37, 111**
See also BPFB 3; BRWS 2; CA 13-14; 97-
100; CANR 13, 34; CAP 1; DLB 14, 207;
DLBY 1987; EWL 3; MTCW 1, 2; MTFW
2005; RGEL 2; TEA

Rank, Otto 1884-1939 .... **TCLC 115**

Rankin, Ian 1960- .... **CLC 257**
See also BRWS 10; CA 148; CANR 81, 137, 171, 210; DLB 267; MTFW 2005

Rankin, Ian James
See Rankin, Ian

Ransom, John Crowe 1888-1974 .. **CLC 2, 4, 5, 11, 24; PC 61**
See also AMW; CA 5-8R; 49-52; CANR 6, 34; CDALBS; CP 1, 2; DA3; DAM POET; DLB 45, 63; EWL 3; EXPP; MAL 5; MTCW 1, 2; MTFW 2005; RGAL 4; TUS

Rao, Raja 1908-2006 . **CLC 25, 56, 255; SSC 99**
See also CA 73-76; 252; CANR 51; CN 1, 2, 3, 4, 5, 6; DAM NOV; DLB 323; EWL 3; MTCW 1, 2; MTFW 2005; RGEL 2; RGSF 2

Raphael, Frederic (Michael) 1931- ... **CLC 2, 14**
See also CA 1-4R; CANR 1, 86; CN 1, 2, 3, 4, 5, 6, 7; DLB 14, 319; TCLE 1:2

Raphael, Lev 1954- .... **CLC 232**
See also CA 134; CANR 72, 145; GLL 1

Rastell, John c. 1475(?)-1536(?) .... **LC 183**
See also DLB 136, 170; RGEL 2

Ratcliffe, James P.
See Mencken, H. L.

Rathbone, Julian 1935-2008 .... **CLC 41**
See also CA 101; 269; CANR 34, 73, 152

Rathbone, Julian Christopher
See Rathbone, Julian

Rattigan, Terence 1911-1977 . **CLC 7; DC 18**
See also BRWS 7; CA 85-88; 73-76; CBD; CDBLB 1945-1960; DAM DRAM; DFS 8; DLB 13; IDFW 3, 4; MTCW 1, 2; MTFW 2005; RGEL 2

Rattigan, Terence Mervyn
See Rattigan, Terence

Ratushinskaya, Irina 1954- .... **CLC 54**
See also CA 129; CANR 68; CWW 2

Raven, Simon (Arthur Noel)
1927-2001 .... **CLC 14**
See also CA 81-84; 197; CANR 86; CN 1, 2, 3, 4, 5, 6; DLB 271

Ravenna, Michael
See Welty, Eudora

Rawley, Callman 1903-2004 .... **CLC 47**
See also CA 21-24R; 228; CAAS 5; CANR 12, 32, 91; CP 1, 2, 3, 4, 5, 6, 7; DLB 193

Rawlings, Marjorie Kinnan
1896-1953 .... **TCLC 4, 248**
See also AAYA 20; AMWS 10; ANW; BPFB 3; BYA 3; CA 104; 137; CANR 74; CLR 63; DLB 9, 22, 102; DLBD 17; JRDA; MAICYA 1, 2; MAL 5; MTCW 2; MTFW 2005; RGAL 4; SATA 100; WCH; YABC 1; YAW

Raworth, Thomas Moore 1938- .... **PC 107**
See also CA 29-32R; CAAS 11; CANR 46; CP 1, 2, 3, 4, 5, 7; DLB 40

Raworth, Tom
See Raworth, Thomas Moore

Ray, Satyajit 1921-1992 .... **CLC 16, 76**
See also CA 114; 137; DAM MULT

Read, Herbert Edward 1893-1968 ..... **CLC 4**
See also BRW 6; CA 85-88; 25-28R; DLB 20, 149; EWL 3; PAB; RGEL 2

Read, Piers Paul 1941- .... **CLC 4, 10, 25**
See also CA 21-24R; CANR 38, 86, 150; CN 2, 3, 4, 5, 6, 7; DLB 14; SATA 21

Reade, Charles 1814-1884 .... **NCLC 2, 74**
See also DLB 21; RGEL 2

Reade, Hamish
See Gray, Simon

Reading, Peter 1946- .... **CLC 47**
See also BRWS 8; CA 103; CANR 46, 96; CP 5, 6, 7; DLB 40

Reaney, James 1926-2008 .... **CLC 13**
See also CA 41-44R; CAAS 15; CANR 42; CD 5, 6; CP 1, 2, 3, 4, 5, 6, 7; DAC; DAM MST; DLB 68; RGEL 2; SATA 43

Reaney, James Crerar
See Reaney, James

Rebreanu, Liviu 1885-1944 .... **TCLC 28**
See also CA 165; DLB 220; EWL 3

Rechy, John 1934- ..... **CLC 1, 7, 14, 18, 107; HLC 2**
See also CA 5-8R, 195; CAAE 195; CAAS 4; CANR 6, 32, 64, 152, 188; CN 1, 2, 3, 4, 5, 6, 7; DAM MULT; DLB 122, 278; DLBY 1982; HW 1, 2; INT CANR-6; LLW; MAL 5; RGAL 4

Rechy, John Francisco
See Rechy, John

Redcam, Tom 1870-1933 .... **TCLC 25**

Reddin, Keith 1956- .... **CLC 67**
See also CAD; CD 6

Redgrove, Peter (William)
1932-2003 .... **CLC 6, 41**
See also BRWS 6; CA 1-4R; 217; CANR 3, 39, 77; CP 1, 2, 3, 4, 5, 6, 7; DLB 40; TCLE 1:2

Redmon, Anne
See Nightingale, Anne Redmon

Reed, Eliot
See Ambler, Eric

Reed, Ishmael 1938- . **BLC 1:3; CLC 2, 3, 5, 6, 13, 32, 60, 174; PC 68**
See also AFAW 1, 2; AMWS 10; BPFB 3; BW 2, 3; CA 21-24R; CANR 25, 48, 74, 128, 195; CN 1, 2, 3, 4, 5, 6, 7; CP 1, 2, 3, 4, 5, 6, 7; CSW; DA3; DAM MULT; DLB 2, 5, 33, 169, 227; DLBD 8; EWL 3; LMFS 2; MAL 5; MSW; MTCW 1, 2; MTFW 2005; PFS 6; RGAL 4; TCWW 2

Reed, Ishmael Scott
See Reed, Ishmael

Reed, John (Silas) 1887-1920 .... **TCLC 9**
See also CA 106; 195; MAL 5; TUS

Reed, Lou
See Firbank, Louis

Reese, Lizette Woodworth
1856-1935 .... **PC 29; TCLC 181**
See also CA 180; DLB 54

Reeve, Clara 1729-1807 .... **NCLC 19**
See also DLB 39; RGEL 2

Reich, Wilhelm 1897-1957 .... **TCLC 57**
See also CA 199

Reid, Christopher 1949- .... **CLC 33**
See also CA 140; CANR 89; CP 4, 5, 6, 7; DLB 40; EWL 3

Reid, Christopher John
See Reid, Christopher

Reid, Desmond
See Moorcock, Michael

Reid Banks, Lynne 1929- .... **CLC 23**
See also AAYA 6; BYA 7; CA 1-4R; CANR 6, 22, 38, 87; CLR 24, 86; CN 4, 5, 6; JRDA; MAICYA 1, 2; SATA 22, 75, 111, 165; YAW

Reilly, William K.
See Creasey, John

Reiner, Max
See Caldwell, (Janet Miriam) Taylor (Holland)

Reis, Ricardo
See Pessoa, Fernando

Reizenstein, Elmer Leopold
See Rice, Elmer (Leopold)

Remark, Erich Paul
See Remarque, Erich Maria

Remarque, Erich Maria 1898-1970 . **CLC 21**
See also AAYA 27; BPFB 3; CA 77-80; 29-32R; CDWLB 2; CLR 159; DA; DA3; DAB; DAC; DAM MST, NOV; DLB 56; EWL 3; EXPN; LAIT 3; MTCW 1, 2; MTFW 2005; NFS 4, 36; RGHL; RGWL 2, 3

Remington, Frederic S(ackrider)
1861-1909 .... **TCLC 89**
See also CA 108; 169; DLB 12, 186, 188; SATA 41; TCWW 2

Remizov, A.
See Remizov, Aleksei (Mikhailovich)

Remizov, A. M.
See Remizov, Aleksei (Mikhailovich)

Remizov, Aleksei (Mikhailovich)
1877-1957 .... **TCLC 27**
See also CA 125; 133; DLB 295; EWL 3

Remizov, Alexey Mikhaylovich
See Remizov, Aleksei (Mikhailovich)

Renan, Joseph Ernest 1823-1892 . **NCLC 26, 145**
See also GFL 1789 to the Present

Renard, Jules(-Pierre) 1864-1910 .. **TCLC 17**
See also CA 117; 202; GFL 1789 to the Present

Renart, Jean fl. 13th cent. - .... **CMLC 83**

Renault, Mary 1905-1983 .... **CLC 3, 11, 17**
See also BPFB 3; BYA 2; CA 81-84; 111; CANR 74; CN 1, 2, 3; DA3; DLBY 1983; EWL 3; GLL 1; LAIT 1; MTCW 2; MTFW 2005; RGEL 2; RHW; SATA 23; SATA-Obit 36; TEA

Rendell, Ruth
See Rendell, Ruth

Rendell, Ruth 1930- ...... **CLC 28, 48, 50, 295**
See also BEST 90:4; BPFB 3; BRWS 9; CA 109; CANR 32, 52, 74, 127, 162, 190; CN 5, 6, 7; CPW; DAM POP; DLB 87, 276; INT CANR-32; MSW; MTCW 1, 2; MTFW 2005

Rendell, Ruth Barbara
See Rendell, Ruth

Renoir, Jean 1894-1979 .... **CLC 20**
See also CA 129; 85-88

Rensie, Willis
See Eisner, Will

Resnais, Alain 1922- .... **CLC 16**

Revard, Carter 1931- .... **NNAL**
See also CA 144; CANR 81, 153; PFS 5

Reverdy, Pierre 1889-1960 .... **CLC 53**
See also CA 97-100; 89-92; DLB 258; EWL 3; GFL 1789 to the Present

Reverend Mandju
See Su, Chien

Rexroth, Kenneth 1905-1982 .... **CLC 1, 2, 6, 11, 22, 49, 112; PC 20, 95**
See also BG 1:3; CA 5-8R; 107; CANR 14, 34, 63; CDALB 1941-1968; CP 1, 2, 3; DAM POET; DLB 16, 48, 165, 212; DLBY 1982; EWL 3; INT CANR-14; MAL 5; MTCW 1, 2; MTFW 2005; RGAL 4

Reyes, Alfonso 1889-1959 .... **HLCS 2; TCLC 33**
See also CA 131; EWL 3; HW 1; LAW

Reyes y Basoalto, Ricardo Eliecer Neftali
See Neruda, Pablo

Reymont, Wladyslaw (Stanislaw)
1868(?)-1925 .... **TCLC 5**
See also CA 104; DLB 332; EWL 3

Reynolds, John Hamilton
1794-1852 .... **NCLC 146**
See also DLB 96

Reynolds, Jonathan 1942- .... **CLC 6, 38**
See also CA 65-68; CANR 28, 176

Reynolds, Joshua 1723-1792 .... **LC 15**
See also DLB 104

Scalapino, Leslie 1947-2010 .... **PC 114**
See also CA 123; CANR 67, 103; CP 5, 6, 7; CWP; DLB 193

Scamander, Newt
See Rowling, J.K.

Scammell, Michael 1935- .... **CLC 34**
See also CA 156

Scannel, John Vernon
See Scannell, Vernon

Scannell, Vernon 1922-2007 .... **CLC 49**
See also CA 5-8R; 266; CANR 8, 24, 57, 143; CN 1, 2; CP 1, 2, 3, 4, 5, 6, 7; CWRI 5; DLB 27; SATA 59; SATA-Obit 188

Scarlett, Susan
See Streatfeild, Noel

Scarron 1847-1910
See Mikszath, Kalman

Scarron, Paul 1610-1660 .... **LC 116**
See also GFL Beginnings to 1789; RGWL 2, 3

Sceve, Maurice c. 1500-c. 1564 . **LC 180; PC 111**
See also DLB 327; GFL Beginnings to 1789

Schaeffer, Susan Fromberg 1941- ..... **CLC 6, 11, 22**
See also CA 49-52; CANR 18, 65, 160; CN 4, 5, 6, 7; DLB 28, 299; MTCW 1, 2; MTFW 2005; SATA 22

Schama, Simon 1945- .... **CLC 150**
See also BEST 89:4; CA 105; CANR 39, 91, 168, 207

Schama, Simon Michael
See Schama, Simon

Schary, Jill
See Robinson, Jill

Schell, Jonathan 1943- .... **CLC 35**
See also CA 73-76; CANR 12, 117, 187

Schelling, Friedrich Wilhelm Joseph von 1775-1854 .... **NCLC 30**
See also DLB 90

Scherer, Jean-Marie Maurice
See Rohmer, Eric

Schevill, James (Erwin) 1920- .... **CLC 7**
See also CA 5-8R; CAAS 12; CAD; CD 5, 6; CP 1, 2, 3, 4, 5

Schiller, Friedrich von 1759-1805 ...... **DC 12; NCLC 39, 69, 166**
See also CDWLB 2; DAM DRAM; DLB 94; EW 5; RGWL 2, 3; TWA

Schisgal, Murray (Joseph) 1926- .... **CLC 6**
See also CA 21-24R; CAD; CANR 48, 86; CD 5, 6; MAL 5

Schlee, Ann 1934- .... **CLC 35**
See also CA 101; CANR 29, 88; SATA 44; SATA-Brief 36

Schlegel, August Wilhelm von 1767-1845 .... **NCLC 15, 142**
See also DLB 94; RGWL 2, 3

Schlegel, Friedrich 1772-1829 .... **NCLC 45, 226**
See also DLB 90; EW 5; RGWL 2, 3; TWA

Schlegel, Johann Elias (von) 1719(?)-1749 .... **LC 5**

Schleiermacher, Friedrich 1768-1834 .... **NCLC 107**
See also DLB 90

Schlesinger, Arthur M., Jr. 1917-2007 .... **CLC 84**
See Schlesinger, Arthur Meier
See also AITN 1; CA 1-4R; 257; CANR 1, 28, 58, 105, 187; DLB 17; INT CANR-28; MTCW 1, 2; SATA 61; SATA-Obit 181

Schlink, Bernhard 1944- .... **CLC 174**
See also CA 163; CANR 116, 175; RGHL

Schmidt, Arno (Otto) 1914-1979 ...... **CLC 56**
See also CA 128; 109; DLB 69; EWL 3

Schmitz, Aron Hector 1861-1928 ..... **SSC 25; TCLC 2, 35, 244**
See also CA 104; 122; DLB 264; EW 8; EWL 3; MTCW 1; RGWL 2, 3; WLIT 7

Schnackenberg, Gjertrud 1953- ...... **CLC 40; PC 45**
See also AMWS 15; CA 116; CANR 100; CP 5, 6, 7; CWP; DLB 120, 282; PFS 13, 25

Schnackenberg, Gjertrud Cecelia
See Schnackenberg, Gjertrud

Schneider, Leonard Alfred 1925-1966 .... **CLC 21**
See also CA 89-92

Schnitzler, Arthur 1862-1931 ..... **DC 17; SSC 15, 61; TCLC 4**
See also CA 104; CDWLB 2; DLB 81, 118; EW 8; EWL 3; RGSF 2; RGWL 2, 3

Schoenberg, Arnold Franz Walter 1874-1951 .... **TCLC 75**
See also CA 109; 188

Schonberg, Arnold
See Schoenberg, Arnold Franz Walter

Schopenhauer, Arthur 1788-1860 . **NCLC 51, 157**
See also DLB 90; EW 5

Schor, Sandra (M.) 1932(?)-1990 ..... **CLC 65**
See also CA 132

Schorer, Mark 1908-1977 .... **CLC 9**
See also CA 5-8R; 73-76; CANR 7; CN 1, 2; DLB 103

Schrader, Paul (Joseph) 1946- . **CLC 26, 212**
See also CA 37-40R; CANR 41; DLB 44

Schreber, Daniel 1842-1911 .... **TCLC 123**

Schreiner, Olive 1855-1920 ...... **TCLC 9, 235**
See also AFW; BRWS 2; CA 105; 154; DLB 18, 156, 190, 225; EWL 3; FW; RGEL 2; TWA; WLIT 2; WWE 1

Schreiner, Olive Emilie Albertina
See Schreiner, Olive

Schulberg, Budd 1914-2009 .... **CLC 7, 48**
See also AMWS 18; BPFB 3; CA 25-28R; 289; CANR 19, 87, 178; CN 1, 2, 3, 4, 5, 6, 7; DLB 6, 26, 28; DLBY 1981, 2001; MAL 5

Schulberg, Budd Wilson
See Schulberg, Budd

Schulberg, Seymour Wilson
See Schulberg, Budd

Schulman, Arnold
See Trumbo, Dalton

Schulz, Bruno 1892-1942 .. **SSC 13; TCLC 5, 51**
See also CA 115; 123; CANR 86; CDWLB 4; DLB 215; EWL 3; MTCW 2; MTFW 2005; RGSF 2; RGWL 2, 3

Schulz, Charles M. 1922-2000 .... **CLC 12**
See also AAYA 39; CA 9-12R; 187; CANR 6, 132; INT CANR-6; MTFW 2005; SATA 10; SATA-Obit 118

Schulz, Charles Monroe
See Schulz, Charles M.

Schumacher, E(rnst) F(riedrich) 1911-1977 .... **CLC 80**
See also CA 81-84; 73-76; CANR 34, 85

Schumann, Robert 1810-1856 ...... **NCLC 143**

Schuyler, George Samuel 1895-1977 . **HR 1:3**
See also BW 2; CA 81-84; 73-76; CANR 42; DLB 29, 51

Schuyler, James Marcus 1923-1991 .. **CLC 5, 23; PC 88**
See also CA 101; 134; CP 1, 2, 3, 4, 5; DAM POET; DLB 5, 169; EWL 3; INT CA-101; MAL 5; WP

Schwartz, Delmore (David) 1913-1966 . **CLC 2, 4, 10, 45, 87; PC 8; SSC 105**
See also AMWS 2; CA 17-18; 25-28R; CANR 35; CAP 2; DLB 28, 48; EWL 3; MAL 5; MTCW 1, 2; MTFW 2005; PAB; RGAL 4; TUS

Schwartz, Ernst
See Ozu, Yasujiro

Schwartz, John Burnham 1965- .... **CLC 59**
See also CA 132; CANR 116, 188

Schwartz, Lynne Sharon 1939- .... **CLC 31**
See also CA 103; CANR 44, 89, 160, 214; DLB 218; MTCW 2; MTFW 2005

Schwartz, Muriel A.
See Eliot, T. S.

Schwarz-Bart, Andre 1928-2006 .... **CLC 2, 4**
See also CA 89-92; 253; CANR 109; DLB 299; RGHL

Schwarz-Bart, Simone 1938- . **BLCS; CLC 7**
See also BW 2; CA 97-100; CANR 117; EWL 3

Schwerner, Armand 1927-1999 .... **PC 42**
See also CA 9-12R; 179; CANR 50, 85; CP 2, 3, 4, 5, 6; DLB 165

Schwitters, Kurt (Hermann Edward Karl Julius) 1887-1948 .... **TCLC 95**
See also CA 158

Schwob, Marcel (Mayer Andre) 1867-1905 .... **TCLC 20**
See also CA 117; 168; DLB 123; GFL 1789 to the Present

Sciascia, Leonardo 1921-1989 .. **CLC 8, 9, 41**
See also CA 85-88; 130; CANR 35; DLB 177; EWL 3; MTCW 1; RGWL 2, 3

Scoppettone, Sandra 1936- .... **CLC 26**
See also AAYA 11, 65; BYA 8; CA 5-8R; CANR 41, 73, 157; GLL 1; MAICYA 2; MAICYAS 1; SATA 9, 92; WYA; YAW

Scorsese, Martin 1942- .... **CLC 20, 89, 207**
See also AAYA 38; CA 110; 114; CANR 46, 85

Scotland, Jay
See Jakes, John

Scott, Duncan Campbell 1862-1947 .... **TCLC 6**
See also CA 104; 153; DAC; DLB 92; RGEL 2

Scott, Evelyn 1893-1963 .... **CLC 43**
See also CA 104; 112; CANR 64; DLB 9, 48; RHW

Scott, F(rancis) R(eginald) 1899-1985 .... **CLC 22**
See also CA 101; 114; CANR 87; CP 1, 2, 3, 4; DLB 88; INT CA-101; RGEL 2

Scott, Frank
See Scott, F(rancis) R(eginald)

Scott, Joan
See Scott, Joan Wallach

Scott, Joan W.
See Scott, Joan Wallach

Scott, Joan Wallach 1941- .... **CLC 65**
See also CA 293

Scott, Joanna 1960- .... **CLC 50**
See also AMWS 17; CA 126; CANR 53, 92, 168

Scott, Joanna Jeanne
See Scott, Joanna

Scott, Paul (Mark) 1920-1978 ...... **CLC 9, 60**
See also BRWS 1; CA 81-84; 77-80; CANR 33; CN 1, 2; DLB 14, 207, 326; EWL 3; MTCW 1; RGEL 2; RHW; WWE 1

Scott, Ridley 1937- .... **CLC 183**
See also AAYA 13, 43

Scott, Sarah 1723-1795 .... **LC 44**
See also DLB 39

Shaffer, Anthony 1926-2001 .... **CLC 19**
See also CA 110; 116; 200; CBD; CD 5, 6;
DAM DRAM; DFS 13; DLB 13
Shaffer, Anthony Joshua
See Shaffer, Anthony
Shaffer, Peter 1926- ... **CLC 5, 14, 18, 37, 60,**
291; DC 7
See also BRWS 1; CA 25-28R; CANR 25,
47, 74, 118; CBD; CD 5, 6; CDBLB 1960
to Present; DA3; DAB; DAM DRAM,
MST; DFS 5, 13; DLB 13, 233; EWL 3;
MTCW 1, 2; MTFW 2005; RGEL 2; TEA
Shakespeare, William 1564-1616 . **PC 84, 89,**
98, 101; WLC 5
See also AAYA 35; BRW 1; BRWR 3; CD-
BLB Before 1660; DA; DA3; DAB;
DAC; DAM DRAM, MST, POET; DFS
20, 21; DLB 62, 172, 263; EXPP; LAIT
1; LATS 1:1; LMFS 1; PAB; PFS 1, 2, 3,
4, 5, 8, 9, 35; RGEL 2; TEA; WLIT 3;
WP; WS; WYA
Shakey, Bernard
See Young, Neil
Shalamov, Varlam (Tikhonovich)
1907-1982 .... **CLC 18**
See also CA 129; 105; DLB 302; RGSF 2
Shamloo, Ahmad
See Shamlu, Ahmad
Shamlou, Ahmad
See Shamlu, Ahmad
Shamlu, Ahmad 1925-2000 .... **CLC 10**
See also CA 216; CWW 2
Shammas, Anton 1951- .... **CLC 55**
See also CA 199; DLB 346
Shandling, Arline
See Berriault, Gina
Shange, Ntozake 1948- .. **BLC 1:3, 2:3; CLC**
8, 25, 38, 74, 126; DC 3
See also AAYA 9, 66; AFAW 1, 2; BW 2;
CA 85-88; CABS 3; CAD; CANR 27, 48,
74, 131, 208; CD 5, 6; CP 5, 6, 7; CWD;
CWP; DA3; DAM DRAM, MULT; DFS
2, 11; DLB 38, 249; FW; LAIT 4, 5; MAL
5; MTCW 1, 2; MTFW 2005; NFS 11;
RGAL 4; SATA 157; YAW
Shanley, John Patrick 1950- .... **CLC 75**
See also AAYA 74; AMWS 14; CA 128;
133; CAD; CANR 83, 154; CD 5, 6; DFS
23, 28
Shapcott, Thomas W(illiam) 1935- .. **CLC 38**
See also CA 69-72; CANR 49, 83, 103; CP
1, 2, 3, 4, 5, 6, 7; DLB 289
Shapiro, Jane 1942- .... **CLC 76**
See also CA 196
Shapiro, Karl 1913-2000 ... **CLC 4, 8, 15, 53;**
PC 25
See also AMWS 2; CA 1-4R; 188; CAAS
6; CANR 1, 36, 66; CP 1, 2, 3, 4, 5, 6;
DLB 48; EWL 3; EXPP; MAL 5; MTCW
1, 2; MTFW 2005; PFS 3; RGAL 4
Sharp, William 1855-1905 .... **TCLC 39**
See also CA 160; DLB 156; RGEL 2;
SUFW
Sharpe, Thomas Ridley 1928- .... **CLC 36**
See also CA 114; 122; CANR 85; CN 4, 5,
6, 7; DLB 14, 231; INT CA-122
Sharpe, Tom
See Sharpe, Thomas Ridley
Shatrov, Mikhail CLC 59
Shaw, Bernard
See Shaw, George Bernard
Shaw, G. Bernard
See Shaw, George Bernard
Shaw, George Bernard 1856-1950 ..... **DC 23;**
TCLC 3, 9, 21, 45, 205; WLC 5
See also AAYA 61; BRW 6; BRWC 1;
BRWR 2; CA 104; 128; CDBLB 1914-
1945; DA; DA3; DAB; DAC; DAM
DRAM, MST; DFS 1, 3, 6, 11, 19, 22;

DLB 10, 57, 190, 332; EWL 3; LAIT 3;
LATS 1:1; MTCW 1, 2; MTFW 2005;
RGEL 2; TEA; WLIT 4
Shaw, Henry Wheeler 1818-1885 .. **NCLC 15**
See also DLB 11; RGAL 4
Shaw, Irwin 1913-1984 .... **CLC 7, 23, 34**
See also AITN 1; BPFB 3; CA 13-16R; 112;
CANR 21; CDALB 1941-1968; CN 1, 2,
3; CPW; DAM DRAM, POP; DLB 6,
102; DLBY 1984; MAL 5; MTCW 1, 21;
MTFW 2005
Shaw, Robert (Archibald)
1927-1978 .... **CLC 5**
See also AITN 1; CA 1-4R; 81-84; CANR
4; CN 1, 2; DLB 13, 14
Shaw, T. E.
See Lawrence, T. E.
Shawn, Wallace 1943- .... **CLC 41**
See also CA 112; CAD; CANR 215; CD 5,
6; DLB 266
Shaykh, al- Hanan
See al-Shaykh, Hanan
Shchedrin, N.
See Saltykov, Mikhail Evgrafovich
Shea, Lisa 1953- .... **CLC 86**
See also CA 147
Sheed, Wilfrid 1930-2011 ... **CLC 2, 4, 10, 53**
See also CA 65-68; CANR 30, 66, 181; CN
1, 2, 3, 4, 5, 6, 7; DLB 6; MAL 5; MTCW
1, 2; MTFW 2005
Sheed, Wilfrid John Joseph
See Sheed, Wilfrid
Sheehy, Gail 1937- .... **CLC 171**
See also CA 49-52; CANR 1, 33, 55, 92;
CPW; MTCW 1
Sheldon, Alice Hastings Bradley
1915(?)-1987 .... **CLC 48, 50**
See also CA 108; 122; CANR 34; DLB 8;
INT CA-108; MTCW 1; SCFW 1, 2; SFW
4
Sheldon, John
See Bloch, Robert (Albert)
Sheldon, Raccoona
See Sheldon, Alice Hastings Bradley
Shelley, Mary
See Shelley, Mary Wollstonecraft
Shelley, Mary Wollstonecraft
1797-1851 .... **NCLC 14, 59, 103, 170;**
SSC 92; WLC 5
See also AAYA 20; BPFB 3; BRW 3;
BRWC 2; BRWR 3; BRWS 3; BYA 5;
CDBLB 1789-1832; CLR 133; DA; DA3;
DAB; DAC; DAM MST, NOV; DLB 110,
116, 159, 178; EXPN; FL 1:3; GL 3;
HGG; LAIT 1; LMFS 1, 2; NFS 1, 37;
RGEL 2; SATA 29; SCFW 1, 2; SFW 4;
TEA; WLIT 3
Shelley, Percy Bysshe 1792-1822 .. **NCLC 18,**
93, 143, 175; PC 14, 67; WLC 5
See also AAYA 61; BRW 4; BRWR 1; CD-
BLB 1789-1832; DA; DA3; DAB; DAC;
DAM MST, POET; DFS 96, 110, 158;
EXPP; LMFS 1; PAB; PFS 2, 27, 32, 36;
RGEL 2; TEA; WLIT 3; WP
Shepard, James R.
See Shepard, Jim
Shepard, Jim 1956- .... **CLC 36**
See also AAYA 73; CA 137; CANR 59, 104,
160, 199; SATA 90, 164
Shepard, Lucius 1947- .... **CLC 34**
See also CA 128; 141; CANR 81, 124, 178;
HGG; SCFW 2; SFW 4; SUFW 2
Shepard, Sam 1943- .... **CLC 4, 6, 17, 34, 41,**
44, 169; DC 5
See also AAYA 1, 58; AMWS 3; CA 69-72;
CABS 3; CAD; CANR 22, 120, 140; CD
5, 6; DA3; DAM DRAM; DFS 3, 6, 7,
14; DLB 7, 212, 341; EWL 3; IDFW 3, 4;
MAL 5; MTCW 1, 2; MTFW 2005;
RGAL 4

Shepherd, Jean (Parker)
1921-1999 .... **TCLC 177**
See also AAYA 69; AITN 2; CA 77-80; 187
Shepherd, Michael
See Ludlum, Robert
Sherburne, Zoa (Lillian Morin)
1912-1995 .... **CLC 30**
See also AAYA 13; CA 1-4R; 176; CANR
3, 37; MAICYA 1, 2; SAAS 18; SATA 3;
YAW
Sheridan, Frances 1724-1766 .... **LC 7**
See also DLB 39, 84
Sheridan, Richard Brinsley
1751-1816 . **DC 1; NCLC 5, 91; WLC 5**
See also BRW 3; CDBLB 1660-1789; DA;
DAB; DAC; DAM DRAM, MST; DFS
15; DLB 89; WLIT 3
Sherman, Jonathan Marc 1968- .... **CLC 55**
See also CA 230
Sherman, Martin 1941(?)- .... **CLC 19**
See also CA 116; 123; CAD; CANR 86;
CD 5, 6; DFS 20; DLB 228; GLL 1;
IDTP; RGHL
Sherwin, Judith Johnson
See Johnson, Judith
Sherwood, Frances 1940- .... **CLC 81**
See also CA 146; 220; CAAE 220; CANR
158
Sherwood, Robert E(mmet)
1896-1955 .... **DC 36; TCLC 3**
See also CA 104; 153; CANR 86; DAM
DRAM; DFS 11, 15, 17; DLB 7, 26, 249;
IDFW 3, 4; MAL 5; RGAL 4
Shestov, Lev 1866-1938 .... **TCLC 56**
Shevchenko, Taras 1814-1861 .... **NCLC 54**
Shiel, M. P. 1865-1947 .... **TCLC 8**
See also CA 106; 160; DLB 153; HGG;
MTCW 2; MTFW 2005; SCFW 1, 2;
SFW 4; SUFW
Shiel, Matthew Phipps
See Shiel, M. P.
Shields, Carol 1935-2003 . **CLC 91, 113, 193,**
298; SSC 126
See also AMWS 7; CA 81-84; 218; CANR
51, 74, 98, 133; CCA 1; CN 6, 7; CPW;
DA3; DAC; DLB 334, 350; MTCW 2;
MTFW 2005; NFS 23
Shields, David 1956- .... **CLC 97**
See also CA 124; CANR 48, 99, 112, 157
Shields, David Jonathan
See Shields, David
Shiga, Naoya 1883-1971 .... **CLC 33; SSC 23;**
TCLC 172
See also CA 101; 33-36R; DLB 180; EWL
3; MJW; RGWL 3
Shiga Naoya
See Shiga, Naoya
Shilts, Randy 1951-1994 .... **CLC 85**
See also AAYA 19; CA 115; 127; 144;
CANR 45; DA3; GLL 1; INT CA-127;
MTCW 2; MTFW 2005
Shimazaki, Haruki 1872-1943 .... **TCLC 5**
See also CA 105; 134; CANR 84; DLB 180;
EWL 3; MJW; RGWL 3
Shimazaki Toson
See Shimazaki, Haruki
Shirley, James 1596-1666 .... **DC 25; LC 96**
See also DLB 58; RGEL 2
Shirley Hastings, Selina
See Hastings, Selina
Sholem Aleykhem
See Rabinovitch, Sholem
Sholokhov, Mikhail 1905-1984 ..... **CLC 7, 15**
See also CA 101; 112; DLB 272, 332; EWL
3; MTCW 1, 2; MTFW 2005; RGWL 2,
3; SATA-Obit 36
Sholokhov, Mikhail Aleksandrovich
See Sholokhov, Mikhail

Sholom Aleichem 1859-1916
See Rabinovitch, Sholem
Shone, Patric
See Hanley, James
Showalter, Elaine 1941- .... **CLC 169**
See also CA 57-60; CANR 58, 106, 208;
DLB 67; FW; GLL 2
Shreve, Susan
See Shreve, Susan Richards
Shreve, Susan Richards 1939- .... **CLC 23**
See also CA 49-52; CAAS 5; CANR 5, 38,
69, 100, 159, 199; MAICYA 1, 2; SATA
46, 95, 152; SATA-Brief 41
Shue, Larry 1946-1985 .... **CLC 52**
See also CA 145; 117; DAM DRAM; DFS
7
Shu-Jen, Chou 1881-1936 . **SSC 20; TCLC 3**
See also CA 104; EWL 3
Shulman, Alix Kates 1932- .... **CLC 2, 10**
See also CA 29-32R; CANR 43, 199; FW;
SATA 7
Shuster, Joe 1914-1992 .... **CLC 21**
See also AAYA 50
Shute, Nevil 1899-1960 .... **CLC 30**
See also BPFB 3; CA 102; 93-96; CANR
85; DLB 255; MTCW 2; NFS 9; RHW 4;
SFW 4
Shuttle, Penelope (Diane) 1947- .... **CLC 7**
See also CA 93-96; CANR 39, 84, 92, 108;
CP 3, 4, 5, 6, 7; CWP; DLB 14, 40
Shvarts, Elena 1948-2010 .... **PC 50**
See also CA 147
Sidhwa, Bapsi 1939-
See Sidhwa, Bapsy (N.)
Sidhwa, Bapsy (N.) 1938- .... **CLC 168**
See also CA 108; CANR 25, 57; CN 6, 7;
DLB 323; FW
Sidney, Mary 1561-1621 .... **LC 19, 39, 182**
See also DLB 167
Sidney, Sir Philip 1554-1586 .... **LC 19, 39,
131; PC 32**
See also BRW 1; BRWR 2; CDBLB Before
1660; DA; DA3; DAB; DAC; DAM MST,
POET; DLB 167; EXPP; PAB; PFS 30;
RGEL 2; TEA; WP
Sidney Herbert, Mary
See Sidney, Mary
Siegel, Jerome 1914-1996 .... **CLC 21**
See also AAYA 50; CA 116; 169; 151
Siegel, Jerry
See Siegel, Jerome
Sienkiewicz, Henryk (Adam Alexander Pius)
1846-1916 .... **TCLC 3**
See also CA 104; 134; CANR 84; DLB 332;
EWL 3; RGSF 2; RGWL 2, 3
Sierra, Gregorio Martinez
See Martinez Sierra, Gregorio
Sierra, Maria de la O'LeJarraga Martinez
See Martinez Sierra, Maria
Sigal, Clancy 1926- .... **CLC 7**
See also CA 1-4R; CANR 85, 184; CN 1,
2, 3, 4, 5, 6, 7
Siger of Brabant 1240(?)-1284(?) . **CMLC 69**
See also DLB 115
Sigourney, Lydia H.
See Sigourney, Lydia Howard
Sigourney, Lydia Howard
1791-1865 .... **NCLC 21, 87**
See also DLB 1, 42, 73, 183, 239, 243
Sigourney, Lydia Howard Huntley
See Sigourney, Lydia Howard
Sigourney, Lydia Huntley
See Sigourney, Lydia Howard
Siguenza y Gongora, Carlos de
1645-1700 .... **HLCS 2; LC 8**
See also LAW
Sigurjonsson, Johann
See Sigurjonsson, Johann

Sigurjonsson, Johann 1880-1919 ... **TCLC 27**
See also CA 170; DLB 293; EWL 3
Sikelianos, Angelos 1884-1951 .... **PC 29;
TCLC 39**
See also EWL 3; RGWL 2, 3
Silkin, Jon 1930-1997 .... **CLC 2, 6, 43**
See also CA 5-8R; CAAS 5; CANR 89; CP
1, 2, 3, 4, 5, 6; DLB 27
Silko, Leslie 1948- .... **CLC 23, 74, 114, 211,
302; NNAL; SSC 37, 66; WLCS**
See also AAYA 14; AMWS 4; ANW; BYA
12; CA 115; 122; CANR 45, 65, 118; CN
4, 5, 6, 7; CP 4, 5, 6, 7; CPW 1; CWP;
DA; DA3; DAC; DAM MST, MULT,
POP; DLB 143, 175, 256, 275; EWL 3;
EXPP; EXPS; LAIT 4; MAL 5; MTCW
2; MTFW 2005; NFS 4; PFS 9, 16; RGAL
4; RGSF 2; SSFS 4, 8, 10, 11; TCWW 1,
2
Silko, Leslie Marmon
See Silko, Leslie
Sillanpaa, Frans Eemil 1888-1964 ... **CLC 19**
See also CA 129; 93-96; DLB 332; EWL 3;
MTCW 1
Sillitoe, Alan 1928-2010 . **CLC 1, 3, 6, 10, 19,
57, 148**
See also AITN 1; BRWS 5; CA 9-12R, 191;
CAAE 191; CAAS 2; CANR 8, 26, 55,
139, 213; CDBLB 1960 to Present; CN 1,
2, 3, 4, 5, 6; CP 1, 2, 3, 4, 5; DLB 14,
139; EWL 3; MTCW 1, 2; MTFW 2005;
RGEL 2; RGSF 2; SATA 61
Silone, Ignazio 1900-1978 .... **CLC 4**
See also CA 25-28; 81-84; CANR 34; CAP
2; DLB 264; EW 12; EWL 3; MTCW 1;
RGSF 2; RGWL 2, 3
Silone, Ignazione
See Silone, Ignazio
Siluriensis, Leolinus
See Jones, Arthur Llewellyn
Silver, Joan Micklin 1935- .... **CLC 20**
See also CA 114; 121; INT CA-121
Silver, Nicholas
See Faust, Frederick
Silverberg, Robert 1935- .... **CLC 7, 140**
See also AAYA 24; BPFB 3; BYA 7, 9; CA
1-4R, 186; CAAE 186; CAAS 3; CANR
1, 20, 36, 85, 140, 175; CLR 59; CN 6, 7;
CPW; DAM POP; DLB 8; INT CANR-
20; MAICYA 1, 2; MTCW 1, 2; MTFW
2005; SATA 13, 91; SATA-Essay 104;
SCFW 1, 2; SFW 4; SUFW 2
Silverstein, Alvin 1933- .... **CLC 17**
See also CA 49-52; CANR 2; CLR 25;
JRDA; MAICYA 1, 2; SATA 8, 69, 124
Silverstein, Shel 1932-1999 .... **PC 49**
See also AAYA 40; BW 3; CA 107; 179;
CANR 47, 74, 81; CLR 5, 96; CWRI 5;
JRDA; MAICYA 1, 2; MTCW 2; MTFW
2005; SATA 33, 92; SATA-Brief 27;
SATA-Obit 116
Silverstein, Sheldon Allan
See Silverstein, Shel
Silverstein, Virginia B. 1937- .... **CLC 17**
See also CA 49-52; CANR 2; CLR 25;
JRDA; MAICYA 1, 2; SATA 8, 69, 124
Silverstein, Virginia Barbara Opshelor
See Silverstein, Virginia B.
Sim, Georges
See Simenon, Georges
Simak, Clifford D(onald) 1904-1988 . **CLC 1,
55**
See also CA 1-4R; 125; CANR 1, 35; DLB
8; MTCW 1; SATA-Obit 56; SCFW 1, 2;
SFW 4
Simenon, Georges 1903-1989 .... **CLC 1, 2, 3,
8, 18, 47**
See also BPFB 3; CA 85-88; 129; CANR
35; CMW 4; DA3; DAM POP; DLB 72;

DLBY 1989; EW 12; EWL 3; GFL 1789
to the Present; MSW; MTCW 1, 2; MTFW
2005; RGWL 2, 3
Simenon, Georges Jacques Christian
See Simenon, Georges
Simic, Charles 1938- .... **CLC 6, 9, 22, 49, 68,
130, 256; PC 69**
See also AAYA 78; AMWS 8; CA 29-32R;
CAAS 4; CANR 12, 33, 52, 61, 96, 140,
210; CP 2, 3, 4, 5, 6, 7; DA3; DAM
POET; DLB 105; MAL 5; MTCW 2;
MTFW 2005; PFS 7, 33, 36; RGAL 4;
WP
Simmel, Georg 1858-1918 .... **TCLC 64**
See also CA 157; DLB 296
Simmons, Charles (Paul) 1924- .... **CLC 57**
See also CA 89-92; INT CA-89-92
Simmons, Dan 1948- .... **CLC 44**
See also AAYA 16, 54; CA 138; CANR 53,
81, 126, 174, 204; CPW; DAM POP;
HGG; SUFW 2
Simmons, James (Stewart Alexander)
1933- .... **CLC 43**
See also CA 105; CAAS 21; CP 1, 2, 3, 4,
5, 6, 7; DLB 40
Simmons, Richard
See Simmons, Dan
Simms, William Gilmore
1806-1870 .... **NCLC 3**
See also DLB 3, 30, 59, 73, 248, 254;
RGAL 4
Simon, Carly 1945- .... **CLC 26**
See also CA 105
Simon, Claude 1913-2005 ... **CLC 4, 9, 15, 39**
See also CA 89-92; 241; CANR 33, 117;
CWW 2; DAM NOV; DLB 83, 332; EW
13; EWL 3; GFL 1789 to the Present;
MTCW 1
Simon, Claude Eugene Henri
See Simon, Claude
Simon, Claude Henri Eugene
See Simon, Claude
Simon, Marvin Neil
See Simon, Neil
Simon, Myles
See Follett, Ken
Simon, Neil 1927- .... **CLC 6, 11, 31, 39, 70,
233; DC 14**
See also AAYA 32; AITN 1; AMWS 4; CA
21-24R; CAD; CANR 26, 54, 87, 126;
CD 5, 6; DA3; DAM DRAM; DFS 2, 6,
12, 18, 24, 27; DLB 7, 266; LAIT 4; MAL
5; MTCW 1, 2; MTFW 2005; RGAL 4;
TUS
Simon, Paul 1941(?)- .... **CLC 17**
See also CA 116; 153; CANR 152
Simon, Paul Frederick
See Simon, Paul
Simonon, Paul 1956(?)- .... **CLC 30**
Simonson, Rick CLC 70
Simpson, Harriette
See Arnow, Harriette (Louisa) Simpson
Simpson, Louis 1923- ... **CLC 4, 7, 9, 32, 149**
See also AMWS 9; CA 1-4R; CAAS 4;
CANR 1, 61, 140; CP 1, 2, 3, 4, 5, 6, 7;
DAM POET; DLB 5; MAL 5; MTCW 1,
2; MTFW 2005; PFS 7, 11, 14; RGAL 4
Simpson, Mona 1957- .... **CLC 44, 146**
See also CA 122; 135; CANR 68, 103; CN
6, 7; EWL 3
Simpson, Mona Elizabeth
See Simpson, Mona
Simpson, N(orman) F(rederick)
1919- .... **CLC 29**
See also CA 13-16R; CBD; DLB 13; RGEL
2

Sinclair, Andrew (Annandale) 1935- . **CLC 2, 14**
See also CA 9-12R; CAAS 5; CANR 14, 38, 91; CN 1, 2, 3, 4, 5, 6, 7; DLB 14; FANT; MTCW 1

Sinclair, Emil
See Hesse, Hermann

Sinclair, Iain 1943- .... **CLC 76**
See also BRWS 14; CA 132; CANR 81, 157; CP 5, 6, 7; HGG

Sinclair, Iain MacGregor
See Sinclair, Iain

Sinclair, Irene
See Griffith, D.W.

Sinclair, Julian
See Sinclair, May

Sinclair, Mary Amelia St. Clair (?)-
See Sinclair, May

Sinclair, May 1865-1946 .... **TCLC 3, 11**
See also CA 104; 166; DLB 36, 135; EWL 3; HGG; RGEL 2; RHW; SUFW

Sinclair, Roy
See Griffith, D.W.

Sinclair, Upton 1878-1968 ...... **CLC 1, 11, 15, 63; TCLC 160; WLC 5**
See also AAYA 63; AMWS 5; BPFB 3; BYA 2; CA 5-8R; 25-28R; CANR 7; CDALB 1929-1941; DA; DA3; DAB; DAC; DAM MST, NOV; DLB 9; EWL 3; INT CANR-7; LAIT 3; MAL 5; MTCW 1, 2; MTFW 2005; NFS 6; RGAL 4; SATA 9; TUS; YAW

Sinclair, Upton Beall
See Sinclair, Upton

Singe, (Edmund) J(ohn) M(illington)
1871-1909 .... **WLC**

Singer, Isaac
See Singer, Isaac Bashevis

Singer, Isaac Bashevis 1904-1991 .. **CLC 1, 3, 6, 9, 11, 15, 23, 38, 69, 111; SSC 3, 53, 80; WLC 5**
See also AAYA 32; AITN 1, 2; AMW; AMWR 2; BPFB 3; BYA 1, 4; CA 1-4R; 134; CANR 1, 39, 106; CDALB 1941-1968; CLR 1; CN 1, 2, 3, 4; CWRI 5; DA; DA3; DAB; DAC; DAM MST, NOV; DLB 6, 28, 52, 278, 332, 333; DLBY 1991; EWL 3; EXPS; HGG; JRDA; LAIT 3; MAICYA 1, 2; MAL 5; MTCW 1, 2; MTFW 2005; RGAL 4; RGHL; RGSF 2; SATA 3, 27; SATA-Obit 68; SSFS 2, 12, 16, 27, 30; TUS; TWA

Singer, Israel Joshua 1893-1944 .... **TCLC 33**
See also CA 169; DLB 333; EWL 3

Singh, Khushwant 1915- .... **CLC 11**
See also CA 9-12R; CAAS 9; CANR 6, 84; CN 1, 2, 3, 4, 5, 6, 7; DLB 323; EWL 3; RGEL 2

Singleton, Ann
See Benedict, Ruth

Singleton, John 1968(?)- .... **CLC 156**
See also AAYA 50; BW 2, 3; CA 138; CANR 67, 82; DAM MULT

Siniavskii, Andrei
See Sinyavsky, Andrei (Donatevich)

Sinibaldi, Fosco
See Kacew, Romain

Sinjohn, John
See Galsworthy, John

Sinyavsky, Andrei (Donatevich)
1925-1997 .... **CLC 8**
See also CA 85-88; 159; CWW 2; EWL 3; RGSF 2

Sinyavsky, Andrey Donatovich
See Sinyavsky, Andrei (Donatevich)

Sirin, V.
See Nabokov, Vladimir

Sissman, L(ouis) E(dward)
1928-1976 .... **CLC 9, 18**
See also CA 21-24R; 65-68; CANR 13; CP 2; DLB 5

Sisson, C(harles) H(ubert)
1914-2003 .... **CLC 8**
See also BRWS 11; CA 1-4R; 220; CAAS 3; CANR 3, 48, 84; CP 1, 2, 3, 4, 5, 6, 7; DLB 27

Sitting Bull 1831(?)-1890 .... **NNAL**
See also DA3; DAM MULT

Sitwell, Dame Edith 1887-1964 ..... **CLC 2, 9, 67; PC 3**
See also BRW 7; CA 9-12R; CANR 35; CDBLB 1945-1960; DAM POET; DLB 20; EWL 3; MTCW 1, 2; MTFW 2005; RGEL 2; TEA

Siwaarmill, H. P.
See Sharp, William

Sjoewall, Maj 1935- .... **CLC 7**
See also BPFB 3; CA 65-68; CANR 73; CMW 4; MSW

Sjowall, Maj
See Sjoewall, Maj

Skelton, John 1460(?)-1529 ..... **LC 71; PC 25**
See also BRW 1; DLB 136; RGEL 2

Skelton, Robin 1925-1997 .... **CLC 13**
See also AITN 2; CA 5-8R; 160; CAAS 5; CANR 28, 89; CCA 1; CP 1, 2, 3, 4, 5, 6; DLB 27, 53

Skolimowski, Jerzy 1938- .... **CLC 20**
See also CA 128

Skram, Amalie (Bertha)
1846-1905 .... **TCLC 25**
See also CA 165; DLB 354

Skvorecky, Josef 1924- . **CLC 15, 39, 69, 152**
See also CA 61-64; CAAS 1; CANR 10, 34, 63, 108; CDWLB 4; CWW 2; DA3; DAC; DAM NOV; DLB 232; EWL 3; MTCW 1, 2; MTFW 2005

Skvorecky, Josef Vaclav
See Skvorecky, Josef

Slade, Bernard 1930-
See Newbound, Bernard Slade

Slaughter, Carolyn 1946- .... **CLC 56**
See also CA 85-88; CANR 85, 169; CN 5, 6, 7

Slaughter, Frank G(ill) 1908-2001 ... **CLC 29**
See also AITN 2; CA 5-8R; 197; CANR 5, 85; INT CANR-5; RHW

Slavitt, David R. 1935- .... **CLC 5, 14**
See also CA 21-24R; CAAS 3; CANR 41, 83, 166; CN 1, 2; CP 1, 2, 3, 4, 5, 6, 7; DLB 5, 6

Slavitt, David Rytman
See Slavitt, David R.

Slesinger, Tess 1905-1945 .... **TCLC 10**
See also CA 107; 199; DLB 102

Slessor, Kenneth 1901-1971 .... **CLC 14**
See also CA 102; 89-92; DLB 260; RGEL 2

Slowacki, Juliusz 1809-1849 .... **NCLC 15**
See also RGWL 3

Small, David 1945- .... **CLC 299**
See also CLR 53; MAICYA 2; SATA 50, 95, 126, 183, 216; SATA-Brief 46

Smart, Christopher 1722-1771 .... **LC 3, 134; PC 13**
See also DAM POET; DLB 109; RGEL 2

Smart, Elizabeth 1913-1986 .... **CLC 54; TCLC 231**
See also CA 81-84; 118; CN 4; DLB 88

Smiley, Jane 1949- ...... **CLC 53, 76, 144, 236**
See also AAYA 66; AMWS 6; BPFB 3; CA 104; CANR 30, 50, 74, 96, 158, 196; CN 6, 7; CPW 1; DA3; DAM POP; DLB 227, 234; EWL 3; INT CANR-30; MAL 5; MTFW 2005; NFS 32; SSFS 19

Smiley, Jane Graves
See Smiley, Jane

Smith, A(rthur) J(ames) M(arshall)
1902-1980 .... **CLC 15**
See also CA 1-4R; 102; CANR 4; CP 1, 2, 3; DAC; DLB 88; RGEL 2

Smith, Adam 1723(?)-1790 .... **LC 36**
See also DLB 104, 252, 336; RGEL 2

Smith, Alexander 1829-1867 .... **NCLC 59**
See also DLB 32, 55

Smith, Alexander McCall 1948- ..... **CLC 268**
See also CA 215; CANR 154, 196; SATA 73, 179

Smith, Anna Deavere 1950- ...... **CLC 86, 241**
See also CA 133; CANR 103; CD 5, 6; DFS 2, 22; DLB 341

Smith, Betty (Wehner) 1904-1972 .... **CLC 19**
See also AAYA 72; BPFB 3; BYA 3; CA 5-8R; 33-36R; DLBY 1982; LAIT 3; NFS 31; RGAL 4; SATA 6

Smith, Charlotte (Turner)
1749-1806 .... **NCLC 23, 115; PC 104**
See also DLB 39, 109; RGEL 2; TEA

Smith, Clark Ashton 1893-1961 .... **CLC 43**
See also AAYA 76; CA 143; CANR 81; FANT; HGG; MTCW 2; SCFW 1, 2; SFW 4; SUFW

Smith, Dave
See Smith, David (Jeddie)

Smith, David (Jeddie) 1942- .... **CLC 22, 42**
See also CA 49-52; CAAS 7; CANR 1, 59, 120; CP 3, 4, 5, 6, 7; CSW; DAM POET; DLB 5

Smith, Iain Crichton 1928-1998 .... **CLC 64**
See also BRWS 9; CA 21-24R; 171; CN 1, 2, 3, 4, 5, 6; CP 1, 2, 3, 4, 5, 6; DLB 40, 139, 319, 352; RGSF 2

Smith, John 1580(?)-1631 .... **LC 9**
See also DLB 24, 30; TUS

Smith, Johnston
See Crane, Stephen

Smith, Joseph, Jr. 1805-1844 .... **NCLC 53**

Smith, Kevin 1970- .... **CLC 223**
See also AAYA 37; CA 166; CANR 131, 201

Smith, Lee 1944- .... **CLC 25, 73, 258; SSC 142**
See also CA 114; 119; CANR 46, 118, 173; CN 7; CSW; DLB 143; DLBY 1983; EWL 3; INT CA-119; RGAL 4

Smith, Martin
See Smith, Martin Cruz

Smith, Martin Cruz 1942- .. **CLC 25; NNAL**
See Smith, Martin Cruz
See also BEST 89:4; BPFB 3; CA 85-88; CANR 6, 23, 43, 65, 119, 184; CMW 4; CPW; DAM MULT, POP; HGG; INT CANR-23; MTCW 2; MTFW 2005; RGAL 4

Smith, Patti 1946- .... **CLC 12**
See also CA 93-96; CANR 63, 168

Smith, Pauline (Urmson)
1882-1959 .... **TCLC 25**
See also DLB 225; EWL 3

Smith, R. Alexander McCall
See Smith, Alexander McCall

Smith, Rosamond
See Oates, Joyce Carol

Smith, Seba 1792-1868 .... **NCLC 187**
See also DLB 1, 11, 243

Smith, Sheila Kaye
See Kaye-Smith, Sheila

Smith, Stevie 1902-1971 .... **CLC 3, 8, 25, 44; PC 12**
See also BRWR 3; BRWS 2; CA 17-18; 29-32R; CANR 35; CAP 2; CP 1; DAM POET; DLB 20; EWL 3; MTCW 1, 2; PAB; PFS 3; RGEL 2; TEA

Smith, Wilbur 1933- .... **CLC 33**
See also CA 13-16R; CANR 7, 46, 66, 134,
180; CPW; MTCW 1, 2; MTFW 2005
Smith, Wilbur Addison
See Smith, Wilbur
Smith, William Jay 1918- .... **CLC 6**
See also AMWS 13; CA 5-8R; CANR 44,
106, 211; CP 1, 2, 3, 4, 5, 6, 7; CSW;
CWRI 5; DLB 5; MAICYA 1, 2; SAAS
22; SATA 2, 68, 154; SATA-Essay 154;
TCLE 1:2
Smith, Woodrow Wilson
See Kuttner, Henry
Smith, Zadie 1975- .... **CLC 158**
See also AAYA 50; CA 193; CANR 204;
DLB 347; MTFW 2005
Smolenskin, Peretz 1842-1885 .... **NCLC 30**
Smollett, Tobias (George) 1721-1771 ... **LC 2, 46, 188**
See also BRW 3; CDBLB 1660-1789; DLB
39, 104; RGEL 2; TEA
Snodgrass, Quentin Curtius
See Twain, Mark
Snodgrass, Thomas Jefferson
See Twain, Mark
Snodgrass, W. D. 1926-2009 .... **CLC 2, 6, 10, 18, 68; PC 74**
See also AMWS 6; CA 1-4R; 282; CANR
6, 36, 65, 85, 185; CP 1, 2, 3, 4, 5, 6, 7;
DAM POET; DLB 5; MAL 5; MTCW 1,
2; MTFW 2005; PFS 29; RGAL 4; TCLE
1:2
Snodgrass, W. de Witt
See Snodgrass, W. D.
Snodgrass, William de Witt
See Snodgrass, W. D.
Snodgrass, William De Witt
See Snodgrass, W. D.
Snorri Sturluson 1179-1241 .... **CMLC 56**
See also RGWL 2, 3
Snow, C(harles) P(ercy) 1905-1980 ... **CLC 1, 4, 6, 9, 13, 19**
See also BRW 7; CA 5-8R; 101; CANR 28;
CDBLB 1945-1960; CN 1, 2; DAM NOV;
DLB 15, 77; DLBD 17; EWL 3; MTCW
1, 2; MTFW 2005; RGEL 2; TEA
Snow, Frances Compton
See Adams, Henry
Snyder, Gary 1930- . **CLC 1, 2, 5, 9, 32, 120; PC 21**
See also AAYA 72; AMWS 8; ANW; BG
1:3; CA 17-20R; CANR 30, 60, 125; CP
1, 2, 3, 4, 5, 6, 7; DA3; DAM POET; DLB
5, 16, 165, 212, 237, 275, 342; EWL 3;
MAL 5; MTCW 2; MTFW 2005; PFS 9,
19; RGAL 4; WP
Snyder, Gary Sherman
See Snyder, Gary
Snyder, Zilpha Keatley 1927- .... **CLC 17**
See also AAYA 15; BYA 1; CA 9-12R, 252;
CAAE 252; CANR 38, 202; CLR 31, 121;
JRDA; MAICYA 1, 2; SAAS 2; SATA 1,
28, 75, 110, 163; SATA-Essay 112, 163;
YAW
Soares, Bernardo
See Pessoa, Fernando
Sobh, A.
See Shamlu, Ahmad
Sobh, Alef
See Shamlu, Ahmad
Sobol, Joshua 1939- .... **CLC 60**
See also CA 200; CWW 2; RGHL
Sobol, Yehoshua 1939-
See Sobol, Joshua
Socrates 470B.C.-399B.C. .... **CMLC 27**
Soderberg, Hjalmar 1869-1941 ...... **TCLC 39**
See also DLB 259; EWL 3; RGSF 2
Soderbergh, Steven 1963- .... **CLC 154**
See also AAYA 43; CA 243

Soderbergh, Steven Andrew
See Soderbergh, Steven
Sodergran, Edith 1892-1923 .... **TCLC 31**
See also CA 202; DLB 259; EW 11; EWL
3; RGWL 2, 3
Soedergran, Edith Irene
See Sodergran, Edith
Softly, Edgar
See Lovecraft, H. P.
Softly, Edward
See Lovecraft, H. P.
Sokolov, Alexander V. 1943- .... **CLC 59**
See also CA 73-76; CWW 2; DLB 285;
EWL 3; RGWL 2, 3
Sokolov, Alexander Vsevolodovich
See Sokolov, Alexander V.
Sokolov, Raymond 1941- .... **CLC 7**
See also CA 85-88
Sokolov, Sasha
See Sokolov, Alexander V.
Solo, Jay
See Ellison, Harlan
Sologub, Fedor
See Teternikov, Fyodor Kuzmich
Sologub, Feodor
See Teternikov, Fyodor Kuzmich
Sologub, Fyodor
See Teternikov, Fyodor Kuzmich
Solomons, Ikey Esquir
See Thackeray, William Makepeace
Solomos, Dionysios 1798-1857 .... **NCLC 15**
Solwoska, Mara
See French, Marilyn
Solzhenitsyn, Aleksandr 1918-2008 ... **CLC 1, 2, 4, 7, 9, 10, 18, 26, 34, 78, 134, 235; SSC 32, 105; WLC 5**
See also AAYA 49; AITN 1; BPFB 3; CA
69-72; CANR 40, 65, 116; CWW 2; DA;
DA3; DAB; DAC; DAM MST, NOV;
DLB 302, 332; EW 13; EWL 3; EXPS;
LAIT 4; MTCW 1, 2; MTFW 2005; NFS
6; PFS 38; RGSF 2; RGWL 2, 3; SSFS 9;
TWA
Solzhenitsyn, Aleksandr I.
See Solzhenitsyn, Aleksandr
Solzhenitsyn, Aleksandr Isayevich
See Solzhenitsyn, Aleksandr
Somers, Jane
See Lessing, Doris
Somerville, Edith Oenone
1858-1949 .... **SSC 56; TCLC 51**
See also CA 196; DLB 135; RGEL 2; RGSF
2
Somerville & Ross
See Martin, Violet Florence; Somerville,
Edith Oenone
Sommer, Scott 1951- .... **CLC 25**
See also CA 106
Sommers, Christina Hoff 1950- ...... **CLC 197**
See also CA 153; CANR 95
Sondheim, Stephen 1930- .. **CLC 30, 39, 147; DC 22**
See also AAYA 11, 66; CA 103; CANR 47,
67, 125; DAM DRAM; DFS 25, 27, 28;
LAIT 4
Sondheim, Stephen Joshua
See Sondheim, Stephen
Sone, Monica 1919- .... **AAL**
See also DLB 312
Song, Cathy 1955- .... **AAL; PC 21**
See also CA 154; CANR 118; CWP; DLB
169, 312; EXPP; FW; PFS 5
Sontag, Susan 1933-2004 ... **CLC 1, 2, 10, 13, 31, 105, 195, 277**
See also AMWS 3; CA 17-20R; 234; CANR
25, 51, 74, 97, 184; CN 1, 2, 3, 4, 5, 6, 7;
CPW; DA3; DAM POP; DLB 2, 67; EWL
3; MAL 5; MBL; MTCW 1, 2; MTFW
2005; RGAL 4; RHW; SSFS 10

Sophocles 496(?)B.C.-406(?)B.C. .... **CMLC 2, 47, 51, 86; DC 1; WLCS**
See also AW 1; CDWLB 1; DA; DA3;
DAB; DAC; DAM DRAM; MST; DFS 1,
4, 8, 24; DLB 176; LAIT 1; LATS 1:1;
LMFS 1; RGWL 2, 3; TWA; WLIT 8
Sordello 1189-1269 .... **CMLC 15**
Sorel, Georges 1847-1922 .... **TCLC 91**
See also CA 118; 188
Sorel, Julia
See Drexler, Rosalyn
Sorokin, Vladimir .... **CLC 59**
See also CA 258; DLB 285
Sorokin, Vladimir Georgievich
See Sorokin, Vladimir
Sorrentino, Gilbert 1929-2006 .... **CLC 3, 7, 14, 22, 40, 247**
See also AMWS 21; CA 77-80; 250; CANR
14, 33, 115, 157; CN 3, 4, 5, 6, 7; CP 1,
2, 3, 4, 5, 6, 7; DLB 5, 173; DLBY 1980;
INT CANR-14
Soseki
See Natsume, Soseki
Soto, Gary 1952- ... **CLC 32, 80; HLC 2; PC 28**
See also AAYA 10, 37; BYA 11; CA 119;
125; CANR 50, 74, 107, 157; CLR 38;
CP 4, 5, 6, 7; DAM MULT; DFS 26; DLB
82; EWL 3; EXPP; HW 1, 2; INT CA-
125; JRDA; LLW; MAICYA 2; MAIC-
YAS 1; MAL 5; MTCW 2; MTFW 2005;
PFS 7, 30; RGAL 4; SATA 80, 120, 174;
SSFS 33; WYA; YAW
Soupault, Philippe 1897-1990 .... **CLC 68**
See also CA 116; 147; 131; EWL 3; GFL
1789 to the Present; LMFS 2
Souster, (Holmes) Raymond 1921- .... **CLC 5, 14**
See also CA 13-16R; CAAS 14; CANR 13,
29, 53; CP 1, 2, 3, 4, 5, 6, 7; DA3; DAC;
DAM POET; DLB 88; RGEL 2; SATA 63
Southern, Terry 1924(?)-1995 .... **CLC 7**
See also AMWS 11; BPFB 3; CA 1-4R;
150; CANR 1, 55, 107; CN 1, 2, 3, 4, 5,
6; DLB 2; IDFW 3, 4
Southerne, Thomas 1660-1746 .... **LC 99**
See also DLB 80; RGEL 2
Southey, Robert 1774-1843 .... **NCLC 8, 97; PC 111**
See also BRW 4; DLB 93, 107, 142; RGEL
2; SATA 54
Southwell, Robert 1561(?)-1595 .... **LC 108**
See also DLB 167; RGEL 2; TEA
Southworth, Emma Dorothy Eliza Nevitte
1819-1899 .... **NCLC 26**
See also DLB 239
Souza, Ernest
See Scott, Evelyn
Soyinka, Wole 1934- .. **BLC 1:3, 2:3; CLC 3, 5, 14, 36, 44, 179; DC 2; WLC 5**
See also AFW; BW 2, 3; CA 13-16R;
CANR 27, 39, 82, 136; CD 5, 6; DLB
3; CN 6, 7; CP 1, 2, 3, 4, 5, 6 ,7; DA;
DA3; DAB; DAC; DAM DRAM, MST,
MULT; DFS 10, 26; DLB 125, 332; EWL
3; MTCW 1, 2; MTFW 2005; PFS 27;
RGEL 2; TWA; WLIT 2; WWE 1
Spackman, W(illiam) M(ode)
1905-1990 .... **CLC 46**
See also CA 81-84; 132
Spacks, Barry (Bernard) 1931- .... **CLC 14**
See also CA 154; CANR 33, 109; CP 3, 4,
5, 6, 7; DLB 105
Spanidou, Irini 1946- .... **CLC 44**
See also CA 185; CANR 179
Spark, Muriel 1918-2006 ... **CLC 2, 3, 5, 8, 13, 18, 40, 94, 242; PC 72; SSC 10, 115**
See also BRWS 1; CA 5-8R; 251; CANR
12, 36, 76, 89, 131; CDBLB 1945-1960;
CN 1, 2, 3, 4, 5, 6, 7; CP 1, 2, 3, 4, 5, 6,

5; MBL; MTCW 1, 2; MTFW 2005;
NCFS 4; NFS 27; PFS 38; RGAL 4;
RGSF 2; SSFS 5; TUS; WP

Steinbeck, John 1902-1968 .. **CLC 1, 5, 9, 13,
21, 34, 45, 75, 124; SSC 11, 37, 77, 135;
TCLC 135; WLC 5**
See also AAYA 12; AMW; BPFB 3; BYA 2,
3, 13; CA 1-4R; 25-28R; CANR 1, 35;
CDALB 1929-1941; DA; DA3; DAB;
DAC; DAM DRAM, MST, NOV; DLB 7,
9, 212, 275, 309, 332; DLBD 2; EWL 3;
EXPS; LAIT 3; MAL 5; MTCW 1, 2;
MTFW 2005; NFS 1, 5, 7, 17, 19, 28, 34,
37; RGAL 4; RGSF 2; RHW; SATA 9;
SSFS 3, 6, 22; TCWW 1, 2; TUS; WYA;
YAW

Steinbeck, John Ernst
See Steinbeck, John

Steinem, Gloria 1934- .... **CLC 63**
See also CA 53-56; CANR 28, 51, 139;
DLB 246; FL 1:1; FW; MTCW 1, 2;
MTFW 2005

Steiner, George 1929- .... **CLC 24, 221**
See also CA 73-76; CANR 31, 67, 108, 212;
DAM NOV; DLB 67, 299; EWL 3;
MTCW 1, 2; MTFW 2005; RGHL; SATA
62

Steiner, K. Leslie
See Delany, Samuel R., Jr.

Steiner, Rudolf 1861-1925 .... **TCLC 13**
See also CA 107

Stendhal 1783-1842 .... **NCLC 23, 46, 178;
SSC 27; WLC 5**
See also DA; DA3; DAB; DAC; DAM
MST, NOV; DLB 119; EW 5; GFL 1789
to the Present; RGWL 2, 3; TWA

Stephen, Adeline Virginia
See Woolf, Virginia

Stephen, Sir Leslie 1832-1904 .... **TCLC 23**
See also BRW 5; CA 123; DLB 57, 144,
190

Stephen, Sir Leslie
See Stephen, Sir Leslie

Stephen, Virginia
See Woolf, Virginia

Stephens, James 1882(?)-1950 .... **SSC 50;
TCLC 4**
See also CA 104; 192; DLB 19, 153, 162;
EWL 3; FANT; RGEL 2; SUFW

Stephens, Reed
See Donaldson, Stephen R.

Stephenson, Neal 1959- .... **CLC 220**
See also AAYA 38; CA 122; CANR 88, 138,
195; CN 7; MTFW 2005; SFW 4

Steptoe, Lydia
See Barnes, Djuna

Sterchi, Beat 1949- .... **CLC 65**
See also CA 203

Sterling, Brett
See Bradbury, Ray; Hamilton, Edmond

Sterling, Bruce 1954- .... **CLC 72**
See also AAYA 78; CA 119; CANR 44, 135,
184; CN 7; MTFW 2005; SCFW 2; SFW
4

Sterling, George 1869-1926 .... **TCLC 20**
See also CA 117; 165; DLB 54

Stern, Gerald 1925- .... **CLC 40, 100; PC 115**
See also AMWS 9; CA 81-84; CANR 28,
94, 206; CP 3, 4, 5, 6, 7; DLB 105; PFS
26; RGAL 4

Stern, Richard (Gustave) 1928- ... **CLC 4, 39**
See also CA 1-4R; CANR 1, 25, 52, 120;
CN 1, 2, 3, 4, 5, 6, 7; DLB 218; DLBY
1987; INT CANR-25

Sternberg, Josef von 1894-1969 .... **CLC 20**
See also CA 81-84

Sterne, Laurence 1713-1768 .. **LC 2, 48, 156;
WLC 5**
See also BRW 3; BRWC 1; CDBLB 1660-
1789; DA; DAB; DAC; DAM MST, NOV;
DLB 39; RGEL 2; TEA

Sternheim, (William Adolf) Carl
1878-1942 .... **TCLC 8, 223**
See also CA 105; 193; DLB 56, 118; EWL
3; IDTP; RGWL 2, 3

Stetson, Charlotte Perkins
See Gilman, Charlotte Perkins

Stevens, Margaret Dean
See Aldrich, Bess Streeter

Stevens, Mark 1951- .... **CLC 34**
See also CA 122

Stevens, R. L.
See Hoch, Edward D.

Stevens, Wallace 1879-1955 .... **PC 6, 110;
TCLC 3, 12, 45; WLC 5**
See also AMW; AMWR 1; CA 104; 124;
CANR 181; CDALB 1929-1941; DA;
DA3; DAB; DAC; DAM MST, POET;
DLB 54, 342; EWL 3; EXPP; MAL 5;
MTCW 1, 2; PAB; PFS 13, 16, 35; RGAL
4; TUS; WP

Stevenson, Anne (Katharine) 1933- .. **CLC 7,
33**
See also BRWS 6; CA 17-20R; CAAS 9;
CANR 9, 33, 123; CP 3, 4, 5, 6, 7; CWP;
DLB 40; MTCW 1; RHW

Stevenson, Robert Louis
1850-1894 ...... **NCLC 5, 14, 63, 193; PC
84; SSC 11, 51, 126; WLC 5**
See also AAYA 24; BPFB 3; BRW 5;
BRWC 1; BRWR 1; BYA 1, 2, 4, 13; CD-
BLB 1890-1914; CLR 10, 11, 107; DA;
DA3; DAB; DAC; DAM MST, NOV;
DLB 18, 57, 141, 156, 174; DLBD 13;
GL 3; HGG; JRDA; LAIT 1, 3; MAICYA
1, 2; NFS 11, 20, 33; RGEL 2; RGSF 2;
SATA 100; SUFW; TEA; WCH; WLIT 4;
WYA; YABC 2; YAW

Stevenson, Robert Louis Balfour
See Stevenson, Robert Louis

Stewart, J(ohn) I(nnes) M(ackintosh)
1906-1994 .... **CLC 7, 14, 32**
See also CA 85-88; 147; CAAS 3; CANR
47; CMW 4; CN 1, 2, 3, 4, 5; DLB 276;
MSW; MTCW 1, 2

Stewart, Mary (Florence Elinor)
1916- .... **CLC 7, 35, 117**
See also AAYA 29, 73; BPFB 3; CA 1-4R;
CANR 1, 59, 130; CMW 4; CPW; DAB;
FANT; RHW; SATA 12; YAW

Stewart, Mary Rainbow
See Stewart, Mary (Florence Elinor)

Stewart, Will
See Williamson, John Stewart

Stifle, June
See Campbell, Maria

Stifter, Adalbert 1805-1868 ... **NCLC 41, 198;
SSC 28**
See also CDWLB 2; DLB 133; RGSF 2;
RGWL 2, 3

Still, James 1906-2001 .... **CLC 49**
See also CA 65-68; 195; CAAS 17; CANR
10, 26; CSW; DLB 9; DLBY 01; SATA
29; SATA-Obit 127

Sting 1951- .... **CLC 26**
See also CA 167

Stirling, Arthur
See Sinclair, Upton

Stitt, Milan 1941-2009 .... **CLC 29**
See also CA 69-72; 284

Stitt, Milan William
See Stitt, Milan

Stockton, Francis Richard
1834-1902 .... **TCLC 47**
See also AAYA 68; BYA 4, 13; CA 108;
137; DLB 42, 74; DLBD 13; EXPS; MAI-
CYA 1, 2; SATA 44; SATA-Brief 32; SFW
4; SSFS 3; SUFW; WCH

Stockton, Frank R.
See Stockton, Francis Richard

Stoddard, Charles
See Kuttner, Henry

Stoker, Abraham
See Stoker, Bram

Stoker, Bram 1847-1912 ... **SSC 62; TCLC 8,
144; WLC 6**
See also AAYA 23; BPFB 3; BRWS 3; BYA
5; CA 105; 150; CDBLB 1890-1914; DA;
DA3; DAB; DAC; DAM MST, NOV;
DLB 304; GL 3; HGG; LATS 1:1; MTFW
2005; NFS 18; RGEL 2; SATA 29; SUFW;
TEA; WLIT 4

Stolz, Mary 1920-2006 .... **CLC 12**
See also AAYA 8, 73; AITN 1; CA 5-8R;
255; CANR 13, 41, 112; JRDA; MAICYA
1, 2; SAAS 3; SATA 10, 71, 133; SATA-
Obit 180; YAW

Stolz, Mary Slattery
See Stolz, Mary

Stone, Irving 1903-1989 .... **CLC 7**
See also AITN 1; BPFB 3; CA 1-4R; 129;
CAAS 3; CANR 1, 23; CN 1, 2, 3, 4;
CPW; DA3; DAM POP; INT CANR-23;
MTCW 1, 2; MTFW 2005; RHW; SATA
3; SATA-Obit 64

Stone, Oliver 1946- .... **CLC 73**
See also AAYA 15, 64; CA 110; CANR 55,
125

Stone, Oliver William
See Stone, Oliver

Stone, Robert 1937- .... **CLC 5, 23, 42, 175**
See also AMWS 5; BPFB 3; CA 85-88;
CANR 23, 66, 95, 173; CN 4, 5, 6, 7;
DLB 152; EWL 3; INT CANR-23; MAL
5; MTCW 1; MTFW 2005

Stone, Robert Anthony
See Stone, Robert

Stone, Ruth 1915- .... **PC 53**
See also CA 45-48; CANR 2, 91, 209; CP
5, 6, 7; CSW; DLB 105; PFS 19

Stone, Zachary
See Follett, Ken

Stoppard, Tom 1937- ... **CLC 1, 3, 4, 5, 8, 15,
29, 34, 63, 91; DC 6, 30; WLC 6**
See also AAYA 63; BRWC 1; BRWR 2;
BRWS 1; CA 81-84; CANR 39, 67, 125;
CBD; CD 5, 6; CDBLB 1960 to Present;
DA; DA3; DAB; DAC; DAM DRAM,
MST; DFS 2, 5, 8, 11, 13, 16; DLB 13,
233; DLBY 1985; EWL 3; LATS 1:2;
LNFS 3; MTCW 1, 2; MTFW 2005;
RGEL 2; TEA; WLIT 4

Storey, David (Malcolm) 1933- . **CLC 2, 4, 5,
8; DC 40**
See also BRWS 1; CA 81-84; CANR 36;
CBD; CD 5, 6; CN 1, 2, 3, 4, 5, 6; DAM
DRAM; DLB 13, 14, 207, 245, 326; EWL
3; MTCW 1; RGEL 2

Storm, Hyemeyohsts 1935- ... **CLC 3; NNAL**
See also CA 81-84; CANR 45; DAM MULT

Storm, (Hans) Theodor (Woldsen)
1817-1888 ... **NCLC 1, 195; SSC 27, 106**
See also CDWLB 2; DLB 129; EW; RGSF
2; RGWL 2, 3

Storni, Alfonsina 1892-1938 . **HLC 2; PC 33;
TCLC 5**
See also CA 104; 131; DAM MULT; DLB
283; HW 1; LAW

Stoughton, William 1631-1701 .... **LC 38**
See also DLB 24

Su Yuean-ying
See Su, Chien
Suzuki, D. T.
See Suzuki, Daisetz Teitaro
Suzuki, Daisetz T.
See Suzuki, Daisetz Teitaro
Suzuki, Daisetz Teitaro
1870-1966 .... **TCLC 109**
See also CA 121; 111; MTCW 1, 2; MTFW 2005
Suzuki, Teitaro
See Suzuki, Daisetz Teitaro
Svareff, Count Vladimir
See Crowley, Edward Alexander
Svevo, Italo
See Schmitz, Aron Hector
Swados, Elizabeth 1951- .... **CLC 12**
See also CA 97-100; CANR 49, 163; INT CA-97-100
Swados, Elizabeth A.
See Swados, Elizabeth
Swados, Harvey 1920-1972 .... **CLC 5**
See also CA 5-8R; 37-40R; CANR 6; CN 1; DLB 2, 335; MAL 5
Swados, Liz
See Swados, Elizabeth
Swan, Gladys 1934- .... **CLC 69**
See also CA 101; CANR 17, 39; TCLE 1:2
Swanson, Logan
See Matheson, Richard
Swarthout, Glendon (Fred)
1918-1992 .... **CLC 35**
See also AAYA 55; CA 1-4R; 139; CANR 1, 47; CN 1, 2, 3, 4, 5; LAIT 5; NFS 29; SATA 26; TCWW 1, 2; YAW
Swedenborg, Emanuel 1688-1772 ..... **LC 105**
Sweet, Sarah C.
See Jewett, Sarah Orne
Swenson, May 1919-1989 ...... **CLC 4, 14, 61, 106; PC 14**
See also AMWS 4; CA 5-8R; 130; CANR 36, 61, 131; CP 1, 2, 3, 4; DA; DAB; DAC; DAM MST, POET; DLB 5; EXPP; GLL 2; MAL 5; MTCW 1, 2; MTFW 2005; PFS 16, 30, 38; SATA 15; WP
Swift, Augustus
See Lovecraft, H. P.
Swift, Graham 1949- .... **CLC 41, 88, 233**
See also BRWC 2; BRWS 5; CA 117; 122; CANR 46, 71, 128, 181; CN 4, 5, 6, 7; DLB 194, 326; MTCW 2; MTFW 2005; NFS 18; RGSF 2
Swift, Jonathan 1667-1745 ..... **LC 1, 42, 101; PC 9; WLC 6**
See also AAYA 41; BRW 3; BRWC 1; BRWR 1; BYA 5, 14; CDBLB 1660-1789; CLR 53, 161; DA; DA3; DAB; DAC; DAM MST, NOV, POET; DLB 39, 95, 101; EXPN; LAIT 1; NFS 6; PFS 27, 37; RGEL 2; SATA 19; TEA; WCH; WLIT 3
Swinburne, Algernon Charles
1837-1909 ... **PC 24; TCLC 8, 36; WLC 6**
See also BRW 5; CA 105; 140; CDBLB 1832-1890; DA; DA3; DAB; DAC; DAM MST, POET; DLB 35, 57; PAB; RGEL 2; TEA
Swinfen, Ann CLC 34
See also CA 202
Swinnerton, Frank (Arthur)
1884-1982 .... **CLC 31**
See also CA 202; 108; CN 1, 2, 3; DLB 34
Swinnerton, Frank Arthur
1884-1982 .... **CLC 31**
See also CA 108; DLB 34
Swithen, John
See King, Stephen
Sylvia
See Ashton-Warner, Sylvia (Constance)

Symmes, Robert Edward
See Duncan, Robert
Symonds, John Addington
1840-1893 .... **NCLC 34**
See also BRWS 14; DLB 57, 144
Symons, Arthur 1865-1945 ..... **TCLC 11, 243**
See also BRWS 14; CA 107; 189; DLB 19, 57, 149; RGEL 2
Symons, Julian (Gustave)
1912-1994 .... **CLC 2, 14, 32**
See also CA 49-52; 147; CAAS 3; CANR 3, 33, 59; CMW 4; CN 1, 2, 3, 4, 5; CP 1, 3, 4; DLB 87, 155; DLBY 1992; MSW; MTCW 1
Synge, Edmund John Millington
See Synge, John Millington
Synge, J. M.
See Synge, John Millington
Synge, John Millington 1871-1909 ...... **DC 2; TCLC 6, 37**
See also BRW 6; BRWR 1; CA 104; 141; CDBLB 1890-1914; DAM DRAM; DFS 18; DLB 10, 19; EWL 3; RGEL 2; TEA; WLIT 4
Syruc, J.
See Milosz, Czeslaw
Szirtes, George 1948- .... **CLC 46; PC 51**
See also CA 109; CANR 27, 61, 117; CP 4, 5, 6, 7
Szymborska, Wislawa 1923- ... **CLC 99, 190; PC 44**
See also AAYA 76; CA 154; CANR 91, 133, 181; CDWLB 4; CWP; CWW 2; DA3; DLB 232, 332; DLBY 1996; EWL 3; MTCW 2; MTFW 2005; PFS 15, 27, 31, 34; RGHL; RGWL 3
T. O., Nik
See Annensky, Innokenty (Fyodorovich)
Tabori, George 1914-2007 .... **CLC 19**
See also CA 49-52; 262; CANR 4, 69; CBD; CD 5, 6; DLB 245; RGHL
Tacitus c. 55-c. 117 .... **CMLC 56**
See also AW 2; CDWLB 1; DLB 211; RGWL 2, 3; WLIT 8
Tadjo, Veronique 1955- .... **BLC 2:3**
See also DLB 360; EWL 3
Tagore, Rabindranath 1861-1941 .... **PC 8; SSC 48; TCLC 3, 53**
See also CA 104; 120; DA3; DAM DRAM, POET; DFS 26; DLB 323, 332; EWL 3; MTCW 1, 2; MTFW 2005; PFS 18; RGEL 2; RGSF 2; RGWL 2, 3; TWA
Taine, Hippolyte Adolphe
1828-1893 .... **NCLC 15**
See also EW 7; GFL 1789 to the Present
Talayesva, Don C. 1890-(?) .... **NNAL**
Talese, Gay 1932- .... **CLC 37, 232**
See also AITN 1; AMWS 17; CA 1-4R; CANR 9, 58, 137, 177; DLB 185; INT CANR-9; MTCW 1, 2; MTFW 2005
Tallent, Elizabeth 1954- .... **CLC 45**
See also CA 117; CANR 72; DLB 130
Tallmountain, Mary 1918-1997 .... **NNAL**
See also CA 146; 161; DLB 193
Tally, Ted 1952- .... **CLC 42**
See also CA 120; 124; CAD; CANR 125; CD 5, 6; INT CA-124
Talvik, Heiti 1904-1947 .... **TCLC 87**
See also EWL 3
Tamayo y Baus, Manuel
1829-1898 .... **NCLC 1**
Tammsaare, A(nton) H(ansen)
1878-1940 .... **TCLC 27**
See also CA 164; CDWLB 4; DLB 220; EWL 3
Tam'si, Tchicaya U
See Tchicaya, Gerald Felix

Tan, Amy 1952- ..... **AAL; CLC 59, 120, 151, 257**
See also AAYA 9, 48; AMWS 10; BEST 89:3; BPFB 3; CA 136; CANR 54, 105, 132; CDALBS; CN 6, 7; CPW 1; DA3; DAM MULT, NOV, POP; DLB 173, 312; EXPN; FL 1:6; FW; LAIT 3, 5; MAL 5; MTCW 2; MTFW 2005; NFS 1, 13, 16, 31, 35; RGAL 4; SATA 75; SSFS 9; YAW
Tan, Amy Ruth
See Tan, Amy
Tandem, Carl Felix
See Spitteler, Carl
Tandem, Felix
See Spitteler, Carl
Tania B.
See Blixen, Karen
Tanizaki, Jun'ichiro 1886-1965 ... **CLC 8, 14, 28; SSC 21**
See also CA 93-96; 25-28R; DLB 180; EWL 3; MJW; MTCW 2; MTFW 2005; RGSF 2; RGWL 2
Tanizaki Jun'ichiro
See Tanizaki, Jun'ichiro
Tannen, Deborah 1945- .... **CLC 206**
See also CA 118; CANR 95
Tannen, Deborah Frances
See Tannen, Deborah
Tanner, William
See Amis, Kingsley
Tante, Dilly
See Kunitz, Stanley
Tao Lao
See Storni, Alfonsina
Tapahonso, Luci 1953- .... **NNAL; PC 65**
See also CA 145; CANR 72, 127, 214; DLB 175
Tarantino, Quentin 1963- .... **CLC 125, 230**
See also AAYA 58; CA 171; CANR 125
Tarantino, Quentin Jerome
See Tarantino, Quentin
Tarassoff, Lev
See Troyat, Henri
Tarbell, Ida 1857-1944 .... **TCLC 40**
See also CA 122; 181; DLB 47
Tarbell, Ida Minerva
See Tarbell, Ida
Tarchetti, Ugo 1839(?)-1869 .... **SSC 119**
Tardieu d'Esclavelles,
Louise-Florence-Petronille
See Epinay, Louise d'
Tarkington, (Newton) Booth
1869-1946 .... **TCLC 9**
See also BPFB 3; BYA 3; CA 110; 143; CWRI 5; DLB 9, 102; MAL 5; MTCW 2; NFS 34; RGAL 4; SATA 17
Tarkovskii, Andrei Arsen'evich
See Tarkovsky, Andrei (Arsenyevich)
Tarkovsky, Andrei (Arsenyevich)
1932-1986 .... **CLC 75**
See also CA 127
Tartt, Donna 1964(?)- .... **CLC 76**
See also AAYA 56; CA 142; CANR 135; LNFS 2; MTFW 2005
Tasso, Torquato 1544-1595 .... **LC 5, 94**
See also EFS 2; EW 2; RGWL 2, 3; WLIT 7
Tate, (John Orley) Allen 1899-1979 .. **CLC 2, 4, 6, 9, 11, 14, 24; PC 50**
See also AMW; CA 5-8R; 85-88; CANR 32, 108; CN 1, 2; CP 1, 2; DLB 4, 45, 63; DLBD 17; EWL 3; MAL 5; MTCW 1, 2; MTFW 2005; RGAL 4; RHW
Tate, Ellalice
See Hibbert, Eleanor Alice Burford
Tate, James (Vincent) 1943- ..... **CLC 2, 6, 25**
See also CA 21-24R; CANR 29, 57, 114; CP 1, 2, 3, 4, 5, 6, 7; DLB 5, 169; EWL 3; PFS 10, 15; RGAL 4; WP

Tate, Nahum 1652(?)-1715 .... **LC 109**
    See also DLB 80; RGEL 2

Tauler, Johannes c. 1300-1361 ...... **CMLC 37**
    See also DLB 179; LMFS 1

Tavel, Ronald 1936-2009 .... **CLC 6**
    See also CA 21-24R; 284; CAD; CANR 33;
    CD 5, 6

Taviani, Paolo 1931- .... **CLC 70**
    See also CA 153

Taylor, Bayard 1825-1878 .... **NCLC 89**
    See also DLB 3, 189, 250, 254; RGAL 4

Taylor, C(ecil) P(hilip) 1929-1981 ... **CLC 27**
    See also CA 25-28R; 105; CANR 47; CBD

Taylor, Edward 1642(?)-1729 ..... **LC 11, 163;**
    PC 63
    See also AMW; DA; DAB; DAC; DAM
    MST, POET; DLB 24; EXPP; PFS 31;
    RGAL 4; TUS

Taylor, Eleanor Ross 1920- .... **CLC 5**
    See also CA 81-84; CANR 70

Taylor, Elizabeth 1912-1975 .... **CLC 2, 4, 29;**
    SSC 100
    See also CA 13-16R; CANR 9, 70; CN 1,
    2; DLB 139; MTCW 1; RGEL 2; SATA
    13

Taylor, Frederick Winslow
    1856-1915 .... **TCLC 76**
    See also CA 188

Taylor, Henry 1942- .... **CLC 44**
    See also CA 33-36R; CAAS 7; CANR 31,
    178; CP 6, 7; DLB 5; PFS 10

Taylor, Henry Splawn
    See Taylor, Henry

Taylor, Kamala
    See Markandaya, Kamala

Taylor, Mildred D. 1943- .... **CLC 21**
    See also AAYA 10, 47; BW 1; BYA 3, 8;
    CA 85-88; CANR 25, 115, 136; CLR 9,
    59, 90, 144; CSW; DLB 52; JRDA; LAIT
    3; MAICYA 1, 2; MTCW 2005; SAAS 5;
    SATA 135; WYA; YAW

Taylor, Peter (Hillsman) 1917-1994 .. **CLC 1,**
    4, 18, 37, 44, 50, 71; SSC 10, 84
    See also AMWS 5; BPFB 3; CA 13-16R;
    147; CANR 9, 50; CN 1, 2, 3, 4, 5; CSW;
    DLB 218, 278; DLBY 1981, 1994; EWL
    3; EXPS; INT CANR-9; MAL 5; MTCW
    1, 2; MTFW 2005; RGAL 4; RGSF 2; SSFS 9; TUS

Taylor, Robert Lewis 1912-1998 .... **CLC 14**
    See also CA 1-4R; 170; CANR 3, 64; CN
    1, 2; SATA 10; TCWW 1, 2

Tchekhov, Anton
    See Chekhov, Anton

Tchicaya, Gerald Felix 1931-1988 .. **CLC 101**
    See also CA 129; 125; CANR 81; EWL 3

Tchicaya U Tam'si
    See Tchicaya, Gerald Felix

Teasdale, Sara 1884-1933 .... **PC 31; TCLC 4**
    See also CA 104; 163; DLB 45; GLL 1;
    PFS 14; RGAL 4; SATA 32; TUS

Tecumseh 1768-1813 .... **NNAL**
    See also DAM MULT

Tegner, Esaias 1782-1846 .... **NCLC 2**

Teilhard de Chardin, (Marie Joseph) Pierre
    1881-1955 .... **TCLC 9**
    See also CA 105; 210; GFL 1789 to the
    Present

Temple, Ann
    See Mortimer, Penelope (Ruth)

Tennant, Emma 1937- .... **CLC 13, 52**
    See also BRWS 9; CA 65-68; CAAS 9;
    CANR 10, 38, 59, 88, 177; CN 3, 4, 5, 6,
    7; DLB 14; EWL 3; SFW 4

Tenneshaw, S.M.
    See Silverberg, Robert

Tenney, Tabitha Gilman
    1762-1837 .... **NCLC 122**
    See also DLB 37, 200

Tennyson, Alfred 1809-1892 ... **NCLC 30, 65,**
    115, 202; PC 6, 101; WLC 6
    See also AAYA 50; BRW 4; BRWR 3; CD-
    BLB 1832-1890; DA; DA3; DAB; DAC;
    DAM MST, POET; DLB 32; EXPP; PAB;
    PFS 1, 2, 4, 11, 15, 19; RGEL 2; TEA;
    WLIT 4; WP

Teran, Lisa St. Aubin de
    See St. Aubin de Teran, Lisa

Terence c. 184B.C.-c. 159B.C. ...... **CMLC 14;**
    DC 7
    See also AW 1; CDWLB 1; DLB 211;
    RGWL 2, 3; TWA; WLIT 8

Teresa de Jesus, St. 1515-1582 .... **LC 18, 149**

Teresa of Avila, St.
    See Teresa de Jesus, St.

Terkel, Louis
    See Terkel, Studs

Terkel, Studs 1912-2008 .... **CLC 38**
    See also AAYA 32; AITN 1; CA 57-60; 278;
    CANR 18, 45, 67, 132, 195; DA3; MTCW
    1, 2; MTFW 2005; TUS

Terkel, Studs Louis
    See Terkel, Studs

Terry, C. V.
    See Slaughter, Frank G(ill)

Terry, Megan 1932- .... **CLC 19; DC 13**
    See also CA 77-80; CABS 3; CAD; CANR
    43; CD 5, 6; CWD; DFS 18; DLB 7, 249;
    GLL 2

Tertullian c. 155-c. 245 .... **CMLC 29**

Tertz, Abram
    See Sinyavsky, Andrei (Donatevich)

Tesich, Steve 1943(?)-1996 .... **CLC 40, 69**
    See also CA 105; 152; CAD; DLBY 1983

Tesla, Nikola 1856-1943 .... **TCLC 88**
    See also CA 157

Teternikov, Fyodor Kuzmich
    1863-1927 .... **TCLC 9**
    See also CA 104; DLB 295; EWL 3

Tevis, Walter 1928-1984 .... **CLC 42**
    See also CA 113; SFW 4

Tey, Josephine
    See Mackintosh, Elizabeth

Thackeray, William Makepeace
    1811-1863 ...... **NCLC 5, 14, 22, 43, 169,**
    213; WLC 6
    See also BRW 5; BRWC 2; CDBLB 1832-
    1890; DA; DA3; DAB; DAC; DAM MST,
    NOV; DLB 21, 55, 159, 163; NFS 13;
    RGEL 2; SATA 23; TEA; WLIT 3

Thakura, Ravindranatha
    See Tagore, Rabindranath

Thames, C. H.
    See Marlowe, Stephen

Tharoor, Shashi 1956- .... **CLC 70**
    See also CA 141; CANR 91, 201; CN 6, 7

Thelwall, John 1764-1834 .... **NCLC 162**
    See also DLB 93, 158

Thelwell, Michael Miles 1939- .... **CLC 22**
    See also BW 2; CA 101

Theo, Ion
    See Theodorescu, Ion N.

Theobald, Lewis, Jr.
    See Lovecraft, H. P.

Theocritus c. 310B.C.- .... **CMLC 45**
    See also AW 1; DLB 176; RGWL 2, 3

Theodorescu, Ion N. 1880-1967 ...... **CLC 80**
    See also CA 167; 116; CDWLB 4; DLB
    220; EWL 3

Theriault, Yves 1915-1983 .... **CLC 79**
    See also CA 102; CANR 150; CCA 1;
    DAC; DAM MST; DLB 88; EWL 3

Therion, Master
    See Crowley, Edward Alexander

Theroux, Alexander 1939- .... **CLC 2, 25**
    See also CA 85-88; CANR 20, 63, 190; CN
    4, 5, 6, 7

Theroux, Alexander Louis
    See Theroux, Alexander

Theroux, Paul 1941- .... **CLC 5, 8, 11, 15, 28,**
    46, 159, 303
    See also AAYA 28; AMWS 8; BEST 89:4;
    BPFB 3; CA 33-36R; CANR 20, 45, 74,
    133, 179; CDALBS; CN 1, 2, 3, 4, 5, 6,
    7; CP 1; CPW 1; DA3; DAM POP; DLB
    2, 218; EWL 3; HGG; MAL 5; MTCW 1,
    2; MTFW 2005; RGAL 4; SATA 44, 109;
    TUS

Theroux, Paul Edward
    See Theroux, Paul

Thesen, Sharon 1946- .... **CLC 56**
    See also CA 163; CANR 125; CP 5, 6, 7;
    CWP

Thespis fl. 6th cent. B.C.- .... **CMLC 51**
    See also LMFS 1

Thevenin, Denis
    See Duhamel, Georges

Thibault, Jacques Anatole Francois
    See France, Anatole

Thiele, Colin 1920-2006 .... **CLC 17**
    See also CA 29-32R; CANR 12, 28, 53,
    105; CLR 27; CP 1, 2; DLB 289; MAI-
    CYA 1, 2; SAAS 2; SATA 14, 72, 125;
    YAW

Thiong'o, Ngugi Wa
    See Ngugi wa Thiong'o

Thistlethwaite, Bel
    See Wetherald, Agnes Ethelwyn

Thomas, Audrey (Callahan) 1935- .... **CLC 7,**
    13, 37, 107, 289; SSC 20
    See also AITN 2; CA 21-24R; 237; CAAE
    237; CAAS 19; CANR 36, 58; CN 2, 3,
    4, 5, 6, 7; DLB 60; MTCW 1; RGSF 2

Thomas, Augustus 1857-1934 .... **TCLC 97**
    See also MAL 5

Thomas, D.M. 1935- ..... **CLC 13, 22, 31, 132**
    See also BPFB 3; BRWS 4; CA 61-64;
    CAAS 11; CANR 17, 45, 75; CDBLB
    1960 to Present; CN 4, 5, 6, 7; CP 1, 2, 3,
    4, 5, 6, 7; DA3; DLB 40, 207, 299; HGG;
    INT CANR-17; MTCW 1, 2; MTFW
    2005; RGHL; SFW 4

Thomas, Donald Michael
    See Thomas, D.M.

Thomas, Dylan 1914-1953 . **PC 2, 52; SSC 3,**
    44; TCLC 1, 8, 45, 105; WLC 6
    See also AAYA 45; BRWR 3; BRWS 1; CA
    104; 120; CANR 65; CDBLB 1945-1960;
    DA; DA3; DAB; DAC; DAM DRAM,
    MST, POET; DLB 13, 20, 139; EWL 3;
    EXPP; LAIT 3; MTCW 1, 2; MTFW
    2005; PAB; PFS 1, 3, 8; RGEL 2; RGSF
    2; SATA 60; TEA; WLIT 4; WP

Thomas, Dylan Marlais
    See Thomas, Dylan

Thomas, (Philip) Edward 1878-1917 . **PC 53;**
    TCLC 10
    See also BRW 6; BRWS 3; CA 106; 153;
    DAM POET; DLB 19, 98, 156, 216; EWL
    3; PAB; RGEL 2

Thomas, J. F.
    See Fleming, Thomas

Thomas, Joyce Carol 1938- .... **CLC 35**
    See also AAYA 12, 54; BW 2, 3; CA 113;
    116; CANR 48, 114, 135, 206; CLR 19;
    DLB 33; INT CA-116; JRDA; MAICYA
    1, 2; MTCW 1, 2; MTFW 2005; SAAS 7;
    SATA 40, 78, 123, 137, 210; SATA-Essay
    137; WYA; YAW

Thomas, Lewis 1913-1993 .... **CLC 35**
    See also ANW; CA 85-88; 143; CANR 38,
    60; DLB 275; MTCW 1, 2

Thomas, M. Carey 1857-1935 .... **TCLC 89**
    See also FW

Thomas, Paul
    See Mann, Thomas

Thomas, Piri 1928- .... **CLC 17; HLCS 2**
See also CA 73-76; HW 1; LLW; SSFS 28

Thomas, R(onald) S(tuart)
1913-2000 .... **CLC 6, 13, 48; PC 99**
See also BRWS 12; CA 89-92; 189; CAAS
4; CANR 30; CDBLB 1960 to Present;
CP 1, 2, 3, 4, 5, 6, 7; DAB; DAM POET;
DLB 27; EWL 3; MTCW 1; RGEL 2

Thomas, Ross (Elmore) 1926-1995 .. **CLC 39**
See also CA 33-36R; 150; CANR 22, 63;
CMW 4

Thompson, Francis (Joseph)
1859-1907 .... **TCLC 4**
See also BRW 5; CA 104; 189; CDBLB
1890-1914; DLB 19; RGEL 2; TEA

Thompson, Francis Clegg
See Mencken, H. L.

Thompson, Hunter S. 1937(?)-2005 .. **CLC 9,
17, 40, 104, 229**
See also AAYA 45; BEST 89:1; BPFB 3;
CA 17-20R; 236; CANR 23, 46, 74, 77,
111, 133; CPW; CSW; DA3; DAM POP;
DLB 185; MTCW 1, 2; MTFW 2005;
TUS

Thompson, Hunter Stockton
See Thompson, Hunter S.

Thompson, James Myers
See Thompson, Jim

Thompson, Jim 1906-1977 .... **CLC 69**
See also BPFB 3; CA 140; CMW 4; CPW;
DLB 226; MSW

Thompson, Judith (Clare Francesca)
1954- .... **CLC 39**
See also CA 143; CD 5, 6; CWD; DFS 22;
DLB 334

Thomson, James 1700-1748 .... **LC 16, 29, 40**
See also BRWS 3; DAM POET; DLB 95;
RGEL 2

Thomson, James 1834-1882 .... **NCLC 18**
See also DAM POET; DLB 35; RGEL 2

Thoreau, Henry David 1817-1862 .. **NCLC 7,
21, 61, 138, 207; PC 30; WLC 6**
See also AAYA 42; AMW; ANW; BYA 3;
CDALB 1640-1865; DA; DA3; DAC;
DAC; DAM MST; DLB 1, 183, 223, 270,
298; LAIT 2; LMFS 1; NCFS 3; RGAL
4; TUS

Thorndike, E. L.
See Thorndike, Edward L(ee)

Thorndike, Edward L(ee)
1874-1949 .... **TCLC 107**
See also CA 121

Thornton, Hall
See Silverberg, Robert

Thorpe, Adam 1956- .... **CLC 176**
See also CA 129; CANR 92, 160; DLB 231

Thorpe, Thomas Bangs
1815-1878 .... **NCLC 183**
See also DLB 3, 11, 248; RGAL 4

Thubron, Colin 1939- .... **CLC 163**
See also CA 25-28R; CANR 12, 29, 59, 95,
171; CN 5, 6, 7; DLB 204, 231

Thubron, Colin Gerald Dryden
See Thubron, Colin

Thucydides c. 455B.C.-c.
399B.C. .... **CMLC 17, 117**
See also AW 1; DLB 176; RGWL 2, 3;
WLIT 8

Thumboo, Edwin Nadason 1933- .... **PC 30**
See also CA 194; CP 1

Thurber, James 1894-1961 .... **CLC 5, 11, 25,
125; SSC 1, 47, 137**
See also AAYA 56; AMWS 1; BPFB 3;
BYA 5; CA 73-76; CANR 17, 39; CDALB
1929-1941; CWRI 5; DA; DA3; DAB;
DAC; DAM DRAM, MST, NOV; DLB 4,
11, 22, 102; EWL 3; EXPS; FANT; LAIT

3; MAICYA 1, 2; MAL 5; MTCW 1, 2;
MTFW 2005; RGAL 4; RGSF 2; SATA
13; SSFS 1, 10, 19; SUFW; TUS

Thurber, James Grover
See Thurber, James

Thurman, Wallace (Henry)
1902-1934 .. **BLC 1:3; HR 1:3; TCLC 6**
See also BW 1, 3; CA 104; 124; CANR 81;
DAM MULT; DLB 51

Tibullus c. 54B.C.-c. 18B.C. .... **CMLC 36**
See also AW 2; DLB 211; RGWL 2, 3;
WLIT 8

Ticheburn, Cheviot
See Ainsworth, William Harrison

Tieck, (Johann) Ludwig
1773-1853 ..... **NCLC 5, 46; SSC 31, 100**
See also CDWLB 2; DLB 90; EW 5; IDTP;
RGSF 2; RGWL 2, 3; SUFW

Tiger, Derry
See Ellison, Harlan

Tilghman, Christopher 1946- .... **CLC 65**
See also CA 159; CANR 135, 151; CSW;
DLB 244

Tillich, Paul (Johannes)
1886-1965 .... **CLC 131**
See also CA 5-8R; 25-28R; CANR 33;
MTCW 1, 2

Tillinghast, Richard (Williford)
1940- .... **CLC 29**
See also CA 29-32R; CAAS 23; CANR 26,
51, 96; CP 2, 3, 4, 5, 6, 7; CSW

Tillman, Lynne (?)- .... **CLC 231**
See also CA 173; CANR 144, 172

Timrod, Henry 1828-1867 .... **NCLC 25**
See also DLB 3, 248; RGAL 4

Tindall, Gillian (Elizabeth) 1938- ...... **CLC 7**
See also CA 21-24R; CANR 11, 65, 107;
CN 1, 2, 3, 4, 5, 6, 7

Ting Ling
See Chiang, Pin-chin

Tiptree, James, Jr.
See Sheldon, Alice Hastings Bradley

Tirone Smith, Mary-Ann 1944- .... **CLC 39**
See also CA 118; 136; CANR 113, 210;
SATA 143

Tirso de Molina 1580(?)-1648 .... **DC 13;
HLCS 2; LC 73**
See also RGWL 2, 3

Titmarsh, Michael Angelo
See Thackeray, William Makepeace

Tocqueville, Alexis (Charles Henri Maurice
Clerel Comte) de 1805-1859 .. **NCLC 7,
63**
See also EW 6; GFL 1789 to the Present;
TWA

Toe, Tucker
See Westlake, Donald E.

Toer, Pramoedya Ananta
1925-2006 .... **CLC 186**
See also CA 197; 251; CANR 170; DLB
348; RGWL 3

Toffler, Alvin 1928- .... **CLC 168**
See also CA 13-16R; CANR 15, 46, 67,
183; CPW; DAM POP; MTCW 1, 2

Toibin, Colm 1955- .... **CLC 162, 285**
See also CA 142; CANR 81, 149, 213; CN
7; DLB 271

Tolkien, J. R. R. 1892-1973 ... **CLC 1, 2, 3, 8,
12, 38; TCLC 137; WLC 6**
See also AAYA 10; AITN 1; BPFB 3;
BRWC 2; BRWS 2; CA 17-18; 45-48;
CANR 36, 134; CAP 2; CDBLB 1914-
1945; CLR 56, 152; CN 1; CPW 1; CWRI
5; DA; DA3; DAB; DAC; DAM MST,
NOV, POP; DLB 15, 160, 255; EFS 2;
EWL 3; FANT; JRDA; LAIT 1; LATS
1:2; LMFS 2; MAICYA 1, 2; MTCW 1,

2; MTFW 2005; NFS 8, 26; RGEL 2;
SATA 2, 32, 100; SATA-Obit 24; SFW 4;
SUFW; TEA; WCH; WYA; YAW

Tolkien, John Ronald Reuel
See Tolkien, J. R. R.

Toller, Ernst 1893-1939 .... **TCLC 10, 235**
See also CA 107; 186; DLB 124; EWL 3;
RGWL 2, 3

Tolson, M. B.
See Tolson, Melvin B(eaunorus)

Tolson, Melvin B(eaunorus)
1898(?)-1966 .... **BLC 1:3; CLC 36, 105;
PC 88**
See also AFAW 1, 2; BW 1, 3; CA 124; 89-
92; CANR 80; DAM MULT, POET; DLB
48, 76; MAL 5; RGAL 4

Tolstoi, Aleksei Nikolaevich
See Tolstoy, Alexey Nikolaevich

Tolstoi, Lev
See Tolstoy, Leo

Tolstoy, Aleksei Nikolaevich
See Tolstoy, Alexey Nikolaevich

Tolstoy, Alexey Nikolaevich
1882-1945 .... **TCLC 18**
See also CA 107; 158; DLB 272; EWL 3;
SFW 4

Tolstoy, Leo 1828-1910 ..... **SSC 9, 30, 45, 54,
131; TCLC 4, 11, 17, 28, 44, 79, 173;
WLC 6**
See also AAYA 56; CA 104; 123; DA; DA3;
DAB; DAC; DAM MST, NOV; DLB 238;
EFS 2; EW 7; EXPS; IDTP; LAIT 2;
LATS 1:1; LMFS 1; NFS 10, 28; RGSF
2; RGWL 2, 3; SATA 26; SSFS 5, 28;
TWA

Tolstoy, Count Leo
See Tolstoy, Leo

Tolstoy, Leo Nikolaevich
See Tolstoy, Leo

Tomalin, Claire 1933- .... **CLC 166**
See also CA 89-92; CANR 52, 88, 165;
DLB 155

Tomasi di Lampedusa, Giuseppe
See Lampedusa, Giuseppe di

Tomlin, Lily 1939(?)- .... **CLC 17**
See also CA 117

Tomlin, Mary Jane
See Tomlin, Lily

Tomlin, Mary Jean
See Tomlin, Lily

Tomline, F. Latour
See Gilbert, W(illiam) S(chwenck)

Tomlinson, (Alfred) Charles 1927- .... **CLC 2,
4, 6, 13, 45; PC 17**
See also CA 5-8R; CANR 33; CP 1, 2, 3, 4,
5, 6, 7; DAM POET; DLB 40; TCLE 1:2

Tomlinson, H(enry) M(ajor)
1873-1958 .... **TCLC 71**
See also CA 118; 161; DLB 36, 100, 195

Tomlinson, Mary Jane
See Tomlin, Lily

Tonna, Charlotte Elizabeth
1790-1846 .... **NCLC 135**
See also DLB 163

Tonson, Jacob fl. 1655(?)-1736 .... **LC 86**
See also DLB 170

Toole, John Kennedy 1937-1969 ..... **CLC 19,
64**
See also BPFB 3; CA 104; DLBY 1981;
MTCW 2; MTFW 2005

Toomer, Eugene
See Toomer, Jean

Toomer, Eugene Pinchback
See Toomer, Jean

Toomer, Jean 1894-1967 ... **BLC 1:3; CLC 1, 4, 13, 22; HR 1:3; PC 7; SSC 1, 45, 138; TCLC 172; WLCS**
See also AFAW 1, 2; AMWS 3, 9; BW 1; CA 85-88; CDALB 1917-1929; DA3; DAM MULT; DLB 45, 51; EWL 3; EXPP; EXPS; LMFS 2; MAL 5; MTCW 1, 2; MTFW 2005; NFS 11; PFS 31; RGAL 4; RGSF 2; SSFS 5

Toomer, Nathan Jean
See Toomer, Jean

Toomer, Nathan Pinchback
See Toomer, Jean

Torley, Luke
See Blish, James

Tornimparte, Alessandra
See Ginzburg, Natalia

Torre, Raoul della
See Mencken, H. L.

Torrence, Ridgely 1874-1950 .... **TCLC 97**
See also DLB 54, 249; MAL 5

Torrey, E. Fuller 1937- .... **CLC 34**
See also CA 119; CANR 71, 158

Torrey, Edwin Fuller
See Torrey, E. Fuller

Torsvan, Ben Traven
See Traven, B.

Torsvan, Benno Traven
See Traven, B.

Torsvan, Berick Traven
See Traven, B.

Torsvan, Berwick Traven
See Traven, B.

Torsvan, Bruno Traven
See Traven, B.

Torsvan, Traven
See Traven, B.

Toson
See Shimazaki, Haruki

Tourneur, Cyril 1575(?)-1626 ...... **LC 66, 181**
See also BRW 2; DAM DRAM; DLB 58; RGEL 2

Tournier, Michel 1924- .... **CLC 6, 23, 36, 95, 249; SSC 88**
See also CA 49-52; CANR 3, 36, 74, 149; CWW 2; DLB 83; EWL 3; GFL 1789 to the Present; MTCW 1, 2; SATA 23

Tournier, Michel Edouard
See Tournier, Michel

Tournimparte, Alessandra
See Ginzburg, Natalia

Towers, Ivar
See Kornbluth, C(yril) M.

Towne, Robert (Burton) 1936(?)- ..... **CLC 87**
See also CA 108; DLB 44; IDFW 3, 4

Townsend, Sue 1946- .... **CLC 61**
See also AAYA 28; CA 119; 127; CANR 65, 107, 202; CBD; CD 5, 6; CPW; CWD; DAB; DAC; DAM MST; DLB 271, 352; INT CA-127; SATA 55, 93; SATA-Brief 48; YAW

Townsend, Susan Lilian
See Townsend, Sue

Townshend, Pete
See Townshend, Peter

Townshend, Peter 1945- .... **CLC 17, 42**
See also CA 107

Townshend, Peter Dennis Blandford
See Townshend, Peter

Tozzi, Federigo 1883-1920 .... **TCLC 31**
See also CA 160; CANR 110; DLB 264; EWL 3; WLIT 7

Trafford, F. G.
See Riddell, Charlotte

Traherne, Thomas 1637(?)-1674 .. **LC 99; PC 70**
See also BRW 2; BRWS 11; DLB 131; PAB; RGEL 2

Traill, Catharine Parr 1802-1899 .. **NCLC 31**
See also DLB 99

Trakl, Georg 1887-1914 ...... **PC 20; TCLC 5, 239**
See also CA 104; 165; EW 10; EWL 3; LMFS 2; MTCW 2; RGWL 2, 3

Trambley, Estela Portillo
See Portillo Trambley, Estela

Tranquilli, Secondino
See Silone, Ignazio

Transtroemer, Tomas Gosta
See Transtromer, Tomas

Transtromer, Tomas 1931- .... **CLC 52, 65**
See also CA 117; 129; CAAS 17; CANR 115, 172; CWW 2; DAM POET; DLB 257; EWL 3; PFS 21

Transtromer, Tomas Goesta
See Transtromer, Tomas

Transtromer, Tomas Gosta
See Transtromer, Tomas

Transtromer, Tomas Gosta
See Transtromer, Tomas

Traven, B. 1882(?)-1969 .... **CLC 8, 11**
See also CA 19-20; 25-28R; CAP 2; DLB 9, 56; EWL 3; MTCW 1; RGAL 4

Trediakovsky, Vasilii Kirillovich 1703-1769 .... **LC 68**
See also DLB 150

Treitel, Jonathan 1959- .... **CLC 70**
See also CA 210; DLB 267

Trelawny, Edward John 1792-1881 .... **NCLC 85**
See also DLB 110, 116, 144

Tremain, Rose 1943- .... **CLC 42**
See also CA 97-100; CANR 44, 95, 186; CN 4, 5, 6, 7; DLB 14, 271; RGSF 2; RHW

Tremblay, Michel 1942- .... **CLC 29, 102, 225**
See also CA 116; 128; CCA 1; CWW 2; DAC; DAM MST; DLB 60; EWL 3; GLL 1; MTCW 1, 2; MTFW 2005

Trevanian
See Whitaker, Rod

Trevisa, John c. 1342-c. 1402 .... **LC 139**
See also BRWS 9; DLB 146

Trevor, Frances
See Teasdale, Sara

Trevor, Glen
See Hilton, James

Trevor, William 1928- ... **CLC 1, 2, 3, 4, 5, 6, 7; SSC 21, 58**
See also BRWS 4; CA 9-12R; CANR 4, 37, 55, 76, 102, 139, 195; CBD; CD 5, 6; DAM NOV; DLB 14, 139; EWL 3; INT CANR-37; LATS 1:2; MTCW 1, 2; MTFW 2005; RGEL 2; RGSF 2; SSFS 10, 33; TCLE 1:2; TEA

Triana, Jose 1931(?)- .... **DC 39**
See also CA 131; DLB 305; EWL 3; HW 1; LAW

Trifonov, Iurii (Valentinovich)
See Trifonov, Yuri (Valentinovich)

Trifonov, Yuri (Valentinovich) 1925-1981 .... **CLC 45**
See also CA 126; 103; DLB 302; EWL 3; MTCW 1; RGWL 2, 3

Trifonov, Yury Valentinovich
See Trifonov, Yuri (Valentinovich)

Trilling, Diana (Rubin) 1905-1996 . **CLC 129**
See also CA 5-8R; 154; CANR 10, 46; INT CANR-10; MTCW 1, 2

Trilling, Lionel 1905-1975 ..... **CLC 9, 11, 24; SSC 75**
See also AMWS 3; CA 9-12R; 61-64; CANR 10, 105; CN 1, 2; DLB 28, 63; EWL 3; INT CANR-10; MAL 5; MTCW 1, 2; RGAL 4; TUS

Trimball, W. H.
See Mencken, H. L.

Tristan
See Gomez de la Serna, Ramon

Tristram
See Housman, A. E.

Trogdon, William
See Heat-Moon, William Least

Trogdon, William Lewis
See Heat-Moon, William Least

Trollope, Anthony 1815-1882 .... **NCLC 6, 33, 101, 215; SSC 28, 133; WLC 6**
See also BRW 5; CDBLB 1832-1890; DA; DA3; DAB; DAC; DAM MST, NOV; DLB 21, 57, 159; RGEL 2; RGSF 2; SATA 22

Trollope, Frances 1779-1863 .... **NCLC 30**
See also DLB 21, 166

Trollope, Joanna 1943- .... **CLC 186**
See also CA 101; CANR 58, 95, 149, 191; CN 7; CPW; DLB 207; RHW

Trotsky, Leon 1879-1940 .... **TCLC 22**
See also CA 118; 167

Trotter, Catharine 1679-1749 .... **LC 8, 165**
See also BRWS 16; DLB 84, 252

Trotter, Wilfred 1872-1939 .... **TCLC 97**

Troupe, Quincy 1943- .... **BLC 2:3**
See also BW 2; CA 113; 124; CANR 43, 90, 126, 213; DLB 41

Trout, Kilgore
See Farmer, Philip Jose

Trow, George William Swift
See Trow, George W.S.

Trow, George W.S. 1943-2006 .... **CLC 52**
See also CA 126; 255; CANR 91

Troyat, Henri 1911-2007 .... **CLC 23**
See also CA 45-48; 258; CANR 2, 33, 67, 117; GFL 1789 to the Present; MTCW 1

Trudeau, Garretson Beekman
See Trudeau, G.B.

Trudeau, Garry
See Trudeau, G.B.

Trudeau, Garry B.
See Trudeau, G.B.

Trudeau, G.B. 1948- .... **CLC 12**
See also AAYA 10, 60; AITN 2; CA 81-84; CANR 31; SATA 35, 168

Truffaut, Francois 1932-1984 ... **CLC 20, 101**
See also AAYA 84; CA 81-84; 113; CANR 34

Trumbo, Dalton 1905-1976 .... **CLC 19**
See also CA 21-24R; 69-72; CANR 10; CN 1, 2; DLB 26; IDFW 3, 4; YAW

Trumbull, John 1750-1831 .... **NCLC 30**
See also DLB 31; RGAL 4

Trundlett, Helen B.
See Eliot, T. S.

Truth, Sojourner 1797(?)-1883 ...... **NCLC 94**
See also DLB 239; FW; LAIT 2

Tryon, Thomas 1926-1991 .... **CLC 3, 11**
See also AITN 1; BPFB 3; CA 29-32R; 135; CANR 32, 77; CPW; DA3; DAM POP; HGG; MTCW 1

Tryon, Tom
See Tryon, Thomas

Ts'ao Hsueh-ch'in 1715(?)-1763 .... **LC 1**

Tsurayuki Ed. fl. 10th cent. - .... **PC 73**

Tsvetaeva, Marina 1892-1941 . **PC 14; TCLC 7, 35**
See also CA 104; 128; CANR 73; DLB 295; EW 11; MTCW 1, 2; PFS 29; RGWL 2, 3

Tsvetaeva Efron, Marina Ivanovna
See Tsvetaeva, Marina

Tuck, Lily 1938- .... **CLC 70**
See also AAYA 74; CA 139; CANR 90, 192

Tuckerman, Frederick Goddard 1821-1873 .... **PC 85**
See also DLB 243; RGAL 4

Valera y Alcala-Galiano, Juan
1824-1905 .... **TCLC 10**
See also CA 106
Valerius Maximus CMLC 64
See also DLB 211
Valery, Ambroise Paul Toussaint Jules
See Valery, Paul
Valery, Paul 1871-1945 ... **PC 9; TCLC 4, 15, 231**
See also CA 104; 122; DA3; DAM POET;
DLB 258; EW 8; EWL 3; GFL 1789 to
the Present; MTCW 1, 2; MTFW 2005;
RGWL 2, 3; TWA
Valle-Inclan, Ramon del 1866-1936 .. **HLC 2; TCLC 5, 228**
See also CA 106; 153; CANR 80; DAM
MULT; DLB 134, 322; EW 8; EWL 3;
HW 2; RGSF 2; RGWL 2, 3
Valle-Inclan, Ramon Maria del
See Valle-Inclan, Ramon del
Vallejo, Antonio Buero
See Buero Vallejo, Antonio
Vallejo, Cesar 1892-1938 ... **HLC 2; TCLC 3, 56**
See also CA 105; 153; DAM MULT; DLB
290; EWL 3; HW 1; LAW; PFS 26;
RGWL 2, 3
Vallejo, Cesar Abraham
See Vallejo, Cesar
Valles, Jules 1832-1885 .... **NCLC 71**
See also DLB 123; GFL 1789 to the Present
Vallette, Marguerite Eymery
1860-1953 .... **TCLC 67**
See also CA 182; DLB 123, 192; EWL 3
Valle Y Pena, Ramon del
See Valle-Inclan, Ramon del
Van Ash, Cay 1918-1994 .... **CLC 34**
See also CA 220
Vanbrugh, Sir John 1664-1726 ... **DC 40; LC 21**
See also BRW 2; DAM DRAM; DLB 80;
IDTP; RGEL 2
Van Campen, Karl
See Campbell, John W(ood, Jr.)
Vance, Gerald
See Silverberg, Robert
Vance, Jack 1916- .... **CLC 35**
See also CA 29-32R; CANR 17, 65, 154;
CMW 4; DLB 8; FANT; MTCW 1; SCFW
1, 2; SFW 4; SUFW 1, 2
Vance, John Holbrook
See Vance, Jack
**Van Den Bogarde, Derek Jules Gaspard
Ulric Niven** 1921-1999 .... **CLC 14**
See also CA 77-80; 179; DLB 14
Vandenburgh, Jane CLC 59
See also CA 168; CANR 208
Vanderhaeghe, Guy 1951- .... **CLC 41**
See also BPFB 3; CA 113; CANR 72, 145;
CN 7; DLB 334
van der Post, Laurens (Jan)
1906-1996 .... **CLC 5**
See also AFW; CA 5-8R; 155; CANR 35;
CN 1, 2, 3, 4, 5, 6; DLB 204; RGEL 2
van de Wetering, Janwillem
1931-2008 .... **CLC 47**
See also CA 49-52; 274; CANR 4, 62, 90;
CMW 4
Van Dine, S. S.
See Wright, Willard Huntington
Van Doren, Carl (Clinton)
1885-1950 .... **TCLC 18**
See also CA 111; 168
Van Doren, Mark 1894-1972 .... **CLC 6, 10**
See also CA 1-4R; 37-40R; CANR 3; CN
1; CP 1; DLB 45, 284, 335; MAL 5;
MTCW 1, 2; RGAL 4

Van Druten, John (William)
1901-1957 .... **TCLC 2**
See also CA 104; 161; DLB 10; MAL 5;
RGAL 4
Van Duyn, Mona 1921-2004 .... **CLC 3, 7, 63, 116**
See also CA 9-12R; 234; CANR 7, 38, 60,
116; CP 1, 2, 3, 4, 5, 6, 7; CWP; DAM
POET; DLB 5; MAL 5; MTFW 2005;
PFS 20
Van Dyne, Edith
See Baum, L. Frank
van Herk, Aritha 1954- .... **CLC 249**
See also CA 101; CANR 94; DLB 334
van Itallie, Jean-Claude 1936- .... **CLC 3**
See also CA 45-48; CAAS 2; CAD; CANR
1, 48; CD 5, 6; DLB 7
Van Loot, Cornelius Obenchain
See Roberts, Kenneth (Lewis)
van Ostaijen, Paul 1896-1928 .... **TCLC 33**
See also CA 163
Van Peebles, Melvin 1932- .... **CLC 2, 20**
See also BW 2, 3; CA 85-88; CANR 27,
67, 82; DAM MULT
van Schendel, Arthur(-Francois-Emile)
1874-1946 .... **TCLC 56**
See also EWL 3
Van See, John
See Vance, Jack
Vansittart, Peter 1920-2008 .... **CLC 42**
See also CA 1-4R; 278; CANR 3, 49, 90;
CN 4, 5, 6, 7; RHW
Van Vechten, Carl 1880-1964 ... **CLC 33; HR 1:3**
See also AMWS 2; CA 183; 89-92; DLB 4,
9, 51; RGAL 4
van Vogt, A(lfred) E(lton) 1912-2000 . **CLC 1**
See also BPFB 3; BYA 13, 14; CA 21-24R;
190; CANR 28; DLB 8, 251; SATA 14;
SATA-Obit 124; SCFW 1, 2; SFW 4
Vara, Madeleine
See Jackson, Laura
Varda, Agnes 1928- .... **CLC 16**
See also CA 116; 122
Vargas Llosa, Jorge Mario Pedro
See Vargas Llosa, Mario
Vargas Llosa, Mario 1936- .. **CLC 3, 6, 9, 10, 15, 31, 42, 85, 181; HLC 2**
See also BPFB 3; CA 73-76; CANR 18, 32,
42, 67, 116, 140, 173, 213; CDWLB 3;
CWW 2; DA; DA3; DAB; DAC; DAM
MST, MULT, NOV; DLB 145; DNFS 2;
EWL 3; HW 1, 2; LAIT 5; LATS 1:2;
LAW; LAWS 1; MTCW 1, 2; MTFW
2005; RGWL 2, 3; SSFS 14; TWA; WLIT
1
Varnhagen von Ense, Rahel
1771-1833 .... **NCLC 130**
See also DLB 90
Vasari, Giorgio 1511-1574 .... **LC 114**
Vasilikos, Vasiles
See Vassilikos, Vassilis
Vasiliu, Gheorghe
See Bacovia, George
Vassa, Gustavus
See Equiano, Olaudah
Vassilikos, Vassilis 1933- .... **CLC 4, 8**
See also CA 81-84; CANR 75, 149; EWL 3
Vaughan, Henry 1621-1695 .... **LC 27; PC 81**
See also BRW 2; DLB 131; PAB; RGEL 2
Vaughn, Stephanie CLC 62
Vazov, Ivan (Minchov) 1850-1921 . **TCLC 25**
See also CA 121; 167; CDWLB 4; DLB
147
Veblen, Thorstein B(unde)
1857-1929 .... **TCLC 31**
See also AMWS 1; CA 115; 165; DLB 246;
MAL 5

Vega, Ana Lydia 1946- .... **SSC 150**
See also CA 193; CWW 2; EWL 3
Vega, Lope de 1562-1635 ... **HLCS 2; LC 23, 119**
See also EW 2; RGWL 2, 3
Veldeke, Heinrich von c. 1145-c.
1190 .... **CMLC 85**
Vendler, Helen 1933- .... **CLC 138**
See also CA 41-44R; CANR 25, 72, 136,
190; MTCW 1, 2; MTFW 2005
Vendler, Helen Hennessy
See Vendler, Helen
Venison, Alfred
See Pound, Ezra
Ventsel, Elena Sergeevna
1907-2002 .... **CLC 59**
See also CA 154; CWW 2; DLB 302
Venttsel', Elena Sergeevna
See Ventsel, Elena Sergeevna
Verdi, Marie de
See Mencken, H. L.
Verdu, Matilde
See Cela, Camilo Jose
Verga, Giovanni (Carmelo)
1840-1922 ..... **SSC 21, 87; TCLC 3, 227**
See also CA 104; 123; CANR 101; EW 7;
EWL 3; RGSF 2; RGWL 2, 3; WLIT 7
Vergil 70B.C.-19B.C. .. **CMLC 9, 40, 101; PC 12; WLCS**
See also AW 2; CDWLB 1; DA; DA3;
DAB; DAC; DAM MST, POET; DLB
211; EFS 1; LAIT 1; LMFS 1; RGWL 2,
3; WLIT 8; WP
Vergil, Polydore c. 1470-1555 .... **LC 108**
See also DLB 132
Verhaeren, Emile (Adolphe Gustave)
1855-1916 .... **TCLC 12**
See also CA 109; EWL 3; GFL 1789 to the
Present
Verlaine, Paul 1844-1896 .. **NCLC 2, 51, 230; PC 2, 32**
See also DAM POET; DLB 217; EW 7;
GFL 1789 to the Present; LMFS 2; RGWL
2, 3; TWA
Verlaine, Paul Marie
See Verlaine, Paul
Verne, Jules 1828-1905 .... **TCLC 6, 52, 245**
See also AAYA 16; BYA 4; CA 110; 131;
CLR 88; DA3; DLB 123; GFL 1789 to
the Present; JRDA; LAIT 2; LMFS 2;
MAICYA 1, 2; MTFW 2005; NFS 30, 34;
RGWL 2, 3; SATA 21; SCFW 1, 2; SFW
4; TWA; WCH
Verne, Jules Gabriel
See Verne, Jules
Verus, Marcus Annius
See Aurelius, Marcus
Very, Jones 1813-1880 .... **NCLC 9; PC 86**
See also DLB 1, 243; RGAL 4
Very, Rev. C.
See Crowley, Edward Alexander
Vesaas, Tarjei 1897-1970 .... **CLC 48**
See also CA 190; 29-32R; DLB 297; EW
11; EWL 3; RGWL 3
Vialis, Gaston
See Simenon, Georges
Vian, Boris 1920-1959(?) .... **TCLC 9**
See also CA 106; 164; CANR 111; DLB
72, 321; EWL 3; GFL 1789 to the Present;
MTCW 2; RGWL 2, 3
Viator, Vacuus
See Hughes, Thomas
Viaud, Julien 1850-1923 .... **TCLC 11, 239**
See also CA 107; DLB 123; GFL 1789 to
the Present
Viaud, Louis Marie Julien
See Viaud, Julien
Vicar, Henry
See Felsen, Henry Gregor

Wagoner, David (Russell) 1926- .... **CLC 3, 5, 15; PC 33**
 See also AMWS 9; CA 1-4R; CAAS 3; CANR 2, 71; CN 1, 2, 3, 4, 5, 6, 7; CP 1, 2, 3, 4, 5, 6, 7; DLB 5, 256; SATA 14; TCWW 1, 2

Wah, Fred(erick James) 1939- .... **CLC 44**
 See also CA 107; 141; CP 1, 6, 7; DLB 60

Wahloo, Per 1926-1975 .... **CLC 7**
 See also BPFB 3; CA 61-64; CANR 73; CMW 4; MSW

Wahloo, Peter
 See Wahloo, Per

Wain, John 1925-1994 ...... **CLC 2, 11, 15, 46**
 See also BRWS 16; CA 5-8R; CAAS 4; CANR 23, 54; CDBLB 1960 to Present; CN 1, 2, 3, 4, 5; CP 1, 2, 3, 4, 5; DLB 15, 27, 139, 155; EWL 3; MTCW 1, 2; MTFW 2005

Wajda, Andrzej 1926- .... **CLC 16, 219**
 See also CA 102

Wakefield, Dan 1932- .... **CLC 7**
 See also CA 21-24R, 211; CAAE 211; CAAS 7; CN 4, 5, 6, 7

Wakefield, Herbert Russell
 1888-1965 .... **TCLC 120**
 See also CA 5-8R; CANR 77; HGG; SUFW

Wakoski, Diane 1937- ...... **CLC 2, 4, 7, 9, 11, 40; PC 15**
 See also CA 13-16R, 216; CAAE 216; CAAS 1; CANR 9, 60, 106; CP 1, 2, 3, 4, 5, 6, 7; CWP; DAM POET; DLB 5; INT CANR-9; MAL 5; MTCW 2; MTFW 2005

Wakoski-Sherbell, Diane
 See Wakoski, Diane

Walcott, Derek 1930- . **BLC 1:3, 2:3; CLC 2, 4, 9, 14, 25, 42, 67, 76, 160, 282; DC 7; PC 46**
 See also BW 2; CA 89-92; CANR 26, 47, 75, 80, 130; CBD; CD 5, 6; CDWLB 3; CP 1, 2, 3, 4, 5, 6, 7; DA3; DAB; DAC; DAM MST, MULT, POET; DLB 117, 332; DLBY 1981; DNFS 1; EFS 1; EWL 3; LMFS 2; MTCW 1, 2; MTFW 2005; PFS 6, 34; RGEL 2; TWA; WWE 1

Walcott, Derek Alton
 See Walcott, Derek

Waldman, Anne (Lesley) 1945- .... **CLC 7**
 See also BG 1:3; CA 37-40R; CAAS 17; CANR 34, 69, 116; CP 1, 2, 3, 4, 5, 6, 7; CWP; DLB 16

Waldo, E. Hunter
 See Sturgeon, Theodore (Hamilton)

Waldo, Edward Hamilton
 See Sturgeon, Theodore (Hamilton)

Waldrop, Rosmarie 1935- .... **PC 109**
 See also CA 101; CAAS 30; CANR 18, 39, 67; CP 6, 7; CWP; DLB 169

Walker, Alice 1944- .... **BLC 1:3, 2:3; CLC 5, 6, 9, 19, 27, 46, 58, 103, 167; PC 30; SSC 5; WLCS**
 See also AAYA 3, 33; AFAW 1, 2; AMWS 3; BEST 89:4; BPFB 3; BW 2, 3; CA 37-40R; CANR 9, 27, 49, 66, 82, 131, 191; CDALB 1968-1988; CN 4, 5, 6, 7; CPW; CSW; DA; DA3; DAB; DAC; DAM MST, MULT, NOV, POET, POP; DLB 6, 33, 143; EWL 3; EXPN; EXPS; FL 1:6; FW; INT CANR-27; LAIT 3; MAL 5; MBL; MTCW 1, 2; MTFW 2005; NFS 5; PFS 30, 34; RGAL 4; RGSF 2; SATA 31; SSFS 2, 11; TUS; YAW

Walker, Alice Malsenior
 See Walker, Alice

Walker, David Harry 1911-1992 ...... **CLC 14**
 See also CA 1-4R; 137; CANR 1; CN 1, 2; CWRI 5; SATA 8; SATA-Obit 71

Walker, Edward Joseph 1934-2004 .. **CLC 13**
 See also CA 21-24R; 226; CANR 12, 28, 53; CP 1, 2, 3, 4, 5, 6, 7; DLB 40

Walker, George F(rederick) 1947- .. **CLC 44, 61**
 See also CA 103; CANR 21, 43, 59; CD 5, 6; DAB; DAC; DAM MST; DLB 60

Walker, Joseph A. 1935-2003 .... **CLC 19**
 See also BW 1, 3; CA 89-92; CAD; CANR 26, 143; CD 5, 6; DAM DRAM, MST; DFS 12; DLB 38

Walker, Margaret 1915-1998 .... **BLC 1:3; CLC 1, 6; PC 20; TCLC 129**
 See also AFAW 1, 2; BW 2, 3; CA 73-76; 172; CANR 26, 54, 76, 136; CN 1, 2, 3, 4, 5, 6; CP 1, 2, 3, 4, 5, 6; CSW; DAM MULT; DLB 76, 152; EXPP; FW; MAL 5; MTCW 1, 2; MTFW 2005; PFS 31; RGAL 4; RHW

Walker, Ted
 See Walker, Edward Joseph

Wallace, David Foster 1962-2008 .... **CLC 50, 114, 271, 281; SSC 68**
 See also AAYA 50; AMWS 10; CA 132; 277; CANR 59, 133, 190; CN 7; DA3; DLB 350; MTCW 2; MTFW 2005

Wallace, Dexter
 See Masters, Edgar Lee

Wallace, (Richard Horatio) Edgar
 1875-1932 .... **TCLC 57**
 See also CA 115; 218; CMW 4; DLB 70; MSW; RGEL 2

Wallace, Irving 1916-1990 .... **CLC 7, 13**
 See also AITN 1; BPFB 3; CA 1-4R; 132; CAAS 1; CANR 1, 27; CPW; DAM NOV, POP; INT CANR-27; MTCW 1, 2

Wallant, Edward Lewis 1926-1962 ... **CLC 5, 10**
 See also CA 1-4R; CANR 22; DLB 2, 28, 143, 299; EWL 3; MAL 5; MTCW 1, 2; RGAL 4; RGHL

Wallas, Graham 1858-1932 .... **TCLC 91**

Waller, Edmund 1606-1687 .... **LC 86; PC 72**
 See also BRW 2; DAM POET; DLB 126; PAB; RGEL 2

Walley, Byron
 See Card, Orson Scott

Walls, Jeannette 1960(?)- .... **CLC 299**
 See also CA 242

Walpole, Horace 1717-1797 ..... **LC 2, 49, 152**
 See also BRW 3; DLB 39, 104, 213; GL 3; HGG; LMFS 1; RGEL 2; SUFW 1; TEA

Walpole, Hugh 1884-1941 .... **TCLC 5**
 See also CA 104; 165; DLB 34; HGG; MTCW 2; RGEL 2; RHW

Walpole, Hugh Seymour
 See Walpole, Hugh

Walrond, Eric (Derwent) 1898-1966 . **HR 1:3**
 See also BW 1; CA 125; DLB 51

Walser, Martin 1927- .... **CLC 27, 183**
 See also CA 57-60; CANR 8, 46, 145; CWW 2; DLB 75, 124; EWL 3

Walser, Robert 1878-1956 ..... **SSC 20; TCLC 18**
 See also CA 118; 165; CANR 100, 194; DLB 66; EWL 3

Walsh, Gillian Paton
 See Paton Walsh, Jill

Walsh, Jill Paton
 See Paton Walsh, Jill

Walter, Villiam Christian
 See Andersen, Hans Christian

Walter of Chatillon c. 1135-c.
 1202 .... **CMLC 111**

Walters, Anna L(ee) 1946- .... **NNAL**
 See also CA 73-76

Walther von der Vogelweide c.
 1170-1228 .... **CMLC 56**

Walton, Izaak 1593-1683 .... **LC 72**
 See also BRW 2; CDBLB Before 1660; DLB 151, 213; RGEL 2

Walzer, Michael 1935- .... **CLC 238**
 See also CA 37-40R; CANR 15, 48, 127, 190

Walzer, Michael Laban
 See Walzer, Michael

Wambaugh, Joseph, Jr. 1937- ...... **CLC 3, 18**
 See also AITN 1; BEST 89:3; BPFB 3; CA 33-36R; CANR 42, 65, 115, 167; CMW 4; CPW 1; DA3; DAM NOV, POP; DLB 6; DLBY 1983; MSW; MTCW 1, 2

Wambaugh, Joseph Aloysius
 See Wambaugh, Joseph, Jr.

Wang Wei 699(?)-761(?) . **CMLC 100; PC 18**
 See also TWA

Warburton, William 1698-1779 .... **LC 97**
 See also DLB 104

Ward, Arthur Henry Sarsfield
 1883-1959 .... **TCLC 28**
 See also AAYA 80; CA 108; 173; CMW 4; DLB 70; HGG; MSW; SUFW

Ward, Douglas Turner 1930- .... **CLC 19**
 See also BW 1; CA 81-84; CAD; CANR 27; CD 5, 6; DLB 7, 38

Ward, E. D.
 See Lucas, E(dward) V(errall)

Ward, Mrs. Humphry 1851-1920
 See Ward, Mary Augusta
 See also RGEL 2

Ward, Mary Augusta 1851-1920 ... **TCLC 55**
 See Ward, Mrs. Humphry
 See also DLB 18

Ward, Nathaniel 1578(?)-1652 .... **LC 114**
 See also DLB 24

Ward, Peter
 See Faust, Frederick

Warhol, Andy 1928(?)-1987 .... **CLC 20**
 See also AAYA 12; BEST 89:4; CA 89-92; 121; CANR 34

Warner, Francis (Robert Le Plastrier)
 1937- .... **CLC 14**
 See also CA 53-56; CANR 11; CP 1, 2, 3, 4

Warner, Marina 1946- .... **CLC 59, 231**
 See also CA 65-68; CANR 21, 55, 118; CN 5, 6, 7; DLB 194; MTFW 2005

Warner, Rex (Ernest) 1905-1986 ...... **CLC 45**
 See also CA 89-92; 119; CN 1, 2, 3, 4; CP 1, 2, 3, 4; DLB 15; RGEL 2; RHW

Warner, Susan (Bogert)
 1819-1885 .... **NCLC 31, 146**
 See also AMWS 18; DLB 3, 42, 239, 250, 254

Warner, Sylvia (Constance) Ashton
 See Ashton-Warner, Sylvia (Constance)

Warner, Sylvia Townsend
 1893-1978 .. **CLC 7, 19; SSC 23; TCLC 131**
 See also BRWS 7; CA 61-64; 77-80; CANR 16, 60, 104; CN 1, 2; DLB 34, 139; EWL 3; FANT; FW; MTCW 1, 2; RGEL 2; RGSF 2; RHW

Warren, Mercy Otis 1728-1814 .... **NCLC 13, 226**
 See also DLB 31, 200; RGAL 4; TUS

Warren, Robert Penn 1905-1989 .. **CLC 1, 4, 6, 8, 10, 13, 18, 39, 53, 59; PC 37; SSC 4, 58, 126; WLC 6**
 See also AITN 1; AMW; AMWC 2; BPFB 3; BYA 1; CA 13-16R; 129; CANR 10, 47; CDALB 1968-1988; CN 1, 2, 3, 4; CP 1, 2, 3, 4; DA; DA3; DAB; DAC; DAM MST, NOV, POET; DLB 2, 48, 152, 320; DLBY 1980, 1989; EWL 3; INT

CANR-10; MAL 5; MTCW 1, 2; MTFW
2005; NFS 13; RGAL 4; RGSF 2; RHW;
SATA 46; SATA-Obit 63; SSFS 8; TUS

Warrigal, Jack
See Furphy, Joseph

Warshofsky, Isaac
See Singer, Isaac Bashevis

Warton, Joseph 1722-1800 ... **LC 128; NCLC
118**
See also DLB 104, 109; RGEL 2

Warton, Thomas 1728-1790 .... **LC 15, 82**
See also DAM POET; DLB 104, 109, 336;
RGEL 2

Waruk, Kona
See Harris, (Theodore) Wilson

Warung, Price
See Astley, William

Warwick, Jarvis
See Garner, Hugh

Washington, Alex
See Harris, Mark

Washington, Booker T. 1856-1915 . **BLC 1:3;
TCLC 10**
See also BW 1; CA 114; 125; DA3; DAM
MULT; DLB 345; LAIT 2; RGAL 4;
SATA 28

Washington, Booker Taliaferro
See Washington, Booker T.

Washington, George 1732-1799 .... **LC 25**
See also DLB 31

Wassermann, (Karl) Jakob
1873-1934 .... **TCLC 6**
See also CA 104; 163; DLB 66; EWL 3

Wasserstein, Wendy 1950-2006 . **CLC 32, 59,
90, 183; DC 4**
See also AAYA 73; AMWS 15; CA 121;
129; 247; CABS 3; CAD; CANR 53, 75,
128; CD 5, 6; CWD; DA3; DAM DRAM;
DFS 5, 17; DLB 228; EWL 3; FW; INT
CA-129; MAL 5; MTCW 2; MTFW 2005;
SATA 94; SATA-Obit 174

Waterhouse, Keith 1929-2009 .... **CLC 47**
See also BRWS 13; CA 5-8R; 290; CANR
38, 67, 109; CBD; CD 6; CN 1, 2, 3, 4, 5,
6, 7; DLB 13, 15; MTCW 1, 2; MTFW
2005

Waterhouse, Keith Spencer
See Waterhouse, Keith

Waters, Frank (Joseph) 1902-1995 .. **CLC 88**
See also CA 5-8R; 149; CAAS 13; CANR
3, 18, 63, 121; DLB 212; DLBY 1986;
RGAL 4; TCWW 1, 2

Waters, Mary C. CLC 70

Waters, Roger 1944- .... **CLC 35**

Watkins, Frances Ellen
See Harper, Frances Ellen Watkins

Watkins, Gerrold
See Malzberg, Barry N(athaniel)

Watkins, Gloria Jean
See hooks, bell

Watkins, Paul 1964- .... **CLC 55**
See also CA 132; CANR 62, 98

Watkins, Vernon Phillips
1906-1967 .... **CLC 43**
See also CA 9-10; 25-28R; CAP 1; DLB
20; EWL 3; RGEL 2

Watson, Irving S.
See Mencken, H. L.

Watson, John H.
See Farmer, Philip Jose

Watson, Richard F.
See Silverberg, Robert

Watson, Sheila 1909-1998 .... **SSC 128**
See also AITN 2; CA 155; CCA 1; DAC;
DLB 60

Watts, Ephraim
See Horne, Richard Henry Hengist

Watts, Isaac 1674-1748 .... **LC 98**
See also DLB 95; RGEL 2; SATA 52

Waugh, Auberon (Alexander)
1939-2001 .... **CLC 7**
See also CA 45-48; 192; CANR 6, 22, 92;
CN 1, 2, 3; DLB 14, 194

Waugh, Evelyn 1903-1966 ... **CLC 1, 3, 8, 13,
19, 27, 44, 107; SSC 41; TCLC 229;
WLC 6**
See also AAYA 78; BPFB 3; BRW 7; CA
85-88; 25-28R; CANR 22; CDBLB 1914-
1945; DA; DA3; DAB; DAC; DAM MST,
NOV, POP; DLB 15, 162, 195, 352; EWL
3; MTCW 1, 2; MTFW 2005; NFS 13,
17, 34; RGEL 2; RGSF 2; TEA; WLIT 4

Waugh, Evelyn Arthur St. John
See Waugh, Evelyn

Waugh, Harriet 1944- .... **CLC 6**
See also CA 85-88; CANR 22

Ways, C.R.
See Blount, Roy, Jr.

Waystaff, Simon
See Swift, Jonathan

Webb, Beatrice 1858-1943 .... **TCLC 22**
See also CA 117; 162; DLB 190; FW

Webb, Beatrice Martha Potter
See Webb, Beatrice

Webb, Charles 1939- .... **CLC 7**
See also CA 25-28R; CANR 114, 188

Webb, Charles Richard
See Webb, Charles

Webb, Frank J. NCLC 143
See also DLB 50

Webb, James, Jr.
See Webb, James

Webb, James 1946- .... **CLC 22**
See also CA 81-84; CANR 156

Webb, James H.
See Webb, James

Webb, James Henry
See Webb, James

Webb, Mary Gladys (Meredith)
1881-1927 .... **TCLC 24**
See also CA 182; 123; DLB 34; FW; RGEL
2

Webb, Mrs. Sidney
See Webb, Beatrice

Webb, Phyllis 1927- .... **CLC 18**
See also CA 104; CANR 23; CCA 1; CP 1,
2, 3, 4, 5, 6, 7; CWP; DLB 53

Webb, Sidney 1859-1947 .... **TCLC 22**
See also CA 117; 163; DLB 190

Webb, Sidney James
See Webb, Sidney

Webber, Andrew Lloyd
See Lloyd Webber, Andrew

Weber, Lenora Mattingly
1895-1971 .... **CLC 12**
See also CA 19-20; 29-32R; CAP 1; SATA
2; SATA-Obit 26

Weber, Max 1864-1920 .... **TCLC 69**
See also CA 109; 189; DLB 296

Webster, Augusta 1837-1894 .... **NCLC 230**
See also DLB 35, 240

Webster, John 1580(?)-1634(?) ...... **DC 2; LC
33, 84, 124; WLC 6**
See also BRW 2; CDBLB Before 1660; DA;
DAB; DAC; DAM DRAM, MST; DFS
17, 19; DLB 58; IDTP; RGEL 2; WLIT 3

Webster, Noah 1758-1843 .... **NCLC 30**
See also DLB 1, 37, 42, 43, 73, 243

Wedekind, Benjamin Franklin
See Wedekind, Frank

Wedekind, Frank 1864-1918 .... **TCLC 7, 241**
See also CA 104; 153; CANR 121, 122;
CDWLB 2; DAM DRAM; DLB 118; EW
8; EWL 3; LMFS 2; RGWL 2, 3

Wehr, Demaris CLC 65

Weidman, Jerome 1913-1998 .... **CLC 7**
See also AITN 2; CA 1-4R; 171; CAD;
CANR 1; CD 1, 2, 3, 4, 5; DLB 28

Weil, Simone 1909-1943 .... **TCLC 23**
See also CA 117; 159; EW 12; EWL 3; FW;
GFL 1789 to the Present; MTCW 2

Weil, Simone Adolphine
See Weil, Simone

Weininger, Otto 1880-1903 .... **TCLC 84**

Weinstein, Nathan
See West, Nathanael

Weinstein, Nathan von Wallenstein
See West, Nathanael

Weir, Peter (Lindsay) 1944- .... **CLC 20**
See also CA 113; 123

Weiss, Peter (Ulrich) 1916-1982 .. **CLC 3, 15,
51; DC 36; TCLC 152**
See also CA 45-48; 106; CANR 3; DAM
DRAM; DFS 3; DLB 69, 124; EWL 3;
RGHL; RGWL 2, 3

Weiss, Theodore (Russell)
1916-2003 .... **CLC 3, 8, 14**
See also CA 9-12R; 189; 216; CAAE 189;
CAAS 2; CANR 46, 94; CP 1, 2, 3, 4, 5,
6, 7; DLB 5; TCLE 1:2

Welch, (Maurice) Denton
1915-1948 .... **TCLC 22**
See also BRWS 8; CA 121; 148; RGEL 2

Welch, James 1940-2003 .... **CLC 6, 14, 52,
249; NNAL; PC 62**
See also CA 85-88; 219; CANR 42, 66, 107;
CN 5, 6, 7; CP 2, 3, 4, 5, 6, 7; CPW;
DAM MULT, POP; DLB 175, 256; LATS
1:1; NFS 23; RGAL 4; TCWW 1, 2

Welch, James Phillip
See Welch, James

Weld, Angelina Grimke
See Grimke, Angelina Weld

Weldon, Fay 1931- . **CLC 6, 9, 11, 19, 36, 59,
122**
See also BRWS 4; CA 21-24R; CANR 16,
46, 63, 97, 137; CDBLB 1960 to Present;
CN 3, 4, 5, 6, 7; CPW; DAM POP; DLB
14, 194, 319; EWL 3; FW; HGG; INT
CANR-16; MTCW 1, 2; MTFW 2005;
RGEL 2; RGSF 2

Wellek, Rene 1903-1995 .... **CLC 28**
See also CA 5-8R; 150; CAAS 7; CANR 8;
DLB 63; EWL 3; INT CANR-8

Weller, Michael 1942- .... **CLC 10, 53**
See also CA 85-88; CAD; CD 5, 6

Weller, Paul 1958- .... **CLC 26**

Wellershoff, Dieter 1925- .... **CLC 46**
See also CA 89-92; CANR 16, 37

Welles, (George) Orson 1915-1985 .. **CLC 20,
80**
See also AAYA 40; CA 93-96; 117

Wellman, John McDowell 1945- ...... **CLC 65**
See also CA 166; CAD; CD 5, 6; RGAL 4

Wellman, Mac
See Wellman, John McDowell; Wellman,
John McDowell

Wellman, Manly Wade 1903-1986 ... **CLC 49**
See also CA 1-4R; 118; CANR 6, 16, 44;
FANT; SATA 6; SATA-Obit 47; SFW 4;
SUFW

Wells, Carolyn 1869(?)-1942 .... **TCLC 35**
See also CA 113; 185; CMW 4; DLB 11

Wells, H. G. 1866-1946 . **SSC 6, 70; TCLC 6,
12, 19, 133; WLC 6**
See also AAYA 18; BPFB 3; BRW 6; CA
110; 121; CDBLB 1914-1945; CLR 64,
133; DA; DA3; DAB; DAC; DAM MST,
NOV; DLB 34, 70, 156, 178; EWL 3;
EXPS; HGG; LAIT 3; LMFS 2; MTCW
1, 2; MTFW 2005; NFS 17, 20, 36; RGEL
2; RGSF 2; SATA 20; SCFW 1, 2; SFW
4; SSFS 3; SUFW; TEA; WCH; WLIT 4;
YAW

Wells, Herbert George
See Wells, H. G.

Wells, Rosemary 1943- .... **CLC 12**
See also AAYA 13; BYA 7, 8; CA 85-88;
CANR 48, 120, 179; CLR 16, 69; CWRI
5; MAICYA 1, 2; SAAS 1; SATA 18, 69,
114, 156, 207; YAW

Wells-Barnett, Ida B(ell)
1862-1931 .... **TCLC 125**
See also CA 182; DLB 23, 221

Welsh, Irvine 1958- .... **CLC 144, 276**
See also BRWS 17; CA 173; CANR 146,
196; CN 7; DLB 271

Welty, Eudora 1909-2001 .... **CLC 1, 2, 5, 14,
22, 33, 105, 220; SSC 1, 27, 51, 111;
WLC 6**
See also AAYA 48; AMW; AMWR 1; BPFB
3; CA 9-12R; 199; CABS 1; CANR 32,
65, 128; CDALB 1941-1968; CN 1, 2, 3,
4, 5, 6, 7; CSW; DA; DA3; DAB; DAC;
DAM MST, NOV; DFS 26; DLB 2, 102,
143; DLBD 12; DLBY 1987, 2001; EWL
3; EXPS; HGG; LAIT 3; MAL 5; MBL;
MTCW 1, 2; MTFW 2005; NFS 13, 15;
RGAL 4; RGSF 2; RHW; SSFS 2, 10, 26;
TUS

Welty, Eudora Alice
See Welty, Eudora

Wen I-to 1899-1946 .... **TCLC 28**
See also EWL 3

Wentworth, Robert
See Hamilton, Edmond

Werfel, Franz (Viktor) 1890-1945 .... **PC 101;
TCLC 8, 248**
See also CA 104; 161; DLB 81, 124; EWL
3; RGWL 2, 3

Wergeland, Henrik Arnold
1808-1845 .... **NCLC 5**
See also DLB 354

Werner, Friedrich Ludwig Zacharias
1768-1823 .... **NCLC 189**
See also DLB 94

Werner, Zacharias
See Werner, Friedrich Ludwig Zacharias

Wersba, Barbara 1932- .... **CLC 30**
See also AAYA 2, 30; BYA 6, 12, 13; CA
29-32R, 182; CAAE 182; CANR 16, 38;
CLR 3, 78; DLB 52; JRDA; MAICYA 1,
2; SAAS 2; SATA 1, 58; SATA-Essay 103;
WYA; YAW

Wertmueller, Lina 1928- .... **CLC 16**
See also CA 97-100; CANR 39, 78

Wescott, Glenway 1901-1987 .. **CLC 13; SSC
35**
See also CA 13-16R; 121; CANR 23, 70;
CN 1, 2, 3, 4; DLB 4, 9, 102; MAL 5;
RGAL 4

Wesker, Arnold 1932- .... **CLC 3, 5, 42**
See also CA 1-4R; CAAS 7; CANR 1, 33;
CBD; CD 5, 6; CDBLB 1960 to Present;
DAB; DAM DRAM; DLB 13, 310, 319;
EWL 3; MTCW 1; RGEL 2; TEA

Wesley, Charles 1707-1788 .... **LC 128**
See also DLB 95; RGEL 2

Wesley, John 1703-1791 .... **LC 88**
See also DLB 104

Wesley, Richard (Errol) 1945- .... **CLC 7**
See also BW 1; CA 57-60; CAD; CANR
27; CD 5, 6; DLB 38

Wessel, Johan Herman 1742-1785 .... **LC 7**
See also DLB 300

West, Anthony (Panther)
1914-1987 .... **CLC 50**
See also CA 45-48; 124; CANR 3, 19; CN
1, 2, 3, 4; DLB 15

West, C. P.
See Wodehouse, P. G.

West, Cornel 1953- .... **BLCS; CLC 134**
See also CA 144; CANR 91, 159; DLB 246

West, Cornel Ronald
See West, Cornel

West, Delno C(loyde), Jr. 1936- .... **CLC 70**
See also CA 57-60

West, Dorothy 1907-1998 ...... **HR 1:3; TCLC
108**
See also AMWS 18; BW 2; CA 143; 169;
DLB 76

West, Edwin
See Westlake, Donald E.

West, (Mary) Jessamyn 1902-1984 ... **CLC 7,
17**
See also CA 9-12R; 112; CANR 27; CN 1,
2, 3; DLB 6; DLBY 1984; MTCW 1, 2;
RGAL 4; RHW; SATA-Obit 37; TCWW
2; TUS; YAW

West, Morris L(anglo) 1916-1999 ..... **CLC 6,
33**
See also BPFB 3; CA 5-8R; 187; CANR
24, 49, 64; CN 1, 2, 3, 4, 5, 6; CPW; DLB
289; MTCW 1, 2; MTFW 2005

West, Nathanael 1903-1940 ...... **SSC 16, 116;
TCLC 1, 14, 44, 235**
See also AAYA 77; AMW; AMWR 2; BPFB
3; CA 104; 125; CDALB 1929-1941;
DA3; DLB 4, 9, 28; EWL 3; MAL 5;
MTCW 1, 2; MTFW 2005; NFS 16;
RGAL 4; TUS

West, Owen
See Koontz, Dean

West, Paul 1930- .... **CLC 7, 14, 96, 226**
See also CA 13-16R; CAAS 7; CANR 22,
53, 76, 89, 136, 205; CN 1, 2, 3, 4, 5, 6,
7; DLB 14; INT CANR-22; MTCW 2;
MTFW 2005

West, Rebecca 1892-1983 ... **CLC 7, 9, 31, 50**
See also BPFB 3; BRWS 3; CA 5-8R; 109;
CANR 19; CN 1, 2, 3; DLB 36; DLBY
1983; EWL 3; FW; MTCW 1, 2; MTFW
2005; NCFS 4; RGEL 2; TEA

Westall, Robert (Atkinson)
1929-1993 .... **CLC 17**
See also AAYA 12; BYA 2, 6, 7, 8, 9, 15;
CA 69-72; 141; CANR 18, 68; CLR 13;
FANT; JRDA; MAICYA 1, 2; MAICYAS
1; SAAS 2; SATA 23, 69; SATA-Obit 75;
WYA; YAW

Westermarck, Edward 1862-1939 . **TCLC 87**

Westlake, Donald E. 1933-2008 ... **CLC 7, 33**
See also BPFB 3; CA 17-20R; 280; CAAS
13; CANR 16, 44, 65, 94, 137, 192; CMW
4; CPW; DAM POP; INT CANR-16;
MSW; MTCW 2; MTFW 2005

Westlake, Donald E. Edmund
See Westlake, Donald E.

Westlake, Donald Edwin
See Westlake, Donald E.

Westlake, Donald Edwin Edmund
See Westlake, Donald E.

Westmacott, Mary
See Christie, Agatha

Weston, Allen
See Norton, Andre

Wetcheek, J. L.
See Feuchtwanger, Lion

Wetering, Janwillem van de
See van de Wetering, Janwillem

Wetherald, Agnes Ethelwyn
1857-1940 .... **TCLC 81**
See also CA 202; DLB 99

Wetherell, Elizabeth
See Warner, Susan (Bogert)

Whale, James 1889-1957 .... **TCLC 63**
See also AAYA 75

Whalen, Philip (Glenn) 1923-2002 .... **CLC 6,
29**
See also BG 1:3; CA 9-12R; 209; CANR 5,
39; CP 1, 2, 3, 4, 5, 6, 7; DLB 16; WP

Wharton, Edith 1862-1937 ... **SSC 6, 84, 120;
TCLC 3, 9, 27, 53, 129, 149; WLC 6**
See also AAYA 25; AMW; AMWC 2;
AMWR 1; BPFB 3; CA 104; 132; CDALB
1865-1917; CLR 136; DA; DA3; DAB;
DAC; DAM MST, NOV; DLB 4, 9, 12,
78, 189; DLBD 13; EWL 3; EXPS; FL
1:6; GL 3; HGG; LAIT 2, 3; LATS 1:1;
MAL 5; MBL; MTCW 1, 2; MTFW 2005;
NFS 5, 11, 15, 20, 37; RGAL 4; RGSF 2;
RHW; SSFS 6, 7; SUFW; TUS

Wharton, Edith Newbold Jones
See Wharton, Edith

Wharton, James
See Mencken, H. L.

Wharton, William 1925-2008 ..... **CLC 18, 37**
See also CA 93-96; 278; CN 4, 5, 6, 7;
DLBY 1980; INT CA-93-96

Wheatley, Phillis 1753(?)-1784 .... **BLC 1:3;
LC 3, 50, 183; PC 3; WLC 6**
See also AFAW 1, 2; AMWS 20; CDALB
1640-1865; DA; DA3; DAC; DAM MST,
MULT, POET; DLB 31, 50; EXPP; FL
1:1; PFS 13, 29, 36; RGAL 4

Wheatley Peters, Phillis
See Wheatley, Phillis

Wheelock, John Hall 1886-1978 .... **CLC 14**
See also CA 13-16R; 77-80; CANR 14; CP
1, 2; DLB 45; MAL 5

Whim-Wham
See Curnow, (Thomas) Allen (Monro)

Whisp, Kennilworthy
See Rowling, J.K.

Whitaker, Rod 1931-2005 .... **CLC 29**
See also CA 29-32R; 246; CANR 45, 153;
CMW 4

Whitaker, Rodney
See Whitaker, Rod

Whitaker, Rodney William
See Whitaker, Rod

White, Babington
See Braddon, Mary Elizabeth

White, E. B. 1899-1985 .... **CLC 10, 34, 39**
See also AAYA 62; AITN 2; AMWS 1; CA
13-16R; 116; CANR 16, 37; CDALBS;
CLR 1, 21, 107; CPW; DA3; DAM POP;
DLB 11, 22; EWL 3; FANT; MAICYA 1,
2; MAL 5; MTCW 1, 2; MTFW 2005;
NCFS 5; RGAL 4; SATA 2, 29, 100;
SATA-Obit 44; TUS

White, Edmund 1940- .... **CLC 27, 110**
See also AAYA 7; CA 45-48; CANR 3, 19,
36, 62, 107, 133, 172, 212; CN 5, 6, 7;
DA3; DAM POP; DLB 227; MTCW 1, 2;
MTFW 2005

White, Edmund Valentine III
See White, Edmund

White, Elwyn Brooks
See White, E. B.

White, Hayden V. 1928- .... **CLC 148**
See also CA 128; CANR 135; DLB 246

White, Patrick 1912-1990 . **CLC 3, 4, 5, 7, 9,
18, 65, 69; SSC 39; TCLC 176**
See also BRWS 1; CA 81-84; 132; CANR
43; CN 1, 2, 3, 4; DLB 260, 332; EWL 3;
MTCW 1; RGEL 2; RGSF 2; RHW;
TWA; WWE 1

White, Patrick Victor Martindale
See White, Patrick

White, Phyllis Dorothy James
See James, P. D.

White, T(erence) H(anbury)
1906-1964 .... **CLC 30**
See also AAYA 22; BPFB 3; BYA 4, 5; CA
73-76; CANR 37; CLR 139; DLB 160;
FANT; JRDA; LAIT 1; MAICYA 1, 2;
NFS 30; RGEL 2; SATA 12; SUFW 1;
YAW

Williams, Joy 1944- .... **CLC 31**
See also CA 41-44R; CANR 22, 48, 97, 168; DLB 335; SSFS 25

Williams, Norman 1952- .... **CLC 39**
See also CA 118

Williams, Paulette Linda
See Shange, Ntozake

Williams, Roger 1603(?)-1683 .... **LC 129**
See also DLB 24

Williams, Sherley Anne
1944-1999 .... **BLC 1:3; CLC 89**
See also AFAW 2; BW 2, 3; CA 73-76; 185; CANR 25, 82; DAM MULT, POET; DLB 41; INT CANR-25; SATA 78; SATA-Obit 116

Williams, Shirley
See Williams, Sherley Anne

Williams, Tennessee 1911-1983 . **CLC 1, 2, 5, 7, 8, 11, 15, 19, 30, 39, 45, 71, 111; DC 4; SSC 81; WLC 6**
See also AAYA 31; AITN 1, 2; AMW; AMWC 1; CA 5-8R; 108; CABS 3; CAD; CANR 31, 132, 174; CDALB 1941-1968; CN 1, 2, 3; DA; DA3; DAB; DAC; DAM DRAM, MST; DFS 17; DLB 7, 341; DLBD 4; DLBY 1983; EWL 3; GLL 1; LAIT 4; LATS 1:2; MAL 5; MTCW 1, 2; MTFW 2005; RGAL 4; TUS

Williams, Thomas (Alonzo)
1926-1990 .... **CLC 14**
See also CA 1-4R; 132; CANR 2

Williams, Thomas Lanier
See Williams, Tennessee

Williams, William C.
See Williams, William Carlos

Williams, William Carlos
1883-1963 .... **CLC 1, 2, 5, 9, 13, 22, 42, 67; PC 7, 109; SSC 31; WLC 6**
See also AAYA 46; AMW; AMWR 1; CA 89-92; CANR 34; CDALB 1917-1929; DA; DA3; DAB; DAC; DAM MST, POET; DLB 4, 16, 54, 86; EWL 3; EXPP; MAL 5; MTCW 1, 2; MTFW 2005; NCFS 4; PAB; PFS 1, 6, 11, 34; RGAL 4; RGSF 2; SSFS 27; TUS; WP

Williamson, David (Keith) 1942- ..... **CLC 56**
See also CA 103; CANR 41; CD 5, 6; DLB 289

Williamson, Jack
See Williamson, John Stewart

Williamson, John Stewart
1908-2006 .... **CLC 29**
See also AAYA 76; CA 17-20R; 255; CAAS 8; CANR 23, 70, 153; DLB 8; SCFW 1, 2; SFW 4

Willie, Frederick
See Lovecraft, H. P.

Willingham, Calder (Baynard, Jr.)
1922-1995 .... **CLC 5, 51**
See also CA 5-8R; 147; CANR 3; CN 1, 2, 3, 4, 5; CSW; DLB 2, 44; IDFW 3, 4; MTCW 1

Willis, Charles
See Clarke, Arthur C.

Willis, Nathaniel Parker
1806-1867 .... **NCLC 194**
See also DLB 3, 59, 73, 74, 183, 250; DLBD 13; RGAL 4

Willy
See Colette

Willy, Colette
See Colette

Wilmot, John 1647-1680 .... **LC 75; PC 66**
See also BRW 2; DLB 131; PAB; RGEL 2

Wilson, A. N. 1950- .... **CLC 33**
See also BRWS 6; CA 112; 122; CANR 156, 199; CN 4, 5, 6, 7; DLB 14, 155, 194; MTCW 2

Wilson, Andrew Norman
See Wilson, A. N.

Wilson, Angus 1913-1991 .... **CLC 2, 3, 5, 25, 34; SSC 21**
See also BRWS 1; CA 5-8R; 134; CANR 21; CN 1, 2, 3, 4; DLB 15, 139, 155; EWL 3; MTCW 1, 2; MTFW 2005; RGEL 2; RGSF 2

Wilson, Angus Frank Johnstone
See Wilson, Angus

Wilson, August 1945-2005 .... **BLC 1:3, 2:3; CLC 39, 50, 63, 118, 222; DC 2, 31; WLCS**
See also AAYA 16; AFAW 2; AMWS 8; BW 2, 3; CA 115; 122; 244; CAD; CANR 42, 54, 76, 128; CD 5, 6; DA; DA3; DAB; DAC; DAM DRAM, MST, MULT; DFS 3, 7, 15, 17, 24; DLB 228; EWL 3; LAIT 4; LATS 1:2; MAL 5; MTCW 1, 2; MTFW 2005; RGAL 4

Wilson, Brian 1942- .... **CLC 12**

Wilson, Colin 1931- .... **CLC 3, 14**
See also CA 1-4R; CAAS 5; CANR 1, 22, 33, 77; CMW 4; CN 1, 2, 3, 4, 5, 6; DLB 14, 194; HGG; MTCW 1; SFW 4

Wilson, Colin Henry
See Wilson, Colin

Wilson, Dirk
See Pohl, Frederik

Wilson, Edmund 1895-1972 .. **CLC 1, 2, 3, 8, 24**
See also AMW; CA 1-4R; 37-40R; CANR 1, 46, 110; CN 1; DLB 63; EWL 3; MAL 5; MTCW 1, 2; MTFW 2005; RGAL 4; TUS

Wilson, Ethel Davis (Bryant)
1888(?)-1980 .... **CLC 13**
See also CA 102; CN 1, 2; DAC; DAM POET; DLB 68; MTCW 1; RGEL 2

Wilson, Harriet
See Wilson, Harriet E. Adams

Wilson, Harriet E.
See Wilson, Harriet E. Adams

Wilson, Harriet E. Adams
1827(?)-1863(?) ..... **BLC 1:3; NCLC 78, 219**
See also DAM MULT; DLB 50, 239, 243

Wilson, John 1785-1854 .... **NCLC 5**
See also DLB 110

Wilson, John Anthony Burgess
See Burgess, Anthony

Wilson, John Burgess
See Burgess, Anthony

Wilson, Katharina CLC 65

Wilson, Lanford 1937- .. **CLC 7, 14, 36, 197; DC 20**
See also CA 17-20R; CABS 3; CAD; CANR 45, 96; CD 5, 6; DAM DRAM; DFS 4, 9, 12, 16, 20; DLB 7, 341; EWL 3; MAL 5; TUS

Wilson, Robert M. 1941- .... **CLC 7, 9**
See also CA 49-52; CAD; CANR 2, 41; CD 5, 6; MTCW 1

Wilson, Robert McLiam 1964- .... **CLC 59**
See also CA 132; DLB 267

Wilson, Sloan 1920-2003 .... **CLC 32**
See also CA 1-4R; 216; CANR 1, 44; CN 1, 2, 3, 4, 5, 6

Wilson, Snoo 1948- .... **CLC 33**
See also CA 69-72; CBD; CD 5, 6

Wilson, Thomas 1523(?)-1581 .... **LC 184**
See also DLB 132, 236

Wilson, William S(mith) 1932- .... **CLC 49**
See also CA 81-84

Wilson, (Thomas) Woodrow
1856-1924 .... **TCLC 79**
See also CA 166; DLB 47

Winchelsea
See Finch, Anne

Winchester, Simon 1944- .... **CLC 257**
See also AAYA 66; CA 107; CANR 90, 130, 194

Winchilsea, Anne (Kingsmill) Finch
1661-1720
See Finch, Anne
See also RGEL 2

Winckelmann, Johann Joachim
1717-1768 .... **LC 129**
See also DLB 97

Windham, Basil
See Wodehouse, P. G.

Wingrove, David 1954- .... **CLC 68**
See also CA 133; SFW 4

Winnemucca, Sarah 1844-1891 .... **NCLC 79; NNAL**
See also DAM MULT; DLB 175; RGAL 4

Winstanley, Gerrard 1609-1676 .... **LC 52**

Wintergreen, Jane
See Duncan, Sara Jeannette

Winters, Arthur Yvor
See Winters, Yvor

Winters, Janet Lewis
See Lewis, Janet

Winters, Yvor 1900-1968 .. **CLC 4, 8, 32; PC 82**
See also AMWS 2; CA 11-12; 25-28R; CAP 1; DLB 48; EWL 3; MAL 5; MTCW 1; RGAL 4

Winterson, Jeanette 1959- .... **CLC 64, 158; SSC 144**
See also BRWS 4; CA 136; CANR 58, 116, 181; CN 5, 6, 7; CPW; DA3; DAM POP; DLB 207, 261; FANT; FW; GLL 1; MTCW 2; MTFW 2005; RHW; SATA 190

Winthrop, John 1588-1649 .... **LC 31, 107**
See also DLB 24, 30

Winthrop, Theodore 1828-1861 ... **NCLC 210**
See also DLB 202

Winton, Tim 1960- .... **CLC 251; SSC 119**
See also AAYA 34; CA 152; CANR 118, 194; CN 6, 7; DLB 325; SATA 98

Wirth, Louis 1897-1952 .... **TCLC 92**
See also CA 210

Wiseman, Frederick 1930- .... **CLC 20**
See also CA 159

Wister, Owen 1860-1938 ..... **SSC 100; TCLC 21**
See also BPFB 3; CA 108; 162; DLB 9, 78, 186; RGAL 4; SATA 62; TCWW 1, 2

Wither, George 1588-1667 .... **LC 96**
See also DLB 121; RGEL 2

Witkacy
See Witkiewicz, Stanislaw Ignacy

Witkiewicz, Stanislaw Ignacy
1885-1939 .... **TCLC 8, 237**
See also CA 105; 162; CDWLB 4; DLB 215; EW 10; EWL 3; RGWL 2, 3; SFW 4

Wittgenstein, Ludwig (Josef Johann)
1889-1951 .... **TCLC 59**
See also CA 113; 164; DLB 262; MTCW 2

Wittig, Monique 1935-2003 .... **CLC 22**
See also CA 116; 135; 212; CANR 143; CWW 2; DLB 83; EWL 3; FW; GLL 1

Wittlin, Jozef 1896-1976 .... **CLC 25**
See also CA 49-52; 65-68; CANR 3; EWL 3

Wodehouse, P. G. 1881-1975 ..... **CLC 1, 2, 5, 10, 22; SSC 2, 115; TCLC 108**
See also AAYA 65; AITN 2; BRWS 3; CA 45-48; 57-60; CANR 3, 33; CDBLB 1914-1945; CN 1, 2; CPW 1; DA3; DAB; DAC; DAM NOV; DLB 34, 162, 352; EWL 3; MTCW 1, 2; MTFW 2005; RGEL 2; RGSF 2; SATA 22; SSFS 10

Wodehouse, Pelham Grenville
See Wodehouse, P. G.

Woiwode, L.
See Woiwode, Larry

Literary Criticism Series
Cumulative Topic Index

This index lists all topic entries in Gale's *Children's Literature Review* (CLR), *Classical and Medieval Literature Criticism* (CMLC), *Contemporary Literary Criticism* (CLC), *Drama Criticism* (DC), *Literature Criticism from 1400 to 1800* (LC), *Nineteenth-Century Literature Criticism* (NCLC), *Short Story Criticism* (SSC), and *Twentieth-Century Literary Criticism* (TCLC). The index also lists topic entries in the Gale Critical Companion Collection, which includes the following publications: *The Beat Generation* (BG), *Feminism in Literature* (FL), *Gothic Literature* (GL), and *Harlem Renaissance* (HR).

Topic Index

Topic Index

Topic Index

Topic Index

TCLC Cumulative Nationality Index

TCLC-249 Title Index

ISBN-13: 978-1-4144-7029-0
ISBN-10: 1-4144-7029-0

90000

9 781414 470290